R. Gupta's®

Popular Master Guide

IFS

Indian Forest Service

MAIN EXAMINATION

AGRICULTURE

PAPER I & II

CONDUCTED BY:

UNION PUBLIC SERVICE COMMISSION (UPSC)

Dr. B.B. Singh

Ph.D., FISEP, FSLW, Former Assistant Professor

N.D. University of Agril. & Tech. Kumarganj, Faizabad (U.P.)

2027

EDITION

RAMESH PUBLISHING HOUSE, NEW DELHI

Published by

O.P. Gupta *for* Ramesh Publishing House

Admin. Office

12-H, New Daryaganj Road, Opp. Officers' Mess,
New Delhi-110002 ✆ 23275224, 23245124

E-mail: info@rameshpublishinghouse.com

For Online Shopping: www.rameshpublishinghouse.com

Showroom

- Balaji Market, Nai Sarak, Delhi-110006 ✆ 23282525 📱 9354373464
- 4457, Nai Sarak, Delhi-110006

Book Code: R-1238

ISBN: 978-81-7812-934-1

Price: ₹ 790

Printed at: Deepak Offset, Delhi

CONTENTS

SCHEME OF THE MAIN EXAMINATION

The main examination for the Indian Forest Service comprises:

(A) The written examination consisting of the following papers:-

Paper I	General English	300 marks
Paper II	General Knowledge	300 marks
Paper III **Paper IV** **Paper V** **Paper VI**	Any two subjects to be selected from the list of the optional subjects. Each subject will have two papers.	200 Marks for each paper

(B) Interview for Personality Test —Maximum marks: 300

LIST OF OPTIONAL SUBJECTS

1. Agriculture
2. Agricultural Engineering
3. Animal Husbandry & Veterinary Science
4. Botany
5. Chemistry
6. Chemical Engineering
7. Civil Engineering
8. Forestry
9. Geology
10. Mathematics
11. Mechanical Engineering
12. Physics
13. Statistics
14. Zoology

Provided that the candidate will not be allowed to offer the following combination of subjects:

(a) Agriculture and Agricultural Engineering

(b) Agriculture and Animal Husbandry & Veterinary Science

(c) Agriculture and Forestry

(d) Chemistry and Chemical Engineering

(e) Mathematics and Statistics

(f) Of the Engineering subjects viz. Agricultural Engineering, Chemical Engineering, Civil Engineering and Mechanical Engineering not more than one subject.

GENERAL INSTRUCTIONS

1. All the question papers for the examination will be of conventional (Essay) type.

2. All question papers must be answered in English. Question papers will be set in English only.

3. The duration of each of the papers referred to above will be 3 hours.

Previous Years' Paper

Indian Forest Service (Main) Exam, 2025

SUBJECT–AGRICULTURE

(Exam held on 23-11-2025)

PAPER-I

Instructions: *There are EIGHT questions in all, out of which FIVE are to be attempted, question Nos. 1 & 5 are compulsory. Out of the remaining SIX questions, THREE are to be attempted selecting at least ONE question from each of the two Sections A and B. Attempts of questions shall be counted in sequential order. Unless struck off, attempt of a question shall be counted even if attempted partly. Any page or portion of the page left blank in the Question-cum-Answer Booklet must be clearly struck off. All questions carry equal marks. Answers must be written in ENGLISH only.*

SECTION-A

1. (*a*) Enlist the types of soil structure and explain the prism-like structure.

(*b*) Explain the term "hedgerow intercropping'. Give an account of its advantages.

(*c*) Explain the biotic and abiotic factors in the ecosystem.

(*d*) How have short duration varieties of crops contributed in increasing food grains production in India?

(*e*) Calculate the residual sodium carbonate (RSC) content of the irrigation water and give comments for the use of irrigation purpose.

Given:

Carbonate (CO_3^{2-}) is 1.5 meqL^{-1}

Bicarbonate (HCO_3^{1-}) is 4.0 meqL^{-1}

Calcium (Ca^{2+}) is 2.6 meqL^{-1}

Magnesium (Mg^{2+}) is 2.0 meqL^{-1}

Ans. (*a*) Soil structure refers to the natural arrangement of primary soil particles—sand, silt and clay—into secondary units known as aggregates or peds. This arrangement governs important physical properties of soil such as porosity, permeability, aeration, water movement, root penetration and resistance to erosion, and hence plays a decisive role in soil fertility and agricultural productivity.

The **main types of soil structure** are:

- Granular (crumb) structure
- Blocky structure
- Platy structure
- Prismatic structure
- Columnar structure
- Single-grained structure
- Massive structure

Prism-like (Prismatic) structure is characterized by vertically oriented, elongated soil peds resembling prisms or pillars, separated by well-defined vertical cracks. The tops of these prisms are usually flat or slightly angular, which distinguishes them from columnar structures. This structure develops mainly in the **B horizon** due to **clay illuviation**, shrink–swell behavior of clay minerals and repeated wetting and drying cycles. Prismatic structure facilitates downward movement of water and allows deeper root penetration, but lateral movement of water is relatively restricted. It is commonly observed in clay-rich soils of semi-arid to sub-humid regions and significantly influences subsoil drainage and nutrient movement.

Prismatic: *Vertical columns of soil that might be a number of cm long. Usually found in lower horizons.*

Prismatic

Ans. (*b*) **Hedgerow intercropping** is an agroforestry-based land-use system in which rows of perennial woody plants such as trees or shrubs are grown as hedgerows, while annual agricultural crops are cultivated in the alleys between these hedgerows. The hedgerows are generally planted along contours or across slopes and are periodically pruned to reduce competition with crops. The pruned biomass is incorporated into the soil or used as mulch.

This system is widely practiced in tropical and subtropical regions, particularly on sloping lands, to combine crop production with soil and water conservation. The woody species used in hedgerow intercropping are often fast-growing, deep-rooted and frequently nitrogen-fixing, which helps in maintaining soil fertility and ecological balance.

Advantages of Hedgerow intercropping: The hedgerows act as physical barriers that reduce runoff velocity and effectively control soil erosion. Regular addition of pruned biomass improves soil organic matter content, enhances soil structure and stimulates microbial activity. When leguminous species are used, biological nitrogen fixation enriches the soil nitrogen status. Mulching with prunings conserves soil moisture by reducing evaporation losses and improving infiltration. Deep-rooted hedgerow species also recycle nutrients from deeper soil layers and return them to the surface through leaf fall and prunings. Over time, the system supports sustained agricultural productivity and may provide additional benefits such as fodder, fuelwood or green manure, contributing to diversified farm income.

Ans. (*c*) An ecosystem is a functional unit of nature in which living organisms interact among themselves and with the surrounding physical environment. These interactions are governed by two broad sets of components known as **biotic factors** and **abiotic factors,** both of which are essential for the structure, functioning and stability of an ecosystem.

Biotic factors refer to the **living components of an ecosystem**. They include all organisms that directly or indirectly influence one another through feeding relationships, competition and cooperation. Biotic factors are commonly grouped into three functional categories. **Producers** are autotrophic organisms such as green plants, algae and photosynthetic bacteria that synthesize organic food using solar energy through photosynthesis and form the base of the food chain. **Consumers** are heterotrophic organisms that depend on producers or other consumers for food; they include herbivores, carnivores and omnivores at different trophic levels. **Decomposers**, mainly bacteria and fungi, break down dead organic matter and waste materials into simpler inorganic substances, thereby recycling nutrients back into the ecosystem. Together, biotic factors regulate energy flow, nutrient cycling and population dynamics within the ecosystem.

Abiotic factors comprise the **non-living physical and chemical components of the ecosystem** that influence the survival, growth and distribution of organisms. These include **climatic factors** such as light, temperature, rainfall, humidity and wind, which control photosynthesis, metabolism and species distribution. **Edaphic factors** like soil texture, structure, moisture, pH and nutrient content determine plant growth and soil-based productivity. **Physiographic factors** such as altitude, slope and topography influence microclimate and habitat conditions. Additionally, **chemical factors** including availability of oxygen, carbon dioxide, minerals and salinity play a crucial role in regulating biological processes.

Biotic and abiotic factors are closely interlinked, and any change in one component brings about corresponding changes in the other, thereby maintaining the dynamic equilibrium of the ecosystem.

Ans. (*d*) Short duration varieties of crops are those that **complete their life cycle in a relatively shorter time** compared to traditional varieties. The introduction and large-scale adoption of such varieties in India, particularly since the Green Revolution, have played a crucial role in increasing overall food grains production by improving cropping intensity, resource use efficiency and yield stability.

One of the most significant contributions of short duration varieties is the **increase in cropping intensity**. Because these crops mature quickly, farmers are able to grow **two or even three crops in a year on the same piece of land**, especially in irrigated areas. This multiple cropping system has substantially increased annual food grains output without expanding the cultivated area. Short duration varieties also fit well into diverse crop rotations, allowing better utilization of available land and time.

Short duration crops contribute to **efficient use of water and inputs**. Their shorter growing period reduces total water requirement, making them particularly suitable for regions with limited or uncertain water availability. Faster maturity also lowers exposure to drought, floods and terminal heat stress, thereby reducing the risk of crop failure and stabilizing production. In addition, these varieties allow better synchronization of fertilizer application with crop demand, improving nutrient use efficiency.

Another important contribution is the **reduction in pest and disease incidence**. Since the crop remains in the field for a shorter duration, the window for pest and disease attack is reduced, leading to lower yield losses and, in some cases, reduced dependence on chemical pesticides. Early maturity also enables timely harvesting, reducing post-harvest losses caused by adverse weather.

Short duration varieties have also facilitated the **spread of modern agricultural practices**, including mechanization and improved crop management, by allowing timely field operations. Collectively, these factors have significantly enhanced food grains production in India while supporting sustainability and resilience in agricultural systems.

Ans. (*e*) Residual Sodium Carbonate (RSC) is an index used to assess the **suitability of irrigation water**, particularly with respect to the hazard posed by carbonate and bicarbonate ions in relation to calcium and magnesium. High RSC water tends to precipitate calcium and magnesium in the soil, increasing the relative dominance of sodium and thereby adversely affecting soil structure and permeability.

The formula for calculating RSC is:

$RSC = (CO_3^{2-} + HCO_3^-) - (Ca^{2+} + Mg^{2+})$ [all concentrations in meq L^{-1}]

Substituting the given values:

$CO_3^{2-} + HCO_3^- = 1.5 + 4.0 = 5.5$ meq L^{-1}

$Ca^{2+} + Mg^{2+} = 2.6 + 2.0 = 4.6$ meq L^{-1}

RSC = 5.5 − 4.6 = **0.9 meq L^{-1}**

Comment on suitability for irrigation: An RSC value **less than 1.25 meq L^{-1}** indicates that the irrigation water is **safe for use** and does not pose a significant sodicity hazard. Since the calculated RSC is **0.9 meq L^{-1}**, the given irrigation water is **suitable for irrigation purposes** and is unlikely to cause adverse effects on soil physical properties or crop growth.

2. **(*a*) Differentiate between agroforestry and social forestry. Give an account of agroforestry systems in India.**

(*b*) Describe the microbiological aspects of organic matter decomposition.

(*c*) Discuss the effects of climatic elements on crop productivity in India.

Ans. (*a*) Agroforestry and social forestry are both land-use approaches involving trees, but they differ fundamentally in **objectives, scale, management and beneficiaries**.

Agroforestry is a land-use system in which **woody perennials (trees or shrubs) are deliberately integrated with agricultural crops and/or livestock on the same unit of land**, either simultaneously or sequentially. Its primary objective is to **enhance overall productivity, sustainability and resource-use efficiency of farmland** while maintaining ecological balance. Agroforestry is mainly practiced on **private agricultural lands**, and management decisions are taken by individual farmers. It directly contributes to farm income through food, fodder, fuelwood, timber and other tree-based products, while also improving soil fertility, moisture conservation and microclimatic conditions.

Social forestry, on the other hand, refers to the **raising of trees on non-agricultural lands such as village commons, wastelands, roadsides, canal banks and degraded forest lands**, primarily to meet the **basic needs of rural and urban communities** for fuelwood, fodder, small timber and environmental improvement. It is generally implemented through **government or community-led programmes**, with broader social objectives such as reducing pressure on natural forests, generating employment, rehabilitating degraded lands and improving environmental quality. Unlike agroforestry, social forestry does not necessarily involve crop cultivation alongside trees.

Thus, while agroforestry focuses on **integrated production systems on farmlands**, social forestry emphasizes **community welfare and ecological restoration on common or public lands.**

Agroforestry systems in India: India has a long tradition of agroforestry, shaped by diverse agro-climatic conditions, farming practices and socio-economic needs. One of the most widespread systems is the **agrisilvicultural system**, where agricultural crops are grown along with trees such as poplar, eucalyptus, neem or teak. This system is common in the Indo-Gangetic plains and parts of central and southern India, where trees provide timber and fuelwood while crops ensure regular income. Another important system is **agrisilvipastoral agroforestry**, which integrates trees, crops and livestock. Trees provide shade and fodder, crops supply food grains, and livestock contribute manure and income. This system is especially prevalent in semi-arid and dry regions. **Silvipastoral systems**, involving trees and pasture grasses, are widely practiced in arid and hilly regions for fodder production and soil conservation.

India also practices **horti-agroforestry**, where fruit trees such as mango, guava or citrus are combined with seasonal crops, and **home**

garden systems, particularly in Kerala and northeastern states, which are highly diverse, multistoried and sustainable. Collectively, these agroforestry systems contribute significantly to food security, livelihood diversification, soil and water conservation, and climate resilience in Indian agriculture.

Ans. (*b*) Organic matter decomposition in soil is a **biologically mediated process** through which dead plant and animal residues are broken down into simpler substances, ultimately leading to the release of nutrients and formation of stable soil organic matter (humus). This process is primarily governed by **soil microorganisms**, whose activity determines the rate, pathway and completeness of decomposition.

The **microbiological aspects of organic matter decomposition** involve the coordinated action of different groups of microorganisms, mainly **bacteria, fungi and actinomycetes**, each playing distinct roles at various stages. **Bacteria** are the most abundant decomposers and are particularly effective in breaking down **simple, readily decomposable compounds** such as sugars, amino acids and proteins. They dominate the early stages of decomposition, especially under moist, warm and well-aerated soil conditions. Certain bacteria also carry out specific biochemical transformations such as ammonification, nitrification and denitrification during decomposition.

Fungi play a crucial role in decomposing **complex and resistant organic materials**, including cellulose, hemicellulose and lignin. Their filamentous growth allows them to penetrate plant residues and soil aggregates, making them especially important in forest soils, acidic soils and under low moisture conditions. Fungi are also major contributors to humus formation due to their ability to synthesize stable organic compounds.

Actinomycetes represent an intermediate group between bacteria and fungi and become prominent during the later stages of decomposition. They are particularly effective in breaking down **complex polymers** such as chitin and lignin derivatives and are responsible for the characteristic earthy smell of soil. Their activity contributes significantly to the stabilization of organic matter.

Microbial decomposition involves the secretion of **extracellular enzymes** such as cellulases, proteases and ligninases, which convert complex organic compounds into simpler molecules. During this process, a portion of carbon is released as **carbon dioxide through respiration**, while nutrients such as nitrogen, phosphorus and sulfur are **mineralized** into plant-available forms. The remaining resistant fraction undergoes **humification**, leading to the formation of stable humus.

Thus, soil microorganisms regulate nutrient cycling, energy flow and soil fertility through the decomposition of organic matter, making microbiological activity central to soil health and ecosystem sustainability.

Ans. (*c*) Crop productivity in India is strongly influenced by **climatic elements**, as agriculture in the country is largely dependent on natural weather conditions, particularly the monsoon. Variations in climate directly affect crop growth, development, yield and stability of agricultural production.

Rainfall is the most critical climatic factor influencing crop productivity in India. The spatial and temporal distribution of rainfall determines the success of rainfed agriculture, which accounts for a large proportion of cultivated area. Adequate and well-distributed rainfall during the cropping season ensures proper germination, nutrient uptake and vegetative growth. Conversely, deficient rainfall leads to drought stress, reduced yields and crop failure, while excessive rainfall causes waterlogging, soil erosion, nutrient leaching and spread of pests and diseases.

Temperature plays a key role in regulating physiological processes such as photosynthesis, respiration, transpiration and enzyme activity. Each crop has an optimum temperature range for growth and yield. High temperatures beyond tolerance levels cause heat stress, accelerate crop maturity and reduce grain filling, particularly in wheat and pulses. Low temperatures and frost damage sensitive crops such as vegetables, oilseeds and fruit crops, especially in northern India during winter.

Solar radiation and light intensity influence photosynthetic activity and biomass production. Adequate sunlight promotes higher dry matter accumulation and yield. Cloudy conditions during critical growth stages reduce photosynthesis and adversely affect crops like rice and sugarcane. Day length also affects flowering and maturity in photoperiod-sensitive crops.

Humidity and wind further modify crop productivity. High humidity favors the incidence of fungal and bacterial diseases, while low humidity increases evapotranspiration demand, leading to moisture stress. Wind affects pollination, transpiration and lodging of crops; strong winds may cause physical damage to standing crops.

Overall, the interaction of climatic elements governs cropping patterns, choice of crops and productivity levels in India, making climate a decisive factor in agricultural sustainability and food security.

3. (*a*) Discuss the cultivation of wheat in respect of the following:

(*i*) Species

(*ii*) Crop rotation

(*iii*) Sowing time

(*iv*) Nutrient management

(*v*) Weed management

(*b*) Give the characteristics of weeds. Discuss the role of exotic weeds on biodiversity with suitable examples.

(*c*) Enlist the various ways of nitrogen losses from soil-plant system. Explain the denitrification losses of nitrogen.

Ans. (*a*) Wheat is one of the most important cereal crops of India and forms the staple food for a large part of the population. Its successful cultivation depends on appropriate varietal choice, timely sowing and proper crop and nutrient management practices.

(*i*) **Species:** The commonly cultivated wheat species in India belong to the genus *Triticum*. The most important species is **Triticum aestivum**, also known as bread wheat, which accounts for the major share of wheat area and production due to its wide adaptability and high yield potential. **Triticum durum** (durum wheat) is grown in limited areas, mainly under irrigated conditions, and is preferred for making semolina and pasta products. **Triticum dicoccum** (emmer wheat) is cultivated on a small scale in parts of southern India and hilly regions, mainly under traditional farming systems.

(*ii*) **Crop rotation:** Crop rotation plays an important role in maintaining soil fertility and reducing pest, disease and weed problems in wheat cultivation. Wheat is commonly grown in rotation with legumes and other crops such as **rice–wheat, maize–wheat, cotton–wheat**, and **pigeon pea–wheat** systems. Inclusion of legumes like gram or mungbean improves soil nitrogen status and enhances wheat productivity. Proper rotation also helps in efficient utilization of soil moisture and nutrients.

(*iii*) **Sowing time:** Timely sowing is critical for obtaining high wheat yields. In north India, wheat is generally sown during **October to November**, immediately after the harvest of kharif crops. Early sowing ensures better tillering and root development, while delayed sowing exposes the crop to high temperatures during grain filling, leading to yield reduction. In central and eastern India, sowing time may extend slightly depending on climatic conditions.

(*iv*) **Nutrient management:** Wheat is a nutrient-responsive crop and requires balanced fertilization for optimum yield. Nitrogen is the most important nutrient and is applied in split doses to ensure availability during critical growth stages. Phosphorus is essential for root development and early growth, while potassium improves disease resistance and grain quality. Secondary nutrients and micronutrients such as sulfur, zinc and iron are also important, particularly in deficient soils. Integrated nutrient management involving fertilizers, organic manures and crop residues helps maintain soil health and sustain productivity.

(*v*) **Weed management:** Weeds compete with wheat for nutrients, moisture and light, especially during the early growth period. Common weeds include **Phalaris minor**, **Chenopodium album** and **Avena ludoviciana.** Effective weed management involves a combination of **cultural practices** (such as proper seed rate and timely irrigation, and **chemical control** using selective herbicides applied at appropriate stages. Timely weed control during the first 30–45 days after sowing is crucial to prevent yield losses.

Overall, adoption of recommended cultivation practices ensures higher productivity and sustainability of wheat cultivation in India.

Ans. (*b*) Weeds are unwanted and undesirable plants that grow along with cultivated crops and compete with them for essential resources. Their characteristics enable them to survive, spread rapidly and dominate agricultural as well as natural ecosystems.

Characteristics of weeds: Weeds generally possess **high reproductive capacity**, producing a large number of seeds that ensure their persistence. Many weeds have **dormant seeds** capable of surviving in the soil for several years and germinating when conditions become favorable. They show **rapid growth and early maturity**, allowing them to complete their life cycle quickly and escape control measures. Most weeds have **wide ecological adaptability**, enabling them to thrive under varied soil, moisture and climatic conditions. They often possess **efficient dispersal mechanisms** through wind, water, animals or human activities. Many weeds also exhibit **vegetative reproduction** through rhizomes, stolons or tubers, making their eradication difficult. In addition, several weeds show **resistance to pests, diseases and herbicides**, which further enhances their survival.

Role of exotic weeds on biodiversity: Exotic weeds are plant species introduced deliberately or accidentally from outside their natural range. Once established, many of these species become invasive and exert a **negative impact on native biodiversity**. Exotic weeds often grow aggressively and form dense monocultures that suppress native plant species by competing for light, nutrients, water and space. This leads to a **decline in species richness and alteration of natural plant communities**.

For example, *Lantana camara*, introduced as an ornamental plant, has invaded forests and grasslands across India, replacing native understory vegetation and disrupting wildlife habitats. *Eichhornia crassipes* (water hyacinth), introduced as an ornamental aquatic plant, chokes water bodies, reduces oxygen levels, affects aquatic biodiversity and disrupts fisheries.

Ans. (*c*) Nitrogen is an essential plant nutrient, but it is also the most **dynamic and loss-prone element** in the soil–plant system. Because nitrogen undergoes several biological and physicochemical transformations, a significant proportion applied through fertilizers or organic sources is lost before being utilized by crops.

The **various ways of nitrogen losses from the soil–plant system** include:

- **Leaching losses** – downward movement of nitrate nitrogen beyond the root zone with percolating water, common in light-textured soils and high rainfall or irrigated conditions.
- **Volatilization losses** – loss of nitrogen as ammonia gas, particularly from surface-applied urea or ammonium fertilizers under high pH, high temperature and moist conditions.
- **Denitrification losses** – microbial reduction of nitrate nitrogen to gaseous forms under anaerobic conditions.
- **Crop removal** – nitrogen uptake and removal through harvested produce.
- **Runoff and erosion losses** – removal of nitrogen along with surface soil and runoff water.
- **Immobilization** – temporary unavailability of nitrogen due to microbial assimilation during decomposition of high C:N ratio residues.

Denitrification losses of nitrogen: Denitrification is a **biological process** in which **nitrate nitrogen (NO_3^-)** is reduced to gaseous forms such as **nitric oxide (NO), nitrous oxide (N_2O) and molecular nitrogen (N_2)** by anaerobic microorganisms. This process occurs mainly in **waterlogged or poorly aerated soils**, where oxygen supply is limited and microorganisms use nitrate as an alternative electron acceptor for respiration.

Denitrification is favored by several conditions: high soil moisture or flooding, availability of **readily decomposable organic matter**, presence of **nitrate nitrogen, warm temperatures,** and **neutral to slightly alkaline soil reaction**. Paddy fields, compacted soils and poorly drained areas are particularly susceptible to denitrification losses. Among the gaseous products, nitrous oxide is of special concern as it is a **potent greenhouse gas,** contributing to climate change.

Denitrification results in a **permanent loss of nitrogen from the soil–plant system,** reducing fertilizer use efficiency and crop productivity. Proper water management, balanced fertilization and use of nitrification inhibitors help minimize such losses.

4. (*a*) Give an account of different sources of soil and water pollution in India.

(*b*) Write short notes on the following:

(*i*) Agroclimatic zones

(*ii*) Reddening of leaf in cotton

(*iii*) Retting in jute

(*iv*) Additive intercropping

(*v*) Relay cropping

(*c*) Describe the causes of micronutrients deficiency in Indian soils.

Ans. (*a*) Soil and water pollution in India has emerged as a serious environmental problem due to rapid population growth, industrialization, urbanization and intensive agricultural practices. Multiple anthropogenic sources contribute to the degradation of soil quality and contamination of surface and groundwater resources.

Sources of soil pollution: Agriculture is a major source of soil pollution in India. Excessive and indiscriminate use of **chemical fertilizers, pesticides, herbicides and fungicides** leads to accumulation of toxic residues in soils, adversely affecting soil microorganisms and long-term soil fertility. Repeated application of poor-quality irrigation water, especially in arid and semi-arid regions, causes **salinity and sodicity**, degrading soil structure and productivity.

Industrial activities contribute significantly to soil pollution through the disposal of **solid wastes, fly ash, heavy metals and toxic chemicals**. **Urban solid waste dumping**, including plastics, biomedical waste and electronic waste, also contaminates soils around cities and towns. Mining activities further degrade soils through removal of topsoil and deposition of mine tailings.

Sources of water pollution: Water pollution in India arises from both point and non-point sources. **Domestic sewage** is the largest contributor, especially in urban areas, where untreated or partially treated wastewater is discharged into rivers, lakes and canals, leading to organic pollution and eutrophication. **Industrial effluents** containing toxic chemicals, acids, dyes, oils and heavy metals are discharged into surface water bodies, severely affecting aquatic ecosystems and human health.

Agricultural runoff is a major non-point source of water pollution. Runoff carrying **nitrates, phosphates, pesticides and sediments** from agricultural fields enters rivers and groundwater, causing nutrient enrichment and contamination. **Thermal pollution** from power plants alters water temperature, affecting aquatic life. In coastal areas, **oil spills, port activities and saline intrusion** further degrade water quality. Religious and cultural practices, such as idol immersion and mass bathing in rivers, also contribute to localized water pollution.

Ans. (*b*)

(*i*) **Agroclimatic zones** are geographical regions delineated on the basis of **climate, soil characteristics, physiography, water resources and cropping patterns**, with the objective of optimizing agricultural planning and sustainable land use. The concept recognizes that agricultural potential and constraints vary significantly across regions due to differences in temperature, rainfall, humidity, soil type and length of growing period.

Each agroclimatic zone is characterized by a relatively uniform set of climatic conditions that influence **crop suitability, productivity and risk**. For example, arid and semi-arid zones are suited for drought-tolerant crops like millets and pulses, whereas humid and per-humid zones favor rice, plantation crops and horticulture. Hill and mountain agroclimatic zones support temperate fruits and specialized cropping systems.

(*ii*) **Reddening of leaf in cotton** is a physiological disorder commonly observed in cotton-growing regions of India, particularly during the later stages of crop growth. It is characterized by the development of **reddish or purplish coloration on cotton leaves**, starting from the margins and gradually spreading over the lamina. The disorder adversely affects photosynthesis, boll development and ultimately seed cotton yield.

The primary cause of leaf reddening is **nutrient imbalance**, especially **deficiency of potassium and magnesium**, which are essential for carbohydrate translocation and chlorophyll stability. Under potassium deficiency, sugars accumulate in leaves, leading to the formation of anthocyanin pigments that impart a red color. Magnesium deficiency further accelerates chlorophyll breakdown, intensifying reddening symptoms. In many cases, **nitrogen deficiency at later growth stages** also contributes indirectly by limiting vegetative vigor.

Reddening of leaves results in **reduced photosynthetic efficiency**, premature leaf senescence and poor boll filling, leading to yield reduction. Proper **balanced fertilization**, timely application of potassium and magnesium, maintenance of adequate soil moisture and selection of tolerant varieties help in minimizing the incidence of leaf reddening in cotton.

(iii) **Retting in jute** is a crucial post-harvest biological process by which the **fibres are separated from the woody stem** of the jute plant. It involves controlled microbial decomposition of the cementing materials—mainly **pectin, hemicellulose and gums**—that bind the fibre bundles to the stem tissues. Proper retting is essential for obtaining **good quality jute fibre** with desirable strength, colour and luster.

Traditionally, retting is carried out by **submerging harvested jute bundles in clean, slow-moving or stagnant water** such as ponds, canals or ditches. The bundles are kept under water with the help of weights, ensuring uniform soaking. Under warm and anaerobic conditions, **microorganisms, particularly bacteria**, multiply and secrete enzymes that break down the non-fibrous materials surrounding the fibre. The retting period generally lasts **2–3 weeks**, depending on water temperature, microbial activity and stem thickness.

Proper retting results in **easy separation of fibres**, yielding soft, strong and uniformly coloured fibre. **Under-retting** leads to hard, coarse fibres that are difficult to extract, while **over-retting** weakens the fibre, reduces strength and causes dull coloration. Therefore, careful monitoring of retting duration is essential.

In recent years, improved retting techniques such as **ribbon retting** and **enzyme-based retting** have been developed to reduce water requirement, improve fibre quality and minimize environmental pollution. Retting thus plays a decisive role in determining the commercial value of jute fibre.

(iv) **Additive intercropping** is a type of intercropping system in which a **secondary (intercrop) is introduced into an existing main crop without reducing the population of the main crop**. In this system, the base crop is planted at its **normal recommended spacing and density**, and the intercrop is added in between or within the rows, thereby increasing total plant population per unit area. It leads to **higher total yield per unit area**, provides **additional income and risk buffering** in case the main crop fails, and improves **nutrient use efficiency**, especially when legumes are used as intercrops due to their nitrogen-fixing ability.

The objective of additive intercropping is to **maximize total productivity and resource use efficiency** by utilizing otherwise under-utilized space, light, nutrients and time. The intercrop is usually a **short-duration, low-growing or complementary crop**, such as pulses or legumes, which does not compete aggressively with the main crop. For example, **black gram or green gram grown in sugarcane, cotton or maize fields** is a common additive intercropping practice.

(v) **Relay cropping** is a multiple cropping system in which a **second crop is sown into a standing first crop before it is harvested**, so that both crops overlap for a part of their growth period. Unlike mixed or intercropping, the crops are grown **sequentially with partial temporal overlap**, rather than simultaneously for the entire season.

The main objective of relay cropping is to **efficiently utilize time, residual soil moisture, nutrients and growing season**, especially in regions where the cropping window is short. The succeeding crop is usually sown when the first crop reaches its reproductive or maturity stage, thereby avoiding delays caused by land preparation after harvest. A common example in India is **lathyrus or lentil sown in standing rice**, particularly in eastern India, where the relay crop germinates using residual soil moisture after rice harvest.

Relay cropping offers several advantages. It helps in **increasing cropping intensity and total land productivity** without additional tillage operations. The system reduces turnaround time between crops and enables better utilization of residual soil fertility and moisture. It is particularly beneficial in rainfed areas where moisture availability is limited after harvest of the main crop. Relay cropping also helps in **reducing soil erosion and weed infestation**, as the soil remains covered for a longer period.

Ans. (*c*) Micronutrient deficiencies have become increasingly widespread in Indian soils and now constitute a major constraint to crop productivity and nutritional security. Although micronutrients are required by plants in small quantities, their deficiency severely affects growth, yield and quality of crops. The causes of micronutrient deficiency in Indian soils are both **natural and management-induced**.

One of the primary causes is the **intensive cultivation of high-yielding crop varieties** following the Green Revolution. These varieties remove large amounts of nutrients from the soil, and while macronutrients like nitrogen, phosphorus and potassium are replenished through fertilizers, **micronutrients are often neglected**, leading to gradual depletion of soil reserves.

Imbalanced and continuous use of chemical fertilizers is another major factor. Excessive application of NPK fertilizers without micronutrient supplementation accelerates deficiencies of zinc, iron, boron and other micronutrients. High phosphorus application, in particular, induces **zinc deficiency** due to antagonistic interactions in soil and plant uptake.

Soil properties and reaction play a significant role. Large areas of Indian soils are **calcareous, alkaline or sodic**, especially in arid and semi-arid regions, where micronutrients such as iron, zinc, manganese and copper become insoluble and unavailable to plants. In contrast, **acidic soils** of eastern and northeastern India often show boron and molybdenum deficiencies due to leaching losses.

Low organic matter content in many Indian soils is another important cause. Organic matter acts as a reservoir and chelating agent for micronutrients. Continuous cropping, residue removal and inadequate use of organic manures have reduced soil organic carbon, thereby lowering micronutrient availability.

Leaching losses due to high rainfall and irrigation, particularly in light-textured sandy soils, lead to deficiencies of boron and molybdenum. **Soil erosion** further removes nutrient-rich topsoil, aggravating micronutrient depletion.

Additionally, **poor-quality irrigation water**, containing high bicarbonates or salts, affects micronutrient solubility and uptake. Thus, the combined effects of intensive agriculture, soil characteristics, climatic factors and improper nutrient management are responsible for widespread micronutrient deficiencies in Indian soils.

SECTION-B

5. (*a*) **Explain the steps of extension education process as per Leagans (1967).**

(b) Describe the factors affecting the types of farming.

(c) How does bunding help in soil and water conservation? Enlist the different types of bunds used for conservation.

(d) Describe the advantages of cooperative marketing in agriculture.

(e) Explain the term 'critical stage of water need of crops'. Give the critical stages of water need of maize, wheat, groundnut and cotton.

Ans. (*a*) According to **Leagans (1967)**, extension education is a **systematic, continuous and problem-oriented process** through which desirable changes in the knowledge, skills, attitudes and practices of people are brought about. The extension education process follows a logical sequence of steps, each step being closely linked with the next to ensure effectiveness and sustainability of extension programmes.

Analysis of the situation: This step involves a thorough understanding of the existing conditions of the people and their environment. This includes studying the socio-economic background of farmers, their needs, problems, resources, farming systems, level of knowledge and prevailing attitudes. Proper situation analysis helps extension workers identify real and felt needs rather than assumed problems.

Programme Planning: Based on the information gathered during situation analysis, clear objectives are formulated and priorities are set. Suitable extension programmes, activities and teaching methods are selected, keeping in view local conditions, available resources and time constraints. Planning ensures that extension efforts are purposeful and well-directed.

Programme Implementation: At this stage, the planned activities are put into action. Extension teaching methods such as demonstrations, meetings, field visits, training programmes and mass media are used to transfer knowledge and skills to farmers. Effective implementation requires proper coordination, leadership and participation of the target group.

Evaluation: Evaluation involves assessing the extent to which the objectives of the extension programme have been achieved. It measures changes in knowledge, attitude, skills and adoption of recommended practices among farmers. Evaluation helps in identifying strengths, weaknesses and gaps in the programme.

Reconsideration and Revision: Based on evaluation findings, necessary modifications are made in objectives, methods or content of the programme. This step ensures feedback, continuity and improvement of extension efforts, making the process dynamic rather than static.

Thus, the extension education process as described by Leagans is a **cyclic and continuous process**, aimed at bringing about planned change and rural development through systematic educational efforts.

Ans. (*b*) The **type of farming** practiced in a region is determined by a combination of **physical, socio-economic and technological factors**. These factors influence farmers' decisions regarding crop selection, intensity of cultivation, use of inputs and overall farming systems.

Climatic factors play a dominant role in shaping farming types. Rainfall amount and distribution, temperature, humidity and length of growing season determine whether farming is rainfed or irrigated, single-crop or multiple-crop, and whether crops, livestock or mixed farming will dominate. For example, arid regions favor pastoral or dryland farming, while humid regions support intensive crop cultivation.

Soil factors such as soil type, fertility, depth, texture and drainage strongly influence farming patterns. Fertile alluvial soils encourage intensive and commercial farming, whereas shallow, poor or eroded soils restrict cultivation and promote extensive or subsistence farming. Soil reaction and nutrient status also determine crop suitability.

Relief and topography affect mechanization, irrigation and erosion risk. Plains favor intensive, mechanized agriculture, while hilly and mountainous areas support terrace farming, horticulture or shifting cultivation due to slope limitations.

Availability of water resources is a critical determinant. Regions with assured irrigation support intensive farming, multiple cropping and cultivation of water-intensive crops, whereas areas dependent on rainfall adopt extensive or dry farming systems.

Socio-economic factors such as population pressure, size of landholdings, labor availability, capital resources and land tenure systems significantly affect farming types. Small holdings and high population pressure encourage subsistence farming, while large holdings and capital availability promote commercial and mechanized farming.

Technological factors including use of improved seeds, fertilizers, machinery, irrigation technologies and pest management influence farming intensity and productivity. Advanced technology enables intensive and specialized farming systems.

Market access and infrastructure also play an important role. Proximity to markets, transportation facilities and price incentives encourage commercial farming, horticulture and cash crop cultivation, whereas remote areas remain dominated by subsistence farming.

Thus, the interaction of environmental conditions, resource availability and socio-economic factors determines the type of farming practiced in any region.

Ans. (*c*) **Bunding** is an important mechanical soil and water conservation practice in which **earthen embankments (bunds)** are constructed across the slope or along field boundaries to control runoff, conserve moisture and prevent soil erosion. It is widely adopted in rainfed and irrigated agriculture, particularly in regions receiving moderate to high rainfall.

Role of bunding in soil and water conservation: Bunding helps in **reducing the velocity of surface runoff** by obstructing the free flow of rainwater over the land surface. When runoff velocity is reduced, the **soil-carrying capacity of water decreases**, thereby minimizing soil erosion and loss of fertile topsoil. Bunds act as barriers that **impound rainwater temporarily**, allowing more time for infiltration into the soil profile. This leads to **improved soil moisture storage**, which is crucial for crop growth, especially in rainfed areas.

By conserving rainwater within the field, bunding enhances **groundwater recharge** and improves the effectiveness of rainfall. It also helps in **reducing nutrient losses**, as fertilizers applied to the field are not washed away with runoff. In sloping lands, bunding contributes to **land leveling and stabilization**, making cultivation easier and more productive. Overall, bunding improves crop yield, water-use efficiency and long-term soil health.

Types of bunds used for soil and water conservation:

- **Contour bunds** – constructed along contour lines across the slope to reduce runoff velocity and soil erosion in gently sloping lands.
- **Graded bunds** – provided with a gentle gradient to safely dispose excess runoff while still controlling erosion, suitable for areas with higher rainfall.
- **Field bunds** – built along field boundaries mainly to retain rainwater and prevent soil loss in agricultural fields.

- **Peripheral bunds** – constructed around the field to prevent entry or exit of runoff water.
- **Stone bunds** – made of stones, commonly used in rocky or hilly terrains where soil bund construction is difficult.
- **Contour stone bunds** – stones laid along contour lines to check runoff and erosion in arid and semi-arid regions.

Thus, bunding is an effective and economical practice for conserving soil and water, improving moisture availability and sustaining agricultural productivity.

Ans. (*d*) **Cooperative marketing** in agriculture refers to the collective organization of farmers for the **sale, storage, processing and distribution of agricultural produce**. Under this system, farmers pool their produce through cooperative societies, enabling them to market their commodities more efficiently and profitably than as individual sellers. Advantages of cooperative marketing are as follows:

Elimination of middlemen: By selling produce collectively, farmers reduce dependence on traders and commission agents, thereby receiving **better and more stable prices** for their produce. This strengthens the bargaining power of small and marginal farmers who otherwise have little influence in the market.

Better price realization and reduced price fluctuation: By regulating the supply of produce to the market and providing storage facilities, cooperatives help farmers sell their produce when market prices are favorable.

Reduction in marketing costs: Collective transport, storage, grading and packaging lower per-unit costs which improves the quality of produce and fetches higher market prices.

Access to credit and inputs: Farmers can obtain short-term loans against stored produce and receive inputs such as seeds and fertilizers at reasonable rates. In addition, cooperatives promote **processing and value addition**, increasing farmers' income and employment opportunities in rural areas.

Market transparency cooperative marketing: Disseminates price information and protects farmers from exploitation. It encourages mutual help, democratic participation and economic empowerment, contributing to the overall development of the agricultural sector.

Ans. (*e*) The **critical stage of water need of crops** refers to the **specific growth period during which adequate soil moisture is essential for normal physiological development and yield formation**. Moisture stress at these stages causes **irreversible yield reduction**, even if water is supplied adequately at other stages. These stages generally coincide with periods of **active cell division, flowering, pollination and grain or boll development**, when water requirement is highest.

Different crops have different critical stages depending on their growth pattern and reproductive biology.

Critical stages of water need of important crops:

Maize: The most critical stages are **knee-high stage, tasseling and silking**, and **grain filling**. Among these, tasseling–silking is the most sensitive stage, as moisture stress during this period affects pollination and kernel formation, leading to severe yield loss.

Wheat: Crown root initiation (CRI) stage is the most critical stage in wheat, which occurs about 20–25 days after sowing. Adequate moisture at this stage is essential for root development and tiller formation. Other important stages include **tillering, flowering and grain filling**.

Groundnut: Groundnut requires adequate moisture during **flowering and pegging**, followed by **pod development**. Moisture stress during pegging prevents proper penetration of pegs into the soil, while stress during pod formation reduces kernel size and yield.

Cotton: In cotton, the critical stages are **square formation, flowering and boll development**. Moisture stress during these stages leads to shedding of squares and flowers, poor boll setting and reduced lint yield.

Thus, identification and proper management of irrigation during the critical stages of crops is essential for efficient water use and achieving optimum crop productivity.

6. **(*a*) Explain the concept of M-Agriculture (M-Krishi) in extension. Give its advantages, services and applications.**

   (*b*) Why is farm planning necessary? Describe its limitations.

   (*c*) Give the classification of gullies in soil erosion. Discuss it based on the dimension of the gully.

Ans. (*a*) **M-Agriculture (Mobile Agriculture or M-Krishi)** refers to the use of **mobile phone–based technologies and services** to support agricultural extension, information dissemination and farm decision-making. It is an extension approach that leverages **mobile communication tools such as SMS, voice calls, mobile apps and interactive platforms** to deliver timely, location-specific and farmer-centric agricultural information. M-Agriculture aims to bridge the information gap between research institutions, extension agencies and farmers, especially in remote and resource-poor areas.

The concept of M-Krishi is based on the premise that mobile phones have high penetration even among small and marginal farmers in India, making them an effective medium for **last-mile extension delivery**. Through mobile platforms, farmers can access real-time advisories related to crops, weather, markets, pests, diseases and farm management practices.

Advantages of M-Agriculture: M-Agriculture enables **timely and cost-effective dissemination of information**, reducing dependence on face-to-face extension visits. It ensures **wide outreach**. M-Agriculture supports **two-way communication**, allowing farmers to seek clarifications and expert advice. It enhances **decision-making efficiency**, reduces risk and promotes adoption of improved technologies.

Services provided under M-Agriculture: M-Agriculture offers a wide range of services such as **weather forecasts and early warnings**, crop-specific advisories, pest and disease alerts, nutrient and irrigation management tips, and market price information. Some platforms provide **voice-based advisory services**, expert consultations, reminders for farm operations, and access to government schemes and subsidies.

Applications of M-Agriculture: M-Agriculture is applied in **crop management**, precision farming, disaster management, market intelligence, and extension education. It supports **climate-smart agriculture** by delivering real-time advisories and helps in improving productivity, profitability and sustainability of farming systems. Thus, M-Agriculture has emerged as a powerful extension tool in modern agricultural development.

Ans. (*b*) **Farm planning** is a systematic process of organizing and allocating the available resources of a farm—such as land, labor, capital and management—in the most efficient manner to achieve the objectives of the farmer. It involves deciding the type and combination of crops, livestock enterprises and farm operations so as to maximize income, ensure efficient resource use and maintain sustainability.

Necessity of farm planning: Farm planning is necessary to ensure **optimum utilization of limited farm resources**. By scientifically allocating land, labor and capital among competing enterprises, farm planning helps avoid waste and inefficiency. It assists farmers in **maximizing farm income** by selecting profitable crop combinations and appropriate production techniques suited to local agro-climatic conditions.

Farm planning helps in **risk reduction and stability of income**, particularly in agriculture where production is subject to climatic uncertainties, price fluctuations and pest outbreaks. Diversification through proper planning reduces dependence on a single crop and safeguards farmers against total crop failure. It also facilitates **balanced use of inputs**, preventing overuse or underuse of fertilizers, water and labor.

Another important necessity is **long-term sustainability**. Farm planning promotes soil conservation, crop rotation and integrated farming systems, thereby maintaining soil fertility and ecological balance. It also aids in **credit planning**, enabling farmers to estimate capital requirements and repayment capacity realistically.

Limitations of farm planning: Despite its advantages, farm planning has certain limitations. One major limitation is **uncertainty in agriculture**, such as unpredictable weather conditions, pest incidence and market price volatility, which can disturb even the best-prepared plans. **Small size of landholdings**, common in India, restricts flexibility in enterprise selection and diversification.

Lack of **adequate and timely information**, including price forecasts and weather predictions, also limits effective farm planning. Many farmers face **capital constraints**, making it difficult to implement recommended plans. In addition, **traditional attitudes and resistance to change** may prevent farmers from adopting scientific farm plans. Limited access to technical guidance and extension services further reduces the effectiveness of farm planning.

Thus, while farm planning is essential for efficient and sustainable farm management, its success depends on supportive institutional, economic and environmental conditions.

Ans. (*c*) **Gullies** are deep and wide channels formed as a result of **advanced stage of water erosion**, where surface runoff concentrates and removes large quantities of soil. Gully erosion represents a serious form of land degradation, as it renders land unfit for cultivation and disrupts drainage patterns. Gullies are classified on several bases, but **classification based on the dimensions of the gully** is most commonly used for planning control measures.

Classification of gullies based on dimensions:

Small gullies: Small gullies are shallow channels with a **depth generally less than about 1 metre and relatively narrow width**. They often develop from enlarged rills when runoff continues unchecked. Though small in size, they indicate the onset of severe erosion and can be controlled easily through agronomic measures, contour bunding or vegetative barriers. If neglected, they gradually deepen and widen into larger gullies.

Medium gullies: Medium gullies have a **depth ranging approximately from 1 to 3 metres**, with wider beds and steeper side slopes. They usually form due to continuous flow of runoff over a longer period. Medium gullies cause considerable loss of fertile topsoil and restrict farm operations. Control measures for medium gullies include **engineering structures** such as check dams, drop structures, combined with vegetative stabilization of side slopes.

Large gullies: Large gullies are very deep and wide erosion channels, often **exceeding 3 metres in depth**, and may extend for long distances. They are highly destructive and permanently remove productive land. Large gullies often develop into ravines if left uncontrolled. Their reclamation requires **major mechanical and engineering interventions**, such as masonry check dams, gully plugs, diversion channels and afforestation. Natural recovery is extremely slow in such gullies.

Thus, classification of gullies based on their dimensions helps in assessing the severity of erosion and selecting appropriate soil and water conservation measures for effective land reclamation.

7. (*a*) **Classify the irrigation water based on salinity and sodium hazards. List the crops according to their degree of salt tolerance.**

(*b*) **Explain watershed management and describe in detail its objectives.**

(*c*) **Explain the term 'contract marketing'. Give its advantages and risk factors.**

Ans. (*a*) The quality of irrigation water has a significant influence on soil properties, crop growth and long-term agricultural sustainability. Irrigation water is commonly classified based on its **salinity hazard** and **sodium hazard**, as both excess soluble salts and sodium adversely affect soil structure, permeability and crop performance.

Classification of irrigation water based on salinity hazard: Salinity hazard is assessed using **Electrical Conductivity (EC)** of irrigation water, which indicates the total concentration of soluble salts.

- **Low salinity water (C_1):** EC < 0.25 dS m^{-1}. Such water is safe for irrigation of most crops on almost all soils.
- **Medium salinity water (C_2):** EC between 0.25 and 0.75 dS m^{-1}. It can be used for irrigation with moderate leaching and is suitable for crops having moderate salt tolerance.
- **High salinity water (C_3):** EC between 0.75 and 2.25 dS m^{-1}. This water requires good drainage and salt-tolerant crops to avoid yield reduction.
- **Very high salinity water (C_4):** EC > 2.25 dS m^{-1}. It is generally unsuitable for irrigation except under special management practices and for highly salt-tolerant crops.

Classification of irrigation water based on sodium hazard: Sodium hazard is evaluated using **Sodium Adsorption Ratio (SAR)**, which reflects the tendency of sodium to replace calcium and magnesium in soil.

- **Low sodium water (S_1):** SAR < 10. Suitable for all soils and crops without any risk of sodicity.
- **Medium sodium water (S_2):** SAR 10–18. Can be used with caution on fine-textured soils; adequate drainage is required.
- **High sodium water (S_3):** SAR 18–26. Harmful to soil structure; suitable only for coarse-textured soils and salt-tolerant crops.
- **Very high sodium water (S_4):** SAR > 26. Generally unsuitable for irrigation due to severe sodicity hazards.

Classification of crops based on degree of salt tolerance:

- **Salt-sensitive crops:** These crops show yield reduction even at low salinity levels. Examples include **beans, onion, carrot, citrus, apple and strawberry**.
- **Moderately salt-tolerant crops:** These crops can tolerate moderate salinity without significant yield loss. Examples include **wheat, rice, maize, sorghum, soybean and groundnut**.
- **Salt-tolerant crops:** These crops can withstand relatively high salinity levels. Examples include **cotton, barley, sugar beet, date palm and spinach**.

Thus, proper classification of irrigation water and selection of crops according to their salt tolerance are essential for maintaining soil health and sustaining agricultural productivity.

Ans. (*b*) **Watershed management** is an integrated and holistic approach to the **development and conservation of land, water and vegetation resources** within a defined natural drainage area known as a watershed. A watershed is a geo-hydrological unit in which all surface runoff drains to a common outlet. Watershed management aims at **optimum utilization of natural resources on a sustainable basis** while minimizing land degradation and improving the socio-economic conditions of the people living in the watershed.

Watershed management involves coordinated use of **soil and water conservation measures, water harvesting, afforestation, pasture development, crop management and community participation**. It treats land and water as interrelated resources and emphasizes conservation at the source, especially in rainfed and drought-prone areas.

Objectives of watershed management:

Soil and water conservation: By reducing runoff velocity and promoting infiltration, watershed management helps in minimizing soil erosion, conserving fertile topsoil and preventing land degradation. This ensures long-term sustainability of agricultural land.

Efficient utilization and conservation of water resources: Watershed management aims to harvest rainwater, enhance groundwater recharge, stabilize stream flow and ensure availability of water for irrigation, domestic use and livestock throughout the year. This is particularly important in areas facing water scarcity.

Increase agricultural productivity and farm income: Improved soil moisture availability, better land use practices and adoption of suitable cropping systems enhance crop yields and reduce the risk of crop failure in rainfed regions.

Ecological restoration and environmental protection: Through afforestation, pasture development and vegetative barriers, watershed management improves vegetation cover, restores degraded lands, enhances biodiversity and improves microclimate.

Livelihood improvement and socio-economic development of rural communities: By generating employment through watershed activities, improving availability of fodder, fuelwood and water, and encouraging community participation, it strengthens rural livelihoods and social cohesion.

Thus, watershed management is a comprehensive strategy for sustainable natural resource management, agricultural development and rural prosperity, especially in fragile and rainfed ecosystems.

Ans. (*c*) **Contract marketing** refers to a marketing arrangement in which **farmers and buyers (such as agribusiness firms, processors or exporters) enter into a prior agreement** for the production and sale of agricultural produce. The contract generally specifies conditions related to **price, quantity, quality standards, delivery time and place**, and sometimes also includes provision of inputs, technical guidance and credit by the buyer. Contract marketing aims to reduce uncertainty for both producers and buyers by linking production directly with markets.

Advantages of contract marketing: One of the major advantages is **assured market and price stability** for farmers. Since the price and buyer are fixed in advance, farmers are protected from market price fluctuations and distress sales. Contract marketing also provides **access to quality inputs, technology and extension support**, as contracting firms often supply seeds, fertilizers, pesticides and technical know-how to ensure desired quality and yield.

Contract marketing reduces **marketing risks and costs**, as farmers do not have to spend on transportation, storage and middlemen. It encourages **adoption of improved production practices**, leading to higher productivity and better quality produce. For buyers, contract marketing ensures **regular supply of uniform-quality raw material**, facilitating efficient processing and export.

Risk factors of contract marketing: Despite its benefits, contract marketing involves certain risks. Farmers may face **exploitation due to unequal bargaining power**, especially when contracts are complex or poorly regulated. In some cases, buyers may reject produce on quality grounds, leading to disputes and income loss. There is also the risk of **side-selling by farmers** when market prices rise above the contract price, undermining trust.

Production risks such as **crop failure due to pests, diseases or climatic uncertainties** can make it difficult for farmers to meet contractual obligations. Delayed payments, lack of transparency and weak legal enforcement further limit the effectiveness of contract marketing.

Thus, while contract marketing offers significant opportunities for market integration and income stability, its success depends on fair contracts, institutional support and effective regulatory mechanisms.

8. (*a*) Explain the term 'irrigation scheduling'. Give the account of the factors influencing the frequency of irrigation in crops.

(*b*) Describe the characteristics of the developed agricultural market.

(*c*) Explain farm budgeting and describe its types.

Ans. (*a*) **Irrigation scheduling** refers to the scientific determination of **when to irrigate and how much water to apply** to a crop so that soil moisture is maintained within an optimum range for plant growth. The objective of irrigation scheduling is to **maximize water-use efficiency and crop yield** while avoiding problems such as moisture stress, waterlogging, nutrient leaching and wastage of water. Proper irrigation scheduling ensures that water is supplied at the right time, in the right quantity and at the critical stages of crop growth.

The **frequency of irrigation**—that is, the interval between successive irrigations—is influenced by several interacting factors related to soil, crop, climate and management practices.

Soil factors play a major role in determining irrigation frequency. Soil texture and structure influence **water-holding capacity and infiltration rate**. Sandy soils have low water-holding capacity and require frequent but light irrigations, whereas clay soils retain more water and therefore need irrigation at longer intervals. Soil depth and organic matter content also affect moisture storage.

Crop factors significantly influence irrigation frequency. Different crops have different **root depth, water requirement and critical growth stages**. Shallow-rooted crops such as vegetables require more frequent irrigation, while deep-rooted crops like cotton and sugarcane can withstand longer intervals. The stage of crop growth is also important; irrigation is more frequent during **flowering, fruiting and grain development** stages when water demand is highest.

Climatic factors such as temperature, humidity, wind velocity and solar radiation affect **evapotranspiration rate**. High temperatures, low humidity and strong winds increase water loss from soil and plants, necessitating more frequent irrigation. Rainfall amount and distribution also influence irrigation frequency by supplementing soil moisture.

Management and field factors further modify irrigation frequency. Method of irrigation, land leveling, mulching and use of conservation practices affect water application efficiency and moisture retention. Availability of water, quality of irrigation water and economic considerations also influence irrigation decisions.

Thus, irrigation scheduling integrates soil, crop and climatic factors to ensure efficient and sustainable use of water resources in agriculture.

Ans. (*b*) A **developed agricultural market** is one that functions efficiently to ensure **fair prices to farmers, reasonable prices to consumers, smooth movement of agricultural produce and overall growth of the agricultural economy**. Such a market is characterized by organized infrastructure, transparent practices and effective institutional support.

The important characteristics of a developed agricultural market includes:

Availability of adequate physical infrastructure: This includes well-established market yards, auction platforms, godowns, warehouses, cold storage facilities, grading and processing units, and efficient transportation networks. Proper infrastructure reduces post-harvest losses and improves market efficiency.

Efficient price discovery and transparency: Prices in a developed market are determined through open competition, auction systems or electronic trading platforms, ensuring that farmers receive remunerative prices. Availability of real-time market information regarding prices, arrivals and demand helps farmers make informed marketing decisions.

Standardization and grading of produce: Produce is classified based on quality standards, which facilitates better pricing, enhances consumer confidence and promotes export competitiveness. Grading reduces disputes between buyers and sellers and rewards quality production.

Presence of regulated markets and strong institutional framework: Regulatory mechanisms prevent exploitation of farmers by middlemen, ensure proper weighing, timely payments and fair trade practices. Cooperative marketing societies and farmer producer organizations strengthen farmers' bargaining power.

Access to market services: Service like credit, insurance, storage, processing and extension support is also a hallmark of a developed market. These services reduce distress sales and encourage value addition. Integration with national and global markets through digital platforms further enhances efficiency.

Overall, a developed agricultural market promotes **market efficiency, farmer welfare, consumer protection and sustainable agricultural development** through organized, transparent and competitive marketing systems.

Ans. (*c*) **Farm budgeting** is a systematic method of **planning, estimating and evaluating the income, costs and profitability of farm enterprises** over a specific period of time. It is an important managerial tool that helps farmers and farm managers make rational decisions regarding **resource allocation, enterprise selection and financial planning**. Farm budgeting provides a quantitative basis for comparing alternative farm plans and assessing the economic feasibility of proposed changes in the farm business.

Types of farm budgeting:

Enterprise budgeting: It deals with the **costs and returns of a single crop or livestock enterprise** on the farm. This type of budgeting helps farmers decide whether to continue, expand or replace a particular enterprise.

Partial budgeting: It is used to evaluate the **financial effect of a small change in the existing farm plan**, such as introducing a new crop variety, changing fertilizer level or adopting a new practice. It considers only the additional costs and additional returns associated with the change, making it a simple and quick decision-making tool.

Whole-farm budgeting: It provides a comprehensive analysis of the **entire farm business**, taking into account all enterprises and available resources. It helps in determining the best combination of enterprises that maximizes farm income under given constraints of land, labor and capital.

Cash flow budgeting: It focuses on the **timing of cash inflows and outflows** during a production period. It helps farmers plan for credit needs, repayment schedules and liquidity management, ensuring that sufficient funds are available when expenses arise.

Comparative budgeting: It is used to **compare two or more alternative farm plans or enterprises** to determine which option is more profitable or feasible under prevailing conditions.

Thus, farm budgeting serves as a vital tool for efficient farm management, guiding decision-making, improving profitability and ensuring financial stability of the farm business.

PAPER-II

Instructions: *There are EIGHT questions in all, out of which FIVE are to be attempted, question Nos. 1 & 5 are compulsory. Out of the remaining SIX questions, THREE are to be attempted selecting at least ONE question from each of the two Sections A and B. Attempts of questions shall be counted in sequential order. Unless struck off, attempt of a question shall be counted even if attempted partly. Any page or portion of the page left blank in the Question-cum-Answer Booklet must be clearly struck off. All questions carry equal marks. Answers must be written in ENGLISH only.*

SECTION-A

1. (*a*) **Explain variation along with various components of variation. Discuss the method of plant breeding useful for creation of variability in plants.**

(*b*) **Name the public sector institutions involved in seed sector in India, with their specific roles.**

(*c*) **Discuss the term 'transpiration' and its role in plants.**

(*d*) **Enlist different organelles of a plant cell with suitable diagram and discuss the role of cell wall in a cell.**

(*e*) **Discuss the role of hybrids in enhancing productivity of major cereal crops in India.**

Ans. (*a*) **Variation** refers to the **differences observed among individuals of the same species or population** with respect to one or more characters such as height, yield, maturity, disease resistance or quality traits. Variation is the **raw material of plant breeding**, as it provides the scope for selection and genetic improvement of crops.

Components of variation: The total variation observed in a plant population is known as **phenotypic variation**, which arises due to the combined effects of genetic makeup and environmental influences.

Genetic variation is the heritable component of variation and is caused by differences in the genetic constitution of individuals. It is of prime importance in plant breeding because only genetic variation can be transmitted from one generation to the next.

Environmental variation arises due to differences in external factors such as soil fertility, climate, moisture, management practices and biotic stresses. These variations affect the expression of characters but are **not heritable**.

Plant breeding methods useful for creation of variability:

Hybridization: In this method genetically dissimilar parents are crossed to bring together desirable genes from different sources. Hybridization generates new gene combinations and wide variability in segregating generations, which can be exploited through selection.

Mutation breeding: In this approach, mutations are induced artificially using physical agents like gamma rays and X-rays or chemical mutagens such as EMS. It is particularly useful for improving one or two specific traits, such as disease resistance or plant height, without altering the overall genetic background of a variety.

Polyploidy breeding: It creates variability by increasing the number of chromosome sets using agents like colchicine. Polyploidy often results in larger plant organs, increased vigor and altered physiological traits, especially in ornamental and forage crops.

Introduction of germplasm: It also serves as an important source of variability. Exotic or indigenous germplasm often carries novel genes for yield, quality and stress resistance.

Thus, through hybridization, mutation breeding, polyploidy and germplasm introduction, plant breeders effectively create and utilize variability for crop improvement.

Ans. (*b*) The seed sector in India is supported by a well-structured **public sector institutional framework**, which plays a crucial role in **variety development, seed multiplication, quality control and distribution**. These institutions ensure availability of quality seeds to farmers and support the overall growth of agriculture.

Indian Council of Agricultural Research (ICAR): It is the apex public institution responsible for **basic and applied research in agriculture**, including crop improvement. Through its network of national research institutes and All India Coordinated Research Projects (AICRPs), ICAR develops high-yielding and stress-resistant crop varieties and produces **breeder seed**, which is the initial source in the seed multiplication chain.

National Bureau of Plant Genetic Resources: It functions under ICAR and is responsible for **collection, conservation, evaluation and exchange of plant genetic resources**. It safeguards indigenous and exotic germplasm and supplies genetically pure material for crop improvement programmes.

State Agricultural Universities: These universities play a vital role in **varietal development for specific agro-climatic regions**, production of breeder and foundation seeds, and dissemination of improved seed technologies through extension activities.

National Seeds Corporation: It is a central public sector undertaking involved in **multiplication, certification, processing, storage and marketing of quality seeds** of notified varieties across the country. It acts as a bridge between research institutions and farmers.

State Farms Corporation of India: It is primarily engaged in **large-scale production of breeder and foundation seeds**, particularly for self-pollinated crops, using government-owned farms.

In addition, **State Seed Corporations** operate at the state level to produce and distribute certified seeds suited to local conditions.

Together, these public sector institutions ensure **genetic purity, quality assurance and wide availability of seeds**, forming the backbone of India's seed sector and contributing significantly to agricultural productivity and food security.

Ans. (*c*) **Transpiration** is the physiological process by which **water is lost in the form of water vapour from the aerial parts of plants,** mainly through the stomata of leaves, and to a lesser extent through the cuticle and lenticels. It is an inevitable consequence of gaseous exchange in plants, as stomata must open to allow entry of carbon dioxide for photosynthesis, during which water vapour diffuses out into the atmosphere.

Transpiration occurs in three main forms: **stomatal transpiration**, which accounts for the major portion of water loss; **cuticular transpiration**, which takes place through the waxy cuticle of leaves; and **lenticular transpiration**, occurring through lenticels in woody stems. The rate of transpiration is influenced by both internal factors such as leaf area, stomatal density and opening, and external factors such as temperature, humidity, wind velocity and light.

Role of transpiration in plants: Transpiration plays several vital roles in plant growth and functioning. One of its most important roles is in **ascent of sap**. The continuous loss of water from leaves creates a transpiration pull, which helps in the upward movement of water and dissolved minerals from roots to aerial parts through the xylem. This ensures an uninterrupted supply of essential nutrients to growing tissues.

Transpiration also helps in **regulation of plant temperature**. Evaporation of water from leaf surfaces produces a cooling effect, protecting plants from heat injury, especially under high temperature and intense sunlight conditions. This is particularly important in tropical climates.

Another significant role of transpiration is in **maintaining cell turgidity**, which is essential for cell expansion, growth and mechanical support of herbaceous plants. Adequate transpiration ensures proper water balance within plant cells.

Transpiration further facilitates **nutrient distribution** within the plant by aiding the mass flow of mineral nutrients from the soil to different plant parts. It also indirectly supports photosynthesis by maintaining stomatal function and enabling continuous gas exchange.

Thus, transpiration is a crucial physiological process that supports water transport, temperature regulation, nutrient movement and overall growth and survival of plants.

Ans. (*d*) A **plant cell** is a highly organized structural and functional unit containing several specialized **organelles**, each performing specific functions essential for the survival, growth and metabolism of the plant.

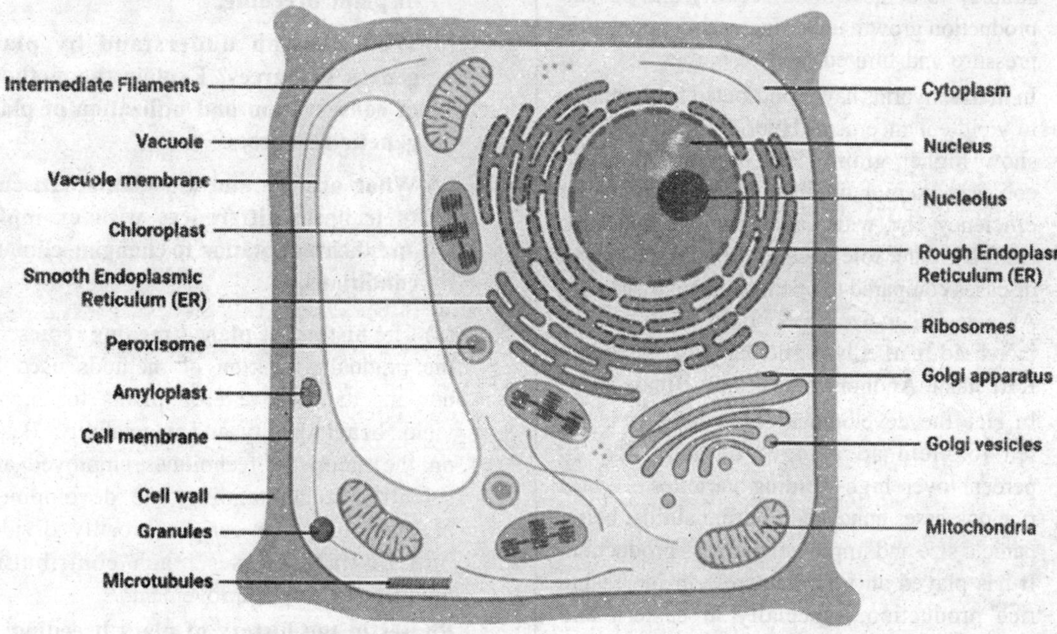

Fig.: *Plant Cell Stucture*

Role of cell wall in a plant cell: The **cell wall** is a non-living, rigid structure composed mainly of **cellulose, hemicellulose and pectin**, and is unique to plant cells. Its primary role is to provide **mechanical strength and structural support**, enabling plants to maintain shape and rigidity. The cell wall protects the cell from mechanical injury and pathogen attack.

The cell wall plays a crucial role in **maintaining cell turgidity**. It also facilitates **cell-to-cell interaction and transport** through structures like plasmodesmata, allowing movement of water, nutrients and signaling molecules between adjacent cells.

Additionally, the cell wall influences **cell growth and differentiation** by regulating the direction and extent of cell expansion. It also acts as a **barrier against toxic substances** and contributes to overall plant defense. Thus, the cell wall is fundamental to the structural integrity, protection and physiological functioning of plant cells.

Ans. (*e*) Hybrids have played a significant role in **enhancing the productivity of major cereal crops in India** by exploiting the phenomenon of **heterosis (hybrid vigor)**, whereby the first-generation (F_1) progeny exhibits superior performance over its parents in terms of yield, vigor, adaptability and stress tolerance. The adoption of hybrid cereals has been an important component of India's strategy to achieve food security and sustain production growth under increasing population pressure and limited land resources.

In **maize**, hybrids have contributed substantially to yield enhancement. Hybrid maize varieties show higher grain yield due to improved cob size, kernel number, better nutrient-use efficiency and wider adaptability. They also exhibit greater tolerance to drought, pests and diseases compared to open-pollinated varieties. As a result, maize productivity in India has increased markedly particularly in states like Karnataka, Andhra Pradesh and Bihar.

In **rice** the development of **hybrid rice** has led to yield advantages of about 15–20 percent over high-yielding varieties. Hybrid rice possesses enhanced tillering ability, better panicle size and improved biomass production. It has played an important role in increasing rice production, especially in eastern and northern India, where yield gaps were large.

In **sorghum and pearl millet**, hybrids have been highly successful due to the natural cross-pollinated nature of these crops. Hybrid pearl millet and sorghum varieties exhibit improved grain yield, better fodder quality and resistance to biotic and abiotic stresses. These hybrids have been particularly beneficial in arid and semi-arid regions, contributing to food and fodder security.

Hybrid cereals also promote **uniformity, early maturity and better response to inputs**, enabling farmers to adopt intensive and mechanized farming practices. However, their success depends on assured seed supply, proper crop management and favorable agro-climatic conditions.

Overall, hybrids have significantly contributed to increasing cereal productivity in India by enhancing yield potential, stability and resilience, thereby strengthening national food security.

2. (*a*) **Write the various phases of history of plant breeding and describe the importance of genetic engineering phase of plant breeding.**

(*b*) **What do you understand by plant genetic resources? Explain the methods of conservation and utilization of plant genetic resources.**

(*c*) **What are C_3 and C_4 plants? Discuss their basic differences with examples and their adaptation to changing climatic conditions.**

Ans. (*a*) The **history of plant breeding** represents the gradual evolution of methods used by humans to improve crop plants for higher yield, better quality and adaptability. Based on the nature of techniques employed and scientific understanding, the development of plant breeding can be broadly divided into **distinct phases**, each contributing uniquely to crop improvement.

Phases in the history of plant breeding:

Domestication and selection phase: This phase began with the origin of agriculture. Early farmers unconsciously selected plants with desirable traits such as larger seeds, non-shattering ears and better taste. This mass selection laid the foundation for cultivated crops.

Classical plant breeding phase: This phase developed after the rediscovery of Mendel's laws in the early 20th century. This phase involved systematic **hybridization and selection**, use of pure-line selection, pedigree breeding and backcross breeding. It led to the development of high-yielding varieties with improved agronomic traits.

Mutation breeding phase: In this phase genetic variability was artificially induced using physical and chemical mutagens. This phase helped in improving specific traits such as disease resistance, plant height and maturity without altering the overall genetic background of varieties.

Polyploidy and cytogenetics phase: It contributed to understanding chromosome behavior and manipulation of chromosome number to develop improved varieties, especially in crops like wheat and ornamental plants.

Genetic engineering (biotechnology) phase: This is the most recent and advanced phase which marks a major shift from conventional breeding methods.

Importance of the genetic engineering phase of plant breeding: The genetic engineering phase is highly significant because it allows **direct transfer of specific genes across species barriers**, which is not possible through conventional breeding. This has greatly expanded the genetic base available for crop improvement. Traits such as **insect resistance, herbicide tolerance, disease resistance and abiotic stress tolerance** have been successfully introduced into crops through genetic engineering.

Genetic engineering enables **precision breeding**, as specific genes of known function can be inserted without disturbing other desirable traits of elite varieties. This reduces the time required for varietal development compared to traditional breeding methods, which involve repeated crossing and selection over many generations.

This phase has also contributed to **enhanced crop productivity and reduced input use**, as seen in insect-resistant Bt crops that lower pesticide requirements. It supports development of crops with **improved nutritional quality**, such as biofortified crops, thereby addressing malnutrition.

Overall, the genetic engineering phase represents a transformative stage in plant breeding, offering powerful tools to meet challenges of food security, climate change and sustainable agriculture.

Ans. (*b*) **Plant genetic resources (PGR)** refer to the **genetic material of plant origin that has actual or potential value for present and future generations**. They include seeds, planting materials or tissues containing genes that determine important traits such as yield potential, quality, resistance to pests and diseases, and tolerance to abiotic stresses like drought, salinity and heat. They also form the **biological foundation of agriculture and food security**, as all crop improvement depends on the availability and diversity of these genetic materials.

Plant genetic resources comprise **landraces, modern cultivars, obsolete varieties, wild relatives of crops, breeding lines and genetic stocks**. In countries like India, which is one of the centres of origin and diversity for several crops, conservation and proper utilization of PGR are critically important.

Methods of conservation of plant genetic resources: Conservation of PGR aims to protect genetic diversity from erosion and loss. It is carried out mainly through **in situ** and **ex-situ** approaches.

- **In situ conservation** involves the conservation of plant genetic resources **in their natural habitats or traditional farming systems**. This includes conservation of wild relatives of crops in forests, protected areas and biosphere reserves, as well as on-farm conservation of landraces by farmers. In situ conservation allows continuous evolution and adaptation of genetic resources under natural conditions.

- **Ex situ conservation** involves conservation of genetic resources **outside their natural habitats**. The most common method is **seed storage in gene banks**, where seeds are stored under controlled temperature and humidity to maintain viability for long periods. For crops with recalcitrant seeds or vegetatively propagated crops, methods such as **field gene banks, in vitro conservation and cryopreservation** are used. Botanical gardens also play a role in ex situ conservation.

Methods of utilization of plant genetic resources: Utilization of PGR is mainly carried out through **plant breeding and crop improvement programmes**. Genetic resources are used as sources of genes for **high yield, quality improvement, resistance to pests and diseases, and tolerance to abiotic stresses**. Wild relatives and landraces often possess unique genes that are absent in modern cultivars and are therefore used in hybridization and pre-breeding programmes.

Plant genetic resources are also utilized in **direct cultivation**, especially in marginal environments where traditional varieties perform better than improved varieties. Additionally, PGR are used in **biotechnological applications**, such as genetic engineering and molecular breeding, to transfer specific desirable genes into elite varieties.

Thus, effective conservation and systematic utilization of plant genetic resources are essential for sustainable agriculture, crop improvement and long-term food security.

Ans. (*c*) **C_3 and C_4 plants** are classified on the basis of the **pathway through which carbon dioxide (CO_2) is fixed during photosynthesis**. The classification reflects fundamental differences in their photosynthetic mechanisms, anatomical features, efficiency of CO_2 utilization and adaptation to environmental conditions.

C_3 plants: C_3 plants are those in which the **first stable product of photosynthesis is a three-carbon compound**, 3-phosphoglyceric acid (PGA). CO_2 fixation occurs directly through the enzyme **RuBisCO** in the mesophyll cells via the Calvin cycle. This pathway is the most primitive and widespread form of photosynthesis.

C_3 plants are typically adapted to **cool, moist and temperate climates** where light intensity and temperature are moderate. However, RuBisCO also has oxygenase activity, leading to **photorespiration**, especially under high temperature, high light intensity and low CO_2 conditions. Photorespiration causes loss of fixed carbon and reduces photosynthetic efficiency.

Examples of C_3 plants include **wheat, rice, barley, soybean, potato and most temperate grasses**.

C_4 plants: C_4 plants are characterized by a specialized photosynthetic pathway in which the **first stable product is a four-carbon compound**, oxaloacetic acid (OAA). CO_2 fixation initially occurs in the mesophyll cells through the enzyme **PEP carboxylase**, which has a high affinity for CO_2 and no oxygenase activity. The CO_2 is then transported to bundle sheath cells, where it is released and re-fixed by RuBisCO in the Calvin cycle. This spatial separation of CO_2 fixation and reduction is associated with **Kranz anatomy**.

C_4 plants are well adapted to **high temperature, high light intensity and dry environments**. The C_4 pathway effectively suppresses photorespiration, resulting in **higher photosynthetic efficiency, better water-use efficiency and greater productivity** under stress conditions.

Examples of C_4 plants include **maize, sorghum, pearl millet, sugarcane and several tropical grasses**.

Basic differences and adaptation to changing climatic conditions: C_3 plants perform better under **lower temperatures and higher atmospheric CO_2 concentrations**, but they are more sensitive to heat and drought stress due to high photorespiration and lower water-use efficiency. In contrast, C_4 plants are better adapted to **warming climates**, as they maintain high photosynthetic rates even at elevated temperatures and low CO_2 levels. Their efficient CO_2 fixation mechanism and reduced transpiration make them more resilient to **climate change–induced heat and moisture stress**.

Thus, while C_3 plants dominate cooler regions, C_4 plants are likely to gain increasing importance under **future climatic scenarios** characterized by higher temperatures and variable rainfall.

3. (*a*) Explain gene pool concept along with different groups of gene pools. Name the scientist who proposed centres of origin along with the total number of centres of origin of plants in the world.

(*b*) Describe the suitable methods of plant breeding along with their application for development of disease-resistant varieties in crops, with suitable examples.

(*c*) Write the various laws of heredity given by Mendel. Discuss the significance of the law of dominance in plant breeding.

Ans. (*a*) The **gene pool concept** refers to the **total genetic diversity available within a species and its related forms**, which can be utilized in plant breeding for crop improvement. It represents the entire range of genes and alleles that exist in cultivated plants and their related wild and weedy relatives. The concept is fundamental in determining the **ease or difficulty of gene transfer** during breeding programmes.

Groups of gene pools: Based on crossability and fertility of hybrids, gene pools are classified into three groups.

The **primary gene pool (GP_1)** includes the cultivated species itself and its wild or weedy forms that can **freely intercross** with it, producing fertile offspring. Gene transfer within this pool is easy using conventional breeding methods. For example, cultivated wheat and its closely related forms belong to the primary gene pool of wheat.

The **secondary gene pool (GP_2)** consists of species that are **closely related but not fully crossable** with the cultivated species. Crosses are possible, but hybrids may show reduced fertility or require special techniques such as embryo rescue. Genes from this pool are often used for introducing disease resistance or stress tolerance.

The **tertiary gene pool (GP_3)** includes **distantly related species** that do not naturally cross with the cultivated species. Gene transfer from this pool is extremely difficult and usually requires advanced techniques such as chromosome manipulation, somatic hybridization or genetic engineering. Despite the difficulty, this pool is an important source of novel genes.

Thus, the gene pool concept helps plant breeders identify **appropriate genetic resources and breeding strategies** for crop improvement.

Centres of origin of plants: The concept of **centres of origin of cultivated plants** was proposed by **Nikolai Ivanovich Vavilov**, a Russian scientist and plant geneticist. According to Vavilov, centres of origin are geographical regions where crops were first domesticated and where **maximum genetic diversity** of those crops and their wild relatives is found.

Vavilov initially identified **eight primary centres of origin**, which were later expanded to **twelve centres of origin of cultivated plants** in the world. These centres include regions such as China, India, Central Asia, the Near East, the Mediterranean, Ethiopia, Central America and South America.

The concept of centres of origin is of great significance in plant breeding, as these regions serve as **rich reservoirs of genetic variability**, essential for crop improvement and conservation of plant genetic resources.

Ans. (*b*) Development of **disease-resistant varieties** is one of the most important objectives of plant breeding, as diseases cause heavy yield losses and increase dependence on chemical control. Various **plant breeding methods** have been successfully used to incorporate resistance genes into crop plants, depending on the nature of resistance, inheritance pattern and availability of genetic variability.

One of the most widely used methods is **selection**. When disease resistance is controlled by one or few major genes and sufficient natural variability exists, resistant plants can be selected directly from local landraces or populations. **Mass selection and pure line selection** have been used to develop disease-resistant varieties in self-pollinated crops. For example, rust-resistant wheat lines have been developed through selection from traditional populations.

Hybridization followed by selection is the most important and commonly used method for developing disease-resistant varieties. In this method, a disease-resistant parent is crossed with a high-yielding but susceptible variety, and desirable recombinants are selected in segregating generations. This approach helps in combining disease resistance with superior agronomic traits. For instance, resistance to **leaf rust and stem rust in wheat** and **blast resistance in rice** has been developed using this method.

Backcross breeding is particularly suitable when resistance is governed by a single major gene and the objective is to transfer resistance into an already well-adapted variety. This method has been extensively used for incorporating **bacterial blight resistance in rice** and **rust resistance in wheat** without altering the desirable characteristics of popular varieties.

Mutation breeding is useful when resistance genes are not available in the existing gene pool or when minor modifications are required. Mutations induced by physical or chemical mutagens create new genetic variation, some of which may confer disease resistance. For example, **powdery mildew-resistant barley varieties** and disease-tolerant rice lines have been developed through mutation breeding.

Wide hybridization involves crossing cultivated crops with their wild relatives, which often possess strong resistance to diseases. Although such crosses may face fertility barriers, they serve as valuable sources of novel resistance genes. Resistance to **late blight in potato** and **rusts in wheat** has been obtained from wild species using this approach.

In recent years, **biotechnological methods**, including marker-assisted selection and genetic engineering, have strengthened conventional breeding by enabling precise identification and transfer of resistance genes. Thus, through a combination of classical and modern breeding methods, durable disease-resistant crop varieties have been successfully developed to ensure stable agricultural productivity.

Ans. (*c*) The **laws of heredity**, proposed by **Gregor Johann Mendel**, explain the fundamental principles governing the inheritance of characters from parents to offspring. These laws were derived from Mendel's experiments on garden pea (*Pisum sativum*) and form the foundation of classical genetics and plant breeding.

Laws of heredity given by Mendel: The **Law of Dominance** states that when two contrasting alleles of a character are present together in a heterozygous condition, only one allele expresses itself, known as the dominant allele, while the other remains unexpressed and is called recessive. As a result, the phenotype of the hybrid resembles that of the dominant parent.

The **Law of Segregation** states that the two alleles of a gene separate or segregate from each other during gamete formation, so that each gamete carries only one allele. This ensures that alleles remain discrete and do not blend, and normal diploid condition is restored at fertilization.

The **Law of Independent Assortment** states that alleles of different genes assort independently of one another during gamete formation, provided the genes are located on different chromosomes or are sufficiently far apart on the same chromosome. This law explains the occurrence of new combinations of traits in offspring.

Significance of the law of dominance in plant breeding: The law of dominance is of great practical importance in plant breeding because it explains the **expression of desirable traits in hybrids**. When favorable dominant genes are present, they can mask undesirable recessive alleles, allowing breeders to achieve improved performance in the first generation itself. This principle forms the genetic basis of **hybrid vigor (heterosis)**, which is extensively exploited in crops such as maize, rice, sorghum and pearl millet.

The law of dominance helps breeders in **selection and fixation of traits,** as recessive traits can be identified and fixed only in homozygous condition through careful breeding. It also aids in predicting the outcome of crosses and planning breeding strategies, especially when dealing with monogenic traits such as disease resistance, dwarfness or quality characters.

Thus, the law of dominance provides a scientific basis for hybrid development, selection of superior genotypes and efficient utilization of genetic variability in plant breeding programmes.

4. (*a*) Describe cytoplasmic inheritance along with sex-linked, sex-limited and sex-influenced characters with suitable examples.

(*b*) Define various parameters of field and seed standards adopted in quality seed production programmes in cross-pollinated crops in India.

(*c*) Write the various types of male sterility available in plants and describe the commercial application of male sterility in vegetable seed production.

Ans. (*a*) Inheritance of characters in organisms is not always governed solely by nuclear genes following Mendelian principles. Certain traits are controlled by genes located outside the nucleus or are associated with sex chromosomes or sex expression. These include **cytoplasmic inheritance, sex-linked, sex-limited** and **sex-influenced characters**, each having distinct genetic mechanisms and significance.

Cytoplasmic inheritance: Cytoplasmic inheritance refers to the transmission of characters controlled by **genes present in the cytoplasm rather than in the nucleus**. These genes are usually located in organelles such as **mitochondria and chloroplasts**, which are inherited predominantly from the female parent through the egg cytoplasm. As a result, cytoplasmic inheritance generally shows **maternal inheritance** and does not follow Mendelian segregation ratios.

A classic example in plants is **leaf variegation in Mirabilis jalapa (four o'clock plant)**, where green, white or variegated leaves depend on the type of plastids present in the egg cell. Another important agricultural example is **cytoplasmic male sterility (CMS)** in crops like maize, rice and sorghum, which is widely exploited in hybrid seed production.

Sex-linked characters: Sex-linked characters are controlled by genes located on the **sex chromosomes**, most commonly the X chromosome. Because males and females differ in their sex chromosome composition, the inheritance and expression of these traits differ between sexes. In X-linked traits, males express the character even if the allele is recessive, as they possess only one X chromosome.

Examples include **colour blindness and haemophilia in humans**. In plants, sex-linked inheritance has been reported in dioecious species, such as **sex-linked leaf colour traits in spinach**.

Sex-limited characters: Sex-limited characters are traits that are **controlled by autosomal genes but expressed only in one sex**, even though the genes are present in both sexes. Their expression depends on the physiological environment associated with a particular sex. Examples include **milk production in female cattle** and **egg laying in hens**, which are not expressed in males despite having the same genes. In plants, sex-limited traits are seen in dioecious species where certain floral or reproductive traits are expressed only in male or female plants.

Sex-influenced characters: Sex-influenced characters are traits controlled by **autosomal genes whose expression differs in dominance or intensity between males and females**. The same genotype produces different phenotypes depending on the sex of the individual.

A common example is **pattern baldness in humans**, which is dominant in males but recessive in females. In animals, horn development in sheep is another example, where horns are dominant in males but recessive in females.

Ans. (*b*) In **quality seed production programmes of cross-pollinated crops in India**, strict **field standards and seed standards** are prescribed to maintain **genetic purity, physical purity and physiological quality** of seed. These standards are framed and implemented under the Indian seed certification system to prevent genetic contamination caused by natural cross-pollination.

Field standards for cross-pollinated crops

Field standards are requirements that must be met **during crop growth in the field** before seed harvest.

Isolation distance: Isolation distance is the **minimum distance required between a seed crop and any other crop of the same species or related species** to prevent foreign pollen contamination. Since cross-pollinated crops are highly prone to pollen flow, larger isolation distances are prescribed compared to self-pollinated crops.

- Breeder seed requires the **maximum isolation distance**, followed by foundation and certified seed.
- Example: In maize, isolation distance is very high due to wind pollination.

Off-types: Off-types are plants that **do not conform to the varietal characteristics**. The permissible percentage of off-types is kept **very low** in cross-pollinated crops to preserve genetic uniformity.

- Breeder seed has **zero or negligible tolerance**.
- Certified seed allows slightly higher tolerance.

Pollen shedders (in hybrids): In hybrid seed production involving male sterility, pollen shedders in female rows are **strictly limited**, as they cause self-pollination and reduce hybrid purity.

Objectionable weeds: Presence of weeds that can **cause admixture or act as alternate hosts** is either completely prohibited or kept within very low limits.

Roguing: Timely removal of off-types, diseased plants and pollen shedders at different growth stages is mandatory.

Seed standards for cross-pollinated crops: Seed standards are assessed **after harvest and processing** to ensure quality of the seed lot.

Physical purity: Minimum percentage of pure seed required, ensuring freedom from inert matter, weed seeds and other crop seeds. Generally, **higher purity standards** are prescribed.

Germination percentage: Minimum germination capacity to ensure good field establishment. Cross-pollinated crops generally require **moderate to high germination standards** depending on crop species.

Genetic purity: Genetic purity ensures that the seed belongs to the **true variety or hybrid**. In cross-pollinated crops, genetic purity standards are very stringent due to higher risk of contamination.

Moisture content: Safe moisture limits are prescribed to maintain seed viability during storage, usually **8–10%**, depending on crop and storage conditions.

Seed health: Seeds must be free from **designated seed-borne diseases**, especially those affecting large areas.

Significance

These field and seed standards together ensure that **cross-pollinated crops retain varietal identity, high yield potential and uniform performance**, which is essential for farmer confidence and sustainable seed systems in India.

Thus, strict adherence to field and seed standards forms the backbone of **quality seed production programmes in cross-pollinated crops**.

Ans. (*c*) **Male sterility** refers to the **inability of a plant to produce functional pollen**, while the female reproductive organs remain normal and fertile. Male sterility is of great significance in plant breeding because it facilitates **controlled cross-pollination without the need for manual emasculation**, thereby reducing cost and labour and ensuring genetic purity of hybrids.

Types of male sterility in plants

Genetic male sterility (GMS): Genetic male sterility is controlled by **nuclear genes**, usually governed by a single recessive gene. Male-sterile plants segregate in the progeny and require identification and removal of fertile plants for maintenance. Although useful, its commercial application is limited due to difficulty in maintaining pure male-sterile lines. GMS has been reported in crops like tomato and chilli.

Cytoplasmic male sterility (CMS): Cytoplasmic male sterility is controlled by **cytoplasmic (mitochondrial) genes** and is maternally inherited. Male sterility is stable and does not segregate, making it highly suitable for hybrid seed production. However, fertility cannot be restored unless a specific restorer gene is present. CMS systems are widely used in crops such as onion, carrot and cabbage.

Cytoplasmic–genetic male sterility (CGMS): CGMS is controlled by an **interaction between cytoplasmic genes and nuclear restorer genes**. In this system, male sterility is expressed in the absence of restorer genes and fertility is restored when restorer genes are present. CGMS is the most commercially exploited system, as it allows easy maintenance of male-sterile lines and large-scale hybrid seed production. It is extensively used in crops like onion, carrot, radish and several cereals.

Environmental-sensitive genic male sterility (EGMS): In this type, expression of male sterility is influenced by **environmental factors** such as temperature or photoperiod. It includes thermo-sensitive and photo-sensitive male sterility. EGMS systems are useful in two-line breeding programmes, though their use requires precise environmental control.

Commercial application of male sterility in vegetable seed production

Male sterility has revolutionized **hybrid vegetable seed production** by eliminating the need for hand emasculation. In vegetables such as **onion, carrot, cabbage, cauliflower, radish and tomato**, CMS and CGMS systems are widely used. Male-sterile female lines are planted alongside fertile male lines in suitable row ratios. Since the female plants do not produce pollen, all seeds set on them are **hybrid seeds resulting from cross-pollination**.

The major advantages include **reduction in labour cost**, **higher genetic purity of hybrids**, **large-scale seed production**, and **uniform hybrid performance**. Male sterility also ensures effective exploitation of **heterosis**, leading to higher yield, better quality and improved adaptability of vegetable crops.

Thus, male sterility is a cornerstone technology in modern vegetable seed production, enabling economical and efficient development of high-yielding hybrid varieties.

SECTION-B

5. (*a*) **Describe the plug-tray nursery production technology in vegetables, along with its advantages.**

(*b*) **Enlist the major fungal and bacterial diseases of Solanaceous vegetables along with their effective management.**

(*c*) **What are the different types of fungi invasions in storage of pulses in India? Explain the different methods of their control.**

(*d*) **Write a short note on microbial toxins.**

(*e*) **Discuss the prime features of National Food Security Act, 2013.**

Ans. (*a*) **Plug-tray nursery production technology** is a modern and scientific method of raising vegetable seedlings in **small individual cells (plugs)** of plastic trays using a **soilless or sterilized growing medium** under controlled conditions. This technology ensures production of **healthy, uniform and vigorous seedlings**, which are essential for achieving high yield and better crop establishment in vegetables.

In this system, plastic plug trays having a fixed number of cavities (commonly 50, 98, 104 or 128 cells) are used. Each cell is filled with a **light, porous and sterile growing medium**, usually a mixture of cocopeat, vermiculite and perlite. Seeds are sown individually in each cavity, ensuring one seedling per cell. After sowing, trays are kept in protected structures such as **polyhouses, shade nets or net houses**, where temperature, humidity and moisture are managed properly. Irrigation is done through fine misting or micro-sprinklers to avoid disturbance of seeds and seedlings.

Seedlings raised through plug-tray technology develop a **compact and intact root ball**, as roots are confined within the cell. This minimizes root damage during transplanting and ensures quick establishment in the main field. Crops like **tomato, brinjal, chilli, capsicum, cabbage, cauliflower and onion** are commonly raised using this method.

Advantages of plug-tray nursery production: One of the major advantages is the **production of uniform and healthy seedlings**, which leads to uniform crop growth and maturity in the field. The use of sterile growing media and protected conditions significantly **reduces the incidence of soil-borne diseases and pests**, lowering seedling mortality.

Plug-tray seedlings experience **minimal transplanting shock**, as the root system remains intact, resulting in better survival rate and faster establishment. This technology allows **efficient use of seeds**, which is particularly important for costly hybrid seeds, as each seed is sown separately and wastage is avoided.

Another important advantage is **better nursery management and space efficiency**, as a large number of seedlings can be raised in a small area. The nursery period is shortened, enabling **early and timely transplanting**, which ultimately improves crop productivity. Additionally, plug-tray technology supports **round-the-year seedling production** under protected conditions.

Thus, plug-tray nursery production technology plays a vital role in modern vegetable cultivation by ensuring quality planting material, higher yield potential and efficient use of resources.

Ans. (*b*) Solanaceous vegetables such as **tomato, brinjal (eggplant), chilli and capsicum** are highly susceptible to several **fungal and**

bacterial diseases, which cause serious yield and quality losses. Effective management requires an **integrated approach** combining cultural, chemical and biological methods.

Major fungal diseases and their management

Early blight (Alternaria solani): Common in tomato and potato, characterized by concentric ring spots on leaves. Management includes use of **disease-free seed**, crop rotation, removal of infected plant debris and spraying of **protective fungicides** such as mancozeb or chlorothalonil.

Late blight (Phytophthora infestans): Severe disease of tomato and potato causing rapid leaf and fruit rot under cool, humid conditions. Management involves growing **resistant varieties**, ensuring proper drainage, and timely application of **systemic fungicides** like metalaxyl + mancozeb.

Fusarium wilt (Fusarium oxysporum): A soil-borne disease causing yellowing and wilting of plants, common in tomato and brinjal. Management includes **soil solarization**, use of resistant varieties, seedling treatment with **Trichoderma**, and crop rotation.

Powdery mildew (Leveillula taurica / Oidium spp.): Causes white powdery growth on leaves of chilli and capsicum. Management involves maintaining proper spacing, avoiding excess nitrogen, and spraying **sulphur or systemic fungicides.**

Major bacterial diseases and their management

Bacterial wilt (Ralstonia solanacearum): A devastating disease of tomato, brinjal and chilli causing sudden wilting without yellowing. Management includes use of **wilt-resistant varieties**, crop rotation with non-host crops, soil solarization and avoidance of waterlogging.

Bacterial leaf spot (Xanthomonas spp.): Seen in tomato and chilli, producing small water-soaked lesions on leaves and fruits. Management involves use of **disease-free seed**, seed treatment with hot water or chemicals, and spraying of **copper-based bactericides**.

Bacterial canker (Clavibacter michiganensis): A serious disease of tomato causing leaf scorching and stem cankers. Management includes strict sanitation, seed treatment, crop rotation and application of **copper fungicides with antibiotics** where permitted.

Integrated disease management approach

Effective control of fungal and bacterial diseases in solanaceous vegetables depends on:

- Use of **resistant or tolerant varieties**
- **Healthy nursery management** and seed treatment
- Crop rotation and field sanitation
- Balanced fertilization and proper irrigation
- Judicious use of fungicides and bactericides
- Adoption of biological control agents

Thus, timely identification and integrated management of fungal and bacterial diseases are essential for sustainable production of solanaceous vegetables.

Ans. (*c*) Stored pulses in India are highly susceptible to **fungal invasion**, particularly under conditions of **high moisture, poor ventilation and warm temperatures**. Fungal infestation not only reduces grain quality and market value but also leads to **loss of viability, discoloration, heating and production of mycotoxins**, posing serious health hazards.

Types of fungal invasions in storage of pulses:

Field fungi invasion: These fungi infect pulses **before harvest or at the time of harvest** and persist into storage. They require relatively high moisture content and are common when harvesting is delayed or drying is inadequate. Important field fungi include *Fusarium*, *Alternaria* and *Cladosporium*. They cause seed discoloration, shrivelling and reduced germination.

Storage fungi invasion: Storage fungi develop **during storage**, even at lower moisture levels than field fungi. They are the most damaging group in stored pulses. Important storage fungi include *Aspergillus* spp. (such as *A. flavus* and *A. niger*) and *Penicillium* spp. These fungi grow rapidly under warm and humid conditions and are responsible for **heating, moulding and mycotoxin production**, especially aflatoxins in pulses.

Advanced deterioration fungi: When storage conditions are extremely poor, secondary fungi invade already damaged grains. These fungi accelerate spoilage, causing complete deterioration of stored pulses.

Methods of control of fungal invasion in stored pulses:

Proper drying: Pulses should be dried to a **safe moisture content (generally below 10%)** before storage. Adequate drying is the most effective method to prevent fungal growth.

Improved storage structures: Use of **moisture-proof, well-ventilated and clean storage structures** such as metal bins, improved godowns and airtight containers prevents moisture ingress and fungal development.

Sanitation and hygiene: Storage premises, bags and containers should be thoroughly cleaned and disinfected before use. Removal of old infested residues helps prevent carryover of fungal spores.

Chemical control: Use of **approved fungicidal seed protectants** or surface disinfectants helps suppress fungal growth. In large-scale storage, fumigation and surface treatment of storage structures may be practiced, following safety guidelines.

Use of botanicals and traditional methods: Neem leaves, neem oil and other plant-based materials are traditionally used in India to reduce fungal and insect infestation in stored pulses.

Environmental control: Maintaining **low temperature and low relative humidity** inside storage facilities significantly reduces fungal activity and prolongs storage life.

Thus, effective management of fungal invasion in stored pulses requires **proper pre-storage drying, scientific storage methods and good storage hygiene**, ensuring both quality preservation and food safety.

Ans. (*d*) Microbial toxins are **toxic substances produced by microorganisms**, mainly bacteria and fungi, as secondary metabolites during their growth and metabolism. These toxins are harmful to humans, animals and plants, even when present in very small quantities, and they pose serious risks to food safety, public health and agricultural productivity.

Microbial toxins are broadly classified into **bacterial toxins** and **mycotoxins** (fungal toxins). **Bacterial toxins** include exotoxins and endotoxins. Exotoxins are actively secreted by bacteria and are highly specific and potent; examples include botulinum toxin and tetanus toxin. Endotoxins are components of the bacterial cell wall, mainly lipopolysaccharides of Gram-negative bacteria, and are released upon cell death, causing fever and inflammatory responses.

Mycotoxins are toxic compounds produced by certain storage and field fungi, particularly species of *Aspergillus*, *Penicillium* and *Fusarium*. Important mycotoxins include **aflatoxins**, **ochratoxins**, **fumonisins** and **zearalen** Aflatoxins, produced mainly by *Aspergillus flavus* and *A. parasiticus*, are among the most dangerous, being **highly carcinogenic and hepatotoxic**. They commonly contaminate cereals, pulses, oilseeds and nuts under warm and humid storage conditions.

Microbial toxins cause a wide range of adverse effects such as **food poisoning, liver damage, immune suppression, reduced growth and even death**. In agriculture, they reduce the quality, marketability and germination capacity of seeds and grains.

Prevention and control of microbial toxins involve **proper drying, safe storage, sanitation, temperature and moisture control**, use of resistant varieties and adherence to food safety regulations. Thus, microbial toxins represent a major concern in food and agricultural systems due to their severe health and economic impacts.

Ans. (*e*) The **National Food Security Act (NFSA), 2013** is a landmark legislation enacted by the Government of India with the objective of **providing food and nutritional security to a large section of the population** by ensuring access to adequate quantity of quality food at affordable prices. The Act adopts a **rights-based approach**, making food security a legal entitlement rather than a welfare measure.

One of the prime features of the Act is the **coverage of population**. It provides food security to **up to 75% of the rural population and 50% of the urban population**, covering nearly two-thirds of India's total population. Beneficiaries are identified under two categories: **Antyodaya Anna Yojana (AAY) households** and **Priority Households (PHH)**.

Under NFSA, **entitled households receive subsidized food grains** through the Public Distribution System (PDS). Priority households are entitled to **5 kg of food grains per person per month**, while AAY households receive **35 kg per household per month**. The subsidized prices are **₹ 3 per kg for rice, ₹ 2 per kg for wheat and ₹ 1 per kg for coarse grains**, ensuring affordability for the poor.

The Act places special emphasis on **nutritional support to women and children**. Pregnant women and lactating mothers are entitled to **free meals during pregnancy and six months after childbirth**, along with a **maternity benefit of not less than ₹ 6,000**. Children in the age group of **6 months to 14 years** are entitled to free nutritious meals through **Integrated Child Development Services (ICDS)** and **Mid-Day Meal Scheme**.

Another important feature is the **women-centric approach**. The eldest woman of the household (18 years or above) is designated as the **head of the household** for the purpose of issuing ration cards, promoting women's empowerment.

The Act also provides for **grievance redressal mechanisms**, transparency and accountability. Provisions for **social audits**, vigilance committees and penalty for non-compliance ensure effective implementation. States are responsible for identification of beneficiaries and delivery of entitlements, while the central government provides food grains and financial assistance.

Thus, the National Food Security Act, 2013 represents a comprehensive and rights-based framework aimed at reducing hunger, malnutrition and poverty, while strengthening India's food distribution system.

6. (*a*) **Describe the package of practices of Pomegranate cultivation in India along with major challenges in its cultivation in arid and semi-arid regions.**

(*b*) **Why are millets called 'Nutri-cereals' ? Discuss the initiatives of Government of India to increase production and consumption of millets in the country.**

(*c*) **Explain seed dormancy and its types, with reasons for induction. Discuss in brief about the mechanisms to break dormancy in seeds.**

Ans. (*a*) **Pomegranate (Punica granatum L.)** is an important commercial fruit crop of India, well adapted to **arid and semi-arid regions** due to its drought tolerance and ability to withstand high temperatures. India is one of the leading producers of pomegranate, with major cultivation in Maharashtra, Karnataka, Gujarat, Andhra Pradesh and Tamil Nadu.

Package of practices for pomegranate cultivation

Climate and soil: Pomegranate thrives best in **hot, dry climates** with cool winters. Dry conditions during flowering and fruit development favor good fruit quality, while excessive humidity encourages disease incidence. The crop performs well in **deep, well-drained loamy soils**, but can also grow in light soils. Slightly alkaline soils are tolerated, though waterlogging is highly detrimental.

Varieties: Popular varieties grown in India include **Bhagwa, Ganesh, Arakta, Ruby and Mridula**, selected for high yield, attractive fruit colour and export quality.

Propagation and planting: Pomegranate is commonly propagated through **hardwood cuttings or air layering**. Planting is usually done at a spacing of **4 m × 4 m or 5 m × 5 m**, depending on soil fertility and management. Proper pit preparation with organic manures improves early establishment.

Training and pruning: Plants are trained to a **multi-stem system** (3–4 stems), which is suitable for dry regions. Regular pruning helps in removal of dead, diseased and crossing branches, improves aeration and enhances fruiting.

Irrigation management: Although pomegranate is drought tolerant, **regulated irrigation** is essential for commercial production. Drip irrigation is widely adopted to conserve water and improve water-use efficiency. Excess irrigation or irregular watering leads to fruit cracking.

Manuring and fertilization: Balanced nutrition is essential for sustained yield. Application of **farmyard manure along with NPK fertilizers** is recommended. Micronutrients such as zinc and boron are important for fruit set and quality, especially in deficient soils.

Flowering regulation (Bahar treatment): To synchronize flowering and fruiting, **bahar treatment** (Mrig, Hasta or Ambe bahar) is practiced by withholding irrigation, followed by pruning and fertilizer application. This is a unique and critical practice in pomegranate cultivation.

Plant protection: Major pests include **anar butterfly and thrips**, while diseases such as **bacterial blight and wilt** are serious constraints. Integrated pest and disease management practices are essential.

Harvesting: Fruits are harvested when they attain full size, colour and sweetness. Proper harvesting ensures good shelf life and market value.

Major challenges in arid and semi-arid regions

One of the major challenges is **water scarcity and erratic rainfall**, which affects flowering, fruit set and size. Improper irrigation leads to **fruit cracking**, a common physiological disorder in dry regions. High temperature and hot winds cause **sunburn and poor fruit quality**.

Soil salinity and poor soil fertility in arid regions limit nutrient availability and root growth. **Micronutrient deficiencies**, especially zinc and boron, are common and affect yield and quality. Another serious challenge is **bacterial blight**, which spreads rapidly under warm conditions and causes severe yield loss. In addition, pest pressure, particularly from anar butterfly, increases under dry conditions.

Thus, while pomegranate is well suited to arid and semi-arid regions, its successful cultivation requires **scientific water management, balanced nutrition, effective bahar regulation and strong plant protection measures** to overcome climatic and biological constraints and achieve sustainable productivity.

Ans. (*b*) Millets are called **"Nutri-cereals"** because, compared to rice/wheat, many millets are **more nutrient-dense**—typically offering **higher dietary fibre**, better **mineral density** (notably iron, calcium, zinc, magnesium in several millets), **better quality protein profile** in many cases, and a **lower/steadier glycaemic response** in several traditional food forms. They also contain valuable bioactive compounds (polyphenols, antioxidants). In addition to nutrition, millets are widely recognised as **climate-resilient crops**—tolerant to drought/heat and suited to rainfed areas—so they support nutrition *and* sustainability.

Government of India initiatives to increase production and consumption of millets

1. **Production-side push (area, seed, technology, demonstrations)**
   - **NFSM Sub-Mission on Nutri-Cereals (from 2018–19):** A dedicated sub-mission under the National Food Security Mission to give focused support for **jowar, bajra, ragi and small millets** through interventions like demonstrations, seed support/minikits, production technologies, etc.
   - **Operational guidelines and yearly allocations under NFSNM/NFSM:** Government issues operational guidelines and allocates resources for components including **nutri cereals/coarse cereals** (e.g., seed minikits and related support).
2. **Price and procurement support**
   - **MSP and procurement of major millets (jowar/bajra/ragi):** Government procurement of these millets and MSP support have been used to incentivize production. Official releases report procurement quantities for key millets over recent years.
3. **Consumption-side push (institutional diets + awareness)**
   - **PM POSHAN (school meals):** The PM POSHAN scheme guidelines explicitly encourage **considering inclusion of millets** (as micronutrient-rich foods) in school menus, subject to local habits and availability—this is a direct pathway to expand demand and normalize millet consumption.
   - **Eat Right India / FSSAI millet promotion:** FSSAI has promoted millets (Shree Anna) under the Eat Right India initiative, especially around the International Year of Millets.
4. **International Year of Millets 2023 and "Shree Anna" campaign**
   - **IYM 2023 as a national movement:** India led global and domestic awareness-building for millets during IYM 2023 through conferences, outreach, value-chain focus and public campaigns under the "Shree Anna" positioning.
5. **Value chain, processing, markets**
   - Alongside production, government and allied ecosystem efforts during the millet push have emphasized **value addition, processing, branding, and market linkages** (so millets are available as convenient foods—flours, ready mixes, snacks—beyond traditional consumption). The IYM 2023 documentation highlights the value-chain and market-development thrust.

Ans. (*c*) **Seed dormancy** is a physiological condition in which a **viable seed fails to germinate even under favourable environmental conditions** such as adequate moisture, oxygen and suitable temperature. Dormancy is an adaptive trait that helps seeds **survive adverse conditions**, ensures proper timing of germination and prevents sprouting at unsuitable periods.

Types of seed dormancy

Primary (innate) dormancy: This dormancy is present in the seed **at the time of its maturation and shedding** from the parent plant. It is genetically controlled and commonly seen in freshly harvested seeds of many crops and wild species.

Secondary (induced) dormancy: Secondary dormancy develops **after seed dispersal** when seeds are exposed to unfavourable environmental conditions such as extreme temperatures, light deficiency or excess moisture. Seeds that have lost primary dormancy may re-enter dormancy under stress.

Exogenous dormancy: Exogenous dormancy is caused by factors **external to the embryo**, mainly due to the seed coat or surrounding structures. It includes:

- **Physical dormancy** due to hard or impermeable seed coat preventing water and oxygen entry (e.g., legumes).
- **Mechanical dormancy** where tough seed coverings restrict embryo expansion.
- **Chemical dormancy** caused by presence of germination inhibitors in seed coat or fruit pulp.

Endogenous dormancy: Endogenous dormancy arises due to conditions **within the embryo itself**. It includes:

- **Morphological dormancy**, where the embryo is underdeveloped at seed maturity.
- **Physiological dormancy**, caused by hormonal imbalance, mainly high abscisic acid and low gibberellins.

Combined dormancy: Some seeds exhibit both exogenous and endogenous dormancy, requiring multiple treatments for germination.

Reasons for induction of seed dormancy

Dormancy is induced to **avoid germination during unfavourable seasons**, such as drought or extreme cold. It ensures **species survival** by spreading germination over time and reduces competition among seedlings. Dormancy also aids in **long-term persistence of seeds in the soil seed bank**, especially in wild species. Environmental stresses during seed development and hormonal control mechanisms also induce dormancy.

Mechanisms to break seed dormancy

Dormancy can be broken naturally or artificially through several methods. **Scarification** (mechanical or chemical) is used to break hard seed coats and allow water uptake. **Stratification**, involving exposure of seeds to low or alternating temperatures under moist conditions, helps overcome physiological dormancy. **Soaking seeds in water or chemicals**, including growth regulators like gibberellic acid, promotes germination by correcting hormonal imbalance. **Light treatment** is effective in photoblastic seeds, while **after-ripening** through dry storage reduces inhibitory substances. In some cases, **removal of seed coat or fruit pulp** is necessary to eliminate chemical inhibitors.

Thus, seed dormancy is a vital biological phenomenon ensuring survival and adaptability of plants, and understanding its types and control mechanisms is essential for seed technology and crop production.

7. (*a*) Describe the major problems in marketing of fruits and vegetables along with important suggestions for stabilization of prices of tomato, onion and potato in India.

(*b*) Write the package of practices of Okra cultivation during *Kharif* season in India.

(*c*) Explain the photoperiodic responses of plants. What is the significance of vernalization in flowering of plants?

Ans. (*a*) Major problems in marketing of fruits and vegetables in India include **high perishability**, which forces quick disposal and leads to distress sale; **seasonal and clustered arrivals**, causing glut-and-crash followed by scarcity-and-spike; **inadequate post-harvest infrastructure** (packhouses, grading lines, cold rooms, ripening chambers, reefer transport), resulting in high quantitative and qualitative losses; **weak primary processing and value addition**, so surplus cannot be absorbed into pulp/puree/dehydrated/frozen forms; **fragmented supply chain with many intermediaries**, raising marketing costs and widening the producer–consumer price spread; **non-uniform grading/standardization and poor packaging**, reducing price realization and export competitiveness; **market information gaps and poor demand forecasting**, so farmers often take planting decisions blindly; **APMC-centric bottlenecks, limited direct marketing**, and poor farmer aggregation; **price volatility due to sudden weather shocks** (rain, heat waves, unseasonal hail) and **pest/disease outbreaks**; and **limited access to institutional storage/credit**, which compels farmers to sell immediately after harvest.

Important suggestions for stabilization of prices of **Tomato–Onion–Potato (TOP)** in India should combine **short-term market intervention** with **medium/long-term structural reforms**:

1. **Production and supply planning (reduce glut/scarcity cycles):** Promote **staggered sowing**, region-wise crop calendars, and varietal planning (early/medium/late groups). Encourage **protected cultivation** and heat-tolerant/disease-tolerant varieties for tomato to reduce sudden supply collapses.
2. **Strengthen aggregation and farmer market power:** Expand **FPO-based procurement, grading, and bulk marketing**, linking FPOs directly with organized retailers, processors and institutions to reduce intermediaries and stabilize farmgate prices.
3. **Post-harvest infrastructure as the core stabilizer:**
   - For **onion and potato**: expand scientific **storage** (ventilated onion storages; cold storages for potato with proper curing and sprout control), packhouses and logistics.
   - For **tomato**: focus more on **rapid aggregation, pre-cooling, short cold chain, and nearby processing**, because long storage is limited.
4. **Processing and value addition to absorb surplus:** Create/expand clusters for **tomato paste/puree/ketchup**, dehydration and aseptic pulp; **onion dehydration/flakes/powder**; and **potato processing** (chips, flakes, frozen products). Processing capacity near production belts converts "glut" into storable forms and prevents price crashes.
5. **Efficient price discovery and real-time intelligence:** Strengthen real-time price/arrival forecasting, advisories, and market intelligence so farmers adjust harvest and sales timing. Wider use of **electronic trading and transparent auctions** reduces manipulation and improves price signals.
6. **Buffer stocking and calibrated market intervention (especially for onion/potato):** Maintain a **strategic buffer** and release it in lean months to cool consumer prices, while procurement in surplus periods supports farmers. For tomato, intervention works best through **procurement for processing/distribution** because storage life is short.
7. **Trade and policy calibration (avoid abrupt shocks):** Use predictable, calibrated decisions on **export/import, stock limits, and movement restrictions**, with clear communication, so markets do not overreact and volatility is reduced.
8. **Targeted consumer-side distribution during spikes:** During sharp price rise, ensure quick movement to consumption centres through **direct retail outlets, mobile vans, and institutional channels**, and encourage substitutes/processed forms temporarily to moderate demand pressure.
9. **Risk management at farm level:** Promote crop insurance coverage for weather/pest shocks, integrated pest management, and climate advisories, since production shocks are a major trigger of TOP price volatility.

In essence, **onion and potato** price stabilization depends strongly on **storage + buffer +**

logistics, while **tomato** stabilization depends more on **near-farm aggregation + quick logistics + processing absorption**, along with better planning, FPO strength, and predictable market interventions.

Ans. (*b*) **Okra (Abelmoschus esculentus L.)** is an important vegetable crop grown extensively during the **kharif season** in India due to its adaptability to warm and humid conditions.

Climate and soil: Okra requires a **warm climate** with optimum temperature ranging from **25–35°C**. It is sensitive to frost and performs best under moderate rainfall conditions. The crop grows well in **well-drained sandy loam to loam soils** rich in organic matter, with a **pH range of 6.0–7.5**. Waterlogging is harmful, especially during early growth.

Varieties: Popular kharif varieties and hybrids include **Pusa Sawani, Parbhani Kranti, Arka Anamika, Arka Abhay, Punjab Padmini and Varsha Uphar**, which are tolerant to yellow vein mosaic virus (YVMV) and suitable for rainy season cultivation.

Land preparation: The field is prepared by **2–3 ploughings** followed by leveling to obtain a fine tilth. Raised beds or ridges are preferred in heavy rainfall areas to ensure proper drainage. Well-decomposed **farmyard manure (20–25 t/ha)** is incorporated during land preparation.

Sowing time and method: For kharif season, sowing is done from **June to July** with the onset of monsoon. Seeds are sown by **dibbling** at a spacing of **45–60 cm between rows and 30 cm between plants**. Seed rate is about **8–10 kg/ha**. Seed treatment with fungicide or bio-agents helps in reducing seed-borne diseases.

Nutrient management: A fertilizer dose of about **100–120 kg N, 60 kg P_2O_5 and 60 kg K_2O per hectare** is generally recommended. Full phosphorus and potassium and half nitrogen are applied as basal dose, while the remaining nitrogen is top-dressed in two splits at 30 and 45 days after sowing.

Irrigation management: During kharif, irrigation is usually not required initially due to rainfall. However, **supplemental irrigation** is provided during dry spells. Proper drainage is essential to avoid water stagnation, which predisposes the crop to diseases.

Weed management: The crop should be kept weed-free during the first **30–40 days,** which is the critical period of crop–weed competition. **Two hand weedings** at 20 and 40 days after sowing are effective. Pre-emergence application of suitable herbicides may be used where appropriate.

Plant protection: Major pests include **shoot and fruit borer, aphids, jassids and whitefly,** while diseases include **yellow vein mosaic virus, powdery mildew and damping-off.** Use of resistant varieties, timely removal of infected plants and integrated pest management practices are essential for control.

Harvesting: Fruits are harvested **45–60 days after sowing**, when they are tender and green. Picking is done at **2–3 day intervals** to maintain quality and encourage continuous fruiting.

Thus, adoption of recommended package of practices ensures **higher yield, better quality pods and profitable kharif okra cultivation** in India.

Ans. (*c*) **Photoperiodic response of plants** refers to the **physiological reaction of plants to the relative length of day and night**, particularly in relation to **flower initiation**. Photoperiodism was first demonstrated by Garner and Allard and is mediated through a light-sensitive pigment system called **phytochrome**, which enables plants to perceive day length.

Based on their photoperiodic responses, plants are classified into the following categories:

Short-day plants (SDP): These plants flower when the **day length is shorter than a critical photoperiod**, meaning they require **long,**

uninterrupted nights for flowering. If the dark period is interrupted by light, flowering is inhibited. Examples include **rice, soybean, tobacco, chrysanthemum and cotton**.

Long-day plants (LDP): Long-day plants require a **day length longer than a critical photoperiod** or **short nights** to induce flowering. Interruption of the dark period promotes flowering in these plants. Examples include **wheat, barley, oats, spinach and radish**.

Day-neutral plants: These plants flower **independent of day length** and are not influenced by photoperiod. Flowering depends mainly on age or physiological maturity. Examples include **tomato, cucumber, sunflower and maize**.

Photoperiodic responses help plants synchronize flowering with favorable environmental conditions, ensuring successful reproduction.

Significance of vernalization in flowering of plants: Vernalization is the process by which **exposure of seeds or young plants to low temperatures for a specific duration induces or accelerates flowering**. It is particularly important in plants that require a cold period to shift from vegetative to reproductive phase.

The primary significance of vernalization lies in **ensuring timely flowering.** In crops like **wheat, barley and rye**, especially winter varieties, vernalization prevents premature flowering before winter and ensures flowering occurs during favorable spring conditions. This protects floral organs from frost damage and enhances reproductive success.

Vernalization also **shortens the vegetative phase**, leading to early flowering and maturity, which is beneficial in regions with short growing seasons. In some biennial plants such as **carrot, beet and cabbage**, vernalization is essential for flower initiation in the second year.

From an agricultural perspective, vernalization enables **adaptation of crops to different agro-climatic regions**, allows manipulation of flowering time, and supports breeding programmes by facilitating seed production. Thus, vernalization plays a crucial role in regulating flowering behavior and improving crop productivity.

8. (*a*) Enlist the major constraints of food procurement in India. How can National and International food policies help in sustainable food security?

(*b*) Explain Integrated Pest Management (IPM). Discuss the biological control of pests and diseases in horticultural crops with special reference to Thrips and Mites.

(*c*) Describe the role of biofortification in horticultural crops in human nutrition, with suitable examples.

Ans. (*a*) Food procurement in India (mainly of rice and wheat through MSP operations and allied procurement for buffer stocks and welfare schemes) faces several structural, operational and policy constraints that affect both efficiency and sustainability.

Major constraints of food procurement in India

1. **Regional concentration of procurement:** Procurement is heavily concentrated in a few states (e.g., parts of NW India for wheat/rice), while many producing states have weak procurement operations; this creates unequal MSP access and regional distortions.
2. **Crop concentration and diet distortion:** Over-emphasis on rice–wheat procurement discourages diversification towards pulses, oilseeds and nutri-cereals, affecting nutrition and sustainability.
3. **Inadequate procurement infrastructure:** Shortage of modern mandis, drying yards, scientific godowns, silos, weighbridges, grading facilities, and logistics leads to delays and quality deterioration.

4. **Quality and standardization challenges:** High moisture, admixture, and variable quality at harvest create frequent rejections or require heavy cleaning/drying; inconsistent quality norms can trigger disputes.
5. **High storage and carrying costs:** Large buffer stocks increase costs of storage, interest, handling, transport and wastage; older godowns and open storage raise spoilage risk.
6. **Post-harvest losses and pest damage:** Inadequate scientific storage and pest management cause quantitative and qualitative losses, reducing effective food availability.
7. **Leakages and inefficiencies in movement/ distribution chain:** Diversion, pilferage and weak tracking reduce the effectiveness of procurement-to-distribution systems.
8. **Delayed payments and administrative bottlenecks:** Farmer payment delays, paperwork, limited procurement windows, and slow grievance redressal reduce farmer confidence and participation.
9. **Limited inclusion of small/marginal farmers:** Many smallholders sell to local traders due to distance, transport costs, small marketable surplus, and limited awareness/access to procurement centres.
10. **Policy unpredictability and operational rigidity:** Sudden changes in procurement norms, stock limits, movement restrictions, or export/import decisions create uncertainty and can disrupt market signals.
11. **Environmental stress in intensive procurement belts:** Groundwater depletion, soil degradation and residue burning in high-procurement regions raise sustainability concerns, indirectly constraining future procurement.

How National and International food policies can help in sustainable food security: Sustainable food security means ensuring **availability, access, utilization (nutrition) and stability** without degrading natural resources. National and international policies can support this in complementary ways:

National food policies (India):

- **Diversify procurement and incentives:** Expand effective MSP/procurement support (or price deficiency/market support) for **pulses, oilseeds, millets** and climate-resilient crops, reducing over-dependence on rice–wheat and improving nutrition.
- **Modernize storage and supply chains:** Invest in **silos, scientific warehouses, cold chains (for perishables), decentralized storage**, and end-to-end digital tracking to cut losses and costs.
- **Smarter buffer stock management:** Maintain **scientific buffer norms**, rotate stocks efficiently, and use transparent release mechanisms to stabilize prices while minimizing excess holding.
- **Strengthen PDS and nutrition delivery:** Improve targeting where needed, reduce leakages, and integrate nutrition goals (diversified food basket, fortified foods where appropriate) to improve utilization outcomes.
- **Promote sustainable production:** Align procurement with **water-smart, climate-smart** practices (micro-irrigation, direct-seeded rice where suitable, crop diversification) so food security does not come at ecological cost.
- **Empower farmer institutions:** Use **FPOs/ cooperatives** for aggregation, quality management and direct procurement access—reducing transaction costs and improving inclusion.

International food policies:

- **Stable and transparent trade frameworks:** Predictable global rules reduce panic restrictions and price spikes; coordinated approaches can reduce volatility in import-dependent countries and during shocks.

- **Early warning and information systems:** International cooperation on **climate, crop forecasts and price monitoring** helps countries plan buffer needs, imports and humanitarian responses in time.
- **Strategic reserves and humanitarian channels:** Collaboration for emergency reserves and rapid food assistance supports stability during disasters, conflicts and extreme weather.
- **Standards and safety harmonization:** Support compliance on food safety, SPS standards, and quality norms to enable smoother trade, reduce rejections and improve food utilization and health outcomes.
- **Support for climate adaptation and resilience:** International financing/ technology partnerships for drought-tolerant seeds, water efficiency, and sustainable agriculture strengthens long-term availability.

In essence, strengthening procurement systems (infrastructure, inclusion, efficiency) while **diversifying both production and the food basket**, and combining this with **predictable trade and coordinated global risk management**, makes food security more stable, nutritious and environmentally sustainable.

Ans. (*b*) **Integrated Pest Management (IPM)** is an **ecologically sound and economically viable approach** to pest management in which **all compatible pest control methods** are integrated to keep pest populations **below the economic injury level (EIL)** while minimizing risks to humans, beneficial organisms and the environment. IPM emphasizes **prevention, monitoring and need-based intervention**, rather than sole dependence on chemical pesticides.

The core principles of IPM include **correct pest identification, regular monitoring and surveillance**, understanding **pest biology and ecology**, use of **economic threshold levels (ETL)**, and adoption of a **combination of cultural, mechanical, biological and chemical methods**, with chemicals used only as a last resort. IPM is particularly important in horticultural crops, which are highly sensitive to pest damage and pesticide residues.

Biological control of pests and diseases in horticultural crops

Biological control is a key component of IPM and involves the **use of living organisms (natural enemies)** such as predators, parasitoids and pathogens to suppress pest populations. It is especially valuable in horticultural crops because it is **eco-friendly, residue-free and sustainable**.

Biological control of Thrips

Thrips are serious pests of horticultural crops like chilli, onion, tomato and ornamentals. They cause damage by **rasping and sucking sap**, leading to leaf curling, silvering and flower drop, and also transmit viral diseases.

Biological control measures against thrips include:

- **Predators** such as predatory mites (*Amblyseius* spp., *Neoseiulus* spp.) that feed on thrips larvae and eggs.
- **Predatory insects** like lacewings (*Chrysoperla* spp.) and minute pirate bugs that actively prey on thrips.
- **Entomopathogenic fungi** such as *Beauveria bassiana* and *Metarhizium anisopliae*, which infect and kill thrips under favorable humidity conditions.

These agents reduce thrips populations effectively when released early and maintained under protected or field conditions with minimal pesticide interference.

Biological control of Mites

Mites, especially spider mites, are major pests of fruit and vegetable crops, causing **yellowing, bronzing, leaf drop and yield reduction,** particularly under hot and dry conditions.

Biological control of mites involves:

- **Predatory mites** such as *Phytoseiulus persimilis* and *Amblyseius* spp., which are highly effective in suppressing spider mite populations.
- **Entomopathogenic fungi** like *Hirsutella thompsonii* and *Beauveria bassiana*, which infect mites and reduce their population.
- Conservation of natural enemies by **avoiding indiscriminate use of broad-spectrum pesticides**, which otherwise destroy beneficial organisms.

Advantages of biological control in IPM

Biological control provides **long-term pest suppression**, reduces pesticide residues in horticultural produce, delays development of pest resistance, and helps maintain **ecological balance**. When integrated with cultural practices, resistant varieties and need-based chemical use, it forms a strong foundation of IPM in horticultural crops.

Thus, IPM, with biological control of pests like thrips and mites, ensures **sustainable pest management, safer food production and environmental protection**.

Ans. (*c*) **Biofortification** is the process of **enhancing the concentration and bioavailability of essential nutrients in crops through plant breeding, agronomic practices or modern biotechnological approaches**. In horticultural crops, biofortification plays a vital role in improving **human nutrition**, as fruits and vegetables are primary sources of vitamins, minerals and health-promoting phytochemicals.

Role of biofortification in human nutrition: Biofortification helps in addressing **hidden hunger**, a condition caused by deficiency of micronutrients such as iron, zinc, vitamin A, iodine and folate, which affects a large population in developing countries, including India. Since horticultural crops are consumed fresh and regularly, biofortified fruits and vegetables offer a **sustainable and cost-effective means of improving dietary quality**, especially for vulnerable groups such as children, women and the elderly.

Biofortified horticultural crops enhance **vitamin intake**, particularly vitamins A, C, folate and antioxidants. For example, **orange-fleshed sweet potato** enriched with beta-carotene significantly improves vitamin A intake and helps prevent night blindness and immune disorders. Similarly, **tomato varieties with higher lycopene content** contribute to better antioxidant intake, reducing risks of cardiovascular diseases and certain cancers.

Biofortification also improves **mineral nutrition**. Vegetables enriched with **iron and zinc**, such as certain varieties of spinach and leafy greens, help combat anemia and support growth and immune function. **Calcium-rich vegetables** like improved varieties of broccoli and amaranthus contribute to bone health.

In addition, biofortified horticultural crops often contain higher levels of **functional compounds** such as flavonoids, anthocyanins and polyphenols. For instance, **purple-fleshed brinjal and carrot** are rich in anthocyanins, which have anti-inflammatory and anti-carcinogenic properties.

Biofortification is advantageous because it **reaches rural populations** who may not have access to supplements or fortified foods, requires minimal behavior change, and integrates nutrition directly into agriculture. Thus, biofortification of horticultural crops plays a crucial role in improving **nutritional security, public health and overall quality of diets** in a sustainable manner.

Previous Years' Paper

Indian Forest Service (Main) Exam, 2024

SUBJECT–AGRICULTURE

(Exam held on 29-11-2024)

PAPER-I

INSTRUCTIONS: *There are EIGHT questions in all, out of which FIVE are to be attempted, Question Nos. 1 & 5 are compulsory. Out of the remaining SIX questions, THREE are to be attempted selecting at least ONE question from each of the two Sections A and B. Attempts of questions shall be counted in sequential order. Unless struck off, attempt of a question shall be counted even if attempted partly. Any page or portion of the page left blank in the Question-cum-Answer Booklet must be clearly struck off. All questions carry equal marks. Answers must be written in ENGLISH only.*

SECTION-A

1. (*a*) Analyse how crop diversification and production are dependent on nature and culture in the Indian context.

(*b*) Describe the criteria of essentiality of plant nutrients given by Arnon.

(*c*) Give an account of criteria for selecting component crops for intercropping system.

(*d*) Explain the term relay cropping. Describe its role in increasing cropping intensity and productivity in rice-fallow areas.

(*e*) Explain soil structure. Describe the factors affecting soil structure.

2. (*a*) Write an account of shift in cropping patterns in different parts of India along with factors responsible for the same.

(*b*) Explain the critical period of crop-weed competition with suitable examples. Describe the factors affecting critical period of crop-weed competition.

(*c*) Describe water erosion. Explain the factors affecting water erosion.

3. (*a*) Explain the term "Agroforestry system". Justify the statement that "Agroforestry systems are more sustainable than cropping systems".

(*b*) Give an account of sources of air, water and soil pollution. Describe the impact of increasing pollution on crops.

(*c*) What is wind erosion? Describe the factors affecting wind erosion.

4. (*a*) Describe the cultivation of sugarcane in respect of the following:

(*i*) Methods of planting

(*ii*) Planting season

(*iii*) Seed cane

(*iv*) Propping

(*v*) Ratooning

(*b*) Differentiate between soil productivity and soil fertility. Explain the factors affecting soil productivity.

(*c*) Explain the biological properties of soil. Write the factors responsible for soil formation.

SECTION-B

5. (*a*) Write an account of factors affecting choice of irrigation methods.
   (*b*) Describe the important measures to measure the size of farm business.
   (*c*) How is marketing of agricultural outputs different from industrial outputs? Explain with examples.
   (*d*) Write a brief historical background of Krishi Vigyan Kendra. Explain the mandates and activities of Krishi Vigyan Kendra.
   (*e*) Establish the relationship between farm manage-ment and other sciences. Explain the ways and means of application of farm management to agriculture and allied sciences.

6. (*a*) Explain the criteria for judging the quality of irrigation water. What problems can be found if poor quality water is used for irrigation?
   (*b*) What is secondary agriculture? Explain with suitable examples how group approach can help small and marginal farmers to improve socio-economic status.
   (*c*) Write a brief account of various extension methods used by extension professionals.

7. (*a*) Enumerate the reasons behind decelerated progress of cooperative societies in India. Briefly describe the role of apex marketing cooperatives in the country—NAFED, NCDC and TRIFED.
   (*b*) Describe scheduling of irrigation based on critical stages, depletion of available soil moisture and climatological approach.
   (*c*) Describe the "Platform of Platforms" (PoP) feature of e-NAM and its implications on enhancing income of farmers.

8. (*a*) Elaborate the features of Farmer FIRST (Farm Innovations, Resources, Science and Technology) Programme.
   (*b*) What are the tools adopted for farm management analysis? Explain with examples.
   (*c*) Write an account of causes of water logging and its adverse effect on crops.

PAPER-II

INSTRUCTIONS: *There are EIGHT questions in all, out of which FIVE are to be attempted, Question Nos. 1 & 5 are compulsory. Out of the remaining SIX questions, THREE are to be attempted selecting at least ONE question from each of the two Sections A and B. Attempts of questions shall be counted in sequential order. Unless struck off, attempt of a question shall be counted even if attempted partly. Any page or portion of the page left blank in the Question-cum-Answer Booklet must be clearly struck off. All questions carry equal marks. Answers must be written in ENGLISH only.*

SECTION-A

1. (*a*) Why is Golgi body called as Golgi body or dictyosome? Briefly describe the mor-phology and functions of Golgi body.
   (*b*) Give a concise account on merits and demerits of mass selection.
   (*c*) Describe the major differences between scientifically produced seed and the grain (when used as seed). Also discuss the quality characteristics of seed.

(d) Explain diffusion pressure and its significance in plants. Also discuss the various factors influencing the rate of diffusion.

(e) Explain the right approaches for breeding of crop varieties for wide adaptability.

2. (a) What do you understand by somatic and meiotic crossing-over? Discuss the mechanism of meiotic crossing-over.

(b) Discuss the technique of producing virus-free nucleus stock in potato.

(c) Briefly discuss the biotechnological approaches for increasing yield and quality of oil.

3. (a) Distinguish between imbibition and permeability. Also discuss the importance of imbibition in plants and the factors affecting it.

(b) What do you understand by spontaneous mutations, induced mutations and mutation rate? Describe the practical applications and significance of mutations in cereal crops.

(c) Enlist the breeding methods for disease resistance in crop plants and discuss hybridization method in detail with suitable examples.

4. (a) What is cytoplasmic-genetic male sterility? Discuss about the development of new male sterile and restorer lines with the help of examples and suitable diagrams. Also explain the limitations of cytoplasmic-genetic male sterility in hybrid seed production of crops.

(b) Write in detail about the mechanism of water absorption in plants. Explain the factors influencing the rate of water absorption.

(c) Explain *in situ* and *ex situ* germplasm conser-vations.

SECTION-B

5. (a) Write in detail about different phases of growth and growth curve. Also explain the determinate and indeterminate types of growth in crops with suitable examples.

(b) Write the symptoms and management of late blight and golden cyst nematode in potato.

(c) Discuss the importance of fruits and vegetables in human nutrition.

(d) Write the symptoms and management of shoot and fruit borer in brinjal and diamondback moth in cabbage.

(e) How is food consumption trend in Indian population changing in relation with availability of crop produces and socio-economic factors?

6. (a) Write in detail about the occurrence, transport, site of synthesis and bioassay of abscisic acid in plants. Also explain the effect of abscisic acid on various plant physiological processes.

(b) Discuss the following in respect of turmeric cultivation:

(i) Climate and soil

(ii) Varieties, seed rate and planting

(iii) Manures and fertilizers

(iv) Cultural operations

(v) Post-harvest processing

(c) Discuss in detail about apple scab and its management.

7. (a) Enumerate the major insect-pests which affect wheat crop produce qualitatively and quantitatively during storage. Describe the preventive and control measures for management of storage insect-pests in cereals.

(b) Discuss the following post-harvest processes with reference to fruits and vegetables:

(i) Curing
(ii) Degreening
(iii) Pre-cooling
(iv) Disinfestation
(v) Sorting and grading

(c) Explain the role of ethylene in plants.

8. (a) Describe the following:
(i) NAFED
(ii) The Targeted Public Distribution System
(iii) Buffer stock operations
(iv) Coffee Board
(v) Food production and nutrition

(b) Give a lucid account on the principal biotic agents and the methods of their use in horticultural crops.

(c) Briefly discuss the methods of lawn making in India.

ANSWERS

PAPER-I

1. (a): Crop diversification and production in India are deeply influenced by both natural factors (like climate, soil, topography) and cultural-historical factors (such as traditions, food habits, and agrarian customs). The interplay of these elements has shaped the agricultural landscape of the country.

Dependence on Nature:

1. **Agro-climatic Zones:** India's division into 15 agro-climatic zones directly influences crop choices. For example, rice thrives in humid Eastern India, while wheat is dominant in the northwestern plains.
2. **Rainfall and Irrigation:** Rain-fed regions (like Bundelkhand) support coarse cereals and pulses, while irrigated zones (like Punjab, Haryana) favour water-intensive crops like paddy and sugarcane. Crop diversification is more visible in rain-fed areas due to risk minimization strategies.
3. **Soil Types:**
   - Black soils in Deccan are suitable for cotton.
   - Red soils in Karnataka and Tamil Nadu favour millets and groundnuts.
   - Alluvial soils in the Indo-Gangetic plains support cereals like wheat and rice.
4. **Topography:** Hilly terrains of the northeast and Jammu & Kashmir support horticulture—tea, apples, and spices—due to climatic suitability and sloped lands.
5. **Climate Change:** Increasing climate unpredictability has driven farmers to diversify into drought-resistant crops and short-duration varieties to manage risks.

Dependence on Culture:

1. **Food Habits and Traditions:** Regional dietary preferences promote specific crops—e.g., rice in South and East India, wheat in the North, and millets in tribal areas.
2. **Religious and Ritual Use:** Some crops like turmeric, sesame, and basil are grown for religious purposes, influencing regional cultivation trends.
3. **Economic and Social Customs:**
   - In tribal regions, shifting cultivation (jhum) is culturally embedded, shaping crop patterns.
   - Cultural reluctance toward meat in some communities promotes pulses and oilseeds over livestock-based farming.
4. **Market Demand and Festivals:** Seasonal crops are aligned with festivals—sugarcane during Pongal, maize during Baisakhi—which ensures local market demand and crop viability.
5. **Government and Institutional Influence:** Green Revolution focused on wheat and rice due to policy emphasis, but current policies (like National Mission on Oilseeds, Millets promotion) are reshaping diversification efforts based on socio-cultural considerations.

1. (*b*): The criteria of essentiality of plant nutrients were established by Daniel I. Arnon and P.R. Stout in 1939 to scientifically define which elements are essential for plant growth and development. According to Arnon, a nutrient is considered essential if it meets three key criteria:

Arnon's Criteria of Essentiality:

1. A deficiency of the element makes it impossible for the plant to complete its vegetative or reproductive cycle.
   - This means that the absence of the nutrient will prevent the plant from reaching maturity or producing viable seeds.
   - For example, without nitrogen, plants cannot synthesize proteins, leading to stunted growth and failed reproduction.
2. The deficiency is specific to the element and cannot be corrected by substituting another element.
   - Each essential element has a unique physiological role that cannot be replaced by any other nutrient.
   - For instance, magnesium is specifically required as the central atom in the chlorophyll molecule; no other element can perform this function.
3. The element is directly involved in the metabolism of the plant.
   - It must take part in biochemical reactions such as enzyme activation, photosynthesis, energy transfer, or osmotic balance.
   - Phosphorus, for example, is involved in ATP synthesis, which is essential for energy transfer within cells.

Importance of Arnon's Criteria:

- These criteria helped distinguish essential elements from beneficial elements (which may promote growth but are not vital for life cycle completion).
- Based on these, 17 elements are currently classified as essential for higher plants, including macronutrients (N, P, K, Ca, Mg, S) and micronutrients (Fe, Mn, Zn, Cu, B, Mo, Cl, Ni).

1. (*c*): Selection of appropriate component crops is crucial for the success of an intercropping system, where two or more crops are grown simultaneously on the same land. Proper crop selection ensures efficient use of resources, minimal competition, better yield, and sustainability.

Criteria for Selecting Component Crops for Intercropping:

1. **Complementarity in Resource Use:**
   - Selected crops should utilize resources (light, water, nutrients) differently—either spatially (different root zones) or temporally (different peak demand periods).
   - **Example:** Deep-rooted pigeon pea with shallow-rooted groundnut.
2. **Difference in Growth Duration:**
   - Mixing short-duration and long-duration crops prevents peak resource competition and ensures efficient land use.
   - **Example:** Intercropping mustard (short-duration) with sugarcane (long-duration).
3. **Contrasting Canopy Structure:**
   - Crops should differ in height and canopy spread to optimize light interception and reduce shading.
   - **Example:** Maize (tall) intercropped with cowpea (low-growing and shade-tolerant).
4. **Mutual Benefits or Facilitation:**
   - Some crops may improve soil fertility (like legumes fixing nitrogen) or act as trap crops/pest deterrents.
   - **Example:** Sorghum + pigeon pea (pigeon pea fixes nitrogen; sorghum provides shade).
5. **Similar Agronomic Practices:**
   - Selected crops should have compatible require-ments for planting time, irrigation, fertilization, and harvesting, to simplify management.
   - **Example:** Wheat + mustard (both grown in rabi season with similar inputs).
6. **Marketability and Economic Value:**
   - Component crops should have good market demand or home utility, ensuring profitability and economic security.
   - Farmers often choose combinations where one crop ensures income (cash crop) while the other offers food security.
7. **Disease and Pest Management Compatibility:**
   - Crops must not share common pests or diseases to avoid cross-infestation.

- **Example:** Avoid intercropping crops from the same family (e.g., tomato + chili).

8. **Growth Habit and Maturity Synchrony:**
   - Crops should have harmonious growth habits (erect vs. spreading) and ideally non-synchronous maturity to ease harvesting.

1. (*d*): Relay cropping is a type of multiple cropping system where the second crop is sown before the harvest of the first crop, allowing both crops to share part of the growing season. This technique enables efficient use of land, time, residual moisture, and nutrients.

Example: Sowing lentil or chickpea into standing rice 10–15 days before rice harvest in Eastern India.

Role in Increasing Cropping Intensity and Productivity in Rice-Fallow Areas:

1. **Utilization of Residual Soil Moisture:**
   - Rice-fallow areas, particularly in eastern India, Chhattisgarh, Jharkhand, Odisha, and eastern U.P., receive good monsoon rains but remain uncropped in rabi due to lack of irrigation.
   - Relay cropping utilizes residual moisture from rice cultivation to raise a second crop like lentil, chickpea, or linseed without irrigation.
2. **Increased Cropping Intensity:**
   - Traditionally mono-cropped (only kharif rice), these lands remain fallow post-harvest.
   - Relay cropping allows an additional rabi crop, increasing cropping intensity from 100% to 200%.
3. **Higher Land Productivity:** By taking two crops from the same land within a year, per hectare productivity increases, boosting total farm output and farmer income.
4. **Reduction in Turnaround Time:** Relay sowing minimizes the gap between harvest and sowing of the next crop, helping in timely establishment of rabi crops, which is critical in areas with short winters.
5. **Improved Soil Health:** Inclusion of legumes like lentils, chickpeas, or mungbean improves soil nitrogen through biological nitrogen fixation and enhances soil structure.
6. **Low-Cost Cultivation:** It reduces field preparation cost for the second crop, as sowing is done with minimal tillage using techniques like utera or paira sowing.
7. **Risk Reduction and Diversification:** Crop diver-sification reduces the risk from climatic vagaries and price fluctuations, making the system more resilient.

1. (*e*): Soil structure refers to the arrangement or grouping of soil particles (sand, silt, clay) into aggregates or peds of various shapes and sizes. It determines the soil's porosity, aeration, water-holding capacity, and root penetration ability—critical for plant growth and soil health.

Factors Affecting Soil Structure:

1. **Soil Texture:**
   - Finer textures (high clay) form stronger aggregates but may lead to compact structures.
   - Sandy soils have loose particles and poor aggregation unless organic matter is added.
2. **Organic Matter:**
   - Organic residues and humus act as binding agents that promote aggregation.
   - Microbial by-products (polysaccharides) also help in forming stable soil peds.
3. **Soil Organisms:**
   - Earthworms, fungi, and bacteria contri-bute to aggregation by excreting sticky substances and creating biopores.
   - Root exudates also stabilize soil particles.

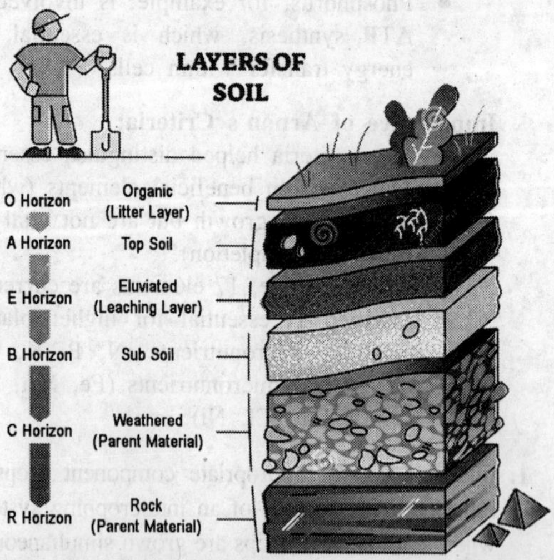

4. **Water Content and Moisture Regime:**
   - Alternating wetting and drying or freezing and thawing enhances aggregate formation.
   - Excessive water (waterlogging) can break down aggregates and lead to dispersion.

5. **Tillage and Mechanical Operations:**
   - Light tillage can improve structure by breaking clods.
   - Excessive or improper tillage destroys soil aggregates and leads to compaction and crusting.

6. **Clay Mineral Type:**
   - 2 : 1 expanding clays (like montmorillonite) shrink and swell, influencing structure significantly.
   - 1 : 1 clays (like kaolinite) have less swelling and more stable structure.

7. **Cation Composition:**
   - Soils rich in divalent cations (Ca^{2+}, Mg^{2+}) tend to flocculate particles and improve structure.
   - High sodium content (Na^{+}) leads to dispersion and poor structure (as in sodic soils).

8. **Cropping and Vegetation:**
   - Continuous cropping without organic inputs can degrade structure.
   - Perennial vegetation and cover crops help maintain good aggregation.

2. (*a*): Cropping pattern refers to the proportion of area under different crops at a point in time and space. Over the decades, India has witnessed significant shifts in cropping patterns, influenced by agro-climatic, economic, technological, and policy-related factors.

Shifts in Cropping Patterns in India (Region-wise):

1. **Northern India (Punjab, Haryana, Western UP):**
   - Shift: From diversified crops (millets, pulses, oilseeds) to rice-wheat monoculture.
   - Reasons:
     - ❑ Green Revolution technologies (HYVs of rice & wheat).
     - ❑ Assured procurement by FCI under MSP.
     - ❑ Expansion of irrigation (canals + tubewells).

2. **Eastern India (Bihar, Odisha, Assam, West Bengal):**
   - Shift: From coarse cereals and pulses to rice dominance in kharif and gradual introduction of vegetables and maize in rabi.
   - Reasons:
     - ❑ Improved irrigation and rural electrification.
     - ❑ Increased awareness of vegetable profitability.
     - ❑ Rising urban demand.

3. **Central India (Madhya Pradesh, Chhattisgarh):**
   - Shift: From coarse cereals to soybean, pulses, and horticulture crops.
   - Reasons:
     - ❑ Market-driven shift toward soybean and oilseeds.
     - ❑ Support from National Food Security Mission (NFSM) for pulses.

4. **Western India (Rajasthan, Gujarat, Maharashtra):**
   - Shift: From traditional drought-resistant crops (bajra, jowar) to oilseeds (groundnut, mustard) and horticultural crops.
   - Reasons:
     - ❑ Watershed development programs.
     - ❑ Drip irrigation support for horticulture.
     - ❑ Market-driven incentives for oilseeds and cotton.

5. **Southern India (Tamil Nadu, Andhra Pradesh, Karnataka):**
   - Shift: From food grains to commercial crops like cotton, sugarcane, tobacco, and fruits.
   - Reasons:
     - ❑ Diversified agro-climate and better rainfall.
     - ❑ Export-oriented production policies.
     - ❑ Shift toward high-value crops due to better returns.

6. **Northeastern States:**
   - Shift: From traditional jhum (shifting cultivation) to settled horticulture, spices, and bamboo-based agroforestry.
   - Reasons:
     - ❑ Government incentives for settled agriculture.
     - ❑ Soil conservation and climate resilience needs.

Factors Responsible for the Shifts:

1. **Technological Changes:** HYV seeds, mechanization, irrigation, and fertilizers.
2. **Government Policies:** MSP regime, input subsidies, crop insurance, and FCI procurement.
3. **Market and Profitability:** Price trends, export demands, contract farming.
4. **Environmental Concerns:** Soil degrada-tion, water table depletion (e.g., rice in Punjab), and climate change have prompted diversification.
5. **Changing Food Habits:** Rising demand for fruits, vegetables, and dairy has pushed farmers toward diversification.
6. **Institutional and Infrastructural Development:** Roads, cold chains, storage, and mandis influence perishable and cash crop cultivation.

2. (*b*): The critical period of crop-weed competition refers to the specific time span in the life cycle of a crop during which weed competition causes the most significant yield loss. Weed removal during this period is essential to prevent irreversible damage to crop productivity.

Examples of Critical Periods (in Days After Sowing – DAS):

Crop	Critical Period (DAS)
Rice (transplanted)	30–45 DAS
Wheat	20–40 DAS
Maize	15–45 DAS
Groundnut	20–45 DAS
Soybean	20–45 DAS
Sugarcane	30–90 DAS
Cotton	20–60 DAS
Chickpea	20–40 DAS

Factors Affecting Critical Period of Crop-Weed Competition:

1. **Crop Species and Growth Rate:**
   - Fast-growing crops (e.g., maize) can suppress weeds earlier, reducing the critical period.
   - Slow-growing crops (e.g., sugarcane) have longer vulnerable periods.
2. **Weed Flora and Density:**
   - Aggressive weeds like *Cyperus rotundus or Parthenium hysterophorus* dominate early and increase competition.
   - High weed pressure shortens the safe delay in weeding.
3. **Soil Fertility and Moisture:** In fertile, moist soils, both weeds and crops grow vigorously, increasing competition intensity early.
4. **Crop Spacing and Plant Population:** Wider spacing allows more room for weeds to grow, potentially extending the critical period.
5. **Climatic Conditions:** Warm and humid weather promotes faster weed emergence, especially in kharif crops, advancing the onset of the critical period.
6. **Type of Cropping System:** Intercropping may suppress weed growth (e.g., maize + cowpea), reducing competition.
7. **Weed Management History:** Fields with a history of poor weed control often have a dense weed seed bank, influencing early competition.

2. (*c*): Water erosion is the detachment, transportation, and deposition of soil particles by the action of rainfall and surface runoff. It is the most widespread type of soil erosion globally and is especially severe in hilly and deforested regions of India.

Factors Affecting Water Erosion:

1. **Rainfall Characteristics:**
   - Intensity and duration determine the erosive power of rain.
   - High-intensity storms cause splash and runoff erosion.
2. **Soil Properties:**
   - Texture: Sandy and silty soils are more prone to detachment.
   - Structure: Well-aggregated soils resist erosion better.
   - Infiltration rate: Soils with low infiltration allow more surface runoff.
3. **Slope and Topography:**
   - Steeper slopes increase runoff velocity, enhancing soil particle detachment.
   - Long slopes allow water to accumulate speed and cause greater erosion.

4. **Vegetative Cover:**
   - Dense vegetation reduces the impact of raindrops and increases water infiltration.
   - Bare land or overgrazed areas are highly vulnerable.
5. **Land Use Practices:**
   - Deforestation, overgrazing, and poor cultivation practices like up-and-down slope ploughing enhance erosion.
   - Conservation tillage and contour farming help reduce erosion.
6. **Runoff Volume and Speed:**
   - Greater runoff leads to increased erosion.
   - Fast-moving water has more kinetic energy to detach and carry soil.
7. **Human Activities:** Road construction, mining, and urbanization disturb soil and increase runoff, making the land erosion-prone.
8. **Soil Moisture Content:** Saturated soils are more prone to erosion due to reduced cohesion between particles.

3. (*a*): An Agroforestry system refers to a land-use management system where trees or shrubs are deliberately integrated with crops and/or livestock on the same land unit, either spatially (side-by-side) or temporally (in rotation). This integration aims to create ecological and economic synergy between components, enhancing productivity and sustainability.

Justification: Agroforestry Systems are More Sustainable Than Cropping Systems

1. **Soil Health Improvement:**
   - Tree roots prevent erosion, reduce nutrient leaching, and improve soil organic matter.
   - Leaf litter adds nutrients and maintains soil biological activity.
2. **Biodiversity Enhancement:** Multiple species coexist in agroforestry, improving ecosystem resilience and encouraging beneficial insects and birds.
3. **Efficient Resource Utilization:**
   - Trees and crops utilize light, water, and nutrients at different depths and times, reducing inter-species competition.
   - For example, deep-rooted trees access ground-water, while shallow-rooted crops use surface moisture.
4. **Microclimate Regulation:** Trees moderate temperature extremes, reduce wind speed, and improve humidity, benefiting sensitive crops.
5. **Carbon Sequestration and Climate Mitigation:** Trees absorb CO_2, helping in climate change mitigation—an advantage absent in sole cropping systems.
6. **Risk Diversification and Economic Stability:** Multiple outputs (fruits, timber, fodder, fuelwood, and crops) reduce dependence on a single commodity and protect against market or climate shocks.
7. **Long-Term Productivity:** While mono-culture cropping systems may degrade soil and water over time, agroforestry maintains ecological balance, supporting sustained productivity.
8. **Water Management:** Trees increase infiltration and reduce runoff, improving groundwater recharge and reducing irrigation demand.
9. **Adaptability in Marginal Lands:** Agro-forestry is viable in degraded or rain-fed areas where cropping alone may fail.

3. (*b*): Pollution refers to the contamination of natural resources—air, water, and soil—due to the release of harmful substances. These pollutants originate from both natural and anthropogenic sources and significantly impact crop productivity and quality.

Sources of Pollution:

1. **Air Pollution:**
   Major Sources:
   - Industrial emissions (SO_2, NO_x, CO, PM)
   - Vehicular exhausts (CO, hydrocarbons, lead, ozone precursors)
   - Burning of fossil fuels (coal, diesel, petroleum)
   - Stubble burning in agriculture (emits CO_2, methane, and particulates)
   - Aerosols and dust storms in arid zones
2. **Water Pollution:**
   Major Sources:
   - Industrial effluents containing heavy metals, acids, and dyes
   - Agricultural runoff containing fertilizers, pesticides, and herbicides
   - Untreated sewage and domestic waste
   - Oil spills and chemical leakage
   - Eutrophication due to nutrient overloading

3. Soil Pollution:

Major Sources:

- Overuse of agrochemicals (pesticides, synthetic fertilizers)
- Solid waste dumping (plastics, metals, e-waste)
- Irrigation with contaminated water
- Mining and smelting activities
- Sewage sludge and fly ash application

Impact of Pollution on Crops:

1. **Air Pollution:**
   - Ozone (O_3): Causes chlorosis, necrosis, and reduced photosynthesis.
   - SO_2 and NO_x: Injure leaf tissues, inhibit growth.
   - Particulate matter: Blocks stomata, interferes with light interception.
   - Acid rain: Alters soil pH, leaches nutrients, and weakens plant health.
2. **Water Pollution:**
   - Salinity and heavy metals (e.g., arsenic, cadmium): Reduce water uptake, cause toxicity.
   - Pathogens and chemicals: Damage roots and disturb hormonal balances.
   - Algal blooms from eutrophication reduce oxygen, affecting aquatic crops like paddy.
3. **Soil Pollution:**
   - Fertilizer buildup: Alters pH, reduces microbial activity.
   - Pesticide residues: Harm beneficial soil organisms (e.g., rhizobia), reducing nutrient cycling.
   - Heavy metals: Accumulate in plant tissues, impairing growth and entering the food chain.

3. (*c*): Wind erosion is the process by which soil particles are detached, lifted, and transported by the wind from one location to another. It is especially severe in arid and semi-arid regions with dry, loose, and bare soils, such as parts of Rajasthan, Gujarat, and the Deccan plateau in India.

Factors Affecting Wind Erosion:

1. **Soil Texture and Structure:**
   - Light-textured soils (sands, sandy loams) are more prone to wind erosion.
   - Poorly aggregated soils with low organic matter detach more easily.
2. **Soil Moisture:** Dry soils are easily lifted by wind, while moist soils resist erosion due to particle cohesion.
3. **Vegetative Cover:**
   - Absence of vegetation exposes soil to direct wind impact.
   - Crops, grasses, and cover crops reduce wind velocity and stabilize soil.
4. **Wind Velocity and Duration:**
   - Higher wind speed increases erosive power.
   - Prolonged winds in open areas cause sustained erosion.
5. **Surface Roughness:**
   - Rough soil surfaces disrupt airflow and reduce erosion.
   - Tilled, smooth surfaces accelerate wind speed near the ground.
6. **Field Size and Orientation:**
   - Large, open fields aligned with prevailing winds face higher erosion risks.
   - Narrow, cross-oriented strips reduce wind run.
7. **Climatic Factors:** Regions with low rainfall and high temperature (e.g., Thar Desert) are more prone to wind erosion.
8. **Human Activities:** Overgrazing, deforestation, and unsustainable tillage remove protective cover and aggravate erosion.

4. (*a*) (*i*): Methods of Planting Sugarcane: Sugarcane is a long-duration cash crop primarily propagated vegetatively through stem cuttings called setts. The choice of planting method depends on climate, soil conditions, water availability, and cropping system. The following are the main methods of sugarcane planting:

1. Flat Bed Method
2. Furrow (Trench) Method
3. Ring Pit Method
4. Space Transplanting Method (STP)
5. Bud Chip Method

4. (*a*) (*ii*): Planting Season of Sugarcane: The planting season of sugarcane varies across India due to climatic differences between tropical and subtropical regions. Sugarcane is a long-duration crop (10–18 months) and can be planted in three major seasons:

1. Autumn Planting (Time : September to October)
2. Spring (or Late) Planting (Time : February to March)
3. Adsali Planting (Time : July to August)
4. Suru Planting (Time : January to February)

4. (*a*) (*iii*): Seed Cane in Sugarcane Cultivation: Seed cane, also known as cane setts, is the vegetative planting material used for propagating sugarcane. Since sugarcane is propagated asexually, stem cuttings from mature, healthy canes are used rather than botanical seeds.

4. (*a*) (*iv*): Propping in Sugarcane Cultivation: Propping is an important cultural practice in sugarcane cultivation that involves tying or supporting sugarcane stalks to prevent them from lodging or falling over due to wind, rain, or the weight of the canes. Lodging reduces photosynthetic efficiency, affects juice quality, and makes harvesting difficult.

Objectives of Propping:

- To prevent lodging of tall, mature canes.
- To ensure erect growth for better light interception.
- To facilitate intercultural operations like weeding, fertilizer application, and harvesting.
- To reduce mechanical damage and loss due to breakage or wind.

4. (*a*) (*v*): Ratooning in Sugarcane Cultivation: Ratooning refers to the practice of growing a new sugarcane crop from the stubble left after harvesting the previous (plant) crop, without replanting. The crop that regenerates from the remaining underground buds of the harvested cane is called the ratoon crop.

Process of Ratooning:

- After harvesting the plant cane, the undisturbed underground portions (buds on stubble) sprout and regenerate new shoots.
- These shoots develop into full-grown canes, forming the ratoon crop.

4. (*b*): Difference Between Soil Productivity and Soil Fertility:

Aspect	Soil Fertility	Soil Productivity
Definition	Soil's capacity to supply essential nutrients to plants in adequate amounts.	Soil's capacity to produce crops under a specific set of management and environment.
Nature	It is a chemical/biological property.	It is a comprehensive term—includes fertility plus other factors like climate, water, etc.
Dependency	Depends mainly on nutrient availability and microbial activity.	Depends on fertility + climate, soil structure, water, topography, and management.
Scope	Narrower in scope—just nutrient-related.	Broader in scope—includes fertility, climate, drainage, human input.
Example	Fertile soil may still be unproductive due to waterlogging or poor structure.	Productive soil ensures high yield with proper management.

Factors Affecting Soil Productivity:

1. **Soil Fertility:**
   - Adequate and balanced availability of essential nutrients like N, P, K, S, Fe, Zn, etc.
   - Influenced by organic matter, microbial activity, and cation exchange capacity (CEC).
2. **Soil Physical Properties:**
   - Texture (loamy soils are best), structure, porosity, bulk density.
   - Affects water retention, aeration, and root penetration.
3. **Soil Water Availability:**
   - Water-holding capacity and drainage affect crop performance.
   - Waterlogged or drought-prone soils are less productive.
4. **Soil pH and Salinity:**
   - Optimal pH (6.5–7.5) enhances nutrient availability.
   - Saline or acidic soils can inhibit growth and nutrient uptake.
5. **Topography:**
   - Steep slopes promote erosion and reduce pro-ductivity.

- Flat to gently sloping lands are more productive due to better moisture conservation.

6. **Climate:**
   - Temperature, rainfall, humidity, and sunlight influence crop suitability and growth duration.
   - Even fertile soil can be unproductive if climate is unfavorable.
7. **Biological Factors:**
   - Presence of beneficial soil organisms (e.g., nitrogen-fixing bacteria, mycorrhizae).
   - Suppression of pests, pathogens, and nematodes improves productivity.
8. **Management Practices:**
   - Timely tillage, irrigation, cropping systems, and nutrient management enhance productivity.
   - Use of high-yielding varieties and pest control is crucial.
9. **Land Use History:**
   - Continuous mono-cropping or overgrazing depletes nutrients and reduces productivity.
   - Crop rotation and organic amendments help restore it.

4. **(c): Biological Properties of Soil:** The biological properties of soil refer to the presence and activities of living organisms—microorganisms, fauna, flora, and roots—that contribute to nutrient cycling, organic matter decomposition, and soil structure.

Factors Responsible for Soil Formation: Soil formation (pedogenesis) is governed by five major factors first described by Hans Jenny:

1. **Parent Material (P):**
   - The rock or mineral material from which soil originates.
   - Determines soil texture, mineral content, pH, and fertility.
2. **Climate (Cl):**
   - Temperature and rainfall control weathering rates, organic matter decay, leaching, and soil profile development.
   - Warm and wet climates accelerate soil formation.
3. **Organisms (O):**
   - Plants, animals, microbes influence organic matter addition, bioturbation, and nutrient cycling.
   - Roots promote weathering of parent material.
4. **Topography (Relief, R):**
   - Influences erosion, drainage, and accumulation of materials.
   - Steep slopes develop shallow soils; flat areas accumulate deep soils.
5. **Time (T):**
   - Longer time allows greater weathering, horizon development, and soil maturity.
   - Young soils are poorly developed; older soils are more differentiated.

5. **(*a*): Factors Affecting Choice of Irrigation Methods:** The choice of irrigation method depends on several technical, economic, climatic, soil, and crop-specific factors. Selecting the appropriate method is essential to ensure efficient water use, uniform crop growth, and higher productivity with minimum water loss.

1. **Soil Type and Properties:**
   - Texture: Sandy soils (high infiltration) are suitable for drip or sprinkler systems; clay soils (low infiltration) suit furrow or basin irrigation.
   - Permeability and structure: Well-drained soils can support most methods; poorly drained soils are better suited for controlled methods like drip.
2. **Topography of the Land:**
   - Flat land: Ideal for surface irrigation (e.g., basin, border strip).
   - Undulating or sloping land: Requires sprinkler or drip systems to avoid erosion and water runoff.
   - Steep slopes may need terracing and contour irrigation.
3. **Water Availability and Source:**
   - Abundant water: Surface methods like flood or furrow irrigation are economical.
   - Limited or costly water: Efficient methods like drip (90–95% efficiency) or sprinkler (70–80% efficiency) are preferred.
   - Water quality: Saline or hard water is better applied through drip to avoid foliar injury.
4. **Crop Type and Rooting Pattern:**
   - Wide-spaced, high-value crops (fruit trees, vegetables): Best suited for drip irrigation.
   - Close-growing cereals (wheat, rice): Suitable for surface or sprinkler irrigation.

- Shallow-rooted crops: Need frequent and light irrigation.
- Deep-rooted crops: Can handle less frequent but heavier irrigation.

5. **Climate and Evapotranspiration Demand:**
   - Arid, hot regions: Drip irrigation reduces evaporation losses.
   - Windy areas: Reduce efficiency of sprinkler irrigation due to drift.
   - Rainfed regions: Supplemental irrigation methods like furrow or surge irrigation are adopted.
6. **Economic and Infrastructure Considerations:**
   - Initial cost: Drip and sprinkler systems are costlier than surface methods.
   - Operational cost: Includes power, labour, and maintenance.
   - Availability of skilled labour: Influences adoption of complex systems like drip.
7. **Cropping Intensity and Farm Size:**
   - Small fragmented holdings: Drip or sprinkler can be customized easily.
   - Large-scale farming: May adopt mechanized surface or pivot sprinkler systems.
8. **Institutional and Government Support:**
   - Subsidies on micro-irrigation systems promote adoption.
   - Government schemes like PMKSY encourage water-saving irrigation techniques.

5. (*b*): **Important Measures to Measure the Size of Farm Business:** The size of a farm business refers to the physical and economic scale of agricultural operations. It provides a basis for comparing farm efficiency, planning expansion, and evaluating viability. The size can be assessed using both physical and value-based criteria.

1. **Land Area (Physical Measure):**
   - Total cultivated land under the operational control of the farmer, measured in hectares or acres.
   - Most basic and commonly used measure.
   - Limitation: Doesn't reflect intensity or productivity; two farms of same size can have vastly different outputs.
2. **Gross Income or Output:**
   - Total value of all produce (crops, livestock, by-products) sold during a year.
   - Indicates economic scale of operations.
   - Helps in classifying farms as small, medium, or large.
   - Limitation: Doesn't account for costs or profitability.
3. **Net Income:**
   - Net returns = Gross Income – Total Costs.
   - More accurate reflection of farm profitability.
   - Useful for comparing different enterprises or time periods.
4. **Capital Investment:**
   - Total value of fixed capital (land, buildings, machinery) and working capital (seeds, fertilizers, labour).
   - Indicates the financial size and intensity of operations.
   - Higher capital suggests larger or more mechanized farms.
5. **Labour Employment:**
   - Number of labourers (family + hired) employed annually.
   - Measured in man-days or labour units.
   - Large farms require more labour, especially for diverse or intensive cropping.
6. **Value of Farm Assets:**
   - Market value of all assets (land, buildings, livestock, machinery).
   - Indicates overall economic worth of the farm business.
   - Used by banks and institutions for credit decisions.
7. **Cropping Intensity:**
   - Cropping Intensity (%) = (Gross Cropped Area / Net Sown Area) × 100
   - Reflects land use efficiency.
   - Higher intensity may indicate better use of available land even on small farms.
8. **Livestock Units:**
   - For mixed farms, size is also measured in Animal Units (AUs).
   - Helps assess scale of dairy or livestock component.
9. **Power and Machinery Use:** Number and type of machinery (tractors, harvesters) indicate technological advancement and operational scale.
10. **Family Labour vs. Hired Labour Ratio:**
    - Large farms depend more on hired labour; small farms rely on family labour.
    - Helps assess the labour structure and sustainability of operations.

5. (*c*): Difference Between Marketing of Agricultural Outputs and Industrial Outputs: The marketing of agricultural outputs is fundamentally different from that of industrial products due to the nature of production, perishability, seasonality, and the profile of producers involved. These differences affect the pricing, storage, transportation, and institutional mechanisms used in both sectors.

Key Differences Between Agricultural and Industrial Marketing:

Aspect	Agricultural Outputs	Industrial Outputs
1. Nature of Product	Perishable, bulky, and seasonal (e.g., fruits, vegetables, cereals)	Non-perishable, standardised, and often durable (e.g., tools, cars)
2. Production Units	Mostly produced by small, scattered farmers	Produced by organized firms or factories in concentrated zones
3. Production Seasonality	Seasonal production, but year-round demand	Generally continuous production based on steady demand
4. Price Fluctuations	Prices fluctuate widely due to weather, yield, and supply-demand gap	Prices more stable and regulated through planned production
5. Market Infrastructure	Limited cold storage, warehousing, and grading facilities	Better developed infrastructure for logistics and quality control
6. Role of Middlemen	Involves many intermediaries (traders, commission agents)	Fewer intermediaries; often direct sales from manufacturer to retailer
7. Marketing Channels	Mostly informal (mandis, village markets, traders)	Organized (distributors, wholesalers, retail chains)
8. Grading and Standardization	Often absent or poorly implemented in agri-marketing	Strict standards and quality control systems in place
9. Transportation	Inadequate and expensive for small farmers	Organized logistics with dedicated networks
10. Government Regulation	MSP, APMC Acts, eNAM, subsidies common	Less intervention, mostly governed by market competition

Examples:

- **Agricultural Marketing:** A tomato farmer in Karnataka sells produce in the local mandi, facing price crash during surplus months and spoilage due to lack of cold storage.
- **Industrial Marketing:** A tractor manufacturer produces machines year-round based on projected demand and distributes them through dealerships with fixed price tags and warranties.

5. (*d*): Historical Background of Krishi Vigyan Kendra:

- The concept of Krishi Vigyan Kendra (KVK) was first proposed by the Education Commission (1964–66) under Dr. D. S. Kothari, which recommended the establishment of vocational education centers in agriculture.
- The idea was developed into a formal proposal by the Indian Council of Agricultural Research (ICAR) in 1973.
- The first KVK was established in 1974 at Puducherry under the administrative control of Tamil Nadu Agricultural University.
- Since then, KVKs have become the frontline extension system of ICAR to apply agricultural research in real field conditions.

Mandates of KVK:

1. Technology Assessment and Demonstration:

- Conduct on-farm testing (OFT) to assess the location specificity of agricultural technologies.
- Demonstrate new and improved technologies through frontline demonstrations (FLDs) on crops, livestock, and other enterprises.

2. Capacity Building and Training:

- Organize training programs for farmers, rural youth, and extension personnel.

- Focus on skill development and vocational training for self-employment in agriculture and allied sectors.

3. **Frontline Extension Work:**
   - Act as a bridge between research institutions and farmers.
   - Provide feedback to research organizations on farmers' problems and local needs.
4. **Knowledge and Resource Center:**
   - Serve as a knowledge hub for latest technologies and practices in agriculture and allied fields.
   - Disseminate information through publications, farm advisories, and ICT tools.

Key Activities of KVKs:

1. **On-Farm Trials (OFT):** Testing new varieties, practices, and inputs under actual field conditions.
2. **Frontline Demonstrations (FLD):** Demonstrating proven technologies on farmer fields to showcase impact.
3. **Training Programs:** Short and long-term courses for farmers, farm women, and youth on various agri-technologies.
4. **Advisory Services:**
   - On-the-spot diagnosis and solutions to crop, soil, or livestock issues.
   - Use of mobile apps, SMS, and radio for quick outreach.
5. **Seed and Planting Material Production:** Production and supply of quality seeds, seedlings, grafts, and bio-inputs.
6. **Field Days, Exhibitions, and Kisan Melas:** Interface between scientists and farmers for knowledge sharing.
7. **Linkage Development:** Coordination with line departments, NGOs, and input agencies for technology diffusion.

5. **(*e*): Relationship Between Farm Management and Other Sciences:** Farm management is an applied science that focuses on the efficient allocation of resources (land, labour, capital, and inputs) for maximum output and profit on a farm. It is interdisciplinary and draws knowledge from multiple sciences to optimize decision-making in agriculture.

1. **Economics:**
   - Provides tools for cost-benefit analysis, input-output relationships, marginal analysis, and profit maximization.
   - Concepts like opportunity cost, risk, and market analysis are core to farm planning.
2. **Agronomy:** Offers knowledge on crop management, soil-water-weed interactions, and nutrient planning, which guides crop selection and land use.
3. **Soil Science:** Helps in understanding soil fertility, classification, pH, and nutrient dynamics, essential for site-specific input use and yield maximization.
4. **Horticulture and Crop Science:** Informs about high-value crops, seasonality, and planting techniques for better economic returns per unit area.
5. **Animal Husbandry:** Supports mixed farming and integrated livestock management, optimizing output through resource recycling.
6. **Agricultural Engineering:** Relates to mechanization, irrigation systems, post-harvest technology, and land leveling—all vital for labour saving and efficiency.
7. **Statistics and Mathematics:** Used in farm records, budgeting, forecasting, regression analysis, and optimization models.
8. **Extension Education:** Aids in technology transfer, training, and adoption of improved farm practices, making management knowledge accessible to farmers.

Application of Farm Management in Agriculture and Allied Sciences:

1. **Resource Optimization:** Farm management applies budgeting, planning, and enterprise selection to use limited land, labour, and capital efficiently across crop-livestock-fishery systems.
2. **Farm Planning and Decision Making:** Helps design optimal cropping systems, calculate cost of production, and decide between enterprises based on comparative profitability.
3. **Risk and Uncertainty Management:** Through tools like enterprise diversification, crop insurance, and market forecasting, it reduces vulnerability to weather or price fluctuations.
4. **Economic Evaluation:** Assesses new technologies or practices (e.g., drip irrigation, organic farming) for economic feasibility using cost-return analysis.
5. **Sustainable Resource Use:** Integrates ecological principles with management (e.g., conservation agriculture, integrated pest management) for long-term sustainability.

6. **Allied Sector Integration:** In fishery, poultry, dairy, or agroforestry, farm management principles help plan mixed enterprises, ensuring continuous income and better resource cycling.

6. (*a*): Criteria for Judging Quality of Irrigation Water: The suitability of water for irrigation depends on its chemical composition, which affects soil health, crop growth, and long-term sustainability. The following are the key criteria:

1. **Electrical Conductivity (EC):**
   - Measures total salt concentration (salinity hazard).
   - EC < 0.7 dS/m – good;
     0.7–3.0 dS/m – permissible;
     >3.0 dS/m – unsuitable for sensitive crops.
   - High EC leads to osmotic stress, reducing water uptake by plants.
2. **Sodium Adsorption Ratio (SAR):**
   - Indicates the relative proportion of sodium to calcium and magnesium.
   - $SAR = Na^+ / \sqrt{[(Ca^{2+} + Mg^{2+})/2]}$
   - SAR > 9 suggests sodicity risk.
   - High SAR causes dispersion of soil particles, reducing permeability and aeration.
3. **Residual Sodium Carbonate (RSC):**
   - $RSC = (CO_3^{2-} + HCO_3^-) - (Ca^{2+} + Mg^{2+})$ (meq/L)
   - RSC > 2.5 meq/L indicates high risk of sodicity, causing calcium and magnesium precipitation.
   - Leads to soil hardening and reduced fertility.
4. **pH of Irrigation Water:**
   - Optimal pH: 6.5–8.5.
   - High pH (>8.5) indicates alkalinity and possible nutrient imbalances.
   - Low pH (<5.5) may increase metal toxicity (Al, Mn).
5. **Specific Ion Toxicity:**
   - Chloride (Cl^-), Boron (B), Sodium (Na^+): Harmful at higher concentrations.
   - Boron > 1 ppm is toxic to most crops.
   - Causes leaf burn, necrosis, and reduced yield.
6. **Total Dissolved Solids (TDS):**
   - Indicates total concentration of salts in mg/L or ppm.
   - TDS < 500 ppm is safe;
     2000 ppm is harmful for most crops.
7. **Bicarbonate and Carbonate Content:**
   - Excess leads to precipitation of calcium, worsening sodicity.
   - Affects soil permeability and plant nutrient uptake.

Problems Caused by Poor Quality Irrigation Water:

1. **Salinity Build-Up:**
   - Increases soil osmotic pressure.
   - Reduces water availability to roots → physiological drought.
2. **Sodicity and Soil Structure Degradation:** High SAR or RSC causes clay dispersion, reduced infiltration, crusting, and poor root growth.
3. **Nutrient Imbalances:**
   - Precipitation of nutrients like Ca^{2+} and Mg^{2+}.
   - Poor uptake of essential elements like K, P, Fe, Zn.
4. **Toxicity to Crops:**
   - Leaf scorch and tip burn due to Na^+, Cl^-, or B accumulation.
   - Sensitive crops (citrus, beans) are more affected.
5. **Reduced Crop Yield and Quality:** Long-term use leads to soil degradation, poor plant health, and reduced productivity.
6. **Soil Alkalinity or Acidity:**
   - Alters microbial activity and nutrient cycling.
   - Impairs soil biological properties.

6. (*b*): What is Secondary Agriculture? Secondary agriculture refers to the processing, value addition, storage, packaging, marketing, and allied services related to primary agricultural produce. It transforms raw farm products into consumable or marketable forms, generating additional income, employment, and entrepreneurship opportunities beyond the farm gate.

Group Approach: Definition and Benefits: A group approach involves collective action by farmers through Self-Help Groups (SHGs), Farmer Producer Organizations (FPOs), Cooperatives, or Farmer Interest Groups to manage resources, marketing, or processing collectively.

How Group Approach Helps Small and Marginal Farmers:

1. **Economies of Scale:**
   - Collective buying of inputs (seeds, fertilizers) reduces costs.
   - Joint marketing fetches better prices by avoiding middlemen.
2. **Better Access to Credit and Infrastructure:** Groups have higher creditworthiness and can secure loans for establishing processing units, cold storage, or transport vehicles.
3. **Value Addition and Processing:** Through SHGs or FPOs, farmers can process produce collectively (e.g., rice milling, turmeric processing), increasing product value and shelf life.
4. **Skill Development and Training:** Group training in food processing, packaging, and marketing enables adoption of new income-generating activities.
5. **Market Linkages and Branding:** Groups can develop local brands and connect to institutional buyers, online platforms, or participate in fairs, boosting income.
6. **Risk Sharing and Empowerment:**
   - Risks of production and marketing are shared, reducing individual vulnerability.
   - Promotes social empowerment, especially for women and youth in SHGs.

6. (*c*): Various Extension Methods Used by Extension Professionals: Extension methods are systematic techniques used by extension professionals to transfer knowledge, technology, and skills to farmers and rural communities. These methods aim to change attitudes, improve practices, and increase productivity in agriculture and allied sectors.

Extension methods are classified based on audience size and mode of communication into three major categories:

1. **Individual Methods:** These involve one-on-one inter-action, ensuring personal attention and tailored advice.
   - Farm and Home Visit: Extension worker visits a farmer's field or home to offer personalized guidance.
   - Personal Letter: Written communication offering specific advice or reminders.
   - Telephone/Mobile Call: Used for direct updates, advisories, or problem-solving.

   Advantages: High credibility, immediate feedback.

   Limitation: Time-consuming and costly for large-scale outreach.
2. **Group Methods:** These are used for interacting with a group of farmers, encouraging group learning and discussions.
   - Method Demonstration: Teaching a skill by showing how to perform it (e.g., seed treatment, compost making).
   - Result Demonstration: Conducted over time to show the result of adopting a new practice (e.g., yield comparison).
   - Group Meetings: Organized to discuss local issues, share experiences, and make collective decisions.
   - Training Programs: Skill-oriented sessions for farmers or rural youth (e.g., dairy, food processing).
   - Field Days/Kisan Goshti: Farmers visit a demonstration plot to observe the performance of new technologies.

   Advantages: Encourages peer learning and participatory interaction.

   Limitation: Less personalized than individual methods.
3. **Mass Methods:** Used to reach a large audience simultaneously through media and ICT tools.
   - Radio and Television: Programs like Krishi Darshan disseminate farm information.
   - Newspapers and Magazines: Publish success stories, advisories, and articles.
   - Pamphlets and Leaflets: Distribute technical information on crop practices or pest control.
   - Exhibitions and Kisan Melas: Showcase technologies, tools, and innovations.
   - Mobile Apps and SMS Services: Real-time weather alerts, market prices, and recommendations.
   - Social Media and YouTube: Widely used for visual demonstrations and farmer engagement.

   Advantages: Cost-effective and fast outreach.

   Limitation: No immediate feedback or interaction.

7. (*a*): Reasons Behind Decelerated Progress of Cooperative Societies in India: Despite being pivotal to rural development and inclusive growth, many cooperative societies in India have not performed to their potential due to the following reasons:

1. **Excessive Government Control:**
   - Political interference in management and elections.
   - Loss of autonomy leads to inefficiency and lack of farmer participation.
2. **Poor Financial Management:**
   - Lack of professional accounting systems.
   - Inability to generate surplus or mobilize adequate working capital.
3. **Lack of Professional Leadership:**
   - Elected leaders often lack management and marketing skills.
   - Training and capacity-building are minimal at grassroots levels.
4. **Limited Marketing and Storage Infra-structure:** Inadequate cold chains, godowns, grading, and transport facilities hinder com-petitiveness.
5. **Low Member Participation:** Many cooperatives function without active participation of members, becoming inactive or dormant.
6. **Corruption and Mismanagement:** Allegations of misappropriation and misuse of funds reduce trust among members.
7. **Credit Recovery Issues:** High incidence of non-repayment of loans, especially in credit cooperatives.
8. **Fragmented and Small Operations:** Many societies serve a limited area and cannot scale operations effectively.

Role of Apex Marketing Cooperatives:

1. **NAFED (National Agricultural Cooperative Marketing Federation of India Ltd.):**
   - **Established:** 1958
   - **Objective:** Promote cooperative marketing of agri-cultural produce.
   - **Key Functions:**
     - ❑ Procurement and distribution of pulses, oilseeds, and horticultural produce.
     - ❑ Market intervention during price crashes under Price Support Scheme (PSS).
     - ❑ Export and import of agri-commodities.
     - ❑ Promotion of FPOs and contract farming.

   Impact: Acts as a national-level stabilizing force to protect farmers from market volatility.
2. **NCDC (National Cooperative Development Corpo-ration):**
   - **Established:** 1963 under an Act of Parliament.
   - **Objective:** Plan and finance programs for cooperative development in agriculture and rural sectors.
   - **Key Functions:**
     - ❑ Provides financial assistance to cooperatives for setting up agro-processing, storage, cold chains.
     - ❑ Promotes cooperative enterprises across sectors like dairy, fisheries, handlooms, livestock.
     - ❑ Supports training and infrastructure development.

   Impact: Enhances rural employment and infrastructure through cooperative-based investments.
3. **TRIFED (Tribal Cooperative Marketing Development Federation of India Ltd.):**
   - **Established:** 1987 under the Ministry of Tribal Affairs.
   - **Objective:** Socio-economic development of tribal people through marketing support.
   - **Key Functions:**
     - ❑ Procurement and promotion of minor forest produce (MFP) and tribal handicrafts.
     - ❑ Runs **TRIBES India** outlets and online platforms to sell tribal products.
     - ❑ Implements Van Dhan Yojana for value addition and income generation through SHGs.

   Impact: Empowers tribal communities by providing assured markets and fair prices.

7. (*b*): Irrigation scheduling refers to determining the right time and amount of water to be applied to crops to maximize productivity and conserve water. It is based on crop water needs, soil conditions, and weather. Three widely used approaches are:

1. **Based on Critical Stages of Crop Growth:**
   - Irrigation is scheduled at specific growth stages when crops are most sensitive to water stress.
   - Missing irrigation at these stages causes maximum yield reduction, even if water is sufficient at other times.

Examples of Critical Stages:

Crop	Critical Growth Stages
Wheat	Crown root initiation (CRI), flowering, milking
Rice	Tillering, panicle initiation, flowering
Maize	Tasseling, silking, grain filling
Groundnut	Pegging, pod formation
Cotton	Flowering, boll development

- Advantages: Saves water, increases water-use efficiency.
- Limitation: Requires crop-specific knowledge.

2. **Based on Depletion of Available Soil Moisture (Soil Moisture Deficit Approach):**
   - Irrigation is scheduled when soil moisture falls below a certain percentage of available water-holding capacity (field capacity – permanent wilting point).
   - Monitoring tools: Tensiometers, gypsum blocks, or soil feel and appearance method.

Typical Depletion Levels for Irrigation:

- Sandy soils: Irrigate at 40–50% depletion
- Loamy soils: At 50–60% depletion
- Clay soils: At 60–70% depletion
- Advantages: Scientifically precise and avoids under- or over-irrigation.
- Limitation: Requires equipment and regular monitoring.

3. **Based on Climatological Approach (Weather-Based):**
   - Irrigation is scheduled using climate data, especially evapotranspiration (ET).
   - The IW/CPE ratio (Irrigation Water/ Cumulative Pan Evaporation) is widely used.

Examples:

- Wheat: IW/CPE = 0.9
- Groundnut: IW/CPE = 0.8
- Pearl millet: IW/CPE = 0.6–0.8
- CPE (mm) is measured using a Class-A Pan Evaporimeter.
- Irrigation is applied when cumulative evaporation reaches a target value.
- Advantages: Dynamic and adjusts for seasonal weather variations.
- Limitation: Needs local climate data and trained personnel.

7. **(c): What is e-NAM?**

The National Agriculture Market (e-NAM) is a pan-India electronic trading platform launched in 2016 by the Government of India to integrate physical agricultural markets (mandis) across the country. It aims to facilitate transparent, competitive, and fair price discovery for farmers by linking buyers and sellers online.

What is the "Platform of Platforms" (PoP) Feature of e-NAM?

Launched in July 2022, the Platform of Platforms (PoP) is a digital ecosystem within e-NAM that integrates various agri-tech platforms, private digital marketplaces, logistics providers, FPO networks, warehousing services, fintech companies, etc., into a unified interface accessible through e-NAM.

Key Features of PoP:

1. **Digital Convergence:** Links 41 service providers offering trading, quality certification, transport, logistics, warehousing, and digital payments into one portal.
2. **Wider Market Access:** Farmers can sell beyond APMCs to e-commerce companies, processors, exporters, and bulk buyers.
3. **Real-Time Services:** Unified access to crop advisory, weather updates, market trends, and price discovery tools.
4. **FPO Integration:** Over 1,000 FPOs integrated into e-NAM PoP, allowing collective marketing and better price negotiation.
5. **One-Stop Solution:** Brings services like soil testing, drone mapping, crop insurance, and supply chain financing under one umbrella.

Implications on Enhancing Income of Farmers:

1. **Competitive Pricing and Better Price Discovery:** Farmers can choose the best buyer across platforms, leading to better realization of produce value.
2. **Reduced Intermediaries:** Direct access to end buyers minimizes dependence on middlemen and reduces price exploitation.
3. **Lower Marketing Costs:** Integration with logistics providers and online payments reduces transportation, loading, and handling costs.
4. **Assured Payment and Transparency:** Digital transactions ensure timely and traceable payments, building trust in market systems.

5. **Access to Storage and Finance:** Farmers can avoid distress sales by linking with warehouse receipt finance, storing produce when prices are low.
6. **Empowerment of FPOs and Small Farmers:** Aggregated selling through FPOs improves bargaining power, logistics efficiency, and market intelligence.
7. **Diversified Buyer Base:** Producers can tap into retail chains, online grocery platforms, processors, and even exporters, expanding sales avenues.

8. (*a*): The Farmer FIRST Programme (FFP) is an innovative initiative launched by the Indian Council of Agricultural Research (ICAR) in 2016 to redefine the agricultural extension approach. It emphasizes a farmer-centric model rather than the traditional top-down, technology-driven transfer system.

Key Features of Farmer FIRST Programme:

1. **Farmer-Centric Research Model:**
   - Unlike traditional systems where research is disseminated to farmers, FFP involves farmers in planning, implementing, and evaluating research.
   - Promotes co-creation of knowledge with mutual respect between scientists and farmers.
2. **Location-Specific and Need-Based Interventions:**
   - Focuses on site-specific farming challenges—soil fertility, water stress, crop diversification, etc.
   - Solutions are tailored based on local agro-ecological conditions and socio-economic realities.
3. **Multidisciplinary Approach:**
   - Involves experts from agronomy, horticulture, animal husbandry, fisheries, social sciences, and engineering.
   - Supports integrated farming systems (IFS) to improve farm profitability and resilience.
4. **Inclusivity:**
   - Ensures participation of women, marginal farmers, and tribal communities.
   - Promotes gender equity and livelihood support through skill training and enterprise development.
5. **Farmer-Led Innovations:**
   - Recognizes, refines, and upscales innovations developed by farmers.
   - Encourages grassroots knowledge to complement scientific inputs.
6. **Integrated Resource Management:**
   - Promotes efficient use of on-farm resources—land, water, livestock, crop residues.
   - Emphasizes sustainable practices and natural resource conservation.
7. **Capacity Building and Institutional Linkages:**
   - Regular training programs, field days, and demonstrations for farmers.
   - Builds synergy with KVKs, ICAR institutes, line departments, NGOs, and private sector.
8. **Participatory Monitoring and Feedback:**
   - Farmers are involved in evaluating technologies and giving feedback.
   - Their responses help in redefining research priorities and refining interventions.

Examples of Interventions under FFP:

- Water-saving techniques in dryland farming.
- Low-cost poultry sheds and dairy improvements.
- Vegetable kits, mushroom units, and backyard poultry for women farmers.
- ICT tools and mobile apps for crop advisory.

8. (*b*): Tools Adopted for Farm Management Analysis with Examples: Farm management analysis involves using systematic tools and techniques to assess the efficiency, profitability, and sustainability of farming operations. These tools help farmers and planners make informed decisions on resource allocation, enterprise choice, input use, and risk management.

1. **Farm Budgeting:**
   - **Definition:** A method of estimating income and expenses for a farm or specific enterprise.
   - **Types:**
     - ❑ Partial Budgeting – To analyze the impact of a small change (e.g., switching from local to hybrid seed).

- ❑ Enterprise Budgeting – Evaluates the cost and return of a specific enterprise (e.g., dairy, maize cultivation).
- ❑ Whole Farm Budgeting – Estimates total income, cost, and profit from all farm enterprises.
- **Example:** A farmer prepares an enterprise budget to calculate profitability of paddy vs. groundnut.

2. Gross Margin Analysis:

- **Definition:** The difference between gross income and variable costs.
- **Formula:**

  Gross Margin = Total Revenue – Variable Costs
- **Use:** Helps in comparing enterprises where fixed costs are constant or hard to allocate.
- **Example:** Comparing gross margin of vegetables (high-value but high-cost) vs. pulses (low-cost, low-value).

3. Break-Even Analysis:

- **Definition:** Identifies the level of output or price at which total revenue equals total cost (no profit, no loss).
- **Use:** Assists in pricing decisions and investment planning.
- **Example:** A dairy farmer calculates that 15 litres/day milk yield is needed to break even.

4. Cost-Benefit Analysis (CBA):

- **Definition:** Compares the total expected cost of a project against its benefits.
- **Use:** For evaluating long-term investments (e.g., installing drip irrigation or building a greenhouse).
- **Example:** Analyzing whether installing solar-powered pump sets gives a better return than diesel ones over 10 years.

5. Linear Programming (LP):

- **Definition:** A mathematical technique used to optimize resource allocation under given constraints.
- **Use:** Helps decide how to maximize profit or minimize cost using limited land, labour, and capital.
- **Example:** Optimizing land allocation among wheat, mustard, and fodder crops within budget and labour limits.

6. Farm Records and Accounting:

- **Types:**
  - ❑ Production records (yield, input use)
  - ❑ Financial records (income, expenses, depreciation)
  - ❑ Labour and machinery records
- **Use:** Tracks profitability, identifies loss-making areas, and aids in planning and audits.
- **Example:** A vegetable farmer maintains daily expense and harvest logs to track net profit per acre.

7. Sensitivity Analysis:

- **Definition:** Examines how changes in key variables (input cost, yield, price) affect profitability.
- **Use:** Essential for risk management and planning under uncertainty.
- **Example:** A farmer assesses how a 10% increase in fertilizer cost would impact maize profitability.

8. Comparative Analysis:

- **Definition:** Comparing performance of two or more farms or enterprises under similar conditions.
- **Use:** Identifies best practices and bench-marks for improvement.
- **Example:** Comparing net income per hectare between irrigated and rainfed paddy farms.

8. (*c*): What is Water Logging?

Water logging is a condition where excess water accumulates in the root zone of the soil, leading to poor aeration and reduced oxygen availability for plant roots. This impairs plant growth and productivity, especially in crops not adapted to water-saturated conditions.

Causes of Water Logging:

1. **Poor Natural Drainage:** Low-lying or flat terrain with impermeable sub-soil layers (clay pan, hard pan) restricts water percolation.
2. **Excessive Irrigation:** Over-irrigation, especially under canal or flood irrigation systems, raises the water table.
3. **Seepage from Canals and Reservoirs:** Leakage from unlined canals and storage structures contributes to groundwater rise and saturation of adjacent areas.

4. **Inadequate Drainage Infrastructure:** Absence or clogging of surface and sub-surface drainage systems prevents removal of excess water.
5. **Heavy Rainfall and Poor Infiltration:** Intense monsoons or cyclonic rains, especially in compacted or poorly-structured soils, cause temporary or permanent water stagnation.
6. **Rise in Groundwater Table:** Continuous recharge from rainfall and irrigation without proper discharge elevates water table above root zone.
7. **Land Use Changes and Urbanization:** Encroachment of natural drainage paths, concrete surfaces, and deforestation reduce infiltration and increase runoff.

Adverse Effects of Water Logging on Crops:

1. **Poor Root Respiration:** Oxygen deficiency inhibits root function and respiration, leading to root suffocation and decay.
2. **Reduced Nutrient Uptake:**
   - Saturated conditions hinder absorption of nutrients like nitrogen, phosphorus, and potassium.
   - Denitrification and leaching further deplete soil fertility.
3. **Stunted Growth and Yield Loss:** Delayed germination, yellowing of leaves (chlorosis), and poor flowering result in low productivity.
4. **Increased Disease Incidence:** Waterlogged soils favor fungal and bacterial root diseases like root rot, wilt, and blight.
5. **Lodging and Poor Soil Structure:**
   - Water-saturated soils become soft, causing lodging (falling over) of tall crops like wheat or sugarcane.
   - Continuous logging leads to soil compaction and loss of structure.
6. **Toxic Gas Accumulation:** Accumulation of CO_2, methane, and hydrogen sulfide in anaerobic soils harms roots and microbes.
7. **Poor Germination and Crop Establishment:** Water stagnation leads to seed rotting and poor seedling emergence in crops like maize or cotton.

PAPER-II

1. (*a*): Why is it called Golgi Body or Dictyosome?

- The Golgi body was first observed in 1898 by Italian cytologist Camillo Golgi in nerve cells using a silver staining technique, hence the name Golgi apparatus or Golgi body.
- In animal cells, it is commonly termed the Golgi body or Golgi apparatus.
- In plant cells, individual units of the Golgi apparatus are scattered and unstacked, and each unit is called a dictyosome.
- Thus, the terms refer to functionally similar structures, with dictyosome used for the plant cell equivalent of the Golgi body.

Morphology of Golgi Body:

- The Golgi apparatus is composed of flattened, membrane-bound sacs known as cisternae.
- It usually has 3 to 8 cisternae, but may vary depending on cell type and activity.
- The structure has a distinct polarity:
  - ❑ **Cis face (forming face):** Oriented towards the endo-plasmic reticulum (ER); receives vesicles from ER.
  - ❑ **Trans face (maturing face):** Faces the plasma membrane and releases processed vesicles.
- It is surrounded by a network of tubules, vesicles, and vacuoles.

Functions of Golgi Body:

1. **Protein Modification and Sorting:**
   - Modifies proteins received from the rough ER by glycosylation, sulfation, phosphorylation, etc.
   - Sorts and packages proteins into secretory vesicles.
2. **Formation of Lysosomes:**
   - Produces primary lysosomes by packaging hydrolytic enzymes.
   - Plays a central role in intracellular digestion.
3. **Secretion:** Involved in exocytosis: Secretes enzymes, hormones, mucins, and poly-saccharides.
4. **Synthesis of Complex Polysaccharides:**
   - Synthesizes cell wall components in plants (e.g., pectin, hemicellulose).

- In animal cells, it synthesizes glycolipids and glycoproteins.

5. **Membrane Recycling and Transport:**
   - Assists in membrane formation and repair.
   - Facilitates retrograde transport to the ER.
6. **Storage and Transport:** Temporarily stores substances like lipids and proteins before transportation.

1. (*b*): **Mass Selection:** Mass selection is a plant breeding method where a large number of phenotypically superior plants are selected from a population and their seeds are bulk-harvested and used to grow the next generation. It is mainly used for cross-pollinated crops and some self-pollinated crops.

Merits of Mass Selection:

1. **Simplicity and Low Cost:**
   - Easy to apply in the field without specialized equipment or facilities.
   - Requires no controlled crossing or hybridization.
2. **Maintains Genetic Variability:** Because many plants are selected, genetic diversity is preserved, ensuring adaptability.
3. **Useful for Local Adaptation:** Ideal for improving landraces or local varieties for specific agro-climatic conditions.
4. **Quick Improvement:** Faster than hybridization-based methods since it doesn't involve multiple generations of backcrossing.
5. **Effective for Traits with High Heritability:** Works well for easily visible and highly heritable traits like seed size, color, plant height, etc.

Demerits of Mass Selection:

1. **Lack of Genetic Purity:** Since it's based on phenotypic selection, genotypic variation remains; not suitable for producing uniform varieties.
2. **No Control Over Pollination:** Especially in cross-pollinated crops, off-type pollination can introduce undesirable traits.
3. **Limited to Certain Traits:** Ineffective for low-heritability traits (like yield), as phenotype may not reflect genotype accurately.
4. **Slower Genetic Gain:** Improvement per cycle is lower compared to pedigree or backcross breeding methods.
5. **Requires Large Population Size:** To be effective, it demands evaluation of a very large number of individuals in each cycle.

1. (*c*):

A. Major Differences Between Scientifically Produced Seed and Grain (When Used as Seed):

Aspect	Scientifically Produced Seed	Grain Used as Seed
Purpose of Production	Specifically produced for planting and propagation	Produced primarily for consumption, occasionally reused as seed
Genetic Purity	High genetic purity maintained through seed certification protocols	No guarantee of genetic purity; often heterogeneous
Physical Purity	Free from inert matter, weed seeds, and off-types	May contain impurities, broken seeds, or other crop seeds
Germination and Vigor	High germination percentage and seedling vigor ($\geq 85\%$ in most cases)	Germination percentage uncertain and often low
Health Status	Free from seed-borne pathogens (after treatment)	May carry diseases, insects, or fungi
Processing and Grading	Properly cleaned, graded, treated, and packaged	Unprocessed and untreated
Storage and Labeling	Stored in ideal conditions with label and lot number	No standard storage or labeling norms
Regulatory Oversight	Regulated under Seed Act, 1966 and Seed Certification Agencies	Not regulated or inspected
Performance Assurance	Ensures uniform field stand, yield, and maturity	Variable performance, inconsistent yield

B. Quality Characteristics of Good Seed:

1. **Genetic Purity:** Seed must be true to its variety or hybrid type, free from off-types and admixtures.
2. **Physical Purity:** Should contain minimal inert matter, weed seeds, and other crop seeds (usually ≥98%).
3. **High Germination Percentage:** Seeds should have germination of ≥85% (varies with crop), ensuring optimal field emergence.
4. **Seed Vigour:** Seedlings emerging from good seed are uniform, healthy, and have good early growth.
5. **Seed Health:** Free from seed-borne pathogens, insects, and pests.
6. **Moisture Content:** Must be below safe limits (generally ≤12% for cereals, ≤8% for oilseeds) to ensure viability during storage.
7. **Uniform Size and Weight:** Seeds should be bold, uniformly sized, and well-developed for consistent sowing and emergence.
8. **Freedom from Objectionable Weeds:** Must be free from noxious and prohibited weed seeds (e.g., *Phalaris minor, Striga*).
9. **Proper Packaging and Labelling:** Certified seed should be packed in approved bags with a label showing lot number, variety, purity, and germination.

1. (*d*): What is Diffusion Pressure?

Diffusion pressure refers to the potential or tendency of molecules to move from an area of higher concentration to an area of lower concentration. It is directly proportional to the concentration of the diffusing substance.

- It is not a measurable physical pressure, but a conceptual representation of the driving force behind molecular movement during diffusion.

Significance of Diffusion Pressure in Plants:

1. **Gas Exchange:** Essential for uptake of CO_2 during photosynthesis and release of O_2 and water vapor during respiration and transpiration.
2. **Absorption and Transport of Minerals:** Helps in passive uptake of ions like K^+, NO_3^-, Cl^- from the soil solution into root cells when their diffusion pressure is higher in soil than in the root.
3. **Translocation of Water and Solutes:** In leaf cells and phloem, diffusion pressure gradients assist in the distribution of assimilates.
4. **Maintaining Cellular Homeostasis:** Helps in equalizing concentrations within and between cells to maintain metabolic balance.
5. **Seed Germination and Growth:** Water and gases diffuse into seeds driven by diffusion pressure, facilitating enzymatic activation and germination.

Factors Influencing the Rate of Diffusion:

1. **Concentration Gradient:** The greater the difference in concentration between two regions, the faster the diffusion.
2. **Temperature:** Higher temperatures increase kinetic energy, thus increasing diffusion rate.
3. **Molecular Size:** Smaller molecules (e.g., oxygen, water) diffuse faster than larger ones (e.g., sugars, proteins).
4. **Permeability of the Membrane:**
   - Semi-permeable membranes regulate which molecules can pass through and at what rate.
   - Lipid-soluble and nonpolar molecules diffuse more easily.
5. **Surface Area:** Larger surface area (e.g., root hairs, leaf stomata) increases diffusion rate.
6. **Thickness of the Diffusion Path:** Thinner membranes or shorter distances result in faster diffusion.
7. **Nature of the Medium:** Diffusion is faster in gases, slower in liquids, and very slow in solids.
8. **Presence of Barriers or Obstacles:** Cell walls, membranes, or cuticles may retard diffusion unless assisted by transport proteins.

1. (*e*): What is Wide Adaptability?

A widely adapted variety is one that performs consistently well across different environmental conditions, including varied climates, soils, and seasons. Breeding such varieties is essential to stabilize yields across diverse agro-ecological zones.

Right Approaches for Breeding Crop Varieties with Wide Adaptability:

1. **Multilocation Testing (MLT):**
   - Definition: Testing genotypes in multiple agro-climatic zones over several seasons.

- Purpose: Identify genotype × environment interactions (G × E).
- Outcome: Varieties with stable performance across zones are selected.
- Example: ICAR's All India Coordinated Research Projects (AICRP) conduct MLT for major crops.

2. Breeding for Stability and Plasticity:

- Use biometrical models like Eberhart and Russell's model to select varieties with:
  - ❑ High mean performance
  - ❑ Low environmental interaction
  - ❑ Regression coefficient near 1
- These are indicators of stability and adaptability.

3. Use of Diverse Parental Material:

- Involves crossing parents from different agro-climatic backgrounds to combine broad genetic bases.
- Enhances the chance of obtaining progeny with tolerance to varied stresses.

4. Marker-Assisted Selection (MAS) and Genomic Selection:

- Identify and introgress genes/QTLs for stress resistance (drought, heat, salinity).
- Use of MAS and genomic prediction models accelerates breeding for wide adaptability.

5. Participatory Plant Breeding (PPB):

- Involving farmers from diverse regions helps in real-world selection under variable conditions.
- Farmers' preferences enhance adaptability and success of the variety.

6. Breeding for Stress Tolerance:

- Target traits that allow crops to withstand biotic (diseases, pests) and abiotic stresses (drought, temperature, flooding).
- Enhances adaptability across stress-prone and favorable zones.

7. Focus on Yield Stability Rather Than Yield Maximum:

- Select varieties with moderate but consistent yields rather than high yield in only optimal conditions.
- Such varieties avoid crop failure under stress or suboptimal inputs.

8. Incorporating Resilience Traits: Traits like early maturity, deep rooting, photoperiod insensitivity, and high tillering support adaptation across geographies.

9. Biotechnology and Crop Modelling Tools:

- Use of crop simulation models to predict varietal performance in multiple virtual environments.
- Helps breeders plan for climate-smart agriculture.

2. (*a*): Somatic and Meiotic Crossing-Over & Mechanism of Meiotic Crossing-Over

Somatic and Meiotic Crossing-Over – Understanding the Difference:

1. Meiotic Crossing-Over:

- Definition: Meiotic crossing-over is the exchange of genetic material between homologous chromosomes during prophase I of meiosis.
- Purpose: It increases genetic variation in gametes and follows Mendelian inheritance patterns.
- Location: Occurs at the pachytene stage of prophase I in germ cells.
- Outcome: Produces recombinant chromosomes, contributing to genetic diversity.

2. Somatic Crossing-Over:

- Definition: A rare event where exchange of genetic material occurs between homologous chromosomes in somatic (non-reproductive) cells.
- First observed: In *Drosophila* by Curt Stern (1936).
- Outcome: May lead to mitotic recombination, genetic mosaics, or patches of mutated tissue.
- Relevance: Important in studies of development, cancer, and DNA repair but does not contribute to heredity.

Mechanism of Meiotic Crossing-Over: Occurs during Prophase I of Meiosis, specifically in the pachytene stage of meiosis I. The process involves the following steps:

1. Synapsis of Homologous Chromosomes (Zygotene):

- Homologous chromosomes align and form pairs called bivalents or tetrads.
- Held together by a proteinaceous structure called the synaptonemal complex.

2. Formation of Chiasmata (Pachytene):

- Non-sister chromatids of homologous chromosomes overlap and exchange DNA segments at specific points called chiasmata.

- Crossing-over usually occurs between chromatids of homologous chromosomes, not sister chromatids.

3. **Enzyme-Mediated Break and Rejoining (Molecular Steps):**
   - **Initiation:** Enzyme Spo11 induces double-strand breaks (DSBs) in one chromatid.
   - **Exonuclease Activity:** Exonucleases create 3' over-hangs by digesting the 5' ends at the break site.
   - **Strand Invasion and Homology Search:**
     - The 3' single-stranded DNA invades the homologous non-sister chromatid.
     - Forms a D-loop (displacement loop), stabilizing the base pairing.
   - **Holliday Junction Formation:**
     - DNA polymerase fills in gaps and ligase seals the strands.
     - Results in formation of Holliday junctions (cross-shaped structures of DNA).
   - **Resolution:**
     - Holliday junctions are resolved by endonucleases.
     - Depending on how the junction is cleaved, the outcome can be a crossover (reciprocal exchange) or non-crossover (gene conversion without recombination).

4. **Terminalization (Diplotene Stage):**
   - Chiasmata move toward the ends of chromosomes (terminalization).
   - Homologous chromosomes begin to separate but remain connected at chiasmata.

2. (*b*): Why Virus-Free Nucleus Stock in Potato?

Potato (*Solanum tuberosum*) is vegetatively propagated through tubers, which accumulate viral infections over generations. These viruses (like PVX, PVY, PLRV) severely reduce yield and quality. Hence, producing virus-free nucleus stock is essential as the starting material for quality seed production.

Steps in Producing Virus-Free Nucleus Stock in Potato:

1. **Selection of Healthy Elite Plants:**
   - Identify and select true-to-type, vigorous, and disease-free mother plants from breeder's field or a recognized germplasm source.
   - Plants should be free from visual symptoms of viral diseases.

2. **Meristem Tip Culture:**
   - Meristematic tissue (0.2–0.5 mm) from apical shoot is excised under a sterile microscope.
   - Reason: Meristem region is virus-free or has very low virus titer, as viruses fail to multiply rapidly in dividing cells.

3. **In Vitro Culture and Multiplication:**
   - Meristem is cultured in Murashige and Skoog (MS) medium with hormones for callus initiation and shoot regeneration.
   - Shoots are rooted to produce complete plantlets.
   - Multiple subcultures are used to multiply the material in controlled tissue culture laboratories.

4. **Virus Indexing and ELISA Testing:**
   - Regenerated plantlets are tested for major potato viruses using:
     - ELISA (Enzyme-Linked Immunosorbent Assay)
     - RT-PCR (for molecular confirmation)
   - Only virus-free plants are selected for further use.

5. **Hardening and Acclimatization:**
   - Virus-free plantlets are transferred to soil or cocopeat in polyhouses to adapt to external conditions.
   - Care is taken to prevent reinfection through aphid-proof net houses.

6. **Mini-Tuber Production:**
   - Acclimatized plants are grown under aeroponics, hydroponics, or soil beds to produce mini-tubers (G0 seed).
   - These mini-tubers are multiplied under strict supervision to form the nucleus seed stock.

7. **Maintenance and Multiplication:** The nucleus stock is used to generate breeder seed, then foundation seed, and finally certified seed under seed certification systems.

2. (*c*): Biotechnology plays a significant role in enhancing both yield and nutritional quality of oilseed crops by targeting genetic, molecular, and cellular traits. These approaches aim to overcome the limitations of traditional breeding and accelerate the development of high-yielding, oil-rich, and quality-improved varieties.

1. **Genetic Engineering for Fatty Acid Modification:**
   - Objective: Modify the composition of fatty acids (increase oleic acid, reduce erucic or saturated fats).
   - Example:
     - ❑ High oleic acid groundnut and soybean through insertion of FAD2 gene mutation.
     - ❑ Low erucic acid mustard (Canola) by silencing FAE1 gene.
   - Benefit: Improves nutritional quality and enhances shelf life of oil.
2. **Gene Editing (CRISPR/Cas9):**
   - Used to precisely knock out or alter specific genes related to oil biosynthesis pathways.
   - Example: Editing DGAT1, WRI1, LPAAT genes to increase oil content in seed tissues.
   - Advantage: No foreign DNA; faster and more precise than conventional transgenics.
3. **Marker-Assisted Selection (MAS):**
   - Utilizes molecular markers linked to oil content and yield traits to accelerate breeding.
   - **Example:** Selection for oil QTLs in groundnut, mustard, and sunflower.
   - Benefit: Enhances selection efficiency without altering plant genome.
4. **Metabolic Engineering:**
   - Manipulates entire metabolic pathways to enhance oil accumulation.
   - Involves genes controlling carbon partitioning, lipid biosynthesis, and transport.
   - **Example:** Overexpression of WRINKLED1 (WRI1) gene to divert carbon into fatty acid synthesis.
5. **Development of Transgenic Crops for Yield Stability:**
   - Introduction of genes conferring resistance to pests, diseases, and abiotic stress ensures stable oilseed yields.
   - Example:
     - ❑ Bt cotton and Bt mustard for reduced pest damage and higher seed yield.
     - ❑ Drought-tolerant soybean using DREB genes.
6. **Tissue Culture and Micropropagation:**
   - Used for rapid multiplication of elite oil-rich genotypes.
   - Also helps in somaclonal variation for identifying superior variants.
7. **Synthetic Biology Approaches:**
   - Design and construct synthetic pathways in non-traditional plants or microbes to produce designer oils or increase lipid yield.
   - Example: Producing omega-3 fatty acids in transgenic Camelina or algae.

3. (*a*): Distinction Between Imbibition and Permeability:

Aspect	Imbibition	Permeability
Definition	The absorption of water by solid colloidal particles (like seeds or cell walls) without forming a solution.	The property of a membrane that allows substances (mainly water) to pass through.
Nature of Process	Passive physical adsorption process involving hydration of hydrophilic surfaces.	It is a transport property of membranes (selective or non-selective).
Examples	Dry seeds absorbing water; wood swelling in water.	Water passing through plasma membrane or cell wall.
Requirement of Semipermeable Membrane	Not required; occurs even without membranes.	Involves semipermeable membranes (especially in osmosis).
Type of Material Involved	Involves hydrophilic colloids (e.g., cellulose, pectin, proteins).	Involves membranes or porous structures controlling passage.

Importance of Imbibition in Plants:

1. **Seed Germination:** First step in germination—dry seeds imbibe water, swell, and activate enzymes for metabolic activity.
2. **Breaking of Seed Dormancy and Seed Coat:** Swelling from imbibition generates pressure (imbibitional force) that ruptures the seed coat.
3. **Water Uptake in Dry Tissues:** Dry plant tissues like wood, gums, or roots absorb water through imbibition.
4. **Ascent of Sap (Early Theory):** Imbibitional forces in cell walls may assist in water movement through xylem during early germination or in desiccated plants.
5. **Cell Expansion and Growth:** Cell wall materials imbibe water, allowing cell enlargement and flexibility.
6. **Swelling of Root Hairs and Germ Tubes:** Fungal spores and pollen tubes also imbibe water during growth and penetration.

Factors Affecting Imbibition:

1. **Nature of Imbibant:** Materials like proteins imbibe more water than cellulose, due to their greater hydrophilicity.
2. **Affinity Between Water and Imbibant:** Greater chemical affinity increases the imbibition capacity (e.g., polar substances imbibe polar solvents like water better).
3. **Temperature:** Higher temperature increases kinetic energy, thus enhancing imbibition rate up to an optimum level.
4. **Concentration Gradient (Diffusion Pressure Deficit):** Imbibition is faster when the surrounding water potential is lower, creating a steep gradient.
5. **Presence of Solutes:** Solutes reduce the water potential of the medium, thereby reducing imbibition (since water moves from high to low potential).
6. **pH and Electrolytes:** Certain ions may alter the imbibition behavior of colloids (e.g., proteins show variable imbibition at different pH due to charge effects).

3. (*b*): Spontaneous Mutations, Induced Mutations, Mutation Rate, and Their Applications in Cereal Crops

1. Spontaneous Mutations:

- **Definition:** Spontaneous mutations occur naturally without any external intervention, due to errors in DNA replication, spontaneous chemical changes, or natural transposon activity.
- **Causes:**
  - ❑ Tautomeric shifts
  - ❑ Replication slippage
  - ❑ Oxidative damage
  - ❑ Natural background radiation
- **Example:** Naturally occurring color variation in maize kernels due to spontaneous gene alteration.

2. Induced Mutations:

- **Definition:** Induced mutations are artificially created by exposing organisms to mutagens, which are physical or chemical agents that alter DNA.
- **Types of Mutagens:**
  - ❑ **Physical:** Gamma rays, X-rays, fast neutrons, UV rays
  - ❑ **Chemical:** EMS (ethyl methanesulfonate), Sodium azide, Colchicine
- **Purpose:** Used in mutation breeding to enhance specific traits in crops like disease resistance, short stature, or high yield.

3. Mutation Rate:

- **Definition:** The frequency at which mutations occur in a gene or genome per generation.
- **Expression:** Usually denoted as mutations per gene per generation (e.g., 10^{-6}/gene/generation).
- **Influenced by:**
  - ❑ Type of mutagen
  - ❑ Exposure time and dose
  - ❑ Target gene characteristics

4. Practical Applications and Significance of Mutations in Cereal Crops:

(*a*) Development of Improved Varieties:

- Induced mutations have led to the release of thousands of high-yielding cereal varieties worldwide.
- **Examples:**
  - ❑ **'Sharbati Sonora' (wheat)** – Mutagenesis improved grain quality.
  - ❑ **'Jagannath' (rice)** – Developed using gamma rays; high yielding and early maturing.
  - ❑ **'Pusa Basmati-1'** – Quality rice variety from induced mutation.

(b) Alteration of Plant Height:

- Semi-dwarf wheat and rice varieties were developed by altering genes related to gibberellin metabolism, making them lodging resistant and high yielding.
- Mutation in 'sd-1' gene in rice helped create short-statured varieties suitable for high inputs.

(c) Disease and Pest Resistance:

- Resistance to diseases like blast in rice and rust in wheat achieved via mutagenesis.
- Broadens the genetic base when natural resistance is absent.

(d) Improving Nutritional Traits:

- Enhancement of protein content (as in 'Atlas 66' wheat mutant) and micronutrient density through targeted mutations.

(e) Stress Tolerance:

- Induced mutations have produced cereal varieties tolerant to drought, salinity, and submergence.

(f) Male Sterility and Hybrid Development: Cytoplasmic male sterile (CMS) lines in sorghum and pearl millet were developed through induced mutations, facilitating hybrid seed production..

3. (c): Breeding Methods for Disease Resistance in Crop Plants:

1. Introduction
2. Selection (Mass & Pure-line selection)
3. Hybridization
4. Backcross Breeding
5. Mutation Breeding
6. Marker-Assisted Selection (MAS)
7. Genetic Engineering and Transgenic Approaches
8. Genomic Selection
9. Polyploidy Breeding

Hybridization Method – Detailed Explanation:

Definition: Hybridization is the mating or crossing of two genetically different parents to combine desirable traits such as disease resistance from one parent and high yield or quality from another.

Steps in Hybridization for Disease Resistance:

1. Selection of Parents:

- One parent must be resistant to the target disease (donor parent), and the other is usually elite but susceptible (recurrent parent).
- Example: Crossing blast-resistant *Moroberekan* with high-yielding susceptible *IR64* in rice.

2. Emasculation and Pollination:

- Emasculation (removal of anthers) is done in the female parent to prevent self-pollination.
- Pollination is performed with pollen from the selected male (resistant) parent.

3. F_1 Generation:

- The F_1 plants are genetically uniform and generally heterozygous.
- Often shows heterosis (hybrid vigor) but not always disease-resistant.

4. Segregation in F_2 and Subsequent Generations:

- F_1 generation is genetically variable.
- Selection begins from F_1 onwards for plants that combine resistance with other agronomic traits.

5. Screening for Disease Resistance:

- Artificial inoculation or natural hot spot screening is used to expose plants to pathogens.
- Selected resistant individuals are advanced through pedigree method, bulk method, or SSD (Single Seed Descent).

6. Testing and Release:

- Advanced lines are tested in multi-location trials.
- Varieties showing stable resistance and high performance are released.

Examples of Hybridization for Disease Resistance:

- **Wheat:** 'HD2967' developed through hybridization for leaf and stripe rust resistance.
- **Rice:** 'Samba Mahsuri-Sub1' developed by hybridization and MAS for BLB resistance and submergence tolerance.
- **Maize:** Resistant hybrids like HQPM-1 bred for resistance to downy mildew and stem borer.
- **Pigeonpea:** 'ICPH 2671' is a hybrid resistant to Fusarium wilt.

4. (a): What is Cytoplasmic-Genetic Male Sterility (CGMS)?

Cytoplasmic-genetic male sterility (CGMS) is a type of male sterility in plants where the inability to produce functional pollen is controlled by the interaction of cytoplasmic factors (mitochondrial genes) and nuclear genes.

- **Cytoplasm:** Sterile (S) or Normal (N) type.
- **Nuclear genes:**
  - **Restorer gene (Rf)** restores fertility in hybrids.
  - **Maintainer gene (rf)** does not restore fertility.

System Components in CGMS:

1. **A-line (Male sterile line):** Has sterile cytoplasm (S) and recessive nuclear gene (rfrf). Used as the female parent.
2. **B-line (Maintainer line):** Has normal cytoplasm (N) and same nuclear genes (rfrf). Used to maintain A-line.
3. **R-line (Restorer line):** Has fertility restorer genes (Rf) and used as the male parent in hybrid production.

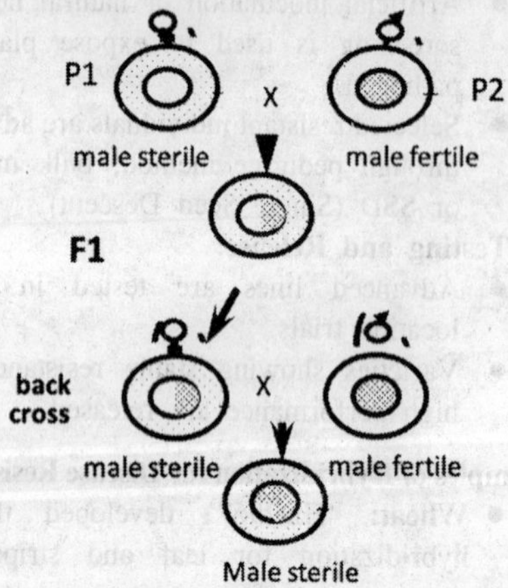

Development of New Male Sterile and Restorer Lines:

1. **Development of A-line (Male Sterile Line):**
- **Cross:** S-rfrf × N-rfrf (maintainer)
- Backcross repeatedly with B-line while selecting sterile plants each generation.
- After 5–6 backcrosses, A-line becomes isogenic to B-line but with sterile cytoplasm.

2. **Development of B-line (Maintainer Line):**
- Select a normal fertile line with nuclear background identical to A-line.
- Must not carry restorer gene (rfrf).

3. **Development of R-line (Restorer Line):**
- Select or breed lines that carry dominant Rf genes.
- Cross R-line with A-line and select progeny that restores male fertility in F_1 hybrid.
- R-lines must have good combining ability and desirable agronomic traits.

Examples of CGMS Use in Crops:

- **Rice:** IR58025A × IR36 (IR hybrids)
- **Sorghum:** 296A × 296B with restorer R-line like 2219R
- **Pearl millet:** Tift 23A × Tift 23B (first CGMS system developed)

Limitations of CGMS in Hybrid Seed Production:

1. **Cytoplasmic Uniformity Risk:** All hybrids share the same cytoplasm; can lead to vulnerability (e.g., Texas cytoplasm in maize caused Southern corn leaf blight epidemic in the USA in 1970s).
2. **Limited Restorer Genes:** Not all genotypes carry functional Rf genes, limiting choice of male parents.
3. **Complex Inheritance:** Interaction between cytoplasmic and nuclear genes is complex, making it harder to breed stable restorers.
4. **Cost and Effort:** Requires separate development and maintenance of A, B, and R lines under controlled conditions.
5. **Environmental Influence:** Expression of sterility or fertility restoration may vary under temperature or photoperiod variations.

4. (*b*): Mechanism of Water Absorption in Plants and Factors Influencing Its Rate

I. Mechanism of Water Absorption in Plants: Water absorption occurs mainly through the root hairs located in the root epidermis, which are in contact with soil water. The process involves two mechanisms:

A. Passive Absorption (Main Mechanism)

- Nature: Physical process; no metabolic energy required.
- Driven by: Transpiration pull from the leaves.
- Mechanism:
  - During transpiration, water evaporates from the leaf surfaces.

- ❑ This creates negative pressure (suction force) in the xylem.
- ❑ Water is pulled upward from the roots to replace the lost water.
- ❑ Roots act as passive conduits.
- Dominant under: High transpiration, well-aerated soils, daytime.

B. Active Absorption (Minor Contribution)

- Nature: Biological process; requires ATP.
- Driven by: Activity of root cells and osmotic gradients.
- Mechanism:
  - ❑ Roots absorb water against a gradient using osmotic potential and active transport.
  - ❑ Root pressure may be generated, especially at night or low transpiration conditions.
  - ❑ Involves water uptake via aquaporins (water channels in plasma membrane).
- Dominant under: Low transpiration, night-time, or waterlogged soil.

Pathways of Water Movement Across Root Tissues:

1. Apoplast Pathway:
- Through cell walls and intercellular spaces.
- Faster but blocked at endodermis by Casparian strip.

2. Symplast Pathway:
- Through cytoplasm of adjacent cells connected by plasmodesmata.
- Water moves cell-to-cell without crossing membranes repeatedly.

3. Transmembrane Pathway: Water crosses multiple membranes, entering and exiting cells.

II. Factors Influencing Rate of Water Absorption

1. Transpiration Rate:
- Higher transpiration leads to stronger pull and increased passive absorption.
- Influenced by light, temperature, wind, and humidity.

2. Soil Water Availability:
- Water must be present in a form available to roots (not bound tightly to particles).
- Water below wilting point cannot be absorbed.

3. Soil Temperature:
- Low temperatures reduce root metabolism and membrane fluidity, slowing absorption.
- Optimal range: 25–35°C.

4. Soil Aeration: Poorly aerated (waterlogged) soils limit oxygen availability, reducing ATP synthesis and root activity.

5. Root Surface Area and Health:
- More root hairs and fine roots increase contact area for absorption.
- Diseases or root pruning reduce efficiency.

6. Osmotic Concentration in Root Cells:
- High solute concentration in root cells helps draw water in by osmosis.
- Affected by nutrient availability and metabolic state.

7. Soil pH and Salinity:
- High salinity causes osmotic stress, making it harder for roots to absorb water.
- Extremely acidic or alkaline soils damage roots and hinder absorption.

4. (*c*): Explanation of In Situ and Ex Situ Germplasm Conservation

1. In Situ Germplasm Conservation

- **Definition:** Conservation of genetic resources in their natural habitat or environment, where the plants or animals continue to evolve and adapt naturally.
- **Purpose:** To maintain genetic diversity dynamically by allowing natural selection and evolutionary processes to continue.
- **Types:**
  - ❑ On-farm Conservation: Farmers conserve traditional crop varieties and landraces in their own fields.
  - ❑ Natural Reserves or Protected Areas: Conser-vation of wild relatives of crops or native species in biosphere reserves, national parks, and sanctuaries.
- **Advantages:**
  - ❑ Enables ongoing evolution and adaptation to changing environments.
  - ❑ Conserves the entire ecosystem, including associated organisms.
  - ❑ Allows farmers to continue selection for traits valuable to them.
- **Disadvantages:**
  - ❑ Risk of loss due to natural disasters, habitat destruction.
  - ❑ Requires continuous management and monitoring.
  - ❑ Genetic erosion can occur if popu-lations become very small.

2. **Ex Situ Germplasm Conservation**
   - **Definition:** Conservation of genetic material outside their natural habitat, usually in controlled environments.
   - **Purpose:** To preserve germplasm for long-term use and breeding programs.
   - **Types:**
     - ❑ **Seed Banks:** Storage of seeds under low temperature and humidity for longevity.
     - ❑ **Field Gene Banks:** Growing plants under field conditions (used when seeds cannot be stored, e.g., clonally propagated crops).
     - ❑ **In Vitro Conservation:** Tissue culture, cryopreser-vation, or slow growth storage in laboratories.
     - ❑ **DNA Banks:** Storage of genetic material as DNA samples.
   - **Advantages:**
     - ❑ Protects against loss of germplasm due to habitat destruction.
     - ❑ Enables preservation of large numbers of accessions in limited space.
     - ❑ Provides germplasm readily available for research and breeding.
   - **Disadvantages:**
     - ❑ Genetic material is static; no natural evolution or adaptation.
     - ❑ Requires regular regeneration to maintain viability.
     - ❑ Expensive to establish and maintain infra-structure.

5. (*a*): Phases of Growth in Plants: Plant growth is a continuous and irreversible increase in size and dry weight. It generally occurs in three main phases:

1. **Lag Phase:**
   - **Characteristics:**
     - ❑ Slow growth rate.
     - ❑ Seed germination, cell division, and metabolic activities are initiated.
     - ❑ Cells increase in size and prepare for rapid division.
   - **Duration:** Variable depending on species and conditions.
   - **Significance:** Preparation stage for rapid growth.
2. **Exponential (Log) Phase:**
   - **Characteristics:**
     - ❑ Rapid increase in growth rate.
     - ❑ Active cell division and elongation.
     - ❑ Maximum rate of dry matter accumu-lation.
   - **Duration:** Most intensive growth phase.
   - **Significance:** Main phase for biomass and yield formation.
3. **Plateau (Stationary) Phase:**
   - **Characteristics:**
     - ❑ Growth slows and finally ceases.
     - ❑ Cells stop dividing and elongating.
     - ❑ Maximum size and dry weight reached.
   - **Significance:** Maturity phase; energy diverted to reproduction and storage.

Growth Curve:
- The growth curve is sigmoid (S-shaped), plotted with growth (length, volume, or dry weight) on the Y-axis and time on the X-axis.
- **Phases of the Sigmoid Growth Curve:**
  - ❑ **Lag phase:** Initial slow growth.
  - ❑ **Exponential phase:** Rapid, nearly constant growth rate.
  - ❑ **Deceleration phase:** Growth rate slows.
  - ❑ **Plateau phase:** Growth ceases.

Determinate and Indeterminate Growth in Crops:

1. **Determinate Growth:**
   - **Definition:** Growth that ceases after reaching a genetically fixed size or stage, often coinciding with flowering or fruiting.
   - **Characteristics:**
     - ❑ Shoot apex terminates in a flower or inflore-scence.
     - ❑ Limited vegetative growth after reproductive phase begins.
     - ❑ Growth curve shows a sharp plateau.
   - **Examples:**
     - ❑ **Grain crops:** Wheat, barley, peas.
     - ❑ **Vegetables:** Bush beans, determinate tomatoes.
   - **Agronomic Importance: Easier to harvest; uniform maturity.**
2. **Indeterminate Growth:**
   - **Definition:** Growth that continues indefinitely, with shoot apex remaining vegetative while lateral flowering occurs.
   - **Characteristics:**
     - ❑ Continuous elongation of shoots even after flowering starts.
     - ❑ Growth curve shows a longer exponen-tial phase and gradual plateau.

- Produces flowers and fruits over an extended period.
- **Examples:**
  - **Crops:** Maize, rice, cotton.
  - **Vegetables:** Pole beans, indeterminate tomatoes.
- **Agronomic Importance:** Extended harvesting period; higher total yield potential but less uniform.

5. (*b*): Symptoms and Management of Late Blight and Golden Cyst Nematode in Potato

1. Late Blight of Potato

Symptoms:

- **Leaves:**
  - Water-soaked, pale green spots appear, which quickly enlarge into brown or black lesions.
  - Lesions often have a water-soaked margin and may be covered with a white fuzzy growth (sporulation) on the underside in humid conditions.
  - Leaves wilt and collapse, leading to defoliation.

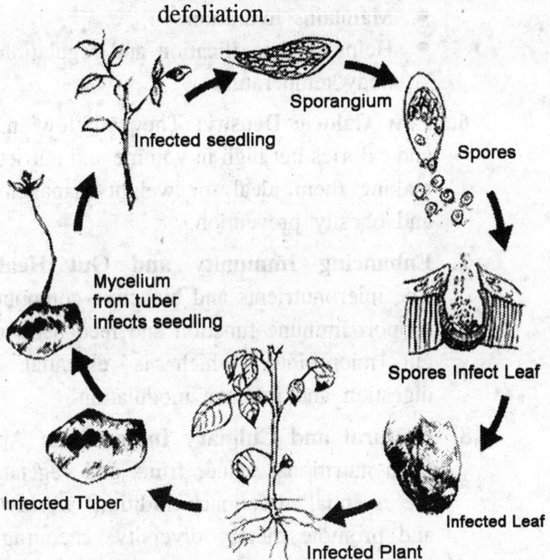

- **Stems:** Dark, sunken lesions develop, often at the base, causing stem breakage.
- **Tubers:**
  - Irregular, dark brown to purplish lesions beneath the skin, which may penetrate deep.
  - Tubers become rotten and foul-smelling.

Causal Agent: Fungus-like oomycete Phytophthora infestans.

Management:

- **Resistant Varieties:** Use late blight-resistant cultivars (e.g., Kufri Jyoti, Kufri Bahar).
- **Cultural Practices:**
  - Crop rotation with non-hosts (e.g., cereals).
  - Avoid overhead irrigation to reduce humidity.
  - Remove and destroy infected plant debris and volunteer potatoes.
  - Ensure proper spacing for air circulation.
- **Chemical Control:** Apply fungicides like Mancozeb, Metalaxyl, or Chlorothalonil at regular intervals, especially during conducive weather.
- **Seed Treatment:** Use certified, disease-free seed tubers.
- **Monitoring:** Regular field inspections and early detection.

2. Golden Cyst Nematode (GCN) of Potato

Symptoms:

- **Above Ground:**
  - Stunted plant growth, yellowing, and wilting under drought stress.
  - Reduced leaf size and poor tuber development.
- **Below Ground:**
  - Presence of small, golden-yellow cysts (egg sacs) on roots, visible as tiny golden grains.
  - Root system is reduced, with fewer and smaller roots.

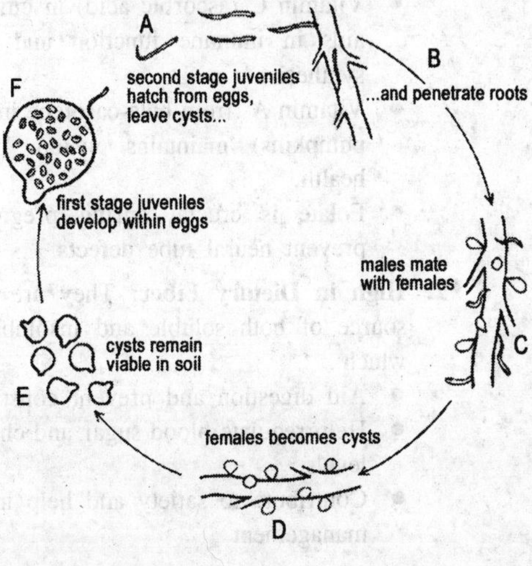

- **Yield Loss:** Can cause 20–50% or more yield reduction.

Causal Agent: Nematode Globodera rostochiensis (Golden cyst nematode).

Management:

- **Resistant Varieties:** Use GCN-resistant varieties like Kufri Jyoti, Kufri Pukhraj.
- **Crop Rotation:** Rotate with non-host crops like cereals (wheat, maize) for 3–4 years to reduce nematode population.
- **Nematicides:** Use nematicides such as Carbofuran or Fenamiphos as soil treatment before planting.
- **Sanitation:** Clean seed tubers and equipment to avoid spreading nematodes.
- **Biological Control:** Use of antagonistic fungi like *Paecilomyces lilacinus*.
- **Soil Solarization:** Solar heating of soil in summer to reduce nematode load.

5. (*c*): Fruits and vegetables are vital components of a balanced diet and play a significant role in human nutrition due to their rich content of essential nutrients, dietary fiber, antioxidants, and phytochemicals. They contribute to overall health, disease prevention, and maintenance of body functions.

1. **Rich Source of Nutrients:** Fruits and vegetables provide essential vitamins (like A, C, E, K, and folate) and minerals (such as potassium, magnesium, and calcium). For example:
   - Vitamin C (ascorbic acid) in citrus fruits aids in immune function and collagen synthesis.
   - Vitamin A (from beta-carotene in carrots, pumpkins) maintains vision and skin health.
   - Folate is crucial during pregnancy to prevent neural tube defects.
2. **High in Dietary Fiber:** They are a major source of both soluble and insoluble fibers which:
   - Aid digestion and prevent constipation
   - Help regulate blood sugar and cholesterol levels
   - Contribute to satiety and help in weight management
3. **Antioxidant Properties:** Fruits and vegetables are abundant in antioxidants such as flavonoids, carotenoids, and polyphenols.

   These:
   - Neutralize free radicals in the body
   - Reduce oxidative stress
   - Lower the risk of chronic diseases like cancer, heart disease, and age-related degeneration
4. **Disease Prevention:** Regular consumption of a variety of fruits and vegetables reduces the risk of:
   - Cardiovascular diseases due to potassium and antioxidant content
   - Certain cancers (e.g., colon, prostate, and stomach) due to phytonutrients
   - Type 2 diabetes, obesity, and hypertension
5. **Hydration and Detoxification:** Many fruits and vegetables (like watermelon, cucumber, orange) have high water content which:
   - Maintains hydration
   - Helps in detoxification and regulation of body temperature
6. **Low Caloric Density:** They are low in fat and calories but high in volume and nutrients, making them ideal for weight management and obesity prevention.
7. **Enhancing Immunity and Gut Health:** The micronutrients and bioactive compounds support immune function and feed beneficial gut microbiota, which is essential for digestion and immune modulation.
8. **Cultural and Culinary Importance:** Apart from nutritional value, fruits and vegetables are essential in culinary traditions worldwide and promote dietary diversity, encouraging healthy eating habits.

Thus, including a variety of seasonal, colorful fruits and vegetables in daily meals is fundamental to ensuring nutrient adequacy, preventing deficiencies, and promoting long-term health and well-being.

5. (*d*): Write the symptoms and management of shoot and fruit borer in brinjal and diamondback moth in cabbage.

1. **Shoot and Fruit Borer in Brinjal (Leucinodes orbonalis)**

Symptoms:

- **Shoot damage:** Larvae bore into tender shoots causing wilting and dieback of the terminal portion, especially in young plants.
- **Fruit damage:** Borer enters through a small hole and feeds internally, leading to:
  - ❑ Premature dropping of fruits
  - ❑ Formation of boreholes with excreta (frass) sticking out
  - ❑ Rotten and unmarketable fruits
- Multiple fruits may be damaged on a single plant, severely reducing yield.

Management:

- **Cultural:**
  - ❑ Use resistant or tolerant varieties like 'Arka Nidhi'.
  - ❑ Remove and destroy affected shoots and fruits regularly to break the life cycle.
  - ❑ Practice crop rotation with non-host crops.
- **Mechanical:** Install pheromone traps (10–12/acre) to monitor and mass-trap male moths.
- **Biological:**
  - ❑ Release egg parasitoid *Trichogramma chilonis* at 1 lakh/acre at weekly intervals.
  - ❑ Apply *Bacillus thuringiensis* (*Bt*) formulations for larval control.
- **Chemical:**
  - ❑ Spray insecticides like cypermethrin (0.005%), deltamethrin (0.0028%), or flubendiamide at recommended intervals.
  - ❑ Use chemicals judiciously and rotate classes to avoid resistance buildup.

2. **Diamondback Moth in Cabbage (Plutella xylostella)**

Symptoms:

- Larval feeding on leaves leads to characteristic small, irregular holes.
- Leaves appear skeletonized in heavy infestation.
- In severe cases, the plant growth is stunted, and heads become unmarketable.
- Larvae may also hide in leaf folds or near the growing tip.

Management:

- **Cultural:**
  - ❑ Grow trap crops like mustard along field borders to attract moths.
  - ❑ Destroy crop residues after harvest to prevent carry-over population.
- **Mechanical:** Use light traps and pheromone traps (15/ha) to monitor adult moth activity.
- **Biological:**
  - ❑ Release parasitoids like *Cotesia plutellae* to parasitize larvae.
  - ❑ Apply biopesticides such as *Bacillus thuringiensis* or neem-based formulations (Azadirachtin 1% EC).
- **Chemical:**
  - ❑ Spray insecticides like spinosad (0.0135%), emamectin benzoate (5 SG at 0.2 g/L), or chlorantraniliprole under severe infestation.
  - ❑ Avoid repeated use of the same insecticide to prevent resistance.

5. (*e*): **How is food consumption trend in Indian population changing in relation with availability of crop produces and socio-economic factors?**

Food consumption patterns in India have undergone significant changes in recent decades, influenced by factors such as agricultural production, income growth, urbanization, lifestyle changes, and market dynamics.

1. **Shift from Cereals to Diversified Diets:** Traditionally, Indian diets were dominated by cereals like rice, wheat, and millets. However:

- With the Green Revolution, wheat and rice became more accessible, causing a decline in the consumption of coarse cereals.
- In recent years, there's a resurgence in millet and coarse grain consumption, driven by awareness of their health benefits and government initiatives like the International Year of Millets (2023).

2. Rise in Fruits, Vegetables, and Protein-Rich Foods:

- Increased awareness of nutrition and lifestyle diseases has led to greater consumption of fruits, vegetables, milk, eggs, and pulses.
- Rising incomes and urbanization are contributing to higher animal protein intake, including poultry, dairy, and fish.
- Government schemes like Mid-Day Meal, Poshan Abhiyan, and National Food Security Act (NFSA) are promoting balanced nutrition.

3. Urbanization and Processed Food:

- Urban populations increasingly consume ready-to-eat and processed foods, fast foods, and packaged snacks.
- This shift is associated with sedentary lifestyles and rising cases of obesity, diabetes, and heart disease.

4. Socio-Economic Factors Influencing Consumption:

- Income levels: Higher income groups tend to consume more fruits, milk, meat, and processed foods, while lower-income groups still depend on staple cereals and pulses.
- Education and health awareness: Educated populations prefer diversified, balanced diets and are more responsive to health campaigns.
- Gender and age: Young populations consume more fast food and beverages, whereas older populations focus on traditional, balanced diets.

5. Changing Agricultural Production Patterns:

- India has increased production of horticultural crops (fruits & vegetables) surpassing food grain production.
- Horticulture, dairy, and fisheries are growing faster than staple food production, matching the shift in demand.
- Market linkages, cold chain infrastructure, and food processing are also evolving to support these trends.

6. Regional and Cultural Variations:

- South India consumes more rice; North India prefers wheat.
- Vegetarianism remains prevalent but meat consumption is rising, especially in urban and coastal areas.
- Religion, festivals, and cultural traditions still influence food choices.

6. (*a*): Write in detail about the occurrence, transport, site of synthesis and bioassay of abscisic acid in plants. Also explain the effect of abscisic acid on various plant physiological processes.

1. Occurrence of Abscisic Acid (ABA): Abscisic acid is a naturally occurring plant hormone found in:

- All higher plants (angiosperms and gymnosperms)
- Algae and some fungi
- Particularly abundant in mature leaves, fruits, seeds, and vascular tissues

It is also produced in response to stress conditions like drought, salinity, and cold, hence called a stress hormone.

2. Site of Synthesis:

- ABA is synthesized mainly in chloroplasts and other plastids of mesophyll cells in leaves.
- Under stress conditions, roots also synthesize ABA, which is transported to shoots to signal water deficiency.
- Biosynthesis involves carotenoid cleavage pathway, where zeaxanthin and violaxanthin act as precursors.

3. Transport:

- ABA is transported through both xylem and phloem, depending on source and demand.
  - ❑ Xylem transport dominates when roots produce ABA during drought.
  - ❑ Phloem transport is seen during seed and fruit development.
- Transport occurs passively in uncharged form or actively via ABA transporters like ABC transporters.

4. Bioassay of ABA: Several bioassays are used to estimate ABA activity:

- Inhibition of seed germination: ABA delays or inhibits germination in seeds like lettuce.

- Stomatal closure test: Applied ABA induces closure of stomata in epidermal peel or intact leaf.
- Inhibition of α-amylase synthesis in barley endosperm: ABA suppresses gibberellin-induced enzyme production.
- Leaf abscission or senescence bioassays are also used.

5. Effects of Abscisic Acid on Plant Physiology:

(*a*) **Seed Dormancy:**
- ABA induces and maintains seed dormancy.
- It inhibits precocious germination (vivipary) in cereals and promotes the accumulation of storage proteins.

(*b*) **Stomatal Closure:**
- ABA triggers the efflux of ions like K^+ from guard cells, causing water loss and closure of stomata.
- It is a key response to water stress, reducing transpiration and water loss.

(*c*) **Inhibition of Growth:**
- ABA acts as a growth inhibitor, countering the actions of growth-promoting hormones like auxins and gibberellins.
- It retards stem elongation and cell division under stress conditions.

(*d*) **Leaf Senescence and Abscission:** Promotes senescence and leaf fall, especially under nutrient or water deficiency.

(*e*) **Fruit Maturation:** ABA regulates fruit ripening, especially in non-climacteric fruits like grapes and citrus by enhancing anthocyanin synthesis and sugar accumulation.

(*f*) **Stress Response:** It activates stress-responsive genes, enhances osmoprotectant accumulation, and increases antioxidant activity under drought, salinity, or temperature extremes.

6. (*b*) (*i*): Climate Requirements for Turmeric Cultivation:

- **Type of Climate:** Turmeric (*Curcuma longa*) thrives in hot and humid tropical climates. It is typically grown in areas with a warm and moist environment.
- **Temperature:** Optimal temperature range is 20°C to 35°C. It cannot tolerate frost or extreme cold conditions.
- **Rainfall:** Requires an annual rainfall of 1000–2000 mm, preferably well-distributed throughout the growing period. It is best suited for rainfed as well as irrigated conditions.
- **Season:**
  - ❑ Turmeric is a Kharif crop sown during April–June depending on onset of monsoon.
  - ❑ It requires about 7 to 9 months from sowing to maturity.
- **Light:** Prefers moderate shade to full sunlight, though partial shade enhances rhizome yield in some varieties.

Soil Requirements for Turmeric Cultivation:

- **Type of Soil:** Turmeric can be grown in a wide range of soils like red loam, clay loam, and alluvial soils, but it performs best in:
  - ❑ Well-drained, friable loamy or sandy loam soils rich in organic matter.
- **Soil pH:** The optimal pH range is 5.5 to 7.5. Slightly acidic soils are preferred.
- **Drainage:** Good drainage is essential as turmeric is highly susceptible to rhizome rot under waterlogged conditions.
- **Soil Preparation:** The field should be deeply ploughed (2–3 times), well-leveled, and made free of clods. Adequate application of compost or FYM (20–25 t/ha) is beneficial.
- **Soil Fertility:** High organic content supports better rhizome development. Supplementary fertilizers (NPK) enhance yield.

6. (*b*) (*ii*): Discuss the following in respect of turmeric cultivation: Varieties, seed rate and planting:

1. Varieties of Turmeric: Turmeric varieties are selected based on yield, curcumin content, disease resistance, and regional adaptability. Prominent varieties include:

- **Erode Local:** Famous for high-quality rhizomes; curcumin content ~2.5–3%.
- **Prabha (IC-31):** Released by IISR; high-yielding with ~5.5% curcumin.

- **Suvarna:** Medium duration; suitable for rainfed conditions; curcumin ~4.7%.
- **Rajendra Sonia:** Developed by RAU, Pusa; suitable for Bihar; curcumin ~5.0%.
- **Roma, Ranga, Rasmi:** Released by OUAT, Odisha; medium to high yielding with curcumin content of 4.5–6%.
- **IISR Alleppey Supreme:** High-yielding, curcumin-rich variety suitable for Kerala and coastal zones.
- **Suguna, Sudarsana, Suvarna:** Developed by Indian Institute of Spices Research (IISR) for different agro-climatic zones.

2. Seed Rate:

- Rhizomes used as planting material (both mother and finger rhizomes).
- Seed rate:
  - ❑ 2000–2500 kg/ha under irrigated conditions
  - ❑ 2500–3000 kg/ha under rainfed or organic farming
- Mother rhizomes are typically preferred for uniform sprouting.
- Use healthy, disease-free, well-developed rhizomes (20–25 g each).

3. Planting:

- **Time of planting:** Best time is April to June, just before the onset of monsoon. In irrigated areas, planting can begin in early summer (April).
- **Method of planting:**
  - ❑ Raised beds, ridges and furrows, or flat beds depending on region and soil type.
  - ❑ Rhizomes are placed horizontally at a depth of 4–6 cm in moist soil.
- **Spacing:**
  - ❑ 30 cm between rows × 25 cm between plants for optimal growth and aeration.
  - ❑ Wider spacing is used in high rainfall zones or when larger rhizomes are expected.
- **Mulching:**
  - ❑ Immediately after planting, fields are mulched with green leaves or straw (about 12–15 t/ha) to conserve moisture and suppress weeds.
  - ❑ Repeat mulching after sprouting and earthing-up.

6. (*b*) (*iii*): Discuss the following in respect of turmeric cultivation: Manures and fertilizers:

1. Importance of Nutrient Management in Turmeric: Turmeric is a heavy feeder of nutrients due to its long duration (7–9 months) and underground rhizome development. Proper application of organic manures and chemical fertilizers enhances rhizome size, yield, curcumin content, and resistance to pests and diseases.

2. Organic Manures:

- **Farmyard Manure (FYM):**
  - ❑ Apply 20–25 tonnes per hectare as a basal dose during land preparation.
  - ❑ It improves soil structure, microbial activity, and moisture retention.
- **Compost or Green Manure:** Can supplement FYM where available.
- **Neem Cake:** @ 1–2 tonnes/ha is often used for soil-borne pest and disease control.
- In organic turmeric farming, organic manures are often supplemented with vermicompost, biofertilizers (Azospirillum, Phosphobacteria), and Trichoderma for plant health and yield.

3. Fertilizer Requirement (Chemical):

- Recommended NPK Dose:
  - ❑ 100–150 kg Nitrogen (N)
  - ❑ 60 kg Phosphorus (P_2O_2)
  - ❑ 60–100 kg Potassium (K_2O) per hectare

Application Schedule:

- **Basal dose (at planting):** Full dose of P (60 kg) + half of K (30–50 kg) + one-third of N (33–50 kg)
- **Top Dressing:** Remaining two-thirds of N and half of K applied in 2 split doses at 60 and 120 days after planting.
- **Micronutrients:**
  - ❑ Zinc, boron, and magnesium can be applied if deficiencies are observed.
  - ❑ Foliar sprays of micronutrients or seaweed extracts enhance rhizome development and stress tolerance.

4. Integrated Nutrient Management (INM):

- Combining organic and inorganic sources is highly beneficial.

- Use of biofertilizers like *Azospirillum* and *Phosphobacteria* at 25 kg/ha each improves nutrient uptake and reduces chemical dependency.

5. **Special Practices:**
   - Mulching after fertilizer application helps conserve moisture and improve nutrient use efficiency.
   - Irrigation after top dressing ensures proper nutrient absorption.

6. (*b*) (*iv*): Cultural operations are essential agronomic practices carried out during the crop growth period to ensure healthy plant development, maximize yield, and minimize pest and weed incidence. In turmeric cultivation, the following major cultural operations are practiced:

1. **Land Preparation:**
   - The field should be ploughed 2 to 3 times to achieve a fine tilth.
   - Ridges and furrows or raised beds are prepared depending on rainfall and soil type.
   - Well-decomposed FYM (20–25 t/ha) is incorporated before planting.
2. **Mulching:**
   - Immediately after planting, the field is mulched with green leaves, paddy straw, or sugarcane trash at 12–15 t/ha.
   - Repeat mulching:
     - ❑ After sprouting (30 days after planting)
     - ❑ After each earthing-up or fertilizer application
   - Benefits: Conserves soil moisture, suppresses weeds, prevents soil erosion, and improves microbial activity.
3. **Irrigation:**
   - Turmeric requires regular irrigation, especially in dry periods.
   - Frequency:
     - ❑ Every 7–10 days during dry months
     - ❑ Reduced frequency during rainy season
   - Over-irrigation should be avoided to prevent rhizome rot.
4. **Weed Management:**
   - Initial 60 days are critical for weed control.
   - Hand weeding is done at 30, 60, and 90 days after planting.
   - Mulching reduces weed growth significantly.
   - In large-scale farming, pre-emergence herbicides like pendimethalin may be used under expert supervision.
5. **Earthing-Up:**
   - Done 2–3 times during the growing season, usually after each weeding and fertilizer top-dressing.
   - Helps in covering the rhizomes, supports plant stability, and improves aeration.
6. **Fertilizer Application:**
   - Split application of N and K fertilizers as top dressing at 60 and 120 days after planting.
   - Followed by earthing-up and light irrigation for better nutrient utilization.
7. **Pest and Disease Management:**
   - Regular field monitoring is essential.
   - Use neem-based sprays, bioagents (like *Trichoderma, Pseudomonas fluorescens*), and organic pesticides in IPM-based systems.
8. **Crop Rotation and Intercropping:**
   - Crop rotation with legumes (e.g., green gram) helps improve soil fertility.
   - Turmeric is often intercropped with maize, chillies, castor, or onions under rainfed conditions.

6. (*b*) (*v*): Discuss the following in respect of turmeric cultivation: Post-harvest processing

Post-harvest processing of turmeric is a critical stage that determines the final quality, market value, and storability of the produce. It involves harvesting, curing, drying, polishing, coloring, and storage. Each step must be carefully managed to preserve curcumin content and rhizome aroma.

1. **Harvesting:**
   - Turmeric is ready for harvest 7–9 months after planting, when:
     - ❑ The leaves and stems start yellowing and drying.
     - ❑ Rhizomes attain maximum size, color, and aroma.

- Harvesting is done manually using a spade or digging fork to avoid damage.
- Rhizomes are separated into mother and finger rhizomes; only finger rhizomes are used for marketing.

2. **Curing (Boiling):**
- Fresh rhizomes are boiled to:
  - ❑ Remove the raw odor
  - ❑ Gelatinize starch
  - ❑ Produce uniform golden-yellow color
- **Method:**
  - ❑ Rhizomes are boiled in water for 30-45 minutes until soft (not overcooked to avoid color loss).
  - ❑ Boiling vessel: Either traditional (mud/metal pot) or improved steam boiling units.
- After boiling, the rhizomes are drained and cooled before drying.

3. **Drying:**
- Boiled rhizomes are sun-dried for 10-15 days on clean drying floors.
- Rhizomes should be turned regularly for uniform drying.
- Proper drying reduces moisture to 8–10%, which prevents fungal infestation during storage.

4. **Polishing:**
- Dried rhizomes are rough and dull; polishing enhances appearance.
- Manual polishing: Rhizomes rubbed against hard surfaces (stone or coir mat).
- Mechanical polishing: Using rotating drums lined with abrasives.
- Polished turmeric is more attractive and fetches better price.

5. **Coloring (Optional):**
- To enhance brightness, rhizomes may be coated with turmeric powder or yellow food-grade color mixed with water and lime.
- Not always preferred for export markets where natural color is demanded.

6. **Grinding (if processed further):**
- Turmeric is ground into fine powder using hammer mills.
- Ground turmeric is immediately packed in airtight containers to retain color and aroma.

7. **Packaging and Storage:**
- Rhizomes are stored in gunny bags or ventilated containers in a cool, dry, and dark place.
- Storage structures should be free from moisture and pests.
- For powdered turmeric, moisture-proof and light-proof packaging is essential.

6. (*c*): Apple scab is one of the most economically important and widespread fungal diseases of apple (*Malus domestica*), caused by the fungus *Venturia inaequalis*. It severely affects fruit quality, marketability, and yield.

1. **Causal Organism:**
- Scientific Name: *Venturia inaequalis*
- Class: Ascomycetes
- Disease Type: Foliar and fruit disease
- Survival: The pathogen survives as pseudothecia (sexual stage) in fallen leaves during winter and releases ascospores in spring.

2. **Symptoms:**

On Leaves:
- Early season lesions appear as olive-green to brown, velvety spots on the upper surface.
- As infection progresses, lesions may become dark, circular or irregular, leading to leaf curling, chlorosis, and premature defoliation.

On Fruits:
- Scabby, black to brown rough lesions on the skin.
- Infected fruits become distorted, cracked, or undersized, leading to poor market value.
- Lesions are usually more prominent on the calyx end and may coalesce in severe cases.

On Twigs (rarely):
- Small dark lesions on young shoots in severe infections.

3. Management of Apple Scab:

A. Cultural Practices:

- **Sanitation:** Collect and destroy fallen leaves and pruned twigs to eliminate overwintering inoculum.
- **Pruning:** Improve air circulation by pruning dense canopy to reduce leaf wetness.
- **Proper spacing** and tree training to reduce humidity buildup in the orchard.

B. Resistant Varieties:

- Use scab-resistant apple cultivars like:
  - Liberty
  - Prima
  - Enterprise
  - Freedom
- However, resistance can break down over time due to pathogen variability.

C. Biological Control:

- Application of compost tea or biological antagonists like *Trichoderma spp.* on fallen leaves to degrade pathogen structures.

D. Chemical Control:

- **Pre-bloom sprays:** Use protectant fungicides like mancozeb, captan, or chlorothalonil at pink bud stage.
- **Post-bloom sprays:** Use systemic fungicides like:
  - Difenoconazole
  - Myclobutanil
  - Trifloxystrobin
  - Fenarimol
- **Spray schedule:** Multiple applications during critical growth stages—bud break to fruit set—based on weather forecasts and disease risk models.
- **Resistance management:** Alternate fungicides with different modes of action to prevent resistance buildup.

E. Forecasting and IPM:

- Use of forecasting models (like Mills' table) to predict infection periods based on temperature and leaf wetness.
- Integrated Pest Management (IPM): Combines cultural, biological, and chemical strategies, guided by disease monitoring.

7. (*a*): Major Insect-Pests Affecting Stored Wheat: Stored wheat and other cereals are highly vulnerable to storage pests, which damage the grains by feeding, contamination, and causing weight loss, reduced quality, and poor germination. The major insect pests include:

1. Lesser Grain Borer (*Rhyzopertha dominica*):

- Most destructive pest of stored wheat.
- Both larvae and adults bore into grains and feed internally.
- Infested grains are hollowed and emit a characteristic musty odor.

2. Rice Weevil (*Sitophilus oryzae*):

- Attacks whole grains.
- Female bores hole in the grain to lay eggs; larvae develop inside.
- Causes severe quantitative and quality loss.

3. Rust-Red Flour Beetle (*Tribolium castaneum*):

- A secondary pest; feeds on broken grains and flour.
- Causes bad odor, discoloration, and mold growth.

4. Khapra Beetle (*Trogoderma granarium*):

- One of the most dreaded pests; larvae cause heavy damage.
- Tolerant to insecticides; feeds on germ and endosperm.
- Contaminates grain with hairs and cast skins, rendering it unfit for consumption.

5. Angoumois Grain Moth (*Sitotroga cerealella*):

- Females lay eggs on grains; larvae bore into grains.
- Damage occurs both during field drying and storage.

Preventive Measures:

1. Pre-Storage Hygiene:

- Clean storage structures (godowns, bins) thoroughly.
- Remove old grain residues and debris.
- Wash with disinfectants like 5% bleaching powder or lime wash.

2. Proper Drying: Grains should be dried to safe moisture content (below 10%) before storage to prevent insect and fungal attack.

3. Sanitation and Sealing:

- Store only clean, uninfested grains.

- Use airtight bins or bags; seal cracks and holes to prevent entry of pests.

4. **Use of Pest-Resistant Packaging:** Employ HDPE bags, double-layered jute bags, or hermetic storage.
5. **Store at Safe Temperature:**
   - Maintain storage temperature below 20°C to restrict insect breeding.
   - Avoid dampness and temperature fluctuations.

Control Measures:

1. **Fumigation:** Phosphine (Aluminum phosphide) is widely used for fumigation.
   - Dosage: 3 tablets per tonne of grain.
   - Exposure: 5–7 days under gas-tight conditions.
   - Highly effective against all life stages of storage insects.
2. **Insecticide Dusting (Preventive):**
   - Malathion 5% dust @ 250 g per 100 kg of grain.
   - Not recommended for grains meant for immediate consumption.
3. **Biological Control:** Use of parasitoids like *Anisop-teromalus calandrae and Theocolax elegans* is being explored for weevil control in eco-friendly storage systems.
4. **Botanicals and Eco-Friendly Alternatives:**
   - Neem seed powder, neem oil (3–5 mL/kg), or other plant-based insect repellents like *Vitex negundo and Pongamia pinnata leaves*.
   - Suitable for small farmers and organic storage systems.

   Integrated Storage Pest Management (ISPM):
   - Combine cleaning, drying, use of botanicals, safe packaging, and timely fumigation.
   - Periodic monitoring of storage for pest detection and early intervention is essential.

7. (*b*) (*i*): What is Curing?

Curing is a post-harvest process primarily applied to certain vegetables and tuber crops (e.g., onion, garlic, potato, sweet potato, yam) to heal surface injuries, dry the outer layers, and prepare the produce for storage or marketing. It improves shelf life, minimizes rot, and enhances quality.

Objectives of Curing:

1. **Healing of Wounds:** Minor bruises, cuts, or harvest injuries are healed as periderm (protective tissue) develops.
2. **Drying of Outer Skin or Neck:** Reduces moisture content from outer layers, preventing microbial infections.
3. **Hardening of Skin:** Forms a protective barrier over delicate tissues.
4. **Prevention of Post-Harvest Losses:** Reduces attack by pathogens and pests during storage.

7. (*b*) (*ii*): What is Degreening?

Degreening is a post-harvest process applied mainly to citrus fruits and some other climacteric fruits to remove the green chlorophyll pigment from the peel, enhancing surface color development and market appeal, without affecting internal ripeness.

Purpose of Degreening:

- Improve the visual quality and uniform ripening of fruits for the market.
- Make fruits more attractive to consumers by bringing out natural pigments like carotenoids (orange, yellow, red).
- Often used when fruits are harvested at physiological maturity but still retain greenish peels due to environmental conditions (low temperature or light).

Fruits Commonly Subjected to Degreening:

- Citrus fruits (e.g., sweet orange, mandarins, lemon)
- Banana
- Tomato (in commercial settings)
- Papaya

7. (*b*) (*iii*): What is Pre-cooling?

Pre-cooling is a post-harvest treatment where the field heat is rapidly removed from freshly harvested fruits and vegetables before storage, packaging, or transportation. It is the first and most essential step in maintaining post-harvest quality and prolonging shelf life.

Purpose of Pre-cooling:

- Removes heat absorbed from sunlight and ambient environment during harvest.
- Slows down respiration, transpiration, and microbial activity, delaying spoilage.
- Preserves texture, flavor, aroma, and nutritional quality.
- Minimizes wilting, softening, decay, and color loss.
- Prepares produce for further cold storage or refrigerated transport.

Fruits and Vegetables That Require Pre-cooling:

- Highly perishable fruits like grapes, strawberries, bananas, apples, peaches
- Leafy vegetables like lettuce, spinach, cabbage
- Other perishables like tomato, capsicum, beans, cauli-flower

7. (*b*) (*iv*): What is Disinfestation?

Disinfestation refers to the post-harvest treatment process aimed at eliminating or killing insect pests, larvae, or eggs present on or within harvested fruits and vegetables. It ensures that produce is free from quarantine pests, safe for consumption, and eligible for export and long-term storage.

Purpose of Disinfestation:

- Prevent infestation during storage, transport, or marketing.
- Comply with quarantine regulations for international trade.
- Avoid physical damage and quality loss caused by insect feeding.
- Enhance shelf life and consumer acceptability.

Common Insect Pests Targeted:

- Fruit flies (e.g., *Bactrocera dorsalis*) in mango, guava
- Mealybugs, thrips, scale insects in citrus, grapes
- Mites and weevils in stored produce

Crop-Specific Examples:

- **Mango:** Hot water treatment or irradiation to meet export standards.
- **Grapes:** Sulphur dioxide pads or fumigation to control mealybugs.
- **Citrus:** Surface washing and fungicide dips to control scale insects and fungal spores.

7. (*b*) (*v*): What is Sorting and Grading?

Sorting refers to the separation of fruits and vegetables based on physical characteristics such as size, shape, color, weight, and maturity.

Grading involves classifying the sorted produce into quality categories according to established standards — for example, Grade A, B, C or Extra Class, Class I, II based on uniformity, defects, and appearance.

Importance of Sorting and Grading:

- Enhances marketability and pricing by ensuring uniform quality.
- Facilitates packaging, labeling, and export compliance.
- Helps in value addition by segregating produce for different end-uses (fresh market, processing, etc.).
- Reduces post-harvest losses by isolating damaged or diseased produce.
- Builds consumer trust by supplying clean and standard-quality produce.

Examples:

- **Mangoes:** Graded based on size (count), color, and surface defects for export.
- **Tomatoes:** Graded as extra, fancy, standard based on firmness, size, and uniform ripeness.
- **Onions:** Sorted by size for storage versus market.

7. (*c*): Ethylene is a simple gaseous plant hormone (chemical formula: C_2H_2) that plays a key regulatory role in plant growth, development, and stress responses. It is unique among plant hormones due to its gaseous nature and acts at very low concentrations.

Major Roles of Ethylene in Plants:

1. Fruit Ripening:

- Ethylene is the primary hormone responsible for ripening of climacteric fruits (e.g., banana, mango, tomato, papaya, apple).
- It induces:
  - ❑ Cell wall softening (via pectinase)

- ❑ Color changes (chlorophyll degradation and carotenoid synthesis)
- ❑ Sugar accumulation (conversion of starch to sugars)
- ❑ Aroma and flavor development

2. **Leaf and Flower Senescence & Abscission:**
   - Ethylene accelerates aging and shedding of leaves, flowers, and fruits.
   - Promotes abscission layer formation, especially under stress or nutrient deficiency.
   - Helps regulate life cycle events in annual plants.
3. **Seed Germination and Dormancy Breaking:** In some species, ethylene helps in breaking seed dormancy, particularly in seeds requiring mechanical weakening of seed coats (e.g., peanut, lettuce).
4. **Triple Response in Seedlings:**
   - In etiolated (dark-grown) seedlings, ethylene triggers a characteristic triple response:
     - ❑ Inhibition of elongation
     - ❑ Radial swelling (thickening of stem)
     - ❑ Horizontal growth (apical hook formation)
   - This response protects emerging shoots during soil emergence.
5. **Stress Responses:**
   - Ethylene production increases under:
     - ❑ Mechanical injury
     - ❑ Flooding, drought, heat, or cold stress
     - ❑ Pathogen attack
   - Acts as a stress signal, triggering protective mechanisms (e.g., defense-related gene expression, ROS production).
6. **Regulation of Sex Expression:**
   - In cucurbits (like cucumber), ethylene promotes femaleness.
   - Application of ethylene-releasing compounds like ethephon increases the number of female flowers and thus yield.
7. **Root Initiation and Nodulation:**
   - Ethylene interacts with auxins to promote adventitious root formation in cuttings.
   - Plays a modulatory role in nodulation in legumes under nitrogen-limiting conditions.
8. **Commercial Applications:**
   - Used in artificial ripening of fruits using ethephon or ethylene gas.
   - Regulates flowering in pineapple and latex flow in rubber trees.
   - Used to synchronize fruit ripening for uniform harvest.

8. (*a*) (*i*): Describe the following: NAFED

NAFED – National Agricultural Cooperative Marketing Federation of India Ltd.

Established: 1958

Headquarters: New Delhi

Ownership: An apex-level cooperative organization under the Ministry of Agriculture & Farmers Welfare, Government of India.

Objectives and Purpose:

NAFED was created to promote cooperative marketing of agricultural produce in India, ensuring fair prices for farmers and stabilization of agricultural markets. It serves as a support system for farmers and a key agency for implementing government procurement and price support operations.

Key Functions of NAFED:

1. **Procurement of Agricultural Produce:**
   - Acts as a central agency for procurement of crops under Price Support Scheme (PSS).
   - Procures crops like pulses, oilseeds, onion, and coarse grains at Minimum Support Price (MSP) to protect farmers from market fluctuations.
2. **Price Stabilization and Buffer Stocking:**
   - Implements the Price Stabilization Fund (PSF) scheme to manage volatility in prices of perishable commodities like onions and pulses.
   - Maintains buffer stocks of key commodities to ensure food availability and price stability.
3. **Promotion of Exports:**
   - Facilitates export of agricultural commodi-ties, ensuring quality certification, packaging, and logistics.
   - Supports farmers and cooperatives in reaching global markets.

4. **Support to Cooperatives:** Provides financial, technical, and marketing assistance to primary and secondary agricultural cooperative societies.

5. **Distribution and Marketing:**
   - Operates wholesale outlets for distribution of pulses, edible oils, and other essentials under schemes like PMGKAY or One Nation One Ration Card.
   - Collaborates with agencies like FCI, TRIFED, SFAC.

6. **Seed and Agri-inputs Distribution:** Supplies certified seeds, biofertilizers, and other inputs to farmers via cooperatives.

8. (*a*) (*ii*): What is TPDS?

The Targeted Public Distribution System (TPDS) is a government-run food security initiative in India, launched in June 1997 by restructuring the earlier universal Public Distribution System (PDS). TPDS aims to provide subsidized food grains specifically to economically weaker sections of the population through a targeted approach.

Nodal Ministry: Ministry of Consumer Affairs, Food and Public Distribution, Government of India.

Objectives of TPDS:

- Ensure food and nutritional security by making basic food commodities affordable for the poor.
- Target subsidies more effectively to the needy (below poverty line or BPL families).
- Reduce leakage, misuse, and wastage associated with the universal system.

Transition to NFSA, 2013:

- TPDS is now implemented under the National Food Security Act (NFSA), 2013, which provides legal entitlement to subsidized food grains.
- Key provisions under NFSA:
  - ❑ 75% rural and 50% urban population are covered.
  - ❑ Beneficiaries entitled to 5 kg food grains/month/person at ₹ 3/kg (rice), ₹ 2/kg (wheat), and ₹ 1/kg (coarse grains).
  - ❑ AAY households continue to receive 35 kg/month.

8. (*a*) (*iii*): What are Buffer Stock Operations?

Buffer stock operations refer to the procurement, storage, and release of essential food grains (primarily wheat and rice) by the government to ensure food security, price stability, and emergency food supply. These operations are carried out through Food Corporation of India (FCI) and other state agencies under the guidance of the Ministry of Consumer Affairs, Food and Public Distribution.

Objectives of Buffer Stock Operations:

1. Ensure food security by maintaining a ready supply for Public Distribution System (PDS) and emergency relief.
2. Stabilize market prices by managing supply during surplus or shortage.
3. Support farmers through Minimum Support Price (MSP) procurement.
4. Meet obligations under welfare schemes, e.g., Mid-Day Meals, Integrated Child Development Services (ICDS), and National Food Security Act (NFSA).

Key Components of Buffer Stock Management:

1. **Procurement:**
   - Food grains are procured from farmers at MSP during harvest seasons.
   - Ensures assured income to farmers and prevents distress sales.
   - Major procuring states: Punjab, Haryana, Madhya Pradesh, Chhattisgarh, Telangana.
2. **Storage:**
   - FCI stores the procured grains in scientifically managed warehouses and godowns.
   - Modern storage includes silos, CAP (Covered and Plinth) storage, and cold storage for perishables.
3. **Distribution:**
   - Stocks are released for:
     - ❑ TPDS and NFSA beneficiaries
     - ❑ Natural calamities/emergency relief
     - ❑ Price stabilization in open market sales (OMSS)
4. **Minimum Buffer Norms:**
   - The government maintains specific buffer norms (in lakh tonnes) to meet national

food requirements at different times of the year (e.g., beginning of April, July, October, and January).

- These norms are periodically reviewed by the Buffer Stocking Policy Committee.

8. (*a*) (*iv*): What is the Coffee Board of India?

The Coffee Board of India is a statutory organization established under the Coffee Act, 1942, functioning under the Ministry of Commerce and Industry, Government of India. It is primarily responsible for the promotion, development, and regulation of coffee production and exports in India.

Headquarters: Bengaluru, Karnataka

Objectives of the Coffee Board:

1. **Promote Coffee Production and Quality Improvement:**
   - ❑ Provide technical assistance, training, and subsidies to coffee growers.
   - ❑ Encourage adoption of modern cultivation practices and high-yielding varieties.
2. **Research and Development:**
   - ❑ Conduct R&D through its Central Coffee Research Institute (CCRI).
   - ❑ Focus on crop improvement, pest and disease control, and sustainability.
3. **Marketing and Export Promotion:**
   - ❑ Promote Indian coffee in international markets through trade fairs, branding, and certifications.
   - ❑ Help improve the global reputation of specialty Indian coffees (like Monsooned Malabar, Robusta Kaapi Royale).
4. **Quality Certification and Grading:**
   - ❑ Conduct grading and cupping to ensure high export standards.
   - ❑ Issue Certificate of Origin for coffee exports.
5. **Welfare of Growers:**
   - ❑ Extend financial support to small and marginal growers.
   - ❑ Operate welfare schemes such as insurance, education, and housing support.
6. **Coffee Statistics and Licensing:**
   - ❑ Maintain data on coffee production, consumption, and exports.
   - ❑ Earlier regulated internal trade through licensing (now liberalized).

8. (*a*) (*v*):

1. **Food Production and Its Importance:** Food production refers to the process of cultivating crops, raising livestock, and managing fisheries to produce food for human consumption. It is the backbone of food security and directly impacts nutritional outcomes in any population.

   India, being an agrarian country, produces a wide range of foods:
   - Cereals (wheat, rice, maize)
   - Pulses and legumes
   - Fruits and vegetables
   - Milk, eggs, and meat
   - Oilseeds and nuts

   A diversified food production system is crucial for meeting the dietary needs of the growing population and ensuring nutritional adequacy.

2. **Link Between Food Production and Nutrition:** While increased food production is essential to meet calorie requirements, nutritional security depends on the quality, diversity, and accessibility of food.

   Key Linkages:
   - Cereal-centric food production (e.g., wheat and rice under Green Revolution) improved energy intake but did not address micronutrient deficiencies.
   - Neglect of pulses, millets, fruits, and vegetables led to imbalanced diets.
   - Livestock and horticulture play a vital role in providing protein, vitamins, and minerals.
   - Promotion of kitchen gardening, backyard poultry, and fish farming improves household nutrition.

8. (*b*): Introduction: In horticulture, biotic agents refer to living organisms (mainly beneficial microbes, insects, and natural enemies) that are used to enhance plant health, boost productivity, and manage pests and diseases. These agents form the foundation of biological control and eco-friendly crop management in sustainable horticulture.

Principal Biotic Agents in Horticultural Crops:

1. **Microbial Biocontrol Agents:**

(*a*) **Fungi:**

- Trichoderma spp.
  - Antagonistic fungus used against soil-borne pathogens like Fusarium, Rhizoctonia, and Sclerotium.
  - Applied as seed treatment, root dip, or soil application in crops like tomato, capsicum, and banana.
- **Beauveria bassiana:** Entomopathogenic fungus effective against whiteflies, aphids, and caterpillars in crops like brinjal, cabbage, and rose.

(*b*) **Bacteria:**

- Bacillus thuringiensis (Bt)
  - A bioinsecticide targeting lepidopteran larvae (e.g., fruit borers, caterpillars).
  - Used as a foliar spray in tomato, okra, cauliflower, and citrus.
- Pseudomonas fluorescens
  - Suppresses bacterial and fungal diseases.
  - Enhances plant growth by inducing systemic resistance.

2. **Beneficial Insects and Parasitoids:**

(*a*) **Predators:**

- **Ladybird beetles (*Coccinella spp.*):** Feed on aphids, mealybugs, and whiteflies in crops like citrus, pomegranate, and guava.
- **Green lacewings (*Chrysoperla carnea*):** Effective predators of soft-bodied pests like thrips and mites.

(*b*) **Parasitoids:**

- **Trichogramma spp.:** Egg parasitoids released in crops like brinjal, chilli, and tomato to control fruit and shoot borers.
- **Encarsia formosa:** Parasitizes whiteflies in protected cultivation (polyhouse-grown vegetables and ornamentals).

3. **Nematode Antagonists:**

- **Paecilomyces lilacinus and Pochonia chlamy-dosporia:** Fungal agents used to manage root-knot nematodes in crops like tomato, cucumber, and banana.

4. **Mycorrhizal Fungi (VAM):**

- Form symbiotic relationships with plant roots.
- Enhance uptake of phosphorus and micronutrients.
- Widely used in fruit crops like citrus, banana, and grape during planting stage.

5. **Biofertilizer Microbes:**

(*a*) **Nitrogen-Fixers:** Azotobacter, Azospirillum – improve nitrogen availability in vegetable and fruit crops.

(*b*) **Phosphate-Solubilizing Bacteria (PSB):** Make fixed phosphorus available to plants, boosting growth in fruit orchards and vegetable nurseries.

(*c*) **Potassium and Zinc Solubilizers:** Promote micronutrient uptake, enhance flowering and fruit set.

8. (*c*): Lawn making refers to the process of establishing a dense, uniform, and green turf using suitable grasses to create aesthetically pleasing open spaces in gardens, parks, institutions, homes, and public places. In India, due to diverse climatic conditions, different methods are used based on region, grass species, and resources.

Essential Steps in Lawn Making:

1. **Site Selection and Preparation:**
   - Choose a well-drained, open sunny area with fertile soil.
   - Remove weeds, stones, and debris.
   - Plough or dig the soil to a depth of 30–45 cm, followed by leveling.
   - Mix well-rotted FYM or compost (5–10 kg/m^2) and sand for drainage improvement.
   - Ensure the surface is smooth and slightly sloped to facilitate water drainage.
2. **Selection of Grass Species:** Grass selection depends on climate, maintenance level, and purpose.

   Common grasses used in India:
   - Doob grass (*Cynodon dactylon*) – drought-tolerant and widely used
   - Mexican grass (*Zoysia tenuifolia*) – fine-textured and shade-tolerant
   - Carpet grass (*Axonopus compressus*) – for shaded and moist areas

- Selection-1 – improved variety of Cynodon for quick coverage

3. Methods of Lawn Establishment in India:

(*a*) Turfing:

- Pre-grown grass sods (turves) are cut and placed over prepared soil.
- Quick establishment and instant green cover.
- Used in public parks, embassies, and official gardens.

(*b*) Dibbling (Root Planting):

- Small rooted grass slips are planted at regular intervals (5–10 cm apart).
- Commonly used in Doob grass lawns.
- Inexpensive but takes time (2–3 months) to form a full lawn.

(*c*) Seeding:

- Grass seeds are sown evenly over the prepared ground.
- Less commonly used due to poor seed availability and longer establishment time.
- Requires regular watering and weed control.

(*d*) Plastering (Rammi method):

- A slurry of grass cuttings mixed with soil and water is spread over the prepared surface.
- Frequently used for Doob grass on slopes or bunds.
- Economical and good for erosion control.

4. Post-Planting Care:

- Regular watering – twice daily initially, then once as lawn establishes.
- First mowing – done when grass reaches 5–6 cm height.
- Rolling – done periodically to keep the surface firm and even.
- Weeding and fertilization – essential during early stages.

Previous Years' Paper

Indian Forest Service (Main) Exam, 2023

SUBJECT–AGRICULTURE

(Exam held on 01-12-2023)

PAPER-I

Note: *There are EIGHT questions in all, out of which FIVE are to be attempted, Question Nos. 1 & 5 are compulsory. Out of the remaining SIX questions, THREE are to be attempted selecting at least ONE question from each of the two Sections A and B. Attempts of questions shall be counted in sequential order. Unless struck off, attempt of a question shall be counted even if attempted partly. Any page or portion of the page left blank in the Question-cum-Answer Booklet must be clearly struck off. All questions carry equal marks. Answers must be written in ENGLISH only.*

SECTION-A

1. (*a*) Elaborate the strategy for increasing production of vegetable oil in India.

(*b*) State the differences between green manuring and brown manuring, and write the advantages of brown manuring.

(*c*) Discuss the effects of abiotic stresses on agricultural production.

(*d*) Give an account of merits and demerits of nanofertilizers with suitable examples.

(*e*) Give an account of agricultural practices affecting sustainability of natural resources.

2. (*a*) Describe the good cultivation practices for short-term initial control of weeds in crops.

(*b*) Give an elaborate account of agronomic practices for managing the problems of environmental pollution.

(*c*) Explain the term 'crop diversification'. Discuss the contribution of high-yielding short-duration varieties in crop intensification and diversification in India.

3. (*a*) Write the characteristics and reclamation of saline soils and sodic soils.

(*b*) Explain various concepts of agroforestry systems and discuss their roles in livelihood security in rural India.

(*c*) Discuss the geographic factors used by the National Bureau of Soil Survey and Land Use Planning (NBSS & LUP) for agroecological zoning in India.

4. Describe the cultivation of maize in respect of the following:

(*i*) Types of maize

(*ii*) Earthing up

(*iii*) Water management

(*iv*) Weed management

(*v*) Harvesting

(*b*) Differentiate between intercropping and mixed cropping. Explain the terms 'additive series', 'replacement series' and 'land equivalent ratio' with examples.

(c) Describe the role of biofertilizers in success of integrated nutrient management and nutrient availability in India.

SECTION-B

5. (a) Describe the causes of soil erosion in brief.

(b) What are the harmful effects of poor drainage on plants?

(c) Enlist and briefly explain the competencies needed by an extension professional.

(d) Why should a farmer maintain farm records? Enlist the records to be maintained by the farmer.

(e) Enlist and explain in brief the problems associated with marketing of agricultural produce in India.

6. (a) Elaborate different *in situ* water conservation techniques by appropriate land configurations.

(b) Enlist the purposes of extension evaluation and explain the degrees of extension evaluation.

(c) Elaborate the institutional infrastructure available for agricultural marketing in India.

7. (a) Describe the role of Self-Help Group (SHG), Cooperative Society and Farmer Producer Company (FPC) in optimization of resource utilization by farming community.

(b) What is commodity-based extension? Explain its characteristics and weaknesses.

(c) Enlist and explain the approaches to increase water-use efficiency in crop fields.

8. (a) Describe the farm management decisions (organizational, administrative and marketing management decisions) to be made by the farmer as a manager of his farm business.

(b) Differentiate between rainfed and dryland agriculture. Describe the technological approaches for improving crop productivity under dryland.

(c) Describe the 'bottom-up approach' adopted under Technology Assessment and Refinement through Institution Village Linkage Programme.

PAPER-II

Note: *There are EIGHT questions in all, out of which FIVE are to be attempted, Question Nos. 1 & 5 are compulsory. Out of the remaining SIX questions, THREE are to be attempted selecting at least ONE question from each of the two Sections A and B. Attempts of questions shall be counted in sequential order. Unless struck off, attempt of a question shall be counted even if attempted partly. Any page or portion of the page left blank in the Question-cum-Answer Booklet must be clearly struck off. All questions carry equal marks. Answers must be written in ENGLISH only.*

SECTION-A

1. (a) Give a brief description of plasma membrane structure (with labelled diagram) and its functions.

(b) What do you understand by passport data of genetic resources? Write its importance in germplasm collection and conservation.

(c) Describe different classes of seeds. What are the essential requirements for production of certified seeds?

(*d*) Discuss in brief the practical significance of plant physiology in agriculture.

(*e*) Explain the methods for linkage detection in recombinant breeding programme.

2. (*a*) What are chromosome structure models? Describe various models with the help of suitable diagrams. Which models are widely accepted and why?

(*b*) Differentiate between the following:

(*i*) Apomixis and Parthenogenesis

(*ii*) Quantitative traits and Qualitative traits

(*iii*) Recurrent Selection for General Combining Ability (RSGCA) and Recurrent Selection for Specific Combining Ability (RSSCA)

(*iv*) Avoidance and Non-Preference

(*v*) Penetrance and Expressivity

(*c*) Write a note on chlorophyll pigments.

3. (*a*) Write in detail about the anatomy and cytology of stomata. Also, explain about the factors affecting stomatal movement.

(*b*) Explain the various parameters of field and seed standards for breeder seed production. Write the field and seed standards for wheat and maize.

(*c*) What are the components of genetic variance? How are these components estimated?

4. (*a*) Write the breeding objectives for improvement of wheat and gram. Describe the pedigree method of breeding for crop improvement.

(*b*) How does CO_2 fixation take place in succulent plants? Why do the stomata open at night and close during the day in CAM plants? Mention the families of Angiosperms in which succulents are available.

(*c*) Give a brief account of genetically modified crops with suitable examples.

SECTION-B

5. (*a*) What is bud dormancy? Explain its causes and the means to break bud dormancy.

(*b*) Write the preparation method of Ready to Serve (RTS) beverages and squashes.

(*c*) Write the causal organisms, nature of damage and management practices for damping off in vegetables.

(*d*) Discuss the preventive measures for management of stored grain pests and diseases.

(*e*) The rice-wheat system has been dominating the national agricultural scenario for the last four decades, in spite of the fact that the water table has been going down year after year. Why?

6. (*a*) Explain the biosynthesis of gibberellins. Also, list the role of gibberellins in plants. With suitable examples, write about the commercial uses of gibberellins in agriculture.

(*b*) Give an account of the area, production and productivity trends with respect to oil seeds and pulses during the last decade in India. What are the agronomic interventions for further boosting up their production?

(*c*) Explain the biological control methods for tomato fruit borer and guava wilt.

7. (*a*) Describe the package of practices for mango cultivation in North India considering suitable varieties for processing, soil and climate requirements, fertilizer requirement, propagation method, management of mango malformation and alternate bearing.

(*b*) Write in detail about the causal organism, nature of damage and management of the following diseases and insect pests:

(*i*) Cotton white fly

(*ii*) Cotton mealy bug

(*iii*) Chickpea pod borer

(*c*) How does photoperiodism influence plant growth and development? Explain with suitable examples.

8. (*a*) Write a note on malnutrition among women and children. How can fruits and vegetables production trends help in mitigating malnutrition?

(*b*) Discuss the cultivation practices for cauliflower considering the following points:

(*i*) Soil and climate requirements

(*ii*) Varieties, seed rate and sowing time

(*iii*) Nursery raising and transplanting method

(*iv*) Management of physiological disorders

(*v*) Harvesting and yield

(*c*) Describe the causal organism, nature of damage and management of the following stored grain pests:

(*i*) Rice weevil

(*ii*) Khapra beetle

ANSWERS

PAPER-I

1. (*a*) Increasing vegetable oil production in India involves a combination of strategies that address various aspects of the value chain, from cultivation to processing and distribution. Here are some strategies to consider:

- **Promotion of High-Yielding Varieties:** Encourage farmers to adopt high-yielding varieties of oilseeds through awareness campaigns and subsidies. Provide farmers with access to quality seeds and promote the cultivation of oilseed crops with high oil content.
- **Research and Development:** Invest in research and development to improve the productivity of oilseed crops. Develop and promote technologies that enhance oil extraction efficiency from oilseeds.
- **Extension Services and Training:** Strengthen agricultural extension services to educate farmers on modern farming practices, including optimal planting techniques, irrigation methods, and pest control.
- Conduct training programs to enhance farmers' skills in oilseed cultivation.
- **Irrigation Infrastructure:** Improve irrigation facilities to ensure consistent water supply for oilseed crops, reducing dependency on rainfall. Promote water-efficient irrigation methods to conserve water resources.
- **Input Subsidies:** Provide subsidies on fertilizers, pesticides, and other inputs to make oilseed cultivation more economically viable for farmers.
- **Financial Incentives:** Introduce financial incentives for farmers engaging in oilseed cultivation to encourage increased production.
- **Crop Diversification:** Promote crop diversification by integrating oilseed cultivation into existing cropping patterns, helping to reduce the risk for farmers and enhance overall agricultural sustainability.
- **Market Linkages:** Strengthen market linkages between farmers and processors to ensure a steady demand for oilseeds. Facilitate the creation of farmer cooperatives to negotiate better prices and improve bargaining power.

- **Processing Infrastructure:** Invest in the development and modernization of oilseed processing units to increase efficiency and reduce post-harvest losses. Encourage private sector investment in oilseed processing facilities.
- **Quality Standards and Certification:** Establish and enforce quality standards for vegetable oils to enhance consumer confidence. Promote certification programs for sustainable and organic oilseed cultivation.
- **Government Policies:** Formulate supportive policies that incentivize oilseed production and processing.
- Monitor and regulate the vegetable oil market to ensure fair practices and prevent price manipulation.
- **Public Awareness Campaigns:** Educate consumers about the nutritional benefits of locally produced vegetable oils to stimulate demand.Foster awareness about the economic and health advantages of using domestically produced oils.

Implementing these strategies will require collaboration between government agencies, agricultural organizations, research institutions, and the private sector. Additionally, continuous monitoring and evaluation will be essential to assess the effectiveness of these measures and make necessary adjustments.

1. (*b*) Differences between Green Manuring and Brown Manuring:

Green manuring: Green manuring incorporates green plant residue into soil with cultivation, commonly with an offset-disc plough. Green manuring aims to kill weeds and control seedset while building soil organic matter and nitrogen status. More than one tillage pass may be required for a successful kill, and cultivation may lead to losses of soil organic matter and cause soil structure damage. In Western Australia, pulses are preferred over cereal crops for green manuring because they add more nitrogen to the soil. Green manuring pulse crops carry the risk of increased nitrous oxide (N_2O) emissions, which may discount increases in soil carbon sequestration. In some locations it may be possible to grow a summer crop – for example, broad-leafed plants such as sunflower and safflower, or grasses such as sorghum and millet – for green manuring, especially on sandplain soils and in higher rainfall areas. However, high water use over summer and high carbon to nitrogen (C:N) ratios, which may tie up nitrogen, can depress subsequent yields.

Brown manuring: Brown manuring is a 'no-till' version of green manuring, using a non-selective herbicide to desiccate the crop (and weeds) at flowering instead of using cultivation. A follow-up treatment may be required to control survivors. The plant residues are left standing, helping to retain surface cover and soil structure. Soil organic matter is increased. A variation on brown manuring is mulching, where the crop or pasture is mowed, slashed or cut with a knife roller and the residue is left lying on the soil surface. This mulch reduces soil moisture loss through evaporation. Mulched residues break down more rapidly than for normal brown manuring because of the increased contact with soil and smaller pieces.

Advantage of Brown Manuring: Brown manuring, also known as green manuring, is an ecologically sound agricultural practice with a myriad of advantages that contribute to sustainable and resilient farming systems. One of the foremost benefits is the enhancement of soil fertility through the incorporation of green plant material, particularly leguminous cover crops. These plants engage in a symbiotic relationship with nitrogen-fixing bacteria, leading to the biological fixation of atmospheric nitrogen. As these cover crops decompose, they release nitrogen into the soil, enriching it and providing a natural and cost-effective alternative to synthetic fertilizers. Economically, brown manuring offers cost reductions as it minimizes the need for synthetic fertilizers and herbicides. The nitrogen-fixing ability of leguminous cover crops reduces the financial burden on farmers while simultaneously contributing to sustainable agriculture. Moreover, by sequestering carbon in the soil, brown manuring plays a role in climate change mitigation, helping to offset the carbon footprint associated with conventional farming practices.

1. **(*c*) Effects of Abiotic Stresses on Agricultural Production:** Abiotic stresses, including factors such as extreme temperatures, drought, salinity, and soil nutrient imbalances, exert significant impacts on agricultural production, posing formidable challenges to global food security. High temperatures and drought, exacerbated by climate change, can lead to reduced crop yields, altered flowering patterns, and increased susceptibility to pests and diseases. Salinity stress, resulting from excessive salt accumulation in soils, hinders plant growth and disrupts essential physiological processes. Unfavorable soil conditions, including nutrient deficiencies or excesses, can impede nutrient uptake by plants, leading to stunted growth and diminished productivity. These abiotic stressors not only directly affect crop physiology but also disrupt the delicate balance of ecosystems, contributing to biodiversity loss and environmental degradation. The repercussions extend beyond immediate crop losses, impacting the livelihoods of farmers and threatening global food supplies. To address these challenges, sustainable agricultural practices, such as precision farming, water management strategies, and the development of stress-tolerant crop varieties through biotechnology, are crucial. Implementing resilient and adaptive agricultural systems becomes imperative to mitigate the adverse effects of abiotic stresses and ensure the long-term sustainability of global food production.

1. **(*d*) Merits and Demerits of Nanofertilizers with Suitable Examples:**

Merits of Nanofertilizers:

- **Enhanced Nutrient Uptake:** Nanofertilizers, due to their nanoscale size, offer increased surface area and improved solubility. This facilitates better nutrient absorption by plant roots, leading to enhanced nutrient uptake and utilization.
- **Controlled Release:** Nanofertilizers can be engineered for controlled and sustained nutrient release, providing a more efficient and targeted delivery of nutrients to plants over an extended period. This helps in minimizing nutrient loss through leaching and runoff.
- **Increased Nutrient Use Efficiency:** The precise nature of nanofertilizers allows for more efficient use of nutrients by crops, reducing the amount of fertilizer needed to achieve optimal yields. This, in turn, can contribute to cost savings for farmers and a reduction in environmental impact.
- **Customization for Specific Crops:** Nanofertilizers can be tailored to meet the specific nutrient requirements of different crops. This customization enables farmers to address the unique needs of their crops, leading to improved overall crop performance.
- **Reduced Environmental Impact:** By minimizing nutrient leaching and runoff, nanofertilizers can help mitigate environmental pollution, preserving water quality and preventing the eutrophication of water bodies.

Demerits of Nanofertilizers:

- **Cost:** The production of nanofertilizers involves advanced technologies and materials, making them more expensive compared to traditional fertilizers. This cost factor may limit widespread adoption, particularly in resource-constrained agricultural settings.
- **Long-Term Environmental Effects:** The long-term environmental impacts

of nanofertilizers are not yet fully understood. Concerns exist regarding the potential accumulation of nanoparticles in soils and their effects on soil health and ecosystems.

- **Regulatory Challenges:** The regulatory framework for nanofertilizers is still evolving. Issues related to safety, labeling, and standardization need to be addressed to ensure the responsible and safe use of nanofertilizers in agriculture.
- **Potential Nanotoxicity:** There are concerns about the potential nanotoxicity of nanoparticles in plants and the food chain. Studies are ongoing to assess the safety of nanofertilizers and their effects on human health.

Examples:

- **Nano-Urea:** Nano-urea is a well-known example of nanofertilizer. It offers controlled release of nitrogen, reducing the risk of nitrogen losses through volatilization and leaching. This leads to increased nitrogen use efficiency and minimized environmental impact.
- **Nano-Phosphorus:** Nanoparticles of phosphorus can enhance phosphorus availability to plants. Nano-encapsulation of phosphorus allows for slow release, improving the efficiency of phosphorus utilization by crops.
- **Nano-Micronutrients:** Nanofertilizers can also be designed to deliver essential micronutrients like iron, zinc, and copper. These nanoparticles ensure precise delivery to plants, addressing micronutrient deficiencies more effectively.

1. **(*e*) Agricultural Practices Affecting Sustainability of Natural Resources:** Agricultural practices play a pivotal role in determining the sustainability of natural resources, influencing the health of ecosystems and the long-term viability of agricultural systems. Unsustainable practices, such as excessive use of chemical fertilizers and pesticides, deforestation for expanded cropland, and monoculture farming, can lead to soil degradation, loss of biodiversity, and water pollution. Overreliance on irrigation without proper water management contributes to the depletion of freshwater resources. Conversely, sustainable agricultural practices, including organic farming, agroforestry, and precision agriculture, prioritize resource conservation. They aim to enhance soil health, reduce reliance on synthetic inputs, and promote biodiversity, fostering resilient ecosystems. By adopting sustainable agricultural practices, farmers can strike a balance between meeting the demands of food production and preserving natural resources, ensuring the long term health of both agricultural landscapes and the environment.

2. **(*a*) Good Cultivation Practices for Short-Term Initial Control of Weeds:** Implementing good cultivation practices is crucial for achieving short-term initial control of weeds in agricultural fields. Firstly, proper soil preparation is essential to create a favorable environment for the desired crops while minimizing weed growth. This involves thorough plowing or tilling to disrupt weed germination and growth. Timely planting and spacing of crops can help create a dense crop canopy that shades the soil, suppressing weed emergence. Additionally, employing cover crops or mulching can act as effective weed barriers, reducing sunlight penetration and hindering weed development. Regular monitoring of fields is vital to identify and address weed issues promptly. Mechanical methods, such as hoeing or shallow cultivation, can be employed selectively to remove emerging weeds without disturbing the crop roots. The integration of these practices not only provides short-term relief from weed competition but also sets the foundation for long-term weed management strategies in sustainable agriculture.

Short-term initial control of weeds in cultivation involves a combination of cultural, mechanical, and chemical practices. Here are some good cultivation practices for short-term weed control:

- **Crop Rotation:** Rotate crops regularly to disrupt the life cycles of weeds that are specific to certain crops.
- Different crops have different nutrient needs, which can help prevent the dominance of particular weed species.
- **Cover Cropping:** Plant cover crops during fallow periods to suppress weed growth.
- Cover crops also add organic matter to the soil and improve soil structure.
- **Mulching:** Apply organic or synthetic mulches around plants to suppress weed growth by blocking sunlight and preventing weed germination.
- Mulching also helps retain soil moisture and regulate temperature.
- **Proper Spacing:** Plant crops at recommended spacing to create a canopy that shades the soil, reducing the opportunity for weeds to germinate and grow.
- **Hand Weeding:** Regularly inspect and manually remove weeds, especially in the early stages of crop growth. Hand weeding is effective for controlling weeds in specific areas without affecting the crop.
- **Cultivation Practices:** Use shallow cultivation to disrupt weed seedlings without bringing buried weed seeds to the surface. Timing is crucial; cultivate when weeds are small and before they have a chance to produce seeds.
- **Herbicide Application:** Consider the judicious use of herbicides for effective weed control. Apply pre-emergence herbicides before weed seeds germinate or post-emergence herbicides when weeds are actively growing. Follow label instructions carefully and consider environmental impact.
- **Integrated Weed Management (IWM):** Combine multiple control methods in an integrated approach.
- IWM involves using cultural, mechanical, biological, and chemical practices in a coordinated manner.
- **Soil Health Management:** Maintain healthy soils through practices such as organic matter addition, proper fertilization, and pH adjustment. Healthy soils promote strong crop growth, making it more difficult for weeds to compete.
- **Timely Planting:** Plant crops at the recommended time to ensure rapid and uniform germination and growth, minimizing the window for weed establishment.
- **Regular Monitoring:** Monitor fields regularly for weed growth and take prompt action to address weed issues. Early intervention is key to preventing weed establishment and spread.

Remember, the best approach to weed control is often a combination of these practices tailored to the specific crop, climate, and local conditions. Integrated weed management is a sustainable and effective strategy for long-term weed control.

2. (*b*) Agronomic Practices for Managing the Problems of Environmental Problems: Implementing strategic agronomic practices is imperative for effectively managing environmental challenges in agriculture. Crop rotation stands out as a foundational approach, disrupting the life cycles of pests and diseases while optimizing soil fertility through the cultivation of diverse crops. Cover cropping, another vital practice, involves planting cover crops during fallow periods to protect the soil from erosion, suppress weed growth, and enhance organic matter content, thereby promoting overall soil health. Conservation tillage methods, such as minimum or no-till practices, play a pivotal role in preserving soil structure, moisture, and carbon sequestration. By minimizing soil disturbance and leaving crop residues on the field, conservation tillage mitigates erosion risks and contributes to sustainable land management. Water management practices, including precision irrigation systems, are crucial for optimizing water use efficiency, preventing wastage, and minimizing the environmental impact associated with excessive water application.

Nutrient management practices aim to optimize fertilizer application, reducing the risk of nutrient runoff and environmental pollution. Soil testing guides the precise application of fertilizers, aligning nutrient inputs with the specific needs of crops. Integrated Pest Management (IPM) strategies prioritize biological control methods, emphasizing the use of natural predators and judicious application of chemical controls only when necessary. This approach minimizes the ecological footprint of pesticides. Agroforestry, characterized by the integration of trees and shrubs into agricultural landscapes, provides multiple environmental benefits, including carbon sequestration, enhanced biodiversity, and improved soil health. Organic farming practices, devoid of synthetic inputs, prioritize the use of natural fertilizers and pesticides, contributing to soil conservation and reduced environmental impact. Precision agriculture, facilitated by advanced technologies like GPS-guided machinery and remote sensing, enables farmers to optimize resource use, reduce inputs, and enhance overall efficiency. Finally, biodiversity conservation practices involve maintaining natural habitats within or around agricultural areas to support diverse ecosystems. This fosters natural pest control mechanisms, reducing the reliance on chemical interventions. Collectively, these agronomic practices form a comprehensive and sustainable approach to managing environmental challenges in agriculture, promoting resilience, and ensuring the long-term viability of agricultural systems.

Certainly, let's delve into more detail on agronomic practices that address environmental problems in agriculture:

Crop Rotation:

- **Objective:** Break the life cycle of pests and diseases, enhance soil fertility, and manage nutrient imbalances.
- **Implementation:** Plan a sequence of different crops in a specific field over successive seasons. Legumes in rotation can fix nitrogen, benefiting subsequent crops.

Cover Cropping:

- **Objective:** Protect soil from erosion, suppress weed growth, enhance organic matter, and improve soil structure.
- **Implementation:** Plant cover crops like clover or rye during fallow periods or between main crops. These plants cover the soil, preventing nutrient leaching and erosion.

Conservation Tillage:

- **Objective:** Reduce soil disturbance to preserve structure, moisture, and sequester carbon.
- **Implementation:** Adopt minimum or no-till practices, leaving crop residues on the field surface. This protects against erosion, retains moisture, and promotes soil health.

Water Management:

- **Objective:** Optimize water use, reduce wastage, and prevent water pollution.
- **Implementation:** Implement precision irrigation methods such as drip or sprinkler systems. Monitor soil moisture levels and adjust irrigation schedules accordingly to meet crop needs.

Nutrient Management:

- **Objective:** Optimize fertilizer application to prevent nutrient runoff and reduce environmental impact.
- **Implementation:** Conduct soil tests to determine nutrient levels. Apply fertilizers based on crop needs and use precision agriculture tools for accurate and efficient application.

Integrated Pest Management (IPM):

- **Objective:** Control pests with minimal environmental impact.
- **Implementation:** Monitor pest populations, introduce natural predators, and use biological control methods. Reserve chemical control for when pest thresholds are exceeded.

Agroforestry:

- **Objective:** Integrate trees and shrubs for multiple environmental benefits.
- **Implementation:** Plant trees along field borders or in rows within fields. Agroforestry systems can enhance biodiversity, sequester carbon, and provide shade for crops.

Organic Farming Practices:

- **Objective:** Eliminate synthetic inputs, promote soil health, and reduce environmental impact.
- **Implementation:** Use natural fertilizers, organic pesticides, and practice crop diversification. Follow organic certification standards to ensure sustainable practices.

Precision Agriculture:

- **Objective:** Improve efficiency, reduce inputs, and minimize environmental impact.
- **Implementation:** Utilize technologies like GPS-guided tractors, drones, and sensors to optimize field-level management. Precision agriculture allows for targeted resource application based on real-time data.

Biodiversity Conservation:

- **Objective:** Promote a diverse and resilient ecosystem for natural pest control.
- **Implementation:** Maintain hedgerows, buffer strips, or natural habitats around fields. These areas support beneficial insects, birds, and other wildlife that contribute to pest management.

By combining these agronomic practices, farmers can develop holistic and sustainable approaches to mitigate environmental challenges associated with agriculture. These practices not only contribute to environmental stewardship but also enhance the overall resilience and productivity of agricultural systems.

2. **(*c*) Crop Diversification:** Crop Diversification is the addition of new crops or cropping systems to agricultural production on a particular farm taking into account the different returns from value-added crops with complimentary marketing opportunities.In the successive years of the green revolution, food security was fulfilled at the national level due to the stupendous efforts of the Indian Council of Agricultural Research (ICAR). This article gives information behind the 2 mains reasons for implementing crop diversification and the changes in area coverage of different crops spread over 2 decades.

The agricultural scientists put emphasis on the implementation of Crop Diversification. This was advocated to the farmers for two main reasons.

- **First Reason:** The prices of food grains like rice and wheat were not encouraging and farmers ended up with very low net returns even during years of bumper production. By concentrating on other crops like cotton, chilli and sunflower the farmers were encouraged to earn higher profits.
- **Second Reason:** The productivity of rice and wheat was poor in some regions like uplands and dry lands due to high moisture stress sensitivity of these crops. Hence by encouraging farmers to diversify to oil seeds and pulse crops and high value medicinal plants which require less quantity of irrigation compared to that of field crops, they would certainly get higher profits.

The Contribution of High Yielding Short Duration Varieties in Crop Intensification and Diversification in India: High-yielding short-duration varieties (HYSDVs) have made substantial contributions to both crop intensification and diversification in India.

These varieties, characterized by shorter growth cycles, enable farmers to cultivate multiple crops within a single agricultural season. This has led to increased cropping intensity, significantly enhancing overall productivity and income for farmers. By allowing for more efficient use of resources such as water and nutrients, HYSDVs contribute to sustainable agricultural practices. Moreover, their adaptability to varying climatic conditions supports resilience in the face of climate change impacts. The timely harvest associated with these varieties reduces vulnerability to adverse weather, pests, and diseases, ensuring better quality produce. Importantly, the cultivation of HYSDVs has facilitated crop diversification, a crucial strategy for risk mitigation and improved agricultural sustainability. Overall, the widespread adoption of HYSDVs has not only boosted agricultural productivity and income but has also played a pivotal role in transforming India's agricultural landscape by fostering intensification and diversification. High-yielding short-duration varieties (HYSDVs) have made significant contributions to crop intensification and diversification in India, positively impacting agricultural productivity and sustainability. Here are some key aspects of their contribution:

- **Increased Crop Productivity:** HYSDVs are designed to have a shorter growth duration, allowing farmers to cultivate multiple crops in a single agricultural season. This enables increased cropping intensity, leading to higher overall productivity and income for farmers.
- **Optimal Resource Utilization:** Short-duration varieties often have specific characteristics that allow for optimal use of resources such as water, nutrients, and sunlight. They are well-suited for regions with limited resources, contributing to efficient resource management and improved agricultural sustainability.
- **Crop Diversification:** HYSDVs promote crop diversification by facilitating the cultivation of multiple crops within a year. This diversification is crucial for risk mitigation, as it reduces the dependence on a single crop and enhances the resilience of agricultural systems to various challenges, including pests, diseases, and climate variability.
- **Adaptability to Changing Climate:** Short-duration varieties are often more adaptable to changing climatic conditions. They provide flexibility in cropping patterns, allowing farmers to adjust their cultivation strategies in response to variations in temperature and precipitation. This adaptability is essential in the face of climate change impacts.
- **Timely Harvest and Reduced Vulnerability:** The shorter growth cycle of HYSDVs allows for timely harvesting, reducing the vulnerability of crops to adverse weather conditions, pests, and diseases. This timely harvest contributes to better quality produce and minimizes post-harvest losses.
- **Enhanced Food Security:** By enabling multiple cropping cycles in a year, HYSDVs contribute to increased food production and enhanced food security. This is particularly important in a country like India with a growing population and increasing food demand.
- **Income Generation:** The ability to cultivate multiple crops within a year translates into increased income opportunities for farmers. HYSDVs not only boost productivity but also contribute to the economic well-being of farmers, especially in regions with limited arable land.
- **Technology Adoption:** The adoption of HYSDVs often goes hand-in-hand with the adoption of other modern agricultural technologies. This includes improved irrigation practices, precision farming techniques, and the use of quality seeds

and fertilizers, fostering a more technologically advanced and sustainable agricultural sector.

In summary, the widespread adoption of high-yielding short-duration varieties in India has played a crucial role in intensifying and diversifying crop cultivation. This has not only improved agricultural productivity and income for farmers but has also contributed to the resilience and sustainability of the Indian agricultural sector in the face of various challenges.

3. (a) Characteristics and Reclamation of Saline and Sodic Soils:

Characteristics of Saline Soils

Saline soils are characterized by the presence of high levels of soluble salts, primarily sodium chloride (common table salt), calcium sulphate, and magnesium sulphate. These soils pose significant challenges to plant growth and agricultural productivity due to their unique properties. Here are the key characteristics of saline soils:

- **Excess Salts:** Saline soils contain elevated concentrations of soluble salts, which can accumulate over time through natural processes such as weathering, irrigation, or poor drainage.
- **Poor Water Infiltration:** High salt content reduces the soil's ability to absorb and retain water. This limitation on water infiltration can lead to waterlogged conditions and hinder the movement of essential nutrients to plant roots.
- **Osmotic Stress:** The presence of excessive salts creates osmotic stress on plant roots. This stress inhibits the uptake of water by plants, leading to dehydration, stunted growth, and diminished crop yields.
- **White Crust Formation:** As water evaporates from the soil surface, salts accumulate and form a white crust. This visible salt deposition is a common feature of saline soils and can hinder plant emergence.
- **High Electrical Conductivity (EC):** Salinity levels are often quantified by measuring the electrical conductivity of the soil solution. High EC values indicate a high concentration of soluble salts.
- **Limited Plant Diversity:** Saline conditions restrict the types of plants that can thrive. Most crops are sensitive to high salt concentrations, and only salt-tolerant plants, known as halophytes, can withstand these conditions.
- **Altered Soil Structure:** Excessive salts can disrupt soil structure, leading to the breakdown of soil aggregates. This alteration in soil structure negatively impacts aeration, root penetration, and overall soil fertility.
- **Reduced Nutrient Availability:** Salinity can interfere with the availability of essential nutrients by displacing them from soil particles. This can lead to nutrient deficiencies in plants, further compromising their growth.
- **Challenges in Soil Reclamation:** Reclaiming saline soils is a complex and challenging process, often requiring leaching to remove excess salts and the addition of amendments such as gypsum to improve soil structure.

Management of Saline Soils

- The management of saline soils, characterized by high concentrations of soluble salts that can severely hinder agricultural productivity, necessitates a multifaceted and strategic approach. One fundamental strategy is leaching, wherein excess salts are flushed from the soil through the application of ample water. However, this method requires efficient drainage systems to prevent waterlogging, a common challenge in saline-prone areas. Gypsum, a calcium sulphate amendment, is often applied to saline soils to replace sodium ions with calcium ions, thereby enhancing soil structure and promoting better water infiltration. The selection of salt-tolerant crops, known as halophytes, is another critical aspect of saline soil management, as these plants can thrive in high-salt environments, contributing to sustainable agriculture in affected regions.

- Additionally, adopting precision irrigation methods, such as drip irrigation, helps minimize surface evaporation and reduce the risk of salt accumulation. Introducing organic matter, such as compost or well-decomposed manure, into saline soils enhances soil fertility, improves structure, and encourages microbial activity, thereby mitigating the adverse effects of salinity. Monitoring soil salinity through regular soil testing is indispensable for making informed management decisions, allowing farmers to adjust practices based on the evolving conditions of the soil. Implementing crop rotation with salt-tolerant and economically viable crops aids in diversifying agricultural activities, improving resilience, and reducing the dependence on a single susceptible crop.
- The reclamation and sustainable management of saline soils also involve comprehensive land-use planning. Strategic agroecological zoning considers factors such as climate, topography, and water availability, helping tailor agricultural practices to specific regions. Furthermore, education and outreach programs play a pivotal role in disseminating knowledge about best management practices among farmers, promoting the adoption of sustainable approaches in saline-prone areas. Overall, the successful management of saline soils requires a combination of scientific understanding, technological interventions, and community engagement to ensure the long-term sustainability of agriculture in these challenging environments.

Characteristics of Sodic Soils

Sodic soils are characterized by elevated levels of sodium ions in comparison to other cations like calcium and magnesium. These soils often exhibit distinct properties that can have significant impacts on soil structure and fertility. Here are the key characteristics of sodic soils:

- **High Sodium Content:** Sodic soils have an excess of sodium ions compared to other essential cations such as calcium and magnesium.
- **Poor Soil Structure:** Sodium ions cause clay particles to disperse, disrupting soil aggregates and leading to poor soil structure. This dispersion negatively affects soil porosity and water infiltration.
- **Alkaline pH:** Sodic soils tend to have an alkaline pH due to the prevalence of sodium ions. The high pH can affect nutrient availability and contribute to soil infertility.
- **Cracking of Soil Surface:** Sodic soils often exhibit large cracks on the soil surface, especially when they dry. These cracks can hinder root growth and reduce water infiltration.
- **Impaired Water Infiltration:** Due to the dispersion of clay particles, water infiltration is hindered, leading to waterlogging and reduced aeration in the soil.
- **High Exchangeable Sodium Percentage (ESP):** The exchangeable sodium percentage represents the proportion of sodium on soil exchange sites. Sodic soils typically have high ESP values.
- **Limited Nutrient Availability:** The high sodium content can displace essential cations like calcium and magnesium from soil particles, affecting nutrient availability for plant uptake.
- **Reduced Cation Exchange Capacity (CEC):** Sodic soils often have a reduced cation exchange capacity, which further limits the soil's ability to hold essential nutrients.
- **Difficulty in Soil Reclamation:** Reclaiming sodic soils is challenging due to the persistence of sodium-induced dispersion

and structural issues. The process usually involves the addition of amendments to replace sodium with more favorable cations.

- **Reduced Microbial Activity:** Sodic conditions can negatively impact soil microbial activity, affecting the decomposition of organic matter and nutrient cycling processes.
- **Altered Soil Physical Properties:** Sodic soils experience changes in physical properties, including reduced aggregate stability, leading to increased susceptibility to erosion.
- **Crop Yield Reduction:** Sodic soils can result in decreased crop yields due to poor soil structure, impaired water and nutrient availability, and challenges in root development.

Management of Sodic Soil

- Sodic soil management involves addressing the challenges posed by high levels of sodium in the soil, which can adversely affect soil structure and plant growth. Sodic soils have poor water infiltration and drainage due to the dispersion of clay particles, leading to the formation of hard, impermeable crusts. To manage sodic soils effectively, several strategies can be employed.
- One common approach is soil amendment with gypsum (calcium sulphate), which helps replace sodium ions with calcium ions, improving soil structure. Additionally, organic matter incorporation can enhance soil fertility and microbial activity, contributing to better soil aggregation. Proper irrigation management is crucial to prevent the accumulation of excess salts, and the use of salt-tolerant crops can be explored. Regular monitoring of soil quality and adopting sustainable agricultural practices are essential components of a comprehensive sodic soil management plan, aiming to enhance both soil health and crop productivity.

3. (*b*) Various Concepts of Agroforestry Systems and Their Role in Livelihood Security in Rural India: Agroforestry is an age old practice, indeed very old. The scientific principles of agroforestry are Farmers of the warmer parts especially have long tradition of growing food crops, trees and animals together for producing multiple range of products. Trees and forests in fact an integral part of the Indian culture. The best of Indian culture was born in the forests. Our rishis who evolved the Hindu philosophy, lived in forests in complete harmony with the nature. In fact, so much has been said about trees in our ancient literature that planting tree was being done by individuals on their own along with agriculture crops. "Krishishukti" written by Maharishi Kashyap, classifies land into several categories and identifies areas which are suitable for planting trees: all wet and dry lands and areas around houses, wells, tanks are specifically identified for tree planting. But foresters and agriculturists, who have traditionally operated within rather rigid disciplinary boundaries concentrating on monoculture production of their preferred commodities of crops, animals and trees used to ignore such combined integrated production systems.

More recently, however, the forest area has receded and resources have shrunk considerably. The people are no longer able to meet their requirements of firewood, fodder, timber, bamboo, etc. from the forest. Due to shortage of wood the prices of these commodities have, therefore, increased manifold. Many forest based industries have been facing problems in supply of raw material. Many farmers quite recently started planting trees on their farm lands to meet these shortages along with agriculture crop; thus from the concept of agroforestry it emerged out:

- agroforestry is a collective name for land use systems involving trees combined with crops and/or animals on the same unit of land. Further it,

- combines production of multiple outputs with protection of production base
- places emphasis on the use of multiple indigenous trees and shrubs
- is particularly suitable for low-input conditions and fragile environments
- involves the interplay of sociocultural values more than in most other land-use systems
- is structurally and functionally more complex than monoculture

Several concepts of agroforestry systems exist, each offering unique benefits and addressing specific environmental or agricultural challenges. Here are some key concepts:

- **Alley Cropping:** Involves planting rows of trees or shrubs in between rows of crops. Trees provide shade and windbreak, reducing soil erosion and improving microclimatic conditions for crops.
- **Silvopasture:** Combines trees or shrubs with livestock grazing areas. Trees offer shade for animals, contribute to forage production, and may provide timber or non-timber forest products.
- **Windbreaks and Shelterbelts:** Planting rows of trees along field edges to reduce wind erosion and protect crops. These systems act as barriers against strong winds, preserving soil moisture and enhancing microclimates.
- **Forest Farming:** Integrates crops and/or livestock with the cultivation of forest crops, such as mushrooms, medicinal herbs, or specialty wood products. Utilizes the forest canopy to enhance production and diversity.
- **Agroforestry for Water Management:** Integrates trees and shrubs to manage water resources effectively. Tree planting along water bodies helps control erosion, improves water quality, and regulates water tables.
- **Homegardens or Multistrata Agroforestry:** Involves cultivating a diverse range of crops, trees, and sometimes livestock in a small area around a household. Provides multiple products for household consumption and income generation.
- **Riparian Buffer Strips:** Involves planting vegetation along watercourses to protect water quality and prevent soil erosion. Trees and shrubs help filter nutrients and sediments from runoff before reaching water bodies.
- **Integration of Agroforestry in Watershed Management:** Incorporates agroforestry practices at the watershed level to address soil conservation, water quality, and biodiversity conservation.
- Aims to balance economic, social, and environmental benefits across an entire watershed.
- **Taungya System:** Involves the temporary cultivation of crops between young trees during the establishment phase of a forest plantation. Provides short-term income for farmers while the trees grow.
- **Social Forestry:** Encourages the involvement of local communities in tree planting and management for both environmental and socio-economic benefits. Fosters community participation in sustainable resource management.

Agroforestry systems can be tailored to specific ecological and socio-economic contexts, offering a flexible and resilient approach to sustainable land use.

Role of Agroforestry Systems in Livelihood Security in Rural India: Agroforestry systems play a significant role in enhancing livelihood security in rural India by providing a range of economic, social, and environmental benefits.

Here are several ways in which agroforestry contributes to livelihood security:

- **Diversification of Income Sources:** Agroforestry allows farmers to diversify their sources of income by integrating trees and shrubs with traditional crops and livestock. Income from the sale of timber, non-timber forest products (NTFPs), fruits, and other agroforestry products adds to the overall household revenue.

- **Enhanced Crop and Livestock Productivity:** The presence of trees in agroforestry systems provides shade, reducing temperature stress on crops and livestock, resulting in increased productivity. Nutrient cycling and improved soil fertility contribute to higher crop yields and better forage for livestock.
- **Timber and Non-Timber Forest Products (NTFPs):** Agroforestry systems often include tree species with economic value, such as teak, sandalwood, and bamboo, which can be harvested for timber and other wood products. NTFPs like fruits, nuts, resins, and medicinal plants contribute to income generation.
- **Soil Conservation and Improved Water Management:** The integration of trees in agroforestry helps prevent soil erosion and improves water retention in the soil. Better water management ensures sustained agricultural productivity, particularly in regions prone to water scarcity.
- **Climate Resilience:** Agroforestry systems contribute to climate resilience by enhancing the adaptive capacity of rural communities. Trees act as windbreaks, reducing the impact of storms and protecting crops, while also providing shade and mitigating temperature extremes.
- **Employment Opportunities:** Agroforestry activities, such as planting, pruning, and harvesting, create employment opportunities for rural communities. Community-based agroforestry initiatives often involve local residents in various stages of the agroforestry cycle.
- **Improved Nutrition:** The diverse range of crops and fruits grown in agroforestry systems contributes to improved household nutrition. Farm families have access to a variety of food products, including fruits, nuts, and vegetables, leading to a more balanced diet.
- **Community Empowerment and Social Cohesion:** Agroforestry projects often involve community participation, empowering local residents to take charge of their natural resources. Social forestry initiatives encourage collective decision-making and foster a sense of ownership and responsibility within communities.
- **Biodiversity Conservation:** Agroforestry promotes biodiversity by providing habitats for various plant and animal species. The conservation of indigenous tree varieties and the preservation of natural ecosystems contribute to overall ecological balance.

In summary, agroforestry systems in rural India contribute significantly to livelihood security by promoting economic sustainability, environmental resilience, and community empowerment. These systems align with the principles of sustainable agriculture, providing a holistic approach to rural development.

3. **(*c*)** The National Bureau of Soil Survey & Land Use Planning (NBSS & LUP) came up with twenty agro-ecological zones based on the growing period as an integrated criteria of effective rainfall, soil groups, delineated boundaries adjusted to district boundaries with a minimal number of regions. The National Bureau of Soil Survey and Land Use Planning (NBSS-LUP) made a comprehensive attempt at agro-ecological regionalisation and the country was divided into 20 regions following the FAO methodology of sequential layering of information on maps (NBSS Publication, 1992).

The National Bureau of Soil Survey and Land Use Planning (NBSS & LUP) employs a comprehensive set of geographical factors for agroecological zoning in India. These factors include climate variables such as temperature, rainfall, and humidity, which help delineate distinct agroclimatic zones. Topography, including elevation, slope, and aspect, plays a crucial role in influencing water drainage, soil erosion, and microclimates, thereby shaping land use recommendations. Soil characteristics, such as texture, structure, and fertility, are considered to understand the diverse edaphic conditions across regions, guiding suitable crop choices and soil management practices. Analysis of land use and cover assists in assessing the current state of agriculture and forestry, aiding in sustainable land use planning. Water resource availability, encompassing rivers, lakes, and groundwater, is factored in to recommend appropriate irrigation strategies. Agroclimatic zones, defined by a combination of climatic and soil-related factors, provide a framework for classifying regions with similar environmental conditions. Additionally, studying existing cropping patterns, ecological regions, and biodiversity further enriches the agroecological zoning process, facilitating tailored recommendations for crops and land use practices in different parts of the country. This holistic approach by the NBSS & LUP ensures that agroecological zoning in India is rooted in a nuanced understanding of the geographical factors that influence agricultural productivity and sustainability. The National Bureau of Soil Survey and Land Use Planning (NBSS & LUP) in India employs various geographical factors for agroecological zoning, aiming to categorize and understand the diverse agroclimatic conditions across the country. These factors help in developing region-specific agricultural recommendations and land use planning strategies.

Some key geographical factors considered include:

- **Climate:** NBSS & LUP considers temperature, rainfall, and humidity patterns to delineate different agroecological zones. Understanding climate variations is crucial for recommending suitable crops and agricultural practices in specific regions.
- **Topography:** The topography of an area, including elevation, slope, and aspect, influences factors such as water drainage, soil erosion, and microclimates. These aspects play a role in determining the suitability of certain crops and land management practices.
- **Soil Types:** Soil characteristics, including texture, structure, depth, and fertility, are crucial for agroecological zoning. Different crops have specific soil requirements, and the NBSS&LUP considers soil information to recommend appropriate crops and soil management practices.
- **Land Use/Land Cover:** Understanding the existing land use and land cover helps in assessing the current state of agriculture, forestry, and other land uses. It aids in planning for sustainable land use practices and identifying areas suitable for specific agricultural activities.
- **Water Resources:** Availability and distribution of water resources, such as rivers, lakes, and groundwater, are essential for agriculture. The NBSS & LUP considers water availability and quality to recommend appropriate irrigation practices and cropping patterns.
- **Agroclimatic Zones:** The Bureau defines agroclimatic zones based on a combination of climatic and edaphic (soil-related) factors. These zones help in classifying regions with similar environmental conditions and recommending suitable crops and agricultural practices for each zone.
- **Cropping Patterns:** Studying existing cropping patterns provides insights into the types of crops traditionally grown in different regions. This information assists in recommending crop diversification strategies and improving overall agricultural sustainability.
- **Ecological Regions:** The NBSS & LUP considers ecological regions, taking into account biodiversity, vegetation types, and ecosystem services. This holistic approach aids in understanding the broader ecological context and promoting sustainable land use practices.

By integrating these geographical factors, the NBSS & LUP creates agroecological zoning maps and provides valuable information for policymakers, farmers, and land use planners. These efforts contribute to informed decision-making in agriculture, leading to sustainable and region-specific land use practices across India.

5. (*a*) **Causes of Soil Erosion:** Soil erosion is a natural process, but human activities often accelerate it, leading to significant environmental and agricultural challenges. Here are some of the main causes of soil erosion:

Water Erosion:

- **Rainfall Impact:** Intense rainfall can dislodge soil particles and create surface runoff, leading to sheet erosion.
- **Surface Runoff:** Excessive water flow across the land surface can transport soil particles, causing rill and gully erosion.

Wind Erosion:

- **Lack of Vegetative Cover:** When land is left bare without adequate vegetation, wind can easily lift and transport loose soil particles.
- **Overgrazing:** Excessive grazing by live-stock reduces vegetation cover, making the soil more susceptible to wind erosion.

Deforestation: Removal of trees and vegetation reduces the root structure that helps bind soil particles. This loss of cover makes the soil vulnerable to erosion, especially during rainfall.

Overcultivation: Continuous or improper plowing and cultivation practices can disturb the soil structure, leaving it exposed and susceptible to erosion. Monoculture (planting the same crop repeatedly) can also contribute to erosion.

Poor Land Management Practices: Improper Irrigation: Poorly designed irrigation systems can lead to waterlogging and salinity, degrading soil structure and increasing vulnerability to erosion.

Inadequate Crop Residue Management: Failure to leave crop residues on the field after harvest reduces soil cover and increases erosion risk.

Urbanization and Construction: Construction activities, such as the clearing of land for buildings and roads, disturb the soil and reduce natural vegetation, increasing the likelihood of erosion. Paved surfaces in urban areas can lead to increased runoff and erosion.

Mining Activities: Open-pit mining and quarrying activities can expose large areas of soil, making them susceptible to erosion. The removal of vegetation and topsoil during mining exacerbates the problem.

Climate Change: Changes in precipitation patterns and increased frequency of extreme weather events, such as heavy rainfall and storms, can intensify soil erosion. Temperature changes may also impact vegetation cover and soil moisture content.

Soil Compaction: Heavy machinery and intensive agricultural activities can lead to soil compaction, reducing porosity and increasing runoff, making the soil more prone to erosion.

Lack of Contour Plowing: Plowing along the contour lines of the land helps to slow down water runoff, reducing the risk of erosion. Without proper contour plowing, water can quickly flow downhill, leading to erosion.

5. (*b*) **Harmful Effects of Poor Drainage on Plants:** Poor drainage can have detrimental effects on plants, compromising their health and overall growth. When water accumulates in the soil due to inadequate drainage, it creates conditions that are unfavorable for plant roots. Excess water can lead to oxygen deprivation in the root zone, impeding root respiration and nutrient uptake. Prolonged waterlogged conditions also create an environment conducive to the growth of harmful soil-borne pathogens, including fungi

and bacteria, which can cause root rot and other diseases. Additionally, poor drainage contributes to soil compaction, limiting the movement of air and nutrients within the soil. As a result, plants may exhibit stunted growth, yellowing of leaves, wilting, and increased susceptibility to pests and diseases. In extreme cases, prolonged waterlogging can lead to the death of plant roots, severely impacting the plant's ability to survive and thrive. Proper drainage management is crucial for maintaining optimal soil conditions, ensuring the well-being of plants, and promoting a healthy and productive garden or agricultural environment.

5. (*c*) Extension professionals play a crucial role in disseminating knowledge and facilitating learning among farmers and communities. To be effective in their roles, they require a diverse set of competencies. Here are some key competencies needed by extension professionals:

- **Subject Matter Expertise:** Extension professionals should have in-depth knowledge of the subject matter they are addressing, whether it's agriculture, horticulture, livestock management, or other relevant fields.
- **Communication Skills:** Clear and effective communication is essential for extension professionals to convey information to diverse audiences. This includes the ability to adapt communication styles for different stakeholders.
- **Educational Background:** A solid educational foundation, often in agricultural sciences or related fields, provides the necessary background to understand and communicate technical information.
- **Interpersonal Skills:** Building positive relationships with farmers, community members, and other stakeholders is vital. Extension professionals should be approachable, empathetic, and able to work well with diverse groups.
- **Adaptability:** The ability to adapt to changing circumstances, technologies, and agricultural practices is crucial. Extension professionals must stay current with new developments in their field.
- **Problem-Solving Skills:** Agriculture often presents challenges and uncertainties. Extension professionals need to be adapt at analyzing problems and providing practical solutions to address the needs of farmers.
- **Technological Literacy:** Proficiency in using modern technologies, including digital tools and communication platforms, is important for effective outreach and knowledge dissemination.
- **Project Management:** Extension professionals often work on various projects and initiatives. Project management skills, including planning, implementation, and evaluation, are valuable in ensuring the success of extension programs.
- **Cultural Competence:** Understanding and respecting cultural diversity is essential, especially when working with communities with different traditions, languages, and practices.
- **Teamwork and Collaboration:** Extension professionals often work in interdisciplinary teams or collaborate with other organizations. The ability to work collaboratively enhances the impact and effectiveness of extension efforts.
- **Monitoring and Evaluation:** Competence in monitoring and evaluating the outcomes of extension programs helps in assessing the effectiveness of interventions and making necessary adjustments for continuous improvement.
- **Facilitation Skills:** Extension professionals need to facilitate learning and participatory processes. This includes organizing workshops, field demonstrations, and other activities that engage farmers in the learning process.

- **Policy Awareness:** Understanding local, regional, and national agricultural policies is important for extension professionals to align their efforts with broader agricultural development goals.
- **Time Management:** Effectively managing time and resources ensures that extension professionals can prioritize tasks, meet deadlines, and maximize their impact.

By possessing these competencies, extension professionals can contribute significantly to the success of agricultural extension services, promote sustainable farming practices, and enhance the livelihoods of farming communities.

5. (*d*) Farmers should maintain detailed farm records as a fundamental aspect of efficient and sustainable agricultural management. These records serve as a vital tool for financial planning, enabling farmers to create realistic budgets, track income sources, and comply with tax regulations. In addition to financial management, accurate records aid in decision-making by providing insights into crop rotations, performance evaluations, and the success of different farming practices. Compliance with regulations, whether related to environmental standards or food safety, is facilitated through meticulous record-keeping. Furthermore, records play a crucial role in risk management, helping farmers navigate unforeseen events such as natural disasters and ensuring a smooth process when filing insurance claims. Succession planning, grant applications, and continuous improvement also benefit from comprehensive farm records. By documenting and analyzing past experiences, farmers can make informed decisions, learn from both successes and failures, and work towards the long-term sustainability and success of their agricultural operations.

Farmers should maintain a variety of records to effectively manage their agricultural operations. While the specific records may vary depending on the type of farming and local regulations, here is a general list of records that farmers may need to keep:

- Financial Records
- Crop Records
- Livestock Records
- Equipment and Machinery Records
- Weather and Climate Records
- Labor Records
- Compliance and Regulatory Records
- Insurance Records
- Records for Grant and Loan Applications
- Succession Planning Records
- Market and Sales Records
- Miscellaneous Records

Maintaining these records systematically helps farmers make informed decisions, comply with regulations, and manage their resources efficiently for sustainable and successful agricultural practices.

5. (*e*) The marketing of agricultural produce in India faces several challenges that impact farmers, traders, and the overall agricultural sector. Here are some key problems associated with the marketing of agricultural produce in India:

- **Fragmented Supply Chain:** India's agricultural supply chain is often fragmented, involving multiple intermediaries between farmers and consumers. This fragmentation can lead to inefficiencies, delays, and increased costs in the marketing process.
- **Lack of Infrastructure:** Inadequate infrastructure, including storage facilities, transportation, and cold chains, hinders the smooth flow of agricultural produce from farms to markets. Poor infrastructure contributes to post-harvest losses and reduces the overall quality of the produce.
- **Limited Market Access for Farmers:** Many farmers, especially smallholders, face challenges in accessing broader markets. Limited market access can result in lower prices for their produce and restrict their ability to negotiate favorable terms.

- **Price Volatility:** Agricultural markets in India often experience price volatility due to factors such as unpredictable weather conditions, market speculation, and insufficient market information. Farmers may struggle to predict and plan based on fluctuating prices.
- **Middlemen Exploitation:** Intermediaries in the supply chain, such as commission agents and traders, may exploit farmers by offering low prices for their produce. This exploitation further reduces the income that farmers receive for their efforts.
- **Quality Standards and Grading Issues:** Compliance with quality standards and grading requirements is a challenge for many farmers. Failure to meet these standards can result in lower prices or rejection of produce in the market.
- **Limited Access to Credit:** Farmers often face challenges in accessing credit for investments in technology, inputs, and storage facilities. Limited credit can constrain their ability to adopt modern agricultural practices and improve productivity.
- **Inefficient Marketing Channels:** The traditional marketing channels are often inefficient and may involve multiple intermediaries, each adding to the overall cost. Streamlining and modernizing these channels can improve efficiency and reduce costs.
- **Seasonal Glut and Scarcity:** Seasonal variations in agricultural production can lead to gluts or scarcities in the market. This imbalance affects prices, and farmers may not receive fair returns during periods of oversupply.
- **Lack of Farmer Producer Organizations (FPOs):** The absence or limited presence of Farmer Producer Organizations hampers collective marketing efforts by farmers. FPOs can enhance the bargaining power of farmers and provide better access to markets.

6. (*a*) *In-situ* water conservation techniques, harmonized with appropriate land configurations, form a crucial strategy for sustainable agriculture. Contour farming involves plowing along the contour lines of the land, mitigating runoff and soil erosion. Terracing, particularly on sloping terrain, creates steps that slow down water flow, minimizing erosion and facilitating water retention in terraced pockets. Check dams, well-suited for areas with intermittent streams, impede water flow, encouraging infiltration and groundwater recharge. Bunding, featuring small embankments along the land contours, captures rainwater, preventing runoff. Ridge and furrow systems on flat or gently sloping land retain water by creating raised ridges and sunken furrows for crops. Check basin farming, where small basins are constructed to capture and hold rainwater, proves effective in flat or nearly flat landscapes. Subsurface dams in areas with seasonal watercourses slow down water flow, aiding groundwater recharge. Farm ponds, excavated on gently sloping land, store rainwater for agricultural use. Cover cropping and mulching, suitable for various terrains, enhance soil structure, reduce evaporation, and control erosion. These techniques, tailored to land configurations, collectively contribute to efficient water use, increased soil health, and sustainable agricultural practices.

In-situ water conservation techniques refer to methods that retain and manage water within the boundaries of a farm or agricultural field, minimizing runoff and improving water use efficiency. Appropriate land configurations play a crucial role in implementing these techniques. Here are different *in-situ* water conservation techniques based on land configurations:

Contour Farming:

- **Land Configuration:** Contour farming involves cultivating along the contour lines of the land.

- **Technique:** Plowing and planting across the slope, rather than up and down, helps slow down water runoff, allowing it to infiltrate the soil. This reduces soil erosion and enhances water retention.

Terracing:

- **Land Configuration:** Terracing involves creating steps or level platforms on sloping land.
- **Technique:** Building embankments across the slope helps slow down water runoff, reducing soil erosion. Terraces act as mini-reservoirs, capturing rainwater and preventing it from flowing downhill too quickly.

Check Dams:

- **Land Configuration:** Suitable for areas with intermittent streams or gullies.
- **Technique:** Constructing low check dams across gullies or small streams helps slow down water flow. This allows water to infiltrate the soil, raising the water table and enhancing groundwater recharge.

Bunding:

- **Land Configuration:** Effective on flat or gently sloping land.
- **Technique:** Creating small embankments or bunds along the contour of the land helps trap rainwater, preventing it from running off. This technique is particularly useful in areas with low rainfall.

Ridge and Furrow System:

- **Land Configuration:** Suitable for flat or gently sloping land.
- **Technique:** Creating ridges and furrows in the field helps retain rainwater. The ridges prevent runoff, allowing water to infiltrate into the furrows where crops are planted.

Check Basin Farming:

- **Land Configuration:** Suitable for flat or nearly flat land.
- **Technique:** Constructing small basins or depressions in the field captures rainwater and prevents runoff. This technique is useful for retaining water around the root zone of plants.

Subsurface Dams:

- **Land Configuration:** Applicable in areas with seasonal streams or watercourses.
- **Technique:** Constructing subsurface dams involves building structures below the ground to impede the flow of water. This helps in recharging groundwater and creating a more stable water supply.

Farm Ponds:

- **Land Configuration:** Suitable for areas with gentle slopes.
- **Technique:** Excavating ponds on the farm collects rainwater for later use. These ponds can store water for irrigation, livestock, and other agricultural needs.

Cover Cropping:

- **Land Configuration:** Applicable in flat or sloping lands.
- **Technique:** Planting cover crops such as legumes or grasses helps improve soil structure and water retention. The cover crops protect the soil from erosion and enhance infiltration.

Mulching:

- **Land Configuration:** Suitable for flat or gently sloping land.
- **Technique:** Applying organic or inorganic mulch on the soil surface helps reduce evaporation, control weeds, and improve water retention. This technique is especially effective in arid and semi-arid regions.

Implementing *in-situ* water conservation techniques with appropriate land configurations not only improves water use efficiency but also contributes to sustainable agriculture by reducing soil erosion and enhancing overall farm productivity. The choice of technique depends on factors such as topography, soil type, and climate conditions.

6. (*b*) **Enlist the Purposes of Extension Evaluation:** Extension evaluation serves various important purposes in agricultural and rural development contexts. The evaluation of extension programs helps assess their effectiveness, efficiency, and overall impact. Here are key purposes of extension evaluation:

Assess Program Effectiveness: Evaluate the extent to which extension programs are achieving their stated objectives and goals. This involves measuring the impact of extension services on farmers' knowledge, skills, and practices.

Improve Program Design and Implementation: Identify strengths and weaknesses in program design and implementation to make informed adjustments. This ensures that extension services are relevant, responsive, and tailored to the needs of the target audience.

Enhance Decision-Making: Provide data and insights that support evidence-based decision-making for program managers, policymakers, and stakeholders. Evaluation results can inform resource allocation, strategic planning, and policy development.

Demonstrate Accountability: Demonstrate accountability to funding agencies, policymakers, and the public by showcasing the outcomes and impacts of extension programs. Evaluation results help build trust and transparency in the use of resources.

Facilitate Learning and Innovation: Create a culture of learning within extension organizations by using evaluation findings to identify successful strategies and areas for improvement. This facilitates ongoing innovation and adaptation to changing agricultural contexts.

Measure Cost-Effectiveness: Evaluate the efficiency of extension programs in terms of cost-effectiveness. This involves assessing the relationship between resources invested and outcomes achieved, helping to optimize resource utilization.

Inform Policy Development: Provide evidence that can influence the development of agricultural and rural development policies. Evaluation results can contribute to the formulation of policies that support sustainable agriculture and rural livelihoods.

Strengthen Stakeholder Engagement: Engage stakeholders, including farmers, in the evaluation process to ensure their perspectives and feedback are considered. This participatory approach enhances the relevance and acceptance of extension services.

Promote Innovation and Technology Adoption: Assess the effectiveness of extension in promoting the adoption of innovative agricultural practices and technologies. Evaluation results can guide efforts to overcome barriers to technology adoption among farmers.

Improve Communication and Extension Strategies: Evaluate the communication strategies employed by extension services to ensure that information reaches the target audience effectively. This includes assessing the accessibility and usability of extension materials and channels.

Document Best Practices: Identify and document successful extension practices and approaches. This information can be shared within the organization and with other extension agencies to promote the replication of successful models.

Measure Social and Economic Impacts: Assess the broader social and economic impacts of extension programs, including changes in income, livelihoods, and community well-being. This helps demonstrate the contribution of extension to overall development goals.

By serving these purposes, extension evaluation contributes to the continuous improvement and effectiveness of agricultural extension services, ultimately benefiting farmers and rural communities.

Degrees of Extension Evaluation

Extension evaluation involves different degrees or levels, each serving a specific purpose in assessing the effectiveness and impact of extension programs. The degrees of extension evaluation can be categorized into three main levels: formative evaluation, summative evaluation, and impact evaluation.

Formative Evaluation:

- **Purpose:** The primary purpose of formative evaluation is to shape and improve the design and implementation of an extension program during its development or early stages.
- **Focus:** Formative evaluation focuses on providing feedback and recommendations for program improvement. It helps identify strengths, weaknesses, and areas for modification.
- **Methods:** Qualitative and quantitative research methods, including focus groups, interviews, and surveys, are commonly used in formative evaluation.
- **Timing:** Conducted before or during the initial phases of program implementation.

Summative Evaluation:

- **Purpose:** Summative evaluation aims to assess the overall effectiveness and impact of a completed extension program. It provides a comprehensive understanding of whether the program achieved its intended outcomes.
- **Focus:** Summative evaluation focuses on measuring the extent to which program objectives were met and determining the overall success or failure of the program.
- **Methods:** Both quantitative and qualitative methods are employed, including surveys, interviews, and data analysis. It often includes comparing the achieved outcomes with the intended outcomes.
- **Timing:** Conducted at the end or after the completion of the program.

Impact Evaluation:

- **Purpose:** Impact evaluation goes beyond measuring program outcomes to assess the broader and long-term effects of the extension program on the target population and the community.
- **Focus:** Impact evaluation examines the social, economic, and environmental changes resulting from the program. It seeks to attribute observed changes to the extension intervention.
- **Methods:** Advanced statistical techniques, control groups, and longitudinal studies are often employed to isolate the impact of the program from other factors.
- **Timing:** Conducted after some time has passed since the completion of the program to capture sustained impacts.

Each degree of evaluation plays a vital role in the overall assessment and improvement of extension programs. Formative evaluation helps refine programs during their development, summative evaluation provides a comprehensive assessment of the program's outcomes, and impact evaluation measures the long-term effects and contributions to broader development goals. Using a combination of these evaluation approaches ensures a thorough understanding of the strengths, weaknesses, and impacts of extension interventions, facilitating evidence-based decision-making and continuous improvement in agricultural extension services.

6. (*c*) Elaborate the Institutional Infrastructure Available for Agricultural Marketing in India: India's institutional infrastructure for agricultural marketing is multifaceted, comprising various entities and systems aimed at facilitating the efficient sale and distribution of agricultural produce. Agricultural Produce Market Committees (APMCs) serve as pivotal entities, established under state regulations, providing regulated market spaces or mandis where farmers can sell their produce. The National Agriculture Market (eNAM) is a significant digital initiative integrating APMCs across states, fostering online trading for farmers and transparent price discovery. Cooperative marketing societies, like Agricultural Marketing Cooperatives (AMCs), play a vital role in collective marketing, reducing the influence of middlemen and ensuring fair returns to farmers. Warehousing Infrastructure Development and Regulatory Authority (WIDRA) oversees the development of storage facilities, crucial for mitigating post-harvest losses. Commission agents and brokers operate within APMCs, connecting farmers with traders, while State Agricultural Marketing Boards (SAMBs) coordinate marketing activities at the state level. Additionally, the emphasis on Cold Chain Infrastructure, Agri-Export Zones (AEZs), and Farmers Producer Organizations (FPOs) further contributes to enhancing market linkages, preserving quality, and empowering farmers in the marketing landscape. Ongoing efforts are directed towards modernizing this institutional framework to meet the evolving needs of India's diverse agricultural sector.

In India, the institutional infrastructure for agricultural marketing comprises a network of organizations and entities that facilitate the sale and distribution of agricultural produce. The key components of this infrastructure include:

Agricultural Produce Market Committees (APMCs): APMCs are established under state-level agricultural marketing regulations. They provide a platform for farmers to sell their produce through regulated market yards or mandis. APMCs aim to ensure fair prices, prevent exploitation of farmers, and regulate the buying and selling of agricultural commodities.

National Agriculture Market (eNAM): eNAM is a pan-India electronic trading platform that integrates APMCs across states. It enables farmers to sell their produce online, promoting transparent price discovery and reducing intermediaries. eNAM enhances market accessibility and provides a wider market reach for farmers.

Cooperative Marketing Societies: Cooperative marketing societies, such as Agricultural Marketing Cooperatives (AMCs), play a crucial role in aggregating produce from farmers and marketing it collectively. These societies aim to eliminate middlemen, reduce transaction costs, and ensure a fair share of profits for the farmers.

Warehousing Infrastructure Development and Regulatory Authority (WIDRA): WIDRA oversees the development of warehousing infrastructure, including cold storage and silos, to address post-harvest storage and management challenges. Efficient warehousing facilities help prevent post-harvest losses and enable better price realization for farmers.

Commission Agents and Brokers: Commission agents and brokers operate in APMCs and facilitate the buying and selling of agricultural commodities on behalf of farmers. They play a role in price negotiation and transaction facilitation, connecting farmers with traders and processors.

State Agricultural Marketing Boards (SAMBs): SAMBs operate at the state level and are responsible for the overall planning, development, and regulation of agricultural marketing activities. They work in coordination with APMCs and other entities to ensure effective marketing infrastructure.

Agri-Export Zones (AEZs): AEZs are designated regions that focus on the production and export of specific agricultural commodities. They aim to integrate farmers, processors, and exporters in a value chain. AEZs promote the development of export-oriented infrastructure, including cold storage and processing facilities.

Cold Chain Infrastructure: The development of cold chain infrastructure, including cold storage units and refrigerated transportation, is crucial for preserving the quality and extending the shelf life of perishable agricultural products.

Farmers Producer Organizations (FPOs): FPOs are formed by farmers to collectively engage in the production,. marketing, and sale of agricultural produce. They empower farmers by providing collective bargaining power in the market. FPOs enhance the market linkages for small and marginal farmers.

Agricultural Marketing Research and Information Network (AMRIN): AMRIN facilitates the collection and dissemination of market information to farmers. Timely information on prices, demand, and market trends helps farmers make informed decisions. Effort. are ongoing to strengthen and modernize this institutional infrastructure to address challenges in agricultural marketing, enhance efficiency, and improve the income and livelihoods of farmers in India.

PAPER-II

1. (*a*) **Plasma Membrane:** Plasma membrane is also referred to as the cell membrane. It is the membrane found in all cells, that separate the inner part of the cell from the exterior. A cell wall is found to be attached to the plasma membrane to its exterior in plant and bacterial cells. Plasma membrane is composed of a lipid layer which is semipermeable. It is responsible to regulate the transportation of materials and the movement of substances in and out of the cell.

Plasma Membrane Functions: This membrane is composed of a phospholipid bilayer implanted with proteins. It forms a stable barrier between two aqueous compartments, which are towards the outside and inside of a cell in plasma membrane. The embedded proteins perform specialized functions which include cell-cell recognition and selective transport of molecules. Plasma membrane renders protection to the cell along with providing a fixed environment within the cell. It is responsible for performing different functions. In order for it allow movement of substances such as white and red blood cells, it must be flexible such that they could alter the shape and pass through blood capillaries. In addition, it also anchors the cytoskeleton to render shape to a cell and in associating with extracellular matrix and other cells to assist the cells in forming a tissue. It also maintains the cell potential. Plasma membrane is responsible for interacting with other, adjacent cells which can be glycoprotein or lipid proteins. The membrane also assists the proteins to monitor and maintain the chemical climate of the cell, along with the assistance in the shifting of molecules across the membrane.

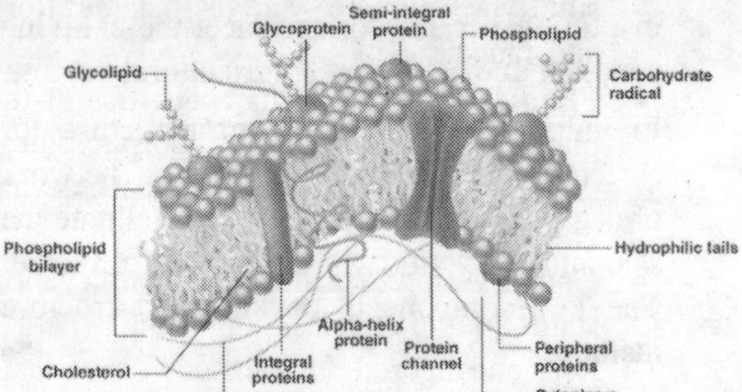

Structure of Plasma Membrane

1. (*b*) **Passport Data of Genetic Resources:** The term "Passport Data" in the context of genetic resources refers to detailed information about a particular germplasm or genetic resource sample. This information is crucial for the documentation, conservation, and utilization of genetic diversity in plant or animal species. Passport data typically includes the following key information:

- **Accession Number:** A unique identifier assigned to each germplasm sample for tracking and reference purposes.
- **Species Name:** The scientific name of the plant or animal species to which the genetic resource belongs.

- **Common Name:** The common name or vernacular name of the species, which may vary based on regions and languages.
- **Collector's Information:** Details about the person or organization who collected the sample, including their name, affiliation, and contact information.
- **Geographic Origin:** Information about the location where the genetic resource was collected, including latitude, longitude, and altitude. This helps in understanding the geographical distribution of the species.
- **Date of Collection:** The date when the genetic resource sample was collected. This information is important for tracking changes over time and assessing the temporal aspects of genetic diversity.
- **Habitat Description:** Details about the natural habitat of the species, including soil type, climate, and associated flora and fauna.
- **Plant Description:** Characteristics of the plant or animal, including morphological traits, growth habits, and any other relevant features.
- **Conservation Status:** The conservation status of the species, indicating whether it is endangered, threatened, or of least concern.
- **Legal and Regulatory Information:** Information about any legal restrictions, permits, or agreements associated with the collection and use of the genetic resource. This may include compliance with international agreements such as the Nagoya Protocol.

Passport data is an essential component of genetic resource documentation, especially in germplasm banks, botanical gardens, and other repositories. It helps in maintaining a comprehensive record of the genetic diversity present in various species, facilitates research and breeding programs, and ensures the sustainable and equitable use of genetic resources while respecting the rights of the providers. This type of information is particularly valuable for biodiversity conservation efforts and sustainable agriculture.

Importance of Passport Data in Germplasm Collection and Conservation: Passport data in germplasm collection and conservation plays a pivotal role in ensuring the effective management, utilization, and preservation of plant and animal genetic resources. This comprehensive information, including unique identifiers, species details, geographic origin, and collector's information, serves as a critical reference for researchers, conservationists, and breeders. Passport data enables the precise identification of each germplasm sample, facilitating efficient tracking and retrieval when needed. It provides valuable insights into the geographic distribution, ecological context, and morphological characteristics of the collected genetic resources. Moreover, this data is essential for assessing the conservation status of species, guiding efforts to protect endangered or threatened plants and animals. Additionally, passport data aids in complying with legal and regulatory requirements, ensuring that the collection and utilization of genetic resources adhere to international agreements and respect the rights of providers, as outlined in agreements like the Nagoya Protocol. Overall, passport data forms the foundation for informed decision-making in genetic resource management, enabling sustainable agricultural practices, biodiversity conservation, and scientific research.

1. (*c*) **Different Classes of Seeds:** The Seed certification program recognizes four classes of seeds- the Nucleus Seed, the Breeder Seed, the Foundation Seed, and the Registered or Certified Seed. The Registered Seed is a category that represents the advancing generations of seed production.
   - **Nucleus Seed:** Nucleus seed represents the initial stage in the seed multiplication process. It is the first generation of seed produced by the plant breeder.

- **Breeder Seed:** Breeder seed is the second stage in the seed multiplication process. It is produced by planting and cultivating nucleus seed.
- **Foundation Seed**: Foundation seed is the third stage in the seed multiplication process. It is produced from breeder seed and serves as the basis for certified seed production.
- **Certified Seed (or Registered Seed):** Certified seed is the final stage in the seed certification process. It is produced from foundation seed and is made available to farmers for planting crops.

Essential Requirement of Production of Certified Seeds: The production of certified seeds is a crucial aspect of ensuring high-quality crops and agricultural productivity. Certified seeds provide farmers with assurance regarding the genetic purity, germination potential, and other quality parameters of the seeds they purchase. To meet the standards for certified seed production, several essential requirements need to be fulfilled. These requirements may vary by country, but the following are common considerations:

- **Genetic Purity:** The seed must exhibit genetic purity, ensuring that it carries the desired characteristics of the parent variety or cultivar. Adequate isolation distances or other measures should be implemented to prevent cross-pollination with other varieties, ensuring genetic integrity.
- **Field Inspection:** Regular and thorough field inspections are necessary during the growing season to monitor crop development and verify compliance with standards. Inspections are conducted by qualified personnel to identify and eliminate off-types, contaminants, and other issues that may compromise seed quality.
- **Seed Source and Pedigree:** Traceability of the seed source is critical. The production should begin with foundation seed obtained from a reliable source with documented genetic purity. Maintaining accurate records of the seed pedigree, including the source of the original seed and subsequent generations, is essential.
- **Seed Germination Testing:** Certified seed must undergo germination testing to ensure a high percentage of viable seeds. This is typically performed by accredited seed testing laboratories. Seeds that do not meet specified germination standards are not eligible for certification.
- **Seed Health:** Certification involves testing for seed-borne diseases and pests. Seeds must be free from pathogens that could negatively impact crop performance. Disease-resistant varieties may be required, and treatments for controlling seed-borne diseases might be necessary.
- **Seed Treatment and Coating:** Seed treatment, if required, should be performed using approved methods and materials. Coating processes should not adversely affect seed germination, and coatings should comply with relevant regulations.
- **Storage and Handling:** Adequate facilities for seed storage must be in place to maintain seed quality during storage. Handling procedures should prevent contamination and damage to the seeds.
- **Labeling and Packaging:** Proper labeling of seed packages is essential to provide information on seed type, genetic characteristics, germination percentage, and other relevant details. Packaging should be secure and protect the seeds from external factors such as moisture, light, and pests.
- **Documentation:** Detailed and accurate records of the entire seed production process, from planting to packaging, should be maintained. Documentation is essential for traceability and to demonstrate compliance with certification standards.
- **Compliance with Regulations:** Adherence to national and international regulations

governing seed certification is mandatory. The entire seed production process should align with the legal requirements and standards set by relevant authorities.

By meeting these essential requirements, producers contribute to the production of high-quality certified seeds, supporting sustainable agriculture and ensuring farmers have access to reliable planting materials.

1. (*d*) Practical Significance of Plant Physiology in Agriculture:

- Plant physiology plays a crucial and practical role in agriculture, serving as a fundamental discipline that bridges the gap between the understanding of plant processes and their direct application to crop production. By delving into the physiological mechanisms governing plant growth, development, and responses to environmental factors, agricultural practitioners can make informed decisions to optimize crop yields, enhance crop quality, and promote sustainable farming practices.
- Understanding the intricacies of plant physiological processes is essential for crop management, especially in the context of optimizing resource use efficiency. Knowledge of how plants absorb, transport, and utilize water and nutrients, for instance, allows farmers to implement precise irrigation and fertilization strategies. This not only conserves resources but also minimizes environmental impact, addressing concerns related to water scarcity and nutrient runoff.
- Plant physiology is also integral in the study of plant responses to biotic and abiotic stressors. By comprehending how plants react to pests, diseases, and adverse climatic conditions, agricultural scientists can develop effective strategies for pest control, disease management, and crop breeding for stress resistance. This knowledge forms the basis for the development of resilient crop varieties that can withstand challenges such as drought, salinity, and extreme temperatures, contributing to global food security.
- Furthermore, plant physiology guides the timing of key agricultural practices, such as planting, harvesting, and post-harvest management. Understanding the physiological processes associated with flowering, fruiting, and maturation helps farmers optimize the timing of these activities, resulting in improved crop yields and quality. It also aids in the development of storage and preservation techniques that maintain the nutritional value of harvested crops, addressing post-harvest losses.
- In the era of climate change, where unpredictable weather patterns pose significant challenges to agriculture, plant physiology becomes a valuable tool for adapting farming practices. By unraveling the physiological responses of crops to changing environmental conditions, farmers can adjust planting calendars, choose suitable crop varieties, and implement innovative cultivation practices to mitigate the impact of climate variability.
- In essence, the practical significance of plant physiology in agriculture lies in its ability to provide a scientific foundation for informed decision-making. From resource management and stress tolerance to optimal timing of agricultural operations, plant physiology empowers farmers and agricultural researchers to address contemporary challenges and work towards sustainable, resilient, and productive agricultural systems.

1. (*e*) Methods for Linkage Detection in Recombinant Breeding Programme: Linkage detection is a crucial step in recombinant breeding programs, as it helps identify and map the genetic loci associated with desirable traits.

The following are common methods used for linkage detection in recombinant breeding programs:

Molecular Markers:

- **Description:** Molecular markers are DNA sequences associated with specific genes or genomic regions. Common types include Restriction Fragment Length Polymorphisms (RFLPs), Random Amplified Polymorphic DNA (RAPD), Simple Sequence Repeats (SSRs), and Single Nucleotide Polymorphisms (SNPs).
- **Methodology:** Molecular markers are used to create genetic maps by identifying associations between marker loci and trait loci. The closer two loci are on a chromosome, the more likely they are to be inherited together.

Quantitative Trait Loci (QTL) Mapping:

- **Description:** QTL mapping involves identifying regions of the genome that are associated with quantitative traits, such as yield, disease resistance, or quality.
- **Methodology:** Researchers cross two individuals with contrasting trait values, and then, using molecular markers, they analyze the inheritance of these markers along with the expression of the quantitative trait. Statistical methods are then applied to identify significant associations.

Association Mapping:

- **Description:** Association mapping looks for associations between molecular markers and traits within natural populations, rather than in controlled crosses.
- **Methodology:** This method utilizes diverse germplasm collections and evaluates the natural variation present in a population. It is particularly useful for crops with complex breeding histories.

Bulked Segregant Analysis (BSA):

- **Description:** BSA is a method that involves grouping individuals based on their phenotypic expression and analyzing pooled DNA samples from these groups.
- **Methodology:** By comparing the frequency of molecular markers in the two bulks, researchers can identify markers linked to the trait of interest. BSA is especially useful for traits controlled by major genes.

Marker-Assisted Selection (MAS):

- **Description:** MAS involves selecting individuals for breeding based on the presence of specific molecular markers associated with desirable traits.
- **Methodology:** Once marker-trait associations are established, breeders can use molecular markers to screen and select individuals with the desired traits more efficiently. This accelerates the breeding process compared to traditional methods.

Genome-Wide Association Studies (GWAS):

- **Description:** GWAS involves scanning the entire genome for associations between molecular markers and traits across diverse populations.
- **Methodology:** GWAS is particularly useful for crops with a high degree of genetic diversity. It allows for the identification of multiple genes and their interactions influencing complex traits.

Genomic Selection:

- **Description:** Genomic selection involves predicting the breeding value of individuals based on their entire genomic information, rather than individual marker-trait associations.
- **Methodology:** Statistical models are used to estimate the genomic value of individuals, making it a powerful tool for predicting complex traits influenced by multiple genes.

These methods, often used in combination, contribute to the efficient identification and utilization of genetic linkage information in recombinant breeding programs, ultimately enhancing the precision and speed of crop improvement efforts.

2. (*a*) **Chromosome Structure Models:** The following points highlight the top four models proposed for chromosome structure. The models are: (*i*) Molecular Model (*ii*) Multi-Stranded Model or Polyneme Chromosome Model (*iii*) General Chromosome Model (*iv*) Folded Fibre Model.

(*i*) **Molecular Model:** This model of chromosome structure was proposed by Taylor and coworkers in 1957, 1963 and is based on the semiconservative replication of eukaryotic chromosome. According to this model, the chromatid consists of only one DNA chain, where several DNA double helices linked end-to-end by protein molecules. Interactions of protein molecules with each other are responsible for coiling and uncoiling of the chromosomes. DNA molecule can be broken by deoxyribonucleases but not by proteolytic enzymes.

(*ii*) **Multi-Stranded Model or Polyneme Chromosome Model:** This model was put forth by Ris in 1961 and Ris and Chandler in 1963. According to this model, the chromosome is multi stranded, *i.e.*, it contains several DNA double helices arranged parallel to each other. Each chromosome is divided into two chromatids, each chromatid is made of two "half chromatids" and each half chromatid is composed of two "quarter chromatids". Each "quarter chromatid" is, in turn, made of four chromatin fibres and each chromatin fibre contains 2 DNA double helices. The diameter of the DNA double helix is 2 nm, and two DNA molecules are associated with protein to make the chromatin fibre. Diameters of chromatin fibres, quarter chromatids, half chromatids and chromatids are 10 nm, 40 nm, 80 nm, and 160 nm, respectively. Thus each chromatid contains 32 DNA molecules, while the metaphase chromosome contains 64 DNA molecules. However, according to the recent studies, the chromosome is definitely not multistranded.

(*iii*) **General Chromosome Model:** This model was proposed by Crick in 1971; it suggests that DNA in a chromatid is a large monomer which runs continuously from one end to the other. Band and inter band regions of chromosomes (especially giant chromosomes) are suggested to have distinct functions. The bands contain globular control DNA, while the inter-bands contain fibrous coding DNA.

(*iv*) **Folded Fibre Model:** DuPraw in 1965 proposed this model on the basis of electron microscopic studies of human chromosomes. According to this model, each chromatid contains single long nucleoprotein complex (Chromatin fibres) in which a single DNA double helix forms the main structure of the axis. This model of chromosome has been widely accepted.

The main features of this model are as follows:

- Before interphase replication, each chromosome consists of a single chromatid made up of a single 200-500 Å thick chromatin fibre; each fibre contains a single long DNA double helix which is associated with proteins and RNA.
- The chromatin fibre (chromatid) replicates during S phase of call cycle to produce two sister chromatids which are held together by the un-replicated regions.
- This pair of sister chromatids folds up to form a visible chromosome at prophase, but sister chromatids are held together by minute un-replicated regions.
- Exact folding and packing patterns of chromatids of different chromosomes are thought to vary in some specific ways.

Thus each metaphase chromatid is composed of tightly folded single chromatin fibre of 200-500 Å diameter. The exact 3-dimensional configuration of nucleoprotein fibre in any given chromatid is not constant. This configuration varies from metaphase to interphase.

It also differs for the same chromosome during mitosis and meiosis, in mature sperm, and from metaphase to metaphase. Non-homologous chromosomes differ not only in their genetic content but also in their 3-dimensional configurations.

This model suggests that in the centromeric region, chromatin fibres are continuous and pass from one arm to the other for each sister chromatid; the sister chromatids are held closely together in this region up to the beginning of their separation during anaphase. This model also suggests that a small amount of DNA is synthesized before the sister chromatids actually separate. The diagrammatic representation of the folded fibre model is given in the Fig.

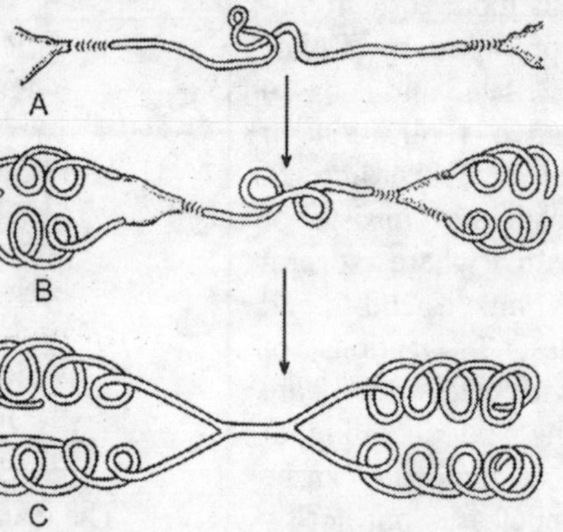

Chromosome replication and structure according to the folded fibre model of DuPraw. A. Unreplicated chromatid is a single 200-500Å chromatin fibre containing a DNA double helix in supercoiled configuration (replication is just being initiated). B. Replication of the chromatid begins at several sites. C. The late replicating segment of the fibre at the centromere serves to hold the sister chromatids together. The chromatin fibre is folded to give the chromatid and chromosome structures visible under light microscope.

The chromatin fibres are proposed to be of "A" and "B" type. The A type fibre is intermediate between the extended DNA double helix and the fully packed B type fibre. DNA double helix is 20 Å in diameter; it associates with histones to form a nucleo-histone fibril.

This fibril folds into a super-helix of 100 Å diameter with a pitch of 120 Å; this is the type A fibre. The 100 Å fibril folds under the influence of divalent cations (Ca^{2+}, Mg^{2+}) to give rise to a branched system of 250 Å fibres.The fully packed fibre is 200-500 Å in diameter and is called a B type fibre. When Ca^{2+} and Mg^{2+} are removed, the 200-500 Å fibres unfold into 100 Å fibrils. The digestion of 100 Å fibrils by proteinase enzymes releases a single 20-30 Å thick stand (DNA double helix) which is susceptible to DNAase.

2. (*b*) (*i*) Differentiate between the Apomixis and Parthenogenesis

Apomixis	Parthenogenesis
Apomixis is a type of asexual reproduction where the embryo develops from the seeds without the process of fertilisation.	Parthenogenesis is a type of apomixis where the egg cells help in the development of an embryo.
It produces a genetically identical clone of the mother cell.	Here, the embryos develop from an unfertilised egg, and the offspring are genetically identical. The apomictic parthenogenesis produces the clone of the mother.
The types of apomixis are–Recurrent apomixis, Non-recurrent, Adventitious and Vegetative apomixis.	The major two types of parthenogenesis are–Natural and Artificial parthenogenesis.

(ii) **Differentiate between Quantitative Traits and Qualitative Traits**

Quantitative Traits	Qualitative Traits
It deals with the inheritance of traits of kind, viz., form, strcture, colour, etc.	It deals with the inheritance of traits of degree, viz., heights of length, weight, number, etc.
Discrete phenotypic classes occur which display discontinuous variations.	A spectrum of phenotypic classes occur which contain continuous variations.
Each quantitative trait is governed by many non-allelic genes or polygenes.	Each qualitative trait is governed by two or many alleles of a single gene.
The phenotypic expression of a gene is not influenced by environment.	Environmental conditions effect the phenotypic expression of polygenes variously.
It concerns with individual matings and their progeny.	It concerns with a population of organisms consisting of all possible kinds of matings.
In it analysis is made by counts and ratios.	In it analysis is made by statistical method.

(iii) **Differentiate between Recurrent Selection for General Combining Ability (RSGCA) and Recurrent Selection for Specific Combining Ability (RSSCA):** Recurrent selection is a breeding technique used to improve quantitative traits in plants or animals over several generations. The terms "Recurrent Selection for General Combining Ability (RSGCA)" and "Recurrent Selection for Specific Combining Ability (RSSCA)" refer to different approaches within recurrent selection. Here's a differentiation between the two:

Recurrent Selection for General Combining Ability (RSGCA):

- **Focus:** RSGCA focuses on selecting parents based on their general combining ability (GCA), which is the average performance of their progeny when crossed with various other individuals.
- **Objective:** The goal is to identify and promote parents that consistently contribute desirable traits to their offspring across a wide range of genetic backgrounds.

Process:

- Progeny from selected parents are evaluated in different combinations over multiple generations.
- Selection is based on overall performance, emphasizing the general combining ability of the parents.
- The emphasis is on improving the average performance of the population.

Recurrent Selection for Specific Combining Ability (RSSCA):

- **Focus:** RSSCA, on the other hand, concentrates on selecting parents based on their specific combining ability (SCA), which is the interaction effect between two parents when they are crossed.
- **Objective:** The goal is to identify parents that exhibit superior performance when specifically combined with certain other parents, emphasizing the interactions between specific pairs of parents.

Process:

- Progeny from selected parents are evaluated in specific combinations to assess their specific combining ability.
- Selection is based on the superior performance of certain parent combinations, focusing on specific interactions that lead to exceptional traits.
- The emphasis is on creating superior hybrids by capitalizing on specific combinations of parental traits.

Selection Criteria:

- **RSGCA:** Selection based on the general combining ability of parents, considering their overall performance across various crosses.
- **RSSCA:** Selection based on the specific combining ability of parents, focusing on their performance in specific combinations with other parents.

Emphasis:

- **RSGCA:** Emphasis on improving the average performance of the population by selecting parents with consistently good general combining ability.
- **RSSCA:** Emphasis on creating superior hybrids by identifying parents that interact exceptionally well in specific combinations, leading to outstanding traits in the offspring.

Genetic Background:

- **RSGCA:** Considers the performance of parents across a broad range of genetic backgrounds.
- **RSSCA:** Focuses on the specific interactions between parents, emphasizing the potential for creating high-performing hybrids in certain combinations.

(*iv*) **Differentiate between Avoidance and Non-Preference:** "Avoidance" and "non-preference" are terms often used in the context of plant-insect interactions, particularly in pest management strategies. These terms describe different mechanisms by which plants may defend themselves against herbivores. Here's an explanation of each term:

Avoidance: Avoidance refers to a plant's ability to deter herbivores through mechanisms that make the plant less attractive or even harmful to the herbivore.

Mechanisms:

- **Chemical Defenses:** Plants can produce secondary metabolites, such as alkaloids, terpenoids, or phenolic compounds, that are toxic or unpalatable to herbivores.
- **Physical Defenses:** Plants may have physical structures like thorns, trichomes, or tough leaves that deter herbivores from feeding.
- **Allelopathy:** Some plants release chemicals into the soil that inhibit the germination or growth of competing plants, reducing herbivore attraction.

Non-Preference (Antixenosis): Non-preference, also known as antixenosis, occurs when a plant is not preferred by herbivores, meaning that the herbivores do not choose to feed on that plant even when it is available.

Mechanisms:

- **Morphological Factors:** The plant may have features such as leaf hairs, textures, or colors that are unappealing or confusing to herbivores.
- **Chemical Factors:** The plant may produce compounds that act as repellents or deterrents, making it less attractive to herbivores.
- **Physical Barriers:** Plants may have physical structures that make it difficult for herbivores to access and feed on the plant.

In summary, avoidance involves active defense mechanisms that make the plant less palatable or even harmful to herbivores, thereby discouraging feeding. On the other hand, non-preference (antixenosis) relies on characteristics of the plant that make it unappealing or less favorable for herbivores, leading them to avoid or not prefer that particular plant in the first place. Both avoidance and non-preference are strategies that contribute to a plant's defense against herbivores and are important considerations in the development of pest-resistant crops and sustainable pest management practices.

(*v*) **Differentiate between Penetrance and Expressivity:** Penetrance and expressivity are terms used in genetics to describe variations in the manifestation of traits or genetic conditions among individuals. Here's a differentiation between penetrance and expressivity:

Penetrance: Penetrance refers to the proportion of individuals with a specific genotype who express the associated phenotype. In other words, it measures the likelihood that a particular gene or mutation will lead to the observable trait.

Example: If a genetic mutation is said to have 80% penetrance, it means that 80% of individuals with the mutation will exhibit the associated trait, while 20% will not.

Expressivity: Expressivity refers to the degree or intensity to which a particular phenotype is expressed in individuals carrying a specific genotype. It describes the variation in the severity or extent of a trait among individuals with the same genetic mutation.

Example: If a genetic condition exhibits variable expressivity, individuals with the same mutation may show different degrees of severity in the associated trait. For instance, a disorder may manifest as mild in some individuals and more severe in others.

In summary, penetrance focuses on the probability of expressing a trait, while expressivity describes the variability in the expression of a trait among individuals with the same genotype. Both concepts are important in understanding the complexity of genetic traits and conditions.

2. **(*c*) Chlorophyll Pigments:** The word chlorophyll is derived from the Greek word khloros (green) and phyllon (leaves). Chlorophyll is a green pigment that acts as a photoreceptor. It is a pigment that perceives light energy and aids in the biochemical process. This exists in many forms, such as chlorophyll a, chlorophyll b, etc. Also, chlorophyll is one of the pigments that aid in the photosynthesis process.The chlorophyll absorbs light energy of red and blue wavelengths. Whereas, the green light is not absorbed and is reflected back. Thus, the leaves appear green.

Chlorophyll pigment is present in chloroplasts. In a chloroplast, thylakoid membranes have chlorophyll pigments embedded in them. The chlorophyll pigments actually capture light energy. Hence light reactions occur in thylakoid membranes.

Type of Chlorophyll

- **Chlorophyll *a*:** This pigment is found in all higher plants. It is the most vital pigment used in photosynthesis. Some algae, cyanobacteria and anaerobic phototrophs also show the presence of chlorophyll *a*. It has a strong rate of absorption. It absorbs violet-blue as well as orange-red light and reflects blue-green light.
- **Chlorophyll *b*:** This type of chlorophyll is seen in green algae and plants. It is an accessory pigment that aids chlorophyll *a*. This pigment usually absorbs the orange-red light and reflects a yellow-green colour. The chlorin ring of this chlorophyll has a CHO. Whereas, the chlorin ring of Chlorophyll-*a* contains CH_3.
- **Chlorophyll *c*:** This pigment is primarily seen in marine algae. Brown algae, Diatoms and Dinoflagellates show the presence of chlorophyll *c*. It is an unusual chlorophyll pigment that has a porphyrin ring. This can be further classified into chlorophyll c_1, c_2 and c_3. The chemical composition and the absorption rate differ in each sub-type.
- **Chlorophyll *d*:** Chlorophyll *d* is present only in red algae and cyanobacteria. These organisms live in deep water, and thus use red light for photosynthesis.
- **Chlorophyll *e*:** This is a rare pigment that is found in some golden algae. Chlorophyll *e* has been identified from the Xanthophytes (yellow-green algae).
- **Chlorophyll *f*:** This pigment was recently found and is known to absorb infrared light. It can absorb light of a wavelength that is over the visible range. Their function is yet to be studied.

Pigments are compounds that give colour to materials around us. The substances that give this colour are also termed as biochromes or biological pigments. They are usually insoluble in water and are of two types – organic (natural) and inorganic (synthetic). Photosynthetic pigments are a type of natural pigment that helps in the process of photosynthesis. Here, let's discuss more about the different types of photosynthetic pigments.

The most widespread pigment in photosynthetic plants is chlorophyll. They are cyclic tetrapyrrole pigments chelated with magnesium. They share structural features with the haem and bile pigments of animals. These chlorophyll pigments can be found in fruits, flowers as well as leaves.

Chlorophyll *a* and chlorophyll *b* are the major types of chlorophylls found in plants. The former is a blue-green pigment and the latter is a yellow-green pigment. They give their characteristic green colour due to the strong absorbance of red and blue light. The other types of chlorophyll include chlorophyll c_1, c_2, c_3, *d*, *e* and chlorophyll *f*.

5. (*a*) **Bud Dormancy:** Bud dormancy is a process in which plant meristems become mostly inactive (physiological processes do not completely stop) to withstand harsh environmental conditions.

Causes of Bud Dormancy:

- **Cold Temperature:** Exposure to chilling temperatures induces dormancy in many plants as a protective response to winter conditions.
- **Breaking Dormancy:** Providing a period of cold stratification, mimicking winter conditions, is often necessary to fulfill the chilling requirement and break dormancy.

Photoperiod (Day Length):

- **Cause:** Shortening day length signals to certain plants that winter is approaching, triggering dormancy.
- **Breaking Dormancy:** Extending the photoperiod using artificial light or selecting plant varieties adapted to longer days can break dormancy.

Plant Hormones (Abscisic Acid - ABA):

- **Cause:** Increased levels of abscisic acid (ABA) contribute to the initiation and maintenance of dormancy.
- **Breaking Dormancy:** Application of gibberellins (GAs) or cytokinins can counteract the effects of ABA and promote bud break.

Chilling Requirement:

- **Cause:** Some plants require a certain amount of chilling hours to break dormancy.
- **Breaking Dormancy:** Ensuring that the chilling requirement is met by exposing plants to the required cold temperatures is essential for breaking dormancy.

Genetic Factors:

- **Cause:** Genetic programming influences the dormancy patterns of different plant species.
- **Breaking Dormancy:** Selecting plant varieties with lower chilling requirements or that are less dependent on specific dormancy-inducing factors can be an effective strategy.

Means to Break Bud Dormancy Intentionally:

Artificial Heating:

Method: Providing controlled warming through greenhouses or heated structures can simulate the onset of spring and break dormancy.

Chilling and Stratification:

Method: Subjecting seeds or plants to a period of chilling (cold stratification) can fulfill the chilling requirement and promote bud break.

Application of Growth Regulators:

Method: Applying plant growth regulators like gibberellins (GAs) or cytokinins can counteract the inhibitory effects of ABA and promote bud break.

Light Manipulation:

Method: Using artificial lighting to extend the photoperiod can prevent the shortening day length that induces dormancy in some plants.

Water Management:

Method: Ensuring adequate water supply can alleviate stress conditions that may contribute to dormancy. However, this approach is context-dependent and may not be universally applicable.

Nutrient Management:

Method: Balancing nutrient levels to avoid deficiencies or imbalances can promote overall plant health and reduce stress-induced dormancy.

Selective Breeding:

Method: Developing plant varieties with reduced chilling requirements or altered responses to environmental cues through selective breeding.

5. (*b*) Preparation Method of Ready to Serve (RTS) Beverages and Squashes

This is a type of fruit beverage containing at least 10% fruit juice and 10% total soluble solids besides about 0.3% acid. It is not diluted before serving and, hence, is known as ready-to-serve (RTS) beverage.

Method of preparation: For the preparation of 10 lts. of RTS beverage, follow the procedure given below:

- Calculate the amount of juice required as per commercial specification

  Required juice = (10/100) × 10 = 1.0 lts
- Measure the TSS using a refractometer (say the TSS is 30%)

  Calculate the total solids content of the juice *i.e.* 0.3 × 1.0 = 0.30 kg
- The final required TSS content in the product is to be say 10%.

  The TSS required to be added to obtain the final product is

  (0.1 × 10 – 0.30) kg = 0.70 kg
- The amount of soluble solids in the form of citric acid and KMS is Citric acid @ 0.3%, in the final produce is 30 g *i.e.* 0.03 kg.
- Amount of solids to be added in the form of sugar is 0.70–0.03 = 0.67kg.
- Add calculated amount of sugar to about 2 lts of water and heat it till it dissolves completely. Add citric acid and juice to the sugar syrup and makeup the volume to 10 lts. Mix it well.
- Heat up to 90°C, fill hot in clean pre-sterilized glass bottles up to brim, seal and cool in the air or fill in bottle, seal and heat process (90°C for 25 min.).

Flow Sheet

FRUIT
(pulp/juice)

↓

MIXING WITH STRAINED SYRUP SOLUTION
(sugar + water + acid, heated just to dissolve)
according to recipe

↓

HOMOGENIZATION

↓

BOTTLING

↓

CROWN CORKING

↓

PASTEURIZATION
(at about 90°C) For 25 Minutes

↓

COOLING

↓

STORAGE

5. (*c*) Causal Organism, Nature of Damage and Management Practices for Damping Off in Vegetables:

Causal Organism and Nature of Damage: Damping-off can be caused by various fungi, including Rhizoctonia species (spp.) and Fusarium spp., or fungus-like organisms called oomycetes (also called water molds), including Phytophthora spp. and Pythium spp. Many of these pathogens have a broad host range and are capable of infecting numerous vegetable hosts.

Symptoms of damping-off may include a failure of seeds to germinate, discoloration and rot of young stems near the soil line, and wilting, collapse, and death of young seedlings. Seedlings with damping-off often have discolored and rotting roots. In high-humidity situations, white, fluffy growth of the causal pathogen may develop on infected tissues.

Damping-off typically affects new plantings. It can occur in just a few seedlings, or it may be more extensive, resulting in poor stand establishment (Figure) and the need to replant. Damping-off commonly occurs in low-lying areas that have poor drainage and hold water. Damping-off may also be a problem in transplant production.

Management

- **Biological Management:** Apply biological products (biofungicides) that are effective against damping-off pathogens. Biofungicides labeled for use in various vegetable crops and against some pathogens that cause damping-off are available. However, data on the efficacy of many biofungicides is limited.
- **Cultural and Environmental Management:** Plant in an appropriate site when environmental conditions are favorable for seedling growth, and follow local planting recommendations for each vegetable. To reduce the potential for damping-off, place seeds/seedlings at the recommended planting depth in soils that drain well and when soil temperatures are warm and soils are not wet. Planting on raised beds can help improve soil drainage in the field. Cool, wet soils slow seed germination and plant growth and favor disease development, whereas warm soil temperatures support plant growth.
- **Do not overwater.**
- **Do not overcrowd plants.**
- **Maintain appropriate environmental conditions in enclosed structures:** When growing transplants or seedlings in enclosed structures, such as greenhouses, maintain temperatures that are favorable for seed germination and plant growth.
- **Sanitation:** Use new or disinfested media, pots, and transplant trays.

5. (*d*) Preventive Measures for Management of Stored Grain Pests and Diseases: Managing stored grain pests and diseases is crucial to ensuring the quality and safety of stored grains. Here are some preventive measures and management strategies:

Clean and Sanitize Storage Facilities:

- Thoroughly clean storage facilities before introducing new grain.
- Remove any remaining grain residues, dust, and debris.
- Sanitize storage bins, silos, and handling equipment to eliminate potential sources of contamination.

Proper Storage Practices:

- Use aeration systems to maintain optimal moisture levels in stored grains, as both excess moisture and dry conditions can promote pest infestations.
- Store grains at recommended temperatures to inhibit the growth of pests and fungi.
- Regularly inspect stored grains for signs of mold, discoloration, or pest activity.

Quality Seed and Pest-Free Grain:

- Start with high-quality, pest-free seed and grain.
- Implement a quality control program to monitor incoming grains for pests, diseases, and contaminants.

- Hermetic Storage:
- Consider using hermetic storage methods, such as airtight containers or bags, to create an oxygen-deprived environment that inhibits pest and fungal growth.

Proper Moisture Management:
- Maintain optimal moisture content for stored grains to prevent the growth of fungi and the development of mycotoxins.
- Use moisture meters to monitor and control moisture levels.

Temperature Control:
- Implement temperature monitoring systems to ensure that stored grains remain within the recommended temperature range.
- Cold storage can slow down insect activity and reduce the risk of infestations.

Pest Monitoring and Trapping:
- Set up insect traps to monitor pest populations.
- Implement a regular monitoring program to detect early signs of infestation.
- Use pheromone traps and other monitoring tools to track and manage pest populations.

Integrated Pest Management (IPM):
- Implement an integrated pest management approach that combines physical, biological, and chemical control methods.
- Use natural enemies of pests, such as predators and parasites, to control infestations.

Regular Inspections:
- Conduct regular inspections of stored grains to identify and address issues promptly.
- Train personnel to recognize the signs of pest infestations and diseases.

Proper Sealing:
- Ensure that storage facilities are properly sealed to prevent entry of pests.
- Repair any cracks, gaps, or openings in storage structures.

Chemical Treatments:
- Consider the judicious use of approved pesticides and insecticides.
- Follow recommended application rates and safety guidelines.
- Rotate chemical treatments to minimize the development of resistance in pest populations.

Training and Education:
- Train personnel on proper storage practices, pest identification, and the importance of preventive measures.
- Promote awareness of the risks associated with poor grain storage and handling practices.

By implementing these preventive measures and incorporating integrated pest management strategies, you can significantly reduce the risk of stored grain pests and diseases, ensuring the quality and safety of the stored grains.

5. **(*e*)** The persistent dominance of the rice-wheat cropping system in the national agricultural scenario over the last four decades, despite a consistent decline in water tables year after year, can be attributed to a complex interplay of economic, climatic, cultural, and infrastructural factors. Rice and wheat, being staple food crops for a significant portion of the population, hold a critical position in meeting the ever-growing demand for food. The adaptability of these crops to diverse climatic conditions, coupled with their high economic viability and established markets, has incentivized farmers to continue their cultivation. Additionally, the extensive infrastructure and supply chains developed for rice and wheat, encompassing storage facilities and distribution networks, make it more convenient for farmers to market their produce.

The economic policies and subsidies provided by the government to support rice and wheat cultivation contribute to the sustained dominance of this cropping system. Farmers, often risk-averse due to uncertainties in market dynamics and the adaptability of alternative crops, may choose to stick with the familiar and economically stable rice-wheat system. Cultural and traditional practices also play a significant role, as the rice-wheat cycle may be deeply ingrained in the agricultural traditions of certain regions.

The challenges associated with crop rotation, which could contribute to water conservation and mitigate pest and disease pressures, are often outweighed by the economic considerations and market demand for rice and wheat. Furthermore, the advancements in agricultural technology, including the development of high-yielding varieties and improved cultivation practices for rice and wheat, have contributed to the sustained productivity of these crops.

Despite the ongoing decline in water tables, farmers may employ certain water management practices, such as efficient irrigation techniques, to cope with water scarcity while still cultivating rice and wheat. There is a need for a comprehensive approach that addresses water conservation, encourages sustainable agricultural practices, and promotes awareness about alternative cropping systems. Government initiatives, research and extension services, and incentives for diversification could play pivotal roles in steering the agricultural sector towards more sustainable and water-efficient practices, ensuring long-term resilience in the face of environmental challenges.

7. **(*a*) Package of Practices of Mango Cultivation in North India:** Mango is considered as king of fruits. Mango Cultivation is the leading fruit crop of India and considered to be the king of fruits. Mango fruit is utilized at all stages of its development both in its immature and mature stage. Raw fruits are used for making chutney, pickles and juices. The ripe fruits besides being used for desert are also utilized for preparing several products like squashes, syrups, nectars, jams and jellies. India occupies first place in mango production of the world and accounts for almost half of the global production and area. Mango occupies 22 per cent of the total area under fruits cultivation comprising of 1.2 million hectares, with a total production of 11 million tonnes. Uttar Pradesh ranks first in Mango production & productivity with share of 23.47% followed by Andhra Pradesh, Karnataka, Telangana, Bihar, Gujarat, Tamil Nadu, West Bengal, Maharashtra and Madhya Pradesh.

Climate: Mango is well adapted to tropical climate. High humidity and cloudy weather at the time of flowering are not favourable as they affect pollination and fruit set and encourage diseases. Rains during flowering are detrimental to the crop.

Soils: Alluvial and sandyloams are ideal for mango cultivation. It can be grown even on lighter soils like chalkas and dubbas when properly manured. Alkaline and saline soils should be avoided. The most desirable soils for mango should be of medium texture, deep (2 to 2.5 m) well drained with low water table (below 180 cms in all seasons) and have a pH range of 6.0 to 7.5. Mango cannot tolerate high soil salt content (not more than 0.05 %).

Manures and fertilizers: To improve the texture of soils, add adequate tank silt and FYM. Sowing of the green manure crop (20 kg sun hemp/10 kg diancha/acre) with the onset of monsoon Fertilizer and incorporating 45 days after sowing. The fertilizers schedule for mango for different ages is as follows:

Age of the tree	Nitrogen	Phosphorus	Potash
First Year	100	100	100
Second Year	200	200	200
Third Year	300	300	300
Fourth Year	400	400	400
Fifth Year	500	500	500
Sixth Year	600	600	600
Seventh Year	700	700	700
Eight Year	800	800	800
Ninth Year	900	900	900
Tenth Year	1000	1000	1000

- Fertilizers should be applied through placement in circular trenches around the trunk. For the 10 years age and above trees the fertilizer should be applied at 1.5 m away from the trunk.
- Manures and fertilizers should be generally done in the beginning of monsoon. Irrigation should be given after the application of fertilizers. Wherever irrigation is available it is advantageous to apply half of the recommended dose of fertilizers after fruit set.
- For the correction of micronutrient deficiency, spraying of $ZnSO_4$ 5g , Boran 2g and 10g urea per liter of water is recommended at the onset of monsoon.
- Spraying of KNO_3 @ 10g/l during November helps in opening of the flower bud and uniform flowering.

Suitable Varieties: Though there are nearly 1000 varieties of mango in India, only following varieties are grown in different states : Alphonso, Bangalora, Banganpalli, Bombai, Bombay Green, Dashehari, Fazli, Fernandin, Himsagar, Kesar, Kishen Bhog, Langra, Mankhurd, Mulgoa, Neelam, Samarbehist, Chausa, Suvarnarekha, Vanaraj and Zardalu. Recently some mango hybrids have been released for cultivation by different institutes / universities. A brief introduction to such varieties is presented below:

- **Mallika:** It is a cross between Neelam and Dashehari. Fruits are medium sized cadmium coloured with good quality, reported to be a regular bearer.
- **Amrapali:** It is a cross between Dashehari and Neelam. It is a dwarf vigorous type with regular and late bearing variety. It yields on an average 16 t/ha and about 1600 plants can be accommodated in one hectare.
- **Mangeera:** It is a cross between Rumani and Neelam. It is a semi vigorous type with a regular bearing habit. Fruits are medium sized with light yellow coloured skin, firm and fibreless flesh and sweet to taste.

  Ratna: It is a cross between Neelam and Alphonso. It is a regular bearer and free from spongy tissue. Fruits are medium sized with excellent quality. Flesh is firm and fibreless, deep orange in colour with high TSS (19-21 Brix).
- **Arka Aruna:** It is a hybrid between Banganapalli and Alphonso with regular bearing habit and dwarf in stature. About 400 plants can be accommodated per hectare. Fruits are large sized (500-700 gm) with attractive skin colour. Pulp is fibreless, sweet to taste (20-22 Brix). Pulp percentage is 73 and the fruits are free from spongy tissue.
- **Arka Puneet:** It is a regular and prolific bearing hybrid of the cross between Alphonso and the Banganapalli. Fruits are medium sized (220-250 gm) with attractive skin colour, having red blush.
- **Arka Anmol:** It is a semi-vigorous plant type from the cross between Alphonso and Janardhan Pasand. It is also a regular bearing and free from spongy tissues.

Propagation: Farmers should always get vegetatively propagated, true to type plants from recognised nurseries. Inarching, veneer grafting, side grafting and epicotyl grafting are the popular methods of propagation in mango.

Pruning: Pruning to remove criss-cross branches may be done so that center of the tree is opened out and inner branches are exposed to sunlight. Pruning of the dried twigs and branches should be done with pruning saw during June-July. Pruning in mango encourages production of new shoots.

Intercultivation: Inter crops like vegetables, low growing field crops and fruits like Phalsa or Papaya can be profitably grown in alleys in young orchards. Red gram is not advisable as it is an alternative host to mealy bug. In old orchards, shade tolerating crops like ginger, turmeric etc., can be taken. Two ploughing in the inter spaces, once at the beginning and another at the end of the monsoon keep the orchard weed free and facilitate rain water percolation.

Pruning: Pruning to remove criss –cross branches may be done so that center of the tree is opened out and inner branches are exposed to sunlight.

Irrigation: Mango responds well to irrigation, particularly at fruit set and developmental phases. The young plants at bearing stage should be irrigated frequently.

- In bearing trees, for obtaining good flowering, irrigation must be stopped at least 2 months before flowering period. Stopping of irrigation creates stress and encourages flower bud formation.
- Irrigation should be given fruit set and thereafter at regular intervals during fruit development period, beginning from fruit set stage to full development stage.
- For better quality irrigation should be stopped 20-30 days before maturity/ harvesting the crop.
- As far as possible irrigation should be given with drip system. Drip irrigation not only conservers water but also increases water use efficiency.
- For conservation of rain water, rows (in rectangular system of planting) should be along the contour in sloppy locations.

Fruit Drop: Fruit drop in mango occurs when the fruits are at pea stage of development. Moisture deficiency, nutrient deficiency and hormonal imbalance are the causes for the mango fruit drop. Fruit drop can be controlled by spraying 2,4 – D at 10 ppm or Naphthalene acetic acid (NAA) at 20 ppm twice at an interval of 15 days during the early stage (peanut stage) of fruit development.

Alternate/Irregular Bearing: Irregular bearing in mango is due to imbalance in nutrient status of the plant. Balanced manuring and fertilizer application and irrigation will keep the tree healthy and vigorous and prevent the irregular bearing. Pruning of weak, dead criss cross shoots to open the canopy of the tree is suggested to regulate the bearing in old trees.

Malformation: One spray of 200 ppm NAA in October followed by deblossoming at bud burst stage in December - January.

Top Working: Top working is done to replace the inferior seedling mango by known variety. The trees are beheaded upto 1.5 m height in August to September months *i.e.,* after receding of heavy rain. Allow 4-5 vigorous shoots to grow. Grafting on the shoots is done by veneer grafting on the shoots of pencil thickness. Once the graft is successful, remove the shoots arising from the seedling tree. Prune the new shoots to get more branches. The young shoots arising from grafts should be protected.

Harvesting and packing: Early harvest of fully developed but not matured fruit starts in April to catch the early Northern markets. However, the fruits harvested without reaching maturity will not ripen properly. Normal harvest commences when few "Patukayalu" or "Shakh" fall from the tree. In case of pickle mangoes, time of harvest is relatively more flexible and any time between stone hardening and attainment of physiological maturity. Harvesting the fruits with a long poll having a net at the end (Gowka) or Dapoli harvester and lowering them gently on a gunny cushion minimizes the injuries. The minimum total soluble content for harvesting without sacrificing the quality is 9.0 in case of Banganpalli and 8.5 for Dashehari. For judging the maturity, fruit samples from various directions of the tree are taken and dropped in a bucket of water, the dipped fruits being indicative of correct maturity. The fruits should be harvested with 7 cm stock and taken to the packhouse in plastic crates. Desapping of the fruits should be done by keeping the fruits in inverted position in the desapping nets for about 3-4 hours. Desapping of mango fruits prevent the sap injury on the fruits. After desapping the stock of the fruits are cut up to 1 cm. The desapped fruits are washed thoroughly in the running water to remove the dirt and other extraneous material. For export, the mango fruits are graded as per the international guidelines of the importing country. The fruits are then packed in the Corrugated fiber board baskets with stock end pointing upward to avoid injury to the fruits.

7. **(*b*) (*i*) Cotton white fly:** Causal organism: *Bemisia tabaci* (Aleyrodidae: Hemiptera)

Nature of damage:

- Appearance of chlorotic spots on the leaves and upward curling of leaves.
- Leaves become reddish, brittle.
- Premature leaf dropping, boll bursting and poor-quality lint due to honey dew secretion.

Management of diseases and insect pests:

- ETL: 5 - 10 /leaf
- Avoid alternate cultivated host crops of the whitefly like brinjal, bhendi, tomato, tobacco and sunflower in the vicinity of cotton crop.
- Removal and destruction of alternate weed hosts like *Abutilon indicum and Solanum nigrum* from the fields and neighbouring areas and maintaining field sanitation.
- Adoption of crop rotation with non-preferred hosts such as sorghum, ragi, maize.
- Timely sowing with recommended spacing, preferably wider spacing and judicious application of recommended dose of fertilizers, particularly nitrogenous and irrigation management is essential to arrest the excessive vegetative growth and pest build up.
- Monitoring the activities of the adult white flies by setting up yellow sticky traps at 1 foot height above the plant canopy.
- Spray any one of the following insecticides when pest population reaches ETL:
- Imidacloprid 17.8% SL 40 – 50 ml/ acre or Buprofezin 25%SC 400 ml/acre or Diafenthiuron 50%WP 240 g/acre or Thiacloprid 21.7%SC 200- 240ml/acre or Flonicamid 50% WG 60 g/acre or Thiamethoxam 25% WG 80 g/acre or Fipronil5% SC 600-800 ml/acre.

7. **(*b*) (*ii*) Cotton mealy bug:** Causal organism: *Phenacoccus solenopsisi and Papaya mealybug Paracoccus marginatus* (Pseudococcidae: Hemiptera)

Nature of damage:

- Vegetative phase exhibit symptoms of distorted, bushy shoots, crinkled and/or twisted bunchy leaves and stunted plants that dry completely in severe cases.
- Late season infestations during reproductive crop stage result in reduced plant vigour and early crop senescence.
- Honeydew secreted by the mealybug encourages development of black sooty mould which adversely affects photosynthetic activity.

Management of diseases and insect pests:

- Remove and destroy the infested plant parts.
- Remove the alternate weeds hosts.
- Release encyrtid parasitoids, Acerophagus papayae @ 100 per village against Paracoccus marginatus and Aenasiusbam bawaeli against Phenococcus solenopsis.
- Use botanical insecticides like neem derivatives such as neem oil 2%, NSKE 5% and Fish oil rosin soap 25 g/lit. of water.
- Spray any one of the insecticides: Flonicamid 50% WG 60 g/acre or Thiamethoxam 25% WG 80 g/acre.

7. **(*b*) (*iii*) Chickpea Pod Borer:** Causal organism: Helicoverpa armigera

Nature of damage:

- Skeletinization of leaves–feeding chlorophyll only leaving veins by young larvae Defoliation

- Feeds flower and green pods
- In green pods–make circular holes and feed the grains and make empty.

Management of diseases and insect pests:

- ETL: 2 early instar larvae/plant 5-8 eggs/ plant
- Pheromone traps for *Helicoverpa armigera* 12/ha
- Bird perches 50/ha
- Hand picking of grown up larvae and blister beetles
- Ha NPV 1.5 × 1012 POB/ha with teepol (1 ml/lit.)

Apply any one of the following (Spray fluid 625 ml/ha)

- Dichlorvos 76 WSC 625 ml/ha
- Neem seed kernel extract 5% (31.0 kg/ha) twice followed by
- Triazophos 40 EC 780 ml/ha
- Neem oil 12.5 lit./ha
- Phosalone 35 EC 1.25 lit./ha

7. (*c*) Photoperiodism is a critical factor that influences the growth and development of plants. It refers to the response of plants to the relative lengths of day and night, which ultimately regulates various physiological processes, including flowering, germination, and dormancy. The duration of light and darkness in a 24-hour period, known as the photoperiod, serves as a signal for plants to undergo specific developmental stages.

There are three main categories of plants based on their photoperiodic responses:

Long-Day Plants (LDP):

- These plants typically flower when the day length is longer than a critical duration. They often initiate flowering in late spring or early summer when days are longer.
- Examples of long-day plants include spinach, lettuce, and radishes.
- In these plants, flowering is inhibited when exposed to short days, such as during the fall or winter.

Short-Day Plants (SDP):

- Short-day plants require a day length shorter than a critical duration for flowering. They often bloom in late summer or early autumn when days are shorter.
- Examples of short-day plants include chrysanthemums, soybeans, and strawberries.
- Exposure to long days inhibits flowering in short-day plants.

Day-Neutral Plants:

- Day-neutral plants are less influenced by day length, and their flowering is not strongly tied to photoperiod.
- Examples of day-neutral plants include tomatoes, roses, and dandelions.
- These plants typically flower based on factors other than day length, such as maturity or environmental conditions.

The influence of photoperiodism on plant growth and development is primarily mediated by the production of specific plant hormones, particularly flowering hormones like gibberellins and florigen. These hormones respond to changes in day length and initiate the molecular and genetic processes leading to flowering.

An example of how photoperiodism influences plant development is the case of the Arabidopsis thaliana, a model plant used in scientific research. Arabidopsis is a long-day plant, meaning it requires relatively longer days to induce flowering. When exposed to short days, Arabidopsis plants delay flowering. This responsiveness to photoperiod has made Arabidopsis a valuable tool for studying the genetic and molecular mechanisms behind flowering and circadian rhythms in plants.

Understanding photoperiodism is crucial for agricultural practices, especially when cultivating crops with specific flowering requirements. Farmers can use this knowledge to optimize planting times, manage crop rotations, and manipulate growing conditions to ensure proper flowering and maximize yield. Additionally, it has implications for greenhouse and controlled-environment agriculture, where artificial lighting can be used to manipulate day length and control the timing of flowering in various crops.

8. (*a*) **Malnutrition among Women and Children:** Malnutrition among women and children is a persistent and multifaceted global challenge that poses severe health, economic, and social implications. Insufficient access to a diverse and nutritious diet, coupled with factors such as poverty, lack of education, and inadequate healthcare, contributes to the prevalence of malnutrition in vulnerable populations. Women and children, particularly in developing countries, are disproportionately affected by this issue, facing a higher risk of undernutrition, stunted growth, and micronutrient deficiencies.

In women, malnutrition can have profound consequences for maternal health and fetal development. Undernourished mothers are more likely to give birth to underweight babies, perpetuating a cycle of intergenerational malnutrition. Additionally, malnourished women face increased risks during pregnancy, including complications during childbirth and higher maternal mortality rates. The impact extends beyond the physical realm, affecting cognitive development and educational attainment, thus perpetuating the cycle of poverty.

Children, being in a critical phase of growth and development, are particularly vulnerable to the long-term effects of malnutrition. Chronic malnutrition can lead to stunted growth, impaired cognitive development, and weakened immune systems, making children more susceptible to infections and diseases. The consequences are not only individual but also societal, as malnourished children are more likely to face challenges in reaching their full potential, limiting their future productivity and contributing to a perpetuation of poverty.

Addressing malnutrition among women and children requires a comprehensive approach that combines nutritional interventions with efforts to improve access to healthcare, education, and economic opportunities. Nutrition education programs can empower communities with the knowledge to make informed dietary choices, while initiatives promoting women's education and economic empowerment can address underlying factors contributing to malnutrition. Access to clean water, sanitation, and healthcare services is crucial in preventing and treating malnutrition, ensuring that both women and children receive the necessary nutrients for their well-being.

On a global scale, the challenge of malnutrition demands collaborative efforts from governments, non-governmental organizations, and the private sector to implement sustainable solutions. Investments in nutrition-sensitive agriculture, social safety nets, and healthcare infrastructure are essential components of a holistic strategy to combat malnutrition and break the cycle of poverty. By prioritizing the nutritional well-being of women and children, societies can build a foundation for healthier, more resilient communities and contribute to the achievement of sustainable development goals.

Fruits and Vegetables Production Trends Help in Mitigating Malnutrition: Fruits and vegetables play a pivotal role in mitigating malnutrition by providing essential vitamins, minerals, fiber, and antioxidants necessary for overall health. Understanding and addressing production trends in these food categories are crucial components of efforts to combat malnutrition globally. Several key factors contribute to the significant impact of fruits and vegetables on nutrition and public health.

- **Diverse Nutrient Profile:** Fruits and vegetables are rich sources of a wide range of nutrients, including vitamin C, vitamin A, potassium, folate, and various phytochemicals. Consuming a diverse array of fruits and vegetables ensures that individuals receive a broad spectrum of essential nutrients, contributing to optimal growth, development, and immune function.

- **Micronutrient Deficiency Prevention:** Many regions grappling with malnutrition face challenges related to micronutrient deficiencies, such as vitamin A, iron, and iodine deficiencies. Fruits and vegetables, being nutrient-dense, can address these deficiencies when incorporated into diets. For example, promoting the cultivation and consumption of vitamin A-rich vegetables like sweet potatoes and leafy greens can combat vitamin A deficiency and associated health issues, including vision problems.
- **Fiber for Digestive Health:** Fruits and vegetables are excellent sources of dietary fiber, which is crucial for digestive health. Fiber helps prevent constipation, regulates blood sugar levels, and contributes to a feeling of fullness, reducing the risk of overeating. Additionally, a diet high in fiber has been linked to a lower risk of chronic diseases, including heart disease and certain types of cancer.
- **Antioxidant Properties:** Antioxidants found in fruits and vegetables help protect cells from oxidative stress, which is linked to chronic diseases and aging. Consuming a variety of colorful fruits and vegetables ensures a diverse range of antioxidants, offering potential protective effects against various health issues.
- **Local Adaptation and Biodiversity:** Encouraging the production and consumption of locally grown fruits and vegetables promotes biodiversity and addresses specific nutritional needs within communities. Local adaptation of agricultural practices to cultivate a variety of crops ensures resilience against environmental challenges and contributes to sustainable food systems.
- **Community Gardens and Nutrition Programs:** Community-based initiatives, such as community gardens and nutrition education programs, can play a crucial role in promoting the cultivation and consumption of fruits and vegetables. These programs empower communities to grow their own nutritious foods, fostering a sense of ownership and sustainability.
- **Global Agricultural Policies and Trade:** International efforts to address malnutrition involve promoting agricultural policies that support the production and trade of fruits and vegetables. Encouraging sustainable farming practices, reducing trade barriers, and ensuring fair prices for farmers contribute to increased availability and accessibility of these nutrient-rich foods.

Efforts to enhance fruits and vegetables production trends should be integrated into broader strategies for addressing malnutrition. This includes education on nutrition, promotion of sustainable agricultural practices, and the development of infrastructure to support the cultivation, storage, and distribution of fruits and vegetables. By recognizing the pivotal role of these foods in combating malnutrition and aligning agricultural policies accordingly, communities and nations can make significant strides toward achieving better health outcomes for all.

8. (*b*) Cultivation Practices for Cauliflower Considering the Following Points:

(*i*) Soil and Climate Requirements: It requires cool moist climate. The early varieties may tolerate higher temperature and long days. This can be grown in plains during September to February. Deep loamy soils with a pH range of 5.5 to 6.6 with higher organic matter content and good drainage are suited for cauliflower cultivation.

(ii) **Varieties, Seed Rate and Sowing Time:**

Varieties: Early: Sabour Agrim, Pusha Meghana and Pusa Kartik sankar in Saharanpur Distt. Mid - Pusa hybrid-2, Pusa sharad, Pusa Paushja, Late-Pusa snowball K-1, Pusa Snowball Kt-25.

Seed Rate: Early 700-800 gm/ha. Mid early 400-500 gm/ha. and late 500-600 gm/ha.

Sowing Time: This variety early maturing and nursery sowing Mid-May-June and transplanting time June to August. July end–August start Mid early seed sowing and Sept.-Oct. Late

(iii) **Nursery Raising and Transplanting Method:**

Nursery Raising: The nursery bed should be thoroughly prepared by adding well rotten FYM or compost @ 4 kg/m^2. Before sowing, the seeds should be treated with Captan or Thiram @ 2.5g/kg seeds to get rid of fungal diseases. The seeds are sown at a spacing of 2-3 cm between seeds and 8-10 cm between lines. The depth of sowing is l-1.5 cm. After sowing, the seeds are covered with a mixture of fine soil and sieved FYM. After this, a light irrigation is provided with a water can. The nursery bed should be kept weed free. **Transplanting and spacing:** Four to six weeks old healthy seedlings having 4-6 leaves should be transplanted. Before transplanting, hardening of seedlings should be done by withholding irrigation for 4-6 days prior to transplanting. Seedlings should be watered a day prior to uprooting and transplanting to avoid damage to the root system.

Spacing: Early season: 45 × 30 cm, Mid season: 60 × 45 cm, Late season: 60 × 60 cm

(iv) **Management of Physiological Disorders:** Cauliflower suffers from a number of physiological disorders, which manifest in different type of disease syndromes. Important physiological disorders, affecting cauliflower are described below:

Riceyness: It manifests in the elongation on peduncle wearing flower buds, rendering curds, granular, loose and somewhat velvety. A premature initiation of floral bud is characterized by riceyness in cauliflower and is considered to be of poor quality for marketing. It can be controlled by cultivation of genetically pure seed and appropriate varieties with recommended cultural practices.

Fuzziness: It appears as the flower pedicels of velvety curds elongate. The anomaly is both hereditary and non-hereditary. Cultivation of cauliflower, out of their normal season encourages fuzziness. Sowing good quality seed in right season under proper cultural practices, minimized fuzziness.

Leafiness: This disorder is commonly seen by formation of small thin leaves from the curd which reduces quality of curd. Prevalence of high temperatures during curding phase aggravates leafiness. Certain varieties are more sensitive to leafiness or bracketing than other. It can be controlled by selection of varieties according to their adaptability.

Browning (Brown Rot or Red Rot): It is caused by boron deficiency which is influenced by soil pH. The availability of boron decreases at neutral soil reaction. This may be controlled by application of borax or sodium borate or sodium tetra borate at the rate of 20 kg/ha a soil application. In case of acute deficiency, spray of 0.25 to 0.50 per cent solution of borax at the rate of 1 to 2 kg/ha depending upon growth, soil reaction and extent of deficiency.

Whiptail: Deficiency of molybdenum causes 'whiptail' syndrome, especially, in highly acidic soils. Because high manganese concentrations in such soils hinder the uptake of molybdenum which seldom occurs when the soil pH is 5.5 or higher. It can be corrected by application of lime or dolomite limestone to raise the soil pH up to 6.5 or higher. Sodium or Ammonium molybdate at the rate of 1-2 kg/ha as soil application can also control "whiptail" of cauliflower.

Buttoning: Development of small curds with inadequate foliage in cauliflower is known as buttoning. It is also referred to as premature heading. The leaves are so small that cannot cover the formed head. Causes of buttoning are:

- Transplanting of more than 6 week-old seedlings.
- Planting as early variety in late vice versa leads buttoning.
- Hot and dry weather is unfavourable for vegetative growth of plants, but favourable for inducing curd formation and inhibits further enlargement. Curds remain very small in size like buttons.
- It can be controlled by using quality seedlings and proper cultural management practices.

(*v*) **Harvesting and Yields:** Early crop is harvesting in Sept. to Nov. and gives yield early 175-195 qt/ha. Mid early harvested in Oct. to Nov. and give the yield 200-250 qt/ha and late crop harvested Dec. to Feb. and give the yield 250-275 qt/ha.

8. (*c*) Causal Organism, Nature of Damage and Management of the Following Stored Grain Pests:

(*i*) **Rice weevil:** Causal Organism, Nature of Damage and Management

Rice weevil: *Sitophilus oryzae, S. zeamais, S. granaries*

Nature of Damage

- Both grub and adults cause the damage.
- Grains are hollowed out; kernels are reduced to mere powder. *S. oryzae* and *S. zeamais* starts its attack in field itself.
- Adults cut circular holes. Heating takes place during heavy infestation, which is known as 'dry heating'

Management

- Removal of infested food products
- Discarding heavily infested material
- Repackaging material into new infection-free containers
- Placing the products in the freezer for several weeks may help to kill adults and larvae

(*ii*) **Khapra beetle:** Causal Organism, Nature of Damage and Management

Causal Organism: *Trogoderma granarium* Everts (Insecta: Coleoptera: Dermestidae)

Nature of Damage: The Khapra beetle, scientifically known as *Trogoderma granarium*, is a highly destructive pest that primarily infests stored grains. Originating from South Asia, this beetle has gained notoriety due to its ability to cause significant damage to stored food products and its resilience to various environmental conditions. The nature of damage inflicted by the Khapra beetle is characterized by both direct feeding on the stored grains and indirect consequences associated with its presence. The Khapra beetle inflicts extensive damage to stored grains through the direct consumption of the grains by larvae, contamination with fecal pellets and hairs, and the potential for mold growth. The economic and trade-related implications, coupled with the beetle's resilience, highlight the need for effective monitoring, quarantine measures, and pest management strategies to prevent and control infestations.

Management: Some fumigants give control at high dosages, even though this beetle is more resistant to fumigants than most stored product pests. High concentrations of fumigant must be maintained over the fumigation period to allow penetration into all cracks and crevices. In an eradication program, both fumigants and surface sprays are used in combination with preventive measures, *e.g.*, good sanitation practices and exclusion.

Previous Years' Paper (Solved)

Indian Forest Service (Main) Exam, 2022

SUBJECT—AGRICULTURE

(Exam held on 25-11-2022)

PAPER-I

INSTRUCTIONS: *There are EIGHT questions in all, out of which FIVE are to be attempted. Question Nos. 1 & 5 are compulsory. Out of the remainin SIX questions, THREE are to be attempted selecting at least ONE question from each of the two Sections A and B. Attempts of questions shall be counted in sequential order. Unless struck off, attempt of a question shall be counted even if attempted partly. Any page or portion of the page left blank in the Question-cum-Answer Booklet must be clearly struck off. All questions carry equal marks. Answers must be written in ENGLISH only. Neat sketches may be drawn, wherever required.*

SECTION–A

1. (*a*) Discuss the influences of human beings and natural resources on ecology and nature.

(*b*) Describe the role of diversification and intensification of the cropping systems in enhancing farm productivity and nutritional security.

(*c*) Enumerate the production technologies of sweet corn and baby corn, which are different from normal maize cultivation.

(*d*) What are different types of noxious weeds? Describe with suitable examples. Enumerate the measures to prevent noxious weed entry in the country.

(*e*) What are the various diagnostic techniques employed in evaluating soil fertility? Enumerate advantages and disadvantages of each technique.

2. (*a*) "Global warming is due to human activities." Justify the statement with appropriate examples.

(*b*) Discuss the factors considered for selection of a cropping system. Suggest efficient and productive cropping system for Indo-Gangetic plains.

(*c*) How do herbicides control weeds selectively? Write down the classification of herbicides with suitable examples?

3. (*a*) Explain the agronomic approaches to reduce the impact of climate change on crops.

(*b*) Describe the multi-storied cropping system. Discuss in detail its advantages and feasibility in horticultural crops.

(*c*) Explain different types of soils in India based on ICAR classification and their main characteristics in relation to crop production.

4. (*a*) Enumerate various types of nitrogenous fertilizers. Briefly describe the role and benefits of neem-coated urea and nano urea in improving nitrogen use efficiency.

(*b*) Enunciate the different types of problematic soils and briefly discuss the RKVY guidelines for reclamation of problematic soils.

(*c*) Describe the ecological benefits of agroforestry system and also substantiate the efforts of the Government for promoting agroforestry in the country.

SECTION–B

5. (*a*) Write down the consequences of soil erosion on our environment. Enlist the various agronomics measures for soil and water conservation and specify the role of cropping systems in controlling soil runoff and erosion.

(*b*) Describe the various means for sustaining crop production with available water resources.

(*c*) Discuss the characteristics of a good farm plan in context of Indian agriculture situation.

(*d*) Describe the role of diversified farming in managing risk and uncertainty.

(*e*) Explain the role of Government in stabilizing the food grains prices in India.

6. (*a*) Explain major constraints of dryland areas. Describe various soil moisture conservation practices and contingent crop plan in dryland areas for sustaining crop productivity.

(*b*) Explain the assumptions and steps for developing an optimum resource use plan using Linear Programming (LP) with suitable examples.

(*c*) Describe the advantages and disadvantages of Lab to Land programme.

7. (*a*) Describe water saving approaches employed in pressurized irrigation systems. Enlist the advantages, disadvantages and applicability of drip and sprinkler irrigation systems.

(*b*) Discuss the causes of high price spread in agriculture commodities and suggest measures to minimize the price spread.

(*c*) Explain the approaches and benefits of market-led extension.

8. (*a*) Describe the functions of National Agricultural Cooperative Marketing Federation (NAFED) and its present role in stabilizing the prices of pulses.

(*b*) Discuss the role of farm mechanization and custom hiring centres on farm production and profitability.

(*c*) Enlist the different risks associated with poor quality irrigation water. Discuss the management practices for effective application of brackish water in crop production.

PAPER-II

INSTRUCTIONS: *There are EIGHT questions in all, out of which FIVE are to be attempted. Question Nos. 1 & 5 are compulsory. Out of the remaining SIX questions, THREE are to be attempted selecting at least ONE question from each of the two Sections A and B. Attempts of questions shall be counted in sequential order. Unless struck off, attempt of a question shall be counted even if attempted partly. Any page or portion of the page left blank in the Question-cum-Answer Booklet must be clearly struck off. All questions carry equal marks. Answers must be written in ENGLISH only. Neat sketches may be drawn, wherever required.*

SECTION–A

1. (*a*) Describe the mode of origin and growth of a cell wall with its functions.

(*b*) Explain the pre- and post-harvest factors affecting the seed quality of a crop during seed production.

(*c*) Describe chemically induced male sterility and its importance in crop improvement and seed production.

(*d*) Discuss various factors affecting enzyme activity in plants.

(*e*) Explain the molecular markers approach in crop improvement.

2. (*a*) Differentiate between the following:

(*i*) *Sex-linked and sex-limited characters*

(*ii*) *C_3 and C_4 plants*

(*iii*) *Epistasis and dominance gene interaction*

(*b*) Explain the method of recurrent selection. Write the importance of combining ability in crop improvement.

(*c*) Explain the mechanism of interphase in mitosis cell division.

3. (*a*) Describe the detailed structure of deoxyribonucleic acid (DNA) as prepared by Watson and Crick with suitable diagram.

(*b*) Describe backcross method of plant breeding and its application in development of biotic stress tolerant or resistant varieties with suitable examples.

(*c*) Discuss the role of public and private sector organization in seed production and marketing in India.

4. (*a*) What is seed treatment? Discuss the role of quality seeds in success of seed production programmes.

(*b*) Explain the methods for creating the variability. How are the types of selection responsible for population improvement in crop plants?

(*c*) What is imbibition? Differentiate between osmosis and diffusion.

SECTION–B

5. (*a*) Describe the preventive and curative methods for management of storage pests in pulses.

(*b*) Describe the principles of fruits and vegetables preservation.

(*c*) Discuss the strengths and weaknesses of Public Food Distribution system in India.

(*d*) Discuss the principles and components of integrated pests and diseases management.

(*e*) Describe the role of brassinosteroids and salicylic acid hormones in agriculture.

6. (*a*) Describe in detail the package of practices for onion cultivation in India.

(*b*) Discuss the growth and development in plants. Describe various parameters for measuring the plant growth.

(*c*) Discuss the high density planting system in fruit crops along with suitable examples and advantages of the system.

7. (*a*) Describe the role of under-utilized fruits and vegetables in human nutrition with suitable examples.

(*b*) Describe the biological control methods of pests and diseases with respect to organic and natural farming.

(*c*) Describe the management of fungal and bacterial diseases of major vagetable crops.

8. (*a*) Discuss the iron and protein malnutrition in India. Describe the dietary pattern for mitigating the above-said malnutrition.

(*b*) Enlist the cut flower ornamental crops grown in India. Describe the off season production technology for chrysanthemum.

(*c*) Discuss the integrated management of nematodes in fruits and vegetables.

ANSWERS

PAPER-I

1. (*a*) **Influences of Human beings and Natural Resources on Ecology:** Human beings and natural resources have significant impacts on ecology, which is the study of the relationships between living organisms and their environment. Human beings and natural resources have complex and varied influences on ecology, with both positive and negative impacts. It is important to manage these impacts carefully to preserve biodiversity and maintain healthy ecosystems for future generations.

Here are some of the ways in which humans and natural resources influence ecology:

- **Habitat destruction:** Human activities such as deforestation, mining, and urbanization destroy natural habitats and cause a loss of biodiversity. This loss of habitat can cause species to become endangered or even go extinct.
- **Pollution:** Humans produce a variety of pollutants such as chemicals, plastics, and greenhouse gases that can damage the environment and harm living organisms. Pollution can also contribute to climate change, which has significant impacts on ecology.
- **Overexploitation of natural resources:** Human beings rely on natural resources such as forests, fisheries, and mineral deposits, but overexploitation can lead to depletion of these resources and damage to ecosystems. For example, overfishing can lead to the collapse of fish populations and damage to marine ecosystems.
- **Introduction of non-native species:** Humans have introduced non-native species to new environments, which can have negative impacts on native species and ecosystems. Non-native species can outcompete native species, disrupt food webs, and spread diseases.
- **Conservation efforts:** On the positive side, human beings can also play a role in preserving and protecting natural ecosystems through conservation efforts such as habitat restoration, protected areas, and sustainable resource management.

1. (*b*) **Role of Diversification and Intensification of the Cropping Systems in Enhancing Farm Productivity and Nutritional Security:** Diversification and intensification of cropping systems can play an important role in enhancing farm productivity and nutritional security. Diversification refers to the practice of growing a variety of crops on the same farm, rather than relying on a single crop. This can provide a number of benefits, such as reducing the risk of crop failure due to weather or disease, improving soil fertility, and providing a range of nutrients in the diet.

Intensification, on the other hand, involves increasing the productivity of a given area of land by improving soil fertility, using improved seed varieties, and adopting better management practices. This can increase yields and improve the quality of crops, which can help to enhance food security and improve nutrition.

Together, diversification and intensification can help to improve the resilience of farming systems, particularly in the face of climate change and other environmental challenges.

They can also help to reduce the reliance on external inputs such as fertilizers and pesticides, which can be costly and harmful to the environment and human health.

In terms of. nutritional security, diversification can help to ensure that a wider range of nutrients are available in the diet, particularly in areas where certain crops may be lacking. For example, in areas where there is a high prevalence of vitamin A deficiency, promoting the cultivation of orange-fleshed sweet potatoes can help to increase the availability of this important nutrient. Similarly, the cultivation of legumes such as beans and lentils can help to increase the availability of protein and other essential nutrients.

Intensification can also play an important role in improving nutritional security by increasing the productivity and quality of crops. For example, the use of improved seed varieties and better management practices can increase the nutrient content of crops, while reducing the risk of contamination by toxins and other harmful substances. Overall, the diversification and intensification of cropping systems can be a powerful tool for enhancing farm productivity and nutritional security. By promoting the cultivation of a wider range of crops and adopting better management practices, farmers can improve their livelihoods, while ensuring that their communities have access to nutritious and healthy food.

1. (*c*) **Production Technologies of Sweet Corn and Baby corn, which are different from normal maize production:** Sweet corn and baby corn are different from normal maize in terms of their physical characteristics and culinary uses. As a result, their production technologies differ from those of normal maize. Here are some key differences between the production technologies of sweet corn and baby corn compared to normal maize:

Planting: Sweet corn and baby corn are typically planted in shorter rows and closer together than normal maize. This is because sweet corn and baby corn have smaller cobs and require less space to grow.

Harvesting: Sweet corn is usually harvested when the kernels are in the milk stage, which is when they are plump and full of juice. Baby corn, on the other hand, is harvested when the ears are still very young and small, typically around 10-15 cm in length.

Fertilization: Sweet corn and baby corn require more nitrogen than normal maize to produce their characteristic sweet flavor. They also require regular irrigation to maintain moisture levels in the soil.

Pest and disease management: Sweet corn and baby corn are susceptible to a range of pests and diseases that are different from those that affect normal maize. These include pests like corn earworm and diseases like smut.

Processing: Sweet corn and baby corn are often processed and packaged differently than normal maize. Sweet corn is often canned or frozen, while baby corn is often pickled or used fresh in stir-fries and other dishes.

Overall, the production technologies for sweet corn and baby corn are more specialized and require different techniques and inputs than normal maize.

1. (*d*) **Different Types of Noxious Weeds:** Noxious weeds are invasive plants that can cause significant economic, environmental, and social damage. There are many types of noxious weeds, but some of the most common ones include:

- **Purple loosestrife** - a perennial plant that invades wetlands and outcompetes native plants, causing significant ecological damage.
- **Japanese knotweed** - a highly invasive plant that can grow up to 10 feet tall and

spread rapidly, damaging infrastructure, buildings, and natural habitats.

- **Giant hogweed** - a tall, herbaceous plant that can cause severe skin irritation and even blindness if its sap comes into contact with skin or eyes.
- **Kudzu** - a vine that can grow up to a foot a day and covers trees, buildings, and other structures, leading to their collapse.
- **Russian olive** - a tree that can grow up to 30 feet tall and has a dense canopy that shades out native plant species, reducing biodiversity.
- **Himalayan blackberry** - a thorny shrub that can grow up to 10 feet tall and form impenetrable thickets, displacing native plant species and impeding access to waterways and other areas.
- **Tamarisk** - a tree that can grow up to 30 feet tall and can displace native plant species and reduce water availability.
- **Saltcedar** - a tree that can grow up to 25 feet tall and is highly invasive in arid regions, displacing native plant species and reducing water availability.
- **Cheatgrass** - an annual grass that can grow up to 3 feet tall and is highly invasive in arid regions, outcompeting native plant species and increasing wildfire risk.
- **Canada thistle** - a perennial plant that can grow up to 5 feet tall and forms dense patches, reducing the productivity of agricultural lands and causing significant economic damage.

Measures to Prevent Noxious Weed Entry in the Country: Preventing the entry of noxious weeds into a country is important to protect the local ecosystem and agricultural industry. Here are some measures that can be taken:

- **Border inspections:** Regular inspections of incoming goods at borders can help identify and intercept noxious weeds before they enter the country. Inspectors should be trained to recognize and identify these invasive plants.
- **Quarantine measures:** Quarantine measures can be put in place to isolate incoming goods that are suspected of containing noxious weeds. Quarantine can be done at the border or at facilities located within the country.
- **Public awareness campaigns:** Educating the public about the dangers of noxious weeds and how to identify them can help prevent their entry into the country. This can be done through media campaigns, public events, and educational programs.
- **Import restrictions:** Restrictions can be placed on the import of goods from countries known to have high rates of noxious weeds. This can help limit the entry of these plants into the country.
- **Monitoring and surveillance:** Regular monitoring and surveillance of high-risk areas, such as ports and airports, can help detect noxious weeds before they become established in the local ecosystem.
- **Early detection and rapid response:** Early detection of noxious weeds is critical to prevent their spread. Rapid response measures, such as eradication or containment, can be implemented as soon as they are detected.
- **Research and development:** Investing in research and development of new technologies and methods to prevent the entry and spread of noxious weeds can help improve prevention efforts.

1. (*e*) Various Diagnostic Techniques Employed In Evaluating Soil Fertility: There are various diagnostic techniques that are commonly used to evaluate fertility of the soils. They are:

Nutrient Deficiency Symptoms

Advantages

- Nutrient deficiency symptoms can provide a quick and inexpensive way to diagnose the nutrient status of plants.
- The visual symptoms can help to identify which nutrient is lacking in the plant, which can help guide fertilizer applications.
- By identifying nutrient deficiencies early, corrective actions can be taken before yield losses occur.
- Nutrient deficiency symptoms can be used to monitor the effectiveness of fertilizer programs and identify potential soil fertility issues.

Disadvantages

- Nutrient deficiency symptoms may not be specific to a particular nutrient and can be influenced by other factors such as water stress or disease.
- It can be difficult to distinguish between nutrient deficiencies and toxicities, which can have similar symptoms.
- Some nutrient deficiencies may not result in obvious visual symptoms until they have reached a severe stage, which can be detrimental to yield and quality.
- Nutrient deficiency symptoms do not provide quantitative information about the nutrient status of the plant or soil, which is important for making informed fertilization decisions.

Plant Analysis Methods

Advantages

- **Direct measurement of plant nutrient status:** Plant analysis provides direct information about the nutrient status of plants, which can help in determining the need for fertilization.
- **Identifying nutrient deficiencies and toxicities:** Plant analysis can help to identify nutrient deficiencies and toxicities at an early stage, allowing for corrective measures to be taken before yield losses occur.
- **Determining nutrient uptake:** Plant analysis can be used to determine the uptake of nutrients by plants and can help to estimate fertilizer requirements.
- **Monitoring fertilizer programs:** Plant analysis can be used to monitor the effectiveness of fertilizer programs and can help in adjusting fertilizer application rates.
- **Indicator of soil fertility:** Plant analysis can serve as an indicator of soil fertility and can help in evaluating the fertility status of different soils.

Disadvantages

- **Variability in results:** Plant analysis results can be influenced by several factors such as plant species, plant age, sampling time, and environmental conditions, leading to variability in results.
- **High cost:** Plant analysis is often expensive and may not be costeffective for routine use on a large scale.
- **Limited information:** Plant analysis provides information on nutrient concentrations in plant tissue but does not provide information on the availability of nutrients in the soil.
- **Limited suitability:** Plant analysis is not suitable for all crops, and in some cases, the use of plant analysis may not provide accurate information about soil fertility.
- **Complex interpretation:** Interpreting plant analysis results can be complex and requires specialized knowledge and expertise.

Biological Tests:

Advantages

- **Direct measurement of soil microbial activity:** Biological tests provide direct information about soil microbial activity, which is a key indicator of soil fertility.

- **Assessing soil quality:** Biological tests can help in assessing soil quality by evaluating the soil's ability to support plant growth and maintain soil health.
- **Assessing soil fertility:** Biological tests can help in assessing soil fertility by measuring soil microbial biomass, enzyme activities, and nutrient cycling processes.
- **Measuring the effect of management practices:** Biological tests can be used to evaluate the impact of management practices, such as fertilizer application, on soil microbial activity and soil health.
- **Sustainability:** Biological tests provide information on the sustainability of soil fertility management practices by evaluating the soil's ability to maintain its fertility over time.

Disadvantages

- **Complexity:** Biological tests are often complex and require specialized knowledge and expertise, which can be a barrier to their widespread use.
- **Variability:** Biological test results can be influenced by several factors, such as soil moisture, temperature, and pH, leading to variability in results.
- **Time-consuming:** Biological tests can be time-consuming and may require several days or weeks to obtain results.
- **Cost:** Biological tests can be expensive, requiring specialized equipment and reagents, which can be a barrier to their use on a large scale.
- **Limited information:** Biological tests provide information on specific aspects of soil fertility, such as microbial biomass and activity, but do not provide a comprehensive picture of soil fertility.

Soil Testing Methods

Advantages

- **Quantitative information:** Soil testing provides quantitative information about soil nutrient levels, which can be used to determine the soil's fertility status and fertilizer requirements.
- **Customized fertilization:** Soil testing can help in customizing fertilizer application rates and methods to match crop nutrient requirements, which can improve fertilizer use efficiency and reduce costs.
- **Improved crop yield and quality:** Soil testing can help in optimizing nutrient management, which can improve crop yield and quality.
- **Monitoring soil fertility over time:** Soil testing can be used to monitor changes in soil fertility over time, which can help in making adjustments to fertilizer programs and soil management practices.
- **Sustainability:** Soil testing can help in promoting sustainable agriculture by optimizing nutrient use efficiency, reducing nutrient losses, and minimizing environmental impacts.

Disadvantages

- **Variability:** Soil test results can be influenced by several factors, such as sampling depth, time, and location, leading to variability in results.
- **Cost:** Soil testing can be expensive, especially when testing for multiple nutrients, which can be a barrier to its widespread use.
- **Time-consuming:** Soil testing can be time-consuming, requiring several days or weeks to obtain results, which can delay decision-making.
- **Limited information:** Soil testing provides information on soil nutrient levels but does not provide information on other important soil properties, such

as soil structure, organic matter content, and soil biology.

- **Sampling difficulties:** Soil testing requires proper sampling procedures to ensure representative soil samples, which can be challenging in some situations.

Modern Approaches of Soil Fertility Evaluation and Fertilizer Recommendation:

Advantages

- **Comprehensive evaluation of soil fertility:** Modern approaches combine several soil testing methods, such as soil chemical, physical, and biological tests, to provide a more comprehensive evaluation of soil fertility.
- **Site-specific nutrient management:** Modern approaches use precision agriculture techniques to customize nutrient management practices to the specific needs of each field, resulting in more efficient nutrient use and reduced environmental impact.
- **Technology-driven:** Modern approaches use advanced technologies, such as remote sensing, GIS, and precision application systems, to collect and analyze data, which improves decision-making and reduces errors.
- **Real-time data collection:** Modern approaches allow for real-time data collection and analysis, which enables timely decision-making and adjustments to fertilizer programs and soil management practices.
- **Sustainability:** Modern approaches promote sustainable agriculture by optimizing nutrient use efficiency, reducing nutrient losses, and minimizing environmental impacts.

Disadvantages

- **Cost:** Modern approaches can be expensive, requiring specialized equipment and expertise, which can be a barrier to their widespread use.
- **Technical expertise:** Modern approaches require specialized knowledge and technical expertise, which can be a challenge for some farmers or consultants.
- **Complexity:** Modern approaches can be complex and require several steps, such as data collection, analysis, and interpretation, which can be time-consuming.
- **Limited availability:** Modern approaches may not be readily available in some regions, limiting their use by farmers and consultants.
- **Risk of overreliance on technology:** Modern approaches rely heavily on technology, which can be a risk if the technology fails or if there is a lack of trust in the data or recommendations.

2. (*a*) Global Warming due to Human Activities: Global warming is the gradual increase in the Earth's average surface temperature primarily caused by human activities, such as the burning of fossil fuels, deforestation, and industrial processes that release large amounts of greenhouse gases (mainly carbon dioxide) into the atmosphere. These greenhouse gases trap heat from the sun and cause the Earth's temperature to rise. The burning of fossil fuels such as coal, oil, and gas for transportation, electricity, and heating is one of the main sources of carbon dioxide emissions. Deforestation and land-use changes also release large amounts of carbon dioxide into the atmosphere. Additionally, industrial processes such as cement production, aluminum production, and fertilizer production also release significant amounts of greenhouse gases. The consequences of global warming are already becoming evident and can have serious implications for our planet, including more frequent and intense heatwaves, droughts, floods, and storms. These events can lead to food and water shortages, displacement of people, and negative impacts on biodiversity and ecosystems. The continued rise in global temperature also threatens to trigger feedback loops, such as melting permafrost, which could further exacerbate global warming. To mitigate global warming, it is important to reduce greenhouse gas emissions by transitioning to clean energy sources, promoting energy efficiency, and implementing policies and practices that support sustainable land use and transportation. We all have a role to play in reducing our carbon footprint and protecting the planet for future generations.

Global warming is largely caused by human activities, primarily the burning of fossil fuels, which release large amounts of carbon dioxide and other greenhouse gases into the atmosphere. Here are a few examples:

- **Transportation:** Cars, trucks, and airplanes are major sources of carbon dioxide emissions. For example, in the United States, transportation accounts for approximately 29% of total greenhouse gas emissions, with cars and trucks being the largest contributors. As more people use cars and air travel, the demand for fossil fuels increases, leading to more emissions.
- **Energy production:** Electricity generation is another major source of carbon dioxide emissions, with the burning of coal, natural gas, and oil being the primary culprits. In many parts of the world, energy production accounts for the largest share of greenhouse gas emissions. For example, in the United States, electricity production is responsible for approximately 25% of total greenhouse gas emissions.
- **Deforestation:** Trees absorb carbon dioxide through photosynthesis, so deforestation - the cutting down and clearing of forests - contributes to global warming by reducing the number of trees that can absorb carbon dioxide. Deforestation is a significant problem in many parts of the world, including the Amazon rainforest and Southeast Asia.
- **Agriculture:** Agricultural activities such as livestock production and the use of fertilizers also contribute to global warming. Livestock such as cows and sheep produce methane, a potent greenhouse gas, as part of their digestive process, and the production of fertilizers involves energy-intensive processes that release greenhouse gases.

2. (*b*) Factors Considered for Selection of a Cropping System:

Climatic Factors: This is the most important factor influencing the cropping pattern. The factors involved are given below:

- **Temperature:** It is one of the most critical factors that influences crop, from when seed is shown up to crop maturity.
- **Rainfall:** Water perform many functions in plants. It dissolves the nutrient in soil which is taken by the root. It promotes turgidity, cell growth and photosynthesis.
- **Day length:** A particular crops requires a definite periods of light and darkness for its growth and development.
- **Humidity:** Different plants required different humidity for their optimum growth and development.

Edaphic Factors: As the plant grows on soil, edaphic factors must be considered. The different factors concerned are:

- **Land elevation:** Particular crops require particular elevation.
- **Soil type:** Most the crops do not grow in sandy soil as its water holding capacity is very low.
- **Soil fertility:** Cropping pattern is designed with consideration to the soil fertility.

- **Soil moisture:** Soil moisture depends on its water holding capacity and this varies with soil type.
- **Soil pH:** Some crops grow well in acidic and some in alkaline. Most of the crop prefer neutral soil. It effects on cropping pattern.

Neutral Factors: These factor occur naturally which can't be checked by man.

- Flood level
- Suspension material on the flood level.
- Social Factors
- Availability of market
- Market Price
- Farmers knowledge and liking
- Growers economic ability
- Lack of courage and initiative to change
- Food habit of the people
- Irrigation Facilities
- Availability of seeds and other materials
- Density of labour
- Credit
- Working animals

Technological Factors

- Limited choice of crops.
- Cost and time consuming
- Limited use of fertilizer
- Poor response of biofertilizer
- Unavailability of organic manure.
- Limited scope of land improvement
- Lack of technological knowledge.

Geosocial Factors

- Demand of food crop
- Food habit
- Market system
- Population density
- Transport and communication
- Custom and tradition
- Willingness and capability to change
- Attitude towards materials things

Historical Factors

- Landlord system
- Capital/money/money lending family/ stock
- Farmers proprietary right system
- Nil cultivation

Efficient and Productive Cropping Systems for Indo-Gangetic Plains: The Indo-Gangetic plains are one of the most productive agricultural regions in the world. To maintain the productivity of this region and ensure sustainable agriculture, efficient and productive cropping systems are crucial. Here are some suggestions for efficient and productive cropping systems for the Indo-Gangetic plains:

- **Rice-Wheat Cropping System:** This is the most common cropping system in the Indo-Gangetic plains. In this system, rice is grown during the kharif season (June-September) and wheat is grown during the rabi season (October-March). The system is highly productive but can lead to soil degradation over time due to excessive use of fertilizers and water. To address this issue, farmers can adopt precision farming techniques such as laser land leveling, zero tillage, and direct seeding of rice.
- **Rice-Maize Cropping System:** In this system, rice is grown during the kharif season and maize is grown during the rabi season. Maize is a high-yielding crop that can be grown using less water and fertilizers than wheat. This system can be a good alternative to the rice-wheat system and can help reduce the environmental impact of agriculture.
- **Cotton-Wheat Cropping System:** In this system, cotton is grown during the kharif season and wheat is grown during the

rabi season. Cotton is a high-value crop that can generate good income for farmers. However, cotton requires a lot of water and fertilizers, which can lead to soil degradation. To mitigate this, farmers can use drip irrigation and precision nutrient management.

- **Sugarcane-Based Cropping System:** Sugarcane is an important cash crop in the Indo-Gangetic plains. In this system, sugarcane is grown during the kharif season and wheat or other crops are grown during the rabi season. Sugarcane requires a lot of water and fertilizers, but it can also generate good income for farmers. To reduce the environmental impact of sugarcane cultivation, farmers can adopt precision irrigation and nutrient management practices.
- **Intercropping:** Intercropping is a technique where two or more crops are grown together on the same piece of land. This can help increase productivity, reduce pest and disease pressure, and improve soil health. Some popular intercropping systems in the Indo-Gangetic plains include rice-wheat-mungbean, maize-wheat-mungbean, and sugarcane-wheat.

2. (*c*) Herbicides Control Weeds Selectively: Herbicides are chemical substances use to control or eliminate unwanted plants, commonly known as weeds. Herbicides can work in various ways, but one of their primary functions is to selectively target and kill specific types of plants while leaving other plants unharmed. This selective control is accomplished through the use of different herbicides that are formulated to target specific types of plants. Selective herbicides work by targeting specific plant characteristics such as leaf shape, size, and color, as well as the way the plant grows and develops. These herbicides are formulated to kill only the plants that have these specific characteristics, while leaving other plants unharmed. For example, some selective herbicides are designed to target broadleaf weeds, which have leaves that are wider than grass leaves. These herbicides will kill the broadleaf weeds but leave the grass unharmed. Selective herbicides are often used in agricultural settings to control weeds in crops. Farmers can use herbicides that are selective to specific types of crops, such as corn or soybeans, to control weeds without damaging the crops themselves. This selective control helps to reduce competition for resources between the crops and the weeds, which can lead to increased yields and more efficient use of resources.

Classification of Herbicides with Suitable Examples:

1. Based on Method of application

- **Soil applied herbicides:** Herbicide act through root and other underground parts of weeds. Eg. Fluchloralin
- **Foliage applied herbicides:** Herbicide primarily active on the plant foliage Eg. Glyphosate, Paraquat

2. Based on Mode of action

- **Selective herbicide:** A herbicide is considered as selective when in a mixed growth of plant species, it kills some species without injuring the others. Eg. Atrazine
- **Non-selective herbicide:** It destroys majority of treated vegetation Eg. Paraquat

3. Based on mobility

- **Contact herbicide:** A contact herbicide kills those plant parts with which it comes in direct contact Eg. Paraquat
- **Translocated herbicide:** Herbicide which tends to move from treated part to untreated areas through xylem/phloem depending on the nature of its molecule. Eg. Glyphosate

4. **Based on Time of application**

- **Pre-plant application (PPI):** Application of herbicides before the crop is planted or sown. Soil application as well as foliar application is done here. For example, fluchloralin can be applied to soil and incorporated before sowing rainfed groundnut while glyphosate can be applied on the foliage of perennial weeds like Cyperus rotundus before planting of any crop.

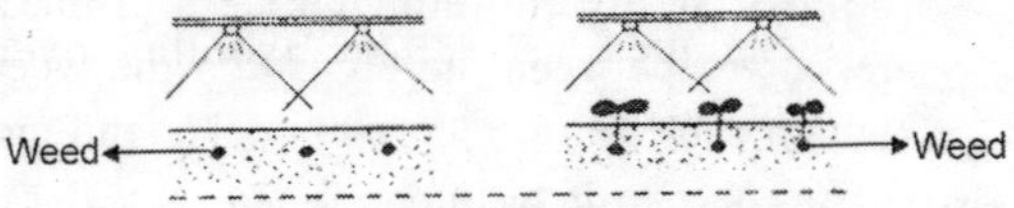

- **Pre-emergence:** Application of herbicides before a crop or weed has emerged. In case of annual crops application is done after the sowing of the crop but before the emergence of weeds and this is referred as pre-emergence to the crop while in the case perennial crops it can be said as pre-emergence to weeds. For example soil application by spraying of atrazine on 3rd DAT to sugarcane can be termed as pre-emergence to cane crop while soil application by spraying the same immediately after a rain to control a new flush of weeds in a inter-cultivated orchard can be specified as pre-emergence to weed. Eg. Atrazine, Pendimethalin, Butachlor, Thiobencarb, Pretilachlor

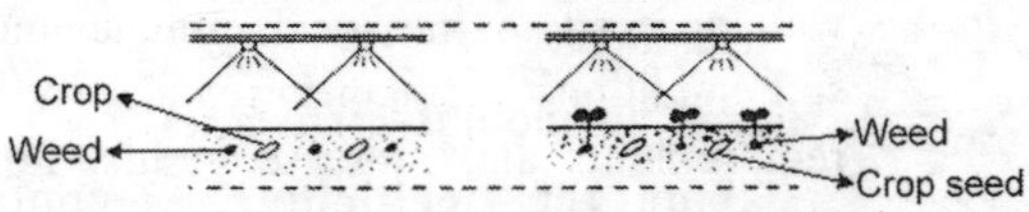

- **Post-emergence:** Herbicide application after the emergence of crop or weed is referred as post-emergence application. When the weeds grow before the crop plants have emerged through the soil and are killed with a herbicide then it is called as early post-emergence. For example spraying 2, 4-D Na salt to control parasitic weed striga in sugarcane is called as post-emergence while spraying of paraquat to control emerged weeds after 10-15 days after planting potato can be called as early post-emergence. Eg. Glyphosate, Paraquat, 2, 4-D Na Salt.

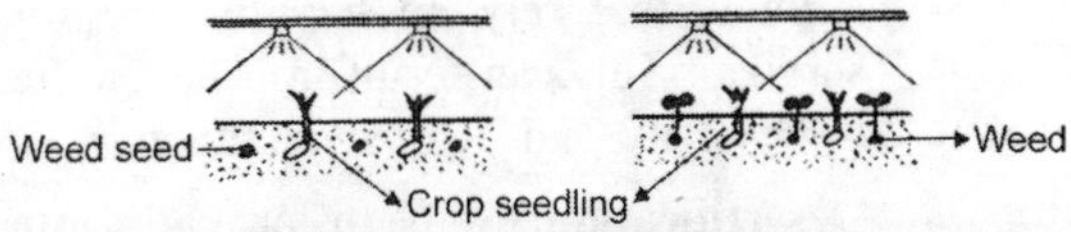

- **Early post emergence:** Another application of herbicide in the slow growing crops like potato, sugarcane, 2-3 week after sowing is classified as early post emergence.

5. **Based on molecular structure**

- Inorganic compounds
- Organic compounds

5. (*a*) **Soil erosion** is a serious environmental issue that can have numerous consequences for our environment. Here are some of the ways soil erosion can impact our environment:

- **Reduced soil fertility:** Soil erosion can remove the nutrient-rich topsoil, which is essential for plant growth. As a result, the soil becomes less fertile, leading to reduced crop yields and decreased agricultural productivity.
- **Water pollution:** Soil erosion can result in sedimentation in nearby rivers and lakes, which can increase the turbidity of the water and reduce the amount of light that can penetrate the water. This can negatively impact aquatic plant and animal life and reduce water quality.
- **Increased flooding:** Soil erosion can lead to the loss of vegetation cover, which can increase the risk of flooding as rainwater is not absorbed by the soil but instead runs off the surface.

- **Climate change:** Soil erosion releases carbon into the atmosphere, contributing to climate change. This is because when soil is disturbed, it releases carbon dioxide and other greenhouse gases that were stored in the soil.
- **Loss of biodiversity:** Soil erosion can lead to the loss of habitat for plants and animals that rely on healthy soil for survival. This can result in a decline in biodiversity and ecosystem function.
- **Desertification:** Soil erosion can cause soil to become compacted and lose its ability to hold water, leading to desertification in some regions. This can result in the loss of land for agriculture and human habitation.

There are various agronomic measures that can be taken to conserve soil and water resources. Here are some examples:

- **Crop rotation:** Crop rotation involves alternating the type of crops grown in a field over time. This can help to maintain soil fertility, reduce erosion, and control pests and diseases.
- **Cover crops:** Cover crops are plants that are grown primarily to protect the soil and improve soil health. They can help to reduce erosion, improve soil structure, and prevent nutrient runoff.
- **Conservation tillage:** Conservation tillage involves leaving crop residues on the soil surface and minimizing soil disturbance during planting. This can help to reduce erosion and maintain soil structure and fertility.
- **Contour farming:** Contour farming involves planting crops along the contours of the land. This can help to slow the flow of water downhill and reduce erosion.
- **Terracing:** Terracing involves constructing broad, flat platforms on steep slopes to create level planting areas. This can help to reduce erosion and improve water infiltration.
- **Agroforestry:** Agroforestry involves integrating trees into agricultural landscapes. This can help to reduce erosion, improve soil fertility, and provide other environmental benefits.
- **Irrigation management:** Proper irrigation management can help to conserve water resources and reduce erosion. This may include using drip irrigation or other water-saving techniques, as well as avoiding over-irrigation.

5. (*b*) Sustaining crop production with available water resources is essential for ensuring food security and livelihoods for millions of people around the world. Here are some various means for sustaining crop production with available water resources:

- **Efficient Irrigation:** Adopting efficient irrigation methods such as drip irrigation, sprinkler irrigation, and micro-irrigation can significantly reduce water usage while improving crop yields.
- **Soil Management:** Good soil management practices such as mulching, cover cropping, and conservation tillage can help to retain moisture in the soil and reduce the amount of water needed for irrigation.
- **Crop Selection:** Choosing crops that are well adapted to the local climate and soil conditions can help to reduce water requirements and increase yields. For example, selecting drought-tolerant crops such as sorghum, millets, and cowpea can help to reduce water requirements.
- **Water Harvesting:** Water harvesting techniques such as the construction of small dams, ponds, and reservoirs can help to store rainwater for irrigation during dry periods.

- **Improved Water Management:** Improving water management practices such as monitoring soil moisture levels and adjusting irrigation schedules accordingly can help to optimize water usage and increase crop yields.
- **Use of Organic Fertilizers:** Organic fertilizers can improve soil structure and water-holding capacity, reducing the need for irrigation.
- **Crop Rotation:** Crop rotation can help to maintain soil fertility and reduce water requirements by alternating between crops with different nutrient and water requirements.

5. (*c*) A good farm plan for Indian agriculture should consider the following characteristics:

- **Crop selection:** The farm plan should take into account the soil type, climate, and water availability in the region to determine the most suitable crops to grow.
- **Soil health:** The plan should also focus on maintaining soil fertility and health, using techniques such as crop rotation, intercropping, and organic farming.
- **Water management:** Given the erratic rainfall patterns in many parts of India, the farm plan should incorporate measures for water conservation, such as rainwater harvesting and drip irrigation.
- **Pest and disease management:** Effective pest and disease management is essential to maximize crop yields. The farm plan should consider integrated pest management techniques, including the use of natural predators and resistant varieties.
- **Financial viability:** The plan should be financially viable and sustainable, taking into account the costs of inputs such as seeds, fertilizers, and labor, as well as potential income from crop sales.
- **Farm mechanization:** The use of appropriate machinery and technology can help reduce labor costs and increase efficiency in farming operations. The farm plan should consider the use of mechanization where appropriate.
- **Market orientation:** The farm plan should consider the demand for crops in the local and national markets, and tailor production accordingly. This can help farmers secure better prices and increase their income.
- **Risk management:** The plan should also consider potential risks, such as weather-related disasters, pest outbreaks, and market fluctuations, and incorporate measures to mitigate these risks.

5. (*d*) Diversified farming is a practice in which farmers grow a variety of crops and/or raise multiple types of livestock on their land. The purpose of diversified farming is to spread risk and reduce uncertainty by creating multiple sources of income from different products. One of the key benefits of diversified farming is that it can help to mitigate the impact of crop failures or livestock losses. For example, if a farmer has only one crop and a disease or weather event destroys that crop, they will suffer a complete loss of income for the season. However, if the farmer has multiple crops, they may still have other crops that were not affected and can continue to generate income.

Similarly, if a farmer is raising only one type of livestock and there is a disease outbreak that affects that particular species, the farmer could suffer a significant financial loss. However, if the farmer is raising multiple types of livestock, they may still have other animals that are unaffected and can be sold or used for breeding. Diversified farming can also help to reduce input costs. By growing multiple crops, farmers can reduce their reliance on expensive inputs like fertilizers and pesticides, as different crops have different nutrient and pest requirements. Additionally, diversified farming can improve soil health and biodiversity, which can reduce the need for costly inputs over time. Diversified farming can help farmers to manage risk and uncertainty by spreading income streams across multiple products, reducing the impact of crop failures or livestock losses, and reducing input costs.

5. (*e*) The Indian government plays an important role in stabilizing food grain prices in the country. There are several measures that the government takes to ensure that food grain prices remain stable and affordable for the common people. Here are some of the key ways in which the Indian government stabilizes food grain prices:

- **Minimum Support Price (MSP):** The government announces a minimum support price (MSP) for various crops every year. The MSP is the minimum price at which the government will buy crops from farmers. This ensures that farmers get a fair price for their crops and are not forced to sell their produce at lower prices to middlemen or traders.
- **Buffer Stocking:** The government maintains buffer stocks of food grains to ensure that there is a sufficient supply of food grains in the market. This helps to stabilize food grain prices during periods of shortages or excess production.
- **Public Distribution System (PDS):** The government runs a public distribution system (PDS) to distribute food grains at subsidized prices to poor families. This ensures that even the poorest families have access to affordable food grains.
- **Export and Import Policies:** The government regulates the export and import of food grains to balance the domestic supply and demand. If there is a surplus of food grains, the government may allow exports to reduce the surplus and stabilize prices. Similarly, if there is a shortage of food grains, the government may allow imports to increase the supply and stabilize prices.

The Indian government plays an active role in stabilizing food grain prices through various measures. However, there are still challenges in ensuring that food grains remain affordable for all sections of society, particularly in times of drought, flood, or other natural disasters.

6. (*a*) Major Constraints of Dryland Areas: Dryland areas are characterized by low and erratic rainfall, high evaporation rates, and a scarcity of water resources. These areas face a range of constraints that limit their ability to support human livelihoods and ecosystem functioning. Here are some of the major constraints of dryland areas:

- **Water scarcity:** Water is the most important resource in dryland areas, and its scarcity is a major constraint to development. Droughts, limited surface water, and declining groundwater resources all contribute to water scarcity in dryland areas.
- **Soil degradation:** Soil erosion, nutrient depletion, and desertification are common in dryland areas, leading to reduced soil fertility and agricultural productivity. These processes can also lead to the loss of biodiversity and ecosystem services.
- **Limited vegetation cover:** The lack of vegetation cover in dryland areas reduces the ability of ecosystems to provide essential services such as carbon sequestration, water infiltration, and soil stabilization. This can result in further soil degradation, desertification, and loss of biodiversity.
- **Climate variability:** Dryland areas are particularly susceptible to climate variability, including droughts, floods, and extreme temperatures. This variability

can affect agricultural productivity, water availability, and natural resource management.

- **Limited infrastructure:** The remote location of many dryland areas can limit access to markets, education, healthcare, and other essential services. This can further constrain economic development and contribute to poverty.
- **Limited institutional capacity:** The lack of strong institutions and governance structures in many dryland areas can hinder effective natural resource management, disaster response, and development planning.

Various Soil Moisture Conservation Practices and Contingent Crop Plant in Dryland Areas for Sustaining Crop Productivity: Dryland areas are characterized by low and erratic rainfall, which poses significant challenges to crop production. To sustain crop productivity in these areas, it is essential to conserve soil moisture and adopt appropriate crop plants that can withstand dry conditions. Here are some soil moisture conservation practices and contingent crop plants that can be used in dryland areas:

- **Conservation tillage:** Conservation tillage practices involve leaving crop residues on the soil surface to reduce water evaporation, soil erosion, and increase organic matter. This practice can help to conserve soil moisture and improve soil structure.
- **Mulching:** Mulching involves covering the soil surface with organic or inorganic materials to reduce evaporation and protect the soil from erosion. Organic mulches, such as crop residues, can also improve soil fertility.
- **Crop rotation:** Crop rotation involves alternating different crops on the same land to improve soil health, reduce pests and diseases, and conserve soil moisture. Crop rotations can help to improve soil structure and reduce soil erosion.
- **Contingent crop plants:** In dryland areas, it is essential to choose crop plants that can tolerate low soil moisture and high temperatures. Crops such as sorghum, millet, cowpea, groundnut, and pigeon pea are well adapted to these conditions and can sustain crop productivity in dryland areas.
- **Water harvesting:** Water harvesting practices involve collecting and storing rainwater for use during dry periods. Techniques such as constructing contour bunds, check dams, and farm ponds can help to conserve soil moisture and improve crop productivity.
- **Drip irrigation:** Drip irrigation involves applying water directly to the root zone of plants, reducing water loss through evaporation and increasing water use efficiency. This practice can help to conserve soil moisture and sustain crop productivity in dryland areas.

6. (*b*) Linear programming is a mathematical technique used to optimize resource allocation and decision-making in many fields, including business, economics, engineering, and agriculture. To develop an optimum resource use plan using linear programming, one need to follow the following steps:

- **Define the objective:** Determine the goal of the plan. This could be maximizing profits, minimizing costs, maximizing efficiency, or maximizing the use of resources.
- **Identify the decision variables:** Identify the factors that affect the objective, such as the amount of resources used or the level of output produced.
- **Develop the constraints:** Develop the constraints that limit the decision variables. These could be physical

4. (*c*) Contour bunding is the construction of small bund across the slope of the land on a contour so that the long slope is cut into a series of small ones and each contour bund acts as a barrier to the flow of water, thus making the water to walk rather than run, at the same time impounding water against it for increasing soil moisture. Contour bunds divide the length of the slope, reduce the volume of runoff water, and thus preventing or minimizing the soil erosion.

Contour bunds are constructed in relatively low rainfall areas, having an annual rainfall or less than 600 mm, particularly in areas having light textured soils. For rolling and flater lands having slopes from 2 to 6% contour bunding is practiced, in red soils.

Design of contour bunds Vertical Interval between bunds (V.I.)

$$\text{V.I.} = \left(\frac{S}{a} + b\right) 0.3$$

where,

S = land slope (%); *a* and *b* are constants

$a = 3$ and $b = 2$ for medium and heavy rainfall zones

$a = 2$ and $b = 2$ for low rainfall zones

Horizontal Spacing in between bunds (H.I)

$$\text{H.I.} = \frac{\text{V.I.}}{S} \times 100$$

Length of bund per hectare (L.B)

$$\text{L.B per ha} = \frac{100S}{\text{V.I.}}$$

$$\text{or } \frac{10{,}000}{\text{H.I.}}$$

Depth of water impounding before the bund (h)

$$h = \sqrt{\frac{D * R}{500}}$$

where, D = vertical interval (*m*)

R = maximum rainwater on area basis (mm)

Actual height of the bund = h + 20% of h as freeboard

Dimensions of the Contour Bund

Type of soil	Bottom width (m)	Top width (m)	Height (m)	Side slope
Gravel soils	1.2	0.3	0.6	0.75 : 1
Red soils	2.1	0.3	0.6	1.5 : 1
Shallow to medium black soil	2.4	0.45	0.75	1.3 : 1
Deep soils	3.3	0.60	0.675	2 : 1

By knowing the cross section area of the bund, the volume of earthwork per hectare and the cost of earthwork per hectare can be determined.

Contour bunds are laid out in those areas which have less rainfall and permeable soils. The major requirements in such areas are prevention of soil erosion and conservation of rain water in the soil for crop use. To maximize the conservation of rainwater in the soil, no longitudinal slope is provided to the field strip. In such a system of bunding, the bunds are designed to be laid out on contours with minor adjustments, wherever necessary.

The main functions of contour bunds are:

- It reduces the length of slope which in turn reduces the soil erosion.
- The water is impounded for some time and gets recharged into the soil which helps in crop cultivation.

The limitations of contour bunds are:

- The contour bunds are suitable for those areas, which receive the annual rainfall less than 600 mm.
- It is not suitable for clayey soils.
- Contour bunding is not suitable on the land slopes greater than 6%.

5. (*a*) Evaluation as applied to the field of extension education, may be defined as "a process of systematic appraisal by which we determine the value, worth or meaning of an activity or an enterprise". It is a method for determining how far an activity has progressed and how much further it should be carried to accomplish objectives. Thus, to an extension worker evaluation means determining the results of his extension programmes in order to know the extent to which objectives have been achieved and why and what changes would be needed in case the programme is planned again, or in its implementation.

Types of evaluation

Self-evaluation: This is to be carried out by every worker as a matter of routine. This requires the self-critical attitude which is so essential for extension work. By this self-critical attitude, the chances of an extension worker growing and continuously improving his professional competency become greater.

Internal evaluation: Evaluation carried to by the agency responsible for the planning and implementation of the programme. Some of the other methods for internal evaluation are: systematic use of diaries and reports of workers, planned visits of staff members to work spot, use of special questionnaires and proforma for observation and inquiry etc.

External evaluation: Evaluation conducted by a person or a committee outside the area of operation. One of the strong features of the Indian Community Development Programme is that simultaneous with its start an independent agency, namely the Programme Evaluation Organization, was established.

5. (*b*) The role of extension worker while living among rural people is to bring necessary change in individual and collective behaviour and motivating them. For this, extension worker is required to have knowledge about psychological factors, extension related training and technological knowledge. In performing his duties an extension worker has to perform work enumerated:

- **To create motivation and feeling:** By motivating rural people for the development of programmes so that they themselves may become anxious to improve their standard of living and make new programmes and implement them for their upliftment.
- **Knowledge of local felt need:** Development programme should be based upon local felt needs. For this extension worker should be aware of requirements and problems of local people.
- **Precedence of instant needs:** In preparing programme, precedence should be given to those work which fulfil instant requirement of people.
- **To create self-belief in rural people:** Till now rural people have no faith upon their own power. They still depend on government assistance for the development work. So, it is important to make them understand or convince them that they can do most of the work through mutual cooperation.
- **Emphasis on self-dependence:** Our villages were self-dependent before British rule. Their needs like food, clothing and housing, were fulfilled in villages itself, but now they have to go outside to fulfil their basic needs and still they are unable to earn enough for themselves.
- **To develop the close relations between research centre and agricultural farm:** A close coordination is to be developed between research centre and agricultural farm. So that scientific information can be given to the farmers and their problems can be addressed to the scientific institution for solution.
- **Full use of present local resources:** In order to enhance the extension work and rural industries like agriculture and cottage industries, it is necessary to efficiently utilities the available local resources so that people can become self-dependent.
- **Plan for all-round development:** Extension worker should organise social, economic and educational development programmes for all round development of the society.

Advantages of Drip Irrigation:

- ***Water Conservation:*** Drip irrigation delivers water directly to the root zone of plants, reducing evaporation and water waste. This results in higher water use efficiency and reduced water consumption compared to other irrigation methods.
- ***Improved Crop Quality:*** Drip irrigation allows for precise water delivery, which helps to maintain optimal soil moisture levels for crops, leading to improved crop quality and yield.
- ***Reduced Labor:*** Drip irrigation systems require less labor compared to other irrigation methods since they can be automated and don't require frequent maintenance.
- ***Reduced Weed Growth:*** Since water is delivered directly to the root zone of plants, the surrounding soil is kept dry, which helps to reduce weed growth.

Disadvantages of Drip Irrigation:

- ***Initial Cost:*** Drip irrigation systems have a higher initial cost compared to other irrigation systems due to the cost of materials and installation.
- ***Clogging:*** Drip irrigation systems are prone to clogging due to the small emitters used to deliver water. This can lead to uneven water distribution and reduced crop yields.
- ***Limited Applicability:*** Drip irrigation is not suitable for all crops, especially those that require higher soil moisture levels, such as rice and sugarcane.

Advantages of Sprinkler Irrigation:

- ***Uniform Water Distribution:*** Sprinkler irrigation systems provide uniform water distribution across a large area, ensuring that all crops receive adequate water.
- ***Cooling Effect:*** Sprinkler irrigation can help to cool the surrounding air, which is beneficial for crops during hot weather conditions.
- ***Reduced Soil Erosion:*** Sprinkler irrigation helps to reduce soil erosion by delivering water in a gentle rain-like manner.
- ***Applicable to a Wide Range of Crops:*** Sprinkler irrigation is suitable for a wide range of crops, including those that require higher soil moisture levels.

Disadvantages of Sprinkler Irrigation:

- ***Water Loss:*** Sprinkler irrigation is prone to water loss due to evaporation and wind drift, which can result in reduced water use efficiency.
- ***Higher Energy Use:*** Sprinkler irrigation requires higher energy use compared to other irrigation methods since it requires a pump to deliver water.
- ***Equipment Damage:*** Sprinkler irrigation systems can be damaged by wind, hail, or other extreme weather conditions, resulting in the need for repairs or replacement.

Here are some general guidelines for the applicability of these irrigation systems:

Drip Irrigation: Drip irrigation is suitable for a wide range of crops, especially those that have a smaller root zone and require lower soil moisture levels. This irrigation system is particularly effective in arid and semi-arid regions with limited water availability. Drip irrigation is commonly used for fruits and vegetables, such as grapes, strawberries, tomatoes, and peppers. It is also used in orchards, vineyards, and nurseries. Drip irrigation is more commonly used on small to medium sized farms.

Sprinkler Irrigation: Sprinkler irrigation is suitable for a wide range of crops, especially those that require higher soil moisture levels and have a larger root zone. This irrigation system is commonly used for field crops such as corn, wheat, and soybeans, as well as for pastures and hay fields. Sprinkler irrigation is also used in orchards and vineyards. It is more commonly used on larger farms where economies of scale make the higher cost of installation and operation more manageable.

In general, drip irrigation is more water-efficient and requires less labor, while sprinkler irrigation is better suited for larger areas and can provide additional benefits such as cooling the surrounding air and reducing soil erosion. The choice of irrigation system should be based on the specific needs of the crop, soil, and climate, as well as the available water resources and farm size.

7. (*b*) Causes of High Price Spread in Agriculture Commodities: The high price spread in agricultural commodities can be attributed to various factors. Here are some of the primary causes:

- **Production and supply factors:** Agricultural commodities are highly dependent on weather conditions, natural calamities, pest attacks, and diseases. Any disruption in the production process can lead to a reduction in supply, resulting in higher prices. Additionally, transportation and storage costs can further add to the price of the commodity.
- **Market inefficiencies:** Agricultural markets are often fragmented and inefficient, with limited infrastructure for storage, transportation, and distribution. This can lead to market distortions and a lack of transparency, which may result in high price spreads.
- **Government policies:** Government policies, such as subsidies, tariffs, and import/export regulations, can affect the price spread of agricultural commodities. For instance, subsidies provided to farmers can lead to higher production and supply, which can reduce the price spread. On the other hand, import tariffs can protect domestic producers but increase the price of imported commodities.
- **Speculation and hoarding:** Speculators and hoarders can contribute to the high price spread of agricultural commodities. They may buy and hold large quantities of the commodity, artificially inflating prices and creating scarcity.
- **Market power:** The concentration of market power among a few dominant players in the agricultural sector can lead to price distortions. These players may exercise market power to manipulate prices and increase their profits.

The high price spread in agricultural commodities is a complex issue influenced by various factors, including production and supply factors, market inefficiencies, government policies, speculation and hoarding, and market power. Addressing these factors through improved market infrastructure, regulatory reforms, and effective policy interventions can help reduce the price spread and promote greater price stability in agricultural markets.

Measures to Minimize the High Price Spread in Agriculture: To minimize the high price spread in agriculture, several measures can be taken. Here are some of them:

- **Improving infrastructure:** Governments can invest in improving transportation, storage, and distribution infrastructure to reduce the cost of moving agricultural commodities from farms to markets. This can lead to a reduction in the price spread.
- **Promoting market transparency:** Governments can promote greater transparency in agricultural markets by mandating the reporting of prices and quantities traded. This can help reduce information asymmetry, and ensure that

important part of market analysis. Some of the key success factors can be listed as under:

- Accessibility to essential and unique resources.
- Competence to reach economies of scale.
- Accessibility to channels of distribution.
- Accessibility to the state-of-the-art technology.

5. (*e*) Types of Sprinkler Irrigation System: In the sprinkler method of irrigation, water is sprayed into the air and allowed to fall on the ground surface somewhat resembling rainfall. The spray is developed by the flow of water under pressure through small orifices or nozzles. The pressure is usually obtained by pumping. With careful selection of nozzle sizes, operating pressure and sprinkler spacing the amount of irrigation water required to refill the crop root zone can be applied nearly uniform at the rate to suit the infiltration rate of soil.

Sprinkler systems are classified into the following two major types on the basis of the arrangement for spraying irrigation water.

1. Rotating head or revolving sprinkler system.
2. Perforated pipe system.

1. Rotating head: Small size nozzles are placed on riser pipes fixed at uniform intervals along the length of the lateral pipe and the lateral pipes are usually laid on the ground surface. They may also be mounted on posts above the crop height and rotated through 90°, to irrigate a rectangular strip. In rotating type sprinklers, the most common device to rotate the sprinkler heads is with a small hammer activated by the thrust of water striking against a vane connected to it.

2. Perforated pipe system: This method consists of drilled holes or nozzles along their length through which water is sprayed under pressure. This system is usually designed for relatively low pressure (1 kg/cm^2). The application rate ranges from 1.25 to 5 cm per hour for various pressure and spacing.

Based on the portability, sprinkler systems are classified into the following types:

- **Portable system:** A portable system has portable main lines, laterals and pumping plant.
- **Semi-portable system:** A semi-portable system is similar to a portable system except that the location of water source and pumping plant is fixed.
- **Semi-permanent system:** A semi-permanent system has portable lateral lines, permanent main lines and sub mains and a stationery water source and pumping plant.
- **Solid set system:** A solid set system has enough laterals to eliminate their movement. The laterals are positions in the field early in the crop season and remain for the season.
- **Permanent system:** A fully permanent system consists of permanently laid mains, sub mains and laterals and a stationery water source and pumping plant.

7. (*a*) Criteria for Scheduling Irrigation: An ideal irrigation schedule must indicate when to apply irrigation water and how much quantity of water to be applied; several approaches for scheduling irrigation have been used by scientist and farmers. These are as under:

1. Soil moisture depletion approach: The available soil moisture in the root is a good criterion for scheduling irrigation. When the soil moisture in a specified root zone depth is depended to a particular level (which is different for different crops) it is too replenished by irrigation. For practical purpose, irrigation should be started when about 50 per cent of the available moisture in the soil root zone is depleted. The available water is the soil moisture, which lies between field capacity and wilting point. The relative availability of soil moisture is not same field capacity to wilting point stage and since the crop suffers before the soil moisture reaches wilting point, it is necessary to locate the optimum point within the available range of soil moisture, when irrigation must be scheduled to maintain crop yield at high level. Soil moisture deficit represents the difference in the moisture content at field capacity and that before irrigation. This is measured by taking into consideration the percentage, availability, tension, resistance etc.

2. **Plant basis or plant indices:** As the plant is the user of water, it can be taken as a guide for scheduling irrigation. The deficit of water will be reflected by plants itself such as dropping, curling or rolling of leaves and change in foliage colour as indication for irrigation scheduling. However, these symptoms indicate the need for water. They do not permit quantitative estimation of moisture deficit. Growth indicators such as cell elongation rates, plant water content and leaf water potential, plant temperature leaf diffusion resistance etc. are also used for deciding when to irrigate.

3. **Climatological approach:** Evapotranspiration mainly depends up on climate. The amount of water lost by evapotranspiration is estimated from Climatological data and when ET reaches a particular level, irrigation is scheduled. The amount of irrigation given is either equal to ET or fraction of ET. Different methods in Climatological approach are IW/CPE ratio method and pan evaporimeter method. In IW/CPE approach, a known amount of irrigation water is applied when cumulative pan evaporation (CPE) reaches a predetermined level. The amount of water given at each irrigation ranges from 4 to 6 cm. The most common being 5 cm irrigation. Scheduling irrigation at an IW/CPE ratio of 1.0 with 5 cm. Generally, irrigation is given at 0.75 to 0.8 ratios with 5 cm of irrigation water.

Table: *Moisture sensitive stages of important crops.*

Sr. No.	Crop	Important Moisture Sensitive Stages
1.	Rice	Panicle Initiation, Flowering
2.	Wheat	Crown Root Initiation, Jointing, Milking
3.	Sorghum	Seedling, Flowering
4.	Maize	Silking, Tasseling
5.	Bajara	Flowering, Panicle Initiation
6.	Nachani	Panicle Initiation, Flowering
7.	Ground Nut	Rapid Flowering, Pegging, Early Pod Formation
8.	Red Gram	Flowering & Pod Formation
9.	Green Gram	Flowering & Pod Formation
10.	Black Gram	Flowering & Pod Formation
11.	Sugarcane	Formative Stage
12.	Sesamum	Blooming stage to Maturity
13.	Sunflower	Two weeks before & after flowering
14.	Safflower	From rosette to flowering
15.	Soybean	Blooming & seed formation
16.	Cotton	Flowering & Ball Formation
17.	Tobacco	Transplanting to Full Bloom
18.	Chilies	Flowering
19.	Potato	Tuber Initiation to Tuber Maturity
20.	Onion	Bulb Formation to Maturity
21.	Tomato	From the Commencement of Fruit Set

4. **Critical growth approach:** In each crop, there are some growth stages at which moisture stress leads to irrevocable yield loss. These stages are known as critical periods or moisture sensitive periods. If irrigation water is available in sufficient quantities, irrigation is scheduled whenever soil moisture is depleted to critical moisture level. Say 25 or 50 per cent of available soil moisture. Under limited water supply conditions, irrigation is scheduled at moisture sensitive stages and irrigation is skipped at non-sensitive stages.

5. **Plant water status itself:** This is the latest approach for scheduling of irrigation. Plant is a good indicator of a soil moisture and climate factors. The water content in the plant itself is considered for scheduling irrigation. It is however, not yet common use for want of standard and low-cost technique to measure the plant water status or potential.

communication, allowing cells to coordinate their activities and respond to external stimuli.

1. (*b*) The Pre and Post-Harvest Factors Affecting the Seed Quality of a Crop during Seed Production: Seed quality is crucial for crop production as it determines the yield, vigor, and uniformity of the plants grown from the seeds. The quality of the seed is affected by various factors that occur both before and after harvest. Here's a brief explanation of pre and post-harvest factors that affect seed quality:

Pre-harvest Factors:

- **Genetics:** The genetic makeup of the parent plants plays a significant role in determining the quality of the seeds produced. The traits such as yield, disease resistance, and seed size are inherited from the parent plants.
- **Environmental conditions:** Climatic conditions such as temperature, moisture, and light during seed development have a significant impact on seed quality. High temperatures, drought stress, and low light intensity can lead to poor seed quality.
- **Soil fertility:** The availability of essential nutrients in the soil affects the growth and development of the plant, which ultimately affects seed quality.
- **Pest and disease management:** Pest and disease infestations can reduce seed quality by affecting the seed development and causing physical damage to the seed.

Post-harvest Factors:

- **Harvesting practices:** Harvesting at the right time, using appropriate tools and techniques, and avoiding physical damage during harvesting can help maintain seed quality.
- **Drying and processing:** Proper drying, cleaning, and processing of the seeds after harvest are critical to maintaining seed quality. Improper drying and cleaning can result in reduced seed viability and vigor.
- **Storage conditions:** Storage conditions such as temperature, humidity, and ventilation can significantly affect seed quality. High temperature and humidity can lead to seed deterioration and loss of viability.
- **Seed treatment:** Treating seeds with fungicides, insecticides, or other chemicals can help protect them from pests and diseases, but if not done correctly, it can also reduce seed quality.

1. (*c*) The Chemically Induced Male Sterility and its Importance in Crop Improvement and Seed Production: Chemically induced male sterility (CIMS) is a plant breeding technique used to produce male-sterile plants by using chemicals or drugs. This technique involves the application of a chemical substance that interferes with the normal development and function of the anther, which is the male reproductive organ of the plant. As a result, the plants become sterile, meaning they are incapable of producing viable pollen.

The importance of CIMS in crop improvement and seed production can be explained in the following ways:

- **Hybrid Seed Production:** CIMS is used in the production of hybrid seeds in crops such as maize, rice, sorghum, and sunflower. Hybrid seeds are created by crossing two genetically distinct parent plants. The use of male-sterile plants in the production of hybrid seeds ensures that self-pollination does not occur, resulting in hybrid seeds with high yield potential, uniformity, and better adaptation to specific environmental conditions.
- **Reduced Risk of Gene Flow:** CIMS can also be used to prevent gene flow

between genetically modified (GM) crops and their non-GM counterparts or wild relatives. By using male-sterile plants in GM crop production, the risk of unwanted gene transfer through pollen is minimized, which helps to maintain the purity of non-GM crops and wild plant populations.

- **Reduced Cost and Time:** CIMS is a cost-effective and time-saving technique in seed production. Compared to other methods of producing male-sterile plants, such as genetic modification or physical manipulation, CIMS is relatively easy to apply and does not require specialized equipment or facilities.
- **Increased Yield Potential:** By using CIMS to produce malesterile plants, plant breeders can focus their efforts on improving the characteristics of the female parent plant, such as yield, disease resistance, and stress tolerance. This can lead to the development of improved crop varieties with higher yield potential and better adaptation to specific environmental conditions.

1. (*d*) **Various Factors Affecting Enzyme Activity in Plants:** Enzyme activity in plants can be affected by a variety of factors, including:

- **Temperature:** Enzymes have an optimal temperature range at which they are most active. This range varies for different enzymes. As the temperature increases, the rate of enzyme catalyzed reactions increases, until the enzyme is denatured and its activity is lost.
- **pH:** Enzymes have an optimal pH range at which they are most active. This range varies for different enzymes. Changes in pH can alter the shape of the enzyme molecule and disrupt its ability to bind to the substrate.
- **Substrate concentration:** The rate of enzyme activity increases with increasing substrate concentration, until a saturation point is reached. At this point, all of the enzyme molecules are bound to substrate molecules and the rate of reaction cannot increase further.
- **Inhibitors:** Inhibitors can reduce or completely block enzyme activity. There are two main types of inhibitors: competitive inhibitors, which bind to the active site of the enzyme and prevent substrate binding, and non-competitive inhibitors, which bind to a site on the enzyme other than the active site and change the enzyme's shape.
- **Co-factors:** Enzymes require certain co-factors, such as metal ions or vitamins, to function properly. The absence or deficiency of these co-factors can reduce enzyme activity.
- **Enzyme concentration:** The rate of enzyme activity increases with increasing enzyme concentration, until a saturation point is reached. At this point, all of the substrate molecules are bound to enzyme molecules and the rate of reaction cannot increase further.
- **Activators:** Activators can increase enzyme activity. They bind to a site on the enzyme and change its shape, making it more likely to bind to substrate molecules.
- **Presence of other enzymes or enzymes with competitive substrates:** Enzymes with competitive substrates or that are involved in the same metabolic pathway can affect the activity of each other.

1. (*e*) **Molecular Markers Approach in Crop Improvement:** Molecular markers are tools used in crop improvement to identify and track the inheritance of specific genetic traits of interest. These markers are essentially genetic landmarks that help plant breeders identify plants with desirable traits and breed them together to produce new crop varieties

PAPER-II

1. (*a*) Mendel's law of independent assortment states that the alleles of two (or more) different genes get sorted into gametes independently of one another. In other words, the allele a gamete receives for one gene does not influence the allele received for another gene.

A good example of independent assortment is Mendelian dihybrid cross. The presence of new combinations - round green and wrinkled yellow, suggests that the genes for the shape of the seed and colour of the seed are assorted independently.

Independent Assortment

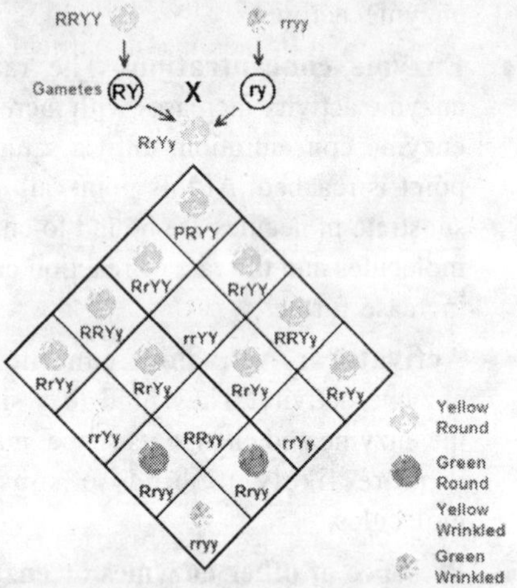

1. (*b*) Mechanisms Promote Cross Pollination: Following mechanism promote cross pollination:

Imperfect flowers (dicliny or unsexuality) Flowers are unisexual i.e., stamens and pistils lie on separate flowers.

- Monoecious plants: e.g., Maize, Castor, Jack, Coconut.
- Dioecious plants: e.g., Papaya, Hemp, Asparagus, Datepalm, etc.

1. **Dichogamy:** Unequal maturation of stamens and pistils in bisexual flowers (Anther and stigma of bisexual flowers mature at different times). They are of two types:

   (*a*) *Protogyny:* Stigma becomes receptive earlier to stamens. *e.g.* Bajra.

   (*b*) *Protandry:* Antherdehisce and release the pollen grains before stigma of the same flower attains receptivity. *e.g.*, Carrot, Marigold.

2. **Herkogamy:** Presence of mechanical barrier between male and female organs of a flower. e.g., Crepes.
3. **Male Sterility:** Seeds are not set due to absence of functional pollen grains. Male sterility determined by (*i*) Genetic factors (e.g. Tomato, Barley, Brinjal and Rice). (*ii*) Cytoplasmic factors (e.g., Onion) and (*iii*) Interaction (e.g. Chili, etc.)
4. **Self Incompatibility:** Male and female gametes are fertile but seeds are not produced when selfed because of some oppositional factors but can set seeds when there is a cross pollination. e.g., Tobacco, Mango, Tomato, Mustard, Radish, Cabbage, etc.

1. (*c*) Quarantine Regulation of Seed Needed: A legal restriction on movement of agricultural commodities for the purpose of exclusion, prevention or delay in the establishment of plants, disease or parasites in the area where they are not present. Plant quarantine is a technique for insuring disease and pest-free plants by isolating them until they are confirmed healthy. Thus, plant quarantine is designed as a safe guard against harmful pests or pathogens exotic to a country or a region and the newly imported plants are isolated to ensure that they are not introducing any foreign parasites. The term quarantine may refer to the quarantine station itself, or to the process of testing and purifying the plant material. A 40 days quarantine period is in rule for isolating the plant material.

Need of Plant and Seed Quarantine:

- A new pest, after arrival and establishment, can rapidly develop into destructive proportions.
- Because of the absence of natural enemies in the new environment.
- Plant pest epidemics could result in the loss of agricultural produce.
- This may adversely affect the food production or an existing export trade.
- Therefore, the main aim of plant quarantine is to prevent the entry of exotic pests into the country by enforcing laws without which it is hard to obtain compliance.

Quarantine Regulation: Whatever the type of introduced plant are, *i.e.* seeds, vegetables, fruits etc. bulk introductions are always risky as thorough examination and treatment in such cases is very difficult and planting area is far too large to prevent the establishment and spread of the introduced pest/disease. Based on these factors, plant quarantine regulates the introductions as follows:

- **Complete embargo/prohibition:** When the pest risk is very high, the safeguards available in the country are not adequate and, therefore, import is prohibited.
- **Post-entry quarantine:** The risk is very high but adequate safeguards in the form of post-entry isolation growing facilities are available.
- **Restricted:** Pest risk is not high and import permit is required stipulating conditions for entry, inspection and treatment.
- **Unrestricted:** Import permit is not required, and material may enter without restriction.

Objectives of the Scheme:

- To prevent the introduction and spread of exotic pests that are destructive to crops by regulating/restricting the import of plants/plant products.
- To facilitate safe global trade in agriculture by assisting the producers and exporters by providing a technically competent and reliable phytosanitary certificate system to meet the requirements of trading partners.

1. (*d*) Factor Affecting Rate of Transpiration in Plants: Different factors affecting the rate of trans-piration are:

Cellular Factors: The cellular factors affecting the rate of transpiration are: • The orientation of leaf, • The water status of the plant, • Structural Peculiarities of the leaf, • Total number and distribution of stomata in a leaf.

Environmental Factors: The environmental factors affecting the rate of transpiration are: • Light, • Humidity, • Temperature, • Atmospheric pressure, • Wind speed or velocity.

Relative Humidity: The amount of water vapour present in the air at a particular time and temperature is expressed as a percentage of the amount required for saturation at the same temperature. The rate of transpiration is inversely proportional to relative humidity. More the relative humidity less is the transpirate rate.

Temperature: A high temperature lowers the relative humidity and opens the stomata even in darkness. As a result, the rate of transpiration increases.

Light: The stomata open during the day and close in the dark. Presence of light is directly proportional to the rate of transpiration.

Air: If the air is still, the transpiration rate is low. This is because the water vapour accumulates around the transpiring organs and reduce the diffusion pressure deficit of the air. If the air is moving, the saturated air around the leaves is removed and the transpiration rate increases.

Water Availability: The transpiration rate is directly proportional to the absorption of water by the roots from the soil. A decrease in water absorption causes the closure of stomata and wilting, thereby reducing the rate of transpiration.

individuals over multiple generations to improve the overall performance of a population. There are different methods of recurrent selection, including mass selection, modified ear-to-row selection, and family selection.

- **Mass selection:** This method involves selecting the best individuals from a population based on their overall performance and using them as parents for the next generation. The selected individuals are then intercrossed to produce the next generation, and the process is repeated over several generations. Mass selection is a simple method and is suitable for populations with high genetic variability.
- **Modified ear-to-row selection:** This method involves selecting the best ears from individual plants and then planting them in rows for the next generation. The best plants from each row are then selected and intercrossed to produce the next generation. Modified ear-to-row selection is suitable for populations with low genetic variability and is commonly used in maize breeding.
- **Family selection:** This method involves selecting the best families of related individuals and using them as parents for the next generation. The selected families are then intercrossed to produce the next generation, and the process is repeated over several generations. Family selection is suitable for populations with moderate genetic variability and is commonly used in breeding self-pollinating crops.
- **Reciprocal recurrent selection:** This method involves selecting superior individuals from two populations and crossing them to produce a hybrid population. The hybrid population is then evaluated, and the best individuals are selected to form two new populations. The process is then repeated over several generations, with each generation involving the selection and crossing of individuals from both populations. Reciprocal recurrent selection is suitable for improving traits that are influenced by both additive and non-additive genetic effects.

  Recurrent selection is a plant breeding method that involves selecting and crossing superior individuals over multiple generations to improve the overall performance of a population. Different methods of recurrent selection can be used depending on the genetic variability of the population and the type of traits being selected for.

Importance of Combining Ability in Crop Improvements: Combining ability refers to the ability of a particular crop line or variety to combine favorably with other varieties or lines, leading to improved crop performance and yield. The concept of combining ability is crucial in crop improvement programs as it allows plant breeders to identify and select the best parental lines for crossing to develop new varieties with improved traits.

Here are some of the key reasons why combining ability is important in crop improvements:

- **Enhancing genetic diversity:** Crossbreeding two or more genetically diverse parental lines with good combining ability can produce offspring with superior genetic characteristics, leading to increased crop productivity and yield.
- **Developing new varieties:** The use of combining ability analysis allows plant breeders to identify the best parental lines for crossing, which can help in the development of new varieties with desirable traits such as disease resistance, drought tolerance, and high yield potential.

- **Minimizing negative effects of inbreeding:** Inbreeding depression can occur when plants are self-fertilized or crossed with closely related individuals. Using parental lines with good combining ability can minimize the negative effects of inbreeding and help maintain the genetic diversity of the population.
- **Accelerating the breeding process:** Combining ability analysis can help breeders to identify the best parental lines for crossing, reducing the time and resources required to develop new varieties.

Combining ability is an important concept in crop improvement programs as it helps plant breeders to develop new varieties with desirable traits, maintain genetic diversity, and accelerate the breeding process.

2. (*c*) Mechanism of Interphase in Mitosis Cell Division: Interphase is the period between two successive mitotic divisions, when the cell grows it, carries out its metabolic activities, replicates its DNA, and prepares for cell division. The interphase is divided into three stages: G1, S, and G2.

During the G1 stage, the cell grows and carries out its metabolic activities. The cell prepares for DNA replication, and the organelles and other cellular components are duplicated. The G1 checkpoint ensures that the cell has enough nutrients and energy to proceed with cell division.

During the S stage, DNA replication takes place, and each chromosome is replicated to form two identical sister chromatids joined at the centromere. The DNA replication checkpoint ensures that DNA replication is complete and accurate.

During the G2 stage, the cell prepares for mitosis by synthesizing proteins and organelles necessary for cell division. The cell undergoes a final check to ensure that DNA replication is complete and accurate before proceeding to the next stage. The G2 checkpoint ensures that the cell is ready to enter mitosis.

After interphase, the cell enters the mitotic phase, which consists of five stages: prophase, prometaphase, metaphase, anaphase, and telophase. During the mitotic phase, the duplicated chromosomes align, separate, and are divided into two daughter cells.

3. (*a*) Detailed Structure of Deoxyribonucleic acid (DNA) as Prepared by Watson and Crick with Suitable Diagram: DNA is a helical, double-stranded molecule with two strands. On the surface, it has two backbones (with alternating glycosyl and phosphate groups) that are linked together on the inside by hydrogen bonds between pairs of nitrogenous bases. The bases are divided into four categories (A, C, G, and T), with A & T and C & G always matching. James Watson and Francis Crick realised that these pairing principles indicated that either strand held all the information needed to build a new copy of the complete molecule and that the aperiodic sequence of bases might offer a "genetic code". Linus Pauling, in 1925, utilised X-ray crystallography to determine the secondary structure of proteins. X-ray crystallography was used for analysing molecular structure. One could see the patterns produced by the X-rays when they were shot through the crystal of a material. The patterns revealed important details about the structure of any molecule of interest. In 1953, Rosalind Franklin, a researcher at Wilkins Lab in the US, used X-ray crystallography to explore the structure of DNA. In the 1950s, while working together at Cambridge, England, Watson and Crick were able to piece together the jigsaw of the DNA molecule using Franklin's discoveries.

Watson-Crick Structure of DNA

- Watson and Crick presented a model for the DNA's double-helix structure.

gametes with short and red alleles. If you create the Punnett square with these gametes, you will see that the classical Mendelian prediction of a 9 : 3 : 3 : 1 outcome of a dihybrid cross would not apply. As the distance between two genes increases, the probability of one or more crossovers between them increases, and the genes behave more like they are on separate chromosomes. Geneticists have used the proportion of recombinant gametes (the ones not like the parents) as a measure of how far apart genes are on a chromosome. Using this information, they have constructed elaborate maps of genes on chromosomes for well-studied organisms, including humans. Mendel's seminal publication makes no mention of linkage, and many researchers have questioned whether he encountered linkage, but chose not to publish those crosses out of concern that they would invalidate his independent assortment postulate. The garden pea has seven chromosomes and some have suggested that his choice of seven characteristics was not a coincidence.

3. (*b*) **Distant Hybridization:** Crossing between two different species of the same genus or two different genera of the same family is called distant hybridization and such crosses are referred to as distant crosses or wide crosses. Wide crossing or distant hybridization has been used in the genetic improvement of some crop plants. It is an effective means of transferring desirable genes into cultivated plants from related species and genera. Distant crosses are more successful in more closely related species or genera than in less closely related species or genera.

Distant Hybridization Used for Developing New Varieties

(*i*) **Wheat-Rye Cross:** The first intergeneric cross was made in the family Gramineae between bread wheat (*Triticum aestivum,* $2n = 42$) and rye (Secale cereale $2n = 14$) by Rimpau around 1890 in Sweden. The F_1 was sterile which was made fertile through colchicine treatment. The amphidiploid ($2n = 56$) was named as Triticale. This combines yield potential and grain quality of wheat and hardiness of rye. Triticale is the best example of the practical achievements of intergeneric hybridization. Now Triticale is commercially grown in countries like Canada and Argentina. Several improved varieties of Triticale have been released for commercial cultivation. Research work on Triticale is in progress at CYMMIT, Mexico.

(*ii*) **Radish Cabbage Cross:** Intergeneric cross between radish (*Raphanus sativus*) and cabbage (*Bassica oleracea*) of the family Cruciferae was made by Karpechenko in 1928 in Russia. The main objective was to combine root of radish with leaves of cabbage. The F_1 was sterile, the doubling of chromosome number by colchicine treatment resulted in development of fertile amphidiploid which was named as *Raphanobrassica* by Karpechenko. But the new species thus developed had roots like cabbage and leaves like radish, which was a useless combination.

(*iii*) **Intergeneric Crosses in Sugarcane:** Several intergeneric crosses have been made in sugarcane. There are eight genera in which intergeneric hybrids have been made with sugarcane (*Saccharum*). These genera include Eccoilopus, Erianthus, Miscanthidium, Miscanthus, Narenga, Rapidum, Sclerostachya and Sorghum (*Sweet sorghums*). Many of the intergeneric hybrids are easily made with the help of male sterility. However, intergeneric hybrids with sugarcane have made little contribution to the development of modern commercial cultivars. Intergeneric hybrids have great potential for the improvement of germplasm.

(*iv*) **Maize-Tripsacum Crosses:** Intergeneric crosses between maize and Tripsacum were also attempted. The basic chromosome number is 10 in maize and 9 in Tripsacum. Crosses are successful in both directions, but hybrids can be more easily produced when Tripsacum is used as the female parent, because the maize pollens are able to produce long pollen tube to reach the ovule. On the other hand, Tripsacum pollen are unable to produce long pollen tube to reach the ovule of maize. Hence when reciprocal cross is made, the maize styles (ear silks) have to be reduced in length by cutting so that the Tripsacum pollen tube can reach the ovule. Now hybrid derivatives of Tripsacum x diploid maize are being utilized in commercial crop improvement programmes.

(*v*) **Intergeneric Crosses in Barley:** Intergeneric crosses of barley (Hordeum) were attempted with some species of Avena, Phleum, Dactylis, Alopercunis, Triticum, Lolium, and Festuca. Seed set was a major problem in these crosses. Application of 2, 4-D prior to pollination followed by gibbrellic acid treatment was found useful in making above intergeneric crosses successful. But none of these intergeneric crosses contributed to cultivar development in barley.

These aspects are briefly discussed below:

(*i*) **Character Improvement:**

- **Disease and Insect Resistance:** Distant hybridization has been instrumental in transferring disease resistance from wild species into cultivated ones. For example, resistance to rust and black arm in cotton; mosaic virus, wild fire, black-fire, blue mould, black root rot, and Fusarium wilt diseases in tobacco; sereh disease in sugarcane; late blight, leaf roll and virus x in potato; rust and eye spot in wheat; and yellow mosaic virus in okra have been transferred from wild species of these crops into cultivated species. In tomato, resistance to bacterial cankar, bacterial wilt, Fusarium wilt, grey leaf spot, leaf moulds Verticillium wilt, curly top virus, mosaic virus has been transferred from wild species to the commercial cultivars. Use of wild root stocks, in commonly grafted crops such as citrus, rubber, grape, pistachio and peach has eliminated many insect pests and diseases of these horticultural crops. Less progress has been made on insect resistance. Resistance to jassids and boll weevil in cotton, leaf chewing insects in peanut, and aphids in strawberry has been transferred from their wild species to cultivars.
- **Improvement in Quality:** In some crops, wild species have been used to improve the quality of cultivated ones. For example, protein content in rice, oats and rye; fibre length in cotton; oil quality in oil palm; carotenoid content in tomato; starch content in potato; leaf quality in tobacco; and oil per cent in oats have been improved through the use of their wild species in the hybridization programme. Teosinte has been used to improve maize for silage. Wild Sorghum has been used to improve green fodder in cultivated species. Wild tobacco has been utilised to reduce nicotine content in cultivated species and flavour of cultivated tea has been improved through the use of wild tea.
- **Improvement in Adaptation:** Adaptation to various environmental conditions has been improved through the use of wild species. For example, tolerance to cold in rye, wheat, onion, potato, tomato, grapes, strawberry and peppermints etc. has been transferred from wild species of these crops in Russia. In wheat, increased winter hardiness has been transferred from Agropyron. In grape, hardier vines

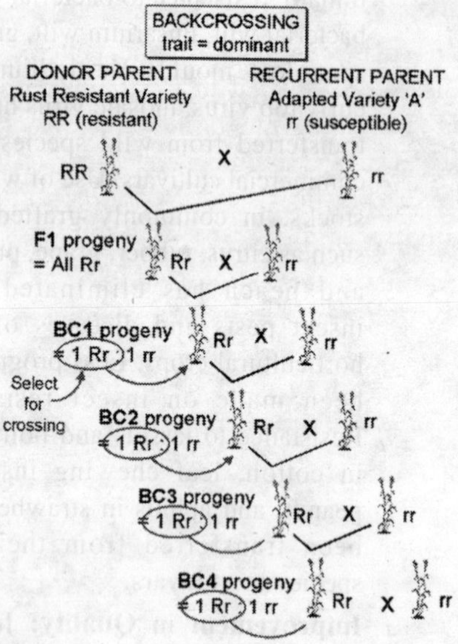

Backcross breeding with a dominant trait.

In contrast, if the genes for rust resistance had been recessive (i.e., ss = resistant) rather than dominant, then the introduced resistant gene is only carried in the heterozygote and would not be detected throughout the backcross program. After each backcross, one would have to self the heterozygote (Ss) in order to produce resistant plants (ss) in the progeny. These resistant plants (ss) are then backcrossed to the recurrent parent (SS)

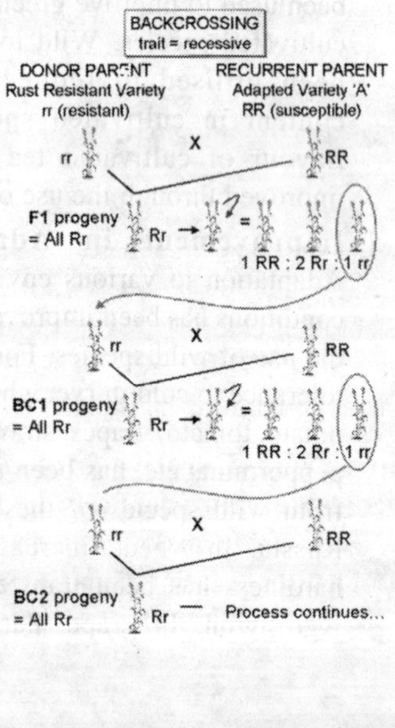

When working with recessive traits, such as this example, Allard (1960) suggested advancing the 1st backcross to the F2 generation followed by selection for the desirable character from the donor parent (ss) and the general features of the recurrent parent. The 2nd and 3rd backcrosses are then made in succession after which the inbreeding with selection phase for ss is repeated. This is followed by the 4th and 5th backcrosses in succession. The BC5F2 that are resistant (SS) are crossed to recurrent parent (SS) for the BC6F1 which is Ss.

The BC7F1 is selfed to get in the BC6F2 : 1/2 SS (susceptible) : 1/2 Ss (susceptible) : 1/2 ss (resistant) backcross with intense selection for both the desired character (ss) and the recurrent parent plant phenotype.

3. (*c*) Role of Public and Private Sector Organizations in Seed Production and Marketing in India:

Seed production and marketing play a crucial role in ensuring food security and sustainable agriculture. In India, both public and private sector organizations have been actively involved in the production and marketing of seeds. These organizations have complementary roles and functions, and their collaboration can significantly contribute to improving seed quality, increasing productivity, and promoting innovation in the agriculture sector. The public sector organizations involved in seed production and marketing in India include the Indian Council of Agricultural Research (ICAR), State Agricultural Universities (SAUs), State Seed Corporations, and the National Seeds Corporation (NSC). These organizations are responsible for conducting research and development activities to develop new seed varieties, testing their efficacy and suitability under different agroclimatic conditions, and promoting their use among farmers. They also produce and distribute highquality seeds to farmers at affordable prices, particularly to small and marginal farmers who cannot afford to buy expensive seeds from the private sector. In addition, they provide technical assistance and training to farmers on seed selection, storage, and usage, as well as on modern farming practices such as integrated pest management and conservation agriculture.

Both public and private sector organizations have complementary roles in seed production and marketing. While the public sector organizations focus on research and development and providing affordable, high-quality seeds to small and marginal farmers, the private sector companies focus on commercializing new seed varieties and providing technical assistance and training on modern farming practices. The collaboration between the two sectors can significantly contribute in improving seed quality, increasing productivity, and promoting innovation in the agriculture sector. In India, both public and private sector organizations play important roles in seed production and marketing.

Public Sector Organizations: The public sector organizations involved in seed production and marketing in India include the Indian Council of Agricultural Research (ICAR), State Agricultural Universities (SAUs), State Seed Corporations, and the National Seeds Corporation (NSC). These organizations are primarily responsible for research and development of new seed varieties, as well as production and distribution of quality seeds to farmers. They also conduct training and extension programs to educate farmers about the benefits of using certified seeds.

Private Sector Organizations: The private sector organizations involved in seed production and marketing in India include seed companies, agro-chemical companies, and agri-input companies. These organizations are mainly focused on producing and marketing high-yielding hybrid seeds, which have higher productivity and better disease resistance compared to traditional varieties. They also provide farmers with technical assistance and training on seed usage and farming practices.

Collaboration between Public and Private Sectors: In recent years, there has been a growing trend towards collaboration between public and private sector organizations in seed production and marketing. This collaboration aims to combine the strengths of both sectors to provide farmers with better quality seeds, as well as to promote the adoption of new technologies and farming practices. For example, the public sector organizations provide technical assistance and research support to the private sector, while the private sector companies invest in research and development and commercialize of new seed varieties.

Both public and private sector organizations play important roles in seed production and marketing in India. The public sector organizations focus on research and development, providing affordable, high-quality seeds to small and marginal farmers, and promoting the adoption of modern farming practices. The private sector companies focus on commercializing new seed varieties, investing in research and development, and providing technical assistance and training on modern farming practices. Collaboration between the two sectors can significantly contribute to improving seed quality, increasing productivity, and promoting innovation in the agriculture sector. This collaboration is essential in achieving food security and sustainable agriculture in India.

5. (*a*) **Preventive and Curative Methods for Management of Storage Pests in Pulses:** Storage pests are a major problem in the storage of pulses, causing significant losses in quantity and quality. The management of

storage pests can be divided into two categories: preventive and curative methods.

Preventive methods include:

- **Hygiene:** Maintaining cleanliness and hygiene in the storage area is the first step in preventing storage pests. Regular cleaning and disinfection of the storage area, containers, and equipment can significantly reduce the pest infestation.
- **Moisture Control:** Most storage pests thrive in damp and humid conditions. Therefore, it is essential to keep the storage area dry and well-ventilated to prevent the growth and multiplication of pests.
- **Temperature Control:** Many pests have specific temperature requirements for their growth and survival. Maintaining the appropriate temperature range in the storage area can prevent pest infestation.
- **Pest Traps:** Installing pest traps in the storage area can help monitor and control the pest population. Sticky traps, pheromone traps, and light traps are commonly used for this purpose.

Curative methods include:

- **Fumigation:** Fumigation is a common curative method for controlling storage pests. It involves the use of chemicals such as phosphine, methyl bromide, or sulfuryl fluoride, which are highly toxic to pests. Fumigation should be carried out by trained professionals, and safety measures should be taken to avoid human exposure to the chemicals.
- **Heat Treatment:** Heat treatment is another curative method that involves exposing the infested pulses to high temperatures for a specific duration. The heat kills the pests and their eggs, preventing further infestation.
- **Cold Treatment:** Cold treatment involves exposing the infested pulses to low temperatures for a specific duration. This method is effective against some pests but may not be suitable for all types.

5. (*b*) Principles of Fruit and Vegetable Preservation:

Preservation means just protecting the foods against spoilage, but scientifically it may be defined as a science that deals with the process of prevention of decay or spoilage of the food are called preservation. In other words, preservation is just controlling the physical, chemical or microbial changes in the food.

- **Physical Changes:** Colour, flavour, texture and taste etc.
- **Chemical Changes:** Carbohydrates, fats, proteins, vitamins and minerals.
- **Microbial changes:** Mould, yeasts and bacteria.

Why do we preserve food?

- To increase the shelf life of the food for increasing the supply.
- To make the fruits and vegetables available throughout the year.
- To add variety to the diet.
- To save time by reducing preparation, time and energy.
- To stabilise the prices of the food in the market.
- To improve the health of the population.

The principles of fruit and vegetable preservation are:

- **Temperature control:** Fruits and vegetables should be stored at cool temperatures to slow down the ripening process and prevent spoilage. The ideal temperature for most fruits and vegetables is between 0 to 5 degrees Celsius.
- **Moisture control:** Fruits and vegetables contain high levels of water, which makes them susceptible to mold and bacterial growth. To preserve them, it's important

to control the moisture content by storing them in a dry and well-ventilated area.

- **Sanitation:** Proper sanitation is essential to prevent the growth of harmful bacteria and maintain the quality of the produce. Fruits and vegetables should be washed thoroughly before preservation to remove any dirt, debris, or bacteria.
- **Chemical treatment:** Chemicals like citric acid and ascorbic acid can be used to preserve fruits and vegetables by preventing discoloration and delaying the growth of bacteria. However, it's important to use these chemicals in the right proportions to avoid altering the taste or texture of the produce.
- **Freezing:** Freezing is a popular method of preserving fruits and vegetables that involves placing them in airtight containers and freezing them at low temperatures. Freezing helps to preserve the texture and flavor of the produce, but it can also cause some loss of nutrients.
- **Drying:** Drying is another method of preserving fruits and vegetables that involves removing the moisture content of the produce by exposing it to low heat. Drying helps to extend the shelf life of the produce, but it can also cause some loss of nutrients.
- **Canning:** Canning involves heating the produce and sealing it in airtight containers to kill bacteria and prevent spoilage. Canned fruits and vegetables can last for months or even years, but they may lose some of their nutritional value during the canning process.

5. (*c*) Strengths and Weaknesses of Public Food Distribution System in India: The Public Food Distribution System (PFDS) in India, also known as the Targeted Public Distribution System (TPDS), is a government-run program that aims to provide subsidized food to the poor and vulnerable sections of the population. While the PFDS has several strengths, it also has some significant weaknesses.

Strengths:

- **Food Security:** The PFDS is a critical source of food security for millions of poor people in India. It provides food grains, such as rice and wheat, at a subsidized rate to people who cannot afford to buy them at market prices.
- **Price stabilization:** The PFDS helps to stabilize the prices of essential food items. By ensuring that food grains are available to people at a fixed price, the government can prevent price hikes during times of scarcity.
- **Employment Generation:** The PFDS creates employment opportunities for people involved in the procurement, storage, and distribution of food grains. It also helps to boost the agricultural sector by providing a reliable market for farmers.
- **Poverty Alleviation:** The PFDS helps to reduce poverty by providing food to people who would otherwise go hungry. It is an important safety net for people who are unable to earn enough to feed themselves and their families.

Weaknesses:

- **Leakage and Corruption:** The PFDS is plagued by corruption and leakages at various levels. The food grains meant for the poor often end up in the hands of middlemen and black marketeers, who sell them at a higher price.
- **Inefficient Management:** The PFDS suffers from inefficient management, particularly at the state and district levels. There are often delays in the procurement, storage, and distribution of food grains, leading to shortages and wastage.

- **Limited Coverage:** The PFDS does not cover all the poor and vulnerable sections of the population. Many people who are eligible for subsidized food grains are left out of the program due to inadequate identification and targeting mechanisms.
- **Low-Quality Food:** The food grains distributed through the PFDS are often of poor quality, with high levels of impurities and adulteration. This can have adverse health consequences for people who consume them regularly.

5. (*d*) Principles and Practices of Integrated Pest and Disease Management: Integrated Pest Management (IPM) is an approach to pest control that aims to minimize the use of pesticides while effectively managing pest populations. IPM relies on a combination of strategies to prevent and control pest problems. The principles and components of IPM include:

- **Pest Identification and Monitoring:** Accurate pest identification is the first step in IPM. Identifying the pest species helps determine the best strategies to manage it. Monitoring the pest population helps to determine the severity of the infestation and to evaluate the effectiveness of the control measures.
- **Prevention:** The best way to manage pest problems is to prevent them from occurring in the first place. Prevention measures can include cultural practices such as crop rotation, sanitation, and exclusion techniques like sealing entry points for pests.
- **Cultural Control:** Cultural control involves modifying the environment to make it less hospitable to pests. Examples include planting pest-resistant crops and selecting varieties that are adapted to local conditions.
- **Biological Control:** Biological control involves using natural predators, parasites, and pathogens to control pest populations. This can include releasing beneficial insects or using microbial pesticides.
- **Chemical Control:** Chemical control involves using pesticides to manage pest populations. IPM aims to minimize the use of pesticides and use them only when necessary, and in a targeted and selective manner.
- **Evaluation:** Evaluating the effectiveness of the IPM program is important to ensure that the chosen strategies are working. Monitoring pest populations and damage levels can help identify when changes to the program are needed.

5. (*e*) Role of Brassinosteroids and Salicyclic acid Hormones in Agriculture: Brassinosteroids and salicylic acid are two types of plant hormones that play important roles in agriculture.

- Brassinosteroids are a class of plant hormones that promote plant growth and development, especially in terms of cell elongation and division. They are involved in various physiological processes such as seed germination, stem elongation, leaf expansion, and flowering. In agriculture, brassinosteroids have been used to improve crop yield and quality, increase stress tolerance, and enhance resistance to pests and diseases.
- One of the major applications of brassinosteroids in agriculture is the improvement of crop productivity. Brassinosteroids have been shown to increase yield and improve quality in a variety of crops, including rice, wheat, corn, and tomato. They can also enhance stress tolerance in plants by improving their ability to withstand environmental stressors such as drought, heat, and cold.
- Salicylic acid is another important plant hormone that plays a key role in plant defense against biotic and abiotic stress. Salicylic acid is involved in the activation of various defense mechanisms, including the production of phytoalexins,

pathogenesis-related proteins, and systemic acquired resistance. These defense mechanisms help plants to resist pathogens and pests.

- In agriculture, salicylic acid has been used to enhance the resistance of crops to various diseases and pests. For example, application of salicylic acid to tomato plants has been shown to enhance their resistance to the fungal pathogen Fusarium oxysporum. In addition to its role in plant defense, salicylic acid is also involved in regulating plant growth and development, including seed germination, root development, and flowering.
- The use of brassinosteroids and salicylic acid in agriculture has the potential to improve crop yield and quality, increase stress tolerance, and enhance resistance to pests and diseases. However, more research is needed to fully understand the mechanisms of action of these hormones and their potential applications in different crops and agricultural systems.

6. (*a*) Package of Practices for Onion Cultivation in India:

Onion is one of the most important bulb crop cultivated commercially throughout the country. The major onion producing states are Maharashtra, Karnataka, Gujarat, Odisha, Andhra Pradesh, Uttar Pradesh, Bihar, etc. Some districts of West Bengal produce onion commercially. Onions is used in making culinary as vegetables and spices both. White onions are processed and exported from India.

Varieties: Agrifound Light Red & NHRDF Red-2 (line355), Pusa Red, Pusa Madhavi, Pusa Riddhi, NHRDF Red-3 (Line 655).

Soil: To get the good yield sandy loam soil having sufficient organic matter is required. It can be well grown on light loam, deep fertile and fertile soil rich in organic matter.

Seed bed preparation: Location of the seed bed should be high land, well drained with ample sunlight and air. Height of the seed bed should be at least 15 cm from the ground level. Soil of the bed is to be dug several times to make it fine and porous. 3-4 kg well rotten FYM or 1 kg vermi compost per sq.m. should be incorporated in the soil. Soil of the bed is to be drenched with Captan or Bavistin @2-3 g/L water or formaldehyde @2 ml/L and then covered with polythene sheet for 5-7 days. Before sowing seed is to be treated with Captan or Bavistin @2-3 g/kg seed or trichoderma viridi @ 4g/kg seed. This practice of soil and seed treatment can help to reduce the seed and soil borne diseases in the seedlings.

Land preparation: One deep plouging is required after that 2-3 ploughing of rotavator.

Climate: The ideal temp. of vegetative growth 12.8-23.0°C for bulb development . It requires little higher temp. i.e. 20-25°C.

Sowing time and seed rate: The seed generally sown in raised nursery bed. The surface beds should be smooth and well leveled.

Oct.-Nov. is best time for seed sowing 10-12 kg. seed sufficient for one ha

Kharif May-June is best time for seed sowing 12-15 Kg./ha.

Seed treatment: Seed treatment with 3 gm Captan

Manure and Fertilizer: Application 20-25tones of FYM/ha. in soil considered adequate. FYM should be applied one month before transplanting and mixed in the soil. A doze of NPK (150:60:60:Kg/ha.) applied better bulb development. Whole quantity of phosphorus, potash and half nitrogen should be mixed in the before transplanting. Rest half doses of nitrogen should be given as top dressing in two equal split doses, first dose should applied at 30 days after transplanting whereas second dose at 45 days after transplanting. The top dressing must be completed before initiation of bulbing.

Transplanting: The best time of transplanting is end Dec. to first week of January. Planting of 15 × 10 cm spacing is considered to be the best.

Weed control: Weed control stomp @ 3.35 liter/ha. just after transplanting

Irrigation: First irrigation after transplanting and their after 10 to 12 days interval

Disease: Purple blotch spray Dithane M-45 @ 0.25 % after mixing sendovit 1.0 ML per liter of water. Insect: Control Thrips spray Dimethoate 2 ML per liter of water.

Harvesting: Mature in 100-120 days after transplanting.

Average yield: 300-400 qt./ha.

Post-harvest handling: It is estimated that 60-65% of onion produced in India is consumed internally, 5% is exported and 30-40% is lost by post harvest damage.

Curing: Sprouting and rotting are common problems in storage since bulbs contain high moisture. The bulbs should be adequately cured for proper development of skin colour and to remove field heat before storage of bulbs. It is done till the neck is tight and outer scales are dried. This will prevent infection of diseases and minimize shrinkage loss. Bulbs are cured either in field or in open shade or by artificial means before storage. During kharif season, bulbs are cured for 2-3 weeks along with top. In rabi, bulbs are cured in field for 3-5 days; tops are cut leaving 2.0-2.5 cm above bulb and again cured for 7-10 days to remove field heat.

Storage: After curing, bulbs are stored in well ventilated rooms by spreading them on dry and damp proof floorings or on racks. Periodical turning of bulbs and removal of rotten and sprouted bulbs is highly essential. A pre-harvest spray of maleic hydrazide (2000-2500 ppm) prevents rotting and sprouting of bulbs stored at room temperature. At BARC, Trombay irradiation of bulbs with very low doses (4000-9000 krads) of gamma rays is effective for preventing sprouting and enhancing storage life of onion bulbs. Bulbs harvested from kharif crop do not store well for long period. At 0-2-2.2°C under cold storage, bulbs can be stored for long period. NHRDF and NAFED are erected storage structures in Nasik for helping farmers. Three types of storage structures, are Panipat type 2-tiered, 3-tier onion store and 2-tier model were established by Government itself after investing heavily.

Grading: These necked, bolted and decayed bulbs are removed. Cured bulbs are graded based on size, and depending on market to which it is sent. Big sized onion is in demand in New Delhi, medium sized in Kolkata, Patna and small sized onion in North Eastern regions of the country.

Marketing: Between farmers and consumers, several intermediaries are involved in marketing of onions. After entry of NAFED in onion trade, farmers' co-operatives are playing a key role in marketing. Lasalgoan is the biggest onion market in India. November - June is the peak period of onion in market.

Export: India is the third biggest exporter of onion, next to Netherlands and Spain, in world. Major export is to Gulf countries, Malaysia, Singapore, Sri Lanka and Bangladesh. Export of onion is channelised through NAFED. Depending on preference of colour and size of bulbs, different varieties are exported. Middle East countries prefer light red to dark red bulbs. In Malaysia preference is for dark red bulbs. In America and Japan, demand is for yellowish or brown onion having mild pungency. Europe and Japan markets prefer large sized bulbs while in Singapore, demand is for small onions. Onion accounts for major share (nearly 75%) of vegetables exported from India.

6. (*b*) Growth and Development in Plants: Growth is defined as a vital process that brings about a permanent and irreversible change in any plant or its part in respect to its size, form, weight and volume. Growth is restricted only to living cells and is accomplished by metabolic processes involving synthesize of macromolecules, such as nucleic acids, proteins, lipids and polysaccharides at the expense of metabolic energy. Growth at cellular level is also accompanied by the organization of macromolecules into assemblages of membranes, plastids, mitochondria, ribosome and other cell organelles. Cells do not definitely increase in size but divide, giving rise to daughter cells. An important process during cell division is synthesis and replication of nuclear DNA in the chromosomes, which is then passed into the daughter cells. Therefore, the term growth is used to denote an increase in size by cell division and cell enlargement, together with the synthesis of new cellulose materials and the organization of cellular organelles

"Development" and "growth" are sometimes used interchangeably in conversation, but in a botanical sense they describe separate events in the organization of the mature plant body. Development is the progression from earlier to later stages in maturation, e.g. a fertilized egg develops into a mature tree. It is the process whereby tissues, organs, and whole plants are produced. It involves: growth, morphogenesis (the acquisition of form and structure), and differentiation. The interactions of the environment and the genetic instructions inherited by the cells determine how the plant develops. Growth is the irreversible change in size of cells and plant organs due to both cell division and enlargement. Enlargement necessitates a change in the elasticity of the cell walls together with an increase in the size and water content of the vacuole. Growth can be determinate-when an organ or part or whole organism reaches a certain size and then stops growing-or indeterminate-when cells continue to divide indefinitely. Plants in general have indeter-minate growth.

Various Parameters for Measuring the Plant Growth: Growth in plants being a quantitative phenomenon can be measured in relation to time. It can be measured in terms of:

- Increase in length or growth - in case of stem and root;
- Increase in area or volume - in case of leaves and fruits;
- Increase in the number of cells - in algae, yeast and bacteria.

Direct Method: Heredity we know that growth generally takes place at the apical region of plant. So growth in length can be directly measured by means of an ordinary measuring scale at any particular interval of time.

Auxanometer: For more accurate measurement of length, we can use the specially designed equipment called auxanometer (Fig.). We can use it to measure the rate of growth of shoot length of plants. A thread is tied to the tip of stem of a potted plant and the thread is hung on the pulley of auxanometer. The other end of the thread is tied to a weight. The pulley is fixed with a long needle, which slides over a graduated arc. As the stem grows in length the weight pulls the thread down. The movement of the needle is read on the scale of arc.

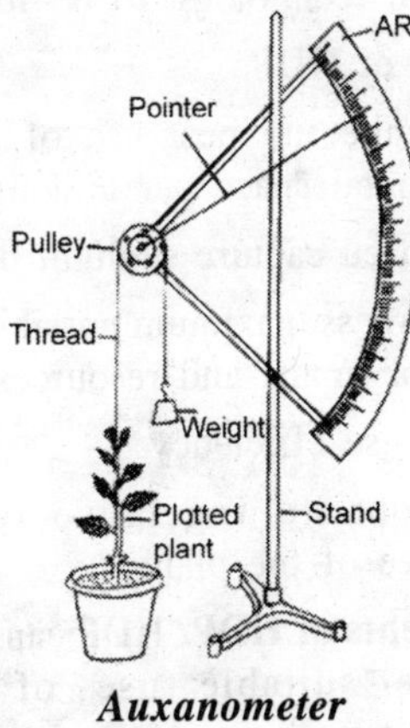

Auxanometer

6. (*c*) High Density Planting System in Fruit Crops along with Suitable Examples: High density planting is defined as planting at a density in excess which gives maximum crop yield at maturity if the individual tree grows to its full natural size. HDP system is normally understood as a system in which a higher number of plants are accommodated within a unit area in comparison to the conventional planting density.

High density planting technique is a modern method of fruit cultivation involving of fruit trees densely, allowing small or dwarf tree with modified canopy for better light interception and distribution and ease of mechanized field operation. HDP gives higher yield as well as return/unit area. It is possible by regular pruning and use of bio regulators for maintaining the size and shape of the tree. It is well known that the diversity in soil and climate conditions in India permits growing of a large variety of Tropical, Subtropical and Temperate fruits in different regions, due to which India is regarded as a horticultural paradise. In recent years, the concept of fruit production is undergoing a change where emphasis is being given to higher production per unit area. High density planting system is the fastest way of reducing the gestation period and increasing the productivity of the orchards. The choice of the system of planting in the orchard depends on topography, crop variety, plant density, production technology to be followed.

Principle of HDP

- To make the best use of vertical and horizontal space per unit time.
- Increased capture sunlight per unit area.
- To harness maximum possible returns per unit of inputs and resources.
- Land use efficiency.
- Appropriate vegetative reproductive balance of the plants.

Components of HDP: HDP can be achieved with the suitable use of following components:

- Dwarf scion varieties
- Dwarf rootstocks and inter-stocks
- Training and pruning
- Use of growth regulators

Advantages of High Density Planting System in Fruit Crops

High Density Planting System (HDPS) is a modern agricultural technique used in fruit crops that involves planting trees at much higher densities than traditional orchards. Here are some advantages of HDPS in fruit crops:

- **Increased yield:** HDPS maximizes the use of available space and resources, resulting in higher yields per unit area. With more trees per hectare, the overall yield of fruit per unit area is significantly increased.
- **Early bearing:** HDPS systems promote early bearing in fruit crops, allowing growers to harvest fruit earlier than traditional orchards. This can lead to earlier returns on investment and a more rapid return on the cost of planting and maintaining the orchard.
- **Improved fruit quality:** HDPS provides better light distribution, resulting in better fruit quality and increased fruit size. The trees in a HDPS orchard are pruned to maintain a compact size, leading to more efficient use of nutrients and water resources, which in turn enhances the quality of the fruit.
- **Increased efficiency:** HDPS requires less labor for planting, pruning, thinning, and harvesting, as compared to traditional orchards. This leads to lower labor costs, which can be a significant advantage for growers.
- **Enhanced pest and disease management:** In HDPS, trees are pruned to maintain a compact size, making it easier to manage pests and diseases. HDPS can also reduce the spread of diseases by allowing for better air circulation and sunlight penetration.
- **Sustainable use of land:** HDPS maximizes the use of land by increasing the number of trees per unit area. This leads to more efficient use of resources such as land, water, and fertilizers. In turn, this can lead to more sustainable and environmentally friendly farming practices.

Previous Years' Paper (Solved)

Indian Forest Service (Main) Exam, 2021

SUBJECT—AGRICULTURE

(Exam held on 04-03-2022)

PAPER-I

INSTRUCTIONS: *There are EIGHT questions in all, out of which FIVE are to be attempted. Question Nos. 1 & 5 are compulsory. Out of the remainin SIX questions, THREE are to be attempted selecting at least ONE question from each of the two Sections A and B. Attempts of questions shall be counted in sequential order. Unless struck off, attempt of a question shall be counted even if attempted partly. Any page or portion of the page left blank in the Question-cum-Answer Booklet must be clearly struck off. All questions carry equal marks. Answers must be written in ENGLISH only. Neat sketches may be drawn, wherever required.*

SECTION–A

1. (*a*) Establish the relationship between Nature, Indian culture and Indian agriculture.

(*b*) List down the principles of ecology.

(*c*) Enlist different groups of soils found in India and discuss any one in detail.

(*d*) Explain various concepts of agroforestry and discuss their benefits towards sustainable development.

(*e*) Describe technological options for stabilizing agricultural production in rainfed areas.

2. (*a*) Environmental pollution is hazardous to crops. Describe with examples.

(*b*) Describe the role of organic matter in maintaining soil productivity.

(*c*) Enlist the problems of dryland agriculture and describe soil constraints in detail.

3. (*a*) Enlist the methods of weed control and discuss the physical control of weeds in detail.

(*b*) Discuss Integrated Farming System (IFS) with suitable examples. How can IFS improve livelihoods of small and marginal farmers?

(*c*) Enlist the factors for conserving moisture and improving the productivity of soil and describe the vegetative cover factor in detail.

4. (*a*) What is Land Equivalent Ratio (LER)? Give advantages and disadvantages of LER.

(*b*) Discuss the factors affecting phosphate fixation in soil.

(*c*) Write a short note on contour bunding to prevent soil erosion.

SECTION–B

5. (*a*) Describe three distinct phases of evaluation of extension programmes and the need for extension evaluation.

(*b*) Enlist and briefly explain the roles to be played by Agricultural Extension professionals to ensure quality extension services.

(*c*) Enumerate the ways and means of how farm planning helps the cultivators to bring efficiency in farming.

(*d*) Enlist and explain various dimensions of market.

(*e*) Describe the types of sprinkler irrigation systems.

6. (*a*) Classify and briefly explain different types of trainings offered according to the stage of career of extension professionals.

(*b*) Write the causes of waterlogging. Describe in brief about system of surface drainage.

(*c*) Enlist and explain advantages and problems of farm budgeting.

7. (*a*) Describe the criteria for scheduling irrigation in detail.

(*b*) Describe the motives behind Cooperation. Explain three-tier structure of Cooperative Credit Society.

(*c*) Enumerate key functions of State Agricultural Management and Extension Training Institute (SAMETI).

8. (*a*) Describe the implications of strong linkages between ATMA and KVK in strengthening extension services.

(*b*) Enlist different hazards associated with irrigation water quality and discuss the management practices for efficient use of saline water for irrigation.

(*c*) Enumerate and explain factors affecting cost of marketing of agricultural produce.

PAPER-II

INSTRUCTIONS: *There are EIGHT questions in all, out of which FIVE are to be attempted. Question Nos. 1 & 5 are compulsory. Out of the remaining SIX questions, THREE are to be attempted selecting at least ONE question from each of the two Sections A and B. Attempts of questions shall be counted in sequential order. Unless struck off, attempt of a question shall be counted even if attempted partly. Any page or portion of the page left blank in the Question-cum-Answer Booklet must be clearly struck off. All questions carry equal marks. Answers must be written in ENGLISH only. Neat sketches may be drawn, wherever required.*

SECTION–A

1. (*a*) What is the principle of independent assortment in inheritance of genes? Describe the experiment used by Mendel.

(*b*) Explain the mechanisms which promote cross-pollination.

(*c*) Why is quarantine regulation on seeds needed? Explain the actions to be recommended for this purpose.

(*d*) Describe the factors affecting the rate of transpiration and its significance in crop production.

(*e*) Discuss the genetic basis of heterosis and inbreeding depression.

2. (*a*) What is polyploidy? Define the ways in which polyploidy can occur.

(*b*) What is micropropagation? Discuss its advantages. Name the types of explants used in micropropagation in important crops.

(*c*) Explain how synthetic varieties are produced and indicate their merits.

3. (*a*) Differentiate between linkage and crossing over. Did Mendel recognize the phenomenon of linkage? Explain.

(*b*) What is distant hybridization? Explain how it is used for developing new varieties.

(*c*) What are the characters of purelines? Describe the procedure for pureline selection with achievements made in agriculture.

4. (*a*) Describe somaclonal variation and its importance. Discuss the causes and factors influencing such variation.

(*b*) What is dormancy of seed? Explain the causes of seed dormancy and methods to break the dormancy.

(*c*) Discuss the photosynthetic pigments in plants and the factors influencing photosynthesis.

SECTION–B

5. (*a*) What are plant growth regulators? Explain the functions of auxins in plants and mechanism of their action.

(*b*) Describe the package of practices for banana cultivation in North India.

(*c*) What are the challenges in fruit and vegetable marketing in India? Suggest suitable remedial measures.

(*d*) Define acellular plant pathogens and discuss their mode of natural transmission. Name five acellular pathogens and symptoms induced by them in potato.

(*e*) Discuss the national plan for supply and distribution of food grains.

6. (*a*) Describe the procedures involved in Hi-tech nursery production.

(*b*) What are baculovirus and entomopathogenic fungi? Discuss their role in pest management.

(*c*) Discuss the relation of food production to national dietary pattern and protein-energy malnutrition.

7. (*a*) Discuss the following :

(*i*) Physiological disorders in cauliflower

(*ii*) Physiological disorders in tomato

(*iii*) Quincunx system of orchard planting

(*b*) Describe the biology, nature of damage and management of the following stored grain pests:

(*i*) Lesser grain borer

(*ii*) Pulse beetle

(*iii*) Rice moth

(*c*) Describe the influence of photoperiodism and vernalisation in flowering of plants.

8. (*a*) Explain the methods to prolong vase-life of cut flowers.

(*b*) Describe the following:

(*i*) Neonicotinoid insecticide

(*ii*) Systemic fungicide

(*iii*) Insecticide granules

(*c*) Describe the systematic position, nature of damage and management of the following:

(*i*) Chilli thrips

(*ii*) Fall armyworm

(*iii*) Citrus greening

ANSWERS

PAPER-I

1. (*a*) Originally the term agriculture is derived from two Latin words 'Ager' and 'Cultura'. Ager means land and cultura means cultivation *i.e.*, tilling the soil and preparing it for planting of crops. Putting the two words together *i.e.*, land and cultivation, agriculture could be regarded as land cultivation. In modern day farming, this definition is no longer acceptable as agriculture means much more than land cultivation. Modern agriculture therefore could be defined as the production of crops and rearing of animals for the purpose of producing food for man's use and raw materials for industries. Agriculture is the process of producing food, feed, fiber and many other desired products by the cultivation of certain plants and the raising of domesticated animals (livestock). Agriculture's primary role is that it gives food to the people, provides raw material for industry, employment to many people, capital for agrarian development, surpluses for national economy if practised quite efficiently. Agriculture has been the strongest and the foundational culture of India. Yes, once upon a time more than eighty percent of the population was involved in agriculture and that number has fallen to just about 50% today. However, farming and agriculture has always moved beyond being mere means to livelihood.

1. (*b*) **The Ten Principles of Ecology**

- **Evolution organizes ecological systems into hierarchies:** Individual organisms combine into populations, populations combine into species, species combine into higher taxa like genera and phyla. Each can be characterized by its abundance and diversity (number of kinds) in each ecosystem or study plot. How and why abundance and diversity vary in time and space is the basic question of ecology.
- **The sun is the ultimate source of energy for most ecosystems:** Life runs on the carbon-rich sugars produced by photosynthesis; every ecosystem's sugar output depends on how much solar energy and precipitation it receives.
- **Organisms are chemical machines that run on energy:** The laws of chemistry and physics limit the ways each organism makes a living and provide a basic framework for ecology. The supply of chemical elements and the sugars needed to fuel their assembly into organisms limit the abundance and diversity of life.
- **Chemical nutrients cycle repeatedly while energy flows through an ecosystem:** The atoms of elements like C, N, P, and Na go back and forth from spending time in living to spending time in dead parts of an ecosystem. But the photons of solar energy can be used only once before they are lost to the universe.
- **$dN/dt = B - X + I$:** The rate that a population's abundance in a given area increases or decreases reflects the balance of its births, deaths, and net migration into the area. Individuals with features that improve their ability to survive (*i.e.*, not die) and make copies of themselves will tend to increase in that population.
- **$dS/dt = D - X + I$:** The rate that the diversity of species in an area changes reflects the balance of the number of new

forms that arise, those that go extinct, and those that migrate into the area. Individuals and species that have features allowing them to survive and reproduce in a local environment will tend to persist there.

- **Organisms interact—do things to each other—in ways that influence their abundance:** Individual organisms can eat one another, compete for shared resources, and help each other survive. Each pair of species in an ecosystem can be characterized by the kind and strength of these interactions, measured as their contribution to dN/dt.
- **Ecosystems are organized into webs of interactions:** The abundance of a population is influenced by the chains of interactions that connect it to the other species in its ecosystem. This often leads to complex behaviour, and a key challenge in ecology is to determine what patterns of abundance and diversity can be predicted.
- **Human populations have an outsized role in competing with, preying upon, and helping other organisms:** Humans are one of millions of species embedded in Earth's ecosystems. The ability of humans to change the planet, abetted by our large population size and technological prowess, increases our ability to shape the biosphere's future. Humans, through principles 1-8, are currently changing the climate, re-arranging its chemistry, decreasing populations of food, moving around its species, and decreasing its diversity.
- **Ecosystems provide essential services to human populations:** These include products like timber, fiber and food, regulating water and air quality, and cultural benefits like recreation. A key goal of ecology is to use principles 1-9 to preserve ecosystem services.

1. (*c*) Major Soil Groups available in India: Some of the major soil groups available in India are: 1. Alluvial Soils 2. Black Soils 3. Red Soils 4. Laterite and Lateritic Soils 5. Forest and Mountain Soils 6. Arid and Desert Soils 7. Saline and Alkaline Soils 8. Peaty and Marshy Soils. India is a country of vast dimensions with varied conditions of geology, relief, climate and vegetation. Therefore, India has a large variety of soil groups, distinctly different from one another. Different criteria have been applied to classify Indian soils, the outstanding being geology, relief, fertility, chemical composition and physical structure, etc.

Alluvial Soils: Alluvial soils are by far the largest and the most important soil group of India. Covering about 15 lakh sq km or about 45.6 per cent of the total land area of the country, these soils contribute the largest share of our agricultural wealth and support the bulk of India's population.

Most of the alluvial soils are derived from the sediments deposited by rivers as in the Indo-Gangetic plain although some alluvial soils in the coastal areas have been formed by the sea waves. Thus, the parent material of these soils is all transported origin. The streams bring with them the products of weathering of rocks from the mountains and deposit them in the low-lying areas. The alluvial soils are yet immature and have weak profiles.

They differ in consistency from drift sand to rich loams and from silts to stiff clays. A few occasional kankar beds are also present. However, pebbly, stony or gravelly soils are rare in this group. The chemical composition of the alluvial soils makes this group of soils as one of the most fertile in the world. The proportion of nitrogen is generally low, but potash, phosphoric acid and alkalies are adequate, while iron oxide and lime vary within a wide range. The porosity and texture provide good drainage and other conditions favourable for bumper crops. These soils are easily replenished by the recurrent river floods and support uninterruped crop growth.

The widest occurrence of the alluvial soils is in the Great Indo-Gangetic Plain starting from Punjab in the west-to-West Bengal and Assam in the east. They also occur in deltas of the Mahanadi, the Godavari, the Krishna and the Cauvery, where they are called deltaic alluvium. Along the coast they are known as coastal alluvium. Some alluvial soils are found in the Narmada and Tapi valleys. Northern parts of Gujarat also have some cover of alluvial soils. Geologically, the alluvium of the Great plain of India is divided into newer or younger khadar and older bhangar soils. The khadar soils are found in the low areas of valley bottom which are flooded almost every year.

They are pale brown, sandy clays and loams, more dry and leached, less calcareous and carbonaceous *i.e.,* they are less kankary. Bhangar, on the other hand, is found on the higher reaches about 30 metres above the flood level. It is of a more clayey composition and is generally dark coloured. A few metres below the surface of the bhangar are beds of lime nodules known as kankar. Along the Shiwalik foothills, there are alluvial fans having coarse, often pebbly soils. This zone is called bhabar. To the south of the bhabar is a long narrow strip of swampy lowland with silty soils. It covers an area of 56,600 sq km and is called tarai. The tarai soils are rich in nitrogen and organic matter but are deficient in phosphate. These soils are generally covered by tall grasses and forests but are suitable for a number of crops such as wheat, rice, sugarcane, jute and soyabean under reclaimed conditions. Due to their softness of the strata and fertility the alluvial soils are best suited to irrigation and respond well to canal and well/tube-well irrigation. When properly irrigated, the alluvial soils yield splendid crops of rice, wheat, sugarcane, tobacco, cotton, jute, maize, oilseeds, vegetables and fruits.

1. (*d*) Concept of Agroforestry

Agroforestry is the art and science of growing woody and non-woody plants together on the same unit of land for range of benefits.

Agroforestry is the use of land for a combination of agriculture and forestry. In other words, the practice of growing tree crops or some other fast growing trees along with the main crop. Agroforestry is one of the important sustainable land management techniques, involving a combination of different agricultural, horticultural, forestry, and livestock practices. Sometimes it is closely related to community forestry and homestead forestry.

Agroforestry Benefits Towards Sustainable Development

1. Environmental/ecological benefits:

- Better protection of crops and lives from environmental hazards such as flood, drought, cyclone etc.
- Conserved biodiversity.
- Improved microclimate—such as reduce soil temperature, reduces evaporation of soil moisture.
- Purification of air and water.
- Reduce use and chemical fertilizer.
- Reduce pressure on forests.
- Protect lands through reduction of surface run-off and soil erosion.
- Increase soil nutrients through of addition decomposition of litterfall.
- More efficient recycling of nutrients by deep-rooted trees.
- Improve soil structures through the constant addition of organic matter from decomposed litter.

2. Economic benefits:

- Diversifies the range outputs a given area.
- Increase the value of outputs from a given area of land.
- Reduces in incidence of total crop failure, common to single or monocropping systems.

- Spread the needs for labour inputs more evenly through the year.
- Provides productive use of underutilized land, labour and capital.
- Increases in levels of farm incomes due to improved and sustained productivity.

3. **Social benefits:**
   - Improved in rural living standards from sustained employment higher incomes.
   - Improved in nutrition and health due to increased quality and diversity of food outputs.
   - Stabilization and improvement of upland communities through elimination of the need to shift sites of farm activities.

4. **Biological benefits:**
   - Increase crop productivity.
   - Sustain crop productivity.
   - Produce diversified foods.
   - Increase forest productivity.
   - Increase fruit supply.
   - Decrease weed infection.

Agroforestry systems tend to protect soil from several adverse effects. Most agroforestry systems constitute sustainable land use and improve soils in a number of ways:

- Reduction of loss of soil by reducing surface run-off.
- It adds C through decomposable biomass.
- Enrich the soil through biological nitrogen fixation.
- It improves soil physical conditions by increasing water holding capacity.
- It helps in nutrient recycling that conserve soil.
- It protects the natural flora and fauna within the soil.

1. (*e*) Rainfed areas account for nearly 57 per cent of the agricultural land in India. These areas assume special significance in terms of ecology, agricultural productivity and livelihoods for millions. With proper management, rainfed areas have the potential of contributing a larger share to food grain production. In-fact the potential is such that there is more opportunity for faster agricultural growth here than in irrigated areas.

- Rainfed agriculture is a type of farming that relies on rainfall for water. It provides much of the food consumed by poor communities in developing countries.
- Rainfed areas in India are highly diverse, ranging from resource rich areas to resource-constrained areas.
- Some of the resource rich areas are highly productive and have experienced widespread adoption of technology. However, most of the areas are resource constrained and dry areas.
- In the resource constrained and dry areas, the farming is a survival mechanism rather than a growth oriented activity.
- Rainfed agriculture contributes to 60 per cent of the value of agriculture GDP of India.
- Rainfed agriculture is practiced under a wide variety of soil types, agro-climatic and rainfall conditions ranging from 400 mm to 1600 mm per annum.
- Rainfed Crops are prone to breaks in the monsoon during the crop growth due to water stress.
- This water stress may be due to variability of rainfall, delay in sowing, diversity in crop management practice and variability of the soil type.
- The prolonged breaks can result in partial or complete failure of the crops.

Rainfed Area Development Programme (RADP) that Stabilizing Agricultural Production

- Rainfed Area Development Programme (RADP) was implemented as a sub-scheme under Rashtriya Krishi Vikas Yojana (RKVY).

- To improve quality of life of farmers, especially, small and marginal farmers by offering a complete package of activities to maximize farm returns.
- Increasing agricultural productivity of rainfed areas in a sustainable manner by adopting appropriate farming system based approaches.
- To minimise the adverse impact of possible crop failure due to drought, flood or uneven rainfall distribution through diversified and composite farming systems.
- Restoration of confidence in rainfed agriculture by creating sustained employment opportunities through improved on-farm technologies and cultivation practices.
- Enhancement of farmer's income and livelihood support for reduction of poverty in rainfed areas.
- The basic endeavour of this programme is to encourage exploitation of different farming systems based on the natural resource endowments created by the farmer or by schemes like the Mahatma Gandhi National Rural Employment Guarantee Act (MNREGA), Rashtriya Krishi Vikas Yojana (RKVY), National Horticulture Mission (NHM).

2. (*a*) Crops are source of fiber, fuel, shelter, and nutrition. During photosynthesis, they absorb carbon dioxide from the air and release oxygen, which humans and other animals need to breathe. Most plants are capable of removing pollutants from the environment through bioaccumulation and incorporating them in their tissues. While these abilities are good news for us, as plants are helpful in mitigating impacts of pollution in the environment where we live, making it safer and cleaner, even they have their limits and get affected by pollutants to a varying degree.

How does pollution affect Crops in general?

Pollution is a widespread problem affecting the world as a whole. It comes in many forms including air, land, and water pollution and from a variety of sources including industry, commercial, and transportation sectors. Some forms of pollution are clearly visible, other forms are invisible to the naked eye. Pollution does not only affect animals and humans, it has many negative effects on plants as well. As a matter of fact, plants reveal toxins in the environment sooner than their effects would show on our health. This is because in most cases pollutants alter plant metabolism and make plant weak and vulnerable to disease or pest infestation. Some of the recognizable signs of these processes include leaf damage (yellowing, falling leaves or injuries), poor growth, root damage, and inability to photosynthesize properly which results in stunted growth and diminishing productivity.

Environmental Pollution is Hazardous to Crops

The impact of air pollution on crops: Air pollution comes from many sources such as smokestack from factories, burning of fossil fuels for energy, emissions from transport, agriculture (livestock) or even fumes from paints, varnish, VOCs, or during the solid waste management such as waste incineration or gas leakage from landfills that are not sanitary. The effects of air pollution on plants can be either direct or indirect.

Direct effect is when toxins harm plants by depositing on them directly from the air and affecting their leaf metabolism and uptake of carbon, which they need to build their body and get energy to live. The chemicals responsible for direct pollution include ozone and nitrogen oxides.

Indirect effect happens via soil and starts at the roots. Some air pollutants, like heavy metals (lead, cadmium, mercury) from industrial activities, fall on the ground and change soil chemistry and pH. Plants then have problems with obtaining enough nutrients they need to thrive. Plants usually show damage in a variety of ways, including visible signs of damage like necrotic lesions on leaves, stunted plant growth, changing in leaf colour including chlorosis (aka yellowing leaves), reddening, bronzing, mottling.

Effects of particulate matter or dust on plants: Particulate matter are very fine particles that get stirred in the air from different sources (industries, agriculture). Particulate matter does mechanical harm to plants. Small particles fall on the leaves and reduce light penetration or even block the opening of stomata, thus preventing their proper function. Smaller particles even enter stomata and interact with the biochemistry of plant metabolism this way. Things can get as far as actually preventing the plant from properly photosynthesizing. Plants that are affected by this pollution could lose the most affected leaves or fade due to the inability to photosynthesize. Leaves can also sustain chemical injuries, lesions, if the deposited dust reacts with water from the environment. Alkaline dust turns to toxic for plants when reacting with water. Imagine that someone applies thick coating of irritative substance on your skin and you are unable to remove it. That is probably how plants feel in this situation, since they are unable to remove the dust coating. During the long-term exposure plants are under stress. Some fruit trees like peaches and cherries, for example, experience shorter flowering periods and drop fruits too soon. Their overall productivity is reduced.

Effects of photochemical smog on plants: Photochemical smog occurs during chemical reactions among nitrous oxides from industrial activities and VOCs originating either from vegetation or human activities. The chemical reactions are driven by sunlight, that's why the name - photochemical smog. Everyone of us is probably even familiar with this type of pollution. Photochemical smog creates that orange haze over cities in the summer, which also correlates with the time when most plants are flowering. One of the resulting products of these chemical reactions is ground level ozone, which has dangerous impact on vegetation.

Ozone pollution - the harmful effect of ozone on plant growth: The ground level ozone is formed when volatile organic compounds react with nitrogen oxides in the presence of sunlight. You can easily recognize the orange-tinged smog one sees in urban areas when nitrogen oxides and volatile organic compounds, emissions from industrial facilities, chemical solvents, motor vehicle exhaust or gasoline vapors cook together in the sunlight. Ground level ozone is major pollutant that greatly affects terrestrial plants and does lot of harm to agricultural crops. So much that there have been numerous studies, which measure its effect on crops, carried out throughout the years. It is, for example, known that crops like soybean and peanut are more sensitive to ozone than corn or wheat. Ozone damages plants by preventing photosynthesis and obstructing stomata, restricting respiration and stunting plant growth. When plants are exposed to this ozone throughout the season, they first exhibit signs of damage on their leaves in the form of tiny light and dark spots, later followed by bronzing and reddening. Later, leaves turn pale due to the lack of photosynthetic activity (chlorosis) and may die out.

How acid rain affects plants?

One harmful pollutant that damages plants is acid rain. Acid rain is formed when one or both of sulphur dioxide and nitrogen oxides react with water, oxygen, and other chemicals in the atmosphere, process which often happens in the presence of fossil fuel combustion. This leads to the formation of sulphuric acid and nitric acid. Acid rain comes in two main forms: wet and dry. Wet rain is any form of precipitation involving water, and could include snow, fog, hail, rain, or dew. Dry deposition occurs when acid particles are formed in the atmosphere in the absence of water. These can then attach themselves to particles in the air and are deposited on the ground during events such as dust-storms. When acid rain reaches earth's surface, it causes damage to the soil, water, and plants. Not only does direct exposure to acid rain directly damage plants, it damages leaves and makes it harder for the plant or tree to photosynthesize and regulate the exchange of gasses.

Acid rain also affects the quality of soils, as it pollutes them and indirectly damages plants by dissolving and washing away nutrients they need and minerals from the soil (for example, magnesium, sodium, potassium, and calcium) on which the plants rely. When acid rain deposits in water, it's pH drops, and water becomes acidic. Plants that are not tolerant to acidity would suffer immediately by not being able to utilize such water. Acid rain may also impair the efficiency of nutrient and water uptake by plants when changing chemistry of soils by mobilizing metals like toxic aluminum, which affects plant metabolism.

Water pollution toxicity to plants: Water pollution is degraded water, toxic for the flora and fauna. It occurs when harmful chemicals or microorganisms or waste or too much sediment contaminates sources of freshwater and groundwater. Water pollution happens in various ways, such as sewage leakage, industrial spills, direct discharge into water bodies, biological contamination, or farm runoff (including pesticides, fertilizers). Contamination of water has many negative effects on plants that reflect this delicate relationship. Sometimes there is an excess of nutrients in water, like in case of agricultural runoff with high concentration of nitrogen and phosphorus, which causes an excess in plant growth. Plants grow leaves and thin branches too fast, while their root system remains too undeveloped and cannot provide enough nutrients for plant to successfully mature and reproduce. After the initial green boom, plants become weak and vulnerable to disease or weather. For example, pH higher than 7.5 could lead to insufficient intake of iron. Plants deprived of iron experience iron chlorosis. Iron deprived plants have yellow leaves with dark green veins. Over time, leaves could turn to white.

Soil pollution effects on vegetation: Sources of soil pollution can be direct, for example, from dumping toxic chemicals directly on to a site, or indirect like deposition of toxic chemicals from particulate matter that come from air pollution. Air pollutants can travel long distances and do not respect any boundaries or regions of a special ecological significance. It can be surprising how far particles can actually travel when blown with the wind. They can contaminate soils even hundreds of miles away from the origin of pollution. Acid rain also belongs to soil pollutants that affect crop.

In other cases, crop get poisoned by toxic substances stored in contaminated soils. For example, pesticides, that leak to vegetation surrounding agricultural fields, can severely burn plant leaves when in contact with them or worse intoxicate the plants and kill them. Everything in nature is interconnected. Pollution of all kinds can damage crop and cause harm to the environment. Once a plant has been weakened, it makes them more susceptible to disease and insect infestation. This is also true for crops or other plants we rely on for food. Animals who eat polluted plants ingest these pollutants and have health problems. It is important to know that pollution causes a variety of damage to the planet as a whole.

2. (*b*) People often think of organic matter as the plant and animal residues incorporated into the soil. They see a pile of leaves, manure, or plant parts and think, "Wow! I'm adding a lot of organic matter to the soil." This is actually organic material, not organic matter. Organic matter causes soil to clump and form soil aggregates, which improve soil structure. With better soil structure, infiltration of water through the soil improves, in turn improving the soil's ability to take up and hold water. Organic matter is stable in the soil; it has been decomposed until it is resistant to further decomposition. Usually, only around 5% of it mineralises yearly. That rate increases if temperature, oxygen, and moisture conditions become favourable for decomposition, which often occurs with excessive tillage. It is the stable organic matter that is analysed in the soil test.

Soils that have developed under forest vegetation usually have comparably low organic matter levels. There are at least two reasons for this:

- Trees produce a much smaller root mass per acre than grass plants.
- Trees do not die back and decompose every year. Instead, much of the organic material in a forest is tied up in the tree instead of being returned to the soil.

Soils that formed under prairie vegetation usually have native organic matter levels at least twice as high as those formed under forest vegetation. Organic material is anything that was alive and is now in or on the soil. For it to become organic matter, it must be decomposed into humus.

Role of organic matter in maintaining Soil Fertility: Organic matter causes soil to clump and form soil aggregates, which improve soil structure. With better soil structure, infiltration of water through the soil improves, in turn improving the soii's ability to take up and hold water.

Organic matter is stable in the soil; it has been decomposed until it is resistant to further decomposition. Organic matter (O.M.) plays a significant role in crop production and soil health. Building and maintaining a healthy soil that has more O.M. can aid in providing a stronger foundation for higher crop yields and resiliency to environmental stresses. Higher soil O.M. levels often translate into sustainable systems that produce higher, more consistent yields and greater long-term profitability.

The importance of soil organic matter in relation to soil fertility and physical conditions is widely recognised. However, organic matter contributes to the fertility or productivity of the soil through its positive effects on the chemical, physical, and biological properties of the soil.

In the formation of a fertile soil, organic substances play a direct role, as they are the sources of plant nutrients which are liberated in available forms during mineralization. The functions of organic matter depend on the process of decomposition, and hence the production of a large quantity of residues as well as their subsequent decay in the soil is necessary for good soil and crop management.

The role of organic matter in soil is so varied and extensive that it makes one think of the claims printed on old-time patent medicine labels; fortunately, these for organic matter are all true:

1. Organic matter influences the soil colour. Due to presence of adequate amount of organic matter in soil, the colour will be brown to dark brown or black.
2. Organic matter binds soil particles (sand, silt and clay) into structural units called aggregates. These aggregates help to maintain porous, open and granular condition. Hence organic matter has a profound effect on the improvement of soil structure and thereby soil maintains favourable condition of aeration and permeability. Organic matter supplies polysaccharides (long chain sugars) which also help for the genesis of good soil structure.

3. The rate of infiltration and percolation of water is enhanced by the application of organic matter in the soil. Drainage condition of soils can also be improved with the application of organic matter.
4. Water holding capacity (WHC) is increased by the application of organic matter. The amount of available water in sandy and loamy soils increases with the application of organic matter.
5. Organic matter reduces plasticity, cohesion, stickiness etc. in soils containing appreciable amounts of clay.
6. Organic matter increases the ability of the soil to resist erosion. It also reduces the surface run-off by providing good infiltration.
7. Organic matter affects the densities of soil especially bulk density of soil which in turn influence the soil porosity favourably.
8. Organic matter reduces losses of surface soil by wind erosion by forming granules with soil particles.
9. The presence of coarse organic matter on the soil surface provides mulching and thereby lower soil temperature during the summer season and keeps the soil warmer in winter season. It also acts as an insulator, retarding heat movement between the atmosphere and the soil.
10. During decomposition of organic matter various organic acids and CO_2 liberate in the soil which help to reduce alkalinity of soil.
11. Organic matter has high cation adsorption capacity. It has two to thirty times more cation adsorption capacity than that of mineral soil colloids. Besides this, organic matter accounts for 30 to 90 per cent of the adsorbing power of mineral soils. Since organic matter possesses different functional groups, it has been estimated that 54 per cent of the exchange positions in soil organic matter were attributable to carboxyl groups, 36 per cent to phenolic and enolic hydroxyl groups, and 10 per cent to imide nitrogen groups.
12. Organic matter also acts as a buffering agent. Due to such buffering effect it reduces the likelihood of damage to plant roots from excessive acids, alkalies or salts, whether naturally present in the soil or added to it in the form of fertilizers and thus stabilizes the soil pH.
13. Organic matter has solubilizing effect on some mineral compounds present in the soil. The simplest form of action of organic substances on the mineral part of the soil is the dissolution of mineral compounds by the root exudates (CO_2 and organic acids) and by various products derived from microbial activity which ultimately bring about the conversion of a number of chemical elements into forms available to plants.
14. Organic matter can be considered as a store house of various nutrients; essential to plant growth. Organic matter is the source of 90-95 per cent of the nitrogen in unfertilized soils. In addition, organic matter supplies available phosphorus, sulphur, and some other micronutrients like Fe, Mn, Cu and Zn etc. to the soil and thereby increases the nutrient regime as well as improves the soil health. Organic matter should be regarded as a positive asset to high crop production.
15. Organic matter temporarily absorb heavy metal pollutants (lead, cadmium etc.) which are usually derived from applied waste waters used for irrigation. Adsorption of pollutants helps clean contaminated water.
16. Organic matter serves as a source of energy for both macro- and micro-organisms and helps in performing various beneficial functions in soil (e.g. nitrogen fixation, mineralization etc.).

17. Organic matter acts as a chelate. A chelate (keylate) is any organic compound than can bound to a metal (usually Fe, Zn, Cu, Mn etc.) by more than one bond and form a ring or cyclic structure by that bonding. The soluble chelates probably help mobilize these micro-nutrients, increasing their availability to plants and mobility in soils.
18. Various organic substances like vitamins, antibiotics and growth-promoting compounds namely auxin are produced by different micro-organisms during decomposition of various organic matter. Auxins enhance the growth of plants by influencing seed germination, root growth etc. Fungi toxic substances derived from organic matter may minimise the incidence of diseases.
19. Organic matter interact with organic pesticides and it can sorb N and S oxides from the atmosphere which have implications with respect to both the yields of crop plants and the quality of the environment respectively.

2. (*c*) The Problems of Dryland Agriculture: The dynamics of dryland farming are different and harsh than irrigated farming. So the problems of dryland agriculture are also unique. Water is the chief requirement for cropping. The crops in dryland or arid lands have to face the challenge of shortage of water more frequently. Rainfall is the sole option for them to get water. Though groundwater is available, however it is a common phenomenon that dryland farmers are poorer than other farmers. It is challenging for them to get access to the groundwater. That is why crop failure is quite common in drylands leaving the farmers and habitants worse off. Either they have to rely on previous stored grains or to buy from market, which is for sure expensive for them. Having said that, water shortage is not the only problem faced by dryland farming community, there are several other problems of dryland agriculture. In this article, i am going to discuss few of these problems of dryland agriculture for beginners to get better insight of the issue.

1. **Moisture Stress, Dryness and Uncertainty:** The rainfall in dryland is erratic and has no pattern. In some years, there is plenty of rainfall, while sometime drought prevails in the area. Farmers have no opportunity to take necessary steps on soil for moisture conservation. This result in dryness of soil-crop roots fail to harness moisture, even if they are lush and lengthy, eventually crop failure occur. Farmers do not have enough resources to gamble with nature. So they crop half-heartedly and get nominal production and yield. This issue can be addressed by providing the farmers with necessary weather forecasting advisory, so that they can schedule their cropping activities accordingly to get maximum benefit from available water.
2. **Water Storage:** Water storage facilities are seldom available in areas where dryland agriculture prevails and this is a serious problem of dryland agriculture. It is more prevalent in developing nations of Asia, Africa and some countries of South America. Water is lost in several ways including evaporation, runoff or used by weeds. As mentioned earlier, problem of dryland agriculture is that there may be no rain or high intensity torrential rain. So there is an opportunity available to save this water. But due to lack of indigenous physical and financial resources along with less state level interest in dryland agriculture, water is wasted. This water can be stored in ponds or ditches or even in the soil. If government support is not available, farmers can form a community at village level and pool resources to have a localized water storage infrastructure to use water during dire need.

3. **Marketing Problems of Dryland Produce:** Marketing is another problem of dryland agriculture. Farmers usually grow same type of crops. At crop maturity, farmers want to market their produce as it is difficult to store it due to lack of storage facilities. This enables the traders and middleman to have upper hand on them and thus the agricultural produce is sold in difficulty and at low price. An option for dryland farmers is to cultivate different crops in a season or also they can pool money to build local level storage facilities.
4. **Limited Liberty of Crop Selection:** This is a serious concern for dryland farmers. There are very limited crops that have the adaptability to grow in arid or dryland conditions. However, it is also an opportunity for them. Oil seeds have greater adaptability and resistance to grow in dryland conditions. If cultivation of oil seed crops is done properly and carefully, these crops can earn handy cash for farmers and can be sold quickly. In this way, farmers can buy other products and food items of their need.
5. **Vigilant and Judicious Fertilizer Application:** We are too much dependent on fertilizer. First, it was needed to increase the output of crops. However, now it is a must need due to weaker soil conditions. The fertility and availability of organic matter in soil has depleted over the past few decades and it is more severe in arid lands. Thus, this increases the problems of dryland agriculture many folds. Moreover, the irrigated farmers have a defined schedule of farming activities specially the irrigation. So they have the liberty to apply fertilizer and schedule it accordingly. In case of dryland farmers, it is a difficulty to manage fertilizer application. In case of applying fertilizer through broadcasting for basal or top-dressing, it is useless without availability of moisture and it is wasted.
6. **Quality of Crop Produce:** The above-mentioned problems of dryland agriculture put a big question mark on the quality of crop produced in dryland or arid conditions. Grain quality is the biggest issue as it is of inferior quality due to underdevelopment. On the other hand, the plant growth is also affected, often termed as stunted. This result in less fodder production and farmers get less return on their produce from the market.

These are few common problems of dryland agriculture and farming community. The ultimate responsibility is on government shoulder for backing the farmers in these areas. This is because of the poverty and lack of resources which is common in arid or dryland farming system. Moreover, the current changing climate is another threat to this form of cropping system. Last but not least, extensive research for new crop varieties, innovative water resource management and introduction of unique cropping practices can aid in lessening problems of dryland agriculture.

Soil Constraints: Poor physical properties of soil are major constraints in dryland regions. Poor physical properties are exacerbated by low organic matter and contribute to low water-holding capacity, which makes it more difficult to deal with the detrimental effects of erratic and limited precipitation.

The different soil groups found in dry areas are black soils, red soils and alluvial soils. The limitations for agricultural production are different in different soil groups. The predominant group of alluvial soils where problems for agricultural production are not as acute as in red and black soils.

The different soil constraints for agricultural production are:

(*a*) **Inadequate availability of moisture from the sun:** The moisture retention capacity of soils in arid regions is shallow due to shallow depth, especially in alfisol (red soils), low rainfall and low organic matter.

(*b*) **Low organic matter content:** The organic matter content in most soils under conditions of dry earth content is very low (<1%) due to the high temperature and low addition of organic fertilizers.

(*c*) **Poor soil fertility:** Due to the low accumulation of organic matter and the loss of the upper fertile layer due to soil erosion, arid soils have a poor state of fertility. Most arid soils are deficient in nitrogen and zinc.

(*d*) **Soil deterioration due to erosion:** In India about 175 m.ha of land are subject to various degradations, among which the predominant soil erosion. Erosion causes the loss of the upper fertile soil, leaving a poor subsoil for growing crops.

(*e*) **Soil crust problem:** In the case of red earth, the formation of hard surface soil layers makes it difficult for seedlings to appear, which ultimately affect the plant population.

(*f*) **Presence of hard layers and deep cracks:** The presence of hard layers in the soil and deep cracks affects crop production especially in the case of black soils.

4. (*a*) Land Equivalent Ratio: The FAO defines land equivalent ratio (LER) as: the ratio of the area under sole cropping to the area under intercropping needed to give equal amounts of yield at the same management level. It is the sum of the fractions of the intercropped yields divided by the sole-crop yields.

For a scenario where a total of ***m*** crops are intercropped, the land equivalent ratio LER can be calculated as:

$$LER = \sum_{i=1}^{m} \frac{IY_i}{SY_i}$$

where, *m* is the number of different crops intercropped,

IY_i is the yield for the ith crop under intercropping, and SY_i is the yield for the ith crop under a sole-crop regime on the same area.

Example:

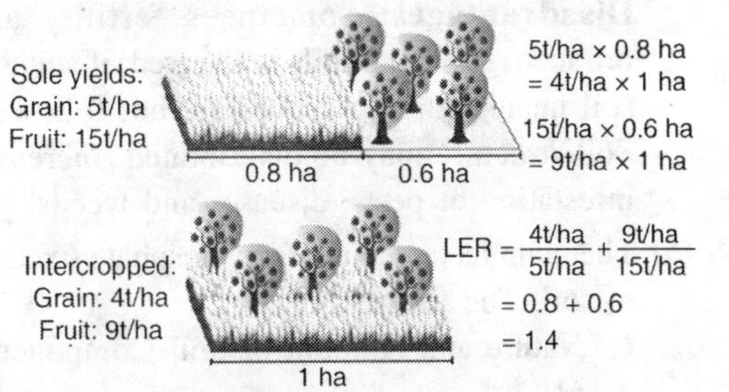

The table in this section provides yield values for a hypothetical scenario intercropping a grain crop with a fruit tree crop.

The first two columns state the yields for intercropping (IY) and sole yields (SY). The third column, *equivalent area*, column calculates the area of sole cropping land required to achieve the same yield as 1 ha of intercropping, at the same management level.

Crop	Intercropped Yield IY (kg/ha)	Sole Yield SY (kg/ha)	Equivalent area (ha)
Grain	4,000	5,000	0.8
Fruit	9,000	15,000	0.6
Land equivalent ratio			1.4

The land equivalent ration can be calculated as

$$LER = \sum_{i=1}^{m} \frac{IY_i}{SY_i} = \frac{IY_{grain}}{SY_{grain}} + \frac{IY_{fruit}}{SY_{fruit}}$$

$$= \frac{4,000}{5,000} + \frac{9,000}{15,000}$$

$$= 0.8 + 0.6 = 1.4$$

An interpretation of this result would be that a total of 1.4 ha of sole cropping area would be required to produce the same yields as 1 ha of the intercropped system.

Advantages: The land equivalent ratio can be used whenever more than one type of yield can be obtained from the same area. This can be intercropping of annual crops (e.g. sorghum and pigeonpea) or combination of annual and perennial crops e.g. in agroforestry systems (e.g. jackfruit and eggplant).

Disadvantages: Sometimes fertility and productivity of the soils is lowered, if suitable soil management practices are not followed. Soil structure may be deteriorated. Increases infestation of pests, diseases and weeds.

4. (*b*) The main factors that affect phosphate fixation in soil. The factors are:

1. Nature and Amount of Soil Components
2. pH
3. Other Ions
4. Organic Matter
5. Temperature
6. Over Liming.

I. Nature and Amount of Soil Components: Adsorption and desorption reactions are affected by the type of surfaces contacted by phosphorus in the soil solution. However, there are various other following soil components that affects phosphate fixation.

(*a*) **Hydrous Oxides of Iron and Aluminium:** These substances have the ability to fix phosphates through adsorption on their surfaces. Aluminium and iron oxides can occur as discrete particles in soils or as coatings or films on other soil particles. They occur as their both amorphous and crystalline hydroxy compounds in soil. When iron and aluminium oxide compounds is soil are less crystalline, the phosphate fixing capacity of the soil be more because of greater surface areas. However, crystalline hydrous oxides are usually capable of fixing more phosphorus than layer silicates.

(*b*) **Type of Clay:** The clay fraction of soil is likely to be the main site of phosphate fixation. The nature of the clay mineral is also important with regards to phosphate fixation. Phosphorus is retained or fixed to a greater extent by 1 : 1 than by 2 : 1 clay and this may be due to the higher amounts of hydrated oxides of Fe and Al associated with 1 : 1 type clays. The phosphate fixing capacity of clay minerals may be found in the following order:

Montmorillonite > Vermiculite > Kaolinite > Muscovite.

(*c*) **Amount of Clay:** Soils containing large quantities of clay will fix more phosphorus than that of soils containing small amount of clay.

(*d*) **Amorphous Colloids:** Amorphous aluminosilicate minerals like allophane have a large negative charge which is partly or entirely balanced by complex aluminium cations. Phosphorus becomes adsorbed by reacting with this aluminium.

(*e*) **Calcium Carbonate:** Calcium carbonate ($CaCO_3$) exerts significant influence on phosphate fixation. Usually, higher the content of $CaCO_3$ in soil, the higher is the fixation of phosphate. Phosphate may be adsorbed on the surface of calcium carbonate particles. The solubility of phosphatic minerals has also been found to be depressed in the presence of $CaCO_3$ (due to formation of less/soluble tricalcium phosphate and latter carbonate apatite).

II. pH: Soil pH has a profound influence on the amount and manner in which soluble phosphorus becomes fixed. Between pH 4.0 and 8.0, H_2PO_4 and HPO_4^- are the principal phosphate ions in soil. Above pH 9.0, PO_4^{3-} dominates but $H_2PO_4^-$ is still present. Different mechanisms of phosphate fixation operate at different pH levels. At pH 2-5 the fixation is chiefly due to the formation of Fe and Al-phosphates. Al pH 4.5-7.5, phosphates are fixed on the surface of the clay colloids and at pH 6-10 phosphate is precipitated usually by Ca and Mg. So the fixation of phosphate in relation to different soil pH is presented in Fig.

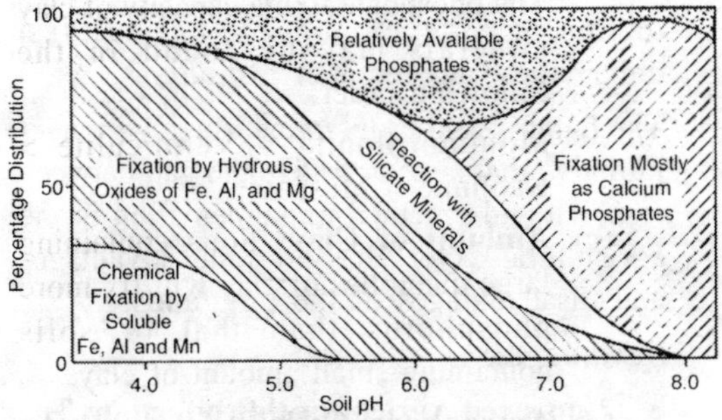

Fig. *Fixation of Phosphorus in relation to different soil pH*

III. Other Ions: Both cations and anions affect fixation of phosphorus.

Cations: Divalent cations enhance phosphate adsorption than that of monovalent cations. The concentration of exchangeable Al also influences the phosphate fixation indirectly through precipitation and adsorption as follows:

Cation exchange:

$$\text{CLAY}\left]\begin{matrix}Al^{3+}\\ \\ Al^{3+}\end{matrix}\right. + 3\,Ca^{2+} \rightleftharpoons \text{CLAY}\left]\begin{matrix}Ca^{2+}\\ Ca^{2+}\\ Ca^{2+}\end{matrix}\right. + 2\,Al^{3+}$$

Hydrolysis:

$$Al^{3+} + 2H_2O \rightarrow Al(OH)_2^+ + 2H^+$$

Precipitation and/or Adsorption:

$$Al(OH)_2^+ + H_2PO_4^- \rightarrow Al(OH)_2H_2PO_4$$

$$(K_{sp} = 2.8\ \tilde{A} - 10^{-29})$$

Anions: Both inorganic and organic anions can compete in varying degrees with phosphate anion for the same adsorption sites resulting in some cases in a decrease in the adsorption of added phosphorus or a desorption of fixed phosphorus. Anions are hydroxyl, silicic acid, sulphate and molybdate etc.

IV. Organic Matter: During decomposition of organic matter various organic acids are produced which solubilize phosphates and other phosphate bearing minerals and thereby lower phosphate fixation. The decrease in phosphate fixation due to presence of sufficient organic matter in soils may be described by the following reactions:

- By the formation of phosphohumic complexes that are easily assimilated by plants.
- Through the replacement of the phosphate by the humate ion (anion exchange reaction).
- Forming coating on sesquioxide particles by humus to form a protective cover and thus reduce the phosphate fixing capacity of the soil.

Organic matter plays an important role in influencing the phosphate fixation in soils. It is evident that organic matter decreases the fixation of phosphate in soils.

V. Temperature: Temperature affects the speed of chemical reaction. High temperatures are expected to slightly increase the solubility of phosphatic compounds like apatites (hydroxy and carbonate), octacalcium phosphate, variscite, strengite etc. Mineralization of phosphorus from soil organic matter, crop residues and other organic wastes etc. are enhanced with the increase in temperature by stimulating the activity of appropriate microorganisms. Phosphorus fixation generally increases with the increase in temperature.

VI. Over liming: Over liming increases the fixation of phosphorus by forming more insoluble compound in soil. Besides phosphate, molybdate (MoO_4^{2-}) and borate (BO_3^{3-}, HBO_3^-, $B(OH)_4^-$) anions also fix in the soils of mostly acidic reaction. Majority of the factors discussed earlier for the fixation of phosphates in soil also affects the fixation of molybdenum and boron in soils.

limitations, such as the amount of resources available or the capacity of a machine, or other constraints, such as legal regulations or environmental policies.

- **Formulate the objective function:** Formulate an equation that represents the objective in terms of the decision variables. This equation could be a linear combination of the decision variables.
- **Solve the linear program:** Solve the linear program using linear programming techniques, such as the simplex method or the interior point method.
- **Interpret the results:** Interpret the results of the linear program and make decisions based on the solution.

For example, suppose a farmer has 100 acres of land to plant two crops: wheat and corn. Each acre of wheat requires 2 units of fertilizer and 1 unit of labor, while each acre of corn requires 1 unit of fertilizer and 2 units of labor. The farmer has 150 units of fertilizer and 180 units of labor available. The objective is to maximize the total revenue from the crops, with wheat selling for \$200 per acre and corn selling for \$300 per acre.

The decision variables are the number of acres of wheat and corn to plant, which can be represented by x and y, respectively. The constraints are:

$2x + y \leq 150$ (limit on fertilizer)

$x + 2y \leq 180$ (limit on labor)

$x \geq 0,\ y \geq 0$ (non-negative requirement)

The objective function is:

Maximize $Z = 200x + 300y$

Solving the linear program using linear programming techniques will result in the optimum resource use plan, which in this case is to plant 50 acres of wheat and 60 acres of corn, resulting in a total revenue of \$33,000.

6. (*c*) Advantages and Disadvantages of Lab to Land Programme: Launched in 1979 as a part of golden jubilee celebrations of ICAR. The programme intended to improve the economic condition of small, marginal farmers and landless agricultural labourers fast ... SC's and ST's by transfer of improved technology developed by agricultural universities and research institutions.

The Lab to Land Programme is a government initiative that aims to bridge the gap between research and practical implementation in the agricultural sector. Here are some advantages and disadvantages of the program:

Advantages:

- **Improved Agricultural Production:** The Lab to Land Programme helps farmers to implement the latest agricultural technologies and practices to enhance productivity and yield. This can lead to increased income and improved livelihoods for farmers.
- **Better Research and Development:** The program allows researchers to work closely with farmers, providing them with access to real-world problems, which can lead to more relevant and impactful research.
- **Knowledge Sharing:** Through the program, farmers can share their traditional knowledge and experience with researchers, while researchers can share their scientific knowledge with farmers. This can lead to improved communication and collaboration between the two groups.
- **Environmentally Sustainable:** The program can help farmers to adopt environmentally sustainable practices, leading to a reduction in negative environmental impacts and improved environ-mental outcomes.

Disadvantages:

- **Limited Coverage:** The program may not reach all farmers due to limited resources, which can lead to unequal access to the benefits of the program.

- **Implementation Challenges:** Implementation of the program can be challenging, especially in rural areas where infrastructure is limited, and farmers may not have access to technology or information.
- **Insufficient Funding:** The program may not receive adequate funding, leading to difficulties in providing necessary resources and support to farmers.
- **Resistance to Change:** Some farmers may be resistant to change, preferring to stick with traditional practices rather than adopting new technologies and practices.

The Lab to Land Programme has the potential to bring significant benefits to the agricultural sector, but it requires adequate funding, infrastructure, and support to be successful.

7. (*a*) **Water Saving Approaches Employed in Pressurized Irrigation Systems:** Pressurized irrigation systems are used to distribute water through pipes and emitters, delivering it directly to the crops. These systems are more efficient than traditional flood irrigation methods because they deliver water directly to the roots of the plants, reducing evaporation and water waste.

Here are some water-saving approaches that can be employed in pressurized irrigation systems:

- **Drip Irrigation:** Drip irrigation is a type of pressurized irrigation that delivers water directly to the root zone of plants. It uses emitters that are placed near the plants and release water at a slow and steady rate. This approach reduces water use by up to 50% compared to flood irrigation.
- **Irrigation Scheduling:** Irrigation scheduling involves determining the appropriate time and amount of water to apply to the crops. This approach is based on factors such as crop type, soil type, and weather conditions. By applying the right amount of water at the right time, farmers can reduce water waste and optimize crop yields.
- **Pressure Regulation:** Pressure regulation involves using pressure regulators to maintain a constant pressure throughout the irrigation system. This helps to reduce water waste by preventing water from being over-sprayed or under-sprayed due to pressure fluctuations.
- **Irrigation Efficiency:** Irrigation efficiency is a measure of how much of the water applied to crops is actually used by the plants. By increasing irrigation efficiency through techniques such as soil moisture monitoring and proper system maintenance, farmers can reduce water waste and improve crop yields.
- **System Upgrades:** Upgrading irrigation systems with more efficient components can also help to reduce water use. For example, replacing old pipes and emitters with newer, more efficient models can improve water delivery and reduce water waste.

Pressurized irrigation systems offer many opportunities to save water and improve crop yields. By employing these approaches, farmers can reduce water waste, optimize crop yields, and promote sustainable agriculture.

Advantages and Disadvantages and Applicability of Drip and Sprinkler Irrigation Systems

Drip and sprinkler irrigation systems are two popular methods for watering crops. Each system has its advantages and disadvantages, and their applicability depends on various factors such as crop type, soil type, climate, and water availability.

- **Reconstruction of village:** Work should be done for the development of education, health, transportation, electricity, water etc in villages, so as to encourage educated people to stay in villages.
- **Change in social attitude:** The rural environment in India is filled with jealousy, hatred, ill felling and conflicts. Selfishness is increasing day by day and it is harmful for the society and the country. "Extension worker should try to bring change in this mental attitude of people so that they can sacrifice their selfishness for the welfare of the society and country and may become partners in the reconstruction of the country.

5. (*c*) If necessity is the mother of invention, scarcity of resources is the mother of farm planning. The fact of scarcity makes it necessary for the farmer to make the most what he has in their efficient utilization. Farmer can make optimum utilization of scarce productive resources. The farm planning, of course, may be annual or long range planning. Annual planning obviously is meant for ensuing agril year. In case of long range planning, long range objectives are involved, covering a longer period over the next 5 to 10 years.

The importance of farm planning can be examined through its helpfulness (or usefulness). In view of this following things are very important (Advantages).

- It enables the farmer to achieve his objectives in relation to his farm and family in a more organized manner.
- Farm planning enables a careful examination of the existing resources and their best allocation.
- It helps farmer to take decisions in relation to selection of crops, hectarage under different crops and kind and number of live-stock to be maintained.
- It helps the farmer to identify the input and credit needs.
- It helps in estimating future cost and returns.

To have a best farm plan, some steps are needed to follow while farm planning is prepared. They are:

- **Preparing the Farm map:** The general lay out of the farm, number and shape, irrigation channels can be shown in the farm map.
- **Recording the History of the Farm:** It is very important to obtain the information pertaining to utilization of resources and their efficiency. What was the crop rotations followed previously, etc on the basis of this information planning in respect of crops to be grown, crop rotations to be followed; requirement of credit along with their sources etc can be possible.
- **Planning Bullock and Human Labour Requirement:** Next a calendar of farm operations should be prepared and bullock and human labour requirements determined for different months. A labour schedule should be developed as to guide a farmer to appraise the amount of labour need in relation to the availability.
- **Planning the Land Use and Soil Conservation Practices:** When a full picture of the resources and their appraisal is obtained, the next step in farm planning is to adopt such practices which would lead to the best use of land.
- **Planning Live stock Programme:** Live stock and crop production is having supplementary relationship. The size of live stock depends upon size of farm, cropping intensity, availability of irrigation etc. If irrigation water is ample naturally cultivator can grow fodder crops through out year and he can maintain milch animals more.
- **Planning the Marketing of Produce:** Only production is not sufficient to maximize the returns, good price for the

produce is also important. Therefore, study of market conditions, prices etc. are essential to decide the time of selling. Similarly the agency through which marketing is to be done must be identified in view of getting maximum shares in consumers price.

5. (*d*) **Various dimensions of a market as including:** Market analysis helps us to determine the market situation in terms of its attractiveness or otherwise. Organizations weigh their strengths and weaknesses relating it to the opportunities and threats, to understand their capability to respond to the market changes, based on such analysis.

- Market size (current and future)
- Market growth rate
- Market profitability
- Industry cost structure
- Distribution channels
- Market trends
- Key success factors

Market Size: Market size is determined based on the current and future sales potentiality of an organization. It is determined by browsing through the information from various sources.

Market Growth Rate: Extrapolating the past data into the future, market growth rate can be ascertained in an organization. This is, however, very crude form of estimation of market growth rate, as it cannot account for the fluctuations or any variation in the growth pattern that may occur in future time period for change in any factor or factors, which may influence the market growth.

Market Profitability: Profitability levels in any organization, to a great extent, are market dependent. Organizations may have different levels of profitability in different market situation, which depends on number of factors. Michael Porter, through his five competitive forces, explained the way to measure the market situation. This framework of competitive forces, to a large extent influences the market profitability.

Industry Cost Structure: Industry cost structure is an important determinant of organizational success or failure. Here, again we can refer Porter's value-chain concept, which helps an organization to add value to products and services, without, however altering the cost. At times, it can even reduce the costs while increasing the customers' satisfaction.

Distribution Channels: Distribution channels facilitate in reaching the products to the end-users on real time basis. Some of the distributions systems, which organizations need to consider while doing market analysis are as under:

- **Understanding of the Existing Distribution Channels:** This helps us to understand how direct the products reach to the customers.
- **Trends and Emerging Channels:** This helps us to asses to what extent new channels can enhance the competitive advantage for the organization.
- **Power Structure of Channels:** Understanding the power structure of channels is very important aspect of market analysis. Organizations with high brand equity can weaken the channels power, as they dictate their terms.

Market Trends: Fluctuations in the market trends could be both an opportunity and threat for an organization. Market trends may be industry specific or general. Industry-specific market trends influence those organizations that falls under the same industry category. General market trends, however, affect all organizations, irrespective of their industry group. Such trends may be in terms of price sensitivity, nature of demand or even regional trends.

Key Success Factors: Key success factors are those which help an organization to achieve its market objectives. It also forms an

prices reflect market fundamentals.

- **Encouraging competition:** Governments can encourage greater competition in agricultural markets by breaking up monopolies or oligopolies, and promoting the entry of new players. This can reduce the market power of dominant players and create more efficient and competitive markets.
- **Implementing market-based policies:** Governments can implement market-based policies such as price stabilization funds and futures markets to stabilize prices and reduce price volatility. This can help reduce the price spread and provide greater price stability for farmers.
- **Promoting sustainable agriculture:** Sustainable agricultural practices such as crop rotation, agroforestry, and conservation tillage can help reduce the cost of production and improve yields. This can help reduce the price spread and make agricultural production more efficient and sustainable.
- **Investing in research and development:** Governments can invest in research and development to improve crop varieties, reduce pest and disease outbreaks, and improve the efficiency of production. This can lead to higher yields, lower production costs, and a reduction in the price spread.

Reducing the high price spread in agriculture requires a multipronged approach that addresses the underlying causes of the problem. Governments, farmers, and other stakeholders must work together to promote greater efficiency, transparency, and sustainability in agricultural markets, and ensure that prices reflect market fundamentals.

7. (*c*) The Approaches and Benefits of Market-led Extension: Market-led extension is an approach to agricultural extension that focuses on promoting market-oriented production practices to increase farm productivity and profitability. This approach is centered on the belief that farmers should produce what the market demands and that extension services should provide the necessary information and support to help farmers meet these demands. Market-led extension is a valuable approach to agricultural extension that focuses on promoting market-oriented production practices to increase farm productivity and profitability. By focusing on market demand and promoting partnerships with the private sector, this approach can help farmers access markets, increase their incomes, and contribute to sustainable agricultural development.

Here are some of the key approaches and benefits of market-led extension:

Approaches:

- **Value chain analysis:** Market-led extension involves analyzing the entire value chain from production to consumption to identify opportunities and challenges for farmers. This approach helps farmers understand the market demand for their products and the specific quality requirements needed to meet that demand.
- **Farmer-to-farmer learning:** Market-led extension often uses peer-to-peer learning strategies to disseminate information and encourage the adoption of new practices. Farmers learn from each other by sharing experiences and knowledge, which helps to build social capital and strengthens the community.
- **Partnership with the private sector:** Market-led extension involves partnerships between the private sector and extension services to provide farmers with access to markets, credit, and technology. This approach can increase the efficiency of the extension system

and promote the adoption of new practices and technologies.

Benefits:

- **Increased productivity:** Market-led extension focuses on increasing farm productivity by promoting market-oriented production practices. Farmers who adopt these practices can increase their yields, improve product quality, and reduce production costs.
- **Increased profitability:** By producing crops that meet market demand, farmers can increase their profitability and income. Market-led extension also promotes value addition, which can help farmers capture more value from their products.
- **Improved market access:** Market-led extension promotes linkages between farmers and markets, which can help farmers access better prices, credit, and technology. This approach can also help farmers manage market risks by providing information on market trends and demand.
- **Sustainability:** Market-led extension promotes sustainable agricultural practices by promoting the adoption of technologies that improve soil health, reduce water use, and enhance biodiversity. This approach can help farmers produce more food while reducing their impact on the environment.

PAPER-II

1. (*a*) The cell wall is an extracellular structure that surrounds and provides support and protection to plant cells, fungi, and some bacteria. It is a complex structure composed of various molecules, including cellulose, hemicellulose, pectin, and lignin. The mode of origin and growth of the cell wall varies depending on the type of organism.

Mode of Origin: In plants, the cell wall is formed during cytokinesis, the final stage of cell division. During cytokinesis, a new cell plate forms between the two daughter cells, which eventually fuses with the existing cell wall to form a complete cell wall. The cell wall grows as the plant cell expands, and new cell wall material is synthesized and deposited by the cell.

In fungi and some bacteria, the cell wall is continuously remodeled and expanded as the cell grows. The cell wall is composed of chitin and glucans in fungi, and peptidoglycan in bacteria. These organisms have enzymes that can break down and rebuild the cell wall as needed, allowing the cell to adapt to changing environmental conditions.

Functions: The cell wall has several important functions, including:

- **Structural support:** The cell wall provides mechanical support to the cell, helping it maintain its shape and resist external forces.
- **Protection:** The cell wall protects the cell from physical damage, pathogens, and environmental stresses such as drought or extreme temperatures.
- **Regulation of water and solute uptake:** The cell wall helps regulate the movement of water and solutes into and out of the cell, maintaining cellular homeostasis.
- **Cell-to-cell communication:** The cell wall contains proteins and other molecules that are involved in cell-to-cell

7. (*b*) **Motive Behind Cooperation:** A practical motivation for the creation of agricultural cooperatives is related to the ability of farmers to pool production and/or resources. In many situations within agriculture, it is simply too expensive for farmers to manufacture products or undertake a service. Cooperatives provide a method for farmers to join in an 'association', through which a group of farmers can acquire a better outcome, typically financial, than by going alone. This approach is aligned to the concept of economies of scale and can also be related as a form of economic synergy, where "two or more agents working together to produce a result not obtainable by any of the agents independently".

Three Tier Structure of Cooperative Credit Society: A credit union is a member-owned financial cooperative, democratically controlled by its members. The Co-operative Credit Institutions in India can be classified as under a three-tier structure—Primary Credit Societies at the bottom; Central Co-operative Bank at the middle; and State Co-operative Bank at the top. A credit union is a member-owned financial cooperative, democratically controlled by its members, and operated for the purpose of promoting thrift, arranging credit at competitive rates, and providing so many other financial services to its members. The Co-operative Credit Institutions in India can be classified as under a three-tier structure.

- Primary Credit Societies at the bottom
- Central Co-operative Bank at the middle
- State Co-operative Bank at the top

The primary societies are functioning in the various towns and villages, the Central Banks at the district headquarters and the State Co-operative Banks at the state capitals forming the apex of the system.

The Reserve Bank of India assists the co-operative structure by providing concessional finance through **NABARD** in the form of General Lines of Credit for lending to agricultural & allied activities. Thus, the whole system is integrated with the Banking structure of the country.

(*i*) **The Primary Agricultural Credit Societies:** A primary society is an association of borrowers and non-borrowers residing in a particular locality and taking interest in the business affairs of one another. As membership is practically open to all inhabitants of a locality, people of different status are brought together into the common organization.

(*ii*) **Central Co-operative Banks:** A Central Co-operative Bank is a federation of primary societies in a specified area. Where membership of a Central Co-operative Bank is restricted to primary societies only, it is known as a 'banking union'. Nowadays, individuals are also admitted as members of almost all Central Co-operative Banks.

(*iii*) **State Co-operative Banks:** At the top of the co-operative banking, there are State Co-operative Banks, organized with the object of attracting deposits from the rich urban classes. These Banks are also more suitably equipped to serve as channel between the co-operative movement and the joint stock banks.

Cooperative Credit: The major deficiencies in the working of the cooperative societies are as follows:

- The essence or basic features of cooperative banking system must be a larger reliance on resources mobilised locally and a lesser and lesser dependence on higher credit institutions. However, many PACSs are at present dependent on CCBs and have failed miserably in mobilising rural savings. Overall, this has made the cooperatives a "mediocre, inefficient and static system".
- The cooperative credit institutions are plagued by the problem of high level of over-dues. These over-dues have clogged

the process of credit recycling since they have substantially reduced the capacity of cooperatives to grant loans.

- The rural cooperative institutions have a high level of NPAs.
- A large number of rural cooperative credit institutions have incurred substantial losses.
- The Primary Agricultural Credit Societies is the most important link in the short-term cooperative credit structure. However, most of them are too small in size to be economical and viable. Besides, several of them are also dormant while some are defunct.
- Because of their strong socio-economic position and grip over the rural economy, big landowners have cornered greater benefits from cooperatives. This is the opposite of what the planners intended.
- There are considerable regional disparities in the distribution of credit by cooperative societies with six States (Gujarat, Maharashtra, Karnataka, Kerala, Punjab and Tamil Nadu) accounting for 70 per cent of the short-term loans provided by the PACSs as of end-March 2010.
- The powers which vest in the government under the cooperative laws and rules are all-pervasive. Over the years, State has come to gain almost total financial and administrative control over the cooperatives, in the process stifling their growth. Instead of strengthening the base, a weak base was vastly expanded as per plan targets and an immense governmental and semi-governmental superstructure was created.

7. (*c*) Functions of State Agricultural Management and Extension Training Institute (SAMETI): State Agricultural Management and Extension Training Institute is an autonomous state level Institute with a mandate of conducting capacity building programmes for Extension Functionaries in the State. Training courses are organized on Agricultural Technology, Extension Management, Gender mainstreaming, Extension Reforms and Information Technology. SAMETI also aims to provide extension management input for extension functionaries of Agriculture and Line Departments. Apart from conducting training programmes, SAMETI facilitates infrastructure to conduct workshops and reviews.

Key Functions of SAMETI:

- Provide capacity building support in Extension Management related areas to the extension functionaries from public, private and non-governmental sectors.
- Provide consultancy in the areas like project planning, appraisal, implementation, monitoring & evaluation, etc.
- Develop and promote application of management tools for improving the effectiveness of Agricultural Extension services.
- Organize need based training programmes for middle level extension functionaries.
- Develop modules on Management, Communication, Participatory Methodologies etc., as a sequel to the feedback from training programmes.
- Organize Annual Workshop involving all the agricultural related training.
- Coordinate with MANAGE in organizing PGDAEM, STRY, ACABC, DAESI programme.
- Supervision of Smooth implementation of ATMA Scheme.
- In order to ensure regular training and skill upgradation of State and District/Block level extension functionaries and for reaching out to the grass root level extension functionaries and farmers through field visits.
- Sub-Mission on Agricultural Extension (SMAE) or Support to State Extension Programmes for Extension Reforms (ATMA Scheme) in the State is monitored and supervised by SAMETI.

with desired traits. Molecular markers are DNA sequences that vary in length and can be found in specific locations in the genome. These markers can be used to identify regions of the genome that are linked to desirable traits such as disease resistance, drought tolerance, or higher yields.

There are several types of molecular markers used in crop improvement including Restriction Fragment Length Polymorphism (RFLP), Simple Sequence Repeat (SSR), Amplified Fragment Length Polymorphism (AFLP), Single Nucleotide Polymorphism (SNP), and Insertion/Deletion (InDel) markers.

The use of molecular markers in crop improvement allows breeders to identify desirable traits early in the breeding process, reducing the time required to develop new varieties. The molecular markers approach also enables breeders to select for traits that may be difficult to observe, such as resistance to pests and diseases, or traits that are influenced by multiple genes. The use of molecular markers in crop improvement has greatly enhanced the efficiency and precision of crop breeding, resulting in the development of new crop varieties that have increased yields, improved quality, and better resistance to biotic and abiotic stresses.

2. (*a*) Differentiate between the following:

(*i*) **Sex-linked and sex-limited characters**

In agriculture, sex-linked and sex-limited traits refer to genetic traits that are related to the sex of an organism and have practical applications in breeding programs.

Sex-linked traits in agriculture are traits that are determined by genes located on the sex chromosomes of an organism. For example, in some species of fish, sex determination is based on the presence or absence of a Y chromosome, similar to humans. In birds, sex is determined by the Z and W chromosomes, with males having ZZ and females having ZW chromosomes. Some sex-linked traits in agriculture include feather color, growth rate, and disease resistance.

Sex-limited traits, on the other hand, are traits that are expressed in only one sex, even though both sexes may carry the genes for the trait. For example, milk production in dairy cows is a sex-limited trait, as only female cows can produce milk, while male cows cannot. In addition, egg production in chickens is a sex-limited trait, as only female chickens can lay eggs, while male chickens cannot. Other examples of sex-limited traits in agriculture include wool production in sheep, antler size in deer, and meat quality in beef cattle.

In agriculture, understanding the genetics of sex-linked and sex-limited traits is important for developing breeding programs that aim to produce animals with desired traits. For example, selecting breeding animals based on their genetic makeup for a particular sex-linked trait can help to increase the frequency of the desirable allele in the population. Similarly, selecting breeding animals based on the expression of sex-limited traits can help to improve the productivity and profitability of the farm.

(*ii*) **C_3 and C_4 Plants:**

C3 and C_4 plants are two different types of photosynthetic pathways used by plants. The main difference between C_3 and C_4 plants lies in the way they capture and store carbon dioxide during photosynthesis.

C_3 plants are the most common type of plants and include the majority of agricultural crops such as wheat, rice, and soybeans. These plants use the Calvin cycle, a process that occurs in the mesophyll cells of the plant leaves.

During the Calvin cycle, carbon dioxide is fixed into a 3-carbon compound, hence the name C_3. C_3 plants are more efficient at photosynthesis under cool and moist conditions with moderate light intensity. However, they are less efficient under high temperatures and intense light, as they tend to lose more water due to increased transpiration rates.

C_4 plants, on the other hand, include a smaller number of plant species, such as maize, sugarcane, and sorghum. These plants use the C_4 pathway, which involves two distinct types of cells, mesophyll, and bundle sheath cells. During the C_4 pathway, carbon dioxide is initially fixed into a 4-carbon compound by mesophyll cells, which then transport the compound into bundle sheath cells. The carbon dioxide is then released, refixed by Rubisco, and enters the Calvin cycle. C_4 plants are more efficient at photosynthesis under high temperatures, intense light, and low water conditions, as they have a mechanism to concentrate carbon dioxide around Rubisco, which reduces water loss through transpiration.

The main difference between C_3 and C_4 plants lies in their photosynthetic pathways. C_3 plants use the Calvin cycle to fix carbon dioxide, while C_4 plants use the C_4 pathway to fix and concentrate carbon dioxide before it enters the Calvin cycle.

***(iii)* Epistasis and dominance**

Epistasis and dominance are two types of gene interactions that can occur between two or more genes that influence a particular trait. The main difference between epistasis and dominance gene interaction lies in the way they affect the expression of the phenotype.

Epistasis occurs when one gene affects the expression of another gene, either by enhancing or suppressing its expression. In other words, the expression of one gene is dependent on the presence or absence of another gene. Epistasis can result in modified ratios of phenotypes that are expected from Mendelian inheritance. For example, in Labrador Retrievers, the coat color is determined by two genes, one gene that controls pigment production, and another gene that controls pigment deposition. The expression of the pigment deposition gene is dependent on the presence of the pigment production gene. Hence, the pigment production gene is said to be epistatic over the pigment deposition gene.

Dominance gene interaction, on the other hand, occurs when one allele of a gene masks or suppresses the expression of another allele of the same gene. This interaction is commonly observed in a cross between two homozygous individuals with different alleles. One allele (dominant) is expressed, and the other allele (recessive) is not. For example, in humans, the ability to roll the tongue is a dominant trait, and the inability to roll the tongue is a recessive trait. If an individual has at least one dominant allele, they will be able to roll their tongue, regardless of the presence of the recessive allele.

Epistasis occurs when one gene affects the expression of another gene, while dominance gene interaction occurs when one allele of a gene masks or suppresses the expression of another allele. Epistasis results in modified ratios of phenotypes, while dominance gene interaction results in the expression of one allele over another.

2. *(b)* Method of Recurrent Selection: Recurrent selection is a plant breeding method that involves selecting and crossing superior

Surface Area of the Leaves: A leaf having more surface area will show more transpiration rate than the leaf with a lesser surface area.

Significance of Transpiration in Plants: The significance of transpiration is explained below:

- Transpiration helps in the conduction of water and minerals to different parts of the plants.
- Due to the continuous elimination of water from the plant body, there is a balance of water maintained within the plant.
- It maintains osmosis and keeps the cells rigid.
- A suction force is created by transpiration that helps in the upward movement of water in the plants.
- Certain hydrophilic salts are accumulated on the surface of the leaves, which keeps the leaves moist.
- It maintains the turgidity of the cells and helps in cell division.
- Optimum transpiration helps in the proper growth of the plants.
- The cooling effect of a tree is due to the evaporation of water from its leaves.

1. (*e*) Genetic Basis of Heterosis and Inbreeding Depression: Heterosis, hybrid vigor, or outbreeding enhancement is the improved or increased function of any biological quality in a hybrid offspring. An offspring is heterotic if its traits are enhanced as a result of mixing the genetic contributions of its parents. Inbreeding depression refers to the decrease or loss of fitness and strength which is mainly caused due to inbreeding. In simpler form, the mating between the relatives in a small population is common and this may lower the population's ability to persist and reproduce which is referred to as inbreeding depression.

3. (*a*) Differentiate between linkage and crossing over

Linkage	Crossing Over
Ensures that the genes stay in a chromosome to inherit together	Crossing over enables the separation of genes in a chromosome and separates it into various gametes
The strength of the genetic linkage between 2 genes is thought to be inversely proportional to the distance between them in the chromosome	The probability of two genes crossing over is directly proportional to the distance between them in the chromosome
The strength of the linkage between 2 genes can increase if the distance between them decreases	The probability of two genes crossing over decreases if the distance between them decreases
Ensures the continuity of the parental trait in the offspring	Causes alternations in the parental traits in the offspring
Reduces the probability of variation through sexual reproduction	Increases the probability of introducing variability in sexual reproduction

Did Mendel Recognize the Phenomenon of Linkage?

The main drawback in Mendelian experiments is that linkage was not defined by Mendel. In his cross, the characters which he studied were located on different chromosomes. Otherwise, if it was located on the same chromosome, linkage would have occurred and the results obtained and interpreted by Mendel would show some difference.

Linked Genes Violate the Law of Independent Assortment: Although all of Mendel's pea characteristics behaved according to the law of independent assortment, we now know that some allele combinations are not inherited independently of each other. Genes that are located on separate non-homologous chromosomes will always sort independently. However, each chromosome contains hundreds or thousands of genes organized linearly on chromosomes like beads on a string. The segregation of alleles into gametes can be influenced by linkage, in which genes that are located physically close to each other on the same chromosome are more likely to be inherited as a pair. However, because of the process of recombination, or "crossover," it is possible for two genes on the same chromosome to behave independently, or as if they are not linked. To understand this, let's consider the biological basis of gene linkage and recombination.

TtIi (top parent) × TtIi (side parent)

	TI	*Ti*	*tI*	*ti*
TI	*TTII*	*TTIi*	*TtII*	*TtIi*
Ti	*TTIi*	*TTii*	*TtIi*	*Ttii*
tI	*TtII*	*TtIi*	*ttII*	*ttIi*
ti	*TtIi*	*Ttii*	*ttIi*	*ttii*

Figure: *Unlinked genes assort independently: This figure shows all possible combinations of offspring resulting from a dihybrid cross of pea plants that are heterozygous for the tall/dwarf and inflated/constricted alleles.*

Homologous chromosomes possess the same genes in the same linear order. The alleles may differ on homologous chromosome pairs, but the genes to which they correspond do not. In preparation for the first division of meiosis, homologous chromosomes replicate and synapse. Like genes on the homologous align with each other. At this stage, segments of homologous chromosomes exchange linear segments of genetic material. This process is called recombination, or crossover, and it is a common genetic process. Because the genes are aligned during recombination, the gene order is not altered. Instead, the result of recombination is that maternal and paternal alleles are combined onto the same chromosome. Across a given chromosome, several recombination events may occur, causing extensive shuffling of alleles.

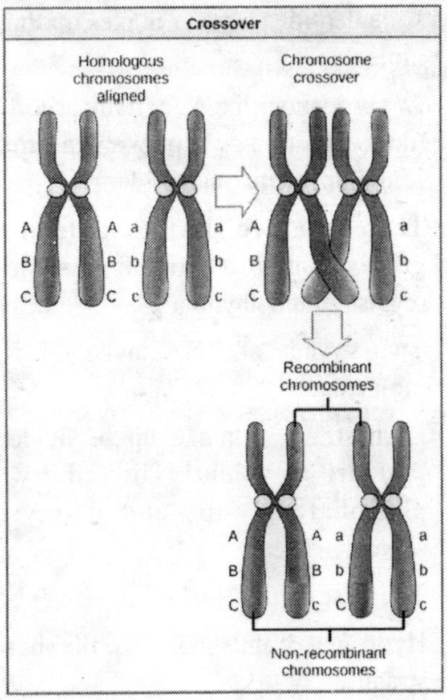

Figure: *Linked genes can be separated by recombination: The process of crossover, or recombination, occurs when two homologous chromosomes align during meiosis and exchange a segment of genetic material. Here, the alleles for gene C were exchanged. The result is two recombinant and two non-recombinant chromosomes.*

When two genes are located in close proximity on the same chromosome, they are considered linked, and their alleles tend to be transmitted through meiosis together. To exemplify this, imagine a dihybrid cross involving flower colour and plant height in which the genes are next to each other on the chromosome. If one homologous chromosome has alleles for tall plants and red flowers, and the other chromosome has genes for short plants and yellow flowers, then when the gametes are formed, the tall and red alleles will go together into a gamete and the short and yellow alleles will go into other gametes. These are called the parental genotypes because they have been inherited intact from the parents of the individual producing gametes. But unlike if the genes were on different chromosomes, there will be no gametes with tall and yellow alleles and no

- A nucleotide polymer makes up the DNA molecule.
- A nitrogenous base, a five-carbon sugar (deoxyribose), and a phosphate group are found in each nucleotide.
- There are two purines (adenine and guanine) and two pyrimidines in the DNA (cytosine and thymine).
- Two strands of DNA make up a DNA molecule.
- Each strand is made up of nucleotides that are covalently linked by their phosphate groups and deoxyribose sugars.
- The bases grow out of this backbone.
- Hydrogen bonds connect the bases of strands.
- Adenine is always linked with thymine, while cytosine is always linked with guanine.
- The two strands wrap around each other in a shape termed the 'double helix' because of the bonding.

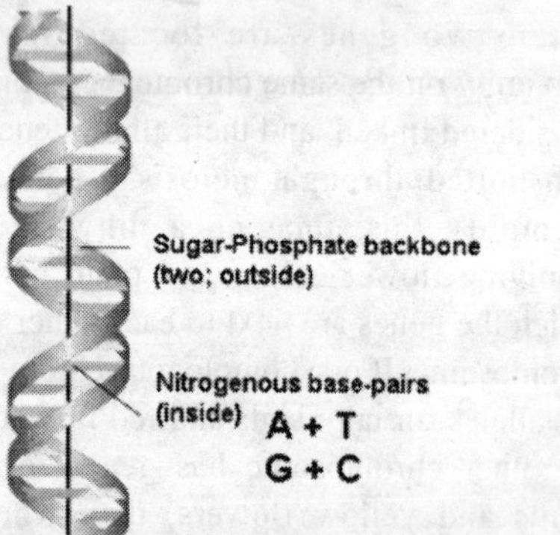

Watson and Crick Structure of DNA

- The second nucleic acid found in the cells is ribonucleic acid (RNA). RNA is a nucleotide polymer with a single strand.
- It also contains sugar ribose instead of deoxyribose and nucleotide uracil instead of thymine.
- RNA molecules play a role in the formation of proteins using DNA's genetic code.
- Prokaryotes have a single circular chromosome with double strands.
- Eukaryotes have chromosomes that include double-stranded linear DNA molecules.
- Nucleosomes are formed when the DNA helix wraps around proteins.
- Protein coils get progressively more coiled, and the chromosomes become even more coiled throughout mitosis and meiosis to make movement easier.
- Chromosomes feature two unique regions that may be differentiated by staining and are determined by whether the DNA in a region is expressed (euchromatin) or not (heterochromatin).

Features of the Watson-Crick Structure of DNA: The Watson-Crick model of DNA has the following important characteristics:

- In a DNA molecule, a right-handed double-helix is made up of a series or strands of two polynucleotides spirally wrapped around each other and twisted along a common path.
- The two strands run in opposing directions, with the fifth ending of one chain facing the third ending of the other. In other words, they are antiparallel.
- The sugar-phosphate backbones remain on the exterior, while the purines and pyrimidines bases are located at the centre of the helix.
- The two series are kept together by hydrogen bonds formed between the purines and pyrimidine bases of the opposing strands.
- Adenine (A) will always couple with thymine (T) through two hydrogen interactions, while guanine (G) will

always pair with cytosine (C) via three hydrogen bonds. This complementary nature is known as the rule of the base pair. As a result, the two chains are complementary to each other.

- The base sequence varies throughout a polynucleotide chain. A certain sequence of bases carries genetic information.
- The constitution of the base of the DNA follows Chargaff's assumptions (E.E. Chargff, 1950), according to which A = T and G = C. As a corollary, $\sum$ purines (A + G) = $\sum$ pyrimidines (C + T). Also, (A + C) = (G + T). The rules also put forth the ratio of (A + T) and (G + C) as constants for a species (range 0.4 to 1.9).
- The DNA has a diameter of 20 nm, or 20Å. The adjoining bases are 0.34 nm or 3.4Å along the axis apart. The length of a full helix turn is 3.4 nm or 34Å, implying that there are 10b/turning.
- A small groove, called the minor groove (1.2 nm), and a deep groove, known as the major groove (2.2 nm), run across the DNA helix.

3. (*b*) Backcross Method of Plant Breeding and its Application in Development of Biotic Stress Tolerant or Resistant Varieties with Suitable Diagram:

With all of the advances in molecular biology, it may seem surprising to find out that traditional plant breeding methods are still needed in the development of plant varieties. Today, the backcross procedure is most often used to move a transgene from a good tissue culture variety that was used in transformation to an elite experimental line or variety. It turns out that for many crops, once the transgene is in the crop species crossing is more efficient than transformation procedures. Backcrossing is more efficient than transforming the elite line because most transformation protocols are optimized for a specific (often poorly adapted and lower yielding) laboratory line. Many elite lines (which are high yielding) are not amenable for transformation. Hence genetic engineers transform their lab line and breeders backcross the trangene from the lab line into the elite line.

The backcross method has been used extensively for transferring qualitative characters (characters with clear phenotypes that are easy to identify in cross progeny) such as disease resistance. It is effective in both self and cross pollinated crop species.

The actual procedure for back crossing is almost self-explanatory. In back crossing you have a donor parent (has a gene of interest) and a recurrent parent (an elite line that could be made better by adding the gene of interest). The donor parent is crossed to the recurrent parent. The progeny of this cross is then crossed to the recurrent parent (it is 'crossed back' to the recurrent parent, hence the term back cross). The progeny of this cross is selected for the trait of interest and then crossed back to the recurrent parent. This process is repeated for as many back crosses as are needed to create a line that is the recurrent parent with the gene of interest from the donor parent. The goal of backcrossing is to obtain a line as identical as possible to the recurrent parent with the addition of the gene of interest that has been added through breeding.

In the end, keep only the individuals homozygous for the resistance gene. To obtain them, self Rr plants from BC4. The resulting offspring will be 1RR : 2Rr : 1rr. Progeny testing would be needed to identify RR from Rr plants. Progeny testing is where the genotype of a parent plant is determined by genotypes of the line's progeny. In the case of RR plant, the progeny will all be RR (no segregation for the gene/trait). However in the case of an Rr plant, the progeny will segregate 1/4 RR : 1/2 Rr : 1/4 rr. Therefore, the progeny of RR plants will be uniformly resistant to leaf rust, while the progeny of Rr plants will segregate for resistance and susceptibility.

have been developed through the use of wild species *Vitis amurensis* in the breeding programme. In sugarcane, cold tolerance has been transferred from wild species in USA. Drought tolerance in peas and wheat, salt tolerance in tomato, tolerance to calcareous soils and photo insensitivity in Pennisetum have been achieved through the use of their wild species in the breeding programmes.

- **Improvement in Yield:** Improvement in yield has also been achieved through the use of wild species in some crops. For example, in oat yield increase of 25-30% over the recurrent parent was obtained from a cross between *Avena sativa* × *A. sterilis.* High yielding transgressive segregants were obtained after 4 backcrosses. Increase in yield has been reported in several crops such as Vigna, Zea, Ribes, Vanilla, Arachis, potato and tobacco through interspecific hybridization. In tobacco, yields were increased by the use of wild species *Nicotianci debneyi.* Yields of sugarcane and octaploid strawberries have been increased by the use of their wild species.
- **Mode of Reproduction:** Use of wild species in the hybridization programmes sometimes leads to alteration in the mode of reproduction. The male sterility is the most common alteration in the mode of reproduction which results from interspecific hybridization. Cytoplasmic male sterility (CMS) is an economic device for hybrid seed production. CMS has been discovered in crosses between wild and cultivated species in wheat, cotton, barley, tobacco, potato, sunflower and ryegrass. The CMS has been transferred to cultivated species of these crops. Apomictic genes have been transferred from maize — Tripsacum cross to maize and from wild species of Beta to cultivated species. The cleistogamy and self-fertility traits of wild Secale have been transferred to cultivated rye (*Secale cereale*).
- **Other Characters:** There are several other desirable characters which have been transferred from wild species to cultivated plants. For example, wild species have been used to transfer dark green colour and excellent leaf texture in lettuce and bright red thin flesh in red peppers. Semi-dwarf wheat has obtained from *Triticum* × *Agropyron* hybrid derivatives. Short statured oil palms resulted from interspecific hybrids. Earliness has been achieved from use of wild species in soybean.

(ii) **Hybrid Varieties:** Improved hybrid cultivars have been developed through the use of wild species mainly in sugarcane, potato and some forage crops. Most of the modern cultivars of sugarcane and potato are the derivatives of interspecific hybridization. In cotton, commercial interspecific hybrids have been developed both at tetraploid and diploid levels but between cultivated species only. Some of the varieties of upland cotton (MCU 2, MCU 5, Deviraj, Devitej, G 67, Khandwa 1, Khandwa 2, Badnawar 1 PKV081, Rajat and Arogya) are derivatives of interspecific hybridization. A hybrid between Pearl-millet and napier grass has been developed which has become very popular by virtue of its high fodder yield potential and superior fodder quality.

(iii) **New Crop Species:** Sometimes, distant hybridization and polyploidy lead to creation of new crop species. Nicotiana digluta has been synthesized from a cross between *N. tabacum* and *N. glutinosa.* Triticale is the example of new crop which has evolved from an intergeneric cross between *Triticum aestivum* and *Secale sereale* and combines good characters of both the species.

3. (*c*) **Characters of Purelines:** Johannsen (1903, 1926), a Danish biologist, developed the concept of pure-line theory working with Princess variety of common bean (*Phaseolus vulgaris*). The common bean is a self-pollinated species. Johannsen isolated 19 different lines on the basis of seed weight form the original seed of the princess variety. Each of the 19 isolated lines had characteristic mean weight of seed. The line No. 1 with largest seed had a mean weight of 640 mg and the line No. 19 with smallest seed showed mean seed weight of 350 mg. There were seeds of various sizes within each line but the variability within the line was much lesser than the original seed lot. When the seeds in each line were separated into various classes of 100 mg difference and grown separately, the seeds of different classes within a pure-line produced progeny with the same mean weight. In other words, the largest and smallest seed from a line produced progeny with the same mean weight.

He concluded that:

(*i*) continuous inbreeding (selfing) leads to homozygosity,

(*ii*) variation within a pure-line results from environmental factors only,

(*iii*) selection within a pure line is not effective because all the plants in a pure-line have exactly the same genotype, and

(*iv*) selection in the original population is effective because the plants have genetic variation.

The main effect of self-pollination is increase in homozygosity. The homozygosity refers to the proportion of homozygous individuals in a population. Thus there is difference between homozygous and homozygosity. The term homozygous is used for individuals having like alleles on the corresponding locus and homozygosity refers to the proportion of homozygous plants in a population.

- All plants within a pure line have the same genotype.
- The variation with in a pureline is environmental and nonheritable.
- Purelines become genetically variable with time due to natural hybridization, mutationand mechanical mixtures.

Procedure of Pureline Selection with Achievement Made in Agriculture

First year: An old variety or landrace is used for pure line selection. Population they selected for pureline selection is homozygous. Single plant is selected and harvested separately superior plants must be selected from the mixed population. About 1000-2000 plants are selected depending on the available resources.

Second year: The individual progenies are grown separately with proper spacing the top 15-20 progenies are selected and they are bulked. Poor, defective, weak and segregating progenies are discarded. Selection should be based on simply inherited character like plant type, plant height, grain type, flowering and maturity duration disease resistance this process may be repeated.

Third year: Seed of the individual plant progenies are not enough to conduct a replication trail. So, they are grown in unreplicated trial with check.

Fourth year: Replicated yield trials are conducted using the best available check variety. This may be repeated for 2-3 year. All the observation are recorded.

Fifth to Eighth year: Promising strains are evaluated at several locations along with strains or check. The best progeny / strain is released as a new variety and its seed multiplication in initiated for distributed to the farmer.

Advantages: Maximum possible improvement over original variety. Uniform and more attractive, easily identifiable.

Disadvantages: This method can isolate only superior genotypes, it can not create new genotypes. And not applicable in cross pollinated crop. Poor adaptability due to narrow genetic base vulnerable for new diseases and pests.

4. (*a*) **Somaclonal Variation:** Larkin and Scowcroft (1981) proposed the term somaclone to describe the plants originating from any type of tissue culture. Genetic variation found to occur between somaclones in plant tissue cultures was called somaclonal variation. This variation includes aneuploids, sterile plants and morphological variants, sometimes involving traits of economic importance in case of crop plants. The usefulness of variation was first demonstrated through the recovery of disease resistant plants in potato (resistance against late blight and early blight) and sugarcane (resistance against eye-spot disease, Fiji disease and downy mildew).

Causes of Somaclonal Variation: There are three main reasons to causes the somaclonal variation.

- ***Physiological causes:*** The somaclonal variation developed due to physiological activity such as plant hormone, plant growth regulators, and culture conditions of the media. This type of variation caused when the sample expose a longer time in a particular conditions.
- ***Genetic causes:*** The most of the somaclonal variations developed due to genetic reason. The genetic causes govern by changes in chromosomal number (Euploidy, Aneuploidy, Polyploidy, Monoploidy) chromosomal structure (deletion, inversion, duplication, translocation), gene mutation (transition, transversion, insertion, deletion), plasma gene mutation (self-replicating genetic particle postulated to be in the cytoplasm of a cell, as like in mitochondria) and DNA sequences (Changes in DNA, protein) etc.
- ***Biochemical causes:*** This is developed by some biochemical elements such as nitrogen metabolism, antibiotics resistance, carbon metabolism and lack of photosynthetic ability.

Table-1 : *Crop improvement through somaclonal variation*

Sl. No.	Plant	Trait improved
1.	Apple (*Malusx domestica* Borkh.)	Resistance to *Erwinia amylovora*
2.	Brinjal (*Solanum melongena* L.)	Stress tolerant somaclone selection
3.	Banana (*Musa acuminate* L.)	Semi dwarf and resistant to Fusarium wilt
4.	Capsicum (*Capsicum annuum* L.)	Yellow fruited var. Bell sweet
5.	Potato (*Solanum tuberosum* L.)	Somaclones for heat tolerance
6.	Rice (*Oryza sativa*)	Submerge tolerance
7.	Wheat (*Triticum aestivum*)	Resistance to *Bipolaris sorokiniana*

Table-2: *Variety developed through somaclonal variation*

SN	Crop	Variety	Released year	Characteristics	Developed by
1.	Sugarcane	Co 94012 (Phule savitri)	2006	High yield, red rot and smut diseases resistant	MPKV, Rahuri
		VSI 434	2016	High cane and sugar yield, high sucrose content and moderately resistant to smut, grassy shoot and red rot diseases	VSI, Pune
2.	Rice	Dama	1992	Haploid somaclone, salinity tolerance	Heszky and Simon-Kiss, Hungary

Factors Influencing Somaclonal Variants: Some of the important factors that influence development of somaclonal variants by without *in vitro* selection and with *in vitro* selection are briefly described.

Genotype and explant source: The nature of genotype of the plants influences the frequency of regeneration and frequency of production of somaclones. Explants can be taken from any part of plant — leaves, roots, internodes, ovaries etc. The source of explant is very critical for somaclonal variations. For instance, potato plants regenerated from callus of rachis and petiole are much higher (~50%) compared to those regenerated from callus of leaves (~12%).

Duration of cell culture: In general, for many plant cultures, somaclonal variations are higher with increased duration of cultures. For example, it was reported that genetic variability increased in tobacco protoplasts from 1.5 to 6% by doubling the duration of cultures.

Growth hormone effects: The plant growth regulators in the medium will influence the karyotypic alterations in cultured cells, and therefore development of somaclones. Growth hormones such as 2, 4-dichlorophenoxy acetic acid (2, 4-D) and naphthalene acetic acid (NAA) are frequently used to achieve chromosomal variability.

Besides the factors discussed above, selection of somaclones with in vitro selection are dependent on the following parameters:

- Selection propagule (cells, protoplasts, calli).
- Selection agent (toxin, herbicide, amino acid analogue).
- Technique used for selection.
- Stability of resistant substance.
- In vivo testing procedure.
- Ability for regeneration of plants.

4. (*b*) Dormancy of Seed: Dormancy is a delaying mechanism which prevents germination under conditions which might prove to be unsuitable for establishment. As long as the seed remains viable the possibility exists that it may eventually find itself more favourably placed. Seed dormancy can be defined as the state or a condition in which seeds are prevented from germinating even under the favourable environmental conditions for germination including, temperature, water, light, gas, seed coats, and other mechanical restrictions. In many species seeds are incapable of germinating because of some inhibitory factor(s). Such seeds even placed under suitable environments of germination are unable to germinate. Sometimes the seeds are quiescent. Such seeds do not germinate because of the lack of favourable environmental conditions. This condition may vary from days to months and even years. These conditions are the combination of light, water, heat, gases, seed coats and hormone structures.

Causes for Seed Dormancy

- Factors
  - Environmental
    - negative or positive light requirement
    - high temperature
    - absence of water
  - Internal
    - seed coat (no gas exchange)
    - seed coat (mechanical effects)
    - immature embryo
    - low ethylene
    - inhibitor present (coumarin, para-ascorbic acid, etc.)
    - growth promoters absent
  - Timing mechanism
    - after ripening
    - loss of inhibitor
    - appearance of growth promoter

- **Light Requirements:** Some seeds require a definite light treatment before they can germinate. Such seeds supposedly possess inhibitors(s) which are disintegrated by light.
- **Temperature (Thermodormancy):** In seeds of many plant species pretreatment with low temperature quickens germination whereas high temperature inhibits their germination. Stratification is a process where seeds are layered in some trays and cold air is blown over them for several weeks or months. The chilling may-affect embryo or seed-coat or both the parts of the seeds. It seems at low

temperature Abscisic acid (ABA) present in the seeds is broken down. In some seeds seed-coat causes dormancy and stratification decreases the ABA level. On the contrary chilling promotes Gibberellic acid (GA) synthesis.

- **Seed coat effect:** Dormancy in some seeds is due to the occurrence of hard seed coat. Once removed the seeds start germinating. Possibly biochemical or physiological processes may be involved in such a dormancy. In some instances, seed coat is hard and impervious to oxygen. If in such instances the seed coat is broken and oxygen supplied, there is stimulation of seed germination. Seed coat, if hard and impervious, may also prevent diffusion of inhibitors.
- **Immature embryo:** In Ranunculus and some members of orchidaceae dormancy is due to immature embryos.
- **Inhibitors:** Seeds of some species may contain inhibitors which act as germination inhibitors. These inhibitors may be located in the seed coat, glumes or some parts of the fruit, endosperm, embryo, etc. Coumarin, para-ascorbic acid, etc. are some of the very common inhibitors. On the contrary, KNO_3, kinetin, GA counteract these inhibitors and promote seed germination. Some seeds show secondary dormancy *i.e.,* due to the lack of suitable environmental conditions they fail to do so.

Methods of Breaking Seed Dormancy: The different methods of breaking dormancy are mentioned below:

(*a*) **The natural breaking of Seed Dormancy:** Nature of dormancy stops when the embryo gets appropriate environment such as adaptive moisture and temperature. The seed coat that exists in many species becomes permeable due to the rupturing of smoothing action of natural agents like microorganism, temperature, and abrasion by the digestive tract of birds and animals that feed on these seeds. Other natural methods include:

- Completion of the over-ripening period.
- Leaching of inhibitors present in the seed coat.
- Inactivation of inhibitors by the supply of cold, heat, and light.
- Leaching of the excess and highly concentrated solutes from the seeds.
- Production of growth hormones which can neutralize the effect of inhibitors.

(*b*) **Artificial Overcoming of Seed Dormancy:** Some of the artificial methods used for breaking seed dormancy are listed below:

- Action with hot water for termination of waxes, surface inhibitors, etc.
- Rupturing of seed coats by filing, chipping, or threshing through machines.
- Exposure to heat, cold or light, depending upon the type of seed dormancy.
- By applying Hydraulic pressure for 5 to 20 minutes in order to weaken the tough seed coats.
- Seed coats are treated with concentrated sulphuric acid for removing all traces of the mineral acid.

Treatment to Break Dormancy in Seeds

There are separate treatments to overcome dormancy and they are further divided into the following groups:

Seed coat treatment: These treatments make a hard seed coat permeable to water or gases either by softening or cracking. This process is called scarification. The treatment can be either chemical or physical in nature.

Embryo treatments:

- ***Mechanical Scarification:*** Seeds having very hard seed coat when scratched with some abrasive material, softens the coat and makes it pervious to water.

- ***Chemical Scarification:*** Dipping of seeds in strong acids like H_2SO_4 or some organic solvents e.g. acetone, alcohol or even dipping in boiling water breaks dormancy by weakening the seed coat.
- In some instances, seeds subjected to high oxygen pressure also germinate.
- Immature embryo dormancy may be broken when embryos are allowed to complete their development.
- Through the application of some chemical like potassium nitrate, gibberellin, kinetin etc., it is possible to counteract the inhibition on seed germination. Cyanide, azide, thiourea also induce germination.

4. (*c*) Photosynthetic Pigments in Plants: A pigment is a generic term for a molecule that absorbs light and has a colour. Plants contain many pigments, giving rise to the various colours we see. Flowers and fruits obviously contain a large number of organic molecules that absorb light. Leaves, stems and roots also contain a variety of pigments. Such pigment molecules include anthocyanins, flavanoids, flavines, quinones and cytochromes, just to name a few. However, none of these should be considered a photosynthetic pigment. Photosynthetic pigments are the only pigments that have the ability to absorb energy from sunlight and make it available to the photosynthetic apparatus. In land plants, there are two classes of these photosynthetic pigments, the chlorophylls and the carotenoids. The ability of chlorophyll and carotenoid molecules to absorb the energy of light and use it effectively is related to their molecular structure and to their organization within the cell.

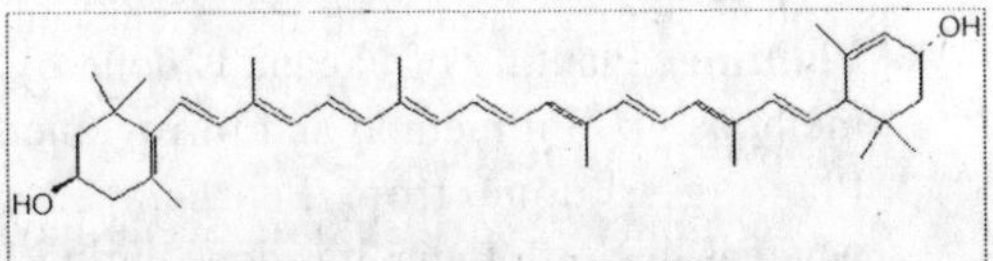

Lutein, an carotenoid hidroxilado tipico

Structure A: *Molecular structure of lutein, a carotenoid.*

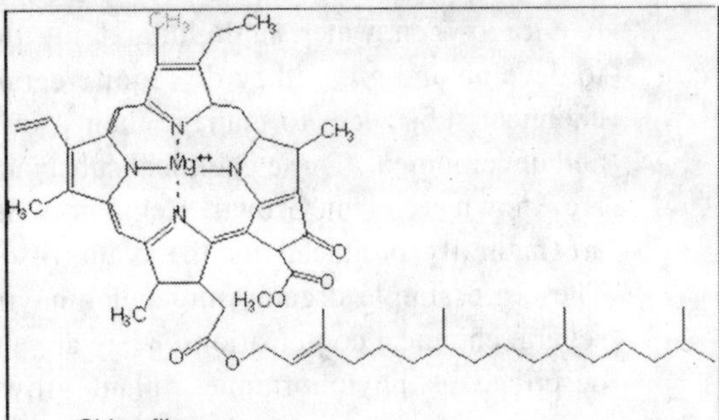

Chlorofila a

Structure B: *Molecular structure of chlorophyll.*

Examine the molecular structure of representative chlorophyll and carotenoid molecules in Figures: Structure A and B. Notice the linear system of conjugated double bonds in the carotenoid (lutein) and the zig-zag of conjugated double bonds in the large ring structure. of the chlorophyll. These systems of conjugated double bonds are responsible for the ability to absorb light energy from photons.

Factors Influencing Photosynthesis: Various factors influence/affect the photosynthesis process. These are:

- **Light Intensity:** More the light, the more will be the rate of photosynthesis. Similarly, low light will lead to a low rate of photosynthesis.
- **The Concentration of CO_2:** A higher CO_2 concentration rate in a plant also accelerates the photosynthesis process. The required amount of CO_2 is 300-400 PPM.
- **Temperature:** If the temperature is between the range of 25 to 35 degrees Celsius, photosynthesis takes place effectively.
- **Water:** An essential amount of water is required for stomatal opening, and it's a key factor in the process of photosynthesis.
- **Pollution:** The increasing rate of polluting particles in the atmosphere block the pores of somatic cells, and the intake of carbon dioxide becomes difficult.

5. (*a*) Plant Growth Regulators: As the plants require oxygen, water, sunlight, and nutrition to develop and grow, they do require certain chemical substances to manage their growth and development. These chemical substances are known as Plant Growth Regulators and are naturally produced by the plants itself. These are simple organic molecules having several chemical compositions. They are also described as phytohormones, plant growth substances, or plant growth hormones. They can accelerate as well as retard the rate of growth in plants. Plants growth hormones or plant growth regulators exhibit the following characteristics:

- Differentiation and elongation of cells.
- Formation of leaves, flowers, and stems.
- Wilting of leaves.
- Ripening of fruit.
- Seed dormancy, etc.

Generally, there are five types of plant hormones, namely, auxin, gibberellins (GAs), cytokinins, abscisic acid (ABA) and ethylene. In addition to these, there are more derivative compounds, both natural and synthetic, which also act as plant growth regulators.

Functions of Auxins in Plants and Mechanism of Their Action:

- Facilitate flowering in plants.
- Used in the process of plant propagation.
- Used by gardeners to keep lawns free from weeds.
- Involved in the initiation of roots in stem cuttings.
- Prevention of dropping of leaves and fruits at early stages.
- Regulate xylem differentiation and assists in cell division.
- Auxins are widely used as herbicides to kill dicot weeds.
- Used to produce fruit without preceding fertilization.
- Promote natural detachment (abscission) of older leaves and fruits.
- Apical dominance may occur in which the growth of lateral buds is inhibited by the growth of apical buds.
- These are produced by the apex of root and shoot.

The plant hormone auxin triggers complex growth and developmental processes. Its underlying molecular mechanism of action facilitates rapid switching between transcriptional repression and gene activation through the auxin-dependent degradation of transcriptional repressors.

5. (*b*) Package of Practices of Banana Cultivation in North India

The botanical names of banana are *Musa cavendish* and *Musa paradisiaca*, which belongs to the family Musaceae.

Climate: Being a tropical crop, banana requires warm, humid and rainy climate. The optimum temperature range is 10 to 40°C and the relative humidity is 90% or above. It is highly susceptible to frost and cannot tolerate arid conditions. Strong desiccating winds cause considerable reduction in the growth of the plant and yield and quality of fruits.

Soil: Banana is a heavy feeder crop/. Therefore, fertility of soil is very important. Rich, well drained, fertile, free working, soils with plenty of organic matter are best suited for cultivation. The optimum range of pH of soil should be 6 to 8.

Propagation: Commercial edible bananas do not produce viable seeds. So, the banana is commonly propagated by suckers and sword suckers with narrow leaves. Rhizomes whole or in bits from fruited and non-fruited plants with at least one sound bud can be successfully used as propagating material.

Planting: Planting of banana is done by two methods viz. Pit method and furrow method. Planting is done from February to May whereas in North India, it is done during July-August. In South-India, it can be done any time of year except summer. Tall varieties should be planted at 3 × 3 m whereas dwarf ones at 2 × 2 m apart.

Manuring: Banana is a heavy feeder and responds well to manuring. Banana is a quick growing and short-lived plant. Therefore, it is more beneficial, if quick growing fertilizers are applied. In Tamil Nadu, application of 100 g of N, 30 g of P_2O_5 and 300 g of K_2O per plant to be supplied in three doses during the second, third and fifth months is recommended. In Maharashtra, 100 g N, 40 g P_2O_5 and 100 g K_2O per plant is recommended. Out of these, P_2O_5 and K_2O is applied at the time of planting and N is given is three split doses: third, fourth and fifth month after planting.

After Cares:

- **Desuckering:** Desuckering is an important operation in banana cultivation. In this, the unwanted suckers, which develop near the base of the plant, are removed. Cutting the suckers from ground level and then pouring the kerosene (2-3 drops) to kill the growing point of pseudostem does it.
- **Propping:** It is an essential cultural practice to give proper support to the plants with bamboos. It is done to avoid falling down of plants due to high winds.
- **Wrapping:** To protect the fruits from sunburn, hot wind and dust the bunch is covered. Wrapping is also done to improve the colour of the fruit.

Harvesting and Yield: Harvesting of banana is done 12 to 15 months after planting in dwarf and 15 to 18 months after planting in tall varieties. Signs of maturity of banana fruits are, fruit becomes plumpy and angles are filled in completely, when tapped gives metallic sound, drying off of top leaves and change in colour of fruits from deep green to light green. Tall varieties like Poovan yield 15-25 tonnes/ha, while Dwarf Cavenshish yield 25-50 tonnes/ha. It can be stored at temperature slightly above 55°F and relative humidity of about 85-95% for about three weeks.

Varieties: Poovan, Dwarf Cavendish or Basarai, Robusta or Harisal, Rasthali or Mutheli, Rajeli or Nendran, Sonakela and Safed Velchi.

Plant Protection: Important diseases of banana are:

Panama wilt: Control Measures: Eradication of the infected plants. Growing resistant varieties like Dwarf Cavendish. Soil drenching with Vapam @ 0.85% and mercuric chloride @ 3000 PPM in nursery.

Bunchy Top: It is caused by the virus, which is transmitted by an aphid *Pentalonia nigroneruosa*. Symptoms: Infected plants have short, narrow, erect leaves with short petiole. Plants remain slanted.

Control Measures: Infected plants should be uprooted and burnt. Spraying of 2-4, D to control weeds.

Root stock weevil: Damaging stage is adult and grub.

Symptoms of damage: Grub bores into stem which is affected by fungi or bacteria.

Control measures: Use healthy suckers and rhizomes. Before planting treat the pit with 0.65%. Lindane 60-80 g/pit. Soak the sucker in 0.1% Lindane solution, spray 0.05% endosulfan.

5. (*c*) **Challenges in Fruit and Vegetable Marketing in India and its Remedial Measures:** Losses and wastage of fresh produce; Transportation facilities; Demand and market information etc. are the factors which constitutes serious challenges for Fruits and Vegetables sector and are affecting the overall growth of the agricultural development of India. There are numerous factors which will act as roadblocks for the efficient supply chain of Fruits and Vegetables sector in India. In a process of finding out the dimensions to different factors, the authors have made an effort to summarize these factors and categorized them as Cold Chain issues, Fragmented Supply Chain issues, Linkage and Integration issues, Infrastructural issues, Packaging issues, Technological issues,

Farmer's knowledge and awareness issues, Quality and Safety issues, Processing issues, Supply chain efficiency issues, Financial issues, Post-harvest losses issues, Transportation issues, Information issues.

The following are some of the measures to be followed for improving the existing system of fruit and vegetable marketing in the country:

(*i*) Establishment of regulated markets.

(*ii*) Establishment of co-operative marketing societies.

(*iii*) Extension and construction of additional storage and warehousing facilities for agricultural produce of the farmers.

(*iv*) Expansion of market yards and other allied facilities for the new and existing markets.

(*v*) Provision is made for extending adequate amount of credit facilities to the farmers.

(*vi*) Timely supply of marketing information's to the farmers.

(*vii*) Improvement and extension of road and transportation facilities for connecting the villages with mandis.

(*viii*) Provision for standardisation and grading of the produce for ensuring good quality to the consumers and better prices for the farmers.

(*ix*) Formulating suitable agricultural price policy by the Government for making a provision for remunerative prices of agricultural produce of the country.

5. (*d*) Acellular Plant Pathogens and Their Mode of Natural Transmission

Infectious, acellular pathogens. Obligate intracellular parasites with host and cell-type specificity. DNA or RNA genome (never both) Genome is surrounded by a protein capsid and, in some cases, a phospholipid membrane studded with viral.

Most acellular plant viruses are transmitted by vectors from one host to another. Virus transmission by a vector is often characterized by some degree of specificity. Numerous studies suggest the involvement of a virus-ligand interaction in transmission specificity. The coat protein (CP) and its derivatives (read through CP and minor CP), and nonstructural proteins, such as a helper component (HC) or a transmission factor, are major viral determinants of transmission specificity. A number of virion-binding vector proteins have been identified as potential receptors.

Five Cellular Pathogens and Symptoms induced by them in Potato

- Potato virus Y (PVY) is a Potyvirus, causes stipple streak. The necrotic strain generally causes mild foliage symptoms, but necrosis in the leaves of susceptible potato varieties.
- Potato virus S (PVS) is a Carlavirus, if plant infected early in the season, show a slight deepening of the veins, rough leaves, more open growth, mild mottling, bronzing, or tiny necrotic spots on the leaves. PVS is transmitted by aphids non-persistently.
- Potato virus X (PVX) is the type member of the Potyvirus family of plant viruses. Plants often do not exhibit symptoms, but the virus can cause symptoms of chlorosis, mosaic, decreased leaf size, and necrotic lesions in tubers.
- PVX can interact with PVY and PVS to cause more severe symptoms and yield loss than either virus alone. The source of this virus is infected tubers.
- Potato Spindle Tuber Viroid (PSTVd) causes mild foliar symptoms including smaller leaves that curl downward, giving the plant a more upright growth habit. Plants can also be stunted, and leaves can be grey and distorted. The stems are often more branched, with the branches having sharp angles on the stem. Tubers become narrow and spindle or oblong in shape, or more rounded than expected for a particular variety, and have prominent eyebrows.

5. (*e*) National Plan for Supply and Distribution of Food Grains

PDS is a public service infrastructure which is managed, controlled and financed by the government. Hence, it aims to attain three social objectives: (1) Ensuring fair remuneration for the farmers, thus, promoting agriculture; (2) Safeguard poor people by providing food grains at affordable prices, and (3) Efficient use of tax payers money. Off the three social objectives, determining the fair remuneration for framers as sourcing partners is completely driven by the policy design. Since, the sourcing activity also aimed at providing protection to the farmers, rather than strategic sourcing from the low cost, high quality and reliable vendor. While, the second and third objective focusing on a reliable customer service and efficient system respectively, can be handled through supply chain operations.

The public distribution system means the system of management of food economy and distribution of food grains at affordable price. This scheme provides staple food grains, such as wheat, rice, sugar & kerosene through a network of public distribution shops in the whole country. This scheme is run by ministry of consumer affairs, food and public distribution. Basic motive behind this scheme is to provide food the weaker section of the country at the cheaper/affordable rates.

PDS distributes commodities worth more than ₹ 30,000 crore annually to about 160 million families and is perhaps the largest distribution network of its kind in the world. The main agency providing food grains to the PDS is the Food Corporation of India (FCI) set up in 1965. The primary duty of the Corporation is to undertake the purchase, storage, movement, transport, distribution and sale of food grains and other foodstuffs. It ensures on the one hand that the farmers get remunerative prices for their produce and on the other hand, the consumers get food grains from the central pool at uniform prices fixed by the Government of India.

7. (*a*) (*i*) Physiological Disorder in Cauliflower

1. **Browning:** Sometimes there is a appearance of water soaked lesions in the steam, leaf and on the surface of the curd which later become rusty and brown in colour. This symptoms is mainly observed when there is a deficiency of boron in plant or in soil. To get rid out of this, soil application of Borax @ 10-15 kg/ hectare is recommended. This dose of fertilizer may differ from country to country, type of soil, time of application, methods of application & various other factors. If there is acute deficiency, spraying of Borax solution @0.25% to 0.5% is generally recommended. This means 2.5 to 5 gram of borax fertilizer on 1 liter of pure water. Spraying of fertilizer should be done at the time of early morning or at the time of evening.
2. **Whiptail:** This disorder is caued due to the deficiency of Molybdenum. Young cauliflower plants become chlorotic in nature and may turn white, particularly along the leaf margins, leaves also become cupped and wither. Whiptail develops with high nitrate supply and low molybdenum. So in acidic soil, heavy application of nitrogenous fertilizers should be avoided. Application of 1.5 kg sodium or ammonium molybdate per hectare is recommended mixed with fertilizers or irrigation water when the plants are set in the field.
3. **Buttoning:** Buttoning is generally known as the development of small curds with inadequate foliage in cauliflower. It is also referred as premature heading. The causes of buttoning are transplanting over-aged seedlings, poor nitrogen supply, and wrong selection of cultivars which means transplantation of early season variety on late season and vice-versa. Maintenance of adequate supply of nutrients and good plant population checks the disorders.

4. **Ricyness:** In this disorder velvety or granular appearance on the surface of the curd is seen. Due to higher or lower temperature than the optimum temperature required for a particular variety, temperature fluctuation at the time of curd development, poor seed stock generally causes ricyness. Selection of proper variety and transplanting at right time controls this malady.
5. **Hollow stem:** Hollowness is caused by boron deficiency and higher supply of nitrogen. It can be controlled by spraying of borax @ 15-20 kg/ha. in normal types of hollowness, spacing the plants in closer is suggested.
6. **Fuzziness:** The flower pedicels become velvety and curd elongates. The cultivation of the cultivars out of their normal growing season encourages this disorder. Sowing of good quality of seed in right times under proper cultural practices minimizes the fuzziness.

(*ii*) Physiological Disorders in Tomato

1. Fruit Cracking

Symptoms: Cracking on the surface of the fruit at the stem end is a common occurrence. It is developed mostly in fully ripe fruit than in mature green or breaker stage. Sudden water availability causes rapid fruit expansion leading to fruit cracking.

Causes:

- High temperature and high light intensity.
- Excessively rapid fruit growth cracking.
- Some cultivars crack more than other because of genotypic differences.
- Boron deficiency (especially calcareous soil).
- Fruit exposed to sunlight leads to more concentric cracking.

Management:

- Soil application Borax @ 15-20 kg/ha.
- Spraying of borax 0.25% 2-3 times fruiting stage to ripening stage.
- Maintaining plants at low to medium soil moisture so preferable to grow in the greenhouse.

Blossom End Rot (BER)

Symptoms: The water soaked area near the bottom or blossom end of the fruit. The area usually develops rapidly eventually resulting in a blackened, dry, sunken leathery spot. BER affects the blossom end of the placenta and adjacent locular contents as well as the outer wall. It can most easily be identified by a discoloured, sunken spot at the blossom end of the fruit.

Causes: BER is not caused by any single factor but a combination of one or more factors intensifying the effect it includes high salinity high $MgSO_4$, NH_4 and/ or K concentration. Accelerated growth rate, unfavourable moisture relationships.

Management:

- Cultural practices, such as the use of polyethylene mulch maintain adequate soil moisture, and avoiding varieties that are most susceptible to BER will help reduce the incidence.
- Misting or fogging inside the greenhouse reduces the incidence.
- Foliar spray of $CaCl_2$ solution 0.5%@ time of fruit developed was an effective control.

Puffiness

Symptoms: Puffiness refers to the existence of open cavities between the outer walls and the locular content in one or more locules and is also known as hollowness or boxiness.

Causes:

- Nonfertilization of ovules
- Embryo abortion after normal fertilization
- High temperature and high soil moisture are predisposing factors.

Management:

- Maintenance of normal temperature.
- Spraying of Borax or Solubor 10-15 ppm at the peak flowering time.

Sunscald or Sunburn

Symptoms: Green fruits exposed to direct sunlight ripen unevenly so that yellow patches appear on the side of the tomato fruit when it ripens. Symptoms are most likely to appear at the mature green to breaker stage of development. The lesions are infected by secondary infection of fungus which shows black dark spots making tomatoes units for consumption.

Causes:

- High fruit pericarp temperature 40°C
- In bright sunlight, surface temperature may be more than 10°C highest then the air temperature.

Management:

- The best protection against sunscald is to utilize cultivars with enough foliage to cover the fruit and to provide enough water and pest protection to maintain the healthy foliage.
- Crop are planted at higher densities are less susceptible.
- Cultivation of indeterminate /semi-determinate varieties without staking.

Blotchy Ripening

Symptoms: This disorder also known as the gray wall is recognized as grayish appearance caused by partial collapse of the wall tissue hence the term gray wall. The affected area remain green or yellow are usually found nearly at the stem end of the tomato fruit.

Causes: K deficiency.

Management:

- Use of balanced fertilizer dose (after soil testing) in the crop prevents the occurrence of blotchy ripening.
- Adjust planting date to achieve favourable light intensity for good fruit development.

Cat Face

Symptoms: Cat face is a disorder characterized by gross deformity of tomato fruit, which usually renders them unmarketable. The defect is usually located on the blossom end of the fruit cat face is a commonly observed in first harvest.

Causes: In the field air temperature of 17/10°C for a week are sufficient to induce abnormal flower development. Low temperature during the sensitive period increases the no. of locales in the fruit. The time of greatest sensitivity for an individual flower is well before anthesis.

Control:

- Maintenance of sufficient soil moisture balance.
- Recommended cultural practices should be adopted.

Gold Fleck or Gold Speck

Symptoms: Gold speck or flecks are often observed around the calyx and should of mature fruit particularly in a summer season. In green fruit, the speck is white and less abundant. The specks decrease the attractiveness of the fruit and significantly shorten its shelf life. Cells containing a granular mass of tiny calcium salt crystals, probably calcium oxalate appears as a golden colour.

Causes: These specks are considered to be symptoms of excess calcium in the fruit. Increasing the P level also increased calcium uptake rate and increased speckling.

Control: Cultivars resistant to BER tend to be more susceptible to gold spots. Increasing the electrical conductivity of the nutrient solution reduced the gold speck incidence.

(*iii*) Quincunx System of Orchard Planting:

This system of planting fruit trees is similar to square system, except that a fifth tree is planted at the centre of each square. As a result, the tree number in an unit area becomes almost double the number in the square system. The additional tree in the centre is known as "filler". The fillers are usually quick growing, early maturing and erect type fruit trees like banana, papaya, pomegranate, etc., which are removed as soon as the main fruit trees planted at the corner of the square come into bearing. The planting of filler trees provides an additional income to the grower in the early life of the orchard.

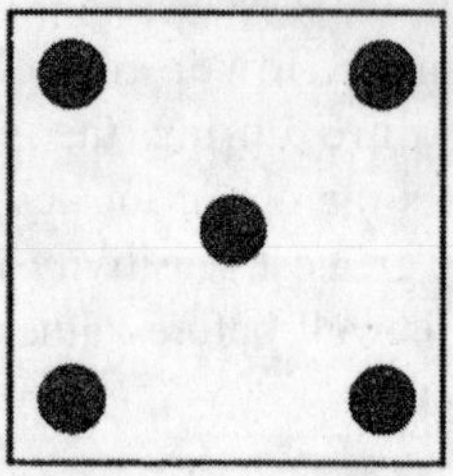

7. (*b*) (*i*) Lesser Grain Borer

Nature of Damage: Lesser grain borers mainly attack wheat, corn, rice and millet. Both the larvae and adults are primary pests. They bore irregularly shaped holes into whole, undamaged kernels and the larvae, immature stages, may develop inside the grain. Larval and adult feeding in and on grain kernels may leave only dust and thin brown shells. A sweet, musty odor is often associated with infestations of this insect.

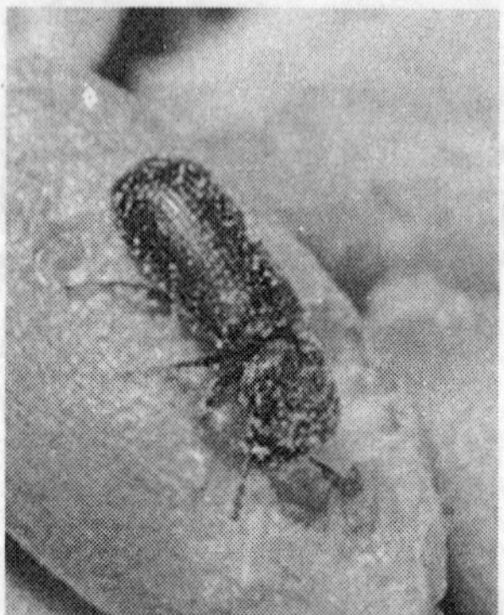

The adults (pictured right) are 0.1 inch long, brown to black beetles with cylindrical bodies and numerous small pits on the wing covers. The head is directed downward and covered by the prothorax, so that is not visible when the insect is viewed from above. The creamy white larva is a c-shaped grub with a small dark head that is partly retracted into the thorax.

Biology: The female deposits her eggs in clusters of 2 to about 30 on kernels. Most of the newly-hatched larvae chew into kernels and complete their entire development there. However, the larvae can feed on fines or can develop as free-living insects in the grain. There are four larval stages. Development from egg to adult requires about 25 days under ideal conditions of 93°F and 12% moisture. Both the larvae and adults produce a large amount of frass or waste. Larval fecal pellets are pushed out of the kernel and large amounts can accumulate in the grain. The adults are winged and may fly to spread infestations.

Management: Prevention is always the most economical and efficient method of controlling these pests. Once they are distributed within the grain mass, fumigation is the only method of relieving the problem.

(*ii*) Pulse Beetle

Biology: Breeding occurs from March to September female lays as many as 300-400 cylindrical and glistening white eggs in 20-60 day after mating. They are glued to the grains in batches, Larvae (grubs) hatch out in 5-9 days. Their body is long and constricted, and dirty white in colour. They crawl about and feed on the flour, or bore into slightly damaged grains and feed inside them. Larval life lasts for 22-52 days. Full-grown larvae are curved. They pupate inside the grains, or in the grain flour, Pupal stage lasts for nearly 7 days. Adults emerge from within the grains after making rounded holes. There would be 5 or 6 generations in a year.

Nature of Damage

- Adults and larva cause serious damages to pulses and grains.
- They bore into pulses and grains and feed inside them making tunnels.
- This severely hollows out and damages pulses and in heavy infestation, a considerable amount of frass is formed, which forms the food for the young larva.

Management

- Thoroughly dry grains and other food products before storage.
- Clean and disinfect godowns, flour mills, storage bins, bags, etc. before storing food products.
- Destroy infested food products.
- Treat food products with mild insecticides before storage.
- Periodic fumigation with methyl bromide, ethylene dibromide, etc. to kill larva and adults.

(*iii*) Rice Moth (*Corcyra cephalonica*)

Biology: The **rice moth** (*Corcyra cephalonica*) is a moth of the family Pyralidae. This small moth can become a significant pest. Its caterpillars feed on dry plantstuffs such as seeds, including cereals (e.g. rice). Other recorded foods are flour and dried fruits. This moth attacks grains, especially rice, but will also eat oil seeds, cocoa beans, dried fruit and spices. It lays up to 160 eggs on or near a food source. The larval stage lasts 15-20 days in favourable conditions and the larvae will produce masses of strong webbing which it uses to form a dense cocoon in order to pupate. This stage will last 7-10 days.

Nature of damage:

- The larva feeds on the grains and pollutes them with frass, moult and dense webbings.
- It attacks rice, sorghum, other millets whole cereals, deals, processed products of cereals, pulses oilseeds, nuts, dry fruits and milled spices.

Management

Before storing (No Chemicals)

- Before storage the intact grain must be separated from broken or injured grain.
- Grain must be cleaned off and free from any insect pests or refuges.
- Grain must be well dried (Moisture level should be at 8-10%) so that insects cannot infest the grain.
- Godown or container should be cleaned and must be free of cracks or crevices. All cracks and crevices in the godown should be filled up with cement.
- Godown should be had free ventilation so that grain may remain dry.
- Old bags and other containers should not be allowed inside the godown.
- Essential are the regular inspection of stored products and the adoption of appropriate control measure when pests are round.

Use of Chemicals

- Two tablets of Phostoxin (Aluminium phosphide) each of 3 g per 1 ton grain are very much useful protective measure in large godowns.
- Fumitox tablet can be used @ 4-6 tabs/1000 kg seeds.
- Grain should be stored by mixing 10% Sevin or Malathion dust @ 1 lbs/40 mounds (only for seed purpose) or 1 lbs/80 mounds (for general consume).
- Grain bins and containers (Jute bag or other bags) should be treated with Malathion 50 E @0.25 ml/L or Fenitrothion 50 EC @ 0.25 ml/L or Deltamethrin 2.5% @ 0.75 g/L water before storing the grains.
- Use of mixture of 120 g of the powder of Neem+ Nishida+ Bishkatali per mound of grain (only for seed purposes).

Curative/Remedial Measures

- Seed should be treated with Ethylene dichloride (ED) or Carbon tetrachloride (CT) @ 1-1.5 lbs/15 mounds.
- DDVP/Vapona @1-2 oz/100 cft area.
- Dusting with 10% Sevin/Malathion @ 8 oz/100 cft of stock.
- Use of Methyl bromide (MB) @ 1-1.5 lbs/1000 cft area, an exposure period of 24 hrs.
- Dusting with Agrocide-3 @ 8 oz/100 square feet of stock surface.

- Applying EDCT (Ethylene dichloride with Carbon tetrachloride) 3 : 1 killopter or DDVP (Dimethyl dichlorovinyl phosphate) @ 1-2 oz/1000 cft.

7. (c) Influence of Photoperiodism and Vernalisation in Flowering Plants

Photoperiodism: The plants in order to flower require a certain day length i.e., the relative length of day and night which is called as photoperiod. The response of plants to the photoperiod expressed in the form of flowering is called as photoperiodism. Depending upon the duration of the photoperiod, they classified plants into three categories.

1. **Short Day Plants (SDP):** These plants require a relatively short-day light period (usually 8-10 hours) and a continuous dark period of about 14-16 hours for subsequent flowering. Some examples of these plants which are also known as long-night-plants are Maryland Mammoth variety of tobacco (*Nicotiana tabacum*), Biloxi variety of Soybeans (*Glycine max*), Cocklebur (*Xanthium pennsylvanicum*).
2. **Long Day Plants (LDP):** These plants require a longer day light period (usually 14-16 hours) in a 24 hours cycle for subsequent flowering. Some examples of these plants which are also called as short night plants are *Hyoscyamus niger* (Henbane) Spinacea (spinach) Beta vulgaris (Sugar beet).
3. **Day Neutral Plants:** These plants flower in all photoperiods ranging from 5 hours to 24 hours continuous exposure. Some of the examples of these plants are tomato, cotton, sunflower, cucumber and certain varieties of peas and tobacco. During recent years certain intermediate categories of plants have also been recognised. They are:

   Long-Short Day Plants: These are short day plants but must be exposed to long days during early periods of growth for subsequent flowering. Some of the examples of these plants are certain species of *Bryophyllum*.

   Short-Long Day Plants: These are long day plants but must be exposed to short days during early periods of growth for subsequent flowering. Some of the examples of these plants are certain varieties of wheat (*Triticum*) and rye (*Secale*).

Photoperiodic Induction: Plants may require one or more inductive cycles for flowering. An appropriate photoperiod in 24 hours cycle constitutes one inductive cycle. If a plant which has received sufficient inductive cycles is subsequently placed under unfavourable photoperiods, it will still flower. Flowering will also occur if a plant receives inductive cycles after intervals of unfavourable photoperiods (i.e., discontinuous inductive cycles). This persistence of photoperiodic after effect is called as photoperiodic induction.

- An increase in the number of inductive cycles results in early flowering of the plant. For instance, Xanthium (a short day plant) requires only one inductive cycle and normally flowers after about 64 days. It can be made to flower even after 13 days if it has received 4-8 inductive cycles. In such cases the number of flowers is also increased.
- Continuous inductive cycles promote early flowering than discontinuous inductive cycles.

Perception of the Photoperiodic Stimulus and Presence of a Floral Hormone:

It is now well established that the photoperiodic stimulus is perceived by the leaves. As a result, a floral hormone is produced in the leaves which is then trans located to the apical tip, subsequently causing the initiation of floral primordia.

That the photoperiodic stimulus is perceived by the leaves can be shown by simple experiments on cocklebur (*Xanthium pennsylvanicum*), a short day plant. Cocklebur plant will flower if it has previously been kept under short-day conditions (Fig. A). If the plant is defoliated and then kept under short day condition, it will not flower (Fig. B). Flowering will also occur even if all the leaves of the plant except one leaf have been removed (Fig. C).

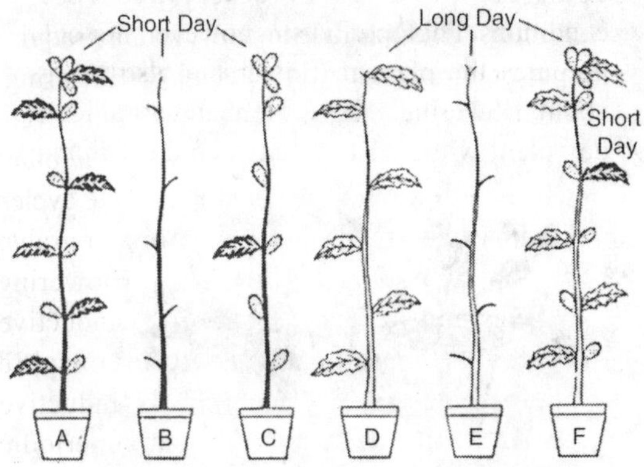

Fig. *Experiment on cocklebur plants to show that photoperiodic stimulus is perceived by the leaves. Flowering occurs even if a single leaf is exposed to appropriate photoperiod.*

If a cocklebur plant whether intact of defoliated, is kept under long day conditions it will not flower (Fig. D, E). But, if even one of its leaves is exposed to short day condition and the rest are under long day photoperiods, flowering will occur (Fig. F). The photoperiodic stimulus can be transmitted from one branch of the plant to another branch.

For example, if in a two branched cocklebur plant one branch is exposed to short day and other to long day photo period, flowering occurs on both the branches (Fig. A). Flowering also occurs if one branch is kept under long day conditions and other branch from which all the leaves except one have been removed is exposed to short day condition (Fig. B). However, if one branch is exposed to long photoperiod and the other has been defoliated under short day condition, flowering will not occur in any of the branches (Fig. C).

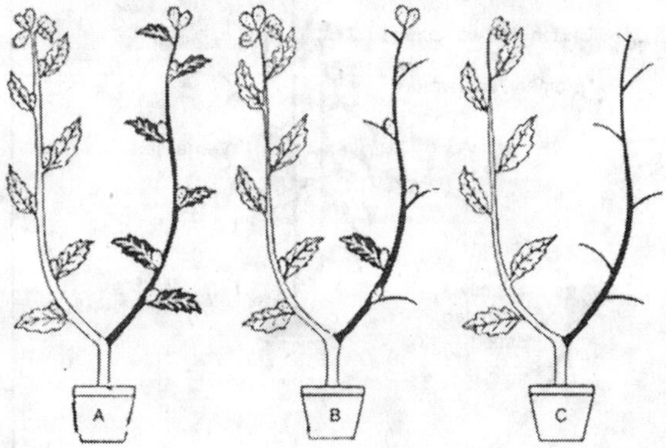

Fig. *Experiments on cocklebur plants to show that the photoperiodic stimulus can be tansmitted from one branch of the plant to another.*

According to a scheme proposed by Brian (1958), a gibberellin like hormone is produced in the leaves during the photoperiod. The whole scheme is diagrammatically shown below:

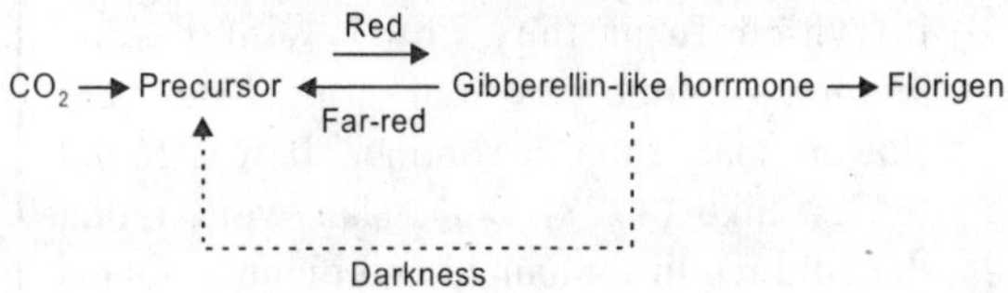

Vernalization: Vegetative during the warm season, receive low temperature during winter, grow further and then bear flowers and fruits. Requirement of low temperature prevents precocious reproductive development in autumn. It allows the plant to reach vegetative maturity before reproduction can occur. The condition occurs in winter varieties of some annual food plants (e.g., Wheat, Barley, and Rye), some biennial (e.g., Cabbage, Sugar beet, Carrot) and perennial plants (e.g., Chrysanthemum). Many plants do not come to flower before they experience a low temperature. These plants remain the annual winter plants also possess spring varieties. The spring varieties are planted in spring. They come to flower and bear fruits prior to end of growing season. If the winter varieties are sown similarly, they fail to flower and produce fruits before the end of growing season.

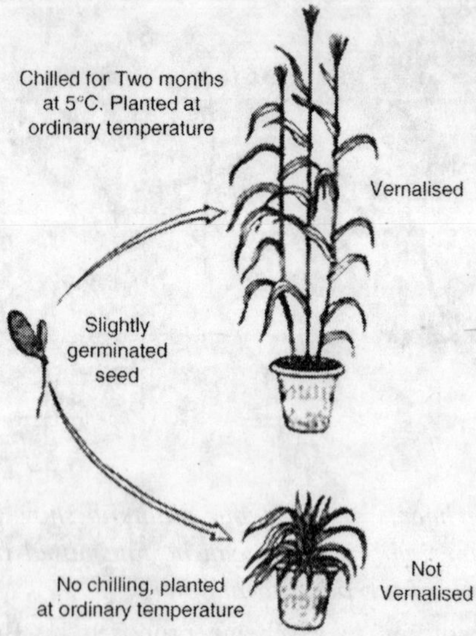

Fig. *Experiment to show effect of vernalization on Winter Rye.*

They are planted in autumn, form seedlings in which form they cover winter. The seedlings resume growth in spring. They bear flowers and fruits in summer. It was found by Lysenko (1928), a Russian worker that the cold requiring annual and biennial plants can be made to flower in one growing season by providing low temperature treatment to young plants or moistened seeds. He called the effect of this chilling treatment as vernalization. The stimulus of vernalization is perceived only by the meristematic cells, e.g., shoot tip, embryo tips, root apex, developing leaves, etc.

Mechanism of Vernalization: The stimulus received by the actively dividing cells of shoot or embryo tip travels to all parts of the plant and prepare it to flower. The stimulus has been named as vernalin. It can be passed from one plant to another through grafting in case of Henbane but not in others. However, the chemical has not been separated. In some plants cold treatment can be replaced by gibberellins. Vernalization prepares the plant to flower. The induction of flowering depends upon the presence of other favourable conditions. Photoperiodism, however, not only prepares the plant to flower but also brings about flowering. Thus, Henbane is a long-day plant which also requires cold treatment.

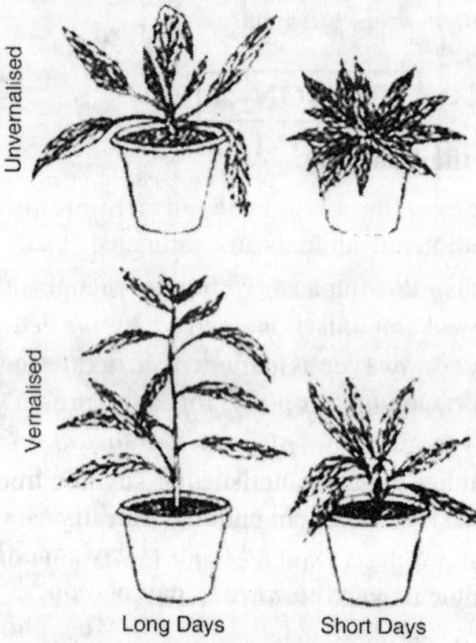

Fig. *Effect of vernalization and photoperiods on Henbane.*

Previous Years' Paper (Solved)

IFS–Agriculture Main Examination, 2020

(Exam held on 05/03/2021)

PAPER-I

INSTRUCTIONS: *There are* ***Eight*** *questions in all, out of which* ***Five*** *are to be attempted. Candidates should attempt question nos.* ***1*** *and* ***5*** *which are compulsory, and out of the remaining* ***six*** *questions,* ***three*** *are to be attempted selecting at least* ***one*** *question from each of the two Sections* ***A*** *and* ***B****. All questions carry equal marks. Answers must be written in English only.*

SECTION–A

1. Answer the following:

(*a*) Discuss the effect of environmental pollution on animals and humans.

(*b*) Discuss the impact of climate change on livestock and fisheries.

(*c*) Why do we consider soil structure an important soil property for crop production?

(*d*) What are the characteristics of suitable tree species for non-conventional forestry?

(*e*) What are the advantages and limitations of biological weed control?

2. Answer the following:

(*a*) Illustrate with examples the abiotic components in the ecosystem that influence crop growth.

(*b*) Discuss the herbicide selectivity phenomenon with the factors affecting it.

(*c*) What is the importance of millets in climate resilient agriculture?

(*d*) Discuss the major factors for achievement of self-sufficiency in pulse production in India.

3. Answer the following:

(*a*) Clasify the natural resources and suggest the conservation strategies.

(*b*) How does the soil acidity affect crop production?

(*c*) Enumerate the applications of remote sensing in agriculture.

(*d*) Discuss the factors affecting crop-weed competition.

4. Answer the following:

(*a*) Enlist and discuss the types of soil erosion and water conservation management option in Indian perspective.

(*b*) Discuss the applications of agro-forestry for socio-economic development.

(*c*) Discuss the physical, chemical and biological weathering of rocks and minerals.

(*d*) Discuss about contingent planning for rainfed farming.

SECTION–B

5. Answer the following:

(*a*) Discuss the measures to enhance water-use efficiency and water-productivity in agriculture.

(*b*) Discuss in detail the drainage methods in water-logged soil.

(*c*) Explain how Agricultural Technology Management Agency (ATMA) approach as Extension Reform to provide extension services is different from previous extension approaches.

(*d*) What is farm planning? Enlist the characteristics of good farm plan. Explain the techniques of farm planning.

(*e*) Describe the implications of the Farmers' Produce Trade and Commerce (Promotion and Facilitation) Act of 2020 on Indian agriculture.

6. Answer the following:

(*a*) What are the advantages of good quality of the irrigation water? Mention its significance.

(*b*) Illustrate with examples the effect of water and soil pollution on agro-ecosystem.

(*c*) Describe the effects of marketing of agricultural produce by farmers' groups, rather than individually. Explain the advantages and limitations of farmers producer organizations (FPOs) from farmers' perspective.

(*d*) Explain the impact of Extension Training on agricultural production in India. Describe how adoption of educational approach will bring the desirable changes in stakeholders.

7. Answer the following:

(*a*) Enlist the effects of farm mechanization on rural employment in India.

(*b*) Enumerate the role of cooperatives in agricultural economy in India.

(*c*) Describe the Government intervention in agricultural marketing and policy related issues.

(*d*) Enumerate the role played by Extension Science in making stakeholders innovative during post-Independence and post-Green Revolution era.

8. Answer the following:

(*a*) Enlist and explain the first-line extension activities of the Indian Council of Agricultural Research (ICAR) and discuss the current status.

(*b*) Describe how extension ensures agricultural development.

(*c*) Elaborate the term 'supply chain management' and discuss its importance in emerging agri-business sector.

(*d*) Explain the importance of agricultural trade in national economy and enumerate the factors affecting agricultural trade.

PAPER-II

INSTRUCTIONS: *There are **Eight** Questions in all, out of which **Five** are to be attempted. Candidates should attempt question nos. **1** and **5** which are compulsory, and out of the remaining **six** questions, **three** are to be attempted, selecting at least **one** question from each of the two Sections A and **B**. Answers must be written in English only.*

SECTION–A

1. Answer the following:

(*a*) What is cell? Enlist different organelles of plant cell with a brief description of mitochondria.

(*b*) What do you mean by heterosis? Describe the genetic basis of heterosis.

(*c*) Describe the agronomic and genetic principles of quality seed production.

(*d*) Explain in detail the Krebs cycle.

(*e*) Explain the molecular marker approach in crop improvement.

2. Answer the following:

(*a*) Describe the role of Cytoplasmic Genetic Male Sterility (CGMS) and Self-incompatibility (SI) systems in hybrid seed production.

(*b*) What do you mean by vertical and horizontal resistance? Give an account of basic principles behind these resistances.

(*c*) What do you mean by conservation of plant genetic resources? Explain their contribution in crop improvement in India.

3. Answer the following:

(*a*) Distinguish between the following, giving suitable examples:

(*i*) Breeder seed and Certified seed

(*ii*) Natural selection and Artificial selection

(*iii*) Cytoplasmic and Cytoplasmic-genetic male sterility

(*b*) Write the various methods of plant breeding. Describe backcross method with its importance in development of crop varieties.

(*c*) Describe the role of mutation in development of disease resistant varieties of crops.

4. Answer the following:

(*a*) Describe the various chromosome structural aberrations with the help of suitable diagrams and discuss their effects on organisms.

(*b*) Describe various steps involved in seed certification. Give an account of institutions associated with the production of certified seeds in India.

(*c*) Explain various mechanisms for water transport in plants.

SECTION–B

5. Answer the following:

(*a*) Write down the physiological effects of auxin in plants.

(*b*) Describe plug-tray technology for seedling production in vegetables.

(*c*) Describe the principles of fruits and vegetables preservation.

(*d*) Describe the major storage pests of pulses and their control measures.

(*e*) Discuss the strengths and weaknesses of public food-grain distribution system in India.

6. Answer the following:

(*a*) Describe the package of practices for 'papaya' cultivation in northern India.

(*b*) Describe the incidence and management of 'leaf curl' and 'mosaic' virus diseases in 'Chilli' and 'Okra' crops.

(*c*) Give a detailed account of constraints in sustaining the food-grain production in India.

7. Answer the following:

(*a*) Differentiate between the following:

(*i*) Formal and Informal styles of gardens

(*ii*) Pollinator and Pollinizer

(*iii*) Insect vectors and Predators

(*b*) Write a detailed note on incidence and management of fruit fly in 'cucurbits' and 'guava'.

(*c*) Describe various factors for seed dormancy and methods for breaking the dormancy.

8. Answer the following:

(*a*) Describe the year-round production technology of 'Chrysanthemum'.

(*b*) Describe the production technology for off-season vegetables in India.

(*c*) Discuss the integrated management practices for insect-pests and diseases in crops.

ANSWERS

PAPER-I

SECTION-A

1. (*a*) Effects of Environmental Pollution on Animals and Humans

Environmental pollution is a major global problem posing serious risk to animals and humans. It is defined as the human alteration of chemical or physical characteristics of the environment to a degree that is harmful to living organisms. Rapid pace of urbanization, industrialization and indiscriminate and improper use of chemicals such as pesticides and drugs have resulted in increased contamination and degradation of the environment leading to adverse health effects on living beings and problems associated with residues in food of animal origin. Recent emergences in environmental related toxicity in man and animals and detection of chemical residues in food products at an increasing frequency have underlined the impact of pollution on biotic component. The deleterious health effects may be observed in the form of overt clinical signs and higher morbidity and mortality or as subtle or subclinical effects. Pesticide toxicity, plumbism, mercury poisoning and fluorosis are some of the commonly encountered overt toxic problems due to pollution in domestic animals. The low level of exposure to pollutants is often associated with chemical residues in animal system, and subtle or subclinical effects. These include oxidative stress, immunotoxicity, carcinogenicity, teratogenecity and endocrine disruption. Wild animals, like their domestic counterparts also suffer from adverse effects of pollution. Eggshell thinning in birds of prey due to DDT residues and heavy mortality amongst fish and birds due to contamination of aquatic ecosystem with mercury, oil spills or acid rains are some of the notable examples of impact of pollution on wild life. Recently, decline in vulture population in Indian subcontinent has been linked to drug residues. This has drawn the attention of researchers and environmentalist owing to drastic decline in the population of an important raptorial bird species and resultant ecological degradation. Besides deleterious health effects on animal and wildlife, chemical pollutants also pose public health concerns because of contamination of human food chain. Noise and other physical pollutants are also reported to cause adverse effects on health and physiology. Exposure to high levels of environmental pollution can cause a variety of adverse health outcomes. It increases the risk of respiratory infections, heart disease and lung cancer. Both short- and long-term exposure to air pollutants have been associated with health impacts. More severe impacts affect people who are already ill. Children, the elderly and poor people are more susceptible. The most health-harmful pollutants - closely associated with excessive premature mortality - are fine PM 2.5 particles that penetrate deep into lung passageways.

1. (*b*) Impact of Climate Change on Livestock and Fisheries

Climate change is a major threat to the sustainability of livestock systems globally. Consequently, adaptation to, and mitigation of the detrimental effects of extreme climates has played a major role in combating the climatic impact on livestock. There is little doubt that climate change will have an impact on livestock performance in many regions and as per most predictive models the impact will be detrimental. Climate change may manifest itself as rapid changes in climate in the short term (a couple of years) or more subtle changes over decades. Generally, climate change is associated with an increasing global temperature. The difficulty facing livestock is weather extremes, *e.g.* intense heat waves, floods and droughts. In addition to production losses, extreme events also result in livestock death. Animals can adapt to hot climates, however the response mechanisms that are helpful for survival may be detrimental to performance. In this article we make an attempt to project the adverse impact of climate change on livestock production. The most significant direct impact of climate change on livestock production comes from the heat stress. Heat stress results in a significant financial burden to livestock producers through decrease in milk component and milk production, meat production, reproductive efficiency and animal health. Thus, an increase in air temperature, such as that predicted by various climate change models, could directly affect animal performance.

Most of the production losses are incurred via indirect impacts of climate change largely through reductions or non-availability of feed and water resources. Climate change has the potential to impact the quantity and reliability of forage production, quality of forage, water demand for cultivation of forage crops, as well as large-scale rangeland vegetation patterns. In the coming decades, crops and forage plants will continue to be subjected to warmer temperatures, elevated carbon dioxide, as well as wildly fluctuating water availability due to changing precipitation patterns. Climate change can adversely affect productivity, species composition, and quality, with potential impacts not only on forage production but also on other ecological roles of grasslands. Due to the wide fluctuations in distribution of rainfall in growing season in several regions of the world, the forage production will be greatly impacted. With the likely emerging scenarios that are already evident from impact of the climate change effects, the livestock production systems are likely to face more of negative than the positive impact. Also climate change influences the water demand, availability and quality. Changes in temperature and weather may affect the quality, quantity and distribution of rainfall, snowmelt, river flow and groundwater. Climate change can result in a higher intensity precipitation that leads to greater peak run-offs and less groundwater recharge. Longer dry periods may reduce groundwater recharge, reduce river flow and ultimately affect water availability, agriculture and drinking water supply. The deprivation of water affects animal physiological homeostasis leading to loss of body weight, low reproductive rates and a decreased resistance to diseases. More research is needed into water resources' vulnerability to climate change in order to support the development of adaptive strategies for agriculture. In addition, emerging diseases including vector borne diseases that may arise as a result of climate change will result in severe economic losses.

Fisheries are a major source of food for the majority of poor and vulnerable communities. Climate change poses a significant threat to fisheries in the region. The potential impacts of climate change on fisheries are categorized as physical and biological changes: physical changes include water surface temperature rise, sea level rise, increasing water salinity and ocean acidification; biological changes include changes in primary production and changes in fish stock distribution. Such changes could lead to disruptions in the food chains of aquatic flora and fauna, habitat destruction, depletion in food stock and prey-predator composition, destruction of coastal fish landing, and risk to processing and marketing sites. These negative effects when combined together are going to have adverse impacts on the already strained resource, thereby reducing fish production. Depletion of fish stock and reduction in fish production could threaten the livelihoods of many vulnerable fisher communities and the food security.

Production from marine capture fisheries has been stagnant duringthe past 10 years because of overfishing, unregulated fishing, habitat destruction and pollution; climate change may exacerbate this situation. Warming of water may impact fish diversity, distribution, abundance and phenology. Acidification of water will affect calciferous animals. Storms, floods and drought will severely impair fisheries. Sea level rise will lower fish production and damage the livelihoods of communities. Some tropical fish stocks may face regional extinction. Some others may move towards higher latitudes. Coastal habitats and resources are likely to be impacted through sea level rise, warming sea temperatures, extremes of nutrient enrichment (eutrophication) and invasive species. Most fish species have a narrow range of optimum temperatures related to their basic metabolism and availability of food organisms. Even a difference of 1°C in seawater may affect their distribution and life processes. At shorter time scales of a few years, increasing temperature may result in changes in distribution, recruitment and abundance. Species with short-life span and rapid turnover such as plankton and small pelagic fishes are most likely to experience such changes. At intermediate time scales of a fewy ears to a decade, changes in distribution, recruitment and abundance of many species may be acute. Changes in abundance will alter the species composition. At longer time scales of multidecade, changes in net primary production and transfer to higher trophic levels are possible. Investigations carried out by the Indian Council of Agricultural Research show that different Indian marine species will respond to climate change as follows:

- Changes in species composition of phytoplankton may occur at higher temperature;
- Small pelagic may extend their boundaries;
- Some species may be found in deeper waters as well; and
- Phenological changes may occur.

1. (*c*) Soil structure refers to the arrangement of solids and pore spaces within soil. Solids, formed from organic compounds and mineral ions clump together to form aggregates. The gaps between these aggregates are the pore spaces. For soil used in agriculture, a 'well-structured soil' will have a continuous network of pore spaces to allow drainage of water, free movement of air and unrestricted growth of roots. Typically, a 'good' agricultural soil is thought to consist of around 50% solids, 25% air and 25% water, but this will vary according to soil type. A good soil structure is important to allow air and water into the soil which are vital for healthy plant growth. It will improve drainage and reduce soil erosion caused by excess surface run-off. Without structure, soils will suffer from anaerobism, waterlogging and nutrient lock-up and, ultimately, plants will die.

Soil structure supports biodiversity by providing a diverse range of habitats for the many organisms that live within it. In turn, soil organisms, such as earthworms, can directly alter the structure of the soil. Plant root systems release compounds which can bind soil particles together. The relationship between soil structure and soil communities is complex and different groups of organisms respond differently to changes in soil structure. Compacted soil can prevent crop root growth and reduce the yield of crops. The presence of earthworms, which have been known to improve soil structure, are linked to increased crop yields. The pore size and distribution affect aeration, water holding capacity, and drainage capacity of soil. Compacted soil reduces the ability of water to vertically infiltrate the soil and thus increases surface runoff and the risk of flooding. Soil structure and climate change mitigation. Soil is the largest terrestrial store of organic carbon, and contains twice as much carbon as the atmosphere. Soil carbon sequestration refers to the long-term accumulation of carbon in soil. Land management practices affect soil structure and carbon sequestration. Practices such as reduced till and growth of soil cover crops have been shown to increase levels of soil organic carbon.

From the point of view of agriculture, the soil offers support to plants and acts as a reservoir of water and nutrients. However, in addition to being a physical medium, the soil may be considered a living system, vital for producing the food and fiber that humans need and for maintaining the ecosystems on which all life ultimately depends. Soils directly and indirectly affect agricultural productivity, water quality, and the global climate through its function as a medium for plant growth, and as regulator of water flow and nutrient cycling.

The physical properties of the soil are very important for agricultural production and the sustainable use of soil. The amount and rate of water, oxygen, and nutrient absorption by plants depend on the ability of the roots to absorb the soil solution as well as the ability of the soil to supply it to the roots. Soil biological properties have a greater role to play in agricultural crop production. Soils host a complex web of organisms which can influence soil evolution and specific soil physical and chemical properties. It includes two basic kind of soil microbes *i.e.*, macro and microorganisms. Soil biology means the soil microbes present in the soil like bacteria, fungi, nematodes, earthworms etc. Soil properties are more important to produce good quality food as well as quantity too. Our aim is to take care of soil, the soil will take care us.

1. (*d*) While selecting tree species for non-conventional forestry systems, the following desirable characteristics should be taken into consideration. Though all desirable characters are not found in a single species, but their multiple uses are taken care of.

- Tree species selected should not interfere with soil moisture. Tree species selected for agroforestry should have very less water requirement
- Tree species should not compete for plant nutrients and should not utilize more plant nutrients
- They should help in building soil fertility
- Tree species should not compete for sunlight and should not interrupt sunlight falling on the crops.
- Tree species should have high survival rate and easy establishment and should have the ability to regenerate lateral roots within a short period of time after transplanting.
- Tree species should have fast growing habit and easy management and fast-growing species such as *Poplar*, *Casuriana*, *Leucaena leucocephala* etc. are important species which provide lot of opportunities to be planted in AFS.
- A tree species selected for agroforestry combinations must have a wider adaptability.
- Some tree species, because of their inherent growth habit and adaptability, are especially helpful in providing protection for soils, crops and livestock. Poplars (*Populus* spp.), Willows (*Salix* spp.), *Casurina equisetifolia*, etc. for example, have been extensively used in soil erosion control because of their extensive root system and ability to grow in water-logged soils.

- Tree species should have nutrient cycling and nitrogen fixation attributes and most leguminous trees and some non-leguminous ones, such as *Acacia, Leucaena* and *Prosopis* as well as *Casuarina* spp. fix the atmospheric nitrogen.
- Tree species should have their multiple uses and should yield more than one of the main produces like fuelwood, leaf fodder, edible fruit, edible flower and fibre.

1. (*e*) Biological control of weeds is the deliberate use of natural enemies to reduce the density of a particular weed to a tolerable level. The objective of biological weed control is not eradication but simply the reduction of the weed population to an economically low level. In fact, for biological control to be conti-nuously successful, small numbers of the weed host must always be present to assured the survival of the natural enemy. Benefits are several-fold. Biological control is permanent, energy-efficient, nonpolluting, and inexpensive relative to other methods.

Advantages of Biological Control:

- Biological control is a very specific strategy. The vast majority of the time, whatever predator is introduced will only control the population of the pest they are meant to target, making it a green alternative to chemical or mechanical control methods. For example, whereas weed killing chemicals can also destroy fruit-bearing plants, biological control allows the fruit to be left uninterrupted while the weeds are destroyed.
- Natural enemies introduced to the environment are capable of sustaining themselves, often by reducing whatever pest population they are supposed to manage. This means that after the initial introduction, very little effort is required to keep the system running fluidly. It also means that biological control can be kept in place for a much longer time than other methods of pest control.
- Biological control can be cost effective in the long run. Although it may cost a bit to introduce a new species to an environment, it's a tactic that only needs to be applied once due to its self-perpetuating nature.
- Most important of all, it's effective. Whatever pest population you want controlled will no doubt be controlled. Because the predator introduced will be naturally inclined to target the pests, very often you'll see the pest population dwindle.

Disadvantages of Biological Control:

- Biological control can be fickle. Ultimately, you can't control whatever natural enemy you set loose in an ecosystem. While it's supposed to manage one pest, there is always the possibility that your predator will switch to a different target - they might decide eating your crops instead of the insects infesting them is a better plan! Not only that, but in introducing a new species to an environment, there runs the risk of disrupting the natural food chain.
- It's a slow process. It takes a lot of time and patience for the biological agents to work their magic on a pest population, whereas other methods like pesticides work provide immediate results. The upside to this is the long-term effect biological control provides.
- If you're looking to completely wipe out a pest, biological control is not the right choice. Predators can only survive if there is something to eat, so destroying their food population would risk their own safety. Therefore, they can only reduce the number of harmful pests.
- While it is cheap in the long run, the process of actually setting up a biological control system is a costly endeavour. A lot of planning a money goes into developing a successful system.

2. (*a*) Abiotic factors like humidity, temperature, moisture, wind, rain, flood and many more destroy the crop raise. Abiotic factors like hot, cold, drought, salinity, etc. affect crop production. Resistant variety can withstand these factors and give a high yield. Abiotic factors include water, sunlight, oxygen, soil and temperature.

- Water (H_2O) is a very important abiotic factor - it is often said that "water is life." All living organisms need water. Plants must have water to grow. Even plants that live in the desert need a little bit of water to grow.
- Sunlight is the main source of energy on Earth, which makes it an extremely important abiotic factor. Sunlight is necessary for photosynthesis, the process by which plants convert carbon dioxide (CO_2) and water to oxygen (O_2) and sugar - food for the plants that later becomes food for animals. Without the sun, plants could not live, and without plants, animals could not live!
- Like water, oxygen (O_2) is another important abiotic factor for many living organisms. Without oxygen, humans would not be able to live! This is true for the many other living organisms that use oxygen. Oxygen is produced by green plants through the process of photosynthesis, and is therefore directly linked to sunlight.
- Soil is often considered an abiotic factor since it is mostly made up of small particles of rock (sand and clay) mixed with decomposed plants and animals. Plants use their roots to get water and nutrients from the soil. Soils are different from place to place - this can be a big factor in which plants and animals live in a certain area.
- Temperature is an abiotic factor that is strongly influenced by sunlight. Temperature is a key factor in plant growth and development. Along with the levels of light, carbon dioxide, air humidity, water and nutrients, temperature influences plant growth and ultimately crop yields. All these factors should be in balance.

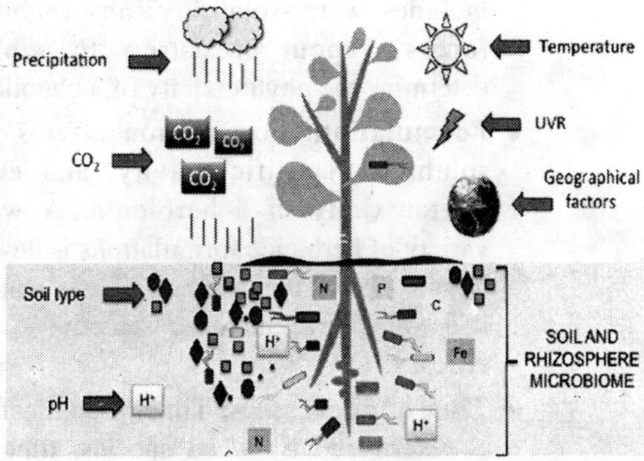

Fig. *Abiotic Factors and Crop Growth*

Abiotic factors impact crop production in the subsequent ways:

- Sunlight aids in photosynthesis.
- Water and minerals from the soil along with gases are the raw materials for the synthesis of food and energy.
- Suitable temperature is required for the proper growth of the plant and various processes such as transpiration. Rainfall is required for natural irrigation of plant.

2. (*b*) Herbicide Selectivity Phenomenon

- Herbicide selectivity referred to the phenomenon where the chemicals kill the target plant species in a mixed plant population without harming or only slightly affecting the other plants. The differential response of the plant to herbicide is called selectivity of herbicide.
- In other words, herbicides harm or kill weeds whereas crop plants are not affected due to selectivity. The susceptibility or tolerance of different plants is called selectivity. Many plant injuries occur wheat and barley tolerate growth regulator herbicide such as 2, 4 - D, and MCPA.

Factors Affecting Herbicide Selectivity

- **Chemical and physical properties of the herbicide:** Herbicides of one chemical family differ from another chemical family. The herbicide is characterized by different physical and chemical properties. This includes water-solubility, absorbability forces, vapour pressure, etc. which determine the phytotoxicity of a chemical.
- **Formulation:** Formulation affects the solubility, specific gravity, and even phytotoxicity of a herbicide. A wide variety of herbicide formulations is design to suit a particular method of application and to achieve increase selectivity and efficacy.
- **Time of application:** Time of application is determined by weed species, time of germination of weed and crop plants, and growth stage of weed. Generally, the time of application falls into three categories - pre-planting, pre-emergence, and post-emergence I relation to crop and weed.
- **Placement of herbicide:** Herbicides are soil-applied and foliage applied. Soil-applied herbicides are applied at pre-planting, and pre-emergence while foliar-applied herbicides are applied at post-emergence. The choice of selecting herbicide for soil or foliage depends on weed - crop situation, type of herbicide, herbicide efficacy, and cost of application.
- **Rate of application:** A herbicide that is selective at a lower rate may become non-effective when applied at a higher rate. For every herbicide, there is an optimum rate at which it maintains its selective characteristics and this rate varies from one weed or crop species to another.
- **Plant morphology:** Plant morphology has a prominent role in determining herbicide selectivity. The amount of spray retained by the foliage influence the amount of chemical available for entry into the plant. The various morphological characters of plant that affect herbicide entry. The morphological characters are leaf size and shaped leaf arrangement, waxiness of leaf, and thickness of cuticle. A thick cuticle prevents herbicide absorption and a thin cuticle which permits greater herbicide absorption.
- **Stages of plant development:** Stages of plant development affect the ability of herbicides to enter the plant. Plant in the germination or young seedling stage is more susceptible to soil-applied herbicides than the later stage. Similarly, perennial weeds are more sensitive to foliage applied herbicide during the active growth period than before or later stage.
- **Cultivation practices:** Various pre-planting and post-planting cultivation practices followed before herbicide application could make tolerate plant sp. Susceptible to a particular herbicide after application. Tillage practice brings out the dormant weed seed roots and stolon to the topsoil layer and exposes them to the sunlight resulting in germination. Thereby increasing their susceptibility to an herbicide applied to the soil or foliage.
- **Absorption:** Once an herbicide is applied its entry into the plant is facilitated by absorption through the root, shoot, and stem. Absorption is influenced by the morphological characteristics of plants. The rate of absorption and amount of chemical which entered the plant varies with plant species and stages of plant growth. This differential absorption from one plant species to another determines herbicide selectivity.
- **Translocation:** When an herbicide enters the plant, it must be translocated to the site of action for it disrupts the metabolic activities of the plant. The translocate herbicide moves from the site of entry to the site of action via the phloem and xylem, but contact herbicide moves very

little or not of all from the point of entry. Many physiological and environmental factors of plants cause differential movement of herbicide to the site of action. This germinates the selectivity of herbicides.

- **Physiological difference of plant species:** After reaching the site of action an herbicide affects one or many metabolic activities related to plant growth and survivability. The physiological tolerant of a plant species variety largely depends upon the genetic makeup of the plant taxonomy, morphotoxicant and phosphological characters.
- **Metabolism:** When any herbicide enters the plant, its metabolism depends on the physical and chemical properties of the plant. The capacity of the plant to affect the metabolic conversion of the applied chemical molecules. The herbicide metabolism and its differences among plant species from the basis of herbicide selectivity.
- **Environmental factor:** The selectivity of a herbicide is also influenced by the environmental factor under which the plant grows. These environmental factors are light, temperature, rainfall, humidity, wind, etc.

2. (*c*) Panicoids (subfamily: *panicoideae*) are a group of C_4 grasses, which include agronomically important crops such as sorghum and maize, bioenergy feedstocks including sugarcane and miscanthus, nutri-cereals such as millets, and biofuel crops including switchgrass, napier grass and guinea grass. Among these, millets are known for their climate-resilient features including adaptation to a wide range of ecological conditions, less irrigational requirements, better growth and productivity in low nutrient input conditions, less reliance on synthetic fertilizers, and minimum vulnerability to environmental stresses. Also, millets are nutritionally superior to other major cereals as they are rich in dietary fibers, resistant starches, vitamins, essential amino acids, storage proteins and other bioactive compounds. These attributes have made millets a crop of choice for cultivation in arid and semi-arid regions of the world; however, the less attempt has been made to study the climate-resilient features of millets compared to other major cereals. Among millets, foxtail millet (*Setaria italica*) and its wild progenitor, green foxtail (*S. viridis*) are extensively studied since they are considered as models for studying the traits related to C_4 photosynthesis, stress biology, and bioenergy characteristics.

Millets are climate-resilient crops adaptable to wide variety of ecological conditions requiring less water for irrigation with better growth and productivity in low nutrient soils. They require low artificial fertilizers application and show minimal vulnerability to environmental stresses. There is need to revive the importance of millet groups as health foods to enhance food and nutritional security. Millets contain high amounts of proteins, fiber, niacin, thiamine and riboflavin, methionine, lecithin and little of vitamin E. They are rich in minerals like iron, magnesium, calcium and potassium also. Millets due to their nutritive value have potential health benefits to prevent cancers, decrease the occurrence of cardiovascular diseases, reduce tumor proliferation, lower blood pressure, risk of heart diseases, cholesterol content, rate of fat absorption, delayed gastric emptying and increased gastrointestinal bulk. Value-addition to millet grains as ready-to-eat and ready-to-cook items offers good opportunity to farmers for enhanced income generation, promotes production and marketing leading to nutritional security, employment and revenue generation.

The exceptional tolerance of millets toward diverse abiotic stresses including drought, salinity, light and heat makes them a tractable system to study their stress-responsive traits at the cellular, molecular and physiological levels. Several morpho-physiological and biochemical studies in millets have shown their stress adaptation strategies. It is realized that millets hold great promise for food security and nutrition amid ever-increasing agricultural costs, climate change and burgeoning mouths to feed worldwide. They are nutritious, possess additional health benefits, requires significantly fewer input costs for cultivation and are naturally tolerant to most biotic and abiotic stresses. These features accentuate millets as crops of choice for the world population amid growing concerns about climate change.

2. (*d*) Pulses, supplemented with cereals, provide a perfect mix of vegetarian protein of high biological value. India is the largest producer, importer and consumer of pulses, accounting for 25% of global production from 35% of global area under pulses. The productivity of pulses in India is less than half of the productivity levels in the USA and Canada, as the pulses are mainly grown under rainfed condition in India in the areas with high rainfall variability. The persistent and growing demand-supply gap is putting pressure on prices and this good source of vegetarian protein is turning inaccessible to the poor. The production of pulses in India has caught in the vicious cycle of low and uncertain yields, poor per hectare returns resulting in farmers' least preference to grow pulses on irrigated and fertile parcel of land, thereby leading to unstable and low yields. Inadequate adoption of production technology, higher price volatility, production risk and low level of irrigation are the important influencing factors responsible for stagnation in the productivity of these crops. The country would require 39 million tonnes of total pulses by 2050, which will require pulses production to grow at an annual rate of 2.2%. To fulfil the growing requirement, the country has to produce enough pulses as well as remain competitive to protect the domestic production.

It is imperative to develop and adopt more efficient crop-production technologies along with favourable policies and market support to encourage farmers to bring more area under pulses. In order to provide the nutritional security to the poor masses relying on vegetarian diet, making pulses affordable through boosting domestic production of pulses is the best alternative. In order to augment the supply of pulses to poor masses, under the current scenario supply through public distribution system will not only distribute pulses to poor at affordable prices and enhance nutritional security, but will also lead to stabilize prices and provide boost to the farmers through assured procurement. The lack of an assured market is one of the major issues in the poor performance of pulses. Government procurement would provide adequate marketing support to growers. Alternative marketing arrangements through contract farming, farmer producer company model, needs to be promoted.

Major Factors Responsible for Low Yield of Pulses in India

- Delayed sowings/plantings;
- Low seed rate resulting in poor crop stands;
- Poor weed management during crop growth;
- Inefficient irrigation and rainwater management;
- Large scale monoculture and non-inclusion of pulses in cropping systems;
- Lack of consideration of previous cropping in the same field;
- Inadequate plant protection;
- Non-availability of seeds of HYVs at affordable price and at the appropriate time;

- Lack of more efficient N using genotypes;
- Imbalanced use of fertilisers;
- Poor management for secondary and micronutrient, mainly S, Zn, Mn, Fe and B.

Suggestions for Sustainable and Self-Sufficient Production of Pulses in India

- New research efforts should be initiated to achieve a breakthrough in the productivity.
- Innovative ideas need to be implemented instead of conducting routine research and material evaluation.
- Scientists to work for development of shorter duration, widely adaptable and biotic and abiotic stress resistant varieties to boost the production of pulses.
- Modernization of pulse breeding programme, supporting genetic gains through transgenic technology, enhancing biological nitrogen fixation through development of super nodulating plant types and breeding short duration varieties for achieving self-sufficiency in pulses.
- Extension workers and agriculture technology information centers should work more towards development and dissemination of newer technologies.

3. (*a*) Natural Resources

- Natural resources are resources that exist without any actions of humankind. This includes the sources of valued characteristics such as commercial and industrial use, aesthetic value, scientific interest and cultural value. On Earth, it includes sunlight, atmosphere, water, land, all minerals along with all vegetation, and animal life.
- These are the resources that are found in the environment and are developed without the intervention of humans. Common examples of natural resources include air, sunlight, water, soil, stone, plants, animals and fossil fuels. Natural resources are naturally occurring materials that are useful to man or could be useful under conceivable technological, economic or social circumstances or supplies drawn from the earth, supplies such as food, building and clothing materials, fertilizers, metals, water and geothermal power. For a long time, natural resources were the domain of the natural sciences.

Classification of Natural Resources: Based on the availability are two types of natural resources:

- **Renewable:** Resources that are available in infinite quantity and can be used repeatedly are called renewable resources. Examples: Forest, wind, water, etc.
- **Non-Renewable:** Resources that are limited in abundance due to their non-renewable nature and whose availability may run out in the future are called non-renewable resources. Examples include fossil fuels, minerals, etc.

Most Important Natural Resources

- **Air:** Clean air is important for all the plants, animals, humans to survive on this planet. So, it is necessary to take measures to reduce air pollution.
- **Water:** 70% of the Earth is covered in water and only 2% of that is freshwater. Initiative to educate and regulate the use of water should be taken.
- **Soil:** Soil is composed of various particles and nutrients. It helps plants grow.
- **Iron:** It is made from silica and is used to build strong weapons, transportation and buildings.
- **Forests:** As the population increases, the demand for housing and construction projects also increases. Forests provide clean air and preserve the ecology of the world.

Conservation Strategies of Natural Resources

- The modern lifestyle and the advance in technology have had a very bad impact on natural resources. Natural resources like coal and petroleum are depleting at a very fast rate, and once they are depleted, we will have to depend on other sources of energy. Therefore, it is very necessary for us humans to act in a way that ensures the conservation of natural resources.

- There are thousands of ways of conserving natural resources. The main idea of conservation is to use natural resources with optimization, and do not waste any natural resources. All you have to do is to act according to the situation so that the use of natural resources is minimal.
- For instance, using bicycles or walking sometimes saves a lot of fuel. Using public transport (city buses and metro trains) also helps in saving a lot of oil. Saving water while bathing, cleaning, etc. help in water conservation.
- Fossil fuels are the fuels that are obtained from the remains of dead organisms. Some examples of fossil fuels are Coal, Natural gas, Oil. Since the quantity of fossil fuels is not unlimited in nature, they are not going to last forever. If we continue to use them, or rather waste them like the way we are doing now, they will soon get depleted.
- Some ways of conservation of fossil fuels are already taken care of. Several countries have started using green energy - hydropower and solar power.
- Power can be generated using water, or sunlight, or wind, and this saves a lot of precious fossil fuels like coal. Environment and Natural resources are precious, and we must all make efforts to conserve them.

3. (*b*) Soil acidity - effects on crop production

- Acidic soils cause significant losses in production and where the choice of crops is restricted to acid tolerant species and varieties, profitable market opportunities may be reduced. In pastures grown on acidic soils, production will be reduced and some legume species may fail to persist.
- Acidic soils create production problems by limiting the availability of some essential plant nutrients and increasing that of the soil solution's toxic elements, such as aluminum and manganese, the major cause of poor crop performance and failure in acidic soils.
- The effects of soil acidity on crop growth tend to be insidious, in that it is in the root zone where the major impact occurs. Damage caused to the root system and the unfavourable soil chemistry associated with excessive acidity, are translated into poor crop growth, with their frequently being no classical leaf symptoms as are often apparent with deficiencies of, for example, N or K.
- Specific detrimental effects of soil acidity include the following:
  - **Aluminium and manganese toxicities:** Aluminium and occasionally high amounts of manganese, released from clays as the soil acidifies are toxic to plant roots and result in poor and abnormal root development. Typically, roots become thick and stubby and there is little development of the all-important fine roots. The resultant inefficient root systems limit yields through poor water and nutrient uptake. Importantly, in seasons of reduced rainfall, aluminium toxicity greatly magnifies the effects of drought. Where subsoils are also acidic, the situation with regard to moisture supply is aggravated further in that moisture reserves in the subsoil are largely unavailable to plants because of restricted root penetration into the lower soil layers. Under these conditions it is not uncommon to see plants displaying symptoms of drought stress even on

relatively moist soils. Researchers have found that the degree to which plant roots are affected by aluminum toxicity depends on the relationship between the quantity of aluminium and the quantity of bases (principally calcium and magnesium), rather than on the level of aluminium alone. The aluminium toxicity hazard is therefore represented on soil test reports by the soil acid saturation index - this being a far more reliable indication of the acidity hazard than soil pH.

- **Deficiencies of calcium and magnesium:** Levels of calcium and magnesium in acid soils are often very low, and may pose a limitation to plant growth. In particular, adequate supplies of calcium in the soil are of critical importance for root growth. The combination of high aluminium and very low calcium levels in subsoils is a widespread yield-limiting factor in grain-producing areas.
- **Micronutrient deficiencies:** Deficiencies of micronutrients, in particular molybdenum and zinc, frequently limit plant growth on acid soils. In the case of molybdenum, most soils contain adequate reserves of this nutrient for plant growth, but its availability for plant uptake is minimised under acid conditions.
- **Soil biological activity:** Acid soil conditions impact negatively on soil biological activity. Evidence of this is the retardation in the breakdown of surface-applied organic matter (*e.g.*, trash) on acid soils. Interestingly, most earthworm species are sensitive to soil acidity, and liming frequently results in a rapid increase in earthworm populations. Agricultural crops do not all respond in the same way to acid soil conditions, but vary widely in their tolerances to soil acidity. Certain vegetables and temperate legumes are highly sensitive to acid soil conditions, while crops such as cowpeas and sugarcane are highly tolerant. Nevertheless, severe soil acidity has been shown to limit the growth of all species, including the highly tolerant ones. Thus, the management of soil acidity is an essential component of sustainable production practices, regardless of the crop grown.
- **Microbial activity:** Low pH in topsoil's may affect microbial activity, most notably decreasing legume nodulation. The resulting nitrogen deficiency may be indicated by reddening of stems and petioles on pasture legumes, or yellowing and death of oldest leaves on grain legumes. Rhizobia bacteria are greatly reduced in acid soils. Some pasture legumes may fail to persist due to the inability of reduced Rhizobia populations to successfully nodulate roots and form a functioning symbiosis.

3. (*c*) Applications of Remote Sensing in Agriculture

Remote sensing is the process of acquiring information about the Earth's surface by measuring its reflected and emitted radiation without coming into direct contact with the object. In much of remote sensing, the process involves an interaction between incident radiation and the targets of interest. The most useful electromagnetic radiation in remote sensing includes visible light (VIS), near infra-red (NIR) and shortwave infrared (SWIR), to thermal infrared (TIR) and microwave bands. Passive remote sensing sensors record incident radiation reflected or emitted from the objects while active sensors emit their own radiation, which interacts with the target to be investigated and returns to the measuring instrument.

Remote sensing is the acquisition of information about an object or any phenomenon without making any physical contact with the object. It is a phenomenon that has numerous applications including photography, surveying, geology, forestry and many more. But it is in the field of agriculture that remote sensing has found significant use.

There are many applications of remote sensing:

- **Crop production forecasting:** Remote sensing is used to forecast the expected crop production and yield over a given area and determine how much of the crop will be harvested under specific conditions. Researchers can be able to predict the quantity of crop that will be produced in a given farmland over a given period of time.
- **Assessment of crop damage and crop progress:** In the event of crop damage or crop progress, remote sensing technology can be used to penetrate the farmland and determine exactly how much of a given crop has been damaged and the progress of the remaining crop in the farm.
- **Horticulture, Cropping Systems Analysis:** Remote sensing technology has also been instrumental in the analysis of various crop planting systems. This technology has mainly been in use in the horticulture industry where flower growth patterns can be analyzed and a prediction made out of the analysis.
- **Crop identification:** Remote sensing has also played an important role in crop identification especially in cases where the crop under observation is mysterious or shows some mysterious characteristics. The data from the crop is collected and taken to the labs where various aspects of the crop including the crop culture are studied.
- **Crop acreage estimation:** Remote sensing has also played a very important role in the estimation of the farmland on which a crop has been planted. This is usually a cumbersome procedure if it is carried out manually because of the vast sizes of the lands being estimated.
- **Crop condition assessment and stress detection:** Remote sensing technology plays an important role in the assessment of the health condition of each crop and the extent to which the crop has withstood stress. This data is then used to determine the quality of the crop.
- **Identification of planting and harvesting dates:** Because of the predictive nature of the remote sensing technology, farmers can now use remote sensing to observe a variety of factors including the weather patterns and the soil types to predict the planting and harvesting seasons of each crop.
- **Crop yield modelling and estimation:** Remote sensing also allows farmers and experts to predict the expected crop yield from a given farmland by estimating the quality of the crop and the extent of the farmland. This is then used to determine the overall expected yield of the crop.
- **Identification of pests and disease infestation:** Remote sensing technology also plays a significant role in the identification of pests in farmland and gives data on the right pests control mechanism to be used to get rid of the pests and diseases on the farm.
- **Soil moisture estimation:** Soil moisture can be difficult to measure without the help of remote sensing technology. Remote sensing gives the soil moisture data and helps in determining the quantity of moisture in the soil and hence the type of crop that can be grown in the soil.
- **Irrigation monitoring and management:** Remote sensing gives information on the

moisture quantity of soils. This information is used to determine whether a particular soil is moisture deficient or not and helps in planning the irrigation needs of the soil.

- **Soil mapping:** Soil mapping is one of the most common yet most important uses of remote sensing. Through soil mapping, farmers are able to tell what soils are ideal for which crops and what soil require irrigation and which ones do not. This information helps in precision agriculture.
- **Monitoring of droughts:** Remote sensing technology is used to monitor the weather patterns including the drought patterns over a given area. The information can be used to predict the rainfall patterns of an area and also tell the time difference between the current rainfall and the next rainfall which helps to keep track of the drought.
- **Land cover and land degradation mapping:** Remote sensing has been used by experts to map out the land cover of a given area. Experts can now tell what areas of the land have been degraded and which areas are still intact. This also helps them in implementing measures to curb land degradation.
- **Identification of problematic soils:** Remote sensing has also played a very important role in the identification of problematic soils that have a problem in sustaining optimum crop yield throughout a planting season.
- **Crop nutrient deficiency detection:** Remote sensing technology has also helped farmers and other agricultural experts to determine the extent of crop nutrients deficiency and come up with remedies that would increase the nutrients level in crops hence increasing the overall crop yield.
- **Reflectance modeling:** Remote sensing technology is just about the only technology that can provide data on crop reflectance. Crop reflectance will depend on the amount of moisture in the soil and the nutrients in the crop which may also have a significant impact on the overall crop yield.
- **Determination of water content of field crops:** Apart from determining the soil moisture content, remote sensing also plays an important role in the estimation of the water content in the field crops.
- **Crop yield forecasting:** Remote sensing technology can give accurate estimates of the expected crop yield in a planting season using various crop information such as the crop quality, the moisture level in the soil and in the crop and the crop cover of the land. When all of this data is combined it gives almost accurate estimates of the crop yield.
- **Flood mapping and monitoring:** Using remote sensing technology, farmers and agricultural experts can be able to map out the areas that are likely to be hit by floods and the areas that lack proper drainage. This data can then be used to avert any flood disaster in future.
- **Collection of past and current weather data:** Remote sensing technology is ideal for collection and storing of past and current weather data which can be used for future decision making and prediction.
- **Crop intensification:** Remote sensing can be used for crop intensification that includes collection of important crop data such as the cropping pattern, crop rotation needs and crop diversity over a given soil.
- **Land mapping:** Remote sensing helps in mapping land for use for various purposes such as crop growing and landscaping. The mapping technology used helps in precision agriculture where specific land soils are used for specific purposes.
- **Water resources mapping:** Remote sensing is instrumental in the mapping of

water resources that can be used for agriculture over a given farmland. Through remote sensing, farmers can tell what water resources are available for use over a given land and whether the resources are adequate.

- **Precision agriculture:** Remote sensing has played a very vital role in precision agriculture. Precision agriculture has resulted in the cultivation of healthy crops that guarantees farmers optimum harvests over a given period of time.
- **Climate change monitoring:** Remote sensing technology is important in monitoring of climate change and keeping track of the climatic conditions which play an important role in the determination of what crops can be grown where.
- **Compliance monitoring:** For the agricultural experts and other farmers, remote sensing is important in keeping track of the farming practices by all farmers and ensuring compliance by all farmers. This helps in ensuring that all farmers follow the correct procedures when planting and when harvesting crops.
- **Soil management practices:** Remote sensing technology is important in the determination of soil management practices based on the data collected from the farms.
- **Air moisture estimation:** Remote sensing technology is used in the estimation of air moisture which determines the humidity of the area. The level of humidity determines the type of crops to be grown within the area.
- **Crop health analysis:** Remote sensing technology plays an important role in the analysis of crop health which determines the overall crop yield.

3. (*d*) Factors Affecting Crop Weed Competition

Factors affecting crop weed competition are summarized as under:

- **Period of weed growth:** It is important to note that when the crop-weed competition is critical; when the weed must be removed and when they may be allowed to grow without fear of any appreciable crop damage. The weeds that germinate and grow at the same time as the crop seeds are most successful competitors. If weeds are controlled at early period of crop growth, the optimum crop yield could be harvested which may be quite close to the maximum. The critical weed free period may, however, vary somewhat with the crop situation. Weeds should be removed at an early stage or at younger stages otherwise they compete severely. A little delay in weeding results in infestation of the crop for major parts of their critical growth periods. In situations, where weeds germinate late (as in dry land wheat/sorghum), late-stage weeding is more useful than their early weeding. The same is also true for crops like grams and peas that are irrigated for considerable period after planting. There is less competition when weeds are either removed early or they germinate slowly because crop plant become sturdy and can tolerate competition. On other hand, when the weeds germinate along with crops, the crop plants are usually smothered by the weed completely *e.g.* direct sown rice suffers severe competition from the weeds than the transplanted crop of rice.
- **Intensity of weeds:** In general, increase in the weed intensity results in reduction of the growth and yield of crops. There has to be some minimum amount of weed growth in terms of either population or yield in the field to exert a minimum biological stress on the crop performance. To maintain zero weed growth is too costly and cannot be achieved.
- **Weed species:** Different weeds differ in their ability to compete with the crop at similar density levels. This is primarily

because of difference in their growth habits as well as due to the allelopathic affects which they may exert on the germination and growth for the crop *e.g.* at early stage of growth, Cocklebur (*Xanthium strumarium*) is a better competitor of crops than many grass weeds because it posses broad leaves that shade the ground heavily. In dry areas Canada thistle (*Cirsium arvense*) and Field bind weed (*Convolvulus arvensis*) are more competitive than annual weeds because of their deep roots and early heavy shoot growth.

- **Soil fertility:** Since weeds compete with crops for mineral nutrients, particularly nitrogen. Addition of fertilizers, manures and other amendments will lessen weed-stress on crop. Methods and time of application of fertilizer to the crop fields are important in determining whether the added fertilizers will suppress or increase weed growth in fields. Band application of fertilizer will also decide the weed growth. Application of fertilizer early in the crop season when weed growth is negligible is more beneficial to crop than when weeds are already grown up. Weeds can grossly alter the fertilizer response curves of the crops.
- **Soil moisture status:** Water supplied to weedy crop fields either through irrigation or through rainfall is equally accessible to both the crop and weeds. Irrigation is expected to increase the yields of both the crops and weed, if the fields are initially under stress. Increase in yield of the crop (weedy and weed free) by rains or irrigation have been found to differ with the crop and weed species, weed growth etc. Higher water use efficiency of the crops has been noted in weed free plots than in the weedy plots because of higher level of crop yield in the weed free plots. Time of rain or first irrigation after planting of the crops is an important factor determining the intensity of the crop weed competition *e.g.* If a crop is irrigated when the plants are 15 cm tall it can compete with weed that germinated with 1st irrigation or rain, whereas when fields are irrigated immediately after planting of crops it induces early flush of weed which is highly detrimental to the crop growth. In water logged soils, many weeds survive much better than the most crop plants and compete severely with them.
- **Soil Reaction:** Some of the weed species tolerate abnormal soil reactions much better than others. Some weeds grow vigorously on abnormal pH soil, where majority of our crop plant will be stunted in growth. Weed crop competition is more intense on high or low pH soils than on normal pH soils. Addition of soil amendments to raise or lower the pH soils, therefore vigorate crop growth, tilting the balance of weed crop competition in favour of the crops.
- **Climate influence:** Climate and seasonal variations are greatly responsible for inducing wide differences in weed-crop competitions. Adverse weather conditions *e.g.* drought, excessive rain, continuous rain, extreme of temperature intensify the weed crop interference, since most of our crop varieties are highly susceptible to such climate influence whereas the weeds are tolerant to these stresses. Weeds germinate at different times at different places. Weed emergence in the fields is more rapid in soils kept continuously wet by rainfall than those that dried three days after planting. The differences in germination of weed are narrowed as the temperature increases because the weed seeds absorb enough moisture in the first three days wet period itself before the soil dries up.

Cropping Practices: It includes:

- **Date and method of planting of crop:** Longer the period or interval between the emergence of crops and weeds lesser will be the weed crop interference. Weed seeds germinate most readily from top 1.25 cm of soil or up to 2.5 cm depth. Only few weeds such as Barnyard grass and cocklebur may germinate even from 10 cm depth of soil. Therefore, a planting method that dries the top 3-5 cm of soil rapidly is enough to deny weed seeds the opportunity to absorb moisture for their germination which usually post pones weed emergence until 1st irrigation is given. By this time, the crop plants are well established to compete with the late maturing weeds. In other cases, when the planting method which leaves the top most soil wet, weed seeds absorb enough moisture to germinate which induces severe weed crop competition.

- **Crop density and rectangularity:** In low plant population resulting from low seed rate, faulty germination or loss of crop seedlings, weed growth is dense and weed crop competition intense. Wide row spacing may also induce dense weed growth. It can weaken the crop plants and intensify weed crop interference further. Square planting should be ideal in reducing the intra-plant competition in crops. Competition among individuals of same species of plant is comparatively weaker than competition among individual of different species.
- **Crop species and varieties:** Crops and varieties differ in their habitat often to weeds to grow as well as in their ability to with stand weed competition. Such differences among crop species may result from either their inherent morphological and physiological features or from differences in their cultivation requirements *e.g.* Barley is found more tolerant to interference by weeds than wheat and wheat more tolerant than oats. Linseed is more sensitive to the presence of weed than to other winter grains. High tolerance of barley to crop weed competition may be due to development of extensive seminal and crown roots during its first three weeks after planting. Fast canopy forming and tall crops suffer less from weed competition than slow growing or short stature crop. Dwarf varieties of crops are more susceptible to weed crop competition than the tall because initially they grow slowly.

SECTION-B

5. (*a*) Agriculture is the largest consumer of water and total evapotranspiration from global agricultural land could double in next 50 years if trends in food consumption and current practices of production continue. There is an imminent need to improve the water use efficiency or more importantly the water productivity. Agriculture is the largest consumer of water and total evapotranspiration from global agricultural land could double in next 50 years if trends in food consumption and current practices of production continue. There is an imminent need to improve the water use efficiency or more importantly the water productivity. During the last 50 years, the original concept of 'water-use efficiency' has been considerably enhanced to include 'crop productivity or value per drop of water'. In its broadest sense it relates to the net socio-economic and environmental benefits achieved through the use of water in agriculture.

The more commonly used concept of 'water productivity' and its measurement at various scales is a robust measure of the ability of agricultural systems to convert water into food. Increasing water productivity is particularly important where water is scarce compared with other resources involved in production. While water productivity increases with increase in water supply up to a certain point, water supply also improves fertilizer-use efficiency by increasing the availability of applied nutrients. Improving water use efficiency or enhancing agricultural water productivity is a critical response to growing water scarcity, including the need to leave enough water in rivers and lakes to sustain ecosystems and to meet the growing demands of cities and industries.

Measure to Improve Water-Use Efficiency

Conservation of water

- Reduce conveyance losses by lining channels or, preferably, by using closed conduits.
- Reduce direct evaporation during irrigation by avoiding midday sprinkling. Minimize foliar interception by under-canopy, rather than by overhead sprinkling.
- Reduce runoff and percolation losses due to overirrigation.
- Reduce evaporation from bare soil by mulching and by keeping the inter-row strips dry.
- Reduce transpiration by weeds, keeping the inter-row strips dry and applying weed control measures where needed.

Enhancement of crop growth

- Select most suitable and marketable crops for the region.
- Use optimal timing for planting and harvesting.
- Use optimal tillage (avoid excessive cultivation).
- Use appropriate insect, parasite and disease control.
- Apply manures and green manures where possible and fertilize effectively (preferably by injecting the necessary nutrients into the irrigation water).
- Practise soil conservation for long-term sustainability.
- Avoid progressive salinization by monitoring water-table elevation and early signs of salt accumulation, and by appropriate drainage.
- Irrigate at high frequency and in the exact amounts needed to prevent water deficits, taking account of weather conditions and crop growth stage.

Improved practices at field level relate to changes in crop, soil and water management. They include: selecting appropriate crops and cultivars; planting methods (*e.g.* on raised beds); minimum tillage; timely irrigation to synchronize water application with the most sensitive growing periods; nutrient management; drip irrigation; and improved drainage for water table control. In its broadest sense, water productivity (WP) is the net return for a unit of water used. Improvement of water productivity aims at producing more food, income, better livelihoods and ecosystem services with less water. There is considerable scope for improving water productivity of crop, livestock and fisheries at field through to basin scale. Practices used to achieve this include water harvesting, supplemental irrigation, deficit irrigation, precision irrigation techniques and soil-water conservation practices. Practices not directly related to water management impact water productivity because of interactive effects such as those derived from improvements in soil fertility, pest and disease control, crop selection or access to better markets.

Water depletion occurs when water evaporates from moist soil, from puddles between rows and before crop establishment. All cultural and agronomic practices that reduce these losses, such as different row spacings and the application of mulches, improve water productivity. The irrigation method also affects these evaporative losses. Drip irrigation causes much less soil wetting than sprinkler irrigation. The significance of soil improvement in enhancing water productivity is often ignored. However, integrated crop and resource management practices, such as improved nutrient management, can increase water productivity by raising the yield proportionally more than it increases evapotranspiration. This principle applies to both irrigated and rainfed agriculture. Integrated weed and integrated pest management have also contributed effectively to yield increases. There is considerable scope for improving water productivity, but not everywhere. The scope for improvement remains in many rainfed, irrigated, livestock and fisheries systems in many regions of the world. Many farmers in developing countries could raise water productivity by adopting proven agronomic and water management practices. Many promising pathways for raising water productivity are available over the continuum from fully rainfed to fully irrigated farming systems.

At large river-basin scales with diverse and interacting uses and users, the water productivity issues become increasingly complex. Options for improving water productivity include reallocation and co-management of the resources among the high-value uses while maintaining a healthy ecosystem. Appropriate water accounting procedures need to be put in place to identify the opportunities for water savings. Large gains in water productivity can be achieved by growing suitable crops in places where climate and management practices enable high water productivity and selling them to places with lower water productivity. Presently, there is great scope for increasing economic water productivity by increasing the value generated by water use and decreasing the associated costs. However, a number of key drivers including climate change, urbanization, changes in diets and populations, and change in prices of commodities (outputs) and inputs (seeds, fertilizers, energy, etc.) will require that systems need to rapidly respond to take advantage of potential gains in water productivity.

There are four primary ways to increase the productivity of water in a basin context:

- Increasing the productivity per unit of ET at the plant-, field and farm-scale,
- Minimizing nonproductive depletion of water flows by reducing water flows to sinks, minimizing salinization and pollution of return flows and discharging polluted water to sinks;
- Improving management of existing irrigation facilities and reusing return flows by controlling, diverting and storing drainage flows; and
- Reallocating and co-managing water among uses by reallocating water from lower value to higher value uses within and between sectors, identifying and managing committed outflows for the environment and for downstream water allocation, co-managing among multiple uses, recognizing multiple uses, and reaping multiple benefits while mitigating adverse impacts and incorporating aquaculture, fisheries, and livestock considerations into basin management.

5. (*b*) **Drainage:** The adverse effects of waterlogging can be reduced to some extent by supplying nitrogenous fertilizers. The best method of avoiding waterlogging is by providing suitable drainage. Waterlogging and salt accumulation are major constraints to sustainable agricultural production in most countries of the world, especially in developing countries (including India). In India, drainage problem is acute in the states of Punjab and Haryana, while it also prevails in the command areas of other states. Broadly speaking, waterlogging is a situation of an agricultural land when the root zone gets saturated. Such a condition restricts normal air circulation, reduces the oxygen level and increases carbon dioxide level in the root zone. On the other hand, salt affected soils are those in which the concentration of salts in the root zone adversely affects the normal

root activity. Both the waterlogging and salt affected soils produce detrimental effects on crop growth and yield as well as cause environmental degradation.

Waterlogging and salinity of agricultural lands are caused due to natural causes or artificial causes (i.e., human interventions). Important natural causes are high rainfall during the rainy season, unfavourable topography, backwater entry from rivers, seawater intrusion, high evaporation during long dry periods, and the salts present in the soil. On the contrary, important human factors are unscientific management of land and irrigation water, use of poor-quality water for irrigation, adoption of unscientific and non-sustainable cropping pattern, and obstruction of natural outlets because of urbanization and construction of highways and railways.

Agricultural Drainage: Agricultural drainage is the provision of a suitable system for the removal of excessive irrigation or rain water from the land surface so as to provide suitable soil conditions for better plant growth.

Advantages of agricultural drainage

1. Provision of drainage facilitates early sowing of the crop.
2. Agricultural land can be used for a long time without any deterioration due to damaged soil structure and salt concentration.
3. Drainage lowers underground water table so as to facilitate increased root zone depth. Drainage improves soil aeration and increases soil temperature.

Conventional Drainage Techniques

The conventional engineering-based techniques most commonly used to drain excess water from land are: surface drainage, horizontal subsurface drainage and vertical subsurface drainage.

Surface drainage is described as 'the removal of excess water from the soil surface in time to prevent damage to crops and to keep water from ponding on the surface'. The term surface drainage applies to situations where overland flow is the major component of the excess-water movement to major drains or natural streams. The technique normally involves the excavation of open trenches/ drains. It could also include the construction of broad-based ridges or beds, as grassed waterways, with the water being discharged through the depressions between ridges. Surface drainage is most commonly applied on heavier soils where infiltration is slow and excess rainfall cannot percolate freely through the soil profile to the water table. The technique has also been applied in more permeable soils to de-water areas having a shallow groundwater table. It is the most important drainage technique in the humid and subhumid zones.

Horizontal subsurface drainage involves the removal of water from below the surface. The field drains can either be open ditches, or more commonly a network of pipes installed horizontally below the ground surface. These pipes used to be manufactured of clay tiles, with the water entering the pipes through the leaky joints (thus the term tile drains). In 1968 flexible corrugated plastic drainage pipe was introduced and this product is now widely used around the world. In spite of the different material used, the term tile drains are still in common use. Horizontal subsurface drainage has been found to be an effective technique. It controls the rise of groundwater tables and enables productive agriculture. Drawbacks are that it is relatively expensive to install, operate and maintain. Also, the disposal of drainage water that can contain high concentrations of pollutants (nutrients and/or toxic elements such as boron) can create problems.

Vertical subsurface drainage involves the removal of groundwater through pumped boreholes or tube wells, either in single or multiple-well configurations. The common problem with this technique is that deeper, often more saline water can be mobilized which can cause disposal problems. Also, as the water is commonly used for irrigation rather than disposal, salt is recycled through the soil profile and inevitably groundwater salinities will increase over time.

Drainage for agricultural land is provided by surface and subsurface drainage.

Surface Drainage:

1. Surface drainage is the simplest and the most common method.
2. Drainage is achieved by digging open drains at suitable intervals and depth.
3. Irrigation channels also serve as drainage channels.

Advantages of surface drainage

1. Provision of surface drainage is cheap.
2. The defects in the open drainage can be seen easily and rectified.
3. It requires less available fall or grade to have an adequate outlet.

Disadvantages in surface drainage system

1. Considerable amount of land is wasted for open drains.
2. These drains cause hindrance to field preparation and intercultivation.
3. The drains get silted and periodical desilting is necessary.
4. Weed growth in the drains is heavy and this has to be removed.
5. Open drains are damaged by rodents and farm animals.

Different Methods of Surface Drainage

Random Field Ditch Method: Standing water may be present in the field at several places distributed randomly. These depressions or micro ponds are connected by mean of shallow channels or ditches and these are led into an outlet.

Land Smoothing: The elevated area is cut off and excess soil is spread over low areas so that the surface is even with uniform slope. Excess surface run off is collected and conveyed into the field ditches provided at the lower end of the field.

Bedding: Small furrows are formed at known intervals parallel to the slope for draining out water. These furrows are known as dead furrows and land between these furrows is known as beds. Small ridges or bunds are made at the centre of the bed with gradual slope to drain water into the dead furrows.

Parallel Field Ditch system: It is almost similar to bedding system except for deep drains and uneven interval between drains.

Broad Bed and Furrow Method: The field is laid out with beds and wide furrows across the slope. About 0.5 per cent slope is provided for the furrows for free drainage. Crops are sown on the beds and furrows help in drainage of water when there is excess rain.

Alternative approaches

Vertical drainage with reuse of the extracted groundwater for irrigation is effective where the groundwater is of good quality and easily accessible (well-developed aquifers). However, this approach does not remove salts from the region. The long-term sustainability of vertical drainage without drainage disposal for salt-balance is therefore questionable. Horizontal drainage also has a proven record, as it controls the rise in the groundwater table and enables productive agriculture.

5. (*c*) A number of extensions programmes have been implemented over the years during both pre- and post-Indian Independence for the delivery or transfer of agricultural technology to the farmers through non-formal education some of which include the Gurgaon project, Marthandam project, Sriniketan project, NES, CDP, IADP, Training and Visit Extension Programme etc. These projects have ensured all round holistic development of the rural populace.

The Training and Visit Programme saw much success. However, owing to certain drawbacks of this programme, the

Government of India through the Ministry of Agriculture and the assistance of MANAGE, Hyderabad designed a new Extension Pilot Project correcting these limitations and adding some more reforms. Thus, with much success achieved through this pilot project, the GoI officially launched the new Centrally Sponsored Scheme called "Support to State Extension Programmes for Extension reforms" and started setting up of Agricultural Technology Management Agency (ATMA) in 588 rural districts in India in 2005 to implement this scheme. ATMA in Nagaland was set up in 2005 first in three districts- Kohima, Dimapur and Mokokchung and later replicated in all the rest districts by 2008.

Under the scheme grants-in-aid is released to the States/UTs with an objective to support State Governments efforts in revitalizing the extension system and making available the latest agricultural technologies in different thematic areas to increase production in agriculture & allied sectors through a Cafeteria of Activities which include Farmers Training, Demonstrations, Exposure Visits, Kisan Mela, Mobilization of Farmers Groups, Setting up of Farm School, Innovative Technology Dissemination, Research-Extension Linkages etc.

The Agricultural Technology Management Agency (ATMA) aims to facilitate and strengthen extension delivery system in the state through gap filling mode so as to ensure effective and all-round location specific technology transfer to the farmers through participatory approach thereby making extension system farmer driven and farmer accountable. In order to address the key constraints faced by extension system in the country with respect to reducing capacity of public extension services, its lack of decentralized and demand driven focus, the Innovations in Technology Dissemination component of National Agricultural Technology Project (NATP) was implemented in seven States in the country namely, Andhra Pradesh, Bihar, Himachal Pradesh, Jharkhand, Orissa, Maharashtra and Punjab through four project districts in each State. This component aimed at pilot testing new institutional arrangements for technology dissemination at district level and below in order to move towards an integrated extension delivery. The project process involved adopting bottom-up planning procedures for setting the research and extension agency in order to make the technology dissemination farmer driven and farmer accountable. The extension delivery was oriented towards group approach catering to the location specific requirement of the farmers. Gender concerns have been given adequate emphasis under the project. It functions as a registered society at District level and serves as a focal point for integrating research and extension activities and helps in decentralizing the management of agricultural technology transfer.

The purpose of NATP's innovation in Technology Dissemination Component is to pilot test new organizational arrangements and operational procedures not merely strengthen the existing extension system. One key concept or goal is to decentralize decision-making to the district level through the creation of Agricultural Technology Management Agency (ATMA). A second goal is to increase farmer input into programme planning and resource allocation, especially at the Block level, and to increase accountability to stakeholders. A third major goal is to increase programme coordination and integration, so that the programme thrust such as farming System innovations, Farmer organization, Technology gaps and Natural Resource Management can be more effectively and efficiently implemented.

The ATMA at district level would be increasingly responsible for all the technology dissemination activities at the district level. It would have linkage with all the line departments, research organizations, non-governmental organizations and agencies associated with agricultural development in the district. Research and Extension units within the project districts such as ZRS or substations, KVKs and the key line Departments of Agriculture, Animal Husbandry, Horticulture and Fisheries etc. would become constituent members or Key stakeholders of ATMA. Each Research-Extension (R-E) unit would retain its institutional identity and affiliation but programmes and procedures concerning district-wise R-E activities would be determined by ATMA Governing Board to be implemented by its Management Committee (MC).

This Scheme was approved on 29th March, 2005. The Scheme has made extension system farmer driven and farmer accountable. 237 Agricultural Technology Management Agency (ATMA) at district level have been set up to operationalise the extension reforms with active participation of farmers / farmer groups, NGOs, Krishi Vigyan Kendras, Panchayati Raj Institutions and another Stakeholder operating at district level and below. The release of funds is based on Strategic Research and Extension Plan (SEWP)/ State Extension Work Plans (SEWPs) prepared by the State Governments. State level Extension Plans have been developed keeping in mind the strategic extension needs of the farmers. 252 districts across all the States/UTs in the country were covered under the scheme during the 10th Plan. The objectives of ATMA are to strengthen research - extension - farmer linkages,to provide an effective mechanism for co-ordination and management of activities of different agencies involved in technology adaption / validation and dissemination at the district level and below. The beneficiaries of ATMA are individual, community, women, farmers/ farm women groups.

5. (*d*) **Farm Planning:** Farm planning is a decision making process in the farm business, which involves organization and management of limited resources to realize the specified goals continuously. Farm planning involves selecting the most profitable course of action from among all possible alternatives.

Characteristics of a Good Farm Plan

A good farm plan generally should have the following characteristics:

- An element of flexibility in a farm plan is essential to account for changes in the environment around the farm.
- A farm plan should maximize the resource use efficiency at the farm.
- It should provide for the attainment of the objectives of profit maximization through optimum resource use and balanced combination of farm enterprises.
- Risk and uncertainty can be accounted for in a good farm plan.
- The plan helps in timely acquisition and repayment of farm credit.

Steps in Farm Planning

The various steps involved in planning are discussed below:

Planning: This includes the identification and definition of the problem, collection of information, identifying alternative solutions and analyzing each alternative. Planning is the basic management function as it means deciding on a course of action, procedure or policy. The control function is a source of new infor- mation, as the results of the initial plan become known.

Implementation: Once the planning process is completed, the best alternative must be selected and action should be taken to place the plan into operation. This requires the acquisition and organization of necessary land, labour, capital and other inputs. An important part of the implementation function is the financing of the necessary resources.

Control: This provides for observing the results of the implemented plan to see if the specified goals and objectives are being met. Many things can cause a plan to go "off its track". Price and other changes, which occur after the implementation of the plan, can cause the actual results to deviate from the expected. Control requires a system for making regular checks on the plan and monitoring progress and results as measured against the established goals. The dashed line in the chart represents the continuous flow of information from the control function back to planning, an important part of the total system. Without some feedback procedure, the information obtained by the control system is of no use in making corrections in the existing plan or improving future plans. This feedback sets up a continuous cycle of planning, implementation, monitoring and recording progress, followed by a reevaluation of the plan and the implementation procedures using the new information obtained through the control function.

Techniques of Farm Planning

With a proper understanding of the planning environment and use of precise input-output data along with true and realistic constraints, sophisticated techniques give better results. However, common sense in the planning process could lead to fairly good results. Some of the farm planning techniques are as listed below:

1. Budgeting
2. Linear Programming

Budgeting is most informal of all the planning techniques and the level of sophistication gradually increases as we move from budgeting to linear programming.

Budgeting: It may be defined as a detailed physical and financial statement of a farm plan or of a change in farm plan over a certain period of time. Farm budgeting is a method of analyzing plans for the use of agricultural resources at the command of the decision-maker. In other words, the expression of farm plan in monetary terms through the estimation of receipts, expenses and profit is called farm budgeting.

Types of Farm Budgeting: The following are the different types of farm budgeting techniques:

- Partial Budgeting.
- Enterprise Budgeting.
- Cash flow Budgeting.
- Complete Budgeting.

Linear Programming: George Dantzing (1947) developed the simplex method for optimal transport of ammunition quickly with minimum cost. Linear programming is a mathematical method of analysis, which finds the "best" or optimal combination of business activities to meet a certain objective.

Three components are needed to solve a problem with linear programming technique. They are:

- a desire to maximize or minimize some objective,
- a set of activities or processes available to accomplish this objective, and
- a set of constraints or restrictions that limit one's ability to achieve this objective.

Basic assumptions of Linear Programming

- ***Proportionality or linearity:*** Linear relationship exists between activity and resource. For example, if one acre requires 30-man days, 100 kgs of nitrogen and ₹ 60 of other variable expenses to produce 20 quintals of maize output, then 10 acres of maize would require exactly 10 times of each resource to produce 200 quintals of output.
- ***Additivity:*** The total amount of resources used by several enterprises on the farm must be equal to the sum of resources used by each individual enterprise. Hence no interaction is possible. The same is true for the products also.

- ***Divisibility:*** Fractions can be used and enterprises can be produced in fractional units. Resources and products are infinitely divisible.
- ***Non-negativity:*** None of the activity is negative.
- ***Finiteness:*** Number of activities and constraints are finite.
- ***Certainty:*** Almost all planning techniques assume that resources, supplies, input-output coefficients and prices are known with certainty.

5. (*e*) The Farmers' Produce Trade and Commerce (Promotion and Facilitation) Act, 2020

- **Freedom to the Farmers:** The Act provides the farmers the freedom of choice related to sale and purchase of produce.
- **Liberation from the Cess:** The farmers will not be charged any cess or levy for sale of their produce under this Act. Further there will be a separate dispute resolution mechanism for the farmers.

Benefits

- **Promotes trade:** It promotes barrier-free inter-state and intra-state trade and commerce outside the physical premises of markets notified under State APMCs.
- **Better price:** It will open more choices for the farmer, reduce marketing costs for the farmers and help them in getting better prices.
- **One nation, one market:** The Act will help create One India, One Agriculture Market and will lay the foundation for ensuring golden harvests for our hard-working farmers.

The Farmers (Empowerment and Protection) Agreement of Price Assurance and Farm Services Act, 2020

Feature: Aims to provide for a national framework on farming agreements that protects and empowers farmers to engage with agri-business firms, processors, wholesalers, exporters or large retailers for farm services.

Benefits

Level playing field: The new legislation will empower farmers for engaging with processors, wholesalers, aggregators, wholesalers, large retailers, exporters etc., on a level playing field without any fear of exploitation.

Transfers the risk: It will transfer the risk of market unpredictability from the farmer to the sponsor and also enable the farmer to access modern technology and better inputs.

Attracts private sector: This legislation will act as a catalyst to attract private sector investment for building supply chains for supply of Indian farm produce to national and global markets, and in agricultural infrastructure.

Eliminates intermediaries: Farmers will engage in direct marketing thereby eliminating intermediaries resulting in full realization of price.

Amendments to Essential Commodities Act (1955)

India has become surplus in most agri-commodities but farmers have been unable to get better prices due to lack of investment in cold storage, processing and export. The imposition of the curbs on stocking of farm produce and regulation of the prices of commodities, etc. under Essential Commodities Act (ECA) are some of factors responsible for less entrepreneurial spirit and thus less investment in the farm sector.

Benefits of Amendments: The amendment would deregulate the commodities such as cereals, edible oils, oilseeds, pulses, onions and potatoes. It will help to lessen the fears of private investors of excessive regulatory interference in their business operations. Any limits under ECA over these commodities will be imposed only in exceptional circumstances such as war, famine, extraordinary price rise and natural calamity.

The freedom to produce, hold, move, distribute and supply will lead to harnessing economies of scale and attract private sector/foreign direct investment into the agriculture sector. It will help drive up investment in cold storages and modernization of the food supply chain. The amendment is expected to help both farmers and consumers while bringing in price stability. It will also create a competitive market environment and also prevent wastage of agri-produce that happens due to lack of storage facilities. It is considered as a step towards transformation of agriculture and raising farmers' income.

Significance of these Acts

- The reforms are expected to accelerate growth in the sector through private sector investment in building infrastructure and supply chains for farm produce in national and global markets.
- They are intended to help small farmers who don't have means to either bargain for their produce to get a better price or invest in technology to improve the productivity of farms.
- The legislation on contract farming will allow farmers to enter into a contract with agri-business firms or large retailers on pre-agreed prices of their produce.
- It will also help farmers of regions with surplus produce to get better prices and consumers of regions with shortages, lower prices.
- It will promote the creation of Farmer Producer Organisations (FPO) on a large scale and will help in creating a farmer-friendly environment for contract farming where small players can benefit.
- Competition is the best protector of stakeholders whether it is consumer or the farmers. Having a variety of buyers will protect farmers from exploitation and by having more sellers (farmers), consumers can buy better products at better deals.

Farmers Protest and Issues Involved

- ***Federal Angle:*** The provisions in the Farmers' Produce Trade and Commerce (Promotion and Facilitation) Act, 2020, provides for unfettered commerce in designated trade areas outside APMC jurisdictions.
    - ❑ Apart from this, the Act empowers the Centre government to issue orders to States in furtherance of the law's objectives.
    - ❑ However, matters of trade and agriculture being the part of subjects on the State list, have caused resentment in States.
- ***Lack of Consultation:*** First the ordinance route and now the hastily attempt to pass the Acts without proper consultation adds to the mistrust among various stakeholders including farmers.
    - ❑ Also, by allowing 'trade zones' to come up outside the APMC area, farmers have become apprehensive that the new system would lead to eventual exit from the minimum support price.
- ***Absence of any regulation in non-APMC mandis:*** Another issue that is raised by the farmers is that it gives the preference for corporate interests at the cost of farmers' interests.
    - ❑ In absence of any regulation in non-APMC mandis, the farmers may find it difficult to deal with Corporates, as they solely operate on the motive of profit seeking.
- ***Non-Favourable Market Conditions:*** While retail prices have remained high, data from the Wholesale Price Index (WPI) suggest a deceleration in farm gate prices for most agricultural produce.
    - ❑ With rising input costs, farmers do not see the free market-based framework providing them remunerative prices.
    - ❑ These fears gain strength with the experience of States such as Bihar which

abolished APMCs in 2006. After the abolition of mandis, farmers in Bihar on average received lower prices compared to the MSP for most crops.

Impact on Stakeholders

- ***Farmers:*** The farmer is now the producer and the seller of his own produce and will be free to enter into agreement with private trade directly.
- ***Consumers:*** The consumers would now get the produce as much lower costs.
- ***Middlemen:*** Although the role of middlemen is not going to end completely, their hold on the trade will not be as strong.
- ***State governments:*** The state govt. of states such as Punjab and Haryana will be adversely affected as there will be a huge loss in annual revenue collection.

It may be concluded that:

- The above-mentioned legislation basically aims at creating additional trading opportunities outside the APMC market yards to help farmers get remunerative prices due to additional competition. It proposes an electronic trading in transaction platform for ensuring a seamless trade electronically.
- None of the legislation affects the Minimum Support Price in any way as the MSP is an administrative decision not a law.
- Agricultural Produce & Market Committee (APMC) will still be available as a choice to sell their products.
- The sale, lease or mortgage of farmers' land is totally prohibited and farmers' land is also protected against any recovery.

6. (*a*) Advantage of Good Quality of Irrigation Water

Knowledge of irrigation water quality is critical to understanding management for long-term productivity. Irrigation water quality is evaluated based upon total salt content, sodium and specific ion toxicities. In many areas of Colorado, irrigation water quality can influence crop productivity. Salt-affected soils develop from a wide range of factors including: soil type, field slope and drainage, irrigation system type and management, fertilizer and manuring practices, and other soil and water management practices. In Colorado, perhaps the most critical factor in predicting, managing, and reducing salt-affected soils is the quality of irrigation water being used. Besides affecting crop yield and soil physical conditions, irrigation water quality can affect fertility needs, irrigation system performance and longevity, and how the water can be applied. Therefore, knowledge of irrigation water quality is critical to understanding what management changes are necessary for long-term productivity. The quality of irrigation water available to farmers and other irrigators has a considerable impact on what plants can be successfully grown, the productivity of these plants, and water infiltration and other soil physical conditions. The first step in understanding how an irrigation water source can affect a soil-plant system is to have it analyzed by a reputable lab.

Irrigation, the addition of water to lands via artificial means, is essential to profitable crop production in arid climates. Irrigation is also practiced in humid and sub-humid climates to protect crops during periods of drought. Irrigation is practiced in all environments to maximize production and, therefore, profit by applying water when the plant needs it.

6. (*b*) Effect of Water Pollution on Agroecosystem: Over the past few decades, the increase in population and advances made in farming technology has increased the demand for crops and livestock from the agricultural industry. This growth in agricultural production has resulted in an increase in contaminants polluting soil and waterways. The increase in contaminants has prompted efforts to reduce the amount of pollutants in waterways in order to improve overall water quality.

Agriculture in many parts of the world is highly efficient in producing and delivering high-quality products to consumers. However, when agricultural activities are not well-monitored and managed, certain practices can negatively affect water quality.

Agricultural Runoff: According to the U.S. Environmental Protection Agency (EPA), nonpoint source (NPS) pollution is pollution that comes from many diffuse sources, unlike pollution from point sources such as industrial and sewage treatment plants. "Polluted runoff is created by rainfall or snowmelt moving over and through the ground. As the runoff moves, it picks up and carries away natural and human-made pollutants, finally depositing them into watersheds via lakes, rivers, wetlands, coastal waters, and even our underground sources of drinking water". In 2002, in the National Water Quality Inventory report to U.S. Congress, the states reported that agricultural nonpoint source (NPS) pollution is the leading cause of river and stream impairment and the second leading cause of impairment in lakes, ponds, and reservoirs.

Agricultural activities that cause nonpoint source pollution include:

Overgrazing: Overworking the land (for example, plowing too often).

Poorly managed and ineffective application of pesticides, irrigation water, and fertilizer.

Effects: Agricultural water can become contaminated through a variety of ways and can potentially spread bacteria, viruses, and parasites to crops and animals.

Crop Production: Fresh fruits and vegetables come in contact with water during various stages of the production process. Contaminated water that is used during crop production, harvesting, and processing can lead to health issues.

Below is a list of the potential food production points where contaminated water sources can affect crop production:

Chemical Application: Crops with contaminated water used for pesticide or herbicide application. Water used for mixing chemicals should be of appropriate quality.

Irrigation: Irrigating crops with contaminated water. Water used for irrigation should be of appropriate quality.

Food Processing: Wash crops in the final wash process with quality water. Water should be of drinking water quality and should not be recycled.

People who consume fruit or vegetables that were exposed to contaminated water are at risk of developing a foodborne illness. Some of the bacteria that are spread through water within the United States include *E. coli, Salmonella* spp., *Shigella* spp., *Cryptosporidium, Giardia, Toxoplasma, Norovirus,* and *Hepatitis A virus.* Irrigation of foods imported from international locations can spread these and other microbes (for example, Cyclospora) not usually found in developed countries. Small amounts of any of these organisms can cause foodborne illness. In order to keep microbes out of water sources, growers should use practices that are appropriate for their operation and make sure that they are using the best quality water. Water quality is also important in ensuring post-harvest quality by decreasing decay.

Animal Health: It is important that livestock are provided with adequate amounts of quality water, free of contamination. Contaminated water can contain disease-causing organisms which can rapidly spread if animals are drinking from the same trough. If there is reason to question the quality of the water that is provided to livestock, it is important to test the water to ensure its safety. There are many chemicals and microorganisms that can be potentially dangerous to livestock. Some chemicals include nitrates, sulphates, and chemicals found in pesticides like DDT, Chlordane, and Endrin. Certain microorganisms such as blue-green algae, *Cryptosporidium,* or *Staphylococcus,* can be toxic to animals and cause symptoms like diarrhea, lack of coordination, labored breathing, or death. Ill animals can then release millions of infectious microbes into the soil that can further contaminate other water sources.

Effect of Soil Pollution on Agroecosystem: Soil pollution is not only the problem in India but it is a global problem. It causes harmful effect on the soil and the environment at large. Contamination of soil will decrease the agricultural output of a land. Major soil pollution after effects are:

- **Inferior Crop Quality:** It can decrease the quality of the crop. Regular use of chemical fertilizers, inorganic fertilizers, pesticides will decrease the fertility of the soil at a rapid rate and alter the structure of the soil. This will lead to decrease in soil quality and poor quality of crops. Over the time the soil will become less productive due to the accumulation of toxic chemicals in large quantity.
- **Harmful Effect on Human Health:** It will increase the exposure to toxic and harmful chemicals thus increasing health threats to people living nearby and on the degraded land. Living, working or playing in the contaminated soil can lead to respira-tory diseases, skin diseases, and other diseases. Moreover, it can cause other health problems.
- **Water Sources Contamination:** The surface run-off after raining will carry the polluted soil and enter into different water resource. Thus, it can cause underground water contamination thereby causing water pollution. This water after contamination is not fit for human as well as animal use due to the presence of toxic chemicals.
- **Negative Impact on Ecosystem and Biodiversity:** Soil pollution can cause an imbalance of the ecosystem of the soil. The soil is an important habitat and is the house of different type of microorganisms, animals, reptiles, mammals, birds, and insects. Thus, soil pollution can negatively impact the lives of the living organisms and can result in the gradual death of many organisms. It can cause health threats to animals grazing in the contaminated soil or microorganisms residing in the soil.

Therefore, human activities are responsible for the majority of the soil pollution. We as humans buy things that are harmful and not necessary, use agricultural chemicals (fertilizers, pesticides, herbicides, etc.), drop waste here and there. Without being aware we harm our own environment. Therefore, it is very important to educate people around you the importance of environment if they are not aware. Prevention of soil erosion will help to cease soil pollution. Thus, it is our small steps and activities that can help us to achieve a healthier planet for us. Therefore, it is essential for industries, individuals and businesses to understand the importance of soil and prevent soil pollution and stop the devastation caused to plant and animal life.

6. (*c*) Marketing is any activity that leads you to sell a product. When you decide what products to sell, what price to ask, where and how to sell them, and how to promote them, you are marketing. Your strategy is your means of doing something—how you will meet your objectives of selling this year's crop. Depending on the type and size of your farm, and whether you are farming full or part time, you have several options for how to market your operation. Selling at a farmer's market is a distribution and sales strategy that is ideal if you are a small or medium-sized agricultural producer. It can also be a stepping stone to larger markets if you want to grow, but with the popularity of these markets, many farmers sell at a different market every weekend within a reasonable distance from their farms. It allows you to sell several types of produce, provide recipes and offer taste samples. Another benefit is that market operators or local communities handle much of the promotion, saving you time and money.

Try community-supported agriculture as a sales and pricing strategy if you are a smaller operation that needs reliable cash flow to sustain your operation. With a CSA, you offer shares in your farm to as many people as your farm can support. They pay for their shares each year before your crops is harvested, in exchange for a set amount of food. It can be one box of vegetables, or a box a week—depending on their subscription or membership, and how much you can produce. Promote your CSA with online tactics such as social media, a website and emails.

An Agricultural Produce Market Committee (APMC) is a marketing board established by state governments in India to ensure farmers are safeguarded from exploitation by large retailers, as well as ensuring the farm to retail price spread does not reach excessively high levels. APMCs are regulated by states through their adoption of an Agriculture Produce Marketing Regulation (APMR) Act.

Until 2020, the first sale of agriculture produce could occur only at the market yards (mandis) of APMCs. However, after 2020 with the passing of the Farmers' Produce Trade and Commerce (Promotion and Facilitation) Act, which allowed farmers to sell outside APMC mandis as well as across different states of India. Prior to independence in 1947, the major concern of Government policy related to agricultural marketing was to keep the prices of food for the consumers and agro-raw materials for the industry in check. However, after independence, there came a need to protect the interest of farmers and to provide them incentive prices to augment the production of agricultural commodities. Common throughout the country were problems of local money lenders extorting high amounts of foodgrains from the farmer, at throwaway prices, as interest. Recognizing the defects that farmers faced—such as losses in terms of undue low prices, higher costs of marketing, and considerable physical losses of the produce in the agricultural marketing system—the Indian Government introduced several mandatory regulations in hopes of establishing a mechanism to monitor the market conduct. Regulation and development of primary agricultural produce markets was taken up as an institutional innovation, and construction of well laid out market yards was considered as an essential requirement for regulating the practices in primary wholesale markets.

APMCs operate on two principles:

- Ensure that farmers are not exploited by intermediaries (or money lenders) who compel farmers to sell their produce at the farm gate for an extremely low price.
- All food produce should first be brought to a market yard and then sold through auction.

Each state that operates APMC markets (mandis) establish their markets in different places within their borders, geographically dividing the state. Farmers are required to sell their produce via auction at the mandi in their region. Traders require a license to operate within a mandi. Wholesale and retail traders (*e.g.* shopping mall owners) and food processing companies cannot buy produce directly from a farmer.

PAPER-II

SECTION-A

1. (a) Cell: The cell is the basic unit of life in all organisms. Like humans and animals, plants are also composed of several cells. The plant cell is surrounded by a cell wall which is involved in providing shape to the plant cell. Apart from the cell wall, there are other organelles that are associated with different cellular activities. Plant cells are eukaryotic cells with a true nucleus along with specialized structures called organelles that carry out certain specific functions. Plant cells are eukaryotic cells that vary in several fundamental factors from other eukaryotic organisms. Both plant and animal cells contain nucleus along with similar organelles. One of the distinctive aspects of a plant cell is the presence of a cell wall outside the cell membrane.

Organelles of Plant Cell: The major organelles and cellular structures include: • Nucleolus • Nucleus • Ribosome • Vesicle • Rough endoplasmic reticulum • Golgi apparatus • Cytoskeleton • Smooth endoplasmic reticulum • Mitochondria • Vacuole • Cytosol • Lysosome • Centriole.

Mitochondria are membrane-bound organelles present in the cytoplasm of all eukaryotic cells, that produces adenosine triphosphate (ATP), the main energy molecule used by the cell. Popularly known as the "Powerhouse of the cell," mitochondria (singular: mitochondrion) are a double membrane-bound organelle found in most eukaryotic organisms. They are found inside the cytoplasm and essentially functions as the cell's "digestive system". They play a major role in breaking down nutrients and generating energy-rich molecules for the cell. Many of the biochemical reactions involved in cellular respiration take place within the mitochondria. The term 'mitochondrion' is derived from the Greek words *"mitos"* and *"chondrion"* which means "thread" and "granules-like" respectively. It was first described by a German pathologist named Richard Altmann in the year 1890.

Structure of Mitochondria

The mitochondrion is a double-membraned, rod-shaped structure found in both plant and animal cell. Its size ranges from 0.5 to 1.0 micrometre in diameter. The structure comprises an outer membrane, an inner membrane, and a gel-like material called the matrix. The outer membrane and the inner membrane are made of proteins and phospholipid layers separated by the intermembrane space. The outer membrane covers the surface of the mitochondrion and has a large number of special proteins known as porins. It is freely permeable to ions, nutrient molecules, energy molecules like the ADP and ATP molecules.

Cristae: The inner membrane of mitochondria is rather complex in structure. It has many folds that form a layered structure called cristae, and this helps in increasing the surface area inside the organelle. The cristae and the proteins of the inner membrane aids in the production of ATP molecules. The inner membrane is strictly permeable only to oxygen and to ATP molecules. A number of chemical reactions take place within the inner membrane of mitochondria.

Mitochondrial Matrix: The mitochondrial matrix is a viscous fluid that contains a mixture of enzymes and proteins. It also comprises ribosomes, inorganic ions, mitochondrial DNA, nucleotide cofactors, and organic molecules. The enzymes present in the matrix play an important role in the synthesis of ATP molecules.

Functions of Mitochondria: The most important function of mitochondria is to produce energy through the process of oxidative phosphorylation. It is also involved in the following process:

- Regulates the metabolic activity of the cell.
- Promotes the growth of new cells and cell multiplication.
- Helps in detoxifying ammonia in the liver cells.
- Plays an important role in apoptosis or programmed cell death.
- Responsible for building certain parts of the blood and various hormones like testosterone and oestrogen.
- Helps in maintaining an adequate concentration of calcium ions within the compartments of the cell.
- It is also involved in various cellular activities like cellular differentiation, cell signalling, cell senescence, controlling the cell cycle and also in cell growth.

1. (*b*) Heterosis: Heterosis, hybrid vigor, or outbreeding enhancement is the improved or increased function of any biological quality in a hybrid offspring. An offspring is heterotic if its traits are enhanced as a result of mixing the genetic contributions of its parents. These effects can be due to Mendelian or non-Mendelian inheritance. When a population is small or inbred, it tends to lose genetic diversity. Inbreeding depression is the loss of fitness due to loss of genetic diversity. Inbred strains tend to be homozygous for recessive alleles that are mildly harmful (or produce a trait that is undesirable from the standpoint of the breeder). Heterosis or hybrid vigor, on the other hand, is the tendency of outbred strains to exceed both inbred parents in fitness. Selective breeding of plants and animals, including hybridization, began long before there was an understanding of underlying scientific principles. In the early 20th century, after Mendel's laws came to be understood and accepted, geneticists undertook to explain the superior vigor of many plant hybrids. Two competing hypotheses, which are not mutually exclusive, were developed.

Genetic Basis of Heterosis: Genetic basis of heterosis. *Dominance hypothesis.* Scenario A. Fewer genes are under-expressed in the homozygous individual. Gene expression in the offspring is equal to the expression of the fittest parent. *Overdominance hypothesis.* Scenario B. Over-expression of certain genes in the heterozygous offspring. (The size of the circle depicts the expression level of gene A).

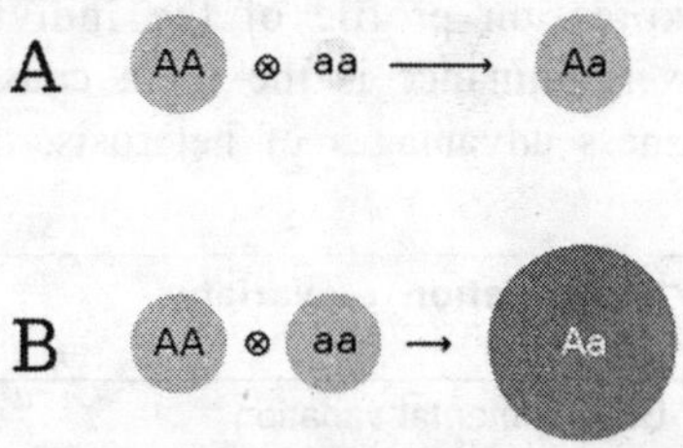

- **Dominance hypothesis:** The dominance hypothesis attributes the superiority of hybrids to the suppression of undesirable recessive alleles from one parent by dominant alleles from the other. It attributes the poor performance of inbred strains to loss of genetic diversity, with the strains becoming purely homozygous at many loci. The dominance hypothesis was first expressed in 1908 by the geneticist Charles Davenport. Under the dominance hypothesis, deleterious alleles are expected to be maintained in a random-mating population at a selection-mutation balance that would depend on the rate of mutation, the effect of the alleles and the degree to which alleles are expressed in heterozygotes.
- **Overdominance hypothesis:** Certain combinations of alleles that can be obtained by crossing two inbred strains are advantageous in the heterozygote. The overdominance hypothesis attributes the heterozygote advantage to the survival of many alleles that are recessive and harmful

in homozygotes. It attributes the poor performance of inbred strains to a high percentage of these harmful recessives. The overdominance hypothesis was developed independently by Edward M. East (1908) and George Shull (1908). Genetic variation at an over dominant locus is expected to be maintained by balancing selection. The high fitness of heterozygous genotypes favours the persistence of an allelic polymorphism in the population.

Dominance and overdominance have different consequences for the gene expression profile of the individuals. If overdominance is the main cause for the fitness advantages of heterosis, then there should be an over-expression of certain genes in the heterozygous offspring compared to the homozygous parents. On the other hand, if dominance is the cause, fewer genes should be under-expressed in the heterozygous offspring compared to the parents. Furthermore, for any given gene, the expression should be comparable to the one observed in the fitter of the two parents.

1. (*c*) Genetic purity of seed can be maintained by reducing factors that cause deterioration. Genetic principles can be discussed on following heading:

- Deterioration of variety • Maintenance of genetic purity

S.No.	Deterioration of variety	Explanation (Arise when)	Maintenance of genetic purity
1.	Developmental variation	Grown in different environment, soil, climate	Growing seeds in their adaptation and growing season.
2.	Mechanical mixture	At sowing time, harvesting time if presence of off seeds	Rogue the seed fields. Care should be given during seed production, harvesting, threshing and further handling
3.	Mutation	Can't be detected, not so serious	Remove mutant plant Increase of true to type stock of seed
4.	Natural Crossing	Natural crossing with undesirable type, diseased plant or off type plant	Maintenance of isolation distance.
5.	Minor Genetic Variation	It often appears in cross pollinated crops	Care should be given during maintenance of nucleus and breeders seed
6.	Selective Influence of Diseases	New variety easily gets infected with diseases. Vegetative propagating stocks gets more infected with pathogens.	Production of disease free stocks in seed production programme.
7.	The Techniques of the Plant Breeder	Premature release of variety Heritable variation Environmental conditions	Careful handling and adaptation of techniques by breeders

Agronomic Principles of Seed Production

- Selection of suitable agro-climatic condition
- Selection of field and its preparation
- Selection of variety
- Isolation of seed crops
- Seed treatment
- Time and method of planting

- Nutrition of the seed crop
- Seed rate (lower seed rates for easy rouging)
- Depth of sowing (small seeds sown upper, larger seeds at more depth)
- Weed control (clean seedbed, clean weed, use herbicide if required)
- Irrigation of seed crop (moderate irrigation, stop 2 weeks before)
- Pollination control (rearing honey bees aid)
- Field inspection (one at flowering and another on grower request)
- Rouging (rogue at vegetative, flowering and maturity stage)
- Plant protection (disease and insect control)
- Harvesting of seed crop (fully matured seed)
- Drying of seeds (dry seeds upto 9-12%)
- Storage of seed (less than 21°C)
- Seed packaging (seed packed in cotton, jute bag or plastic bag)

1. (*d*) The Krebs Cycle, also called the *citric acid cycle,* is the second major step in oxidative phosphorylation. After glycolysis breaks glucose into smaller 3-carbon molecules, the Krebs cycle transfers the energy from these molecules to electron carriers, which will be used in the electron transport chain to produce ATP. Most organisms use glucose as a major fuel source, but must break down this glucose and store the energy in ATP and other molecules. The Krebs cycle is contained within mitochondria. Within the mitochondrial matrix, the reactions of the Krebs cycle add electrons and protons to a number of electron carriers, which are then used by the electron transport chain to produce ATP.

The Krebs cycle starts with the products of glycolysis, which are two three-carbon molecules known as pyruvate. This molecule is acidic, which is why the Krebs cycle is also called the tricarboxylic acid cycle (TCA). Throughout a number of reactions, these molecules are further broken down into carbon dioxide. Energy from the molecules is moved to other molecules, called electron carriers. These molecules carry the stored energy to the electron transport chain, which in turn creates ATP. Then, the cell uses this ATP to power various cellular reactions, such as the activation of enzymes or transport proteins. The Krebs cycle is the second of 4 different processes which must happen to extract the energy from glucose. Altogether, the Krebs cycle consists of 9 sequential reactions.

Krebs Cycle Products: The first step of utilizing glucose, glycolysis, produces a few ATP as well as the molecules which will be processed with the Krebs cycle. During glycolysis, a single glucose molecule is split into two smaller, three-carbon molecules called pyruvate. Pyruvate is then converted to *acetyl CoA*. Acetyl CoA is then utilized within the Krebs cycle to produce several major products. In turn, these products then drive the formation of ATP, the cell's main energy source. Before the first stages of the Krebs cycle, pyruvate is converted into acetyl CoA. During this process, one molecule of CO_2 and one molecule of the electron carrier NADH are produced. The Krebs cycle involves converting this acetyl CoA into carbon dioxide. During the steps of the cycle, two molecules of CO_2 are released, in addition to 3 more molecules of NADH, one of $FADH_2$, and one of GTP. So, for every 1 pyruvate molecule added, the Krebs cycle will produce:

- 2 molecules of CO_2
- 3 molecules of NADH
- 1 molecule of $FADH_2$
- 1 molecule of GTP

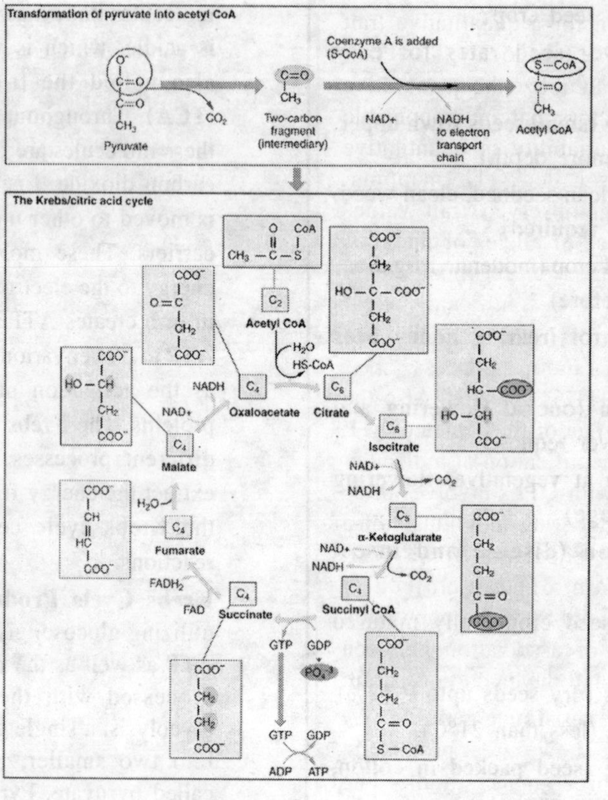

A molecule of glucose contains 2 pyruvate molecules, so 1 glucose molecule will produce double the amount of products listed above as it moves through the Krebs cycle. These products will then be converted to ATP in later stages of aerobic respiration. Carbon dioxide is the only "waste" product and must be removed from the cell. Large organisms must remove carbon dioxide from all their cells. In these animals, carbon dioxide is typically exchanged in the gills or lungs for oxygen, which helps drive the final stages of aerobic respiration.

Krebs Cycle Steps: The Krebs cycle has 9 main reactions, which happen quickly in succession. The image below shows these reactions.

Note that citrate is the first molecule created after acetyl CoA is added. This is why the Krebs cycle is also known as the citric acid cycle. The products of the cycle are in the image above. This process is known as a "cycle" because it always ends on oxaloacetate which can be combined with a new acetyl CoA to produce a new molecule of citrate for each cycle.

1. (*e*) Molecular markers: Molecular markers are specific fragments of DNA that can be identified within the whole genome. Molecular markers are found at specific locations of the genome. They are used to 'flag' the position of a particular gene or the inheritance of a particular character. Molecular markers are phenotypically neutral.

Application of DNA Markers in Crop Improvement

QTL mapping: Some of the most difficult tasks of plant breeders relate to the improvement of traits that show a continuous range of values. Genetic factors that are responsible for a part of the observed phenotypic variation for a quantitative trait are called quantitative trait loci (QTLs Plant breeders would like to utilize the quantitative traits for genetic factors that are responsible for the observed variability in quantitative traits. In a process called QTL mapping, association between observed trait values and presence/absence of alleles of markers, that have been mapped onto a linkage map is analysed. When it is significantly clear that the correlation that is observed did not result from some random process, it is proclaimed that a QTL is detected. Also the size of the allelic effect of the detected QTL can be estimated. Identification of molecular makers associated with QTLs involves three basic steps namely, scoring individuals of a random segregating population for a QTL trait; determination of the molecular genotype of each member of the population and determination of association between any of the markers and the quantitative trait.

Tagging of disease resistance genes: DNA based markers have shown great promise in expediting plant breeding methods. The identification of molecular markers closely linked with resistance genes can facilitate expeditious pyramiding of major genes into elite background, making it more cost effective. Once the resistance genes are tagged with molecular marker the selection of resistant plant in the segregating generations becomes easy.

Tagging of male sterility genes: A cytoplasmic male sterile system is desirable for use in hybrid seed production, as it eliminates the need for hand emasculation. CMS is a maternally inheritable trait characterized by the inability to produce viable pollen but without affecting the female fertility, and it is often associated with mitochondrial DNA rearrangements, mutations and editing. Several restorer locus have been identified using RAPD and STS in different crop and DNA markers linked to these locus enable the molecular study of the CMS system.

Diversity evaluation: Stability and identity of crop variety has assumed great importance for predicting plant breeder's right/farmers right. Traditionally, evaluation and conservation of bio-diversity/genetic variability is based on comparative anatomy, morphology, embryology, physiology, etc., which provide informative data but of low genetic resolution. Recent advances in molecular biology have provided powerful genetic tools, which can provide rapid and detailed genetic resolution. Molecular marker-based genotyping involves the development of marker profile unique to an individual. This unambiguous pattern of crop varieties obtained using DNA a marker is termed as "DNA Fingerprinting".

Heterosis breeding: Another important application of DNA marker is their prediction of heterosis in hybrids. Evaluation of hybrids for heterosis or combining ability in field is expensive. Molecular markers have been used to correlate genetic diversity and heterosis in several cereal crops (like rice, oat, and wheat). It has been reported that measures of similarity based on RFLP and pedigree knowledge could be used to predict superior hybrid combinations.

Hybrid seed purity testing: To determine the hybrid seed quality it is to be verified that the designated cross has occurred, the number of self-pollination between the female parents meet the necessary purity and the product has adequate quality.

Gene pyramiding: It is essentially a way of determining and introducing multiple genes which impart resistance to an independent insect/microbial pest, or impart resistance to a single pest through independent host pathways. One strategy for increasing the durability of resistance is to incorporate multiple resistance genes into a single variety.

Pyramiding of Bt genes: The insecticidal cry (crystal) genes from *Bacillus thuringiensis* (Bt) have been used for insect control both as biopesticides and in transgenic plants. Discovery of new insecticidal genes is of importance for delaying the development of resistance in target insects. The diversity of B tstrains facilitates isolation of new types of cry and vip (vegetative insecticidal protein) genes. PCR is a useful technique for quick and simultaneous screening of Bt strains for classification and prediction of insecticidal activities. PCR together with other methods of analysis such as RFLP, gene sequence determination, electrophoretic, immunological and chromatographic analysis of Cry proteins and insect bioassays for evaluation of toxicity have been employed for identification of new insecticidal proteins.

Map based cloning of genes: The first step of map-based or positional cloning is to identify a molecular marker that lies close to the gene of interest. Initially gene search is done with a small mapping population and subsequently, a highly saturated genetic map is prerequisite to clone a gene. With reference to an initial marker, the region around that original molecular marker is saturated with high density markers. A large number of individuals are screened to find a marker which rarely recombines with the gene of interest.

Uses of DNA markers

(*a*) **DNA fingerprinting**

- To establish distinctness among biological entities
- Genetic diversity studies
- Evolutionary studies

(*b*) **Molecular mapping**

- To prepare saturated genetic map
- Chromosome identification

(*c*) **Map based cloning of genes**

(*d*) **Marker Assisted Selection**

- QTLs
- Disease resistance

(*e*) **Construction of genetic map**

3. (*a*) (*i*) **Breeder Seeds:** A breeder's seed is an offspring of nucleus seed. A breeder is a person (qualified plant breeder) or organization who raises plant primary for breeding purpose. While nucleus seed is genetically pure; the Breeder seeds are produced by mutual multiplication of three different lines which are denoted by A line, B line and R line. A line is female, while B and R line are male sterile. The seeds from offsprings with best and desired quality are selected and certified as Breeder seeds. Such seeds are protected by legal rights called as Breeder's rights. The Breeder seed is further multiplied into the foundation and certified seeds. In our country, Breeder seeds are produced Indian Council of Agricultural Research, National Seeds Corporation, States Farms Corporation and agricultural universities in India.

Certified Seeds: This is the last stage, which actually reaches to a farmer. Certified seed is the progeny of foundation seed and must meet the standards of seed certification prescribed in the Indian Minimum Seeds Certification Standards, 1988. It is the progeny of the foundation seed. Its production is so handled to maintain genetical identity and physical purity according to standards specified for the crop being certified. It should have the minimum genetical purity of 99%. Certified seed may be the progeny of certified seed, provided this reproduction does not exceed two generations beyond foundation seed and provided that if certification agency determines the genetic and physical purity, if not be significantly altered. In case of highly self-pollinated crops certification of one further generation may be permitted. Certified seed produced from certified seed shall be eligible for further seed increase under certification, except in case of highly self-pollinated crops, where certification of one further generation may be permitted. Certification tags issued once for certified seed not eligible for further seed increase under certification.

3. (*a*) (*ii*) Natural Selection: Natural selection is the differential survival and reproduction of individuals due to differences in phenotype. It is a key mechanism of evolution, the change in the heritable traits characteristic of a population over generations. To be more general, natural selection is a process that results in some animals and plants with certain characteristics being better adjusted than others to their natural environment. Those plants and animals then have a higher chance to survive, reproduce, and increase their population more than the ones that are less adapted to their environment. The better adapted plants and animals are therefore able to pass on their advantageous characteristics (coded for by genes) to their offspring through inheritance. A Green Treefrog on the bark of a tree is easier for a predator to find, compared to a Green Treefrog on a green leaf. So, Green Treefrogs that go into habitats where they are not camouflaged are more likely to be eaten by predators.

Artificial Selection: Artificial selection is done to enhance the quality of a trait, or whatever desirable characteristics we need in that trait. By taking an example we will be able to understand it much better. Suppose we need to grow the flowering plant, with some special character of our desire. For this, we will cross breed of the desired characters of a plant and ultimately if the situations favour, it will result in a plant with new and required characters. Though being a fast process than natural selection, the chances of survival are lesser and the new ones get totally different from their native generations as well. Thus, we can say that artificial selection doesn't make a species stronger and fit for survival. This process is dangerous and is much in trend, due to the higher demands of good quality of fruits, vegetables, and pets such as cow, dog, buffalo. The Brassicas are great examples of artificial selection. Cabbage, broccoli, cauliflower, *Brussels sprouts,* collards, and kale are all members of the same species, Brassica oleracea. Gardeners have cultivated flowers has roses and orchids, carefully manipulating heredity to produce the "perfect" hybrid.

Key Differences Between Natural and Artificial Selection

- Natural selection involves the natural process of selection, promoting the fittest one for all time of unpleasant situations; Artificial selection involves the artificial process where the selection is done favouring the desired characters in the new organisms.
- Natural selection is a long and slow process; whereas it is an artificial process and so it takes less time to complete, selection of characters is done artificially hence chances of surviving new breed is at risk whether it is a plant, or animals or any other organism.
- Natural selection is controlled by nature; the artificial selection is controlled and coordinated by humans only.
- Natural selection is performed on all the types organisms; Artificial selection is processed on some selective organisms of human's desires.
- In the natural selection, organisms are totally based on the adaptable character and the one who is able to

cope up with all types of natural conditions. In the artificial selection is done on the basis of the required character.

- Natural selection results in the transformation of the entire population of a species; Artificial selection brings out the new variety of that species.
- Natural selection occurs in all kind of natural populations and it is a natural selection process; whereas Artificial selection occurs in domestic populations and it is a man-made selection.

3. (*a*) (*iii*) **Cytoplasmic sterility:** Male sterility in plants is often cytoplasmically based and maternally inherited. Male sterile plants produce no functional pollen, but do produce viable eggs. Cytoplasmic male sterility is used in agriculture to facilitate the production of hybrid seed. Joseph Gottlieb Kölreuter was the first to document male sterility in plants. In the 18th century, he reported on anther abortion within species and specific hybrids. Cytoplasmic male sterility (CMS) has now been identified in over 150 plant species. Male sterility is more prevalent than female sterility. This could be because the male sporophyte and gametophyte are less protected from the environment than the ovule and embryo sac. Male-sterile plants can set seed and propagate. Female-sterile plants cannot develop seeds and will not propagate. Manifestation of male sterility in CMS may be controlled either entirely by cytoplasmic factors or by interactions between cytoplasmic factors and nuclear factors. Male sterility can arise spontaneously via mutations in nuclear genes and/or cytoplasmic or cyto-plasmic-genetic. In this case, the trigger for CMS is in the extranuclear genome - (mitochondria or chloroplast). The extranuclear genome is only maternally inherited. Natural selection on cytoplasmic genes could also lead to low pollen production or male sterility. Male sterility is easy to detect because a large number of pollen grains are produced in male fertile plants. Pollen grains can be assayed through staining techniques (carmine, lactophenol or iodine).

Cytoplasmic Genetic Male Sterility

- This type of sterility differs from cytoplasmic sterility only in that the offspring of male sterile plants can be male fertile when certain stocks are used as pollinators. Thus, cyto-plasmic sterile plants are converted to fertile plants by crossing with the plants with restorer genes. Production of sorghum hybrids is possible through utilization of cytoplasmic genetic male sterility. MSJCK 60 A (Male sterile combining kafir 60) is a male sterile line of sorghum, which contains the kafir chromosomes.
- Inbred lines are converted to male sterile lines by a number of back crosses using MSJCK 60 or any male sterile as female parent and inbred line to be converted as recurrent pollen parent. The newly synthesized male sterile inbred line is designated as line A. The original male fertile line is designated as line B. There is no other difference between A and B lines except that A is male sterile and B male is fertile, which should be a pollen producing line.
- Line A is grown in an isolated field and it is wind pollinated by B. Thus, male sterile line A will be maintained generation to generation. Line B is maintained by self-pollination Male sterile inbred line A is grown in an isolated field and wind pollinated by unrelated inbred R which is male fertile line which possess pollen restoring genes.

- The seeds of the above single cross may be sold to farmer with the advice not to take advance generation from the year grown plants.

3. (*b*) Various Methods of Plant Breeding: The Crop improvement has been achieved through several methods such as: • Selection • Hybridization • Plant Introduction and acclimatization • Mutation breeding • Breeding for disease resistance.

Backcross Method: In backcross method of breeding, the hybrid and the progenies in subsequent generations are repeatedly backcrossed to one of the parents. As a result, the genotype of the backcross progeny becomes increasingly similar to that of the recurrent parent. The objective of backcross method is to improve one or two specific defects of a high yielding variety.

Application of backcross method: This method is commonly used to transfer disease resistance from one variety to another. But it is also useful for transfer of other characteristics.

1. **Intervarietal transfer of simply inherited characters.**

   e.g., Disease resistance, seed coat colour

2. **Intervarietal transfer of quantitative characters.**

   e.g., Plant height, Seed size, Seed shape.

3. **Interspecific transfer of simply inherited characters**

   e.g. Transfer of disease resistance from related species to cultivated species.

   e.g. Resistance to black arm disease in cotton from wild tetraploid species into *G. hirsutum*

4. **Transfer of cytoplasm:** This is employed to transfer male sterility. The female parent will be having the sterile cytoplasm and recurrent parent will be used as male parent.

   e.g. Sesamum malabariucum × *S.indicum*

   Female parent   Recurrent parent

5. **Transgressive segregation:** Backcross method may be modified to produce transgressive segregants. The F_1 is backcrossed to recurrent parent for 2 to 3 times for getting transgressive segregants.

6. **Production of isogenic lines.**

7. **Germplasm conversion:** *e.g.* Production of photo insensitive line from photo sensitive germplasm through back crossing. This was done in the case of sorghum. Popularly known as conversion programme.

Procedure for Backcross Method: The Plan of backcross method would depend upon whether the gene being transferred is recessive or dominant. The plan for transfer of a dominant gene is simpler than that for a recessive gene.

First Year	Non-Recurrent Parent B Resistant to rust	×	Recurrent Parent A Susceptible to rust
	F_1 Rr Resistant	×	rr BC_1
rr	Rr	×	rr BC_2
rr	Rr	×	rr BC_3
rr	Rr	×	rr BC_4
rr	Rr	×	rr BC_5

Backcross upto 6th or 7th generation. After 7th BC rust resistant lines are Self pollinated. Harvest is done on single plant basis.

8th Section

(*a*) Individual plant progenies grown

(*b*) Homozygous plants having resistance and resembling parent A are selected Harvested and bulked

9th season

Yield trials.

10th season

Seed multiplication and distribution

Importance in Development of Crop Varieties: A breeding method used to move one or an only a few desirable genes from an agronomically poor crop line to an elite line. This is done by crossing a donor parent to an elite line, and crossing offspring with the 'desired gene(s)' back to the elite parent. Backcrossing and/or convergent back-crossing have been used for transferring resistance to desirable agronomic back-grounds. ... The backcross method is also being used for producing disease-resistant inbred lines to be used as parents in hybrid breeding programs for various crops.

3. (*c*) Role of Mutation in Development of Disease Resistant Varieties of Crop

Plant breeding has been the most successful approach for developing new crop varieties since domestication occurred, making possible major advances in feeding the world and societal development. Crops are susceptible tc a large set of pathogens including fungi, bacteria, and viruses, which cause important economic losses; the enhancement of plant resistance plays an important role in adjusting crop production to meet global population increases. Mutation is a sudden heritable change in the genotype of an organism. The process by which the change does occur is called mutation and the individual in which it is observed is called mutant.

Mutation occurs in natural population but at a very low rate, which is called spontaneous mutation, but the mutation can be induced by chemical or physical mutagen is called induced mutation. Utilisation of characters which are the result of induced mutation in crop improvement programme is known as mutation breeding. The development of dwarf wheat and rice varieties that led to the green revolution are classic examples of mutation breeding achieved through successful exploitation of the mutant genes—Norin in case of wheat and dee-gee-woo-gen in rice, which affect a large constellation of characters responsible for their superior agronomic responses. Approaches to disease control that depend on resistant varieties and agrochemicals are usually highly effective whenever they are deployed. However, due to the high evolutionary potential of many plant pathogens, novel genotypes no longer sensitive to the resistance gene or the phytosanitary product can rapidly emerge via mutation or recombination. When this happens, particular disease control approaches can rapidly be rendered ineffective as the novel genotypes increase in frequency through natural selection and quickly spread to other locations, causing failure of control over large geographic areas. An understanding of interactions between plants and communities of bacteria, fungi, and other microorganisms has been a major area of investigation for many years. The advent of high-throughput molecular technologies has made a more complete inventory of the pathogens associated with particular crops possible, and provided insight into how these communities may be affected by environmental factors and the crop genotype. Disease involves a complex inter-play between a host plant and a pathogen, and the resistance/susceptibility response can involve several components. Natural and induced mutations may change the interaction and inhibit certain steps in the mechanism of infection. Nevertheless, mutation breeding methods have been quite successful in improving disease resistance, and traditional plant breeding has been used to generate new crop varieties for decades. Numerous mutants have been developed through mutation induction, showing enhanced resistance to various diseases.

During the early part of the era of mutation breeding largely through radiations, the technique was used as a tool for improvement of traditional traits like yield, resistance to disease and pest etc., in various agricultural crops. During recent decades, tremendous progress has been made in the research of plant molecular biology and biotechnology, particularly plant genomics. As a result, we are witnessing new impulses in plant mutation research for crop improvement, from fundamental studies of mutagenesis to reverse genetics. Breeders are now aware of the newer potentialities and far-reaching implications of induced mutation for crop improvement and are able to use it with more sophistication and efficiency than before. Induced mutagenesis is gaining importance in plant molecular biology as a tool to identify and isolate genes and to study their structure and function. Mutation techniques for crop improvement have also been integrated with other molecular technologies such as molecular marker and high throughput mutation screening techniques. Mutation breeding for crop improvement is entering into a new era: molecular mutation breeding (Shu *et al.,* 2012). Therefore, mutation breeding will continue to play a significant role in crop improvement and solving the issues related to world food security in the coming years and decades.

During the last five decades, several countries including China, India, Pakistan, Bangladesh, Vietnam, Thailand, Italy, Sweden, USA, Canada and Japan took up extensive crop improvement programmes through the use of induced mutagenesis and mutation breeding and made spectacular accomplishments in evolving several superior mutant varieties in large number of important agricultural crop species including cereals, pulses, oilseeds, vegetables, fruits, fibres and ornamentals. A wide range of haracters including yield, maturity, quality and tolerance to biotic and abiotic stresses have been improved in the mutant varieties developed so far.

5. (*a*) Physiological Effects of Auxin in Plants

- **Cell Elongation:** The primary physiological effect of auxin in plants is to stimulate the elongation of cells in shoot. A very common example of this can be observed in phototropic curvatures where the unilateral light unequally distributes the auxin in the stem tip (i.e., more auxin on shaded side than on illuminated side). The higher concen-tration of auxin on the shaded side causes the cells on that side to elongate more rapidly resulting in bending of the stem tip towards the unilateral light.
- **Apical Dominance:** It has been a common observation in many vascular plants especially the tall and sparsely branched ones that if the terminal bud is intact and growing, the growth of the lateral buds just below it remained suppressed. Removal of the apical bud results in the rapid growth of the lateral buds. This phenomenon in which the apical bud dominates over the lateral buds and does not allow the latter to grow is called as apical dominance. Skoog and Thimann (1934) first pointed out that the apical dominance might be under the control of auxin produced at the terminal bud and which is transported downward through the stem to the lateral buds and hinders their growth. They removed the apical bud of broad bean plant and replaced it with agar block. This resulted in rapid growth of lateral buds. But, when they replaced the apical bud with agar block containing auxin, the lateral buds remained suppressed and did not grow.
- **Root initiation:** The higher concentration of auxins inhibits the elongation of the root but the later branch roots get continuously increased which means that more the concentration of auxins more will be the growth of lateral branch roots. Root initiation is done by auxins. The application of AA in lanolin paste is of great importance and this is greatly used for the formation of roots in economically useful plants which are propagated by cuttings.
- **Vascular differentiation:** In tissue culture experiments it has been confirmed that auxins induce the differentiation in plants. Cytokines are known to participate in vascular differentiation too so it is under control of both auxin and cytokinin.

- **Parthenocarpy:** It is the process of development of fruits which fertilization and these fruits are called as parthenocarpic fruits. Auxin can induce the formation of these fruits. Generally, this process is not uncommon and more concentration of auxins are found in ovaries of plants which produce fruits only after fertilization. In the latter cases, the concentration of auxins increases after pollination and fertilization.
- **Cambial activity:** Degree of cambial activity is directly proportional to auxin concentration (Avery *et al.* 1947). Auxins promote cell division within the cambial region.
- **Leaf abscission:** The concentration of IAA in cells near or within the abscission zone appears to delay the abscission process.

5. (*b*) The production of good quality seedlings is very much essential for getting higher yield and quality of any crop. The population of the country is constantly increasing day by day. Therefore, the daily requirement of vegetables / flowers will also grow simultaneously. Hence, there is need for overall development and expansion in vegetable/ flower production. It has now been realized that to achieve higher production levels, productivity has to be increased through the adoption of hybrid varieties and improved production technology. Presently, the commercial vegetable growers are quite aware about the importance of hybrid varieties as they are high yielding, uniform in maturity and can tolerate the effect of abiotic and biotic stresses and have better quality produce as compared to standard varieties/cultivars. Though the seeds of many hybrids are made available to the farmers, they lack the technical knowhow of producing quality seedlings. Hence, the production and timely distribution of quality seedlings of vegetables / flowers would be a greater scope to meet the growing demand. With this background the technology "Pro tray production of vegetable seedlings" is developed.

Technology description

Seedling production using pro trays: Seedling production of F_1 hybrids of tomato, chillies, capsicum, cauliflower and brinjal as well as flowering annuals, using pro trays with coco peat as media could be used. Presently the seedlings of vegetables are raised and distributed to the beneficiaries. Sterilized commercial coco peat is being used as growing media, as it reduces the incidence of seedling diseases and contains right amount of moisture in it. The coco peat is a by-product of coir industry and it has high water holding capacity as, it contains low nutrients and high lignin content.

Raising and Management: The seedling tray (pro tray) is filled with the growing medium (coco peat). A small depression (0.5 cm) is made with fingertip in the centre of the cell of the pro tray for sowing. One seed per cell is sown and covered with medium. Coco peat with 300 to 400 per cent moisture is used and hence no immediate irrigation is required until germination. After sowing 10 trays are kept one over other for 3 to 6 days, depending on the crops. The entire stack will be covered using polyethylene sheet to ensure conservation of moisture until germination. The stacked trays are spread once the germination commences to avoid etiolation. The trays are irrigated lightly every day depending upon the prevailing weather conditions by using a fine sprinkling rose can. Drenching the trays with fungicides as a precautionary measure against seedling mortality is also being done. Spraying of 0.3 per cent (3g / litre) water soluble fertilizer using poly feed (19 all with trace elements) twice (12 and 20 days after sowing) for enhance the growth of the seedlings. The seedlings at right stage of planting are hardened by withholding irrigation and reducing the shade before transplanting or selling to the growers. Systemic insecticides are sprayed 7-10 days after germination and before trans-planting for managing the insect vectors. The seed-lings would be ready in about 21-30 days for trans-planting to the main field depending upon the crop.

Benefits of preparing seedling through pro-tray technique:

- By this method, seedlings get ready in less time.
- The number of seeds used for planting is very low because in this technique the seeds are sown in different sections and every seed gives healthy seedling.
- Seedlings can be protected from soil borne diseases and pests.
- When seedlings are ready in beds then at the time of transplanting the roots gets damaged up-to 10-15%, but in this technique there is no chances of seedling dying.
- By this technique the seedling gets established in the main field after transplanting in a very short time.
- By using protected structures any vegetable crop can be prepared at any time with this technique.
- By this way, prepared seedlings can be transported to long distances after packing.
- Less fertilizer and irrigation are needed in this technique.
- By following this method all the plants grow at the equal rate so that after transplanting the growth rate in the main field is also equal.
- By this method the use of costly hybrid varieties can be done efficiently.

5. (*c*) Principles of Fruits and Vegetable Preservation

Drying fruits and vegetables means removing the water from the produce. Bacteria needs water to survive, so the drying process helps prevent the food from going bad. ... Processing of fruits and vegetables is very important to produce products for direct consumption and as food ingredients. During processing, the main objectives are to preserve the colour, flavour, texture, and nutrition while prolonging the shelf life of perishable fruits and vegetables. The drying process can be done most efficiently in two ways - with a dehydrator or with an oven. Summer is a great time for lovers of fresh, local fruits and vegetables. The choices available in stores and local farm shops is simply staggering. These seven ways to preserve summer fruits and vegetables are all effective - and can all be done in the comfort of your own home.

Drying: Drying fruits and vegetables requires removing the water content. As bacteria needs water to survive, the drying process ensures that food doesn't go bad over time. However, unlike other preservation methods, drying completely changes both the texture and taste of the food. Once food has been successfully dried, it can be stored in ambient conditions. The simplest way to dry summer fruits and vegetables for the winter is to use a dedicated dehydrator. Simply load the machine with your food, and select the appropriate setting. Most modern dehydrators have a range of settings for different sizes and textures. If your fruits or vegetables still feel sticky or spongy once the drying process is complete, they aren't ready - and require further drying. Food generally needs to be 95% dehydrated before it can be stored safely. If you don't want to buy a dehydrator, you can dry fruits and vegetables using your existing oven - but the results can be a little hit or miss. Thinly slice your fruit or vegetable, and soak in a solution of lemon juice and water in equal parts. After 10 minutes, line a baking tray with parchment paper, and place the slices onto it. Put the tray in a preheated oven at a temperature of between 130-160 degrees. If you're drying citrus fruit, the temperature should be at the lower end of this scale. Rotate the baking tray every hour, and continue cooking until the slices are pliable and have a leathery texture.

Canning: The term "canning" is a little misleading. If you're canning at home, you're probably using mason jars or something very similar. This relatively simple method of preservation involves sealing food in a sterile, airtight environment. Both cooked and raw food can be successfully canned using heat to sterilize and seal the jar. To can your fruits and vegetables at home, you'll need a pressure canner, along with canning jars, seals, rings, lids, a funnel and a large pot for blanching. The principle involves killing bacteria inside the jar with heat. Steam pressure is applied to the airtight container that leaves a sterile vacuum in which food can stay safe and relatively fresh for several months.

Pickling: Pickling fruits and vegetables creates an inhospitable environment for bacteria. Potentially dangerous pathogens simply can't survive the acidity of vinegar, which means food can be kept safe and edible for years. Pickling is one of the simpler methods of food preservation, but it drastically changes the flavour of most fruits and vegetables. The process involves creating a pickling solution of white vinegar, salt and sugar, which is brought to a boil in a pan. The fruits and vegetables are placed in an airtight jar, and the solution is poured on top until all of the food is submerged. The jar is then sealed and stored for several days - as many as seven, for particularly chunky summer vegetables such as zucchini.

Fermenting: The fermentation process involves converting carbohydrates to alcohol or organic acids. To get the process going, you need to introduce salt, whey or a dedicated starter culture to water - creating the brine solution in which the food will ferment. Fermenting summer fruits and vegetables is relatively easy, but it's important to ensure that they're cut into small and even chunks or slices. The food is put into an airtight container, and the brine is poured on top. It's important to ensure that all of the food remains submerged in the brine until the fermentation process has finished. If you're fermenting fruit, the process should take around 48 hours. However, because of their lower sugar content, vegetables tend to take a little longer.

Freezing: Freezing your summer fruits and vegetables is the easiest and quickest way to ensure they last throughout the winter. However, the process of freezing and thawing can damage softer fruits like strawberries - changing their texture completely. It's also worth remembering that freezing doesn't kill all bacteria; many become dormant until defrosted. If you decide to freeze your fruits and vegetables, it's usually best to freeze them first on a metal tray. Once they're completely hard, transfer them to sterile, airtight freezer bags. If you're freezing starchy vegetables such as potatoes, blanch them in iced water before placing them in the freezer. And if you're storing fruits that can turn brown, such as apples, treat them with ascorbic acid first.

Oil Packing: The use of vegetable oils to preserve summer fruits and vegetables makes it harder for bacteria to develop - but it also adds a completely different dimension to the flavour. Ideal for preserving tomatoes, eggplants, herbs, onions and olives, oil packing creates anaerobic conditions (basically no air) with the addition of acid, usually vinegar. Most people use airtight mason jars to preserve fruits and vegetables these days, but sealable food bags can work just as well.

Salting: The hypertonic properties of salt make it very difficult for bacteria to survive. Organisms die or become deactivated through dehydration, which means food can be stored for long periods in ambient temperatures. To salt your vegetables at home, place them in a large baking pan and submerge them in water. Add salt to the water until you notice it beginning to deposit on your vegetables - this is an indication that the saturation point has been reached. At this point, you should refrigerate the vegetables in the water for a week or so. Complete the process by draining the brine away and covering your vegetables with more salt, and store in a cool dry place until dried.

5. (*d*) In India, post-harvest losses caused by unscientific storage, insects, rodents, microorganisms etc., account for about 10 per cent of total food grains. The major economic loss caused by grain infesting insects is not always the actual material they consume, but also the amount contaminated by them and their excreta which make food unfit for human consumption. About 500 species of insects have been associated with stored grain products. Nearly 100 species of insect pests of stored products cause economic losses.

Pulse beetle: *Callosobruchus maculatus* (chinensis) (Bruchidae: Coleoptera)

Distribution and status: USA, Mauritius, Formosa, Africa, China, the Philippines, Japan, Indonesia, Sri Lanka, Myanmar and India.

Host range: Gram, mung (*Phaseolus aureus*), moth (*Phaseolus aconitifolius*), peas, cow peas, lentil and arhar (*Cajanus cajan*), cotton seed, sorghum and maize.

Bionomics: Larva is whitish with a light-brown head. The mature larva is 6-7 mm long. The adult beetle measuring 3-4 mm in length, is oval, chocolate or reddish brown and has long serrated antennae, truncate elytra, not covering the pygidium. The pest breeds actively from March to the end of November. It hibernates in winter in the larval stage. A single female lays small, oval, scale like 34-113 eggs at the rate of 1-37 per day. Egg period is 6-16 days, larval period 10-38 days. The hibernating larvae take 117-168 days to complete their development. The pupal stage lasts 4-28 days. The adult escapes by cutting a circular hole in the seed coat and such grains can be spotted easily. The average life-span of an adult is 5-20 days. The insect passes through 7-8 overlapping generations in a year.

Damage symptoms: The adult and grub feed on the grain by making a small hole. Infested stored seed can be recognized by the white eggs on the seed surface and the round exit holes with the 'flap' of seed coat. Kabuli types are particularly susceptible.

Minor Pests of Stored Grains: The other insect species recorded as minor pests on stored grains and products in India are the; the cadelle, *Tenebroides mauritanicus* (Trogossitidae: Coleoptera) and the black fungus beetle, *Alphitobius laevigatus* (Tenebrionidae: Coleoptera).

Management of Storage Pests

The effective management of storage pests may be ensured by drying the grains properly before storage, storing new grains in the clean godowns or receptacles and plugging all cracks, crevices and holes in the godowns thoroughly. If infestation of grain has already taken place, then application of chemicals becomes necessary.

Surface treatment: Disinfect old gunny bags by dipping them in 0.0125 per cent fenvalerate 20EC or cypermethrin 25EC for 10 minutes and drying them in shade before filling with grains or use new gunny bags. Disinfect empty godowns or receptacles by spraying 0.05 per cent malathion emulsion on the floor, walls and ceiling.

Seed treatment: Mixing of malathion 5 per cent at the rate of 250 g per quintal of seed is recommended. The grains may also be treated with/25 ml of malathion 50 EC or 2 ml of fenvalerate 20 EC or 1.5 ml of cypermethrin 25EC or 14 ml of deltamethrin 2.8 EC per quintal of seed by diluting in

500 ml of water. Against pulse beetle (dhora), cover the pulses stored in bulk with 7 cm layer of sand or sawdust or dung ash.

Fumigation: Metallic drums or wooden boxes can be used for fumigating small quantities of grain. In India, ethylene dichloride and carbon tetrachloride mixture has been recommended for fumigation of foodgrains in storage at farm level, and hydrogen phosphide in the form of aluminium phosphide or methyl bromide for protection in warehouses, godowns and silos.

Integrated Management of Stored Produce Pests

The control methods of stored produce pests can be categorized into preventive and curative measures.

Preventive Measures

- Brush the cracks, crevices and corners to remove all debris in the godown.
- Clean and maintain the threshing floor/ yard free from insect infection and away from the vicinity of villages.
- Clean the machines like harvester and thresher before their use.
- Made the trucks, trolleys or bullock carts free from infestation.
- Clean the godowns / storage structures before storing the newly harvested crop to eliminate various bio stages of pest hiding.
- Provide a metal sheet upto a height of 25 cm at the bottom of the wood in doors to arrest the entry of rats.
- Fix up wire meshes to windows, ventilators, gutters, drains etc., to prevent entry of rats, birds and squirrels.
- Remove and destroy dirt, rubbish, sweepings and webbings etc from the stores.
- Close all the rat burrows found in godown with a mixture of broken glass pieces and mud plastered with mud / cement.
- Plaster the cracks, crevices, holes found on walls, and floors with mud or cement and white wash the stores before storing of grains.
- Provide dunnage leaving gangway or alleyway of 0.75 to 1 m all around to maintain good storage condition.
- Store the food grains in rat and moisture proof storage structures.
- Disinfest the storage structures receptacles by spraying malathion 50 EC @ 3 lit 100 m before their use.

Curative Measures: Curative measures includes:

- Ecological method
- Physical methods
- Cultural methods
- Mechanical methods
- Chemical methods

5. (*e*) **Public Distribution System:** The Public Distribution System contribute significantly in the provision of food security. Public Distribution System in the country enables the supply of food grains to the poor at a subsidized price. It also helps to control open - market prices for commodities that are distributed through the system. Government accords great importance to the objective of measuring outcomes of PDS so as to ensure that equal distribution system serves up the purpose for which it was set up. The goal of Public Distribution System does not limit itself with the distribution of rationed articles. Making available sufficient quantities of essential commodities at all times, in places accessible to all, at prices affordable to all and protection of the weaker section of the population from the malicious spiral of rising prices is prime objective of public distribution system.

Major goals of public distribution system are as under:

- Make goods available to consumers, especially the disadvantaged/vulnerable sections of society at fair prices.

- Rectify the existing imbalances between the supply and demand for consumer goods. Check and prevent hoarding and black marketing in essential commodities.
- Ensure social justice in distribution of basic necessities of life.
- Even out fluctuations in prices and availability of mass consumption goods.
- Support poverty-alleviation programmes, particularly, rural employment programmes, (SGRY/SGSY/IRDP/ Mid-day meals, ICDS, DWCRA, SHGs and Food for Work and educational feeding programmes.

The food grains offered to recipients under TPDS are procured from agrarians at MSP. The MSP is the price at which the FCI purchases the crop directly from farmers; typically the MSP is higher than the market price. This is intended to provide price support to farmers and incentivise production. It is done by the central government. They procure the food materials from the Food Corporation of India and the State Agencies at Minimum Prices.

Currently procurement is performed in two ways:

- **Centralised procurement:** Centralised procurement is done by the FCI, where FCI purchases crops directly from farmers.
- **Decentralised procurement:** Decentralised procurement is a central scheme under which 10 states/Union Territories (UTs) procure food grains for the central pool at MSP on behalf of FCI. The scheme was launched to inspire local procurement of food grains and minimise expenditure incurred when transporting grains from surplus to deficit states over long distances. These states directly store and distribute the grains to beneficiaries in the state. Any surplus stock over the state's requirement must be handed over to FCI. In case of a shortage in procurement against an allocation made by the centre, FCI meets the deficit out of the central pool.

Strengths of Public Food Grain Distribution System in India

- India's Public Distribution System is a broad network. The concept of Public Distribution System in India emerged during 1942 for the first time in revised form as a result of shortage of food grains during World War. Subsequently, Government started intrusion in release of food to the people.
- Public Distribution System in India is more than half—a century old as rationing was first introduced in 1939 in Bombay by the British Government as a measure to ensure equitable distribution of food grains to the urban consumers as a result of increasing prices. Thus, rationing in crisis period particularly during shortage was the historical antecedent to the national policy of stabilization and management of food grains. After independence in 1947, major aim of Government of India has been to deliver food security to all the inhabitants of India. With this objective, Public distribution system was started by Ministry of Consumer Affairs, Food and Civil Supplies.
- Public Distribution System is a network whereby accessibility of vital supplies is guaranteed which can be easily accessed by the consumers in every part of the country. This is a transaction system where food grain and other needed items are made available to the people of the state at fair price to meet their minimum needs.
- Regular and timely availability of supplies is assured through close monitoring system to make Public Distribution System an effective instrument against various forces in the open market and to keep under check the inflator tendencies.
- Certain supply on fixed and affordable prices also keeps in control the variable trends of market due to vagaries of

whether and subsequent changing prospects of crops. Public Distribution System serves as a steady stable check on market forces and work as an effective soothing factor.

- In order to efficiently manage and distribute food grains, the government of India has created Ministry of Consumer Affairs, Food and Public Distribution. The ministry has been divided into two departments specifically Department of Food and Public Distribution and Department of Consumer Affairs. The department of food and public distribution is further divided into two parts for the purchase and storage of food grain.
- When appraising Public Distribution System in India, it has been found that among all states, Tamil Nadu has done marvellous job in implementing the PDS as universal system for the cause of eliminating poverty and improving standard of living of the people living below the poverty line. Timely supply of essential commodities is the basic element for the success of the Public Distribution System. Infrastructure *i.e.,* Fair Price Shops (FPS), godown facilities and employees are other requisites of the PDS.
- In 1997, the government launched the Targeted Public Distribution System (TPDS) to resolve the problems of poor communities. The prime aim of TPDS is to provide subsidised food and fuel to the poor through a network of ration shops.
- Food grains such as rice and wheat that are provided under TPDS are procured from farmers, allocated to states and delivered to the ration shop where the beneficiary buys his entitlement. The centre and states share the responsibilities to identify the poor, procuring grains and delivering food grains to beneficiaries. In September 2013, Parliament passed the National Food Security Act, 2013.
- The Act relies largely on the existing TPDS to deliver food grains as legal entitlements to poor households. This made a shift by making the right to food a justiciable right. In order to understand the implications of this Act, the note maps the food supply chain from the farmer to the beneficiary, identifies challenges to implementation of TPDS, and debated alternatives to improve TPDS.

Weakness of Public Food Grain Distribution System in India: The problems of Public Distribution System have not been undeviating in the nation. In some states, the administration is weak and dishonest. In these states, deficiencies regarding huge shortage of stocks, fake supply entries in ration cards, diversion of commodities for sale to open market and bogus ration cards are recorded. Public Distribution System suffers from irregular and poor quality of food grain made available through Fair Price Shops. In general, the public distribution system has following limitations.

- Identification of poor by the states is not fool proof. A large number of poor and needy persons are left out and a lot of fake cards are also issued.
- Fair Price Shop owner gets fake Ration cards and sell the food grains in the open market.
- People do not get the permitted amount of food grains from the Fair price shop.
- Diversion of Food grains by Fair Price Shops holder and mediator.
- Many times, good quality food grains are replaced with poor quality cheap food grains.
- Public distribution system includes only few food grains such as wheat and rice, it does not fulfil the requirement of complete nutrition.
- Uneven distribution of Food generations, procurement and distribution. For example: north eastern states are very far

from Punjab and Haryana, from where wheat is procured. To transport food grains from Punjab to far flung areas in North east will entail cost and time both.

- Main problem involved in the operation of public distribution system is the issue of containing the food subsidy to reasonable levels. Other major issues which confront the system include the issue of targeting the system to benefit the actual poor and restricting the coverage of public distribution system to only the major commodities. De-centralization of operations and devolving to the states the key decision-making powers as regards the operation of public distribution system are some major issues that needs to be addressed.
- Government agencies can reform the system by introducing innovative ideas such as food stamps and food credit/debit cards to facilitate better working of the system with a view to reduce malpractices like diversion and reducing the costs of food delivered to the poor.
- Though government has taken several measures to improve public distribution system like decentralised procurements, introduction of UIDAI etc. but still these measures are not completely espoused. More measures like universalization of public distribution system are need of the hour.

6. (*a*) Package of Practices for Papaya Cultivation in Northern India

Family: Caricaceae

It belongs to "Caricaceae" family and "Carica" genus. It is a fast growth plant which has long fruiting period and contains high nutritional value. India is known as the largest producer of papaya. It can be grown in pots, greenhouse, polyhouse and containers. It also has health benefits such as it helps to relieve constipation, cancer, helps in lowering cholesterol, and helps in fighting with cancer cells. It is a rich source of Vitamin A and C. Papaya is the most preferred fruit for kitchen gardens. Normally it is planted as a filler plant in orchards of fruit trees with long juvenile period. Papaya plants come into bearing within a year of planting.

Origin: Papaya originated in tropical America. Portuguese introduced papaya in India from Malacca during 1611. At present it is cultivated throughout the world in tropical and sub-tropical climate. It do not tolerate freezing temperature and frost.

Area and Production: The papaya plant has short life, hence the area under cultivation varies greatly in different years. In India it is cultivated over an area of 97.7 thousand hectares with annual production of 3628.9 thousand MT. In Punjab it is being grown as filler plant in mango and litchi orchards. No data is available for production/average.

Uses: Papaya is eaten as fresh fruit. It is a rich source of vitamin A (2020 IU per 100 g) and sufficient vitamin C (40 mg/l00g). It also contains sufficient amount of Calcium and other minerals. The yellow colour of the pulp is due to caricaxanthin. Papaya contains vitamin by, 100 gm of pulp riboflavin 250 mg 100 gm of pulp, 0.6% proteins and 9% of carbohydrates. It contains papain a protein digesting enzyme. Papain is prepared by collecting latex from the unripe papaya fruits. Unripe fruits can be used as vegetable. Ripe fruits are used for making of Jam, Jelly, and Ice-Cream, etc.

Botany: Four genera belong to family caricaceae. Only Carica papaya produces edible fruits in genera Carica. Papaya plant is dioecious in nature but hermaphrodite forms also occur. It is dicot with straight, and soft stem. Plant is usually un-branched but branches develop where apex get damaged. Leaves are long stalked and fan like. Papaya fruit is climacteric in nature. Fruit is usually berry containing no or many seeds depending on the cultivar and climate. Shape of fruit also varies from oblong to spherical.

Climate: It requires warm and humid climate without frost. Low temperature affects the fruit and plant growth. Both foliage and fruit get damaged near 0°C. Hence, plants have to be protected by covering with gunny bags under North Indian conditions. It is also very sensitive to water logged conditions.

Soil: Papaya as a filler is grown from plains to sub mountains areas. It like soils which are well drained, rich in organic matter with near normal pH. Water stagnation for few days can be harmful.

Cultivars/Varieties:

Pusa Delicious: A selection from progenies of variety 'Ranchi', its plants are gynodioecious, *i.e.,* both pistillate and hermaphrodite and medium in size. Plant start fruiting at a height of LIO meter from ground level. The plants may grow to a height of 2 m. The fruits size is large with oblong to oval in shape. Flesh deep orange with 10% TSS. Average yield per plant 40 kg.

Punjab Sweet: The plants are dioecious and may grow up to 1.90 meter high. Fruit bearing starts at a height of 1.0 m from ground. Fruits are of large size and oblong in shape with pointed tip. Flesh colour is deep yellow. TSS of pulp ranges between 9.0 to 10.5 per cent. The average yield per plant 50 kg. It is least susceptible to citrus mite (*Entetranychus orientalis*).

Honey Dew: This variety is suited for North Indian conditions. The plants are of medium height and bear fruit heavily on the trunk. Plants are dioecious in nature, but the proportion of male plants is low. The fruits are large in size, elongated in shape with few or no seed. Flesh is sweet (TSS 8.0%) with pleasant flavour. This cultivar is also known as Madhu Bindu.

Coorg Honey Dew: This is a selection from Honey Dew. The plant is tall and bears heavily. Most of the plants are hermaphrodite. A few may produce only pistillate flowers. The fruits are large, variable in shape. The flesh is thicker but TSS (6.0%) is less than Honey Dew.

Co-I: The plants are unisexual with male and female plants occurring separately. The plant is of medium height and start bearing low on the trunk. The fruit shape is round with golden yellow skin and orange coloured flesh. Fruits are podium in size. TSS of pulp is 7%. Average yield per plant is 40 kg.

Pusa Nanha: This is mutant of a local type cultivar developed at IARI. The plants are dioecious in nature. The plants are dwarf and grow up to 1.06 m height. Average yield per plant is 35 kg. This cultivar is preferred for close plantation.

Pusa Giant: Plants are of dioecious in nature. Plants can with stand strong winds. Plants start bearing at 1.0 m height. The plants come into bearing after a year. It bears large fruits weighing over 2 kg per fruit. The fruits are more suited to vegetable making and canning industry.

Propagation: Papaya is propagated through seeds. Seeds are extracted from ripe fruits and are rubbed with little sand to remove the white layer in which seed is enclosed. The seeds are washed and air dried before packing in polythene bags and stored at room temperature before sowing. The seeds loose viability in about 45 days, so due care should be given before extraction of seeds. Seeds can be sown any time from March to September. However, due to severe winter in North India, the seeds should be sown during July to September, when the seedling are of 20-30 cm in height and can easily be protected from frost and freeze of winter. Prepare a mixture of farmyard manure plus soil and sand in equal proportions. Use this mixture to fill the polythene bags of size 25 × 10 cm having 8 to 10 small holes on lower part of the bag for drainage of excess water. Sow two to three seeds per bag 2-3 cm deep. It will be better if seeds are treated with 3 g of Captain per kg of seed before sowing.

After the emergence of seedlings drench them with Captain solution @ 2 g per litre of water t-j prevent damping off disease. Remove the extra seedling from the bag. Each bag should have only one healthy seeding. The plants become ready for transplanting in the field 40-50 days.

Planting: Pits of 50 cm × 50 cm × 50 cm should be dug one month before transplanting is intended to be carried out. The planting is done as filler or at 1.5 m × 1.5 m apart. Fill the pits with an equal mixture of well rotten farmyard manure and soil. To control white ants add 30 g lindane 5% dust while filling the pits. Transplant 2-3 seedling 15 cm apart per pit. While planting the polythene bags should be removed. Apply height irrigation. Uproot the extra male plants. Keep only one plant per pit when these have started flowering. Keep about 10 per cent male plant population scattered throughout the orchard. There will be 4356 plants per hectare.

Intercropping: Papaya is itself planted as filler in mango, litchi and guava orchards because, it stays in the field for 2-3 years only. However, if papaya is planted enblock then shallow rooted vegetables like onion, garlic, turnip, cauliflower can be grown for the first year. No crop should be grown after one year. Intercrop should not compete for nutrition with papaya plants.

Irrigation: Papaya is very sensitive to water logged conditions. Avoid flooding periodically. Divide the field into segments. Apply light irrigation at 6-7 days interval in summer and 15 to 20 days interval in winter depending on soil condition. If rain is there avoiding irrigation. Water should not stay near the stem of plants to prevent collor rot.

Manuring and Fertilization: Papaya needs more nutrition due to its short juvenile period. It prefers soils with good organic matter. Apply 20 kg of farm yard manure by mixing with 200 g of urea 400 g of muriate of potash in February or March every year per plant. A very high dose of fertilizers has been recommended in other states which do not hold good under Punjab conditions. The male plants should not be fertilized at all. The manure and fertilizer mixture should be mixed within a radius of 40 cm around the plants.

Weed Control: Weeding should be done regularly to keep the basins free of weeds when the papaya is planted as a filler in orchards. Two hoeings one in February-March and other in July-August are sufficient to check the growth of weeds. No weedicides should be sprayed since papaya is a shallow rooted fruit crop and plants can be damaged.

Frost Protection: In North India, frost usually occurs in the months of December and January. Sometime late frost may occur in February also. Papaya is very sensitive to frost due to broad leaves and succulent stem. To save the young papaya plants from winter, the plantation should be done during October or November so that plants could be provided protection easily. Cover the plants with Sarkanda thatches or by pegging three support around the plants and covering with white polythene bags of the size of plants in first winter. Care should be taken that bags do not touch the foliage. Few holes may be provided in upper portion of bags for aeration. In the second-year thick gunny bags are wrapped around the fruits and apex during winter season.

Harvesting and Fruit Handling: Papaya plants tend to over bear. Fruits are so crowded that they do not get proper space for development. Fruit thinning should be done to get well sized fruits. Proper size is attained after 5-6 months of flowering. Near ripening fruits change colour from green to yellowish green. Fruits should be harvested at maturity. After harvesting the fruit should be placed in single layer and covered with straw till ripening. For distant markets it should be packed in baskets by placing straw below and newspaper along with gunny bag above to avoid bruising of fruits. Papaya is a climacteric fruit hence; it can be artificially ripened by dipping fruits in 500 ppm ethephon. At ripening fruits attain golden yellow colour of skin.

6. (*b*) Chilli

Chilli Leaf curl Virus Disease: Symptoms of Chilli Leaf Curl Virus are characterized by upward curling of leaf margins, yellowing of veins and reduction of leaf size. Additionally, leaf veins become swollen with shortening of internodes and petioles. Older leaves become leathery and brittle. If plants are infected during the early season, their growth will be stunted, resulting in significant yield reduction. Fruit formation in susceptible cultivars is rudimentary and distorted. The virus causes similar symptoms as the feeding damage of thrips and mites. Symptoms are caused by begomovirus, which is primarily transmitted through whiteflies in a persistent manner. They are characterized as 1.5 mm long, waxy white wings with a pale-yellow body and are frequently found on the lower side of the leaves. The spread of the disease dependson the wind condition, which will indicate how far the whiteflies can travel. Whiteflies are most problematic in the mid-to-late season. Since the disease is not seed-borne, the virus persists in the landscape via alternative hosts (such as tobacco and tomato) and weeds. Some additional factors that can favour the development of the disease are recent rainfall, infected transplants, and the presence of weeds. In nurseries, chilli plants are most prone to infection during the seedling and vegetative stages

- Leaves curl towards midrib and become deformed.
- Stunted plant growth due to shortened internodes and leaves greatly reduced in size.
- Flower buds abcise before attaining full size and anthers do not contain pollen grains.
- The virus is generally transmitted by whitefly. So, control measures of whitefly in this regard would be helpful.

Management

- Use the available plant-resistant species and extract seeds only from virus-free plants.
- Raise at least two rows of a barrier crop such as maize, sorghum or pearl millet around your elds.
- Control whitey population and protect particularly seedlings from them by establishing nylon nets over the nursery plants.
- Monitor regularly to detect early infections by looking for symptoms of curled leaves and stunted growth.
- Position a number of sticky yellow traps or sheets in your eld that attracts whiteflies.
- Control the vector by growing the seedlings under the net, which can also prevent whiteflies attack the seedlings.
- Ensure a weed-free eld and surroundings.
- Collect and destroy early infested plants by burning them.
- Plow deep or burn all plant debris after harvest.
- Encourage beneficial insects by growing mixed cropping.

Chilli Mosaic Virus

- Light green and dark green patches on the leaves.
- Stunted plant growth during early stages.
- Yellowing, chlorotic ring spots on leaves and fruits.

Management

- Collect and destroy early infested plants by burning them.
- Plow deep or burn all plant debris after harvest.
- Raise 2 rows of maize or sorghum for every 5 rows of chilli crop against wind direction. Recommendations given for aphids may be adopted for controlling the vector.
- Encourage beneficial insects by growing mixed cropping.
- Control measures are not known for majority of viral diseases.

- Hence, mechanical, cultural methods are mostly recommended.
- The infected plants should be uprooted and burnt or buried to avoid further infection.
- Avoid monoculture of chilli crop.
- Selection of healthy and disease - free seed.
- Suitable insecticidal sprays reduce the incidence of viral diseases, since majority of viral diseases are transmitted by insect vectors.
- Soaking seeds in a solution containing 150 g Trisodium orthriphosphate per litre of water for 30 minutes inhibits seed-borne inoculum.
- Treated seed should be washed with fresh water and dried before sowing.
- Nursery beds should be covered with nylon net or straw to protect the seedlings from viral infection.
- Raise 2-3 rows of maize or sorghum as border crop to restrict the spread of aphid vectors.
- Apply Carbofuran 3G @ 4-5 Kg/acre in the main field to control sucking complex and insect vectors selectively.
- If it is not possible spray the crop with systemic insecticides. Dimethoate 2 ml of Acephate 1 g per litre of water.
- Collect and destroy infected virus plants as soon as they are noticed.

Okra: Okra, *Abelmoschus esculentus,* is an herbaceous annual plant in the family Malvaceae which is grown for its edible seed pods. Okra plants have small erect stems that can be bristly or hairless with heart-shaped leaves. The leaves are 10-20 cm (4-8 in) long with 5-7 lobes. The plant produces flowers with five white to yellow petals which are 4-8 cm (1.6-3.1 in) in diameter. The seed pod is a capsule up to 25 cm (10 in) long, containing numerous seeds. Okra can grow 1.2-1.8 m (4-6 ft) tall and as an annual plant, survives only one growing season. Okra may also be referred to as lady's fingers and is believed to have originated in Ethiopia.

Leaf curl Virus Disease of Okra

On lower surface of leaves we will see a small pin head enations. This enation become warty and rough in structure at later stage. Reduce in leaf size. The stem, lateral branches and leaf petioles become twisted along enation. Leaves appear thick and leathery. In severely infected plants the emerging leaves shows bold enations and curling. And produce few deformed fruits. The virus is transmitted by white fly.

Management

- Rogue infected plants at very low disease incidence and destroy by burning or burying.
- Place yellow sticky traps at different locations in the field to attract white flies.
- Spray with 5 table spoons of dish washing soap in 20 litres of water at 7-14 days intervals.
- Spray neem seed water extract (5% concentration, w/v) to control vectors just after their appearance (second and third sprays must be applied at 14 days intervals).

Mosaic Virus of Okra

- Bhendi yellow vein mosaic virus (BYVMV) or okra yellow vein mosaic (OYVMV) is a viral disease caused by monopartite Begomovirus affecting okra plants. It was first found in 1924 in Bombay, India, and Sri Lanka. It is the major limitation of the production of okra.
- This disease is transmitted by whitefly. Okra with mosaic virus of this type first develops a mottled appearance on the leaves that is diffuse. As the plant grows, the leaves start to get interveinal yellow colouring. The okra fruit will develop yellow lines as they grow and become dwarfed and malformed.
- Species: Bhendi yellow vein mosaic virus. Genus: Begomovirus.

Symptoms

- Yellowing of the entire network of veins in the leaf blade is the characteristic symptom.

- In severe infections the younger leaves turn yellow, become reduced in size and the plant is highly stunted.
- The veins of the leaves will be cleared by the virus and intervenal area becomes completely yellow or white.
- In a field, most of the plants may be diseased and the infection may start at any stage of plant growth.
- Infection restricts flowering and fruits, if formed, may be smaller and harder.
- The affected plants produce fruits with yellow or white colour and they are not fit for marketing.
- The virus is spread by whitefly.

Management

- By selecting varieties resistant to yellow vein mosaic like Parbhani Kranti, Arka Abhay, Arka Anamika, and Varsha Uphar, the incidence of the disease can be minimised.
- The virus is transmitted by the whitely (*Bemisia tabaci*).
- Parbhani Kranti, Janardhan, Haritha, Arka Anamika and Arka Abhay can tolerate yellow vein mosaic.
- For sowing during the summer season, when the whitefly activity is high, the susceptible varieties should be avoided.
- Spraying monocrotophos 1.5 ml/litre of water can restrict the disease spread.
- Synthetic pyrethroids should not be used because it will aggravate the situation.
- It can be controlled by application of Chlorpyriphos 2.5 ml + neem oil 2 ml/lit of water.

6. (*c*) Majority of farmers are far away from cities living in remote villages. Unlike cities these villages lack good roads and good transport systems which can connect these villages to viable markets. Cold storage transport is scarcely available. There are very less food processing units near the fields and farms. Most of our farming depends on rain water even now. However, in past decade government has been trying to architect new canals and facilitate proper advanced irrigation systems. This still has achieved very little to nothing. These are some of the reasons which inhibit farmers to sell their produce to right market. Some of the major problems and their possible solutions have been discussed as follows. Indian agriculture is plagued by several problems; some of them are natural and some others are manmade.

Small and fragmented land-holdings: The seemingly abundance of net sown area of 141.2 million hectares and total cropped area of 189.7 million hectares (1999-2000) pales into insignificance when we see that it is divided into economically unviable small and scattered holdings. The average size of holdings was 2.28 hectares in 1970-71 which was reduced to 1.82 hectares in 1980-81 and 1.50 hectares in 1995-96. The size of the holdings will further decrease with the infinite Sub-division of the land holdings. The problem of small and fragmented holdings is more serious in densely populated and intensively cultivated states like Kerala, West Bengal, Bihar and eastern part of Uttar Pradesh where the average size of land holdings is less than one hectare and in certain parts it is less than even 0.5 hectare. Rajasthan with vast sandy stretches and Nagaland with the prevailing 'Jhoom' (shifting agriculture) have larger average sized holdings of 4 and 7.15 hectares respectively. States having high percentage of net sown area like Punjab, Haryana, Maharashtra, Gujarat, Karnataka and Madhya Pradesh have holding size above the national average. Further it is shocking to note that a large proportion of 59 per cent holdings in 1990-91 was marginal (below 1 hectare) accounting for 14.9 per cent of the total operated area. Another 19 per cent were small holdings (1-2 hectare) taking up 17.3 per cent of the total operated area. Large holdings (above 10 hectare) accounted for only 1.6 per cent of total holdings but covered 17.4 per cent of the operated area. Hence, there is a wide gap between small farmers, medium farmers (peasant group) and big farmers (landlords). The main reason for this sad state of affairs is our inheritance laws. The land belonging to the father is equally distributed among his sons. This distribution of land does not entail a collection or consolidated one, but its nature is fragmented. Different tracts have different levels of fertility and are to be distributed accordingly. If there are four tracts which are to be distributed between two sons, both the sons will get smaller plots of each land tract. In this way the holdings become smaller and more fragmented with each passing generation. Sub-division and fragmentation of the holdings is one of the main causes of our low agricultural productivity and backward state of our agriculture. A lot of time and labour is wasted in moving seeds, manure, implements and cattle from one piece of land to another. Irrigation becomes difficult on such small and fragmented fields. Further, a lot of fertile agricultural land is wasted in providing boundaries. Under such circumstances, the farmer cannot concentrate on improvement. The only answer to this ticklish problem is the consolidation of holdings which means the reallocation of holdings which are fragmented, the creation of farms which comprise only one or a few parcels in place of multitude of patches formerly in the possession of each peasant. But unfortunately, this plan has not succeeded much.

Seeds: Seed is a critical and basic input for attaining higher crop yields and sustained growth in agricultural production. Distribution of assured quality seed is as critical as the production of such seeds. Unfortunately, good quality seeds are out of reach of the majority of farmers, especially small and marginal farmers mainly because of exorbitant prices of better seeds.In order to solve this problem, the Government of India established the National Seeds Corporation (NSC) in 1963 and the State Farmers Corporation of India (SFCI) in 1969. Thirteen State Seed Corporations (SSCs) were also established to augment the supply of improved seeds to the farmers. High Yielding Variety Programme (HYVP) was launched in 1966-67 as a major thrust plan to increase the production of food grains in the country. The Indian seed industry had exhibited impressive growth in the past and is expected to provide further potential for growth in agricultural production: The role of seed industry is not only to produce adequate quantity of quality seeds but also to achieve varietal diversity to suit various agro-climatic zones of the country. The policy statements are designed towards making available to the Indian farmer, adequate quantities of seed of superior quality at the appropriate time and place and at an affordable price so as to meet the country's food and nutritional security goals. Indian seeds programme largely adheres to limited generation system for seed multiplication. The system recognises three kinds of generation, namely breeder, foundation and certified seeds. Breeder seed is the basic seed and first stage in seed production. Foundation seed is the second stage in seed production chain and is the progeny of breeder seed. Certified seed is the ultimate stage in seed production chain and is the progeny of foundation seed.

Manures, Fertilizers and Biocides: Indian soils have been used for growing crops over thousands of years without caring much for replenishing. This has led to depletion and exhaustion of soils resulting in their low productivity. The average yields of almost all the crops are among the lowest in the world. This is a serious problem which can be solved by using more manures and fertilizers. Manures and fertilizers play the same role in relation to soils as good food in relation to body. Just as a well-nourished body is capable of doing any good job, a well-nourished soil is capable of giving good yields. It has been estimated that about 70 per cent of growth in agricultural production can be attributed to increased fertilizer application. Thus, increase in the consumption of fertilizers is a barometer of agricultural prosperity. However, there are practical difficulties in providing sufficient manures and fertilizers in all parts of a country of India's dimensions inhabited by poor peasants. Cow dung provides the best manure to the soils. But its use as such is limited because much of cow dung is used as kitchen fuel in the shape of dung cakes. Reduction in the supply of fire wood and increasing demand for fuel in the rural areas due to increase in population has further complicated the problem. Chemical fertilizers are costly and are often beyond the reach of the poor farmers. The fertilizer problem is, therefore, both acute and complex. It has been felt that organic manures are essential for keeping the soil in good health. The country has a potential of 650 million tonnes of rural and 160 lakh tonnes of urban compost which is not fully utilized at present. The utilization of this potential will solve the twin problem of disposal of waste and providing manure to the soil. The government has given high incentive especially in the form of heavy subsidy for using chemical fertilizers.

Irrigation: Although India is the second largest irrigated country of the world after China, only one-third of the cropped area is under irrigation. Irrigation is the most important agricultural input in a tropical monsoon country like India where rainfall is uncertain, unreliable and erratic India cannot achieve sustained progress in agriculture unless and until more than half of the cropped area is brought under assured irrigation. This is testified by the success story of agricultural progress in Punjab, Haryana and western part of Uttar Pradesh where over half of the cropped area is under irrigation! Large tracts still await irrigation to boost the agricultural output. However, care must be taken to safeguard against ill effects of over irrigation especially in areas irrigated by canals. Large tracts in Punjab and Haryana have been rendered useless (areas affected by salinity, alkalinity and water-logging), due to faulty irrigation. In the Indira Gandhi Canal command area also, intensive irrigation has led to sharp rise in sub-soil water level, leading to water-logging, soil salinity and alkalinity.

Lack of mechanisation: In spite of the large scale mechanisation of agriculture in some parts of the country, most of the agricultural operations in larger parts are carried on by human hand using simple and conventional tools and implements like wooden plough, sickle, etc. Little or no use of machines is made in ploughing, sowing, irrigating, thinning and pruning, weeding, harvesting threshing and transporting the crops. This is specially the case with small and marginal farmers. It results in huge wastage of human labour and in low yields per capita labour force. There is urgent need to mechanise the agricultural operations so that wastage of labour force is avoided and farming is made convenient and efficient. Agricultural implements and machinery are a crucial input for efficient and timely agricultural operations, facilitating multiple cropping and thereby increasing production. Some progress has been made for mechanising agriculture in India after Independence. Need for mechanisation was specially felt with the advent of Green Revolution in 1960s. Strategies and programmes have been directed towards replacement of traditional and inefficient implements by improved ones, enabling the farmer to own tractors, power tillers, harvesters and other machines. A large industrial base for manufacturing of the agricultural machines has also been developed.

Soil erosion: Large tracts of fertile land suffer from soil erosion by wind and water. This area must be properly treated and restored to its original fertility.

Agricultural Marketing: Agricultural marketing still continues to be in a bad shape in rural India. In the absence of sound marketing facilities, the farmers have to depend upon local traders and middlemen for the disposal of their farm produce which is sold at throw-away price. In most cases, these farmers are forced, under socio-economic conditions, to carry on distress sale of their produce. In most of small villages, the farmers sell their produce to the money lender from whom they usually borrow money. According to an estimate 85 per cent of wheat and 75 per cent of oil seeds in Uttar Pradesh, 90 per cent of Jute in West Bengal, 70 per cent of oilseeds and 35 per cent of cotton in Punjab is sold by farmers in the village itself. Such a situation arises due to the inability of the poor farmers to wait for long after harvesting their crops. In order to meet his commitments and pay his debt, the poor farmer is forced to sell the produce at whatever price is offered to him. The Rural Credit Survey Report rightly remarked that the producers in general sell their produce at an unfavourable place and at an unfavourable time and usually they get unfavourable terms. In the absence of an organised marketing structure, private traders and middlemen dominate the marketing and trading of agricultural produce. The remuneration of the services provided by the middlemen increases the load on the consumer, although the producer does not derive similar benefit.

Inadequate storage facilities: Storage facilities in the rural areas are either totally absent or grossly inadequate. Under such conditions the farmers are compelled to sell their produce immediately after the harvest at the prevailing market prices which are bound to be low. Such distress sale deprives the farmers of their legitimate income.The Parse Committee estimated the post-harvest losses at 9.3 per cent of which nearly 6.6 per cent occurred due to poor storage conditions alone. Scientific storage is, therefore, very essential to avoid losses and to benefit the farmers and the consumers alike. At present there are number of agencies engaged in warehousing and storage activities. The Food Corporation of India (F.C.I.), the Central Warehousing Corporation (C.W.C.) and State Warehousing Corporation are among the principal agencies engaged in this task. These agencies help in building up buffer stock, which can be used in the hour of need. The Central Government is also implementing the scheme for establishment of national Grid of Rural Godowns since 1979-80. This scheme provides storage facilities to the farmers near their fields and in particular to the small and marginal farmers.

Inadequate transport: One of the main handicaps with Indian agriculture is the lack of cheap and efficient means of transportation. Even at present there are lakhs of villages which are not well connected with main roads or with market centres. Most roads in the rural areas are Kutcha (bullock-cart roads) and become useless in the rainy season. Under these circumstances the farmers cannot carry their produce to the main market and are forced to sell it in the local market at low price. Linking each village by metalled road is a gigantic task and it needs huge sums of money to complete this task.

Scarcity of capital: Agriculture is an important industry and like all other industries it also requires capital. The role of capital input is becoming more and more important with the advancement of farm technology. Since the agriculturists' capital is locked up in his lands and stocks, he is obliged to borrow money for stimulating the tempo of agricultural production. The main suppliers of money to the farmer are the money-lenders, traders and commission agents who charge high rate of interest and purchase the agricultural produce at very low price.

7. (*a*) (*i*) **Formal garden styles:** A formal garden is laid out in a symmetrical or geometrical pattern. In this garden, the design is stiff as everything is done in a straight and narrow way. In such gardens, everything is planned in straight lines.

Informal Garden Styles: Informal gardens are characterized by following curves, non-symmetrical arrangements of features and spaces and plants that are allowed to grow into their natural shapes.

Formal Design	Informal Design
Garden Examples: Knot gardens, Versailles	Garden Examples : English landscape gardens, Cottage gardens
Strict symmetry	No symmetry
Central axis	No central axis
Geometric shapes and patterns (Squares, rectangles, circles, triangles)	Irregular patterns- serpentine, curvilinear paths and border edges.
Symmetrical Balance Either side of the central axis is exactly the same so equal balance	Asymmetrical Balance Either side of a viewpoint the mass of plants and structures is balanced. Look at a magazine photo of a garden and you will see this as a well composed picture is always balanced.
Straight lines for paths and borders (You can have perfect circles however)	Serpentine lines and meandering irregular curves
Shrubs and trees have strong form (outline) *e.g.* topiary, clipped hedges. Distinct defined shapes. Plants do not spill over on to paths.	Shrubs and trees are loose and natural-looking with casual shaping, plants spilling out onto paths. Mixed species hedges that are not tightly clipped.
Often used in public garden spaces. (Does look good in a small front garden though)	Often used in private and personal spaces.
Structure of design is clear *e.g.* parterre or knot gardens with strong patterns.	May not 'look' designed at all - this makes them more difficult to design!
Clipped evergreen hedges *e.g. Buxus sempervirens* or *Taxus baccata*	Wild or native mixed hedging *e.g. Crataegus monogyna, Lavandula angustifolia*
Pleached trees *e.g. Tila* (lime) Bay (*Laurus nobilis*) and roses trained as standards.	Trees in natural form Climbing plants, plants left to grow into natural form. Rambling Roses.
Limited plant palette with blocks of plants with the same height (*e.g.* Box edging, bedding displays)	Many diverse plants of different height, forms, colours.
Clean lines *e.g.* dressed stone walls, brick paths, sleek paved areas that match the building.	Rustic fences or natural sculptures, gravel, sliced logs as stepping stones, woven materials or woodchip.
Ornate formal fountains or square, circular rectangular pools with clean stone edges and very few plants. Could also be a rill.	Lake, wildlife ponds or streams with irregular cascades.
Sense of elegance and 'showy'	Sense of relaxation and mystery/reveal
Clear focal points such as urns/water features/statues	More hidden focal points and hidden areas of the garden.
Artificial looking	Natural looking
Formal short lawn with stripes and no weeds. Geometric shape.	Meadow or utility lawn, longer grass, no stripes, irregular shape.
Topography is flat and level or has steps and terraces	Topography may be undulating, irregular.

(*ii*) • A pollinator is an animal that causes plants to make fruit or seeds. They do this by moving pollen from one part of the flower of a plant to another part. This pollen then fertilizes the plant. Only fertilized plants can make fruit and/or seeds, and without them, the plants cannot reproduce. In order to pollinate a plant, the pollinator must touch parts of the flower of the plant. Because of this, animals like bees, hummingbirds and some kinds of butterflies are the best pollinators, because they get their food from the flower of the plant and so brush up against parts of the flower. Other insects such as spiders and flies or wasps may use the flower for a hiding place, or may occasionally scavenge from the flower. These animals can also be pollinators, but they aren't as efficient as bees at their tasks.

- Some kinds of plants, such as soybeans do not require pollinators at all, and some can be pollinated by wind in the ecodome blowing on the plants. But others, such as raspberries or alfalfa won't reproduce or grow fruit without pollination, and many fruit and vegetable plants, such as strawberries reproduce more slowly and produce less fruit without pollinators around.
- Pollinator is the biotic agent that move the pollen to the female plant such as bees, moth, bat, birds etc. They are also called as insect pollinator.
- A pollenizer or polleniser, sometimes pollinizer or polliniser is a plant that provides pollen. In American English, the words pollenizer and pollinator are often confused: A pollinator is the biotic agent that moves the pollen, such as bees, moths, bats, and birds. In UK English it is quite correct to refer to different varieties as 'pollinators'. Bees are normally referred to as 'pollinating insects'. The verb form to pollenize is to be the source of pollen, or to be the sire of the next plant generation. While some plants are capable of self pollenization, the term is more often used in pollination management as a plant that provides abundant, compatible, and viable pollen at the same flowering time as the pollenized plant. For example, most crab apple varieties are good pollenizers for any apple variety that blooms at the same time, and are often used in apple orchards for the purpose. Some apple cultivars produce very little pollen; some produce pollen that is sterile, or incompatible with other apple varieties. These are poor pollenizers. A pollenizer can also be the male plant in dioecious species, such as with kiwifruit or holly.
- Pollinizer is also spell as a pollinizer. Pollinizer is nothing but the plant which provide pollen. Pollinizer are the source of pollen grains for the next generation. Pollinizer can be a male plant in dioecious plant such as kiwi fruit.
- Pollinizers are simply the cultivar which provides viable abundant compatible pollens to female flower... Crab apple is good example of pollinizers for all apple varieties.
- Whereas pollinators are biotic and abiotic factors or mode of transference of pollens. Like wind water birds' insects.

***(iii)* Insect Vectors:** Insect vector biology refers to the field of study focused on the evolutionary, anatomical, physiological, cellular, and molecular mechanisms involved in the transmission of pathogens by insect vectors. Most insect vectors of plant pathogens are hemipteran insects, *e.g.*, aphids, white-flies, and psyllids, that have piercing sucking mouthparts in common. All have a coevolved, mutualistic relationship with intra-cellular, often obligate, microbial partners known as endosymbionts. A disease vector is an agent that carries and transmits infectious pathogen from one organism to another living organism. Insects transmits all types of plant pathogens namely: Virus, Bacteria, Fungus and Phytoplasma.

Insect vector control: Insect vector control is defined as the application of targeted site-specific activities that are cost-effective to manage populations of insects which carry disease-causing organisms. Control of arthropod (insect) vectors is the primary available intervention for some of the most devastating tropical diseases. The most common insect vector control measure adopted over the years has been the use of chemicals in various forms (Chemical control). This involves the application of chemical compounds (mostly synthetic) as repellents or killing agents for insect vectors. Insecticides such as larvicides, adulticides and repellents have been in use to control vectors. For example, larvicides can be used in breeding zones of many insect vectors with aquatic immature stages. Insecticides can be applied to house walls or bed nets, and use of personal repellents can reduce incidence of insect bites and thus infection. The use of pesticides for vector control is promoted by the World Health Organization (WHO) and has proven to be highly effective.

Contemporary Methods of Vector Control: The myriads of challenges associated with chemical control of disease vectors in the tropics have necessitated a call for viable alternative(s) to combat their contributions to disease burden in the regions.

Novel Approaches to Vector Control: Some novel approaches to vector control include: Sterile Insect Technique (SIT), Genetic Modification (GM), Modification of age structure, "New Generation" chemicals, Hormonal control and Integrated Vector Manage-ment (IVM) .

Predators: Predators are mainly free-living species that directly consume a large number of preys during their whole lifetime. Given that many major crop pests are insects, many of the predators used in biological control are insectivorous species. Lady beetles, and in particular their larvae which are active between May and July in the northern hemisphere, are voracious predators of aphids, and also consume mites, scale insects and small caterpillars. The spotted lady beetle (*Coleomegilla maculata*) is also able to feed on the eggs and larvae of the Colorado potato beetle (*Leptinotarsa decemlineata*).

The larvae of many hoverfly species principally feed upon aphids, one larva devouring up to 400 in its lifetime. Their effectiveness in commercial crops has not been studied. The running crab spider *Philodromus cespitum* also prey heavily on aphids, and act as a biological control agent in European fruit orchards. Predatory Polistes wasp searching for bollworms or other caterpillars on a cotton plant. Several species of entomopatho-genic nematode are important predators of insect and other invertebrate pests. Entomopathogenic nematodes form a stress-resistant stage known as the infective juvenile. These spread in the soil and infect suitable insect hosts. Upon entering the insect, they move to the hemolymph where they recover from their stagnated state of development and release their bacterial symbionts. The bacterial symbionts reproduce and release toxins, which then kill the host insect. *Phasmarhabditis hermaphrodita* is a microscopic nematode that kills slugs. Its complex life cycle includes a free-living, infective stage in the soil where it becomes associated with a pathogenic bacterium such as *Moraxella osloensis.* The nematode enters the slug through the posterior mantle region, thereafter feeding and reproducing inside, but it is the bacteria that kill the slug. The nematode is available commercially in Europe and is applied by watering onto moist soil. *Entomopathogenic nematodes* have a limited shelf life because of their limited resistance to high temperature and dry conditions. The type of soil they are applied to may also limit their effectiveness.

Species used to control spider mites include the predatory mites *Phytoseiulus persimilis, Neoseilus californicus,* and *Amblyseius cucumeris,* the predatory midge *Feltiella acarisuga,* and a ladybird *Stethorus punctillum*. The bug *Orius insidiosus* has been successfully used against the two spotted spider mite and the western flower thrips (*Frankliniella occidentalis*). Predators including *Cactoblastis cactorum* (mentioned above) can also be used to destroy invasive plant species. As another example, the poison hemlock moth (*Agonopterix alstroemeriana*) can be used to control poison hemlock (*Conium maculatum*). During its larval stage, the moth strictly consumes its host plant, poison hemlock, and can exist at hundreds of larvae per individual host plant, destroying large swathes of the hemlock.

7. (*b*) Fruit flies are common in homes, restaurants, supermarkets and wherever else food is allowed to rot and ferment. Adults are about 1/8 inch long and usually have red eyes. The front portion of the body is tan and the rear portion is black. Fruit flies lay their eggs near the surface of fermenting foods or other moist, organic materials. Upon emerging, the tiny larvae continue to feed near the surface of the fermenting mass. This surface-feeding characteristic of the larvae is significant in that damaged or over-ripened portions of fruits and vegetables can be cut away without having to discard the remainder for fear of retaining any developing larvae. The reproductive potential of fruit flies is enormous; given the opportunity, they will lay about 500 eggs. The entire lifecycle from egg to adult can be completed in about a week. Fruit flies are especially attracted to ripened fruits and vegetables in the kitchen. But they also will breed in drains, garbage disposals, empty bottles and cans, trash containers, mops and cleaning rags. All that is needed for development is a moist film of fermenting material. Infestations can originate from over-ripened fruits or vegetables that were previously infested and brought into the home. The adults can also fly in from outside through inadequately screened windows and doors. Fruit flies are primarily nuisance pests. However, they also have the potential to contaminate food with bacteria and other disease-producing organisms.

Fruit Fly in Cucurbits: Fruit fly is the most problematic insect pest of the cucumber group plants (cucurbits), which includes cucumber, bitter gourd, pumpkin etc. It attacks young and older stages. Maggots are found in infected fruits, which means the fruits cannot be eaten. Fruit fly damage starts from March and ends in August or September. Female flies lay eggs inside the fruit. The eggs hatch and the maggots damage the fruit. Numerous maggots may be seen within infected fruits. After 7 to 10 days the maggot will drop onto the soil and pupate. The adult fly is pale yellow to brown with transparent wings that each have 2 spots on. Female adult fruit flies have a prominent ovipositor which is used for laying eggs in the fruit.

Symptoms of damage:

- Maggots feed on the pulp of the fruits
- Oozing of resinous fluid from fruits
- Distorted and malformed fruits
- Premature dropping of fruits and also unfit for consumption

Management

- Collect damaged fruits regularly and destroy them in a deep hole or soak in water mixed with a chemical insecticide
- Prepare a food bait to control the flies. Take yellow crushed ripened pumpkin and apply drops of Malathion 50 EC 0.1% solution over it and keep it in different places on the ground near the crop.
- Cover young fruits with newspapers or waste clothes initially if cultivating a small area or in a kitchen garden. The fly will not go into the shaded area under the newspaper or cloth so this will prevent the fly laying eggs.
- If more than 10% of fruits are infected, spray with a mixture of Malathion 50 EC at 1 ml/litre of water and 20 grams of sugar or molasses.
- Do not harvest within 7 days of spraying.
- Treat the soil with Malathion 5% powder 20 kg per Ropani during winter.

- Deep ploughing in winter is recommended as this will damage pupae in the soil.

Fruit Fly in Guava:

Guava is commonly called a poor man's appie in the tropics and known for its delicious, pleasant aroma and outstanding nutritional values throughout the world. It is an excellent source of pectin, phosphorus, calcium, iron, potassium, and sodium with a pleasant aroma. The guava fruit is having a medicinal property and a good source of antioxidant and also having the anticarcinogenic property. Due to various constraints, guava production is severely affected. Among all the known factors, insect pests are of prime importance. The guava is subjected to attack by several kinds of pests and about 80 species of insects have been recorded on guava, but only a few of them have been recognized as a pest of regular occurrence and causing significant damage. Among insect pest, the fruit fly is the major limiting factor in obtaining a good quality of fruits and vegetable and known to cause consi-derable losses. Fruit flies are one of the most diversified and noxious pests on a wide range of tropical and sub-tropical fruits and vegetables. Fruit flies are considered as a highly destructive pest of guava fruit production causing yield losses and quality degrada-tion of the produce. It is recorded, that crop losses caused by fruit fly ranging from 20-80 per cent usually depend upon the crop locality, season and variety.

Guava trees produce sweet smelling fruits with an edible rind, with a creamy white, yellow or pink flesh. When ripe, guavas release a sharp, musky odour that draws fruit flies. Fruit flies are among the world's most serious pests of different horticultural crops due to their direct impact on economy. They are among the most destructive pests. They cause enormous threat to the production of fruits and vegetables throughout the tropical and sub-tropical areas and causes both quantitative and qualitative losses. Fruit flies lay their eggs inside the fruit and the maggots feed on the flesh. As a result, fruits rot and infestation often spread quickly. Most of the damage is caused by the larvae that nourishes inside the fruit during its growth and development. It attacks fruits at different stages of maturity but the harm is more noticeable at harvesting stage. The adult female fruit fly place eggs in the flesh of fruits and vegetables. After emerging the larvae feed on the pulp which looks normal from outside. Fruits finally drops down and is not suitable for sale, therefore reduces orchard productivity. During winter the larvae pupate in soil 5-10 cm deep and flies start developing during April onwards, with extreme population during May to July which overlaps with fruit maturity.

The infestations caused by fruit fly often spread quickly in guava trees which produce sweet-smelling with an edible rind and creamy white, yellow or pink flesh. On the ripening stage of fruit, emit a pungent, musky odor that attracts fruit flies. Adult female fruit flies have a needle-like ovipositor with which they puncture the skin of fruits to lay their eggs in the flesh. Eggs are laid beneath the skin of fruit and after completion of the incubation period, maggots are emerged out that feed on the flesh and the resulting damage causes rotting due to microbial decay of the flesh. When the guava fruit is squeezed, the tiny punctures that leak juice from surface indicate the infestation. At first, the oviposition marks are difficult to detect but as within one to two days the eggs hatch, oviposition marks appear as a distinct spot with a brownish patch around the puncture site.

Symptoms of damage

- Adults and maggots attack semi-ripe fruits
- Oviposition punctures on fruits
- Maggots destroy and convert pulp into a bad smelling
- Discoloured semi-liquid mass

Management

- Fallen and infested rotten fruits should be removed, as they are capable of spreading further infestation. These should be picked up and destroyed by dumping in a 40-60 cm deep pit and must be covered with soil to eradicate all sources of possible breeding sites.

- Fruits should be harvested early when they are mature green. Harvesting guavas before they ripen fully is a good practise for preventing infestation. As fruit flies only attack matured fruits, so early harvesting prevents infestation. As this stage of fruit maturity, crops are not susceptible to attack.
- Overripe fruits should be also picked as these are ideal breeding sites for fruit flies.
- Ploughing the topsoil 5-10 cm deep is good for its control. Due to deep ploughing pupae are exposed to predators, parasites, and direct sunlight.
- Crop and field sanitation is also essential for the control of this pest.
- Guavas should be avoided to extreme and sudden changes in temperature, moisture, fertilizer or soil pH, as unexpected changes may stress plants and draw fruit flies and other pests.
- Pheromone traps such as methyl eugenol capture male flies. Set up methyl eugenol trap in the orchard at the rate of 5 per acre. Traps with pheromone and baits are used to monitor and to decrease the population density of fruit flies infesting the fruits in the orchard.
- Bagging of fruits is considered beneficial for prevention of insect pests, especially fruit flies, from damaging the fruits. The bag provides physical protection from mechanical injuries and act as barrier against pests.
- Fruit fly infestations often spread quickly, but if preventive measures are taken, then the loss can be overcome and its population can be greatly decreased.
- Creating awareness among the farmers is very important as mostly farmers are uneducated and they are unaware about the efficient methods to overcome losses.

7. (*c*) Seed Dormancy: Seed dormancy can be defined as the state or a condition in which seeds are prevented from germinating even under the favourable environmental conditions for germination including, temperature, water, light, gas, seed coats, and other mechanical restrictions. The main reason behind these conditions is that they require a period of rest before being capable of germination. These conditions may vary from days to months and even years. These conditions are the combination of light, water, heat, gases, seed coats and hormone structures.

Importance of Seed Dormancy

- It follows the storage of seeds for later use by animals and man.
- It helps in the dispersal of the seeds through the unfavourable environment.
- Dormancy induced by the inhibitors present in the seed coats is highly useful to desert plants.
- Allows the seeds to continue to be in suspended animation without any harm during cold or high summer temperature and even under drought conditions.
- Dormancy helps seeds to remain alive in the soil for several years and provides a continuous source of new plants, even when all the mature plants of the area have died down due to natural disasters.

Factors of Seed Dormancy:

Impermeability of Seed-Coats to Water: The seed coats of many species are completely impermeable to water at the time of their maturity. This condition is very common in the seeds of many legumes, (*e.g.*, clovers, alfalfa, etc.) of the water lotus, and of the morning glory. Germination fails to occur until water penetrates through the seed coats.

Mechanically Resistant Seed Coats: In some seeds as those of mustard (Brassica), pigweed (Amaranthus), shepherd's purse (Capsella), etc., the seed-coats are so strong that they do not yield to the pressure of the expanding embryo. The embryos of these seeds have no dormant period and will grow readily if the seed coats are removed.

Seed-Coats Impermeable to Oxygen: The two seeds in a fruit of cocklebur (Xanthium) are not equally dormant. Under natural conditions, the lower seed usually germinates in the spring following maturity while the upper seed remains dormant until the next year. The dormancy of these seeds has been demonstrated to result from the impermeability of the seed coats to oxygen.

Rudimentary Embryos: In plants like ginkgo (Ginkgo biloba), European ash (Fraxinus), holly (Ilex) and many orchids, the embryo is unorganized when the seed is shed and attains full development before it germinates.

Dormant Embryos: In many species, although the embryos are completely developed when the seed is ripe, the seed fails to germinate even when environmental conditions are favourable. Dormancy of such seed is a result of the physiological condition of the embryo. The embryos of such seeds will not grow when the seeds first ripen even if the seed coats are removed. During the period of dormancy, some physiological changes called after-ripening occur in the embryo before the seed is capable of germination. The seeds of apple, peach, iris and pine belong to this group. In nature, after-ripening occurs in winter and the seeds formed in autumn germinate the coming spring.

Germination Inhibitors: Germination of seeds is sometimes checked or prevented by the presence of compounds known as inhibitors. These are often substances produced in one or more plant organs. For example, the juice of tomato fruits inhibits the germination of tomato seeds and many other seeds as well. Inhibitors may be present in the embryo (*e.g.*, in Xanthium), endosperm, (*e.g.*, in Iris) or in the seed coat (*e.g.*, in Cucurbita). Abscissic acid (ABA) is one of the most commonly detected inhibitors of germination.

Methods of Breaking Seed Dormancy

The different methods of breaking dormancy are following:

The natural breaking of Seed Dormancy: Nature of dormancy stops when the embryo gets appropriate environment such as adaptive moisture and temperature. The seed coat that exists in many species becomes permeable due to the rupturing of smoothing action of natural agents like microorganism, temperature, and abrasion by the digestive tract of birds and animals that feed on these seeds. Other natural methods include:

- Completion of the over-ripening period.
- Leaching of inhibitors present in the seed coat.
- Inactivation of inhibitors by the supply of cold, heat, and light.
- Leaching of the excess and highly concentrated solutes from the seeds.
- Production of growth hormones which can neutralize the effect of inhibitors.

Artificial Overcoming of Seed Dormancy: Some of the artificial methods used for breaking seed dormancy are listed below:

- Action with hot water for termination of waxes, surface inhibitors, etc.
- Rupturing of seed coats by filing, chipping, or threshing through machines.
- Exposure to heat, cold or light, depending upon the type of seed dormancy.
- By applying Hydraulic pressure for 5 to 20 minutes in order to weaken the tough seed coats.
- Seed coats are treated with concentrated Sulphuric acid for removing all traces of the mineral acid.

Treatment to break dormancy in seeds: There are separate treatments to overcome dormancy, and they are further divided into the following groups:

Seed coat treatment: These treatments make a hard seed coat permeable to water or gases either by softening or cracking. This process is called scarification. The treatment can be either chemical or physical in nature.

Embryo treatments:

- ***Stratification:*** The incubation of seeds at an appropriate low temperature over a moist layer before transferring to a temperature suitable for germination.
- ***High-temperature treatment:*** Incubation at 40-50°C for a few hours to a few days may have an effect in overcoming dormancy in some species. For instance, rice seeds treated with hot water at 40°C for at least 4 hours.

Chemical treatments: Plant growth regulators or other chemicals can be used in induced germination growth regulators.

Previous Years' Paper (Solved)

IFS–Agriculture Main Examination, 2019

PAPER-I

INSTRUCTIONS: *There are **Eight** questions in all, out of which **Five** are to be attempted. Candidates should attempt question nos. 1 and 5 which are compulsory, and out of the remaining **six** questions, **three** are to be attempted selecting at least **one** question from each of the two Sections A and B. All questions carry equal marks. Answers must be written in English only.*

SECTION–A

1. Answer the following in about 150 words each:

(*a*) Discuss the impact of changing climate on cropping pattern and agricultural production.

(*b*) Discuss the importance of diversification and intensification in modern agriculture.

(*c*) What do you mean by dormancy and dissemination of weed seeds? Give their significance in spread and survival.

(*d*) Discuss the importance and scope for drought-tolerant varieties in crops.

(*e*) Discuss the environmental conditions favouring the formation of acidic soils. Give reclamation measures for acidic soils.

2. (*a*) Describe the basis of classification of agro-ecological zones of India. Give the important characteristics and cropping patterns of any two zones.

(*b*) What do you mean by weathering of rocks and minerals? Discuss the role of biological weathering processes.

(*c*) Explain the conditions which lead to wind erosion. Discuss the differences between wind breaks and shelter belts measures of controlling wind erosion.

3. (*a*) Give the improved agro-techniques for rice and chickpea with respect to time of sowing/season, method of sowing/spacing, seed rate, nutrients and weed control.

(*b*) What are the different groups of microorganisms found in soil? How do microbes help in soil aggregation, and thereby improvement in physical properties.

(*c*) Explain the fundamental principles of soil conservation. Discuss the types and role of mulching in soil conservation.

4. (*a*) Why does fertilizer nitrogen have low plant use efficiency? Explain the ways to improve the efficiency of fertilizer nitrogen.

(*b*) Discuss the importance of agro-forestry, social forestry and natural forests in supplementing the income of the farmers.

(*c*) Explain the concepts and benefits of multiple, multi-storey, relay and intercropping.

SECTION–B

5. Answer the following in about 150 words each:

(*a*) Discuss the effective scheduling of irrigation of wheat under normal and limited water conditions.

(*b*) Discuss the economics of organic farming of varied agro-ecological zones of the country.

(*c*) Discuss the importance, scope and objectives of extension education.

(*d*) What is eNAM? How does it safeguard the interests of farm producers?

(*e*) What is Farmer Producer Organisation (FPO)? Discuss its significance for farmers, especially small and marginal farmers.

6. (*a*) What are the importance and characteristics of farm planning?

(*b*) Discuss the structure of agricultural marketing in India. What are the features of the new APMC Act, 2017?

(*c*) What are problems of waterlogged soils for crop production? Give suitable measures for its management.

7. (*a*) What are the consequences of direct use of industrial effluents on human health?

(*b*) What do you understand by custom hiring centres? Discuss their benefits with reference to small and marginal farmers.

(*c*) Enlist the needs and objectives of agricultural price policy.

8. (*a*) What are the benefits of cooperative marketing? Discuss the hindering forces for cooperative movement in India.

(*b*) What are the features of Prime Minister Fasal Bima Yojana? How is it better than the earlier agricultural insurance scheme?

(*c*) Differentiate between training and education. Discuss the role of skill training in empowerment of farm women in SHGs.

PAPER-II

INSTRUCTIONS: *There are **Eight** Questions in all, out of which **Five** are to be atempted. Candidates should attempt question nos.* **1** *and* **5** *which are compulsory, and out of the remaining **six** questions, **three** are to be attempted, selecting at least **one** question from each of the two Sections A and B. Answers must be written in English only.*

SECTION–A

1. Answer the following:

(*a*) What are chromosomal aberrations? Describe the structural aberrations and their genetic significance.

(*b*) Discuss the role of heterosis in crop improvement with suitable examples.

(*c*) Explain the breeding methods of rice crop.

(*d*) Explain the different stages of seed development with suitable diagram.

(*e*) Discuss the role of auxin and cytokinins in plant growth and development.

2. Distinguish between the following:

(*a*) Heterochromatin and Euchromatin.

(*b*) Sex-linked and Sex-limited characters.

(*c*) Pedigree and Bulk method of plant breeding.

(*d*) Growth regulator and Growth inhibitor.

3. Answer the following:

(*a*) Describe the backcross method and its application in agriculture.

(*b*) What are the safeguards for maintenance of genetic purity of seed?

(*c*) Describe the role of transpiration in relation to productivity.

4. Answer the following:

(*a*) Discuss the special types of chromosomes.

(*b*) Discuss the methods of gene transfer to plants. Explain how it is achieved in cotton for insect resistance.

(*c*) Discuss the molecular basis of mutation.

SECTION–B

5. Answer the following:

(*a*) Briefly discuss the package of practices for commercial production of banana.

(*b*) Discuss the principles and components of integrated pest and disease management.

(*c*) Describe the techniques of hi-tech horticulture.

(*d*) Discuss the national initiatives for food and nutrition security.

(e) Define photoperiodism and discuss its mechanism in short-day plants.

6. Answer the following:

(a) Describe the changes that take place in plant during development.

(b) Discuss different types of preservation of fruits and vegetables.

(c) Enlist the insect pests of cruciferous vegetables indicating their nature of damage and management practices.

7. Answer the following:

(a) Discuss high-density planting system in fruit crops with its characteristics and advantages with examples.

(b) Classify insect pests based on their feeding habits with suitable examples.

(c) Describe the nature of damage, life cycle and management of pulse beetle and rice weevil.

8. Answer the following:

(a) Discuss the challenges and opportunities of marketing tomato and onion in India.

(b) What is organophosphate insecticide? Explain its mode of action.

(c) What are the socio-economic characteristics affecting food consumption pattern in India? Discuss them with examples of recent trends.

ANSWERS

PAPER-I

SECTION-A

1. (a) Indian agriculture remains vulnerable to the vagaries of weather, and the looming threat of climate change may expose this vulnerability further. Climate change can reduce farm incomes by 15-18%, and by 20-25% in unirrigated areas.

Agriculture is important in India for the obvious reason of its centrality. It accounts for a large share in GDP (gross domestic product) (16%), and an even larger share in employment (49%). Perhaps it is even more important because, it has the potential to hold back Indian development: poor agricultural performance can lead to high inflation, rural distress, and political restiveness.

Agriculture in India continues to be vulnerable to the vagaries of weather, and the looming threat of climate change has the potential to expose this vulnerability further. A small but growing literature has focused on estimating the impact of weather and climate on economic performance. However, most of these are either cross-country studies, or focus on developed countries, primarily for data reasons, and therefore may not be applicable to a large, climatically diverse country such as India.

There are a couple of important exceptions. Guiteras (2009) finds that crop yields will decline by 4.5-9% in the short-run (2010-2039) and by a whopping 25% in the long-run (2070-2099) in the absence of adaptation by farmers. Further, Burgess *et al.* (2014) find that a one standard deviation increase in high temperature days in a year decreases agricultural yields and real wages by 12.6% and 9.8%, respectively, and increases annual mortality among rural populations by 7.3% in India. By contrast, in urban areas, they find virtually no evidence of an effect on incomes and a substantially smaller increase in the mortality rate.

Climate change is very likely to affect food security at the global, regional, and local level. Climate change can disrupt food availability, reduce access to food, and affect food quality. For example, projected increases in temperatures, changes in precipitation patterns, changes in extreme weather events, and reductions in water availability may all result in reduced agricultural productivity. Increases in the frequency and severity extreme weather events can also interrupt food delivery, and resulting spikes in food prices after extreme events are expected to be more frequent in the future. Increasing temperatures can contribute to spoilage and contamination.

Internationally, these effects of climate change on agriculture and food supply are likely to be similar to those seen in the United States. However, other stressors such as population growth may magnify the effects of climate change on food security. In developing countries, adaptation options like changes in crop-management or ranching practices, or improvements to irrigation are more limited than in the United States and other industrialized nations.

1. (*b*) Importance of Diversification and Intensification in Modern Agriculture

Crop or farm diversification is promoted for various reasons:

(1) for production of diverse food items for better nutrition;

(2) for taking advantage of changing market demands;

(3) for diversifying farm revenues and increasing total farmers' income;

(4) for maximizing the use of different land forms (wetland, dry land, sloping land, forest land, etc.);

(5) for conservation and enrichment of soil;

(6) for coping with changing climate with diverse crops and or animals.

Often, farmers living in uplands near roads may need to diversify into the production of high-value cash crops, development of tree crops and non-timber forest products, the rearing of livestock, the rearing of honey bee and mushroom culture, the development of fishing, and the cultivation of river gardens on receding river banks.

Examples of crop/farm diversification include: diversified cropping systems on different land forms; integrated crop-animal systems; fish farming and aquatic organisms (snails, crabs) and plants (various green and vegetables); and agro-eco-tourism.

The extent of farmer adoption of diversification strategies will depend on the availability of suitable crop species, the availability of labour and the requirement of other facilities to develop new, diverse crops. Other factors which can determine the farmers' choice of diversification options include (*a*) whether their land is located near, or far away from roads, (*b*) market access and demand for new products, and (*c*) whether the farmer has access to different types of land.

Through appropriate diversification of cultivated lands and conservation of natural ecosystems as well as preservation of natural and agro-biodiversity, it is crucial for maintaining the integrity of both natural ecosystems and cultivated agro-ecosystems - both of these landscapes are vital for human welfare and survival.

Crop intensification means growing more number of mono crops in the same piece of land per year. Crop intensification is measured by cropping intensity (CI). In rain fed areas with a short rainy season, you can grow only one crop per year, and the CI is one here. In rain fed areas with a longer rainy season, one main crop is followed by a short duration legume or oil seed crop. Here the CI is 2.0. In irrigated areas, up to 3 crops can be grown with a CI of 3, or 5 crops in two years with a CI of 2.5. Thus, higher the CI, higher is the cropping intensity. While intensifying production, proper crop rotation is critical to optimize crop yields, minimize weeds as well as pests and diseases, maintain soil quality, and maximize water and nutrient use efficiency.

1. (c) Weeds are consistent problems in agriculture because of seed dormancy. Without dormancy, weed seeds would not survive in the soil for any period of time. Also critical are the factors that influence dormancy. These factors which describe seed dormancy also serve to "determine" when the seed has the greatest potential to germinate successfully, and thus survive to replace the seed bank.

Understanding the concepts of seed dormancy and factors that influence the continuation or termination of dormancy thus allowing germination are critical for the development of an effective weed-management program.

Seed dormancy has been described in a number of ways using many different, often synonymous terms. Dormancy has also been categorized into specific types of dormancy, presumably based on different physical and environment (physiological) conditions that cause the different categories of dormancy.

Dormancy has been classically described as the failure for seeds to germinate when environmental conditions are favourable to potentially support development. This failure to germinate is "blocked" by some condition or factor within the seed which, in itself, is not a requirement for germination. Thus, a dormant seed is one that can be prompted to germinate by removing or overcoming a particular condition(s) or factor(s).

Dissemination/Dispersal of Weeds

- A plant seed is a unique genetic entity, a biological individual. However, a seed is in a diapause state, an essentially dormant condition, awaiting the ecological conditions that will allow it to grow into an plant, and produce its own seeds.
- Seeds must therefore germinate in a safe place, and then establish themselves as a young seedling, develop into a juvenile plant, and finally become a sexually mature adult that can pass its genetic material on to the next generation.
- The chances of a seed developing are generally enhanced if there is a mechanism for dispersing to an appropriate habitat at some distance away from the parent plant.
- The reason for dispersal is that closely related organisms have similar ecological requirements. Obviously, competition with the parent plant will be greatly reduced if its seeds have a mechanism to disperse some distance away. Their ability to spread and remain viable in the soil for years makes eradication nearly impossible.
- Seeds have no way to move on their own, but they are excellent travellers. Plants have evolved various mechanisms that disperse their seeds effectively.
- Many species of plants have seeds with anatomical structures that make them very buoyant, so they can be dispersed over great distances by the winds.
- In the absence of proper means of their dispersal, weeds could not have moved from one country to another.
- An effective dispersal of weed seeds and fruits requires two essentials—a successful dispersing agent and an effective adaptation to the new environment.

There are two ways of looking at weed seed dispersal:

- The expanding range and increasing population size of an invading weed species into a new area.
- The part of the process by which an established and stabilized weed species in an area maintains itself within that area. Dissemination includes two separate processes. They are dispersal (leaving

mother plant) and post-dispersal events (subsequent movement). Dispersal of seed occurs in 4 dimensions viz.

- Length
- Width: Land/habitat/soil surface area phenomena
- Height : Soil depth, in the air
- Time: Shatters immediately after ripening (or) need harvesting activity to release seed.

Significance in Spread and Survival

The significance of seed dormancy is to optimize the distribution of germination in time and space. The optimization in time is achieved by spreading the germination of seeds over an extended period of time as expressed both within a specific growing season but also over several growing seasons. Thus, the distribution of seed germination in time improves the probabilities of seeds successfully completing a lifecycle. Often, germination is induced by physical factors such as light and temperature; the interaction of these factors can regulate germination to fit seasonal changes in the environment.

Dormancy allows seeds to germinate when conditions are least hazardous to their successful establishment. Dormancy can also act to secure a suitable place for germination. If seed dormancy is a function of light, deep burial will enforce dormancy. Small seeds that have minimal food reserves that support growth for a short period of time must emerge quickly and establish photosynthesis in order to survive.

Dormancy in space will insure the proper placement of the seed thus optimizing the likelihood of successful seedling development. Spatial dormancy can also a factor with regards to light quality.

Dormancy may be enforced under conditions of poor light quality. The light quality under a heavy plant canopy would poor and thus dormancy does not allow seed germination in an environment where growth conditions would not be favourable.

1. (*d*) Drought tolerance is the ability to which a plant maintains its biomass production during arid or drought conditions. Some plants are naturally adapted to dry conditions, surviving with protection mechanisms such as desiccation tolerance, detoxification, or repair of xylem embolism. Other plants, specifically crops like corn, wheat, and rice, have become increasingly tolerant to drought with new varieties created via genetic engineering.

The mechanisms behind drought tolerance are complex and involve many pathways which allows plants to respond to specific sets of conditions at any given time. Some of these interactions include stomatal conductance, carotenoid degradation and anthocyanin accumulation, the intervention of osmoprotectants (such as sucrose, glycine, and proline), ROS-scavenging enzymes. The molecular control of drought tolerance is also very complex and is influenced other factors such as environment and the developmental stage of the plant. This control consists mainly of transcriptional factors, such as dehydration-responsive element-binding protein (DREB), abscisic acid (ABA)-responsive element-binding factor (AREB), and NAM (no apical meristem).

With the frequency and severity of droughts increasing in recent years, damage to crops has become more serious, lowering the overall yield. However, research into the molecular pathways involving stress tolerance have revealed that over expression of such genes can enhance drought tolerance, leading to projects focused on the development of transgenic crop varieties.

In response to drought conditions, there is an alteration of gene expression, induced by or activated by transcription factors (TFs). These TFs bind to specific cis-elements to induce the expression of targeted stress-inducible genes, allowing for products to be transcribed that help with stress response and tolerance. Some of these include dehydration-responsive element-binding protein (DREB), ABA-responsive element-binding factor (AREB), no apical meristem (NAM), Arabidopsis transcription activation factor (ATAF), and cup-shaped cotyledon (CUC).

The plants in dry environments are subjected to random droughts, and it is generally impossible for them to escape from such adverse conditions. Thus, plants in such environments have the ability to endure water stress through certain biochemical or morphological adaptations and avoidance of cell injury. The mechanism of drought tolerance involves the maintenance of turgor pressure through osmotic adjustment, increase in elasticity in cells, and decrease in cell size by protoplasmic resistance.

1. (*e*) Soil acidity is a natural and induced chemical condition of soils that can:

- decrease the availability of essential nutrients;
- increase the impact of toxic elements;
- decrease plant production and water use;
- affect essential soil biological functions like nitrogen-fixation; and
- make soil more vulnerable to soil structure decline and erosion.

The process of soil acidification is a potentially serious land degradation issue. Without treatment, soil acidification will have a major impact on agricultural productivity and sustainable farming systems and acidification can also extend into subsoil layers posing serious problems for plant root development and remedial action.

In the regions of high rainfall, soils are acidic in their reaction because of the facts that soluble basic salts such as those of Ca, Mg, K, Na, are leached away by drainage water and insoluble acidic residues composed chiefly of oxides and silicates of iron, silicon, aluminium are left which accumulate in pretty high amount. These salts are acidic in reaction, hence the soils are acidic. Besides that reason, there may be other causes also which produce acidity in the soil.

In humid regions where evaporation is less than precipitation, chances for the development of acid soils are good. For the development of acid soils it is also necessary that water percolating down the soil profiles must reach the water table. In India, it is believed that the regions with acid soils must receive more than 750 mm annual rainfall. The regions with annual rainfall 1350 mm may have acid soils with pH value 5.0 or even less than that.

In temperate regions the acid soils can develop even if the rainfall is scanty. In hilly regions where the loss of water through evaporation is very slow due to very low temperature the conditions for the development of acid soils are very favourable, although the rainfall is scanty there.

Reclamation Measures for Acidic Soils

- Acidity of soil is due to predominance of H^+ ions over OH^- ions, the bulk of H^+ ions being held in close association with clay-organic colloid complex. Strong acid soils are not much productive. The soils which are less productive owing to high degree of acidity can be made more productive by liming (application lime).
- When lime is added to moist soil, the soil solution becomes charged with cations and the exchangeable hydrogen and aluminium ions on clay-organic colloid complex as well as the H^+ ions in soil solution are displaced by calcium ions. Hydrogen combines with OH^- to form neutral water or with CO_3 or HCO_3^- to form unstable H_2CO_3, which readily dissociates to form CO_2 and water.

- Acidity of soil can also be corrected by adding exchangeable Mg^{++} to exchange complex. But addition of Ca^{++} or Mg^{++} or both to the soil will not necessarily solve the problem of soil acidity.

2. (*a*) Agro-ecology refers to the study of agricultural ecosystems and their components as they function in themselves and as a part of the larger ecosystem.

The 20 AERs of India and the 60 AESRs with reference to this climate, soil and land use, the distinguishing features of the AESRs are also mentioned. The constraints and potentials with regard to each AER have been analysed for determining suitable cropping systems to reduce deterioration in quality of land.

1. Cold Arid Eco-region with Shallow Skeletal Soils.
2. Hot Arid Eco-region with Desert and Saline Soils.
3. Hot Arid Eco-region with Red and Black Soils.
4. Hot semi-arid eco-region with alluvium derived soils.
5. Hot semi-arid eco-region with medium and deep black soils.
6. Hot semi-arid eco-region with shallow and medium (dominant) black soils.
7. Hot semi-arid eco-region with red and black soils.
8. Hot semi-arid eco-region with red loamy soils.
9. Hot sub-humid (dry) eco-region with alluvium-derived soils.
10. Hot sub-humid eco-region with red and black soils.
11. Hot sub-humid eco-region with red and yellow soils.
12. Hot sub-humid eco-region with red and lateritic soils.
13. Hot sub-humid (moist) eco-region with alluvium-derived soils.
14. Warm sub-humid to humid with inclusion of perhumid eco-region with brown forest and podzolic soils.
15. Hot sub-humid (moist) to humid (inclusion of perhumid) eco-region with alluvium-derived soils.
16. Warm sub-humid eco-region with brown and red hill soils.
17. Warm perhumid eco-region with red and lateritic soils.
18. Hot sub-humid to semi-arid eco-region with coastal alluvium-derived soils.
19. Hot humid perhumid eco-region with red, lateritic and alluvium-derived soils.
20. Hot humid per-humid Island eco-region with red loamy and sandy soils.

1. Cold Arid Eco-region with Shallow Skeletal Soils:

This eco-region represents an area of 15.2 million hectares (mha) in the north-western Himalayas pertaining to Ladakh and Gilgit districts. It occupies 4.7 per cent (329 m ha) of the entire geographical area of India.

Agro-Climate: The climate has mild summer and harsh winter. The mean annual temperature is less than 8°C. The mean annual rainfall is less than 150 mm. The precipitation covers less than 15 per cent of the mean annual Potential Evapotranspiration (PET). The area has aridic soil moisture and cryic soil temperature regime with Length of Growing Period (LGP) being not more than 90 days annually.

Soils: While the very high northern parts of the plateau are permanently covered by snow, the gently sloping to level valleys has skeletal and calcareous soils. The soils are alkaline in reaction and low to medium in organic matter content. The region is represented largely by Ladakh series, which is classified as Typic Cryorthent.

Use of Land: The eco-region has few forest trees. Some 11.2 per cent of the land is in non- agricultural use (inclusive of culturable fallows), current fallow is 1.2 per cent and the net sown area is 2.5 per cent. In the cultivated land, the production per unit area is low. Vegetables are the foremost crops to be grown, followed by millets, wheat, fodder, pulses and barley, these five crops giving yields of 400 to 700 kg/ha. Alfa-alfa is produced among the cultivated fodders. The major fruits grown are apple and apricot. Where the livestock is concerned, the mule is mere common than the sheep, goat and yak which dominate in that order. Pashmina goats graze in the area.

AESRs: (*a*) Eastern aspect of the Ladakh plateau: cold hyper-arid eco sub-region (ESR) shallow skeletal soils; LGP is < 60 days. (*b*) Western aspect of Ladakh Plateau and north Kashmir Himalayas: cold to cool typic-arid ESR; shallow, loamy skeletal soils; LGP is 60-90 days.

2. Hot Arid Eco-region with Desert and Saline Soils:

The hot and arid eco-region covers the western plain, that is south-western parts of Haryana and Punjab, western parts of Rajasthan, the Kachchh peninsula and northern parts of Kathiawar peninsula (Gujarat). The eco-region occupies 9.78 per cent of the entire geographical area (31.9 m ha) of India.

Agro-climate: The region has hot summers and cool winters (arid), with the mean annual precipitation being less than 400 mm. This covers only 15-20 per cent of the annual PET demand which is 1500-2000 mm. The result is that there is a huge water deficit every year. The region has aridic soil moisture and hyperthermic soil temperature regimes. The annual LGP is not more than 90 days.

Soils: The area has sandy soils represented by Thar series. They are moderately calcareous and alkaline in reaction. Pali, Lakhpat and Nihalkhera series occur.

Use of Land: Rainfed mono-cropping is practised. Rainy season crops of short duration, pearl millet, chari (fodder) and pulses, are cultivated in non-saline areas. Where irrigation is available, cotton, sugarcane, mustard, wheat and gram are cultivated. There is sparse, sporadic tropical thorn forest. The forest cover in the region has reduced from 15 per cent to almost 1 per cent, a shocking fall in forest cover.

ASERs:

(*a*) **Marusthali:** Shallow and deep sandy desert soils; LGP is less than 60 days.

(*b*) **Kachchh Peninsula:** A deep loamy saline and alkali soil, LGP is less than 60 days.

(*c*) **Rajasthan Bagar, North Gujarat Plain and south-western Punjab Plain:** Deep, loamy desert soils (inclusion of saline phase); LGP is 60-90 days.

(*d*) **South Kachchh and North Kathiawar Peninsula:** Deep loamy saline and alkali soils; LGP is 60 day.

2. (*b*) The process of disintegration and decomposition of rock and minerals is called as weathering.

Types of Weathering

Physical weathering: Mechanical weathering is the cause of the disintegration of rocks. The primary process in mechanical weathering is abrasion (the process by which clasts and other particles are reduced in size). However, chemical and physical weathering often go hand in hand. For example, cracks exploited by mechanical weathering will increase the surface area exposed to chemical action. Furthermore, the chemical action at minerals in cracks can aid the disintegration process.

Chemical weathering: Chemical weathering involves the change in the composition of rocks, often leading to a 'break down' in its form. This is done through a combination of water and various chemicals to create an acid which directly breaks down the material. This type of weathering happens over a period of time. Chemical weathering may alter a rock's chemical make up by changing the minerals in the rock or it adds some new minerals.

Biological weathering: A number of plants and animals may create chemical weathering through release of acidic compounds, *i.e* moss on roofs is classed as weathering.

The most common form of biological weathering is the release of chelating compounds, *i.e* acids, by plants so as to break down aluminium and iron containing compounds in the soils beneath them. Decaying remains of dead plants in soil may form organic acids which, when dissolved in water, cause chemical weathering. Extreme release of chelating compounds can easily affect surrounding rocks and soils, and may lead to podsolisation of soils.

Man and Animal: The action of man in the disintegration of rocks is well known as he cuts and crushes to build dams, channels and constructs road and buildings. All these activities result in increasing the surface area of rock for attack by chemical agents and accelerate the process of rock decomposition.

Higher plants and their rocks: The roots of tree and other plants penetrate into the joints and crevices of rocks. As they grow, the roots exert a great disruptive force and the hard rock may be broken apart spongy like mass, conserve moisture and check erosion. Some roots go quite deep into the soil and may open a sort of drainage channels.

Micro-organism: In the very early stages of mineral decomposition and soil formation, the lower forms of plants and animals, such as mosses, bacteria, fungi, actinomycetes, etc, play an important role. The extract nutrients from the solid rock, nitrogen from the air and can live with a very small amount of moisture.

As its name suggests, biological weathering is a type of weathering brought about by various activities of living organisms. Along with other types of weathering, biological weathering can contribute to the further degradation of rocks and rock particles by making them more susceptible to other environmental factors, whether be it biotic or abiotic factors.

Living organisms can contribute to the process of weathering in many ways. Depending on the mechanism of how rocks and rock particles are broken down, biological weathering is of two types: by physical means or by chemicals and organic compounds.

Types of Biological Weathering

Living organisms can contribute to the process of weathering in many ways. Depending on the mechanism of how rocks and rock particles are broken down, biological weathering is of two types: by physical means or by chemicals and organic compounds.

Biological Weathering By Physical Means

This is a type of weathering that occurs when a force or pressure is applied to break rocks apart or degrade the minerals in them. By increasing the exposed surface area of rocks, they make it possible for other physical factors to speed up their degradation.

By Plants

Plants can grow anywhere as long as there is water. Roots of trees or plants in general can biologically weather rocks by growing into the cracks and fractures of rocks and soil. As a result, they become more prone to breakage and eventually fall part.

By Animals

Burrowing animals like shrews, moles, earthworms, and even ants contribute to biological weathering. In particular, these animals create holes on the ground by excavation and move the rock fragments to the surface. As a result, these fragments become more exposed to other environmental factors that can further enhance their weathering.

When animals like birds forage for seeds and earthworms, they create holes and erode the upper surface of the soil, thus, contributes to weathering.

An animal called the Piddock shell can drill into rocks in order for it to protect itself. By producing acids that can disintegrate the rock and turn it into fragments, it can create cracks and fractures and eat the minerals found in it.

Biological Weathering By Chemicals/ Organic Compounds

In this type of weathering, living organisms contribute through their organic compounds that contain molecules that acidify and corrode rock minerals. Because of such mechanism, biological weathering is also referred to as organic weathering.

By Plants

When the roots of plants grow deeper into the soil, they tend to create cracks and crevices in marbles and lime stones by producing certain acids that can eventually degrade them.

According to studies, the mere presence of roots in the soil can wear out soil and rocks through the presence of humus. Humus, an organic component of the soil, can increase the availability of water, which then enhances the physical and chemical breakdown of rocks.

When plants die, their roots (and other parts as well) are decomposed and are later on converted to organic matter which produces carbon dioxide. This carbon dioxide (CO_2), when combined with water (H_2O), produces weak carbonic acid which can degrade the surfaces of rocks and rock particles.

By Animals

While ants and termites can contribute to the physical breakdown of rocks, these animals can also contribute to their biological degradation. Aside from creating holes and passages in the ground, these animals also make possible the easy passage of oxygen and water to the soil, which in turn, bring the dissolution of soil, rocks, and rock particles alike.

When animals die, their bodies are converted to substances, which when combined with minerals found in the soil and rocks, can contribute to their degradation.

By Microorganisms

Despite their minute size, some micro-organisms can also break down the largest of rocks and hardest of soil.

One example of such activity is exhibited by lichens. In general, a lichen is a symbiosis between an algae and a fungus.

The minerals in rocks are liberated when a fungus releases chemicals that can break them down. Such minerals are then consumed by the alga, further causing the wearing and development of cracks and gaps on the rock. As a result, cracked rocks become more prone to disintegration.

- Some fungi produce siderophores, a type of chelating agent which can absorb various minerals and nutrients from the soil. By trading cations for hydrogen ions, siderophores make the soil more acidic, hence more prone to degradation.

Role of Biological Weathering Processing

As its name suggests, biological weathering is a type of weathering brought about by various activities of living organisms. Along with other types of weathering, biological weathering can contribute to the further degradation of rocks and rock particles by making them more susceptible to other environmental factors, whether be it biotic or abiotic factors.

Living organisms can contribute to the process of weathering in many ways. Depending on the mechanism of how rocks and rock particles are broken down, biological weathering is of two types: by physical means or by chemicals and organic compounds.

Weathering is responsible for the creation of soil. Below are some other benefits of biological weathering:

1. **Formation of Nutrient Rich Soil :** The very process of weathering is what creates the soil which then allows life to flourish on Earth. It is important to note that without it, minerals cannot be accumulated in the soil, hence, no nutrients will be available for plant and animal consumption.
2. **Creation of Sediments:** When broken, some rock pieces and particles eventually turn into sediments that are formed into different types of sedimentary rocks like sandstones and limestones. Usually, the broken rock pieces become deposited by rivers and are compacted by great pressure, enough to create a sedimentary rock.
3. **Contribution To Land Formation:** Like the formation of sediment rocks, biological weathering can also contribute to the formation of land masses and landscapes. The process tends to be very slow as it needs a lot of time to accumulate soil and rock particles, along with intense pressure to carry it out.

2. (*c*) Wind erosion is a serious environmental problem attracting the attention of many across the globe. It is a common phenomenon occurring mostly in flat, bare areas; dry, sandy soils; or anywhere the soil is loose, dry, and finely granulated. Wind erosion damages land and natural vegetation by removing soil from one place and depositing it in another. It causes soil loss, dryness and deterioration of soil structure, nutrient and productivity losses and air pollution. Suspended dust and dirt is inevitably deposited over everything. It blows on and inside homes, covers roads and highways, and smothers crops. Sediment transport and deposition are significant factors in the geological changes which occur on the land around us and over long periods of time are important in the soil formation process.

Soil movement is initiated as a result of wind forces exerted against the surface of the ground. For each specific soil type and surface condition there is a minimum velocity required to move soil particles. This is called the threshold velocity. Once this velocity is reached, the quantity of soil moved is dependent upon the particle size, the cloddiness of particles, and wind velocity itself.

Wind Breaks : Wind breaks can be both living or inanimate objects. They can range from trees and shrubs, to fences and concrete walls. When positioned perpendicular to the wind, wind breaks will deflect the wind stream and reduce wind velocity. By reducing wind velocities, evaporation will be slowed and a more favorable environment will be provided for the crops.

Shelterbelts: Field shelterbelts can provide extra protection against wind erosion no matter what cropping system is used. They are especially important in dry years when low crop yields result in insufficient residue cover.

Field shelterbelts reduce the wind velocity for distances up to 30 times the height of the trees. They also trap snow, increasing soil moisture for increased crop yields. This yield increase helps to offset yield losses associated with taking land out of crop production for the shelterbelt plantings.

To get the maximum benefit from shelterbelts, you will need to plan the design and species selection, site preparation, weed control for the first years, and pruning and other maintenance. You will need to select a species suitable to your area. New options for shelterbelt weed control - such as plastic, fabric or bark mulches - have reduced the effort needed to establish shelterbelts.

Windbreaks are such structures which break the wind-flow and reduce wind speed while shelterbelts are rows of trees or shrubs planted for protection of crop against wind. They provide a protective shelter against wind and suitable habitat for birds and honeybees as well as produce cattle feed and fuel wood. In the wind erosion areas, windbreaks and shelterbelts are to be planted. They prevent the soil erosion, arrest the desert and protect the agricultural and residential lands from dust-storms. A row of trees and shrubs planted across the winds-direction is the most effective. It reduces the wind speed up to 60-80% on leeward side. The height of tall tree and length of wind break determine the extent of protection provided to soil. Windbreaks and shelterbelts provide the protective shelter against desiccating winds to extent of 5-10 times the height of the tall tree on windward side and up to 30 times on leeward side.

For example a 10-11 meter tall windbreak when encountered by 45-50 km/hr wind, it reduces on windward side to 20-30 km/hr and to 10 km/hr on just leeward side.

The windbreak reduces the wind speed on the leeward side at 200 m away up to 20% only and in the area as at 300 m away, there is no effect at all. Therefore at an interval of 300 m, such windbreaks should be repeated.

To control wind erosion, the capacity of shelterbelt depends upon the speed and direction of wind. In case of high wind speed, the protective area is reduced and in such areas, the interval between two shelterbelts is to be reduced. To counter winds direction, it is necessary to be long length of windbreak so that wind blows across the wind break. Depending upon the porosity of shelterbelt, certain amount of wind passes through it and some deflects & crosses over it. Thus, it does not produce turbulence of air.

Reducing the wind speed reduces the evaporation losses and makes available more water to crops. According to planting pattern of trees and shrubs as shelterbelt, the grasses and shrubs are planted on the outer rows which train the wind to rise much above the ground surface. The inner rows are of small trees which further raise the wind level.

The beneficial effects of the shelterbelts are more clearly seen in drought areas. In such areas windbreaks of 3-7 rows and 15-30 m wide are more effective. It modifies the micro-climate favourable for crop production and shelters for birds, honeybees and pet animals. The windbreaks and shelterbelts should be formed in North-West direction. These shall secure the crops and livestock against cold wave also.

3. (*a*) (1) Rice

- Botanical name: *Oryza sativa* Family: Poaceae (Gramineae)
- *Oryza* has 24 species of which only 2 species (*O. sativa* & *O. glaberima*) is cultivable and rest 22 spp. are wild type. *Oryza sativa* is grown in India and *O. glaberima* is cultivated in Africa.
- *Oryza sativa* is believed to evolve from *O. nivora.*
- Rice is a diploid (2n) crop has chromosome no. of 24.
- Rice contains about 70 per cent carbohydrate and 6-7 per cent protein (*Oryzein*) content.
- *Oryza sativa* has 3 varietal types:

1. *Indica:* Grown in India (Tropical rice)
2. *Japonica:* Grown in Japan (Subtropical rice)
3. *Javanica:* Grown in Indonesia (Wild rice)

- Lodging doesn't occur in *Japonica spp* of rice.
- Rice inflorescence is called as panicle which has 6 numbers of stamens.
- Lemma and Palea together called as *Hull*.
- Stem of rice is called as *Culm*.
- Rice is considered as a self pollinated and short day crop.
- **Rice Growing Regions:**
  1. *North-Eastern Region:* Assam and North eastern states.
  2. *Eastern Region:* Bihar, Chhattisgarh, Madhya Pradesh, Odisha, Eastern UP and WB
  3. *Northern Region:* Haryana, Punjab, Western Uttar Pradesh, Uttarakhand, HP and J& K.
  4. *Western Region:* Gujarat, Maharashtra and Rajasthan.
  5. *Southern Region:* Andhra Pradesh, Karnataka, Kerala and Tamil Nadu.
- Rice favours hot and humid climate.
- Optimum temperature for good crop growth is 30-32ºC.
- Requirement of rainfall throughout growth period is 100-150 cm.
- Rice is grown in three seasons in Eastern and Peninsular India because of uniformity in temperature.
- Clay loam soil with slightly acidic condition (pH 4-6) is best for cultivation of rice.
- Normally, rice is grown at the spacing of 20 cm from row to row and 10 cm from plant to plant.
- **Seasons of rice cultivation:**
  1. *Aus/Autumn/Pre kharif:* Sowing in April-May and harvesting in August-Sept.
  2. *Aman/Kharif/Aghani:* Sowing in June-July and harvesting in October.
  3. *Boro/Summer/Spring:* Sowing in January-Feb and harvesting in April-May.
- Dehusked (unhusked) rice is also known as **Brown rice.**
- **Milling percentage** of rice is 50-55 per cent.
- **Harvest Index** of rice is 0.40.
- Rice (cleaned) is 2/3 of paddy.
- The gene responsible for dwarfness is **Deegee-woo-gene.**
- IR8 was evolved by breeder Henry M. Beachell at IRRI, Manila, Philippines through crossing of Dee-gee-woo-gene × Peta.
- In India, TN1 variety of rice introduced in 1964 by G. V. Ghalam from IRRI.
- IR8 rice variety was introduced in India in 1966 which was higher yielder than TN1.
- First dwarf variety developed on India's rice intervarietal programme was **Jaya** (TN1×T141), which was out yielded of IR8, so also called as **Miracle rice.**
- **Rice plant is transplanted at:**
  1. ***In Kharif season:*** 21-25 days after sowing (3-4 leaf stage)
  2. ***In Rabi season:*** 30-35 days after sowing
  3. ***SRI method:*** 10-12 DAS
  4. ***Depong method:*** 11-14 DAS
  5. ***Dry land areas:*** 30-35 DAS

Methods of Rice Cultivation

1. **Dry or Semi-dry upland cultivation:**
   (*a*) Broadcasting the seed
   (*b*) Sowing the seed behind the plough or drilling.
2. **Wet or lowland cultivation:**
   (*a*) Transplanting in puddled fields.
   (*b*) Broadcasting sprouted seeds in puddled fields.

- Nursery area required for transplanting in 1 ha (10000 m^2):
  Normaily: 1000 m^2 (1:10)
  1. Rice dry bed: 1000 m^2
  2. Rice wet bed: 1250-1500 m^2
  3. SRI method: 100 m^2 (1:100)
  4. Depong method: 40 m^2 (1:250)
- Paira and Utera cropping system are most practiced in Odisha, Bihar and Chhattisgarh.
- Most prominent cropping pattern of rice in India is *Rice-Wheat.*
- Rice prefer nitrogen uptake in Ammonical form (NH_4).
- Best fertilizer as basal dose is DAP followed by SSP.
- Ammonium sulphate is the best fertilizer for top dressing in rice.
- The recommended dose of N, P and K for rice crop is 100, 60 and 40 $kgha^{-1}$.
  Nitrogen Management in Rice
  1. In Direct sown rice : 2 splits
     → ½ at Tillering stage
     → ½ at PI stage
  2. Transplanted and puddled rice : 3 splits
     → ½ as Basal dose
     → ¼ at Tillering stage
     → ¼ at PI stage
  3. Biasi method : 3 splits
     → 30% as Basal dose
     → 35% at Tillering stage
     → 35% at PI stage
- **Azolla** is applied in the rice field for nitrogen fixation and enhance the organic matter in soil.
- **Azospirrillium** is a nitrogen fixing bacterium found on root surface of rice.
- The most important critical stage for irrigation is tillering to flowering. The water supply should be ensured in required amount during panicle initiation to flowering stage.
- The critical stages of rice for both fertilizer application and irrigation are Tillering and Panicle Initiation (PI).
- Rice crop requires 5 irrigations for its life cycle.
- **Rice crop has 5 critical growth stages in respect of irrigation:**
  1. Seedling
  2. Tillering
  3. Panicle Initiation (PI)
  4. Flowering
  5. Dough/Maturity
- Rice crop is a lowest water use efficiency (WUE) and highest water consuming crop, which requires 5000 litre of water to produce 1 kg of yield.
- IW/CPE ratio of rice is 1.20.
- Highest nitrogen loss in rice field occurs due to denitrification process.
- N_2 loss in rice field can be reduced by placing the ammonical fertilizer (NH_4^+) in reduced zone and nitrate fertilizer (NO_3^-) in oxidized zone.
- In low land rice, fertilizer is applied in reduced zone only.
- Mutant variety of rice is Jagannath, Prabhavati.
- World's first high yielding dwarf variety of rice evolved through conversion breeding by IRRI is Pusa Basmati-1.
- Protein rich rice variety is Sabarmati.
- Aroma in rice is due to presence of "Di-acetyl 1 propaline" chemical.
- World first rice hybrid variety was developed by China in 1976, after that India developed rice hybrid variety of APRH-1, APRH-2, KRH-1 and MGR-1 during 1994.
- Hybrid rice was developed by using Cytoplasmic Male Sterility (CMS).
- Gas emitted from rice field is CH_4 (Methane).

➢ Phalguna variety tolerance to Fe toxicity.

Rice Varieties Suitable for Cultivation in Different Condition

❖ Saline-alkaline soil	: CSR-10, CSR-13, CSR-27
❖ Salt tolerant	: Lunishree, TRY1
❖ Post flood situation	: Heera, Kalings-3
❖ Gall midge resistance	: Phalguna, Surekha, Suraksha
❖ BPH resistance	: Aruna, Chandana
❖ BLB resistance	: Ajaya, PR-10
❖ Blast resistance	: Tulsi, IR64
❖ Stem borer resistance	: IR20, Ratna, Sweta, ADJ44
❖ Drought tolerant	: Govind, Sabari
❖ Deep water rice	: Punkaj, Jagannath

- Masuri is a Dormancy resistant rice variety.
- Zinc deficiency of rice can be correctified by applying $ZnSO_4$ @ 25 kg ha^{-1}.
- Integrated Programme for Rice Development (IPRD) was implemented from 1990-91.
- Special Orientation Training Programme on Rice Production Technology: 1997-98
- Most dominated weed species in rice field is *Echinochloa spp.*
- Weeds of rice are controlled by application of:
  1. Butachlor @ 2.0 kg ai/ha PRE.
  2. Propanil @ 3.0 kg ai/ha POST.
- The right stage for harvesting as commonly is when panicles turn into golden yellow and the grains contain about 20-22 per cent moisture.
- Productivity : Highest in
  Japan - 63.00 qt/ha.
  China - 62.00 qt/ha.
  India - 20.00 qt/ha.

Classification of Rice Productivity

❖ High productivity	: Yield more than 25 qt/ha
❖ Medium productivity	: Yield more than 20-25 qt/ha
❖ Medium-Low productivity.	: Yield more than 15-20 qt/ha
❖ Low productivity	: Yield in between 10-15 qt/ha
❖ Very Low productivity	: Yield less than 10 qt/ha

- The critical percentage of moisture for harvesting and storage of paddy is 15 per cent and 10-12 per cent, respectively.
- Rice husk contains 15 to 18 per cent silica, therefore, so it is a potent source of silica for the manufacture of silicates or in glass manufacture.
- Parboiled rice contains vitamin B_{12}.
- **Oil content in rice bran:**
  - Raw rice bran: 12-18 per cent
  - Parboiled bran: 20-28 per cent
  - De-oiled bran: 1-3 per cent

➢ **Disease:**

- Akiochi disease: caused by H_2S toxicity.
- Khaira disease: caused by Zn deficiency.
- Khaira disease first reported by Y.L. Nene at Pantnagar (1966).
- Montek disease: caused by rice root nematode.
- White eye: Fe deficiency.

➢ **Dead heart and white ear** is caused by yellow stem borer of rice.

➢ **Killer disease of rice** is Bacterial Leaf Blight (BLB) and tungro virus.

➢ **Dapog method of rice:**

- Originated and commonly prevalent in Philippines.
- The Dapog nursery is constructed for the raising of seedlings without any

soil. Rice seeds contain sufficient food in the endosperm to permit the young seedlings to grow for up to 14 days without receiving any outside nutrients except air, water, and sunlight.

- 11-14 days old rice seedlings are used for transplanting.
- For nursery sowing, about 1.5 kg sprouted seeds m^2 are required.
- Seedlings from $1m^2$ area are sufficient for transplanting in 200-250 m^2.

➢ Beushening/Biasi in Rice: It is a prominent method of rice cultivation in Chhattisgarh, Bihar and Orissa. Under this system, rice seeds are broadcasted in ploughed field immediately after the onset of monsoon and the standing crop is ploughed 4 to 6 times later when 4 to 5 cm water is standing in the field. The uprooted seedlings are transplanted after biasi which is called as Chalai gap filling.

➢ **Objectives of Biasi**

- To control weeds,
- To create semi puddled conditions,
- To arrest percolation loss of water, and
- Adjust the plant population through chalai.

3.(*a*) (*ii*) Improved Agro-techniques for Chickpea

Growing chickpea is very popular in India, and it is the most important pulse crop of India. Growing chickpea commercially is a good agribusiness in India. And India ranks first in the world in terms of total chickpea production. Haryana, Madhya Pradesh, Maharashtra, Punjab and Uttar Pradesh are the major chickpea producing states in India.The chickpea (Cicer arietinum) is actually a legume of the family Fabaceae, subfamily Faboideae. It is one of the oldest pulse cash crops and cultivated throughout India since ancient times.

Sowing Season: The chickpea plants grow very well in cool climate and it is actually a winter season crop. Sow the seeds from October 10 to 25 for growing chickpea under rainfed conditions. And sow the seeds from October 25 to November 10 under irrigated conditions.

Varieties: There are actually 2 main varieties of chickpea grown in India namely the Bengal gram and the Kabuli Chana. Each variety has different characteristics. The Bengal gram variety can be of black, brown, red or even purple colored. While the Kabuli Chana variety is beige colored.

There are also some high yielding and improved chickpea varieties available. The mostly cultivated and popular chickpea varieties include Avrodhi, BG-2024, BJD-128, Gaurav, Gora Hisari, Haryana Chana, KPG-59, Pusa-Dharwad, Pusa-112, Pusa-212, Pusa-240, Pusa 261, Pusa-372, Pusa-1103, RS-10, ST-4, Sadabahar, Uday, Vijay and many more.

Seed Rate: On average, you will need around 15-18 kg chickpea seeds per acre. Although, exact amount can vary depending on the variety.

Planting: You can sow the chickpea seeds either directly into the field or in rows. For direct sowing, 40-50 plants are desirable per square meter for the Desi/Bengal gram varieties. And 25-35 plants per square meter is ideal for the Kabuli varieties.In case of planting in rows, space the rows about 12-16 inches apart. And sow the seeds at least 4 inches apart. Sow the seeds to about 2 inches deep and water lightly after sowing the chickpea seeds. And the seeds should be treated with fungicide before sowing.

Fertilizing: Applying additional fertilizer actually depends on the fertility of the soil. So, test the fertility of the soil and ask for help from your local agriculture office. In most cases, you don't have to apply additional fertilizer if you have prepared the soil in the above mentioned ways.

Irrigation: The chickpea plants generally require less watering and they grow well in dry soil. And they can be grown mainly as rainfed crop. Although adequate and timely watering can ensure good yield. In case no rains, irrigation is required prior to flowering, at flowering stage and also during the pod developing stage.

Mulching: Mulching will help to prevent most of the weeds from your field, and it will also help to retain moisture into the soil. Try to use organic materials as mulch such as dry leaves, grass clippings, straw, hay or compost.

Controlling Weeds: Weeds consume nutrients from the soil. So controlling them is important. Firstly, remove the weeds from the field while preparing the soil. And then weed again, 4-5 weeks after sowing the seeds. You can either hand control the weeds or by hoeing.

Pests and Diseases: The chickpeas are susceptible to some common pests and diseases just like many other cash crops. Ascochyta blight, cutworms, gram pod borer, grey mold, rust, sclerotinia blight and wilt are some common pests and diseases for the chickpea plants. Try to use organic methods first and then apply chemical methods for controlling these pests and diseases. Consult with an specialist in your area for having better recommendations.

Harvesting: Timely harvesting is very important for getting quality seeds. Generally,. the chickpea crop will be ready for harvesting when the leaves of the plants turn reddish-brown and start shedding from the plants. Pluck the entire plant and then let them dry in sun for about a week. And then thresh either by using a machine or by beating the plants with sticks.

Yield: Exact yield can vary from place to place. And it depends on the practices for growing chickpea. On average, you can expect a yield between 2000 and 2500 kg per hectare.

3.(*b*) Microorganisms which live in soil are algae, bacteria, actinomycetes, bacteriophages, protozoa, nematodes and fungi. A brief description of soil microorganisms has been given below:

1. **Soil Algae:** Soil algae (both prokaryotes and eukaryotes) luxuriantly grow where adequate amount of moisture and light are present. They play a variety of roles in soil. One of the important role of blue-green algae is that it has revolutionised the field of agriculture microbiology due to use of cyanobacterial biofertilizer.

2. **Bacteria:** Bacteria are the smallest unicellular prokaryotes (0.5-1 × i.0-2.0 μm), the most abundant group and usually more numerous than others, the number of which varies between 10^8 and 10^{10} cells per gram soil. However, in an agriculture field their number goes to about 3×10^9/g soil which accounts for about 3 tọnneṣ wet weight per acre.

   Based on regular presence, bacteria are divided into two groups:

   (*a*) Soil indigenous (*i.e.* true resident) or autochthonous, and

   (*b*) Soil invader or allochthonous.

3. **Actinomycetes:** Actinomycetes share the characters of both bacteria and fungi, and they are commonly known as "ray-fungi" because of their close affinity with fungi. They are Gram-positive and release antibiotic substances. However, the earthy odour of newly wetted soils has been found to be a volatile growth product of actinomycetes.

   Population of actinomycetes in soil remains greater in grass land and pasteur soil than in the cultivated land. In temperate zones the number of actinomycetes ranges from 105 to 108 per gram soil.

4. **Bacteriophages:** Bacteriophages as well as plant and animal viruses have been observed in the soil. However, there role has not been clearly understood.

5. **Protozoa:** In moist soil most of the members of microfauna remain in encysted form. The population of each group is 10^3 per gram wet soil. The role of soil protozoa is predatory, as these eat upon bacteria and thereby regulate their population.

6. **Nematodes:** Until the role of nematodes in soil was understood nematology was in infancy stage. In recent years the ecology of nematodes has been greatly advanced. Nematodes derive nutrients for their growth and reproduction from the cell contents and cytoplasm of protozoa, bacteria, fungi, etc. Some common example of protozoa is Colpoda, Pleurotricha, Heteromita, Cercomonas, Oikomonas, Phalansterium, etc

7. **Fungi:** In most of aerated or cultivated soils fungi share a major part of the total microbial biomass because of their large diameter and extensive net work of mycelium. However, population of soil fungi ranges from 2×10^4 to 1×10^6 propagules per gram dry soil and its number differs according to isolation procedure and composition of media.

   Fungi derive nutrients for their growth from organic matters, living animals (including protozoa, arthropods, nematodes, etc.) and/or living plants establishing different types of relationships.

   The root inhabiting fungi are characterized by an expanding parasitic phase on the living host with a little declining saprophytic phase after the death of the invaded host. But the soil inhabiting fungi are characterized by the ability to survive indefinitely as soil saprophyte.

   Success in competitive colonization of substrate by any particular soil fungus depends directly on its competitive saprophytic ability (CSA), inoculum potential at the surface of the substrate, and inversely as the aggregate inoculum potential of the competing fungi.

   Many unspecialized root infecting fungi can probably exist as competitive soil saprophytes in the absence of living host, they have characteristics that confer a high degree of competitive saprophytic ability such as:

   (*a*) a high mycelial growth rate allied to rapid germination of resting propagules when stimulated by nutrient diffusion from a potential substrate,

   (*b*) a sufficient arrangement of tissue-degrading enzymes,

   (*c*) production of fungistatic growth products including antibiotics,

   (*d*) tolerance of those produced by other microorganisms.

3. (*c*) Fundamental Principles of Soil Conservation:

The ultimate objective of soil conservation is to have maximum sustainable level of production from the given land piece along with maintaining the soil loss below the threshold limit. The threshold value of soil loss theoretically reveals the balance between the natural rate of soil formation and the soil erosion.

Also, the objective need to reduce the erosion for checking nutrient loss from the agricultural land, or indirectly to prevent the pollution of water bodies; to decrease the sedimentation rate in reservoirs, rivers, canals and ditches are very important. In longer term, the soil erosion is required to control the land deterioration or it gets to be abandoned which cannot be reclaimed thereafter, because of limited options for future land use. Since, soil erosion is the natural process, therefore, it cannot be prevented, but can be reduced to an acceptable limit. On this aspect, a decision is required to take, that the soil erosion rate should not affect the sustained agricultural production, along with minimizing the environmental impacts.

The chief agents of soil erosion are water and wind.

The actual art of soil conservation is based on certain basic principles which include:

(*i*) Protection of soil from impact of rain drops,

(*ii*) To slow down the water from concentrating and moving down the slope in a narrow path,

(*iii*) To slow down the water movement when it flows along the slope,

(*iv*) To encourage more water to enter into the soil,

(*v*) To increase the size of soil particles,

(*vi*) Reduction in the wind velocity near the ground by growing vegetation cover, ridging the land etc. and

(*vii*) To grow the strips of stubble or other vegetation cover which might catch and hold the moving particles of soil.

Keeping the above said principles in view, ecologists have devised following methods, which can prevent the loss of soil during its erosion.

Types and Role of Mulching in Soil Conservation:

The mulches may be of following types:

(*a*) The natural mulches are borned by nature itself, no man's effort is required.

(*b*) Synthetic Mulches:

Includes organic and inorganic liquids that are sprayed on the soil surface to form a thin film for protecting the soil against various atmospheric happenings, taking place over the top soil surface.

The different synthetic mulching materials are as under:

(*i*) Rasins

(*ii*) Asphalt emulsions

(*iii*) Latex and cut back asphalt

(*iv*) Canvas

(*v*) Plastic and paper products

(*vi*) Polythene and polyvinyle chloride (PVC)

(*vii*) Bitumen emulsions etc.

The plastic mulches are very useful for nurseries in semi-arid and arid regions. Now days, plastic mulches are available in different thicknesses and colours. Cost is also very less. Due to this reason, these mulches can be used at large scale. In respect of soil erosion/soil loss control the plastic mulch could be very promising. By spreading on erosion susceptible soils, the soil loss can be controlled, absolutely. Also, it can be used for moisture conservation and water harvesting, efficiently.

In farm ponds the longevity of stored water can be increased by lining the pond surface using plastic sheets. Apart from above, the plastic mulches are also used with drip system in different crops (horticultural) for moisture conservation and weed control points of view.

The plastic mulching is not suitable for the taller vegetations. In nurseries, the dark coloured plastic mulches make the soil surface very warm during the day hours, because black body absorbs greater heat from the sunlight. This type of characteristics results to lower diurnal and higher nocturnal temperature.

(*c*) Petroleum Mulch: The petroleum mulches are easier to apply and also less expensive. These mulches are available in the form of emulsions of asphalt in water, can be sprayed on the soil surface at ambient temperature to form a thin film in continuous form, that clings the soil, but not penetrate deeply. A thin film of petroleum substance, made so is termed as mulch film.

The mulch film increases the rate of seed germination and also plays a significant role for vigorous growth of seedlings. The surface film is also suitable for erosion control. Also, this mulch is stable against erosion, sufficiently porous to allow water in the soil, but insoluble in water and resistant enough to the weather forces causing it to last as long as necessary for vegetations to become established.

(*d*) **Conventional Mulch:** In few cases the conventional mulches such as hay or straw are more effective than the petroleum mulches. These mulches not only conserve the moisture and reduce the fluctuation of soil temperature, but also protect the soil from rain drop impact and hold the excess surface water in contact with the soil, and thus to increase the infiltration rate, and reduce the runoff and soil erosion.

In addition, during day hours these mulches also absorb as much insulation as bare soil does, but little energy is conducted downward, resulting the surface of the mulch hot and the soil remains cool. On the other hand, during night hours the mulch gets cool down and permits the soil to remain warm. The paper mulches are counted under conventional mulch, are reported to provide a remarkable result.

Paper mulches increase the soil temperature, especially of the surface soil layers. There are several evidences to show that, the paper mulching proves better performance in improvement of soil condition, besides promoting the earthworm activities. However, the toxic contents of chemicals are leached out of the paper, and develops bad effects on soil health should be avoided. The treated papers such as bitumanised have toxic effect on the plants.

(*e*) **Inorganic Mulches:**

(*i*) **Soil Mulch:**

It is an important mulch for the arid and semi-arid regions. Its application should be avoided during summer and rainy seasons, especially. The soil mulch is effective to reduce the evaporation, particularly where the soil is saturated to a lower depth below the top surface or the moisture content is in-excess of field capacity, but not in contact with water-table.

Sometimes, the soil mulches are not effective under ordinary conditions, because large amount of moisture evaporation establishes a protective dry layer of the soil, which if worked, causes excessive soil moisture loss.

In soil mulching, a loose and dry soil layer of 5 to 8 cm thick is established on the soil surface. For this purpose, the land surface is ploughed for the depth as specified above, and left for some-time to get dry; after that by planking operation the tilled soils are planned. In this way a layer of dry soil in loose condition is prepared over the soil surface, which acts as soil mulch.

The soil mulch prepared so, obstructs the capillary loss of water from the lower layers due to following reasons:

(*i*) Lack of contact with moist soil layer lying below to the open atmosphere.

(*ii*) Increase in non-capillary pore spaces.

(*iii*) Resistance to wetting.

These effects are more apparent under isothermal conditions in regards to soil and air temperature. Soil mulching has beneficial effect on soil aeration, also.

The formation of crust on top soil surface is also counted as soil mulching. It results in clogging of the soil pores, which effectively seals the lower horizons from contact with the atmosphere, and also prevents the diffusion of O_2 and CO_2.

The soil mulching becomes more effective, when it is composed of crumbs and clods of proper size not liable to get break down by the impact of subsequent rains. In sandy areas, the soil mulch should be prepared immediately after rains and renewed after subsequent rains.

The general function of mulch is to raise the soil temperature during winter season and to lower the same during summer season, by checking heat conduction through the mulched layer, and thus to maintain the soil temperature at a uniform level. In many cases, the soil mulching also plays an important role to diminish the weeds growth from the soil.

(*ii*) **Stone Mulching:**

It involves the spreading of stone pieces on the ground surface to conserve the moisture and also to reduce the wind erosion. It is a very old practice, followed in arid zones. Soil under the stone pieces tends to be in moist condition, but the soil temperature becomes slightly higher. The soils lying below the stones, harbour small animals and cause high nitrification.

The stone mulching is also used for trapping the dews, particularly in that locations where significant dew fall takes plac Central Arid Zone Research Institute, Jodhpur has reported the use of rubble mulch in combination of small fragments of stones and bricks, provides better result on moisture conservation, as compared to the synthetic mulching and mulching made by the straw materials.

(*f*) **Organic Mulches:** The tree branches, twigs, leaves, leaf litter, grasses, weeds etc. are used as organic mulch to cover the soil surface. The organic mulches are found superior than the artificial mulches in respect of moisture conservation, reduction in evaporation and runoff. By this mulch, the control of evaporation is more effective, particularly when rainfall takes place at frequent intervals, but not found so effective when the rains are few and scattered.

In other words, the infrequent rains and small showers may not be saved at all, but for the intense rains, which result a wet surface for several days with excess surface water for deep percolation, these mulches have better efficiency.

SECTION-B

5. (*a*) **Effective Scheduling of Irrigation of Wheat Under Normal and Limited Water Conditions:**

Adequate soil moisture is required for normal development of the wheat plant at all the stage of growth. The crown root initiation stage and heading stage are critical stages when plant suffers most due to moisture stress. The following schedule of irrigation should be followed by dwarf variety of wheat. In case of dwarf yielding variety as pre, sowing irrigation should be given and crop sown when the field become fit for the operation.

First Irrigation: The first irrigation to be standing crop could be given 20-25 days after sowing, *i.e.* at the crown root initiation stage. In cooler regions like hilly tracts and in late sown wheat, it is desirable to apply first irrigation approximately 25-30 days after sowing. Delay in giving this irrigation should be avoided as it result in upsetting the synchronous tillering in these varieties, subnormal heads, poor root system and finally poor grain yield. It is most critical irrigation.

Second Irrigation: At tillering stage, 40-45 days after sowing.

Third Irrigation: At late jointing stage within 70-75 days after sowing.

Fourth Irrigation: At flowering stage, within 90-95 days after sowing. Irrigation at this stage is also important because during this period plant suffer most from soil moisture deficiency. The grain number and grain size are reduced considerably.

Fifth Irrigation: At dough stage, within 110-115 days after sowing. The total number of irrigations required will vary depending upon soil type, winter rainfall amount of water applied per irrigation.

Under limited supply of water the following irrigation schedule of irrigations should be for the best adopted utilization for available quantity of water.

- Where only one irrigation was possible. Give it crown root initiation CRI stage 20-25 days after sowing.
- Where two irrigation are available, first irrigation should be given at CRI stage and second flowering stage.
- Where three irrigation are possible, first irrigation should be given at CRI stage second at late jointing (boot) stage and third at milk stage. These recommendations strongly stress the importance of irrigation at CRI stage. It has been found that each week delay in first irrigation from CRI stage results in yield reduction of 2-3 quintal per hectare.

5. (*b*) Economics of Organic Farming of Varied Agro-ecological Zones of the Country

India is bestowed with lot of potential to produce all varieties of organic products due to its agro-climatic regions. In several parts of the country, the inherited tradition of organic farming is an added advantage. This holds promise for the organic producers to tap the market which is growing steadily in the domestic market related to the export market. Currently, India ranks 33rd in terms of total land under organic cultivation and 88th position for agriculture land under organic crops to total farming area in the World. The cultivated land under certification is around 2.8 million ha. This includes one million ha under cultivation and the rest is under forest area (wild collection) (APEDA, 2010). Organic farming systems have attracted increasing attention over the last one decade because they are perceived to offer some solutions to the problems currently besetting the agricultural sector. Organic farming has the potential to provide benefits in terms of environmental protection, conservation of nonrenewable resources and improved food quality.

e.g. Economics of paddy (basmati) cultivation

➢ The per acre economics of paddy cultivation in Punjab state both under organic and conventional farming is presented as under. Most of the sample organic farmers in this region are following the concept of 'Natural farming' or 'Zero budgeting'.

➢ The cost of production (variable) per quintal of paddy was ₹ 701 under organic farming (OF) where as ₹ 427 in conventional farming (CF). It is almost 64 per cent higher in OF than CF. The average cost of cultivation of paddy in OF was ₹ 9325 per acre while the same in CF was ₹ 7818 per acre. The cost of cultivation was nearly 19 per cent higher in OF when compared to CF.

➢ Average yield per acre of paddy was 13.35 and 18.36 quintals respectively in OF and CF. The absolute difference between the yield levels was 5.01 quintal per acre. But, the unit price of paddy was higher (30 per cent) in OF relative to CF. There was no significant unit price differences in fodder prices. The average net returns per acre of paddy cultivation were ₹ 17828 and ₹ 20897 respectively in OF and CF. However, the differences between the gross returns per acre of these farming were marginal (₹ 95 only).

➢ Among different cost break-ups, the actual costs on weeding and harvesting operations were significantly higher in OF when compared to CF. It clearly indicates the more labour incentive nature of OF than CF. The relative costs on fertilizer application was higher in OF while the same on plant protection was higher in CF.

➢ The costs on the remaining cost items were more or less equal in both types. Since, many organic farmers are started practicing organic methods from last two or three years, it takes some more time to stabilize or increase the yields further under organic farming. The premium prices for paddy helping the organic farmers in Punjab to cover their higher costs to some extent.

Economics of Paddy Cultivation

	OF	CF	CF=100
Land preparation	1265	1307	97
Seed cost	320	279	115
Sowing cost	1790	1815	99
Fertilizer cost	1955	1760	111
Inter cultivation/Weeding	1245	471	264
Plant protection cost	310	928	33
Irrigation cost	310	72	431
Harvesting cost	1180	771	153
Threshing cost	510	300	170
Marketing cost	440	115	383
Other costs	0	0	-
Total cost of cultivation	9325	7818	119
Yield (Kg)	1335	1836	73
Price (₹)	19.5	15	130
Fodder (Qtl)	11.2	12.5	90
Price (₹)	100	94	106
Total revenue	27153	28715	95
Net returns	17828	20897	85
Cost of production (per Qtl)	701	427	164

5. (*c*) Importance of Extension Education

- Extension uses democratic methods in educating the farmers.
- Extension Helps in adoption of innovations.
- Extension helps in studying and solving the rural problems.
- Extension increases farm yields and improve the standard of living of farmers.
- Extension makes good communities better and progressive.
- Extension contributes to national development programmes.

Scope of Extension Education

It includes all activities of rural development. So extension programmes should be dynamic and flexible. The areas indicating scope of Extension are listed below:

- Increasing efficiency in agricultural production.
- Increasing efficiency in marketing, distribution and utilization of agricultural inputs and outputs.
- Conservation, development and use of natural resources.
- Proper farm and home management.
- Better family living.
- Youth development.
- Leadership development.
- Community and rural development.
- Improving public affairs for all round development.

Objectives of Extension Education:

- To raise the standard of living of the rural people by helping them in right use of their resources.
- To help in planning and implementing the family and village plans for increasing production in various occupations.
- To provide facilities for better family living.
- To provide knowledge and help for better management of farms and increase incomes.
- To encourage the farmers to grow his own food, eat well and live well.

- To promote better social, natural recreational intellectual and spiritual file among the people.
- To help rural families in better appreciation of SWOT in the village.
- To open new opportunities for developing talents and leadership of rural.

5. (*d*) e-NAM:

The National Agriculture Market (NAM) is a pan-India electronic trading portal, which links the existing Agricultural Produce Market Committee (APMC) mandis across the country to form a unified national market for agricultural commodities.

The NAM portal is a single window service for any information and services related to APMC that includes:

- Commodity arrivals and prices
- Buy and sell trade offers
- Provision to respond to trade offers, among other services

The NAM reduces the transaction costs and information irregularity even when the agriculture produce continues to flow through the mandis.

Safeguard the Interests of Farm Producers

The states can administer agriculture marketing as per their agri-marketing regulations, under which, the State is divided into various market areas and each market area is administered by a separate APMC which will impose its own marketing regulation that include fees.

- A nation-wide e-market portal for transparent sale and transactions and price discovery in the regulated markets.
- The States can promote the e-trading as per their APMC Act and enact suitable provision under the act by their State Agricultural Marketing Board/APMC.
- Liberal licensing of traders or buyers and commission agents by State authorities without any pre-condition of physical presence or possession of shop or premises in the market yard.
- One license for a trader valid across all markets in the State.
- Synchronisation of quality standards of agricultural commodities and facility for assessing (quality testing) infrastructure in every market to facilitate informed bidding by buyers.
- Single point tax of market fees on the first wholesale purchase from the farmer.
- Soil Testing Laboratories facility in/or near the particular mandi to help visiting farmers to access this provision in the mandi itself.
- **Farmers:** They can sell products without the interference of any brokers or middlemen thereby making competitive returns out of their investment.
- **Traders:** Traders will be able to do secondary trading from one APMC to another one anywhere in India. Local traders can get access to the larger national market for secondary trading.
- Buyers, Processers & Exporters

Buyers like large retailers, processors or exporters will be able to source commodities from any mandi in India thereby reducing the inter-mediation cost. Their physical presence and dependence on intermediaries will not be needed.

- Consumers

NAM will increase the number of traders and the competition among them increases. This translates into stable prices and availability to the consumers.

- Mandis

There will be a reduction in bookkeeping and reporting system as it will be generated automatically. Monitoring and regulation of traders and commission agents become easy. Transparency in the process eliminates the scope of manipulation of tendering/auctioning process. Market allocation fee will increase due to an accounting of all transactions taking place in the market. It will reduce the manpower requirements as the tendering/auctioning process is carried out electronically. For instance, the system declares the winner of lots within a few seconds. It eliminates information asymmetry as all the activities of an APMC can be known directly from the website.

- Others

NAM aims to improve the marketing aspect of the agriculture sector. With one license for the entire state and single point levy, an entire state becomes a market and the market fragmentation within the same state gets abolished.

5. (*e*) Farmers Producer Organisation" (FPO) and its Significance for Farmers

A Producer Organisation (PO) is a legal entity formed by primary producers, viz. farmers, milk producers, fishermen, weavers, rural artisans, craftsmen. A PO can be a producer company, a cooperative society or any other legal form which provides for sharing of profits/benefits among the members. In some forms like producer companies, institutions of primary producers can also become member of PO.

"Farmers Producer Organisation" (FPO) is one type of PO where the members are farmers. Small Farmers' Agribusiness Consortium (SFAC) is providing support for promotion of FPOs. PO is a generic name for an organization of producers of any produce, *e.g.*, agricultural, non-farm products, artisan products, etc.

Small holders had a mean farm size of 0.5 hectare and that too in 5 to 10 small plots. The small holding size will not produce enough food to support the family. Such small holders constitute the vast majority of farmers in the developing countries including India. Because they are scattered individuals, they have little or no bargaining power or political influence in securing loans from scheduled banks (fewer than 4% of small holders have agricultural credit cards) and very few smallholder farmers carry crop insurance against natural calamities, etc. In addition, smallholders are especially vulnerable to climate change-aggravated weather events, like untimely rains (especially at harvest times), severe droughts and floods, hailstorms and pest infestations, any of which can wipe out their crops. They also continue to suffer from market uncertainties as most agricultural policies (and institutional support) tend to favour large farmers and agricultural or food corporations, *e.g.*, industrial agriculture receives 80% of the farm subsidies and 90% of any research funds.

All of the above constitute an unprecedented agrarian crisis and over the last two decades it has resulted in most (87%) rural households suffering from extreme poverty and serious deprivations - more than 200,000 farmers have committed suicide in India. This agrarian crisis situation is more or less similar in other developing Asian countries, where many rural smallholders suffer from poverty, malnutrition, dispossession of land assets, and death.

Farmer producer organizations were proposed as a way forward to get some form of land consolidation - and an integration of smallholders within an agricultural value chain - which is critical to tackle the problem rural agrarian crisis. Such a consolidation, together with appropriate training and skill development of rural youth for emerging farm and non-farm jobs, would appear to be the key to lifting one billion poor people out of poverty worldwide. In some countries like China, India, Indonesia and Vietnam, smallholder farmers have already begun to come together and form Farmers Producer

Organizations (FPOs), most of which are Farmer Producer Companies (FPCs). For example, in April 2013, the Government of India issued a National Policy and Process Guidelines document on formation of FPOs. This set of Guidelines encouraged State Governments to provide incentives, including credits for and support of the formation and ongoing operation of FPOs in various states. By September 2013, over 500 FPOs had been formed and are now successfully operating throughout the country. Those FPOs which are set up as FPCs enable their members to access financial and other inputs and services, including appropriate technologies for farming. The FPCs also organize collection, processing, storage and marketing of their members' produce in high-value markets at an optimal price. These actions by the FPCs have thus reduced transaction costs and allowed the FPCs to enter into a partnership with private and public sector companies for purposes of supplying farm produce on more equal terms.

8. (*a*) Benefits of the Co-operative Marketing

- Direct contacts with final buyers
- Increase in the bargaining strength
- Credit provision
- Storage opportunities
- Market information
- Transport
- Standardizing and grading
- Influencing the market prizes

Hindering Forces for Cooperative Movement in India

The major hindering forces for cooperative movement in India is the Government. There are also some other problems which are explained below:

(1) Non-accountability: It is like if a child when given too many benefits it gets spoiled. The same is the case with cooperatives in India. The government gave too many benefits to cooperatives like reservation of items, extra benefits like finance facilities so also it was also provided with other support this was a good thing to do, but then there was no further accountability which led to these cooperatives becoming more and more lethargic. Besides as there was no competition they became more and more costly they were not at all efficient and the worst part was that the government allowed them to function like this and pass on the burden of costs to consumers.

(2) Vested interest of some people: A lot of times people who are in position in control of cooperatives are actually people who have joined cooperatives for personal gains. One of the major problems this causes is conflicting of personal interests with the interest of the cooperatives now this affects the performance of the cooperatives in a negative way.

(3) Lack of coordination: Generally what happens in cooperatives is that different cooperatives at different level don't coordinate this makes the work of cooperatives difficult. Coordination is the key to success of any organization. The best example for this is AMUL which works best because of coordination.

(4) The Internal Free Rider Problem: This problem arises when:

(*a*) New members who provide very little capital enjoy the same benefits as long-standing or founding members who have major investments in the cooperative in fixed assets (plant, machinery, equipment) and working capital;

(*b*) When the patronage of new members does not make the cooperative much more efficient or competitive by producing significant economies of scale. New members get a "free ride" on the investments and other efforts of existing members, thereby diluting the returns to existing members. In this situation, new members do not have much incentive to provide capital because it will not appreciate in value and existing members have little incentive to provide capital that will disproportionately benefit new members.

(5) Quality more than Quantity: This is another major problem faced by different cooperatives who go in for quantity this causes a major problem because they think it's a quick way to earn money so this basically affects the productivity.

(6) No Balanced Growth: The cooperatives in northeast areas and in areas like West Bengal, Bihar, Odisha are not as well developed as the ones in Maharashtra and the ones in Gujarat. There is a lot of friction due to competition between different states, this friction affects the working of cooperatives.

(7) Political Interference: Now this is the biggest problem faced by Sugar cooperatives in Maharashtra. The Politicians use the sugar coops as if they are their personal property and also they use it to their political advantage. This is the biggest problem of cooperatives as they use them to increase their vote bank. They also get their own favourites on the boards of such boards so they are on control these cooperatives.

8. Causes of Slow Progress:

***(i)* Lack of Knowledge:** Knowledge of the principles of co-operation is an essential condition for the success of the movement. In most cases, however, this condition was not fulfilled. Members did not understand and appreciate the aims, objectives, and the possibilities of the movement. They joined a society only as 'clients of convenience' and deserted it after their needs were met. There was no genuine urge to develop the movement.

***(ii)* Small Size:** An other reason for the poor performance of the movement was that "a large number of primary agricultural credit societies were neither viable nor even potentially viable and must be regarded as inadequate and unsatisfactory agencies for dispensing production oriented credit."

***(iii)* Rapid Growth:** The qualitative aspect of the movement suffered on account of the 'waves of promotional enthusiasm' which superimposed co-operative societies by the thousands on villages where patient work had not laid the foundations for successful growth. This policy of hurried expansion or 'target hunting' led to the formation of a number of societies which were either still born or suffered an early death.

***(iv)* Uninspiring Leadership:** A major factor responsible for the poor performance of the movement was the lack of "competent leaders on a scale commensurate with the considerable expansion" that took place in the movement. The leadership thrown up by the movement was inadequate, incompetent, faction-ridden and lacking in knowledge, integrity, and dedication. No wonder, that the movement continued to be dominated by money-lenders and others who used its funds to promote their own ends, financial or political.

***(v)* Lack of Supervision, Audit and Inspection:** Another defect was that the co-operative societies were neither strictly supervised nor properly audited. From non-existent or ineffective supervision arose many other weaknesses such as 'book adjustment of debts, bogus loans, misutilisation of credit, and failure to effect recoveries' and window-dressing. Even where accounts were properly audited, audit objections were seldom attended to.

(vi) Lack of Spontaneity: To co-operative movement was officially sponsored in 1904. Ever since its birth, it remained govt., controlled, govt. financed and govt. directed. This rigid official control and interference did great harm in the sense that it provided few opportunities for the people to learn to do things for themselves, to develop a spirit of self-reliance and self-dependence.

In the words of Pandit Nehru, "if govt., money comes, that money is followed by govt. officials the petty official becomes not only the petty boss but big boss." The movement, therefore, functioned at best as a govt., department; it never developed into a genuine people's movement.

(vii) Lack of Proper Atmosphere: Co-operation is a democratic movement based on the principle of equality. But the socio-economic background of the Indian village, especially in areas with long-standing feudal relations, was hardly conducive to its proper functioning and healthy growth.

The caste system, inadequate spread of literacy, and types of land tenures prevailing in certain areas, prevented the co-operative institutions from operating strictly in accordance with democratic principles. This was particularly the case where there were large disparities between members not only in economic terms but also in respect of factors such as influence, authority and social status. The movement would have succeeded had it incorporated a frontal attack on the existing power structure in the village. It instead aimed at improving conditions without disturbing the socio-economic set up. No wonder, the movement failed to take roots or grow rapidly.

(viii) Piecemeal Approach: According to Dr. Gyan Chand, the failure of the movement was largely due to co-operation having been conceived and worked in a 'fragmentary way'. Rural credit, marketing, small industries, better farming, production and distribution of milk, animal husbandry, irrigation, processing all were treated in isolation; the interrelations of these activities or their bearing on one another or on the rural economy as a whole were never kept in mind. This "gravely hampered in the realisation of their potential."

(ix) Defective Loan Policies and Procedures: Loan policies and procedures followed by co-operative institutions were not adopted in accordance with the much publicized crop-loan system. Loans were mostly given on the security of land and not on anticipated crop.

The entire amount was given out in lump sum instead of being paid in instalments; loans were generally given in cash and not in kind. In addition, there were inordinate delays in the disbursement of loans. These defective, cumbersome, and dilatory procedures and policies made the societies unpopular and stood in the way of the speedier growth of the movement.

(*x*) **Structural Obsolescence:** The co-operative organisation was based on the principle of federalism under which local societies were federated into a secondary society which, in turn, federated into a tertiary and finally a national society. Whatever its other advantages, this system, in practice, became 'self-defeating' in as much as the weaknesses of the local unit got pooled at the secondary society level with the result that the secondary institutions, instead of facilitating the working of the primaries, became a drag on them.

(*xi*) **Inefficient Management:** Most of the general ills from which co-operative institutions suffered such as the lack of proper accounting, irregularities of loans, maintenance of records, were largely due to a lack of trained and qualified staff. In 1965-66, only 14% of the societies had full-time paid secretary-manager. Even the working of higher institutions suffered on account of the dearth of trained and qualified personnel. Despite the introduction of training programme, the quality of staff in the cooperative institutions had not attained a high standard of efficiency. Recruitment was not based on merit but on a candidate's capacity to pull wires. That is why there were complaints of inefficiency, graft, corruption and accumulation of over-dues.

(*xii*) **Absence of Self-Help:** One of the major failures of the movement was its inability to develop the habit of thrift and savings amongst its members. This may be seen from the fact that, in 1965-66 the share of borrowings in the working capital of credit societies was 66%, the percentage of owned funds to working capital being only 27%. This means that the movement was not self-sufficient or self-financing but had degenerated into a conduit for channeling stale funds. This too much dependence on slate finances had made the co-operative societies "a semi-state organisation in which there was hardly any initia-tive, auto activity, or autonomy___".

(*xiii*) **Over-Dues:** Another very disquieting feature of the movement was the incidence of over- dues. From a small figure of rupees six crores in 1950-51, they mounted to rupees 125 crores in 1965-66, recording a more than 20 times increase. The proportion of over-dues to out standings also went up from 22% in 1950-51 to 29% in 1965-66.

Even in an advanced state like Maharashtra, over dues constituted 21% of the outstanding loans in 1964-65. It was the failure in this respect (over dues) that mainly accounts for the stagnation in the movement.

(*xiv*) **Vested Interests:** A more disturbing trend, however, was the domination of co-operative institutions by group politics. Communalism and casteism were other factors eating into its vitals.

The result was that either a society did not do much work or there was favouritism and nepotism in the grant of loans restricting the benefits to favoured members. There were instances where members of rival faction persuaded people not to repay their dues.

As commerce pointed out, the sudden rise of over-dues in 1961-62 was directly connected with the general election of 1962. Political interests were thus affecting the working of co-operative institutions in various ways causing credit to be denied to certain groups and providing it to others in violation of all rules in force. This led Jaya Parkash Narain to condemn co-operative societies as "tools of self-aggrandizement."

(xv) Benefit to the Rich: The gravest flaw of the movement was that it had become 'a combination of the strong not for the week but against them.' It had been almost completely captured by the rich and middle farmers with the result that credit went beyond the reach of precisely those who needed it the most but whose assets were scanty.

8. (*b*) Features of Prime Minister Fasal Bima Yojana (PMFBY)

The PMFBY was launched in 2016 and replaces all the prevailing yield insurance schemes in India. The scheme has been launched with an impetus on crop sector. The scheme has extended coverage under localized risks, post-harvest losses etc. and aims at adoption of technology for the purpose of yield estimation. Through increased farmer awareness and low farmer premium rates the scheme aims at increasing the crop insurance penetration in India.

Objective:

Pradhan Mantri Fasal Bima Yojana (PMFBY) aims at supporting sustainable production in agriculture sector by way of :

(*a*) Providing financial support to farmers suffering crop loss/damage arising out of unforeseen events.

(*b*) Stabilizing the income of farmers to ensure their continuance in farming.

(*c*) Encouraging farmers to adopt innovative and modern agricultural practices.

(*d*) Ensuring flow of credit to the agriculture sector; which will contribute to food security, crop diversification and enhancing growth and competitiveness of agriculture sector besides protecting farmers from production risks.

Eligibility Criteria

- **Compulsory Component:** All farmers availing Seasonal Agricultural Operations (SAO) loans from Financial Institutions (*i.e.* loanee farmers) for the notified crop(s) would be covered compulsorily.
- **Voluntary Component:** The Scheme would be optional for the non-loanee farmers.

Coverage of Risks and Exclusions:

Following stages of the crop and risks leading to crop loss are covered under the scheme.

- **Prevented Sowing/ Planting Risk:** Insured area is prevented from sowing/ planting due to deficit rainfall or adverse seasonal conditions.
- **Standing Crop (Sowing to Harvesting):** Comprehensive risk insurance is provided to cover yield losses due to non- preventable risks, *viz.* Drought, Dry spells, Flood, Inundation, Pests and Diseases, Landslides, Natural Fire and Lightening, Storm, Hailstorm, Cyclone, Typhoon, Tempest, Hurricane and Tornado.
- **Post-Harvest Losses:** Coverage is available only up to a maximum period of two weeks from harvesting for those crops which are allowed to dry in cut and spread condition in the field after harvesting against specific perils of cyclone and cyclonic rains and unseasonal rains.

- **Localized Calamities:** Loss/damage resulting from occurrence of identified localized risks of hailstorm, landslide, and Inundation affecting isolated farms in the notified area.

Key Features of PMFBY:

Low Farmer Premium Rates

- The rate of Insurance Charges payable by the farmer will be as per the following table

Sr. No.	Season	Crops	Maximum Insurance Charges Payable By Farmer (% Of Sum Insured)
1	Kharif	All food grain and Oilseed crops (all Cereals, Millets, Pulses and Oilseed crops)	2.0% of SI or Actuarial rate, whichever is less
2	Rabi	All food grain and Oilseed crops (all Cereals, Millets, Pulses and Oilseed crops)	1.5% of SI or Actuarial rate, whichever is less
3	Kharif and Rabi	Annual Commercial/Annual Horticultural crops	5% of SI or Actuarial rate, whichever is less

- **Use of Technology:** The new scheme envisages many new things such as utilizing innovative technologies like satellite imagery, vegetation indices etc. coupled with the mandatory usage of smart phones/hand held devices for increasing the speed and accuracy during yield estimation. In order to minimize the area discrepancy in coverage, the scheme also promotes the digitization of land records.
- **Increased Farmer Awareness :** Efforts are being made to increase the awareness amongst farmers regarding PMFBY so that maximum number of farmers can enroll and avail benefits of the scheme.
- **Better Coverage:** Pradhan Mantri Fasal Bima Yojana (PMFBY) aims at covering the losses suffered by farmers due to reduction in crop yield as estimated by the local appropriate government authorities.
- The scheme also covers pre sowing losses, post-harvest losses due to cyclonic rains and losses due to unseasonal rainfall in India. There is a provision to cover losses due to localized calamities such as inundation also in addition to the previously covered hailstorm and landslide risks.

Better than Earlier Insurance Schemes

While the idea of insuring farmers against crop losses isn't new, the PMFBY is an attempt to plug the holes in the older crop insurance schemes - the National Agriculture Insurance scheme (NAIS) introduced in 1999 and the Modified NAIS (mNAIS) introduced in 2011.

These older schemes didn't find too many takers among farmers, the main dampener being their limited risk coverage. In mNAIS, the premium was capped at 8 to 12 per cent of the sum insured to limit the government's subsidy outgo. Thus, for crops where actuarial rates were higher (that is, the premiums were steeper), insurance companies proportionally reduced the sum insured. Many a time, the 'compensation' fell way short of even the farmer's cost of production.

The Fasal Bima Yojana has done away with this cap on premium. The sum insured per hectare for a farmer is now decided by the District Level Technical Committee and is pre-declared and notified by the State Level

Coordination Committee on Crop Insurance. The farmer also pays less - the premium he shells out is 2 per cent of the sum insured for all kharif crops and 1.5 per cent of it for all rabi crops. For horticulture and commercial crops, the premium is 5 per cent of sum covered. The remaining premium is paid by the government.

Sl. No	Feature	NAIS [1999]	MNAIS [2010]	PM Crop Insurance Scheme
1	Premium rate	Low	High	Lower than even NAIS (Govt to contribute 5 times that of farmer)
2	One Season - One Premium	Yes	No	Yes
3	Insurance Amount cover	Full	Capped	Full
4	On Account Payment	No	Yes	Yes
5	Localised Risk coverage	No	Hail storm, Land slide	Hail storm, Land slide, Inundation
6	Post Harvest Losses coverage	No	Coastal areas- for cyclonic rain	All India - for cyclonic + unseasonal rain
7	Prevented Sowing coverage	No	Yes	Yes
8	Use of Technology (for quicker settlement of claims)	No	Intended	Mandatory
9	Awareness	No	No	Yes (target to double coverage to 50%)

8. (*c*) In general sense, the term training implies the act of imparting a special skill or behaviour to a person, which is commonly offered to employees of operational level. It is not exactly same as education, which is a process of systematic learning something in an institution that develops a sense of judgment and reasoning in employees. It is offered to all employees equally, irrespective of their grades or level in the corporate ladder.

These two are so closely intertwined that with the passage of time the difference between training and education is getting increasingly blurred. Nevertheless, these two terms are different in their nature and orientation. The worker, who takes training, in the organization, is said to have had some education and thus, there is no training, without education.

Training is nothing but learning by doing. It is a well-planned program aimed at developing specific skills and knowledge of the manpower. It is a common concept of human resource development where an attempt is made to improve the performance, productivity and competency of the existing and potential employees through learning. The program is specially designed by the organisation to achieve definite goals.

Training helps in imparting job-related skills in the employees so that they can do the job efficiently and effectively. Training can be on-the-job or off-the-job, paid or unpaid, part time or full time, depending on the contract with the employer.

By the term education, we mean learning in the classroom to acquire certain knowledge. Education does not equal to schooling, but it refers to what a person gains while he is in school or college. It is aimed to deliver knowledge about facts, events, values, beliefs, general concepts, principles, etc. to the students. This helps in developing a sense of reasoning, understanding, judgement and intellect in an individual.

The lessons learned during the process of education helps a person to face future challenges, and it prepares a person for future jobs. Nowadays, education is not confined to classroom learning, but new methods are implemented that offers practical knowledge about the world.

Difference between Training and Education

The significant differences between training and education are mentioned in the following points:

- Training refers to an act of inculcating specific skills in a person. Education is all about gaining theoretical knowledge in the classroom or any institution.
- Training is a way to develop specific skills, whereas education is a typical system of learning.
- Training is completely based on practical application, which is just opposite in the case of education that involves theoretical orientation.
- The concept of training is narrow while the concept of education is comparatively wider.
- Training involves hands-on experience regarding the particular job. On the other hand, education involves learning in the classroom.
- The term of education is longer than the duration of training.
- The training prepares a person for the present job. Conversely, education prepares a person for future job and challenges.
- The purpose of training is to improve the performance and productivity of employees. As opposed to education, where the purpose is to develop a sense of reasoning and judgement.
- During training, a person learns, how to do a specific task. Unlike Education, which teaches about the general concepts.

Comparison between Training and Education

Basis For Comparison	Training	Education
Meaning	The process of inculcating specific skills in a person is training.	Theoretical learning in the classroom or any institution is education.
What is it?	It is a method of skill development.	It is a typical form of learning.
Based on	Practical application	Theoretical orientation
Perspective	Narrow	Wide
Involves	Job experience	Classroom learning
Term	Short term	Comparatively long term
Prepares for	Present job	Future job
Objective	To improve performance and productivity.	To develop a sense of reasoning and judgement.
Teaches	Specific task	General concepts

PAPER-II

SECTION-B

1. (*a*) **Chromosomal Aberrations:** Chromosomal aberrations are abnormalities in the structure or number of chromosomes and are often responsible for genetic disorders. For more than a century, scientists have been fascinated by the study of human chromosomes. It was not until 1956, however, that it was determined that the actual diploid number of chromosomes in a human cell was forty-six (22 pairs of autosomes and two sex chromosomes make up the human genome). In 1959 two discoveries opened a new era of genetics. Jerome Lejeune, Marthe Gautier, and M. Raymond Turpin discovered the presence of an extra chromosome in Down syndrome patients. And C. E. Ford and his colleagues, P. A. Jacobs and J. A. Strong first observed sex chromosome anomalies in patients with sexual development disorders.

Structural Aberrations and Their Genetic Significance: In this category, aberration alters the chromosome structure but do not involve a change in chromosome number. The mechanics signify chiefly a rearrangement through loss, gain or reallocation of chromosomal segments.

However, the structural aberrations of chromosomes can be classified into four common types, which are as follows:

Deletion: The loss of a chromosome segment is known as deletion or deficiency. The deletion of a portion of chromosome is a very rare event. It produces some striking genetic and morphological / physiological consequences. Each deletion gives rise to a distinct set of symptoms which characterizes an abnormality and called as a syndrome.

A specific deletion in chromosome no. 22 produces a condition, called 'Philadelphia 22'; this is associated with chronic myelogenous leukemia. Again, another deficiency in chromosome no. 5 creates 'Cri-du-chat' (cry-of-cat) syndrome where the individuals produce a characteristic mewing cry like cat during childhood. They also possess some unique facial features and exhibit severe physical as well as mental retardations.

Duplication: The presence of an additional chromosome segment (as compared to that of normal number) in a nucleus is known as duplication. In this process, a segment of a chromosome is added to another chromosome; the extra part of the chromosome constitute duplication when this extra-chromosome segment is located immediately after the normal segment following the same orientation (*i.e.* the same gene sequence is maintained), it is called Tandem duplication.

When the gene sequence in the extra-chromosome occurs in a reverse order, it is known as Reverse duplication. The Reverse duplication is almost same as Tandem duplication, but here the additional segment is inverted in order. For example, the sequence will be e d c in place of c d e. Sometimes, the additional segment is found to be located in the same chromosome but away from the normal segment: such cases are termed as displaced duplication. Another case is the Translocation duplication, when the additional chromosome segment is found to be translocated into a non-homologous chromosome.

In general, duplications do not produce any drastic consequences as like deletion in terms of phenotype and survival. It has been postulated that the increase in DNA content per cell accompanied the process of evolution; the origin of new genes with distinct functions was possible only for the event of duplication.

Inversion: When a segment of a chromosome is found to be oriented in reverse direction, it is called inversion. Two breaks are required within a chromosome to get this situation. The segment rotates in 180° angle and reinserted between the breaks. As a result, the linear order of the genes becomes exactly opposite, in comparison to its normal homologous segment.

Suppose, the normal order of a few genes in a segment of the chromosome is ABCDE (in the original chromosome). If an inversion takes place between B and D (*i.e.* BCD segment), the order of the genes in the inverted segment will be ADCBE.

However, inversion may be of two types - Paracentric inversion and Pericentric inversion. If the inverted segment does not contain a centromere, it is termed as Paracentric inversion. But if it contains a centromere, it is called Pericentric inversion.

Translocation: Integration of chromosome segment into a non-homologous chromosome is known as translocation. It involves the transfer of a segment of chromosome to a different part of the same chromosome or a different chromosome. There are three basic types of translocation-simple, reciprocal and shift.

Simple translocation shows an attachment of a small terminal segment of a chromosome to the end of a homologous chromosome or to a non-homologous chromosome. This attachment is not a fusion at all. In Reciprocal translocation, the breakage takes place in two non-homologous chromosomes, and is followed by the reunion of broken segment to the wrong partners. Shift translocation requires at least three breaks in the chromosome. Among these, Reciprocal, and shift are the most common types.

The somatic cells of a diploid organism contain two sets of homologous chromosomes ($2n$ number of chromosomes)

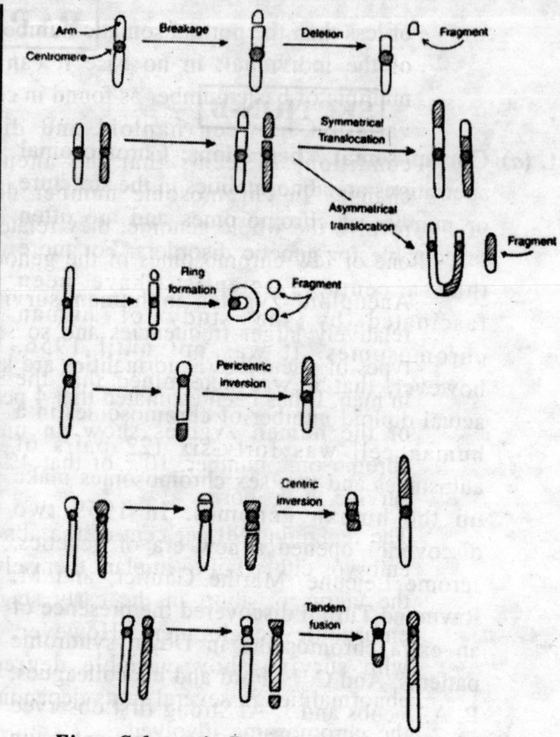

Fig. : Schematic Representation of Aberration (Chromosome Structure) Structural Chromosome Aberration

or in other words, two copies of the same genome are present. But their gametes contain a single genome i.e. haploid number of chromosomes (n). A deviation from the diploid state represents a numerical chromosome aberration which is often referred as heteroploidy. Individuals having the variant chromosome number are known as heteroploids. Heteroploids can be divided into two classes-aneuploidy and euploidy.

Aneuploidy: Some individuals show a loss or a gain of one or few chromosomes as compared to the somatic chromosome number of that species. The situation is known as Aneuploidy. The phenomenon arises due to non-disjunction or abnormal distribution of chromosomes during anaphase of meiosis.

Therefore, the Aneuploid is an organism or a cell having one or few chromosomes more, or less than the normal somatic number (2n) of the individual; in no case it can be a multiple of basic number as found in case of variation between haploid and diploid condition. It seems that the aneuploid changes in chromosome number do not involve the whole genome; they relate only one or few chromosomes of the genome.

Aneuploid zygotes in human survive in relatively larger frequencies and so several types of aneuploid abnormalities are known in man. It has been estimated that 4 per cent of the human zygotes show an unusual chromosome number. 10% of that 4% only survive to be borne.

The remaining 90 per cent of the abnormal embryos either fail to implant themselves in the uterus or abort in the early stages of embryonic development. However, those who survive show variable degrees of abnormalities in several traits depending on the chromosome involved.

Genetic Significance:

- **Role in Evolution:** The study of the karyotypes of different species has revealed interesting facts about the plant kingdom. It has been demonstrated that individuals in wild populations are, to some extent, heterogeneous cytologically and genetically. In some cases, even if the genes are identical they may be ordered in a different way, owing to alterations of the chromosomal segments. These changes have an important bearing on the evolution of species.
- **Genetic Analysis:** Chromosomal aberrations have been very helpful in genetic analysis. Trans-located strains of maize were used to demonstrate that a cytological exchange of chromosome parts results into genetic recombination. In different crop species, translocations, duplications and deficiencies have been used in mapping of gene locus.
- **Role in Plant Breeding:** Aberrations result in altered linkage relationships and this has been exploited for breeding experiments.

1. (*b*) Role of Heterosis in Crop Improvements

- Gains in yield and yield stability offered by heterosis have prompted use of hybrids in several crops.
- Genetic yielding ability has been increased greatly, and thus total production has been increased, with minimal dependence on chemical inputs and maximum use of biological power.
- Enthusiasm and funds have been directed to hybrid breeding, in part because of the proven efficiency of the inbred/hybrid method for producing products that farmers need and want, and in part because private capital was attracted to the profit potential of hybrid breeding and sales.
- The inbred/hybrid method has given breeders greater precision in developing, identifying, and multiplying the best hybrid genotypes in cross-pollinated crops.

Heterosis in Plant Breeding: Heterosis is observed in almost every crop species studied, the application of this phenomenon for its commercial exploitation depends on the expression of the degree of heterosis. This phenomenon is commercially used to produce hybrid or synthetic varieties, which needs the maximisation of its expression and also fixation.

Maximisation of hybrid vigour (HF_1) can be achieved by increasing either 'd' (directional dominance) or 'y' (initial differences in gene frequency between parents), *i.e.*, choosing genetically divergent parents, $HF_1 = \Sigma dy^2$.

Fixation of hybrid vigour is needed for its commercial application which can be done by vegetative propagation, or by stable apomictic reproduction, or by transferring heterozygosity to polyploid or fixation by obtaining structural heterozygotes.

Fixation of heterosis in crops like potato, sweet potato, sugarcane, sugarbeet and many ornamental plants can be achieved by vegetative propagation as there seeds are not essential. Incorporation of genes conditioning vegetative apospory or diploid parthenogenesis in hybrid seed crops may lead to a permanent heterozygote advantage.

Heterozygosity can be maintained or saved from being lost due to segregation by converting diploid heterozygotes into tetraploid or hexaploid. Incorporation of gaudensvelans combination helps to survive only the heterozygotes not the homozygous combination - such mechanism may be introduced in crop plants, thereby hybrid vigour can be fixed with great success.

Heterosis or hybrid vigour have been commercially utilised in both cross pollinated and in some self-pollinated species. In most of the cases the utilisation of this heterosis phenomenon is not successful because of difficulty in production of large quantities of hybrid seeds. This is particularly difficult in self-pollinated species. Few example there the heterosis has been Utilised for improvement of the crop plant are:

Crop Species: Asexually propagated species and also cross pollinated species like maize, jowar, bajra, sunflower, legume, cotton, etc.

Vegetable Crops: Tomato, brinjal, onions, cucurbits, etc.

Fruits: In almost all the fruit trees.

1. (*c*) Rice (Oryza sativa L., $2n = 2x = 24$) is second most widely grown cereal crop and the staple food for more than half of world's population, providing two thirds of calorie intake for more than three billion people in Asia and one-third of calorie intake of nearly 1.5 billion people in Africa and Latin America. It is probably a descendent of wild grass that was most likely cultivated in the foothills of the far Eastern Himalayas.

Some believes that the rice plant may have originated in southern India, then spread to the north of the country and then onwards to China. It then arrived in Korea, the Philippines (about 2000 B.C.) and then Japan and Indonesia (about 1000 B.C.). When Alexander the Great invaded India in 327 B.C., it is believed that he took rice back to Greece. Arab travellers took it to Egypt, Morocco and Spain and that is how it travelled all across Europe.

Portugal and Netherlands took rice to their colonies in West Africa and then it travelled to America through the "Columbian Exchange" of natural resources. But as is traditionally known, rice is a slow starter and this is also true to the fact that it took close to two centuries after the voyages of Columbus for rice to take root in the Americas. Thereafter the journey of rice continues with the Moors taking it to Spain in 700 A.D. and then the Spanish brought rice to South America at the beginning of 17th century.

The Rice Breeding Platform will innovate, develop, and apply modern breeding strategies, tools and technologies to increase rice yield, climate resilience, and enable access to modern breeding technologies for world's rice varietal development programs through knowledge sharing and capacity development.

Improvement in the yield potential of rice is the major strategy to increase world rice production. Various strategies to increase the yield potential include: conventional hybridization, ideotype breeding, heterosis breeding, male sterility, wide hybridization, genetic engineering and molecular marker assisted breeding.

Conventional breeding is still a widely used strategy for developing crop varieties with a higher yield potential. The integration of molecular biology, genomic research, transgenic breeding and molecular marker applications with conventional plant breeding practices has created the foundation for molecular plant breeding and will certainly accelerate rice improvement programs across the world including India. Molecular-assisted selection (MAS) has become integral component of germplasm improvement. A large number of genes for various traits have been tagged with molecular markers to apply MAS for trait improvement. Map-based cloning has resulted in isolation of several genes for resistance to biotic and abiotic stresses as well as yield-related traits. This has opened the possibility of applying MAS for yield enhancement. Recombinant DNA technology has resulted in production of transgenic rice with new genetic traits and for resistance to biotic and abiotic stresses.

1. (*d*) Stages of Seed Development

Parts of a Seed: The seed, along with the ovule, is protected by a seed coat that is formed from the integuments of the ovule sac. In dicots, the seed coat is further divided into an outer coat, known as the testa, and inner coat, known as the tegmen. The embryonic axis consists of three parts: the plumule, the radicle, and the hypocotyl. The portion of the embryo between the cotyledon attachment point and the radicle is known as the hypocotyl. The embryonic axis terminates in a radicle, which is the region from which the root will develop.

Seed Growth: In angiosperms, the process of seed development begins with double fertilization and involves the fusion of the egg and sperm nuclei into a zygote. The second part of this process is the fusion of the polar nuclei with a second sperm cell nucleus, thus forming a primary endosperm. Right after fertilization, the zygote is mostly inactive, but the primary endosperm divides rapidly to form the endosperm tissue. This tissue becomes the food the young plant will consume until the roots have developed after germination. The seed coat forms from the two integuments or outer layers of cells of the ovule, which derive from tissue from the mother plant: the inner integument forms the tegmen and the outer forms the testa. When the seed coat forms from only one layer, it is also called the testa, though not all such testae are homologous from one species to the next.

In gymnosperms, the two sperm cells transferred from the pollen do not develop seed by double fertilization, but one sperm nucleus unites with the egg nucleus and the other sperm is not used. Sometimes each sperm fertilizes an egg cell and one zygote is then aborted or absorbed during early development. The seed is composed of the embryo and tissue from the mother plant, which also form a cone around the seed in coniferous plants such as pine and spruce. The ovules after fertilization develop into the seeds.

Food Storage in the Seed: The storage of food reserves in angiosperm seeds differs between monocots and dicots. In monocots, the single cotyledon is called a scutellum; it is connected directly to the embryo via vascular tissue. Food reserves are stored in the large endosperm. Upon germination, enzymes are secreted by the aleurone, a single layer of cells just inside the seed coat that surrounds the endosperm and embryo. The enzymes degrade the stored carbohydrates, proteins, and lipids. These products are absorbed by the scutellum and transported via a vasculature strand to the developing embryo.

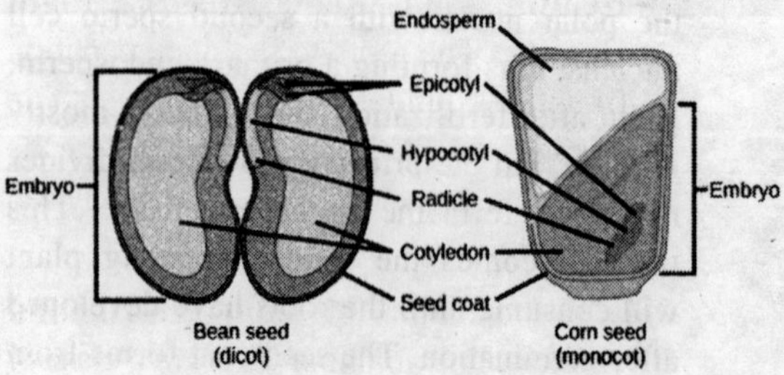

Figure : Monocots and dicots: *The structures of dicot and monocot seeds are shown. Dicots (left) have two cotyledons. Monocots, such as corn (right), have one cotyledon, called the scutellum, which channels nutrition to the growing embryo. Both monocot and dicot embryos have a plumule that forms the leaves, a hypocotyl that forms the stem, and a radicle that forms the root. The embryonic axis comprises everything between the plumule and the radicle, not including the cotyledon(s).*

In endospermic dicots, the food reserves are stored in the endosperm. During germination, the two cotyledons act as absorptive organs to take up the enzymatically-released food reserves, similar to the process in monocots. In non-endospermic dicots, the triploid endosperm develops normally following double fertilization, but the endosperm food reserves are quickly remobilized, moving into the developing cotyledon for storage.

Seed Germination: Upon germination in dicot seeds, the epicotyl is shaped like a hook with the plumule pointing downwards; this plumule hook persists as long as germination proceeds in the dark. Therefore, as the epicotyl pushes through the tough and abrasive soil, the plumule is protected from damage. Upon exposure to light, the hypocotyl hook straightens out, the young foliage ieaves face the sun and expand, and the epicotyl continues to elongate. During this time, the radicle is also growing and producing the primary root. As it grows downward to form the tap root, lateral roots branch off to all sides, producing the typical dicot tap root system.

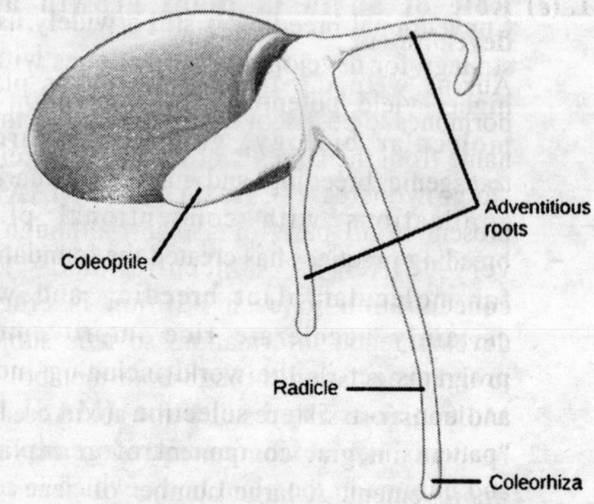

Figure: Monocot seeds: *As this monocot grass seed germinates, the primary root, or radicle, emerges first, followed by the primary shoot, or coleoptile, and the adventitious roots.*

In monocot seeds, the testa and tegmen of the seed coat are fused. As the seed germinates, the primary root emerges, protected by the root-tip covering: the coleorhiza. Next, the primary shoot emerges, protected by the coleoptile: the covering of the shoot tip. Upon exposure to light, elongation of the coleoptile ceases and the leaves expand and unfold. At the other end of the embryonic axis, the primary root soon dies, while other, adventitious roots emerge from the base of the stem. This produces the fibrous root system of the monocot.

Depending on seed size, the time it takes a seedling to emerge may vary. However, many mature seeds enter a period of dormancy marked by inactivity or extremely-low metabolic activity. This period may last for months, years, or even centuries. Dormancy helps keep seeds viable during unfavorable conditions. Upon a return to optimal conditions, seed germination takes place. These conditions may be as diverse as moisture, light, cold, fire, or chemical treatments. Scarification, the softening of the seed coat, presoaking in hot water, or passing through an acid environment, such as an animal's digestive tract, may also be needed.

1. (e) Role of auxin in plant growth and development

Auxins were the first of the major plant hormones to be discovered. They derive their name from the Greek word αυξειν (auxein - "to grow/increase"). Auxin (namely IAA) is present in all parts of a plant, although in very different concentrations. The concentration in each position is crucial developmental information, so it is subject to tight regulation through both metabolism and transport. The result is the auxin creates "patterns" of auxin concentration maxima and minima in the plant body, which in turn guide further development of respective cells, and ultimately of the plant as a whole.

The (dynamic and environment responsive) pattern of auxin distribution within the plant is a key factor for plant growth, its reaction to its environment, and specifically for development of plant organs (such as leaves or flowers). It is achieved through very complex and well-coordinated active transport of auxin molecules from cell to cell throughout the plant body-by the so-called polar auxin transport. Thus, a plant can (as a whole) react to external conditions and adjust to them, without requiring a nervous system. Auxins typically act in concert with, or in opposition to, other plant hormones. For example, the ratio of auxin to cytokinin in certain plant tissues determines initiation of root versus shoot buds.

It has many roles in plant growth and development

- **Stimulating shoot elongation:** Auxins positively influence gibberlins that promote cell elongation. This increases plant length.
- **Controlling seedling orientation:** It was the infamous Charles Darwin and his son Francis who first noticed that seedlings bend toward the light.
- **Stimulating root branching:** When an auxin is applied to a cut stem, the stem will initiate roots at the cut.
- **Healthy Plant Roots, Healthy Plant Growth:** The roots to the plant function like the foundation of a house. The stronger the root system, the stronger the plant and the more likely that plant can overcome environmental stress.

Role of cytokinins in plant growth and development: Cytokinins (CK) are a class of plant growth substances (phytohormones) that promote cell division, or cytokinesis, in plant roots and shoots. They are involved primarily in cell growth and differentiation, but also affect apical dominance, axillary bud growth, and leaf senescence. Folke Skoog discovered their effects using coconut milk in the 1940s at the University of Wisconsin-Madison. There are two types of cytokinins: adenine-type cytokinins represented by kinetin, zeatin, and 6-benzylaminopurine, and phenylurea-type cytokinins like diphenylurea and thidiazuron (TDZ). Most adenine-type cytokinins are synthesized in roots. Cambium and other actively dividing tissues also synthesize cytokinins. No phenylurea cytokinins have been found in plants. Cytokinins participate in local and long-distance signalling, with the same transport mechanism as purines and nucleosides. Typically, cytokinins are transported in the xylem.

It has many roles in plant growth and development

- Regulate cell division in root and shoot.
- Modifies apical dominance and promote lateral bud growth.
- Delay leaf senescence.
- Promotes movement of nutrients.
- Promotes chloroplast development.
- Promotes cell expansion in leaves and cotyledons.
- Helps in Differentiation of vascular tissues.

2. (*a*) The major difference between heterochromatin and euchromatin is that heterochromatin is such part of the chromosomes, which is a firmly packed form and are genetically inactive, while euchromatin is an uncoiled (loosely) packed form of chromatin and are genetically active.

When the non-dividing cells of the nucleus were observed under the light microscope, it exhibited the two regions, on the ground of concentration or intensity of staining. The dark stained areas are said as heterochromatin and light stained areas are said as euchromatin.

Around 90% of the total human genome is euchromatin. They are the parts of chromatin and participate in the protection of DNA in the genome present inside the nucleus. Emil Heitz in the year 1928, coined the term Heterochromatin and Euchromatin.

By focussing on the few more points, we will be able to understand the difference between both types of chromatin.

Comparison Chart

Basis For Comparison	**Heterochromatin**	**Euchromatin**
Meaning	The tightly packed form of DNA in the chromosome is called as heterochromatin.	The loosely packed form of DNA in the chromosome is called as euchromatin.
DNA density	High DNA density.	Low DNA density.
Kind of stain	Stained dark.	Lightly stained.
Where they are present	These are found at the periphery of the nucleus in eukaryotic cells only.	These are found in the inner body of the nucleus of prokaryotic as well as in eukaryotic cells.
Transcriptional activity	They show little or no transcriptional activity.	They actively participate in the process of transcription.
Other features	They are compactly coiled.	They are loosely coiled.
	They are late replicative.	They are early replicative.
	Regions of heterochromatin are sticky.	Regions of euchromatin are non sticky.
	Genetically inactive.	Genetically active.
	Phenotype remains unchanged of an organism.	Variation may be seen, due to the affect in DNA during the genetic process.
	It permits the gene expression regulation and also maintains the structural integrity of the cell.	It results in genetic variations and permits the genetic transcription.

2. (*b*) Distinguish between Sex-linked and Sex-limited Characters: Sex linked inheritance is traits carried in either the X or the Y chromosome. A trait that is due to genes present on the X chromosome is more likely to be expressed in males as they have only one X chromosome. The presence of two X chromosomes in females can suppress its expression when one of them has the genes for the trait and the other does not. X linked traits fall under many categories like recessive, dominant and co-dominant which influence their expression in members of both the sexes. A trait due to a gene in the Y chromosome will only show in males and not in females.

Sex limited inheritance refers to the inheritance of traits that are expressed only in either the male or the female offspring due to their expression being influenced by differences in the anatomy of males and females. For example, if a trait is displayed in organs present only in males, even though a female also inherits the gene, it would not show in her.

2. (*c*) Distinguish between Pedigree and Bulk Method of Plant Breeding

Pedigree Method of Plant Breeding: In pedigree method individual plants are selected from F_2 and their progenies are tested in subsequent generations. A record of the entire parent off spring relationship is maintained and known as pedigree record. The pedigree may be defined as a description of the ancestor of an individual and it generally goes back to some distant ancestor. So each progeny in every generation can be traced back to the F_2 plant from which it is originated.

This method is used for selection from segregating population of crosses in self pollinated crops. It is used for combination or transgressive breeding.

Pedigree advantages

1. Easier to select families-eliminate bad plants early.
2. Select types you want- discard others.
3. Look back on several years data
   (*a*) Computer use essential
   (*b*) Disease, insect, plant type
4. Screen characters in greenhouse and field.
5. Plant breeders can practice their art.
6. Plant breeders can practice their science.
7. Excellent for highly heritable traits (seed size/shape, disease, insect, height, maturity)

Pedigree disadvantages

1. Costly- time, labour-space.
2. Space planting not the same as farmers.

Bulk Method of Plant Breeding: It is a method which can handle segregating generations, in which F_2 and subsequent generations are harvested in bulk to grow the next generation. At the end of bulking period, individual plant selection and evaluation is carried out in the similar fashion as in the pedigree method.

Bulk method of plant breeding completes in following main steps.

Step	Details
Hybridization	Crossing among selected parents
F_1 generation	F_1 seeds (minimum 20) planted. Bulk harvesting is carried out.
F_2 to F_6 generation	F_2 to F_6 are planted, harvested in bulk. Number of plants should be as large as possible. Generally artificial selection is not carried out.
F_7 generation	Generally 30 to 50 thousand F_6 seeds are space planted, selection is carried out based on phenotype and 1000 to 5000 selected ones are harvested separately.
F_8 generation	Individual plant progenies are grown, inferior progenies eliminated. Harvested in bulk.
F_9 generation	Preliminary yield trials with standard varieties as check. Selection is based on yield.
F_{10} to F_{13} generation	Multi location yield trials are conducted using standard varieties as check. Evaluation of performance of lines is done.
F_{14} generation	Seed multiplication for distribution.

Advantages

- Less record keeping
- Easy to handle large numbers
- Natural selection effective (winter-hardiness, disease/insect resistance)
- Little effort needed (cheap)

Disadvantages

- Selected may not be high yielding.
- Environment changes each year.
- Little use of plant breeding skills.

2. (*d*) Plant growth hormones are organic compounds which are either produced naturally within the plants or are synthesized in laboratories. They profoundly control and modify the physiological processes like the growth, development, and movement of plants.

Based on their actions, plant growth regulators are broadly classified into two major groups:

- Plant growth promoters
- Plant growth inhibitors.

Auxins, Gibberellins, and Cytokinins are grouped into Plant growth promoters while Abscisic acid and Ethylene are grouped into Plant growth inhibitors.

Ethylene can be grouped either into the promoters or into the plant inhibitors.

The differences or the distinguishable features of growth regulators of plant and the inhibitors of growth of the plants are listed below in points:

1. Regulator of plant growth are the chemicals which are produced by plants naturally to control the development as well as growth of the plant system. Whereas the inhibitor of plant growth inhibits the growth of the body of plant.
2. Examples of chemicals regulating the growth of plants are : Auxins and Cytokinins. Examples of the chemicals inhibiting the plant growth includes : Abscisic acid.

3. (*a*) Backcross Method: In backcross method of breeding, the hybrid and the progenies in subsequent generations are repeatedly backcrossed to one of the parents. As a result, the genotype of the backcross progeny becomes increasingly similar to that of the recurrent parent. The objective of backcross method is to improve one or two specific defects of a high yielding variety.

Pre-requisite for back cross breeding

1. A suitable recurrent parent must be available which lacks in one or two characteristics.
2. A suitable donor parent must be available.
3. The character to be transferred must have high heritability and preferably it should be determined by one or two genes.
4. A sufficient number of back crosses should be made so that the genotype of recurrent parent is recovered in full.

Application of back cross method

This method is commonly used to transfer disease resistance from one variety to another. But it is also useful for transfer of other characteristics.

1. Intervarietal transfer of simply inherited characters *e.g.* Disease resistance, seed coat colour.
2. Intervarietal transfer of quantitative characters. *e.g.* Plant height, Seed size, Seed shape
3. Interspecific transfer of simply inherited characters *e.g.* Transfer of disease resistance from related species to cultivated species. *e.g.* Resistance to black arm disease in cotton from wild tetraploid species into G. hirsutum
4. Transfer of cytoplasm: This is employed to transfer male sterility. The female parent will be having the sterile cytoplasm and recurrent parent will be used as male parent.

   e.g. Sesamum malabariucum x S. indicum

   Female parent Recurrent parent
5. Transgressive segregation: Back cross method may be modified to produce

transgressive segregants. The F_1 is backcrossed to recurrent parent for 2 to 3 times for getting transgressive segregants.

6. Production of isogenic lines
7. Germplasm conversion
   e.g. Production of photo insensitive line from photo Sensitive germplasm through back crossing. This was done in the case of sorghum. Popularly known as conversion programme.

Procedure for backcross method: The Plan of backcross method would depend upon whether the gene being transferred is recessive or dominant. The plan for transfer of a dominant gene is simpler than that for a recessive gene.

First Year	Non-Recurrent Parent B	x	Recurrent Parent A
	Resistant to rust		Susceptible to rust
	F1 Rr Resistant	x	rr BC1
	rr Rr	x	rr BC2
	rr Rr	x	rr BC3
	rr Rr	x	rr BC4
	rr Rr	x	rr BC5

Back cross upto 6th or 7th generation. After 7th BC rust resistant lines are self pollinated. Harvest is done on single plant basis.

8th Season: Individual plant progenies grown

(*a*) Homozygous plants having resistance and resembling parent A are selected harvested and bulked.

9th season: Yield trials

10th season: Seed multiplication and distribution.

Steps

First Season:

Hybridization: Crossing between parent B donor (Female) and Susceptible parent A recipient (male).

Second Season: Raising the F land backcrossed to recurrent parent A.

Third season: Growing the BClFl. It will be segregating for 1 susceptible (rr) : 1 resistant (Rr). Rust resistant plants are backcrossed with recurrent parent A. This is second backcross.

Fourth Season: Raising BC2 F1 will again segregate in the ratio of 1: 1. Third backcross is done with resistant plants.

Fifth Season to Eighth Season: Raising backcross Fls and crossing resistant plants with recurrent parent is continued up to 7th backcross.

Ninth season : Raising BC7F1 and observing resistant lines. The plants resembling parent A coupled with resistance is selected and harvested on single plant basis.

Tenth Season: Growing the progeny row 8' and observing each row for resistance. Best rows are selected and harvest is done on row basis.

Eleventh Season: The row bulk is raised in yield trial along with check and the best plots are selected.

Twelfth season: Selected plot seeds are multiplied and released as new variety.

Back Cross Method-Transfer of Recessive Gene

I Season	Non recurrent parent B		Recurrent parent A
Hybridization	Resistant		Susceptible
	Rr	x	RR
	F1		Rr

II Season Grow the F1
Rr

III Season Grow F2 RR "Rr" rr x RR BC1
IV Season Grow BC1F1 Rr
V Season Grow BC2F2 RR : Rr : rr x RR BC2
VI Season Grow BC2F1 Rr
VII Season Grow BC2F2 RR : Rr : rr x RR BC3
VIII Season Raise BC3F1
IX Season Raise BC3F2 and it will segregate into 1:2:1 with resistant segregant make Backcross 4 (BC4)
X Season Do as on VIII Season
XI Season do as in IX season

Continue this process still 7th or 8th backcross. After studying 8th BCF2 select plants resembling parent B coupled with resistance. Harvest them on single plant basis. Next season raise them in progeny rows and select beast progenies. Compare them in yield trial and fix the best culture, multiply it and release it as a variety. While selecting plants artificial bombardment for disease is to be done.

Steps

I Season: Make a cross between donor parent A and recurrent parent B and Harvest the hybrid. The donor parents A is resistant which is governed by recessive genes. The susceptibility is governed by dominant gene in parent B.

II Season: Grow the F1 which will be susceptible - Harvest them.

III Season: Grow F2 which will be segregating in the ratio of I :2: I *i.e.* 3/4 susceptible and 1/4 resistant. With the resistant lines (rr) make first backcross with parent A having dominant RR gene. Harvest BCI F1.

IV Season: Grow BCIF1.

V Season: Grow BC1 F2 which will be segregating as we saw in III season. Repeat the process of third season. This will give BC2F1.

VI Season : Grow BC2F1.

VII season: Grow BC2F2 then repeat the process of V Season. This will give BC3F1.

VIII Season: Grow BC3F1.

IX Season: Grow BC3F2 and repeat the process of VII Season. Harvest BC4F.

X season: Grow BC4F1.

XI Season: Grow BC4F2 and repeat the process of IX Season. Harvest BC5F1.

XII, XIII & XIV: Repeat the process and carry out backcross upto 7 time.

XV Season: While studying BC7F2 select single plants having resistance and resembling parent B.

XVI Season: Study the progenies in progeny rows and select best progenies.

XVII Season: Conduct yield trial and select best material.

XVIII Season: Multiply the seeds and distribute it as improved variety with resistance to disease.

Application in Agriculture

The genotype of the new variety is nearly identical with that of the recurrent parent, except for the genes transferred. Thus the outcome of a backcross programme is known beforehand, and it can be reproduced any time in the future.

It is not necessary to test the variety developed by the back cross method in extensive yield tests because the performance of the recurrent parent is already known. This may save upto 5 years time and a considerable expense.

The backcross programme is not dependent upon environment, except for that needed for the selection of the character under transfer. Therefore, off-season nurseries and green - houses can be used to grow 2-3 generation each year. This would drastically reduce the time required for developing the new variety.

Much smaller population are needed in the backcross method than in the case of pedigree method.

Defects, such as, susceptibility to disease, of a well-adapted variety can be removed without affecting its performance and adaptability. Such a variety is often preferred by the farmers and the industries to an entirely new variety because they know the recurrent variety well.

This is the only method for interspecific gene transfers. It may be modified so that transgressive segregation may occur for quantitative' characters.

3. (*b*) Genetic Purity: Genetic purity refers to the percentage of contamination by seeds or genetic material of other varieties or species.

The genetic purity of any commercial agricultural product propagated by seed begins with the purity of the seed planted. In general, the genetic purity of the seed planted must equal or exceed the final product purity standard required, as purity generally decreases with each subsequent generation of propagation. It is virtually impossible to assure that no off-type plants or pollen is present in the seed production field and that all handling and conveyance equipment and storage facilities are completely free of contamination. As a result, commercial planting seed is seldom 100% pure. In practice, practical seed genetic purity standards have been established by state seed laws and by seed certification agencies to ensure that the purchaser receives seed that is within certain purity tolerances. These tolerances are established based on the biology of the species (*i.e.*, self- or cross-pollinated), the type of variety (i.e., open-pollinated, hybrid, synthetic), and market-driven standards for final product quality. Earlier generations of seed (e.g., foundation or registered seed) have stricter standards in order to be able to meet the certified seed purity criteria. The main sources of contamination of a seed crop are the prior crop grown in a field, transfer of pollen from a nearby field, and mixtures during harvesting and handling.

Safeguards for Maintenance of Genetic Purity of Seed: The important safeguards for maintaining genetic purity during seed production are;

1. Control of seed source
2. Preceding crop requirement
3. Isolation
4. Rouging of seed fields
5. Seed certification
6. Grow out test

1. Control of Seed Source : The seed used should be of appropriate class from the approved source for raising a seed crop. There are four classes of seed from breeder seed, which are given and defined by Association of Official Seed Certification Agency (AOSCA).

(*a*) ***Nucleus Seed:*** It is handful of seed maintained by concerned breeder for further multiplication. The nucleus seed will have all the characters that the breeder has placed in it and it is of highest genetic purity. The quantity of nucleus seed is in kilograms.

(*b*) ***Breeder Seed:*** It is produced by the concerned breeder or sponsoring institute and is used for producing foundation seed. It is of 100% genetic purity. The label/tag issued for B/s is golden yellow in colour. The quality of breeder seed is assured by the monitoring team constituted by the govt.

(*c*) ***Foundation Seed:*** It is produced from breeder seed and maintained with specific genetic identity and purity. It is produced on govt. farms or by private seed producers. The quality of foundation seed is certified by certification agency. It has genetic purity of above 98%. The certification tag or label issued for F/s is white in colour.

2. Preceding Crop Requirement: This has been fixed to avoid contamination through volunteer plants and also the soil borne diseases.

3. Isolation: Isolation is required to avoid natural crossing with other undesirable types, off types in the fields and mechanical mixtures at the time of sowing, threshing, processing and contamination due to seed borne diseases from nearby fields. Protection from these sources of contamination is necessary for maintaining genetic purity and good quality of seed.

4. **Rouging of Seed Fields:** The existence of off type plants is another source of genetic contamination. Off type plants differing in their characteristics from that of the seed crop are called as off types. Removal of off types is referred to as roughing.

   The main sources of off types are:

   (*a*) Segregation of plants for certain characters or mutations.

   (*b*) Volunteer plants from previous crops or

   (*c*) Accidentally planted seeds of other variety.

   (*d*) Diseased plants.

   Off type plants should be roughed out from the seed plots before they shed pollen and pollination occurs. To accomplish this regular supervision of trained personnel is required.

5. **Seed Certification:** Genetic purity in seed productions maintained through a system of seed certification. The main objective of seed certification is to make available seeds of good quality to farmers. To achieve this qualified and trained personnel from SCA carry out field inspections at appropriate stages of crop growth. They also make seed inspection by drawing samples from seed lots after processing. The SCA verifies for both filed and seed standards and the seed lot must confirm to get approval as certified seed.

6. **Grow-out Test:** Varieties that are grown for seed production should be periodically tested for genetic purity by conducting GOT to make sure that they are being maintained in true form. GOT test is compulsory for hybrids produced by manual emasculation and pollination and for testing the purity of parental lines used in hybrid seed production.

3. (*c*) Role of Transpiration in Relation to Productivity: Transpiration is the process in which plants release the water inside it in the form of moisture or water vapour. Parts of plants like stems, small pores on leaves, flowers evaporates the water to the atmosphere. Basically, Transpiration is the process in which water is evaporated in the atmosphere from plant leaves and other parts. Some amount of water is consumed by roots and rest is evaporated in the atmosphere. Let us study more about types of Transpiration and Stomata of leaves.

I. Transport of minerals: Usually, high transpiration rates cause high rates of mineral absorption. However, deep understanding of diffusion and differentially permeable membranes point towards the independent absorption of minerals. It is generally held that minerals absorbed by the plant from the soil usually move up through the plant via transpiration stream. The quantum of minerals reaching the leaves is dependent upon the rate of absorption of minerals by the roots rather than the rate of transpiration. Rates of transpiration do not seem to affect the availability of minerals in the leaf. On the contrary when the mineral in the soil are in abundance then the rate of transpiration is vital for their translocation.

II. Lowering of leaf temperature: Transpiration of water from a surface of the leaf lowers the temperature of that organ since the loss of water molecules of a relatively high kinetic energy; the molecules having highest kinetic energy are the first to evaporate. Rough estimates show around that transpiration removes about 600 calories per gram of evaporated water. There are other ways e.g., radiation and convection by which heat is removed. If transpiration stops, there would be an enhanced loss of heat by radiation and convection because of the increased leaf temperature.

III. Optimum turgidity: It is generally argued that there is an optimum level of water potential within the plant. Many and varied functions are slowed down or are rendered inefficient both above or below this level. In the absence of transpiration, plants tend to become over turgid and will cease to grow. Similarly when the water potential becomes highly negative growth also stops.

IV. Bringing water to the top of a plant: It is also suggested that importance of transpiration is embodied in its essentiality to pull water to the top of the trees.

V. Role on growth and development: Winneberger (1958) has observed that the buds of hardy pear cease to grow under conditions of high humidity and that under the same conditions growth of the sunflower plant is reduced to about half of the normal. So it is clear that transpiration is necessary factor in the normal growth of these two plants.Most important point is that cell growth depends on absorption of water which is passively absorbed by the roots of plants due to transpiration pull. Plants showing high rate of transpiration exhibit adequate development of mechanical tissues. Transpiration also shows that plants showing high rate of transpiration exhibit extensive root system.

VI. Involves in improvement in the quality of fruits: Increased sugar and mineral contents of fruits follows high rate of transpiration.

VII. Transpiration help in hardening process: Transpiration induces hardening which imparts resistance of plant to drought.

VIII. Transpiration help in removal of excess water: It has been held that plants absorb far more amount of water than is actually used by the plant. Transpiration removes excess of water.

5. (*a*) Package and practices for Commercial Production of Banana

Agro-climatic requirements: Banana, basically a tropical crop, grows well in a temperature range of 15ºC-35ºC with relative humidity of 75-85%. It prefers tropical humid lowlands and is grown from the sea level to an elevation of 2000 m. above m.s.l.. In India this crop is being cultivated in climate ranging from humid tropical to dry mild subtropics through selection of appropriate varieties. Chilling injury occurs at temperature below 12ºC. High velocity of wind which exceeds 80 km/hr. damages the crop. Four months of monsoon (June to September) with an average 650-750 mm. rainfall are most important for vigorous vegetative growth of banana. At higher altitudes, banana cultivation is restricted to a few varieties like 'Hill banana'. Deep, rich loamy soil with pH between 6.5-7.5 is most preferred for banana cultivation. Soil for banana should have good drainage, adequate fertility and moisture. Saline solid, calcareous soils are not suitable for banana cultivation. A soil which is neither too acidic nor too alkaline, rich in organic material with high nitrogen content, adequate phosphorus level and plenty of potash is good for banana.

Growing and Potential Belts: The state-wise growing belts are given below:

State	Growing belts
Andhra Pradesh	East Godavari, West Godavari, Kurnool, Cuddapah
Assam	Goalpara, Nagaon, Sonitpur, foothills of Garo hills
Gujarat	Surat, Vadodara, Anand, Kheda, Junagadh, Narmada, Bharuch
Jharkhand	Ranchi, Sahebganj
Karnataka	Bangalore, Chitradurga, Shioroga, Hassan, Chikka Mangloor

Kerala	Thiruvananthapuram, Kollam, Pathanamthitta, Alappuzha, Kottayam, Idukki, Ernakulam, Thrissur, Palakkad, Malappuram, Kozhikode, Wynadu, Kannur, Kasargod
Madhya Pradesh	Khandwa, Badwani, Khargaon, Dhar
Maharashtra	Jalgaon, Ahmednagar, Buldhana, Pune, Wardha, Dhule, Nanded, Parbani, Nandurbar, Satara, Sangli, Osmanabad, Buldhana, Akola, Yeothmal, Amravati, Thane, Kulara, Alibag
Odisha	Ganjam, Puri, Khurda, Gajpati, Cuttack, Dhenkanal, Angul, Sundargarh, Sambalpur, Bargarh, Deogarh, Koraput, Keonjhar, Raygada, Mayurbhanj
Tamil Nadu	Thoothukudi, Tiruchirapalli, Coimbatore, Tirunelveli, Karur, Erode, Kanyakumari
West Bengal	Hooghly, Nadia, North 24 Parganas

Varieties Cultivated: Commercially, bananas are classified as dessert types and culinary types. The culinary types have starchy fruits and are used in the mature unripe form as vegetables. Important cultivars include Dwarf Cavendish, Robusta, Monthan, Poovan, Nendran, Red banana, Nyali, Safed Velchi, Basrai, Ardhapuri, Rasthali, Karpurvalli, Karthali and Grand Naine etc.

Land Preparation: Prior to planting banana, green manuring crop like daincha, cowpea etc. may be grown. The land can be ploughed 2-4 times and leveled. Ratovator or harrow is used to break the clod and bring the soil to a fine tilt. During soil preparation basal dose of FYM (about 50 tonnes/ha. before last harrowing) is added and thoroughly mixed into the soil.

Planting

Planting Material: About 70% of the farmers are using suckers as planting material while the rest 30% of the farmers are using tissue culture seedlings. Sword suckers with well developed rhizome, conical or spherical in shape having actively growing conical bud and weighing approximately 450-700 gm are commonly used as propagating material.

Treatment of Planting material: The roots and base of the planting material may be removed. The suckers are dipped in a solution of 0.5% monocrotophos and bavistin (0.1%) before planting.

Planting season: Thus, the important seasons for planting followed in different states of India are:

State	*Planting time*
Maharashtra	• Kharif-June-July • Rabi-October - November
Tamil Nadu	• February-April • November-December
Kerala	• Rainfed-April-May • Irrigated crop-August-September

Spacing

Season	*Spacing*
Kharif	1.5 × 1.5 m., 2 × 2 m. or 2.5 × 2.5 m.
Rabi	1.5 × 1.2 m., 1.5 × 1.37 m.

Planting Method: Pit planting is commonly followed in garden system of cultivation. A pit size of 0.5 × 0.5 × 0.5 m. is normally required. Small pits are dug in case of ridges and furrows. The pits are to be refilled with topsoil mixed with 10 kg of FYM (well decomposed), 250 gm of neem cake and 20 gm of carbofuran. Prepared pits are left open for 15-20 days for solar radiation to kill all the insects, soil borne diseases and for aeration before refilling.

Nutrition: Banana requires high amount of nutrients, which are often supplied only in part by the soil. Nutrient requirement (worked out on all India basis) is 10 kg FYM, 200-250 gm N; 60-70 gm P; 300 gm K/plant. Banana crop requires 7-8 Kg N, 0.7- 1.5 Kg P and 17-20 Kg K per metric ton yield. Traditionally farmers use more of urea and less of phosphorous and potash. Urea is applied in three to four split doses.

Micronutrients: Combined foliar application of $ZnSO_4$ (0.5%), $FeSO_4$ (0.2%), $CuSO_4$ (0.2%) and H_3BO_3 (0.1%) applied at 3, 5 and 7 months after planting helps to increase yield and quality of banana.

Irrigation: Banana being a succulent, evergreen and shallow rooted crop requires large quantity of water for increasing productivity. Water requirement of banana has been worked out to be 1,800-2,000 mm per annum. In winter, irrigation is provided at an interval of 7-8 days while in summer it should be given at an interval of 4-5 days. However, during rainy season irrigation is provided if required as excess irrigation will lead to root zone congestion due to removal of air from soil pores, thereby affecting plant establishment and growth. In all, about 70-75 irrigations are provided to the crop.

Intercultural Operations: The following inter-cultural operations are recommended for optimum productivity of the crop:

(*i*) Spraying of Glyphosate before planting @ 2 lit/ha is carried out to keep the plantation weed free.

(*ii*) Four to five weedings are to be done whenever necessary.

(*iii*) Harrowing the field three to four times to keep the soil loose. Earthing up should be done at 3-4 months after planting raising the soil level around the base of the plant by 10-12". It is better to prepare a raised bed and keep the drip line on bed 2-3" away from the plant. It also helps to protect plants from wind damage and production losses to some extent.

Desuckering: Removal of unwanted suckers is a critical operation in banana for reducing internal competition with the main plant. Small suckers are removed on regular basis upto 7-8 months.

Mulching: Use of wheat straw and banana straw as a mulch material (12.5 kg./plant) in banana orchards is useful in increasing the bunch weight and conservation of soil moisture. The mulch is applied at the beginning of summer (February).

Growth regulators: In order to improve the grade of bunches 2,4 D @ 25 ppm. (25 mg./l.) may be sprayed after the last hand has opened. This also helps to remove the seeds in certain varieties e.g. Poovan and CO-1. Spraying with CCC (1000 ppm.) at 4th, 6th month after planting and plantozyme @ 2 ml./l. at 6th and 8th month after planting helps to achieve higher yield. After full development of bunch, potassium dihydrogen phosphate (0.5%) and urea (1%) or 2,4 D solution (10 ppm.) is to be sprayed on the bunch so that banana size and quality is improved.

Other farm operations: Other farm operations include the following:

(*i*) Removal of dry leaves (green leaves should not be removed).

(*ii*) During the winter months if temperature goes below 10°C, growth of the plant is affected. Under such circumstances, irrigation is to be provided at night or smoking is to be done by inducing fire.

(*iii*) If neem cake of 1 kg. per plant is applied during winter months, the formation of bunch becomes easier.

(*iv*) Plantation should be protected from strong winds by growing tall plants along the farm border.

(*v*) Bamboo poles or eucalyptus poles are used for giving support to the banana plant.

Plant Protection Measures

Insect Pests: The insect pests mostly observed are root stock/rhizome weevil (*Cosmopolites sordidus*), stem borer (*Odioporus longicollis*), thrips, banana beetle (*Nodostoma subcostatum*), banana aphid (*Pentalonia nigronervosa*) and nematodes. Selection of healthy planting material and suitable intercultural operations apart from application of 0.04% endosulfan, 0.1% carbaryl or 0.05% monocrotophos depending upon the type of pest infestation have been found to be effective in controlling the pests.

Diseases: The main diseases reported are panama wilt (*Fusarium oxysporum*), anthracnose (*Gleosporium musarum*), leaf spot (Sigatoka) [*Mycosphaarella musicola* & *Cercospora musae*], shoot rot (*Ceratostomella paradoxa*) and viral diseases. Disease free planting material should be used and the infected plant parts destroyed. Spraying with 1% Bordeaux, copper oxychloride or carbendazim in case of fungal infections has been found to give positive results.

Harvesting and Yield: Banana is harvested when the fruit is slightly or fully mature depending on the market preferences. For long distance transportation, harvesting is done at 75-80 % maturity. The fruit is climacteric and can reach consumption stage after ripening operation.

The planted crop gets ready for harvest within 12-15 months of planting and the main harvesting season of banana is from September to April. Bunches attain maturity from 90-150 days after flowering depending upon variety, soil, weather condition and elevation. Bunch should be harvested when fingers of second hand from top are 3/4 rounded with the help of sharp sickle 30 cm above the first hand. Harvest may be delayed upto 100-110 days after opening of the first hand. Harvested bunch should generally be collected in well padded tray or basket and brought to collection site. Bunches should be kept out of light after harvest, since this hastens ripening and softening. For local consumption, hands are often left on stalks and sold to retailers.

The dwarf varieties are ready for harvesting within 11 to 14 months after planting while the tall varieties take about 14 to 16 months. After harvest of bunch, only leaves are to be cut and plant system is retained for ratoon crop development. This improves the food supply and about 15% can be saved on irrigation. For getting good quality banana, only 7 to 8 berries are to be retained in a bunch.

First ratoon crop would be ready by 8-10 month from the harvesting of the main crop and second ratoon by 8-9 months after the second crop. Thus over a period of 28-30 months, it is possible to harvest three crops i.e., one main crop and two ratoon crop. The yield of banana depends on a number of factors such as variety, plant density, management practices etc.

Post Harvest Management

Grading: Grading is mainly based on size, colour and maturity of the fruits. While grading, smaller fruits are separated from the larger ones in order to achieve uniform ripening. Immature, overripe, damaged and diseased fruits are discarded in the process of grading.

Storage: Mature green bananas can be stored for upto 3 weeks in ethylene free air or upto 6 weeks in a controlled atmosphere at 14°C.

Packing: Wooden or cardboard boxes, rectangular in shape and bamboo baskets are used for packaging and transportation of fruits. In some cases banana bunches are packed in old gunny bags wrapped with banana leaves. Due to poor packing quality the bananas deteriorate and fetch low price.

Marketing: Several intermediaries like wholesalers and commission agents, are involved in marketing of the fruit. Private traders carry out nearly 95% of the trade and even provide credit to farmers for cultivation, but at high rate of interest. Cooperatives account for the balance 5% of the volume of trade.

5. (*b*) Integrated Pest Management (IPM): Integrated Pest Management (IPM) is an ecosystem-based strategy that focuses on long-term prevention of pests or their damage through a combination of techniques such as biological control, habitat manipulation, modification of cultural practices, and use of resistant varieties.

Principles of Integrated Pest Management:

Principle 1: *Prevention and Suppression*

- Prevention is adoption of measures to reduce the chance of occurrence of pest. Suppression is reducing the impact of the pests.
- Prevention and suppression can be done by applying the different techniques.
- It is a method of preventing the spreading of harmful organisms by hygiene measures (e.g. by regular cleansing of machinery and equipment).
- One of the methods of prevention and suppression is crop rotation where it would break the life cycle of the pests.
- Prevention and suppression also include use of adequate cultivation techniques (e.g. stale seedbed technique, sowing dates and densities, under-sowing, conservation tillage, pruning and direct sowing).

Principle 2: *Monitoring*

- Harmful organisms must be monitored by adequate methods and tools, wherever available.
- Monitoring can be done through observations, use of scientifically sound warning, forecasting and early diagnosis systems, advice from professionally qualified advisers, etc.
- Many countries like France, Denmark have adopted this monitoring and forecasting technique.

Principle 3: *Decision making*

- Decision making is done based on the results of the monitoring.
- IPM focuses on threshold-based intervention in most of the cases. Threshold is the defined pest density, or population level, which when exceeded, management should occur.
- However, threshold is difficult to define in most of the cases and in case of tolerant species, decision of intervention is based on the general observations.
- We should also be aware that specific crops, pest life cycle, climatic condition, etc., should be considered before making any kind of decisions.

Principle 4: *Non-Chemical Methods*

- Non-chemical methods are prioritized over chemical methods if they can produce satisfactory results.
- As chemical methods are often not sustainable and creates more pest problems, non-chemical methods are always preferred at first hand as they are more sustainable with less biological and environmental hazards.
- Examples of non-chemical methods include soil-solarization or biological control.
- Use of live natural enemies is one of the major non-chemical (biological) intervention method.
- Other non-chemical methods include biological, physical and ecological methods.

Principle 5: *Pesticide Selection*

- IPM doesn't totally avoid the use of the pesticides.
- When the alternative methods are not properly used then the pesticides are used for pest control.

- The pesticides used however needs to be as specific as possible for the target.
- The pesticides shouldn't possess any threat to the health of human, non-target humans and environment.

Principle 6: *Reduced Pesticide Use*

- Reduced pesticides use refers to the reduction in the frequency and doses of the pesticides.
- This method needs to be supported by the other means of intervention.
- It helps in reducing the side effects of the pesticides.

Principle 7: *Anti- resistant Strategies*

- IPM focuses on the anti-resistance activities as:
- Unmanaged and haphazard use of the pesticides have created the problem of resistance, and
- Pests have developed the resistance and the use of pesticides have less effect on them.
- This is also the major reason for the IPM.
- Anti-resistant strategies include use of combination of different pesticides that has different mode of action, applied in different time.

Principle 8: *Evaluation*

- Evaluation is the important aspect of the IPM program.
- Evaluation is done based on the records of the use of the pesticides, its effects and many more.
- Evaluation is necessary in studying the effectiveness of the plan protective measures and plan further.

Components of Integrated Pest Management: The major components of IPM in increasing order of complexity are as under:

Cultural practices: Cultural methods of pest control consist of regular farm operations in such a way which either destroy the pests or prevent them from causing economic loss. The various cultural practices are as under.

Preparation of nurseries or main fields free from pest infestation by removing plant debris, trimming of bunds, treating of soil and deep summer ploughing which kills various stages of pests.

- Testing of soil for nutrients deficiencies on the basis of which fertilizers should be applied.
- Selection of clean and certified seeds and treating seeds with fungicide or bio-pesticides before sowing for seed borne disease control.
- Selection of seeds of relatively pest resistant/tolerant varieties which play a significant role in pest suppression.
- Adjustment of time of sowing and harvesting to escape peak season of pest attack.
- Rotation of crops with non-host crops. It helps in reduction of incidence of soil borne diseases.
- Proper plant spacing which makes plants more healthy and less susceptible to pests.
- Optimum use of fertilizer. Use of FYM and bio-fertilizers should be encouraged.
- Proper water management as the high moisture in soil for prolonged period is conducive for development of pests especially soil borne diseases.
- Proper weed management. It is well-known fact that most of weeds beside competing with crop for micro nutrients also harbor many pests.
- Setting up yellow pan sticky traps for white flies and aphids at far above canopy height.
- Synchronized sowing. Here community approach is required to sow the crops simultaneously in vast area so that pest may not get different staged crops suitable for its population build up and if pest appears in damaging proportion, control operation could be applied effectively in whole area.
- Growing trap crops on the borders or peripheries of fields. There are certain

crops which are preferred more by a pest species are known as trap crops for that pest. By growing such crops on the border of the fields, pest population develop there which can be either killed by using pesticides or its natural enemies are allowed to develop there for natural control.

- Inter-cropping or multiple cropping wherever possible. All the crops are not preferred by each pest species and certain crops act as repellents, thus keeping the pest species away from preferred crops resulting in reduction of pest incidence.
- Harvesting as close as to ground level. This is because certain developmental stages of insect pests/diseases remain on the plant parts which act as primary inoculum for the next crop season. Hence, harvesting crops at ground level will lessen the incidence of pests in next season.
- Before planting, nursery plants be sprayed/dipped in copper fungicide/ bio pesticide solutions to protect the plants from soil borne diseases.
- While pruning fruit trees, remove crowded/dead/broken/diseased branches and destroy them. Do not pile them in the orchards which may act as source of pest infestation.
- Large pruning wounds should be covered with Bordeaux paste/paint to protect the plants from pest/disease attack.
- Keeping bee hives or placing flower bouquets of pollinizer cultivars facilitate better pollination and subsequent fruit set.
- Selection of high yielding varieties for different crops.
- Selection of comparatively pest resistant/ tolerant varieties.

Mechanical practices:

- Removal and destruction of egg masses, larvae, pupae and adults of insect pests and diseased parts of plants wherever possible.
- Installation of bamboo cage cum bird perchers in the field and placing parasitized egg masses inside them for conservation of natural enemies and withholding of pest species wherever possible.
- Use of light traps and destruction of trapped insects.
- Use of rope for dislodging leaf feeding larvae e.g. caseworm and leaf folders.
- Installation of bird scarer in the field where required.
- Installation of bird perchers in the field for allowing birds to sit and feed on insects and their immature stages viz., eggs, larvae and pupae.
- Use of pheromones for mating disruption and kill zone creation.
- Use of pheromone traps for monitoring and suppression of pest population.
- Use of pheromone traps for mass trapping.

Regulatory practices: In this process regulatory rules framed by Govt. are brought into force under which seeds and infested plant materials are not allowed to enter the country or from one part to other parts of the country. These are known as quarantine methods and are of two types *i.e.* domestic and foreign quarantine.

Biological practices: Biological control of insect pests and diseases through biological means is most important component of IPM. In broader sense, biocontrol is use of living organisms to control unwanted living organisms (pests). In other words, deliberate use of parasitoids, predators and pathogens to maintain pest population at level below those causing economic loss either by introducing a new bioagent into the environment of pest or by increasing effectiveness of those already preset in the field.

Parasitoids: These are the organisms which lay eggs in or on the bodies of their hosts and complete their life cycles on host bodies as a result of which hosts die. A parasitoid may be of different type depending on the host developmental stage in or on which it completes its life cycle. For example, egg, larval, pupal, adult, egg-larval and larval pupal parasitoids. Example are different species of *Trichogramma, Apanteles, Bracon, Chelonus, Brachemeria, Pseudogonotopus etc.*

Predators: These are free living organisms which prey upon other organisms for their food. Examples are different species of spiders, dragon flies, damsel flies, lady bird beetles, Chrysopa species, birds etc.

Bio-pesticides: These are micro-organisms which infest and cause diseases in their hosts as a result of which hosts are killed. Major groups of pathogens are fungi, viruses and bacteria. Some nematodes also cause diseases in some insect pests. Important examples of fungi are different species of Hirsutella, Beauveria, Nomurae and Metarhizium which have been reported to infest and kill large number of insects (upto 90%) in the fields. Among viruses, most important examples are of nuclear polyhedrosis virus (NPV) and granulosis viruses. Outbreak of viruses in armyworms, cut worms, leaf folders, hairy caterpillars and plant hoppers have been reported many times. Among bacteria, Bacillus thuringiensis (B.t.) and B. popillae are very common examples.

Chemical practices: Use of chemical pesticides is the last resort when all other methods fail to keep the pest population below economic loss. Although there is a great advancement in pest management research, yet pesticides would continue to play an important role in crop protection in view of complexity of pest problems. Therefore, use of pesticides should be need based, judicious, based on pest surveillance to minimise not only the cost involved, but also to reduce associated problems. While going for chemical control, we must understand thoroughly what to spray, when to spray, where to spray and how to spray, keeping in mind the following points.

- Pest defender ratio must be observed.
- Relatively safer pesticides should be selected e.g. neem based and biopesticides.
- If pest is present in strips or isolated patches, whole field should not be sprayed.

5. (*c*) Techniques of Hi-tech Agriculture: As high-tech farming mainly refers to agricultural methods using the latest technology, like hydroponics and aerophonics. That is to say growing veggies in water or in the air only without the use of soil and there are also orchid farms and ornamental fish. It is also called agrotechnology here. There are minimal physical inputs to the system, but it is capital intensive since large capital outlay is required to buy specialized equipment, maintenance, training of labour etc. It is also a commercial farming system, farmers invest in them both for local and export markets, technical know-how is a must, for example, for hydroponics computers are used to monitor, it is labour intensive because of the training of lab technicians, scientists, chemists and farm hands. It uses high tech farming methods and technology to increase yields; it has high output and market value because the so called hygienic conditions appeal to all health conscious people out there who do not mind paying more. It is dependent on research and development. Like growing temperate vegetables in a tropical climate or genetic engineering developing disease resistant plants with nice colours or transgenic animals.

Nearly everyone working on the future of modern agriculture is focused on efficiency. A wide range of technologies will enable the transition of modern agriculture in the field. Some technologies will need to be developed specifically for agriculture, while other technologies already developed for other areas could be adapted to the modern agricultural domain such as autonomous vehicles, artificial intelligence and machine vision. If modern agriculture is applied widely in the near future, millions of farmers will be able to benefit from the acquisition of real-time farm information. Farmers need not spend significant amount of time on acquiring farm data and will have access to disaster warnings and weather information when a disaster event occurs.

5. (*d*) **National Initiatives for Food and Nutrition Security:** With a five-fold increase in food grain production from 50 million tonnes in 1950-51 to about 250 million tonnes in 2014-15, India has moved away from dependence on food aid to become a net food exporter. In 2016, the government launched a number of programmes to double farmers' incomes by 2022. These seek to remove bottlenecks for greater agricultural productivity, especially in rain-fed areas. They include: the National Food Security Mission, Rashtriya Krishi Vikas Yojana (RKVY), the Integrated Schemes on Oilseeds, Pulses, Palm oil and Maize (ISOPOM), Pradhan Mantri Fasal Bima Yojana, the e-marketplace, as well as a massive irrigation and soil and water harvesting programme to increase the country's gross irrigated area from 90 million hectares to 103 million hectares by 2017.

The government has also taken significant steps to combat under- and malnutrition over the past two decades, such as through the introduction of mid-day meals at schools, anganwadi systems to provide rations to pregnant and lactating mothers, and subsidised grain for those living below the poverty line through a public distribution system. The National Food Security Act (NFSA), 2013, aims to ensure food and nutrition security for the most vulnerable through its associated schemes and programmes, making access to food a legal right.

To address the linked nutrition and livelihood challenges in India and to ensure that vulnerable groups are not left behind, the UN priority group partners with the government to scale-up nutrition services and improve feeding and caring practices in the home. It assists government efforts to increase the efficiency and effectiveness of the safety nets under the NFSA, and work towards increasing farm incomes for small and marginal farming households. The group provides support the strengthening of agriculture and livelihood dimensions of anti-poverty programmes, particularly the Mahatma Gandhi National Rural Employment Guarantee Act and the National Rural Livelihoods Mission.

In previous years, the group has collaborated with the Ministry of Health and Family Welfare to hold a national consultation on wheat flour fortification, and with the Food Safety and Standards Authority of India to organise a workshop on advocating for a national food fortification policy.

Led by the United Nations Children's Fund (UNICEF), the priority groups members include the Food and Agriculture Organization (FAO), International Fund for Agricultural Development (IFAD), International Labour Organization (ILO), International Organization for Migration (IOM), United Nations Entity for Gender Equality and the Empowerment of Women (UN Women), United Nations Development Programme (UNDP), United Nations Educational, Scientific and Cultural Organization (UNESCO) and World Food Programme (WFP).

5. (*e*) **Photoperiodism and Short Day Plant:** Photoperiodism is the phenomenon of physiological changes that occur in plants in response to relative length of day and night (i.e. photoperiod). The response of the plants to the photoperiod, expressed in the form of flowering is also called as photoperiodism. The phenomenon of photoperiodism was first discovered by Garner and Allard (1920). Depending upon

the duration of photoperiod, the plants are classified into three categories.

1. Short day plants (SDP)
2. Long day plants (LDP)
3. Day neutral plants (DNP)

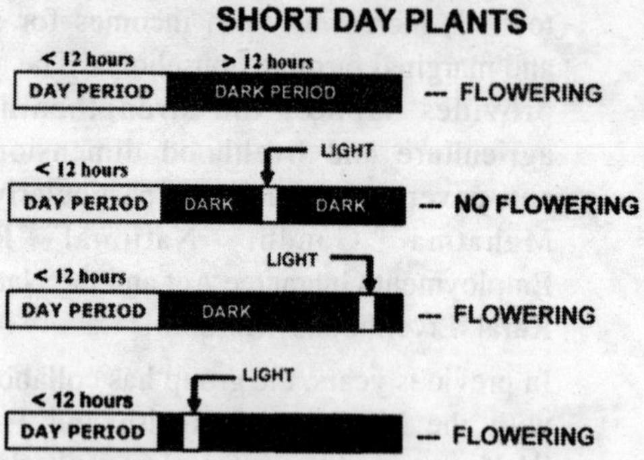

These plants require a relatively short day light period (usually 8-10 hours) and a continuous dark period of about 14-16 hours for subsequent flowering. These plants are also known as long-night plants.

e.g. Rice, coffee, soybean, tobacco and chrysanthemum.

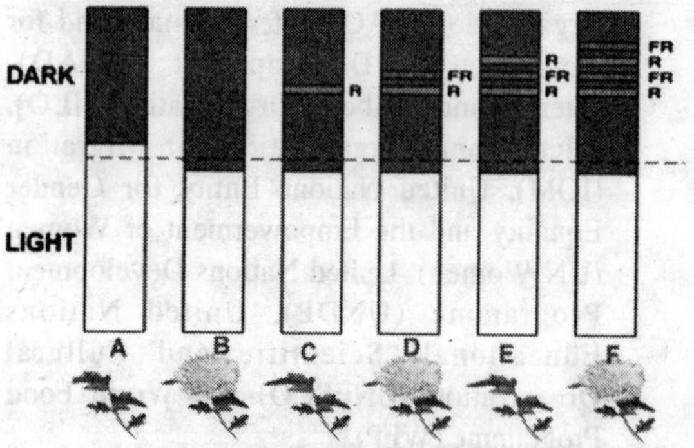

Short Day Plants — Flowering

- In short day plants, the dark period is critical and must be continuous. If this dark period is interrupted with a brief exposure of red light (660-665 nm wavelength), the short day plant will not flower.
- Maximum inhibition of flowering with red light occurs at about the middle of critical dark period.
- However, the inhibitory effect of red light can be overcome by a subsequent exposure with far-red light (730-735 mm wavelength).
- Interruption of the light period with red light does not have inhibitory effect on flowering in short day plants.
- Prolongation of the continuous dark period initiates early flowering.

6. (*a*) Plant development is an umbrella term for a broad spectrum of processes that include: the formation of a complete embryo from a zygote; seed germination; the elaboration of a mature vegetative plant from the embryo; the formation of flowers, fruits, and seeds; and many of the plant's responses to its environment. Plant development encompasses the growth and differentiation of cells, tissues, organs, and organ systems. Plant development shares many similarities with developmental processes in animals, but the fact that plants are nonmotile, photosynthetic organisms requires certain novel developmental processes in addition to the common ones.

Embryo and Seed Development: Embryogenesis, the formation of a multicellular embryo from a single-celled zygote, is one of the most dramatic and best-characterized aspects of plant development. Four key developmental processes take place during embryogenesis. First, the zygote expresses apical-basal polarity, meaning that the apical and basal ends of the zygote cell differ structurally and biochemically. When the zygote divides, it typically divides asymmetrically, giving rise to a small apical cell with dense cytoplasm and a large basal cell with watery cytoplasm. Although these two cells have identical nuclei, their fates differ dramatically. The apical cell gives rise to the embryo itself, while the basal cell gives rise to a short-lived structure called a suspensor and the tip of the root system. The progeny of the apical cell grow and divide to form aspherical mass of cells, the globular-stage embryo. Second, differential growth within the globular embryo gives rise to the "heart" stage embryo, the earliest stage when the precursors of cotyledons, root, and stem can be recognized. This key embryogenic process is called organogenesis. Third, distinctive planes of cell divisions bring about histogenesis, the process by which cells within embryonic cotyledons, root, and stem acquire different shapes, forming the precursors of the plant tissue systems. Last, the apical meristems of the shoot and root systems are formed at the apical and basal ends of the embryo.

After an embryo has reached full size, developmental changes continue to occur at the cellular level. Embryonic cells, particularly those of the cotyledons, begin to synthesize and store the proteins lipids, and starch that will provide the energy and basic building blocks for germination and seedling growth. Next, the embryo begins to desiccate, sometimes losing up to 80 per cent of its previous water content, and enters a phase of dormancy. Development and metabolism are arrested in dormant embryos, and seeds containing dormant embryos can survive for many years (sometimes centuries) and withstand extreme temperatures and drought.

Plant hormones are important regulators of embryogenesis and seed dormancy. The hormones auxin, gibberellic acid, and cytokinin all stimulate growth and are present in the embryo during the stages of embryogenesis. As the embryo matures, these hormones are degraded and abscisic acid is synthesized by the embryo. Abscisic acid provides a developmental signal for the embryo to initiate the synthesis of storage compounds and to undergo desiccation. Abscisic acid is present in dormant seeds and is thought to play an important role in maintaining seed dormancy.

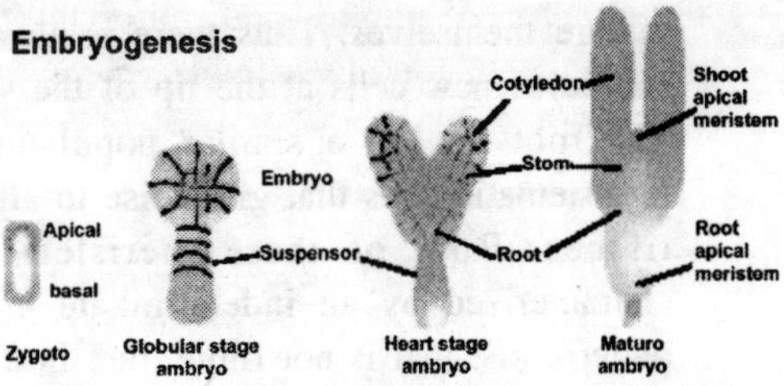

Embryo formation begins with cell division that establishes the apical-basal (top-bottom) axis. Further divisions elaborate on this basic plan, finally forming the cotyledons (seed leaves), as well as the apical meristems of root and shoot.

Germination and Seedling Development: Embryo development and metabolism resume upon seed germination. Given the right combination of water availability, temperatures, and light, the desiccated seed begins to take up water and the embryo begins to grow and metabolize again.

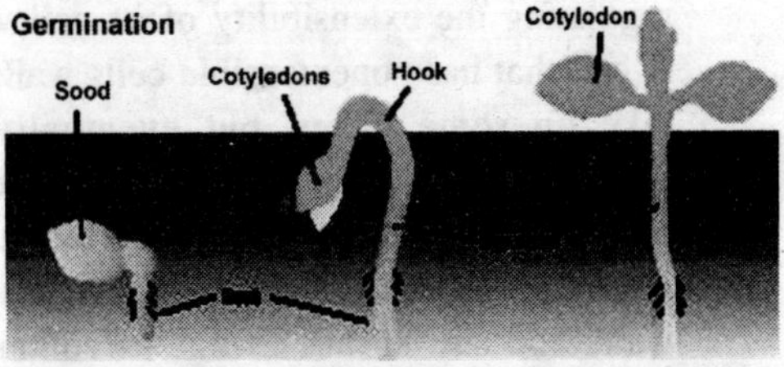

The root is the first portion of the plant to emerge during germination. Growth of the stem behind the cotyledons forms a "hook" that emerges from the soil, followed by emergence of the cotyledons, which begin to photosynthesize to feed further growth.

Apical Meristems and Development: The early stages of germination simply involve the enlargement of the root, hypocotyl, and cotyledons that were preformed in the embryo. Postembryonic development, however, is focused on the apical meristems. The shoot apical meristem is the source of all the leaves, stems, and their component cells formed during the lifetime of the plant. The meristem itself is composed of a small population of perpetually embryonic (meristematic) cells. These cells grow and divide, giving rise to new cells, but never mature themselves. Thus there is always a source of new cells at the tip of the shoot. The root tip has a similar population of meristematic cells that gives rise to all root tissues. Both of these meristems are characterized by an indeterminate growth pattern: one that is not finite, but, in theory at least, could continue throughout the lifetime of the plant. Apical meristems are involved in several distinct developmental processes.

Cell Growth and Cell Division: Growth is defined as an irreversible increase in mass that is typically associated with an increase in volume. Plant cell growth is associated with meristems and must be carefully regulated in order for organogenesis and histogenesis to occur in the appropriate patterns. The plant regulates growth by regulating the extensibility of its cell walls. A cell that has nonextensible cells walls can take up some water, but eventually the physical pressure of the water inside the cell pressing out on the cell wall (the turgor pressure) prevents the entry of additional water and any further change in volume. In contrast, a cell that has extensible cell walls can take up a substantial volume of water and thus increase in size. Turgor pressure that would otherwise prevent water entry momentarily decreases because the walls keep stretching.

Typically cell growth occurs in small increments: (1) wall extensibility increases, reducing turgor pressure; (2) reduced turgor pressure allows water to enter the cell, increasing cell volume; (3) wall extensibility decreases, allowing the cell to build up turgor and preventing further water entry; and (4) the cell undergoes a cycle of synthesis of cytoplasmic and wall components, adding to the cell's mass. This cycle of incremental growth is repeated many times until the cell reaches its final size.

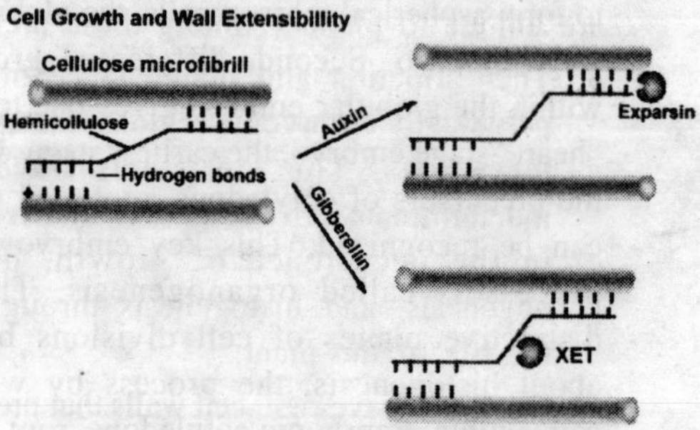

The hormones auxin and gibberellin each promote cell expansion by loosening the bonds between adjacent cell wall molecules. Each hormone acts on a different molecular target.

Differentiation: Differentiation is the process whereby cells, tissues, and organs become different from each other and from their precursors. The concept can be applied to organogenesis since cotyledons, foliage leaves, sepals, and petals may all develop from similar appearing precursors, the leaf primordia. As these organs mature, they become different from each other in size, shape, and the development of distinctive cell types. For instance, the epidermis tissue of petals is sharply differentiated from that of cotyledons, foliage leaves and sepals that are photosynthetic organs. Correlated with a photosynthetic function, the epidermis of these organs is made up of flat, transparent cells that allow the penetration of light into internal tissues. Specialized guard cells that allow CO_2 to enter the leaf are also present. In contrast, the epidermal cells of petals contain brightly colored carotenoid or anthocyanin pigments. These cells also have a papillate shape that imparts a velvetlike sheen to the petal surface. Since petals carry on minimal photosynthesis, they often lack guard cells.

Uniqueness of Plant Development: Although plants share many features of development with animals such as apical-basal polarity, regulation of the balance between cell growth and cell division, formation of distinctive patterns of organs, cells and tissues, and differentiation, some aspects of development are unique to plants. Among these are:

- The formation and maintenance of the perpetually embryonic regions, the apical meristems. The meristems have an indeterminate growth pattern that result in the occurrence of growth, organogenesis, and histogenesis throughout the life of the plant.
- Plant cells have rigid cell walls that prevent cell movement. Thus organogenesis and histogenesis must occur through differential growth and regulation of the planes of cell division. Cell-cell communication is important in plant development, but cell recognition is likely less important than it is in animals since plant cells keep the same neighbours throughout their life.
- Plant cells are totipotent; that is, able to differentiate as a different cell type if given the appropriate stimulus. Totipotency is likely a reflection of the plant's sedentary lifestyle. Plants can't escape predators and other kinds of damage, but they can readily repair wounds and reconnect vascular strands by differentiating the appropriate cell types.

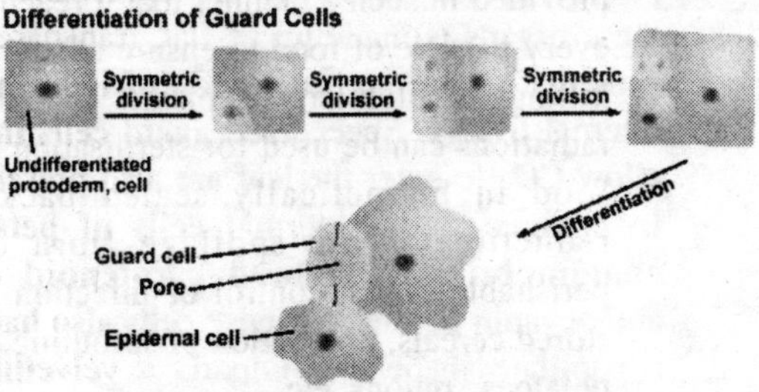

Guard cells regulate passage of gasses into and out of the leaf through pores in the surface. Guard cells form by a series of cell divisions from undifferentiated protoderm, including a final symmetric division that forms the two identical cells.

6. (*b*) Preservation of Fruits and Vegetables: Food preservation can be defined as the science which deals with the methods of prevention of decay or spoilage of food, thus allowing it to be stored in a fit condition for future use. It is better if the following directions are kept in mind to control the spoilage. Most fruits and vegetables are seasonal and perishable in nature. In a good season there may be a glut but because of insufficient transport facilities, lack of good roads and poor availability of packaging materials, the surplus cannot be taken quickly enough to markets in urban areas. Moreover the surplus often cannot be stored for sale in off-season because of inadequate local cold storage facilities. Thus, the cultivator do not get a good price for their produce. Although, the R and D efforts on the development of post-harvest handling has helped in reducing the spoilage, considerable losses continue to occur. Two approaches are possible for solving this problem.

(*i*) One is the creation/expansion of cold storage facilities in the fruit and vegetable producing regions, as also in the major urban consumption centres, to ensure supply of fruit and vegetable throughout year.

(*ii*) Another approach is to process the fruits and vegetable into various products which could be preserved for a long time and add value to the product.

Methods of Preservation:

1. **Asepsis (Absence of infection):** Asepsis means preventing the entry of Micro-organisms. Maintaining of general cleanliness while, picking, grading, packing and transporting of fruits and vegetables increases their keeping quality and the products prepared from them will be of superior quality.
2. **Drying:** Sun-drying or mechanical drying of fruits and vegetables involves complete removal of the moisture from them. They are then treated with sulphur fumes to maintain colour and also to avoid spoilage by Microorganisms. Dates,

grapes, Jack, Peaches, beans, bitter gourd, onions, potatoes etc. are preserved by this method.

3. **Freezing:** When fruits and vegetables are brought suddenly to a very low temperature at which all the chemical reactions stop. But it requires rather expensive equipment and stripping and storing under refrigeration.
4. **Preservation by heating:** This process consists basically the application of heat in varying degrees to the food in close containers for a sufficiently long time to sterilise the contents before they are hermetically sealed. This method of preservation by heat is also known as processing. Canned fruits and vegetables come under this category.

   High temperature used for preservation:

   (*i*) Pasteurization temperature (below 100°C)

   (*ii*) Sterilization temperature (above 100°C).
5. **Preservation by sugar:** No organisms can grow on a substance which contains sugar concentration above 65%, as they get desiccated by osmosis. Jams, jellies, marmalades, candies, crystallized fruits are preserved by this method.
6. **Preservation by salt:** Products which contain about 15% salt makes it most unfavourable for the growth and multiplication of Microorganisms. Salt acts both by osmosis and as a poison on Microorganisms. Pickles of fruits, vegetables and other pickles products are preserved by this method.
7. **Preservation by chemicals:** Chemicals like Benzoic acid SO_2 at specific concentration help to preserve the fruit juices and squashes. Benzoic acid in the form of 0.06-0.10% sodium benzoate is sufficient and is effective against yeasts and its action is effective in the presence of CO_2.

   Potassium matabisulphite (KMS) when added liberates SO_2 which reacts with water to form sulphurous acid. The concentration of SO_2 recommended is 350 PPM. It is more active against moulds, spores and bacteria.
8. **Preservation by fermentation:** Fruit juices containing sugar are fermented to produce alcohol. These fermented substances keep off the spoilage organisms due to the presence of alcohol. 14% alcohol acts as preservative in wines. Wines, beer, vinegar, fermented drinks, fermented pickles etc. are, prepared by these processes.
9. **Preservation by irradiation:** Sterilization of food by ionising radiations is a recently developed method of preservation which is yet to gain acceptance. In the irradiation of food, the radiation dose must be carefully controlled. The WHO and IAEA have recommended that radiation dose of upto 1 kilo rad is not hazardous. Radiation energy must be provided in such a manner that it reaches every particle of food to ensure adequate killing of all microorganisms. Ionizing radiations can be used for sterilisation of food in hermetically sealed packs, reduction of the spoilage flora on perishable foods, control of infection in stored cereals, prevention of sprouting of potatoes, onions etc.

Preservation Products

Jam: Jam is more or less a concentrated fruit pulp possessing a fruity heavy body form. It is rich in flavour. Pectin in the fruit gives it a good set. It contains not less than 68% soluble solids and thus high concentration of sugar facilitate preservation. Jam manufacturer can chose fresh fruit, frozen, chilled or cold stored fruits, fruits or fruit pulp preserved by heat, sulphite, fruits or fruit pulp or dried fruits. Sound fresh fruits free of any damage and for better felling effect, green fruits should be mixed with the ripe fruits. Overripe fruit should not be used. The fruit must be washed thoroughly to remove any adhering dust. Leaves, stalks and other undesirable portions of the fruits must be removed.

Fruit is then subjected to preliminary treatment which varies from fruit to fruit, e.g. apples are peeled, cut into pieces and then pulbed. Strawberries are crushed between rollers but in stone, fruits pacts, they are Lye peeled, stones removed and pulp is cut into pieces.

Addition of sugar: Amount of sugar to be added depends upon the degree of ripeness and acidity of the fruit. To get a minimum of 68.5% of sugar in the jam, generally 55.0 g of sugar is added to every 450 g of fruit.

Addition of acid, colour, and flavour: Generally citric acid, tartaric acid are used to supplement the acidity of fruits for jam making because appropriate combination of Pectin, sugar and acid is essential to give a set to the jam. A good result is obtained if the pH of mixture is about 3.0. Ordinarily, jams do not require addition of flavours of desired, may be added when jam boiling completes. Looking fruit and sugar mixture are boiled to concentrate the soluble solids to about 68.5% and also to bring about necessary degree of inversion of sugar. Determination of soluble solids is easily carried out by using hand refractometer while, boiling is in progress.

Packing: Soon after the end point is reached the jam should be cooled in cooling pan to about 93°C and filled into jars at this temperature either mechanically or by hand. The surface of the jam in the jars should be covered with a thin disc of waxed tissue paper and allowed to cool. The jars should be stored in a dry place. Jams can be prepared from fruits like apple, tomato, papaya, strawberry etc.

Jelly: In Jelly making, pectin is the most essential constituent. This pectin is present in the cell walls of fruit. Precipitation of pectin while boiling causes jelly formation. Precipitation takes places, only when pectin, acid, sugar and water are in equilibrium.

Fruits for jelly: Many fruits are rich in pectin as well as acid and are thus well suited for jelly making. Apple, grape, guava, lemon, orange, plum are rich in pectin and acid.

Selection of fruits: Sufficiently ripe, but not overripe and should have good flavour. Fruits are washed thoroughly with water. Guava and apple, need not be peeled, while fruits like, orange, lemon require peeling before used.

Extraction of pectin: Only a minimum quantity of water should be used to the fruit for a simple extraction of pectin the amount of water required depend or the kind of fruit. To get the desired pectin requirements the fruit should be cooked. The cooking time also varies from fruit to fruit and the time of boiling of fruit required to extract pectin. The pectin extract can be clarified by allowing to settle overnight and the supernatant pectin liquor separated as it may be filtered through a muslin cloth. Aluminium vessels are used for boiling.

Pectin requirement: Usually about 0.5-1.0% pectin of suitable quality in the extract is sufficient to produce a good jelly. If pectin is in excess of this a firm and tough jelly is formed and if it is less the jelly may fail to set. Pectin, sugar, acid and water must be present approximately in the following proportion, pectin (1.0%), sugar (60-65%), fruit acid (1%) water (33-38%). The sugar should be sprinkled on the fruit extract while it is boiling and should be thoroughly mixed by stirring to ensure complete dissolution. During boiling, the scum which rises to the top is removed.

Cooking of Jelly: The mixture is boiled for about 20 minutes and the end point is when the final Brix reaches 65°C. The end point can also be determined by flake test. After reaching the end point, jelly is then cooled slightly and poured into hot and dry containers.

Pickles: The preservations of food in common salt or vinegar is called pickling. Spices and oil may be added. Pickles are good appetizers and add to the partibility of a meal. They aid digestion by stimulating the flow of gastric juices. Salt, vinegar and lactic acid are the three important ingredients used in pickling. These substances when used in sufficient quantities, act as preservatives either singly or collectively.

1. **Salt:** Vegetables don't foremast when covered with a large amount of salt.
2. **Vinegar:** This preservative as pickles, the final percentage should not be below 2%. To avoid dilution of vinegar by water from vegetables they can be kept in a strong vinegar of about (10% concentration).
3. **Lactic acid:** Sufficient quantity of lactic acid, prevents lactic acid bacteria, and any change in the composition of the material is prevented, provided it is air-tight.

6. (*c*) Crucifers are attacked by several pests among which diamondback moth is the most challenging and destructive as it has developed resistance to more than 40 insecticides. Aphids and mustard saw fly are equally destructive under North Indian conditions.

Major pests

1. Diamond back moth: Plutella xylostella (L.) (Plutellidae: Lepidoptera)

Distribution and status: World - wide

Host range: Serious past of Cabbage and cauliflower, but also feeds on other crucifers and solanaceous plants.

Damage symptoms: First instar larvae mine epidermal surface of leaves producing typical white patches. Larvae, second instar onwards feed externally making holes on the leaves and soil them with excreta. Heavy infestations leave little more than the leaf veins.

Bionomics: Yellowish, pinhead sized eggs are laid singly or in batches of 2-40 on the underside of leaves. A female may lay 18-356 eggs in her life time. Egg period 2 - 9 days. Larva: 8-12 mm long, pale yellowish green in colour, pointed at both the ends with fine erect black hairs scattered over the body. Larval period 8-16 days. Pupa is a barrel shaped silken cocoon which is open at both the ends and is attached to the leaf surface. Pupal period 4-5 days. Adult: Small, greyish brown having pale whitish narrow wings with inner margins yellow. Three pale whitish triangular markings on hind margins of each forewing are prominent. At rest, a dorsal median patch of three diamond shaped yellowish white spots clearly visible by joining both forewings. Hind wings have a fringe of long hairs. Adult moth may live for about 20 days. Total life cycle is completed in 15-18 days. There are several generations in a year.

Management: Grow mustard as trap crop. Raise 2 rows of mustard for every 25 rows of cabbage. Sow first mustard crop 15 days prior to cabbage planting or plant 20 days old mustard seedling at the time of cabbage planting. Plant 35 days old cabbage seedlings.

- Install pheromone trap to monitor DBM adults @ 5/ha and 25/ha for mass trapping.
- Apply Bacillus thuringiensis formulation @1 g/L or NSKE 4% spray. Alternate Bt. sero types kurstaki (B.t.k.) and aizawal (B.t.a.)
- Reduce insects colonising on mustard to prevent defoliation of the entire plant by applying dichlorovas 350 at 10 or 15 days interval starting from 15 days after sowing.
- Conserve larval parasitoids viz., Cotesia plutellae in plains and Diadegma semiclausum in hills. Release 40,000 adults / ac, five times @ 8,000 adults/release commencing from 20 days after planting. Also encourage other parasitoids like Apanteles sicarius, Tetrastychus sokolowski (larval), Diadrumus collaris (larval pupal) and Brachymeria excarinata (pupal parasitoids)
- Depending upon the pest intensity, spray any of the following insecticide with 500 - 1000 L water/ha primordial or head initiation stage. Mix teepol or sandovit 0.5 ml/Lt of water whenever sprays are made.

2. Leaf webber: Crocidolomia binotalis (Pyraustidae : Lepidoptera)

Distribution and status: Regular pest of minor status but occasionally reach serious proportions.

Host range: Cabbage, radish, mustard and other cruciferous plants.

Damage symptoms: Young larva feeds gregariously on leaves, later webs together the leaves and feeds. Due to gregarious feeding, rotting of cabbage heads and cauliflower curds are common. Regular pest of minor status but occasionally turn to serious proportions.

Bionomics: Female moth lays 40-100 eggs on underside of the leaves. Egg period 5-15 days. Larva: with red head, brown longitudinal stripes and rows of tubercles on its pale violet body. Larval period 24-50 days. Pupates in soil, pupa is an earthen cocoon. Pupal period 14-40 days. Adult: Small pale brown with forewing having distinct wavy lines and prominent wavy spots. Hind wings semi-hyaline. Life cycle is completed in 43-82 days. More than one generation may be completed in the season.

Management

1. Spray phosalone 50 EC 1.0 L, fenvalerate 20 EC or cypermethrin 10 EC or deltamethrin 28 EC 250 ml, cartap hydrochloride 50 SP 500 ml, spinosad 45 SC 125 ml/ha or azadirachtin 0.03% 2.5-5.0 L/ha. Do not repeat the insecticides with similar mode of action.
2. The pest is regulated by two larval parasitoids viz., Microbracon mellus and Apanteles crocidolmiae

3. Cabbage semilooper: Tircihoplusia ni (Noctuidae: Lepidoptera)

Distribution and status: USA, India and Sri Lanka

Host range: Cabbage, tomato and other cruciferous vegetables.

Damage symptoms: Caterpillars start scrapping and feeding on the leaves initially and later defoliate entire plant leaving midribs and main veins. More damage is evidenced in nurseries than in main field.

Bionomics: Eggs are greenish white, spherical and sculptured and are laid singly on ventral surface of leaves. Adults are stout moths. Head and thorax grey in colour, while abdomen is white with basal tuft of hairs. Pupation takes place in thin transparent cocoons on ventral surface of leaves. Life cycle occupies one month.

Management

1. Hand pick and destroy caterpillars.
2. Use light trap to attract and kill adults.
3. Spray quinolphos 0.5% or endosulfan 0.1 % or malathion 0.1%.

4. Cabbage butterfly: Pieris brassicae (Pieridae: Lepidoptera)

Distribution and status: Throughout India

Host range: cabbage, cauliflower, knol-khol and it may also attack turnip, radish, sarson, toria (Brassica campestris) and other cruciferous plants.

Bionomics: Full-grown pale yellow larva becomes greenish and measures 40-50 mm in length. In adults, the wings are pale white, with a black patch on the apical angle of each fore wing and a black spot on the costal margin of each hind wing. The females have two conspicuous black circular dots on the dorsal side of each fore wing. Males are smaller than the females and have black spots on the underside of each fore wing.

The butterflies are very active in the field and lay, on an average, 164 yellowish conical eggs in clusters of 50-90 on the upper or the lower side of a leaf. Egg period is 3-17 days. The caterpillars feed gregariously during the early instars and disperse as they approach maturity. They pass through five stages and are full-fed in 15-40 days. The larvae pupate at some distance from the food plants, often in barns or on trees. The pupal stage lasts 7-28 days. The butterflies live for 3-12 days and the pest breeds four times during October-April.

Damage symptoms

The caterpillars alone feed on leaves, young shoots and green pods. When young, they feed gregariously but the grown-up caterpillars migrate from one field to another. The first instar caterpillars just scrape the leaf surface, whereas the subsequent instars eat up leaves from the margins inwards, leaving intact the main veins. Often, entire plants are eaten up.

Management

1. When in the gregarious stage, the caterpillars can be easily controlled by picking and destroying the infested leaves.
2. The grown-up caterpillars should be controlled with malathion 5 per cent @ 37.5 kg per ha or by spraying 1.25 L of endosulfan 35 EC or 500 ml of dichlorvos 76 SC in 600-900 L of water per ha.
3. Conserve larval parasitoid Apanteles glomeratus (Braconidae) in the natural populations.

5. Cabbage borer: Hellula undalis (Pyraustidae: Lepidoptera)

Distribution and status: Worldwide, this is sporadic but occasionally serious.

Host range: cabbage, cauliflower, radish, knoll-khol, beet root and the weed Gynadropis pentaphylla.

Damage symptoms: Larva aborts head formation. Caterpillars first mine the leaves later feed on leaves, shoots sheltered within silken passage and finally bore into the stems. They prevent head initiation causing multiple shoots or heads.

Bionomics: Female moth lays oval shaped eggs singly or in clusters on the undersurface of the leaves or some other parts of the plant. Eggs are pearly white when laid which turns pink next day and later brown. Egg period 2-3 days. Larva: Pale whitish-brown in colour with 4-5 purplish brown longitudinal stripes. Larval period 7-17 days. Pupa is a cocoon. Pupal period 6 days. Adult: Pale greyish brown. Forewings have grey wavy lines, a pale apical spot and pale edged dark moon shaped (lunule), hind wings pale dusky with slight fuscous suffusion on apical area. Life cycle is completed in 15-25 days.

Management: Same as for leaf webber.

6. Mustard Sawfly: Athalia lugens (Tenthredinidae: Hymenoptera)

Distribution and status: Widely distributed in Indonesia, Formosa, Myanmar and the Indian Sub-continent.

Host range: Mustard, toria (Brassica campestris), rapeseed, cabbage, cauliflower, knolkhol, turnip, radish, etc

Bionomics: Dark green larvae have 8 pairs of abdominal prolegs. There are five black stripes on the back, and the body has a wrinkled appearance. A full-grown larva measures 16-18 mm in length. The adults are small orange yellow insects with black markings on the body and have smoky wings with black veins. The mustard sawfly breeds from October to March and undergoes pupal diapause during summer. The adults emerge from these cocoons early in October. They live for 2-8 days and lay 30-35 eggs singly, in slits made with saw like ovipositors along the underside of the leaf margins. Egg period is 4-8 days and the larvae feed exposed in groups of 3-6 on the leaves during morning and evening. They remain hidden during the day time and, when disturbed, fall to the ground and feign death. There are 7 instars with a larval period of 16-35 days. Pupation is in water proof oval cocoons in soil and the pupal period is 11-31 days. Lifecycle is completed in 31-34 days. It completes 2-3 generations from October to March.

Damage symptoms: The grubs alone are destructive. They bite holes into leaves preferring the young growth and skeletonize the leaves completely. Sometimes, even the epidermis of the shoot is eaten up. Although the seedlings succumb; the older plants, when attacked, do not bear seed.

Management:

1. Give first irrigation 3-4 weeks after sowing as it reduces the bug population significantly. (*ii*) Spray 1.0 L of malathion 50 EC or 625 ml of endosulfan 35 EC or quinalphos 25 EC in 500-600 L of water per ha once in October and again in March-April.
2. Conserve larval parasitoid Perilissus cingulator Morby (Ichneumonidae) and the bacterium, Serratia marcescens Bizio (Enterobacteriaceae)

7. Cabbage aphid: Brevicoryne brassicae (Aphididae: Hemiptera)

Damage symptoms: Colonies of aphid are found on tender shoots and suck sap from plant tissues. In case of severe infestation plants may completely dry up and die away. On larger plants, feeding damage results in curling and yellowing leaves, stunted plant growth, and deformed heads. White cast skin will be present at the base of the plant.

Management:

1. Set up yellow sticky trap @ 10/ha.
2. Spray any one of the following:
   - Dimethoate 30 EC 1000 ml/ha.
   - Methyl demeton 25 EC 1000 ml/ha.
   - Monocrotophos 36 WSC 625 ml/ha.
   - Neem oil 2.0 L/ha.
   - Azadirachtin 0.03% 2.5-5.0 L/ha
     - ❑ Aphid skin is covered with waxy filaments and for better adherence on aphid body, add wetting agent in spray fluid.

8. Cabbage flea beetle: Phyllotreta cruciferae (Chrysomelidae: Coleoptera)

Distribution and status: Europe, USSR, North and South America, Australia, Japan and India.

Host range: Mustard, raya, taramira, toria, radish, turnip, cabbage, cauliflower, knoll-khol, dahlia, sweet sultan, antirrhinum and sweet peas.

Damage symptoms: Adult beetle feeds on the leaves by making round holes. The stem, flower and even pods may also be attacked. Decaying odour is emitted by the cabbage plants.

Bionomics: The female beetle lays 50-80 creamy white eggs singly in the soil around the host plants. Egg period 5-10 days. The larva is dirty white in colour and 5 mm in length. Larval period 9-15 days. Pupal period 2-4 days. Adult beetle is metallic blue with greenish hue. Beetle measures 1.8-2.0 mm. There are 7-8 generations in a year.

Management: Spray 2.5 kg of carbaryl 50 WP or 2 L of endosulfan 35 EC in 750 litres of water per ha.

Minor pests

- Painted bug: Bagrada hilaris (Pentatomidae: Hemiptera)
- Cutworms: Agrotis ipsilon (Noctuidae: Lepidoptera)
- Thrips: Thrips tabaci (Thripidae: Thysanoptera)
- Aphid: Myzus persicae, Liaphis erysimi (Aphididae: Hemiptera).

Previous Years' Paper (Solved)

IFS–Agriculture Main Examination, 2018

PAPER-I

INSTRUCTIONS: *There are* ***Eight*** *questions in all, out of which* ***Five*** *are to be attempted. Candidates should attempt question nos. 1 and 5 which are compulsory, and out of the remaining* ***six*** *questions,* ***three*** *are to be attempted selecting at least* ***one*** *question from each of the two sections A and B. All questions carry equal marks. Answers must be written in English only.*

SECTION–A

1. Answer the following in about 150 words each:

(*a*) Enlist the agroclimatic zones of India and give their important cropping patterns.

(*b*) What is rainfed farming? Discuss the technologies for stabilizing agriculture production in rainfed areas.

(*c*) Maintenance of soil health needs regular recycling of lignocellulolytic materials to the soil. Justify.

(*d*) What is multiple cropping? Give its significance in increasing the crop production.

(*e*) Discuss the effect of environmental factors on crop distribution and production.

2. Answer the following in about 200 words each:

(*a*) Discuss how the agroforestry system helps in improving the livelihood of rural people.

(*b*) Mention the principles of weed management and give their merits and demerits.

(*c*) Define runoff, give factors affecting it and explain soil loss equation during water erosion.

(*d*) Highlight the effects of environmental pollution on living beings.

3. Answer the following in about 200 words each:

(*a*) Justify the importance of forms of nutrients, their concentrations and ratios to other nutrients in soil for their uptake and crop growth.

(*b*) Discuss how contingent crop planning helps in dryland agriculture.

(*c*) Explain green-house effect and sources of their emission.

(*d*) Describe aquatic weeds and their control management.

4. Answer the following in about 200 words each:

(*a*) Discuss the major constraints in pulse production in India.

(*b*) What is propagation? Give advantages of micro-propagation with reference to plantation plants.

(*c*) What is soil genesis? Discuss the role of factors of soil formation.

(*d*) What soil and water conservation practices are required to be adopted under hilly regions?

SECTION–B

5. Answer the following in about 150 words each:

(*a*) Define and explain consumptive use of water, evapotranspiration and water use efficiency.

(*b*) Discuss the significance of advance farm planning for optimum use of resources.

(*c*) What is agricultural cooperative farming? In what way is cooperative farming helpful to small and marginal farmers?

(*d*) Describe agricultural price policy and instruments of price policy.

(*e*) Discuss the role of farmers' participation in identifying needs of the area for planning and development.

6. Answer the following in about 200 words each:

(*a*) What are drip and sprinkler irrigation? Give their merits and demerits.

(*b*) How does the principle of opportunity cost help farmers to decide what to grow?

(*c*) Explain marketing of farm products and marketing functions.

(*d*) What is programme planning? Explain its evaluation.

7. Answer the following in about 200 words each:

(*a*) How is drainage important? Explain its types.

(*b*) What is farm budgeting? How is it important to farmers?

(*c*) Give different approaches to study marketing and problems in marketing of agricultural produce.

(*d*) How do self-help groups help to provide economic empowerment to rural women?

8. Answer the following in about 200 words each:

(*a*) What is selective mechanization and progress of farm mechanization? Explain advantages and disadvantages of farm mechanization.

(*b*) How is indigenous technical knowledge (ITK) useful to formulate the future programmes?

(*c*) Specify the criteria for time of irrigation.

(*d*) Discuss the importance of farm management and its scope, with characteristics.

PAPER-II

INSTRUCTIONS: *Candidates should attempt question nos.* **1** *and* **5** *which are compulsory, and out of the remaining* **six** *questions,* **three** *are to be attempted, selecting at least* **one** *question from each section. All questions carry equal marks. Answers must be written in English only.*

SECTION–A

1. Answer the following:

(*a*) What is the 'powerhouse' of a cell? Describe its structure and label.

(*b*) Describe the Mendel's law of inheritance by giving suitable example.

(*c*) Describe the process of certified seed production in field crops.

(*d*) Describe the conditions to maintain the seed quality during post-harvest processing and storage.

(*e*) Discuss the role of metal ions in enzyme activity.

2. Distinguish between the following:

(*a*) Seed production in Self-pollinated and Cross-pollinated crops (giving suitable examples).

(*b*) Heterosis breeding and Mutation breeding.

(*c*) Ribonucleic acid and Deoxyribonucleic acid.

(*d*) Enzymes and Plant pigments.

3. Answer the following:

(*a*) Describe the methods and significance of maintenance breeding in seed production system.

(*b*) "C_4 plants are more water-use efficient compared to C_3 plants." Explain by citing suitable examples.

(c) "Transpiration is a necessary evil." Explain and justify the statement.

(d) Describe the significance of male sterility in hybrid seed production. Mention different types of male sterility.

4. Answer the following:

(a) Illustrate the plant and animal cells.

(b) What is the significance of β-oxidation in germinating seeds?

(c) Discuss orthodox and recalcitrant seeds with examples.

(d) Write down the yield components and parameters of cereals, pulses and oilseeds.

SECTION–B

5. Answer/Write on the following:

(a) Discuss the process of minimizing the pesticide residue effects in vegetables.

(b) Seed plot technique for virus-free potato seed production.

(c) Describe the physiological role of gibberellic acid in seed germination process.

(d) Mango malformation.

(e) Importance of carrot and guava in human nutrition.

6. Answer the following:

(a) Calculate the amount of Malathion 50 EC to treat 50 hectares of flower crop @ 800 litres per hectare. The concentration of spray material to be used is 0.01%.

(b) Discuss the problems involved in marketing of vegetables and fruits.

(c) What is pruning? Discuss its principles and significance in fruit crops.

(d) What is biological control of plant diseases? Discuss its principles. Name the important biocontrol agents and their application against important diseases of crops.

7. Distinguish between the following:

(a) Fungal wilt and Bacterial wilt of vegetables.

(b) Insect parasitoids and Predators.

(c) Formal and Informal gardens.

(d) Seed germination and Seed dormancy.

8. Answer the following:

(a) Describe the food production constraints in Indian agricultural system.

(b) Mention the important storage insects of pulses and cereals, and their management practices.

(c) Describe the principles and methods of post-harvest management of important fruits.

ANSWERS

PAPER-I

SECTION 'A'

1. (a) 15 Agro-Climatic Zones in India Categorised by the Planning Commission

(i) Western Himalayan Region
(ii) Eastern Himalayan Region
(iii) Lower Gangetic Plain Region
(iv) Middle Gangetic Plain Region
(v) Upper Gangetic Plains Region
(vi) Trans-Ganga Plains Region
(vii) Eastern Plateau and Hills
(viii) Central Plateau and Hills
(ix) Western Plateau and Hills
(x) Southern Plateau and Hills
(xi) Eastern Coastal Plains and Hills
(xii) Western Coastal Plains and Ghats
(xiii) Gujarat Plains and Hills
(xiv) Western Dry Region
(xv) Island Region

Efficient Cropping Systems for different Agro-climatic Zones of India

	Agro-climatic region	*Soil type*	*Cropping systems*
1.	Western Himalayas (cold-arid) Jammu and Kashmir, Ladakh Plateau	Shallow, sandy to loamy	Rice-Potato-Wheat
2.	Western Kachchh and part of Kathiawar	Desert and saline soils	Sorghum-wheat-millet, Maize-Green manure Maize-wheat-sorghum
3.	Deccan plateau (hot-arid) Andhra Pradesh, Karnataka	Red and black soils	Pigeon pea + sorghum/ groundnut cotton-millet-sorghum
4.	Northern plains and central highlands (semi-arid) Gujarat, Haryana, Madhya Pradesh, Punjab, Uttar Pradesh, Rajasthan	Alluvium derived soils	Maize-green manure Rice-wheat-Maize-wheat Cotton-wheat
5.	Central highlands, Gujarat plains Kathiawar penisula (hot semi-arid)	Medium deep black soils	Groundnut-wheat Rice-sugarcane Rice-wheat
6.	Deccan plateau (hot-semi-arid) Red and black soils	Shallow and Medium black soils Sorghum-safflower cotton-millet Pigeon pea-sunflower	Pearl millet-potato-cotton Cotton-millet-sorghum
7.	Eastern ghats, Tamil Nadu uplands and Deccan plateau (hot semi-arid)	Red loamy soils	Rice-Rice-pulses, Cotton-groundnut Groundnut-sorghum
8.	Northern plain (hot sub humid)	Alluvium derived soil	Rice-wheat, Maize-wheat, Maize-mustard-sugarcane
9.	Central High lands (hot sub-humid)	Black and red soils	Sorghum-wheat, Maize-wheat
10.	Eastern plateau (hot sub-humid) soils	Red and yellow soils	Rice-wheat-green manure Rice-pigeon pea
11.	Eastern plateau and Eastern ghats (hot sub-humid)	Red and lateritic soils	Rice-Rice-Wheat Groundnut-sun flower
12.	Eastern plain (hot sub-humid)	Alluvium derived soil	Rice-wheat, Rice-lentil Rice-chickpea, jute-rice
13.	Western Himalayas (warm sub-humid)	Brown, forest and podzoilic soils	Maize-wheat, finger millet-rice-mustard
14.	Bengal and Assam plains (hot sub humid)	Alluvium derived soils	Rice-wheat-rice Rice-potato-sesame
15.	Eastern Himalayas (warm humid)	Brown and red hill soils	Rice-rice, rice-wheat jute-rice
16.	North-eastern Hills (warm humid)	Red and lateritic soils	Rice-rice, rice-wheat jute-rice
17.	Eastern coastal plains (hot sub humid to semiarid)	Coastal alluvium	Rice-rice, Rice-groundnut, Jute-rice
18.	Western ghats and coastal plains (hot humid)	Red lateritic alluvium derived soils	Rice-rice, Rice-sorghum, Plantation crops
19.	Islands (hot humid)	Red loamy and sandy soils	Rice-rice, Plantation crops

1. (*b*) **Rainfed farming:** Dryland Agriculture refers to growing of crops entirely under rainfed conditions.

Based on the amount of rainfall received, dryland agriculture can be grouped into three categories:

1. **Dry Farming**: Cultivation of crops in areas where rainfall is less than 750 mm per annum
2. **Dryland Farming**: Cultivation of crops in areas receiving rainfall above 750 mm
3. **Rainfed Farming**: Cultivation of crops in regions receiving more than 1,150 mm.

Technologies for Stabilizing Agriculture Production in Rainfed Areas

REDUCING EVAPORATION LOSSES:

Soil moisture is the most limiting factor in dryland agriculture. It is lost as evaporation from the soil surface and as transpiration from the plant surfaces. Evaporation has to be arrested as it is not directly related to productivity whereas transpiration can be reduced to some extent without affecting productivity of plants. The evaporation losses can be reduced by:

1. Mulches 2. Antitranspirants
3. Wind breaks 4. Weed control

REDUCING TRANSPIRATION LOSSES

Antitranspirants: About 99 per cent of the water absorbed by the plants is lost in transpiration. If transpiration is controlled, it may help in maintenance of favourable water balance.

Antitranspirant is any material applied to transpiring plant surfaces for reducing water loss from the plant. These are of four types:

1. Stomatal closing 2. Film forming
3. Reflective 4. Growth retardant

WIND BREAKS AND SHELTERBELTS

Wind breaks are any structures that obstruct wind flow and reduce wind speed while shelterbelts are rows of trees planted for protection of crops against wind. The direction from which wind is blowing is called windward side and direction to which wind is blowing is called leeward side.

Shelterbelts are planted across the direction of wind. They do not obstruct the wind flow completely. Depending upon their porosity, certain amount of wind passes through the shelterbelts while the rest deflects and crosses over the shelterbelts. It thus reduces wind speed without causing turbulence. The protection offered by the shelterbelts is dependent on the height of central tree row in the shelterbelts. Generally, shelterbelts give protection from desiccating winds to the extent of 5 to 10 times their height on windward side and up to 30 times on leeward side. Due to reduction in wind speed, evaporation losses are reduced and more water is available for plants. The beneficial effect of shelterbelts is seen more clearly in drought years. In addition, shelterbelts reduce wind erosion.

WEED CONTROL

1. Promptweed control eliminates the competition of weeds with crops for limited soil moisture.
2. Transpiration rate from weeds is more compared to crops.
3. Effective weed control in dryland agriculture leads to increasing availability of soil moisture to crops.

1. (*c*) Plant-derived cellulosic materials play a critical role when organic wastes are composted to produce a beneficial amendment for topsoil. This review article considers publications dealing with the science of composting, emphasizing ways in which the cellulosic and lignin components of the composted material influence both the process and the product. Cellulose has been described as a main source of energy to drive the biological transformations and the consequent temperature rise and chemical changes that are associated with composting. Lignin can be viewed as a main starting material for the formation of humus, the

recalcitrant organic matter that provides the water-holding, ion exchange and bulking capabilities that can contribute greatly to soil health and productivity. Regular recycling of lignocellulosic materials contribute to air permeability, bulking, and water retention during the composting process. Critical variables for successful composting include the ratio of carbon to nitrogen, the nature of the cellulosic component, particle size, bed size and format, moisture, pH, aeration, temperature, and time. Composting can help to address solid waste problems and provides a sustainable way to enhance soil fertility.

1. (*d*) Multiple Cropping: Multiple cropping is the practice of growing two or more crops in the same piece of land during a single growing season. It helps to harvest as much as possible from the limited land resources provided other resources required for crop production is effectively utilized. It is a form of polyculture and can take in several forms bringing intensification to the existing farming system.

Significance in Increasing Crop Production

The technique of multiple cropping allows farmers to achieve better results by making practical use of resources such as soil, water, fertilisers, etc. Utilisation of nutrients is maximum with multiple cropping as crops having different nutritional requirements grow simultaneously in the same piece of land. Various types of crops can be cultivated in mixed cropping practice, such as food crops, vegetables, fruits, fodder, etc. This helps farmers become self-sufficient in food production while also providing them the option to sell additional products.

Every years, insect and pest attacks destroy a significant amount of agricultural production. This spoilage is particularly due to the susceptibility of specific crops to specific pests. However, some crops are naturally immune to particular pests. Such immune crops synthesise different chemicals that either kill the pest or deflect the pest from them. Cultivating such resistant plants with vulnerable crops protects the vulnerable crops by masking them from the pest. Sometimes, some crops are used to divert the pest from main crops, for example, wheat is always cultivated with canola to divert pests from wheat. The pests attack canola, thus keeping wheat unharmed.

Multiple cropping also helps to maintain soil fertility with suitable crops like legumes in the cropping system. The roots of leguminous plants form a symbiotic association with nitrifying bacteria. The bacteria fix the atmospheric nitrogen in the soil and therefore increase the fertility of the soil.

Multiple cropping also decreases the space available for weeds and restricts their growth. By suppressing weeds, multiple cropping increases the food production.

1. (*e*) Environmental factors that influence the extent of crop agriculture are terrain, climate, soil properties, and soil water. It is the combination of these four factors that allow specific crops to be grown in certain areas. It is seen that the climatic factors should be more interrelated for the betterment of the crop yield. Climate change is the most several problem that world is facing today environmental factor such as water, temperature, fire, light, Nutrients are effect on crop productivity.Today, in order to maximize production, most of the cultivated croplands and grasslands for commercial agriculture are in areas where crops and livestock are well suited to local conditions.

2. (*a*) Agroforestry, as a science and practice, has the potential to contribute to the improvement of rural livelihood, due to the capacity of its various forms to offer multiple alternatives and opportunities to smallholders to enhance farm production and income, while protecting the agricultural environment. The growing food insecurity and deteriorating livelihood situations call for concerted and consorted actions at national and international levels to take advantage of the high potential of agroforestry, among other systems, for promoting best land use practices. However, adoption of agroforestry technologies to effectively improve livelihoods of vulnerable smallholders will need national capabilities to develop and implement appropriate policies and to set up efficient institutions. In this connection, participation of farmers should be central in the process. Traditional practices and indigenous knowledge will play as an important role as extension and training. As well as building on practices used in forestry and agriculture, agroforestry also works towards land protection and conservation through more effective protection of stock, control of soil erosion, salinity and water tables and a higher quality control of timber.

A denser, more-dependable tree covering can provide shelter to livestock during the warmer months allowing the animals can conserve energy. That same tree covering helps block out wind, helping to boost water retention levels that can help produce a more robust crop yield. The agroforestry has brought improvement in socio-economic and ecological conditions of farmers by generating employment, increasing family income, enhancing the crop diversity and reducing dependency on natural forest.

2. (*b*) For designing any weed control programme in a given area, one must know the nature and habitat of the weeds in that area, how they react to environmental changes and how they respond to herbicides. Before selecting a method of weed control one, much have information on the number of viable seeds nature of dispersal of seeds, dormancy of seeds, longevity of buried seeds and ability to survive under adverse conditions, life span of the weed, soil textures moisture and (In case of soil applied volatile herbicides the herbicide will be successful only in sandy loam soil but not in clayey soil. Flooding as a method of weed control will be successful only in heavy soil and net in sandy soil) the area to be controlled.

Principles of weed control are:

(*a*) Prevention

(*b*) Eradication

(*c*) Control

(*d*) Management

Weed control methods are grouped into cultural, physical, chemical and biological. Every method of weed control has its own advantages and disadvantages. No single method is successful under all weed situations. Many a time, a combination of these methods gives effective and economic control than a single method.

MECHANICAL WEED CONTROL

The mechanical methods include tillage, hoeing, hand weeding, digging cheeling, sickling, mowing, burning, flooding, mulching etc.

Merits of Mechanical Method:

1. Oldest, effective and economical method
2. Large area can be covered in shorter time
3. Safe method for environment
4. Does not involve any skill
5. Weeding is possible in between plants
6. Deep rooted weeds can be controlled effectively

Demerits of Mechanical Method:

1. Labour consuming
2. Possibility of damaging crop
3. Requires ideal and optimum specific condition

CULTURAL WEED CONTROL

In cultural methods, tillage, fertiliser application. and irrigation are important. In addition, aspects like selection of variety, time of sowing, cropping system, cleanliness of the farm etc., are also useful in controlling weeds.

Merits of Cultural Method:

1. Low cost for weed control
2. Easy to adopt
3. No residual problem
4. Technical skill is not involved
5. No damage to crops
6. Effective weed control
7. Crop-weed ecosystem is maintained.

Demerits of Cultural Method:

1. Immediate and quick weed control is not possible
2. Weeds are kept under suppressed condition
3. Perennial and problematic weeds can not be controlled
4. Practical difficulty in adoption

BIOLOGICAL WEED CONTROL

Use of living organisms viz., insects, disease organisms, herbivorous fish, snails or even competitive plants for the control of weeds is called biological control. In biological control method, it is not possible to eradicate weeds but weed population can be reduced. This method is not useful to control all types of weeds. Introduced weeds are best targets for biological control.

CHEMICAL WEED CONTROL

Using chemicals, generally referred as herbicides, for the control of weeds is called chemical weed control. In 1944 – discovery of 2,4-D Na salt as a land mark in herbicide usage.

Merits:

1. Herbicide can be recommended for adverse soil and climatic conditions, as manual weeding is highly impossible during monsoon season.
2. Herbicide can control weeds even before they emerge from the soil so that crops can germinate and grow in completely weed-free environment at early stages. It is usually not possible with physical weed comfort.
3. Weeds, which resemble like crop in vegetative phase may escape in manual weeding. However, these weeds are controlled by herbicides.
4. Herbicide is highly suitable for broadcasted and closely spaced crops.
5. Controls the weeds without any injury to the root system of the associated standing crop especially in plantation crops like Tea and Coffee.
6. Reduces the need for pre planting tillage.
7. Controls many perennial weed species.
8. Herbicides control the weed in the field itself or *insitu* controlling where as mechanical method may lead to dispersal of weed species through seed.
9. It is profitable where labour is scarce and expensive.
10. Suited for minimum tillage concept.
11. Highly economical.

Demerits:

1. Pollutes the environment.
2. Affects the soil microbes if the dose exceeds.
3. Herbicide causes drift effect to the adjoining field.
4. It requires certain amount of minimum technical knowledge for calibration.
5. Leaves residual effects.
6. Some herbicide is highly costlier.
7. Suitable herbicides are not available for mixed and inter-cropping system.

2. (*c*) **Runoff** can be described as the part of the water cycle that flows over land as surface water instead of being absorbed into groundwater or evaporating. According to the US Geological Survey (USGS), runoff is that part of the precipitation, snow melt, or irrigation water that appears in uncontrolled surface streams, rivers, drains, or sewers.

Meteorological factors affecting runoff:

- Type of precipitation (rain, snow, sleet, etc.)

- Rainfall intensity
- Rainfall amount
- Rainfall duration
- Distribution of rainfall over the watersheds
- Direction of storm movenent
- Antecedent precipitation and resulting soil moisture
- Other meteorological and climatic conditions that affect evapotranspiration, such as temperature, wind, relative humidity, and season.

Physical characteristics affecting runoff:

- Land use
- Vegetation
- Soil type
- Drainage area
- Basin shape
- Elevation
- Slope
- Topography
- Direction of orientation
- Drainage network patterns
- Ponds, lakes, reservoirs, sinks, etc. in the basin, which prevent or alter runoff from continuing downstream.

Soil-Loss Equation

It is a representation of the combination of factors that lead to soil loss. The Universal soil-loss equation is written as

$$A = RKLSCP$$

where:

R = Rainfall and Runoff Factor

Measures erosive force of rainfall and runoff. Both total rainfall and intensity of particular storms are considered for this factor. A heavy yearly rainfall is less damaging than a series of short intense storms.

K = Soil Erodibility Factor

The erodibility of a soil based on its physical characteristics. Well drained soils have a low soil erodibility factor. The 'structural stability' of the soil also determines its erodibility factor.

L = Length of Slope

Taken together with S, the steepness of slope, L*S is the ratio of soil loss to a plot 22 m long with a 9% slope.

S = Slope

Soil on a steep slope is more likely to be carried in water runoff than soil on flat ground.

C = Cover and Management Factor

This factor represents the influence of cropping systems and management. Forests and grass are the best cover, followed by legumes, then grains such as wheat and oats. The worst type of crops from an erosion point of view are corn, soybeans, and potatoes because there is little cover.

P = Support Practice Factor

This factor represents strategies such as strip cropping, contouring, and terrace systems. P is dependent on slope as well as the practice used.

A is the predicted soil loss in metric tons per hectare per year.

2. (*d*) Pollution is the introduction of harmful contaminants into air, water or soil. These contaminants can have dire effects on entire ecosystems, making life more difficult for humans, plants and animals. Children and the elderly are particularly susceptible to the health effects from these toxins.

Air Pollution: Air pollution consists of solid particles and gases. Many pollutants are carcinogens. People who breathe in these poisons are at a higher risk for asthma and reproductive-system damage. According the US Environmental Protection Agency, birth defects can also be caused by air pollution. Humans are not the only living creatures affected by toxic air pollutants.

Water Pollution: Water is a necessity of life. People and animals need clean drinking water. Farmers need water to irrigate crops.

People enjoy using lakes and rivers for recreation. Unfortunately, this precious resource is easily contaminated by agricultural runoff, mining activities, waste treatment plants and improperly disposed-of industrial waste.

The US Environmental Protection Agency monitors 80 different contaminants that may affect drinking water. Microbial contaminants include bacteria and viruses. Most people can fight off the microbial contaminants, however, people with compromised immune systems can get dangerously ill. Contaminants like solvents, pesticides, radium and arsenic are more sinister. This type of pollution can cause long-term health problems for people. Wildlife can also die from exposure.

Litter is unsightly and dangerous. It often consists of plastic, metal or glass — materials that do not break down easily in the environment. People, especially children, can be seriously injured by a broken bottle or a rusty piece of discarded metal. Medical and sanitary wastes are biohazards that can make people sick. Litter also destroys the beauty of parks and beaches, making people avoid these areas.

Toxic substances from litter also accumulates in fish, exposing the people and animals further up the food chain to these pollutants.

Soil Contamination: Soil contamination consists of either liquid or solid particles mixed with soil. The contaminants may be physically attached to the soil particles or they may be in the spaces between the soil particles. Contamination results when hazardous substances are spilled or buried in the soil. It can also occur when pollutants settle on the soil, such as chemicals or waste from an industrial smokestack.

Plants grown in contaminated soil take up the hazardous substances through their roots. Humans or animals that ingest these plants may get sick. People and animals can also inhale soil contaminants through dust that is present in the air or absorb these hazardous chemicals through their skin.

4. (*a*) Pulses have become a victim of the high handiness of the government. They were not given the importance due to them. They have been given little importance as compared to cereals and other staple crops. Still they are treated as secondary crops. As farmers in the country have low purchasing power, their first priority becomes the staple crops like paddy, wheat and maize. Grown under rain fed conditions:The biggest constraint in pulses production is that these are still cultivated on marginal and degraded lands under rain fed conditions. More than 87% of the area under pulses is rain fed. This is much greater as compared to the area under other crops like Paddy and Wheat which are largely grown under irrigated conditions low production per unit area. In India Pulses have very low production per unit area. As far as productivity is concerned, the highest productivity recorded was of France (4219 kg/ha) followed by Canada (1936 kg/ha), USA (1882 kg/ha), Russian Federation (1643 kg/ha) and China (1596 kg/ha). In India the productivity is around 600-700 kg/ha. This becomes a serious handicap in promoting pulse production. This can be attributed to the hostile weather and the use of local varieties. The seed replacement ratio in pulses is very low. The seed replacement ratio for Chickpea, Uradbean, Mungbean and Pigeon pea was 19, 34, 30 and 22 per cent respectively.

Lack of technical knowhow: The farmers are still unaware of modern production technologies of Pulses. Still practicing the crude and traditional methods without any knowledge of the input doses and time of their application, their yields are far less than the potential yields. This makes their cultivation non remunerative and ultimately the farmers get disillusioned with growing pulses in his fields.

Lack of incentives: There are no incentives to farmers to promote these crops. There is no well defined mechanism for their procurement and marketing as is the case with Paddy or Wheat. The Minimum Support Price which the government announces is also not compatible with the rising cost of cultivation of the crop.

4. (*b*) **Propagation** is the process of growing new plants from a variety of sources: seeds, cuttings, and other plant parts. Plant propagation can also refer to the artificial or natural dispersal of plants.

Advantage of Micropropagation with reference to Plantation Plants: The main advantage of micropropagation is the production of many plants that are clones of each other.

- Micropropagation can be used to produce disease-free plants.
- It can have an extraordinarily high fecundity rate, producing thousands of propagules while conventional techniques might only produce a fraction of this number.
- It is the only viable method of regenerating genetically modified cells or cells after protoplast fusion.
- It is useful in multiplying plants which produce seeds in uneconomical amounts, or when plants are sterile and do not produce viable seeds or when seed cannot be stored.
- Micropropagation often produces more robust plants, leading to accelerated growth compared to similar plants produced by conventional methods - like seeds or cuttings.
- Some plants with very small seeds, including most orchids, are most reliably grown from seed in sterile culture.
- A greater number of plants can be produced per square meter and the propagules can be stored longer and in a smaller area.

4. (*c*) **Soil Genesis:** Soil is the mixture of rock debris and organic materials which develop on the earth's surface. It is biological and chemical composition. Suitable for plant growth. Pedogenesis is the science and study of the processes that lead to the formation of soil and first explored by the Russian geologist Vasily Dokuchaev.

In 1941 the Swiss scientist Hans Jenny, gave formula for soil genesis:

$$\text{Soil} = f(\text{C, PM, R, O, V}) \times \text{Time}$$

(where C = climate, PM = parent material, R = relief/topology, O = fauna, V = flora).

Role of Factors of Soil Formation: There are/five elements which control the pace and direction of soil formation.

1. **Parent Rock**: It is in the texture and fertility, which the parent rock contributes, that the soil formation is controlled by the parent rock. For instance, sandstone and gritstone give coarse and well drained oils, while shale gives finer and poorly drained soils. And, in terms of fertility, limestone rocks produce base-rich soils through the process of calcification. Non-calcareous rocks, on the other hand, are liable to podzolisation and acidity.
2. **Climate:** The climate exercises its influence through temperature and rainfall. High temperature facilitates more bacterial activity, more physical and chemical weathering, but little or no humus. Low temperature, on the other hand, helps form thicker, organic layers. In situations, where evapotranspiration is less than precipitation, pedalfers (rich in aluminium, iron) are formed, while in situations where evapotranspiration exceeds precipitation, pedocals (rich in calcium) are formed.
3. **Biotic Activity:** Plants and animals are the instruments of biotic activity. Plants form a part of the soil profile in the form of humus, which is basically decayed

plant material. Plants check soil erosion through interception of rainwater and by binding the soil with their roots. The plants absorb bases from the lower horizons into their stems, roots and branches and by shedding their mass, the plants again release these bases to the upper horizons. Roots of plants create crevasses and thus enhance leaching. Through transpiration, the plants inhibit percolation and make the rainfall less effective. Plants are also critical for the process of **podzolisation.**

4. **Topography:** Various aspects of topography have their own influence on the process of soil formation. On steep slopes, thinner soils are formed because of the inability of soil constituents to lodge themselves. Location also has its influence— a flat surface on the hilltop may be a material- exporting site, whereas a flat surface in a valley may be a material-receiving site.

   From the point of view of drainage, the hill-slope soils are better drained while the valley soils are poorly drained and may experience gleying. Exposure to the sun may determine the extent of bacterial activity and evapotranspiration and nature of vegetation. These factors further influence soil genesis. Topography also governs the extent and amount of moisture seepage.

5. **Time:** A more porous rock like sandstone or a less massive rock like glacial till, may take less time in soil formation than an impervious rock or a more massive rock like dark basalt.

4. (*d*) Soil and Water Conservation Measures

The water conservation is inseparable from soil conservation. It is the application of all measures necessary to conserve the whole complex of land and water resources. The maximum benefit of a variety can be derived only after maintaining a high fertility level. Therefore, soil and water conservation measures should be primary objective of research programmes. There are two approaches that have been used to reclaim degraded soils and intensify agriculture production system, *i.e.*, engineering approaches and ecological approaches. Mechanical soil and water conservation measures are required for controlling soil erosion, retaining maximum rainfall within the slope and safe disposal of excess run off from the top to the foot hills. These structures are used in case of extreme soil degradation, where other approaches are not possible or slow. The measures useful in controlling are discussed below.

Contour bunds: Bunds are either mechanical or vegetative barrier created across the slope. The purpose is to divert the excess run-off during rain to the waterways and to retain eroded soil. These bunds on steep slopes are created by way of excavating parabolic channels (0.3 m top and 0.2 m deep) on contours and keeping the dug out soil in form of a bund at the lower edge of the channel. These bunds require care in maintenance during first 2 years. Our experience showed that vegetative barrier alone will not serve the purpose on steep slopes. The vertical interval of these bunds may vary from 0.5 to 5 m depending on the land use, soil depth and slope of the land.

Bench terrace: Bench terraces are flat beds constructed across the hill slope; spaces between two contours are levelled by cut and fill method. In micro-watershed involving steep slopes, experiences showed that only at foot hills few benches may be constructed to produce food crops through intensive cropping. The vertical interval of such terraces should not increase more than one meter. Such measures can be adopted where the soil depth is more than 1.0 m. ENVIS Bulletin Vol 14(1) : Himalayan Ecology in case the entire hill slope is to be converted into benches, the construction should start from foot hill.

Half moon terrace: These are level circular beds having 1 to 1.5 m diameter cut into half moon shape on the hill slopes. These beds are used for planting and maintaining sapling of fruits and fodder trees in horticulture/agro-forestry land uses.

Grassed waterways: These are channels laid out preferably on natural drainage lines in the watershed. As far as possible, natural courses should be used without much disturbances for draining out the excess water. At appropriate locations, stilling basin (water pools) should be created with land use of earthen and boulder pitched bunds for temporary detention of run-off water. This structure will also serve the purpose of energy dissipation of flowing run-off water.

Water harvesting ponds: Dug out cum embankment type of water harvesting structure can be used for creating seasonal and perennial ponds at the foot of the micro-watershed for irrigation and fish farming purposes. The above soil and water conservation measures can be created with the use of local resources. On hill slopes, soil and water conservation measures may be followed with horticulture land use system. Other steps required are: Contour bund at 1.0 m to 5 m. vertical interval in all the land uses with common grassed waterways. Bench terraces towards the foot hills for growing vegetable crops (Vertical interval should not increase over 1.0 m.) Half-moons terrace (1 to 1.5 m dia.) for fruit crops. Water storage at appropriate location for irrigation/fish purposes.

Watershed Based Land Use System: Watershed management is the development and management of the watershed resources in such a manner so as to achieve optimum production, which can be sustained without causing deterioration in the resources base or disturbing the ecological balance.

SECTION 'B'

5. (*a*) Consumptive Use of Water: Consumptive water use is water removed from available supplies without return to a water resource system (e.g., water used in manufacturing, agriculture, and food preparation that is not returned to a stream, river, or water treatment plant). Evaporation from the surface of the earth into clouds of water in the air which then falls to the ground as "rain" is excluded from this model. Crop consumptive water use is the amount of water transpired during plant growth plus what evaporates from the soil surface and foliage in the crop area. The portion of water consumed in crop production depends on many factors, especially the irrigation technology.

Evapotranspiration: Evapotranspiration consists of evaporation from soil and water bodies and loss of water from plant leaves, which is called transpiration. It is a major component of the hydrologic cycle and its information is needed to design irrigation projects and for managing water quality and other environmental concerns. The term consumptive use is also sometimes used to denote the loss of water molecules to atmosphere by evapotranspiration. For a given set of atmospheric conditions, evapotranspiration depends on the availability of water. If sufficient moisture is always available to completely meet the needs of vegetation fully covering the area, the resulting evapotranspiration is called potential evapotranspiration (PET). The real evapotranspiration occurring in a specific situation is called actual evapotranspiration (AET).

Water Use Efficiency (WUE): Water use efficiency is defined as yield of marketable crop produced per unit of water used in evapotranspiration.

$$WUE = Y / ET$$

Where, WUE = Water use efficiency (kg/ha/mm of water)

Y = marketable yield (kg/ha)

ET = Evapotranspiration (mm)

If yield is proportional to ET, water use efficiency has to be constant but it is not so. Actually, Y and ET are influenced independently by crop management and environment. Yield is more influenced by crop management practices, while ET is mainly dependent on climate and soil moisture. Fertilization and other cultural practices for high yield usually increase in water use accompanying fertilization is often negligible. Crop production can be increased by judicious irrigation without markedly increasing ET. Under optimum water supply, ET is not dependent on kind of plant canopy provided the soil is adequately covered with crop.

Increasing the amount of plant canopy has therefore little or no effect on ET. Obviously, any practice that promotes plant growth and more efficient use of sunlight in photosynthesis without causing a corresponding increase in ET will increase WUE.

5. (*b*) Significance of Advance Farm Planning for Optimum use of Resources

"The farm plan is a process for deciding in the present what to do in the future about the best combination of crops and livestock to be raised through rational use of resources." When a new enterprise is established a complete and long range planning is undertaken giving basic directions to farming operations, investments patterns, with evaluation of its progress keeping in mind the goals.

The planning process helps to:

1. Identify the goals of the farm business (what you want to accomplish);
2. Identify the farm's inventory and resources (what you have to work with);
3. Assess the farm business and the environment in which it operates (where you are and where you may want to go);
4. Identify the farm's organizational structure (and chart) if it is a larger operation with several employees, employee compensation, allocation of profits, etc.;
5. Analyze the performance of the farm business (how you have done in the past based on the historical financial statements);
6. Decide upon a course of action (what you will do);
7. Implement the strategies (how you will do it); and
8. Evaluate the farm plan (whether it is working).

To be more specific, farm planning does the following:

1. Identifies goals that are attainable and moves the farming operation along the targeted path. Each goal should be SMART. A SMART goal is:
   - **Specific:** a goal that has a specific thing to do and can be defined.
   - **Measurable:** the goal can be measured and can be proven.
   - **Attainable:** the goal is realistic; the farm business can reach the goal.
   - **Rewarding:** the goal will move the farm operation toward what you want it to be.
   - **Timely:** there is a time limit to reach the goal.
2. Identifies all resources that are available to the operation and those that are needed but are not available to the operation. These include physical and natural resources including forages, forbs, water sources, soil types, land resources, and rainfall.
   - Human and personnel resources.
   - Animals and crop resources (forages).
   - Equipment, facilities, barns, computers, fencing.
   - Financial resources.

3. Assesses the farm business and the environment in which it operates. The SWOT analysis can identify the farm operation's Strengths, Weaknesses, Opportunities, and Threats.
4. Evaluates the farm business to determine its production and financial strengths and weaknesses with an emphasis on the financial.
5. Helps the farm manager to decide upon a course of action or strategy for the farming operating such as improving the breeding stock, paying debts, or buying handling facilities.
6. Helps the farm manager implement the strategies that have been identified. The manager must be sure to include all members of the operation in the decisions and explain their responsibilities.
7. Allows the farm plan to be evaluated annually to see if the goals for the year were met and whether they need to be revised or continued into the following year.

5. (*c*) Cooperative farming refers to an organisation in which:

1. Each member-farmer remains the owner of his land individually.
2. But farming is done jointly.
3. Profit is distributed among the member-farmers in the ratio of land owned by them.
4. Wages distributed among the member-farmers according to number of days they worked.

In other words, Cooperative farming = pooling of land and practicing joint agriculture. Cooperative farming is not a new concept in India. Since ancient times, Indian farmers have been giving mutual aid to each other in weeding, harvesting etc. In India, majority of the holdings are too small. About 76.4 per cent of the total holdings in India are below the size of 2 hectares and on these again 28.8 per cent of total operated area is engaged into these marginal and small holdings. Average area operated in the case of marginal farm is only 0.4 hectares and in case of small farm it is about 1.4 hectares only. Cultivation in such a small holding is uneconomic and unprofitable. Under such a situation if these marginal and small holdings can be consolidated and if the small and marginal farmers pool their land, resources and other inputs and then start cultivating their land jointly by forming a co-operative, they can get the benefits of large scale farming.

5. (*d*) Agricultural Price Policy: In India, majority of the holdings are too small. About 76.4 per cent of the total holdings in India are below the size of 2 hectares and on these again 28.8 per cent of total operated area is engaged into these marginal and small holdings. Average area operated in the case of marginal farm is only 0.4 hectares and in case of small farm it is about 1.4 hectares only.

Cultivation in such a small holding is uneconomic and unprofitable. Under such a situation if these marginal and small holdings can be consolidated and if the small and marginal farmers pool their land, resources and other inputs and then start cultivating their land jointly by forming a co-operative, they can get the benefits of large scale farming.

Instruments of Agriculture Price Policy: APP includes the following instruments:

(*i*) MSP and Procurement Prices: The price support policy was initiated by the Government to provide protection to agricultural producers against any sharp drop in farm prices.

(*ii*) Buffer stocks and Public Distribution System: Buffer stock operations are an integral component of agriculture price in India. It is used as an instrument to minimize the fluctuations in the prices of agriculture products.

5. (*e*) Farmers shape our world. Now let us shape theirs. Go organic. Summing the link between organic agriculture and welfare of farmers, renowned actor. Most farmers do some kind of planning on their farms nearly every day. Whole Farm Planning and Development is distinct from other farm planning approaches because it ties all the planning you do together for the *whole* farm. This holistic approach is based on the short and long-term vision you and your family has for itself and the farm. Following the whole farm planning process actively helps beginning farmers tailor farming goals and actions over time to best fit needs and preferences for long-term viability.

The whole farm plan and development is much more than a plan – it is a process for short-term and long-term decision making and evaluation that takes into consideration of the whole farm.

Beginning farmers who use a Whole Farm Planning approach to farm start-up are in a good position to maintain or improve profitability while enhancing their sustainability. Whole Farm Planning can also lead to protection and enhancement of the quality of soil, water, and other natural resources on and near the farm. More importantly, the planning process helps beginning farmers define long and short term goals. These goals can help you improve your chances of a better quality of life at home and in your community.

7. (*a*) During rain or irrigation, the fields become wet. The water infiltrates into the soil and is stored in its pores. When all the pores are filled with water, the soil is said to be saturated and no more water can be absorbed; when rain or irrigation continues, pools may form on the soil surface (Fig.)

Part of the water present in the saturated upper soil layers flows downward into deeper layers and is replaced by water infiltrating from the surface pools.

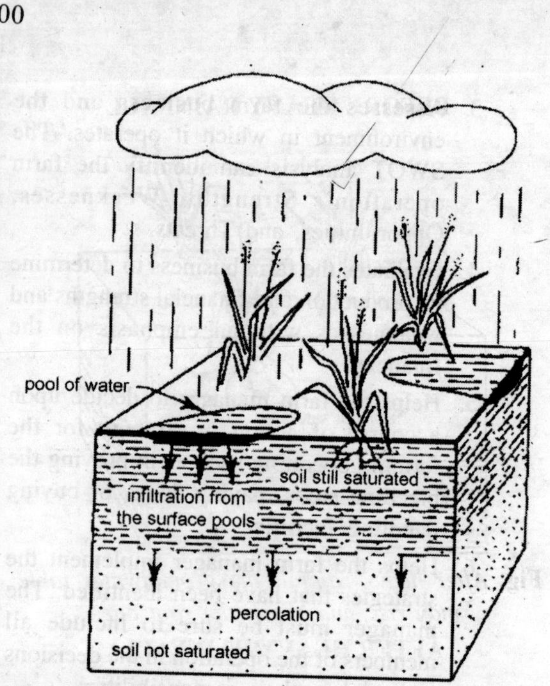

Fig. *During heavy rainfall the upper soil layers become saturated and pools may form. Water percolates to deeper layers and infiltrates from the pools.*

When there is no more water left on the soil surface, the downward flow continues for a while and air re-enters in the pores of the soil. This soil is not saturated anymore. However, saturation may have lasted too long for the plants' health. Plant roots require air as well as water and most plants cannot withstand saturated soil for long periods (rice is an exception). Besides damage to the crop, a very wet soil makes the use of machinery difficult, if not impossible.

The water flowing from the saturated soil downward to deeper layers, feeds the groundwater reservoir. As a result, the groundwater level (often called groundwater table or simply water table) rises. Following heavy rainfall or continuous over-irrigation, the groundwater table may even reach and saturate part of the rootzone. Again, if this situation lasts too long, the plants may suffer. Measures to control the rise of the water table are thus necessary.

BEFORE HEAVY RAINFALL

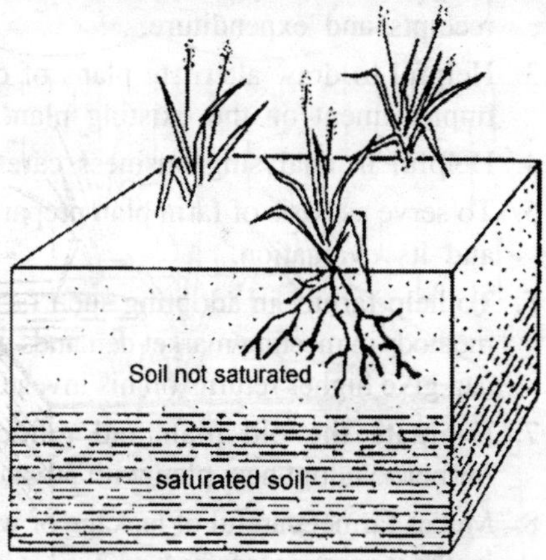

Fig. *After heavy rainfall the groundwater table may rise and reach the rootzone*

AFTER HEAVY RAINFALL

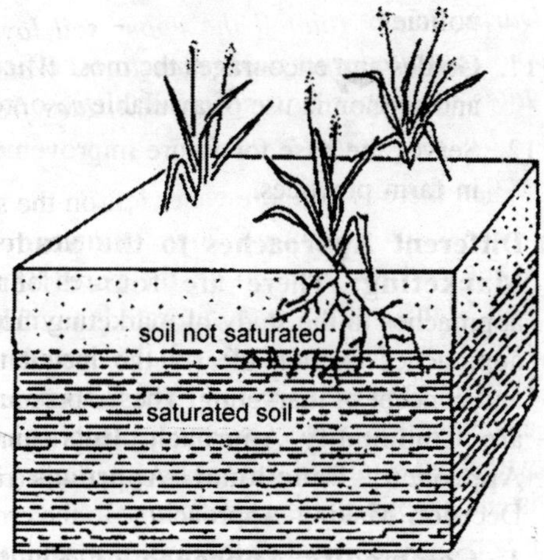

The removal of excess water either from the ground surface or from the rootzone, is called drainage. Excess water may be caused by rainfall or by using too much irrigation water, but may also have other origins such as canal seepage or floods. In very dry areas there is often accumulation of salts in the soil. Most crops do not grow well on salty soil. Salts can be washed out by percolating irrigation water through the rootzone of the crops. To achieve sufficient percolation, farmers will apply more water to the field than the crops need. But the salty percolation water will cause the water table to rise. Drainage to control the water table, therefore, also serves to control the salinity of the soil.

Different types of drainage

1 Surface drainage

2. Subsurface drainage

Drainage can be either natural or artificial. Many areas have some natural drainage; this means that excess water flows from the farmers' fields to swamps or to lakes and rivers. Natural drainage, however, is often inadequate and artificial or man-made drainage is required.

There are two types of artificial drainage: surface drainage and subsurface drainage.

1. **Surface drainage:** Surface drainage is the removal of excess water from the surface of the land. This is normally accomplished by shallow ditches, also called open drains. The shallow ditches discharge into larger and deeper collector drains. In order to facilitate the flow of excess water toward the drains, the field is given an artificial slope by means of land grading (Fig.).

2. **Subsurface drainage:** Subsurface drainage is the removal of water from the rootzone. It is accomplished by deep open drains or buried pipe drains.

   (*i*) **Deep open drains:** The excess water from the rootzone flows into the open drains (see Fig.). The disadvantage of this type of subsurface drainage is that it makes the use of machinery difficult.

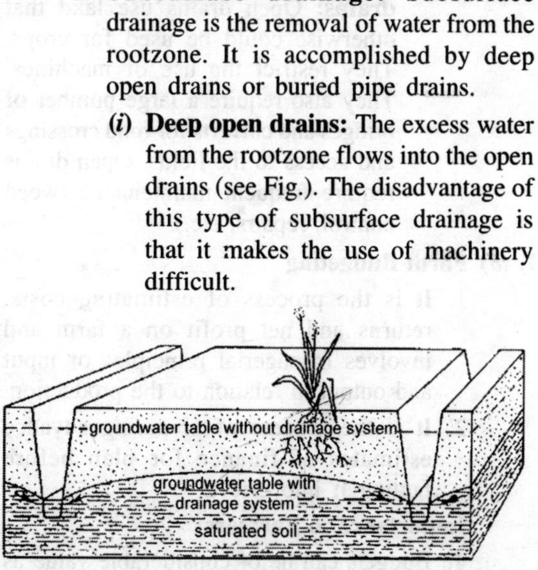

Fig. *Control of the groundwater table by means of deep open drains*

(ii) Pipe drains: Pipe drains are buried pipes with openings through which the soil water can enter. The pipes convey the water to a collector drain.

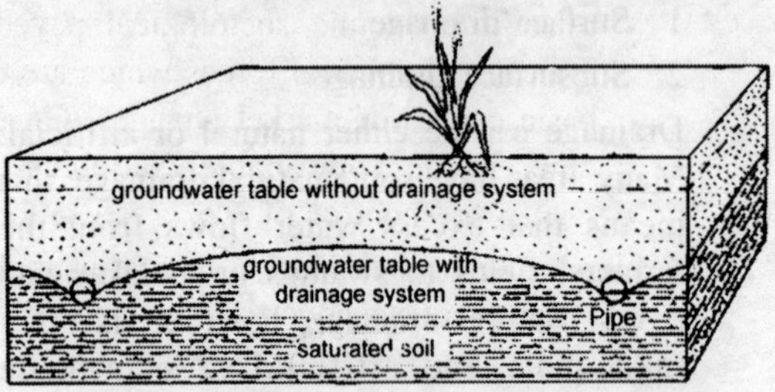

Fig. *Control of the groundwater table by means of buried pipes*

Drain pipes are made of clay, concrete or plastic. They are usually placed in trenches by machines. In clay and concrete pipes (usually 30 cm long and 5 - 10 cm in diameter) drainage water enters the pipes through the joints (see Fig., top). Flexible plastic drains are much longer (up to 200 m) and the water enters through perforations distributed over the entire length of the pipe.

(iii) Deep open drains versus pipe drains: Open drains use land that otherwise could be used for crops. They restrict the use of machines. They also require a large number of bridges and culverts for road crossings and access to the fields. Open drains require frequent maintenance (weed control, repairs, etc.).

7. (b) Farm Budgeting

1. It is the process of estimating costs, returns and net profit on a farm and involves managerial principles of input and output in relation to the production.
2. It is the process of preparing advance estimates of finance for plan before putting it into effect.

Importance to Farmers

1. Budgets can be of considerable value as guide to policy and plans for economic gains.
2. Helpful in preparing statements of receipts and expenditure.
3. Helpful to draw alternate plans of quick improvement on the existing plan.
4. Helpful in analysing business carefully.
5. To serve as basis of farm plan preparation and its evaluation.
6. To help farmer in adopting such farming methods in meeting market demands which can give higher returns on his investment.
7. Evaluate the old plan and guide the farmer to adopt new plan with advantage.
8. Makes farmer careful of leakage or wastes in the operation of farm.
9. Gives a comparative study of receipts, expenses and net earnings on farm.
10. Helps in formulating rational dairy farm policies.
11. Guides and encourages the most efficient and economic use of available resources.
12. Serves the base for future improvements in farm practices.

7. (c) Different Approaches to the Study of Marketing: There are four different approaches to the study of marketing. These approaches explain clearly the mechanism and concept of marketing. These approaches are Commodity Approach, Institutional Approach, Functional Approach and Decision Making Approach.

1. Commodity Approach or Product Approach: This approach refers to the study of a product in detail. The marketing situation of each product chosen for study is examined from such viewpoints as sources and conditions of supply, producer marketing organisations, policies, different middlemen who take part in distributing the product.

Problems with regard to a particular product are studied in detail under this approach. Products of any nature e.g. agricultural products wheat, rice, maize, etc., industrial products like machine tools, lathe-machines, generators, oil engines, etc., and any other products can be covered under this study. In practice, this approach tends to be repetitive and time consuming.

2. **Institutional Approach:** This approach relates to various marketing institutions viz., wholesalers, retailers etc., engaged in marketing. In applying this approach, a thorough study with regard to a particular middleman is undertaken. For example, in retailing, nature and significance of retailing in terms of functions and services performed and rendered by retail institutions like departmental stores, multiple shops, mail order houses etc. Besides wholesalers and retailers, other marketing institutions can be stock exchanges, produce exchanges, banks, regulated markets, etc. In short, it can be said that this approach is applicable on various types of marketing intermediaries.

3. **Functional Approach:** As the very name suggests this approach comprises of the study of various activities or functions performed in the process of marketing of goods and services. It analyses each function in relation to the importance of its performance.

   Various marketing functions are buying, selling, financing, transportation, banking, risk bearing, market information etc. By analysing and studying every function in detail and problems confronted in the performance of each function, it is possible to understand marketing properly.

4. **The Decision Making Approach:** This approach is of vital importance from the viewpoint of marketing management. Various decisions are taken at every level of management. In successful marketing, decision making occupies an important place. The marketing manager should be very expert and competent in his job so that he takes proper decisions for marketing the goods and services. The decision is based on two variables which can be classified as 'uncontrollable' and 'controllable'. Uncontrollable' variables relate to economic, sociological, psychological and political forces which are the basic causes of market changes. On the other hand, 'controllable' variables are within the control of the organisation.

These refer to individual firm's adjustments in prices, products, advertisement and selling policies etc. Both these variables have marked influence on decision making. These variables should be properly interpreted by the marketing manager before taking a decision.

Problems in Agricultural Marketing of Agricultural Produce: Even though India is an agricultural country, still its agricultural marketing has been defective. The Indian farmers are unable to get reasonable price for the products even after their hard work and are fully exploited by the middlemen.

1. Too Many Intermediates
2. Defective Weights and Scales
3. Illiteracy and Lack of Unity among Farmers
4. Lack of Financial Resources
5. Lack of Organised Marketing System
6. Lack of Transport Facilities
7. Lack of Store Houses
8. Lack of Standardization
9. Lack of Awareness of the Market
10. Corrupt Policies of the 'Mandis'

7. (*d*) A woman SHG is a grass-root level voluntary alliance wherein women belonging to same socio-economic strata of the society contribute a fixed amount for a particular time period until the group has enough capital to start its own lending process. These funds are then utilised for lending to other women to help and empower them through support, encouragement and financial assistance so as to allow them to achieve their personal and professional goals for a better future. Women SHG is therefore, a noble initiative in developing countries like

India, especially for the upliftment and welfare of the women in the society.

Five ways through which women SHGs empower rural women

1. **Make rural women aware of their basic rights:** Most of the time, rural women are exploited by their husbands, children and other family members and since they are uneducated and unaware as to whom to approach and how to safeguard their basic rights, they continue to suffer for long. Here, women SHGs become the torchbearers for such women and help them in getting educated and knowing their basic fundamental rights and laws.
2. **Help rural women in getting employment:** The women SHGs' play an instrumental role in arranging for various kinds of trainings for rural women relating to improved farming practices, livestock development, sewing, book keeping and general management. These trainings open up various employment opportunities for the rural women.
3. **Boost self-confidence and enhance social status:** Doing something for the family monetary wise automatically builds the confidence in rural women. Not to forget, being financially independent also enhances the social status of the family to which the women belong and thus, this puts an end to many of the problems that they face.
4. **Increase community participation of the rural women:** Not only women SHGs educate the rural women but also increase their community participation. They help the rural women in knowing their right to vote and even motivate them to take part in the local governance and village development process. This also goes a long way in empowering the rural women.
5. **Spreads awareness about social issues:** Rural India is still plagued by social evils like dowry system, child marriage, caste system, domestic violence, alcoholism and the list is long. Most of the times, it is the rural women which suffer due to such evils prevailing in the society. Thus, SHGs take the task of eliminating these evils very seriously. For that, the first thing they do is promote girl child education as educated women can bring a positive change in the society. The other task they do is conducting campaigns and meetings with the families of the rural women to bring about a change in the thinking of the men. Through these steps, women SHGs indirectly help in empowering the rural women.

PAPER-II

SECTION 'A'

1. (*a*) Mitochondria – Powerhouse of a Cell: Mitochondria are known as the powerhouses of the cell. They are **organelles** that act like a digestive system which takes in nutrients, breaks them down, and creates energy rich molecules for the cell. The biochemical processes of the cell are known as **cellular respiration.** Many of the reactions involved in cellular respiration happen in the mitochondria. Mitochondria are the working organelles that keep the cell full of energy. Mitochondria are small organelles floating free throughout the cell. Some cells have several thousand mitochondria while others have none. Muscle cells need a lot of energy so they have loads of mitochondria. Neurons (cells that transmit nerve impulses) don't need as many. If a cell feels it is not getting enough energy to survive, more mitochondria can be created. Sometimes a mitochondria can grow larger or combine with other mitochondria. It all depends on the needs of the cell.

Mitochondria Structure: Mitochondria are shaped perfectly to maximize their productivity.

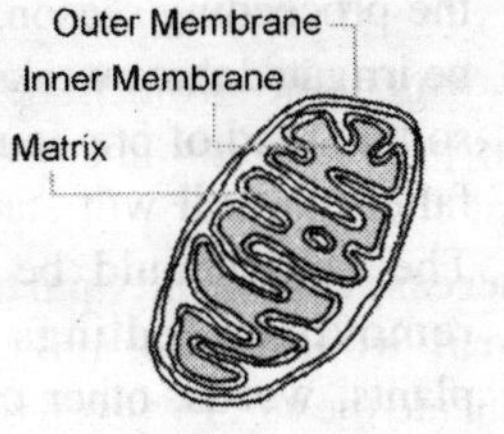

They are made of two membranes. The **outer membrane** covers the organelle and contains it like a skin. The **inner membrane** folds over many times and creates layered structures called **cristae**. The fluid contained in the mitochondria is called the **matrix.** The folding of the inner membrane increases the surface area inside the organelle. Since many of the chemical reactions happen on the inner membrane, the increased surface area creates more space for reactions to occur. If you have more space to work, you can get more work done. Similar surface area strategies are used by **microvilli** in your intestines.

1. (*b*) Laws of Inheritance

Mendel proposed three laws:

- Law of Dominance
- The Law of Segregation
- Law of Independent Assortment

Law of Dominance

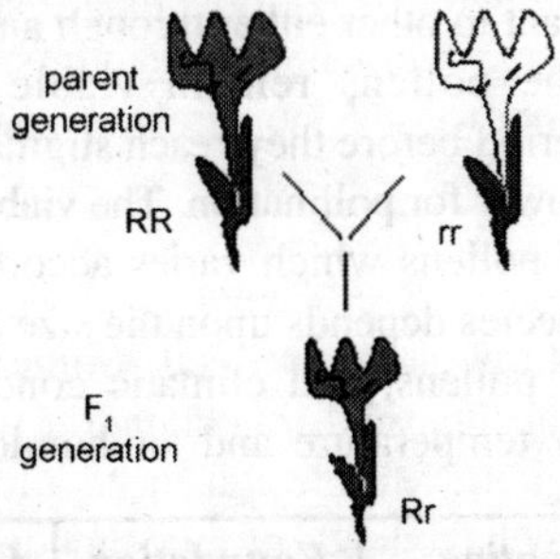

This law states that in a heterozygous condition, the allele whose characters are expressed over the other allele is called the dominant allele and the characters of this dominant allele are called dominant characters. The characters that appear in the F_1 generation are called as dominant characters. The recessive characters appear in the F_2 generation.

Law of Segregation

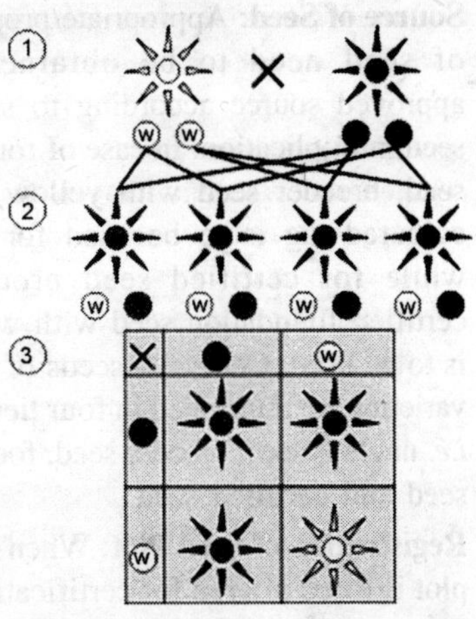

This law states that when two traits come together in one hybrid pair, the two characters do not mix with each other and are independent of each other. Each gamete receives one of the two alleles during meiosis of the chromosome.

Mendel's law of segregations supports the phenotypic ratio of 3:1 *i.e.;* the homozygous dominant and heterozygous offsprings show dominant traits while the homozygous recessive shows the recessive trait.

Law of Independent Assortment

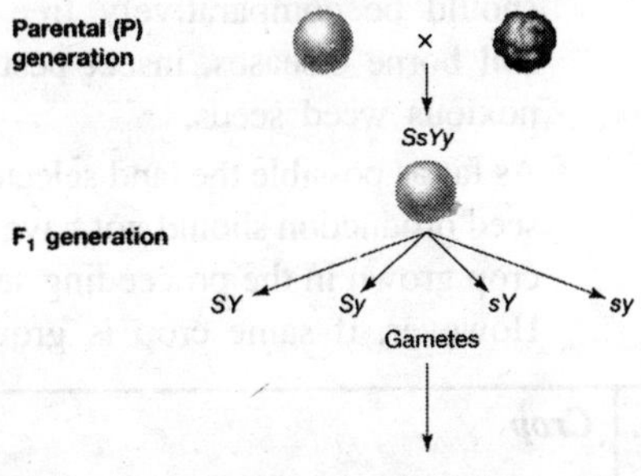

This means that at the time of gamete formation, the two genes segregate independently of each other as well as of other traits. Law of independent assortment emphasizes that there are separate genes for separate traits and characters and they influence and sort themselves independently of the other genes.

1. (*c*) Certified Seed Production in Field Crops

1. **Source of Seed:** Appropriate/proper class of seed need to be obtained from approved source according to stages of seed multiplication. In case of foundation seed, breeder seed with yellow or buff coloured tag is to be used for sowing while for certified seed production, certified foundation seed with white tag is to be used. Generally seeds of notified varieties are multiplied in four tier system *i.e.* nucleus seed, breeder seed, foundation seed and certified seed.
2. **Registration of Seed Plot:** When the seed plot is to be offered for certification, it is necessary to register the said plot for certification with District Seed Certification Officer.
3. **Land Requirement:**
   (*a*) The land selected for seed production should be suitable for that crop. It should be medium to deep and well drained light soils, sandy soils or waterlogged soils should not be selected for seed production as such lands affect crop growth and thereby reduce the seed yields.
   (*b*) The land selected for seed production should be comparatively free from soil borne diseases, insect pests and noxious weed seeds.
   (*c*) As far as possible the land selected for seed production should not have same crop grown in the proceeding season. However, if same crop is grown in the proceeding season, then it should be irrigated three weeks before sowing so that seed of previous crop that had fallen the soil will start germination. The land should be harrowed for removing seedlings of volunteer plants, weeds, other crop plants.
   (*d*) It is desirable to have protective irrigation source.
   (*e*) The selected land should meet isolation requirement.
4. **Isolation Requirement:** Isolation is the separation of seed field from the fields of:
   (*a*) Other varieties or hybrids of same crop.
   (*b*) Same variety of hybrids which do not conforming to varietal requirements.
   (*c*) Other related species which are readily crossable and
   (*d*) Fields affected by designated diseases prevent genetic and disease contamination.

   Space Isolation: Space isolation is the minimum distance kept between the seed plot and neighbouring plot of same crop which prevents natural cross pollination and physical contamination. During pollination, pollens are carried from one plant to other either through air or insects. The pollens remain viable for some period before they reach stigma of female flower for pollination. The viability period of pollens which varies according to the species depends upon the size and weight of pollens, and climatic conditions viz. air temperature and air humidity.

Sr. No.	*Crop*	*Mode of Pollination prescribed (mtrs)*	*Foundation Distance*	*Certified Distance*
1.	Rice, Wheat, Groundnut, Soyabean	Self Pollinated	3	3
2.	Jowar (Open pollinated varieties), Tur, Sunflower	Often cross pollinated	200	100
3.	Cotton, Jute	Often cross pollinated	50	30
4.	Jowar hybrids	Cross pollinated	300	200

Sr. No.	Crop	Mode of Pollination prescribed (mtrs)	Foundation Distance	Certified Distance
5.	Maize (*a*) Inbreeds and single crosses (*b*) Hybrids (*c*) Composites	–	400	–
6.	Mustard, Sunflower	–	400	200
7.	Bajara (Hybrid)	–	1000	200
8.	Lucerne, Berseem	–	400	100
9.	Cole Crops	–	1600	1000
10.	Gram	Self Pollinated	10	5

It is necessary to maintain prescribed isolation distance on all sides of the seed crop throught the cultivation of seed crop.

5. **Cultivation Practices and Plants Protection:** Cultivation practise recommended for the crop are required to be adopted timely so as to get good stand of seed crop and thereby higher seed yields. It consists of:
   (*a*) Good land preparation.
   (*b*) Use of optimum seed rate with timely sowing.
   (*c*) Application of FYM and fertilizers at recommended doses and as per schedule of split application.
   (*d*) Timely weeding and interculturing.
   (*e*) Timely control of pests and diseases.
   (*f*) Timely application of irrigations.
   (*g*) Watching the seed plots from birds, stray animals.
6. **Roughing:** Rouge is an undesirable plant or off type growing in the seed plot. Roughing is the removal of individual plants which differ significantly from the normal type of the variety.
7. **Field Inspection:** As per provisions of seed certification, the seed plots offered for certifications are subjected to field inspection by the staff of seed certification agency. The number of field inspections is usually carried without prior intimation to the seed producer.
8. **Harvesting, Threshing, Drying and Sealing of Raw Seed:** Seed plot should be harvested at proper stage of maturity and only after permission is granted by the field inspector. After harvesting the crop, it should be brought to threshing yard for drying care should be taken to see that there will not be contamination with other varieties in the produce of seed plot. The seed produce be threshed and winnowed for removing major part of inert matter. *i.e.;* Stones, sand, dried twigs, leaves, husk etc. The cleaned seed produce should be bagged in the presence of the field inspectors who ill seal the entire bags ad issue threshing certificate. At the time of sealing, field inspector draw 3 kg sample from each lot. In case of F/S and certified cotton seed for F.T. The seed bags should be transported to authorized seed processing plant for processing along with threshing certificate.
9. **Seed Processing:** Seed lot accepted for processing is processed at the seed draws three samples and sends one sample to seed testing laboratory for testing, one sample kept at his disposal and one sample for concerned seed producer.
10. **Bagging, Tagging:** When the seed lot is passed by seed certification agency on the basis of seed testing laboratory report (STL). The processed and treated seed is bagged and tagged with appropriate tags issued by seed certification officer.

11. Release of Seed Lot: The certified seed lot is released to the seed producer for sale.

Harvesting:

1. The seed crop should be taken from seed certification officer for harvesting the seed plot.
2. The crop is harvested by taking care to ensure that there will be no physical contamination with neighbouring crop.

Drying: The initial moisture content of freshly harvested seed is usually high in between 15 to 25%. It is therefore necessary to dry the seed produce to bring its moisture content to safe level of 12% or less.

Threshing: After proper drying the seed produce is to be threshed by using bullocks, tractors, or suitable thresher. The thresher should be thoroughly cleaned from inside for removing seed of previous crop. The speed of the thresher should be adjusted by choosing appropriate size of pulley so as to prevent mechanical damage to the seed. After threshing, the produce should be winnowed for removing husk, bhusa and other trash material.

All seed processing done under the supervision of Agril. Officer of S.C.A.

1. Drying if seed moisture content is more than 12%
2. Precleaning
3. Grading
4. Seed Treatment
5. Weighing, Bagging
6. Tagging and Sealing
7. Release the seed lot

1. (*d*) Seed Storage Seeds are uniquely equipped to survive, as viable regenerative organisms until the time and place are right for the beginning of a new generation. However, like other form of life, they cannot retain their viability indefinitely and eventually deteriorate and die. Fortunately neither nature nor agricultural practice ordinarily requires seeds to survive longer than the next growing season, though the seeds of most species are able to survive much longer under the proper conditions.

1. Harvesting and threshing

- In vegetables, the harvests are to be taken in different pickings. For getting higher yield, the first and last one or two pickings may be taken for vegetables.
- This may promote further growth of the plant to put for the more number of fruit/pods. In addition, the seed recovery and quality will be poor in the above pickings.
- From the harvested produce the seeds should be extracted following suitable extraction methods *viz*., wet extraction method for tomato, brinjal, bitter gourd, snake gourd and dry extraction method for bhendi, chilli, crucifers, ribbed gourd, pea and beans.

2. Drying and grading

- Direct exposure of the seed to sunlight may affect its quality therefore if necessary seed may be dried under diffused sunlight in a shed with opening on all sides.
- Artificial drying is done by blowing dry air at 70-85°F but never exceeding 110°F. Grading is done with various types of grader.

3. Seed treatment

- Seed treatment with the fungicides and insecticides to arrest the carry over of pathogens and insects with the seed or their fresh entry in to it.

4. Packaging, labelling and sealing

- It is necessary to use right type of containers with (seed moisture content at proper level) labelling and sealing in the prescribed manner.

5. **Movement and storage**
   - Precautions should be taken to avoid seed deterioration while in transit and or in storage.
   - Ideal storage for long term is dry and cool condition.
   - Ideal condition can be maintained if the sum of RH and temperature does not exceed 100.

General principles of seed storage

1. Seed storage conditions should be dry and cool.
2. Effective control of storage pests.
3. Proper sanitation in seed stores.
4. Before placing seeds into storage they should be dried to safe moisture limits, appropriate for storage system.
5. Store only high quality seed *i.e.,* seeds which are well cleaned, treated, with high germination and vigour.
6. Determine seed storage needs in view of period or length of storage time and preveling climate of the area during storage period. Long-term storage requires more exacting conditions of seed storage than short-term storage. Similarly, the regions with favourable storage climate, *i.e.,* one where relative humidity is rather low, require less sophistication than areas of high relative humidity.

1. (*e*) Role of Metal Ions in Enzyme Activity

Metal ion catalysis, or electrostatic catalysis, is a specific mechanism that utilizes metalloenzymes with tightly bound metal ions such as Fe^{2+}, Cu^{2+}, Zn^{2+}, Mn^{2+}, Co^{3+}, Ni^{3+}, Mo^{6+} (the first three being the most commonly used) to carry out a catalytic reaction. This area of catalysis also includes metal ions which are not tightly bound to a metalloenzyme, such as Na^{+}, K^{+}, Mg^{2+}, Ca^{2+}.

Enzymes can catalyze a reaction by the use of metals. Metals often facilitate the catalytic process in different ways. The metals can either assist in the catalytic reaction, activate the enzyme to begin the catalysis or they can inhibit reactions in solution. Metals activate the enzyme by changing its shape but are not actually involved in the catalytic reaction. First, the metal can make it easier to form a nucleophile which is the case of carbonic anhydrase and other enzymes. In this case, the metal facilitates the release of a proton from a bound water to produce a nucleophilic hydroxide ion and start the catalytic reaction. With the polarization of the O-H bond, the acidity of the bound water can increase. Equally important, the metal can promote the production of an electrophile which in turn stabilizes the negative charge on the intermediate. Also, metals can promote binding of the enzyme and substrate by acting as a bridge to increase the binding energy and orient them correctly to make the reaction possible.

Common metals that take part in metal ion catalysts are copper ion and zinc ion. The catalysis of carboxypeptidase A is a prime example of this catalytic strategy. The iron metal ion is also very common—from the binding of oxygen to hemoglobin and myoglobin, to participating as an electron carrier in the cytochromes of the electron transport chain, to even as a detoxifying agent in catalase and peroxidase. Metal ions also have the ability to stabilize transition states, which makes them very useful in catalytic chemistry because it allows them to stabilize unstable intermediates that are still transitioning into a structure that's going to allow them to react with another substrate and form the final product. For example, in the presence of a tetrahedral oxyanion and another oxygen that is attached to a carbonyl functional group nearby that is also about to become nucleophilic as an intermediate, the metal ion can coordinate to these two neighbouring anions and participate in charge stabilization.

2. (a) Distinguish between Seed Production in Self-pollinated and Cross-pollinated Crops

Basis for Comparison	*Self-Pollination*	*Cross-Pollination*
Meaning	The inbreeding process in plants where pollens are transferred from the anthers to the stigma of the same flowers or another flower but of the same plant.	The outbreeding process between the two plants of the same species and different flowers.
It involves	Single plant.	Two different plants of the same species.
Occurs in	Self-pollination occurs in genetically same plants.	Cross-pollination occurs in genetically different plants of the same species.
External pollinating agents	There are no requirements of the pollinating agents.	External pollinating agents are required like water, animals, wind and insects.
Perfect flowers	Self-pollination occurs in perfect flowers only.	It occurs in both imperfect and perfect flowers.
Flowers of the plants	These plants have small flowers.	These types have the scent, nectar and bright-coloured petals.
Pollen grains	Less number of pollen grains are produced.	A large number of pollen grains are produced.
Reproduction	Geitonogamy and autogamy are the two types of the process of reproduction.	Allogamy kind of reproduction occurs here.
Genetic variability	With the self-pollination, pure line progeny is obtained and so no role in genetic variations.	With the cross-pollination, genetic variations and genetic recombinations are observed.
Characters	Desirable characters can be obtained, but undesirable character cannot be eliminated.	Desirable characters can be obtained and undesirable character can be removed.
Offspring	It results in homozygous offspring.	It results in heterozygous offspring.
Examples	Wheat, rice, pea, orchids, barley, tomatoes, peaches, apricot.	Mulberry, maize, pumpkins, strawberries, blackberries, plums, grapes, daffodils, maple, catkins, grasses.

2. (b) Distinguish between Heterosis breeding and Mutation breeding

Heterosis Breeding: Heterosis breeding is used in/all the three groups. However, it is common in cross pollinated and asexually propagated species and rare in self pollinated species. A hybrid variety has homogeneous but heterozygous population. Synthetic and composite varieties are developed in cross pollinated species. Such varieties consist of several homozygotes and heterozygotes and thus constitute a heterogeneous population.

Mutation Breeding: Mutation breeding is common in self pollinated and asexually propagated species and rare in cross pollinated species. A mutant variety differs from parent variety in one or few characters. A mutant differs from a segregant in two main ways. Firstly, the frequency of segregants is very high and that of mutant is extremely low (0.1%). Secondly, mutant differs from parent variety in one or few characters, where as a segregant differs from parent material in several characters.

2. (*c*) Distinguish between Ribonucleic acid and Deoxyribonucleic acid

Comparison *Full Name*	*DNA* *Deoxyribonucleic Acid*	*RNA* *Ribonucleic Acid*
Function	DNA replicates and stores genetic information. It is a blueprint for all genetic information contained within an organism.	RNA converts the genetic information contained within DNA to a format used to build proteins, and then moves it to ribosomal protein factories.
Structure	DNA consists of two strands, arranged in a double helix. These strands are made up of subunits called nucleotides. Each nucleotide contains a phosphate, a 5-carbon sugar molecule and a nitrogenous base.	RNA only has one strand, but like DNA, is made up of nucleotides. RNA strands are shorter than DNA strands. RNA sometimes forms a secondary double helix structure, but only intermittently.
Length	DNA is a much longer polymer than RNA. A chromosome, for example, is a single, long DNA molecule, which would be several centimetres in length when unravelled.	RNA molecules are variable in length, but much shorter than long DNA polymers. A large RNA molecule might only be a few thousand base pairs long.
Sugar	The sugar in DNA is deoxyribose, which contains one less hydroxyl group than RNA's ribose.	RNA contains ribose sugar molecules, without the hydroxyl modifications of deoxyribose.
Bases	The bases in DNA are Adenine ('A'), Thymine ('T'), Guanine ('G') and Cytosine ('C').	RNA shares Adenine ('A'), Guanine ('G') and Cytosine ('C') with DNA, but contains Uracil ('U') rather than Thymine.
Base Pairs	Adenine and Thymine pair (A-T) Cytosine and Guanine pair (C-G)	Adenine and Uracil pair (A-U) Cytosine and Guanine pair (C-G)

2. (*d*) Enzymes

- **Enzymes** are Biological Catalysts. They increase the rate of Metabolic reactions. Almost all Biological Reactions involve Enzymes. All enzymes are Globular Proteins with a specific Tertiary Shape. They are usually specific to only one reaction.
- The part of the Enzyme that acts a **Catalyst** is called the Active Site. The rest of the Enzyme is much larger and is involved in maintaining the specific shape of the Enzyme.
- When a reaction involving an Enzyme occurs, a Substrate is turned into a Product. The Substrate can be one or more molecules. The Active Site of an Enzyme is Complementary to the Substrate it catalyses.
- Some examples of Enzymes are:
  - **Lactase**: Breaks down Lactose into Glucose and Galactose.
  - **Catalase**: Breaks Hydrogen Peroxide down into Water and Oxygen.
  - **Glycogen Synthase**: Catalyses the formation of Glycosidic Bonds between Glucose molecules.
  - **ATP-ase**: Breaks down ATP into ADP, producing energy.

Plant Pigment: Plants have a unique property of capturing the light energy and convert it into sugars through the process called photosynthesis. The process starts with the absorption of light energy by some specialized form of organic molecules, called the pigments. The photosynthesis process makes use of the green pigment called chlorophyll along with some other form of yellow and red pigments.

Some of the other plant pigments include porphyrins, carotenoids, betalains, anthocyanins, etc. All these pigments stimulate the process of chemical reactions by reflecting the wavelengths.

The plant pigments are given below:

- **Chlorophyll:** Chlorophyll is one of the main pigment in the green plants. The green colouring of the plant leaves is due to the pigment called chlorophyll. The chlorophyll pigment is of various kinds such as a, b, c, d, p. All the green plants, cyanobacteria, algae have the pigment chlorophyll "a". The chlorophyll pigment b is found in most of the green algae.
- **Carotenoids:** Carotenoids are the pigments in the form of orange, red, yellow colours. These compounds are insoluble in water and are attached to the membranes of the cell bodies. These biomolecules are antioxidants which promote a good eyesight in the humans.
- **Anthocyanins:** Anthocyanins are a kind of flavonoid pigments meaning "flower blue". These pigments are present in all the tissues of the higher group of plants providing colour in stem, leaves, roots, fruits, and flowers.
- **Flavonoids:** Flavonoids are a kind of yellow pigments that are seen in lemons and oranges. The plastids and cytoplasm in plants consist of this pigment flavonoid. These are the chemicals that help to lower the cholesterol levels and have the antioxidant properties.

SECTION 'B'

5. (*a*) Process of the Minimizing the Pesticide Residue Effects in Vegetables: Pesticide residue refers to the pesticides or metabolic products of the pesticides that may remain in food grains, vegetables and fruits after they are applied to crops. Many of these chemical residues, especially derivatives of chlorinated pesticides, exhibit bioaccumulation which could build up to harmful levels in the body as well as in the environment. Persistent chemicals can be magnified through the food chain and have been detected in products ranging from meat, poultry, and fish, to vegetable oils, nuts, and various fruits and vegetables.

Different types of pesticides are used in different countries for different types of crops to prevent pests, insects, and weeds. Because of the expansion of worldwide trade, more foods which are treated by pesticide are being imported into different countries. These worldwide trades increase the expansion of pesticide residues in different areas of the world and it's the issue of public health concern. There are a number of strategies which can be used to minimize pest and disease problems and reduce pesticide residues in, vegetables.

Organic farming: One of the methods used to reduce the effect of pesticide residue in food is to eat organic foods than non-organic ones. According to standard meta-analyses the frequency of occurrence of detectable pesticide residues was four times higher in non-organic crops than organic crops. There is evidence that indicated organic food consumption can reduce exposure to pesticide residues in food. Organic crops, on average, have higher concentrations of antioxidants and a lower incidence of pesticide residues than the non-organic foods across regions and production seasons. It is advisable to consume foods rich in antioxidant to reduce effects of the chronic disease by suppressing oxidative activity. An increased dietary intake of antioxidant rich foods protect against chronic diseases, including cardio vascular diseases, certain cancers (*e.g.* prostate cancer) and neurodegenerative diseases.

Washing: The second methods reported to reduce pesticide residue is washing. Washing may reduce pesticide residue. Washing with water and various chemical solutions for domestic and commercial applications is necessary to decrease the pesticide residues. The efficiency of the washing treatments on pesticide removal depends on the washing solution, the chemical properties of the pesticide, the surface area, the nature of the vegetable, the length of time the pesticide is in contact with the food, and the formulation and application method of the pesticide. Usually, the pesticide is lodged in the outer wax-like layers and then moves to the inside, making washing and removal of the pesticides less effective.

Processing: An important factor leading to a reduction of any residues left on crops at harvest are processing treatments such as washing, peeling, canning or cooking that the majority of foods receive prior to consumption. Pesticide residue levels in vegetables may change due to processing, such as peeling, boiling, frying, fermentation, grinding. Cooking also reduces pesticide residues in food; boiling may remove 35 - 60% of organophosphate residues and 20 - 25% of organochlorines. Husking and immersing of vegetables are reported to reduce pesticide residues especially organophosphates.

Rational use of pesticides: Rational use of pesticides involves selection of correct pesticides, dosage rates, dilutions, timing, and frequency of application, treatment intervals, and method of application, precautions, and limitations. Rational use of pesticides can be useful to reduce pesticide residues vegetables. In many cases, there may not be any need of a pesticide, particularly where cultural or biological methods are effective.

Use of natural pesticides and bio-pesticides: Bio-pesticides are biodegradable so no harmful residues are produced and are eco-friendly. Bio-pesticides encompasses a broad array of microbial pesticides, biochemical's derived from micro-organisms and other natural sources that confer protection against pest damage. Some insect repellents can also be used for the prevention of pesticide residues accumulation in the vegetables and fruits. Natural pesticides such as extracts and compounds from neem tree are also very useful for the prevention of pesticide residues accumulation in the vegetables.

Implementation and amendment of pesticide-related laws: In India, the agriculture ministry regulates the manufacture, sale, transport, distribution, export, import and use of pesticides under the Insecticides Act, 1968. Still awaiting Parliamentary approval is the Pesticide Management Bill of 2008, which is meant to replace the Insecticides Act, 1968. The pesticide-related laws should be implemented strictly and amended so as to reduce the cases of pesticide residues.

The excess consumption of pesticides contributes in the accumulation of pesticide residues in vegetables associated with variety of human health hazards, including damage to central and peripheral nervous systems, cancer, allergies and hypersensitivities, reproductive disorders, and disruption of the immune system. The impact of pesticide residues can be minimized by preventive measures such as rational use of pesticides, washing and proper processing of vegetable products, practising organic farming, use of natural pesticides and biopesticides, and strict implementation and amendment of pesticide-related laws.

5. (*b*) Seed Plot Technique for Virus Free Potato Seed Production

- Use of healthy seed in vegetative propagated crop like potato is very important.
- Continuous use of same seed stocks year after year without periodic replacement allows infiltration of diseases particularly widely prevalent viruses.

- These viruses readily spread through contact of foliage and roots in the field or through aphid vectors from far off fields or within fields.
- They have debilitating effect and are responsible for bringing down yield potential of infected tubers.
- The high hills were the traditional sources of healthy seed as population of aphids remain low due to low temperature.
- However, hills accounts for only 5% of the area under potato and this was not enough to meet the seed requirement of the plains.
- In 1962, Cockerham (Scotland) came to India to do some studies to increase the potato yield.
- On the basis of data on appearance and build up of aphids in different months, it was found that potato can successfully be grown for seed production in many parts of the plains under low or no aphid condition.
- This led to the development of "Seed Plot Technique" *i.e.* raising the healthy seed crop during low aphid population period available in northern plains.

Steps followed in seed plot technique:

- Planted before the commencement of 10th October.
- Sowing at closer spacing of 45 cm × 15 cm for smaller size potato tubers.
- Two inspections at least should be made to rogue out any diseased or off-type plants during growing season.
- Application of granular systemic insecticides at planting or earthing up.
- When the crop has tuberized well by the middle of December, restrict irrigation and later with hold it completely.
- At the end of December or first week of January, haulm should be cut down before the aphid population builds up to 20 aphids per 100 leaves.
- If the crop is still green destroy the haulms by spraying 2% solution of $CuSO_4$ or cut them.
- The harvesting of tubers is done in mid February to end February.

Modifications

- Hot weather cultivation and green manuring.
- Crop rotation for 2-3 years.
- One or two sprays of systemic insecticides + spray of metalaxyl or mancozeb in December-January.
- Tubers dip treatment with 3% boric acid for 30 minutes after harvest and before storage of the produce.
- The use of this technique helps in meeting the large requirement of healthy seed in country.

5. (*c*) Gibberellins are the plant growth regulators involved in regulating the growth and influencing different developmental processes which include stem elongation, germination, flowering, enzyme induction, etc.

Gibberellins have different effects on plant growth and the stem elongation is the most dramatic amongst all. The stem starts to grow when it is applied in low concentration to a bush. The internodes become so long that the plants become indistinguishable from climbing. The Gibberellins overcome the genetic limitations in different dwarf varieties.

There are more than 70 gibberellins isolated. They are GA1, GA2, GA3 and so on. The GA3 Gibberellic acid is the most widely studied plant growth regulators.

Some seeds that are sensitive to light such as tobacco and lettuce exhibit poor germination in the absence of sunlight. Germination begins rapidly if the seeds are exposed to the sunlight. If the seeds are treated with gibberellic acid, the light requirement can be overcome. The buds that are formed in autumn stay dormant until next spring. This dormancy can be overcome by treating them with gibberellin.

Physiological processes stimulated by active gibberellins depend on their types. Stimulate cell elongation in stem breaks seed dormancy in some plants which requires light for germination. Stimulates alpha-amylase production in germinating cereal grains. Stimulates bolting/flowering in response to long days. Delay senescence in leaves and also in citrus fruits. Induces maleness in dioecious flowers Play a role in development of seedless fruit (parthenocarpic).

5. (*d*) Mango malformation: *Fusarium moliliforme* var. *subglutinans*

Symptoms

- Three types of symptoms: bunchy top phase, floral malformation and vegetative malformation.
- In bunchy top phase in nursery bunching of thickened small shoots, bearing small rudimentally leaves. Shoots remain short and stunted giving a bunchy top appearance.
- In vegetative malformation, excessive vegetative branches of limited growth in seedlings. They are swollen with short internodes forming bunches of various size and the top of the seedlings shows bunchy top appearance.
- In malformation of inflorescens, shows variation in the panicle. Malformed head dries up in black mass and persist for long time.
- Secondary branches are transformed into number of small leaves giving a witches broome appearance.

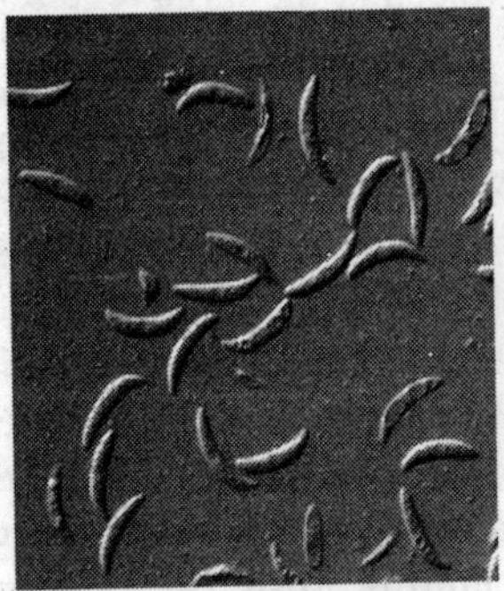

Conidia of *Fusarium moliliforme* var. subglutinans

Malformation on mango inflorescens

Management:

- Diseased plants should be destroyed.
- Use of disease free planting material.
- Incidence reduced by spraying 100-200 ppm NAA during October.
- Pruning of diseased parts along the basal 15-20 cm apparently healthy portions.
- This is followed by the spraying of Carbendazim (0.1%) or Captafol (0.2%).

5. (*e*) Importance of Carrot in Human Nutrition

Naturally sugary, delicious and crunchy, carrots are healthy additions you can make to the vegetable list of your diet. Indeed, these root vegetables come with wholesome health benefiting compounds such as beta-carotenes, falcarinol, vitamin-A, minerals, and antioxidants in ample amounts. Botanically they are the taproots belong to the Apiaceae or umbelliferous family in the genus; **Daucus.** Scientific name: *Daucus carota.* The other close Apiaceae members include parsnips, parsley, dill, cumin, etc.

1. Sweet and crunchy carrots are notably rich in anti-oxidants, vitamins and dietary fiber. They provide only 41 calories per 100 g, a negligible amount of fat and no cholesterol.
2. They are an exceptionally rich source of carotenes and vitamin-A. 100 g fresh carrot contains 8,285 µg of beta-carotene and 16,706 IU of vitamin-A. Studies have

found that flavonoid compounds in carrots may offer to protect from skin, lung and oral cavity cancers.

3. In the humans, carotenes convert into vitamin-A in the liver cells. Beta-carotene is the important carotene type present in these roots. Beta-carotene is one of the powerful natural antioxidants that protect the human body from harmful oxygen-derived free radicals. Also, it also carries out all the functions of vitamin-A such as maintaining good eye health, reproduction (sperm production), maintenance of epithelial integrity, growth and development.
4. Carrots are rich in polyacetylene antioxidant, falcarinol. A research study conducted by scientists at the University of Newcastle on laboratory animals has found that falcarinol in carrots may help fight against cancers by destroying pre-cancerous cells in the tumors.
5. Fresh roots are also good in vitamin-C; provide about 9% of RDA. Vitamin-C is water soluble antioxidant. It helps the body maintain healthy connective tissue, teeth, and gum. Its anti-oxidant property helps the human body protect from diseases and cancers by scavenging action on harmful free radicals.
6. Also, they are exceptionally rich in many B-complex groups of vitamins such as folic acid, vitamin B-6 (pyridoxine), thiamin, pantothenic acid, etc., that acts as co-factors to enzymes during substrate metabolism in the body.
7. Further, they also compose healthy levels of minerals like copper, calcium, potassium, manganese and phosphorus. Potassium is an important component of cell and body fluids that helps controlling heart rate and blood pressure by countering effects of sodium. The human body utilizes manganese as a co-factor for the antioxidant enzyme, *superoxide dismutase*.

Importance of Guava in Human Nutrition:
Guava is low in calories and fats but carry several vital vitamins, minerals, and antioxidant polyphenolic and flavonoid compounds that play a pivotal role in the prevention of cancers, aging, infections, etc. The fruit is a very rich source of soluble dietary fiber (5.4 g per 100 g of fruit, about 14% of DRA), which makes it a good bulk laxative. The fiber content helps protect the colon mucosa by decreasing exposure time to toxins as well as binding to cancer-causing chemicals in the colon.

- Guava-fruit is an excellent source of antioxidant vitamin-C. 100 g fresh fruit provides 228 mg of this vitamin, more than three times the required DRI (daily-recommended intake). Flesh just underneath its thick outer rind composes exceptionally higher levels of vitamin-C than its inner creamy pulp.
- Scientific studies suggest that regular consumption of fruits rich in vitamin-C helps the human body develop resistance against infectious agents and scavenge cancer causing harmful free radicals from the body. Further, it is essential for collagen synthesis within the body. Collagen is one of the chief structural protein in the human body necessary for maintaining the integrity of blood vessels, skin, organs, and bones.
- The fruit is a very good source of Vitamin-A, and flavonoids like beta-carotene, lycopene, lutein and cryptoxanthin. The compounds are known to have antioxidant properties and therefore essential for optimum health. Further, is also critical to maintaining healthy mucosa and skin. Consumption of natural fruits rich in carotene is known to protect from lung and oral cavity cancers.
- 100 g of pink guava fruit provides 5204 µg of lycopene, nearly twice the amount than in tomatoes. (100 g tomato contains 2573 µg of lycopene). Studies suggest that lycopene in pink guavas prevents skin damage from UV rays and offer protection from prostate cancer.

- Fresh fruit is a very rich source of potassium. It contains more potassium than other fruits like banana weight per weight. Potassium is an important component of cell and body fluids that helps controlling heart rate and blood pressure.
- Further, the fruit is also a moderate source of B-complex vitamins such as pantothenic acid, niacin, vitamin-B6 (pyridoxine), vitamin E and K, as well as minerals like magnesium, copper, and manganese. The human body uses manganese as a co-factor for the antioxidant enzyme, superoxide dismutase. Copper required for the production of red blood cells.

7. (*a*) Fungal Wilt of Vegetable: Fungal wilt is a soil-borne pathogen that attacks potato, tomato, eggplant and pepper plants. Disease fungi *(Fusarium oxysporum)* enter through the roots and interfere with the water conducting vessels of the plant. As the infection spreads up into the stems and leaves it restricts water flow causing the foliage to wilt and turn yellow.

Disease symptoms often appear later in the growing season and are first noticed on the lower (older) leaves. As the disease progresses, the younger leaves will also be affected and the plant eventually dies. In many cases, only one branch or side of the plant show symptoms.

Fusarium wilt can survive for years in the soil and is spread by water, insects and garden equipment. The fungal disease develops during hot weather and is most destructive when soil temperatures approach 80°F. Dry weather and low soil moisture encourage this plant disease.

Bacterial Wilt of Vegetable: Cucumbers, melons and occasionally summer squash can suddenly have wilted leaves and stems. A cause can be bacterial wilt, which is a serious disease of cucurbits. It is transmitted principally by striped cucumber beetle feeding. Spotted cucumber beetles, however, are also capable of transmitting the disease. Plants are particularly vulnerable between seedling emergence and the bloom stage. The first symptoms are wilting of individual leaves followed by wilting of individual stems and then of entire plants. Wilted vines may recover at night (regain their turgor) but wilt again the next day. Infected vines die in 7-14 days. Wilted plants should be pulled up and composted. To test for the disease cut a wilted stem, press the side of a knife to the exposed surface and draw it away. If the plant is infected with bacterial wilt disease you may notice white strands of bacterial ooze. You can also immerse a piece of wilted stem in room temperature water and look for a milky discolouration of the water caused by the bacteria. The bacteria overwinters in adult cucumber beetles hibernating around the garden.

7. (*b*) Insect parasitoids: Insect parasitoid is an organism that lives on or in a host organism and ultimately kills the host. Most insect parasitoids are found in the Order Hymenoptera and roughly 10% of all described insect species are parasitoids. In many species eggs are laid within the bodies of other organisms (most commonly other insects) the eggs hatch and feed on the internal organs of the host. Initially the parasitoid larvae feeds on non-essential organs thus feeding without killing the host. Eventually the larvae either feeds on the vital organs killing the host or pupates within the host and then emerges as an adult killing the host. Parasitoids are commonly used in biological control.

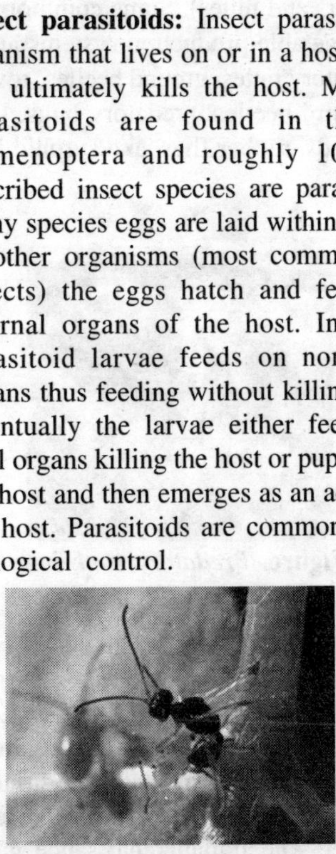

A parasitic wasp, *Peristenus digoneutis,* laying an egg in a plant bug nymph.

A parasitoid is an organism that lives on or in a host organism and ultimately kills the host. Most insect parasitoids are found in the Order Hymenoptera and roughly 10% of all described insect species are parasitoids. In many species eggs are laid within the bodies of other organisms (most commonly other insects) the eggs hatch and feed on the internal organs of the host. Initially the parasitoid larvae feeds on non-essential organs thus feeding without killing the host. Eventually the larvae either feeds on the vital organs killing the host or pupates within the host and then emerges as an adult killing the host. Parasitoids are commonly used in biological control.

Predators: Predators consume one or more living prey insects. Predatory behaviour is widespread among arthropods (insects, spiders and mites). Some common predators in vegetable production systems are spiders, predatory mites, ground beetles, rove beetles, ladybird beetles, predatory bugs, lacewings, mantids, robber flies, and syrphid fly larvae.

Figure. *Predatory stink bug, Tethida barda, and prey.*

7. (*c*) **Formal Garden:** The gardens of Greece and Rome assured an emotional security though their Formal style. The Persian, Moorish gardens of Spain and Moghul gardens were also of the same kind and were strictly formal, symmetrical and geometrical resembling a carpet. The Italian renaissance garden was having intricate geometric designs, sheared trees, trimmed hedges and edges to create formality. The impact of formalism influenced the French and British gardens also in the form of parierre, the much divided flower beds. The Moorish garden of Spain also had the impact of Moghul's architecture and they were formal and geometrical though Moorish gardens were exclusively meant to beautify patios of large mansions.

Features of Formal Garden

1. Plan is made on the paper and land is selected accordingly.
2. The plan is symmetrical with square, rectangular and roads cut at right angles.
3. It had a sort of enclosure or boundary.
4. Flower beds also have geometric designs as in carpets.
5. The arrangement of trees and shrubs are necessarily geometrical and kept in shape by trimming and training.
6. Other features like fountains, water pools, cascades, etc. are used for further attraction.

Informal Garden: Hindu, Buddhist and Japanese garden laid no emphasis on formality.

1. Woodlands (vanams) and running water (streams and rivers) was the main feature around which the garden was created in natural way.
2. Brindavan of Lord Krishna was a woodland.
3. Every temple was provided with irregular shaped lotus tanks. (Latter on such tanks was given masonry boundary either rectangular or square).
4. Japanese developed an intensely national and naturalistic style of its own. It is in Japanese garden, the asymmetric balance has been perfected.
5. The impact of industrial climate drove the Britishers to opt for natural gardens latter.

The further the man is isolated from nature (due to industrial revolution) the deep is the longing to go back to nature. The industrialized cities became concrete jungles with no flavour and aroma of nature and there was emptiness in human life. To avert this, natural gardens was given impetus.

1. The nature's projection of mountains, oceans, rivers and lakes on a larger canvas of earth's surface is informal with all its grandeur. Such grandeur is mimicked in informal gardens omitting the untamed, disastrous and violent side of nature.
2. Lanchlot 'capability' Brown (1716-83): She emphasized the use of coloured flower and foliage, tree form, etc. in natural style.
3. The cottage gardens of UK had the utility with fruits, vegetable and herb plants as well as the beauty that spans from its harmony with surrounding rural scenery.

Feature of Informal Garden

1. This style reflects naturalistic effect of total view and represents natural beauty.
2. It is contrast to formal style.
3. Plan is asymmetrical according to the land available for making the garden.
4. Smooth curvaceous out lines are more appropriate.
5. Water bodies are more irregular in shape.
6. Hillock are made, water falls provided, lakes and islands, cascades, rocks, shola and a rustic hutment are provided to create rural effect. Appropriately grouped plants provide living quality and they are not trimmed.

7. (*d*) Seed Dormancy: A seed dormancy can be defined as the state or a condition in which seeds are prevented from germinating even under the favourable environmental conditions for germination including, temperature, water, light, gas, seed coats, and other mechanical restrictions.

The main reason behind this conditions is that they require a period of rest before being capable of germination. This conditions may vary from days to months and even years. These conditions are the combination of light, water, heat, gases, seed coats and hormone structures.

Seed Dormancy

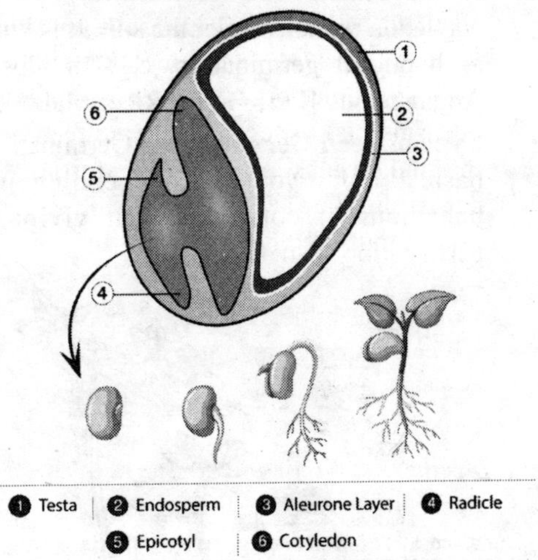

Seed germination: Seed germination is a process in which dormant embryo of seed resumes metabolic activities and grows to produce a seedling. "During germination, the seed absorbs water by imbibition and undergoes swelling. Due to water, hydrolytic enzymes become active and complex organic materials stored in endosperm and/or, cotyledons are converted into simple substances like glucose and maltose. This simple food is utilized by embryo and also by seedling till it becomes photosynthe-tically active.

During growth of embryo, seed coat ruptures, radical comes out through micropyle and develops into root system. The plumule comes out and develops to form the shoot system. The embryo of seed grows in to a sporophyte plant. The radicle produces primary root. The plumule develops short and later on cotyledons degenerates.

In some of the plants cotyledon comes above the surface of the soil during the germination of seed. Such type of germination is called Epigeal germination. e.g. Capsella. This is due to higher growth takes place in hypocotyl region of embryo in seed so cotyledon pushed above the soil surface [Capsella, Castor, French bean etc.]

In some of plants the epicotyl region grow faster during the germination results cotyledon remains under the soil. It is known as hypogeal germination, e.g. In most of Angiosperms [Pea, Gram, Rice, Maize etc]

Type of Seed Germination: Germination is basically of two types, depending upon behaviour of cotyledons but viviparous germination also found:-

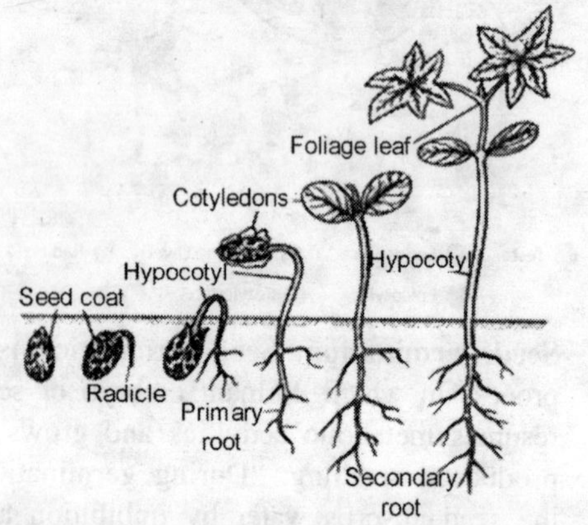

Fig. *Epigeal Germination of Castor Seed*

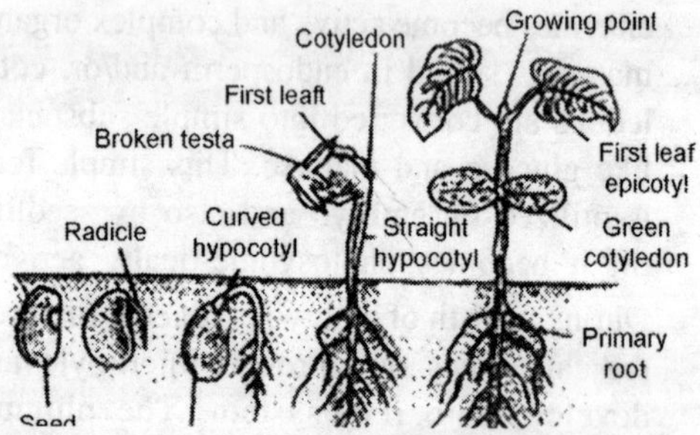

Fig. *Epigeal Germination of Bean Seed*

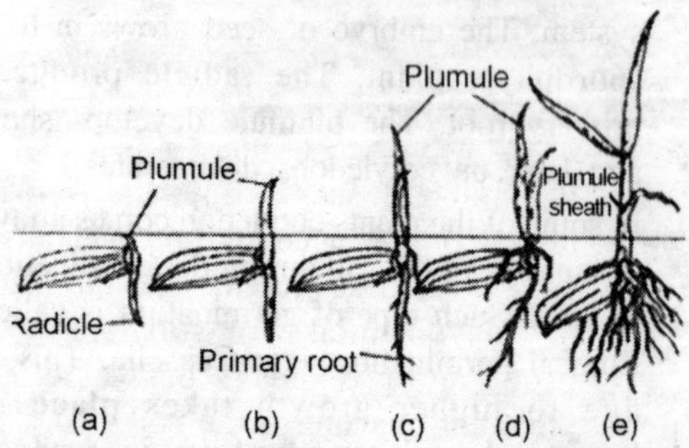

Fig. *Hypogeal Germination of Rice Seed*

8. (*a*) Food production constraints in Indian agricultural system are natural and some others are manmade.

1. Small and fragmented land-holdings: The problem of small and fragmented holdings is more serious in densely populated and intensively cultivated states like Kerala, West Bengal, Bihar and eastern part of Uttar Pradesh where the average size of land holdings is less than one hectare and in certain parts it is less than even 0.5 hectare.

Rajasthan with vast sandy stretches and Nagaland with the prevailing 'Jhoom' (shifting agriculture) have larger average sized holdings of 4 and 7.15 hectares respectively. States having high percentage of net sown area like Punjab, Haryana, Maharashtra, Gujarat, Karnataka and Madhya Pradesh have holding size above the national average.

Further it is shocking to note that a large proportion of 59 per cent holdings in 1990-91 were marginal (below 1 hectare) accounting for 14.9 per cent of the total operated area. Another 19 per cent were small holdings (1-2 hectare) taking up 17.3 per cent of the total operated area. Large holdings (above 10 hectare) accounted for only 1.6 per cent of total holdings but covered 17.4 per cent of the operated area. Hence, there is a wide gap between small farmers, medium farmers (peasant group) and big farmers (landlords).

The main reason for this sad state of affairs is our inheritance laws. The land belonging to the father is equally distributed among his sons. This distribution of land does not entail a collection or consolidated one, but its nature is fragmented.

Different tracts have different levels of fertility and are to be distributed accordingly. If there are four tracts which are to be distributed between two sons, both the sons will get smaller plots of each land tract. In this way the holdings become smaller and more fragmented with each passing generation.

Sub-division and fragmentation of the holdings is one of the main causes of our low agricultural productivity and backward state of our agriculture. A lot of time and labour is wasted in moving seeds, manure, implements and cattle from one piece of land to another.

Irrigation becomes difficult on such small and fragmented fields. Further, a lot of fertile agricultural land is wasted in providing boundaries. Under such circumstances, the farmer cannot concentrate on improvement.

2. **Seeds:** Seed is a critical and basic input for attaining higher crop yields and sustained growth in agricultural production. Distribution of assured quality seed is as critical as the production of such seeds. Unfortunately, good quality seeds are out of reach of the majority of farmers, especially small and marginal farmers mainly because of exorbitant prices of better seeds.

Indian seeds programme largely adheres to limited generation system for seed multiplication. The system recognises three kinds of generation, namely breeder, foundation and certified seeds. Breeder seed is the basic seed and first stage in seed production. Foundation seed is the second stage in seed production chain and is the progeny of breeder seed.

Certified seed is the ultimate stage in seed production chain and is the progeny of foundation seed. Production of breeder and foundation seeds and certified seeds distribution have gone up at an annual average rate of 3.4 per cent, 7.5 per cent and 9.5 per cent respectively, between 2001-02 and 2005-06.

3. **Manures, Fertilizers and Biocides:** Indian soils have been used for growing crops over thousands of years without caring much for replenishing. This has led to depletion and exhaustion of soils resulting in their low productivity. The average yields of almost all the crops are among the lowest in the world. This is a serious problem which can be solved by using more manures and fertilizers.

Manures and fertilizers play the same role in relation to soils as good food in relation to body. Just as a well-nourished body is capable of doing any good job, a well nourished soil is capable of giving good yields. It has been estimated that about 70 per cent of growth in agricultural production can be attributed to increased fertilizer application.

Thus increase in the consumption of fertilizers is a barometer of agricultural prosperity. However, there are practical difficulties in providing sufficient manures and fertilizers in all parts of a country of India's dimensions inhabited by poor peasants. Cow dung provides the best manure to the soils. But its use as such is limited because much of cow dung is used as kitchen fuel in the shape of dung cakes. Reduction in the supply of fire wood and increasing demand for fuel in the rural areas due to increase in population has further complicated the problem. Chemical fertilizers are costly and are often beyond the reach of the poor farmers. The fertilizer problem is, therefore, both acute and complex.

It has been felt that organic manures are essential for keeping the soil in good health. The country has a potential of 650 million tonnes of rural and 160 lakh tonnes of urban compost which is not fully utilized at present. The utilization of this potential will solve the twin problem of disposal of waste and providing manure to the soil.

The government has given high incentive especially in the form of heavy subsidy for using chemical fertilizers. There was practically no use of chemical fertilizers at the time of Independence. As a result of initiative by the government and due to change in the attitude of some progressive farmers, the consumption of fertilizers increased tremendously.

4. **Irrigation:** Although India is the second largest irrigated country of the world after China, only one-third of the cropped area is under irrigation. Irrigation is the most important agricultural input in a tropical monsoon country like India where rainfall is uncertain, unreliable and erratic India cannot achieve sustained progress in agriculture unless and until more than half of the cropped area is brought under assured irrigation.

   This is testified by the success story of agricultural progress in Punjab, Haryana and western part of Uttar Pradesh where over half of the cropped area is under irrigation! Large tracts still await irrigation to boost the agricultural output.

5. **Lack of mechanisation:** In spite of the large scale mechanisation of agriculture in some parts of the country, most of the agricultural operations in larger parts are carried on by human hand using simple and conventional tools and implements like wooden plough, sickle, etc.

   Little or no use of machines is made in ploughing, sowing, irrigating, thinning and pruning, weeding, harvesting, threshing and transporting the crops. This is specially the case with small and marginal farmers. It results in huge wastage of human labour and in low yields per capita labour force.

6. **Soil erosion:** Large tracts of fertile land suffer from soil erosion by wind and water. This area must be properly treated and restored to its original fertility.

7. **Agricultural Marketing:** Agricultural marketing still continues to be in a bad shape in rural India. In the absence of sound marketing facilities, the farmers have to depend upon local traders and middlemen for the disposal of their farm produce which is sold at throw-away price.

   In most cases, these farmers are forced, under socio-economic conditions, to carry on distress sale of their produce. In most of small villages, the farmers sell their produce to the money lender from whom they usually borrow money.

   In order to meet his commitments and pay his debt, the poor farmer is forced to sell the produce at whatever price is offered to him. The Rural Credit Survey Report rightly remarked that the producers in general sell their produce at an unfavourable place and at an unfavourable time and usually they get unfavourable terms.

   In the absence of an organised marketing structure, private traders and middlemen dominate the marketing and trading of agricultural produce. The remuneration of the services provided by the middlemen increases the load on the consumer, although the producer does not derive similar benefit.

   Many market surveys have revealed that middlemen take away about 48 per cent of the price of rice, 52 per cent of the price of groundnuts and 60 per cent of the price of potatoes offered by consumers.

8. **Inadequate storage facilities:** Storage facilities in the rural areas are either totally absent or grossly inadequate. Under such conditions the farmers are compelled to sell their produce immediately after the harvest at the prevailing market prices which are bound to be low. Such distress sale deprives the farmers of their legitimate income.

The Parse Committee estimated the post-harvest losses at 9.3 per cent of which nearly 6.6 per cent occurred due to poor storage conditions alone. Scientific storage is, therefore, very essential to avoid losses and to benefit the farmers and the consumers alike.

At present there are number of agencies engaged in warehousing and storage activities. The Food Corporation of India (F.C.I.), the Central Warehousing Corporation (C.W.C.) and State Warehousing Corporation are among the principal agencies engaged in this task. These agencies help in building up buffer stock, which can be used in the hour of need. The Central Government is also implementing the scheme for establishment of national Grid of Rural Godowns since 1979-80.

This scheme provides storage facilities to the farmers near their fields and in particular to the small and marginal farmers. The Working Group on additional storage facilities in rural areas has recommended a scheme of establishing a network of Rural Storage Centres to serve the economic interests of the farming community.

9. **Inadequate transport:** One of the main handicaps with Indian agriculture is the lack of cheap and efficient means of transportation. Even at present there are lakhs of villages which are not well connected with main roads or with market centres.

10. **Scarcity of capital:** Agriculture is an important industry and like all other industries it also requires capital. The role of capital input is becoming more and more important with the advancement of farm technology. Since the agriculturists' capital is locked up in his lands and stocks, he is obliged to borrow money for stimulating the tempo of agricultural production.

8. (*b*) **Storage Insects of Pulses and Cereals and their Management Practices:** Everywhere in the world stored products are attacked by a number of storage enemies. Three major groups of storage enemies are:

- Fungi
- Insects
- Rats and mice

Insect-Pests of Stored Grains

Insect-Pests

I. Insect-Pests of Stored Grains

(*i*) **Wheat, barley and other grains:** Stored grain insect-pests attack the stored grain products as a result of which the grains lose their nutritive value and germinative capacity. Important insect-pests of these grains are khapra beetle, lesser grain borer, rice weevil, red rust flour beetle and grain moth.

Preventive/Curative measures

1. Store new grains in a clean godown.
2. Fill cracks, crevices and holes with cement.
3. Use brand new gunny bags. Old gunny bags if used, must be disinfected by dipping in Malathion 50 EC (1 part of cythion/ malathion) in 500 parts water for 10 minutes and dried in shade before filling the grains.
4. Disinfect empty godowns in April-May by spraying Malathion 50 EC (1 part of cythion/ malathion) in 100 parts water on floor, walls and ceiling or by using almunium phosphide (celphos/phostoxin) 25 tablets for 100 cubic meter (3600 cubic ft.).
5. Mix 250g Cythion/Malathion 5% dust per quintal grains meant for seed only.

Caution:

1. Where there is infection of khapra, fumigation of godown with Celphos/ Phostoxin (aluminium phosphide) is essential by using double the recommended dose for grains.

2. Do not mix BHC with grains meant for consumption.
3. Fumigate only in air-tight stores. Do not use fumigants in houses.

(*ii*) Pulses: *Gram dhora, mung dhora*

Preventive/Curative measures

Aluminium phosphide (Phostoxin/celphos) @ one tablet of 3 g/metric tonne or 25 tablets/100 cubic metre of space. Do not expose for 7 days.

II. Insect-Pests of Nursery Beds

Cutworms: They are polyphagus and especially damage nursery and newly transplanted seedlings by cutting them at ground level. Dirty grey caterpillars remain in soil at day time and at nigh come out of their hide-outs and damage the crop.

Preventive/Curative measures

1. At sowing time or when the crop is to be transplanted, apply 2.5 ml chlorpyriphos 20 EC/ litre of water in the soil.

III. Non Insect-Pests and Their Control

Root-knot nematodes: Leaves of affected cole crops, tomato, brinjal and bhindi plants become discoloured after the invasion of their roots by the larvae. Occasionally, leaves dry up and plant height is affected. On the roots, distinct galls or knots develop and in case of severe infestation, side roots develop profusely which gradually weaken the plants.

Preventive/Curative measures

1. Flood the soil and destroy alternate weed hosts.
2. Do not take same crop in the same plot regularly. Follow suitable crop rotation.
3. Use carbofuran 3G(Furadon) @ 33 kg/ha before sowing or transplanting.

Field rats and house rats: They cause heavy losses and destroy the stored grains and other products by consuming and contaminating with their excreta, urine, hair and extraneous matter. They also spoil storage bags, clothes *etc.*

Preventive/Curative measures

1. Use traps for catching rats and kill by drowning in water.
2. Close all burrows in the evening and fumigate reopened burrows of field rats with Aluminium (Phostoxin/Celphos) one tablet per hole.
3. Bait with zinc phosphide : smear 19.5 kg wheat, gram, maize or bajra grains with sarson oil and mix with it 500 g zinc phosphide. Put one table spoon of these poisoned grains in and outside the burrow.

Birds: Some birds such as, sparrows, parrots, crows etc. are harmful to grains, crops, vegetables and fruits.

Preventive/Curative measures

1. Scare them a ways by means of mechanical bird scarer.
2. Sparrows can be killed by feeding them soaked wheat grains containing 2% Lebaycid 100 EC (fenthion).
3. Crows can be killed by feeding them on chapatis soaked in water containing 2% Lebaycid 100 EC (fenthion).
4. Destroy eggs and nests during breeding season.

Caution: Soak 1 kg wheat in 1/2 L water containing 2-3 ml Lebaycid 100 EC (fenthion) for 6 hours and then dry under shade. These grains should be spread on cloth late in the evening so that sparrows may eat them early in the morning. Pets, cattle and children should be kept away from baits.

Note: *The quantity of water recommended for different sprays in insect control is according to the conventional high volume sprayers that are in general use. If motorized knapsack sprayer is used, then the amount of water* *would be 40-125 L per hectare. However, the quantity of the insecticide would remain the same in both the cases.*

***Source:** Stored Grain pests (GRDS, Sept. 2010)*

Storage Insects: Insects need food, air and water to live. In many cases stored grain provides a perfect place for insects to live and grow because food, air and water are available in sufficient quantities. This is why some insect species infest stored products.

The two major insect pests in stored grains and pulses are beetles and moths. The larvae of both groups of insects are totally unlike the adult forms. They look a little like worms. Some times you do not discover them because they develop inside the kernel.

Rodents are also carriers of diseases which are harmful to man. People can get these diseases from eating and handling grains contaminated by rodent faeces, urine or parasites which they carry.

Unlike the insects and fungi which infest the storage, rodents will plunder stores whatever the temperature or moisture content of the grain or air.

Preventive Measures Against Insects: Preventive measures against insects and mould start already at the time of growing the crops that will be stored later. In general it can be said that a farmer can influence the occurrence of pests in the stored crops by carefully choosing certain resistant varieties, planting or sowing and harvesting in the optimum season, properly treating the crop before storing, siting the store in a favourable place and keeping it very clean.

Dry and Cool Storage: Prevent the absorption of water when the product is stacked. The product can be placed on plastic or on a layer of tar paper. When the product is stored in bags these should preferably be stored on pallets. Pallets can be made of wooden laths or poles. The bags should always be neatly stacked, in such a way that air can pass through the sacks to dry and cool the grain.

Non-chemical Insect Control: There are many methods to control insects without using chemicals. In general these methods might take more time, but they will cost far less money. Non-chemical control include mechanical methods and adding natural material that have insecticidal or repellent characteristics. There are many natural additives like local plants (or parts of them), minerals or oil, that are useful to control or repel insects damaging stored products. Used in the right way these additives may even have a protective action. In general these methods are only useful in small scale storage.

Insecticides Used for Controlling Storage Insects: Many insecticides are available but only few can be used for protection of stored cereals and pulses. Below we describe a few insecticides which are commonly used.

Malathion: Malathion may be mixed with grain as a dust or sprayed on walls or floors. As a dust it is one of the insecticides most widely used to protect stored cereals and pulses. The product to be dusted must be well dried, otherwise malathion breaks down very rapidly. Malathion is not suitable for disinfecting storage structures because it is unstable on concrete surfaces or white-washed walls.

Between treatment and consumption there should be a period of 12-13 weeks. In that period malathion breaks down completely without leaving harmful residues. Some disadvantages of malathion are:

Malathion is not very effective against the lesser grain borer;

Some insects have already developed resistance against malathion;

This means that the insecticide is no longer killing these insects;

Malathion has a nasty smell;

Malathion is only slightly effective against caterpillars, moths and mites.

Recommendations for use of malathion dust

Shelled maize/rice: 1000 g of malathion 1% dust/1000 kg of cereal.

Threshedbeans: 1000 g of malathion 1% dust/1000 kg of beans.

Corn-cobs: 1000-1500g of malathion 2% dust/1000kg of cobs.

Pirimiphos-methyl: Pirimiphos-methyl is active against beetles, moths and mites. It performs well against species resistant to malathion.

Pirimiphos-methyl is available in different formulations: dusts, wettable powder, emulsion concentrates and fumigants. Trade names are: Actellic, Actellifog, Silosan, Blex.

Recommendations for Use of Pirimiphos-methyl Dust

Shelled maize/rice/beans: Mix 200-500 g of 2% dust/1000 kg produce.

Bromophos: Bromophos has a relative low toxicity (similar to malathion) for human beings and their domestic animals. It is more persistent than malathion on concrete surfaces and therefore it can be used for disinfection of storage buildings. It is also more persistent on warm moist grain.

Bromophos is available as a dust, to mix with the stored product, or as a emulsion concentrate to treat stacks of bags or walls and floors.

Recommendations for Use of Bromophos Dust

Grain: Mix 10-20 g of active ingredient/ 1000 kg produce.

Maize or *beans:* Mix 8-12 g of active ingredient/ 1000 kg produce.

Chlorpyrifos Methyl: Chlorpyrifos methyl has a relative low toxicity for human beings and their domestic animals. It is effective against a wide range of storage pests except against the resistant Lesser Grain Borer. Mixing Chlorpyrifos methyl with Bioresmethrin could make a very effective mixture against many species. The trade name of Chlorpyrifos-methyl is Reldan.

Recommendations for use of Chlorpyrifos methyl dust

Grain: Mix 2.5-4 g of active ingredient/ 1000 kg produce.

Fenitrothion: Fenitrothion is very effective against a wide range of insect pests, although it is not fully effective against the Lesser Grain Borer. It can be used to disinfect storage structures or to protect stored produce.

Recommendations for Use of Fenitrothion Dust

Grain: Mix 4-12 g of active ingredient/ 1000 kg produce.

Corn-cobs: Apply 8-20 g of active ingredient/1000 kg produce.

Bioresmethrin: Bioresmethrin is effective against the Lesser Grain Borer, so it is especially useful in situations where the Lesser Grain Borer has developed resistance against insecticides such as Malathion, Pirimiphos-methyl, Fenitrothion and Chlorpyrifos-methyl. In these cases Bioresmethrin can be mixed with these other insecticides to improve efficiency of the application.

Recommendations for use of Bioresmethrin

Mix 4 g active ingredient of Bioresmethrin + 20 g of active ingredient of Piperonyl-butoxide to treat 1000 kg produce.

Mix 1 g of active ingredient of Bioresmethrin +12 g active ingredient of Fenitrothion to treat 1000 kg produce (especially to control those insects that are developing resistance against Malathion).

Permethrin: Permethrin is available as dust (0.5%) which is a useful formulation. For the protection against the Larger Grain Borer it seems more effective to store and treat shelled maize instead of maize on the cob.

Recommendations for Use of Permethrin

Grain: Apply 1-2 g active ingredient of

Permethrin +10 g active ingredient of Piperonyl butoxide + 4-6 g active ingredient of Pirimiphos-methyl per 1000 kg grain, for a protection of at least 9 months.

Effective Application for Protection Against the Larger Grain Borer

Shelled maize: 2.5 - 5 g active ingredient of Permethrin per 1000 kg of maize.

Shelled maize: 1 g active ingredient of Permethrin + 4 g active ingredient of Pirimiphos-methyl per 1000 kg of produce.

Pyrethrum: Pyrethrum is a botanical insecticide with a low toxicity to human beings and the domestic animals. It has a rapid effect on a wide range of insects, but sometimes after treatment insects can recover. To avoid this Pyrethrum is often mixed with another insecticide, especially Piperonyl-butoxide. The mixture also is cheaper because a lower doses of Pyrethrum can be used.

Pyrethrum is available as oil solutions and solution concentrates. Wettable powders and dusts have a short shelf-life.

Recommendations for Use of Pyrethrum

1.5-2.5 g active ingredient of Pyrethrum +7.5-12.5 g active ingredient of Piperonyl butoxide per 1000 kg grain (ratio of Pyrethrum: Piperonyl butoxide = 1 : 5).

Methoprene: Methoprene is effective against a wide range of storage pests.

Recommendations for Use of Methoprene

5-10 g active ingredient of Methoprene per 1000 kg stored product.

Dichlorvos: Dichlorvos is mainly used to treat the free space in a store or to disinfect infested grain when brought into the store.

8. (*c*) India being the largest producer of fruits and second largest producer of vegetables. But unfortunately the average Indian remains aloof from the basic requirements of fruits and vegetables. As a result of which there is a huge gap between gross production and net availability.

All these is because of the inefficient post harvest management, a significant portion of production is lost after harvest. Post harvest losses accounts to approximately 25 – 30 % of production. Just to feed the bursting population of India, maximising alone the production and productivity will not be enough. Efficient post harvest handling and processing is mere essential to make available more food (fruits) to the mankind.

Sorting or grading: Sorting is done in order to discard rotten, damaged, diseased, mis-shaped and overriped fruits before spreading infection to other healthy commodities. Grading is a form of grouping the fruits according to the firmness, cleanliness, size, weight, colour, shape and maturity.

Washing: The produce is cleaned or washed in order to remove the dirt, dust, insects, moulds, exception – onion, garlic, okra, mushroom are not washed. For surface decontamination, Chlorinated water (100 ppm) is effective after this, the fruits are again washed with clean water.

Curing: Curing is a means of natural wound healing process. It is a process of forming a corky layer against water loss and infection.

Waxing: It is a process of application of waxy layer on the skin of the fruits to reduce moisture loss, shrievelling and to extend the storage life. Paraffin wax, carnauba wax and various resins are common types of waxes used. Waxol is a common coating material.

Pre-cooling: The process of removal of heat from the just harvested fruits particularly during hot weather is called pre-cooling. It helps in decreasing the transpiration rate, respiration rate, ripening providing an ease to transport and storage. The methods are room cooling, forced air cooling, hydro cooling, vacuum cooling etc.

Hot water treatment: It is a process of eradicating or killing the infectious organism on several fruits. For inactivation of infection by *Phytopthora* sp. in tomato and oranges, *Colletotrichum* in papaya, mango and crown rot in banana, dip in hot water at 50 ± 2 degree C for 1-2 minutes. Hot water treatment of mango results in uniform ripening.

Vapour heat treatment: It is termed as an ecofriendly treatment mostly applicable for fruit flies mostly mango. It is initially expensive and cannot be used much by small and marginal farmers. Total treatment time for mangoes is approximately 195 minutes.

Regulation of ripening: Ripening of fruits like mango, banana can be regulated or is carried out in special treatment rooms with controlled temperatures with low application of ethylene. Release of ethylene occurs where fruits along with etherel alkaline solution is placed in a closed chamber. Ripening process is delayed and extension of shelf life is done by removing ethylene from storage atmosphere using ethylene absorbent.

Packaging: Packaging is a process to assemble the produce into convenient units of handling and to protect the produce during distribution, storage and marketing. It is a means of prolonging the storage life. For packaging cushioning materials should be used (paper shreds, paddy straw, thermocole). Packaging of fresh produce is done with bamboo baskets, sacks, wooden or plastic crates etc. corrugated fibre board (CFB) cartons being polar now a days for transport of fruits as they are of lighter weight and cheaper cost. Aseptic packaging, modified atmospheric packaging and controlled packaging are some new innovations of packaging.

Transportation: It is a phase of movement of fruits from one place to another, performed by, means of rail, truck, airplane and ship. Effective transportation doesnot help if there is no proper handling, in many developed countries pallets are used for trading of horticultural produce.

Marketting: Fruits have a high degree of perishability so marketing problems are more in fruits. NHB (National Horticultural Board) provides good market intelligence service for horticultural products. NDDB, HOPCOM are few of marketing organiza-tions for benefit of growers and consumers.

Storage: The process of maintaining life processes of fruits upto a required level till it reaches the consumers avoiding market glut is called storage.

Methods:

1. **Refrigerated storage:** storage of perishable commodities at the lowest temperature without any chilling injury is refrigerated storage, it strongly retards moisture loss and spoilage by microorganisms.
2. **Controlled or modified storage:** it is a process of adjusting the atmospheric composition of air surrounding the fruits different from that of normal air, it involves reduction in O_2 and elevation of CO_2 concentrations.
3. **Hypobaric storage:** it is a form of storage in which the produce is stored in partial vacuum, it is maintained to the desired low pressure by vacuum pump. It is limited to high value crops.
4. **Zero energy cool chamber:** this zero energy cool chamber works on the principle of evaporative cooling using locally available materials like brick, sand and bamboo as compared to surrounding atmosphere the temperature in the chamber is less.

Previous Years' Paper (Solved)

IFS–Agriculture Main Examination, 2017

PAPER-I

INSTRUCTIONS: *There are* ***Eight*** *questions in all, out of which* ***Five*** *are to be attempted. Candidates should attempt question nos.* **1** *and* **5** *which are compulsory, and out of the remaining* ***six*** *questions,* ***three*** *are to be attempted selecting at least* ***one*** *question from each of the two sections A and B. All questions carry equal marks. Answers must be written in English only.*

SECTION–A

1. Answer the following in about 150 words each:

(*a*) What are the climatic parameter affecting crop productivity according to which farmers follow the cropping pattern in the western zone of the country?

(*b*) Justify the plant ecology and edaphic factors influencing sustainable agriculture.

(*c*) What are the problems of herbicide-resistance in wheat crop?

(*d*) Diversification and intensification are important in present day agriculture. Explain.

(*e*) What is the importance of agroforestry and social forestry in the changing environment?

2. Describe the package and practices, viz., planting pattern, sowing time and spacing, weeds and nutrients management and productivity of the following crops:

(*a*) Chickpea

(*b*) Wheat

(*c*) Lucerne

(*d*) Sunflower

3. Answer the following in about 200 words each:

(*a*) What are the essential elements of plant nutrients? State the significance of C : N ratio in crop productivity.

(*b*) Describe crop management practices in the early stage of saline and alkaline soils.

(*c*) Describe phosphorus fixation in relation to soil pH.

(*d*) Soil solarization is an important tool for weed control. Justify.

4. Answer the following in about 200 words each:

(*a*) Describe Dryland technology and Rainfed agriculture for stabilizing production.

(*b*) Define Land Degradation and discuss the major factors affecting it.

(*c*) Explain the need of Integrated Nutrient Management (INM) in present day agriculture.

(*d*) Enumerate the agronomic measure for soil and water conservation and practices adopted by the farmers.

SECTION–B

5. Answer the following in about 150 words each:

(*a*) Discuss the role of Drip/Sprinkler irrigation system in increasing water use efficiency and productivity.

(*b*) Describe Cropping systems, Inter-cropping and Relay cropping in agriculture, with examples.

(*c*) Explain the current water pollution issues in agriculture with suitable remedies.

(*d*) Vermicompost is important in sustainable agriculture. Justify.

(*e*) Discuss Water Harvesting and the role of the Government and NGOs for its promotion.

6. Answer the following in about 200 words each:

(*a*) Explain the short-term and long-term effects of agriculture mechanization.

(*b*) Define Farm Management and explain the role of the farm manager in planning intensive agriculture.

(*c*) Explain about rural employment for women through agriculture.

(*d*) Price fluctuations of agricultural products have an impact on small and marginal farmers. Justify.

7. Answer the following in about 200 words each:

(*a*) What are the problems faced by landless agricultural labourers? What are the steps taken by the Government in order to intervene in the matter?

(*b*) Discuss the role of Krishi Vigyan Kendras (KVK) in transfer of technologies to end users.

(*c*) Explain management of wasteland for promoting agricultural production.

(*d*) What is Contractual Farming? What are its merits and demerits in present day agriculture?

8. Discuss the following in about 200 words each:

(*a*) Role of Farmers' Field School (FFS) in agriculture.

(*b*) Role of Cooperative Societies in agriculture.

(*c*) Importance of Extension Workers in transfer of technology to farmers.

(*d*) Integrated Farming System and its profitability to the farmers.

PAPER-II

INSTRUCTIONS: *Candidates should attempt question nos.* **1** *and* **5** *which are compulsory, and out of the remaining* ***six*** *questions,* ***three*** *are to be attempted, selecting at least* **one** *question from each section. All questions carry equal marks. Answers must be written in English only.*

SECTION–A

1. Answer the following in about 150 words each:

(*a*) Describe the mode of origin and growth of cell wall.

(*b*) Define allopolyploidy. Give its applications in crop improvement.

(*c*) Write the factors affecting seed quality.

(*d*) Enlist the enzymes requiring metal activators.

(*e*) Describe chemically induced male sterility.

2. Answer the following:

(*a*) Distinguish between epistasis and dominance. Explain gene interaction.

(*b*) Amongst the seed sample of a particular crop which would you recommend to grow based on the flowing data?

Samples	*Germination (%)*	*Purity (%)*
A	85	98
B	88	98
C	91	96

(*c*) Discuss the cyclic and non-cyclic photophosphorylation?

3. Distinguish between the following:

(*a*) Diffusion and osmosis.

(*b*) Sex-influenced and sex-limited characters.

(c) Synchrony in following and planting ration of parents.

4. Answer the following:

(a) What is phytochrome? Enlist different processes mediated by phytochrome.

(b) Give the advantages of molecular markers over other genetic markers.

(c) Describe the seed certification and seed quality assurance in India.

SECTION–B

5. Answer the following in about 150 words each:

(a) Importance of pinching in quality production of carnation?

(b) Preventive and curative methods against stored grain pests.

(c) Integrated management of Fusarium and Verticillium.

(d) Entomopathagenic bacteria for pest control.

(e) Describe the reservation methods of important fruits.

6. Answer the following:

(a) Give major insect pest of cauliflower and their management.

(b) Find out the quantity of Chlorpyriphos 20EC for treating an area which requires 1000 litres of spray fluid at 0.02% strength.

(c) Discuss the procurement and processing constructions of food grains.

7. Distinguish between following :

(a) Olericulture and pomology.

(b) Mildew and blights.

(c) Inoculative and augmentative release of natural enemies.

8. Answer the following :

(a) What are the critical component need adequate attentions while planning an orchard?

(b) Discuss Protein-Energy-Malnutrition.

(c) Discuss various methods of training in chrysanthemum.

ANSWERS

PAPER-I

SECTION 'A'

1. (*a*) Agriculture is sensitive to short-term changes in weather and to seasonal, annual and long-term variations in climate. Crop yield is the culmination of a diversified range of factors. Parameters like soil, seed, pest and diseases, fertilizers and agronomic practices exert significant influence on crop yield. The burgeoning population, along with human-induced climate change and environmental problems is increasingly proving to be a limiting factor for enhancing farm productivity and ensuring food security for the rural poor.

Agricultural productivity of the western zone of the country can be affected by climate change in two ways: first, directly, due to changes in temperature, precipitation and/ or CO_2 levels and second, indirectly, through changes in soil, distribution and frequency of infestation by pests, insects, diseases or weeds. Acute water shortage conditions, combined with thermal stress, could adversely affect wheat and, more severely, rice productivity in India even under the positive effects of elevated CO_2 in the future. The mean temperature in India is projected to increase by 0.10°C to 0.3°C in kharif (summer) and 0.3°C to 0.7°C in rabi (winter) by 2010 and to 0.4°C to 2°C in kharif and 1.1°C to 4.5°C in rabi by 2070 (IPCC, 1996). Mean rainfall is projected not to change by 2010 but may increase by 10% during rabi by 2070. At the same time, there is an increased possibility of climate extremes, such as the timing of onset of monsoon and intensities and frequencies of droughts and floods.

The soil system responds to the short-term events such as episodic infiltration of rainfall and also undergoes long-term changes such as physical and chemical weathering due to climatic change. The potential changes in the soil forming factors directly resulting from global climate change would be in the organic matter supply, temperature regimes, hydrology and changes in the potential evapotranspiration. Both the organic matter and carbon to nitrogen ratio(C: N ratio) will diminish in a warmer soil temperature regime. Drier soil conditions will suppress both root growth and decomposition of organic matter and will increase vulnerability to erosion. Increased evaporation from the soil and accelerated transpiration from the plants themselves will cause soil moisture stress.

Signals of climatic change are already visible. Global climate change is going to affect major crops like rice, wheat and maize in India. Climate is the least manageable of all resources. Hence, to avert the ill effects of climate change, more attention has to be paid to other resources and technologies viz., soil, irrigation water, nutrients, crops and their management practices, to sustain the productivity and to ensure food and environmental security to the country. Adaptive measures are to be taken in a timely fashion, both at the farmers' level (backed by strong agriculture/climate research and application oriented outputs) as well as at the policy makers' level to enable the small and marginal farmers to cope with the adversities of climate change.

1. (*b*) Ecological crop and soil management practices can be grouped under one or more of three overall strategies:

- Grow healthy plants with strong defense capabilities
- Stress pests
- Enhance beneficial organisms.

These overall strategies are accomplished by practices that maintain and enhance the habitat both above ground and in the soil. Ecological approaches call for designing the field and farm to take advantage of the inherent strengths of natural systems. Most of this is done prior to, and during, planting a crop and has the goal of preventing problems from developing by contributing to one or more of the three overall strategies.

It is well established—and known by most farmers—that crop rotation can decrease many disease, insect, nematode, and weed pressures.

Edaphic Factors Influencing Sustainable Agriculture

***(i)* Soil**

The word 'soil' is derived from the Latin word *solum* meaning earthy material in which plants grow. The science which deals with the study of soil is called Soil Science, Pedology (pedos = earth) or edaphology (edaphos = soil). The process of formation of soil is called pedogenesis. A soil complex is formed of 5 categories of components, *viz.*, mineral matter, organic matter or humus, soil water, soil air and living organisms. The quality of soil is due to its fertility, texture, structure, organic contents and air-water relationship.

***(ii)* Soil profile**

The vertical layered structure of soil is called the soil profile. There are 4 main horizons in a soil profile.

O - horizon is the organic layer composed of dead organic residues.

A - horizon is the top soil, the upper most layer which contains roots.

B - horizon is the sub soil.

C - horizon is the less weathered parent material.

***(iii)* Topography**

Topography includes the physical features of the earth like altitude, slope, exposure, mountain chains, valleys, plains, etc.

Marked variations in temperature at different altitudes result in the division of earth's vegetation into different zones such as equatorial, tropical rain forests, desert or grasslands, deciduous forests, coniferous forests, tundra, ice and snow of poles.

***(iv)* Minerals**

Minerals are also called as biogenic materials and are essential for the proper growth of organisms. So the type and distribution of plants and animals are determined by specific distribution of minerals. Deficiency or absence or excess of minerals results in abnormal growth or even death of organisms. To derive the required nutrients, organisms are adapted differently.

***(v)* Fire**

Fire has important ill effects on the environment. Fire removes plant cover, burns litter on the soil surface and causes loss of nutrients. Due to forest fires a variety of animal groups die.

***(vi)* Range of tolerance**

Plants and animals show a range of tolerance to environmental factors. The factor, which is present in least amount may become limiting. For example, water availability limits plant growth in deserts.

1. *(c)* International Survey of Herbicide-Resistant Weeds (1995-96) recorded 183 herbicide-resistant weed biotypes (124 different species) in 42 countries. The increase in the number of new herbicide-resistant weeds has remained relatively constant since 1978, at an average of nine new cases per year worldwide. Whilst 61 weed species have evolved resistance to triazine herbicides, this figure now only accounts for one-third of all documented herbicide-resistant biotypes. Triazine-resistant weeds have been controlled successfully in many countries by the use of alternative herbicides. Due to the economic importance of ALS and ACCase inhibitor herbicides worldwide, and the ease with which weeds have evolved resistance to them, it is likely that ALS and ACCase inhibitor-resistant weeds will present farmers with greater problems in the next five years than triazine-resistant weeds have caused in the past 25 years. Thirty-three weed species have evolved resistance to ALS-inhibitor herbicides in 11 countries. ALS-inhibitor-resistant weeds are most problematic in cereal, corn/soybean and rice production. Thirteen weed species have evolved resistance to ACCase inhibitors, also in 11 countries. ACCase inhibitor resistance in *Lolium* and *Avena* spp. threatens cereal production in Australia, Canada, Chile, France, South Africa, Spain, the United Kingdom and the USA. Fourteen weed species have evolved resistance to urea herbicides. Isoproturon-resistant *Phalaris minor* infesting wheat fields in North West India and chlorotoluron-resistant *Alopecurus myosuroides* in Europe are of significant economic importance. Although 27 weed species have evolved resistance to bipyridilium herbicides, and 14 weed species have evolved resistance to synthetic auxins, the area infested and the availability of alternative herbicides have kept their impact minimal. The lack of alternative herbicides to control weeds with multiple herbicide resistance, such as *Lolium rigidum* and *Alopecurus myosuroides*, makes these the most challenging resistance problems. The recent discovery of glyphosate-resistant *Lolium rigidum* in Australia is a timely reminder that sound herbicide-resistant management strategies will remain important after the widespread adoption of glyphosate-resistant crops.

1.(*d*) Agricultural diversification involves movement of resources from low value commodity mix to high value commodity mix. It focuses mainly on horticulture, dairy, poultry and fisheries sector. While most definitions of diversification in developing countries do work on the assumption that diversification primarily involves a substitution of one crop or other agricultural product for another, or an increase in the number of enterprises, or activities, carried out by a particular farm, the definition used in developed countries sometimes relates more to the development of activities on the farm that do not involve agricultural production. For example, one section of the British Department for Environment, Food and Rural Affairs (DEFRA) defines diversification as "the entrepreneurial use of farm resources for a non-agricultural purpose for commercial gain". Using this definition DEFRA found that 56% of UK farms had diversified in 2003. The great majority of diversification activities simply involved the renting out of farm buildings for non-farming use, but 9% of farms had become involved with processing or retailing, 3% with provision of tourist accommodation or catering, and 7% with sport or recreational activities. Others adopt a broader definition, which may include development of new marketing opportunities. In the developing countries such as India, which has been one of the leaders in promoting diversification, the concept is applied both to individual farmers and to different regions, with government programmes being aimed at promoting widespread diversification. The concept in India is seen as referring to the "shift from the regional dominance of one crop to regional production of a number of crops ..... (which takes into account) .... the economic returns from different value-added crops .... with complementary marketing opportunities".

Improving nutrition: Diversifying from the monoculture of traditional staples can have important nutritional benefits for farmers in developing countries.

Intensive farming involves various types of agriculture with higher levels of input and output per cubic unit of agricultural land area. It is characterized by a low fallow ratio, higher use of inputs such as capital and labour, and higher crop yields per cubic unit land area. This contrasts with traditional agriculture, in which the inputs per unit land are lower. The term "intensive" involves various meanings, some of which refer to organic farming methods (such as biointensive agriculture and French intensive gardening), and others that refer to non-organic and industrial methods. Intensive animal farming involves either large numbers of animals raised on limited land, usually confined animal feeding operations (CAFOs), often referred to as factory farms, or managed intensive rotational grazing (MIRG), which has both organic and non-organic types. Both increase the yields of food and fibre per acre as compared to traditional animal husbandry. In CAFO, feed is brought to the seldom-moved animals, while in MIRG the animals are repeatedly moved to fresh forage.

Further information: Sustainable farming, Integrated Multi-Trophic Aquaculture, Zero waste agriculture, and Organic farming. Sustainable intensive farming practices have been developed to slow the deterioration of agricultural land and even regenerate soil health and ecosystem services, while still offering high yields. Most of these developments fall in the category of organic farming, or the integration of organic and conventional agriculture.

1. (*e*) Importance of Agroforestry

(*i*) Salinity is mainly caused by rising water tables. Trees help to lower water tables, acting as pumps to take up water from the soil and then evaporating it to the atmosphere.

(*ii*) Soil erosion or loss results from the action of wind and water on unprotected soils. The forest canopy, roots and leaf litter all have a role in controlling soil erosion.

(*iii*) Through water removal, established trees can substantially reduce water logging in their immediate area, which may result in improved land uses, *e.g.*, pasture or crop.

(*iv*) Agroforestry can have immense benefits for the environment and the farmer (a detailed breakdown of agroforestry's main benefits can be found on AgriInfo's site).

(*v*) For farmers, the ability to maintain some sort of control over land and production in the face of climate change means agroforestry could hold huge promise for the agricultural sector.

(*vi*) On an environmental level, agroforestry's ability to help prevent soil erosion while simultaneously aiding water retention and promoting soil fertility could help provide a solution for areas where rainfal is irregular or might become irregular due to climate change while dense plantations of trees would also help to absorb CO_2 and regulate local temperature.

Importance of Social Forestry

(*i*) Betterment of environment

(*ii*) Reduction of pollution

(*iii*) Providing the basic needs of rural and urban people for fuel, small timber, manure leaf and other economic products nearer to home

(*iv*) Providing raw materials for industries such as wood, wool, packing cases, slate frames, fibre, tamarind extract, oil seeds, pulping and husking material

(*v*) Provide shelter for insectivorous birds on the farms

(*vi*) Protection from wind

(*vii*) Conservation of moisture

(*viii*) Prevention of soil erosion

(*ix*) Fullest utilization of land unsuitable for cultivation

(*x*) Employment opportunities in rural and urban area

(*xi*) Reduction of noise

(*xii*) Recreation

(*xiii*) Reduction of pressure on national forests

(*xiv*) Achievement of self-sufficiency by the villages

(*xv*) Improvement of rainfall by induction precipitation

2. (*a*) Chickpea

Botanical name*:* *Cicer* spp.

Cicer aeritinum – Desi/Brown Chickpea/ Kala Chana

Cicer kabulium – Kabuli/White Chickpea

Family: Papilionaceae (Leguminaceae)

- Chickpea is also known as Gram or Bengal gram.
- Gram is originated in South-West Asia (Afghanistan).
- Chickpea consists of more than 1/3 of the area and 40 per cent of the total production of pulses in India.
- Chickpea is called as King of Pulses and contains 22-23 per cent protein content.
- The sour taste in leaf of chickpea is due to presence of Maleic and Oxalic acid.
- Its leaves are recommended for intestined disorder patient, due to presence of Maleic and Oxalic acid.

Types of Chickpea:

Desi: It has small, darker seeds and a rough coat, cultivated mostly in the Indian subcontinent, Ethiopia, Mexico, and Iran. The desi type is used to make Chana Dal, which is a split chickpea with the skin removed.

Kabuli: It has lighter/white coloured, larger seeds and a smoother coat, mainly grown in Southern Europe, Northern Africa, Afghanistan, Pakistan and Chile, also introduced during the 18th century in India.

- Desi chickpeas have markedly higher fibre content than Kabulis and hence a very low glycemic index which may make them suitable for people with blood sugar problems.
- Chickpea is a self-pollinated and long-day plant.
- Chickpea is usually considered a dry-land crop.
- Chickpea has tape root system.
- It favours moderate rainfall with mild cold weather.
- Chickpea requires a loose and well aerated rough seedbed.
- Light alluvial soil is best for cultivation of gram.
- Chickpea may be cultivated as a sole crop, or mixed with barley, lathyrus (grasspea), linseed, mustard, peas, corn, coffee, safflower, potato, sweet potato, sorghum, or wheat.
- In India, chickpea is also grown as a catch crop in sugarcane fields and often as a second crop after rice.
- When chickpea is grown as mixed crop, it checks blight disease.
- Shelling percentage is 49 per cent.
- The optimum time of sowing of chickpea is 15th to 20th October.

Seed rate:

- Early sown – 75-80 kg/ha
- Late sown – 80-100 kg/ha

NPK requirement (kg/ha):

- Normally – 20 : 60 : 30
- Rainted – 15 : 20 : 15

Important varieties of Chickpea:

Recently released from IARI	PDM-11, BG 2024
Popular varieties released from ICAR	Pusa-209, DG-203
Desi variety	JG-11, CO-3, RS-10, GCP-11
Kabuli variety	Pusa-1003, K-551
Early maturing and medium sized grain	Chaff chaff, JG-62
Medium duration and high yielding	L-550, C-104, NP-58, RS-11, G-130
Suitable variety for late sown Culinary purpose	Radhey, Uday, Haryana chana 1 C 104
Both early and late planting	Mahamaya 2
Rainfed condition	Vishal, Anubhav
Drought resistant (Most suitable)	NP-58
Resistant to drought and wilt	G 24
Resistant to Blight	C-235, Gaurav, Pusa 256, Sadbhavana
Resistant to Wilt	JG-74, JG-315, BG-256, Awarodhi
Resistant to Pod borer	PBG 3

- Phosphorus should be applied at below or side of the seed to increase the gram yield.
- The critical stages for irrigation is
  (*i*) Pre-flowering/Late vegetative phase
  (*ii*) Pod development
- **Nipping in Chickpea:** It is a process of plucking/tipping of apical buds with some young leaves once from each plant at a height of 12 to 15 centimetre (30-40 DAS) to check luxuriant growth and encourage more branching and fruit development.
- Late planting of chickpea is done to protect the seedlings from wilt disease. In such type of delayed planting, seed rate is increased by 25 per cent to obtain a good yield.
- Sowing depth for checking wilt disease is 8-10 cm.
- Most important pest of gram is Pod borer (Helicoverpa armigera), which is controlled by Endosulphan 0.07 per cent at fruiting stage.

Yield: Rainfed condition – 500 to 600 kg/ha

Irrigated condition – 1200 - 1500 kg/ha

2. (*b*) Wheat

- **Botanical name:** *Triticum* spp.; **Family:** Poaceae
- Wheat is the largest staple food crop of world.
- India stands 2nd position in production of wheat after China.
- Generally, wheat is a self-pollinated, C_3 and hexaploid plant.
- The national average productivity of wheat is 26.5 qt/ha.

Triticum spp:

T. aestivum	→ 2n = 42	Mexican dwarf wheat, everywhere grown, evolved by Dr. N.E. Borlaug of Mexico, covered 87 per cent of total wheat area.
T. vulgare	→ 2n = 42	Tall wheat for Rainfed condition, typical wheat for alluvial soil.
T. durum	→ 2n = 28	Marconi wheat, very old spp., best for drought condition, used for Suji preparation, covered 12 per cent of total wheat area.
T. dicocum	→ 2n= 28	Emmer wheat, used for Uppumav preparation, popularly grown in south India, covered 1 per cent of total wheat area.
T. spherococum	→ 2n= 14	Indian dwarf/Club wheat, very short & compact heads
T. monococum	→ 2n= 14	Einkorn wheat

- The common bred wheat, *T. aestivum*, is the most important species, occupying more than 90 per cent of the wheat area and 87 per cent of the total wheat production in the country.
- UP covers maximum area and production of wheat in India, whereas in productivity, Punjab gets 1st position.

Sowing:

1. **Sowing date:**

Irrigated: Timely sowing	: 2nd week of Nov.
Irrigated: Late sowing	: 15 Dec.
Rained: Timely sowing	: 15 Oct – 15 Nov.
Rained: Late sowing	: 15 Nov – 15 Dec.
In North-West plain zone	: up to 25th Dec.
In Central zone	: up to 10th Dec.
In Peninsular zone	: up to 30th Nov.

2. **Sowing depth:** The dwarf wheats should be sown only at 5-6 cm depth as they have shorter coleoptiles. Seeding depth of 8-10 cm results in poor germination and reduced yield.

3. **Seed rate:**

Particulars	***Row to Row Spacing***	***Seed Rate (kg/ha)***
Timely sown wheat	22.5 - 23.0 cm	100 -125
Late sown wheat	15- 18 cm (25% more of timely sown)	125 -150

Irrigation Management:

- Water requirement of wheat is 45-65 cm through its life cycle.
- Average no. of irrigation required is 6.
- For dwarf wheat – 30-60 cm
- Deshi wheat – 15-20 cm
- In light soil – 5 irrigation, each of 5 cm
- In heavy soil – 4 irrigation, each of 6 cm
- IW/CPE ratio is 0.90
- Percentage irrigated area of wheat in India is 85 per cent

Irrigation Management according to number of irrigation availability:

Critical Growth Stages	***No. of Irrigation Available***				
1. Crown root initiation (20-25 DAS)	✓	✓	✓	✓	✓
2. Tillering stage (40-45 DAS)				✓	✓
3. Late jointing stage (60-65 DAS)			✓		✓
4. Flowering stage (80-95 DAS)		✓		✓	✓
5. Milking stage (110-115 DAS)			✓	✓	✓
6. Grain filling/Dough stage (120-125 DAS)					✓

* DAS: Days after sowing.

Fertilizer management:

Particulars	***NPK (kg/ha)***	
Irrigated: timely sowing	100:60:40	½ – – – – N
Late sowing	80:50:30	– do –
Unirrigated :	30:20:10	Complete basal application
Semi irrigated	60:40:20	½ N as basal application + ½ at CRI stage

* For obtaining 50 qt ha–1 production, wheat crop uptake 125, 45 and 165 kg NPK/ha.

Wheat Varieties:	
Single gene dwarf	Sonalika, UP-262, WL-711, Girja
Double gene dwarf	Kalyansona, UP-215, Arjun, Pratap, Janak
Triple gene dwarf	Jawahar, Jyoti, Hira, Moti, Sangam, UP-301, UP-319
Late sown	Sarbati sanora, Sonalika, Safed lerma, UP-301, Sanora-64, Raj 3765, UP-2425, UP-2338
Rainfed timely sown	C-306, Sujata, Mukta, K-8027, HW 2004, N59
Marconi wheat	Jayraj, Meghdoot, Malvika, HD-4530, Bansi
Bred wheat	C-306, C-3, K-65, K-68,
Chapati wheat	DWR-39, HI-977, HW-65, Kalyansona, NP824, NP 891
For Central zone	HI-1077, GW-190
Important varieties during Green revolution	HD-2329, Kalyansona and Sonalika,
For salt affected soil	Lok1, Raj 3077, KRL 1-4, PBW 19
Baking purpose	K 65, K 68, NP 880, UP 310, UP 319, Sarbati sanora
Biscuit purpose	Sonalika, HD 2285, PBW 175, HD 2285, Larma roja, Safed larma, Chhoti larma
Rainfed areas	C -306, Sujata, Shera, Mukta
Partially irrigated	GW 2004, GW 1034, GWV 17, HI 1277
Timely sown irrigated	Arpa, Ratan, Bilasa, Lok1, GW190, GW147, GW273, GW273, Kanchan, Swati
Late sown irrigated	Lok1, Swati, GW173, Jayraj 1555, Raj 911, Meghdoot, Sonali
Resistant to	HD 2189, HD 2285
Blight and Rust	UP 2425, PBW 273, WH 29
Shoot fly	HUW 243, HUW 468
Heat tolerant	Raj 3765
Leaf blight	HD 2643
Drought	K 68, Narmada, NP 890

- Most suitable cropping system for wheat crop is mixed cropping (wheat + mustard and wheat + chickpea).
- Four to Five rows of wheat grown in two rows of sugarcane is a popular intercrop practice.
- Relay cropping of wheat in an early planted potato crop is a high bonus cropping system.
- To obtain maximum yield of wheat, 500 tillers per m^2 is required.

Weeds of wheat crop:

1. Objectionable weed – Convolvulus arvensis
2. Associated weed – Phalaris minor, Avena fatua and Chenopodium album

3. Horrible weed– Sorghum halepense
4. Satellite weed – Phalaris minor & Avena fatua
   - *Phalaris minor* is found with dwarf wheat.
   - Common herbicide used to control wheat weeds is 2, 4-D.
   - Grain and straw ratio in Mexican dwarf wheat is 1:1.5.

2. (*c*) Lucerne

1. Botanical name	*Medicago sativa*
2. Family	Leguminoceae
3. Origin	South West Asia
4. Optimum temperature required	20 - 22°C
5. Sowing time	October
6. Sowing method	Broadcasting
7. Seed rate	20 - 25 kg/ha
8. Seed treatment	By Rhizobium meliloti culture
9. Varieties	Moopa, Rambler, Anand-2, 3, Sirsa 1, 8, 9, Type- 8, 9, NDRI – 1, 2, IGFRI-5, 54, 244
10. Weeds	Cuscuta reflexa (Doddar/amarbel – parasitic weed)
11. NPK	20-25:60-75:0-0 kg/ha
12. Cutting	First cutting at 50-55 days after sowing and subsequent cutting is taken at 20-30 days after previous cutting
13. Forage yield	800 - 1100 qt/ha
14. Glucosides found	Saponins
15. Physiological disorder	"Lucern yellowing" (due to boron deficiency)

2. (*d*) Sunflower

Botanical name: *Helianthus annus*

Family: Compositae

- Helios = Sun and Annus = Flower
- Auxin activity is more in apical portion of flower.
- Sunflower is a **day neutral crop**.
- It has high seed multiplication ratio (>1:80).
- Sunflower has high quality edible oil (45-50 per cent).
- Sunflower has no unsaturated fatty acid content, so it is **safe for heart patients**.
- The head of sunflower is called as **'Capitulai'**.
- Sunflower has ray and disc floret, in which Ray floret is for beautifulness (attraction of pollination) and Disc floret forms seed and have male & female flowers.
- **Chaffiness** means non-filling of seed.

Sowing time:

Kharif: July to 1st week of August
Rabi: November 1st to 2nd week
Summer: February 2nd week

Seed rate: 5-7.5 kg/ha

Spacing:

Kharif: 45 × 30 cm
Rabi: 50 × 20 cm
Summer: 60 × 30 cm

Irrigation:

Kharif: no need

Rabi: 3-4 irrigation

Summer: 5-6 irrigation

Critical stages:

1. Seedling stage (10-12 DAS)
2. Bud initiation/Button/Knee high stage (30-35 DAS)
3. Flowering stage (50-55 DAS)
4. Seed development stage (70-90 DAS)

Varieties:

- Modern, MSFH-8,17, Jwalamukhi, KBSH-1, JS-1, Sunrise selection, EC 68413
- Sunflower is intercropped with groundnut, Arhar, urad etc.
- **Weed management:** Pendimethalin @ 1.5 kg ai/ha followed by hoeing at 30 DAS.
- Sunflower is matured at 90-120 days after sowing, when 10 per cent of head become brown and the disc floret attached to the tip of the head drop down the crop.
- Yield: 20-30 qt/ha

4. (*a*) Dry Land Technology: Indian agriculture is traditionally a system of Rainfed agriculture. Out of 143 million hectares of net cropped area, about 72% is Rainfed production about 45% of food grains and 75 - 80% of pulses and oil - seeds and a number of important industrial crops. Considering the present rate of development of irrigation facilities and also water potentiality of the country, express estimate that at any point of time 50% of cropped area in India will remain under Rainfed farming system.

Such vast areas as of now consume hardly 25% of total fertilizer consumption of the country. Due to poor level of management, crop productivity is also very low resulting in socio-economic backwardness of the people.

Definition: The different definitions of dry farming given by various express are described below:

1. Dry farming is an improved system of cultivation in which maximum amount of moisture is conserved in low and untimely rainfall for the production of optimum Quantities of crop on economic and sustames basis.
2. Dry farming in short, is a programme of soil and water management designed to conserve the maximum quantity of water on a particular piece of land.
3. Dry farming is the profitable production of useful crops without irrigation on land that receive annually a rainfall of 500 mm or less.
4. In a more specific way dry farming may be defined as an efficient system of soil and crop management in the regions of low land and uneven distributed rainfall.

Dry Land Vs Rainfed Agriculture

Constituents	*Dryland farming*	*Rainfed farming*
1. Rainfall (mm)	< 750	>75
2. Moisture	Shortage	Enough/Sufficient
3. Growing season	<200	>200
4. Growing regions	Arid and Semiarid & up lands of sub humid & humid regions.	Humid and slub humid regions
5. Cropping system	Single crop or inter-cropping	Inter-cropping or double cropping
6. Constraints	Wind and water erosion	Water erosion

Rainfed Farming

Growing of crops on natural preciption without irrigation.

Dry farming areas: Dry farming areas (as per the IV five year plan) are those areas receiving an annual rainfall ranging from 375 to 1125 mm and very limited irrigation facilities. Areas which receive less than 375 mm of average rainfall are considered as absolutely arid or desert areas, which require special treatment. As many as 128 districts in the country falls under category of dry farming areas as defined above. Out of these 25 dists from the states of Rajasthan, Sourashtra and rainshadow region of Maharashtra and Karnataka belong to very high intensity dryfarming areas (*i.e.*, rainfall ranges from 375 to 750 mm and irrigated area belong 10% of the cropped area.)

As the Encylopedia Britanmputs Dry land farming consists of making the best use of limited water supply by storing in the soil and much of the rainfall as possible and by going suitable crop plants those make the best use of this moisture.

The major physiographic regions observed in India namely:

(*i*) Mountain region

(*ii*) Indogangatic alluvial plains

(*iii*) Peninsular or Deccan plateau

(*iv*) Coastal plains

National Agricultural Research Project (NARP) launched in 1979 by ICAR with soft loan support from International Development Agency (IDA) of World Bank. Where in state Agricultural Universities were advised to divide each zone/state into subzons (NARP). Accordingly 120 sub zone map based primarily on rainfall, existing cropping pattern and administrative units was prepared.

4. (*b*) Land degradation:

(*i*) Loss of natural fertility of soil because of loss of nutrients.

(*ii*) Less vegetation cover

(*iii*) Changes in the characteristic of soil.

(*iv*) Pollution of water resources from the contamination of soil through which water sweeps into ground or runoff to the water bodies.

(*v*) Changes in climatic conditions because of unbalanced created in the environment.

Major Feature affecting Land Degradation

(*a*) **Deforestation:** Deforestation is taking place at a faster rate due to increasing demands of timber, fuel and forest products which results into degradation of land resources.

(*b*) **Overgrazing:** Overgrazing refers to excessive eating of grasses and other green plants by cattle. It results into reduced growth of vegetation, reduced diversity of plant species, excessive growth of unwanted plant species, soil erosion, and degradation of land due to cattle movement.

(*c*) **Agricultural practices:** The modern agricultural practices, excessive use of fertilizers and pesticides has adversely degraded the natural quality and fertility of the cultivation land.

(*d*) **Industrialization:** Development of industries for the economic growth of the country leads to excessive deforestation and utilization of land in such as way that it has lost its natural up gradation quality.

(*e*) **Urbanization:** Increasing growth of population and demand for more residential areas and commercial sectors is also one of the reasons for land degradation.

4. (*c*) Integrated Nutrient Management (INM): Integrated Nutrient Management (INM) refers to maintenance of soil fertility and plant nutrient supply to an optimum level for sustaining the desired crop productivity through optimisation of the benefits from all possible sources of plant nutrients in an integrated manner.

Integrated Plant Nutrient system is the management and conservation of natural resource base and the orientation of technological and institutional agencies in such a manner as to ensure the attainment and continuing satisfaction of human needs for the present and future generations - FAO.

Components

On-site resource generation: On-site generation of resources stipulates recycling of crop residues, animal manure etc.

Mobilisation of off-site nutrient resources: The mobilisation of off-site nutrient resources stipulates the addition of chemical nutrients from outside sources.

Resources integration: The resources responsible for on-site generation of nutrients and energy have to be appropriately integrated with chemical forms of nutrients and other management factors which enhances productivity.

Resources management: All the sources have to be appropriately managed at the optimum level of efficiency. In practical terms, the integrated nutrient supply system stipulates the management of the farming system as a whole, involving cattle, poultry, animals and plant resources and the use of chemicals for their conversion into food-grains and other forms of food.

Schemes like the 'Balanced and integrated use of fertilisers' have been designed by Govt. of India with the aim of promoting the use of organic manures and bio-fertilisers. The scheme is also designed to encourage the processing and production of compost from urban waste and bio-fertiliser.

Integrated Plant Nutrient Management at farm level

It is only after they have made improvements in the biological, physical and hydrological properties of their soils that farmers can expect to get the full benefits from the supply of additional plant nutrients, in the form of inorganic fertilizer, to their crops. At the farm field level IPNM therefore calls for an integrated and synergistic approach which involves:

Matching the land use requirements of individual agricultural enterprises with the land qualities present in the areas where they are undertaken - *i.e.,* the biological, chemical and physical properties of the soil, and the local climatic conditions (temperature, rainfall etc);

Seeking to improve yields by identifying and overcoming the most limiting factors in order of their diminishing influence on yield;

Better plant management, especially: (*i*) improved crop establishment at the beginning of the rains, so as to increase protective ground cover thereby reducing splash erosion, enhancing infiltration and biological activity; and (*ii*) timely weeding to reduce crop yield losses from competition for nutrients and soil moisture;

Combinations of complementary crop, livestock and land husbandry practices which maximize additions of organic materials and recycle farm wastes, so as to maintain and enhance soil organic matter levels (ideally at levels of at least 50-75% of those under natural vegetation);

Land management practices that ensure soil moisture conditions are favourable for the proposed land use (*e.g.,* moisture harvesting/conservation in low rainfall areas, drainage in high rainfall areas);

The replenishment of soil nutrients lost by leaching and/or removed in harvested products through an integrated plant nutrition management approach that optimizes the benefits from all possible on- and off-farm sources of plant nutrients (*e.g.,* organic manures, crop residues, rhizobial N-fixation, P and other nutrient uptake through root mycorrizhal fungi infestation, transfer of nutrients released by weathering in the deeper soil layers to the surface via tree roots and leaf litter, rock phosphate, inorganic fertilizer etc);

Combinations of crop, livestock and land husbandry practices that reduce rainfall impact, improve surface infiltration, and reduce the velocity of surface runoff thereby ensuring any soil loss is below the 'tolerable' level for the soil type;

Conservation tillage, crop rotation, agroforestry and restorative fallow practices that maintain and enhance the soils physical properties through maintaining an open topsoil structure, and breaking any subsoil compacted layer (hoe/plough pan) thereby encouraging root development and rainfall infiltration (*e.g.*, use of ox drawn chisel ploughs, double dug beds, pasture leys, interplanting of deep rooted perennial crops/ trees and shrubs).

4. (*d*) The main agronomic measures are: 1. Conservation Tillage 2. Deep Tillage 3. Conservation Farming 4. Contour-Farming 5. Mulching 6. Growing of Cover Crops 7. Strip Cropping 8. Mixed Cropping.

Conservation Tillage:

(*a*) This umbrella term can include reduced tillage, minimum tillage, no-till, direct drill, mulch tillage, stubble-mulch farming, trash farming, strip tillage, plough-plant.

(*b*) With advanced soil conservation programmes, the concept of conservation tillage is the main theme of the recommendations for cropland.

(*c*) The application is mainly in mechanized high production farming with good rainfall, or for the control of wind erosion where there is large-scale mechanized cereal production. It is less applicable to low input level crop production, or subsistence agriculture.

(*d*) The principles are equally effective in any conditions – to maximize cover by returning crop residues and not inverting the top soil, and by using a high crop density of vigorous crops.

(*e*) Conservation tillage also has the advantage of reducing the need for terraces or other permanent structures. However there are several disadvantages which hinder the application of conservation tillage in semi-arid conditions.

(*f*) Dense plant covers may be incompatible with the well-tested strategy of using low plant populations to suit low moisture availability.

(*g*) Crop residues may be of value as feed for livestock.

(*h*) Planting through surface mulches is not easy for ox-drawn planters although there may be no problem with hand job planters.

Deep Tillage:

(*a*) One of the reasons for low yields in semi-arid areas is the limited amount of moisture available to crop roots.

(*b*) The available moisture will be increased if the rooting depth is increased and it has been shown that in some cases deep tillage can help, for example on the dense sandy soils.

(*c*) Deep tillage is beneficial for some crops but not all, and on some soils but not all.

(*d*) Deep tillage requires greater draught power which is usually in short supply in semi-arid areas.

(*e*) Ripping or sub soiling can be beneficial, either to increase the porosity of the soil, or to break a pan which is reducing permeability.

(*f*) The deep placement of fertilizer can also be used to encourage more rooting at depth, but again the application of this technique to subsistence farming will be difficult.

Conservation Farming:

(*a*) It includes any farming practice which improves yield, or reliability, or decreases the inputs of labour or fertilizer, or anything else leading towards improved land husbandry, which we have defined as the foundation of good soil conservation.

(*b*) It includes strip cropping, crop rotations, alternate cropping, mixed cropping and interplanting, surface and mulching, organic mulches, deep planting of varieties, dry seeding etc.

Contour-Farming:

(*a*) During intense rain storms, the soil cannot absorb all the rain as it falls. The excess water flows down the slope under the influence of gravity. If farming is done up and down the slope, the flow of water is accelerated, because each furrow serves as a rill.

The major part of the rain is drained away without infiltrating into the soil. The top fertile soil, along with plant nutrients and seeds, is washed off. All this results in a scanty and uneven growth of a crop.

(*b*) "A simple practice of farming across the slope, keeping the same level, as far as possible is technically called contour-farming.

(*c*) The ridges and the rows of the plants placed across the slope form a continual series of miniature barriers to the water moving over the soil surface. The barriers are small individually, but as they are large in number, their total effect is great in reducing run-off, soil erosion and loss of plant nutrients."

Mulching:

(*a*) Surface mulches are used to prevent soil from blowing and being washed away, to reduce evaporation, to increase infiltration, to keep down, to improve soil structure and eventually to increase crop yields.

(*b*) Inter-culture kills weeds and produces five or seven cm thick soil mulch which helps to reduce evaporation from the top soil.

(*c*) It also breaks the surface crust which forms after each downpour.

Growing of Cover Crops:

(*a*) Cultivated legumes, in general, furnish a better cover and hence better protection to cultivated land against erosion than ordinary cultivated crops.

(*b*) The crops and the cropping systems will naturally vary from region to region, depending on the soil and climatic conditions.

(*c*) The mostly preferred cover crops are green gram, black gram, cowpea, groundnut etc.

Strip Cropping: Strip cropping is the system of growing alternate strips of erosion permitting crops (row crop such as maize, jowar, bajra, cotton etc.) and erosion resisting crops (close growing crops such as green gram, black gram, moth, groundnut etc.) in the same field. This practice reduces the velocity of runoff and checks the eroded soil from being washed away.

Mixed Cropping:

(*i*) Mixed cropping is the growing of 2 or more crops simultaneously in the same field without any definite row pattern. This is done by mixing their seeds.

(*ii*) Important objectives of mixed cropping are a better and continuous cover of the land, good protection against the beating action of the rain, almost a complete protection against soil erosion and the assurance of one or more crops to the farmer.

SECTION 'B'

5. (*a*) **Role of Drip Irrigation System in Increasing Water Use Efficiency and Productivity:** Drip irrigation is a controlled, slow application of water to soil over a long period of time, usually lasting several hours. The water flows under low pressure through plastic pipe/tubing laid along each row of plants. It reduces water loss by up to 60 per cent.

Flow rate needs to be adjusted so there is no flooding or runoff.

- Apply enough water to wet the soil to a depth of 4-6 inches
- Avoid frequent light applications of water
- Water in early daylight hours

Source of clear water that flows at a rate of at least 2 to 5 gallons per minute with at least 30 to 40 pounds of pressure. If using a rain barrel, raise or elevate it to increase the pressure.

- Locate the area to be irrigated as close as possible to water source. Use a 5/8-inch or 3/4-inch hose to get from house faucet to the header in the area to be irrigated
- Determine the layout of the area to be irrigated. Make a sketch using graph or grid paper draw the area and the tubing needs.
- Have a plan when you shop and take it with you.
- When buying irrigation equipment, avoid mixing brands of fittings, hoses and emitters unless they are compatible.
- Emitter selection and performance are keys to the success of all drip irrigation systems. Some emitters perform satisfactorily underground, while other tube is used only above ground. Emitter clogging is a major problem in drip irrigation. They clog easily.

Role of Soil System Sprinkler Irrigation System in increasing water use efficiency

In the sprinkler method of irrigation, water is sprayed into the air and allowed to fall on the ground surface somewhat resembling rainfall. The spray is developed by the flow of water under pressure through small orifices or nozzles. The pressure is usually obtained by pumping. With careful selection of nozzle sizes, operating pressure and sprinkler spacing the amount of irrigation water required to refill the crop root zone can be applied nearly uniform at the rate to suit the infiltration rate of soil.

- Elimination of the channels for conveyance, therefore no conveyance loss
- Suitable to all types of soil except heavy clay
- Suitable for irrigating crops where the plant population per unit area is very high. It is most suitable for oil seeds and other cereal and vegetable crops
- Water saving
- Closer control of water application convenient for giving light and frequent irrigation and higher water application efficiency
- Increase in yield
- Mobility of system
- May also be used for undulating area
- Saves land as no bunds etc. are required
- Influences greater conducive micro-climate
- Areas located at a higher elevation than the source can be irrigated
- Possibility of using soluble fertilizers and chemicals
- Less problem of clogging of sprinkler nozzles due to sediment laden water.

5. (*b*) **Cropping System:** The cropping pattern used on a farm and its interactions with farm resources, other farm enterprises and available technology which determine their makeup.

Farming System: An appropriate combination of farm enterprises *viz.*, cropping system, livestock, poultry, fisheries and the means available to the farmer to raise them for increasing profitability.

Mixed Farming

1. A system of farming on a particular farm which includes crop production, raising livestock, poultry, fisheries, bee keeping etc. to sustain and safety as many needs of the farmer as possible. The objective is subsistence while higher profitability without altering ecological balance is important in farming system.
2. Cropping pattern which involve the raising of crops, animals and or trees.

Ratooning: One of the important methods of intensive cropping, allowing the stubbles of the original crop to strike again after harvesting and to raise another crop.

Live Mulch System: Live mulch crop production involves planting a food crop directly into a living cover of an established cover crop without tillage or the destruction of the fallow vegetation.

Mixed Cropping: Growing of two or more crops simultaneously and intermingled without row arrangements, where there is significant amount of intercrop competition.

Sole Cropping/Solid Planting

1. It is opposite of intercropping.
2. "One crop variety grown alone in pure stands at normal density in a field".

Monoculture

The repetitive growing of the same sole crop on the same land.

Multiple Cropping

1. "The growing of more than one crop on the same land in one year".
2. Types of multiple cropping:
   (*a*) Inter cropping
   (*b*) Mixed cropping
   (*c*) Sequential/non-overlapped cropping
   (*d*) Relay/overlapped cropping

(*a*) Inter Cropping: "Growing of two or more crops simultaneously in alternate rows or otherwise in the same area, where there is significant amount of inter crop competition".

Example: Planting a deep rooted crop with a shallow rooted crop or planting a tall crop with shorter crop.

Advantages of Inter Cropping

1. Greater stability of yield over different seasons
2. Better use of growth resources
3. Better control of weeds, pests and diseases
4. One crop provides physical support to the other crop
5. One crop provides shelter to the other crop
6. Erosion control through providing continuous leaf cover over the ground surface
7. It is the small farmers of limited means who is most likely to benefit.

Disadvantages of Inter-cropping

1. Yield decrease because of adverse competition effect
2. Allelopathic effect
3. Creates obstruction in the free use of machines for inter cultural operations
4. Large farmers with adequate resources may likely to get less benefit out of inter-cropping.

(*b*) Mixed Cropping: Cultivation of two or more than two crops simultaneously on the same piece of land without any definite row pattern or fixed ratio.

1. Scientific study of mixed cropping was firstly done by La-Flitze in 1929.
2. Mixed cropping is commonly practiced in Dryland areas of India.
3. Sowing of seeds is generally by broadcasting method.

4. Main objective is to lessen the risk of total crop failure, and to satisfy the farmers in food and fodder.
5. Mixed cropping needs irrigation through out the year.

(c) **Sequential/Non-overlapped Cropping:** Growing of two or more crops in quick succession on the same piece of land in a farming year. The swing of the succeeding crop and harvesting of the preceding crop may be done simultaneously or in a quick succession *e.g.*, Just after the harvest of Maize, Potato is sown and just after digging of potato, Chilli is sown.

(*d*) **Relay/Overlapped Cropping:** Relay planting is inter planting or inter sowing of seeds/seedlings of the succeeding crop before harvesting the preceding/maturing crop.

1. Generally 2nd crop is planted after the first crop has reached its reproductive stage of growth *e.g.*, Potato is planted before the harvest of Maize and Radish is sown before harvesting of Potato.
2. Paira (Bihar & WB) and Utera (MP) cropping are also referred as an example of relay cropping. Paira/Utera cropping means sowing of Lathyrus or Lentil before the harvest of rice in lowland area with an objective to use the residual moisture of rice field.

5. (*c*) Any undesirable change in the physical and chemical properties of water which adversely effects living systems is known as water pollution.

- **Modern agriculture:** In modern agriculture, excess of chemical fertilizers and pesticides are supplied to the crops, which cause water pollution.
- **Industries:** The industrial waste is discharged into water – bodies. Toxic chemicals are present in industrial waste. *e.g.*, Paper, Chemical, Food processing, Paint, Leather, Sugar, Industries, Mining.
- **Household activities:** Domestic activities also cause water – pollution.
- **Marine pollution:** Due to accidental leakage of oil during its transport, in the sea *i.e.*, oil spillage and dumping of waste of the coastal cities in the sea are the major cause of marine pollution.

Categories of Sources of Water Pollution

1. Point sources: Point sources are the identified single location of water pollution. *e.g.*, sewerage systems, industrial effluent.
2. Diffused or non-point sources: Their location cannot be easily identified *e.g.*, the entry of scattered pollutants such as fertilizers and pesticides from a farm to nearby water-body.

Types of Water Pollutants

Water pollutants are divided into three major categories: Physical, chemical and biological agents

(*i*) Physical agents: It mainly includes the physical factors *e.g.*, heat released into water-bodies causes thermal pollution.

(*ii*) Chemical agents: Chemical wastes released into water bodies from chemical, metallurgical and food processing plants, textile paper and sugar mills, rubber and plastic industries, oil refineries, tanneries and other industries are categorized as below:

(*a*) Organic chemicals: *e.g.*, Hydrocarbons and compounds containing benzene are hazardous and cause water pollution. Cellulose fibers, carbohydrates, proteins, oils, fasts, phenols, organic acids, aromatic compounds, antibiotic etc. are the examples.

(*b*) Inorganic chemicals: *e.g.*, Arsenic, fluorides, nitrates are the source of arsenecosis, fluorosis and mithmaeglobaenemia respectively. Metals, chlorides, CN–, SCN–, FeOx, Cu, Cd, Hg and Cr acids and alkalis are the examples.

(*c*) Fertilizers *e.g.*, Chemical fertilizers cause eutrophication in water-bodies.

(*iii*) Biological agents: Certain micro-organisms present in water are the source of water-borne and water-induced diseases. *e.g.*, protozoa and bacteria may degrade water quality. Escherichia coli is the bacteria present in fecal matter, when enters in water body makes the water unfit for drinking.

Effects of Water Pollution

Various water pollutants are so toxic that they cause death of living organisms (due to their toxicity). Thus, they come under the category of hazardous waste. The list of adverse effects of water pollution is given below:

- **Eutrophication:** In modern agriculture, chemical fertilizers are supplied to the crops. The water runoff with chemical fertilizers will reach to the nearby water-body. Small water plants grow in excess known as algal bloom. This prevents inter-mixing of atmospheric oxygen to dissolved oxygen in water. The water plants and animals start dying due to lack of dissolved oxygen. The dead parts will deposit at the bottom of the water body. The process is known as eutrophication. The water body is known as eutrophic water body. *e.g.*, Chilka lake in Odisha.
- **Thermal pollution:** Due to discharge of industrial waste, temperature of water body increases.
- **Biomagnification:** The concentration of toxic chemical increase several times when it is transferred from one tropic level to another *e.g.*, (minamata disease in Japan) the people died when consumed Mercury contaminated fish in Japan. Mercury containing chemical is accidentally released in the bay of Minamata in Japan immediate death of people occur known as minamata disease.
- The bad smell comes out of the polluted water body.
- Penetration of sunlight decreases in polluted water body, reducing the plant's ability to photosynthesize.
- **Biological Oxygen Demand (BOD):** The amount of dissolved oxygen required by micro-organisms to decompose the organic matter present in the waste water is known as Biological Oxygen Demand. BOD increases due to water pollution.

Control Measures of Water Pollution

Wastewater Treatment: The waste water from industries should be treated before discharging into the water-bodies.

Bioremediation: Water hyacinth absorbs toxic chemicals from water-body, the process of detoxification with the help of living organisms is known as bioremediation.

Sustainable Agriculture: Integration of traditional and modern agricultural techniques reduces water pollution *e.g.*, agroforestry, terrace-farming.

5. (*d*) Vermicomposting is a modified and specialised method of composting - the process uses earthworms to eat and digest farm wastes and turn out high quality compost in two months or less. Vermicompost is not a biofertiliser as is touted by some, merely improved compost.

Vermicompost can also be used to make compost tea. Vermicompost tea is useful as a prophylactic against pests and diseases, for pest repelling and as a foliar spray. A by-product of vermicomposting called vermiwash (which can be collected if there is a tap at the base of the vermicompost tank) also serves the same purpose.

An important point to note in case of vermicomposting but widely ignored, is to carry out proper sieving of the compost before applying it in the fields. The most efficient and widely-used earthworms in vermicomposting are not indigenous and if the worms and casts find their way to the fields, they will quickly colonise and dominate the local species. Farmers can also use indigenous earthworm species, collecting them from their fields using collection baits and introducing the earthworms into heaps. In the usual way vermicomposting is practiced in India and most other places around the world, it is both labour-intensive and requires some infrastructure. As a result, while a small farm can use this method to compost most of its wastes, a larger farm often finds it expensive and difficult to compost most of its wastes through vermicomposting. We have after some experimentation developed a methodology through which these issues are resolved - labour, time, managerial inputs, infrastructure and the usage of exotic worms. We offer training and consultancy services on composting and vermicomposting, including enrichment techniques, low-cost methods and improved methodologies. To know more, please read the sections on consultancy and training, specialised areas of consultancy and training and production of organic inputs.

The most widely used vermicomposting system, worldwide, is the 'bed' method, which involves applying thin layers of sanitised and partially matured compost, to the surface of beds containing high densities of earthworms. New layers of waste are applied to beds on a regular basis and the earthworms move upwards into the fresh waste to feed and to process the material. Earthworm numbers increase as more waste is applied until a limiting density is reached. The earthworms are then harvested or the beds are divided. Harvesting earthworms by hand can be a very time consuming business and although in principle trammel screens would be suitable, these are seldom used. The top 100 mm to 150 mm of the compost bed soil is removed regularly and is the worm compost sold.

It is difficult to compare directly composting with vermicomposting in terms of the time taken to produce stable and mature composted products. With vermicomposting, particles of waste spend only a few hours inside the earthworm's gut and most of the decomposition is actually carried out by micro-organisms, either before or after passing through the earthworm. Hence, earthworms accelerate waste decomposition rather than being the direct agent. With windrow composting, it usually takes at least six to twelve weeks to produce stable compost, and research suggests that vermicomposting takes about the same length of time. However, processing rates will depend on many factors such as the system being used, the nature of the wastes and the ratio of earthworms to waste.

5. (*e*) Water Harvesting and the Role of the Government and NGOs for its Promotion: Rainwater harvesting is the gathering, or accumulating and storing, of rainwater.

Rainwater harvesting has been used to provide drinking water, water for livestock, water for irrigation or to refill aquifers in a process called groundwater recharge. Rainwater collected from the roofs of houses, tents and local institutions, or from specially prepared areas of ground, can make an important contribution to drinking water. In some cases, rainwater may be the only available, or economical, water source. Rainwater systems are simple to construct from inexpensive local materials, and are potentially successful in most habitable locations. Roof rainwater is usually of good quality and does not require treatment before consumption. Household rainfall catchments systems are appropriate in areas with an average rainfall greater than 200 mm per year, and no other accessible water sources.

Systems of Rain Water Harvesting

There are a few systems of rain water harvesting. They include:

- Roof Catchments System
- Ground Catchments System
- Subsurface Dyke
- Ground water recharge

Roof catchments systems channel rainwater that falls onto a roof into storage via a system of gutters and pipes. The first flush of rainwater after a dry season should be allowed to run to waste as it will be contaminated with dust, bird droppings etc. Roof gutters should have sufficient incline to avoid standing water. They must be strong enough, and large enough to carry peak flows. Storage tanks should be covered to prevent mosquito breeding and to reduce evaporation losses, contamination and algal growth. Rainwater harvesting systems require regular maintenance and cleaning to keep the system hygienic and in good working order.

Ground catchments systems channel water from a prepared catchment area into storage. Generally, they are only considered in areas where rainwater is very scarce and other sources of water are not available. They are more suited to small communities than individual families. If properly designed, ground catchments can collect large quantities of rainwater.

Rain Water Harvesting as a Government Policy

The Government has been promoting the adoption of 'Rainwater harvesting' as a mass movement. 'Rainwater Harvesting' is also an important component for achieving the goals of 'Water Security'. 'Shelter Security' and 'Ecological Security' enunciated in the Hon'ble Chief Minister's 15 Point programme. Universal adoption of Rainwater Harvesting by government departments, Non-Governmental organizations (NGOs) and people would go a long way in improving the ground water levels in the states as well as in meeting the immediate requirements of the people for fresh water. Considerable success has been achieved in propagating the beneficial effects of Rainwater Harvesting and the Government departments, NGOs, industries and individuals are now involved in this task of Rainwater Harvesting. Several government departments have issued separate guidelines for the implementation of Rainwater Harvesting by their respective departments. It is, therefore, considered necessary, at this stage, to issue comprehensive guidelines to coordinate the activities of various agencies involved in Rainwater Harvesting to maximize the benefits and bring about synergy.

Roof Water Harvesting by Government Departments/ Public Sector Undertakings/ Aided Institutions:

1. All Government departments/Public Sector Undertakings/Aided Cooperative institutions buildings constructed hereafter shall provide for Rainwater Harvesting.
2. All departments shall prepare an action plan for equipping the existing buildings of the departments/Public Sector Undertakings/aided/cooperative institutions with Rainwater Harvesting structures, within a period of 3 years.
3. Rented buildings occupied by the government departments/Public sector undertakings shall also be provided with Rainwater Harvesting structures and the owners of the rented buildings shall be asked to complete the task within a period of 3 years.

4. The buildings mentioned in the 3rd point provided with Rainwater Harvesting structures, shall prominently display a signboard approved by the Municipal Administration and Water Supply department for this purpose, indicating that the building is provided with Rainwater Harvesting structures.

Rainwater Harvesting by the NGOs and Public:

Both persuasive and legislative measures shall be used for ensuring the provision of Rainwater Harvesting structures in all buildings.

Information, Education and Communication (IEC):

IEC is an important component in persuading public to adopt Rainwater Harvesting. As they are the direct beneficiaries of these structures, more information dissemination will be sufficient to make them construct Rainwater structures. While the Chennai Metropolitan Water Supply and Sewage Board will be the nodal agency for the IEC campaign within the Chennai Metropolitan area, the respective district collectors shall coordinate the IEC activities in the districts.

Managing freshwater scarcity constitutes to be one of the biggest responsibilities of governance everywhere in the world, and thus, local management of this resource is an indispensable component. Many countries have national water laws. In India, however there are no national laws as such, though there is a national water policy. The National Water policy 2002 is a cogent and comprehensive document and forms a basis that could be converted into a law.

Ground water exploitation is inevitable in Urban areas. But the groundwater potential is getting reduced due to urbanization resulting in over exploitation. Hence, a strategy to implement the groundwater recharge, in a major way need to be launched with concerted efforts by various Governmental and Non-Governmental Agencies and Public at large to build up the water table and make the groundwater resource, a reliable and sustainable source for supplementing water supply needs of the urban dwellers.

Recharge of groundwater through storm run off and roof top water collection, diversion and collection of run off into dry tanks, play grounds, parks and other vacant places are to be implemented by Special Village Panchayats/Municipalities/Municipal Corporations and other Government Establishments with special efforts.

The Special Village Panchayats/ Municipalities/Municipal Corporations will help the citizens and builders to adopt suitable recharge method in one's own house or building through demonstration and offering subsidies for materials and incentives, if possible.

8. (*a*) Role of Farmer's Field School (FFS) in Agriculture

- Farmer Field School (FFS) is non-formal educational activity.
- All learning is a group activity and field based.
- Empowers farmers to solve their field problems by themselves.
- Fosters participation, interaction and joint decision making.
- Farmers learn by carrying out activities through constant observation

The Farmer Field School is a form of adult education, which evolved from the concept that farmers learn optimally from field observation and experimentation. It was developed to help farmers tailor their Integrated Pest Management (IPM) practices to diverse and dynamic ecological conditions.

In regular sessions from planting till harvest, groups of neighbouring farmers observe and discuss dynamics of the crop's ecosystem. Simple experimentation helps farmers further improve their understanding of functional relationships (*e.g.*, pests-natural enemy population dynamics and crop damage-yield relationships). In this cyclical learning process, farmers develop the expertise that enables them to make their own crop management decisions. Special group activities encourage learning from peers, and strengthen communicative skills and group building.

IPM Farmer Field Schools were started in 1989 in Indonesia to reduce farmer reliance on pesticides in rice. Policy-makers and donors were impressed with the results and the program rapidly expanded. Follow-up training activities were added to enhance community-based activities and local program ownership. Eventually, IPM Farmer Field School programs for rice were carried out in twelve Asian countries and gradually branched out to vegetables, cotton and other crops. From the mid-nineties onwards, the experience generated in Asia was used to help initiate IPM Farmer Field School programs in other parts of the world. New commodities were added and local adaptation and institutionalization of these programs was encouraged. At present, IPM Farmer Field School programs, at various levels of development, are being conducted in over 30 countries worldwide.

These diverse programs have generated a variety of data on the impact of the IPM Farmer Field School. Such data generally are presented in project reports that have a limited circulation. Impact studies that are published in official literature tend to focus on specific aspects of impact. Impact studies varied in focus, approach, methodology and robustness. Some lack description of metho's. The nature of impact studies typically varies with the developmental stages of programs. Pilot projects often compared pesticide use and yields or profits of field plots grown with IPM practices and those under regular farmer practice, to demonstrate the merit of the approach. More advanced projects evaluated the adoption of IPM practices, studied expertise or recorded the developmental impacts resulting from farmer empowerment.

Principles

- "Grow a healthy crop" allows plants to recover better from environmental or pest injury, avoids nutrient deficiencies related with pest attack (insects and disease), and promotes natural defences to many insects and diseases inherent in plants. Proper crop and plant management methods used [Academic term: cultural controls].
- "Conserve natural enemies" provides free biological control of insects and diseases. Parasites, predators and pathogens have long been recognised to control pest insects, but recent research shows microbial antagonists, and competitors of plant diseases are also important. Vertebrate natural enemies are also essential for control systems. Conservation usually implies avoiding inappropriate pesticide applications (herbicides, fungicides and insecticides all have impact on insect and disease natural enemies) or improving soil organic matter necessary for beneficial soil micro-organisms. Natural enemy habitat protection and development are more active methods of conserving natural enemies (*e.g.*, owl houses, mulching for spiders, floral nectaries for parasites). Inoculation or inundation of reared natural enemies may be possible under special circumstances but usually only after conservation efforts have already been implemented. [Academic term: biological control].

- "Observe crops regularly" means informed decision making for appropriate interventions to be made quickly for water, soil, and plant management. Inputs used are based on an ecologiceconomic assessment. [Academic term: Input analysis].
- "Farmers become experts" in their own fields is crucial for long-term management of soils, pests and crops. Expertise implies a basic understanding of the agro-ecological system, and decision making processes. Simple rules and directives may provide short-term benefits but cannot sustain long-term local developments.

Characteristics of Farmer's Field School:

- **Farmers as Experts:** Learning by doing is the training approach used. Farmers learn by carrying out for themselves the various activities related to the particular farming practice they want to study and learn about. This could be related to annual crops, livestock/fodder production, orchards or forest management. The key thing is that farmers conduct their own field studies. Their training is based on comparison studies (of different treatments) and field studies that they, not the extension/ research staff conduct. In so doing they become experts on the particular practice they are investigating.
- **The Field is the Primary Learning Material:** All learning is based in the field. The field is where the farmers learn. Working in small sub-groups they collect data in the field, analyse the data, make action decisions based on their analyses of the data, and present their decisions to the other farmers in the field school for further discussion, questioning, and refinement.
- **Extension Workers as Facilitators Not Teachers:** The role of the extension worker is very much that of a facilitator rather than a conventional teacher. Once the farmer know what it is they have to do, and what it is that they can observe in the field, the extension worker takes a back seat role, only offering help and guidance when asked to do so. Presentations during meetings are the work of the farmers not the extension worker, with the members of each working group assuming responsibility for presenting their findings in turn to their fellow farmers. The extension worker may take part in the subsequent discussion sessions but as a contributor, rather than leader, in arriving at an agreed consensus on what action needs to be taken at that time.
- **The curriculum is Integrated:** The curriculum is integrated. Crop husbandry, animal husbandry, horticulture, silviculture, land husbandry are considered together with ecology, economics, sociology and education to form a holistic approach. Problems confronted in the field are the integrating principle.
- **Trainings Follows the Seasonal Cycle:** Training is related to the seasonal cycle of the practice being investigated. For annual crops this would extend from land preparation to harvesting. For fodder production would include the dry season to evaluate the quantity and quality at a time of year when livestock feeds are commonly in short supply. For tree production and such conservation measures as hedgerows and grass strips training would need to continue over several years for farmers to be able to see for themselves the full range of costs and benefits.
- **Regular Group Meetings:** Farmers meet at agreed regular intervals. For annual crops such meetings may be every 1 or 2 weeks during the cropping season. For other farm/forestry management practices

the time between each meeting would depend on what specific activities need to be done, or be related to critical periods of the year when there are key issues to observe and discuss in the field.

- **Learning materials are learner generated:** Farmers generate their own learning materials, from drawings of what they observe, to the field trials themselves. These materials are always consistent with local conditions, are less expensive to develop, are controlled by the learners and thus can be discussed by the learners with others. Learners know the meaning of the materials because they have created the materials.
- **Group dynamics/team building:** Training includes communication skill building, problem solving, leadership, and discussion methods. Farmers require these skills. Successful activities at the community level require that farmers can apply effective leadership skills and have the ability to communicate their findings to others.

8. (*b*) Role of Cooperative Societies in Agriculture: The role of cooperative sector is extremely important in agriculture sector, as it supplies agricultural credit and funds and has the potential to deliver goods and services in vital areas where state and private sectors have not been able to do very much. At all the forums, we always cry that water table is declining, soil health is degraded, so with the cooperative department till date their main focus was to arrange the supply of the inputs which are considered very crucial for the agriculture sector,". Small and marginal farmers are able to take up new technologies and even go in for alternative farming, as credit is easily available at Cooperative Banks. Many educated unemployed youth too have benefited from self-employment schemes run by the cooperative societies. "There is tremendous scope for employment. We need passion to improve the conditions in farming. So there is no doubt that a number of people can get employment,". Dairy farming is one of the main thrust areas of economic development. Agriculture continues to be an extremely important sector of India's economy and the cooperative movement has a crucial role to play in bringing about its transformation.

Agricultural cooperatives facilitate small producers' access to:

- Natural resources such as land and water.
- Information, knowledge and extension services. Role of cooperatives in agriculture in Africa.
- Markets, food, and productive assets such as seeds and tools.
- Policy and decision making.

Cooperative development in many countries has shown that farmers who are effectively organized can be benefited from aggregated links to markets and services, from accessing centralized services that can help them achieve higher yields and higher incomes, and from speaking with a collective voice to advocate for their needs. At a global level, countries with the highest share of cooperatives in marketed outputs also have high average yields for staple crops like rice and wheat, as well as substantial cash crop exports.

Cooperatives are used by the government and NGOs to extend training and other capacity building initiatives. Many stakeholders use cooperative structures to build capacity in post harvest handling techniques as well as commodity.

8. (*c*) Importance of Extension Workers in Transfer of Technology to Farmers: Agriculture is the science of cultivating crops and rearing animals for the benefit of man and also includes other processes such as processing, storage and marketing of agricultural produce. The agricultural sector is essential in the economic development and poverty alleviation drive of many sectors. The importance of this sector is more pronounced in developing countries.

The role of an agricultural extension worker involves disseminating information on agricultural technologies and improved practices to farm families and ensuring farmers' capacity building through the use of a variety of communication methods and training programmes. Without it, farmers would lack access to the support and services required to improve their agriculture and other productive activities. It is through education and communication that agricultural extensionists are able to bring changes in farmers' knowledge, attitudes and skills which help to put farmers in a frame of mind that is conducive for adopting proven agricultural innovations.

The role of extension education in agriculture is summarised as under:

- Making the adoption of new technology possible.
- To help the farmer to accept new agricultural technology for obtaining higher yields.
- Extension workers' carry out field demonstrations about new technology.
- Helps the farmers to visualize farming as a profitable occupation.
- Helps farmers to understand their own situation, resources and critical analysis helps them to take rational decisions for the best use of the available resources.
- Trains the local leaders.
- Helps getting necessary inputs.
- Helps in decision-making.
- Helps to change attitude.
- To bring about this change through education.
- It helps in achieving cooperation of people.
- It develops, strengthens and organizes groups, institutes and people to achieve their aims.
- Extension helps the planners, policy-makers and administrators with local conditions and latest technologies suited to it.
- Job of extension is to bridge the gap between the scientists on the one hand and the farmer's on the other. This is done by taking new farm technology and innovations to the farmers' door and helping him to adopt them.

8. (*d*) Integrated Farming System and its Profitability to the Farmers: Integrated Farming System is a whole organic farm management system which aims to deliver more sustainable agriculture. It is a dynamic approach which can be applied to any farming system around the world. It involves attention to detail and continuous improvement in all areas of a farming business through informed management processes. Integrated Farming combines the best of modern tools and technologies with traditional practices according to a given site and situation. In simple words, it means using many ways of cultivation in a small space or land.

Profitability of Integrated Farming System to the Farmers

- **Productivity:** IFS provides an opportunity to increase economic yield per unit area per unit time by virtue of intensification of crop and allied enterprises.
- **Profitability:** Use waste material of one component at the least cost. Thus, reduction of cost of production and form the linkage of utilization of waste material, elimination of middleman interference in most input used. Working out net profit B/C ratio is increased.

- **Potentiality or Sustainability:** Organic supplementation through effective utilization of by-products of linked component is done thus providing an opportunity to sustain the potentiality of production base for much longer periods.
- **Balanced Food:** We link components of varied nature enabling to produce different sources of nutrition.
- **Environmental Safety:** In IFFS waste materials are effectively recycled by linking appropriate components, thus minimize environment pollution.
- **Recycling:** Effective recycling of waste material in IFFS.
- **Income Rounds the year:** Due to interaction of enterprises with crops, eggs, milk, mushroom, honey, cocoons silkworm. Provides flow of money to the farmer round the year.
- **Adoption of New Technology:** Resources farmer (big farmer) fully utilize technology. IFS farmers, linkage of dairy/mushroom/sericulture/vegetable. Money flow round the year gives an inducement to the small/original farmers to go for the adoption technologies.
- **Saving Energy:** To identify an alternative source to reduce our dependence on fossil energy source within short time. Effective recycling technique the organic wastes available in the system can be utilized to generate biogas. Energy crisis can be postponed to the later period.
- **Meeting Fodder crisis:** Every piece of land area is effectively utilized. Plantation of perennial legume fodder trees on field borders and also fixing the atmospheric nitrogen. These practices will greatly relieve the problem of non–availability of quality fodder to the animal component linked.
- **Solving Fuel and Timber Crisis:** Linking agro-forestry appropriately the production level of fuel and industrial wood can be enhanced without determining effect on crop. This will also greatly reduce deforestation, preserving our natural ecosystem.
- **Employment Generation:** Combing crop with livestock enterprises would increase the labour requirement significantly and would help in reducing the problems of under employment to a great extent IFS provide enough scope to employ family labour round the year.
- **Agro – industries:** When one of produce linked in IFS are increased to commercial level there is surplus value adoption leading to development of allied agro – industries.
- **Increasing Input Efficiency:** IFS provide good scope to use inputs in different component greater efficiency and benefit cost ratio.

PAPER-II

SECTION 'A'

1. (*a*) Most of the plant cells are provided with tough rigid cell wall and this is taken as an outstanding point of difference between plant and animal cells.

Naked protoplasts are noticed in lower groups of plants. The reproductive cells of higher plants as a rule lack walls.

The cell wall was actually noticed by the early workers long before the more important matter protoplasm was recognised. Naturally, it received considerable attention then. With the discovery of protoplasm the wall obviously lost much of its importance.

In recent years, the cell wall has again attracted serious attention of the investigators. In fact, spectacular advances in the technique of investigations, in application of X-rays, polarized light photography and electron microscope, and increasing commercial importance of cellulose have given new impetus in investigations on the wall.

The cell wall is usually looked upon as a secretory product of the protoplast. In that sense it ought to be a non-living membrane surrounding the protoplast. It protects the protoplast from adverse external influences, delimits the same, gives mechanical stability to the cells and also imparts shape to the cells.

But the very fact that wall is secreted by protoplast and that an intimate relationship exists between the two have led some workers to believe that it may not be completely non-living.

Formation of the cell wall and the process thereof has got to be sought in the method of cell division. During mitosis two daughter nuclei are constructed after having gone through a series of complicated changes.

The nuclear division is then followed by cytoplasmic division (cytokinesis). In this process protoplasmic matters accumulate in the equatorial region in form of small droplets, which cohere in course of time and form a continuous plate called cell plate.

This plate undergoes physical and chemical changes and is ultimately converted into the intercellular substance, the middle lamella. In fact, middle lamella is the 'cement' between the two cells.

By proper chemical treatment middle lamella may be dissolved, when the cells lose the cementing material and become isolated. Middle lamella is optically inactive and colloidal in nature. It is composed of pectates of calcium and often magnesium.

The protoplast goes on secreting cell wall materials on the middle lamella, and ultimately a soft, delicate and plastic wall is formed. This is primary cell wall. It consists mainly of cellulose and pectic compounds and may also contain other polysaccharides. This is really the first formed cell wall, which may persist in many cells as the only wall. The primary wall is optically active.

Primary cell wall gets more and more stretched during the growth of the cell. In course of time secondary cell wall materials are deposited on the primary wall. It may happen that primary walls of the adjacent cells become fused with the intercellular substance and form the common layer between the two cells.

In that case, middle lamella is not purely the cementing material. Some workers have attributed the term compound middle lamella to such layer.

1. (*b*) **Allopolyploidy** Allopolyploids are also called alloploids. They are a combination of genomes from different species (Acquaah, 2007). They result from hybridization of two or more genomes followed by chromosome doubling or by the fusion of unreduced gametes between species (Acquaah, 2007; Chen, 2010; Jones et al., 2008; Ramsey and Schemske, 1998). This process is key in the process of speciation for angiosperms and ferns (Chen, 2010) and occurs often in nature. Economically important natural alloploid crops include strawberry, wheat, oat, upland cotton, oilseed rape, blueberry and mustard (Acquaah, 2007; Chen, 2010). To differentiate between the sources of the genomes in an alloploid, each genome is designated by a different letter. For example, the origin of the cultivated mustards (Brassica spp) has been well explained by Nagaharu in the triangle of U with each species represented by a distinct letter (Bellostas et al., 2007; Nelson et al., 2009).

Application of Autopolyploidy in Crop Improvement

- Triploids. Triploids are produced by hybridization between tetraploid and diploid strains. They are generally highly sterile, except in a few cases. This feature is useful in the production of seedless watermelons. In certain species, they may be more vigorous than the normal diploids, *e.g.*, in sugarbeets.
- Seedless watermelons are grown commercially in Japan. They are produced by crossing tetraploid (4x, used as female) and diploid (2x, used as male) lines, since the reciprocal cross (2x × 4x) is not successful. The triploid plants do not produce true seeds; almost all the seeds are small, white rudimentary structures like cucumber (Cucumis sativus) seeds. But a few normal sized seeds may occur, which are generally empty. For good fruit setting, pollination is essential. For this purpose, diploid lines are planted in the ratio 1 diploid; 5 triploid plants. There are several problems, viz, genetic instability of 4x lines, irregular fruit shape, a tendency towards hollowness of fruits, production of empty seeds and the labour involved in triploid seed production (by hand-pollination).
- Triploid sugarbeets (*B. vulgaris*) produce larger roots and more sugar per unit area than do diploids, while tetraploids produce smaller roots and lower yields than diploids. Apparently, 3x is the optimum level of ploidy in sugarbeets. Triploid sugarbeet varieties have been grown commercially in Europe and Japan, but their popularity is declining rapidly. The triploid varieties are mixtures of triploid, diploid and other ploidy level plants. Seed production of triploid sugarbeet is difficult because the beet flower is small. Triploid seed may be produced in one of the following two ways: (1) using 4x plants as female and 2x as male or (2) using 4x as male and 2x as female. The first combination gives lower seed yield but a higher proportion of triploids, while the second gives higher seed yield but a lower proportion of triploids. Commercial triploid sugarbeet seed is produced by interplanting 4x and 2x lines in the ratio 3:1, and seed from both 4x and 2x plants is harvested. This seed consists of about 75% triploid (3x) seeds. Triploids sugarbeet may give 10-15 per cent higher yields than diploids.
- Pusa Giant Berseem is the first autopolyploid variety released for general cultivation in India. It yields 20-30 per cent more green fodder than the diploid berseem varieties.

1. Autoploypoidy is more likely to succeed in species with lower chromosome

numbers than in those with higher chromosome numbers.

2. Cross-pollinating species are generally more responsive than self pollinating species.

3. Crops grown for vegetative parts are more likely to succeed as polyploids than those grown for seeds.

Application in Crop Improvement

1. Aneuploids are useful in the studies on effects of loss or gain of an entire chromosome or a chromosome arm on the phenotype of an individual.

2. Aneuploids are useful in locating a linkage group and a gene to a particular chromosome. By using a secondary or tertiary trisomic, the gene may be located to one of the two arms of a chromosome, or even to a part of the chromosome arm. The most important application of aneuploids is in locating genes on particular chromosomes; this will be considered in some detail.

3. Aneuploids are useful in identifying the chromosome involved in translocations.

4. They are useful in the production of substitution lines. Chromosome substitution may be desirable for studying the effects of individual chromosomes of a variety or for the transfer of the genes carried by specific chromosomes or a variety into another one.

1. (*c*) QUALITY SEED

Factors Affecting Seed Quality

Genetic Factors

- Seed size
- Bulk density
- Differences in dormancy levels

Seed Selection

- **Selecting seeds using water**

Good quality seed

Physical or Environmental Factors

- Quality of seed at the point of sowing
- Injury during planting and establishment
- Growing conditions during seed development
- Nutrition of the mother plant.

1. (*d*) Metal ions play important roles in the biological function of many enzymes. The various modes of metal-protein interaction include metal-, ligand-, and enzyme-bridge complexes. Metals can serve as electron donors or acceptors, Lewis acids or structural regulators. Those that participate directly in the catalytic mechanism usually exhibit anomalous physicochemical characteristics reflecting their entatic state. Carboxypeptidase A, liver alcohol dehydrogenase, aspartate transcarbamoylase and alkalin phosphatase exemplify the different roles of metals in metalloenzymes while the nucleotide polymerases point to the essential role of zin in maintaining normal growth and development.

Table I

Metals Present in Naturally Occurring Metalloenzymes

Metal	*Enzyme Function*
Cobalt	Transcarboxylation
Copper	Oxidoreduction
Iron	Oxidoreduction
Manganese	Various
Molybdenum	Oxidoreduction
Nickel	Urease
Selenium	Peroxidase
Zinc	Various

1. (*e*) Male sterility is defined as an absence or non-function of pollen grain in plant or incapability of plants to produce or release functional pollen grains. The use of male sterility in hybrid seed production has a great importance as it eliminate the process of mechanical emasculation.

Chemical Induced Male Sterility

The chemical which induces male sterility artificially is called as male gametocide. It is rapid method but the sterility is non-heritable.

In this system A, B and R lines are not maintained. Some of the male gametocides used are gibberellins (rice, maize), Sodium Methyl Arsenate (rice) and Maleic hydrazide (wheat, onion).

3. (*a*) Osmosis is the spontaneous net movement of water across a semi-permeable membrane from a region of low solute concentration to a more concentrated solution, up a concentration gradient.

DIFFUSION refers to the movement of any chemical from one place to another. Diffusion is also the movement of molecules — solute or particles.

They move from a region in which they are in higher concentration to regions of lower concentration. A good example of diffusion is food colouring.

If you place a drop of red food colouring in a beaker of water eventually the entire beaker of water will have a red tint. The food colouring moved through the water until it was equally distributed throughout the beaker. Diffusion takes place along a concentration gradient. A concentration gradient exists until the diffused substance is evenly distributed.

The other everyday examples of diffusion:

(*i*) Sugar will diffuse through tea until the entire cup of tea is sweet. We stir to speed up the process.

(*ii*) The odour of food cooking diffuses through the kitchen. If you open the kitchen door it will spread through the next room.

The movement of these molecules is said to be passive. No energy needs to be provided. The natural kinetic energy of the particles supplies the energy.

OSMOSIS exclusively refers to the movement of water across a membrane is a special example of diffusion. It is the diffusion of a substance through a semi-permeable membrane from a more dilute solution to a more concentrated solution. This process is also passive since no external energy is needed.

A semi-permeable membrane is a barrier that permits the passage of some substances but not others. Cell membranes are described as selectively permeable because not only do they allow the passage of water but also allow the passage of certain solutes (dissolved substances).

Some Examples of Osmosis:

1. Absorption of water by plant roots.

2. Reabsorption of water by the proximal and distal convoluted tubules of the nephron.
3. Reabsorption of tissue fluid into the venule ends of the blood capillaries.
4. Absorption of water by the alimentary canal — stomach, small intestine and the colon.

3. (*b*) Distinguish between Sex Influenced/Sex Limited and Sex Linked Inheritance: Sex limited inheritance refers to the inheritance of traits that are expressed only in either the male or the female offspring due to their expression being influenced by differences in the anatomy of males and females. For example, if a trait is displayed in organs present only in males, even though a female also inherits the gene, it would not show in her.

Sex influenced inheritance is the difference in display of traits due to a differing biological environments as males and females like the presence of specific sex hormones. For example, the genes that result in baldness may be present in both males as well as in females but are more likely to be expressed in males as a result of the male sex hormones.

Sex linked inheritance is traits carried in either the X or the Y chromosome. A trait that is due to genes present on the X chromosome is more likely to be expressed in males as they have only one X chromosome. The presence of two X chromosomes in females can suppress its expression when one of them has the genes for the trait and the other does not. X linked traits fall under many categories like recessive, dominant and co-dominant which influence their expression in members of both the sexes. A trait due to a gene in the Y chromosome will only show in males and not in females.

3. (*c*) Synchrony of Flowering

Synchronous flowering refers to the phenomenon of coincident, simultaneous flowering of all population of a given species in a large region. It may involve many plants, but not necessarily all plants of that species.

Many plant species need pollinators in order to cross-pollinate and produce seeds; for this reason the production of flowers in various plant is relatively synchronized and all mature individuals of the same species bloom at the same time, in spite of the variations in environmental conditions across a region. While such synchrony could be generated by responses to weather factors, it may represent an evolved response to optimize reproductive success.

Synchronous flowering of a species across a region may enhance fertilization and seed set during years with strong flowering responses as a higher concentration of flowers increases the probability of pollination. In addition, synchronous flowering may reduce the proportion of seeds attacked by seed predators due to predator satiation The resulting pattern is selectively advantageous in reducing the proportion of seeds lost to predators.

Planting Ratio of Parents

The ratio in which the male and female parental lines are planted in hybrid seed production or maintenance of the cytoplasmic male sterile line is known as planting ratio of parents.

SECTION 'B'

5. (*a*) Carnation is a half hardy perennial with branching stems and tumid joints. Leaf blades are simple, entire and usually narrow. Each stems form a terminal flower and hence inflorescence is generally a terminal cyme.

The flowering shoots of carnation are marketed in two forms, standard form and spray or miniature form. Perpetual flowering and green house carnations are of modern origin.

Pinching of Carnation

Pinching is an important operation in the successful production of quality carnation. There are generally two types of pinching used:

(*i*) **Single pinch:** This method facilitates more rapid flowering but all stems flower at same time. After the establishment of plants, about 3 – 4 weeks after planting, the apex shoot is pinched leaving on the 5th – 6th pair of leaf or leaving 5 – 6 lateral shoots to develop.

(*ii*) **Pinch and half method:** After initial pinch, one half of the breaks from the first pinch are pinched a second time about three to five weeks after first pinch.

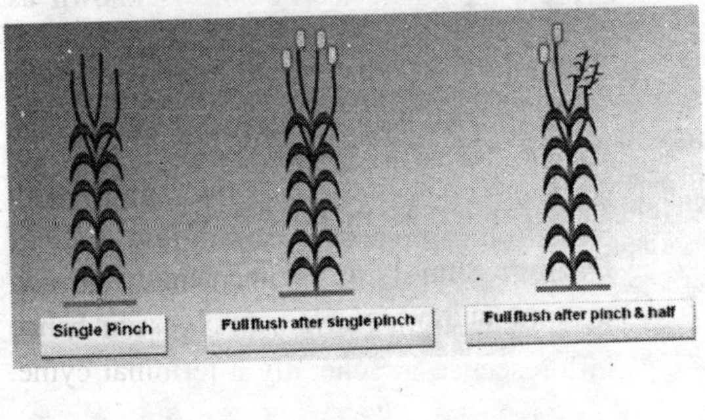

This method result in lower yields in first flush compared to single pinch method, it will result in more even and stable production over time follows pinching with spray of fungicides.

5. (*c*) It is an ecology-based approach aiming minimizing damage caused by diseases through 'the combined use of all available disease control measures, either simultaneously or in a sequence, through actions taken prior and after establishing the crop'. In this chapter, we propose and develop a strategy for the integrated management for Fusarium wilts, one of the most devastating and challenging type of diseases impairing agricultural production worldwide, based on the:

(*i*) use of pathogen-free planting material;

(*ii*) site selection to avoid planting into high risk soils;

(*iii*) reduction or elimination of F. oxysporum inoculum in soil;

(*iv*) use of biocontrol agents for protection of healthy planting material from infection by resident or incoming inoculum subsequent to planting;

(*v*) use of resistant cultivars regardless the level of resistance; and

(*vi*) choice of cropping practices to avoid conditions favouring infection of the plant. The integrated management of Fusarium wilt diseases is difficult because complexities of target pathosystems are overlaid on the inherent complexities of the management strategy itself. Much research is still needed on population biology and genetic diversity in Fusarium wilt pathogens, disease risk prediction, disease-incidence-yield losses relationships, biological control, biotechnological breeding for disease resistance.

Integrated Management of Verticillium

Verticillium wilt caused by *Verticillium dahliae* (fungus). Maple is one of the most common hosts. Ash, barberry, buckeye, catalpa, cherry, dogwood, elderberry, elm, Kentucky coffee tree, lilac, linden, magnolia, maple, plum, redbud, rose, Russian olive, smoketree, spirea, sumac, viburnum, and weigela are some of the trees and shrubs susceptible to verticillium wilt.

Symptoms of chronic infection include: sudden wilting, leaf yellowing or scorching in a portion of the crown, often on one side. Foliar symptoms are most likely to appear during July and August, when plants are under water stress. Other symptoms of chronic infection include undersized foliage, poor growth, abnormally heavy seed set and twig and branch dieback. Plants may also become severely infected, wilt and collapse in a short period of time. Acutely infected plants may show; leaf curling or browning; foliage or areas between veins abnormally colored red or yellow; partial defoliation; wilting and branch dieback, often on only one branch or side of the tree or shrub. Verticillium wilt can also cause sudden death of a tree or shrub.

Confirm your field diagnosis by sending a sample to MSU Diagnostic Services for positive identification. Fungicides are not effective against this disease. Avoid using a susceptible host as a replacement when replanting in an area where a plant has died of verticillium wilt. Avoid using wood chip mulch made from trees or shrubs that died from verticillium wilt, as recent research suggests that the fungus may remain viable in wood chips for considerable periods of time. Trees and shrubs reported as resistant to verticillium wilt that could be considered as replacements include: arborvitae, fir, juniper, larch, pine, spruce, yew, birch, beech, boxwood, ginkgo, hawthorn, hickory, honeylocust, hophornbeam, katsura, mountain ash, bur and white oaks, pear, sweetgum, sycamore, walnut and willow.

5. (*d*) Entomopathogenic Bacteria for Pest Control

- Microbial pesticides which consist of bacteria, entomopathogenic fungi or viruses (and sometimes includes the metabolites that bacteria or fungi produce). Entomopathogenic nematodes are also often classed as microbial pesticides, even though they are multi-cellular.

The scientific community working in the field of insect pathology is experiencing an increasing academic and industrial interest in the discovery and development of new bioinsecticides as environmentally friendly pest control tools to be integrated, in combination or rotation, with chemicals in pest management programs. In this scientific context, market data report a significant growth of the biopesticide segment. Acquisition of new technologies by multinational Ag-tech companies is the center of the present industrial environment. This trend is in line with the requirements of new regulations on Integrated Pest Management. After a few decades of research on microbial pest management dominated by Bacillus thuringiensis (Bt), novel bacterial species with innovative modes of action are being discovered and developed into new products. Significant cases include the entomopathogenic nematode symbionts Photorhabdus spp. and Xenorhabdus spp., Serratia species, Yersinia entomophaga, Pseudomonas entomophila.

5. (*e*) Preservation Methods of Important Fruits

Drying: Sum-dying or mechanical drying of fruit and vegetables involves complete removal of the moisture from them. They are then treated with sulphur fumes to maintain colour and also to avoid spoilage by micoorganisms. Dates, grapes, jack, peaches, beans, bitter gourd, onion, potatoes etc., are preserved this method.

Freezing: When fruits and vegetables are brought suddenly to a very low temperature at which all the chemical reactions stop. But it requires rather expensive equipment and shipping and storing under refrigeration.

Preservation by Heat: It consists basically of the application of heat in varying degree to the food in closed containers for a sufficient long time to sterilize contents before they are hermetically sealed. This method of preservation by heat is also known as processing. Canned fruits and vegetable come under this category.

Preservation by Sugar: No organism can grow in a substance which contains sugar concentration above 65% as microorganisms get desicated at higher concentration by osmosis. Jams, jellies, marmalades and crystallized fruits are preserved by virtue of the above said principle.

Preservation by Salt: A product which contains above 15% salt make it most unfavorable for the growth and multiplication of microorganisms. Pickles are preserved by this method.

Preservation by Chemical: Chemical like benzoic acid and sulphur-di-oxide at specific concentration help to preserve the fruit juice, squashes or cordials. Benzoic acid in the form of 0.06 to 0.10% sodium benzoate is sufficient and is effective against yeast and its action is effective in the presence of CO_2 Potassium metabolism (KMS) when added liberate sulphur-di-oxide which reacts with water to from sulphorous acid. The concentration of SO_2 is recommended around 350 ppm. It is more active against, spores and bacteria.

Preservation by Fermentation: Fruits juice containing sugar are fermented to produce alcohol. These fermented substances keep off the spoilage organism due to the presence of alcohols. *e.g.*, wine making. Methods and techniques involved in the preservation of selected products like jam, jelly, squashes, syrup and pickle.

7. (*a*)

Olericulture	***Pomology***
It refers to the study of vegetables. Vegetable in horticultural science is an edible herbaceous plant or part their of which commonly used for culinary purpose or as salads. **Vegetables:** roots, stems, leaves, flowers, or fruit. All fruits are vegetables, but not all vegetables are fruits.	**Pomology** refers to the study of fruits crops. A fruit in horticultural science represented a plant the product of which is edible in ripening. Fruits crops are classified as woody plants and herbaceous plants. The woody plants may be trees, shrubs or vines. Fruits borne on herbaceous perennial plants.

7. (*b*) Distinguish between Mildews and Blights

Mildew is a form of fungus. It is distinguished from its closely related counterpart, mold (British English: mould), largely by its colour: moulds appear in shades of black, blue, red, and green, whereas mildew is white. It appears as a thin, superficial growth consisting of minute hyphae (fungal filaments) produced especially on living plants or organic matter such as wood, paper or leather. Both mould and mildew produce distinct offensive odours, and both have been identified as the cause of certain human ailments.

In horticulture, mildew is either species of fungus in the order Erysiphales, or fungus-like organisms in the family *Peronosporaceae*. It is also used more generally to mean mould growth. In Old English, mildew meant honeydew (a substance secreted by aphids on leaves, formerly thought to distill from the air like dew), and later came to mean mould or fungus.

Blight refers to a specific symptom affecting plants in response to infection by a pathogenic organism. It is a rapid and complete chlorosis, browning, then death of plant tissues such as leaves, branches, twigs, or floral organs. Accordingly, many diseases that primarily exhibit this symptom are called blights. Several notable examples are:

- Late blight of potato, caused by the water mold Phytophthora infestans (Mont.) de Bary, the disease which led to the Great Irish Famine
- Southern corn leaf blight, caused by the fungus *Cochliobolus heterostrophus* (Drechs.) Drechs, anamorph *Bipolaris maydis* (Nisikado & Miyake) Shoemaker, incited a severe loss of corn in the Unied States in 1970.
- Chestnut blight, caused by the fungus Cryphonectria parasitica (Murrill) Barr, has nearly completely eradicated mature American chestnuts in North America.
- Fire blight of pome fruits, caused by the bacterium *Erwinia amylovora* (Burrill) Winslow et al., is the most severe disease of pear and also is found in apple and raspberry, among others.

7. (*c*) Distinguish between Inoculative and Augmentative Releases of Natural Enemies: The principal way that antagonists of plant pathogens are used is by releasing them either where the plant pathogen already occurs or, prophylactically, on the plant surfaces, where they can protect the plant from infection by the pathogen. While all antagonists have been called biopesticides, those applied prophylactically are often called bioprotectants instead. Some plant pathologists have called all of these mass applications of antagonists "introductions" but this general term could be used in reference to several strategies, including classical biological control, or inoculative or inundative releases. So what do we call releases of antagonists against plant pathogens? Using our definitions for release strategies, an inundative release would occur when control is achieved exclusively by the organisms themselves that have been released. Thus, for an inundative release of insect natural enemies to succeed, large numbers of natural enemies are usually released. In contrast, most releases of microbial antagonists fit the definition of inoculative releases. Microorganisms increase so quickly that it is not the released organisms that are effective against the host but rather the generations of microbes produced after release that increase to colonize the complete habitat, sometimes producing antibiotics as they increase. We have defined inoculative releases as releases of natural enemies that need to multiply to be effective and that will thus control the pest for a more extended period than an inundative release. Antagonists that are applied in large amounts either as protectants to prevent infection by a pathogen or as biopesticides to control pre-existing pathogens must grow to colonize the sites where they will be active; in this way both types of applications (applied preventively or after disease is present) fit our definition of inoculative release. While the exact length of a so-called "extended period" of control can be subjective, many antagonists can protect against or inhibit plant pathogens for longer than an immediate effect. Therefore, in the vast majority of cases, releases of antagonists to control plant pathogens are inoculative releases; antagonists that are released inoculate the area to be protected, much as aliquots of microbes are used to inoculate media, and these microbes then increase and spread throughout the area necessary for colonization. Antagonists of plant pathogens first began to be developed for augmentative release in 1962.

8. (*a*) Establishment of an orchard is a long-term investment and deserves a very critical planning. The selection of proper location and site, planting system and planting distance, choosing the varieties and the nursery plants have to be considered carefully to ensure maximum production.

Location and Site

Proper selection of site is important. Selection may be made based on the following criteria.

1. The location should be in a well established fruit growing region because one could get the benefit of experience of other growers and also get the benefit of selling the produce through co-operative organizations with other fruit growers.
2. There should be a market close to the area.
3. The climate should be suitable to grow the chosen fruit crops.
4. Adequate water supply should be available round the year.

Before a grower selects a site for establishing a new orchard, he must have assessed the following factors:

1. Suitability of soil, its fertility, the nature of subsoil and soil depth.
2. Site must have proper drainage and no water stagnation during rainy season.
3. Irrigation water must be of good quality.
4. There must be proper transport facilities either by road or rail within the reach.
5. Whether the climatic conditions are suitable for the fruits to be grown and are whether site is free from the limiting factors such as cyclones, frost, hailstorms and strong hot winds.
6. Whether there are seasonal gluts or over production in any particular period of the year.
7. Whether there is assured demand in the market for the fruits to be grown.
8. Whether his orchard is a new venture or whether there are already other growers.
9. Availability of labour.

Preliminary Operations

After selecting the suitable location and site, some preliminary operations have to be done. Trees are felled without leaving stumps or roots. The shrubs and other weedy growth are also cleared. Deep ploughing is essential to remove big roots. The lands should be thoroughly ploughed, leveled and manured. Levelling is important for economy of irrigation and preventing soil wash. In the hills, the land should be divided into terraces depending upon the topography of the land and the levelling is done within the terraces. Terracing protects the land from erosion. If the soil is poor, it would be advisable to grow a green manure crop and plough it *in situ* so as to improve its physical and chemical conditions before planting operations are taken up.

Planning of an Orchard

A careful plan of the orchard is necessary for the most efficient and economic management. The following points should be borne in mind in preparing the plan:

1. Optimum spacing to accommodate maximum number of trees per unit area.
2. Stores and office building in the orchard should be constructed at the centre for proper supervision.
3. Wells should be located at convenient places in different parts at the rate of one well for 2 to 4 hectares.
4. Each kind of fruit should be assigned in a separate block.
5. Fruits ripening at the same time should be grouped together.
6. Pollinators should be provided in deciduous fruits. In deciduous fruit trees, there are some varieties which require pollen from another variety to set fruits in them, otherwise, they will be barren. Such pollen donors are known as pollinators. Every third tree in every third row should be planted with a pollinator.
7. Irrigation channels should be laid along the gradients for most economical conduct of water. For every 30 m length of channel, 7.5 cm slope should be given.
8. Roads should occupy minimum space for the economy of transport. The clearance between wind break and first row of trees is advantageous for the road.
9. Short growing trees should be allotted at the front and tall at the back for easy watching and to improve the appearance.
10. Evergreen trees should be in the front and deciduous ones behind.
11. Fruits attracting birds and animals should be close to the watchman's shed.
12. A good fence is essential. Live fencing is economic and cheap to other kind of fences. The plants suitable for live fencing should be drought resistant, easy to propagate from seed, quick growing, have dense foliage, should stand severe pruning and should be thorny. Agave, *Prosopis juliflora, Pithecolobium dulce* and *Thevetia* if closely planted in 3 rows would serve as a good live fencing.
13. Wind breaks, rows of tall trees planted close together around the orchard, are essential to resist velocity of wind which cause severe ill-effects particularly moisture evaporation from the soil. Since the wind breaks are very effective in reducing the wind velocity and minimizing the damage to the fruit trees and to other crops, their presence in regions where strong winds prevail is of paramount importance. A wind break ordinarily has its maximum effectiveness for a distance about four times as great as its height but has some effect over twice about that distance.

The most effective windbreak is a double row of tall trees alternately placed. There should be at least as much as space between the windbreak and the first row of the fruit trees as between fruit trees. It is preferable to dig a trench of 90 cm deep at a distance of 3 m from the windbreak trees and prune and cut all the roots exposed and again fill up the trenches. This may be repeated for every 3 or 4 years in order to avoid the competition between the wind breaks and fruit trees for moisture and nutrition.

Trees suitable for windbreak should be erect, tall and quick growing, hardy and drought resistant and mechanically strong and dense to offer maximum resistance to wind. The trees which are suitable for growing as wind breaks are *Casuarina equisetifolia, Pterospermum acerifolium, Polyalthia longifolia*, Eucalyptus *globulus, Grevillea robusta, Azadirachta indica* etc.

8. (*b*) Protein-Energy Malnutrition

Definition: Protein-energy malnutrition (PEM) is a potentially fatal body-depletion disorder. It is the leading cause of death in children in developing countries.

Description: PEM is also referred to as protein-calorie malnutrition. It develops in children and adults whose consumption of protein and energy (measured by calories) is insufficient to satisfy the body's nutritional needs. While pure protein deficiency can occur when a person's diet provides enough energy but lacks the protein minimum, in most cases the deficiency will be dual. PEM may also occur in persons who are unable to absorb vital nutrients or convert them to energy essential for healthy tissue formation and organ function.

Although PEM is not prevalent among the general population of the United States, it is often seen in elderly people who live in nursing homes and in children whose parents are poor. PEM occurs in one of every two surgical patients and in 48% of all other hospital patients.

Types of Pem: Primary PEM results from a diet that lacks sufficient sources of protein and/or energy. Secondary PEM is more common in the United States, where it usually occurs as a complication of AIDS, cancer, chronic kidney failure, inflammatory bowel disease, and other illnesses that impair the body's ability to absorb or use nutrients or to compensate for nutrient losses. PEM can develop gradually in a patient who has a chronic illness or experiences chronic semi-starvation. It may appear suddenly in a patient who has an acute illness.

Kwashiorkor: Kwashiorkor, also called wet protein-energy malnutrition, is a form of PEM characterized primarily by protein deficiency. This condition usually appears at the age of about 12 months when breastfeeding is discontinued, but it can develop at any time during a child's formative years. It causes fluid retention (edema); dry, peeling skin; and hair discolouration.

Marasmus: Primarily caused by energy deficiency, marasmus is characterized by stunted growth and wasting of muscle and tissue. Marasmus usually develops between the ages of six months and one year in children who have been weaned from breast milk or who suffer from weakening conditions like chronic diarrhoea.

Causes and Symptoms: Secondary PEM symptoms range from mild to severe, and can alter the form or function of almost every organ in the body. The type and intensity of symptoms depend on the patient's prior nutritional status and on the nature of the underlying disease and the speed at which it is progressing.

Mild, moderate, and severe classifications have not been precisely defined, but patients who lose 10-20% of their body weight without trying are usually said to have moderate PEM. This condition is also characterized by a weakened grip and inability to perform high-energy tasks.

Losing 20% of body weight or more is generally classified as severe PEM. People with this condition can't eat normal-sized meals. They have slow heart rates and low blood pressure and body temperatures. Other symptoms of severe secondary PEM include baggy, wrinkled skin; constipation; dry, thin, brittle hair; lethargy; pressure sores and other skin lesions.

Kwashiorkor: People who have kwashiorkor often have extremely thin arms and legs, but liver enlargement and ascites (abnormal accumulation of fluid) can distend the abdomen and disguise weight loss. Hair may turn red or yellow. Anemia, diarrhoea, and fluid and electrolyte disorders are common. The body's immune system is often weakened, behavioural development is slow, and mental retardation may occur. Children may grow to normal height but are abnormally thin.

Kwashiorkor-like secondary PEM usually develops in patients who have been severely burned, suffered trauma, or had sepsis (tissue-destroying infection) or another life-threatening illness. The condition's onset is so sudden that body fat and muscle mass of normal-weight people may not change. Some obese patients even gain weight.

Marasmus: Profound weakness accompanies severe marasmus. Since the body breaks down its own tissue to use as calories, people with this condition lose all their body fat and muscle strength, and acquire a skeletal appearance most noticeable in the hands and in the temporal muscle in front of and above each ear. Children with marasmus are small for their age. Since their immune systems are weakened, they suffer from frequent infections. Other symptoms include loss of appetite, diarrhoea, skin that is dry and baggy, sparse hair that is dull brown or reddish yellow, mental retardation, behavioural retardation, low body temperature (hypothermia), and slow pulse and breathing rates.

The absence of edema distinguishes marasmuslike secondary PEM, a gradual wasting process that begins with weight loss and progresses to mild, moderate, or severe malnutrition (cachexia). It is usually associated with cancer, chronic obstructive pulmonary disease (COPD), or another chronic disease that is inactive or progressing very slowly.

Some individuals have both kwashiorkor and marasmus at the same time. This most often occurs when a person who has a chronic, inactive condition develops symptoms of an acute illness.

Hospitalized Patients: Difficulty chewing, swallowing, and digesting food, pain, nausea, and lack of appetite are among the most common reasons that many hospital patients don't consume enough nutrients. Nutrient loss can be accelerated by bleeding, diarrhoea, abnormally high sugar levels (glycosuria), kidney disease, malabsorption disorders, and other factors. Fever, infection, surgery, and benign or malignant tumours increase the amount of nutrients hospitalized patients need. So do trauma, burns, and some medications.

Diagnosis: A thorough physical examination and a health history that probes eating habits and weight changes, focuses on body-fat composition and muscle strength, and assesses gastrointestinal symptoms, underlying illness, and nutritional status is often as accurate as blood tests and urinalyses used to detect and document abnormalities.

Some doctors further quantify a patient's nutritional status by:

(*i*) Comparing height and weight to standardized norms

(*ii*) Calculating body mass index (BMI)

(*iii*) Measuring skinfold thickness or the circumference of the upper arm

Treatment: Treatment is designed to provide adequate nutrition, restore normal body composition, and cure the condition that caused the deficiency. Tube feeding or intravenous feeding is used to supply nutrients to patients who can't or won't eat protein-rich foods.

In patients with severe PEM, the first stage of treatment consists of correcting fluid and electrolyte imbalances, treating infection with antibiotics that don't affect protein synthesis, and addressing related medical problems. The second phase involves replenishing essential nutrients slowly to prevent taxing the patient's weakened system with more food than it can handle. Physical therapy may be beneficial to patients whose muscles have deteriorated significantly.

Prognosis: Most people can lose up to 10% of their body weight without side effects, but losing more than 40% is almost always fatal. Death usually results from heart failure, an electrolyte imbalance, or low body temperature. Patients with certain symptoms, including semi-consciousness, persistent diarrhoea, jaundice, and low blood sodium levels, have a poorer prognosis than other patients. Recovery from marasmus usually takes longer than recovery from kwashiorkor. The long-term effects of childhood malnutrition are uncertain. Some children recover completely, while others may have a variety of lifelong impairments, including an inability to properly absorb nutrients in the intestines and mental retardation. The outcome appears to be related to the length and severity of the malnutrition, as well as to the age of the child when the malnutrition occurred.

Prevention: Breastfeeding a baby for at least six months is considered the best way to prevent early-childhood malnutrition. Preventing malnutrition in developing countries is a complicated and challenging problem. Providing food directly during famine can help in the short-term, but more long-term solutions are needed, including agricultural development, public health programs (especially programs that monitor growth and development, as well as programs that provide nutritional information and supplements), and improved food distribution systems. Programs that distribute infant formula and discourage breastfeeding should be discontinued, except in areas where many mothers are infected with HIV.

Every patient being admitted to a hospital should be screened for the presence of illnesses and conditions that could lead to PEM. The nutritional status of patients at higher-than-average risk should be more thoroughly assessed and periodically re-evaluated during extended hospital stays or nursing home residence.

8. (*c*) Training in Chrystanthemum

Chrystanthemum can be trained for various decorate and attractive forms:

(*i*) **Standard:** For better shape of the plants and attractive extra large flower large flowered chrysanthemums are trained as standards producing 1-3 blooms/plant. For this suckers are planted in January. All care in taken for proper development if the plant. The plants are transplanted several times in bigger posts and finally into 25 cm posts in August. There plants bloom in November-December are normally very tall need care throughout the year. The lower portion of the plant looks bare as the older leaves drops. According to recent culture methods for developing better standard plants are developed from cuttings in July. It avoid unnecessary caring of plants for about six months.

(*ii*) **Sen rin ttukuti:** It is a Japanese style of chrysanthemum culture. It means growing thousand blooms. In this, plants is designed to a geometric shape (6-10 centimeter circle in stepped manner) and it is trained in such a way that about 200-300 height of 153-183 can and a diameter of 183-294 mm. Varieties suitable for this should have vigorous growth habit in all direction incurve or reflex type with medium-sized blooms long pedicel and uniform blooming habit.

(*iii*) **Bush form:** This is a specific cultural practice for small flowered chrysanthemums. The plant is given a bush appearance by specific pinching and training. The blooms are arranged compactly to give an effect of a floral carpet. Medium sized cultivative having profuse branching habit are suitable for bush korean, anemone, button, charm, stellate, decorative and quilled bloomed are most suitable.

(*iv*) **Cascade forms:** The plants trained in cascade from give to effect of water fall in blooming stage. This is also a Japanese art of chrysanthemum culture. The stem is made to bend down above the rim of the contained. This training method give an excellent looks of the blooms.

(*v*) **Fan form:** This is also a type of training of small flowered chrysanthemums. In final form, it looks like a hand fan.

Previous Years' Paper (Solved)

IFS–Agriculture Main Examination, 2016

PAPER-I

INSTRUCTIONS: *There are **Eight** questions in all, out of which **Five** are to be attempted. Candidates should attempt question nos. **1** and **5** which are compulsory, and any three of the remaining questions, selecting at least one question from each section. All questions carry equal marks. Answers must be written in English only.*

SECTION–A

1. Answer the following in about 150 words each :

(*a*) Describe the basis of classification of agro-ecological zones of India. Give the important characteristics of any two zones with their states/regions and major cropping patterns.

(*b*) Differentiative between multi-storey cropping and relay cropping. Write their importance.

(*c*) What is the physiological effect of low temperature on seed germination? What are its remedies?

(*d*) Describe the integrated weed control measures involving both pre- and post-emergence herbicides in rice and cotton.

(*e*) How can we manage erosion and run-off in valley land?

2. Write short notes on the following in about 200 words each:

(*a*) Bio-fertilizers and bio-herbicides and their benefits.

(*b*) Biological nitrogen fixation bacteria and their modes of action.

(*c*) Role of phosphorus solubilizing and/or mobilizing organisms in crop production.

(*d*) Azolla, its production technology and role in rice culture.

3. Give the recommended package of practices for wheat, maize, pigeon-pea and potato under the following heads :

(*a*) Time of sowing/season

(*b*) Spacing pattern

(*c*) Seed rate

(*d*) Nutrient management

(*e*) Weed control

4. Explain the following in about 200 words each :

(*a*) Agro-forestry and its benefits.

(*b*) Cloning technology for propagation of forest tree species.

(*c*) Role of social forestry in the present situation of global warming.

(*d*) Green house gases (GHG), their effects on crop production and possible remedical measures.

SECTION–B

5. Answer the following in about 150 words each :

(*a*) How is plant growth affected by water-logging conditions? Suggest suitable measures to improve crop productivity under these situations.

(*b*) Explain run-off losses of irrigation water and their management.

(*c*) What are the various irrigation systems followed in crop production? Describe the merits and demerits of the system you prefer the most.

(*d*) What measures are taken for increasing economic viability of farming?

(*e*) What is crop diversification? What are the factors affecting it?

6. Describe the following in about 200 words each :

(*a*) Important characteristics of dryland and rainfed farming.

(*b*) Constraints of pulse production in India and measures to improve their production and productivity.

(*c*) Polyhouse technology and its impact on farmers' prosperity.

(*d*) Stabilization of agricultural product prices.

7. Answer the following in about 200 words each :

(*a*) What is the need of farm mechanization in the present situation?

(*b*) Mention the benefits of advance planning in agriculture.

(*c*) What is the basis of classification of water for irrigation?

(*d*) Write a short note on Lab-to-Land programme.

8. Discuss the following in about 200 words each :

(*a*) Role of SAUs and NGOs in effective dissemination of agricultural technologies.

(*b*) Need for survey of extension programmes in agriculture and its method of survey.

(*c*) Role of APMC for the benefits of farming community.

(*d*) Important characteristics of sodic soils and their reclamation.

PAPER-II

INSTRUCTIONS: *Candidates should attempt question nos.* **1** *and* **5** *which are compulsory, and any three of the remaining questions, selecting at least one question from each section. All questions carry equal marks. Answers must be written in English only.*

SECTION–A

1. Answer the following in about 150 words each :

(*a*) Differentiate between IAA and IBA. Give their role in Agriculture.

(*b*) Describe testing, release and notification of crop varieties.

(*c*) Describe meristem culture and production of virus-free plants.

(*d*) Describe the role of micro and macro-mutations in crop improvement.

(*e*) Give the importance of 'economic threshold' and 'economic injury level' in integrated pest management.

2. Distinguish between the following :

(*a*) Gametogenesis and sporogenesis.

(*b*) Photoperiodism and vernalization.

(*c*) Isolation and Roguing in seed plots.

(*d*) Interspecific and intergeneric hybrids.

3. Answer the following :

(*a*) Enlist various types of male sterility. Describe briefly about cytoplasmic male sterility.

(*b*) Discuss engineering plants for tolerance to insect damage.

(*c*) Discuss food grain procurement and distribution constraints in India.

(*d*) What are vascular wilts? Give main pathogens associated with this disease.

4. Answer the following :

(*a*) Give the differences between outer and inner mitochondrial membrane.

(*b*) Explain crassulation acid metabolism. How they are better suited to extreme desiccation?

(*c*) Enlist the factors affecting enzyme activity and give the importance of hydrogen-ion concentration.

(*d*) What is abscisic acid? Give physiological roles of ABA.

SECTION–B

5. Answer the following in about 150 words each :

(*a*) Give the factors affecting post-harvest life of flowers.

(*b*) Discuss drying, dehydration and concentration in preservation of fruits and vegetables.

(*c*) Give the major insect pests of tomato and their management.

(*d*) What are rapid methods of testing seed viability?

(*e*) Why *Sitophilus oryzae* and *Rhyzopertha dominica* are important?

6. Answer the following :

(*a*) What is disease occurrence and epidemic? List different components of integrated disease management.

(*b*) Give definition and concept of biological control. How the biological control of *Agrobacterium tumefaciens* has been achieved?

(*c*) What are the possible reasons for slow adoption of integrated pest management?

(*d*) Give important varieties of aonla and discuss their harvesting and post-harvest management.

7. Distinguish between the following :

(*a*) Back cross and Test cross.

(*b*) Rhizobial inoculant and Microbial toxin.

(*c*) Surface treatment and Fumigation.

(*d*) Germination and Dormancy.

8. Write short notes on the following :

(*a*) Design and layout of lawns and gardens.

(*b*) Food production and national dietary pattern.

(*c*) National and International food policies.

(*d*) Management of storage pests in pulses.

ANSWERS

PAPER-I

SECTION 'A'

1. (*a*) The Agro-climatic Zones of India

The planning commission, divided the country into 15 broad agro-climatic zones based on physiographic and climate. The emphasis was given on the development of resources and their optimum utilization in a suitable manner within the framework of resource constraints and potentials of each region.

Agro-climatic Zones of India (Planning Commission, 1989)

1. **Western Himalayan Region :** Ladakh, Kashmir, Punjab, Jammu etc.

   Brown soils & silty loam, steep slopes.
2. **Eastern Himalayan Region :** Arunachal Pradesh, Sikkim and Darjeeling. Manipur etc. High rainfall and high forest covers heavy soil erosion, Floods.
3. **Lower Gangatic Plains Regions :** West Bengal Soils mostly alluvial & are prone to floods.
4. **Middle Gangatic Plains Region :** Bihar, Uttar Pradesh, High rainfall, 39% irrigation, cropping intensity 142%.
5. **Upper Gangatic Plains Region :** North region of U.P. (32 dists) irrigated by canal & tube-wells good ground water.
6. **Trans Gangatic Plains Region :** Punjab, Haryana, Union territory of Delhi, Highest sown area irrigated high.
7. **Eastern Plateaus & Hills Region :** Chhota Nagpur, Garhjat hills, M.P. W. Banghelkhand plateau, Odisha, soils Shallow to medium sloppy, undulating Irrigation tank & tube-wells.
8. **Central Plateau & Hills Region :** Madhya Pradesh.
9. **Western Plateau & Hills Region :** Sahyadry, M.S. M.P. Rainfall 904 mm, Sown area 65%, forest 11%, irrigation 12.4%.
10. **Southern Plateau & Hills Region :** Tamil Nadu, Andhra Pradesh, Karnataka, Dry land Farming 81%, Cropping Intensity 11%.
11. **East Coast Plains & Hills Region :** Tamil Nadu, Andhra Pradesh, Odisha. Soils, alluvial, coastal sand, Irrigation.
12. **West Coast Plains & Hills Region :** Saurashtra, Maharashtra, Goa, Karnataka, Tamil Nadu, Variety of cropping Pattern, rainfall & soil types.
13. **Gujarat Plains & Hills Region :** Gujarat (19 districts). Low rainfall arid zone. Irrigation 32% well and tube-wells.
14. **Western Dry Region :** Rajasthan (9 districts). Hot, Sandy desert rainfall erratic, high evaporation. Scanty vegetation, famine droughts.
15. **The Island Region :** Eastern Andaman & Nicobar, Western Lakshdweep. Typical equatorial, rainfall 3000 mm (9 months) forest zone undulating.

Demarcation of Climatic Zones and Cropping Patterns (National Symposium on Cropping Patterns in India, 1972)

Climatic zones of India in terms of mean annual temperature and moisture indices.

Sub-Zone No.	*Mean annual temp. ºC*	*Temp. situation*	*Zone No.*	*Moisture Index*	*Moisture situation*
B	25-28	hot	2	-60 to -80	Semi-dry
C	20-25	Mild	3	-40 to 60	Dry
D	10-20	Cold	4	-20 to -40	Slightly dry
E	10 or less	Very Cold	5	0 to -20	Slightly moist
—	—	—	6	0 to 50	Moist
—	—	—	7	50 to 100	Wet
—	—	—	8	Greater than 100	Extremely wet.

Distribution of Important Crops in Various Soil-climatic Zone in India

Moisture index zone	*Thermal zone*	*Soil type*	*Districts in the climatic zone**	*Percentage of area under irrigation*	*Distribution of crops in the zone***
2	**3**	**4**	**5**	**6**	**7**
1	B	Desert soil	Bikaner, Jaisalmer, Jodhpur, Barmer	1	Bajra (62), Jowar (3), Wheat (2), Til (2)
1	C	Desert soil	Ganganagr	29	Gram (32), Wheat (14), Bajra (13), Cotton (6), Mustard (5), Barley (2)
1	E	Skeletal soil	Ladakh	100	Ragi (26), Wheat (18), Barley (6)
2	A	Mixed red and black soil	Kurnool, Raichur, Mahbub Nagar	6	Jowar (29), Groundnut (14), Cotton (14), Rice (6), Bajra (4), Ragi (2)
2	B	Desert soil	Churu, Jalore, Banaskantha	5	Bajra (42), Jowar (6), Wheat (4), Til (3), Gram (2)
2	B	Alluvial soil	Jaipur	23	Bajra (24),Gram (14), Barley (13), Wheat (7), Jowar (4), Maize (4), Til (3)

* *Whenever a district falls under more than one zone, it is included in the zone, where the greater protection of its area lies.*

** *Figures in bracket gives the percentage of area under the crop concerned to total cropped area.*

1. (*b*) Multistorey Cropping

Other names of multistoried cropping are multi-layer cropping and multi-tier cropping. It is one kind of intercropping. Growing plants of different height in the same field at the same time is termed as multistoried cropping. It is mostly practiced in orchards and plantation crops for maximum use of solar energy even under high planting density. It is the practice of different crops of varying heights, rooting pattern and duration to cultivate together. The objective of this system of cropping is to utilize the vertical space more effectively. In this system, the tallest components have foliage of strong light and high evaporative demand and shorter components with foliage requiring shade and or relatively high humidity.

Income per unit area increase substantially with this system and ensures a more evenly distribution of income and employment throughout the year from harvesting different crops in different season.

Minimize risks of crop yield loss. This system enables a steady supply of farm products the whole round the year.

Generates jobs & provides better labour use pattern.

Helps to maximize land use. All growing space is used as crop fit together vertically (tall, medium & short), horizontally (all planting spots occupied) and underground (deep-rooted and shallow-rooted plants).

Reduces the impacts of hazards like high intensity rainfall, soil erosion and landslides.

Efficiently utilizes the soil moisture at different depths of soil and catch solar energy at different heights.

Natural resources are utilized properly. Efficiency in water use. Enrich in fertility status of soils.

Improve the soil characteristics and adds organic matter to soil.

Effective utilization of leaching materials.

It helps in effective weed control.

It provides partial guaranty against market glut of single commodity. Efficient cultivation of a range of products is possible. Crops can be grown according to market preference.

Higher production as the cultivation process is accelerated.

Better and more consistent crop quality.

Maintain an ecological balance.

A mix of tree and plant species that could grow well in the multi-storied system.

There are several secondary outputs from the system.

Increase biodiversity which reduces pest and disease pressure.

Provide micro-climate conditions that benefit crops underneath.

Examples of Some Multistoried Cropping Pattern

Mango + guava + cowpea

Coconut + black pepper + cacao + pineapple

Coconut + jackfruit + coffee + papaya + pineapple

Coconut + papaya + pineapple

Coconut + coffee + papaya + pineapple

Coconut + coffee + black pepper

Coconut + banana + coffee

Coconut + banana + black pepper

Coconut + papaya + pineapple + peanut

Coconut + banana + taro

Coconut + banana + ginger

Coconut + banana + pineapple

Coconut + banana

Coconut + pasture

Mango + pineapple

Mango + papaya + pineapple

Mango + pasture

Arecanut + betel vine + papaya + pigeon pea + pineapple + ginger

In Relay cropping second crop is planted even before the first crop is harvested. Thus, both crops share some part of the season. In

India, rice-cauliflower-onion-summer gourd is one example of relay cropping:

Pigeon pea + sesame + ground nut

Maize + green gram + groundnut

Pigeon pea + upland rice + black gram

Amaranth + lady's finger + colocasia

Spinach + radish + onion

Brinjal + lady's finger + basella + colocasia

Eucalyptus + papaya + berseem

Sugarcane + potato + onion (seed crop)

Sugarcane + mustard + potato

Relay Cropping

Relay planting is inter planting or inter sowing of seeds/seedlings of the succeeding crop before harvesting the preceding/ maturing crop. Generally 2nd crop is planted after the first crop has reach its reproductive stage of growth e.g. Potato is planted before the harvest of Maize and Radish is sown before harvesting of Potato Paira (Bihar & WB) and Utera (MP) cropping are also referred as an example of relay cropping. Paira/Utera cropping means sowing of Lathyrus or Lentil before the harvest of rice in lowland area with an objective to use the residual moisture of rice field.

1. (*c*) Germination is the growth of a plant contained within a seed; it results in the formation of the seedling, it is also the process of reactivation of metabolic machinery of the seed resulting in the emergence of radicle and plumule. The seed of a vascular plant is a small package produced in a fruit or cone after the union of male and female reproductive cells. All fully developed seeds contain an embryo and, in most plant species some store of food reserves, wrapped in a seed coat. Some plants produce varying numbers of seeds that lack embryos; these are called empty seeds and never germinate. Dormant seeds are ripe seeds that do not germinate because they are subject to external environmental conditions that prevent the initiation of metabolic processes and cell growth. Under proper conditions, the seed begins to germinate and the embryonic tissues resume growth, developing towards a seedling.

Seed germination depends on both internal and external conditions. The most important external factors include right temperature, water, oxygen or air and sometimes light or darkness. Various plants require different variables for successful seed germination. Often this depends on the individual seed variety and is closely linked to the ecological conditions of a plant's natural habitat. For some seeds, their future germination response is affected by environmental conditions during seed formation; most often these responses are types of seed dormancy.

Temperature affects cellular metabolic and growth rates. Seeds from different species and even seeds from the same plant germinate over a wide range of temperatures. Seeds often have a temperature range within which they will germinate, and they will not do so above or below this range. Many seeds germinate at temperatures slightly above 60-75°F (16-24°C) [room-temperature if you live in a centrally heated house], while others germinate just above freezing and others germinate only in response to alternations in temperature between warm and cool. Some seeds germinate when the soil is cool 28-40° F (–2-4°C), and some when the soil is warm 76-90° F (24-32°C). Some seeds require exposure to cold temperatures (vernalization) to break dormancy. Some seeds in a dormant state will not germinate even if conditions are favourable. Seeds that are dependent on temperature to end dormancy have a type of physiological dormancy. For example, seeds requiring the cold of winter are inhibited from germinating until they take in water in the fall and experience cooler temperatures. Four degrees Celsius is cool enough to end dormancy for most cool dormant seeds, but some groups, especially within the family Ranunculaceae and others, need conditions cooler than –5°C. Some seeds will only germinate after hot temperatures during a forest fire which cracks their seed coats; this is a type of physical dormancy.

Most common annual vegetables have optimal germination temperatures between 75-90°F (24-32°C), though many species (e.g. radishes or spinach) can germinate at significantly lower temperatures, as low as 40 F° (4°C), thus allowing them to be grown from seeds in cooler climates. Suboptimal temperatures lead to lower success rates and longer germination periods.

As the air temperature starts to warm up in early spring you may like to get a head start with your sowing and accelerate the warming of the soil. If you have a mulch on your soil for the winter you can temporarily remove the mulch. The dark coloured soil will absorb all wavelengths of light and convert them into heat, warming the soil much faster. Another alternative is to leave the mulch on and cover the bed with a plastic sheet or glass pane. On a sunny day, this will provide considerable heat. Of course you can also remove the mulch and use the sheet or glass on the bare soil and this has the added benefit of germinating any seeds in the patch that can be pulled before you start sowing.

1. (*d*) Weeds have been existing on the earth ever since the man started domesticating/cultivating plants and animals around 10,000 B.C. Weeds have been recognized as a problem since then and the battle against weeds is a never ending one and often the costliest agronomic input for successful crop production. Between humans and continuing food supply, there stand four natural hazards, e.g. weather, weeds, insect pests and plant diseases. Sometimes these hazards work independently and many times they work hand in hand. Weeds are the most underestimated crop pests in tropical agriculture although they cause maximum reduction/loss in the yields of crops than other pests and diseases. Of the total annual loss of agricultural produce from various pests in India, weeds roughly account for 37%, insects for 29%, diseases for 22% and other pests for 12% . They decrease quantity and quality of produce/food, fibre, oil, forage/fodder, animal products (meat and milk) and cause health hazards for humans and animals. Thus weed control is indispensable in every crop production system.

Knowledge of weed seed characteristics, morphology, ontogeny, nature of competition and degree of association with crops are prerequisite for suggesting some efficient weed control measures. It makes the users/scientists quite acquainted with the nature and spectrum of weeds existing in the crop fields and accordingly guides them to adopt certain measures. Identification and naming of a particular weed based on its genus, species or certain biological characters may not be much useful to users since weed control usually, unless specific weed problem in certain area, aims at composite weed culture and not on individual species of weeds. Therefore, some common characteristics of the species, which are clearly visible and easily understandable by users, are to be exploited for making of their classes/groups and for recommending suitable control measures.

Rice

Critical period of weed control : 20-30 DAT.

Cultural method : 1. Hand weeding, 2. Hand pulling, 3. Pudding, 4. Flooding.

Mechanical method : 1. Weeder (Float), 2. Conoweeder/Rotary weeder

Chemical method : Apply pendimethalin 1.0 kg/ha on 5 days after sowing or Pretilachlor + safener (Sofit) 0.45 kg/ha on the day of receipt of soaking rain followed by one hand weeding on 30 to 35 days after sowing.

Biological method : 1. Hirsch - Manniella spinicaudata is a rice root nematode which controls most upland rice weeds, 2. Azolla

Remarks : I. Substitution and preventive method: (*a*) Stale seed bed technology, (*b*) Land preparation, (*c*) Water management.

Cotton

Critical period of weed control : First 45 days.

Cultural method : 1. One hand weeding on 45 DAS will keep weed free environment upto 60 DAS, 2. Hoe and hand weed between 18th to 20th day of sowing, if herbicide is not applied at the time of sowing.

Chemical method : 1. Diuron (0.5-1.5 kg/ha), Monuron (1-1.5 kg/ha), Fluchloralin (1-1.5 kg/ha) applied as preemergence/preplanting.

1. (*e*) Soil Erosion

Soil Erosion is an important natural process, resulting in the redistribution of the products of geologic weathering and both soil formation and soil loss. The world's landscapes have been sculptured by Soil erosion process. There are many kinds of soil erosion. Based on the rate of soil loss, there are two main kinds of soil erosion.

1. **Normal or Natural Geologic Soil Erosion:** It occurs by natural or normal conditions by itself without involvement of man. Natural or normal soil erosion, it is very slow process and equilibrium between loss of soil and built-up soil is hardly lost, unless there is some major disturbance by foreign agent.
2. **Accelerated Soil Erosion:** This type of removal of soil is rapid and never keeps pace with the soil formation. It is a most serious type of loss, generally caused by an interference of an agency like other animals and man.

Mechanism of Soil Erosion

Based on the agents of soil erosion, different kinds have been recognized. They are Sheet erosion, Rill erosion and Gully erosion. In Sheet erosion, the soil is removed by water in the form of their covering from over large area. The sheet is lost more or less uniformly. In Rill erosion, soil is removed with full force, the run off water moving rapidly over the soil surface cutting finger like grooves, appearing as their channels or streams called as rills. In Gully erosion, became still wider and deeper due to heavy rains. Moreover, several rills coverage towards steep slope forming wider channels of water gullies.

Slip Soil Erosion of Land Slide

Due to hydraulic pressure caused by heavy rains increases the weight of the rocks at cliffs that passes under the gravitational force and finally slip down. This is called as land slide or slip soil erosion.

Riparian Soil Erosion or Stream Bank Erosion

During floods, the rivers splash their water against the river banks cutting through them particularly at curves, water strikes with great speed and the bank of river caves in alongside.

In case of wind erosion, salty soil carried in the form of small leaps is known as saltation. The small particles of soil blown up by wind as fine dust is called as suspension. It may be surface creep, when heavy particles of soil are simply pushed or spread along the surface by wind.

Control of Soil Erosion

There are three methods to control of soil erosion. They are: 1. Biological methods, 2. Mechanical methods.

Other methods

Biological Methods: By the use of plant or vegetation cover.

A. Agronomic Practices: Natural protection by growing vegetation in a manner that reduces soil loss.

(*a*) *Contour Farming:* Oldest methods useful in areas with low rainfall. It is the preparation of the field with alternate burrows and ridges known as contours.

(*b*) *Mulching:* It is effective against wind as well as water erosion. Some such plants as maize stalks, cotton stalks, potato tops etc., are use as mulch.

(*c*) *Crop Rotation:* It decreases soil loss and preserves the productivity of land. The same crop year after year depleted the soil minerals.

(*d*) *Strip Cropping:* It involves the planning of crop in rows or strips to check flow of water. It may be contour strip cropping, so that the water used is minimal.

B. Dry Farming: The practice is useful for crop plants grown in low and moderate rainfall areas where ordinary farming is at risk. Crop production, animal husbandry and growing grazing fields are the only possibility of checking the soil erosion.

C. Agrostological Methods: Grasses such as Cyonodon dactylon are utilized as erosion restricting plants. They act as stabilizers when grown in fully and sodding.

(*a*) *Lay Farming:* This aims to grow grasses in rotation with the field crops which helps in building up the structure of soil, preventing soil erosion and improving its fertility.

Mechanical Methods : These methods are used as supplements to biological methods. They are:

A. Basin Lifting: To construct small basin along the contours to retain water, which also reduces its velocity.

B. Contour Terraining: To construct a channel along the slope to intercept and divert the runoff water. This may be:

(*a*) *Channel Terrace:* To dig channels at suitable intervals and the excavated soil deposited as a wide, low ridge along the lower ridge of the channel.

(*b*) *Broad Based Ridge Terrace:* To construct ridge along both the sides of the channel.

(*c*) *Bench Terrace:* To construct a number of platforms along contours or suitable graded lines across the slope.

Other Methods

A. Gully Control: By constructing bunds, dams, drains or diversion channels.

B. Protection from Stream Bank: The growth of the vegetation along the side of the riverbank. The construction of drains, concrete or store embedding etc. for checking the cutting and caving of riverbanks.

C. Afforestation: Trees like Casuarina, mangroves, badam, soap nut trees and cashew trees are planted along shores which control the soil erosion and reduce the Tsunami and other heavy floods.

3. (*a*) Time of sowing season of the following crops:

Wheat : Rabi (winter)
Maize : Kharif (monsoon)
Pigeon pea : Rabi (winter)
Potato : Rabi (winter)

3. (*b*) Spacing pattern of the following crops:

Wheat : 22.5 cm (R × R)
Maize : 60 × 25 cm
Pigeon pea : 30 × 10 cm
Potato : 50 × 20 & 60 × 25 × 25 cm

3. (*c*) Seed rate of the following crops:

Wheat : 100-125 kg/h
Maize : Hybrid 20-25 kg/h, composite 75-100 kg/ha
Pigeon pea : 75-100 kg/ha
Potato : 10-15 qt/ha

3. (*d*) Nutrient Management in Wheat

Nutrients play an important role in the wheat production.

Well rotten farmyard manure (FYM) or compost should be applied at the rate of 15 to 20 tons after every two years.

The above will provide partially the requirement of nitrogen and will keep the soil physical properties in good condition.

Fertilizer Application : These nutrients can also be supplied from other fertilizers available in the market. All sources of nitrogen and phosphorus available are equally efficient.

Apply potassium to soils testing low in this nutrient.

When 55 kg of DAP or 125 kg of Nitrophosphate is used, reduce the dose of urea by 20 kg and 50 kg, respectively.

Time and Method of Fertilizer Application : Drill 1/2 dose of N and whole of P and K at sowing and broadcast the remaining N with the first irrigation. If Nitrophosphate is used as source of P, omit nitrogen application at sowing.

Nitrogen : Most limiting nutrient

Highly soluble and highly mobile

Rapid transformation into leachable forms

Losses may be as a gas (volatalisation) when nitrate is exposed to anaerobic condition and leaching

N loss is very high in flooded soils

Nitrogen Content of Various Fertilizers (%)

Ammonium Sulphate 20%

Ammonium Sulphate Nitrate 26%

Urea 46%

Ammonium Chloride 25%

Calcium Ammonium Nitrate 25%

Nitrophos 14%

Dia Ammonium Phosphate 18%

Sulphur : Wheat crop suffers from sulphur deficiency when sown in sandy soils.

The deficiency is more severe when the winter rains continue for a long time in the early growth period.

The symptoms first appear on the younger leaves with fading of the normal green colour. This is followed in the veins.

The topmost leaves become light yellow except for the tip, while the lower leaves retain green colour for a longer time.

This is distinctly different from the nitrogen deficiency where the yellowing starts with the lower leaves. The plants are short in size with fewer tillers.

Sulphur Content of Various Fertilizers (%)

Ammonium Sulphate 24%

Single Super Phosphate 12%

Paramphos 15%

Zinc : Zinc deficiency generally appears in light soils under intensive cropping.

If recommended dose of zinc sulphate has been applied to the kharif crop, its application may be omitted to the following wheat crop.

Paddy responds more to zinc application, therefore zinc should be applied to paddy and its residue is sufficient to meet the requirement of the following wheat crop.

However, if zinc has not been applied to paddy and zinc deficiency is expected/ appears whose symptoms are a stunted and bushy crop with leaves chlorotic in the middle, which later break and keep hanging.

Application of 25 kg of zinc sulphate per acre which will be enough for 2-3 years.

Zinc deficiency can also be corrected by foliar spray of 0.5% zinc sulphate (21% Zinc).

Prepare the solution for spray by dissolving 1 kg zinc sulphate and 1/2 kg unslaked lime in 200 litres of water. This solution is sufficient for spraying an acre of wheat once. Two or three sprays at 15-day intervals are needed.

Manganese : Manganese deficiency generally appears in light soils under intensive cropping especially in rice-wheat rotation.

The symptoms appear on the middle leaves as interveinal chlorosis with light grayish yellow to pinkish brown or buff coloured specks of variable size confined largely to 2/3 lower portion of the leaf; Later, the specks coalesce forming a streak or band in between the veins which remain green. In acute deficiency whole of the plant may become dry.

At earing stage, the symptoms become prominent flag leaf.

In manganese deficient soils, give one spray of 0.5% manganese sulphate solution (1 kg manganese sulphate in 200 litres of water) 2-4 days before first irrigation and two to three sprays afterwards at weekly intervals on sunny days.

Nutrient Management in Maize

Of the several inputs essential for crop production, fertilizer/nutrient management is of paramount importance.

Widespread deficiency of N.P.K. and micro-nutrients like zinc show the need to apply for getting optimum yield of maize.

The maize plant is a heavy feeder, requiring an intelligent fertilizer programme. It requires a lot of nitrogen, phosphorus, potassium and zinc.

It responds very well to heavy nitrogen fertilisation, at a concentration that would normally cause lodging of other cereal crops.

The nutrients are to be replenished through balanced fertilizer application and integrated use of nutrients. These principles are not new to crop production but assumes significant importance in view of steep hike in fertilizer prices and abolition of subsidies. Hence, there is need to get acquainted with N.P.K. and Zn nutrition and their management as they are not replenished in sufficient quantities to produce optimum corn yields.

Organic Manures

A Judicious application of organic manure such as well rotten compost or FYM at the rate of 10-12 t/ha about 25 days before sowing the crop has been found to be most ideal for an increased crop yields.

Chemical Fertilizers

Nitrogen : Maize plants throughout the cropping season take up nitrogen.

There is gradual increase in the requirement of nitrogen by the growing maize crop, the highest nitrogen requirement being exhibited at the flowering stage. Subsequently, the demand for nitrogen starts declining.

Therefore, it is utmost important that adequate nitrogen supply should be ensured from germination to the flowering stage.

Phosphorus : It is the next most important plant nutrient after nitrogen which is found deficient in most maize growing areas of Karnataka.

It has beneficial effect on root growth and maximum root development is completed until knee high stage. Thus, the nutrient should be applied initially at the early stages.

Potassium : It is essential for vigorous growth of the plant and for so many other metabolic activities. The young seedling does not need much potassium, but the rate of uptake jumps upto a peak level during three weeks prior to tasseling.

Fertilizer Management : Maize requires a regulated and assured supply of nutrients particularly nitrogen throughout its growing period right from seedling stage to grain filling stage.

The nitrogen utilization pattern is found to be increased from seedling of knee-height and reaches to the peak at tasseling stage when the plants remove nearly 4-5 kg N/ha/day.

Plants respond to a dose of 120 to 150 kg N/ha and so is the recommendation for hybrids and composite varieties, however, in certain cases the economical yield of maize grains has been obtained even upto the application of 200 kg N per hectare.

The best results from applied nitrogen may be achieved when nitrogen is applied in three splits viz., 1/3rd at sowing, 1/3rd at knee-heigh stage (about 35-40 days after sowing) and remaining 1/3rd at tasseling stage. Amongst the method of fertilization placement below the seed and side dressing of nitrogen at second and third split applications gave the best results. The crop needs relatively lesser nitrogen when grown during winter season, which may be accounted for higher uptake and lower loss of the nutrient from the field. Similarly, during spring season when the crop is taken after potato, peas or gram it needs low nitrogen contents. On an average it is found that 100 to 125 kg N/ha becomes sufficient but the mode of application should be same as in kharif season.

The average uptake of minerals by a corn crop of 5000 kg grain/ha yield, is 105 kg N, 50 kg P_2O_5, 75 kg K_2O, 10 kg CaO, 10 kg MgO and 6 kg S. In addition, micro-nutrients such as manganese, zinc, boron and copper are absorbed in the order of 100 g/ha.

Nutrient Management in Pigeon-pea

Pigeon-pea requires heavy doses of the nutrients, hence care should be taken that the crop does not suffer due to lack of nutrients. A crop of pigeon-pea yielding 2 t/ha grains and 5.4 t/ha sticks removed 115 kg N and 16 kg P on sandy loam soils of AIRI. Various agronomic factors (Cultural, manurial and cropping system) influence the uptake of nutrients.

Nitrogen : Being a legume, it does not require much nitrogenous fertilizers. However, there is general agreement that a starter dose of 10-30 kg N/ha gives positive response in most of the soils depending upon the initial N status of the soil. On sandy loam soils which are poro in N and organic matter, a starter dose of 20-25 kg N/ha has increased the yield.

On the red and laterite soils of Medak, red soils of Sundergarh, mixed red and black soils of Phulbani districts, the responses of pigeon-pea to 20 kg N/ha ranged from 1.40-5.20 q/ha over control yields ranging from 3 to 6 q/ha. A response of 6.70 q/ha over control yield of 4.90 q/ha in Medak with variety Hy.3C. Positive response of rabi pigeon-pea 'Bahar' to 40-60 kg/ha in Bihar.

Culture : Soils with high fertility do not response to culture. However, light textured soil with low in organic matter content, newly reclaimed, eroded and flooded lands show positive response to culture.

The necessity of seed inoculation with culture for legume, which is grown for the first time in a field, has been known for a number of year. More effect strain of Rhizobia can increase yield and protein content of legume to an extent of 20 per cent.

Phosphorus : The importance of adequate supply of phosphorus for higher yields of pigeon-pea has long been recognized. In one of the earliest experiments. Good response of pigeon-pea to phosphorus fertilization in Hawaii specially in upland and also recommended a dose of 350 to 1000 kg/ha of acidulated rockphosphate.

In India, responses to phosphorus have been generally positive and in some cases highly significant realised that phosphorus improved all growth and yield attributes, root and nodule development. 15.0 and 27.5 q/ha of grain yield without and with 60 kg P_2O_5/ha, respectively. However, further increase in the level of phosphorus did not increase the yield.

Potassium : Pigeon-pea normally do not respond to potassium application unless grown on the soils low in available potassium. However, on cultivators fields, the response to 20 kg K_2O_3/ha over 20 kg N + 40 kg P_2O_5/ha ranged from 0.90-2.0 q/ha except in Jalaun district where there was no response to potassium.

Micronutrients : The work on the response of pigeon-pea to micro nutrients has been very limited. Most of pigeon-pea cultivars show susceptibility to zinc deficiency. Soil application of 2-4 ppm zinc or foliar spray of 0.5 per cent zinc-sulphate with 0.05 per cent lime has proved effective in controlling zinc deficiency.

Agrawal observed varietal differences in pigeon-pea of Zn deficiency. He found that varieties Pant A-3 and Prabhat were more tolerant to Zn deficiency than other varieties.

Benefits from Rhizobium biofertilizers

Supplies nitrogen to legume crop.

Low cost technology.

Saves cost on nitrogen fertilizer.

Improves soil fertility.

Improves yield of cereal intercrop.

Improves yield of cereal rotation crop.

Nitrogen fixation needs adequate phosphorus fertilisation.

Control legume root-nodule eating insects for higher nitrogen fixation.

Rhizobium inoculation is a low cost technology.

Use Rhizobium save urea.

Optimum soil moisture for higher nitrogen fixation.

Air has 35,000 tonnes nitrogen over an acre of land, you can use it only with the help of microbes.

Legume protein is solar protein.

Rhizobium uses solar energy for nitrogen fixation.

Inputs required (for hectare)

	Irrigated	*Rainfed*
Seed Tubers	1500-2000 kg	1500-2000 kg
Organic Manure	25 t	25 t
Fertilizers		
Nitrogen	125 kg	75 kg
Phosphorous	100 kg	75 kg
Potassium	125 kg	100 kg

Integrated Nutrient Management in Potato

The optimum doses of nitrogen, phosphorus and potassium vary greatly with the length of growing season, fertility status of the soil, soil type, cultivar, geographical location and the environmental factors.

The use of chemical fertilizers involves non-renewable sources of energy.

This calls for utilization of nutrients from renewable energy sources like farm yard manure (FYM).

However, very little information is available for Karnataka state on effect of organic, inorganic and combination of both on the yield and yield parameters of potato and its economics.

The research conducted in this respect in Karnataka have produced following results:

Amongst the different fertility levels tested in the study, the economic optimum dosage was found to be 60 kg N + 50 kg P_2O_5 + 60 kg K_2O + 50 t FYM/ha by considering the cost benefit ratio with yield compared to the earlier recommended practices.

3. (*e*) Weed control in Wheat, Maize, Pigeon-pea and Potato

Wheat

For weed management in wheat, post-emergence application of 2,4-D 0.8 kg/ha or Carfentrazone 25 g/ha at 30 DAS (where Phalaris minor is not a problem) or Isoproturon 0.75-1.0 kg/ha or Sulfosulfuron 25 g/ha as POE when *Phalaris minor* and wild oat are also problematic and Pre-emergence application of Pendimethalin 1.0 kg/ha are recommended.

Application of Clodinafop + Metribuzin 60 + 122.5 g/ha at 28 DAS or Sulfosulfuron + Metribuzin 25 + 150 g/ha at 28 DAS were found equally effective for reducing the weed count and weed dry weight and producing similar grain yield to that of weed free plot.

Application of Pinoxaden + Carfentrazon ethyl 50 + 20 g/ha at 28 DAS has also been found equally effective for reducing the weed count and weed dry weight and producing similar grain yield to that of weed free plot.

Pigeon-pea

For effective weed control in pigeon-pea, pre-emergence application of Pendimethalin

1 kg/ha or post-emergence application of Quizolofob ethyl 40 g/ha at 15-20 DAS or Fluchloralin 1.0 kg/ha as pre-emergence and its soil incorporation are recommended.

Maize

Atrazine 1.5 kg/ha as pre-emergence + 2,4-D 0.8 kg/ha as post-emergence or Pendimethalin 1.0 kg/ha as pre-emergence followed by 2,4-D 0.8 kg/ha as post-emergence are recommended for effective weed management in maize (kharif and rabi).

Potato

The pre-emergence application of 0.5 kg/ha metribuzine followed by one earthing up at 25 DAP has been found the most effective and remunerative for controlling weeds in the field of potato and for higher productivity and net return of the system.

4. (*a*) Agro-forestry

(*i*) Agro-forestry is sustainable land management system which increases the overall yield of land, combines the production of crops (including tree crops) and forest plants and/or animals simultaneously or sequentially on the same unit of land and applied management practices that are compatible with cultural practices of local population. —King and Chandler (1978).

(*ii*) Agro-forestry as a land use unit of land and applies management practices that are compatible with the cultural practices of local population.—Nair (1979).

Benifits of Agro-forestry : Agro-forestry has some components as follows (Nair, 1989)

(*i*) It is deliberate growing of woody perennials on the same unit land as agricultural crops and/or animals either in some form of spatial mixture or in sequence.

(*ii*) There must be significant interaction (Positive/negative) between the woody and non-woody components of the system either ecological and/or economical.

(*iii*) This is a production system which tends to harmonize the production of various components and also maximizes the production from a given unit of land.

(*iv*) The production and use is sustainable and makes use of modern technologies and traditional local experience and is compatible with the social and cultural life of the local population.

(*v*) It is a long-term land management systems and cycles of agro-forestry system is more than one year.

(*vi*) Agro-forestry is a more complex form of land management both ecologically and economically than other agricultural or forestry systems.

Characteristic Features of Agro-forestry

The success of agro-forestry programme depends on the selection of suitable tree spaces. While selecting the tree species for Agro-forestry, some criteria should be taken into consideration as follows :

1. Tree species capable of meeting different needs of the people should be selected.
2. Tree should have erect growth habit and factor rate of stem elongation. Tree having fast growing habit should be preferred.
3. Trees having broad leaves should not be selected for Agro-forestry.
4. Trees of leguminous family should be preferred as they fix atmospheric nitrogen and enrich the soil. Besides this, leaves of most of leguminous plant are small in size, decompose fact, adding large quality of humus and nutrients to the soil. So, the leguminous plant do not compete with agricultural crops for nutrients.
5. Tree should have the ability of tolerance to relatively high incidence of pruning. The pruned branches and leaves are used as fuel wood and fodder respectively.
6. Tree species having coppicing ability should be preferred. Because the farmers

need not replant after cutting the trees for fuel woods and poles.

7. Trees having the character of erect branches and smaller leaflets should be preferred so that sunlight can penetrate through the canopy.
8. Trees having no allelopathic effect on other crop should be preferred.
9. Tree should produce wood of high caloric value that burns without sprays of toxic smoke.
10. Tree should be free from disease pathogen and should not work as alternative host for pests of commercial crops.

4. (*b*) Cloning Technology

Clonal selection and deployment is receiving attention as an intensive forest management tool for increased wood production. Many pulp, paper and other wood based industries are now establishing clonal forestry programme after the promulgation of 1988 National Forest Policy. The new policy under para 4.9 has given clear indication that the forest based industries must prefer to raise required raw materials by themselves. The industries should establish direct relationship with individual growers of raw material by providing them credit, technical advice, harvesting and transport services. The policy also indicated that small and marginal farmers have to be encouraged to grow wood species required in forest based industries in their marginal and sub-marginal lands. This has created excellent scope for establishing plantations of industrial importance using clonal propagation. Many wood based industries in particular, pulp and paper industries are involved in plantation establishment programme using clonal forestry approaches in the recent past. However, there is no systematic approach for clonal forestry establishment and also there is growing interest to develop in future industrial wood plantations through clonal forestry approaches. The need to all stakeholders is a readymade reference material incorporating the strategies, methods, and experiences of stakeholders in the area of clonal forestry.

Clonal Technology for Propagation of Forest Trees Species

(*a*) ***Production of quality planting stock:*** In the intensive management of forests it is very important of develop fast and economical methods of raising superior planting stock. The somatic propagation of trees has an edge over raising of stock through seeds. These techniques have also become important in forestry owing to their potential in propagating trees, which possess superior traits, in an effort to increase volume and quality of production.

(*b*) ***Propagation of problem trees:*** There are many tree species, which normally produce little or no viable seeds, and some tree seeds have poor germination capacity. Such trees can easily be propagated vegetatively. Propagation by vegetative means is easy, more rapid and economical than by seed. In some tree species, germination is very poor or slow or there may exist complex dormancy problems or the seed may lose its viability very quickly. Moreover, seedlings of many species grow slowly and take a long time to reach marketable size. In all these cases, use of vegetative multiplication is a more convenient method of propagation.

(*c*) ***Maintenance of genetic uniformity:*** Most of the tree species are cross-pollinated and naturally they are highly heterozygous. The progenies of such cross-pollinated trees are not true to type and loose many of their unique characteristics. Hence, asexual clonal propagation helps in maintaining the genetic characteristics of each species.

(*d*) ***Production of disease free plants:*** Certain tree species are often susceptible to some pests and diseases and others may be partially or entirely resistant. Vegetative approaches using grafting will help to produce resistant clones.

(*e*) ***Early flower induction:*** Vegetatively propagated plants are precocious in bearing *i.e.*, Flower earlier than seed propagated plants. This will help to reduce the rotation of the tree species and also to increase the productivity. This will ultimately help to speed up the reproductive cycle for accelerated breeding and testing.

(*f*) ***Clonal repository:*** Vegetative propagation helps to preserve the genotypes in clonal banks. This will also help to evaluate genotypes and their interaction with the environment through clonal testing. This method of propagation will help to conserve and multiply the valuable trees in a centralized area such as in a laboratory or green house for intensive study and breeding.

(*g*) ***Maintenance of genetic gain:*** Vegetative propagation ultimately helps to capture maximum genetic gains when used for regeneration in operational planting programme.

Operational Use of Clonal Propagation

The clonal multiplication reproduces clones, which contain all the genetic information of the parent tree. The term clone is used to mean a genetically uniform plant material derived from a single individual and propagated exclusively by vegetative means. Before going for clonal propagation, the first step is selection of genetically superior tree or elite tree or mother tree. After selecting the trees, the clonal materials are collected and used for propagation. The cultural requirements of all the individual members of a clone are under a particular site of environment conditions. Environment can modify the growth and development of individual members of a clone. Clones are less broadly adopted. Eventhough each members of a clone has the same genotypes, the individual genotypes can possess a considerable ability for adoption to differing adverse environments. It is possible to select clones that posses greater adoptability than that possessed by the seedling. A forest tree needs great adaptability mainly to survive and to reproduce.

4. (*c*) Role of Social Forestry in the present situation of Global Warming

The impacts of climate change will be felt most strongly in the least developed countries that have limited abilities to cope and adapt.

Forests store large amounts of carbon which are released into the atmosphere by deforestation or degradation. An estimated one-fifth of global CO_2 emissions comes from the forest sector. In fact, 97% of Cambodia's CO_2 emissions come from its forest sector. Indonesia is considered to be one of the biggest contributors to global CO_2 emissions, with the majority of its emissions produced by land use, land use change, and forestry.

Climate change mitigation and adaptation strategies nonetheless rely on forests. Managing forests sustainably and enhancing the extent and condition of forest cover can increase carbon sequestration. This fundamental principle underlies international mitigation mechanisms. Forest resources furthermore support climate change adaptation by helping diversify livelihoods, thereby reducing the vulnerability of rural peoples to natural disasters. Accordingly, forest management will be integral to addressing climate change.

Reducing Emissions from Deforestation and Forest Degradation (REDD+) is an effort to valuate forest carbon and generate financial incentives for forest protection. Much as its namesake suggests, it reduces emissions from deforestation and forest degradation. In addition, it promotes sustainable forest management (SFM) as well as the conservation and enhancement of forest carbon. As such, REDD+ has the potential to increase recognition of customary land rights, encourage participation of local people in forest management, and provide financial resources for continued development and poverty reduction. Conversely, it has just as much potential to further exclude rural and indigenous people from forest resources. Governments and private companies may restrict forest access and resource use in order to secure the potentially high volume of financial flows from REDD+ for their own benefit.

A range of REDD+ pilot projects are already taking place throughout ASEAN countries. These projects contribute to a growing body of experience and knowledge on the systems and structures needed to reduce deforestation and forest degradation while engaging local communities. However, the international community of policymakers and practitioners has yet to address the myriad of challenges that REDD+ development and implementation present.

REDD+ countries will need comprehensive legal and policy frameworks to govern national and local forest management. Existing laws and policies may require updating or amending to determine how REDD+ strategies are managed, implemented, and monitored; to recognize customary rights; and to delineate how the potential benefits will be shared.

Awareness and understanding of REDD+ among local people must also be enhanced. Free, Informed and Prior Consent (FPIC) of forest-dependent people will help foster their participation, which in turn, will be critical in enabling them to claim an equitable share in the potential REDD+ benefits.

Future financial rewards from REDD+ will need to be made available to forest-dependent communities to reward them for forest protection and compensate them for lost revenues. To this end, the development of robust mechanisms for benefit-sharing is crucial. Profitable land use strategies - such as timber production, industrial agriculture, palm oil production, or mining—are powerful economic drivers of deforestation and can act as powerful disincentives to forest protection.

Sustainable Forest Management (SFM) aims to balance the forest's economic, environmental, and social functions and ensure their continued benefits. Social forestry, which emphasizes the role of local people in forest management, is a key strategy for SFM in many ASEAN countries. Social forestry thereby presents an opportunity to link sustainable forest management, forest protection, biodiversity conservation, and improved livelihoods, as well as climate change mitigation strategies like REDD+.

The current status of social forestry across ASEAN varies from country to country. In some places, social forestry is established with large areas of forestland officially managed by local people. In other places, existing national policies and legal frameworks for local forest management remain weak. Still others have established the necessary laws and policies, but lack institutional capacity for effective implementation. The varying conditions suggest that REDD+ may meet similarly varying degrees of success across the region.

Many ASEAN countries are moving forward with REDD+ with pilot projects. These projects are generating a growing body of knowledge and experience on the implementation of REDD+, the role of social forestry, and the engagement of local people. ASFN could help disseminate this information in order to support the development of effective policy and institutional capacity. Regional activities may include producing communications materials on social forestry best practices in ASEAN languages; facilitating regional learning and sharing events; and conducting study visits to pilot project sites in other countries.

Such an exchange of information will also help coordinate regional action on climate change adaptation. Because forests and climate change transcend government sectors and administrative boundaries, local and national agencies must synchronize their policies, strategies, and actions. ASFN could act as a regional body for coordinating relevant policies and programs across and within ASEAN countries.

ASFN could also support capacity building of government institutions and stakeholders at all levels to effectively design, develop, implement, and monitor REDD+ projects. This might consist of a series of trainings and workshops that provide a platform for the dynamic exchange of knowledge and experience.

Finally, the role of social forestry in climate change adaptation has received little attention. It will be an important area for future research, which ASFN may be able to support.

4. (*d*) Greenhouse gases are a group of compounds that are able to trap heat (longwave radiation) in the atmosphere, keeping the Earth's surface warmer than it would be if they were not present. These gases are the fundamental cause of the greenhouse effect. Increases in the amount of greenhouse gases in the atmosphere enhances the greenhouse effect which is creating global warming and consequently climate change.

Greenhouse gases allow sunlight (shortwave radiation) to pass through the atmosphere freely, where it is then partially absorbed by the surface of the Earth. But some of this energy bounces back out towards space as heat. Of the heat emitted back to space, some is intercepted and absorbed by greenhouse gases in the atmosphere. This is because these compounds are made of three or more atoms. This molecular structure allows them to absorb some of the escaping heat and then re-emit it towards the Earth which increases global temperatures.

The ability of these gases to trap heat is what causes the greenhouse effect. So, the more greenhouse gases you have in the atmosphere, the more heat stays on Earth. This process, which is very similar to the way a greenhouse works, is why the gases that can produce this effect are collectively known as greenhouse gases.

There are 2 ways that a greenhouse gas (often abbreviated GHG) can enter our atmosphere. One of them is through human activities. The main human sources of GHG emissions are: fossil fuel use, deforestation, intensive livestock farming, use of synthetic fertilizers and industrial processes. The other is through natural processes like animal and plant respiration.

Forcing greenhouse gases take many years to leave the atmosphere. CO_2, CH_4, N_2O and the fluorinated gases are all well-mixed gases in the atmosphere. They do not react to change in either temperature or air pressure and thus do not get removed easily like water that condenses to become rain or snow. Their long atmospheric lifetimes allows them to have a lasting effect of green house gases on crop production, global warming and climate change.

Water vapour on the other hand has a residence time of a few days. It is a highly active component of the climate system that responds rapidly to change in conditions by either condensing into rain or snow, or evaporating to return to the atmosphere. Thus, the impact of the greenhouse effect is primarily circulated through water vapour, and it acts as a fast feedback, accentuating the warming provided by the forcing greenhouse gases.

CO_2 and the other forcing greenhouse gases are the key gases within the Earth's atmosphere that sustain the greenhouse effect and control its strength. In fact, the greenhouse effect would collapse were it not for the presence of CO_2 and the other non-condensing greenhouse gases.

Greenhouse gases greatly affect the temperature of the Earth. Without them, surface temperatures would be on average about 32.5°C colder than the present average of 14.4°C (57.9°F), 6 making life on Earth as we know it not possible. Greenhouse gases are not, inherently, a bad thing. But the growing concentration of greenhouse gases in the atmosphere has been raising average temperatures around the world.

CO_2, CH_4 and N_2O are emitted to the atmosphere through natural processes as well as human activities (use of fossil fuels, industrial production, etc). The fluorinated gases on the other hand, are created and emitted almost exclusively through human activities.

Since the Industrial Revolution, which began in the 18th century, human activities have been a major source of all forcing greenhouse gases. Human activities have led to a sharp and dangerous increase of these gases within the Earth's atmosphere, so much so that the growth of all forcing greenhouse gas (GHG) concentrations is now directly controlled by humans.

SECTION 'B'

5. (*a*) Plant Growth Affected by Waterlogging Conditions: Waterlogging occurs when roots cannot respire due to excess water in the soil profile. Water does not have to appear on the surface for waterlogging to be a potential problem. Improving drainage from the inundated paddock can decrease the period at which the crop roots are subjected to anaerobic condition. While raised beds are the most intensive management strategy, they are also the most effective at improving drainage. Waterlogged soils release increased amounts of nitrous oxide (N_2O), a particularly damaging greenhouse gas.

Waterlogging occurs whenever the soil is so wet that there is insufficient oxygen in the pore space for plant roots to be able to adequately respire. Other gases detrimental to root growth, such as carbon dioxide any ethylene, also accumulate in the root zone and affect the plants.

Plants differ in their demand for oxygen. There is no universal level of soil oxygen in its root zone will vary with its stage of growth.

Low levels of oxygen in the root zone trigger the adverse effects of waterlogging on plant growth. Waterlogging of the seedbed mostly affects germinating seeds and young seedling. Established plants are most affected when they are growing rapidly. Therefore, if a soil becomes waterlogged in July, final yields may not be greatly reduced. Soils are cold, the demand for oxygen is low and plant growth is slow at this time of year. Prolonged waterlogging during the warmer spring period could be more detrimental, however the probability for this to occur is much lower than waterlogging in July.

When plants are growing actively, root tips begin to die within a few days of waterlogging. The shallow root systems that then develop limit the uptake of nutrients (particularly nitrogen) and water, particularly when the soil profile starts to dry in spring. As a result plants may ripen early and grains may not fill properly. Nitrogen is lost from waterlogged soils by leaching and denitrification (degassing). Denitrification leads to the gaseous loss of nitrous oxide (N_2O) into the atmosphere, which is a major greenhouse gas. These losses, together with the lowered ability of plants to absorb nutrients from waterlogged soil, cause the older leaves to yellow. Waterlogging also directly reduces nitrogen fixation by the nodules of legume crops and pastures.

Measures to Improve Crop Productivity Under Waterlogging Conditions

Drainage can be improved on many sites and is the first thing to consider once a waterlogging problem has been identified. Options might vary from shallow surface drains to more intensive drainage using wide-spaced furrows, to the intensive drainage form of raised beds. The efficiency of surface drainage increases in that order as does the degree of management. Consult your local adviser for further advice.

5. (*b*) Run-off losses of irrigation water and their management

Incorporating a crop demand-dependent irrigation schedule saves water without affecting crop yields. In order to efficiently apply water to the root zone, estimate the water demand based on soil type, precipitation, crop needs and soil moisture retention. The process for developing an irrigation schedule is described below.

- **Determine your soil type:** Soil characteristics help to determine effective irrigation application rates, durations and frequencies. For instance, sandy soils may require more frequent but shorter- duration applications.
- **Determine weekly precipitation amounts:** Install a rain gauge in a central location. Although local radio and TV weather services can give you general precipitation rates for the week, site-specific information is more accurate.
- **Determine each crop's water quantity needs:** Contact your county cooperative extension service for irrigation demand information for individual crops.
- **Monitor soil moisture to determine whether irrigation is necessary:** If the soil moisture content is adequate for the crop's water quantity needs, no additional water application is required. Soil moisture can be measured with tensiometers, electrical resistance blocks ("gypsum", "ceramic" or "moisture" blocks) or neutron probes.
- **Measure the output from your irrigation devices:** Use flow meters or gauged water pans to measure the output of sprinklers and drip irrigation heads.

Combine the five pieces of information above to determine a week-by-week irrigation schedule.

Update the schedule as weather and soil moisture conditions change.

Recheck soil moisture 1-2 days after irrigation to determine depth of applied water and uniformity. If water penetration is too deep, too shallow, or spotty adjust your irrigation schedule to correct it.

The following miscellaneous water efficiency practices and techniques will help further reduce water use.

Employ mulches wherever possible.

Develop an irrigation maintenance program. Routinely inspect all water lines, valves and pumps for leaks. Keep replacement and repair parts on hand. Inspect sprinkler nozzles to ensure they are operating properly and are distributing the water uniformly. Evaluate irrigation system pressures to better control application rates.

Collect stormwater and irrigation runoff in a series of ditches or drains that return the excess water to a storage pond.

Incorporate moisture retentive polymers in the soil. Though traditionally used in container plantings, these polymers are presently being tested by some growers and golf courses to cut down on irrigation demands.

Water early in the morning to reduce evaporation losses.

Practice conservation tillage. Conservation tillage encompasses minimal or no tilling and leaves at least 30 per cent of the previous season's crop residue in the field. Although conservation tillage was originally devised to prevent soil erosion, a side benefit is increased soil water storage capabilities.

Till the land along the topographic contours to reduce runoff.

Incorporate organic matter such as compost into the soil. Organic matter retains moisture and is especially effective in sand and clay soils.

Incorporate cover crops for winter and fallow times to improve the soil and reduce water and soil losses caused by runoff. When tilled under, cover crops also add organic matter to the soil.

Practice deficit irrigation where feasible. This method involves stressing plants by reducing water applications. Be aware that this practice typically reduces crop yields and may lower the quality of some products. However, the water savings may be more valuable than the crop losses.

Use computer software to aid irrigation scheduling.

Use pressure regulators for uniform water distribution throughout irrigation systems.

Use timers, automatic shut off valves, rain sensors and other such devices to help ensure over-watering does not occur.

Limit the volume of water used for frost protection for late maturing crops such as pumpkins.

Investigate alternative irrigation water sources, such as treated municipal wastewater treatment plant effluent, treated industrial effluent, on-site gray water systems, and holding tanks for rain-water or greenhouse irrigation water. State and federal regulations that restrict the reuse of water from certain sources should be investigated and permits obtained where applicable.

Water Conservation for Greenhouse, Nursery Stock, and Potted Plant Irrigation

Water-efficient methods for irrigating greenhouse plants include hand watering, micro irrigation and sub-irrigation techniques. Micro-irrigation and sub-irrigation techniques minimize losses through accurate application and recycling designs.

Micro-irrigation techniques are capable of applying water accurately at rates that do not result in runoff or overflow waste. See the section of this fact sheet titled "Irrigation Technology and Methods" for a more complete description of micro-irrigation.

5. (*c*) **Irrigation :** Irrigation is the artificial application of water to land for growing crops or trees.

Irrigation is the artificial application of water for the purpose of supplying moisture essential to plant growth (Hansen *et al.*, 1980).

Various Irrigation Systems

Surface method

Sub-surface method

Micro methods

1. Surface Irrigation Methods

(*a*) Flooding

(*b*) Check basin

(*c*) Ring basin

(*d*) Border strip

(*e*) Furrow method

(*f*) Surge method

(*a*) Flooding

1. Used for lowland rice and other crops.
2. Water is allowed from the channel into the field without much control on either sides of the flow.
3. It covers the entire field and move almost unguided.
4. The height of bunds around the field should be 15 cm for effective use of rainfall.
5. It is a minimum labour intensive method.
6. Most suitable to irrigated saline soils.

Advantage

1. Less labour required.
2. No extra care required.
3. Large stream can be easily managed.

Disadvantage

1. Uneven distribution of water.
2. Low water application efficiency.

(*b*) Check Basin

1. Most common method of surface irrigation.
2. The field is divided into small plots surrounding by small bunds on all four sides.
3. Water from head channel is supplied to the field channel one after another.
4. Each field channel supplied water to 2 row of check basin and water is applied to one basin after another.
5. The size of check basin ranges from 4 m × 3 m to 6 m × 5 m depending upon stream size and soil texture.

Advantages

1. Uniformly water application.
2. Suitable for those fields which are quite large and not easy to level the entire field.

Disadvantage

1. More labour required for field layout and irrigation.
2. Wastage of field/land is more under irrigations and bunds. Mostly 5 per cent of land is waste for making bunds.

(*c*) Ring Basin Method

1. Basins around the trees are made.
2. It is suitable for fruit trees.
3. It enhances the water use efficiency and fewer losses.
4. Basins are generally round in shape and occasionally square shaped.
5. Basins are small when the fields are young and the size is increased with age of trees.
6. Basins are connected by channel irrigation.

(*d*) Border Strip Method

1. Field divided into number of strips by bunds of around 15 cm height.
2. These parallel earth ridges (called border) are formed to guide the flow of the water across the field.
3. Length of strip ranges from 30 m - 50 m, while width is from 3 m - 5 m.
4. The slope ranges from 0.1-1 per cent.
5. Water from the channel is allowed into each strip at a time.
6. This method is suitable for close growing crops and medium to heavy texture soils, but not suitable for sandy soils.

Advantages

1. Large irrigation streams can be efficiently used.
2. This method gives highest water use efficiency than other surface irrigation methods.

Disadvantages

1. No uniform distribution of water.
2. This method can not applied for sandy soil.

(*e*) Furrow Method

1. Furrows are formed along or across the slope and water from pipes is diverted into the furrows.
2. Water infiltrate from the bottom and sides of the furrow moving downward and laterally to wet the soil.
3. Water is allowed into 3-5 furrows at a time from open ditches and or pipes.
4. This method is adapted to crops grown with ridges and furrows.
5. This method is suitable for crops *i.e.*, Sorghum, cotton, maize, tobacco, potato, sugarcane etc.

(*f*) Surge Method

1. Intermittent application of water to the field surface under gravity flow which results in a series of "On and Off" modes of constant or variable time spans.

Advantages

1. Infiltration uniformity is increased.
2. Deep percolation is reduced compared to continuous water application due to intermittent wetting and drying process.

2. Sub-surface Irrigation Method

Through underground perforated pipes or through deep trenches at 15-30 m. intervals water gradually wet root zone through capillary movement.

Advantages

1. Evaporation loss is less due to dry surface.
2. Less weed management.
3. Deep trenches should be made for drainage.

Disadvantages

1. Deep percolation through trenches.
2. Maintenance of pipe lines is difficult.
3. High initial cost.

3. Micro Irrigation Methods

(*a*) Sprinkler irrigation

(*b*) Drip Irrigation

(*a*) Sprinkler Irrigation

1. Water is applied as spray or as rain over the crop.
2. Rate of water delivery is > 1000 litre/hrs.
3. It operates at the pressure of > 2.5 bar and through water as a spray upto the distance of > 10 m.

Advantages

1. Uniform distribution of water.
2. Saving of water from 25-50 per cent.
3. Saving of land 10-20 per cent.
4. Irrigation area is increased by 1-2 times with the same amount of the water.
5. No risk of runoff and erosion.
6. Suitable for undulating land and steep sloppy.
7. Suitable for areas where water and labour scarcity.
8. Suitable for saline soils to leach salts.

Disadvantages

1. Not followed under high wing velocity (>12 km/hour).
2. High initial costs.
3. High energy is required (0.50 to >10 kg/cm^2).
4. More spreading of diseases.
5. Can not be used for rice and jute crops.

(*a*) Drip Irrigation : Discovered in Israel

1. It is also known as trickle irrigation.
2. Discharge rate of water per dripper is 1-4 litre/hrs.
3. It consists of main line, sub pipe line, laterals and emitters.
4. The discharge is from emitters.
5. The irrigation interval is 1-4 days.
6. It saves 50-70 per cent water.

Advantages

1. Well suited for areas of acute water shortage.
2. Minimization of soil erosion and deep percolation and runoff losses.
3. Water is maintained at field capacity.
4. Salt concentration is less.
5. No land levelling is necessary.
6. Herbigation and Fertigation can also be applied.
7. Less disease and weed infestation.

Disadvantages

1. Clogging of emitter.
2. Damage to lateral systems due to rodents and other animals.
3. Salt accumulation near plants due to lack of sufficient moisture for leaching.
4. High initial cost.
5. Most suitable for wider spaced orchard crops and sugarcane.
6. Inadequate root development.

5. (*d*) Economic viability means that market operation is sustainable regarding current and projected revenues. The revenues will be greater than or equal to all current and planned expenditures. In simple terms, any project or activity that can financially support itself is economically viable. Using farming as an example, economic viability refers to the ability and capacity of a farm to 'make a living' annually.

Part of the concept of economic viability is the implicit recognition that the enjoyment of ? and effort put into ? a project determines how a project or business grows and how often workers are replaced.

For economic viability to work, it must often span generations. Workers must stay on top of best practices and share that information appropriately. In the farming example, this would include sharing with other farmers in the region as well as the community.

The basic economic viability of farming is a key indicator of genuine progress in agriculture. Economic well-being is typically and conventionally measured in terms of the total gross income accruing to the agricultural sector. In this report, a number of more nuanced and therefore more accurate measures of economic well-being are included, taking into account the multiplier effects of economic activity, price indices, and measures of net income, equity, and debt, all of which more precisely indicate farmers' actual economic and financial situation than do gross receipts.

As noted above, however, indicators always and by definition reflect underlying social goals and values. Thus, the indicator selection in this section must also reflect the fundamental economic goals for agriculture that are alluded to in the quotations above and that include thriving farms, fair prices, circulating wealth within the region, and a sufficient return on investment to ensure economic and financial viability.

5. (*e*) The introduction of new cultivated species and improved varieties of crop is a technology aimed at enhancing plant productivity, quality, health and nutritional value and/or building crop resilience to diseases, pest organisms and environmental stresses. Crop diversification refers to the addition of new crops or cropping systems to agricultural production on a particular farm taking into account the different returns from value-added crops with complementary marketing opportunities. Major driving forces for crop diversification include:

- Increasing income on small farm holdings
- Withstanding price fluctuation
- Mitigating effects of increasing climate variability
- Balancing food demand
- Improving fodder for livestock animals
- Conservation of natural resources
- Minimising environmental pollution
- Reducing dependence on off-farm inputs
- Depending on crop rotation, decreasing insect pests, diseases and weed problems
- Increasing community food security.

Farmer experimentation with new varieties. Farmers have introduced new and improved species over centuries, mainly in regions that constitute world centres of cultivated crop diversification, such as Meso-America, the Andes, Africa and parts of Asia, in response to environmental stress conditions. There are many thousands of existing varieties of all of the important crops, with wide variation in their abilities to adapt to climatic conditions. Agricultural researchers and extension agents can help farmers identify new varieties that may be better adapted to changing climatic conditions, and facilitate farmers to compare these new varieties with those they already produce. In some cases, farmers may participate in crossing select seeds from plant varieties that demonstrate the qualities they seek to propagate to develop new varieties with the characteristics they desire.

The introduction of new crop species to diversify the crop production systems needs to take into account the following:

Availability and quality of resources including irrigation, rainfall and soil fertility.

Access to technologies such as seed, fertiliser, water, marketing, storage and processing.

Household related factors covering food and fodder self-sufficiency requirement as well as investment capacity.

Price and market related factors including output and input prices as well as trade policies and other economic policies that affect these prices either directly or indirectly.

Institutional and infrastructure related factors covering farm size and tenancy arrangements, research, extension and marketing systems and government regulatory policies.

6. (*a*) Dryland Farming

Indian agriculture is traditionally a system of Rainfed agriculture. Out of 143 million hectares of net cropped area, about 72% is Rainfed production about 45% of food grains and 75-80% of pulses and oil-seeds and a number of important industrial crops. Considering the present rate of development of irrigaticn facilities and also water potentiality of the country, express estimate that at any point of time 50% of cropped area in India will remain under Rainfed farming system.

Such vast areas as of now consume hardly 25% of total fertilizer consumption of the country. Due to poor level of management, crop productivity is also very low resulting in socio-economic backwardness of the people.

Definitions

The different definitions of dry farming given by various express are described below:

1. Dry farming is an improved system of cultivation in which maximum amount of moisture is conserved in low and untimely rainfall for the production of optimum quantities of crop on economic and sustained basis.
2. Dry farming in short, is a programme of soil and water management designed to conserve the maximum quantity of water on a particular piece of land.
3. Dry farming is the profitable production of useful crops without irrigation on land that receive annually a rainfall of 500 mm or less.
4. In a more specific way, dry farming may be defined as an efficient system of soil and crop management in the regions of low land and uneven distributed rainfall.

Table: Dryland Vs. Rainfed Farming

Constituents farming	*Dryland farming*	*Rainfed farming*
1. Rainfall (mm)	< 750	> 75
2. Moisture	Shortage	Enough/ Sufficient
3. Growing season	< 200	> 200
4. Growing regions	Arid and Semiarid & up lands of sub humid & humid regions.	Humid and sub humid regions.
5. Cropping system	Single crop or inter-cropping	Inter-cropping or double cropping.
6. Constraints	Wind and water erosion	Water erosion.

Dryland Farming: Problems of Crop Production

Dry farming crops are characterized by very low and highly variable and uncertain yields. Crop failures are quite common.

These are mainly due to the following causes.

(*i*) ***Inadequate and Uneven Distribution of Rainfall :*** In general, the rainfall is low and highly variable which results in uncertain crop yields. Besides its uncertainty, the distribution of rainfall during the crop period is uneven, receiving high amount of rain, when it is not needed and lack of it when crop needs it.

(*ii*) ***Late Onset and Early Cessation of Rains :*** Due to late onset of monsoon, the sowing of crop are delayed resulting in poor yields. Sometimes the rain may cease very early in the season exposing the crop to drought during flowering and maturity stages which reduces the crop yields considerably.

(*iii*) ***Prolonged Dry Spells during the Crop Period :*** Long breaks in the rainy season is an important feature of Indian monsoon. These intervening dry spells when prolonged during crop period reduces crop growth and yield and when unduly prolonged crops fail.

(*iv*) ***Low Moisture Retention Capacity :*** The crops raised on red soils, and coarse textured soil suffer due to lack of moisture whenever prolonged dry spells occur due to their low moisture holding capacity. Loss of rain occurs as runoff due to undulating and sloppy soils.

(*v*) ***Low Fertility of Soils :*** Drylands are not only thirsty, but also hungry too. Soil fertility has to be increased, but there is limited scope for extensive use of chemical fertilizers due to lack of adequate soil moisture.

Rainfed Farming

Dry farming areas (as per the IV five year plan) are those areas receiving an annual rainfall ranging from 375 to 1125 mm and very limited irrigation facilities. Areas which receive less than 375 mm of average rainfall are considered as absolutely arid or desert areas, which require special treatment. As many as 128 districts in the country falls under category of dry farming areas as defined above. Out of these 25 districts from the states of Rajasthan, Sourashtra and rain shado region of Maharashtra and Karnataka belong to very high intensity dryfarming areas (*i.e.* rainfall ranges from 375 to 750 mm and irrigated area belong 10% of the cropped area.)

As the Encyclopedia Britannica puts dryland farming consists of making the best use of limited water supply by storing in the soil and much of the rainfall as possible and by going suitable crop plants those make the best use of this moisture.

The major physiographic regions observed in India are namely:

(*i*) Mountain region

(*ii*) Indo-gangatic alluvial plains

(*iii*) Peninsular or Deccan plateau &

(*iv*) Coastal plains.

6. (*b*) Constraints to increase pulse production in India

Production of major pulses is constrained by both biotic/abiotic stresses and socio-political problems. The main biotic stresses that block pulse productivity include various pests. We note here that legume crops are rich in N and P and it makes them attractive for insect pests and disease. Most of the pulses in India are grown in low fertility, problematic soils and unpredictable environmental conditions. More than 87% of the area under pulses are in rainfed.

In these areas, issue is of availability of water. Thus, areas of pulse production in India are subject to drought and heat stress of arid and semi-arid regions, which brings down its yield. Further, the arid and semi-arid areas of the country face problem of alkaline and acidic soils. Since long, governments gave little importance to pulses in comparison to staples. Only in recent times, government started providing MSP support to pulses viz. Gra, Lentil, Urad, Tur and Moong, despite of this, farmers in India treat pulses as secondary crops. The cost input in case of pulses is higher in comparison to staple crops. Farmers have low purchasing power and they would give first priority to staple cereals and cash crops. Due to this, pulses in our country continue to be grown on poor soils with low inputs.

6. (*c*) The return are good as polyhouse enables you to grow crops throughout the year irrespective of season. Also the quality of produce is better than the open field cultivation. The yield under polyhouse or greenhouse cultivation can be achieved to the level of 4 to 8 times as compared to the open field crop cultivation. Various research trials conducted at agro research centers in northern India that indicates that tomato (November planting) capsicum (Planted in mid September) and cucumber (planting mid October) under polyhouse produced 1550 kg, 1500 kg and 1100 kg per 100 square meter. The duration of these vegetable crops were 4 to 10 months and more than 90% of total yield were obtained during of-season (during winter before the start of summer) which fatches higher market price (2-4 times than normal season price.)

Further, the crop duration can be extended up to the July or August with the application of micro irrigation and fertilizers and yield can be achieved to the level of 20-25 kg/ square meter. Therefore, it is possible to harvest a single crop round year with minimum additional applications and inputs and higher returns can be generated. Further cut flowers like Gerbera, Rose, Carnations, Lilly, Antherium and Orchids can be grown under poly houses/Net houses giving high profits and top quality produce. This is the reason why the potential of floriculture under protected cultivation is huge for Indian and global markets.

It is possible to get back the initial investment on polyhouse within a period of 4 to 5 years. If a cultivator/entrepreneurs go for polyhouse for nursery production of high yielding vegetable plants/Flower plants in an area where large scale vegetable/flower cultivation is done, in such situation he can get back his investment within 2 to 3 years by providing quality planting materials to flower growers vegetable. Minimum preferred or recommended project with right economic viability and long terms sustainability is around 1 to 2 acres.

6. (*d*) Factors leading to rise of prices of agricultural products mainly include tension of supply-demand relationship, promotion of production cost and circulation cost, and speculation of Refugee Capital (Hot Money). Factors leading to low price and difficult sales of agricultural products mainly include asymmetry of supply-demand information, lack of risk management tools for prices of agricultural products and decentralized and small-scaled operation of farmers. On the basis of these factors, this paper presents following counter-measures and suggestions for stabilizing prices of agricultural products: firstly, building long-effect mechanism for production and sales of agricultural products; secondly, expand the production and increase supply of agricultural products; thirdly, control the rising range of production cost for agricultural products; fourthly, enhance organization level of farmers; fifthly, promote innovation and development of risk management tools for prices of agricultural products.

PAPER-II

SECTION 'A'

1. (*a*) Indole-3-acetic acid (IAA, 3-IAA) is the most common, naturally occurring, plant hormone of the auxin class. It is the best known of the auxins, and has been the subject of extensive studies by plant physiologists. IAA is a derivative of indole, containing a carboxymethyl substituent. It is a colourless solid that is soluble in polar organic solvents.

IAA is predominantly produced in cells of the apex (bud) and very young leaves of a plant. Plants can synthesize IAA by several independent biosynthetic pathways. Four of them start from tryptophan, but there is also a biosynthetic pathway independent of tryptophan. Plants mainly produce IAA from tryptophan through indole-3-pyruvic acid. IAA is also produced from tryptophan through indole-3-acetaldoxime in Arabidopsis thaliana.

In rats, IAA is a product of both endogenous and colonic microbial metabolism from dietary tryptophan along with tryptophol. This was first observed in rats infected by Trypanosoma brucei gambiense. and correlation with protein intake has been confirmed in 2015. Humans did not excrete IAA.

As all auxins, IAA has many different effects, such as inducing cell elongation and cell division with all subsequent results for plant growth and development. On a larger scale, IAA serves as signaling molecule necessary for development of plant organs and coordination of growth.

Since IBA is not soluble in water, it is typically dissolved in 75% or purer alcohol for use in plant rooting, making a solution of between 10,000 and 50,000 ppm. This alcohol solution is then diluted with distilled water to the desired concentration. IBA is also available as a salt, which is soluble in water. The solution should be kept in a cool, dark place for best results.

This compound had been thought to be strictly synthetic; however, it was reported that the compound was isolated from leaves and seeds of maize and other species. In maize IBA has been shown to be synthesized *in vivo* using IAA and other compounds as precursors. This chemical may also be extracted from any of the Salix (Willow) genus.

In plant tissue culture IBA and other auxins are used to initiate root formation *in vitro* in a procedure called micropropagation. Micropropagation of plants is the process of using small samples of plants called explants and causing them to undergo growth of differentiated or undifferentiated cells. In connection with cytokinins like kinetin, auxins like IBA can be used to cause the formation of masses of undifferentiated cells called callus. Callus formation is often used as the first step process in micropropagation where the callus cells are then caused to form other tissues such as roots by exposing them to certain hormones like auxins that produce roots. The process of callus to root formation is called indirect organogenesis whereas if roots are formed from the explant directly it is called direct organogenesis.

In a study of Camellia sinensis the effect of three different auxins, IBA, IAA and NAA were examined to determine the relative effect of each auxin on root formation. According to the result for the species IBA was shown to produce a higher yield of roots compared to the other auxins. The effect of IBA is in concurrence with other studies where IBA is the most commonly used auxin for root formation.

1. (*b*) Testing Release and Notification of Crop Varieties

Improved varieties play a critical role in agricultural development of a country. Hence, primary objective of crop science research is development of improved varieties in different crops. In India, new improved varieties of crops are developed by Crop Research Institutes of Indian Council of Agricultural Research, State Agricultural Universities and few Private Seed Companies. These varieties are tested (evaluated) for a minimum period of three years, before consideration of release for cultivation. The important characters for which the new varieties are evaluated/tested are:

(*a*) Yield

(*b*) Resistance to disease and pests

(*c*) Quality of product

(*d*) Resistance to adverse environmental factors (*viz.* drought)

(*e*) Adaptation to different agro-climatic conditions.

Variety Release

The scientist in-charge of the culture will propose the culture for release as a variety. There is a proforma for variety release. This proforma will contain all the information about the culture viz., parentage. Parent's morphology, cultures morphology, key characters of the culture for identification, agronomic practices, pest and disease resistance, quality characters and yield trial result.

The variety release proposal will be discussed by Director of Research and Scientists. After approval, the proposal will be presented before variety release committee.

Notification of the variety

For certified seed production, the variety is to be notified by the central variety release committee, Delhi. After release of the variety for notification purpose the information will be furnished in the prescribed proforma. At that time details about all India trial will also be furnished. After notification only, a variety can be multiplied under certified seed production.

1. (*c*) A meristem is the tissue in most plants containing undifferentiated cells (meristematic cells), found in zones of the plant where growth can take place.

Meristematic cells give rise to various organs of the plant and keep the plant growing. The shoot apical meristem (SAM) gives rise to organs like the leaves and flowers, while the root apical meristem (RAM) provides the meristematic cells for the future root growth. SAM and RAM cells divide rapidly and are considered indeterminate, in that they do not possess any defined end status. In that sense, the meristematic cells are frequently compared to the stem cells in animals, which have an analogous behaviour and function.

The term meristem was first used in 1858 by Karl Wilhelm von Nägeli (1817-1891) in his book Beiträge zur Wissenschaftlichen Botanik ("Contributions to Scientific Botany"). It is derived from the Greek word merizein, meaning to divide, in recognition of its inherent function.

In general, differentiated plant cells cannot divide or produce cells of a different type. Therefore, cell division in the meristem is required to provide new cells for expansion and differentiation of tissues and initiation of new organs, providing the basic structure of the plant body.

Meristematic cells are incompletely or not at all differentiated, and are capable of continued cellular division (youthful). Furthermore, the cells are small and protoplasm fills the cell completely. The vacuoles are extremely small. The cytoplasm does not contain differentiated plastids (chloroplasts or chromoplasts), although they are present in rudimentary form (proplastids). Meristematic cells are packed closely together without intercellular cavities. The cell wall is a very thin primary cell wall.

Maintenance of the cells requires a balance between two antagonistic processes: organ initiation and stem cell population renewal.

Apical meristems are the completely undifferentiated (indeterminate) meristems in a plant. These differentiate into three kinds of primary meristems. The primary meristems in turn produce the two secondary meristem types. These secondary meristems are also known as lateral meristems because they are involved in lateral growth.

At the meristem summit, there is a small group of slowly dividing cells, which is commonly called the central zone. Cells of this zone have a stem cell function and are essential for meristem maintenance. The proliferation and growth rates at the meristem summit usually differ considerably from those at the periphery.

Meristems also are induced in the roots of legumes such as soybean, Lotus japonicus, pea, and Medicago truncatula after infection with soil bacteria commonly called Rhizobium. Cells of the inner or outer cortex in the so-called "window of nodulation" just behind the developing root tip are induced to divide. The critical signal substance is the lipo-oligosaccharide Nod-factor, decorated with side groups to allow specificity of interaction. The Nod factor receptor proteins NFR1 and NFR5 were cloned from several legumes including Lotus japonicus, Medicago truncatula and soybean (Glycine max). Regulation of nodule meristems utilizes long distance regulation commonly called "Autoregulation of Nodulation" (AON). This process involves a leaf-vascular tissue located LRR receptor kinases (LjHAR1, GmNARK and MtSUNN), CLE peptide signalling, and KAPP interaction, similar to that seen in the CLV1,2,3 system. LjKLAVIER also exhibits a nodule regulation phenotype though it is not yet known how this relates to the other AON receptor kinases.

Generally plant shoot apical meristems are virus free. This is because the spread of virus in the plant tissue does not keep up (is slow) vis a vis the fast meristem growth if it is actively producing new leaves/flowers. To get rid of viruses in a chronically infested plant the technique of "meristem culture" (Tissue culture) is used. Here, the meristem dome is surgically excised and planted aseptically on a synthetic medium. The meristem grows into a virus-free shoot that is rooted to get a virus free plant. This is a commercial application.

1. (*d*) Role of Micro and Macro Mutations in Crop Improvement:

A mutation is any change in the sequence of the DNA encoding a gene. Most of these mutations are recognized because the phenotype of the organism has changed. Morphological mutants affects the outward appearance of an individual. Plant height mutations could changes a tall plant to a short one, or from having smooth to round seeds. Biochemical mutations have a lesion in one specific step of an enzymatic pathway. For some mutations to be expressed, the individual needs to be placed in a specific environment. This is called the restrictive condition. But the individual grow in any other environment (known as permissive condition), the wild type phenotype is expressed. These are called conditional mutations.

Micro-mutation is a small-scale or highly localized mutation; especially one involving alternation at a single gene locus. A macromutation is a mutation of large phenotypic effect; one that produces a phenotype well outside the range of variation previously existing in the population. Mutations with effects in early stages of development can have large phenotypic consequences.

The role of micro and macro-mutations in crop improvement are summarized as under:

(*i*) When a variety is exceptionally good except for one or few characters.

(*ii*) When recessive characters is desirable and transfer of that character from wild species is difficult.

(*iii*) When a desirable character is linked with an undesirable character.

(*iv*) If there is no known source of resistance gene in the available germplasm.

(*v*) To create variability.

(*vi*) To development of male sterile line.

(*vii*) To create variations in vegetatively propagated plants.

1. (*e*) Although the economic injury level (EIL) and the economic threshold (ET) are fundamental integrated pest management (IPM) concepts, they are often confused. This is understandable, as the concepts are closely related and the definitions of EIL and ET can be expressed differently depending on context. You will see various versions of the following definitions:

Economic injury level : The smallest number of insects (amount of injury) that will cause yield losses equal to the insect management costs.

Economic threshold : The pest density at which management action should be taken to prevent an increasing pest population from reaching the economic injury level.

EILs are usually expressed as a pest density and are developed from yield-loss relationships derived from field research studies. The EIL has been described as the break-even point, the level of pest a plant can tolerate, among other things. The main thing is that we want to manage the pest population before it reaches the EIL. That is where the ET comes in.

The ET is the practical rule used to determine when to take management action. In fact, some refer to the ET as the action threshold. It is essentially a prediction of when a pest population is going to reach the EIL. It is assumed that once the ET is reached, there is a high probability that the pest population will reach the EIL if no management action is taken.

Establishing an ET is complex. It incorporates the EIL as well as other factors which require a thorough understanding of the pest's population dynamics in the specific crop. Pest and crop phenology, pest population growth and injury rates, and the practical aspects of management tactics all have to be considered when establishing ETs.

Unfortunately, a complete understanding of the pest and crop biology and ecology is rarely available, and a certain level of subjectivity is a part of establishing ETs. For example, sometimes the ET is simply set at 80% of the EIL, as it is with bean leaf beetle on soybean. In this case, the ET is relatively close to the EIL. On the other hand, for an insect such as the soybean aphid that has an exponential population growth rate, the ET is well below the EIL and at a level where no damage occurs.

Because ET development is complex and dependent on the specific agro-ecosystem, one should have an understanding of how ETs are determined before altering them. Simply raising or lowering ETs to account for changes in the market may not be appropriate.

2. (*a*) Gametogenesis

The production of male and female gametes in the microspores and the megaspores, respectively, is known as gametogenesis.

Microgametogenesis: This refers to the production of male gamete or sperm. During the maturation of pollen, the microspore nucleus divides mitotically to produce a generative and a vegetative or tube nucleus. The pollen is generally released in this binucleate stage. When the pollen lands onto the stigma of a flower, it is known as pollination. Shortly after pollination, the pollen germinates. The pollen tube enters the stigma and grows through the style. The generative nucleus now undergoes a mitotic division to produce two male gametes or sperms. The pollen, along with the pollen tube, is known as microgametophyte. The pollen tube finally enters the ovule through a small pore, micropyle, and discharges the two sperms into the embryo sac.

Megagametogenesis: The nucleus of a functional megaspore divides mitotically to produce four or more nuclei. The exact number of nuclei and their arrangement vary considerably from one species to another. In most of the crop plants, megaspore nucleus undergoes three mitotic divisions to produce eight nuclei. Three of these nuclei move to one pole and produce a central egg cell and two synergid cells; one synergid is situated on either side of the egg cell. Another three nuclei migrate to the opposite pole to give rise to antipodal cells. The two nuclei remaining in the centre, the polar nuclei, fuse to form a secondary nucleus. The megaspore thus develops into a mature megagametophyte or embryo sac. The development of embryo sac from a megaspore is known as megagametogenesis. The embryo sac generally contains one egg cell, two synergids, three antipodal cells (all haploid), and one diploid secondary nucleus.

Sporogenesis

Productions of microspores and megaspores is known as sporogenesis. Microspores are produced in anthers (microsporogenesis), while megaspores are produced in ovules (megasporogenesis).

Microsporogenesis: Each anther has four pollen sacs, which contain numerous pollen mother cells (PMCs). Each PMC undergoes meiosis to produce four haploid cells or microspores. This process is known as microsporogenesis. The microspores mature into pollen grains mainly by a thickening of their walls.

Megasporogenesis: Megasporogenesis occurs in ovules, which are present inside the ovary. A single cell in each ovule differentiates into a megaspore mother cell. The megaspore mother cell undergoes meiosis to produce four haploid megaspores. Three of the megaspores degenerate leaving one functional megaspore per ovule. This completes megasporogenesis.

2. (*b*) Photoperiodism

The circadian clock enables organisms to determine the time of day at which a particular molecular or biochemical event occurs. Photoperiodism, or the ability of an organism to detect day length, makes it possible for an event to occur at a particular time of year, thus allowing for a seasonal response. Circadian rhythms and photoperiodism have the common property of responding to cycles of light and darkness.

Precisely at the equator, day length and night length are equal and constant throughout the year. As one moves away from the equator toward the poles, the days become longer in summer and shorter in winter. Not surprisingly, plant species have evolved to detect these seasonal changes in day length, and their specific photoperiodic responses are strongly influenced by the latitude from which they originated.

Photoperiodic phenomena are found in both animals and plants. Plant responses controlled by day length are numerous, including the initiation of flowering, asexual reproduction, the formation of storage organs, and the onset of dormancy. Perhaps all plant photoperiodic responses utilize the same photoreceptors, with subsequent specific signal transduction pathways regulating different responses. Because it is clear that monitoring the passage of time is essential to all photoperiodic responses, a timekeeping mechanism must underlie both the time-of-year and the time-of-day responses. The circadian oscillator is thought to provide an endogenous time-measuring mechanism that serves as a reference point for the response to incoming light (or dark) signals from the environment.

Vernalization

Many species, especially many biennial and perennial are induced or promoted to flower by low temperature. Lysenko (1938) used term vernalization for a low temperature promotion of flowering in plants. The low temperature requirement for flowering was first noticed by Klippart in 1857 while working with two varieties of wheat—the winter wheat and the spring wheat. The winter wheat is sown in winter and produces flower in summers. The spring wheat is sown in the spring and produces flower in summers. He observed that if the germinated seeds of winter wheat are treated with low temperature they can behave as spring wheat. He concluded that winter wheat require low temperature (0-5°C) for subsequent flowering, the phenomenon known as vernalization.

Vernalization is the process whereby flowering is promoted by a cold treatment given to a fully hydrated seed (*i.e.*, a seed that has imbibed water) or to a growing plant. Dry seeds do not respond to the cold treatment. Without the cold treatment, plants that require vernalization show delayed flowering or remain vegetative. In many cases, these plants grow as rosettes with no elongation of the stem.

Winter annuals, such as the winter forms of cereals (which are sown in the fall and flower in the following summer), respond to low temperature very early in their life cycle. They can be vernalized before germination if the seeds have imbibed water and become metabolically active. Other plants, including most biennials (which grow as rosettes during the first season after sowing and flower in the following summer), must reach a minimal size before they become sensitive to low temperature for vernalization. The effective temperature range for vernalization is from just below freezing to about 10°C, with a broad optimum usually between about 1 and 7°C (Lang, 1965). The effect of cold increases with the duration of the cold treatment until the response is saturated. The response usually requires several weeks of exposure to low temperature, but the precise duration varies widely with species and variety.

Vernalization can be lost as a result of exposure to devernalizing conditions, such as high temperature, but the longer the exposure to low temperature, the more permanent the vernalization effect. Vernalization appears to take place primarily in the shoot apical meristem. Localized cooling causes flowering when only the stem apex is chilled, and this effect appears to be largely independent of the temperature experienced by the rest of the plant. Excised shoot tips have been successfully vernalized, and where seed vernalization is possible, fragments of embryos consisting essentially of the shoot tip are sensitive to low temperature.

2. (*c*) Isolation in Seed Plots

The crop raised for seed production should be separated from field of the same crop species by a minimum distance, which varies from one crop to the other. This distance is known as the isolation distance. Isolation is essential to prevent pollination from unwanted pollen in the case of cross pollinated species and to avoid mechanical mixtures and chance of cross pollination in self pollinated species. The isolation distance varies from 3 m in self-pollinated crops like rice, wheat etc. to 400 m in case of hybrid maize. Maintaining isolation is often difficult for farmers for various reasons. In such case, isolation distance may considerably be reduced by planting border rows or by harvesting seed from the central part of the plot and leaving surrounding crops of minimum isolation distance, declaring non-seed will serve the purpose. A larger field for seed production is better than a smaller plot in relation to maintain isolation, distance.

Roughing in Seed Plots

Roughing is the removal of plants which are off-type that is phenotypically different from the plants of the variety under production. It is an important aspect of seed production and is necessary to prevent out-crossing and mechanical mixtures.

The off-type plants are to be regularly removed from the field either by uprooting or by cutting at the ground level.

2. (*d*) Hybrids involving different species of the same genus are called interspecific hybridization (also called intra-generic). Common examples include Mule (male donkey × female horse), Hinny (male horse × female donkey), Liger (male lion × female tiger). Note that in mules and hinnies, the common genus the parents belong to is Equus and in liger, its Panthera.

Hybrids involving different genera are called intergeneric hybridization. Examples include Sheep-Goat hybrid (*Ovis aries* × *Capra hircus*), Mule (*European goldfinch* × *Domestic canary*), Cama (male dromedary camel × female Llama).

Intervarietal, also called intraspecific hybridization is when the hybrid is between parents of the same species but belonging to different populations, breeds or cultivars.

Intervarietal hybridization involves parents of same species as in the most common hybridization we know.

Interspecific hybridization means hybridization between two parents from different species. For ex-cross between lion and tiger. Both belong to the genus Panthera.

Intergeneric hybridization means cross between parents of different genus as in a cross between a cat and a dog. Cat belongs to Felis genus and dog belongs to Canis genus.

Inter generic hybrids are rare.

Horse × Donkey = mule (sterile).

Human × Chimpanzee = no viable off spring.

Inter specific – well we all are inter specific Homo sapiens male × Homo sapiens female "Varieties" or "Cultivars" are below species level. These are the terms of breeders/ professional. There is a tendency to preserve varieties by selfing and other means. Varieties can howerever cross breed. *Triticum aestivum* var kharcha 65 × *T. aestivum* HD 2329 will produce a fertile wheat plant.

SECTION 'B'

5. (*a*) Flowers are highly perishable unlike other horticultural or agricultural crops. Owing to poor keeping quality, the post-harvest losses in floriculture are significantly higher than any other sector. Although there has been significant increase in the area, production and productivity of flower crops in the last two decades, there is an urgent need to minimize the huge post-harvest losses in terms of the value of the produce which are estimated to be 30-40 per cent of farm value.

The post-harvest behaviour of flowers is an outcome of the physiological processes, occurring in leaves, stem, flower bud, leafless peduncle or scape connecting bud to the stem. Some of these processes may act independently to affect the senescence and vase life of cut flowers but most of them are inter-related. The nature and extent of post-harvest damage in cut flowers is typical for each crop and/or cultivar. The post-harvest losses become important especially when dealing with the export of fresh flowers to distant and foreign market. Therefore, patient, soft and expert handling of flowers is of utmost importance after harvest.

The harvest quality of flowers depends upon mainly three factors:

1. Pre-Harvest Factors

Genetic or inherent makeup: Post-harvest lasting quality of flower species and cultivars vary considerably due to differences in their genetic make-up. Gladiolus varieties White Prosperity, Sancerre, Suchitra, Eurovision, Nova Lux, Rose Supreme and Trader Horn possess the better vase-life.

Growing conditions: Most cut flower crops require well-lighted conditions. On the contrary, too high light intensities cause scorching and dropping of leaves and abscission of petals. Flower crops are also specific in their temperature requirements. Flowers also require adequate nutrients for good longevity. High nitrogen doses should be avoided as they increase susceptibility to diseases. For example, iron deficiency is commonly observed in gladiolus in north India, causing heavy yield losses. Flowering crop should also be grown away from the industries which release toxic effluent, gases, damaging the foliage as well as flowers. Flowers damaged by pathogens, insects and pests also show high ethylene production resulting in poor vase-life.

2. Harvest Factors

The most important factors for harvest are when, how and where.

"When" the plant material will reach the optimum stage of development and when, during the day, to harvest. Each plant material has its own best harvest stage and this can vary depending on the use and market for the plant material. Materials for preserving usually are harvested more mature than those for fresh, wholesale markets. Some general rules of thumb for when to harvest are: spike type flowers—harvest when one-fourth to one-half of the individual florets are open, daisy type flowers—harvest when flowers are fully open. Further, the best time of day for harvesting flowers is the coolest part of the day and when there is no surface water from dew or rain on the plants.

Right stage, method and time of harvesting of flowers are of considerable importance to ensure their long vase-life. The stems should be cut with sharp knives or secateurs. Hardwood stems should always be given slanting cut to expose maximum surface are to ensure rapid water absorption. The flowers of dahlia and poinsettia release latex upon cutting. To overcome such problem, stems should be given a dip in hot water (80-90° C) for a few seconds.

The flowers of rose, carnation, gladiolus, tuberose, daffodils, lily, iris, freesia and tulip should be harvested at bud stage since their buds continue to open in water.

The flowers of snapdragon, harvesting of flowers at bud stage is always preferred as their buds have long vase-life, are less sensitive to ethylene, easy to handle during storage and transport and are less prone to diseases and pests.

3. Post-Harvest Factors

Water relations: The termination of life of the harvested flowers depends on water uptake and transport, water loss and the capacity of the flower tissue to retain its water. A water deficit and wilting develops when the transpiration exceeds absorption of water. The rate of water uptake of cut flowers depends on transpiration pull, temperature and composition of solutes. Disruption of water columns in stem vessels by air embolism and resistance to water flow in stems, also develop water deficit condition. Acidification of water and addition of wetting agent and flower food in the holding solution markedly improve water uptake of cut flowers.

Respiration: The rate of respiration depends on quantity of carbohydrates available in the harvested flowers, temperature and the use of certain chemicals to regulate it. With higher temperature, there is faster rate of respiration and burning of the tissue. Consequently, the life of flowers is shortened.

Relative humidity: It has bearing on the transpiration rate. Higher the humidity in the air, less is the transpiration rate and vice-versa.

Growth regulators: Post-harvest life of flowers can be controlled by growth regulators. Water relation changes associated with flower senescence are also influenced by growth regulators. Cytokinins delay senescence of some cut flowers. Depending upon the concentrations, GA in some cases promotes longevity of flowers, while this is also used in bud opening solution. The IAA promotes ethylene production of isolated carnation petals. In contrast, the senescence and abscission of poinsettia flowers is delayed by auxin.

Preservative solutions: Preservatives in the form of tablets or powder are prepared from a mixture of chemicals-sugars, germicides, salts and growth regulators. Various types of conditioners are sugar and biocide, antiethylene compound, and hydrated compound. The flowers like gladiolus, carnation, chrysanthemum and freesia are benefitted most by the pre-treatment. Antiethylene compounds in preservative solutions reduce the action of ambient ethylene as well as autocatalytic production of ethylene by fresh cut flowers. Fresh cut flowers responding to silver thiosulphate are carnation, orchids, gypsophila, gladiolus, gerbera, snapdragon, alstromaeria, agapanthus, anemone and sweet pea. Greatest improvement in cut flower quality and longevity is obtained when DICA or DDMH were combined with sucrose.

Precooling and storage: Precooling is essential for removing field heat from flowers. This is done either by forced air cooling or hydrocooling to bring down temperature from 200-300°C to 10°C in a relatively short period. Other methods are room cooling and vacuum cooling. Flowers can be stored for a longer period at low temperature. There are two methods of cold storage—wet and dry. Wet method is short-term storage, in which cut stems are dipped in water. Dry storage is more labour-intensive method and costly. The controlled atmosphere based on reduction of respiration rates, conservation of respirable substrates during storage, and delay in ethylene-triggered changes cause senescence. It involves the use of increased level of CO_2 and decreased levels of O_2 in the atmosphere, low storage temperature and prevention of the build-up of endogenous ethylene.

Packing and transporting: Packaging ensures garden fresh of flowers to the consumers. Lower rate of transpiration, respiration and cell division during transportation, are essential for long storage life and keeping quality. Before packing, flowers should be dried. They should be treated with systemic insecticides and miticides. Packing must ensure protection of flowers against physical damage, water loss and external conditions detrimental to transported flowers. Boxes made of corrugated fibre boards are good. Flowers sensitive to geotropic bending must be transported in an upright position. The flowers should be transported at an optimal low temperature. The relative humidity of the air during pre-cooling and shipment of cut flowers should be maintained at the level of 95-98%. Lack of light during prolonged transportation particularly at high temperature causes yellowing of leaves in many flowers. Shipment of flowers is usually done by truck, air and sea. For short distance and time period shorter than 20 hr, cut flowers may be transported in insulated trucks without refrigeration after pre-cooling and proper packing. Air shipment is quickest and usually the temperature is not controlled during the flight. The flowers should be pulsed with STS prior to air shipment.

5. (*b*) Drying, Dehydration and Concentration of Fruits and Vegetables

Removal of moisture by applying heat is called "Drying". Dehydration is drying by artificial heating under controlled temperature, humidity and air flow. The basic drying processes are classified as sun drying, atmospheric dehydration and vacuum dehydration. Sun drying is still in use. These methods are accompanied by removing water. Moisture may be removed from foods by any of the methods.

Dehydrating (below 5%) moisture helps to preserve nutritive value of the product although heat-labile vitamin losses are more. Low moisture preserved material can be fortified with vitamins under proper storage conditions. The dried products have more shelf life in properly packed and stored.

Retention of nutrients and overall quality is better in modern methods of dehydration such as freeze drying, vacuum drying, osmotic or solar dehydration as there are little changes in physio-chemical composition.

Sun drying of fruits and vegetables is practiced by solar energy widely in tropical and sub-tropical regions. In indirect solar drying, the fruits and vegetables are spread on trays, which are kept in a close compartment or cabinet drier. In solar drier, the air is heated by direct sunrays and carried to the drier from bottom and goes out from the top of chimney. The drying conditions are influenced by the temperature and velocity of the air flow. These solar driers may be with chimney or with amber coloured glass. For drying fruits and vegetables at home, the home drier is ideal.

5. (*c*) Major Insect Pests of Tomato

Tomatoes are subject to attack by a large number of insect pests from the time plants first emerge in the seed bed until harvest. Aphids, flea beetles, leafminers, and spider mites threaten young plant-bed tomatoes. In the field, flea beetles, aphids, leafminers, stink bugs, and fruitworms cause minimal damage to the foliage. However, severe damage may result either from their feeding on the fruit or by spreading certain diseases.

Greenhouse tomatoes have many of the same pests as field tomatoes. Tiny pests such as aphids, whiteflies, leafminers, and spider mites are more likely to infest greenhouse crops than beetles, grubs, or caterpillars. Occasionally, moths enter through holes in screens or fans and lay eggs in the greenhouse. Even in screened greenhouses, armyworms, fruitworms, and loopers may be brought into the greenhouses on plants.

Tomato Pest Control

BT Organic Insect Control for Your Tomatoes

Kill Bad Bugs using natural methods

How would you like to kill bugs BEFORE they have a chance to kill your plants?

If that sounds good to you, keep reading because we've got exactly what you're looking for.

How to Identify Tomato Pests

Don't let these pests destroy your plants! Home tomato growers across the country face a variety of insect pests that will eat the plants, damage the fruit and leave the plant vulnerable to disease.

You should know about the tomato pests that can kill your plants before you get your first tomato so that you know what to look for and can stop the destruction before it starts!

Root-Knot Nematodes

Have you ever pull up a troubled plant and found knots on the roots? Most likely root-knot nematodes are the root of your problems.

Nematodes are microscopic roundworms that live in the dirt. Many of them are actually beneficial and are used to control pests including grubs, fleas, aphids, beetles, fungus gnats and other pests that inhabit the soil.

Beneficial Insects for Tomato Plants

Before you reach for the broad spectrum insecticides remember that not all insects are bad. In fact only 2% of the insect population is destructive and some insects are really good because they feast on the "bad insects." Many insecticides will kill those good bugs and leave your garden vulnerable to a re-infestation of crop destroying critters.

BT (Bacillus thuringiensis) for Natural Pest Control

Many of the pests that make a meal out of your tomato plants can be controlled by the judicious use of BT *(Bacillus thuringiensis).* BT, which is actually a microbial disease, is not toxic to people, animals, birds or even beneficial insects. It biologically targets tomato plant destroying pests including army worms, loopers, and the dreaded tomato hornworm. The larvae of the pest eats the BT, the spores dissolve releasing toxins into the bloodstream, the toxins multiply and the pest is poisoned. Thus, you have a safe and natural "pesticide" which does not harm your tomatoes or the surrounding environment.

Integrated Pest Management for Tomato Plants

Too often home gardeners reach for chemical controls without really knowing what they are and if they are really necessary. Integrated Pest Management (IPM) was developed to provide an environmental friendly way to control pests.

5. ***(d)*** The Tetrazolium Chloride (TZ) test is often called the quick germination test. It's a chemical test used to determine seed viability, and results are usually available within 24 to 48 hours.

The TZ test can give you an early and quick snapshot of seed viability but is not a replacement for the more comprehensive seed germination test.

In Canada, the TZ test is not officially recognized by the CFIA (except for western wheatgrass where the TZ result may be added to the germination for a final germination total). In the United States, the TZ test can be used as a replacement for a germination test, although a follow-up germination test is usually recommended.

This test has a long history. Early research and development done by Professor Dr. Georg Lakon, Dr. Helene Blat and professor Dr. W. Lindenbein, led to the formation of the tetrazolium committee with the International Seed Testing Association (ISTA) in 1950.

In 1974, Professor R.P. Moore became chairman of the committee. In 1983 he presented a handbook to the ISTA Congress in Ottawa, which has become the standard that all official seed laboratories use.

Advantages of the TZ test are:

A rapid evaluation of seed viability.

Detect seed weaknesses before they become evident in germination tests.

Timely guidance in quality control programs.

5. (*e*) Sitophilus oryzae

The adults are around 2 mm long with a long snout. The body colour appears to be brown/black, but on close examination, four orange/red spots are arranged in a cross on the wing covers. It is easily confused with the similar looking maize weevil, but there are several distinguishing features.

Adult rice weevils are able to fly, and can survive for up to two years. Females lay 2-6 eggs per day and up to 300 over their lifetime. The female uses strong mandibles to chew a hole into a grain kernel after which she deposits a single egg within the hole, sealing it with secretions from her ovipositor. The larva develops within the grain, hollowing it out while feeding. It then pupates within the grain kernel and emerges 2-4 days after eclosion.

An adult emerges from inside a grain of rice

Male S. orzyae produce an aggregation pheromone ((4S,5R)-5-Hydroxy-4-methyl-heptan-3-one) to which males and females are drawn. A synthetic version is available which attracts rice weevils, maize weevils and grain weevils. Females produce a pheromone which attracts only males.

Control of weevils involves locating and removing all potentially infected food sources. Rice weevils in all stages of development can be killed by freezing infected food below –17.7°C (0°F) for a period of three days, or heating to 60°C (140°F) for a period of 15 minutes.

Rhyzopertha dominica (Fabricius)

Adults 2-3 mm long, body reddish-brown and shiny, cylindrical, head not visible from above. Pronotum tuberculate and elytra with punctate, parallel-sided striations. Larvae whitish with a brown head, thoracic segments broad, posteriorly narrow, elderly larvae with head and thorax recurved ventrally, about 5 mm long.

The females lay 200-500 eggs on grains. The larvae initially feed on frass and then on cereal seeds and on foods and animal feed, and can bore into intact kernels. At 34°C complete development requires about 3 weeks and humidity content of above 9%. The pest cannot develop below 20°C or above 38-40°C. The adults, which are good flyers, can live for several months. The males produce a pheromone that attracts both genders.

This borer is a major pest of stored products throughout the tropics, sub-tropics, Australia and the USA. Due to the trade in products and its ability for prolonged flights it also occurs in temperate countries. The pest feeds mostly on stored cereal seeds as well as on beans, ginger, cassava chips, biscuits and many others. The feeding of larvae and adults reduce grain weight, causing losses of up to 40%, and can turn rice to dust. Damaging the seed germ reduces germination rates and may be followed by secondary pests and fungi. However, R. dominica often occurs along with other stored food pests, thus it is difficult to evaluate its individual damage and the accompanying control costs.

7. (a) Back cross

In back cross, F1 hybrid is crossed back with any of the parent, either dominant or recessive. Back crosses are used to increase useful traits in a population. For example, certain crop plant hybrids are backcrossed with wild species to obtain its useful traits such as disease resistance. However, this process may dilute the other useful traits of hybrid. In order to overcome this disadvantage, hybrids are backcrossed repeatedly with its parent plants over few generations to receive their good traits back into the new hybrids.

Test cross

In test cross, F1 hybrid is crossed back with the recessive parent. In other words, test cross is the cross between a dominant phenotype (TT or Tt) and a homozygous recessive (tt). **Mendel** was the first person to perform the test cross to identify whether an individual is heterozygous or homozygous for dominant character. Other than discovering heterozygosity, test cross is also useful to check the purity of the gametes produced by parents.

If homozygous dominant F1 hybrid (TT) is crossed with the recessive parent, it will always result receive 100% heterozygous tall hybrids.

If heterozygous dominant F1 hybrid (Tt) is test crossed with the recessive parent, only 50% will be tall and the rest 50% will be dwarf.

Major difference between Test cross and Back cross

All test crosses are considered as backcrosses, but all backcrosses are not the test crosses.

During backcross, F1 hybrid is crossed back with any of the parents, either homozygous or heterozygous. However, during test cross, F1 hybrid is always crossed back with the recessive parent.

7. (b) Rhizobial Inoculants

Legumes have the ability to form a mutually beneficial (symbiotic) relationship with certain soil bacteria of the type or genus Rhizobia. These bacteria can take nitrogen from the air and make it available to the plant. Legumes have the ability to form a mutually beneficial (symbiotic) relationship with certain soil bacteria of the type or genus Rhizobia. The benefit to the plant, and thus to the grower, is that these bacteria can take (fix) nitrogen from the air (in soil spaces) and make it available to the plant via symbiotic nitrogen fixation. The amount of nitrogen fixed can meet the needs of the plant and leave nitrogen in the soil.

Microbial Toxins

Microbial toxins are toxins produced by micro-organisms, including bacteria and fungi. Microbial toxins promote infection and disease by directly damaging host tissues and by disabling the immune system. Some bacterial toxins, such as Botulinum neurotoxins, are the most potent natural toxins known. However, microbial toxins also have important uses in medical science and research. Potential applications of toxin research include combating microbial virulence, the development of novel anticancer drugs and other medicines, and the use of toxins as tools in neurobiology and cellular biology.

7. (c) Surface Treatment and Fumigation

Fumigation is a method of pest control that completely fills an area with gaseous pesticides—or fumigants—to suffocate or poison the pests within. It is used to control pests in buildings (structural fumigation), soil, grain, and produce, and is also used during processing of goods to be imported or exported to prevent transfer of exotic organisms. This method also affects the structure itself, affecting pests that inhabit the physical structure, such as woodborers and drywood termites.

Process

Fumigation generally involves the following phases: First the area intended to be fumigated is usually covered to create a sealed environment; next the fumigant is released into the space to be fumigated; then, the space is held for a set period while the fumigant gas percolates through the space and acts on and kills any infestation in the product, next the space is ventilated so that the poisonous gases are allowed to escape from the space, and render it safe for humans to enter. If successful, the fumigated area is now safe and pest free.

Tent fumigation (tenting)

Structural fumigation techniques differ from building to building, but in houses a rubber (usually the tent is made of plastic/pvc coated canvas material) tent(s) are often placed over the entire house while the pesticides are being released into the vacant residence.

This process is called tent fumigation or "tenting". The sealed tent concentrates the poisonous gases and prevents them from escaping into the neighbourhood. The process can take up to a week depending on the fumigant used, which is in turn dependent on the temperature and the pest.

Chemicals

Methyl bromide was among the most widely used fumigants until its production and use was restricted by the Montreal Protocol due to its role in ozone depletion.

Widely used fumigants include:

1,3-dichloropropene

dazomet (methyl isothiocyanate precursor)

chloropicrin

DBCP (banned worldwide)

formaldehyde

hydrogen cyanide

iodoform

methyl isocyanate

phosphine

sulphuryl fluoride

Safety

Fumigation is a hazardous operation. Generally it is a legal requirement that the operator who carries out the fumigation operation holds official certification to perform the fumigation as the chemicals used are toxic to most forms of life, including humans.

- Post-operation ventilation of the area is a critical safety aspect of fumigation. It is important to distinguish between the pack or source of the fumigant gas and the environment which has been fumigated. While the fumigant pack may be safe and spent, the space will still hold the fumigant gas until it has been ventilated.

7. (*d*) Germination and Dormancy

The embryo, contained within the seed, is the next generation of plant. Thus successful seed germination is vital for a species to perpetuate itself. Germination commences when the dry seed, shed from its parent plant, takes up water (imbibition), and is completed when the embryonic root visibly emerges through the outer structures of the seed (usually the seed or fruit coat). Thereafter, there is seedling establishment, utilizing reserves stored within the seed, followed by vegetative and reproductive growth of the plant, supported by photosynthesis.

The seed is metabolically inactive (quiescent) in the mature, dry state and can withstand extremes of drought and cold. For example, dry seeds can be stored over liquid nitrogen at –150 degrees Celsius (–238 degrees Fahrenheit) for many years without harm. Upon hydration of a seed, metabolism commences as water enters its cells, using enzymes and structural components present when the seed was dry. Respiration to provide energy has been observed within minutes of water uptake. Mitochondria that were stored in the dry seed are involved, although initially they are somewhat inefficient because of damage sustained during drying and rehydration. During germination they are repaired and also new organelles are synthesized. Protein synthesis also commences rapidly in the imbibing seed.

Mature seeds of some species are incapable of germinating, even under ideal conditions of temperature and hydration, unless they receive certain environmental stimuli; such seeds are dormant. Breaking of this dormancy may be achieved in several ways, depending upon the species. Frequently, dormancy is lost from seeds as they are stored in the dry state for several weeks to years, a phenomenon called dry after-ripening. But many seeds remain dormant in a fully imbibed state; they are as metabolically active as non-dormant seeds, but yet fail to complete germination. Dormancy of these seeds may be broken by one or more of the following:

1. light, sunlight being the most effective;
2. low temperatures (1 to 5 degrees Celsius [33.8 to 41 degrees Fahrenheit]) for several weeks;
3. day/night fluctuating temperatures of 1 to 10 degrees Celsius (41 to 50 degrees Fahrenheit);
4. chemicals, such as nitrate in the soil, or applied hormones (gibberellins) in the laboratory; and
5. fire.

Dormancy mechanism operate to control the germination of seeds in their natural environment and to optimize the conditions under which the resultant seedling can become established. Dormant seeds that require light will not germinate unless they are close to the soil surface; hence germinated seeds will not expend their stored reserves before they can reach the surface and become photosynthetically independent seedlings.

8. (*a*) Design and Layout of Lawns and Gardens

Besides the landscape gardening the other two familiar terms is gardening *i.e.,* formal and informal gardens.

Formal Gardens : A formal garden is laid out in a symmetrical or geometrical pattern. In formal garden everything is planted in straight lines.

If there is a plant on the left hand side of a straight road, a similar plant must be planted at the opposite on the right hand side.

Informal Gardens : In an informal garden, the whole design looks informal, as the plans and the features are arranged in a natural way without following any hard and fast rules.

However, here also the work has to proceed according to a set and well throughout plan; otherwise the creation will not be artistic and attractive. The reason behind it is to imitate nature.

Wild Garden : It is a recent style of gardening, namely, wild gardening.

Wild garden was expounded by William Robinson in the last decade of the nineteenth century.

The famous garden style of India the "Mughal Gardens" are nothing but a replica of the ancient Persian Gardens.

Different Features of a Garden

Garden Walls : From safety or beauty point of view it may be necessary to erect a brick, concrete or stone wall along the periphery of the garden.

A compromise is to have a low brick or concrete or stone wall of say 60-90 cm height to put over it some grills, so that the view is not totally obscured from outside.

Fencing : Fences are a utility item essentially needed for making the boundary and for protection.

Fences are also put to separate one part of the garden from the other. Materials such as wood, bamboo, wire, wire nettings and chain-link fences may be used for the purpose.

Steps : Sometimes steps become necessary to have steps in garden, as for example, when a path goes from one level to the other or one has to climb or get down from the terrace garden.

Steps can be made of various materials like concrete, stone, wood, gravel etc.

Garden Drives and Paths

A garden must have a carriage drive leading to the house and garage besides several other paths or walks leading to different parts of the garden.

A good garden drive or path is to provide a flat, dry and good passage for persons/ vehicles. Garden path are generally made of gravel, paving-stones, crazy-paying, bricks or grass.

Hedge

A hedge is a line of closely spaced shrubs and tree species planted and trained to form a barrier or to mark the boundary of an area. Hedges used to separate a road from adjoining fields or one field from another, and of sufficient age to incorporate larger trees are known as hedge grows.

Edging

Edging is lining of borders of flower beds, paths, lawn and shrubbery with brick, concrete, living plants etc.

Edging may be formal, made of stone, bricks, tiles, etc. informal edges consisting of living plants.

Arches

Arches are supports provided for climbers. It should be at least two meter height and one meter wide. The breadth depends upon the paths over which it is constructed but should not be less than one meter. Arches may be made of wood, metal, stones or concrete structures.

Arches are generally constructed near the gate or over paths in the garden. An arch should be at least 2 to 2.5 m high and the portions above may be painted green.

Pergolas

It may be defined as a series of arches joined together. Pergolas are generally constructed over pathway, which add beauty to a garden. A pergola is a useful resting place during the summer months in a tropical country. The path below remains cool to the creepers growing above.

Topiary

Topiary is the horticultural practice of training live perennial plants by clipping the foliage and twigs of trees, shrubs and sub-shrubs to develop and maintain clearly defined shaped, perhaps geometric or fanciful.

It is an art of trimming plants into different shapes *i.e.,* birds, animals, domes, umbrella etc.

Rock garden

Rock and soils are arranged in such a fashion that condition is created for the growth of different plants.

A rock garden is artificial in the sense that it is man-made. But a well prepared and well managed rock garden should become one of the most attractive and interesting features of the garden.

Carpet bed

The term carpet bedding means covering an area, preferably a bed or a series of beds, with dense low, growing herbaceous plants according to a set design carpet beddings look better when arranged in a slope or a slanting.

Carpet bed can often utilized for creating figures or letters (*e.g.* Swastika (卐) or a wheel (⊕) or other designs like a map of country or a state *etc.*) are cutout with the help of plants having different growth habits or having different coloured leaves.

Flower beds

The flower beds can be planted with winter flowering annuals sown during September-October or summer flowering ones sown during February-March and rainy season flowers sown during April-June.

Idea of creating flower beds in the garden is to display the flowers in the best way as possible. The shape of flowerbed should be simple designs such as circles, rectangles, squares, ellipses are easier to maintain.

Shrubbery

Growing of shrubs is a group is known as shrubbery. If it should be properly selected, the shrubs in the shrubbery will provide flowers throughout the year.

More suitable places for the shrubbery in the garden are centre part and corner of the garden.

Borders

It is defined as beds, which are more in length than breadth and contain plants of heterogeneous character.

Borders are of three types *i.e.,* herbaceous border, annual mixed border and mixed border.

Arbour

It is a hut like structure having more than eight entrances. It acts as resting place for visitors.

Suitable place of construction of arbour is preferably highest part of the garden so that visitors can see overall structure and beauty of garden.

Garden Bridges

Garden bridges are necessity item is a garden to cross the stream or pond and it should be developed harmoniously with landscape.

Garden bridges are made up of stone, wood or concrete materials. The shape, size, and materials of the bridge depend upon the type of water barrier it is to transverse.

Bonsai

Bonsai is a Japanese art form using miniature trees grown in containers. The word *bonsai* is often used in English as an umbrella term for all miniature trees in containers or pots.

It is an art of growing trees, plant proportionately in smaller containers occasionally in combination with rocks of many forms, by treating them with certain technique in order to reproduce in miniature appearances found in nature.

Lawn

A lawn is an area of soil covered land planted with grasses or rarely other durable plants such as clover which are maintained at a short height with a lawnmower and used for aesthetic and recreational purposes.

Lawn is also called as green carpet. Lawn may be defined as a piece of land thickly covered with uniformly green soft grass. It is like a cushion velvet carpet giving pleasure both to sight and feeling. Lawn-mower was invented by Edwin Budding in 1930 in England.

8. (*b*) Food is any substance consumed to provide nutritional support for the body. It is usually of plant or animal origin, and contains essential nutrients, such as fats, proteins, vitamins, or minerals. The substance is ingested by an organism and assimilated by the organism's cells to provide energy, maintain life, or stimulate growth.

Food Production and Consumption Trends in India

As per the 2010 FAO World agriculture statistics, India is the world's largest producer of many fresh fruits and vegetables, milk and major spices. India is the second largest producer of wheat and rice, the world's major food staples. The details of production and procurement of food grains are summarised as under.

Recommended Dietary Intakes of Nutrients for Indians

Group	Particulars	Calories	Proteins (g)	Calcium (mg)	Iron (mg)	Vitamin A retinol (mg)	Thiamin (mg)	Riboflavin (mg)	Niacin (mg)	Ascorbic acid (mg)	Vitamin I.U.
Man	Sedentary work	2400						1.2	1.4	16	
	Moderate work	2800	55g	400 -500	24	750	3000	1 .4	1.7	19	40
	Heavy work	3900						2.0	2.3	26	
Woman	Sedentary work	1900						1.0	1.1	13	
	Moderate work	2200	45g	400 -500	32	750	3000	1.1	1.3	15	40
	Heavy work	3000						1.5	1.8	20	
	Pregnancy										
	II half	+300	+14	—	40	750	3000	+0.2	+0.2	+2	40
	Lactation -		+25	1150	32	1150	4600	+0.3	+0.4	+5	80
	0-6 months	+550						+0.2			
	7-12 months	+400		500 -600	1 mg /kg	400	—	59 mcg/ kg	71 mcg/ kg	780 mcg/ kg	
Infants	0-6 months	118/kg	2.0/kg		300	1200	54 mcg/ kg	65 mcg/ kg	780 mcg/ kg	20	200
	0-12 months	108/kg	1.7/kg								
Children		1 year		17							
		2 years	1220	18							
		3 years		20	400- 500	15-20	250	1000	0.6	0.7	8
		4-6 years	1720	22							
		7-9 years	2050	33			300	1200	0.9	1.0	11
	Boys										
	10-12 years	2420	41			400	1600	1.0	1.2	14	
	Girls										
	10-12 years	2260				600	2400	1.2	1.5	16	
Adole- scents	13-15 yrs.										
	Boys	2500	55	600-700	25			1.1	1.4	15	40
	Girls	2200	50		35	—	3000	1.4	1.7	19	
	16-18 yrs.										
	Boys	2820	60		25	—	3000	1.3	1.6	18	
	Girls	2200	50		35			1.1	1.3	15	

8. (*c*) National Food Policy of India

International Food Policy : According to the report of the International Food Policy Research Institute (1992), Washington, food security is basically defined as access by all people, at all times, to the food, needed for a healthy life. The food security concept thus addresses people's risk of not having access to the required food (*i.e.*, food insecurity). These risks can broadly encompass the major demands of crop production and productivity improvement, efficient public distribution systems, employment generation for poverty alleviation; and last but not the least, household food security ensuring enough food to meet adequate dietary intake of all its members.

The latest estimates of the FAO in its Bulletin published on the state of food in security in the world have indicated that roughly about 826 million people are undernourished-of them, 729 million people in the developing world, and 34 million in the developed world. The report, in analyzing region-wise depth of hunger regime, has critically observed that 'to develop lasting solution to end hunger, it is important to know not only how many people are hungry but how hungry they are'. The daily diets of the 826 million chronically hungry people in the world lack an average intake shortage of 100-400 kilocalories, diminishing their ability to lead an active life.

The greater the depth of this hunger, the greater is the vulnerability to the nutrition-related health risk. The food security, thus in its true sense of the word, as derived from the Latin word 'Secures', means free from care and anxiety and hence implies not only access to but right to food.

8. (*d*) Pulses, which constitute an important part in the daily diet of mostly the vegetarian population, suffer a great damage by insects during storage. In this review, different control measures such as chemical treatment, physical treatment, and biological control of insects in stored pulses are discussed in brief. Chemicals like methyl bromide, malathion, and dichlorvos are being phased out. In these circumstances, new age chemicals like carbonyl sulphide and sulphuryl fluoride are gaining acceptance. Carbon dioxide and biogas generated from cow dung can be used as fumigation measures. Natural products like vegetable oil, inert dusts, plant extracts like essential oils, lectins, proteins, and leaf powders, which have insecticidal and antimicrobial activity, have been used as fumigants for traditional storage worldwide.

Simple technologies like sun drying and repeated sieving can be adopted by small-scale farmers and traders. Maintaining low oxygen, high carbon dioxide, or pure nitrogen atmosphere in the storage environment is also proving to be beneficial preventive methods. Hot air and irradiation are being used, while dielectric heating is still in the stage of development in many of the developed countries for insect control. Developing countries are beginning to consider the use of these methods to control stored product insects.

YOUR SPACE

IFS AGRICULTURE

PAPER-I

1. ECOLOGY

ECOLOGY AND ITS RELEVANCE TO MAN

Ecology

The term ecology comes from two Greek words Oikos (= house of dwelling place) and logos (= study of). Ecology is the study of plants in reciprocal relationship with their environment. Odum (1971) defines "ecology as the study of structure and function of ecosystem".

The two aspects of ecology are :

(*i*) **Autoecology :** Ecology of individuals. The interrelationships of individual species and its environment are studied under this sub-division.

(*ii*) **Synecology :** It is the study of inter-reaction between all the living organisms in a natural community.

MAN AND THE BALANCE OF NATURE

The biosphere is a vast ecosystem. All organisms within biosphere interact between themselves and with their environment to keep the system running. Energy flows through the system while materials keep on cycling. The material inputs into the system just equals the output. Thus, a delicate balance is maintained between the biotic and abiotic components and biosphere as a whole, remains in a state of homeostasis. It can adjust to small changes in the balance caused due to natural forces.

Man is a part of this system as a consumer. He is governed by the same laws of nature as other organisms. But unlike others he is a newcomer and is the most intelligent. He is found in all biomes and can reach any part of the biosphere. He has gained extraordinary knowledge and prowess through his brainpower and tool making skill. It has enabled him to alter many aspects of nature for his own comforts. This has created serious environmental problems, which threaten the balance of nature; hence cannot be ignored. These problems result primarily from two factors :

(1) Man's increasing population density, which has placed a tremendous burden on the carrying capacity of total world ecosystem.

(2) The many technological developments that release into the biosphere a variety of undesirable wastes.

As a consequence of these, the life supporting systems of biosphere like air, water and land are getting polluted at an alarming rate. The biogeochemical cycles are disturbed and the natural environment is changing very rapidly. If left unchecked it will make the biosphere inhospitable for man and many other organisms and may lead to mass extinctions. The only way out of this problem is conservation and wise management of our natural resources.

Natural Resources

Natural resources can be defined as– things/materials of nature, that can be put to some use by human beings for their growth, development, and other necessities are called as **"Natural Sources"**.

For example, air, water, soil, forests, animals, minerals, metals, energy and other substances are some examples of natural resources that are utilized by human beings. At present, total global production is nearly enough to match the human demand for energy, materials *etc.*, if we judiciously distribute the resources available to us.

The resources are not equally distributed throughout the world. We can realise the value of resource only when it is rather scarce. Over exploitation threatens most of our natural resources now. All the natural resources can be divided into :

(*i*) Exhaustible natural resources

(*ii*) Inexhaustible natural resources

(i) Exhaustible Natural Resources:

The resources which are consumed or exhausted through continuous use or misuse. **Exhaustible natural resources** can be further divided into two–

(*a*) Renewable natural resources

(*b*) Non-renewable natural resources

(ii) Inexhaustible Natural Resources:

Inexhaustible natural resources are those which can not be exhasuted through continuous use or misuse *e.g.*, air and sunlight etc.

RENEWABLE RESOURCES

The natural resources which are consumed/exhausted/depleted through continuous use and can be recovered by very hard efforts taken up for long periods are called **Renewable Resources,** for *e.g.* soils, forests, groundwater etc. In other words, we can say that all renewable resources are replenished through natural cycles or manually. Forest is maintained themselves and manually. Similarly fresh water is available through cycles and manually too.

Most of the removable resources are interdependent to each other. Forests maintained the environment/climate, plants need to check soil erosion and soil is needed for plants. Air and insects are needed for pollination. Wood, fibre, fodder, fruits, vegetables, milk etc. are developed directly or indirectly by recent photosynthetic activity. Thus the renewal of these resources will continue at as long as photosynthesis continues on this planet. These resources are the life support system which can fulfil all human needs. But its productivity/ renewability is limited or depend upon availability of water, nutrients and environmental conditions.

NON-RENEWABLE RESOURCES

Non-renewable resources are not replenishable or we can not get back our coal and petroleum reserves in our life time, if ones they are consumed/exhausted completely. Non-renewable resources are metals (iron, copper, zinc etc.), coal, oil deposits, minerals, stone, mineral salts (Phosphate, nitrates carbonates etc.) etc.

Coal, petroleum and natural gas are called as *'FOSSIL FUELS'* because they are formed from dead remains of plants and animals buried in the earth long long ago. They are called fuels because they are burnt to give off energy. Coal have a high heating value, hence it is a useful fuel. Since fossil fuels are non-renewable sources of energy, therefore, it is essential to explore more and more alternatives. Today we are utilizing solar energy, wind energy, ocean, geothermal and atomic energy as an alternative sources of energy.

FOREST RESOURCES

India is one of the 10 mega diversity countries, commanding 9% of the world's biodiversity and supporting 17.5% of the major forest types, varying from alpine pastures in the Himalayas to temperate sub tropical, tropical forests and mangroves in the coastal areas. But nearly half of the country's area is degraded, affected by problems of soil degradation and erosion. Sixty per cent forests are located in ecologically sensitive zones. These forests need to be managed in a way to ensure that they are ecologically protected and maintained, as well as sustained at the highest productivity level to meet the growing population's burgeoning demands for fuel, food, fodder and timber.

INDIA

Total land area (thousand ha)	299.419
Total forest area 2007 (thousand ha)% of total land area	66.005/22.9
Natural forest 2007 (thousand ha)	52.385
Total change in forest cover 2002-07 (thousand ha)/annual change (%)	38/0.1
Population total 2007 (million)/ Annual rate of change 2002-07(%)	960.2/1.6
Rural population 2007 (%)	70.6
GNP per person 2005 in US$	340

Source: Forest Survey of 2007.

India has a large and diverse forest resource. Its forest types vary from tropical rainforest in the north-east, to desert and thorn forests in Gujarat and Rajasthan; mangrove forest in West Bengal, Orissa and other coastal areas; and dry alpine forests in the western Himalaya. The most common forest types are tropical moist deciduous forests, tropical dry deciduous forests, and wet tropical evergreen forests.

According to the Forest Survey of 2007, the country has 86.5 million ha of forest. The degraded area was 36.13 million ha and there was another 15.72 million ha of scrub; thus, in total 41.85 million ha of forests were degraded or open.

DEFORESTATION

Deforestation is the loss or continual degradation of forest habitat due to either natural or human related causes. Agriculture, urban sprawl, unsustainable forestry practices, mining, and petroleum exploration all contribute to human caused deforestation. Natural deforestation can be linked to tsunamis, forest fires, volcanic eruptions, glaciation and desertification. The effects of human related deforestation can be mitigated through environmentally sustainable practices that reduce permanent destruction of forests or even act to preserve and rehabilitate disrupted forestland.

The term deforestation is often the source of disagreement between various interest groups. Conservation groups often use broad definition while groups seeking to maintain the status quo often use a narrow definition.

Deforestation defined broadly can include not only conversion to non-forest, but also degradation that reduces forest quality—the density and structure of the trees, the ecological services supplied, the biomass of plants and animals, the species diversity and the genetic diversity. Narrow definition of deforestation is; the removal of forest cover to an extent that allows for alternative land use.

Definitions can also be grouped as those which refer to changes in land cover and those which refer to changes in land use.

Land cover measurements often use a per cent of cover to determine deforestation. This type of definition has the advantage in that large areas can be easily measured, for example from satellite photos.

WATER RESOURCES

Water is a crucial natural resource, its availability greatly influences the health of the people and development potential of the area. Water as a resource in relation to its needs is becoming increasingly scarce. Proper assessment of the availability of this resource from surface and sub surface sources is crucial for its proper planning, development and efficient management.

Water Resources of India

India is a country of vast biological, geographic, and climatic diversity. It has total geographic area of 329 Mha; excluding bodies of water, India's total land area is estimated at 297 Mha.

India is bordered in the north by the 2,500- kilometer long Himalayan Mountains. Melting snow and glaciers provide a continuous flow for numerous rivers running south from the Himalayas into the vast Indo-Gangetic Plain, which is dominated by the Ganges River and its tributaries. Heavy rains are typical in the Himalayas during the monsoon months between June and October, causing frequent floods. Southern India consists largely of the Deccan Plateau, which is flanked by the Western Ghats running along the west coast and the smaller Eastern Ghats on the east coast. The Deccan rivers are rainfed and fluctuate in volume; many of these rivers are not perennial.

India receives average annual precipitation of 4000 km^3, out of which 700 km^3 is immediately lost to the atmosphere, 2150 km^3 soaks into the ground, and 1150 km^3 flows as surface runoff.

India is one of the few countries in the world endowed with abundant land and water resources. Average annual precipitation including snowfall over the country is 4000 billion cubic meters (BCM). In addition, it receives another 200 BCM from rivers flowing in from other countries. Average annual water resources in various river basins are estimated to be 1869 BCM, of which the utilizable volume of water has been estimated to be 1086 BCM including 690 BCM of surface water and 396 BCM of ground water. The rest of the water is lost by evaporation of flows into the sea and goes waste. The utilization of water is expected to be 784 to 843 BCM by the year 2025. Though the present utilization level is only about 50%, the availability of water is highly irregular. It is not available in places of need, at times of need and in required quantities.

In the major part of the country, rainfall is the only sources for water which is available mainly during the monsoon season lasting for less than 3 months. Due to tropical climate and its geographical, location, the country experiences vast spatial and temporal variation in precipitation. About one-third of the country's area is drought prone. The south and western parts comprising the states of Rajasthan, Gujarat and Andhra Pradesh. Madhya Pradesh, Maharashtra, Tamil Nadu and Karnataka are the drought prone states. On the other hand, north and north eastern regions including states of Uttar Pradesh, Bihar, West Bengal and Assam (Asom) are subjected to periodic floodings.

Surface Water : There are twenty river basins in which 12 are major basins having drainage areas of 20,000 km^2. The annual average runoff estimated to be 1952.87 BCM. The storage built up in various river basins through major and medium irrigation projects is about 173.73 BCM. The major and medium irrigation projects under construction and identified would account for 75.42 BCM and 132.3 BCM respectively taking the total to Rs. 381.45 BCM. If minor irrigation structures are included the total storage goes upto 420 BCM. However, it is estimated that about 49.5 BCM and 75.2 BCM capacities of the existing reservoirs will be lost through siltation by the year 2020 and 2025 AD respectively. Total live storage capacity of all reservoirs would be about 462 km^3.

Ground Water Resources : Replenishable ground water resources assessed is of the order of 431.32 BCM and utilisable groundwater resources as 395.6 BCM of which 325.6 BCM is available for irrigation and the rest for domestic and industrial uses (Central Ground Water Board 1995). Thus the total utilisable Ground Water resource amounts to about 92% of potential replenishment.

According to a standard definition for water availability if it falls below 1000 m^3/capita/year water supply begins to hamper health, economic development and human beings resulting in scarcity conditions requiring to take up immediate remedial measures. At less than 500 m^3/capita/year, water supply is primary constraint to life. So many river basins are already facing water stress requiring remedial measures.

According to the initial estimates of the Central Ground Water Board an additional quantity of about 10,081 km^3 of static ground water can be exploited. Generally static water is not regular replenished on annual basis, its one time use is only possible as a short time strategy. Further experience indicates that large scale use of static water or its mining is usually associated with surface settlement which may cause heavy damages to properties of land and soils and may, possibly, trigger seismic activities. Therefore, any appreciable use of static ground water on regular basis, is not foreseen till the middle of the 21st century.

OVER EXPLOITATION OF WATER

The exploitation of groundwater resources more than its annual replenishment has caused the continuous declining of water levels, declining of well yield, drying of shallow wells, deterioration of groundwater quality, sea water intrusion into coastal aquifers and high cost of energy required to lift the water from great depths which becomes uneconomical for poor farmers to continue agriculture.

Though India is blessed with a good water resources, but its distribution over the country is not uniform/proper. Even in the high rainfall areas like Meghalaya and Kerala water scarcity is felt in summer months due to over exploitation of water and mismanagement. There is large amount of rainfall annually flowing out as runoff to sea. The annual replenishment to groundwater resources is getting reduced due to reduction in natural recharge mechanism by man's interaction besides recurring droughts.

There is uneven distribution of water resources coupled with over utilization of groundwater resources has resulted in imbalance between recharge and development. There exists gap between available utilizable water resource and future need of water for the country. Due to over utilization of water, Punjab, Haryana, Tamil Nadu and Gujarat and the states where the water tables have declined steeply. In Gujarat more than 90% wells water table dropped by 0.5 meters to 9.5 meters. In Haryana, the average depth of groundwater is fallen by 1 to 33 cm annually in different parts of the state.

MINERAL RESOURCES

Minerals, being the vital raw material for many basic industries, play an important role in the industrialisation and overall developments of nation. Minerals are the definite chemically bonded substances, created through chemical processes between organic and inorganic matters present in the earth's crust. They may be solid or liquid. Since the prosperity of a nation depend upon the proper use of minerals, hence they should be conserved and should not be misused. Govt., should promote the research in this field of mining minerals.

The history is hundreds year old. Iron, steel, copper, zinc, lead, gold, silver, cobalt etc. metals were extracted from minerals in India. But now, building materials coal, iron ore, mangenese ore, gold, petroleum, natural gas, copper ore, ilmenite, glass sand, lead and zinc ores, chromite, gypsum, dolomite, bauxite etc. are produced from minerals in India. The minerals from metals like bismuth, cadmium, graphite, platinum, tungsten, tin, silver, gold are extracted, are in least quantity.

Types of Minerals

Minerals available in earth crust can be divided into three types :—

1. Metallic minerals,
2. Non-metallic minerals and
3. Mineral fuels

1. Metallic Minerals—We cannot extract metal directly from minerals. There is difference between minerals and ores. Therefore, for extracting metals, minerals are treated by different processes before extraction. Metallic minerals are generally found in combined state. According to availability of metals, metallic minerals are further divided into following three types:—

(a) *Ferrous alloys* : Most common metal (which is used largely) is iron. Other than iron are aluminium, lead, zinc, copper etc. All are found in rich quantities, found in native as well as in combined state. Iron pyrite, lynonite, haematite, magnetite are examples of ferro alloys. Certain other metals, non-metals are contaminated with these as impurities.

(b) *Non-ferrous alloys* : The minerals/alloys of this type contain the metals like titanium, antimony, arsenic, beryllium, copper, zirconium, cerium, lithium etc. These metals are costlier than proceeding metals. Here the iron found as an impurities.

(c) The minerals/alloys containing very least quantity of metals whose extraction is costlier. These metals are generally used in jewellary *e.g.* gold, platinum, silver, etc.

2. Non-metallic Minerals—Minerals, whose yield product are other than metals come in this head. They are called the non-metals. They are further divided on the basis of physical properties and they are found in different parts of the country like Krishna district in Andhra and Mysore in Karnataka.

Bauxite deposits are found in western Jharkhand, southwest Kashmir, Central Tamil Nadu, and parts of Kerala, U.P., Maharashtra and Karnataka.

India also produces third quarters of the world's **mica.** Belts of high quality mica are, Jharkhand, Andhra and Rajasthan. **Gypsum** reserves are in Tamil Nadu and Rajasthan. **Nickel ore** is found in Cuttack and Mayurbanj in Orissa.

Silimanite reserves are in Sonapahar of Meghalaya and in Pipra in M.P. **Copper ore** bearing areas are Agnigundala in Andhra, Singhbhum in Jharkhand, Khetri and Dartiba in Rajasthan and parts of Sikkim and Karnataka.

The Ramagiri field in Andhra, Kolar and Hutti in Karnataka are the important **gold mines.**

The Panna **diamond belt** is the only diamond producing area in the country, which covers the districts of Panna, Chatarput and Satna in Madhya Pradesh, as well as some parts of Banda in Uttar Pradesh.

Petroleum deposits are found in Assam (Asom) and Gujarat. Fresh reserves were located off Mumbai. The potential oil bearing areas are Assam (Asom), Tripura, Manipur, West Bengal, Punjab, Himachal, Kutch and the Andamans.

India also possesses the all valuable and important nuclear **uranium** as well as some varieties of **rare earths.**

A quarter of all mining is carried out in the southern part of Orissa. Gold, silver and diamonds make up a small part of other natural resources available in India. The gemstones are found in Rajasthan. Major portion of the energy in India is generated from coal. It is estimated that India has around 120 billion tons of coal in reserve, enough to last for around 120 years. Huge reserves of the petroleum have been found off the coast of Maharashtra. Gujarat and Madhya Pradesh.

Energy Sources

There are following two types of energy sources:

1. Inexhaustible Energy Sources— These sources are continuously replenished by natural processes. For example, solar energy, wind energy, bio-energy, hydropower etc. These energy systems convert such energy in to a form which we can use. Renewable energy sources are essentially flows of energy. At present total potential of 126000 MW assessed by different non-conventional energy sources.

At present, most important non-conventional energy source is wind energy, for which a capacity of 1800 MW has been set up in the country. There is also a large potential for tapping of ocean energy, geo thermal energy and tidal power, but the techno-economic viability for power generation from these sources has still to be established.

2. Exhaustible Energy Sources— Examples of this are coal, petroleum, natural gas and nuclear power. These are traditional sources available to us. All these sources are limited and takes millions of years for formation. As a result of unlimited use, they will exhaust one day. Therefore, we should conserve these for longer period.

In addition to commercial fuels, coal, oil—natural gas and power. India consumes large quantities of traditional fuels. The traditional energy sector is not well documented. Firewood, dung cake and agricultural wastes constitute the primary source of energy for cooking in over 90 per cent of rural households. These fuels are also used for water heating and space heating. Traditional fuels also comprise an important source of energy in over 30 per cent of ubran households and their use is most prevalent among the lower income categories.

(1) Renewable Energy Sources

Here we will discuss the application potential of commercially viable renewable energy sources are as follows :

Table 1. Renewable Energy Potential in India

Energy Source	*Estimated potential*
Hydropower	86,000 MW
Ocean thermal power	50,000 MW
Wave energy	20,000 MW
Tidal power	10,000 MW
Wind energy	45,000 MW
Solar energy	5×10^{15} kWh/year
Bio-energy	18,000 MW Biomass

***(i)* Solar Energy :** Solar energy is the most readily available and free source of energy since prehistoric times in a most primitive manner. It is estimated that solar energy equivalent to over 15000 times the world's annual commercial energy consumption reaches the earth every year. It is non-polluting helps in lessening green house effect. Solar energy can be utilised through two different routes, as solar thermal route and solar electric route. Solar thermal energy is used for cooking, heating, drying, timber seasoning, distillation electricity generation, cooling, refrigeration, cold storage etc. Solar photovoltaic uses sun's heat to produce electricity for lighting home and building, running motors, pumps, electric appliances, lighting streets, village electrification, powering of remote telecommunication and railway signals etc.

***(ii)* Wind Energy :** Wind energy is basically harnessing of wind power to produce electricity. The kinetic energy of the wind is covered to electrical energy. Since airflow from warmer to cooler regions, this causes, what we call winds and it is these air flows that are harnessed in windmills and wind turbines to produce power. Wind power is not a new development as this power in the form of traditional windmills—for grinding corn, pumping water, sailing ships have been used for centuries. The basic wind energy conversion device is the wind turbine. These turbines are generally of two types—vertical axis wind turbines and horizontal axis wind turbines depending upon the rotation of axis.

Wind electric generators (WEG) convert kinetic energy available in wind to electrical energy by using rotor, gearbox and generator.

India has been rated as one of the most promising countries for wind power development with an estimated potential of 20,000 MW. India ranks fifth in the world in wind power generation. There are 208 wind potential stations in India.

(*iii*) **Hydro Energy :** Potential energy of falling water, captured and converted to mechanical energy by water-wheels, powered the start of the industrial revolution. Wherever sufficient change in elevation could be found, rivers and streams were dammed and mills were built. Water under pressure flows through a turbine causing it to spin. The turbine is connected to a generator, which produces electricity.

In India, the potential of small hydropower is estimated about 10,000 MW. Small hydropower is a reliable, mature and proven technology. It is non-polluting and does not involve setting up of large dams or problems of deforestation, submergence and rehabilitation. Hill regions of India, particularly the Himalayan belts are endowed with rich hydel resources with tremendous potential.

(*iv*) **Bio-Energy :** Biomass is a renewable energy resource divided from the carbonaceous waste of various human and natural activities. It is derived from numerous sources, including the by-products from the wood industry, agricultural crops, raw material from the forest, household wastes etc.

(*v*) **Hydrogen Energy :** Hydrogen is a clean fuel and energy storage medium for various applications. Hydrogen can be produced by biological conversions of various organic effluents like distillary, starch etc. and as by-products in chemical processes.

Hydrogen contained in metal hydrides can be used in vehicles. The centre for Hydrogen energy, Banaras Hindu University has synthesised metal hydrides, graphite nanofibres, which exhibit a very high storage capacity of the order of 40% through catalytic decomposition.

(*vi*) **Tidal and Ocean Energy**

Tidal Energy : Tidal electricity generation involves the construction of a barrage across an estuary to block the incoming and outgoing tide. The head of the water is then used to drive turbines to generate electricity from elevated water in the basin as in hydro electric Dam. A tidal range of at least 7 m is required for economical operation and for sufficient head of water for the turbines.

Ocean Energy : Ocean covers more than 70% of earth surface making them world's largest solar collector. Ocean energy draws on the energy of ocean waves tides or on the thermal energy stored in the ocean. The sun warms the surface water a lot more than the deep ocean water, and this temperature difference stores thermal energy. The ocean contains two types of energy thermal energy from the sun's heat and mechanical energy from the tides and waves.

(*vii*) **Geothermal Energy :** The Earth's population lives between two great sources of energy the hot rocks beneath the surface of the earth and the sun in the sky. Geothermal energy is based on the core of the earth, which is very hot and it is possible to make use of this geothermal energy. These are areas containing volcanoes, hot springs, geysers, and methane, under the water in the oceans and seas.

(2) Lignite

Lignite reserves in the country are estimated to be about 29.72 billion tonnes.

Eighty per cent is located in Tamil Nadu. Lignite is also mainly utilized to produce electricity.

(3) Petroleum and Natural Gas

India's oil and gas reserves are 732 million tonnes and 768 billion cubic metres, respectively (2006). The bulk of oil and natural gas resources are located in offshore areas where exploration, drilling and production are expensive, leading to much higher costs of domestic crude oil and natural gas as compared to imported oil and gas. Exploration for hydrocarbons has so far been limited to onland and shallow water offshore areas.

Deep water exploration has now been included under the New Exploration Licensing Policy (NELP) and these areas were offered through competitive bidding routes. The success of the New Exploration Licensing Policy has been demonstrated by recent findings of natural gas in deep waters. The discoveries in deep water have opened up vast areas for exploration and exploitation but require specialized technologies and large scale investments.

(4) Nuclear Power

The Nuclear power programme in India is based on natural uranium and indigenous thorium reserves. Nuclear power generation started in India in 1969 with the commissioning of Tarapur Atomic Power Plant with a capacity of 2 × 200 and 20 MW based on Boiling Water Reactor (BWR) Technology. This power station is currently under operation and supplies power to the western grid. Subsequent nuclear power projects in India have been based on Pressurized Heavy Water Reactor Technology (PHWR). The first such nuclear project was set up in Rajasthan with external assistance from Canada. Subsequently, this plant has been fully indigenized and further developed. At present Pressurized Heavy Water Reactors are in operation in Kalpakkam near Chennai, at Narora in Uttar Pradesh, and Kakrapara in Gujarat, all of them being totally indigenous.

Available reserves of natural uranium can support a nuclear programme of 10,000 MW based on Pressurized Heavy Water Reactor Technology. The Nuclear Power Programme in India is under the control of Department of Atomic Energy and its Nuclear Power Corporation. The current nuclear capacity is 2225 MW based on BWR/PHWR technology and constitutes 2.65 per cent of the total installed capacity.

COMMERCIAL ENERGY SOURCES

Commercial as well as non-conventional energy sources, are converted to electricity which is the most convenient and favoured secondary energy source. The main sources of electricity production in the country are coal, hydropower, natural gas, nuclear energy and renewable energy sources, which are as follows :—

Coal

Coal reserves in the country comprise about 192 billion tonnes (2006). About 85 per cent of the coal reserves are non-cooking coal, the rest being cooking coal. Coal reserves are unevenly distributed in the country, with the bulk reserves located in the eastern states of Jharkhand, West Bengal and Orissa. Central India, including Madhya Pradesh, Chhattisgarh and Andhra Pradesh, also possess sizeable coal reserves of the order of 22 per cent of the total.

Soil

The word *"SOIL"* is derived from the latin word *"SOLUM"* meaing ground. Here, the word soil is used in a strictly scientific sense. Soil is defined as a thin layer of earth's crust which serves as a natural medium for the growth of plants. Soil is formed by weathering process of parental material rocks. Soil differs from parental material in the morphological, physical, chemical and biological properties.

Generally it is said that, it is a mixture of mineral constituents and of organic matter, which later consists, more or less of the decomposed residues of plant materials and to a lesser extent of animal remains and excreta.

There are various types of soils like red, black, yellow, alluvial etc. Depth of soil is variable and it differs in texture like coarse, find, soils serve as reservoirs of nutrients and soil's flora. The most characteristic constituents of soil are the colloidal organic matter and colloidal clay. Soil organic matter and particles conserve soil moisture for crops, plantation, soil living organisms. Soil provides even mechanical anchorage and favourable tilth. The components of the soil are mineral material, organic material, water and air the proportion which vary.

Since, the main interest of soils to men is for growing his crops, it is necessary to learn also about the physical and chemical properties of the soils. Because for growing with success particular crop is dependent. In soil studies, the following physical properties are important :—

(*i*) Specific gravity
(*ii*) Pore space
(*iii*) Plasticity
(*iv*) Cohesion
(*v*) Colour
(*vi*) Texture
(*vii*) Soil temperature
(*viii*) Permeability

LAND RESOURCES

In India, our life depend on land resources such as food, fibre, fuel and other basic amenities. Therefore, it is the valuable gift of nature to human beings. Top layer of the land is called soil, which is renewable resource and essential for survival of life. Though it is life support system, but it is overused which causes environmental problems. The existing land use pattern in different regions in India has been evolved as the result of the action and interaction of the various factors, *i.e.*, physical characteristics of land, the institutional frame work, the structure of other resources available and the location of the region in relation to other aspects of the economic development *e.g.*, those relating to transport as well as to industry and trade.

Out of the total geographical area of 328 million hectares, the land use statistics are available for roughly 306 million hectares, constituting 93% of the total land available for cultivation is approximately 14 million hectares. But it is reducing day by day. The earth is made up of three principal layers cores, mantle and crust. Cores are inner most fluid layers. Mantle is the middle layer and curst is the upper most layer.

The land area is classified into 9 categories: they are (*i*) forests, (*ii*) land put to non-agricultural use (*iii*) barren land unculturable land (*iv*) permanent pastures and other grazing lands (*v*) misc. tree crops and groves (*vi*) culturable waste (*vii*) fallow land (*viii*) current fallow (*ix*) net area sown.

TYPES OF SOILS IN INDIA

Soils widely vary in their characteristics and properties. The different types of soil are as follows :

1. **Alluvial Soil :** This include the deltaic alluvium calcareous alluvial soils, Coastal alluvium and Coastal sands. It is the most important soil group of India contributing the largest share to its agricultural wealth. This soil are derived from the deposition laid by the numerous tributaries of the Indus, Ganges and the Brahmputra systems. These streams draining the Himalayas. Geologically, alluvium is divided in to Khadar generally light coloured sandy and

Bhanger generally dark and full of "Kankar".

2. **Black Soil :** These soils vary in depth from shallow to deep. The typical soil derived from Deccan trap is the "Regur" or black cotton soil. It is common in Maharashtra, western parts of Madhya Pradesh, A.P., Gujarat and Tamil Nadu. It is comparable with the "Chernozems of Russia and Spairie soil of U.S.

3. **Red Soil :** The ancient crystalline and metamorphic rocks on meteoric weathering have given rise to the red soils. The red colour is due to the wide diffusion of iron rather then to a high proportion of it. The soils grade from poor thin gravelly and light coloured varieties of the plains and valleys. They are poor in nitrogen, phosphorus, lime, potash, iron oxide. The soils comprise vast areas of Tamil Nadu, Karnataka, Goa, Daman and Diu, M.P., Orissa, Chhotanagpur, Bihar, West Bengal, U.P. etc.

4. **Laterites and Lateritic Soil :** It is a formation peculiar to India and some other countries. It is a mixture of the hydrated oxides of aluminium and iron with small amounts of manganese oxide and tatania, etc. These soils are poor in lime, magnesia nitrogen, potassium oxide but humus and P_2O_5 is high.

5. **Desert Soil :** The most predominant component of this soil is quartz but feldspar and hornblende grains also occur with a fair proportion of calcareous grains. Some of these soils contain high percentage of soluble salts, possess high pH, a very high percentage of calcium carbonate and are poor in organic matter.

6. **Problem Soil :** These are the soils which owing to land and soil characteristics, cannot be economically used for the cultivation of crops without adopting proper reclamation measures. High eroded soils, revive lands, soils on steeply sloping lands, etc., constitute one set of problem soil.

7. **Acid Soil :** Soil having pH below 7 are considered to be the acidic, but those which have pH less than 5.5 and which respond to liming may be considered to qualify to be designated as acid soil.

Role of Society in Conservation of Natural Resources :

Planning of a suitable strategy for the conservation of our natural resources and most judicious execution of planned strategies is called as Conservation Management. Environmental planning, evaluation, monitoring, and impact assessment are methods of conservation management. The Indian philosophy of conservation is to keep "Harmony with Nature". Therefore, we have to learn to live with nature. For this every individual has to play his role to conserve the nature and natural resources.

It should not be optional but for all *i.e.,* old, young, rich, poor, industrialist, common man, consumer, businessman, resident of a posh colony, slum dweller. Everybody should take part in this work. Voluntary organisations are doing some work in this regard but it is not sufficient. Some important roles of individuals in maintaining peace, harmony and equity in nature are as :

1. People should at once stop the over utilization of natural resources instead they must be properly used.
2. Instead of deforestation, representation should keep in mind. We should take help from the Govt. for plantation programmes. Everybody should take part in plantation and care the plants.

3. We should protect wildlife. Though hunting is not allowed even then the persons are doing so. For this educated young should teach the lesson of wildlife act.
4. Mixed cropping, crop rotation, and proper use of fertilizer, insecticide, pesticides should be taught to farmers. Encourage the use of manures, biofertilizers and organic fertilizers.
5. We should make habit for waste disposal, compose and to restore biodiversity.
6. Try to educate local people for the protection and judicious use of natural resources.
7. Install rain water harvesting system in houses / colonies.
8. We should recycle the waste and waste water for agriculture purposes.
9. We must develop energy saving methods to avoid wastage of energy. We should remember *energy saved is energy produced.*
10. Use drip irrigation and sprinkling irrigation to improve irrigation efficiency and reduce evaporation.
11. Utilize renewable energy sources as much as possible. Encourage use of solar cooker, pump etc.

Sustainable Resource Management : Land, water, climate, flora and fauna are the basic natural resources for agricultural development. Unfortunately, these are subject to various kinds of deteriorating influences. Since agricultural development cannot subsist or deteriorating natural resource base, it is imperative to develop strategies for conservational improvement of resources. The concept of substainable resource management implies that needs of the present should be met without endangering the ability of the resources to meet needs of the future.

Irrigated agriculture covering 48 million hectares of land area is producing about 2.5 ton of foodgrains. This is very low and the realizable potential is much higher. This gap should bridged.

Rainfed areas of about 92 million hectares has a productivity of only about one tonne hectare. There are sufficient indications that by exploiting all available modern technology this could be doubled, by strictly following the soil reclamation technologies. Similarly, available fallow lands could be remedied and made to contribute to the overall production.

Agriculture and ecology are mutually interactive. The positive aspects of this interact must be maximised, while the negative aspects have to be monitored and remedied. Assess the impact of the different kinds of solid, liquid and gaseous pollutants and agrochemicals that affect the quality of land, water and atmosphere and developing remedial measures become important.

In an international dialogue at the M.S. Swaminathan Research Foundation, Chennai was observed that to meet the challenge of increasing food availability now and in the future demands equal attention on production systems and on the larger issues of food security. Science must work in partnership with farmers to create a new agriculture and in endeavour, the efforts would aim towards transformation of the most marginalised, farm into agents of poverty alleviation and environmental management through the blending traditional and frontier technologies in socially equitable, economically viable and environmentally viable ecological technologies and management systems and provide increasing productivity per unit of land, water, energy, labour and investment. Part of this involve focussing research on neglected minor millets, grains, legumes and tubers which perform tolerably well in times of environmental stress. Also, research should be focussed areas such as arid, semi-arid, coastal and mountain areas.

I. PHYSICAL AND SOCIAL ENVIRONMENT AS FACTORS OF CROP DISTRIBUTION AND PRODUCTION

The important factors covered by environment are moisture, atmospheric temperature, light, movement of air, edaphic, biotic and social conditions. Crop yield is the product derive from the interaction of genotype and environment. If the yield is to be satisfactory, either crop environment has to be changed to meet the requirements of the crop, or the crop should changed to fit into the prevailing environment in which it has to grow. The scientists working on this challenge to bring mutual adjustment between crop and environment.

Manipulation of Physical Factors:

1. **Moistures :** Soil moisture is very important in the growth of a plant. In crop husbandry, to get good yield, choice of a crop to suit the available soil moisture is a prerequisite. Paddy growing is restricted to heavy rainfall and moisture saturated regions, while maize is grown in moderato but well distributed rainfall areas and millets are confined to low rainfall tracts.
2. **Physical and Social environment as a factors for crop growth :** In a region, a crop has to be grown in a particular season and in particular soil conditions (Kharif and rabi). *e.g.* Coffee and tea are hill plantations; but tea needs higher elevation than coffee for better performance. Accordingly they get distributed. In north Bihar, maize yields better than wheat in the rabi season. But because of strong western winds in February, in eastern Uttar Pradesh, maize cannot be grown (to avert crop damage) even though both the regions come in the same crop belt.
   In the same crop, a particular variety may suit better, because of its tolerance to drought or frost or pest as these factors are induced in crop breeding. These have to be preferred to other varieties. The seasonal factor can be manipulated. In the same crop plant, there are short, medium and long duration varieties which have to be sown according to monsoon conditions.
3. **Irrigation :** Each crop has a critical growth stage and development stage, when the crop should not have adverse moisture level. Prompt irrigations should be provided, and if liberal water supply is available, multiple cropping can also be undertaken.
4. **Moisture conservation :** For raising good crops in rainfed areas, conservation of moisture is very essential. Bunding, shallow beds, basin listing, fallowing, weed control and mulching are useful measures. Contour bunding and terracing according to the slope of the land have to be done. Application of organic manure to the soil helps in moisture conservation.
5. **Cultural practices :** The practices in sequence for raising a good crop are the following : Timely sowing, proper placement of seeds at the recommended depth, deep placement of phosphatic and potassic fertilisers, split application of nitrogen, timely control of weeds, application of irrigation water at the critical stages

of growth, and control of pests and diseases. Any setback in timely operations of these cultural factors affects adversely the normal correlation between climate and the crop development stages and finally the yield.

6. **Drainage :** Provision of surface and underground drainage, removes the surplus water and helps the timely preparation of land for sowing.

7. **Temperature :** Temperature manipulation to suit a crop can be done by :

   (*a*) Fixing the date of sowing the seeds to meet the temperature requirements of crops for germination and growth of crop.

   (*b*) Choice of variety for the particular period of sowing viz. early or late escape frost of very high temperature at the critical stage of development.

   (*c*) Growing seedlings of valuable crops providing adequate temperature for germination, if necessary in glass houses.

8. **Light :** For the photosynthetic mechanism in plants to funciton, when carbohydrates are prepared and moved to fill the grains, light is very essential. The following points have to be kept in mind for providing enough light requirements:

   For optimum plant population, the seed rate, spacing between plants, whether the crop should be solo or mixed or inter-cropped have to be decided. Similarly the sowing and harvesting time should be such, that the plants receive enough day length; selection of the variety of plant most efficient in light utilization, branching habit in mixed-cropping and the duration of the various components in the mixture or inter-crop are also to be considered prior to the commencement of seedling.

9. **Wind breaks :** Crops are badly damaged by high wind velocity. In fruit crops, not only the fruits drop, but the fruit plants also are uprooted. Hence, a wind break is very essential.

10. **Soil and moisture factors :** Each crop has a definite requirement for a specific component of the environment. For example, rice, wheat and maize require sufficient moisture at least 15 days before flowering till the milk (dough) stage and also till the grain filling is over. Bajra and Sorghum are relatively resistant to moisture stress because of their xerophytic nature. Though the total water requirement of these two crops is the same as wheat or maize, millets are suited to dry land conditions.

    Soil texture is also important for a crop. Groundnut needs a sandy loam, paddy, clay soil and cotton, a deep black soil. Wheat, maize and bengal gram require loam and clay loams.

    A seed bed is to be prepared fine, to bring the soil structure to a level when there will be better aeration and moisture absorption.

    pH has to be regulated by application of lime wherever necessary. The above are some of the methods of creating favourable environments for crop growth.

11. **Biotic factors :** Companion crops in inter-cropping and mixed-cropping systems, microbial flora and fauna in

the soil, diseases and pests of the crops and weeds comprise the biotic environment of cultivated crops.

Manipulation of these biotic factors is possible by controlling competition from weeds, as well as the companion crops and also the plants of the same crop by adjusting the plant population.

By adopting integrated pests and diseases management, the crops can be saved from damage. Appropriate soil management helps in increasing the microbial flora in the soil around the root zone, increasing the yield.

12. **Social Environment:** People change their preference for growing more remunerative crops with the improvement in their standard of living. With a change in consumers preference, the importance of a particular crop gets enhanced, and the grower puts more area under that crop. Relative price relationship and easy marketability have great influence on the adaptability of a crop.

    As an example, the dwarf high-yielding wheat replacing barley and other grains in rabi season and also paddy in eastern India in the fallow period can be quoted. Dwarf wheat gives more yield, it has price support, fertilisers are available, income level of the people has gone up.

    High-yielding varieties of rice are replacing maize and kharif pulses in the entire North India where new irrigation facilities are introduced.

    Groundnut, being more profitable is replacing bajra in some parts of Gujarat.

13. **Minimum Tillage :** Tillage is required to improve the physical conditions of the soils and maintain a conducive air-water-temperature-plant root relationship. The seedling environment zone also known as the 'row zone' and the inter-row zone which is the spacing between two rows of crops are to be kept free of weeds and in a stirred condition by using suitable inter-cultivating implements with bullock power or tractor power. There will be proper aeration and adequate water absorption during the rain. Loss of soil due to erosion is prevented by the row crops.

II. CLIMATIC ELEMENTS AS FACTORS OF CROP GROWTH; IMPACT OF CHANGING ENVIRONMENT ON CROPPING PATTERN

The climate of a region is linked with the annual rainfall, range of temperature and the soil formation; ultimately climate decides what crops to be grown, in which zone, in which season and what should be the duration of crop. Under this broad grouping, there are years when the crops are successful and years when they fail, The main contributory cause is, the nature of distribution of rainfall or the spread of the rainy days during the crop growth. Even with lesser rainfall, the crop will give good yield if the rains are well distributed. If the rain is torrential and received in the course of a few days or in the off season, crops cannot survive as there is more damage than beneficial effect and the crops have to pass through an unduly long rainless period later.

The **Statement I** appended, gives the agro-climatic regions of the country and the states covered by each region, annual rainfall, range of temperature, types of soils met within the region.

Statement II gives the climatic zones of India in terms of mean annual temperature and moisture indices.

Statement III shows the distribution of important crops in various soil-climatic zones in India.

The environmental influence on crop distribution has been brought out by the three statements given below :

Statement I

Agro-climatic Region	*States covered*	*Annual Rainfall*	*Temperature Range*	*Major Soil Groups*
1	*2*	*3*	*4*	*5*
1. Humid western Himalayan region	Jammu and Kashmir, Himachal Pradesh and Kumaon, and Garhwal divisions of Uttarakhand	1500 mm	Jan: 0-4°C July: 5-30°C	Submontane soils, hill soils and tarai soils
2. Humid Bengal Assam Basin	West Bengal and Assam	2000 mm	Jan: 10-25°C July: 25-41°C	Riverine alluvium, tarai soils, laterite soils, red-yellow loams, red sandy or gravelly soils
3. Humid eastern Himalayan region and Bay Islands	Arunachal Pradesh, Nagaland, Manipur, Mizoram, Tripura, Meghalaya and Andaman and Nicobar Islands	2000 mm	Jan: 11-24°C July: 25-33°C	Red loamy soils, laterite soils, red-yellow and alluvial soils
4. Sub-humid Satluj-Ganga alluvial plains	Punjab, U.P, Bihar and Delhi Territory	1000-1500 mm	Jan: 6-23°C July: 25-41°C	Calcareous alluvial soils, riverine alluvium, saline and alkaline soils, red-yellow loam, red sandy or gravelly soils and mixed red and black soils
5. Sub-humid to humid eastern and south eastern uplands	Orissa, Andhra Pradesh and Eastern Madhya Pradesh	750-1500 mm	Jan: 16-28°C July: 27-36°C	Laterite soils, red-yellow loams, red sandy or gravelly soils, mixed red and black soils, deltaic alluvium, deep black soils, red loamy soils and coastal alluvium

1	2	3	4	5
6. Humid to semiarid Western Ghats and Karnataka Plateaus	Karnataka, Tamil Nadu, Union Territory of Puducherry and Lakshadweep Islands	750-2000 mm	Jan: 20-29°C July: 28-38°C	Laterite soils, red sandy or gravelly soils, deltaic alluvium, coastal alluvium and red loamy soils
7. Semiarid Lava Plateaus and Central Highlands	Maharashtra, Western and Central Madhya Pradesh, Goa and Union Territory of Daman and Diu	500-1000 mm	Jan: 13-29°C July: 20-42°C	Riverine alluvium, coastal alluvium, mixed red and black soils, skeletal soils, deep-to-shallow black soils and red sandy or gravelly soils
8. Arid western plains	Haryana, Rajasthan, Gujarat and Union Territory of Dadra and Nagar Havelli	250-750 mm	Jan: 5-22°C July: 28-45°C	Alluvium, deep and medium soils and medium-deep black soils.

Statement-II

Demarcation of Climatic Zones and Cropping Patterns (National Symposium on Cropping Patterns in India, 1972)

Water is an important resource and the cropped land is classified into rainfed or irrigated Krishnan and Singh (1972) have demarcated soil-climatic zones of India by superimposing the mean index (P – P.E.) × 100/P.E. and mean temperature (Max + Min)/2 (isopicths) where P.E. is the mean annual potential evapotranspiration compute. Thornthwaite's method and P is the mean annual precipitation, both expressed in the same unit undermentioned scale was adopted in defining climatic zones in terms of moisture and temperature.

Climatic zones of India in terms of mean annual temperature and moisture indices

Sub-Zone No.	*Mean annual temp. °C* $\frac{(Max + Min)}{2}$	*Temp. situation*	*Zone No.*	*Moisture Index* $\frac{(P - P.E.)\,100}{P.E.}$	*Moisture situation*
A	28 or more	Very hot	1	Less than – 80	Extremely dry
B	25-28	Hot	2	– 60 to – 80	Semi-dry
C	20-25	Mild	3	– 40 to – 60	Dry
D	10-20	Cold	4	– 20 to – 40	Slightly dry
E	10 or less	Very cold	5	0 to – 20	Slightly moist
			6	0 to 50	Moist
			7	50 to 100	Wet
			8	Greater than 100	Extremely wet.

Statement-III

Distribution of important crops in various soil-climatic zone in India (After Krishnan and Singh, 1972)

S.No.	*Moisture index zone*	*Thermal zone*	*Soil type*	*Districts in the climatic zone**	*Percentage of area under irrigation*	*Distribution of crops in the zone***
1	*2*	*3*	*4*	*5*	*6*	*7*
1.	1	B	Desert soil	Bikaner, Jaisalmer, Jodhpur, Barmer	1	Bajra (62) Jowar (3) Wheat (2) Til (2)
2.	1	C	Desert soil	Ganganagar	29	Gram (32) Wheat (14) Bajra (13) Cotton (6) Mustard (5) Barley (5) Jowar (2)
3.	1	E	Skeletal soil	Ladakh	100	Ragi (26) Wheat (18) Barley (6)
4.	2	A	Mixed red and black soil	Kurnool, Raichur, Mahbub Nagar	6	Jowar (29) Groundnut (14) Cotton (14) Rice (6) Bajra (4) Ragi (2)
5.	2	B	Desert soil	Churu, Jalore Banaskantha	5	Bajra (42) Jowar (6) Wheat (4) Til (3) Gram (2).
6	2	B	Alluvial soil	Jaipur	23	Bajra (24) Gram (14) Barley (13) Wheat (7) Jowar (4) Maize (4) Til (3)
7	2	B	Grey brown soil	Sikar, Jhunjhunu, Pali, Nagpur	9	Bajra (36) Jowar (8) Til (6) Gram (5) Wheat (5) Barley (3)
8	2	B	Coastal and deltaic alluvium	Kutch, Jamnagar, Junagarh,	7	Groundnut (30) Bajra (23) Jowar (18)

1	*2*	*3*	*4*	*5*	*6*	*7*
				Bhavnagar Rajkot, Amreli		Cotton (9) Wheat (3) Til (2)
9.	2	B	Medium and deep black soil	Bijapur, Galbarga	2	Jowar (45), Bajra (10) Cotton (10) Groundnut (10) Wheat (4) Tur (4) Linseed (2) Gram (2)
10.	2	C	Alluvial soil	Bhatinda, Hissar Mohindergarh, Ferozepur	36	Gram (34) Bajra (17) Wheat (15) Cotton (8) Mustard (4)
11.	2	C	Grey brown Soil	Ajmer, Sirohi	28	Wheat (14) Jowar (12) Bajra (12) Til (11) Maize (9) Barley (7) Gram (7) Cotton (2)
12.	3	A	Red soil	Nalgonda, Salem, Tiruchirapalli	25	Jowar (20) Rice (18) Bajra (13) Groundnut (11) Ragi (6) Castor (5) Cotton (2)
13.	3	A	Mixed red and black soil	Khammam, West Godavari, Krishna, Cudappah, Nellore, Madurai, Ramanathapuram, Tirunelveli, Warangal	40	Rice (32) Jowar (19) Groundnut (8) Cotton (5) Bajra (6) Til (4)
14.	3	A	Medium and deep black soil	Guntur	27	Rice (24) Jowar (19) Tobacco (9) Bajra (6) Groundnut (5)
15.	3	B	Red soil	Hyderabad, Anantapur	13	Jowar (21) Groundnut (13) Rice (10) Bajra (5) Castor (5) Cotton (3) Gram (2)

1	*2*	*3*	*4*	*5*	*6*	*7*
16.	3	B	Alluvial soil	Gurgaon, Alwar, Tonk, Bharatpur, Mathura, Agra, Mainpuri, Kanpur, Farrukhabad, Etawah	24	Gram (17) Mustard (15) Wheat (14) Bajra (14) Jowar (8) Barley (7) Maize (4) Rice (3) Tur (2) Sugarcane (2)
17.	3	B	Grey brown soil	Mensana, Surendranagar Kaira, Ahmedabad	8	Cotton (26) Bajra (18) Jowar (15) Wheat (9) Rice (5) Groundnut (4) Tobacco (3)
18.	3	B	Mixed red and black soil	Jalaun, Hamirpur, Ratlam, Mandasur, Medak, Bellary, Chitradurga, Coimbatore	14	Jowar (22) Gram (10) Cotton (10) Wheat (9) Groundnut (7) Rice (5) Til (4) Bajra (3) Ragi (3) Maize (3) Sugarcane (2) Linseed (2) Tur (2)
19.	3	B	Medium and deep black soil	Bhind, Datia, Shivpuri, Kotah, Sabarkantha, Panch Mahals, Jhabua, Dhar, West Nimar, East Nimar, Baroda, Dhulia, Jalgaon, Buldana, Akola, Amravati, Parbhani, Aurangabad, Nasik, Ahmednagar, Bir, Sholapur, Osmanabad, Bidar	5	Jowar (25) Cotton (16) Wheat (9) Groundnut (8) Gram (7) Rice (4) Maize (3) Tur (2)

1	*2*	*3*	*4*	*5*	*6*	*7*
20.	3	C	Red soil	Karnataka	11	Ragi (25) Jowar (16) Rice (11) Groundnut (5) Tur (2) Tobacco (2) Til (2)
21.	3	C	Alluvial soil	Gurdaspur, Amritsar, Kapurthala, Jalandhar, Ludhiana, Sangrur, Patiala, Karnal, Rohtak, Delhi, Meerut, Bulandshahr, Etah, Aligarh	14	Wheat (25) Gram (13) Maize (8) Bajra (7) Sugarcane (5) Cotton (4) Rice (4) Jowar (3) Barley (3) Mustard (2)
22.	3	C	Red and Yellow soil	Udaipur, Dungarpur, Banswara	14	Maize (32) Rice (8) Gram (12) Wheat (10) Til (7) Barley (6) Cotton (3)
23.	3	C	Mixed red deep black soil	Chittorgarh, Dharwar	15	Jowar (19) Cotton (16) Wheat (16) Maize (10) Groundnut (8) Gram (5) Rice (4)
24.	3	C	Medium and deep black soil	Puen, Satara, Sangli, Belgaum	8	Jowar (33) Bajra (18) Rice (4) Wheat (3) Cotton (3) Gram (2)
25.	4	A	Red soil	Visakhapatnam, Srikakulam, Chittor, Ganjam, North Arcot, South Arcot, Chingleput	50	Rice (48) Groundnut (14) Ragi (8) Bajra (6) Jowar (3) Til (2)
26.	4	A	Coastal and deltaic alluvium	East Godavari	57	Rice (58) Jowar (6) Til (5) Bajra (3)

1	2	3	4	5	6	7
27.	4	A	Mixed red and black soil	Karimnagar	27	Rice (24) Jowar (23) Til (11) Maize (11) Groundnut (10)
28.	4	B	Red soil	Kolar	17	Ragi (45) Groundnut (10) Jowar (8) Tur (3) Bajra (3)
29.	4	B	Mixed red and black soil	Tikamgarh, Jhansi, Adilabad	14	Jowar (26) Til (13) Wheat (12) Gram (9) Rice (7) Cotton (5)
30.	4	B	Alluvial soil	Hardoi, Sitapur, Unnao, Lucknow, Barabanki, Fatehpur, Raibarelli, Allahabad, Pratapgarh, Faizabad, Sultanpur, Varanasi, Ghazipur, Ballia, Azamgarh, Shahabad, Patna, Monghyr, Gaya	29	Rice (28) Gram (13) Wheat (12) Barley (11) Tur (4) Sugarcane (3) Jowar (3) Bajra (2)
31.	4	B	Shallow black soil	Betul		Jowar (17) Wheat (16) Gram (10) Tur (8) Groundnut (5) Rice (4) Maize (3)
32.	4	B	Medium and deep black soil	Thalawar, Wardha, Nizamabad, Baroda, Broach		Cotton (30) Jowar (27) Rice (9) Wheat (6) Gram (3) Tur (3) Maize (3) Groundnut (2)

1	*2*	*3*	*4*	*5*	*6*	*7*
33.	4	C	Red soil	Chikmagalur, Hassan, Mandya, Tumkur, Bangalore	20	Ragi (32) Rice (15) Jowar (4) Groundnut (3)
34.	4	C	Alluvial soil	Ambala, Saharanpur, Muzaffarnagar, Badaun, Moradabad, Shahjahanpur	21	Wheat (25) Gram (13) Rice (10) Bajra (7) Maize (6) Barley (3) Tur (2)
35.	4	C	Mixed red and black soil	Banda	14	Gram (30) Wheat (17) Jowar (13) Til (9) Tur (5) Linseed (4) Bajra (3) Barley (2)
36.	4	C	Medium and deep black soil	Ujjain, Shajapur, Dewas, Indore	2	Wheat (29) Jowar (28) Cotton (18) Gram (8) Bajra (5) Tur (4)
37.	4	C	Partly alluvial and partly brown hill soil	Jammu, Kathua	35	Wheat (35) Rice (20) Maize (13) Bajra (8) Barley (4) Gram (2) Til (2).
38.	5	B	Red soil	Belangir, Purulia, Bankura, Kalahandi, Baudh Kandhamal, Puri, Bhubaneshwar, Keonjhar, Dhenkanol	20	Rice (66)
39.	5	B	Alluvial soil	Nadia, Hooghly, Bhagalpur	26	Rice (53) Gram (9) Jute (6) Maize (5) Wheat (2)

1	*2*	*3*	*4*	*5*	*6*	*7*
40.	5	B	Laterite soil	Midnapur, Birbhum	45	Rice (86)
41.	5	B	Red and yellow soil	Bilaspur, Raipur, Santhal Parganas, Hazaribagh, Palamau, Dhanbad, Murshidabad, Burdwan, Malda	16	Rice (6) Maize (4) Gram (4) Jute (2)
42.	5	B	Mixed red and black soil	Singhbhum, Chanda, Bhandara, Shahdol, Sidhi	10	Rice (47) Jowar (8) Wheat (5) Til (4) Linseed (4) Gram (3) Maize (3) Barley (2)
43.	5	B	Medium and deep black soil	Nagpur, Hoshangabad	3	Wheat (29) Jowar (24) Cotton (9) Gram (8) Tur (7) Til (5) Rice (3)
44.	5	C	Alluvial soil	Hoshiarpur, Bijnor, Rampur, Bareilly, Pilibhit, Kheri, Bahraich, Gonda, Basti, Gorakhpur, Deoria, Muzaffarpur, Darbhanga, Saharsa	12	Rice (29) Wheat (16) Gram (7) Maize (7) Sugarcane (6) Barley (5) Mustard (4)
45.	5	C	Red and yellow soil	Raigarh, Surguja, Mirzapur	7	Rice (47) Gram (4) Linseed (4) Wheat (3) Barley (3) Til (3) Mustard (3)
46.	5	C	Mixed red and black soil	Chattarpur, Panna, Satna, Rewa	5	Wheat (21) Rice (19) Gram (13) Jowar (6)

1	*2*	*3*	*4*	*5*	*6*	*7*
						Til (6) Linseed (6) Barley (5) Tur (3)
47.	5	C	Medium and deep black soil	Raigarh, Sehore, Vidisha, Sagar, Guna, Damoh, Durg	2	Wheat (42) Jowar (18) Gram (12) Cotton (4) Maize (13) Linseed (3) Til (2)
48.	6	B	Red soil	Bastar, Sundargarh	9	Rice (68)
49.	6	B	Coastal and deltaic alluvium soil	24 Parganas	76	Rice (80) Jute (5)
50.	6	B	Alluvial soil	Howrah	23	Rice (78) Jute (5)
51.	6	B	Mixed red and black soil	Balaghat	25	Rice (58) Linseed (10) Wheat (4) Gram (3)
52.	6	C	Alluvial soil	Nowgong, Champaran, Purnea	11	Rice (57) Jute (11) Wheat (4) Barley (4) Mustard (3) Maize (3)
53.	6	C	Red and yellow soil	Ranchi	2	Rice (62) Ragi (6)
54.	6	C	Shallow black soil	Seoni	6	Wheat (21) Rice (20) Gram (10) Jowar (4) Linseed (4)
55.	6	C	Mixed red and black soil	Mandla		Rice (23) Wheat (12) Gram (6) Maize (5)
56.	6	C	Medium and deep black soil	Chindwara, Narasinghpur, Jabalpur	2	Wheat (20) Jowar (15) Rice (10) Tur (3), Til (2) Gram (2)

1	2	3	4	5	6	7
57.	7	B	Coastal alluvium and partly laterite soil	Thana, Kolaba Ratnagiri, N. Kanara, S. Kanara, Cannanore, Trichur, Kozhikode, Ernakulam, Kottayam, Alleppy, Quilon, Trivandrum	19	Rice (41) Ragi (3) Figures for Kerala only Coconut (24) Pepper (3)
58.	7	C	Alluvial soil	Darrang	18	Rice (70) Mustard (7) Jute (5)
59.	7	C	Terai soil	Dehradun	28	Wheat (21) Rice (17) Maize (12) Mustard (8) Ragi (7) Til (5) Sugarcane (4) Gram (3)
60.	7	C	Red and yellow soil	Tripura	18	Rice (68) Jute (4) Cotton (3)
61.	8	C	Alluvial soil	Lakhimpur, Kamrup, Goalpara, Coochbehar	31	Rice (64) Jute (8) Mustard (5)
62.	8	B	Brown hill soil and Terai soil	Mandi, Mahasu, Almorah, Garhwal, Tehri	13	Wheat (29) Rice (18) Ragi (14) Barley (9) Maize (9) Mustard (7)
63.	8	D	Sub-montane soil	Udhampur, Chamba, Kangra	15	Maize (36) Wheat (28) Rice (11) Barley (7).

* Whenever a district falls under more than one zone, it is included in the zone, where the greater portion of its area lies.

** Figures in bracket gives the percentage of area under the crop concerned to total cropped area.

2. ENVIRONMENTAL POLLUTION

Environment:

Everything which surrounds us may collectively be termed as the environment.

Definition : *Pollution is an unfavourable alteration of our environment.* It is harmful to human life and that of other desirable species. It can be natural or man-made. The agents that cause environmental pollution are called **pollutants**. These when injected into biosphere in large quantities affect the normal functioning of ecosystems and have adverse effects on plants, animals and man.

Types of Pollution :

(1) Air pollution

(2) Water pollution

(3) Soil pollution

(4) Radioactive pollution

(5) Noise pollution.

1. AIR POLLUTION

Air pollutants consists of suspended particles and harmful gases. Some the gases react in the atmosphere to prodece extremely toxic secondary pollutants. Air pollution can be defined as :

A change in the quality and composition of air due to emissions other than oxygen into the atmosphere is called air pollution.

Emissions of about 1×10^{12} tonnes enter the atmosphere annually. Out of it, about 5×10^{8} tonnes or 0.05 per cent arise directly from human activities. These are usually released over populated cities and industiral centres. As a result the ambient air quality over the residential areas is spoiled. Their local concentration often becomes very high with severe consequences.

Table 1. Average ambient air quality of some major Indian cities

	Air pollutants (μg/m³ Air)*			
City	***Suspended Particulate Matter (SPM)***	***Respirable Suspended Particulate Matter (RSPM)***	SO_2	NO_2
Delhi	300	118	10	42
Ahmedabad	150	130	13	23
Bangalore	105	70	9	42
Chennai	310	40	7	5
Hyderabad	150	50	6	25
Kolkata	250	110	8	27
Mumbai	240	80	7	10
Pune	240	105	25	18
Bhubaneshwar	230	90	5	48

* Data based on CPCB and other pbulications. National Ambient Air Quality Standard (NAAQS) for residential and other areas as fixed in Status Report 2004 is 60 mg/m³ each for SO_2, NO_2 and RSPM and 140 mg/m³ for SPM. As per the Environmental Sustainability Index (ESI), the ranking of India is at 101 out of 146 countries. Other sources of air pollutions are industrial processes, agricultural and natural sources like volcanic eruptions, forest fires and natural inorganic and organic decays.

EFFECTS OF AIR POLLUTION

1. Smog and Photochemical Smog

Smog is a combination of smoke and fog. A classic smog is chaused when a mixture of smoke and SO_2 released by burning of fossil fuel. Photochemical smog formed from nitrogen oxides (NOx) and hydrocarbons in presence of sunlight. Automobile exhausts, release nitrous oxide (NO) alogn with small amount of nitrogendioxide (NO_2). These are also released from coal power plants and industrial manufacturing factories. Hydrocarbons are released into atmosphere through incomplete combustion and other man-made sources such as petrol, paints, solvents, pesticides etc. and biogenic sources such as pine and citrus tree emission.

2. Acid Rain

Due to higher atmospheric concentration of sulphur oxides (SOx), and nitrogen oxides (NOx), is very high. These compounds undergo atmospheric oxidation and hydrolysis to form sulphuric and nitric acids.

$$2SO_2 + O_2 \longrightarrow 2SO_3$$

$$SO_3 + H_2O \xrightarrow{\text{Sunlight}} H_2SO_4$$

$$2NO + O_2 \longrightarrow 2NO_2$$

$$4NO_2 + 2H_2O + O_2 \longrightarrow 4HNO_3$$

Acid rain deteriorates monuments and buildings. It damages vegetation, kills useful soil microbes, prevents seed germination and reduces soil fertility. It pollutes inland water bodies, adversely affecting aquatic life and often causes fish-kills.

3. Effects on Human Health and Animals

Air pollution generally causes many respiratory disorders, lung diseases including lung cancer, allergies and eye irritations. The exact nature of disease often depends on the type of pollutant. Coal miners often suffer from **black lung** disease. **Asbestosis** results from exposure to air borne asbestos. Cotton dust causes **byssinosis** among textile workers.

The general effects of air pollution on livestock are similar to man. Fluorides and arsenic in air cause series injuries to cattle.

Table 2. Effects of continuous exposure to various levels of carbon monoxide

CO level ppm	*% conversion of O_2Hb to COHb*	*Effects on humans*
10	2	Impairment of judgement and visual perception
100	15	Headache, dizziness, weariness
250	32	Loss of consciousness
750	60	Death after several hours
1000	66	Rapid death

Table 3. Effect of Exposure to various levels of NO_2 on human heath

Level of NO_2, ppm	*Duration of exposure*	*Effects on human health*
50-100	Up to 1 hour	Inflammation of lung tissue for 6-8 weeks
150-200	—	Bronchiolitis fibrosa obliterans - fatal result within 3-5 weeks of exposure
500 or more	2-10 days	Death

4. Depletion of Ozone Layer

Ozone layer protects the earth from harmful UV radiations, most of which are screened out by it. A group of air pollutants called chlorofluorocarbons (CFCs) or "Freon" gas threaten to disrupt this layer. The CFCs are compounds containing chlorine and fluorine. They are used as propellants in aerosol sprays and as refrigerants. Due to depletion in ozone layer UV radiation reach on earth, resulting the more skin diseases specially skin caner in human and other harmful effects like mutations.

5. Green House Effect

The main atmospheric component involved in green house effect process is CO_2 gas. Together with water vapour in the atmosphere it has established the temperature equilibrium for this planet. Over the years the average temperature of earth has remained constant because of constancy in the CO_2 concentration in the atmosphere. But in the recent past there has been a rise in the CO_2 concentration from 280 ppm to 330 ppm. About one-fourth of this rise has occurred in the last decade and the rising trend continues unabated. It has happened due to excessive burning of fossil fuels and destruction of forest. At this rate of rise the CO_2 concentration in the atmosphere will be doubled by 2020 AD. It may lead to rise in the global temperature by 2 to 4 degrees because of the green house effect. As a result of this, the glaciers and polar ice caps would melt increasing the flow in rivers and raising the sea level. Most islands would submerge and coastal plains would be flooded.

6. Effects on Plant/Vegetation

Air pollution reduces crop yield. Plants growing in polluted areas often show symptoms of injury general debility and premature ageing. Fluorides destroy leaf tissues.

SO_2 is injurious to plants. Exposure to high levels of the gas causes destruction of leaf tissue (leaf necrosis) and damage of the edges of leaves and the areas between leaf veins. Chronic exposure ot SO_2 leads to chlorosis, *i.e.,* bleachng or yellowing of the normally green portions of leaves. As relative humidity increases, plant injury also is enhanced. Such injury becomes maximum when the stomata (small openings in surface tissue which provide for interchange of gases with the atmosphere) are open, *i.e.,* during daytime. It is known that long-term low-level exposures to SO_2 are more dangerous for crops than short-term high-dose exposures.

SO_2 causes acid rains which also damage plants, besides aquatic lives in rivers and lakes.

CONTROL MEASURES OF AIR POLLUTION

1. Using improved designs of industrial burners and combustion equipment.
2. Creating a general awareness among people to keep the atmosphere free of pollution.
3. Separating the pollutants from harmless gases before their release into atmosphere. Devices such as gravity setting tanks, porous filters, cyclone collectors and electrostatic precipitators etc. can do this effectively.
4. More area should be put under forests with dense vegetation and canopy cover. Deforestation should be minimised.
5. Trees should be planted around each industry forming a 'green belt' of thick stand of trees surrounding it to absorb and minimize the pollution load.
6. Enacting and enforcing strict environmental laws covering all types of pollutants and their sources.
7. General switch over fossil fuels to renewable natural energy sources such as sunlight, water, wind, tidal power, etc.

2. WATER POLLUTION

Water pollution has become a very serious problem. Most of our surface water resources like ponds, streams, lakes and rivers etc. are highly polluted. Even the ground water is not free from pollution in many areas. This has accentuated problem of potable drinking water supply and has resulted in epidemics of water borne diseases. Water pollution can be defined as "Any contamination of water that makes it unsuitable for human."

Sources of Water Pollution

1. Sewage : Sewage contains human and animal body wastes, food residues, detergents etc. and many harmful micro-oganisms. Most of the chemical pollutants in sewage are biodegradable.

2. Industrial Discharge : Discharges of wastewater from industries directly into lakes and rivers are the main cause of their pollution. Directly discharge of hot water from industrial cooling, particularly from thermal and nuclear power plants causes severe thermal pollution.

3. Agricultural Runoff : Excess fertilizers are carried to ground water by leaching. Fertilizers, insecticides, pesticides etc. mix with surface water bodies by drainage and surface runoffs. Many pesticides like the organochlorine compounds are non-degradable. These are carried off through rainwater into surface water bodies and cause pollution.

4. Oil and Radioactive Wastes : Large amounts of crude oil, grease and petroleum products are added to seawater by sinking ships, tankers, broken pipelines, off shore oil wells etc. These cause oil-spills, which affect the marine ecosystem adversely.

EFFECTS OF WATER POLLUTION

(i) Toxicity : The industiral effluents and residual insecticides, pesticides etc. are highly toxic to man and animals. They may damage the liver, kidneys, reproductive system, respiratory system, nervous system and may cause death.

(ii) Eutrophication : Addtion of excessive plant nutrients through sewage and agricultural runoffs causes severe eutrophications. Rich growths of micro-organisms consume most of the dissolved oxygen. Fish and aquatic organisms of the bottom become deprived of oxygen and die.

(iii) Turbidity and Silting : Slit and other particulate pollutants increase turbidity of water; decrease light penetrability and productivity of aquatic bodies.

(iv) Water Borne Diseases : Bacterial contamination of water results in many epidemics of water borne diseases like typhoid, amoebic dysentary etc.

(v) Calefaction : Hot water discharges in river, lakes increase the temperature beyond normal limits. This is called calefaction. It has a severe disruptive effect on aquatic ecosystems.

CONTROL MEASURES OF WATER POLLUTION

(i) Treatment of Industrial Effluents : Industrial effluents should be properly treated to remove all pollutants, and should be cooled before their discharge into water bodies.

(ii) Sewage Treatment : Sewage must be treated properly and pure water only should be released into water bodies.

(iii) Recycling of Wastes : Wastes should be recycled whenever possible and their direct disposal into bodies of water should be banned. For example, body wastes of cattle can be used in "gobar gas plants" to produce fuel and manure.

(iv) Proper Agricultural Practices : Chemical fertilizers, non-degradable insecticides, pesticides etc. must be used judiciously, only in amounts absolutely necessary for the crop.

3. SOIL POLLUTION

Biological wastes are degradable and cause very little pollution of soil. Many solid chemical wastes like aluminium cans, plastics, polythene bags etc. are non-degradable or degrade very slowly. Urban areas contribute for most of the solid wastes. It is estimated that about 10 million urban population in India proudce about 15 million tons of solid wastes per year. Soil is the receptor of large quantities of waste products—domestic, human, animal, industrial and agricultural.

Combustion of sulphur-containing fuels emits SO_2 and finally leaves sulphate on the soil. Nitrates from the atmosphere are deposited on the soil. Particulate lead from automobile exhausts also settles on soil along both sides of highways with heavy automobile traffic. High levels of Pb, Zn, etc. are observed on soils near lead and zinc mines, etc.

Fertilizers and pesticides applied to crop are largely retained by the soil. They become part of environmental cycles by sorption by the soil, leaching into water, etc. Pesticides undergo degradation in soil, through the processes of biodegradation, chemcial degradation, or photochemical reactions.

Soil pollution alters the physical, chemical and biological properties of the soil. As a result the soil losses fertility and becomes unproductive.

Soil pollution can be controlled through proper waste disposal and by controlling air and water pollution.

4. RADIOACTIVE POLLUTION

Radioactivity is the spontaneous emission of protons or alpha (α) particles, electrons or beta (β) particles, and gamma rays (uncharged) as a result of disintegration of unstable atomic nuclei. These emissions are called ionizing radiations and are extremely harmful to protoplasm.

Sources of Radioactive Pollution

The major sources of radioactive pollutants are atomic explosions and radioactive wastes from reactors and nuclear power stations. Atomic explosions use uranium 235 and plutonium 239 for fission and hydrogen or lithium as fusion material. The explosion makes materials in the surrounding radioactive.

Effects of Radioactive Pollution

Radiation in high doses can cause instant death. Sub-lethal doses induce mutations, leukaemia, cancers, bone tumours, and child mortality. The mutated genes persist in the population for a very long time affecting several generations. After-effects of the first-atom bomb explosion in 1945 in Hiroshima are still observed in Japan. There, is in fact no safe limit of radiation and no cure for radiation damage. The radioactive pollution increases the risk associated with radiation.

Control Measures of Radioactive Pollution

The radioactive pollution can be minimised if all nuclear explosions are banned. Very stringent safety measures should be enforced in all nuclear establishments. All countries must adopt safe radioactive waste disposal measures. Release of radioactive isotopes with long half-life into the environment must be prohibited.

5. NOISE OR SOUND POLLUTION

Noise is unpleasant sound. Frequency of sound is measured in Hertz (Hz). The range of human hearing is in the range of 50 Hz 15000 Hz. The intensity of sound is measured in decibels (dB). One dB is equivalent to the faintest sound audible to human ear.

Sources of Noise Pollution

Vehicular traffic, running of machines, overcrowded streets, booming of jet planes, dynamite blasting, firing of crackers, loud pop music, blaring horns, music and public address systems etc. are some common sources of noise pollution.

Effects of Noise Pollution

Prolonged exposure to loud noise leads to permanent loss of hearing. It also causes many psychosomatic disorders and may affect the unborn babies. The manifestations of noise pollution include: increased level of serum cholesterol, high blood pressure, dilation of pupil of the eye, digestive spasms, headache and disturbed secretions of endocrine glands.

Control Measures of Noise Pollution

Noise pollution can be controlled by avoiding noisy machines and gadgets. Noisy industries and aerodromes can be acoustically zoned or restricted away from residential area. Trees can absorb sound to a very large extent. Therefore, several rows of trees should be planted on roadsides, and around industries and airports. use of noisy horns, loudspeakers etc. in residential areas should be discouraged.

Questions From Previous Year's Papers

Q. 1. Give a brief account of point and non-point sources of air pollutants.

Q. 2. Enumerate the major effects of air pollutants on vegetation. Against each of the effects, name an air pollutant which is responsible.

Q. 3. Write short notes on the following, each not exceeding 150 words.

(a) B.O.D.

(b) Acid rain

3. CROPPING PATTERNS

Basic concept of various types of cropping systems viz. sequential and inter-cropping, crop planning, different input-cum-operations regarding successful raising of crops like selection of suitable crop variety, tillage practices, fertilizer schedules, irrigation and plant protection are briefly summarised as under :

I. CROP

Community of plants grown for economical use are known as crop. Crop plants are grouped into following three main classes according to range of cultivation :

(*i*) **Garden crops :** Crop plants that are grown on small scale in garden such as kitchen gardens *e.g.*, onion, brinjal etc.

(*ii*) **Plantation crops :** Crop plants that are grown on a large scale on estates. They are permanent in nature *i.e.* harvesting continues for a prolonged period from a single planting *e.g.* tea, coffee, cocoa etc.

(*iii*) **Field crops :** Crop plants that are grown on a large scale. They are mostly seasonal *e.g.*, wheat, rice, maize etc.

A. Botanical Classification

Crops are classified on the basis of morphological similarities or on the basis of family of the crop plants *e.g.*

(*i*) Poaceae (Gramineae) *e.g.* rice, wheat, oat, barley etc.

(*ii*) Leguminaceae *e.g.* pea, pigeonpea, black gram, green gram etc.

(*iii*) Cucurbitaceae *e.g.* sweet guard, bitter guard, pumpkin, cucumber etc.

(*iv*) Cruciferae *e.g.* mustard, toria, cabbage, radish etc.

(*v*) Malvaceae *e.g.* cotton, lady's finger etc.

(*vi*) Solanaceae *e.g.* potato, tobacco, tomato, brinjal etc.

(*vii*) Tiliaceae *e.g.* jute etc.

(*viii*) Compositae *e.g.* sunflower, safflower, niger etc.

(*ix*) Chenopodiaceae *e.g.* sugarbeet, spinach etc.

(*x*) Pedaliaceae *e.g.* sesame etc.

(*xi*) Euphorbiaceae *e.g.* castor etc.

(*xii*) Liliaceae *e.g.* onion, garlic etc.

B. Commercial Classification :

(*i*) Food crops *e.g.* rice, wheat, green gram, soybean, groundnut etc.

(ii) Feed crops *e.g.* napier, maize, berseem, lucern, oat, jowar, stylo etc.

(*ii*) Industrial crops *e.g.* cotton, sugarcane, sugarbeet, tobacco, jute etc.

C. Economic or Agricultural Classification :

1. **Cereals :** Cereals are the cultivated grasses used as staple food *e.g.* rice, wheat, maize etc.

2. **Millets :** Millets are small grained cereals which are of minor importance as food *e.g.* bajra, ragi, sawan, cheena etc.

3. **Oil seeds :** Those crops which are rich in fatty acids and are used to extract vegetable oil to meet various requirements *e.g.* mustard, sunflower, castor, linseed, groundnut etc.

4. **Pulses :** Seeds of leguminous crop plants are used as food. They produce

dal after splitting *e.g.* green gram, black gram, bengal gram, peas, lentil etc.

5. **Feed or forage :** It refers to vegetative matter fresh or preserved utilized as feed for animal forage *e.g.*, berseem, jowar, napier, cowpea, grasses etc.
6. **Fiber crops :** Crop plants grown for fibre yield. Fibre may be obtained from bark *e.g.* sunhemp or from seed *e.g.,* cotton.
7. **Sugar crops :** Crop grown for production of sugar *e.g.* sugarcane etc.
8. **Starch crops :** Crops grown for production of starch *e.g.* potato, sweet potato etc.
9. **Drug crops :** Crops that are used for the preparation of medicines *e.g.* tobacco, mint etc.
10. **Narcotics :** Crop plants or their products used for stimulating nervous system *e.g.* tobacco, coffee, opium etc.
11. **Spices and condiments :** Crop plants or their products used to flavour, taste or colour *e.g.* cumin, ginger, chillies, onion, coriander etc.

D. Seasonal Classification : Crops are grouped under the following seasons in which they are cultivated :

1. **Kharif crops :** Crop plants grown during June-July to September-October *e.g.* rice, maize, castor, groundnut etc.
2. **Rabi crops :** Crop plants grown during October-November to January-February *e.g.* wheat, linseed, mustard, lentil, berseem etc.
3. **Zaid or summer crops :** Crop plants grown during February-March to May-June *e.g.* black gram, green gram, cowpea, sunflower etc.

E. Classification according to ontogeny : Crop plants are grouped according to their life cycles in following manner :

1. **Annual crops :** Crop plants that complete their life cycle (seed to seed) within a season or year *e.g.* rice, maize bajra, wheat, mustard etc.
2. **Biennial crops :** Crop plants that complete their life cycle (seed to seed) within two years. In first year, growth is purely vegetative and during second year, it produces a flower stalk from the crown *e.g.* sugarbeet, carrot etc.
3. **Perennial crops :** Crop plants that live for three or more years. They may be seed bearing or non-seed bearing *e.g.* sugarcane, napier, sweet potato ginger etc.

F. Classification based on special purpose crops : Crop plants which are grown with the intention of serving specific purpose in addition to obtaining yield. The crops can be grouped into following groups :

1. **Catch crops or emergency crops :** These are crops cultivated to 'catch' the forthcoming season. They replace a main crop that has failed due to biotic or climatic or management hazards and utilize the remaining period of the season. They are short growing in nature *e.g.* green gram, black gram, cowpea, toria etc.
2. **Cover crops :** The crops whose plants are able to protect the soil surface from erosion (wind, water or both) through their ground covering foliage *e.g.* black gram, khesari, green gram, soybean etc.
3. **Nurse crops :** These crop plants help in the nourishment of other crops by providing shade and acting as climbing sticks *e.g.* rai in peas, jowar in cowpea etc.

4. **Smoother crops :** These crop plants are able to smoother or suppress the population and growth of weeds by providing suffocation (curtailing movement of air and light) *e.g.* barley, mustard, cowpea etc.
5. **Guard or barrier crops :** These plants help to protect another crop from trespassing or restrict the speed of wind and thus damage *e.g.* Safflower in gram, sunhemp around the sugarcane field.
6. **Restorative crops :** These crops provide a good harvest alongwith enrichment or restoration or amelioration of the soil *e.g.* legume crops.
7. **Exhaustive crops :** These are crop plants which are growing in the field and exhaust the fertility because of a more aggressive nature *e.g.* sesame, linseed, mustard etc.
8. **Paira crops :** Those crops which are sown a few days or weeks before the harvesting of the standing mature crop *e.g.* berseem in paddy, lentil in paddy, sweet guard in potato etc.
9. **Cash crops :** These crop plants are grown for sale to earn hard cash. The processing of such crops after harvest is beyond the means of individual farmers *e.g.* sugarcane, jute, cotton, tobacco etc.
10. **Trap crops :** These crop plants are grown to trap soil borne harmful biotic agents *e.g.* parasitic weeds. Orobanche and striga are trapped by solanaceous and sorghum crops, respectively.
11. **Brake crops :** These crops are grown to break the continuity of the agro-ecological situation of the field under multiple cropping systems Growing potato, pulses or oilseeds in rice, rice-wheat etc.
12. **Mulch crops :** These crop plants are grown to conserve the soil moisture from bare ground by their thick and multi-layered foliage, trailing habit *e.g.*, cowpea, Atylosia etc.
13. **Sod or turf crops :** These crop plants belong to the grass family and have sod type tillers with motted foliage and roots close to the soil surface. They are grown to conserve soil from erosion particularly in non-arable areas *e.g.* marbel grass, Doob grass etc.
14. **Truck crops :** These crop plants are grown for distant market and yielded in tonnes. It requires transport vehicles to supply the produce to market *e.g.* berseem, potato, lady's finger, brinjal, spinach, radish etc.
15. **Silage crops :** These crop plants are grown to be preserved in pits (Silo pits) in a succulent condition by a process of natural fermentation for feeding live-stock during off seasons *e.g.*, maize, jowar, bajra etc.
16. **Ley crops :** These include any crop or combination of crop plants which are grown for grazing immediately or feeding livestock in future *e.g.* marbel grass + berseem, dinanath grass + cowpea etc.
17. **Green manuring crops :** These crop plants are grown to be incorporated into the soil to increase the fertility of the soil *e.g.* dhaincha, sunhemp, green gram etc.
18. **Augmenting crops :** When sub-crops are sown to supplement the yield of the main crops, the sub-crops are known as augmenting crops *e.g.* mustard with berseem, Chinese cabbage with mustard etc.
19. **Alley crops :** When arable crops are grown in alleys formed by trees or shrubs established mainly to hasten soil

fertility restoration, to enhance soil productivity and to reduce soil erosion, they are known as alley crops *e.g.* sweet potato, black gram, turmeric and ginger in between the rows of eucalyptus subabool etc.

20. **Avenue crops :** These crop plants are grown along the farm roads and fences *e.g.* pigeonpea, sisal etc.
21. **Riparian crops :** These crop plants are grown along irrigation and drainage channels or water bodies *e.g.* paragrass, dhaincha etc.
22. **Energy crops :** These crop plants are grown to obtain liquid energy *e.g.* ethanol, alcohol and crops like sugarcane, potato, maize, barley etc.

II. CROPPING SYSTEM

Cropping system is a kind and sequence of crops grown on a given piece of land over a period of time. It varies from region to region at macro-level and economic and eco-edaphic factors. Cropping system represents cropping pattern used on a farm and their interaction with farm resources other farm enterprises and available technology which determine their make up.

Cropping Pattern

Cropping pattern means the proportion of area under various crops at a point of time in a unit area. It includes yearly sequence and spatial arrangement of crops and fallow in an area. Individual crops are the components of a given cropping pattern. The plot-wise record of crops grown in each season of a year gives a complete picture of the cropping pattern of a particular locality or geographical area.

Types of Cropping System :

(A) Sequential or rotational cropping: It refers to the growing of different crops in recurring succession on the same piece of land in a specific period of time. It is one of the means of diversification in cropping in different seasons of the year or in different years. There are certain principles to select the crops for rotational cropping. It is further divided in to the following :

1. Single cropping : It refers to the growing of only one crop on a piece of land year after year. It may be due to climatological, socio-economic conditions and specialization of farmer to grow a particular crop *e.g.* in canal irrigated areas, rice is main crop.

2. Multiple cropping : Growing of more than one crop on a same piece of land in recurring succession in one calendar year is known as multiple cropping. The main objective of multiple cropping is to obtain maximum production per unit time and per unit area.

Pre-requisites of Multiple Cropping

1. Adequate supply of available water
2. Sufficient and timely availability of manures and fertilizers
3. Adequate and timely availability of seed and plant protection materials
4. Use of shortduration varieties
5. Tillage implements
6. Development of market for produce of new crops
7. Better understanding of scientific agriculture
8. Utilization of crop residue

Multiple cropping may be double cropping, triple cropping and realy cropping.

(*i*) **Double cropping :** Growing of two crops on the same piece of land in recurring succession in one calendar year.

(*ii*) **Triple cropping :** Growing of three crops on the same piece of land in recurring succession in one calendar year.

(*iii*) **Relay cropping :** It is analogous to relay race where a crop hands over the land to the next crop in quick succession. In this system, a succeeding crop is grown before the harvesting of preceding crop and four crops are taken during one calendar year on the same piece of land.

Rotation Intensity : Average number of crops grown in a rotation per year is called rotation intensity. It is represented in percentage and one crop in a year is considered to be 100%. It is calculated with the help of the following formula :

$$\text{Rotation Intensity (\%)} = \frac{\text{Number of crops grown in rotation}}{\text{Number of years of rotation}} \times 100$$

B. Inter/mixed Cropping :

(*i*) Inter Cropping : Inter-cropping can be defined as the growing of two or more crops simultaneously on the same area of land in a definite row arrangement. In inter-cropping, there is a greater utilization of interspaced area, the spatial distribution of light, nutrients, moisture, air and microenvironment of both the rhizospheres and phyllospheres and the temporal use of resources during slow growth phase of crop by subsidiary crops.

Systems of Inter-cropping :

1. **Inter-cropping in additive series :** In this system of inter-cropping, base crop (one component crop) is grown with 100% plant population with recommended spacing and seed rate and another component crop (inter-crop) is adjusted between the rows of base crop *e.g.* sugarcane + wheat, sugarcane + potato, sugarcane + mustard, pigeonpea + green gram etc.
2. **Inter-cropping in replacement series :** In this system of inter-cropping, few rows or plants of one component crop are replaced by few rows or plants of another component crop. *e.g.* potato + mustard (3:1), potato + wheat (3:3), wheat + mustard (9:1), etc.
3. **Inter-cropping in both series :** In this system, both the inter-cropping systems are included *e.g.* sugarcane + chickpea + mustard etc. Inter-cropping may be divided into four groups :

A. Parallel cropping : Under this cropping system, two crops are selected which have different habits and zero competition between each other and both of them express their full potential *e.g.* black gram or green gram with maize etc.

B. Companion cropping : The yield of both crops is equal to their pure crops *e.g.* sugarcane + wheat, sugarcane + mustard etc.

C. Synergistic cropping : The yield of both crops grown together is higher than their pure crops *e.g.* sugarcane + potato etc.

D. Multi-storeyed cropping : Growing of plants of different heights in the same field at the same time is termed as multi-stroeyed cropping *e.g.* eucalyptus + papaya + berseem, sugarcane + potato + onion (seed), sugarcane + potato + mustard etc.

Management of inter-cropping : Important aspects are selection of suitable varieties of component crops, planting geometry (row ratio) of component crops, nutrient management and irrigation management.

Assessing yield advantage in inter-cropping :

(*i*) LER

(*ii*) Crop yield equivalent

(*iii*) Economics

(*iv*) Relative crowding coefficient

(*v*) Aggressivity

(*vi*) Competition index

Some of the above are given below:

1. Crop Equivalent Yields (CEY) : The yield of different inter-crops are converted into equivalent yield of one crop based on price of produce. It is estimated as follows :

$$\text{CEY} = \frac{\text{Yield of I crop} \times \text{price rate}}{\text{Price rate of II crop}}$$

2. Land Equivalent Ratio (LER): It is relative land area under sole crop that is required to produce the yield achieved in inter-cropping. It is calculated with the help of following formula:

$$\text{LER} = \frac{\text{Yield of component crop A in inter-cropping}}{\text{Yield of component Crop A in pure-cropping}} + \frac{\text{Yield of component crop B in inter-cropping}}{\text{Yield of component crop B in pure-cropping}}$$

If the LER is more than 1, then inter-cropping is advantageous.

3. (*i*) On economic basis : The total monetary value of economic produce and by-products obtained from the crop raised in the inter-cropping and sole-cropping are calculated based on the local market prices. Net return is obtained by substracting cost of cultivation from gross income. If net income is more in inter-cropping than sole-cropping, inter-cropping may be recommended.

(*ii*) Mixed cropping : Mixed cropping, is a process of growing two or more crops together in the same piece of land without any set row arrangement. The seeds of different crops are mixed together and then sown either in lines or broad casted. This system causes problems in performing agricultural operations and harvesting of crops. This system covers the risk under adverse climatic conditions *e.g.* wheat + gram, wheat + mustard, pigeonpea + jowar etc. There are various principles and advantages of this system.

The success of inter-cropping/mixed cropping depends on allelopathic effect of component crops.

Allelopathy : It refers to the phenomenon of biochemical interaction between root excreted chemical compounds and decomposed products of root and shoot residues. It includes autotoxicity, teletoxicity, synergisticity etc.

III. CROPPING SCHEME OR CROPPING PLAN

The plan according to which crops are raised on individual plot in fixed period with an object of getting maximum yield from each crop without impairing the fertility of soil is called cropping scheme. It is prepared in advance for ascertaining the availability of inputs.

Steps for preparation of cropping scheme :

(*i*) Assumption and limitation

(*ii*) Selection of crops according to season

(*iii*) Framing of crop rotation

(*iv*) Skeleton of cropping scheme

(*v*) Summary of cropped area

(*vi*) Cropping intensity

Cropping intensity is calculated with the help of following formula:

$$\text{Cropping intensity} = \frac{\text{Total cropped area}}{\text{Net cultivated area}} \times 100$$

IV. FUNDAMENTALS RELATED TO RAISING OF CROP

A. Selection of Suitable Variety

The basic principle is to select the variety according to agro-climatic regions and cropping systems.

B. Tillage Operations

The objectives of tillage operations are to provide loose and friable soil, to conserve moisture for longer period, to provide aeration, to provide aeration, to control weeds and to mix fertilizers in soil. Minimum and zero tillage are recommended for different crops.

(*i*) **Minimum tillage (reduced tillage):** This refers to the growing of a crop with least possible soil disturbance which involves controlling unwanted vegetation by other than mechanical means or by minimum use of tillage equipments.

(*ii*) **Zero tillage :** Zero tillage is a system in which mechanical soil manipulation is reduced to traffic and seedbed preparation only (Baeumer and Bakermans, 1973).

C. Seed and Sowing

(*i*) **Quality of seed :** Good quality of seed should be used for sowing. Seed should be of pure variety (certified), mature, free from insect-pest and diseases and have good germination capacity.

(*ii*) **Seed treatment :** It should be done according to the crop *e.g. Rhizobium* inoculation in pulses.

(*iii*) **Seed rate :** It is decided according to methods of sowing and cropping systems.

(*iv*) **Methods of sowing :** Field crops are sown in various methods.

(*a*) **Broad casting :** In this method, required quantity of seed is broad-casted uniformly on the entire area.

(*b*) **Line sowing :** Required quantity of seed is sown in rows opened by plough or seed drill. It is further divided into :

(*i*) **Regular method :** Sowing of seed is done in every furrow.

(*ii*) **Border method :** Three rows are sown and every fourth row is kept unsown and unfertilized

(*iii*) **Skip method :** Two rows are sown and every third row is kept unseeded and unfertilized but seed and fertilizer of 3rd row is adjusted on two sown rows.

(*iv*) **Dibbling :** Sowing of seed is done with the help of dibbler.

D. Optimum Plant Population

It refers to that plant population per unit area which gives maximum economical yield. The optimum plant population is adjusted by different plant geometries (ratio of rows and plant spacing) like square, rectangular, extreme rectangular and irregular etc. It depends on method of sowing of field crops.

E. Fertilizer Schedules

It includes doses sources time and method of fertilizer application.

(*i*) **Doses of fertilizer :** The correct or optimum doses of nutrients are given through various sources of fertilizers.

(*ii*) **Sources :** Various types of nitrogenous, phosphatic and potassic fertilizers as well as fertilizers containing secondary and micro-nutrients should be selected according to cropping systems.

(*iii*) **Time of application :** Time of application of manures and fertilizers are basal and topdressing.

(*iv*) **Method of fertilizer application :** The basic knowledge about method of fertilizer application is essential.

(*a*) **Solid form :**

1. **Broadcasting method :** Fertilizer is uniformly broadcasted in the entire area.
2. **Placement :** Fertilizer is placed in a certain depth irrespective of the position of seed/plant.
   (*i*) Plough sole placement
   (*ii*) Deep placement
   (*iii*) Sub-soil placement
3. **Localized placement :** Fertilizer is placed close to the seed/seedling/plant

(*i*) Contact placement or combine drilling.

(*ii*) Row placement

(*iii*) Side dressing

(*iv*) Pellet application

(*b*) Liquid Form :

1. Starter solution
2. Direct application to soil
3. Foliar application
4. Application through irrigation water.

V. IRRIGATION

The artificial application of water to the soil for the purpose of supplying moisture essential for plant growth is known as irrigation.

(*i*) Time of irrigation : According to critical stages or time interval or based on climatological approach in different crops.

(*ii*) Number of irrigation : It is decided according to the crop. Pulses and oil seeds require only 1 or 2 irrigations and wheat requires 5 irrigations.

(*iii*) Methods and systems of irrigation :

(A) **Surface method :** Water is applied directly to the soil surface from the channel located at the upper reach of the field. It is divided into flooding, border strip method, checkbasin, basin or ring method and furrow method etc.

(B) **Sub-surface :** Water is applied to the sub-surface soil through underground perforated pipes. Water gradually wets root zone through capillary movements.

(C) **Sprinkler irrigation :** Water is applied as spray or as rain over the crop with the help of pipelines.

(D) **Drip-irrigation :** Water is applied to the soil from a dripper at an extremely low pressure with the help of pipe lines. Water diffuses by capillary action in the soil.

Suitability of method depends on crop, availability of sources of water and landscape.

(*iv*) Depth of irrigation : Generally 5 to 6 ha cm water is recommended to most of the crops. Depth of irrigation is decided according to method of irrigation and crop.

VI. PLANT PROTECTION

(*i*) **Weed control :** Knowledge about the number and time of inter-cultural operations is essential. In most of the crops, up to 45 days, crop should be free from weeds.

(*ii*) **Chemical weed control :** It includes doses, time, method and selection of herbicides. Thus, fundamental ideas about these points in weedicides are essential.

(*iii*) **Diseases and their control :** Knowledge about important diseases of the crop and their control measures is essential.

(*iv*) **Insect-pests and their control :** Knowledge about the important insects of the crop and their control measures is essential.

In the present era, conscepts of integrated weed management, disease and pest managements have been developed. Thus, their concepts must be clear.

VII. HARVESTING OF PRODUCE

Crop should be harvested at physiological maturity. Thus, knowledge about symptoms of physiological maturity of the important crops is necessary.

VIII. THRESHING

Crop produce should be collected from the field as early as possible and it should be threshed properly after suitable proper drying.

Supervision and management of inputs is most essential.

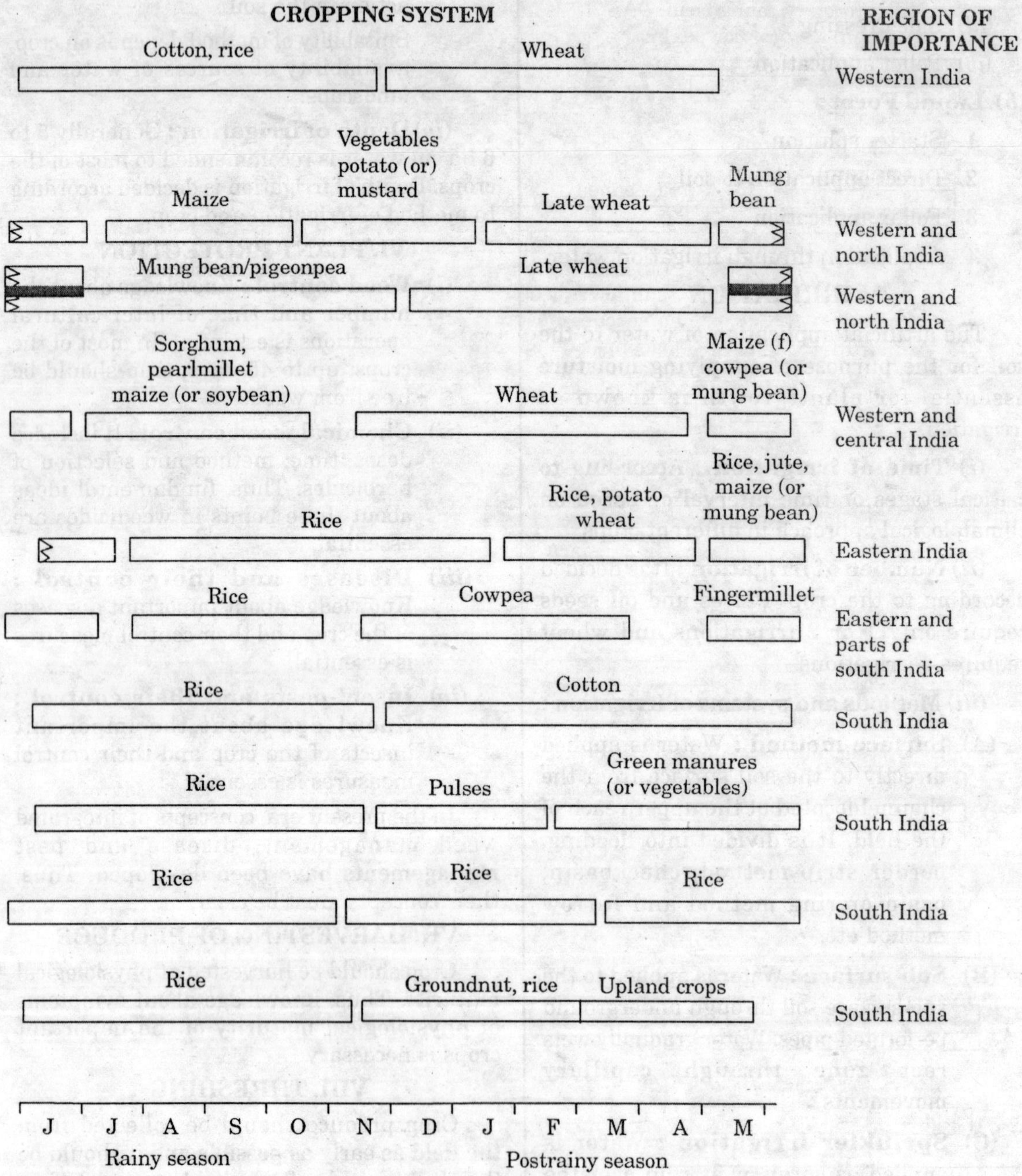

Fig. 1. Major cropping systems of irrigated areas in India.

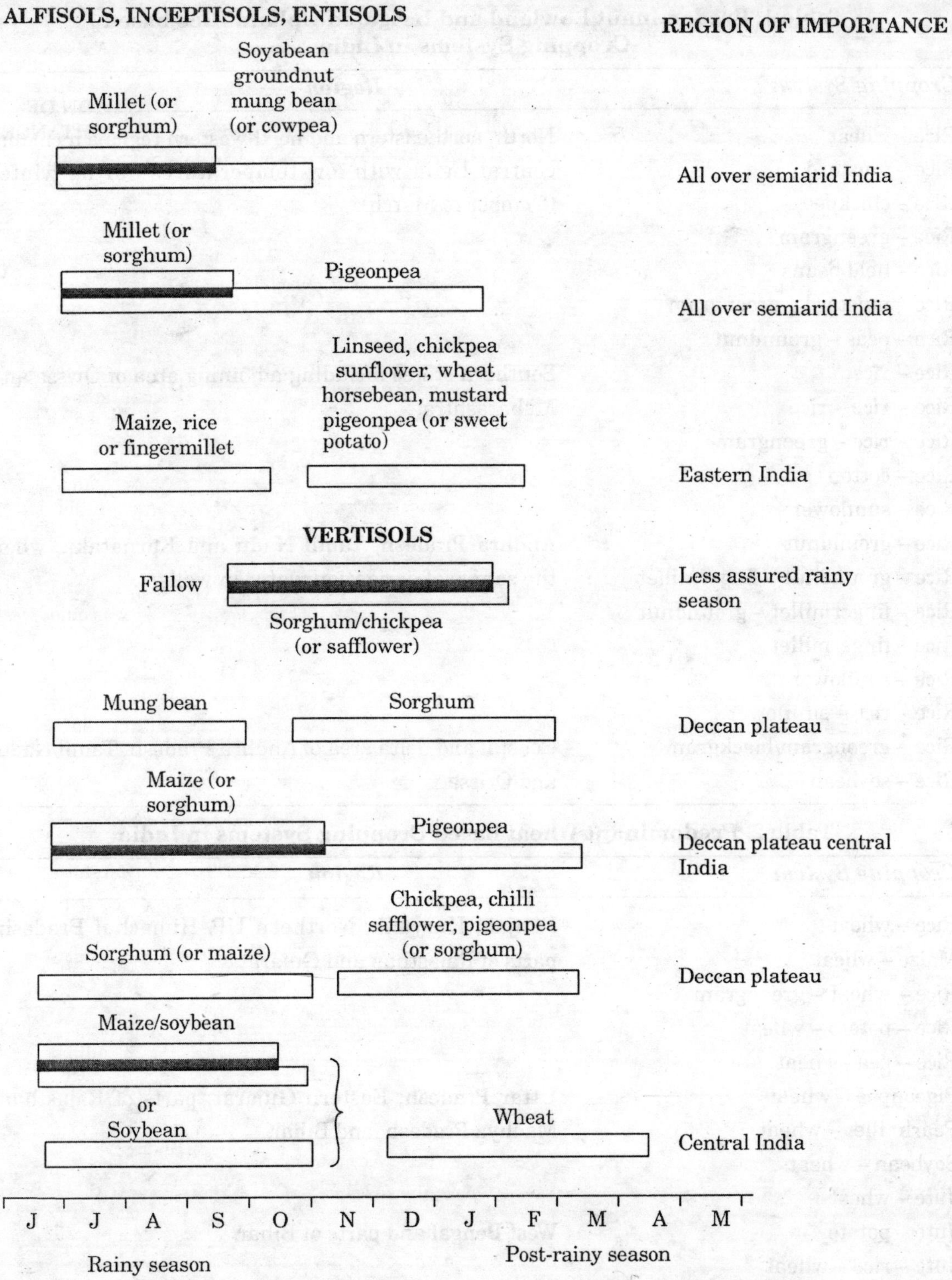

Fig. 2. Major cropping systems of rainfed areas in India.

Table 1: Predominant Lowland and Irrigated Upland Rice based Cropping Systems in India

Cropping System	*Region*
Rice – wheat Rice – mustard Rice – chickpea Rice – greengram Rice – field beans Rice – mustard – greengram Rice – peas – groundnut	North, northeastern and northwestern regions including central India with low temperatures during winter (October to March).
Rice – rice Rice – rice – rice Rice – rice – greengram Rice – cotton Rice – sunflower	Southern states including adjoining area of Orissa and Maharashtra.
Rice – groundnut Rice – groundnut – fingermillet Rice – fingermillet – groundnut Rice – fingermillet Rice – sunflower Rice – rice – sunflower	Andhra Pradesh, Tamil Nadu and Karnataka, when the source of irrigation water in wells.
Rice – greengram/blackgram Rice – soybean	Coastal and delta area of Andhra Pradesh, Tamil Nadu and Orissa.

Table 2. Predominant Wheat based Cropping Systems in India

Cropping System	*Region*
Rice – wheat Maize – wheat Rice – wheat – greengram Rice – potato – wheat Rice – pea –wheat	Punjab, Haryana, Northern UP, Himachal Pradesh, parts of Rajasthan and Gujarat.
Pigeonpea – wheat Pearlmillet – wheat Soybean – wheat	Uttar Pradesh, Eastern Gujarat, parts of Rajasthan, Madhya Pradesh and Bihar.
Jute – wheat Jute – potato Jute – rice – wheat	West Bengal and parts of Bihar.

Table 3. Broad Guidelines for Contingency Crops Planning for Delayed Onset of Monsoon under Rainfed Conditions

Zone/ region	*June to mid-July*	*Mid-August*	*Mid-September*	*Mid-October*	*Mid-November*
1	*2*	*3*	*4*	*5*	*6*
		CENTRAL REGION			
Red Soil					
Varanasi	Upland rice Maize Pearlimillet Blackgram Greengram Sesame Pigeonpea	Short duration rice Pearlmillet Blackgram Greengram Fodder sorghum and maize	—	Chickpea Barely Wheat Lentel Mustard Linseed Safflower	Wheat Mustard Lentil Linseed
Rewa	Rice Greengram Pigeonpea Groundnut Sesame Blackgram Soybean	Short duration rice Pigeonpea Groundnut Soybean	—	Wheat Safflower Barley Linseed Chickpea Lentil	Wheat Barley Chickpea Mustard
Agra	Pearlmillet Blackgram Greengram Pigeonpea Groundnut Cluster bean Cowpea	Pearlmillet Sunflower Greengram Cluster bean Cowpea	—	Mustard Barley Chickpea Safflower Lentil	—
Black Soil					
Indore	Maize Sorghum Groundnut Soybean Pigeonpea	Sunflower Pigeonpea Soybean	Safflower	Chickpea	Wheat
Jhansi	Sorghum Pigeonpea Soybean Groundnut Maize	Soybean Blackgram Pearlmillet Fodder sorghum Cowpea	—	Chickpea Safflower Mustard	Mustard Chickpea

1	2	3	4	5	6
Submontane Soil					
Dehradun	Maize Rice Soybean	Rice Soybean	Maize Toria	Wheat Barley Chickpea	Barley Chickpea
			SOUTHERN REGION		
Red Soils					
Hyderabad	Sorghum + pigeonpea Castor Pearlmillet	Fingermillet Castor Sunflower Pigeonpea	Greengram Cowpea Horsegram	Horsegram Greengram Blackgram	—
Anantapur	Groundnut + pigeonpea Sorghum Castor	Pearlmillet Castor Pigeonpea Sunflower	Pearlmillet Fodder Sorghum Greengram	Horsegram Blackgram Greengram	—
Bangalore (Bengluru)	Groundnut Maize Fingermillet Sunflower Pigeonpea	Fingermillet Sunflower Pigeonpea	Foxtailmillet Cowpea Horsegram Safflower Direct seeding of fingermillet Sunflower	Horsegram Cowpea Safflower	—
Black Soils					
Bellary	Greengram Blackgram Soybean	Soybean Cowpea Field bean	Sorghum Field bean Safflower	Sorghum Sunflower Safflower	Coriander Chickpea Safflower
Nandyal	Desi cotton Foxtailmillet Soybean Sesame Greengram	American and Hybd cotton Sunflower Pigeonpea	Coriander Sorghum Safflower Coriander Sunflower	Chickpea Coriander Blackgram Greengram	Greengram Blackgram Cowpea
Bijapur	Greengram Blackgram Pigeonpea Pearlmillet	Foxtailmillet Cotton Sunflower	Sorghum Safflower Sunflower	Sorghum Safflower Chickpea	—
Kovilpatti	—	—	Sorghum Pearlmillet	Cotton Sorghum	Coriander Sesame

1	2	3	4	5	6
			Foxtailmillet Cotton Pigeonpea	Foxtailmillet Greengram Blackgram Cowpea	
		EASTERN REGION			
Red Soils					
Ranchi	Mesta Fingermillet Sorghum Maize Groundnut Greengram Blackgram Soybean Rice Potato	Transplanted Fingermillet Soybean Cowpea	Toria	Safflower Linseed Lentil	Wheat
Bhubaneshwar region	Pigeonpea Mesta	Transplanted Fingermillet	Pigeonpea Greengram Blackgram	Horsegram	—
Black Soil					
Solapur	Groundnut Pearlmillet Pigeonpea Greengram Blackgram Cowpea Kidneybean	Foxtailmillet Pigeonpea Kidneybean Castor	Sunflower Sorghum Foxtailmillet Greengram Blackgram Horsegram	Sorghum Safflower Chickpea	Fodder Sorghum Chickpea Safflower
Akola	Sesame Pearlmillet Sorghum Cotton Groundnut Pigeonpea Sunflower	Sorghum Sunflower Cowpea Greengram Blackgram	Safflower Cowpea Greengram Blackgram	Safflower Chickpea	—

1	*2*	*3*	*4*	*5*	*6*
Rajkot	Sorghum Pearlmillet Groundnut Castor Cotton Sesame	Cotton Castor Greengram Blackgram Clusterbean	Greengram Blackgram Cowpea Cluster bean	—	—
Udaipur	Sorghum Maize Pigeonpea Cowpea	Greengram Blackgram Cowpea Soybean	—	Chickpea Safflower Mustard	Mustard Chickpea
Desert Soils					
Dandtiwada	Pearlmillet Sorghum Fingermillet Pigeonpea Castor Clusterbean Greengram	Transplanted Pearlmillet Fingermillet Castor Sunflower	Tobacco Sunflower	Tobacco	—
Jodhpur	Pearlmillet Greengram Cowpea Clusterbean Mothbean Castor Sesame	Greengram Cowpea Sunflower Castor Clusterbean Mothbean Transplanted Pearlmillet	—	—	—
		NORTHERN REGION			
Submontane Soil					
Hoshiarpur region	Maize Pearlmillet Groundnut Soybean Blackgram	Pearlmillet Fooder crops Cowpea	—	Wheat Barley Mustard Chickpea	Barley Mustard Chickpea

1	2	3	4	5	6
Rakh Dhiansar region	Maize Sorghum Pearlmillet Greengram Blackgram Cowpea Sesame Castor	Greengram Blackgram Cowpea Sunflower	—	Wheat Barley Rapeseed Linseed Chickpea Lentil	Wheat Barley Chickpea Lentil
Desert Soils					
Hissar	Pearlmillet Clusterbean Greengram Mothbean	Transplanted Pearlmillet Clusterbean Cowpea	Clusterbean Cowpea	Chickpea Taramira Rapeseed Safflower	Mustard Taramira

PACKAGE OF PRATICES FOR PROUDCUTION OF IMPORTANT CROPS GROWN DURING RABI AND KHARIF SEASONS IN DIFFERENT REGIONS OF THE COUNTRY

Rice :

Botanical name	:	*Oryza sativa L.*
Family	:	Gramineae or Poacea
Origin	:	India
Climate	:	The average temperature required for crop period ranges from 21 to 37°C.
Soil	:	Clay or clay loam having pH 5.5 to 6.5.

Improved Agronomic Practices :

Land preparation : One ploughing with S.T.P. and two to three intercross ploughings with harrow or cultivator followed by planking.

Methods of Sowing/Transplanting :

1. Direct sowing

2. Transplanting

System of Cultivation :

1. Dry or semi-dry upland cultivation

(*a*) Broadcasting the seed

(*b*) Sowing the seed behind the plough or drilling

Seed rate – 55 to 60 kg/ha.

2. Wet or lowland cultivation

(*a*) Transplanting in Puddled soils

(*b*) Broadcasting of sprouted seeds in puddle soils

Time of Sowing/Transplanting :

In North India it is grown only in Kharif season but in South India it is grown in Kharif, Rabi and summer seasons.

Kharif : *(1) Rainfed areas :* At start of monsoon.

(2) Irrigated Condition : 25th June to 15th July.

Rabi : October – November

Summer : February – March

Raising of Nursery :

Select a fertile well drained upland field near the source of irrigation. For transplanting one hectare area, about 500-600 m^2 area for normal and about 750-1000 m^2 area for late planting is enough. Seed rate for bold grain varieties is 40 to 45 kg/ha while for fine varieties 30 to 35 kg/ha seed is enough. After puddling, field should be divided into narrow beds of 1.25 m width and any convenient length with 30 cm wide drainage channel between seed beds. Fertilizer should be applied @ 100 kg N + 50 kg P_2O_5 + 25 kg zinc sulphate + 200 kg Gypsum/ha. According to need, frequent irrigation should be provided. Seed should be treated with thiram @ 3 g/kg of seed.

Methods of Raising Seedlings :

(i) Wet bed method

(ii) Dry bed method

(iii) Dapog method

Transplanting :

After puddling, transplanting should be done at 20 cm × 10 cm distance with two to three seedlings/hill. The optimum age of seedlings for transplanting is 3 to 4 weeks for short duration and 4 to 5 weeks for medium and long duration varieties. In abnormal, soils, 45 days old seedlings should be transplanted.

Varieties :

(A) Unirrigated :

1. **Direct sowing :** Saket-4, Govind, Narendra-118 and Ashwani.
2. **Transplanted :** Saket-4, Govind, Prasad, Narendra-80 and Ashwani.

(B) Irrigated :

1. **Early maturing (100 to 120 days):** Govind, Ashwani, Narendra-2, Narendra-118, Ratna, Pusa-169, Prasad and R-50.
2. Medium maturing (120 to 140 days) : Narendra-356, Pant-4, Pant-10, Pant-12, Sita, Sarjoo-52, Jaya, IR-8, Pusa-166, Malviya-36 and PNR-381.
3. **Late maturing (more than 140 days):** T-9, Mahsuri, T-23, Cross-116, T-100 and Pankaj.

(C) Scented rice : T-3, Kasturi, PB-1, HB-1, Basmati-370, N-12 and Pakistan Basmati-217

(D) Usar soil rice : Lakara (T-22A), Usar-1, Usar-2, CSR-10, CSR-13, Saket-4, Jhona-349, Jaya, IR-8 and Sarjoo-52.

(E) Low Land Rice :

1. Upto 30 cm deep water : T-100, Cross-116, Mahsuri, Jallahari, Sona, Pankaj and Swarna.
2. 30 to 50 cm deep water : Chakiya-59, Madhukar and Jalpriya.
3. More than 120 cm deepwater; Jalnidhi and Jalmagna.
4. Flooded conditions : Madhukar Chakiya-59 and Badh Awarodhi.

Fertilizer Management :

1. Desi variety : 60 kg N + 30 kg P_2O_5 + 30 kg K_2O/ha.
2. High yielding varieties : 120 kg N + 60 kg P_2O_5 + 60 kg K_2O + 25 kg Zinc Sulphate + 200 kg Gypsum/ha. 1/2 N + full P_2O_5 + K_2O, zinc sulphate and gupsum as basal. Remaining 1/2 N should be applied in two splits at tillering and before panicle initiation stage.

Water Management :

The water requirement is high during initial seedling period. Covering 10 days tillering to flowering is the most critical stage when crop should not be subjected to any moisture stress. Generally 5 cm water should be maintained up to dough stage.

Weed Management :

Weed should be removed twice at 20 to 25 and 50 to 60 days after transplanting through weeding. Broad and narrow leaved weeds can be controlled by application of Butachlore (50 EC) @ 3 to 4 litres or pendimethiline (30 EC) @ 3.3 litres per hectare in 800 to 1000 litres of water within 3 to 4 days of transplanting. Only broad leaved weeds can be controlled by 2-4, D Sodium salt @ 625 g/ha mixed in 800 to 1000 litres of water applied at 20 days after transplanting.

Plant Protection Measures :

(A) Diseases :

1. Blast : Caused by *Pyricularia oryzae.*

Control :

(*i*) Seed treated with any organic mercurial compound should be sown.

(*ii*) Grow resistant varieties like - IR-8, IR-20, IR-24, Jaya and Ratna.

(*iii*) Spray 0.1 % Hinosan 50 EC or Benlate or Bavistin.

2. Brown spot : Caused by *Helminthosporium oryzae.*

Control :

(*i*) Treated seed should be sown.

(*ii*) Resistant varieties like - IR-24, Krishna, Bala and Sabarmati should be grown.

(*iii*) 3 to 4 spraying of zineb or maneb @ 0.25% at 10 to 12 days interval should be done.

3. Stem rot : Caused by *Leptospheria salvinii.*

Control :

(*i*) Destroy infected plants.

(*ii*) Avoid standing water in the field for longer period.

4. Sheath blight : Caused by *Corticium saskaii*

5. Bacterial leaf spot : Caused by *Xanthomonas oryzae.*

Control :

(*i*) Use disease free seed.

(*ii*) To check the blight phase of disease, use Agrimycin-100 (75 g) and 500 g copper oxychloride.

6. Kharia disease : Caused due to zinc deficiency.

Control :

Spray mixture of 5 kg zinc sulphate and 2.5 kg lime mixed in 1000 litres of water in nursery at three times.

(B) Insect pests : Stem borer, gall midge, rice hispa, leaf roller, armyworm, Gandhi bug, mole cricket, green leaf hopper and plant hopper are the common insects.

Control :

(*i*) Dusting of malathion 5% @ 20 to 25 kg/ha two to three times should be done.

(*ii*) Spray Dimecron 100 EC @ 1.5 litre/ha] mixed in 800 to 1000 litres of water.

Yield :

1.	Short duration	45 to 55 q/ha
2.	Mid late	60 to 65 q/ha
3.	Scented	30 to 35 q/ha

Wheat :

Botanical name	:	*Triticum aestivum L.*
Family	:	Gramineae or Poaceae
Origin	:	South Western Asia

Climate :

Wheat can be cultivated from the sea level to as high as 3300 meter. The optimum temperature for better germination is 20 to 25° C and for ripening 14 to 15° C.

Soil : Clay loam with good water holding capacity.

Varieties :

1. For Bhaber and Tarai Region :

Sowing time	:	Second fortnight of October.
Unirrigated	:	C-306
Sowing time	:	First fortnight of November.
Unirrigated	:	C- 306, K-78, PBW-175 and K-8027.
Irrigated	:	UP-2338, CPAN-3004 (Sangam), PBW-215, WH-896, WH-542,

PBW-343, UP-2382 and HD-2687.

Sowing time : Second fortnight of November.

Irrigated : K-68, CPAN-3004, UP-2338, PBW-342, UP-2382 and HD-2687.

Sowing time : Late sown up to 25 December.

Irrigated : UP-2338, WH-291, Malviya-234, Raj-3077, Raj-3765, PBW-373, UP-2425 and PBW-343.

2. Western plains region : Same as Bhaber and Tarai Region.

3. Central western region : Same as Bhaber and Tarai Region.

4. South western semi-arid region : Same as Bhaber and Tarai Region.

5. Central plain region :

Sowing time : Second fortnight of October to second fortnight of November.

Unirrigated : C-306, K-8027 (maghar), K-8962 (Indra), K-9465 (Gomti), K-88, UP-2338, WH-542, K-9006 (Ujiyar) CPAN-3004 (Sangam), HP-1731 (Raj laxmi), NW-1012, UP-2382, K-9107 (Deva), HUW-468 and PBW-343.

Sowing time : For khader soils, second fortnight of November.

Unirrigated : K-78 and K-8027.

Irrigated : DL-784-3, UP-2338, K-88, CPAN-3004, K-9107 (Deva), K-9006 (Ujiyar), UP-2382, HP-1721, NW-1012, HUW-468 and PBW-343.

Sowing time : Late sown up to 25 December.

Irrigated : HUM-234, K-8020 (Triveni), HD-2643, UP-2338, HP-1633 (Sonali), HO-1744, NW-1014 and UP-2425.

North Eastern Plains Region :

Sowing time : Second fortnight of October to first fortnight of November.

Unirrigated : C-306, K-8027, K-8962 (Indra) and K-9465

Irrigated : U.P.-2003, K-88, DL-784-3, K-9107, HUW-206, HP-1731, K-9006, NW-1012, UP-2382 and HUW-486.

Sowing time : Second fortnight of November.

Irrigated : DL-784-3, UP-2338, K-88, Malviya-206, UP-2003, K-9107, HP-1731, K-9006, NW-1012, UP-2382 and HUW-268.

Sowing time : Late sown upto 15 December.

Irrigated : HD-2285, HP-1209, HUW-234, HP-1633, HP-1744 NW-1014, K-8020, HD-2643 and UP-2425.

7. Eastern plain and Vindhya region :

Sowing time : Same as North eastern plains :

8. Usar soils

Irrigated : KRL-1-4, Raj-3077, Lok-1 and PBW-65.

9. Bundelkhand :

Sowing time : Second fortnight of October.

Unirrigated : K-8027, C-306, Sujata and K-8962.

Irrigated : DL-803, GW-190, HD-2236, Raj-1555, HI-838, HI 8498, K-88, K-9107, UP-2382 and WH-147

Sowing time : Late sown upto 15 December.

Irrigated	:	HI-784, Malviya-234, HP-1633, DL-788-2 and UP-2425.

For Bundelkhand Region :

Timely sown	:	Kalyan Sona, Jairaj HD-4530 and Raj-911
Late sown	:	C-306, Mukta, Meghdoot and NP-401
Salt-affected area	:	WH-157 and KRL 1-4

Crop Rotation :

(*i*) Paddy-wheat	1 year
(*ii*) Maize-potato-wheat	1 year
(*iii*) Maize-toria-wheat-moong	1 year
(*iv*) Maize-wheat-Sugarcane-Ratoon	3 years

Field preparation : One ploughing with S.T.P. and 2 to 3 harrowing followed by planking

Seed and Sowing

(*i*) Seed rate :

Timely sown	:	100 kg/ha
Late sown	:	125 kg/ha
Rainfed area	:	100 to 125 kg/ha
Dibler sown	:	25 kg/ha

(*ii*) Time of sowing : First fortnight of November

Late- upto 25th December

(*iii*) Spacing :

Normal sown	:	20 to 22.5 cm
Late sown	:	15 to 18 cm
Rainfed sown	:	20 to 23 cm

(*iv*) Depth :

Dwarf varieties	:	5 cm
Semi dwarf	:	5-6 cm
Late sown crop	:	4 cm

(*v*) Method of sowing : Kera or Pora method, mostly broadcasting but scientifically by seed cum fertilizer dril.

Fertilizer and its Application :

Condition	*N,P_2 O_5 and K_2O kg/ha*			*Time & Method of application*
(*i*) Irrigated	120	60	60	1/2 of N % total P and K applied at 5 cm below the seed, remaining 1/2 N at Ist irrigation
(*ii*) Late sown	100	80	40	1/2 of N and total P and K applied at 5 cm below the seed, remaining 1/2 N at 1st irrigation.
(iii) Rainfed	40	20	—	Total NPK should be applied at 8-10 cm deep in soil before sowing

Irrigation : Total need of water of 44 to 46 cm for complete life cycle.

No. of Irrigation	*Stage*	*DAS*
Ist	CRI	20 to 25
IInd	Tillering	40 to 45
III rd	Late jointing	70 to 75
IVth	Flowring	90 to 95
Vth	Dough stage	100 to 110

But if only one irrigation is possible then at CRI 20 to 25 DAS. When only two irrigations are available then Ist at CRI and 2nd at flowering. When only three irrigation are available then Ist at CRI, 2nd at late jointing and 3rd at milking stage.

Weed Control :

For Broad leaves : 2,4-D-sodium salt @ 625 g dissolved in 600 to 800 litre of water and spray at 30 to 35 DAS.

For monocot weeds : Isoproturon 75% WP @ 1 kg dissolved in 400 to 600 litre of water and spray at 30 to 35 DAS.

Disease and Pest Control :

Rusts : For black rust, brown rust and yellow rust spray Dithane M-45@ 0.2%.

Loose smut : Seed treatment with Vitavax @ 2.5 g/kg seed.

Karnal bunt : Seed treatment with Agrosan G.N. @ 2.5 g/kg seed.

Powdery mildew : Dithane M-45 @ 0.2%.

Insect pest : Aldrin dust @ 20 to 25 kg/ha should be mixed in soil at last ploughing.

Rodents : Aluminium phosphide, 1 tablet (0.5 g) should be kept into each burrow at morning time and burrow should be closed.

Harvesting : At proper stage of harvesting when grain contain about 20 to 25% moisture, crop is harvested by sickle manually but recently combines are also available for this purpose.

Grain yield : Dwarf irrigated condition-45 to 55 q/ha.

Rainfed condition-20 to 25 q/ha.

Straw yield : 1.5 to 2 times of grain yield.

Chickpea :

Botanical name : *Cicer arietinum* L.

Family : Leguminosae of Fabaceae.

Origin : South Western Asia.

Climate : Average rainfall 65 to 100 cm and temperature 12 to 15°C.

Soil : Loam, heavy loam, Mar and Paruva with good drainage conditions having 6.5 to 7.5 pH.

Varieties :

1. **Timely sown :** Pusa-256, K-850, Awrodhi, KWR-108, Pant G-114, JG-315, KGD-1168, Sadabahar, Radhey and Karnal gram-1.
2. **Late sown** : Uday, Pant G-186 and PDG 84-10.
3. **Kabuli** : L-550, Pusa-267, K-4 and K-5.

Field preparation : Ist ploughing with S.T.P. and two ploughings with desi plough or cultivator followed by planking should be done.

Seed treatment : (*i*) Thiram @ 2.5 g/kg seed.

(*ii*) *Rhizobium* culture-1 packet/10 kg seed.

Seed rate : Timely sown- 80 to 90 kg/ha.

Late sown-100 to 125 kg/ha.

Sowing Time :

1. **Normal sown :** Unirrigated-2nd to 3rd week of October Irrigated-Second week of November.
2. **Late sown** : 1st week of December

Spacing : (*i*) Unirrigated and Late Sown- 30 cm apart.

(*ii*) Irrigated-45 cm apart.

Fertilizer : 20 kg N + kg P_2O_5 + 25-30 kg sulphur per hectare should be given.

Irrigation : First at 45 to 60 days after sowing (before flowering) and second at grain formation stage.

Weed control : Spray 2 litres Flucchlorine 45 EC mixed in 800 to 1000 litres of water before sowing or 3.3 litres Pendimethiline 30 EC just after sowing.

Diseases :

***(i)* Wilt :** Caused by a fungus *Fusarium orthocerus.*

Control :

1. Mixed cropping with linseed.
2. Grow resistant variety like-Awarodhi.

***(ii)* Blight :** Caused by a fungus *Sclerotinia sclerotiorum*

Control : Treat the soil with a mixture of Brassicol and Captan @ 10 kg/ha.

Insect pests : Cut worm and gram pod borer.

Control : Spray Endosulphan 35 EC @ 1.25 litres mixed in 1000 litres of water/ha.

Yield : Timely sown - 25 to 30 q/ha.
Late sown - 20 to 25 q/ha.
Kabuli - 25 to 30 q/ha.

Pigeonpea :

Botanical Name	:	*Cajanus cajan* L. Millssp.
Family	:	Leguminosae or Fabaceae
Origin	:	Africa.
Climate	:	Tropical and sub tropical.
Soil	:	Fertile well drained loamy soils.

Varieties :

1. **Early :** -T-21, UPAS-120, Pusa-6, ICPL-151 and Prabhat.
2. **Late :** T-7, T-17, Bahar, Amar, Narendra-1 and Azad.

Seed Treatment:

1. Seed should be treated with Thirum. @ 2g/1kg of seed.
2. *Rhizobium* culture @ 1 packet/10 kg of seed.

Seed rate	:	Early - 12 to 15 kg/ha. Late - 15 to 20 kg/ha.
Spacing	:	Early - 45 cm × 20 cm Late - 60 cm × 30 cm
Sowing time	:	Early - April to June Late - July
Fertilizer	:	15 kg N + 40 – 45 kg P_2O_5/ha.

Weed control : Spray Pendimethiline 30 EC @ 3.0 litres mixed in 800 to 1000 litres of water just after sowing.

Diseases :

***(i)* Wilt :** Caused by a fungus *Fusarium oxysporum.*

Control : 1. Crop rotation and mixed cropping with jowar.

2. Grow resistant variety like Mukta.

***(ii)* Stem rot :** Caused by a fungus *Phytophthora dischsleri.*

Control : Good drainage facilities should be provided.

***(iii)* Sterility mosaic :** Caused by virus and spreads through *Eriophyid* mite.

Control : Mite should be controlled by spraying 0.1% metathorax.

Insect pests : Pod borer, pod fly, hairy caterpillar and leaf hopper.

Control : Spray Endosulphan 35 EC @ 1.5 litres mixed in 800 to 1000 litres of water per hectare.

Yield : Early- 16 to 20 q/ha.
Late- 25 to 30 q/ha.

Sugarcane :

Botanical name	:	*Saccharum officinarum* L.
Family	:	Gramineae or Poaceae
Origin	:	India

Importance and Uses :

Sugarcane is the main source of sugar in India and world. It account for about 50% of total sugar production in the world. The sugar recovery is about 10 and 11%.

Climate : The crop requires hot and humid climate for optimum growth. Optimum temperature for its germination and growth is 26 to 32°C. The average annual rain-fall is 75 to 120 cm. The pH of soil should be between 6 and 8.

Soil : Well drained loam soil.

Season of Planting :

(1) Adsali planting - June to July

(2) Autumn planting - 10th Oct. to 25th Oct.

(3) Spring planting - Feb. to March

(4) Summer planting - April to May

Verieties :

1. For Western U.P. :

(*i*) **Early :** CoJ-64, CoS-8436, CoS-88230, CoS-87216 and Co- 687.

(*ii*) **Medium and late :** CoS-8816, CoS-91269, CoS-95270, CoS-94257 and CoS -747

2. For Central U.P. :

(*i*) **Early :** CoS-687, CoJ-64, Bo-47 and CoS-8436.

(*ii*) **Medium and late :** CoS- 8407, CoS-8439, 8432, UP-15, CoS-767, 91269 and 86218.

3. For Eastern U.P. :

(*i*) **Early :** Co-687, CoS-8436, Bo-47 and CoS-416.

(*ii*) **Medium and late :** CoS-8432, Co-617, Bo-54, Bo-70, U.P.-15 and CoS-8407.

Improved Agronomic Practices :

Field preparation : One ploughing with S.T.P. and five to six ploughings with local plough followed by planking should be done. There must be enough moisture at the time of planting.

Selection of seed : Healthy seed should be used which is free from pest and diseases. The top one-third portion of cane has buds of high viability and is best for sowing.

Seed rate : About 35000 to 40000 three budded sets are needed to plant one hectare area which can be obtained from about 70 to 80 quintals of cane.

Seed treatment : The seed sets should be dipped into 0.5% solution of Agalol (3%) or 0.25% solution of Aretan (6%) or Tafasan (6%) before planting.

Methods of Planting :

1. Flat planting
2. Furrow planting
3. Trench method

Spacing : 60-75 and 90 cm apart

Manures and fertilizers : 120 to 150 kg, N, 80 to 100 kg P_2O_5 and 60 to 80 kg K_2O/ha - 1/3 dose of N and full doses of P and K should be given as basal at sowing in furrows and remaining nitrogen should be given at two split doses, 1/3 at tillering and 1/3 at growing period or at earthing.

Irrigation : In summer season at 10 to 15 days and in winter season 25 to 30 days interval. Irrigation should be given at 50% available moistur soil.

Weed Control :

(*i*) Mechanical methods can be practised effectively during premonsoon period.

(*ii*) Spray 2.00 kg a.i. Simazine or Atrazine mixed in 800 to 1000 litres of water per hectare just after planting.

Earthing and tying : Earthing should be done in the month of June to July which prevents from lodging of the crop. Tying should be done in August when crop reaches about 2 metres height.

Diseases :

1. Red rot : Caused by *Colletotrichum falcatum*.

Control : (*i*) Treated seed should be sown.

(*ii*) Resistant variety like CoJ- 64 should be grown.

2. Wilt : Caused by *Cephalosporium sacchari.*

Control :

(*i*) Seed should be treated with Agalol or Aretan before planting.

(*ii*) No ratoon should be kept.

3. Albino (grassy shoot) : Caused by virus.

Control :

(*i*) Resistant variety like CoS - 8432 and Co - 62399 should be grown.

(*ii*) Seed should be treated with hot water at 50°C for 22 minutes before planting.

4. Red stripe : Caused by *Xanthomonas rubrilineans.*

Control :

(*i*) Drainage facilities should be provided.

Insects pests : Early shoot borer, pyrilla root borer, Gurdaspur borer, top borer, pyrilla, black bug and sugarcane white fly are the common insects.

Control : Spray 1.5 litres of Endosulphan 35 EC or Nuvacron 40 EC mixed in 800 litres of water per hectare.

Harvesting : Maturity of cane can be identified through arrowing drying of leaves and by brix per cent when it become between 17 and 18 %.

Yield : The average yield is 400 to 500 q/ha.

High yielding varieties -800 to 1000 q/ha.

Groundnut:

Botanical name : *Arachis hypogaea*

Family : Leguminoseae

Origin : Brazil (South Africa)

Among the oilseed crops, groundnut has first place in India. Groundnut oil is primarily used in manufacture of vegetable oil. Seed contains about 45% oil and 26% protein.

Classification : It is divided in two groups.

(*i*) Erect or bunch type.

(*ii*) Trailing or spreading type.

Climatic requirement : Annual average rainfall of atleast 50 cm. The best temperature for growth is 21 to 26°C.

Soil : Well drained sandy and sandy learn soils. (*i*) Erect or bunch type- T-64, G-201 varieties (Kaushal), Chitra (semi spreading).

(*ii*) Spreading type - T-28, Chandra, H-13, Prakash, Ambar.

Field preparation : One ploughing with soil turning plough followed by two harrowings would be sufficient to achieve a good surface tilth upto 12 to 18 cm depth. One or two summer ploughing will minimize the weed and insect pests to great extent in problem areas.

Seed and sowing

Seed treatment : Selected kernels should be treated with 5 g of Thiram or Captan or Ceresan per kg of Kernels to check the various seed and soil borne diseases. Seed should be inoculated with proper strain of *Rhizobium* culture where groundnut is to be grown for the first time.

Seed rate :

(*i*) Bunch type - 90 kg/ha.

(*ii*) Spreading type - 55 to 75 kg/ha.

Spacing :

(*i*) Bunch type - 40 × 20 cm or 30 × 20 cm.

(*ii*) Spreading type - 45 × 20 cm or 60 × 20 cm.

Time of sowing : Mid-June to mid-July.

Manures and fertilizers : 10 to 15 tonnes F.Y.M or Compost 15 to 20 days before sowing. 20 kg N + 30 kg P_2O_5 + 45 kg K_2O + 200 kg Gypsum + 4 kg Borax/ha.

Full N, P, K + 1/2 Gypsum as a basal and rest 1/2 Gypsum + full Borax as top dressing after three weeks of sowing followed by light hoeing.

Irrigation : Two irrigations if rains do not occur, Ist at pegging and 2nd at pod formation stage.

Weed control and earthing : Ist weeding and hoeing at 15 to 20 days after sowing and IInd at 30 to 35 days after sowing followed by earthing. For chemical weed control, Pendimethiline 30 EC 3.3 litre/ha or Alachlore 50 EC 4 litre/ha with 600 to 800 litres of water 3 to 4 days after sowing should be sprayed.

Digging : Crop should be harvested after complete maturity when kernel colour becomes pink.

Disease :

(*i*) **Tikka :** This disease is caused by two species of fungus :

1. *Cercospora personata,* and
2. *Cercospora arachidicola.*

Control :

1. Spray 2 kg Zineb with 1000 litres of water 4 times.
2. Treated seed should be sown with Thirum @ 3g/kg of seed.

(*ii*) **Seed and pre-emergence rot:**

Control : Seed should be treated with Thiram @ 3 g/kg seed.

(*iii*) **Sclerotium rot :** This disease is caused by fungus *Sclerotium rolfsii.*

Control : Seed should be treated with Brassicol @ 3%.

(*iv*) **Characoal rot :** This disease is caused by virus transmitted through aphids.

Control : For control of aphid, spray Metasystox 25 EC @ 1 litre with 1000 litres of water/ha.

Insect :

1. Termite :

Control : Mix 5% Aldrin dust @ 25 kg/ha in soil at last ploughing,

2. Bihar Hairy Caterpillar :

Control : Spray Thiodan 35 EC or Ekalux 25@1 millilitre/litre of water.

Yield :

1. Bunch type - 15 to 20 q/ha.
2. Spreading type - 20 to 30 q/ha.

Tomato :

Botanical name	:	*Lycopersicon esculentum*
Family	:	Solanaceae
Origin	:	Tropical America

Composition (100 g fruit) :

Moisture : 93.1 g	Carbohydrate: 3.6 g
Protein : 1.9 g	Vitamin A : 32 i.u.
Fat : 0.1 g	Vitamin C : 31 mg

Climate requirement : Tomato is a warm season crop. Tomato pollen grains germinate best at 29.4°C, good at 21.1°C and poorly at 10°C. It cannot be grown successfully in regions of higher rainfall sensitive to frost.

Soil : Clay loam and silt-loam soils of 6 to 7 pH are well suited for higher yields. Light soil is good for early crop.

Varieties :

Determinate type : Punjab Chhuhara, Roma, KS-1, Punjab Keshri, Pusa early dwarf, Pusa Gaurav, Hisar Lalima, Pusa red plum, K-S-1, S-12, S-32, K-S-118.

Indeterminate type : Best of all, Pant Bahar, Pusa Rubi, S-120, Sioux, Arka Vikash, Arka Saurabh, Pant T-3.

Hybrids : ARTH-4, MTH-6, ARTH-3, Arka Vardhan, Pusa Hybrid-2, KT-4, NA-601, NA-501, DTH-4.

Disease resistant : WR-5, LE-79-5.

Seed and sowing : Nursery beds are prepared in June/July.

(*i*) **Seed rate :** 500 g seed for 1 ha transplanting.

Hybrid -300g seeds are sufficient.

(*ii*) **Time of transplanting :** 3 to 4 week old seedlings should be transplanted.

(*iii*) **Distance :** Early 60 cm × 4 cm.

Angurlata - 90 cm × 60 cm (Kitchen garden) (1.0 m × 30 cm).

About 25000 plants should be planted in one hectare field.

Manuring : 100 kg FYM at last polishing.

40 : 40 : 40 kg NPK/ha is needed for good cropping.

Time of application : 1/2 N + Full dose of P and K should be applied as basal and rest 1/2 N should be top dressed 30 days after transplanting.

Method of application : Band placement 7.5 to 10 cm deep on both sides of row before making furrows.

Irrigation : In summer season, at 8 to 10 days interval and in winter at 20 to 25 days interval.

Interculture Operation :

Weed control : Two hoeing should be done at regular interval for providing condition free from weeds, proper aeration and root development. Application of Pendimethiline 1 kg per ha or Oxyflorefen 0.25 kg per ha should be done before planting of crop.

Disease Control :

(*i*) **Damping off :** Caused by *Pyphium apheridermatum.*

Control: Disease may be controlled by soil sterilization in the field condition with spraying of Formaldehyde @ 1 lit. dissolved in 270 litre of water. Planting should be done 2 weeks after spraying.

(*ii*) **Bacterial blight :** Caused by *Pseudomonas solanacearum.* It is soil borne disease. Resistant varieties should be grown.

(*iii*) **Early blight:** Caused by *Alternaria solani* Black spot with concentric rings appear on leaf.

Control : Spray 0.2% Dithane M-45.

(*iv*) **Fruit rot:** Caused by *Phytophora licopersici*. Brownish spot occur on fruits.

Control : Spray Difolatan 0.3% at weekly interval.

(*v*) **Powdery mildew :** Caused by *Odium* spp.

Control : Wettable sulphur 0.25% should be sprayed at weekly interval.

(*vi*) **Leaf curl virus :** Spray 0.05% Malathion at 10 days interval.

(*vii*) **T. M.V. :** It can be controlled by spray of 0.2% Monocrotophos.

(*viii*) **Sun injury:** Avoid the defoliation leading to exposure of fruits to sun.

Pest Control :

(*i*) **Epilachna beetle :** Spray 0.2% Phosphamidon at weekly interval.

(*ii*) **Root knot nematode:** Caused by *Meloidogyne incognita.*

Nursery control : Apply Carbofuran @ 0.3 g a.i./m^2.

Seed soaked with 0.1% Dimethoate solution should be sown.

Harvesting and Yield :

(*i*) **Pink stage :** Most suited for local market.

(*ii*) **Ripe stage :** Home and table use.

(*iii*) **Full ripe stage :** For processing purpose.

Yield : 250 q/ha average yield but excellent crop may give 400 q/ha yield.

Seed production: To get true to type seed, no other tomato variety should be grown at least within 50 m around. The crushed fruits are allowed to ferment for 1 to 2 days and then put in water whose pulp and skin float and seed settle down at bottom. Average seed yield is 143 kg/ha. For obtaining 1 kg seed, 160 to 210 kg tomato is required.

Mango

Botanical name	:	*Mangifera indica*
Family	:	Anacardiaceae
Origin	:	Indo-Burma region

Area and production : Mango is grown all over world. U.P. has the largest area and production followed by Bihar, A.P., W.B., Tamil Nadu and Orissa. The average fruit production in India is 8 to 10 ton /ha which is lower than world's productivity 14 to 16 ton/ha. Total area in India is 12.2 lakh ha. Mango covers 42% of area in India and contributes about 70% of world production.

Climate : Ideal temperature for better growth is 24 to 26°C. It requires frost free weather at flowering and sufficient heat at ripening. Mango can be grown at 1400 metre altitude. Mango thrives will in tropical and sub-tropical climate.

Soil : Well drained deep loam soil and deep alluvial soil with 5.5 to 7.5 pH.

Varieties :

A. Monoembryonic:

(a) Table Varieties :

(*i*)North India :

- Early - Bombay green, Bombay yellow, Gopal Bhog, Rataul, Gaurjeet.
- Mid - Dashehri, Langra, Gulab Khash, Krishna Bhog, Malihabadi, Safeda.
- Late - Samarbahist Chausa, Taimuria, Ram Kela.

(*ii*) Southern India :

- Mid - Alphanso (export variety), Rumani, Banganpalli.
- Late - Neelam, (regular bearer), Mulgoa.
- Early - Swarna Rekha (colour variety).

(b) Sucking varieties : - Raspunia, Mithuwa Ghazipur, Hardilaziz, Lucknow Safeda.

3. Polyembryonic: – Olour, Goa, Salem, Chandra Kiran, Bellary, Bappakai, Kurankan, Maza Gaon, Neleswar.

Some New Hybrids :

Amrapali	-	Dashehri × Neelam (IARI dwarf, Regular bearing).
Mallika	-	Neelam × Dashehri (IARI, regular).
Sindhu	-	Ratna × Alphanso (seedless, regular).
Ratna	-	Neelam × Alphanso.
Arka Aruna	-	Banganpalli × Alphanso (dwarf, kitchen garden, regular bearing and fruit size 500 g and free from spongy tissue).
Arka puneet	-	Alphanso × Banganpalli (regular bearer, free from spongy tissue and good for processing).
Arka Anmol	-	Alphanso × Janardan Prasad (Semi vigorous, regular, free from spongy tissue).
PKM-1	-	China Swarna Rekha × Neelam (regular, cluster fruiting, Tamil Nadu Agri. University).
PKM-2	-	Neelam × Malgoa, (regular).
M.D.C.H.-1	-	Bear twice in a year after 6th month of planting.
S.T.H-1	-	Bear twice in a year after 6th month of planting.

Totapari and Banglora are used for juice and pulping purpose.

Propagation : Cleft or veneer grafting is a better method for mango propagation and is commercially practiced with 80 to 90% success.

Planting :

(*i*) **Time of planting :** (*a*) Rainy season (15th July to September).

(*b*) Spring season (15th Feb. to March).

(*ii*) **Method of planting :** Pit method size of pit 0.5 × 0.5 metre).

(*iii*) **Distance of planting :** High density – 2.5 × 2.5 metre, 1600 plants/ha.

(*iv*) **System of planting :** Square system, 100 plants/ha. It is the popular system all over the world. Another is hexagonal 115 plant/ha. One year old plant should be planted.

Manuring:

Upto 10 years old plant : N-100 g, P_2O_5-50 g, K_2O 100 g per plant per year is recommended.

After 10 years old plant : 1 kg N, 500 g P_2O_5 and 1kg K_2O/plant/year, should be given.

Time of application : 1/2 amount of NPK should be given in July-August and rest 1/2 during February to March.

Irrigation : Modified ring system is preferred for mango orchard at 7-10 days interval during summer and every 2 to 3 weeks during winter. In case of bearing plants, irrigation should be avoided during flowering.

Intercropping : Papaya, phalsa, plum, peach pine apple & leguminous vegetables should be taken as inter-crops.

Pruning and training : Healthy 3 to 4 shoots should be allowed and remaining weak shoots should be removed. The branches touching the ground should also be pruned.

Flowering & fruiting : The time of flowering is January to February. The crop is cross pollinated. The flowers vary between 1000 to 6000 depending upon varieties. Flowering period is 2 to 3 weeks. Furit setting can be improved by application of NAA 200 ppm at bud initiation.

Fruit drop : In the mango orchard, the fruit drop is serious problem. For reducing it, application of growth regulator NAA 25 ppm or 2, 4 to D, 10-15 ppm during peak stage. Spraying of urea @ 2% results into high yield.

Harvesting and yield : Fruits mature about 90 days after setting. Commonly fruits are harvested from April to June.

Yield : Age 5 to 8 years - 200 to 300 fruits tree.

Age 9 or above - 300 to 500 fruits tree.

Age 15 or above - 1500 to 2000 fruits tree

High density plants - 22 tons/ha. After 9th and 10th year.

Average yield in India 8.31 to 8.70 tons/ha.

Disorders:

(1) Black tip : Common in Punjab, UP, Bihar and West Bengal. Fruits are affected due to SO_2 gas fruits turn black.

Control : Spray Borax 0.6% at flowering and setting.

(2) Spongy tissue : It is common in Alphanso variety. Spongy tissue develop in the pulp.

Control : (*i*) Harvest of fruits should be done at 3/4 maturity stage.

(*ii*) Post harvest dipping of fruits in 500 ppm Ethephon solution reduces spongy tissue.

(3) Malformation : It was first reported in 1801 by Maries in India. This is caused by a fungus *Fusarium monilifomae.*

Control : (*i*) Spray NAA 200 ppm in the month of October.

(*ii*) Spray NAA 200 ppm followed by deblossoming at bud burst stage.

(5) Internal necrosis : It is caused due to boron deficiency.

Control : Spray 0.5% Borax after fruit setting twice at monthly interval.

(6) Alternate bearing : Alternate bearing is a major problem in mango orchard.

Control : Regular fruit bearing varieties namely, Amrapali, Mallika, Totapari, Neelam, Romani and Bangalora should be planted.

Pest :

(1) Mango mealy bug *(Drosicha mangiferae) :* This is very serious pest of mango.

Control : (*i*) Carbaryl dust 5% @ 250 g/tree should be used.

(*ii*) Polythene banding or sticky banding with grease and coaltar in 1:2 ratio at lower side of trunk should be used.

(2) Mango hopper or jassids *(Amritodus etkinsoni) :*

Control : Spray Monocrotophos 0.4% or Demecron 0.05% at the time of panicle emergence and again at peak stage.

(3) Fruit fly *(Daucus dorsalis) :*

Control : Spray Savin 0.2% or 0.1% protein hydrolysate during April.

(4) Bark eating caterpillar *(Indarbela auedrinotata):*

Control : Plugging the hole with cotton petrol mix & plastering the hole.

Diseases :

(1) Powdery mildew *(Odium mangiferae):*

Control: Spray sulphur 0.2% or sulfex 0.2 % at 10 days interval.

(2) Anthracnose *(Coletrotrichum gloesporoides) :*

Control : Spray Bordeaux mixture 3:3:50 or Blitox 0.3% or Bavistin 0.1% in the month of February to April and September to November.

Questions From Previous Year's Papers

Q. 1. Write on the following packages of practices viz., major growing regions, varieties, time and method of sowing, spacing and seed rate, manure and fertilizer requirement of the following crops :

(a) Wheat

(b) Cotton

(c) Groundnut

(d) Sugarcane

Q. 2. (a) Define Intercropping System. Enlist the advantages and disadvantages of intercropping system. Support your answer with suitable examples.

(b) Which are the pre-requisites of successful intercropping system?

Q. 3. (a) Give time of sowing and harvesting time, seed rate and yield per hectare of crops namely wheat, cotton, potato, brinjal and carrot.

Q. 4. (a) What are the features of good cropping system?

(b) Suggest procedures for assessing suitability of different multiple cropping systems.

Q. 5. Furnish a detailed account of the features of agroclimatic zones of India.

Q. 6. Describe the climate and soil requirement of tea, cotton and cashew.

Q. 7. Explain with concrete examples whether sequence cropping against monoculture does help farmer in crop production.

Q. 8. "Wheat cultivation in India is a gamble of temperature" Explain. Write brifefly about the packages of practices of dwarf wheat for achieving high yield with judicious uses of inputs.

Q. 9. Write in tubular form the scientific names, sowing time, harvesting time, variety, seed rate, manure and fertiliser dose, irrigation requirements of rice, corn, peanut, green gram, black gram, sesamum, sugarcane and berseem.

Q. 10. Differentiate between the following pairs in not more than 150 words each :

(a) Multiple cropping and multistorey cropping system

(b) Diversified farming and mixed farming.

(c) Crop rotation and ratoon cropping.

(d) Intercropping, sequential cropping and relay cropping.

(e) Tall indica and semidwarf high yielding variety of rice.

(f) Plants available and unavailable water in soil.

(g) Sensitive and tolerant stages of growth in cereal crops.

Q. 11. Write short notes on the following in about 150 words each :

(a) Intercropping

(b) Constraints in the production of food grains

(c) Package of practices for paddy cultivation

(d) Benefits of crop-rotation in intensive cropping.

(e) Raising of oranamental flower crops.

(f) Importance of package of practices of cultivation of vegatable crops.

(g) Crop rotation

(h) Curing of tobacco

(i) Silking, tasseling, arrowing, pegging.

Q. 1.2 (a) What are biological determinants of a cropping system? Discuss briefly the influence of each one of them on crop yield.

(b) Explain which qualities possessed by Bajra have made it a very significance crop in semi-arid regions.

(c) What is mid-season correction in a crop cycle? Elaborate the answer with concrete examples.

Q. 13. (a) List out different methods adopted for sugarcane planting.

(b) Suggest suitable schedule of manuring, time and method of application for a 12-month sugarcane crop.

(c) Explain why sugarcane yields in northern India are generally lower than those in the south.

Q. 14. (a) What is crop-cafetaria? How does it help farmer in his crop planning? Suggest two examples each for Kharif and Rabi Programmes under irrigation.

(b) Describe salient features of Berseem cultivation with reference to phosphate fertilization.

Q. 15. Write short notes on the following :

(a) Soil inoculation

(b) Fertilizer ratio

(c) Desuckering in tobacco

(d) Staggered planting

4. FORESTRY

IMPORTANT FEATURES

Forests are important for the life and prosperity of man and nations. It provides him with his basic necessities, such as food, fibres and shelter. Besides human requirements, it is a wealth of raw materials for industries. These help the country to maintain its economic standards.

Forests are renewable resources and contribute substantially to economic development besides this it play a major role in enhancing the quality of environment. Forest Survey of India (FSI) and its Zonal offices are mainly engaged in collection of data on scientific lines through country wide.

According to State Forests Report 2005, the total forests cover of the country as per 2005 assessment is 677.088 km^2 and this constitutes 20.60 per cent of the total geographical area of the country. Of this 54,569 km^2 (1.66%) is very dense forest 332.647 km^2 (10.12%) is moderately dense forest, while 289.872 km^2 (8.82%) is open forest cover. The scrub account for 38,475 km^2 (1.17%).

The State/UT wise forest cover in the country shows that Madhya Pradesh with 76.013 km^3 has the largest area under forest cover, followed by Arunachal Pradesh (67,777 km^2), Chhattisgarh (55,863 km^2), considering the geographic area under forest cover, Mizoram has the maximum percentage of 88.63% followed by Nagaland (82.75%), Arunachal Pradesh (80.93%) and Andaman and Nicobar Islands (80.36%), Andhra Pradesh has the largest area under scrub (9.862 km^2).

Integrated Forest Protection Scheme: Integrated Forest Protection Scheme (IFPS) was being implemented during the Xth Five Year Plan and being continued during XIth Plan. The Planning Commission has suggested to rename the scheme "as Intensification of Forest Management" during 11th Five Year Plan. It is proposed to broadbase the scheme by including following two new components in addition to the existing components of IFPS *i.e.,* Infrastructure Development and Forest Fire Control Management.

New Components :

1. Conservation and Restoration of Unique Vegetation and Ecosystems.
2. Protection and Conservation of Sacred Groves.

INPORTANCE AND SCOPE OF FORESTS

Forests are important for the life and prosperity of man and country. It provides large number of goods to both rich and poor. Importance of forest are summarized as under:

(*a*) Environment : Forest is a biotic community where plants, animals and micro organisms live in harmony. Forests have a major role in reducing atmospheric pollution. They act as sink for the polluting gases.

Forests act as water shed and thus help in maintaining hydrological cycle. Forests are also important in prevention of soil erosion by wind and water. It also improves porosity and fertility of soil by addition of humus.

(*b*) Essential Oils : Many essential oils are used in the manufacture of soaps, cosmetics, pharmaceuticals, confectionary, incense etc. Essential oils are obtained from forests plants for *e.g.,* rosha grass, khas, sandal wood etc.

(*c*) **Wood :** Wood is useful as building material for construction. It is the major forest product. It is used as a raw material for doors, windows furniture, sports goods bullockcarts etc.

(*d*) **Fuel wood :** In developing countries, it is a major source of fuel for domestic purposes.

(*e*) **Bamboos :** Bamboos are used as raw materials in paper and rayon industries. These grow in forests and are useful in rafters, roofing, walling floor mating, basketary, cartwood etc.

(*f*) **Forest industries :** Industries like paper and news print, plywood, fibre board, match industry, resin and turpentine etc. are forest based.

(*g*) **Animal based products :** Tusser and Moga silk, lac, honey, wax etc. are result of activities of forest insects. The other useful products include horns, ivory, hides etc.

(*h*) **Some other forest products :** Useful products such as tanning materials, dyes, resins, gum, drugs, spices and insecticides are also obtained from forests plants.

(*i*) **The tribal life :** The tribal population living in and around forests obtains its food, fibre, timber, medicines, etc. from the forest plants and animals.

EFFECTS OF DEFORESTATION

The following are the major effects of deforestation :

(*i*) Loss of economic balance of the country.

(*ii*) Loss of important and useful wild life.

(*iii*) Increase in soil erosion, leading to increased recurrence of floods and droughts.

(*iv*) Deterioration of economy and quality of life.

Agro-Forestry

Agro-Forestry is primarily a system where agriculture and forestry are practiced either simultaneously or separately on the same unit of land and has affinities with taungya system of regenerating forests which in Burmese means cultivation of trees and crops. Agriculture in forest is called agro-forestry. Dr. King and Chandler defined it as a sustainable land management system which increases the use of the land combines the production of crop (including tree crops) and forest plants and/or animals–simultaneouly or sequentially, on the same unit of land and applies management practices that are compatible with the cultural practices of the local population. It is localised in its concept.

The main feature of the multistoreyed production of different species of economic plants with suitable plant geometry. Agro-forestry is 6–F programme because it provides *i.e.*, **Food** for man, **Feed** for livestocks, **Fibre** for clothing, **Fuel** for village and urban homes, **Furniture** timber and **Funds** for the poor forest **Villagers** and is govt. development programmes.

Necessity of Agro-forestry :

(*i*) Ecological balance.

(*ii*) Fresh oxygen through photosynthesis.

(*iii*) Acts as windbreaks.

(*iv*) Creates employment opportunity.

(*v*) Continuous supply of fuel and fodder.

Objectives of Agro-forestry :

(*i*) Economically superior land use with intensive agro forestry systems on fertile soils of small and marginal farmers.

(*ii*) Production of basic needs of farmers namely, food, fruit, fodder, fuel etc. from their own piece of land.

(*iii*) Enhancement of land productivity and sustainability in lands affected by low soil fertility, high erosion and high soil degradation.

(*iv*) Diversifield and or more sustainable production at a higher level from the available resources.

Components of Agro-forestry :

The essential aim of the components of agro-forestry is to conserve and improve the site and to optimise the combined production. The different types and component of agro-forestry are–

1. Sylvo-Pastoral Systems : Such land management systems in which forests are managed for the production of wood as well as for rearing of domesticated animals.

Sylo-Pastoral System : Silviculture + Pasture Managements.

2. Agro-sylvo-pastoral Systems : Agl. crops + Forest crops + Pasture management.

3. Agri-horti-Silviculture Systems : Agl.crops + horticulture + silviculture.

4. Multipurpose Forest Tree Production Systems : Forestry for the multipurpose benefits or uses.

5. Agri-Silviculture : The growing of agricultural crops along with the forest crops is known as agri-silviculture. Agri-silviculture = Agl. crops + Forest crops (silviculture).

• SOCIAL FORESTRY

Social forestry means plantation of such trees which are useful for community development. The word 'Social forestry' was first time used by Westoby in 1968. He defined as "social forestry is a forestry which aims at producing flow of protection and recreational benefits for the community".

Principles of Social Forestry :

1. Principle of forest area extension : It aims to increase the forest area by rehabilitating wastelands while producing biomass both for industrial and local uses.

2. Principle of democracy : Social forestry implies the culturing of trees by the people, for the people and of the people.

3. Principle of Govt. Based programme: It is primarily a govt. based programme. Sometimes social forestry is also tagged as 'sick land for sick people'.

4. Principle of employment : It is a continuous process discouraging the migration of labour to the urban habitats.

5. Principle of Poverty-Eradication : It is single largest developmental strategy to eradicate poverty by providing the job.

Objectives of Social Forestry

(*a*) Ecological and environmental balance and purity.

(*b*) Fostering of agro-based industries in rural areas for absorption of people in gainful employment.

(*c*) Easy and abundant availability of fuel and firewood for the families, foodder for their domestics and timber wood for domestic use.

Components of Social Forestry Programmes :

1. Farm Forestry : Objectives of encouraging farmers to plant and raise trees on their own plot of land through free or subsidised supply of seedlings. In dry areas, trees are grown around the farm.

2. Rural Forestry : For the benefit of the community as a whole through massive plantations along roadside and canal banks, around tanks and ponds and on fallow and uncultivable lands. It is also called **Extension forestry** as this results in extending forests beyond the existing.

3. Urban forestry : Forestry in the urban areas *i.e.*, on the useless land near govt. buildings, schools, colleges and universities, roadsides, hospitals, recreation gardens, municipal areas etc. Community woodlands are planted by particular communities themselves on land of their own or on that pooled by themselves and benefits of which are shared by them equally.

With a vigorous programme of social forestry, India may land into a new green revolution through which it will be possible to increase wood in the villages.

Questions From Previous Year's Papers

Q. 1. Justify the role of agroforestry in meeting the human needs. How do you plan for new agroforestry programmes for wasteland development?

Q. 2. Enumerate the theory and priciple of landscape gardening. What are the main types of landscape gardening? Discuss.

Q. 3. Differentiate between the social forestry and Agro-forestry in not more than 150 words each.

Q. 4. What do you understand by social-forestry? State the advantages of social forestry.

5. WEED MANAGEMENT

Weed is a plant growing at a place and time where it is not desired. Thus, any plant other than groundnut in a sole crop of groundnut is a weed. While all weeds are unwanted plants, all unwanted plants at a particular situation may not be weeds in other situations. As long as a plant is growing at a place and time without interfering with man's activities, all unwanted plants may not be weeds. Common definitions for **weed** found in literature are :

- A plant out of place
- A plant interfering with the intended use of land
- A plant with negative value
- A plant growing with desired plant
- An uninvited guest.

Depending on their migration into crop lands, association with specific crop, problems created, survival etc. weeds are named differently.

Parasitic weed : A weed that depends partially or fully for its growth on its host plant.

Obligate weed : A cropland weed incapable of surviving in a wild community.

Objectionable weed : A problem weed, whose seed once mixed with crop seed is extremely difficult to separate.

Noxious weed : An undesirable troublesome weed difficult to control.

Facultative weed : Weed of wild community origin, escaping sometimes to cropland.

Alien weed : Weed not native of country.

Associated weed : Non-parasitic weed association with a specific crop.

Satellite weed : A weed that has become an integral part of a crop ecosystem.

Weeds have been part of agriculture scene since man started cultivating crop plants and weed management is an integral part of crop production with the introduction of improved cultivars.

Weed management is an approach in which weed prevention and weed control have companion roles. It implies a systems approach in which all available tools are used to reduce the propagule seedbank, prevent weed emergence and minimise competition from weeds growing with desired plants. Thus, weed management has both immediate and long term objectives.

Common Weeds

About 30,000 species of weeds have been listed in the world, out of which nearly 18,000 cause serious damage in different ways resulting in considerable losses to agricultural production. Eighteen weeds identified as the most serious in the world are listed in Table 1.

Table 1. Eighteen Most Serious Weeds in the World

Common name	*Scientific name*	*Growth habitat and kind of plant*
Smooth pig weed	*Amaranthus hybridus*	A–B
Spiny amaranth	*Amaranthus spinosus*	A–B

Common name	*Scientific name*	*Growth habitat and kind of plant*
Wild oat	*Avena fatua*	A–G
Common lambsquarters	*Chenopodium album*	A–B
Field bind weed	*Convolvulus arvensis*	P–B
Bermuda grass	*Cynodon dactylon*	P–G
Yellow nut sedge	*Cyperus esculentus*	P–S
Purple nut sedge	*Cyperus rotundus*	P–S
Crabgrass	*Digitaria sanguinalis*	A–G
Jungle rice	*Echinochloa colonum*	A–G
Barnyard grass	*Echinochloa crusgalli*	A–G
Water hyancinth	*Eichhornia crassipes*	P–B
Goose grass	*Eleusine indica*	A–G
Cogon grass	*Imperata cylindrica*	P–G
Sour paspalum	*Paspalum conjugatum*	P–G
Common purslane	*Portulaca oleracea*	A–B
Itch grass	*Rottboellia exaltata*	A–G
Johnson grass	*Sorghum halepense*	P–G

A = Annual. P = Perennial. B = Broad leaved. G = Grass. S = Sedge.

Table 2. Most Common Weeds in Crop Fields of India (Sankaran and Mudaliar 1991)

Monocot species	*Dicot species*
Annuals	**Annuals**
Barnyard grass (*Echinochloa crusgalli*)	Goat weed (*Ageratum conyzoides*)
Crabgrass (*Digitaria sp*)	Pig weed (*Amaranthus sp*)
Foxtail (*Setaria sp*)	Black jack (*Bidens pilosa*)
Sandbur (*Cenchrus sp*)	Cox comb (*Celosia argentia*)
Wild oat (*Avena fatua*)	Lambsquarters (*Chenopodium album*)
Goose grass (*Eleusine indica*)	Wild carrot weed (*Parthenium hysterophorus*)
Torpedo grass (*Panicum repens*)	Common purslane (*Portulaca oleracea*)
Canary grass (*Phalaris minor*)	Horse purslane (*Trianthema portulacastrum*)
Crowfoot grass (*Dactyloctenium aegyptium*)	
Perennials	**Perennials**
Bermuda grass (*Cynodon dactylon*)	Canada thistle (*Circium arvense*)
Thatch grass (*Imperata cylindrica*)	Day flower (*Commelina benghalensis*)
Johnson grass (*Sorghum halepense*)	Field bind weed (*Convolvulus arvensis*)
Quack grass (*Agropyron repens*)	White horse nettle (*Solanum elaeagnifolium*)
Nut grass (*Cyperus rotundus*)	

Yield Losses Due to Weeds :

Among the annual agricultural losses in India, weeds account for 33 per cent, insects 20 per cent, diseases 26 per cent and others 21 per cent. The annual economic losses account for Rs. 2000 crores in the country (Kulshrestha and Parmer 1992). Estimates (Bhan 1997) show that average crop yield reductions due to weeds vary from 12 to 72 per cent depending upon the crop (Table 3).

Table 3. Average Reduction in Yield Due to Weeds in India (BHAN 1997)

Crop	*Yield reduction (%)*
Rice	41.6
Wheat	16.0
Maize	39.8
Millets	29.5
Soybean	30.5
Gram	11.6
Pea	32.9
Linseed	34.9
Groundnut	33.8
Sugarcane	34.2
Sugarbeet	70.3
Cotton	47.5
Carrot	72.5
Onion	68.0
Potato	20.1

Reduction in yield due to weeds is highest in carrot (72.5%) followed by sugarbeet (70.3%), onion (68%), cotton (47.5%) and rice (41.6%).

Crop Pests and Disease Incidence

Weeds act as alternate hosts to pests and pathogens in off-season which infect the crop later and cause severe damage.

Crop	*Pest/disease*	*Weed host*
Rice	Stemborer	*Echinochola, Panicum*
Maize and tomato	Stalk borer, bettle and cutworm	*Chenopodium album*
Castor	Hairy caterpillar	*Crotolaria sp*
Citrus	Fruit moth	*Tinospora cordifolia*
Tomato	Wilt	*Amaranthus sp, Portulaca oleracea*
Banana	Virus and nematodes	*Commelina sp*
Wheat	Black rust	*Agropyron repens*

Fallow land weeds	*Abutilon indicum*
	Achyranthes aspera
Grassland or pasture land weeds	*Argemone mexicana*
	Celosia argentea
Playground weeds	*Euphorbia hirta*
	Kyllinga erecta
Rail and road side weeds	*Lantana camara*
	Datura stramonium
Lawns and public garden weeds	*Gyperus rotundus*
	Gomphrena celosioides
Soil reaction	
Saline soil weeds	*Salsola* sp
	Suaeda maritima
Alkaline soil weeds	*Cressa erecta*
	Sporobolus diander
Acid soil weeds	*Rumex acetosella*
	Pteridium aquilinum
Dependence on Other Hosts	
Total parasite	*Cascuta reflexa*
Semiparasite	*Striga* sp
Independent	*Cyperus rotundus*

Crop-Weed Association

Some weeds prefer to grow in crop-fields only and some of them have a distinct association with some specific crops. Irrespective of crop-weed association, weeds compete with crop plants (crop-weed competition) for all the growth factors.

Climatic, edaphic and biotic factors of environment determine the distribution of species, their competitive ability, prevalence and intricate relationships. Crops grown under specific agroecological situations have their characteristic weeds. Major factors contributing to crop-weed association and similarity in climatic needs, seed size, seed germination, tillage needs, cropping and harvest practices. As weeds do not belong to a particular plant species, atleast some weed species enjoy the favour of a crop field habitat and flourish along with crop plants. Some of the weeds always associated with specific crops are summarised in the following table 4:

Table 4

Crop	*Associated weeds*
Rice	*Echinochloa colonum, E. crusgalli*
Wheat	*Chenopodium album, Phalaris minor*
Maize	*Eclipta alba, E. colonum*
Barley	*P. minor, Avena fatua, C. album*
Sorghum	*Striga lutea, Tridax procumbens*
Chickpea	*Croton sparsiflorus, Cleome viscosa*
Blackgram	*Solanum nigrum, Physalis minima*
Mustard	*Cleome viscosa, Spergula arvensis*
Groundnut	*Phyllanthus niruri, Ageratum conyzoides*
	Celosia argentea, Acanthospermum hispidum
Potato	*C. album, Anagallis arvensis*
Cotton	*C. rotundus, Abutilon indicum*
	Digera arvensis, Tephrosia purpurea
Tobacco	*Orabanche indica, C. rotundus*

Crop– Weed Competition

Struggle for survival and existence is called competition. Competition occurs when each of the two or more organisms seeks the measure it wants of any particular growth factor and when the immediate supply of that factor is below the combined demand of the organisms. Water, nutrients, light and space are the major factors for which competition usually occurs. Competition between crop plants and weeds is most severe when they have similar vegetative habits and common demands for available growth factors. Dominance of a habitat by the crop or weed depends on the rapidity of seed germination, seedling establishment and subsequent growth and development.

Differences in photosynthetic area, root development and its growth largely determine the competitiveness of plants. The degree of weed competition is determined by the weed species infecting the crop, density of infestation and duration of infestation. Weed species differ among themselves in competitive ability. Annual monochoria– (*Monochoria vaginalis*) is more severe competitor than another grass *Echinochloa crusgalli* in rice crop. If weeds are controlled within two or three weeks of emergence, their influence on final crop yield is minimal. Weeds are capable of absorbing just as much as much as or at times even bigger amounts of nutrients and water than crop plants. It has been reported that for every 1.0 per cent increase in yield, weed infestation should be eliminated to the extent of 3 per cent in barley, 2 per cent in wheat, 0.5 per cent in maize, 3 per cent in tomato and 8 per cent in apple.

Soybean has lower competitive ability with *Cyperus rotundus* followed by groundnut, blackgram, greengram, sorghum and maize. It clearly shows that crops differ appreciably in competitive ability with weeds.

Critical Period of Crop-Weed Competition

The critical period for crop-weed competition is the period from sowing upto which the final crop has to be maintained in a weed free environment for remunerative crop production. Differences in final crop yield due to weeding at this period and that due to weed free environment throughout the crop period will be marginal. The crop canopy in the early period of growth is inadequate to smother the weed growth. By early reproductive phase, the crop develops leaf area adequate to smother the weed growth. Hence, weed competition in crop field is invariably severe in early stages of crop growth than at later stages. Generally, in a crop of 100 days duration, the first 35 days after sowing should be maintained weed free for optimum yield. Critical periods of weed competition for major crops are given in Table 5.

Table 5. Critical Periods of Crop-Weed Competition and Yield Losses

Crops	*Critical period (DAS)*	*Reduction in grain yield (%)*
Cereals		
Direct seeded rice	15–45	15–90
Transplanted rice	30–45	15–40
Wheat	30–45	20–40
Maize	15–45	40–60
Sorghum	15–45	15–40
Pearlmillet	30–45	15–60
Pulses		
Pigeonpea	15–60	20–40
Greengram	15–30	25–50
Blackgram	15–30	30–50
Cowpea	15–30	15–30
Chickpea	30–60	15–25
Peas	30–45	20–30
Lentil	30–60	20–30
Oilseeds		
Soybean	20–45	40–60
Groundnut	30–50	40–50
Sunflower	30–45	30–50
Castor	30–60	30–35
Safflower	15–45	35–60
Sesame	15–45	15–40
Rapeseed-mustard	15–40	15–30
Linseed	20–45	30–40
Commercial crops		
Sugarcane	30–120	20–30
Potato	20–40	30–60
Cotton	15–60	40–50
Jute	30–45	50–80
Vegetable crops		
Cauliflower	30–45	50–60
Cabbage	30–45	50–60
Okra	15–30	40–50
Tomato	30–45	40–70
Onion	30–75	60–70

Effect of Weeds on Crops

There are several reports on the allelopathic effect of weeds on crops :

(*i*) Seed exudates of *Avena fatua* (wild oat) affect germination and early growth of wheat.

(*ii*) Leaf and inflorescence of *Amaranthus spinosus* affect the vegetative growth of fingermillet and maize.

(*iii*) Leaves and inflorescence extract of *Trianthima portulacastrum and Parthenium hysterophorus* affect the gemination and seedling growth of sorghum.

(*iv*) Tubers of *Cyprus esculentus* affect the growth of maize and groundnut.

(*v*) Leaf extracts of *Camelina alyssum* (flax weed) greatly reduce the yield of flax.

Effect of Crops on Weeds

There is evidence in support of crop plants showing allelopathy on weeds. Root exudation of maize inhibits the growth of *Chenopodium album* and *Amaranthus retroflexus.* Cold water extracts of wheat straw reduced the germination and growth of *Ipomea* sp and *Abutilon indicum.*

Effect of Weeds on Weeds

Certain allelopathic effect of weeds on other weed plants has been reported. This phenomenon helps the weed to dominate in that environment. Extract of leaves, leachates and decaying leaves of *Polygonum orientale* contains flavonoids which are toxic to germination and growth of *Ameranthus spinosus.* Decaying rhizomes of *Sorghum halepense* affect the growth of *Setaria viridis, Digitaria sanguinalis* and *Amaranthus* sp. Whole plant extracts of *Amaranthus viridis, Trianthima portulacastrum* and *Flavaria australasica* affect the germination of *Echinochloa colonum.*

METHODS OF WEED CONTROL

Different methods are followed to prevent, eradicate or control the weeds. Preventive measures eliminate majority of weed species.

(1) Preventive Measures

They aim at preventing introduction and spread of specified weed species in areas that are not currently infested with these plant species. No weed control programme can be successful if adequate preventive measures are not taken to minimise weed infestation. Introduction of weeds in crop fields can be prevented by :

(*i*) Using weed free crop seed and seedlings,

(*ii*) Not using fresh or partly decomposed FYM or compost,

(*iii*) Proper cleaning of farm machinery before moving from infested to clean area,

(*iv*) Following legal and quarantine measures to check interstate and intercountry movement of noxious weeds.

(*v*) Keeping the irrigation and drainage channels free from weeds, and

(*vi*) Keeping the field bunds and fence lines free from weeds.

(2) Eradication Methods

Eradication infers that a given weed species, its seed and vegetative parts, has been killed or completely removed from a given area and that the weed will not reappear unless reintroduction to the area. This may be desirable and economical when the weed species is extremely noxious (weed specified by law) and persistent as to make cropping difficult and uneconomical or preclude bringing new area under plough. Eradication of perennial weeds cannot be accomplished in one season or year, as viable seeds and underground plant propagules may remain dormant in soil for years. Underground parts can be destroyed by tillage and/or with postemergence translocated herbicides or soil sterilants. A soil sterilant may, however, render the soil unfit for crop production for several years.

3. Control Methods

The process of minimising cropped field from weed infestation for remunerative crop production is called **weed control**. It aims at limiting unwanted plant growth, both in space and time, without any attempt to eliminate from the scene. The extent to which the weed growth is desired to be limited depends on the cost of weed control and the expected benefits. Weed control methods can be broadly grouped into cultural, biological and chemical methods.

4. Cultural Methods

Cultural methods of weed control can be subdivided into mechanical and crop management methods.

(A) Mechanical Methods

Mechanical and/or physical methods are being employed ever since man began to grow crops. They include hand hoeing, hand pulling, tillage, digging, sickling, burning, flooding and mulching. Choice of each method depends on the location, extent and habitat of weeds.

(*i*) **Hand hoeing :** Hand hoe has been the simplest weeding tool for centuries. Hoeing is particularly effective on annuals and biennials as weed growth can be completely destroyed. In case of perennials, it can destroy only top growth. It is effective on creeping perennials, which have shallow root system.

(*ii*) **Hand pulling :** It is physical removal or pulling out of weeds by hand. It is very effective against annual and biennial weeds, as they do not regenerate from pieces of roots left in the ground. It is very economical where weeds are scattered around that makes herbicide use uneconomical or herbicides are not effective on a particular weed species.

(*iii*) **Tillage :** Weed control by tillage is achieved primarily by Burial of small annual weeds under soil with tillage implements or tools. Disruption of intimate contact between weed plant and soil for water and nutrients, and injury of root and stem of weeds leading to their reduced competitiveness or regenerative capacity.

(*iv*) **Digging :** It is very useful to remove underground propagating parts of perennial weeds from deeper layers of soil. Digging is followed by hand pulling of the weed. Digging, a labour intensive method, is restricted to perennial weed control in small areas where other methods are not effective.

(*v*) **Sickling :** Sickling by hand is used to remove top weed growth, to prevent weed seed production and to starve the underground parts. It is specially ideal on sloppy lands, where root system has to be left in the field to minimise soil erosion. If the soil condition does not permit use of implements or tools for controlling weeds, especially at critical stages, sickling is usually followed. Herbicide needs can be considerably brought down by sickling before applying the herbicide.

(*vi*) **Burning :** It is an economical and simple means of weed control. It is used to dispose of accumulated vegetation, destroy dry tops of matured weeds, kill green weed growth when other methods are impracticable, and destroy buried weed seeds and other propagating plant parts.

Fire is used to burn crop residues and weeds after the harvest of crops like sugarcane, cotton, potato, maize, etc. When burning is used for selective control of annual broadleaf weeds and grasses in widely spaced crop rows, it is known as flame cultivation.

(*vii*) **Flooding :** Weed infested field is ploughed deep and flooded with 20–30 cm standing water for 5 to 10 weeks. It is successful against weed species sensitive to longer periods of submergence in water. Flooding is an efficient method of weed control for some perennial weeds like *Cyperus* sp, *Cynodon dactylon* and *Convolvulus arvensis.* Lowland rice is usually rotated with other irrigated crops for controlling such problem weeds.

(*viii*) **Mulching :** It has smothering effect on weeds by restricting the photosynthesis. Mulching is effective against annual weeds and some perennial weeds like *Cynodon dactylon, Sorghum halepense,* etc. Mulching with straw, hay, paper and films is successful in cash crops. Availability and cost of the materials limit its large scale use.

(*ix*) **Soil solarisation :** High soil temperature can suppress weed seed germination and kill weed seedlings. During the process of heating soil surface, termed solarisation, soil temperature is raised above thermal depth point for most weed seeds and seedlings.

(x) Chemical stimulants

Chemicals that stimulate germination of both viable and dormant seed include growth regulators respiratory inhibitors, nitrogen compounds, etc. Ethylene can be used to control striga by stimulating its seed gemination. Nitrates such as ammonium nitrate are known to cause increased emergense of wild oats, *Elusine indica, Echinochloa colonum* etc. Sodium azide is known to stimulate oat seed germination. Striga is a chemical stimulant of parasitic weeds, striga, orobanche etc.

(B) Crop Management

Crop management practices are directed in favour of crops and suppressing weed growth. Such management practices are : good seedbed preparation to minimise early weed infestation such that the crop dominate the weeds, timely sowing, optimum stand establishment and adequate fertiliser use leading to vigorous crop for better competition with weeds (selective crop stimulation), weeding before the weeds produce seeds for minimising weed infestation in the succeeding season, crop rotation for controlling crop associated weeds, including smother crops such as legumes in intercropping systems.

Line sowing for using intercultivation implements, and summer ploughing to desiccate the weed seed and vegetative propagules by exposing them to hot sun. Bank placement of fertilizers nearer to crop rows.

5. Biological Methods

It involves utilisation of natural living organisms (bioagents) such as insects, pathogens and competitive plants to limit the weed infestation. The objectives of biological control are not eradication, but reduction and regulation of the weed population below the level of economic injury. A bioagent may be either specific or non-specific. Specific bioagent attacks only one or two specific weeds, while the non-specifics feed upon a variety of vegetation. The specific bioagents include, primarily insects and plant pathogens. The choice of pests and pathogens should meet certain criteria before they can be decleared successful as bioagents. Important criteria are:

- Host specificity,
- Fast damaging ability,
- Adaptability to new environment,
- Fasting ability for long period during periods of declining weed population,
- Efficient reproduction, and
- Freedom from natural enemies.

Merits of Biological Control :

The merits of biological control are relative cheapness, comparatively long lasting effects and least harm on the environment and the non-target organisms. Some outstanding examples of successful biological control of weeds are :

(*i*) **Bioherbicides** using pathogens such as fungi, bacteria and virus are also used as biocontrol agents.

(*ii*) Release of *Dactylopius tomentosus* (scale insect) controlled *Opuntia dillenii* (prickly pear) in many parts of India.

(*iii*) *Lantana camara* (lantana weed) in Andhra Pradesh of India has been effectively controlled by a moth *Crocidosema lantana* and a bug *Teleonemia scrupulosa.*

(*iv*) *Zygogramma bicolorata* beetle feeds on parthenium plants during rainy season.

(*v*) In Florida, *Alternanthera philoxaroides* (alligator weed) is controlled by flea beetle *Agasiees hygrophila.*

(*vi*) *Salvinia molesta* (water fern) is controlled by *Crytobagous* sp (curculinoid weevil). *Nyphula responsalis* defoliate water fern besides pistia, typha, azolla and *Marsilea* sp.

(vii) Control of *Eichhornia crassipes* (water hyacinth) using *Necochetina eichhorniae, N. bruchi* (hyacinth weevils) and *Sameodes albiguttalis* (hyacinth moth).

Competitive Plants

The weed, *Parthenium hysterophorus* is suppressed by *Cassia sericea*. Plant leachates of *C. sericea* have kaolines which accumulate in the soil and interfere with the germination and growth of parthenium only. *Brachiaria mutica* (paragrass) is highly competitive to the growth of *Typha* sp in ditches. Some success has been achieved in biological control of weeds in crop fields.

Chemical Methods

Use of chemicals for weed control offer great potential in crop production. Chemical weed control functions on the basis that certain chemicals are capable of killing some plants (weeds) without significantly affecting other plants (crops). Such chemicals are called **herbicides.**

Chemical weed control has been largely a post World War II development. A part from introduction of dinoseb in 1933, MCPA and 2, 4–D in 1945, it is now around 60 years since the first effective organic herbicide was marketed. At global level, the usage of herbicides is higher than any other agrochemical. The percentage of herbicide consumption is 43 as against 31 per cent with insecticides, 21 per cent with fungicides and 5 per cent with other agrochemicals. In India, although 2, 4–D was first tested as early as in 1946, chemical concept of weed control struck deeper roots only when tea growers began using herbicides on a commercial scale in late 1970s. In India, consumption of insecticides is more (75%) as compared to herbicides (13%), fungicides (8%) and other agrochemicals (4%). Herbicide market in India has grown about eight folds in the past 15 years. Chemical weed control has some definite advantages over other methods.

(i) Most effective compared with other methods of weed control,

(ii) Suitable for adverse soil and climatic conditions,

(iii) Reduces the need for repeated cultural operations during the crop season,

(iv) Provides early season or zero day weed control,

(v) Highly suitable for closely spaced crops,

(vi) Controls the weeds without any mechanical injury to the associated standing crop, and

(vii) Controls even many perennial weeds which cannot be effectively controlled by other methods.

Some of the drawbacks with chemical control of weeds are that they must be applied at proper time, they have harmful residues which may affect succeeding crops and require minimum technical knowledge.

Classification of Herbicides

No classification is perfect, more so the classification of herbicides which is periodically modified as and when new herbicides are developed. Herbicides are classified based on their method of use (soil and foliage applied) mode of action (systemic or translocated and non-systemic or contact herbicides) and chemical key structure (aliphatic, aromatic, dinitrophenol, etc). Some herbicide molecules contain more than one classifying key structure and they are put into the group most likely to be contributing activity.

Any approved herbicide is known by three names : common name, chemical name and trade name. Common name of herbicide is a technically accepted abbreviation of its chemical name. Chemical name reads out its full molecular structure. Trade names refer to their formulations offered by the chemical companies for the consumer.

Previous Questions Papers

Q. 1. What is weed? How does it compete with crop plant? To what extent it causes yield loss of field crops? What do you mean by critical period of weed competition in field crop? List the weeds associated with rice and wheat crop and suggest suitable control measures with minimum environmental pollution.

Q. 2. (a) What are plants' essential elements? What are the criteria of essentiality? Write briefly about role, deficiency symptoms of nitrogen, phosphorus and sulphur along with remedial meausres there of.

(b) Name three nitrogenous, two phosphatic and two potassic straight fertilisers along with their primary nutrient content, physical characteristics and suitablility for application to different plants and soil types.

(c) Outline an effective plan of eradication of parthenium (PARTHENIUM HYSTERO-PHORUS) weed.

Q. 3. Define integrated weed management. Briefly discuss the role of bioagents for weed control. Suggest an appropriate and cost effective integrated weed management system for a rained crop.

Q. 4. (a) What are the special characteristics of weeds? How are they harmful in crop production? Write on their methods of dissemination.

(b) How are herbicides classified? Describe briefly the methods of herbicidal application.

Q. 5 Write shortsnotes on the following. Each not exceeding 150 words :

(a) Selectivity of herbicides.

(b) Intercropping.

(c) Bioherbicides.

(d) Crop-weed competition.

(e) Herbicide safeners.

(f) Allelopathy effects of weeds.

(g) Biological weed control.

Q. 6. Differentiate between the following pairs in not more than 150 words each.

(a) Selective and non-selective herbicide.

(b) Chemigation and fertigation.

6. SOIL AND PLANT NUTRIENTS

The farmer looks upon the soil as a habitat for plants, since it provides physical anchorage to crops besides serving as reservoir of nutrients and water needed for growth and development. From the dawn of agriculture, farmers recognised goods soils, being attracted to productive soils of river valleys. They followed several management practices like inclusion of legumes in the cropping systems, application of dung and wood ashes for realising optimum yield, however, without any scientific base. During seventeenth and eighteenth centuries, there were blossoming scientific investigations and the stage was set for the application of science to the improvement of agriculture.

Concept of Soil : Pedological and edaphological. **Pedology** is the study of soil as a natural body and does not focus on soil's immediate practical use. Origin of the soil, its classification and its description is examined in pedology. Soil is treated as biochemically weathered and synthesised product of nature. **Edaphology** is the study of soil in relation to higher plants.

Physical, Chemical and Biological Properties :

Development of soil and its physical, chemical and biological properties have significant bearing on crop production. Soil physical properties are extremely important in determining how soils can and should be used. Soil management practices—tillage, crop sequences, organic amendments, irrigation practices, etc. followed are primarily aimed at optimum physical characteristics—crumb structure, optimum ratio of capillary to noncapillary pores, retentivity and release of soil moisture, root growth, fixation and release of nutrients, etc. An improvement in soil structure alters the bulk density, relative proportion of macro and micro pore space, infiltration and water retentivity and air-water relations to the advantage of crop productivity.

Availability and transformation of nutrients is largely a function of soil chemical and biological properties. The most outstanding characteristic of soil solution is its reaction : whether it is acidic, alkaline or neutral. Soil reaction is largely controlled by soil colloids and their associated exchangeable cations. Colloids are also the mechanism for soil buffering, giving stability to most plant-soil systems. Knowledge of soil chemical characters is essential to know how soil reaction is controlled, how it influences the supply and availability of plant nutrients and soil microbial activities.

Biological activities are vital to the cycle of life on earth. They digest plant and animal residues incorporated in to the soil, release carbon dioxide in to the atmosphere for recycling through higher plants and simultaneously create humus vital to good physical and chemical soil conditions. During decomposition, soil organisms release essential plant nutrients in inorganic forms for plant absorption. Activities of some macro-organisms such as earthworms, rodents, ants, snails, etc. have significant effect on soil physical properties. Microbial requirements are factors in determining the success of most soil management systems.

Table 1. Elements of Earth's Crust

Element	*Percentage*
Oxygen	47.02
Silicon	28.06
Aluminium	8.16
Iron	4.64
Calcium	3.50
Magnesium	2.62
Potassium	2.35
Sodium	2.63
Titanium	0.41
Hydrogen	0.17
Carbon	0.12
Phosphorus	0.09
Sulphur	0.07
Manganese	0.07
Barium	0.05
Strontium	0.02
Chromium	0.01
Nickel	0.01
Lithium	0.01
Chlorine	0.01
Fluorine	0.01

Mineralisation of Organic Sulphur : Important group of sulphur oxidising micro-organisms are the autotrophic bacteria belonging to genus *Thiobacillus*. Most common form is *T. thiooxidans*

$$-(HS) + 2O_2 \longrightarrow SO_4^{2-} + H^+ + \text{energy}$$

Phosphorus Compounds : Organic phosphorus is simplified soil micro-organisms. *Bacillus megatherium* var *phosphaticum* increase the plant availability of native and applied soil phosphorus. Other organisms associated with phosphate solubility are *Pseudomonas striata, Bacillus polymxa, Aspergillus awamori* and *Penicillium digitatum*. Increase in available soil phosphorus results primarily from the decomposition of organic phosphorus compounds, especially in neutral to alkaline soils.

Availability of other elements such as iron and manganese depends on microbial activity. These elements are oxidised by autotrophic organisms to their higher valence in which forms their solubilities are low. This keeps iron and manganese in insoluble and non-toxic forms even under acidic conditions.

Fixation of Atmospheric Nitrogen

Biological nitrogen fixation is the biochemical process through which atmospheric nitrogen is converted into inorganic forms by several species of bacteria, a few actinomycetes and blue-green algae. The overall effects of the nitrogen fixation process is to reduce elemental nitrogen to ammonia.

$$N_2 + 6H + 6e^- \xrightarrow[\text{Fe, MO}]{\text{Nitrogenase}} 2NH_3$$

Ammonia combines with organic acids to form amino acids and proteins.

$$NH_3 + \text{organic acid} \rightarrow \text{amino acids} \rightarrow \text{proteins}$$

The site of nitrogen reduction is the enzyme *nitrogenase,* a two-protein complex of a large ion, a molybdenum containing member and a smaller companion containing iron. Different systems of biological nitrogen fixation are given in Table 2.

Table 2. Different Systems of Biological Nitrogen Fixation

N fixing system	*Organisms involved*	*Plants inoculated*	*Site of fixation*
Symbiotic			
Legumes	Bacteria (*Rhizobium*)	Legumes	Root nodules
Nonlegumes	Actinomycetes (*Frankia*)	Nonlegumes (angiosperms)	Root nodules

N fixing system	*Organisms involved*	*Plants inoculated*	*Site of fixation*
Associative morphological involvement	Blue-green algae, bacteria	Higher plants and microbes	Leef and root nodules, lichens
Nonmorphological involvement	Blue-green algae, bacteria	Higher plants and microbes	Rhizosphere, Phillosphere
Nonsymbiotic	Blue-green algae, bacteria	Plants not involved	Soil, water independent plants

Symbiotic fixation with legumes : Legume-*Rhizobium* symbiotic relationship is the major biological source of nitrogen in agriculture. A given *Rhizobium* species will inoculate specific legumes only.

Process of Soil Formation

The undercomposed and more or less chemically weathered mineral or organic matter from which the column of soil is developed by pedogenic processes is called **parent material.** Parent material of mineral soils are weathered mineral rocks and that of organic soils are mostly plant residues preserved by low oxygen because of excessive wetness, as in shallow lake.

They process of transformation of solid rocks into soil is known as **weathering.** Weathering of minerals consists of physical, chemical and biological processes of disintegration and decomposition. Physical weathering brought about by the mechanical action of various weathering agents is designated as **disintegration** and chemical weathering as **decomposition.** Distintegration results in a decrease in size of rocks and minerals without appreciably affecting their composition. During decomposition, however, definite chemical changes takes place, soluble minerals are released and new materials are synthesised, some of which are resistant end products.

1. Mechanical Processes

Temperature : During the day, the rocks are heated up and cooled below air temperature during night. Some of the minerals within a given rock expand more than others due to heat. Similarly, some minerals contract more than others when cooled. This alternate expansion and contraction due to diurnal change in temperatures set up differential stresses which eventually produce cracks and rifts leading to break down of rock into pieces.

Rocks conduct heat slowly. As such, the outer rock surface is often warmer or colder than the inner. This differential heating and cooling sets up lateral stress that may cause surface layers to peel away from the parent mass. This phenomenon is referred to as **exfoliation,** which at times is sharply accelerated by the freezing of included water.

Water, ice and wind : These are the most potent agents in weathering of rocks. Water that flows over the surface, loaded with sediments has tremendous cutting power as observed from the fomation of ravines and valleys due to erosion. Rock fragment moving along with running water exerts grinding action on rocks leading to their disintegration.

Ice is an erosive detachment and transporting agency of tremendous capacity. Water present in chinks and crevices of rock, when freezes, expands in volume and exerts tremendous pressure due to which the rock splits and broken into small stones. The abrasive action of glaciers as they move under their own weight disintegrates rocks and minerals. Wind also exerts and abrasive action when it carries fine debris. Dust storms transfers huge quantities of material from one area to another. As dust is transferred and deposited, abrasion of one particle against other occurs.

Plants and animals : Simple plants such as mosses and lichens grow on exposed rock. They catch dust and encourage further plant growth.

2. Chemical Processes

Presence of water, oxygen, organic and inorganic acids that result from microbial breakdown of plant residues accelerate the process.

Hydrolysis is a chemical weathering process in which a mineral combines with water to form an acid and a base. Hydrolysis of orthoclase is a good example that frequently occurs in soils.

$$KAlSi_3O_8 + HOH \longrightarrow HAlSi_3O_8 + KOH$$

(Orthoclase mineral) slowly soluble) (water) (acid silicate clay more soluble) (Potassium hydroxide very soluble)

Hydration is combining of water molecules within the structural lattice of a mineral to form a different mineral. Common example is hydration of hematite to limonite.

$$2Fe_2O + 3HOH \longrightarrow 2Fe_2O_3.3H_2O$$

(hematite, red, firm) (water) (limonite, yellow, softer, more easily decomposed)

Oxidation in mineral weathering is combination of a chemical with oxygen or loss of one or more electrons to form an ion or an atom.

$$2S + 3O_2 + 2H_2O \longrightarrow 2H_2SO_4$$

(Slowly soluble mineral sulphur) (oxygen) (water) (bilogically oxidised sulphuric acid)

$$Zn + O_2 \longrightarrow ZnO_2$$

(Slowly soluble mineral zinc) (oxygen) (chemically oxidised zinc oxide, readily soluble.

Reduction is a chemical reaction in which oxygen is removed from a mineral. It also means a decrease in positive valence or an increase in negative valence. In other words, reduction is the addition of electrons to an atom or ion. Change of ferric iron (Fe^{3+}) to ferrous iron (Fe^{2+}) due to low soil oxygen because of excessive wetness.

$$Fe_2O_3 + H_2 \longrightarrow 2FeO + H_2O$$

(ferric oxide) (ferrous oxide)

Carbonation is a common process by which carbon dioxide of air combines with water to form carbonic acid, which react with carbonates forming more soluble bicarbonates.

$$CO_2 + HOH \longrightarrow H_2CO_3$$

(carbon dioxide in air) (water) (carbonic acid)

$$H_2CO_3 + CaCO_3 \longrightarrow Ca(HCO_3)_2$$

(carbonic acid) (calcite, slowly soluble) (calcium bicarbonate, very soluble)

3. Biological Processes

Biological weathering comprises the action of living things that disintegrate and decompose minerals and organic matter into products. Important agents of biological weathering are people, animals, earthworms and microbes such as algae, fungi and bacteria. People hasten physical weathering by tillage and related soil manipulation and chemical weathering by applying lime and fertilisers. Animals such as rats and mice dig burrows leading to formation of smaller minerals by abrasion. Earthworms eat organic matter along with fine clay minerals. Their excreted casts are ideal environment for faster chemical and microbial weathering of minerals. Algae growing on barren minerals upon death are subjected to the action of bacteria and fungi. Decaying organic residues release carbon dioxide, which after change as carbonic acid degrade minerals by carbonation.

Bacteria, most concerned with mineral breakdown in soil formation are classified as **chemoautotrophs.** Memebrs of this group obtain their carbon from carbon dioxide and energy from oxidation of such mineral substances as nitrogen, iron or sulphur.

$$2NH_4^+ + 3O_2 \xrightarrow{\text{Nitrosomonas}} 2NO_2^- + 4H^+ + H_2O$$

(ammonium) (oxygen) (nitrite) (hydrogen) (water)

$$2NO_2^- + O_2 \xrightarrow{\text{Nitrobacter}} 2NO_3^- +$$

(nitrite) (oxygen) (nitriate)

$$4Fe^{+2} + O_2 + 4H^+ \xrightarrow[\text{ferro-oxidans}]{\text{Thiobacillus}} 4Fe^{3+} + 2H_2O$$

(ferrous ion) (oxygen) (hydrogen) (ferric ion)(water)

$$2S + 3O_2 + 2H_2O \xrightarrow[\text{thio-oxidans}]{\text{Thiobacillus}} 2H_2SO_4$$

(mineral sulphur) (oxygen) (water) (sulphuric acid)

Soil Forming Factors

Simultaneously with disintegration and decomposition of minerals, new materials are synthesized. These include the soil clay minerals formed from the physico-chemical breakdown products of rock minerals. In addition, other minerals are formed by various organisms. As of 1981, 31 such minerals had been identified. Twenty five are synthesized by animals, 11 by protoctists, 8 by monerans, 7 by vascular plants and 4 by fungi.

At any one time and place on the land mass of the earth, there are five factors at work making soil from parent material.

1. Climate (cl) — temperature and precipitation
2. Organisms (o) — human beings, vegetation, soil animals and microbes
3. Parent material (p)
4. Topography or relief (r) and
5. Time (t).

Soil (s) = *f* (*cl, o, p, r, t* .....)

Modern System of Classification

Tho soil survey staff of United States Department of Agriculture (1975) proposed a new system of soil classification called the Seventh Approximation. This is based on present soil properties which are the consequence of soil genesis. There are six categories of classification in soil taxonomy : order, suborder, great group, subgroup, family and series. These categories are similar to those used for the classification of plants.

Order : This category is largely on the basis of soil forming processes as indicated by the presence or absence of specific diagnostic horizons. There are eleven soil orders in soil taxonomy. Nine of eleven orders are mineral soils. The eleventh order (Andisols) is only recently added.

Orders		Major Characteristics
1. Entisols	—	Young soils with little profile development.
2. Inceptisols	—	Embrionic soils with few diagnostic features, no horizon of illuvial clays, moisture adequate for crops in most years.
3. Mollisols	—	Dark coloured surface horizons, high base saturation, relatively high organic matter.
4. Alfisols	—	Relatively low in organic matter, relatively high in base saturation, an illuvial horizon of silicate clays, moisture adequate for crop growth.
5. Ultisols	—	Low in base saturation, highly weathered, an illuvial horizon of silicate clays, moisture adequate for crop growth in most years.
6. Oxisols	—	No illuvial horizon of silicate clays, no weatherable minerals, clay very inactive.
7. Vertisols	—	High in swelling clays, deep, cracks when soil is dry.
8. Aridisols	—	Relatively low in organic matter, few horizons, inadequate moisture for crop growth.
9. Spodosols	—	An illuvial horizon of amorphous aluminium

		and organic matter with or without amorphous iron.
10. Histosols	—	Peat or bog, more than 30 per cent organic matter.
11. Andisols	—	From volcanic ejecta, dominated by allophane or aluminium humic complex.

Suborder : These are subdivisions or orders that suggest genetic homogeneity. Moisture content, climatic environment and vegetation which helps to determine the nature of genetic processes, also helps to determine the suborders in which a given soil is found. There are 47 soil suborders in the US system of soil taxonomy.

Great groups : There are about 230 known great groups in the world. These are classified primarily on the basis of :

(*i*) Similarities in kind, arrangement and degree of expansion of horizons,

(*ii*) Similarities in soil moisture and soil temperature regimes, and

(*iii*) Similarities in degree of base saturation.

Subgroup : Great groups have been divided into three subgroups :

(*i*) First subgroup possesses only the properites of the concerned great group,

(*ii*) Second subgroup possesses some of the properties of other subgroups, great group, suborders and orders in addition to properties of concerned great group, and

(*iii*) Third subgroup possesses some properties that have not been found in any other great groups, suborders and orders in addition to properties of the concerned great group.

Family : Subgroups have been divided into families on the basis of similarities in physical and chemical properties affecting their response to management practices, especially to the penetration of plant roots. Important properties considered are soil texture, clay minerals, soil reaction, annual mean soil temperature and rainfall. About 6600 soil families are recognised in US.

Series : Families are subdivided into lowest category of the systems called series. One series may be differentiated from another in a family through differences in one or more but not necessarily all of the soil properties. Series are established mainly on the basis of profile characteristics. The soil series have been divided into **phases** which describes soil texture, percentage slope, stoniness, wetness, erosion, soluble salts, etc.

Genetic System of Classification

The basis of Russian pedologists genetic classification is genesis or origin of the soil and its subsequent development. The soil is looked upon as the result of five main soil forming factors : parent material, climate, organisms, topography and time. The soils inherit their properties from the parent material in the initial stages of soil formation. However, the inherited characters gradually disappear and the soils are dominated by acquired character from climate and vegetation.

According to genetic systems, soils of the world have been classified into three orders.

Zonal Soils : Climate and vegetation largely determine the soil characters. Soils developed from different parent material under similar climate and vegetation possess same general properties.

Intrazonal Soil : Local conditions like drainage, soluble salts, etc. determines the general characteristics of this order. The characteristic due to climate and vegetation are usually masked to a great extent by the local conditions.

Azonal soils : Soils of this order does not posses well developed profile.

Role of Macro-And Micro-Nutrients

Element	*Obtained in the form of*	*Specific role in Plants*	*Deficiency symptoms*
1. Nitrogen	NO_2^-, NO_3^-	Constituent of proteins, vitamins, hormones, nucleic acids, coenzymes, ATP, chlorophyll etc.	Stunted growth, chlorosis, development of anthocyanin.
2. Phosphorus	HPO_4^-	Constituent of nucleic acids, phospholipids, coenzymes, nucleotides, NAD^+, $NADP^+$ etc.	Poor growth, leaves dull green, premature fall of leaf and flower buds and delayed seed germination.
3. Potassium	K^+	Involved in protein synthesis in opening and closing of stomata, activates enzymes and helps in maintenance of turgidity of cells.	Yellow edges of leaves, inward curving of leaves, premature death.
4. Calcium	Ca^{2+}	As calcium pectate in the middle lamella of the cell wall, activates certain enzymes involved in selective permeability of cell membranes.	Stunted growth, disintegration of apical meristems and chlorosis.
5. Magnesium	Mg^{2+}	Constituent of chlorophyll, maintains ribosome structure, activates enzymes in phosphate metabolism.	Interveinal chlorosis
6. Sulphur	SO_4^{2-}	Constituent of amino acids (methionine, cysteine and cystine), vitamins, ferredoxin etc.	Chlorosis, rolling of tips and leaf margins.
7. Iron	Fe^{3+}	Constituent of ferredoxin, cytochromes, activates catalase, required for synthesis of chlorophyll.	Chlorosis
8. Manganese (trace)	Mn^{2+}	Activates some enzymes necessary for O_2 evolution in photosynthesis.	Chlorosis, grey spots on leaves
9. Molybdenum (trace)	Mo^{3+} or Mo^{4+} or MoO_2^{2+}	Activates certain enzymes in nitrogen metabolism and ascorbic acid synthesis.	Slight retardation of growth, whiptail in crucifers, loosening of cauliflower head.
10. Boron (trace)	Bo_3^{3-} or $B_4O_7^{2-}$	Calcium metabolism, pollen germination, cell differentiation, carbohydrate translocation.	Suppression of flower formation, leaves becomes coppery in testure, heart rot or brown heart of Sugar beet and Turnip.

Element	*Obtained in the form of*	*Specific role in Plants*	*Deficiency symptoms*
11. Copper (trace)	Cu^{2+}	Constituent of several oxidising enzymes, plastocyanin, cytochrome oxidase.	Dieback, brown heart disease, blackening of potato tuber, reclamation of leguminosae.
12. Zinc (trace)	Zn^{2+}	Activates various enzymes especially carboxylases, part of carbonic anhydrase and various dehydrogenases involved in synthesis of growth hormone auxin (IAA).	Little leaf disease, mottle leaf disease of apple and citrus, white bud, stunted growth, interveinal chlorosis.
13. Chlorine (trace)	Cl^-	Photolysis of water, with Na^+ and K^+ helps in maintaining solute concentration and anion-cation balance in cells, activatior of amylase.	Wilting, stunting of roots and swollen root tips, flower abscission, reduced fruiting bronze coloured leaves.

Role of NPK and their deficiency Symptoms in Plants :

Nitrogen, phosphorus and potassium are the three major elements found essential for the growth and development of plants.

Nitorgen :

Nitrogen ranks as prima dona in the realm of plant nutrition. It is a major structural constituent of the cell. The essential nature of nitrogen for plants was at-first established by **Theodore de Saussure** in 1804. The major functions assigned to it in plant nutrition are as follows.

Functions in Plants :

1. It is a structural constituent of proteins. With the exception of water, proteins are the main constituents of protoplasm-the basis of life. Protoplasmic proteins, acting together, synthesize not only themselves but other organic compounds of the plant. 21 amino-acids form the building blocks of plants proteins. Proteins in the plant cells of vegetative parts are primarily functional in nature. Nitrogen is an essential constituent of purines, pyrimidines, enzymes and co-enzymes. Purines and pyrimidines are found in nucleic acids. RNA and DNA, essential for protein synthesis and for respiration-energy carrier adenosine tri-phosphate (ATP). As a constituent of nucleoproteins, nitrogen is also present in chromosomes and genes-the heredity material. Enzymes along with co-enzymes regulate metabolic processes. Thus, functional proteins serve both as catalysts and director of the metabolism.
2. As an essential constituent of porphyrines, nitrogen is found is duch metabolically important compounds as the chlorophyll and cytochrome enzymes essential in photosynthesis and respiration.
3. Nitrogen is found in plant hormones (IAA), vitamins and cytokinins exerting regulatory effects on growth and metabolism of plants.
4. Nitrogen is also an integral component of alkaloids and a number of plant glucosides.

Physiological Effects of Nitrogen Supply on Plant :

1. Carbohydrate Utilization

With increasing N-supply to plants, the carbohydrate content tends to decrease. Additional N-supply promotes growth of additional tissues which consume carbohydrates synthesized during photosynthesis. Thus, starch percentage in wheat and sugar content in sugar beet is depressed following excess N-supply.

2. Succulence

Excessive N-supply promotes thin-walled succulent tissues which decrease the mechanical strength of hemp fiber and thus deteriorates its quality. The shelf-life of potato and apple also decreases with excessive N-supply.

3. Root Growth

In general, high N-supply promotes more growth of plant shoots than that of roots, increasing thereby ratio of shoot to root.

4. Fruiting

An optimum C:N ratio in tomato and mango is essential for higher and regular fruit-production. An excessive N-supply promotes vegetative growth and decreases fruiting. Biennial bearing in apple and mango can be controlled by optimization of C : N ratio through N-supply.

5. Lodging

Plants become susceptible to lodging with nitrogen supply due, to action of nitrogen in increasing plant height, weight and leaf area without simultaneous increase in stalk-strength decreasing thereby resistance to breaking.

6. Time of Maturity

Nitrogen fertilization often delays the maturity of plants by promoting succulence and higher moisture content in grain.

7. Incidence of Diseases

In general, nitrogen promotes disease incidence (mildews and rusts) by promoting succulence and lodging in plants and through raising the relative humidity around the plants.

Forms Available to Plants

1. Inorganic-N : NO_3 and NH_4^+ Some plants like rice, crotons etc. prefer NH_4^+- over NO_2^- -N.
2. Organic-N : Amino acids and urea.
3. Molecular-N : N_2- utilized by lower plants only such as certain groups of bacteria (symbionts and non-symbionts) and blue-green algae.

Deficiency Symptoms of Nitrogen in Crops:

I General Symptoms :

Small leaves, stems thin, upright with few lateral shoots giving a sparse growth appearance. Pale, yellowish green leaves which may develop yellow, red or purple. Being a nutrient mobile within the plant, symptoms are most pronounced on older leaves and appear there at first.

II. Specific Symptoms for Selected Crops:

Plant	Visual Symptoms
1. Maize	Leaf tip yellowing in older leaves the yellowing progresses along the mid-rib towards the leaf base, leaf margins remain green for comparatively longer peroid, stalks slender.
2. Cotton	'Firing' of lower leaves; plants light green lower leaves yellow drying to brownish colour, stalk little branched and slender.
3. Potato	Leaf margins of lower leaflets fade to a yellow; yellowing and shedding of

	lower leaves; stems few and slender growth upright; tubers small.	and margins prematurely; order leaves reddish purple; leaves narrow; stems thin; tillering retarded.
4. Sugarcane	Leaves yellowish green to yellow, drying at tips	

Critical values for N-deficiency in selected crop tissues:

Crop	*Tissue to be sampled*	*Stage of growth*	*Critical limit for N(%)*
1. Rice	3rd leaf from top	3 to 6 weeks after transplanting	1.4
2. Maize	Entire fully developed leaf below the whorl	Before silking	3.0
3. Potato	Leaves; 4th node from top	40 to 45 days old	6.00
4. Sugar cane	(*a*) 8th to 10th internode	-	.025
	(*b*) Leaf blades 3,4,5,6 from the top	-	1.00
5. Orange	Leaves	4 to 7 months, bloom cycle from non-fruiting terminals	

Indicator Plants for N Deficiency :

Maize, apple, peach and citrus are good indicators for nitrogen deficiency.

Phosphorus :

Like nitrogen, phosphorus plays an important role as a structural component of the cell constituents and metabolically active compounds. C. Sprengel (1839) was the first to demonstrate phosphorus as an essential element for the higher plants and using controlled culture method. Ville (1981) established its essential nature to higher plants.

Functions in Plants:

1. As a constituent of structural and storage compounds the phosphorus in organic form is present in phytin, phospholipds and nucleic acids. While phytin stores phosphorus in seeds, phospholipids are an important constituent of cell membranes. Nucleoproteins constitute the genetic material and control the nature of protein synthesis.
2. Besides cell membranes, it is a structural component of chloroplasts and mitochondria.
3. As a constituent of ATP, phosphorus plays a vital role in energy transformations and metabolic processes of plants including photosynthesis, glycolysis, respiration and fatty acid synthesis in plants.
4. As a constituent of coenzymes NAD and NADP, phosphorus plays an important role in oxidation-reduction reactions in which hydrogen transfer takes place.
5. Although inorganic P is present in small amounts in plants, it is in a continuous state of flux with Org-P changing frequently from one form to

another. Inorganic P provides P to the organic-P pool in plants and P leaves the plant as inorganic-P. Thus, the rate of metabolic processes are limited by the availability of inorganic P ions for binding in organic forms.

PHYSIOLOGICAL EFFECTS OF PHOSPHORUS SUPPLY ON PLANTS

1. Root Growth

Phosphorus promotes lateral as well as fibrous root growth which increases the feeding zone of plants and improves the uptake of nutrients. The favourable effect of P on root growth is much more conspicuous in tuber-roots (sweet-potato) where translocation of carbohydrates to storage tissues proceeds for longer periods in P-fertilized plots than in P-deficient plants.

2. Development and Maturity

Tasselling and silking in maize, flowering in tomato, panicle emergence in cereals are earlier with ample supply of phosphorus. Earlier maturity of wheat with an ample supply of phosphorus may help the crop to escape damage from the boll weevil.

3. Disease Incidence

Phosphorus decreases fungal disease incidence in crops such as barley mildew and fungal root rots in seedling stage (*Pythium* root rot of wheat). Thus, phosphorus counteracts largely the ill-effects of nitrogen decreasing the infection.

4. Plant Growth and Yield

Phosphorus supply to crop plants is important during early growth stages. It promotes tillering, number of panicles and test-weight of grains in cereals improving thereby yield of the crop. It also improves grain : straw ratio in cereals.

5. Lodging

It provides strength to the stem and decreases incidence of crop lodging.

6. Symbiotic N-fixation in Legumes

Phosphorus supply improves nodulation and N-fixation in legumes through improved rhizobial activity. It, in turn, improves grain yield and better crop quality through higher protein content of the crop. The fodder quality of berseem is also improved through better palatability and higher protein content of crop.

7. Availability of Secondary and Micronutrients to Plants

Availability of S and Mo to plants increases with an ample supply of phosphorus to plants. However, availability of Zn to plants decreases with high-P supply.

FORMS AVAILABLE TO PLANTS

1. Inorganic Forms

(*i*) $H_2PO_4^-$ and (*ii*) $HPO_4^=$

$H_2PO_4^-$ is the dominant form below pH 6.7. Between pH 6.7 and 9.0 the divalent $HPO_4^=$ form is predominant and above pH 9.0, trivalent $PO_4^=$ becomes more importnat but its availability to plants is little, if any. Maximum availability of P to plants is between 6.0 and 7.0 soil pH.

2. Organic Forms :

(*i*) Phytin-absorbed directly by the plants.

(*ii*) Nucleic acid-broken down at root surface and phosphorus absorbed either as inorganic or organic-P.

Organic forms contribute little to P-availability of plants.

Deficiency Symptoms of Phosphorus in Crops:

Similar to N, P is also mobile within the plants.

I. General Symptoms

In general, symptoms of phosphorus deficiency are not particularly pronounced or specific.

(*i*) Extreme P deficiency may result in some yellowing of older leaves.

(*ii*) Common symptom is dark-green or bluish-green colour which may be tinted with bronze or purple in lower leaves; stunted plant growth.

(*iii*) Similar to N, P deficient plants have thin stems, small leaves, premature defoliation beginning with lower leaves, delayed and reduced flowering.

(*iv*) Sickle-leaf of plants with chlorosis of leaf except for mid-rib.

(*v*) Under P-deficiency, fruits become soft, pulpy and sour. Keeping quality of fruits and potato is much reduced. Under conditions of deficiency both P and N are withdrawn from older tissues and translocated to meristmetic tissues where metabolism is more rapid.

II. Specific Symptoms for Selected Plants

Plant	Visual symptoms
1. Maize	Leaves purple green during early growth, growth is spindly, slow maturity, irregular ear formation.
2. Cotton	Leaves dark green; stunted plant growth; delayed maturity.
3. Potato	Forward roll and marginal leaf burn; defoliation of older leaves; spindly and upright growth; tubers may have brown internal lesions.
4. Sugar cane	Leaves show narrow bluish-green lines; older ones turn yellow and show tip die-back; stalks slender with short internodes and stunted growth.
5. Tomato	Leaves olive green with purple casts on lower side, stems slender; foliage sparse plants stunted.

Critical Values of Phosphorus for P-deficiency in Selected Crops

Crop	*Tissue to be sampled*	*Stage of growth*	*Critical limit for P(%)*
Rice	3rd leaf from top	3 to 6 weeks after transplanting	0.08
Maize	Entire fully developed leaf below the whorl	Before silking	0.25
Potato	Petioles of 4th to 6th leaf from the top	4 weeks after emergence	0.004 (fresh wt.) (2% Acetic acid extraction)
Sugarcane	(a) 8th to 10th internode-	0.25	
	(b) Leaf blades 3,4,5,6 from top	-	0.08
Pea	Shoots	Early bloom stage	0.11 to 0.16 (2% Acetic acid extract)
Wheat	Grain	Harvest	0.39

Indicator Plants for P Deficiency

Roman lettuce, tomato and maize are good indicators of phosphorus deficiency.

Potassium

Potassium is the third major plant nutrient which, unlike nitrogen and phosphorus, is present almost entirely in the cell sap of the plants in ionic form (K^+). However, a small fraction of potassium is adsorbed by the proteins which is in consonance with the current view that potassium functions in enzymatic reactions. Within the cell, potassium (K^+) is found in cytoplasm and vacuole and to a lesser extent in nucleus in the ionic form.

The essential nature of potassium to higher plants was first reported by C. Sprengel (1839) and experimentally established by Birnar and Lucanus (1866).

Function in Plants

1. It promotes the deposition of cellulose and lignin on the cell walls and increases the proportion of hard sclerenchymatous tissues which in turn decreases crop lodging and incidences of plant diseases. Stem rot disease of rice and dead heart disease of maize can be appreciable controlled with an ample K-supply to crops.
2. It improves the size, firmness and keeping quality of tomato and prevents fruit cracking in general. It also improves the aroma and burning quality of hukkah tobacco.
3. It improves dought resistance in crops. It helps in better utilization of N by plants.
4. It improves the ammonification, nitrification and N-fixation in soils by influencing the activity of micro-flora directly or indirectly.
5. It is required in coupling of amino-acids to form peptide bonds and thus contributes in protein synthesis particularly in pulses and legumes.
6. Potassium catalyses the activity of a number of enzymes involved in carbohydrate and nucleic acid metabolism in plants.
7. It has a favourable effect on photosynthesis while its deficiency increases the rate of respiration in plants. Thus, it helps in improving sugar and starch content in sugarcane, potato; sweet-potato and maize.
8. It also catalyses the activity of enzymes involved in fatty-acid synthesis and helps to improve the oil content in crops.
9. It plays an important role in the maintenance of cellular organization, permeability of cellular membranes, hydration of protoplasm and balance of the electrical charge within the cell.

Besides, it also affects the following :

1. Water Relations

Potassium improves the turgidity of plants with an increased supply. It is due to lowered transpiration and higher Na^+ absorption resulting in osmotic effects.

2. Carbohydrate and Nitrogen Metabolism

Being essential for the action of enzymes involved both in carbohydrate and nitrogen metabolism, potassium deficiency leads to accumulation of free amino-acids, reduced photosynthesis and increased rate of respiration. Sucrose content in sugarcane and sugar beet decreases with K-stress in plants. Potassium helps to improve diameter and wall thickness of cotton fiber. The test weight of wheat and maize grain decreases under K-stress.

3. Root Lodging

Potassium supply to maize increases the number of brace roots/plant and the surface area of soil within the ambit of brace roots. Thus, it helps to anchor the plant firmly in the ground reducing lodging thereby.

4. Crop Quality

Potassium is often termed as an element for 'crop quality'. The effects of K-deficiency on the quality of selected crops are summarized below:

- Potato – Tubers hollow in center, darken after cooking.
- Apple – Do not colour well.
- Tomato – Premature dropping, poor colouration and por keeping quality, decrease in acidity.
- Tobacco – Aroma and fire holding capacity impaired.
- Peas – Seed coat toughened.
- Barley – Brewing quality impaired.
- Cabbage – Heads are not solid.
- Citrus – Low acidity and ascorbic acid (Vit-C).
- Soybean – Decrease in oil content.

5. Time of Maturity

K-deficiency delays maturity of oats, soybean and maize. However, deficiency of K causes early maturity in cotton.

6. Disease Resistance

K-deficiency increases the severity of cotton wilt (*Fusarium oxysporum* f. vasiinfectum), cereal-rust, tobacco mosaic virus (TMV), potato rot (*Phytophthora infestans*) and alternaria in cotton and tobacco. An ample supply of K helps to minimize the incidence of disease and in some cases helps the crops to escape the disease.

7. Resistance to Low Temperatures

Plants deficient in K are prone to low temperature frost injury than those supplied well with K *e.g.*, potato and alfalfa presumably due to greater carbohydrate accumulation by the K-sufficient plants.

Forms of Potassium Available to Plants:

K^+ ions only.

Deficiency Symptoms of K in Plants :

Potassium is also an element mobile within the plant. Thus, in plants under K-stress, potassium is translocated from older tissues to new growth.

I. General Deficiency Symptoms in Plants:

1. Browning and death of leaf margins (leaf scorch) or tips (tip burn) but in some plants appearance of brown spots in interveinal areas.
2. Leaves narrow and wrinkled with leaf margins curling towards upper or lower surface.
3. Deficiency of K in plants results in an accumulation of putrescine and/or agmatine which impart characteristic visual symptoms of K-deficiency in plants.
4. Leguminous crops develop 'off-white' small granules along the leaf margins under K-stress.
5. Deficiency of K decreases root activity in plants resulting in almost doubling of shoot root ratio.
6. Browning and death of leaves is preceeded by less marked symptoms wherein leaves turn bluish green purple of orange followed by shrinking, collapse and browning of individual cells when viewed under a microscope.

II. Specific Deficiency Symptoms of K for Selected Plants

Plant	Visual Symptoms
1. Rice	Leaves bluish green when young; older leaves show irregular chlorotic and necrotic areas turning red with brown at tips; ears long and thin; grain formation poor.
2. Wheat	Leaves bluish green; older leaves turn yellow, then brown and finally die at tips and margins; eventually entire leaf dies resulting in scorch symptom, stalks short and weak; grain shriveled; tillering profuse; panicles reduced.
3. Maize	Yellow or yellowish streaks on leaves; lower or older leaves corrugated followed by tip and marginal scorch; ears poorly filled at the tip ends; short internodes in stalk; plants weak and may blow down.
4. Potato	Leaves are bluish green at first; older leaves turn yellowish followed by necrosis and browning at the tips and margins; leaf-lets cupped and crowded; stalks (haulms) slender with short internodes; may collapse prematurely; tubers flesh bluish.
5. Sugar cane	Young leaves dark-green at first turning pale yellow with maturity with reddish mid-rib on the upper surface; older or lower leaves die back at tips and margins with minute interveinal chlorotic spots followed by necrotic spots; stalks short.

Critical Values of K for Potassium Deficiency in Crops:

Crop	*Tissue to be sampled*	*Stage of growth*	*Critical limit for K (%)*
1. Rice	3rd leaf from top	3 to 6 weeks after transplanting	1.08
2. Maize	6th from base	Silking stage	1.00
3. Potato	Petioles	Mid season	7.00
4. Sugar cane	3rd to 6th leaf sheaths	-	2.25
5. Pea	Leaves from 8th node	Pre-bloom	1.30
6. Cotton	Petioles, youngest mature	130 days	1.00

Indicator Plants for K-Deficiency

Potato, alfalfa, tobacco and cucurbit. Occasionally, cotton, tomato and maize are good indicators of K deficiency.

Management of Soil Acidity

Acidic soils are usually managed for crop production by the application of carbonates, oxides or hydroxides of calcium and magnesium compounds referred to as **agricultural limes.**

When lime is added to the moist acidic soils, it charges the soil solution with calcium ions (Ca^{2+}). These Ca^{2+} ions exchange with hydrogen (H^+) ions in the exchangeable complex. The H^+ ions combine with OH^- ions to form H_2O or with CO_3^{-2} to form unstable H_2CO_3 which readily changes to H_2O and CO_2.

$$^{H^+}_{H^+}\boxed{\text{Micelle}} + Ca(OH_3)_2 \leftrightarrow Ca^{2+}\boxed{\text{Micelle}} + 2H_2O$$

$$^{H^+}_{H^+}\boxed{\text{Micelle}} + Ca(HCO_3)_2 \leftrightarrow Ca^{2+}\boxed{\text{Micelle}} + 2H_2O + 2CO_2$$

$$^{H^+}_{H^+}\boxed{\text{Micelle}} + CaCO_3 \leftrightarrow Ca^{2+}\boxed{\text{Micelle}} + H_2O + CO_2$$

$$^{H^+}_{H^+}\boxed{\text{Micelle}} + CaO \leftrightarrow Ca^{2+}\boxed{\text{Micelle}} + H_2O$$

Liming Materials

Material selected for reclaiming acid soils must be cheap and effective in reducing the hydrogen ion concentration. The two metallic cations best suited for this purpose are calcium and magnesium, specially calcium meet the requirement perfectly. Potassium and sodium are also effective. However, potassium is very expensive and sodium compounds disperse the soil colloids leading to poor physical condition of the soil. Calcium and magnesium salts of strong acids are not ideal, since the adsorbed hydrogen ion is exchanged with cation of such salt as calcium sulphate leading to formation of a strong acid in the soil solution.

$$H^+\boxed{\text{Micelle}} + CaSO_4 \leftrightarrow Ca^{2+}\boxed{\text{Micelle}} + 2H^+ + SO_4^{2-}$$

The soil complex may be charged with active calcium, but pH of the soil solution may decrease. Hence, salts like gypsum and calcium chlorides are not suitable for liming.

Calcium Oxide (CaO) : It is also known as unslaked lime, burnt lime, quick lime or oxide of lime. It is manufactured by roasting calcite limestone in a furnace. Pure material has a neutralising value or calcium carbonate equivalent (CCE) of 179 per cent compared with pure calcium carbonate.

Calcium Hydroxide ($Ca(OH)_2$) : It is referred to as slaked lime, hydrated lime or builders' lime. It is prepared by hydrating calcium oxide. Chemically pure compound has neutralising value of 136, making it common liming material.

Calcium and Calcium-Magnesium Carbonates: Calcium carbonate ($CaCO_3$) and calcium-magnesium carbonate [$CaMg(CO_3)_2$] are usually mined by open pit method. Neutralising value of chemically pure calcium carbonate has been fixed at 100 per cent.

Basic Slag ($CaSiO_3$) : It is a by-product of the pigiron manufacture. In addition to its phosphorus content, it has a neutralising value of 60-70 per cent.

Beneficial Effects of Liming

Liming minimises the adverse effects of soil acidity on crop growth. The main effects of lime on acid soils are :

(*i*) Increases the availability of phosphorus, calcium and magnesium,

(*ii*) Reduces the toxicity of aluminium, manganese and iron,

(*iii*) Increases the availability of nitrogen through nitrogen fixation and nitrification,

(*iv*) Increases organic matter decomposition,

(*v*) Improves the multiplication of beneficial soil bacteria, and

(*vi*) Improves soil physical condition.

Salt Affected Soils

Soils of arid and semiarid regions contain excessive concentration of either soluble salts or exchangeable sodium or both due to inadequate leaching of base forming cations. The pH is usually 7 or above with exchangeable complex dominated by calcium and magnesium ions. Irrigated soils in low rainfall regions also develop soil salinity and alkalinity due to accumulation of salts in surface layers through evaporating water. The accumulated salts are primarily chlorides and sulphates of calcium, magnesium, sodium and potassium. Weathering of rocks and minerals, rainfall, ground water and irrigation are the sources of these salts.

Salinity is usually expressed in terms of electrical conductivity (EC) which is measured in decisiemens per meter (dS m^{-1}). Formerly it used to be expressed in mmho cm^{-1}. Since 1 S is 1 mho, 1 dS m^{-1} is 1 mmho cm^{-1}. Sodium status is usually characterised in two ways : exchangeable sodium percentage and sodium adsorption ratio.

Exchangeable Sodium Percentage (ESP) : It indicates the degree of exchangeable complex saturated with sodium.

$$\text{ESP} = \frac{\text{Exchangeable sodium (Cmol kg}^{-1})}{\text{Cation exchange capacity (Cmol kg}^{-1})} \times 100$$

Sodium Adsorption Ration (SSR) : It indicates comparative concentrations of Na^+, Ca^{2+} and Mg^{2+} in soil solution.

$$\text{SAR} = \frac{Na^+}{\sqrt{\frac{1}{2}(Ca^{2+}+Mg^{2+})}}$$

where (Na^+), (Ca^{2+}) and (Mg^{2+}) are concentrations (Cmol kg^{-1}) of sodium, calcium and magnesium ions in soil solution.

Classification of Salt Affected Soils

Using the EC and ESP characteristics and soil pH, salt affected soils are classified as saline, saline-sodic and sodic (Table 3).

Table 3. Characteristics of Saline, Saline-Sodic and Sodic Soils

Soil	*pH*	*EC(dS m^{-1})*	*ESP*
Saline	<8.5	>4	<15
Saline-sodic	<8.5	>4	>15
Sodic	>8.5	<4	>15

Sodic Soils and Plant Growth

Saline and saline-sodic soils affect plant growth due to their high soluble salt concentration. Sodic soils dominated by active sodium exert detrimental effect on plants in four ways.

(1) High concentration of sodium carbonate and bicarbonate leads to cell collapse due to passage of water from cell into concentrated soil solution,

(2) Toxicity of bicarbonate and other anions,

(3) Low micronutrient availability due to high pH of the soil, and

(4) Oxygen deficiency in root zone due to breakdown of soil structure (deflocculation).

The limits of tolerance of plants to salts in soil may vary depending on rainfall, physical makeup of the plant and climate. Relative tolerance of crops to salinity (saline soils) and sodicity (sodic soils), however, may give some general idea.

Table 4. Relative Tolerance of Crops to Salinity and Sodicity

Saline Soils			*Sodic Soils*		
Tolerant	*Semi-tolerant*	*Sensitive*	*Tolerant*	*Semi-tolerant*	*Sensitive*
Barley	Pomegranate	Cirtus	Rice	Wheat	Groundnut
Sugar beet	Wheat	Gram	Sugar beet	Barley	Cowpea
Rape	Rice	Peas	Paragrass	Oats	Lentil
Cotton	Sorghum	Groundnut	Sugarcane	Peas	
	Maize	Lentil	Cotton	Maize	
	Sunflower	Cowpea	Millets	Gram	
	Potato				

Management of Saline and Sodic Soils

Saline soils with appreciable amounts of neutral soluble salts high in calcium and magnesium can be easily managed as the problem is to bring down the salt concentration only. Sodic soils need replacement of exchangeable sodium besides reducing the concentrantion of soluble salts.

Saline Soils : Flooding and draining the flooded water after 3 to 4 days of flooding can leach down the soluble salts below root zone depth. Two to three such treatments can make the soil suitable for most crops. **Leaching Requirement** (LR) is that fraction of water that must be leached through the soil root zone depth to control the salinity at a specified level. This is simply the ratio of equivalent depth of drainage water to the depth of applied water which can be expressed as fraction or per cent.

$$LR = \frac{\text{Electrical conductivity of applied water (ECa)}}{\text{Electrical conductivity of drainage water (ECd)}}$$

If the ECd in root zone is to be maintained below 4 dS m^{-1} and ECa is 2 dS m^{-1}.

$$LR = \frac{2}{4} = 0.5 \text{ or 50 per cent}$$

Fifty per cent of applied water must pass through the root zone for maintaining desired salt balance in the root zone depth. However, several other factors need consideration at field level.

Provision of adequate drainage can minimise the adverse effects of salinity. Sowing the seed on the sides of ridges rather than on the top application of acid forming fertilisers, use of organic manures and proper irrigation schedule can reduce the risk of crop production on saline soils.

Sodic Soils : Basic principle in reclamation of sodic soils is replacement of exchangeable sodium by calcium and leaching out the relased sodium salt from the root zone. Availability and low cost makes gypsum an important amendment for reclamation.

$$\begin{matrix}Na^+\\Na^+\end{matrix}\boxed{\text{Micelle}} + CaSO_4 \leftrightarrow Ca^{2+}\boxed{\text{Micelle}} + NaSO_4\downarrow$$

Since the process is reversible, sodium sulphate should be leached out from the sphere of exchange. The amount of gypsum required to lower the ESP of a sodic soils to a desired level is known as **gypsum requirement** (GR). It depends on purity and solubility of gypsum, clay minerals present in the soil and the extent to which the exchange process takes places in the soil.

Laboratory method is used for assessing the GR of sodic soil. Weighed quantity of sodic soil 5g is shaken with 100 ml saturated gypsum solution of known Ca^{2+} concentration and the filtrate analysed for Ca^{2+} and Mg^{2+}.

$$GR = \frac{(C_1 - C_2) \times 100 \times 100}{1000 \times 5}$$

$$= (C_1 - C_2) \times 2 \text{ meq of } Ca^{2+}\ 100\ g^{-1} \text{ of soil}$$

where, C_1 is the concentration (meq 1^{-1}) of Ca^{2+} in gypsum solution and C_2 is the concentration of Ca^{2+} plus Mg^{2+} in the filtrate.

Elemental sulphur and sulphuric acid can also be used where sodium carbonate content is more. Sulphur upon biological oxidation yields sulphuric acid which not only changes sodium corbonate to less harmful sodium sulphate, but also decreases the alkalinity.

$$Na_2CO_3 + H_2SO_4 \leftrightarrow CO_2 + H_2O + Na_2SO_4\downarrow$$

$$\begin{matrix}Na^+\\Na^+\end{matrix}\boxed{\text{Micelle}} + H_2SO_4 \leftrightarrow \begin{matrix}H^+\\H^+\end{matrix}\boxed{\text{Micelle}} + Na_2SO_4\downarrow$$

Several other material are also used for reclaiming sodic soils. Gypsum equivalents of amendments used for reclamation of sodic soils as per Central Soil Salinity Research Institute, Karnal (CSSRI) are given below.

Amendment	Gypsum equivalent
Gypsum	1.00
Calcium chloride	0.85
Sulphur	0.19
Sulphuric acid	0.57
Iron sulphate	1.62
Aluminium sulphate	1.29

Effective management practices are essential in the early state of exploitation of saline and alkali soils, such as:

(*i*) Growing salt tolerant crops,

(*ii*) Growing shallow rooted crops that tolerate high soil moisture conditions,

(*iii*) Heavy irrigation before planting,

(*iv*) Using higher seed rate,

(*v*) Keeping the land under cultivation without leaving it fallow for long, especially in hot, dry climates,

(*vi*) Using fertilisers containing calcium,

(*vii*) Heavy rates of organic manures application, and

(*viii*) Planting on the bottom side of the furrow.

Reclamation of Saline and Saline-Alkali Soils

Leaching and Amending Stage : Saline soils are leached by ponding an appreciable depth of water with adequate drainage. The objectives and measures to be considered in the course of leachig are:

(*i*) Removal of excess salts to the depth of deepest root system of the crops in rotation,

(*ii*) Reduction of ground water salinity to below the critical level,

(*iii*) Lowering the ground water table sufficiently to remove the danger of it resalinising the soil; and

(*iv*) Avoiding alkalisation of saline-alkali soils by application of gypsum late in leaching and when the rate of infiltration slows down. Gypsum should not be applied before leaching to avoid its removal with other soluble salts.

Cultivation and Improvement Stage: Protection of leached and amended soil against resalinisation or realkalisation can be achieved by:

(*i*) Securing drainage to keep ground water table below the critical depth,

(*ii*) Continuing periodic leaching to maintain the desired salt balance in the soil,

(*iii*) Starting to grow salt tolerant crops or those needing high irrigation water, such as rice, and

(*iv*) Land levelling, furrow irrigations, preplanting/seeding flooding, etc.

Physical, chemical and biological soil properties can be improved by :

(*i*) Deep ploughing to loosen compacted layer for improving soil structure, and

(*ii*) Application of organic manures and balanced fertiliser use to improve soil fertility.

Reclamation of alkali soils depends mainly on the addition of suitable fertilisers after loosening the compacted layers and breaking hard pans, in addition to periodic flooding and drying with effective drainage. The cost and time of reclamation increase as texture becomes heavier and clay fraction becomes dominated by montomorillonite type. It is not necessary to use chemicals as a source of soluble calcium in calcareous soils. Calcium carbonate may be converted into more soluble form through application of acids or high rates of organic manures including green manures.

Process in Reclamation of Saline and Alkali Soils

Reclamation of saline and alkali soils include some basic processes, such as leaching, drainage, application of chemicals, fertilisers and deep ploughing.

Leaching of Salts : Leaching efficiency depends mainly on soil characteristics, sufficiency and suitability of leaching water constituents and depth of ground water and prevailing climatic conditions. Important points to be considered are :

(i) Internal leaching should be preferred where calcium salts are high in the crust. Surface leaching may be done where there is a dense accumulation of sodium salts in the crust,

(ii) Internal flooding and drying are especially useful in leaching slowly permeable soils,

(iii) Basins should be levelled after ploughing and before leaching,

(iv) Leaching may be completed while growing some salt tolerant crops, and

(v) Leaching is not complete until salts have been removed to the desired soil depth to below the critical level.

Drainage : Provision of adequate drainage is a basic principle in reclamation of saline and alkali soils.

(i) Appropriate drainage depth should be determined. Drainage depth increases as ground water salinity increases. Where deep drainage network cannot be installed, drain spacing should be closer,

(ii) Open drainage are preferable in early stages of reclamation, especially in soils of low permeability, and

(iii) Effective maintenance of drainage system is essential at all the stages of leaching, amelioration, improvement and cultivation.

Chemicals : Several chemicals such as gypsum, calcium chloride, sulphur, sulphuric acid and ferrous sulphate are used for soil amelioration. While applying chemicals, the following points need consideration.

(i) To ensure the highest efficiency of exchange between soluble calcium and exchangeable sodium, soluble salts have to be leached out of the soil profile before chemicals are used.

(ii) Chemicals like gypsum migrate slowly from surface to subsoil. Hence, they should be evenly distributed and carefully mixed with soil by deep ploughing, and

(iii) Use of chemicals, preferably accompanied by periodic flooding and drying improves physical and biological characteristics of the soil.

Deep Ploughing and Subsoiling : It is important to plough before leaching the soil. It helps to mix surface substances with the soil. Deep ploughing helps chemicals to reach lower depths and to improve soil permeability. Thus, it aids to leaching and stimulating chemical reactions in the soil.

Use of Saline and Alkali Soils

Where reclamation of saline and alkali soils is not possible, some crops may still be grown up to certain degree of salinity or alkalinity.

Adequate Water and Inadequate Drainage

(i) Avoid over irrigation to prevent rise of ground water table,

(ii) Apply water at short intervals and in small quantities, and

(iii) Grow salt tolerant crops, shallow rooted and those that tolerate high soil moisture regime.

Adequate Drainage and Unsuitable Water

(i) Use higher water rates to cover leaching requirements, keeping in mind that its salinity should not exceed that of soil saturation extract, and

(ii) Chemicals should be used if the SAR and residual sodium carbonate in irrigation water are high.

Inadequate Drainage and Unsuitable Water

Whenever available, rain water should be used. Land may be used as pasture or growing salt resistant plants such as palm trees.

Soil Amendments

Soil **amendments** are substances that influence the plant growth by producing in the soil one or more of the beneficial effects.

(*i*) Changing the soil reaction (pH) to suit the crop needs,

(*ii*) Increasing the availability of plant nutrients,

(*iii*) Improving the soil physical condition, and

(*iv*) Counteracting the effects of injurious substances.

There are three types of soil amendments: materials used for correcting soil acidity, correcting alkaline soils and soil conditioners for improving soil structure.

Soil **conditioners** are materials added to improve or maintain physical condition of the soil. Synthetic materials like polyvinylites, polyacrylates, cellulose gums, lignin derivatives and silicates have been developed for stabilising soil aggregates.

Questions From Previous Year's Papers

Q. 1. (a) Explain the phenomenon of ion exchange in soils. Elaborate the mechanism for the movement of ions in relation to soil and plants.

(b) What type of plant root appears to have the greater CEC legumes or cereals? Elaborate.

(c) Calculate the quantity of urea diammonium phosphate (18–16–0) and muriate of potash required for 25m × 20m size potato plot to supply nutrient at the rate of 150-92-100 kg N, P_2O_5 and K_2O per hectare.

Q. 2. (a) What are the indicators of soil fertility? How these could be used effectively for measuring fertility of soil?

(b) Outline the approaches which could be adopted for efficient use of fertilizers under rainfed farming.

Q. 3. (a) Discuss the relationship between cropping system and soil management. Substantiate your discussion with concrete examples.

(b) Discuss the problem of zinc deficiency in rice crop and how it is removed?

Q. 4. What is nutrient fixation? Briefly discuss the phosphorus and potassium fixation in soil. Explain in detail the important management practices to increase the availability and efficient use of phosphorus and potassium in soils.

Q. 5. What is integrated nutrient management? How do you plan for such a system to monsoon season lowland rice crop?

Q. 6. (a) What are the important physical and chemical properties of soil?

(b) State the important factors responsible for soil formation and explain effects of climate on soil formation.

Q. 7. (a) What do you mean by essential plant nutrient and how are they classified?

(b) How do plants get nutrients from soil?

(c) What are the available forms of plant nutrients?

(d) Discuss the role of N and P in plant growth, development, production and quality of produces.

Q. 8. What is denitrification? Discuss the factors that promote denifrification is soil.

Q. 9. Write short notes on the following, each not exceeding 150 words :

(a) Water harvesting.

(b) Leaching reqirements.

(c) Azolla as biofertilizers

(d) Organic farming.

(e) VAM-Mycorrhizae

(f) Soil fertility evaluation.

Q. 10. Write short notes on the following, each not exceeding 150 words :

(a) Symbiotic nitrogen fixation in non-leguminous plants.

(b) Foliar fertilization to crops.

(c) Major classes of soil forming rocks.

(d) Forms of soil water.

(e) Biofertilizers.

(f) Carbon : Nitrogen ratio.

Q. 11. Write short notes on the following, each not exceeding 150 words :

(a) Vermicompost.

(b) Soil profile.

(c) Nitrogen fixation in soil.

(d) Effect of mulching.

(e) Integrated nutrient management system.

(f) Soil-plant-water relationships.

(g) Soil amendments and conditioners.

Q. 12. Distinguish between/among (a-c) :

(a) Saline and alkali soil

(b) Acid equivalent and basic equivalent of fertilizers

(c) Aerobic, semiaerobic and anaerobic decomposition of organic matter.

(d) Ammonifying bacteria and denitrifying bacteria.

Q. 13. Differentiate between the following pairs in not more than 150 words each :

(a) Particle density and bulk density of soil.

(b) Soil fertility and productivity.

(c) Nitrification inhibitors and slow release nitrogen fertilizers.

(d) Soil pH and soil Eh

(e) Soil permeability and Hydraulic conductivity.

(f) Weathering and withering processes.

(g) Saline and alkaline soils.

(h) Kaolinite montomrillonite clay mineral.

7. SOIL CONSERVATION

SOIL EROSION

Soil erosion is the process of detachment of soil particles from the top soil and transportation of the detached soil particles by wind and/or water. The detaching agents are falling rain drop, channel flow and wind. The transporting agents are flowing water, rain splash and wind.

Out of 328.7 M ha of India's geographical area, about 162 M ha is subjected to erosion (Table 1).

Table 1 : Extent of Soil Erosion (Velayutham and Bhattacharya 2000.)

Type of erosion	*Degree of erosion*				*Area affected (M ha)*	
	Slight	*Moderate*	*Strong*	*Extreme*	*Total*	*Per cent*
Water erosion					148.2	45.3
Loss of top soil	27.3	99.8	5.4	—	135.5	40.3
Terrain deformation	—	11.8	—	4.6	16.4	5.0
Wind erosion					13.5	4.1
Loss of top soil	0.3	5.5	0.4	—	6.2	1.9
Loss of top soil/terrain deformation	—	4.6	—	—	4.6	1.4
Terrain deformation/over flowing	—	—	2.7	—	2.7	0.8
Total	27.6	121.7	5.8	4.6	**162.4**	**49.4**
Total geographical area					328.7	

Water erosion is the major problem causing loss of top soil and/or terrain deformation in about 148 M ha (45%) of the geographical area of the country. **Wind erosion** is dominant in western regions covering 13.5 M ha (4.1%) of the total area. Wind erosion causes loss of top soil in 1.9 per cent, terrain deformation in 1.2 per cent and over blowing and shifting of sand dune in 0.5 per cent of the affected area.

— Arid areas have severe wind erosion, semiarid regions are subjected to sheet and gully erosion and ravines are serious problem in Yamuna and Chambal region. Floods, stream bank cutting and sand deposition have degraded lands of north-east region with heavy rainfall. South and southeast are characterized by undulating terrain with severe erosion in black and red laterite soils.

It has been estimated that a total of more than 5000 Mt of topsoil is being eroded every year in India. Of this about 1600 Mt (30%) of the total eroded area is permanently getting lost in to the sea. It has been shown that the loss of soil by erosion on unprotected soil is often as much as 125 t ha^{-1} annually and may go as high as 300 t ha^{-1} in an year. It takes about 400 to 1000 years to build up a layer of 3 cm top soil. Every cm of soil that is eroded means the loss of a thousand years of nature's work.

TYPES OF EROSION

Geological and accelerated erosion are the two major types of erosion. **Geological erosion** is said to be in equilibrium with the soil forming process. It takes place under natural vegetative cover completely undisturbed by biotic factors. This long time slow process has developed the present topographic features like stream channels, valleys, etc. through weather abnormalities such as intense rainfall and biotic interference.

Accelerated erosion is due to disturbance in natural equilibrium by the activities of man and animals through land mismanagement, destruction of forests, over grazing, etc. Soil loss through erosion is more than the soil formed due to soil forming process.

WATER EROSION

Water and wind are the main agencies responsible for soil erosion. Loss of soil from land surface by water, including runoff from melted snow and ice is usually referred to as **water erosion**. The major erosive agents in water erosion are impacting raindrops and runoff water flowing over the soil surface. Erosion and sedimentation embody the processes of detachment, transportation and deposition of soil particles. **Detachment** is dislodging of soil particles from soil mass by the erosive agents.

Transportation is movement of detached soil particles (sediment) from their original location. The sediment moves along the stream and part of it may eventually reach the ocean. Some sediment is usually deposited at the base of the slopes, reservoirs and flood plains along the way.

TYPES OF WATER EROSION

Water erosion occurs in stages identified as sheet, rill, gully, ravine, landslide and stream bank erosion.

Sheet Erosion

It is the uniform removal of surface soil in thin layers by sheet, or overland flow of water. The breaking action of raindrop combined with surface flow is the major cause of sheet erosion. It is the first stage of erosion and is least conspicuous.

Rill Erosion

When runoff starts, soil is lost from small but well defined channels or streamlets (rills) by water when there is concentration of surface flow. Raindrop impact does not directly detach any particles below flow line in rills but it increases the detachment and transportation capacity of the flow. Rill erosion starts when the runoff exceeds 0.3 to 0.7 mm s^{-1}. Most of the upland sediment load is transported down slope in the rills. This is the second stage of erosion. Rills are small channels which can be removed by timely normal tillage operations.

Gully Erosion

It is the advanced stage of water erosion. Size of the unchecked rills increase due to runoff. Gullies are formed when channelised runoff from vast sloping land is sufficient in volume and velocity to cut deep and wide channels. Gullies are the spectacular symptoms of erosion. If unchecked in time, no scope for arable crop production.

Ravines

Prolonged process of gully erosion leads to ravines, typically found in deep alluvial soils. They are deep and wide gullies indicating advanced stage of gully erosion. The side slopes of gullies fail and blocks of soil mass slough into the flow. The slope stability depends on soil strength and subsurface moisture regime.

Stream Bank Erosion

Stream banks are eroded by water either flowing over the sides of a stream or scouring at the base. Erosion of the bank is due to surface flow leading to scouring and under cutting the soil below the water surface. Small streams, torrents, etc. are subjected to stream bank erosion.

Land Slides

Land slides and land slips occur during wet season in mountain slopes. The quantity of sediment moved from hill sides by mass movement is far higher than that due to gullies. Debris from land slides causes obstruction to roads, choking of bridges, etc., thus blocking traffic and communications. Land slide debris deposited in fields make them unfit for cultivation.

FACTORS AFFECTING WATER EROSION

(*i*) Rainfall

Erosion is directly a function of rainfall and runoff. Amount, intensity, duration and distribution of rainfall influence runoff and erosion.

High intensity rains of longer duration cause severe erosion. Greater the intensity larger the size of raindrop. Velocity of falling raindrop varies from 4-5 m s^{-1} for one mm drop to about 9 m s^{-1} for 5 mm drop. Rainfall intensity more than 5 cm hr^{-1} is considered severe. Total energy of raindrops falling over a hectare land with rainfall intensity of 5 cm hr^{-1} is equal to 625 HP. Two-thirds of the energy is used in sealing soil pores. Runoff may occur without erosion, but there is never water erosion without runoff.

(*ii*) Soils

A highly erodable soil may erode 10 times faster than a less susceptible soil to the same moderate to intense rainfall. Soil properties influencing soil erodability include primary particle size, distribution, organic matter, structure, iron and aluminium oxidies and initial moisture content.

Soil erodability index (K) representing the soil loss per unit of EI_{30} as measured on standard bare soil plot of 22 m long with 9 per cent slope is used to predict soil erodability by water.

(*iii*) Biotic Interference

The natural balance is disturbed and destructive forces of nature operate only when the man with his plough and cattle enter the scene. Removal of vegetal cover for cultivation, disturbances of slopes, misuse of forest area by burning, overfelling, overgrazing, etc. result in accelerated erosion whose extent depends on the degree and nature of human interference.

(*iv*) Topography

Water flows slowly over a gentle slope and faster over a steeper one. If the velocity of a stream is increased, its eroding power is increased to the square of its velocity (if the velocity is doubled, the erosive power will increase 4 times that of the original velocity). A rapid current carries more quantity of material of a given size than a slow current. If the velocity is doubled, the quantity of material of a given size that can be carried is increased about 32 times the quantity of material that the original current was capable of carrying (the amount varies as the fifth power of velocity). Not only does the quantity of material increase with increase in velocity but the size of particle also increases. If the velocity is doubled, the size of particles that can be transported is increased about 64 times the size of those particles that the current carried at its original velocity (size of particles varies as the sixth power of velocity).

Length of slope is also an important factor of water erosion. If the slope is long, large quantity of rain will fall on it and if the rate of rainfall exceeds the rate of infiltration, there will be large accumulation of water at the base leading to problems. If the slope is short, there will be less accumulation of water at the base.

(*v*) Soil Surface Cover

Cover include plant canopy and material like mulches and plant residues in contact with soil surface reducing erosion. The canopy intercepts raindrops and reduces its impact on soil. Soil surface covers also reduce the velocity of runoff as they act as obstruction to the flow. Plant roots bind the soil particles and addition of organic matter through organic surface covers improves soil aggregation to resist break down.

LOSSES DUE TO EROSION

When once the soil is lost by erosion, none of the management practices including inputs can mitigate the loss of soil. Dryland agriculture will not be remunerative when once the rain water is lost by runoff. The adverse effects of water erosion are loss of fertile top soil, loss of rain water, nutrient losses, silting up of reservoirs, damage to forests, reduced ground water potential, damage to reservoirs and irrigation channels, and adverse effect on public health.

3 WIND EROSION

Erosion of soil by the action of wind is known as **wind erosion**. It is a serious problem on lands devoid of vegetation. It is more common in arid and semiarid regions. It is essentially a dry weather phenomenon stimulated by soil moisture deficiency. The process of wind erosion consists of three phases : initiation of movement, transportation and deposition. About 33 M ha in India is affected by wind erosion.

MECHANISM OF WIND EROSION

Lifting and abrasive action of wind results in some detachment of tiny soil particles from the granules or clods. The impact of these rapidly moving particles dislodge other particles from clods and aggregates. These dislodged particles are ready for movement. Movement of soil particles in wind erosion is initiated when the pressure by the wind against the surface soil grains overcomes the force of gravity on the grains. Certain minimum wind velocity is needed to initiate movement of soil particles. The velocity at which movement of most erodable soil particles is initiated is known as **minimum fluid threshold velocity**. It depends on the size and weight of soil particles and the friction provided by neighbouring particles. This threshold velocity is the lowest for grains of 0.1 to 0.15 mm dia. Velocities exceeding about 3 km hr^{-1} are turbulent and are responsible for initiating the process of wind erosion. As the wind velocity increased beyond this minimum, bigger particles start moving till the movement of almost all the size of particles in a soil containing only erodable fractions is initiated. This critical velocity is known as **maximum fluid threshold velocity**. In practice, no maximum fluid threshold velocity exists as the soils contain both erodable and non-erodable fractions together.

Minimum wind velocity necessary for initiating the movement of most erodable soil particles (about 0.1 mm dia) is about 16 km hr^{-1} at a height of 30.5 cm. Most practical limit under field conditions, where a mixture of sizes of single grained material present is about 21 km hr^{-1} at a height of 30.5 cm. Particles of about 0.1 mm dia have a size-weight relationship which is most conducive to initiate the movement. In general, transportation of soil particles by wind takes place in three stages: (*i*) saltation, (*ii*) suspension and (*iii*) surface creep.

FACTORS AFFECTING WIND EROSION

Factors that affect the amount of erosion from a given field are soil clodiness, surface roughness, water stable aggregates and soil crust, wind and soil moisture, field length, organic matter, vegetative cover, topography and soil.

Soil Clodiness

Soil clods resist wind erosion as they are large enough to resist the forces of wind, besides acting as barrier to other erodable materials. Coarse textured sandy loams, loamy sands and sands are most susceptible to erosion and break down. These soils form clods only when cultivated while moist and firm. Such clods are readily broken down by rain. The clodiest and least erodable soils are the loams, silt loams, clay loams and silty clay loams if they have 20-30 per cent clay and silt ranging from 0.005 to 0.01 mm in size. The proportion of soil aggregates that are more than 0.84 mm dia can be used as a simple index of wind erodability of soils.

Surface Roughness

In addition to clods, soil aggregates and ridges, depressions formed by tillage also alter the wind speed by absorbing and deflecting part of the wind energy away from the erodable soil. Rough surface also trap saltating particles. A smooth soil surface is generally more erodable by wind than a rough one because of being less effective in slowing the wind velocity near the ground. Although, a smooth surface reduces wind turbulence, its effect in reducing wind erodability is not compensated by the increased surface velocity. In general, greater the surface roughness, lower the wind velocity against the ground and lower is the rate of erosion.

Field Length

Erosive winds vary highly in direction and seldom follow field boundaries. Hence, the amount of soil lost from a given field cannot be determined by the width and length of field alone. Distance across the field along the direction of prevailing wind must be known. Fields with their broad sides at right angles to, and their narrow sides parallel with, the prevailing wind direction will have the minimum overall rate of erosion. Field orientation is of little consequence where erosive winds blow equally from all directions. If a barrier is present on the windward side of the field, the distance it fully shelters from the wind must be substracted from the total distance across the field along the prevailing direction when computing the soil loss.

Water Stable Aggregates and Surface Crust

Greater the quantity of fine particles dispersible by water, greater the degree of cementation among the structural units and greater is the mechanical stability. Mechanical stability tends to reduce wind erosion by resisting the break down of non-erodable units to smaller erodable particles. Soil crust formed by dispersion of surface soil are more compact and mechanically stable against wind action than soil below.

Wind and Soil Moisture

Wind velocity and turbulence influence wind erosion. Wind speed of about 12 km hr^{-1} is necessary to initiate soil movement. At higher speed, soil movement is proportional to the cube of wind velocity. Wind velocity of 8-10 ms^{-1} can carry 490 Mt of soil ha^{-1} on a 100 m front. Turbulence of wind influences the capacity of atmosphere to transport soil particles.

Soil

Sands erode easily because they contain high proportion of particles of saltation size with little binding material. Clayey soil are highly variable with respect to wind erosion. Those containing higher proportion of water dispersible fine particles tend to puddle are resist wind erosion relative to those with less water dispersible particles.

Vegetative Cover

Living or dead vegetative matter protects the soil surface from wind action by reducing wind speed and by preventing much of the direct wind force from reaching erodable soil particles. It also reduces erosion by trapping soil particles. The finer and denser the residue, the more it slows the wind and the more it reduces find erosion.

Organic Matter

Numerous cementing substances responsible for binding soil particles together are produced in the initial stage of organic residues decomposition by soil microorganisms. These cementing products are not easily water soluble and hence increase the size of aggregates or clods large enough to resist wind erosion.

Topography

Level land is usually more liable to wind erosion than rolling land as the wind encounters less resistance. However, erosion on knolls and ridges is more as wind presses against such areas instead of flowing parallel to the surface. Small depressions catch saltating particles and reduce wind erosion.

LOSSES DUE TO WIND EROSION

The USSR and subsaharian Africa have been subjected to severe damage by wind erosion. Fertile Indo-Gangetic alluvial plains have been converted into sandy desert. Important losses due to wind erosion are fertile top soil is lost, fertile soils are converted into unproductive sandy soils due to drifting sand, and yield losses due to abrasive action of wind driven soil particles, especially on broad leaved crops.

SOIL AND WATER CONSERVATION MEASURES

Soil conservation is using and managing the land based on the capabilities of the land itself involving application of the best management practices leading to profitable crop production without land degradation.

CONTROL OF WATER EROSION

Water erosion occurs simultaneously in two steps: detachment of soil particles by falling raindrops and transportation of detached soil particles by flowing water. Therefore, water erosion can be minimised by preventing the detachment of soil particles and their transportation. Principles of water erosion control are :

(*i*) Maintenance of soil infiltration capacity, (*ii*) Soil protection from rainfall, (*iii*) Control of surface runoff, and (*iv*) Safe disposal of surface runoff.

Agronomic Measures

In soil and water conservation programme, agronomic measures (conservation agronomy) have to be considered in coordination with others for their effectiveness. These measures are effective on gentle slopes up to 9 per cent.

Choice of Crops : Row crops (erosion permitting crops) such as sorghum, maize, pearlmillet, etc., are not as effective as soil conserving crops (erosion resistant crops) such as cowpea, groundnut, greengram, blackgram, etc.

Land Preparation : Land preparation including post-harvest tillage influence intake rate of water, obstruction to surface flow and consequently the rate of erosion. Deep ploughing or chiselling have been found effective in reducing erosion.

Contour Cultivation : All the cultural practices such as ploughing, sowing, intercultivation, etc. across the slope reduce the soil and water loss.

Cropping Systems : Monocropping of erosion permitting crops accelerate soil and water loss year after year. Intercropping erosion permitting and erosion resistant crops or their rotation have been found effective for soil and water conservation. As the legumes (cowpea, greengram, horsegram, blackgram) are effective for soil conservation due to their smothering effect, they should be sown in time to develop adequate canopy by the time of peak rate of runoff.

Stripcropping : It involves growing of few rows of erosion resisting crops and erosion permitting crops in alternate strips on contour with the objective of breaking long strips to prevent soil loss and runoff. Erosion resisting crops reduce the transporting and eroding power of water by obstructing runoff and filtering the sediment from the runoff to retain in the field.

Mulching : It reduces soil loss considerably by protecting the soil from direct impact of raindrop and reducing the sediment carried with runoff. A minimum plant residue ground cover of 30 per cent is necessary to keep runoff and soil loss within acceptable limits. As most of the plant remains are used as cattle fodder, availability of organic residues for mulching is the major limitation under conditions of scarce fodder.

Organic Manures and Fertilizer : Organic manures, besides supplying nutrients, improve soil physical conditions. Fertilizers improve vegetative growth (canopy) which aids in erosion control. Improvement in soil structure improves rate of infiltration leading to reduced runoff.

Mechanical Measures

When agronomic measures alone are not adequate, mechanical measures are adopted to supplement the agronomic measures. Thus, the mechanical and agronomic measures are not the two alternatives, but are complementary which should be used together. Important principles to be kept in view while planning for mechanical measures according to Rama Rao (1962) are :

(*i*) Increasing the time of concentration to allow more runoff water to be absorbed and held by the soil,

(*ii*) Interrupting a long slope into several short ones to maintain a critical velocity of runoff, and

(*iii*) Protection against damage due to excessive runoff.

Mechanical measures consist of construction of mechanical barriers across the direction of the flow of water to retard or retain the runoff for reducing soil and water loss. These measures include contour bunding, graded bunding, bench terracing, construction of grade stabilisation structures, etc. A **bund or terrace** is an earthen embankment or a depression or a combination of both constructed across the land slope to control runoff and minimise soil erosion by reducing the length of slope. By reducing the slope, the velocity of runoff is not allowed to attain a critical value which initiate scouring. In the case of bench terracing, however, both the length and degree of slope are reduced.

Contour bunding : It is most popular in the country. Contour bunding consists of narrow based trapezoidal bunds on contour to impound runoff water behind them such that it can gradually infiltrate into the soil for crop use. It is, generally, recommended for areas receiving less than 600 mm rainfall and for permeable soils upto slopes of about 6 per cent in agricultural lands.

Contour Trenching : It consists of excavating trenches along the contour. They are practiced on hill slopes as well as on degraded lands for soil and water conservation. These trenches break the slope length, reduce the velocity of runoff leading to retarded scouring and carrying capacity. Water retained in trenches aids in conserving moisture for sowing and planting. Trenching can be practiced on slopes not exceeding 20 per cent. Trenches are usually 60 × 45 cm with a spacing of 10-30 m between trenches. The trenches are half refilled diagonally with excavated material and the remaining half of the soil form spoil bank on which planting is done.

Gully Control : Gully erosion starts as small rills and gradually develops into deeper crevices due to erosion of bed, sliding and mass movement of the sides and water fall erosion at the head.

Forestry Measures

Perennial vegetation such as trees and grasses can be successfully used for economic utilization of degraded lands besides reducing soil and water loss. Effectiveness of perennial vegetation in reducing the impact of raindrop on soil surface and minimising the velocity of runoff of surface flow has been well established.

A large number of tree species were introduced for evaluating their performance under different agroclimatic conditions of the country. Tree species found economical are :

- *Pinus kesia*
- *Pinus patula* (Pinus)
- *Eucalyptu camaldulensis* (Eucalyptus)
- *Acacia mearnsii* (Acacia)
- *Acacia nilotica*
- *Acacia tortilis*
- *Moliodora*
- *Leucaena latisilqua* (Subabul)

The desirable characters of grass for soil and water conservation are perennial nature, drought resistance, rhizomniferous, good canopy, deep root system, prostrate habit and usefulness in cottage industry. Some of the useful grasses and legumes are :

Grasses

Chloris guyana, Cenchrus ciliaris, Cynodon dactylon, Dicanthium annulatum, Heteropogon contortus, Eragrostis curvula, Panicum antidotale, Andorpogan haltei, Panicum virgatum and Iseilema laxum.

Legumes

Centrosema pubescence, Stylosanthus hamata and Arylosia scarbaceoides.

Vegetative Barriers : These are closely planted grass or shrub rows along the contour for erosion control in agricultural lands. They check the velocity of runoff and retain the sediment by acting as barrier to runoff. Khus (*Vittveria zelanica*) is the most recommended plant for this purpose, unsuccessfully.

CONTROL OF WIND EROSION :

Greatest damage by wind erosion occurs during summer months in dry regions, where soil surface is bare and wind velocity is at its peak. Basic principles of wind erosion control are :

(i) Reducing wind velocity at ground surface, sufficient to prevent it being able to pickup soil particles,

(ii) Increasing the size of soil aggregates or covering the soil with a non-erodable surface,

(iii) Traping the saltating soil particles, and

(iv) Keeping the soil moist so that soil particles moving by saltation loose their momentum at the surface.

DRYLAND AGRICULTURE

Dryland constitute about 72 per cent of the total cropped area of 143 M ha in the country contributing to about 42 per cent of total food production. Almost all the coarse grains and about 75 per cent of pulses and oilseeds come from dryland agriculture. By 2025 AD, India has to produce about 380 Mt of food grains, as against the present 210 Mt, to feed the estimated population of about 14 billion.

Even after the utilisation of all our water resources for irrigation, about half of the cultivated area will remain rainfed. As there is hardly any scope for increasing the area under cultivation, it is really a colossal task for meeting the future food needs. It is against this background that the role of dryland agriculture gained importance.

Very often, the words dry farming, dryland farming and rainfed farming are used synonymously to indicate similar farming situation. Clearly, all the three exclude irrigation.

Dry Farming

Dry farming is cultivation of crops in regions with annual rainfall less than 750 mm. Crop failure is most common due to prolonged dry spells during the crop period. These are arid regions with a growing season (period of adequate soil moisture) less than 75 days. Moisture conservation practices are necessary for crop production.

Dryland Farming

Dryland farming is cultivation of crops in regions with annual rainfall more than 750 mm. Inspite of prolonged dry spells, crop failure is relatively less frequent. These are semiarid tracts with a growing period between 75 and 120 days. Moisture conservation practices are necessary for crop production. However, adequate drainage is required especially for Vertisols.

Rainfed Farming

Rainfed farming is crop production in regions with annual rainfall more than 1150 mm. Crops are not subjected to soil moisture stress during the crop period. Emphasis is often on disposal of excess water. These are humid regions with growing period more than 120 days.

In dry farming and dryland farming, emphasis is on soil and water conservation, sustainable crop yields and limited fertilizer use according to soil moisture availability. In rainfed agriculture, emphasis is on disposal of excess water, maximum crop yield, high levels of inputs and control of water erosion.

PROBLEMS OF DRYLAND AGRICULTURE

In India, the problem of crop production in drylands are more numerous and varied as it is practiced under a wide range of climate and soil conditions. These problems can be broadly grouped in to two : vagaries of monsoon and soil constraints.

VAGARIES OF MONSOON

On the basis of average annual rainfall, the country can be divided into three zones : (*i*) low (less than 750 mm), (*ii*) medium (750-1150 mm) and (*iii*) high (more than 1150 mm) rainfall zones.

Dryland area is nearly equally distributed among the three. Areas with less than 1150 mm (arid and semiarid) are the problem areas for crop production. Main characteristics (features) of rainfall influencing crop production are its variability, intensity and distribution, late onset of monsoon, early withdrawal of monsoon and prolonged dry spells during the crop period.

Variable Rainfall

Annual rainfall varies greatly from year to year. Table 2 indicate annual rainfall and its coefficient of variation. Generally, higher the rainfall, less is the coefficient of variation. In other words, crop failures due to uncertain rains are more frequent in regions with lesser rainfall.

Table 2. Mean Annual Rainfall and Coefficient of Variation in Selected Locations

Location	*Annual rainfall* Mean (mm)	*CV (%)*
Hissar (Haryana)	451	31
Anantapur (AP)	565	30
Ludhiana (Punjab)	661	50
Sholapur (Maharashtra)	708	28
Kovilpatti (TN)	749	27
Anand (Gujarat)	869	40
Bangalore (Karnataka)	888	20
Ranichauri (UP)	1264	22
Jabalpur (MP)	1308	24
Ranchi (Jharkhand)	1338	16
Mohanpur (WB)	1389	19

Intensity and Distribution

In general, more than 50 per cent of total rainfall is usually received in 3 to 5 rainy days. Such intensive rainfall results in substantial loss of water due to surface runoff. This process also accelerates soil erosion. Distribution of rainfall during the crop growing season is more important than total rainfall in dryland agriculture.

Prolonged Dry Spells

Breaks of monsoon for 7-10 days may not be a serious concern. Breaks of more than 15 days duration especially at critical stages for soil moisture stress leads to reduction in yield. Drought due to break in monsoon may adversely affect the crops in shallow soils than in deep soils.

Late Onset of Monsoon

If the onset of monsoon is delayed crops/varieties recommended to the region cannot be sown in time. Delayed sowing leads to uneconomical crop yields.

Early Withdrawal of Monsoon

This situation is equally or more dangerous than late onset of monsoon. Rainy season crops will be subjected to terminal stress leading to poor yields. Similarly, post-rainy season crops fail due to inadequate available soil moisture, especially during reproductive and maturity phases.

MONSOON AND LENGTH OF CROP GROWING SEASON

In the Central Arid Zone Research Institute, Jodhpur, maps of India showing the normal duration and commencement and cessation dates of the crop growing season with nil or slight water stress under dryland farming with normal rainfall were prepared by Krishnan and Thanvi in 1972. These were computed by the climatological water budgeting approach of Thornthwaite and Mather (1955), taking into account soil storage values for various major soil types of the country and using mean monthly potential evapotranspiration values computed by Penman's method.

DATES OF COMMENCEMENT

Commencement of the crop growing season is, generally, much ahead of the normal onset of the south-west monsoon in Bengal, Bihar, Orissa, Madhya Pradesh, Assam (Asom), Kerala and Karnataka, due to considerable pre-monsoon thunder showers. This feature is specially marked in Karnataka, Kerala, West Bengal and Assam. The beginning of the growing season in the west peninsula varies from April in Kerala to the first week of June in north Maharashtra. The gradient is from east to west in north India. It varies from 1 April in Assam to later than 15 July in western Rajasthan. In Tamil Nadu, the growing season begins only in September/October in the Ramanathapuram and Tirunelveli districts, etc which receive rainfall mainly during the north-east monsoon.

Some of the economic species promising under rainfed conditions include :

Medicinal Plants

Cassia angustifolia (cassia)
Mucuna purients (mucana)
Ocimum basilicum (ocimum)
Cammiphora wightii (camphor)
Plantago ovata (isobagol)
Withania sommifera (aswaganadha)

Essential Oil Plants

Pelargonium graveolens (geranium)
Pogostemon pachouli (patchouli)

Economic Plants

Jatropha carcus (jatropha)
Murraya kounigii (curry leaf)
Agave sisilana (agave)
Lawsonia inermis (henna)

WATERSHED MANAGEMENT

Degradation of environment in drylands is basically attributable to the increasing biotic pressure on the fragile ecosystem in the absence of appropriate management practices to augment and conserve the land and water resources. There are outstanding examples of success at Religon Sidhi and Adgaon in

Maharashtra, Kabbalnal and Mittemari in Karnataka and Jhabue in Madhya Pradesh, all of which show that dryland agriculture can be remunerative.

PRINCIPLES OF WATERSHED MANAGEMENT

Main principles of watershed management based on resource conservation, resource generation and resource utilization are :

(*i*) Water harvesting for supplemental irrigation,

(*ii*) Alternate land use systems for efficient use of marginal lands,

(*iii*) Ensuring sustainability of the ecosystem,

(*iv*) Maximising farm income through agricultural related activities such as dairy, poultry, sheep and goat farming,

(*v*) Improving infrastructural facilities for storage, transport and agricultural marketing,

(*vi*) Setting up of small scale agroindustries,

(*vii*) Improving socio-economic status of farmers.

(*viii*) Minimising silting up of tanks, reservoirs and lower fertile lands,

(*ix*) Protecting vegetative cover throughout the year,

(*x*) *In situ* conservation of rain water,

(*xi*) Safe diversion of surface runoff to storage structures through grassed water ways,

(*xii*) Stabilisation of gullies and construction of check dams for increasing ground water recharge,

(*xiii*) Increasing cropping intensity through inter and sequence cropping,

(*xiv*) Protecting fertile top soil,

(*xv*) Utilising the land based on its capability

COMPONENTS OF WATERSHED MANAGEMENT PROGRAMME

The main components of watershed programme are :

(*i*) Crop management,

(*ii*) Alternate land use systems,

(*iii*) Soil and water conservation, and

(*iv*) Water harversting.

Soil and Water Conservation

Conservation measures in arable lands can be broadly categorised in to three categories : (*i*) permanent, (*ii*) semi-permanent, and (*iii*) temporary.

(*i*) Permanent Measures : These measures are for improving relief, physiography and drainage features of watershed aimed at controlling soil erosion, regulating surface runoff and reducing peak flow rates. Bunds, terraces and waterways are the permanent measures in watershed management project.

(*ii*) Semi-Permanent Measures : These are usually inter-bund treatements in conventionally bunded area. They are adopted to minimize the velocity of overland flow. Such measures may lost 2 to 5 years.

Small section/key line bunds of about 0.1 m^2 across the slope at half of the vertical bund spacing can serve the purpose. They can be renovated once in 2-3 years depending on the necessity. Strip levelling of about 4 to 5 m strips of land above the bund across the major land slope help in reducing the velocity of surface flow. One or two live beds of 2-3 m width on contour or on grade can also serve the purpose. Similarly one or two vegetative/live barriers of close growing grasses or legumes along the bund and at mid length of slope can filter the runoff water or slow down overland flow. *Khus* grass is widely recommend as vegetative barrier.

***(iii)* Temporary Measures :** These are simple treatment for *in situ* moisture conservation and needs remade or renovation every year. Simple practices like contour farming, compartmental bunding, broad bed and furrows, dead furrows and mulching the recent past.

Water Harvesting

Farm ponds, check dams, percolation wells and minor tanks for water harvesting have been effective not only for reducing erosion and storing excess water during peak periods of monsoon but also for improving ground water table and recharging the downstream wells.

Crop Management

- Crops and varieties to suit length of cropping season,
- Optimum seeding time,
- Fertiliser schedules and balanced use of plant nutrients for crops and cropping systems identified,
- Weed management and package of practices for aberrant weather, and contingent crop planning.

AGRONOMY OF RAINFED CROPPING SYSTEMS

Agronomy of rainfed cropping systems include all practices controlled by the farmer that contribute to productivity of crops. Many management decisions are influenced by climate, inherent soil properties and socioeconomic constraints. Each decision on crop and cultivar, land preparation, fertilizers and other agronomic practices will have impact on other factors as well. Intercropping is the major system in rainfed agriculture, although ratooning is practiced under unfavourable rainfall during the season.

CROPS AND CULTIVARS

Crop combinations depend on climate, local preferences and other site specific factors. Farmers combine crops with differences in :

Stress tolerance, Crop duration, Density response, Plant morphology, Resistance to pests and pathogens, and Root system and Yield stability.

Questions From Previous Year's Papers

Q. 1. What is acid soil? How is it formed? What are its harmful effects? Write briefly about the methods of reclamation of an acid soil.

Q. 2. (a) Discuss the significance of soil conservation under dryland farming. Suggest measures which could be adopted by small and marginal farmers under Indian conditions.

(b) Describe the practices which could be recommended to farmers for conservation and efficient of rain water.

Q. 3. What are the various types of soil erosion? Describe the agronomic measures of soil erosion control.

Q. 4. What are the causes of infertlity of acid lateritic soils? Suggest measures for reclamation and management of such soils and enumerate the advantages of such measures.

Q. 5. Write short notes on :

(a) Azolla as biofertilizer

(b) Conservation tillage.

8. IRRIGATIONS

IRRIGATION AND WATER USE EFFICIENCIES

Irrigation water losses to the subsoil include canal seepage and infiltration beyond root zone in the field. The magnitude of irrigation losses is difficult to predict, being extremely variable depending on a great number of hardly controllable factors of which skill in handling irrigation water is not the least important. Other factors of importance are soil and topography. In very permeable soils, percolation losses will be large, surface field losses on the other hand are of little importance. In poorly permeable soils, percolation losses will be low and surface losses relatively high. A similar relationship exists for soil slope. With increasing slope, the risk of excessive infiltration losses becomes less, but the surface losses increase. Method of irrigation is also an important characteristic to be taken into account in estimating irrigation losses.

Application of least amount of water required to bring the root zone depth up to field capacity is considered an efficient irrigation. If the amount exceeds that actually needed for replenishment, the irrigation efficiency is low. Surface irrigation system should be able to apply an equal depth of water all over the field without causing any erosion. After the water is allowed to enter the plot, it will advance towards the end of plot. Recession of water starts from the beginning of the plot after water is shut off. Most of the time, it becomes necessary to stop the inflow of water when the water front reaches a particular length of the plot, so that irrigation of the remaining length is completed with the water already introduced. The reduction of stream size partly or fully is known as cut-back. Difference between the advance and recession periods at any point is known as opportunity time. To minimise the percolation losses, the opportunity time should be uniform all through the plot and also equal to the time required to put the required depth of water into the soil.

Efficiency is a measure of output obtainable from a given input. Some of the costs associated with irrigation and some of the benefits associated with it cannot be quantified in precise economic or financial terms. What is referred as irrigation efficiency by engineers is the net amount of water added to the root zone divided by the amount of water taken from the source. Difference between the net amount of water added to the root zone and the amount withdrawn from source represents seepage and evaporative losses during conveyance to the crop as well as deep percolation losses beyond root zone and runoff from the field. Therefore, control of irrigation should begin at the source to limit withdrawal of water in excess of the rate of replenishment and extend through its conveyance and delivery to the field.

In order to obtain an equal distribution of water over the field in gravity irrigation, field percolation losses should theoretically be in the order of atleast 10 per cent. Actual field percolation losses, even when the field is properly levelled and irrigation properly done, will usually be much higher, especially in rainy season. On the other hand, these losses may be less during peak period in summer, indicating deficit local water supply. In not too permeable soils (infiltration rate 2-10 cm hr^{-1}), field percolation losses for properly carried out gravity irrigation may be estimated at 20-30 per cent of the field supply on an average over year; 30 – 50 per cent during wet season and 10-20 per cent in dry season. For better permeable soils, these values will be higher and the infiltration rate of 15 cm hr^{-1} is sometimes accepted as the limit above which gravity irrigation is no longer possible due to excessive losses. For unlined canals in permeable soils, seepage losses may account to 20-30 per cent of the total irrigation supply.

Where water is made available to the farmer on fixed charges regardless of the actual amount used, the tendency of farmers is to take as much water as they can. This results in over irrigation, which not only wastes water but also leads to problems of waterlogging, disposal of excess water, leaching of nutrients and elevation of water table requiring expensive drainage. The major control of irrigation rests in the hands of irrigator in the field, where we can still witness greatest efficiency.

IRRIGATION EFFICIENCIES

Irrigation Efficiency

It is the ratio, usually expressed as per cent of the amount of irrigation water transpired by plants, that evaporated from soil, that necessary to regulate salt concentration in soil solution and that of consumptive use to the total volume of water delivered, or pumped for irrigation.

$$Ei = \frac{Wet + Wsc - ER}{Wsr} \times 100$$

where, Ei = irrigation efficiency (%),

Wet = amount of irrigation water per unit area of land lost in evapotranspiration, including that necessary for land preparation and nursery,

Wsc = amount of water per unit area of land required for regulating salt concentration in soil solution,

ER = effective rainfall, and

Wsr = amount of water per unit area of land that is stored in a reservoir or diverted for irrigation.

Overall irrigation efficiency indicates how effectively the available irrigation water is used for crop production. It is as low as about 20 per cent in Indian irrigation projects.

Water Conveyance Efficiency

It indicates the losses of water that occur while water is conveyed from source to the point of utilization. It is the ratio between water delivered to the irrigated plot and total quantity delivered at the source.

Water conveyance efficiency (Ec) =

$$\frac{\text{Water delivered to the plot } (Wp)}{\text{Water delivered from the source } (Wr)} \times 100$$

Water Application Efficiency

It is the ratio between the quantity of water stored in the root zone and the water delivered to the plot.

Water application efficiency (Ea) =

$$\frac{\text{Water stored in the root zone } (Ws)}{\text{Water delivered to the plot } (Wp)} \times 100$$

Water Distribution Efficiency

It is a measure of uniformity of water distribution within the field.

$$Ed = \left[1 - \frac{Y}{d}\right] \times 100$$

where, Ed = water distribution efficiency,

Y = average numerical deviation

in depth of water stored from average depth stored during irrigation, and

d = average depth of water stored during irrigation.

Water Storage Efficiency

This concept gives an insight into how completely the required water has been stored in root during irrigation. It is the ratio between water stored in the root zone and water needed in the root zone prior to irrigation.

Water storage efficiency (E_s) =

$$\frac{\text{Water stored in root zone during irrigation } (W_s)}{\text{Water needed in the root zone prior to irrigation } (W_n)} \times 100$$

Project Irrigation Efficiency

It is the percentage of irrigation water stored in the root zone soil depth and available for crop consumptive use to the amount of water delivered at the source of supply. When water is measured at farm head gate or well, it is called farm irrigation efficiency and when measured at inlet to the field, it is called field irrigation efficiency.

Operational Efficiency

It is the ratio of actual project efficiency, relative to the operational efficiency of an ideally designed and managed system using the same irrigation method and management. Defective design and poor management leads to low operational efficiency.

Economic Irrigation Efficiency

It is the ratio of total net or gross farm returns compared to total returns expected with ideally operated system under ideal conditions. As it relates to input and output, it is a measure of overall efficiency of the project.

WATER USE EFFICIENCIES

Consumptive Use Efficiency

It is a measure of the water that has been actually used by the crop from the total water depleted from root zone. It includes water used for metabolic processes also besides ET.

Consumptive use efficiency =

$$\frac{\text{Consumptive use of water by crop } (W_{cu})}{\text{Water depleted from root zone } (W_d)} \times 100$$

Water Use Efficiency

It relates crop yield to water use. It is the ratio between marketable crop yield and water used in evapotranspiration.

Water use efficiency (WUE) =

$$\frac{\text{Marketable crop yield } (Y)}{\text{Evapotranspiration } (ET)}$$

Field Water Use Efficiency

It is the ratio of crop yield to the amount of water used in the field, which include ET, deep percolation and that used in plant metabolic processes. Since water used in metabolic processes is very small, field water use efficiency (FWUE) is the ratio between marketable yield and water used in ET plus deep percolation (DP) losses.

$$FWUE = \frac{Y}{ET + DP}$$

CRITERIA OF SCHEDULING IRRIGATION

An ideal irrigation schedule for optimum yield must indicate correct timing (when to irrigate) and amount of irrigation water at each irrigation. Scheduling irrigation is the process of determining when to irrigate and how much water to apply. There are several approaches for determining when to irrigate the crop. The approaches can be broadly classified into three groups.

(1) Soil moisture regime approaches,

(2) Climatological approaches, and

(3) Plant indices.

1. SOIL MOISTURE REGIME APPROACHES

In these methods, soil moisture content is estimated to know the deficit in available soil moisture at which it is proposed to irrigate based on predetermined soil moisture content to bring the soil to field capacity. Soil moisture content is estimated either by direct gravimetric method or indirect measurements such as tensiometers, resistance blocks, neutron probe etc.

Soil moisture content can be judged by feel and appearance of the soil, with experience. Soil samples from root zone depth are formed into balls, tossed gently into the air and caught in hand. While accuracy of judgement improves with experience, Table 1 may serve as a guide for estimating the available soil moisture. Based on the allowable depletion in available soil moisture (DASM) irrigations can be scheduled at 25, 50 or 75 per cent DASM.

2. CLIMATOLOGICAL APPROACH

An integrated approach to SPAC is essential for an ideal irrigation schedule. Potential rate of water loss from a crop is primarily related to evaporative demand of the atmosphere. The PET can be estimated with any of the methods elaborated. Irrigation can be scheduled if allowable depletion of moisture in the root zone and evapotranspiration during the crop period is known.

Pan evaporation (E_{pan}) is used to determine the amount of irrigation water to be applied in the ratio of irrigation water (IW) and cumulative pan evaporation (CPE) from USWB Class A pan, usually known as IW/CPE ratio method. IW/CPE ratio of 1.0 indicates scheduling irrigation with quantity of irrigation water equal to that lost in evaporation. If 5 cm water is applied when the cumulative pan evaporation is 10 cm, the IW/CPE ratio will be 0.5 (5/10 cm).

Table 1. Guide for Judging the Amount of Available Soil Moisture Range

Available soil moisture range	*Coarse texture (loamy sand)*	*Moderately coarse (sandy loam)*	*Medium texture (loamy and silt loam)*	*Fine texture (clay loam and silty clay loam)*
Field capacity (100 per cent)	On squeezing, no free water appears on soil, but wet outline is left on hand	Similar symptoms	Similar symptoms	Similar symptoms
75 per cent to 100 per cent	Tends to stick together slightly, sometimes forms a very weak ball under pressure	Forms weak ball, breaks easily, do not slick	Forms a ball, is very pliable, slicks readily	Easily ribbons out between fingers, has slick feeling
50 per cent to 75 per cent	Appears to be dry, do not form a ball with pressure	Tends to form a ball under pressure but seldom holds together	Forms a ball some what plastic, sometimes slick slightly with pressure	Forms a ball, ribbons out between thumb and forefinger

Available soil moisture range	*Coarse texture (loamy sand)*	*Moderately coarse (sandy loam)*	*Medium texture (loamy and silt loam)*	*Fine texture (clay loam and silty clay loam)*
25 per cent to 50 per cent	As above, but ball is formed by squeezing very firmly	Appears to be dry, do not form a ball unless squeezed very firmly	Some what crumbly but holds together with pressure	Some what pliable, forms a ball under pressure
0 to 25 per cent	Dry, loose, single grained, flows through fingers	Dry, loose, flows through fingers	Powdery dry, sometime slightly crusted but easily broken down into powdery conditions	Hard, baked, cracked, sometimes has loose crumbs on surface.

The ratio is usually fixed anywhwere between 0.5 and 1.0. Smaller ratio indicates irrigation at longer intervals and larger ratio indicate frequent irrigations.

3. PLANT INDICES

Any plant character, related directly or indirectly to plant water deficit which responds readily to integrated influence of soil, water, plant and evaporative demand of the atmosphere may serve as a criterion for timing of irrigation to crops.

Visual Plant Symptoms

Visual signs of plants wilting can be used to schedule crop irrigation. Farmers frequently use dropping, curling and rolling of sensitive plant as an indication for plant water deficit. Distinct change in foliage colour is also used to time irrigation, especially to bean. In these methods, the crop has already suffered before exhibiting wilting or change in foliage colour reflecting the influence of water deficits on final yield.

Profile Modification

This method also known as soil cum sand mini plot technique is used for timing irrigation to crops. The principle involved in this method is to reduce artificially, the available water holding capacity (W.H.C.) of soil in root zone depth in the mini plot by mixing sand with it. Plants on sand mixed mini plot show moisture stress symptoms earlier than plants in rest of the area. Usually, an area of 1.0 m^2 is selected in the field and a pit of 1.0 m depth is excavated in layers of about 15 cm depth. Each layer of soil is mixed with 5 per cent by volume of sand and the pit refilled in the same sequence of layers as excavated by compacting each layer to bring bulk density of soil in the mini plot as that of the surrounding area. Symptoms of plants in the mini plot indicate time for irrigating the crop.

Increased Plant Stand

An area of about 1.0 m^2, preferably in a high spot, is sown with the same crop to maintain about four times the plant population compared with that in the surrounding area. Crop with high stand establishment wilts earlier than the crop in the rest of the field indicating timing of irrigation.

Reduction in growth rate of sensitive plant organs may indicate irrigation need of crops. In the case of orange plants, irrigation is given when the growth rate of fruit circumference falls below 0.2 to 0.3 mm day^{-1}. Since stem elongation of crops like sugarcane, tomato and cotton is highly correlated with water stress, it is possible to use this character as an indication of irrigation needs. Relative leaf water content, plant water potential, stomatal resistance and plant temperature which can adequately reflect the internal water balance of the plant may be used as potential indicators for scheduling crop irrigation. After fixing timing of irrigation, the next step is to determine how much water to apply. Irrigation water applied should bring the soil to field capacity. As such the quantity of irrigation water to be applied to the soil at each irrigation depends on :

(i) Effective rainfall and/or ground water contribution during the interval between two irrigations,
(ii) The amount of available soil moisture (ASM) in the effective root depth at the start of irrigation or the level of available soil moisture depletion (DASM) considered for irrigation,
(iii) The application losses, and
(iv) Additional quantity of irrigation water if any, required to leach the soils beyond the root zone depth.

NET IRRIGATION REQUIREMENT

It is the depth of irrigation water, exclusive of effective rainfall, ground water contribution and available soil moisture level considered for timing the irrigation, that is required to meet the consumptive use requirement for crop production. It is the amount of irrigation water required just to bring the soil moisture content in the root zone depth to field capacity. Thus, the net irrigation requirement is the difference in soil moisture content between field capacity and the soil moisture content in the root zone before application of irrigation water.

$$NIR = \frac{M_{fc} - M_{bi}}{100} \times BD \times D_s$$

where, NIR = net irrigation requirement (cm),

M_{fc} = soil moisture content (%) at field capacity,

M_{bt} = soil moisture content (%) before irrigation,

BD = soil bulk density, and

D_s = depth of soil (cm) considered.

GROSS IRRIGATION REQUIREMENT

It is the amount of irrigation water that must be applied to the soil surface to meet the net irrigation requirement for each irrigation. Hence, gross irrigation requirement (GIR) is the net irrigation requirement plus water application losses or the total amount of irrigation water to be applied through irrigation.

$$\text{Gross irrigation requirement} = \frac{\text{Net irrigation requirement}}{\text{Efficiency of irrigation system}}$$

IRRIGATION INTERVAL

Number of days between two successive irrigations during the peak period of consumptive use of the crop is known as irrigation interval. It depends on consumptive use rate and amount of available soil moisture in the root zone depth between field capacity and starting moisture level for irrigation. It is a function of both the crop and soil. For a given crop, light shallow soils require more frequent irrigations than fine textured heavy soils. Moisture use rate increases with increase in leaf area and as the days become hotter.

IRRIGATION PERIOD

Irrigation period refers to the number of days that can be allowed for applying one irrigation to a given design area during the peak period consumptive use of the crop under consideration. It is the basis for capacity and equipment design. Irrigation systems are to be designed in such a way that the irrigation period is not greater than the irrigation interval.

Irrigation period =

$$\frac{\text{Net amount of moisture between starting of irrigation and lower limit of moisture delpetion}}{\text{Peak period moisture use rate of the crop}}$$

In most cases, irrigation system is designed in such a way that the irrigation interval is roughly equal to irrigation period. This may cause problem in completing an irrigation in rainy season, if start of irrigation is delayed too long following rainfall. When the soil is at its field capacity following the rain, the entire crop area will be uniformly reduced to the same moisture level. If the crop has to be irrigated at 50 per cent DASM, it may not be possible to irrigate the entire area before the crop experience soil moisture stress.

IRRIGATION WATER MANAGEMENT

Hansen *et al* (1980) defined irrigation as artificial application of water for the purpose of supplying moisture essential to plant growth. They further stated that irrigation is application of water to the soil for other purposes also.

(*i*) To add water to the soil for supplying the moisture essential for plant growth,

(*ii*) To provide crop insurance against short duration droughts,

(*iii*) To cool the soil and atmosphere, thereby making more favourable environment for plant growth,

(*iv*) To reduce the hazards of soil piping, and

(*v*) To soften tillage pans.

Irrigation water management can be defined as the integrated process of intake, conveyance, regulation, measurement, distribution, application and use of irrigation water to farms and drainage of excess water, with proper amounts and at right time for the purpose of increasing crop production and water economy in conjunction with improved agricultural practices.

In recent years, revolutionary developments have taken place in the science and art of irrigation water management. Comprehensive understanding of soil-plant-water regimes as affected by climate and irrigation made it possible to establish and maintain nearly optimum soil moisture conditions continuously. Proper water management can raise yields while minimising waste (runoff, evaporation, excessive seepage), reducing drainage needs and promoting integration of irrigation with inputs.

SOIL-PLANT-WATER RELATIONSHIPS

Soil-plant-water relationships deal with those physical properties of soils and plants that influence the movement, retention and use of water that must be considered to plant efficient irrigation system. They are mutually dependent and conditions in any region are the result of their interaction.

WAYS AND MEANS OF REDUCING RUN-OFF LOSSES OF IRRIGATION WATER

Under permanent cultivation system, where lands are level, and adequate preparations would have been made to keep the land protected from water and wind erosion, there will not be run-off loss due to irrigation (though heavy rains with direct impact on the land can induce run-off loss).

Slopy land beyond 2% slope are not irrigated but crops are grown under rainfed conditions. Slopy lands are terraced to prevent damage due to soil erosion.

Any land under wet cultivation has strong bunds to hold the irrigation water, and when there is surplus water, openings are made to let out the unwanted water gently.

In respect of garden land irrigated by wells, beds or ridges and furrows are made for raising crops or vegetables. Even here, run-off loss is very remote, as the field is in a protected condition.

Regarding dry land cultivation particularly in undulating tracts, there is a possibility of run-off losses caused by rain water. As there is no irrigation for dry land, the run-off loss due to irrigation does not arise.

METHODS OF IRRIGATION

There are three main ways of applying irrigation water :

(1) Run the water over the soil surface and allow it to infiltrate, a method known as surface irrigation,

(2) Spray the water into the air and allow it to fall on to plants and soil as simulated rainfall, a method called sprinkler irrigation, and

(3) Apply the water directly to the root zone, a method known as drip or subirrigation.

SURFACE IRRIGATION

Surface irrigation (gravity irrigation) is the most ancient method of irrigation and this method still holds good for more than 95 per cent of the irrigated area in the world. It can be defined as the process of introducing a stream of water at the head of a field and allowing gravity and hydrostatic pressure to spread the flow over the surface throughout the field. To move forward, the flowing water must have a downward slope in the direction of flow. This is, generally, provided by running water over a sloping land surface, but in the irrigation of level land the water must build its own slope (from deepest at entry to near zero depth at advancing front). The soil surface thus serves the dual role of water conveyance and distribution. As it conveys the water, it controls the spreading pattern and hence the opportunity time for water to infiltrate. Spatial and temporal variability in infiltrability of the soil translates into non-uniformity of water distribution into the root zone.

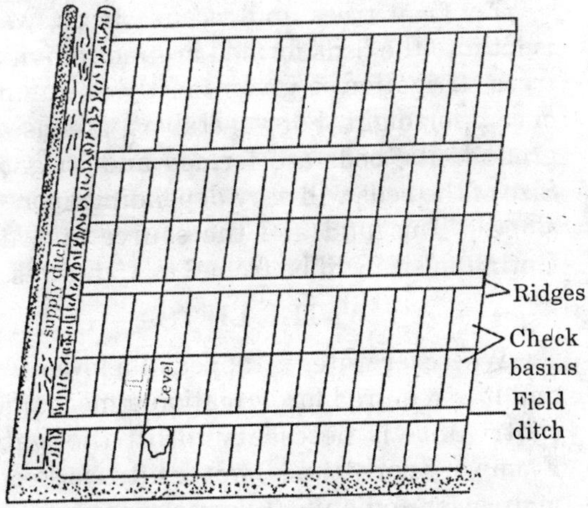

Fig 1. Check basin method of irrigation.

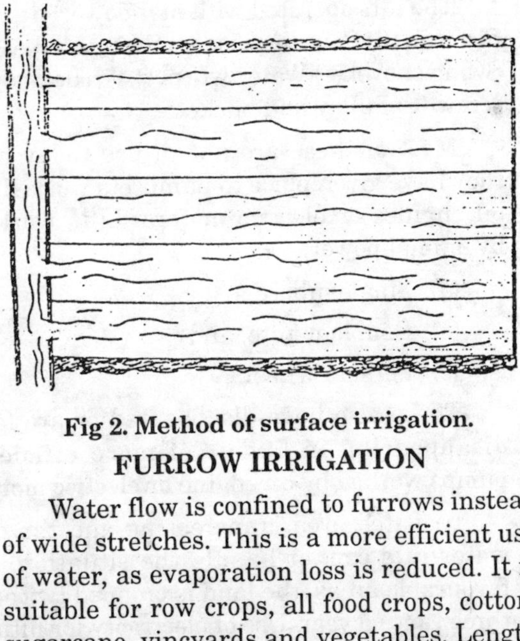

Fig 2. Method of surface irrigation.

FURROW IRRIGATION

Water flow is confined to furrows instead of wide stretches. This is a more efficient use of water, as evaporation loss is reduced. It is suitable for row crops, all food crops, cotton, sugarcane, vincyards and vegetables. Length of the furrow can be 30 metres or even more. Very long furrows cause greater loss of water because of deep percolation and excessive soil erosion at the head of the field. Furrows of 10 to 30 cm in depth and at a spacing of 1 to 2 metres are formed, depending upon the nature of the crop. Uniform crop maturity is noticed under furrow irrigation.

BED METHOD

For fruit trees and coconut trees, water is let into the beds formed around individual trees. Irrigation is given mostly in summer once a fortnight. For vegetables, greens and groundnuts, beds are formed and irrigated. Size of the beds will vary depending upon the slope of the land and the source of water. Optimum size will be from 6 to 15 metres.

WATER LIFTS

Wherever water is tapped at a lower level and it is required for irrigation a mechanical contrivance is necessary to lift the water. From very early times, water lifts worked by manpower and animal-power are being used to irrigate crops, fruits and vegetables.

The lifts operated with manpower are : (*a*) Picottah (b) Counterpoise (*c*) Swing basket (*d*) Swing shovel (*e*) Water wheel (*f*) Archemedian screw (*g*) Pulley and bucket.

Most of these are not in use today and they have given place to pumpsets worked by oil engines or electric motors. Lifts worked by animal power:

(*a*) Single mhote

(*b*) Double mhote, and

(*c*) Persian wheel.

These also have disappeared or are fast disappearing in favour of more efficient pumps worked by oil engine or electric motor.

Irrigated area is increasing and the old water lifts cannot handle the situation. In favourable areas, the land is cropped twice or three times a year. Use of electricity for lifting water commenced since five decades in different parts of the country, as and when they generated electricity for domestic and industrial use.

A word of caution is very necessary at this juncture regarding over-exploitation of ground-water. Electric motors and oil engines work the pumpsets installed everywhere without consideration of adequate water availability, whether there are strong springs or weak springs etc., to replenish the water that has been pumped out.

People spend a lot of money in digging a well an fixing a pump – then they fail because water supply is not adequate. They repeatedly deepen the well and even then with very limited success. Deep bores are also sunk and submersible pumps are installed. This draws water from surrounding area to a few square kilometers, rendering the existing wells dry in that area depleting the underground water and turning the region barren.

A policy decision is necessary to restrict the use of electric and oil engine pumpsets to regions where underground water is plentiful. The other arid regions should continue to have wells fitted with lifts worked by bullock power or wind mills, etc., so that there may be continuous water supply in the well as only a limited quantity of water can be lifted with these contrivances to keep cultivation going.

There is gradual decline in the quantity of annual rainfall year after year. When rain is received it is erratic, and either deficient or ends up in causing floods and bringing disaster. To cope up with the limited water in the tanks, ponds and wells, economy in the use of water for irrigation is a necessity. "Sprinkler irrigation" and "Drip irrigation" are becoming popular.

Sprinkler Irrigation : Water is a very important 'input' in crop production. All other inputs like good seeds, fertilisers, etc., will go to waste, if there is no proper irrigation.

Economy in the use of water is becoming increasingly important on account of frequent failure of rains and limited water resources for crop production.

Sprinklers conserve water up to 50% and irrigate a larger area with the same quantity of water. There is no wastage through seepage in channels, over-irrigation or drainage off the field.

The water is pumped through pipelines and sprayed over the crop, similar to rain. The central water and power commission has estimated the losses during irrigation as follows:

Flow of water through

1.	lined channels	54%
2.	channels not lined	71%
3.	sprinkler irrigation	18%

All crops can be handled by sprinkler irrigation, including orchards, where intercropping can also be done. The distribution of water is even and plants in higher reaches on slopes, etc., can be irrigated without the need for levelling the land.

Channels and bunds are not necessary, hence cost of labour is saved. Sandy soils and also black cotton soils, besides the intermediate types of soils, like loams, gravelly, etc., can be irrigated with equal ease. Operations cost is comparatively less than other systems of irrigation though the initial investment is more. If there is a good supply of water in a pond or well, sowing operations can be taken up in time without waiting for rains. At present plantations like Coffee-Tea-Cardamom are making use of sprinkler irrigation; besides, a number of progressive farmers also use it. The initial cost of installation and the miniature size of farms, absence of wells in all farms are the factors standing in the way of rapid spread of sprinkler irrigation in India.

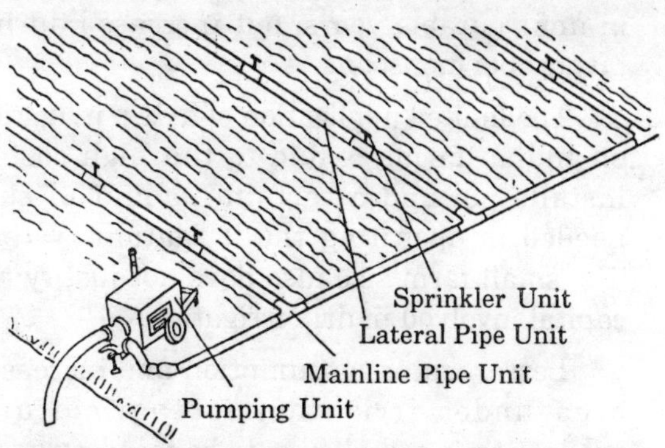

Fig. 3. Typical Sprinkler Irrigation System

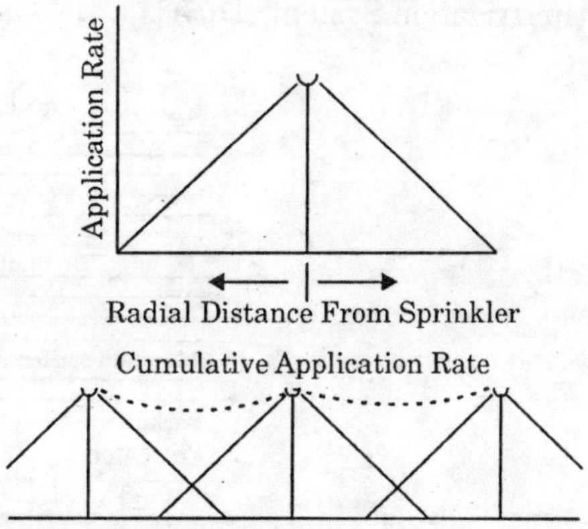

Fig. 4. Distribution Patterns for Single and Overlapping Sprinklers

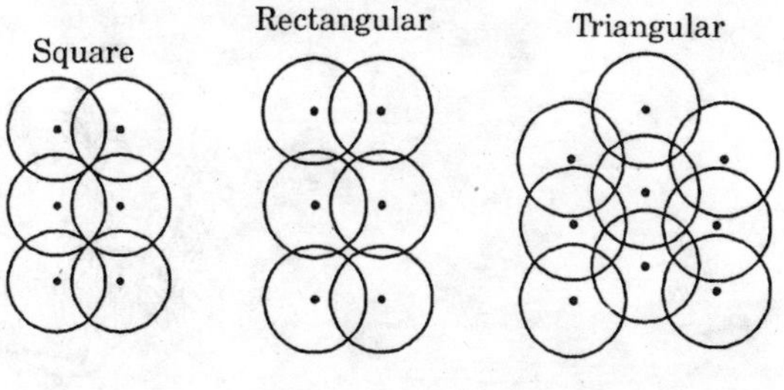

Fig. 5. Alternative Arrangements of Sprinkler Grids

Drip Irrigation : Economic water use is a necessity, particularly since two decades as the water sources are shrinking due to very frequent drought years.

Considering the food needs of the country, production of food is not only to be maintained in unfavourable years, but increased during favourable monsoons.

The limited application of a drip irrigation on Indian farms is due to the high cost of installation and a certain amount of skill needed in operating the irrigation system. The small farm size also does not justify the capital involved in drip irrigation.

Lesser water consumption and increased area under irrigation for agricultural production is a challenge to be faced now and in the coming decades.

The new irrigation technology known as 'Drip Irrigation System' (DIS) is widely adopted in Israel, Egypt, USA, Australia, Africa, Greece and to a lesser extent in many more countries, of which India is one.

Advantages of the Drip Irrigation are:

1. Saving in quantity of water applied
2. Economy due to low cost distribution
3. Reduction in seepage losses
4. Increased yield due to optimum water and nutrient supply.

Suitability : This system is suitable for tree crops, vegetables, cotton, sugarcane, banana, grapes, limes, coconut, etc. The pipes can be laid in all soils from sandy to heavy clay.

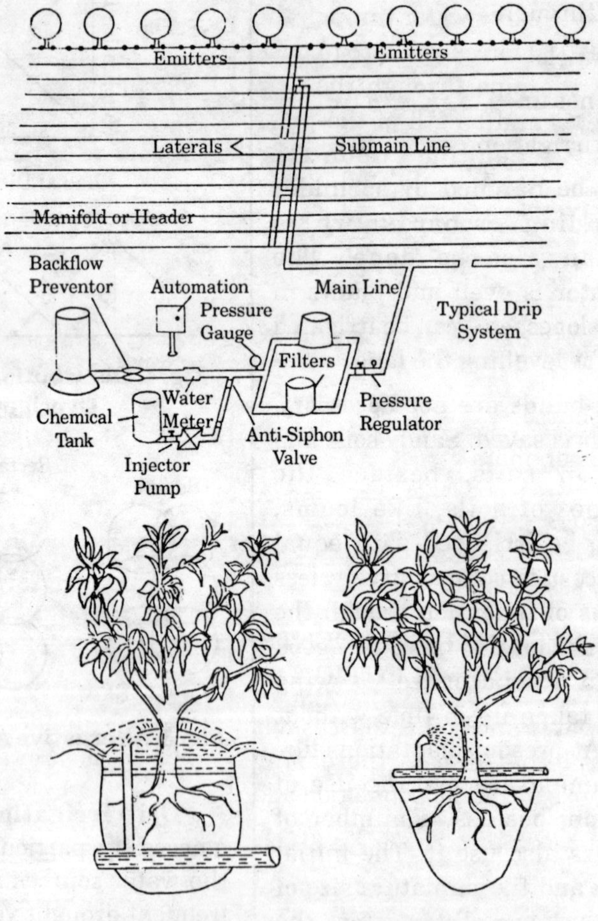

Fig. 6. Drip irrigation system

It is particularly helpful where water availability is low and the land has to be put to fruitful use.

Rationale in the system: Water is required only for the root zone of any crop and this is achieved in this system. There is no surplus wetting of soil, and no surface evaporation.

In water conveyed through open channels for a length of 200 m, there is a percolation loss of 20% (this is a research finding).

Method of Irrigation : Water from the source is conveyed through flexible alkathene pipes to the root-zone of the crop. Hydraulic pressure is needed to carry water through the pipes against frictional forces and also to push the water out of the pipe through the drip holes. The diameter and length of the pipes are adjustable depending upon the requirement to get a uniform distribution of water in all the places. A water delivery head of 1 to 2 metres is sufficient to supply water to the mains and laterals.

The components of the drip irrigation system are:

1. A water source
2. Main and sub-main
3. Laterals
4. Drippers
5. Other accessories

EFFECT OF INDUSTRIAL EFFLUENTS ON SOIL AND WATER POLLUTION :

Pollution of water and soil resources has been greatly exploited due to increasing industrialization, urbanization, population and broad spheres of human activities. Effect of industrial effluents on soil and water are summarised as under :

(i) Effluents containing acids and alkalies make the water corrosive.

(ii) Industrial effluents has direct impact on the soil properties such as texture, structure and filtration rate.

(iii) Due to eutrophication algal attain high degree of dominance due to over fertilization. Algal and rooted weeds interfere with the hydro-electric power, clog the filters, retard the water flow and affect the water quality and water work.

(iv) Soils with high exchangeable sodium become hard on drying and difficult to work for obtaining good tilth.

(v) Soil salinity affects cell division, cell elongation and protein synthesis.

(vi) High content of chloride, Sodium, boron, sulphate and bicarbonate in water cause toxicity to the plant, leading to the poor growth and yield.

(vii) Excessive soluble salt concentration in the root zone restrict plant water uptake leading to physiological drought.

(viii) High concentration of calcium reduces the uptake of potassium by the plant. Higher concentration of magnesium induces calcium deficiency. High sulphate content reduces uptake of calcium and increase sodium uptake leading to sodium toxicity.

Questions From Previous Year's Papers

Q. 1. (a) Define irrigation and irrigation application efficiency. Describe different methods of application of irrigation to field crop merits and demerits of each method. Also indicate suitability of each method for different crops.

(b) Calculate the net irrigation requirement for raising moisture content of soil to field capacity (32%) from the existing moisture content 23% before irrigation in the 70 cm root zone depth of maize field having uniform bulk density of 1.2 g/cc. Also find out the gross irrigation requirement and time to apply in 5 hectares maize field when irrigation efficiency is 80% and discharge rate of the supply source is 10 litres per second.

Q. 2. (a) Explain with concrete examples whether sequence cropping against monoculture does help farmer in crop production.

(b) Distinguish between the following :

(i) Irrigation requirement and consumptive use of water.

(ii) Drought tolerance and drought resistance in crops.

Q.3. Write short critical notes, in about 150 words each on any four of the following :

(a) Drainage coefficient

(b) Drip irrigation

(c) Land drainage

(d) Potential evapotranspiration.

Q. 4. Define water-use efficiency. Explain in detail appropriate measures for improving water-use efficiency in canal-irrigated and well-irrigated soils.

Q. 5. Why are certain crop growth stages most sensitive to soil moisture stress? Suggest water management practices for wheat and groundnut crips at times of variable water supplies.

Q. 6. Discuss the scope of micro-irrigation in Indian Agriculture. State the types of micro-irrigation and explain merits and demerits of drip irrigation system.

Q. 7. (a) How is water important in crop production?

(b) What are the factors you will consider for selecting methods of irrigation?

Q. 8. (a) How will you calculate irrigation requirement and water requirement of a crop?

(b) Enumerate the merits and demerits of sprinkler irrigation.

Q. 9. Write sort critical notes, not more than 150 words each, the followings.

(a) Irrigation interval.

(b) Watershed management.

(c) Water hervesting in dry lands.

Q. 10. Differentiate between the following pairs in not more than 150 words each.

(a) Water requirement and irrigation requirement

(b) Surface and sub surface drainage.

9. AGRICULTURAL ECONOMICS

INTRODUCTION

Economics has been defined by various Economists:–

Smith : Economics is the science of wealth.

Marshall : It is defined as the study of human behaviour in the daily business of life *i.e.,* economic and non-economic activities.

Robins : Human wants are unlimited and the study or choice making behaviour. It is Modern definition.

Pigue : Emphasis given to the human welfare.

Factors of Production :

(1) **Land :** Anything above the earth surface which is free given by the nature. It is fixed.

(2) **Labour :** Labour is an active factor.

(3) **Capital :** It is a passive factor. All capital is wealth but all wealth is not capital. Capital is the part of wealth used for further regenerating wealth.

(4) **Organisation and**

(5) **Enterprise :**

Reward of land ⟶ Rent

Reward of Labour ⟶ Wages

Reward of Capital ⟶ Interest

Reward of Enterprise ⟶ Profit

But according to modern Economists, the subject matter of Economics is grouped into two heads *i.e.,* Micro-Economics and Macro-Economics.

(*a*) **Micro-Economics :** Such activities and services of Consumption, Production, Exchange and Distribution concerned with individual units (viz. single industry, single farm, single consumer etc.) *i.e.,* at micro-level; are grouped under Micro-Economics.

(*b*) **Macro-Economics :** It deals with the whole economic set-up and related additions or averages *e.g.,* total production, total income, total employment, total expenditure, total savings, price level and economic development of whole economic set-up.

Subject Matter of Economics :

(1) Consumption

(2) Production

(3) Exchange

(4) Distribution, and

(5) Public Finance.

Cooperatives in India :

History :

(1) **1904 Act :**Cooperative movement in India started in 1904 when cooperative credit societies act was passed. Father of cooperative movement in India was F. Nicholson.

Limitation of 1904 Act : No any provision for the formation of non-credit societies.

(2) **1912 act :** Provision for the formation of non-credit societies with the aim to improve the economic status of its member as well as to meet the daily requirement. There was provision for the formation of central cooperative society also (no provision in 1904 act).

(3) The Govt. appointed a committee under Sir Macglan in 1914 and it observed that people were had the impression that cooperatives were mainly the govt. agencies. Therefore, he recommended :–

(*a*) for the proper education of the cooperative principles so as that members may participate efficiently.

(*b*) the formation of cooperative banks to help the primary cooperative societies.

(*c*) to form the provincial cooperative society in each state.

(*d*) for careful scruting of members before granting loans.

(4) In 1944, Govt. appointed an agricultural finance sub-committee under Prof. D. R. Gadgil to study the cooperative movement and to give suggestion for their improvement.

(5) In 1945, Govt. appointed a Cooperative Planning Committee which submitted its report in 1946.

(6) In 1951, All India Rural Survey Committee Report was published. The chairman of the committee was A.D. Gorwala. Its recommendations are :–

(*a*) Organisation of large size cooperative society,

(*b*) Organisation of Marketing Cooperatives,

(*c*) Assistance from Govt. in the form of loans and subsidies to the society,

(*d*) adoption of system of controlled credit, and

(*e*) Establishment of SBI as institution which may assist the Cooperative Society through its rural branches.

(7) In 1954, the All India Rural Cooperative Society recommended for the formation of large size society.

(8) 3rd Indian Cooperative Congress held at New Delhi in April 1958 and recognised the importance of cooperative sector.

(9) Indian National Congress in 1959 at Nagpur session accepted the resolution of Agrarian Economy and resolution brought a radical change in the policy and programme of cooperative movement.

(10) Multipurpose Cooperative societies were first established in 1939 in Orissa.

(11) The year 1954 is a landmark in the history of rural credit and Rural Credit policy in India.

(12) 'Cooperation' is originated in Europe. Britain is the homeland of cooperative store movement.

RBI and SBI :

Reserve Bank of India came into existence on 1st April 1935 with the RBI act 1934 and has been nationalised on Jan 1, 1949. Mr. Osporne A. Smith was the first Governor of RBI.

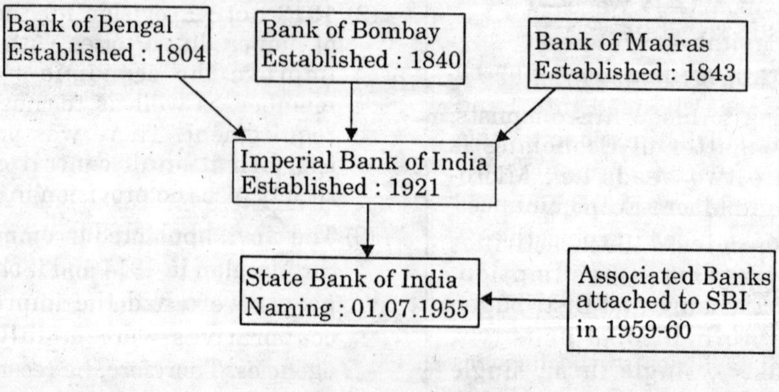

Finance According to Period

(*a*) **Short Term Loan:** Such loan is granted for one season of crop *i.e.*, for 1 to $1^{1/2}$ years.

(*b*) **Medium Term Loan :** Such loan is granted for the period of one year to 5 years.

(*c*) **Long Term Loan :** Such loan for the period of 5 to 30 years.

Structure of Cooperative Banking :

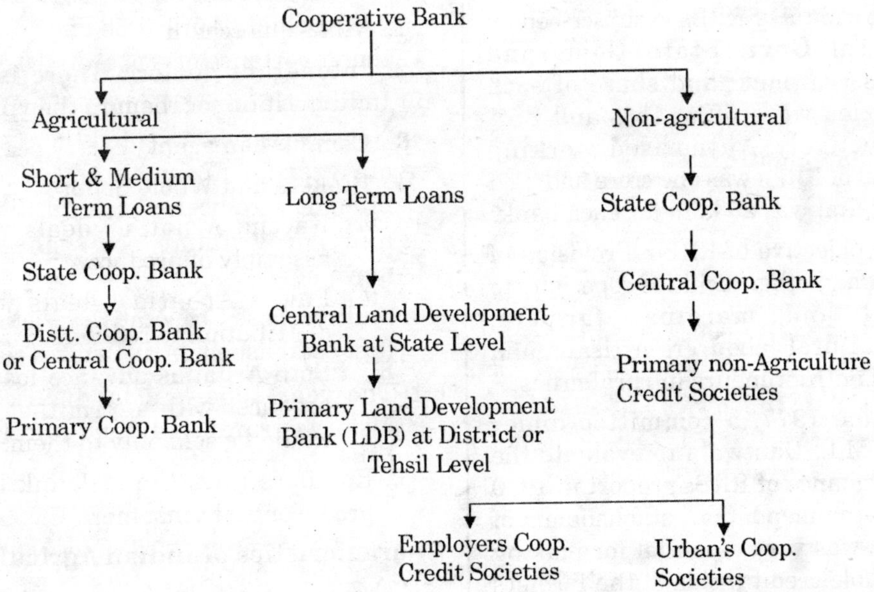

Land Development Bank (LDB)

First mortgage bank was established in 1920 at Jhang (Punjab). But real beginning started by the establishment of central land mortgage bank in 1929 at Madras– for centralising the issue of debentures and for coordinating the working of primary land development banks in the state.

In the beginning of 3rd five year plan, the name of this bank was changed into Land Development Bank (LDB) in order to give credit facilities to the farmers for development of Agriculture. LDB finances long term loans for the following objectives:–

(*a*) The settlement of old debts.

(*b*) Improvement of agricultural lands

(*c*) Giving credit facilities to the farmers for purchasing irrigation equipments and tractors.

Crop Loan Scheme :

This scheme was one of the recommendations of All India Rural Credit Survey Committee Report in 1954. Mr. B.L. Mehata also recommended the need for crop loan in 1960. The crop loan is sanctioned as a cash and kind both. In most of the states cash crop loan is sanctioned in one-third of the total loan.

Regional Rural Banks (RRBs)

(1) Committee on Rural Banks headed by M. Narasimhan (1975).

(2) RRB came into existence as a result of measures taken under 20 point economic programme in 1975 by **Indira Gandhi.**

(3) First of all RRBs were established in U.P. (Muradabad and Gorakhpur), Haryana (Bhiwani), Rajsathan (Jaipur) and in W. B. (Malda District). Syndicate Bank, SBI, Punjab National Bank, United Commercial Bank (UCO) and United Bank of India were sponsored bank respectively. The share capital of RRBs is subscribed by Central Govt, State Govt. and sponsored bank; and share of each agencies were 50%, 15% and 35% respectively. Authorised working capital of RRBs was one crore and paid up capital was 25 lakh for each bank.

(4) Main objective of RRBs: Provision of credit and other facilities especially to small and marginal farmers, agricultural labourers artisans and small entrepreneurs in rural areas.

(5) In June 1977, a committee under Prof. M.L. Dantwala to evaluate the performance of RRBs', report in 1980 and recommendation establishment of RRBs was very essential for making available credit needs of the farmers and weaker people even in those areas where primary cooperative credit societies were functioning.

Taccavi : It is the name of Govt. Loan which is given by the govt. in case of famine and distress condition.

Marketing Services

Marketing Services or Functions are the activities performed by different institutions or agencies which are involved in the process of marketing.

The marketing services are:–

1. Selling
2. Buying of assembling
3. Traffic Management of Transportation
4. Storage
5. **Financing :** It is the provision and management of money and credit to get goods from the hands of producer to the consumer. Financing is presently the most important function.
6. Risk Management : It is also the most important function today.
7. Standardization and grading.

Market Agencies

1. Village merchant
2. Intenerant dealer : There is lack of competition for them in the village
3. Commission agent
4. Brokers and Whole Seller
   (*a*) Kaccha Arhatia : deals with the assembly of produce,
   (*b*) Pakka Arhatia : deals with the distribution to retailers.
   Both Arhatias advance loan to the producer with a term that produce would be sold only to them.
5. Retailers : are the last link between producer and consumer.

Characteristics of Indian Agriculture :

These are the following characteristics of Indian agriculture :–

1. Low Land Productivity of Agriculture
2. Low Labour Productivity in Agriculture
3. Uncertainty in Agriculture
4. Small holdings in India : The average holding size in USA is 158 ha, 188 ha in Canada and 1933 ha in Australia whereas average size of land holdings in India is only about 1.8 ha.
5. Uneven distribution of land : Only 10% people have ownership on 51.7% of total cultivated land where as 10% farmers have only 0.18%.
6. About 14% rural people are landless.
7. Mixed farming
8. Regional specialisation of crops
9. Dependence on Monsoon

10. Subsistence farming
11. Prevalence of foodgrain crops
12. Traditional methods of cultivation still practiced
13. Population pressure on agricultural land
14. Labour dominance.

Problems in Indian Agriculture :

Problems of Indian agriculture are the resultant of natural, social and economic reasons. Followings are problems:–

1. Smaller land holdings
2. Division and sub-division of land holdings
3. Low soil fertility status
4. Natural hazards
5. Lack of education
6. Lack of organisation in farmers
7. Lack of Capital
8. Indebtness of Indian farmers
9. Uncertainty of rainfall and problems in irrigation
10. Excess Population Pressure on agriculture.
11. Faulty land ownership
12. Uneven land distribution
13. Lack of timely payments to cane-producers.
14. Lack of transportation and communication
15. Lack of cold stores, godowns and processing units.
16. Lack of electricity, oils and fuels
17. Lack of highly productive animals
18. Irrational views of the farmers
19. Dependence of fate by the farmers
20. Lack of manures and fertilizers
21. Lack of modern agricultural equipments
22. Lack of suitable and proper seeds
23. Lack of production technique
24. Lack of agricultural research
25. Ups and downs in agricultural price
26. Faulty agricultural marketing systems
27. Lack of proper agriculture planning.

Economic Holding :

The size of holding which provides full employment to the farm family and provides a reasonal standard of living is termed as Economic Holding.

According to Central Land Reforms Committee, the economic holding size for a family (having 5 members) is :–

(*i*) 10 acres *i.e.,* 4 ha. for irrigated land, or

(*ii*) 27 acres *i.e.,* 10.9 ha. for partially irrigated land, or

(*iii*) 54 acres *i.e.,* 21.85 ha. for non-irrigated land.

On the basis of ownership of agriculture land holding, there are three types of common farmers in India :–

1. **Marginal Farmers :** Such farmers who have less than one hectare unirrigated land are called marginal farmers. Marginal farmers constitute 51% of the total farm holdings.
2. **Small Farmers :** Such farmers has one to two (1 – 2) hectare unirrigated land and constitute 19% of the total farm holdings in India.
3. **Agricultural Labour :** Such farmers are landless and having no any landed property.

Agriculture Price

In agricultural sector, conditions of Perfect Competition are more prevalent than that of any other market.

Conditions for Perfect Market

1. Large no. of buyers and sellers.
2. Product produced by all sellers is homogenous.

3. Both sellers and buyers have perfect knowledge about price.
4. No legal or institutional restrictions on buyers and sellers.

A competition that is not pure is called Imperfect Competition. It exists in two forms :–

(a) Monopolistic Competition : Many producers but each produces and sells differentiated products. Each one has a monopoly on its own product.

(b) Oligopoly : A few sellers, dealing in homogenous or differentiated product is small, complete interdependence among the sellers with regard to their price output policies.

There is extreme case also *i.e.,* (3) Monopoly means practically one seller or producer.

Practically all these three market conditions do not prevail in agricultural sector.

Marketable Surplus : The portion of the total produce in stock which the farmer is willing to sell.

Marketed Surplus : The portion which is actually brought to the market at a particular time for sale.

Agriculture Price Commission came into existence in 1965.

Price Elasticity : ⇒

$$E_p = \frac{\text{Relative Change in Quantity}}{\text{Relative Change in Price}} = \frac{\frac{\Delta Q}{Q}}{\frac{\Delta P}{P}}$$

Completely Inelastic Demand : When demand completely unresponsive to the price change *i.e.,* $E_p = 0$.

(i) Relatively Inelastic Demand : When the increase in quantity sold is proportionately smaller than the decrease in price *i.e.,* $0 < E_p < 1$.

(ii) Unit Elasticity : When proportionate change in the quantity demanded is just equal to the proportionate change in its price *i.e.,* $E_p = 1$.

(iii) Elastic Demand : When proportionate change in quantity demanded is more than proportionate price change *i.e.,* $E_p > 1$.

Cost Concepts

The cost is the outlay of funds for productive services. There are many cost concepts used in agricultural economics and farm management *i.e.,* Cost A_1, Cost A_2, Cost B; and Cost C working or variable or operational cost and fixed costs; Explicit and Implicit cost; opportunity cost; labour costs etc.

Cost A_1 : It consists of following 16 items of costs :

1. Value of hired human labour (Permanent and Casual)
2. Value of owned bullock labour
3. Value of hired bullock labour
4. Value of insecticides and fungicides
5. Irrigation charges (both of the owned and hired tubewells, pumping sets etc.)
6. Canal-water charges
7. Land revenue, cesses and other taxes
8. Depreciation on farm implements
9. Value of owned machinery
10. Hired machinery charges
11. Value of fertilizers
12. Value of manure
13. Value of seed
14. Depreciation on farm buildings, farm machinery and irrigation structures.
15. Interest on the working capital
16. Miscellaneous expenses.

Cost A_2 = Cost A_1 + Rent paid for Leased Land

Cost B = Cost A_2 + Imputed Value of Owned Land (less land revenue paid there upon)

+ Imputed interest on Owned Fixed Capital (Excluding land)

Cost C = Cost B + Imputed Value of Family Labour where cost C is the cost of cultivation.

It mean Cost C consist of 20 Items viz.

Cost C = Cost A_1 (having 16 items) +
(17) Rent Paid for Leased land +
(18) Imputed value of owned land (less land revenue paid there upon) +
(19) Imputed interest on owned fixed capital (excluding land) +
(20) Imputed value of family labour

or Cost C = Cost A_1 + (17th + 18th + 19th + 20th items)

or Cost A_1 = Cost C – [17th + 18th + 19th + 20th items]

⇒ Cost A_1 = Cost C – Rent paid for leased land – Imputed value of owned land – Imputed Interest on owned fixed capital – Imputed value of family labour.

⇒ Cost B = Cost C – Imputed value of Family labour.

⇒ Cost A_2 = Cost B – Imputed value of owned land – Imputed interest on owned fixed capital.
= Cost B – [Imputed value of owned land + imputed interest on owned fixed capital]

⇒ Cost A = Cost C – [Imputed value of Family labour + Imputed value of owned land (less land revenue paid there upon) + Imputed interest on owned fixed capital (excluding land)]

Net Income = Gross Return – Cost C,

Cost of Production $= \dfrac{\text{Cost C}}{\text{Output}}$.

Cost of Production means how much fund is outlayed to produce unit output for example to produce 10 quintals the cost of cultivation (Cost C) incurred by a framer is Rs. 900, then the cost of production will $\dfrac{900}{10}$ = Rs. 90/q Rupee Ninety per quintal.

Variable Cost or Prime Cost : It is the cost of using the variable inputs. Such variable inputs are directly related to the production. Examples of variable cost are cost of seed, feed, fertilizer, water, labour hired occasionally, interest on current investment, current repair replacement, diesel etc. Here, expenses are the function of farm output.

Farming Expenses = *f* (farm output)

It means higher the production, higher will be the variable cost. Variable cost is also known as Prime Cost or Special Cost or Direct Cost.

Fixed Cost or Overhead Cost : Such cost does not change in magnitude as the amount of the production process changes and are incurred even when production is not under taken. These are Sunk Cost and may be cash or non-cash fixed costs. The examples of fixed cash cost are Land taxes, Interest, Insurance premiums, annually hired labour etc. Whereas the non-cash fixed costs are depreciation on capital investment, cost of family labour and costs of management, machinery equipment, interest on capital management.

Implicit and Explicit Cost : Implicit cost is the money value of those inputs which are supplied by the farmer himself. Whereas Explicit cost is the actual money expenses directly incurred in raising a farm commodity and monetary estimates of implicit costs. Explicit cost is also known as accounting cost. Both Explicit Cost and Implicit Cost together constitute Economic Cost.

Economic Cost = Accounting (Explicit) Cost + Implicit Cost

Opportunity Cost or Social/ Alternative Cost : The farm resources have normally a number of alternative uses. For example a farmer raises paddy on his farm instead of maize, it means the farmer utilises the other opportunity by giving up the first alternative. Here, the Social Cost of raising paddy will be the amount of maize sacrificed in the process.

Cost Elements

The cost has different elements but broadly two categories viz. :

Fixed Cost and Variable Cost. The cost elements are derived from these two costs.

1. Total Cost (TC) :

   TC = Total Fixed Cost + Total Variable Cost

   = TFC + TVC ⇒ **TC = FC + VC**

   = Explicit Cost + Implicit Cost

   In the beginning total production cost is lower but increases gradually. When total cost is less than the Gross Income at the farm, the profit will be maximum.

2. Average Total Cost/Average Total Unit Cost :

   Average Total Cost (ATC) or Average total unit cost (ATUS) is also known as simply Average Cost (AC)

   $$\text{A.C. or ATC/ATUC} = \frac{\text{TC}}{\text{Output (Q)}}$$

   ATC is called unit cost of production.

3. Total Fixed Cost (TFC or FC)

4. Average Fixed Cost (AFC) :

   $$\text{AFC} = \frac{\text{TFC}}{\text{Output (Q)}} = \frac{\text{FC}}{\text{Q}}$$

   Fixed Cost per unit production is called Average Fixed Cost.

5. Total Variable Cost (TVC or VC) : It is also called Prime Cost, Special Cost or Direct Cost.

6. Average Variable Cost (AVC) :

   $$\text{AVC} = \frac{\text{TVC}}{\text{Unit of Output (Q)}} = \frac{\text{VC}}{\text{Q}}$$

   The Variable Cost per unit production is called AVC.

7. Marginal Cost (MC)

   $$\text{MC} = \frac{\text{Increase in Variable Cost}}{\text{Increase in Output}} = \frac{\Delta\text{VC}}{\Delta\text{Q}}$$

The additional increase in Variable Cost with the additional increase in output is called Marginal Cost or Additional Cost.

Marginal Fixed Cost is always zero because Fixed Cost does not change with the change in output. Therefore, Marginal Cost is necessarily Marginal Variable Cost and the change in Fixed Cost (FC) will not effect Marginal Cost (MC) for example the cost of producing few more vegetables by farming a given amount of land more intensively, is not affected by the amount of rent paid for the fixed amount of land.

Assets :

(*a*) **Fixed Assets :** Such assets are difficult to convert into cash to meet any current obligations *e.g.* land, buildings etc.

(*b*) **Working Assets :** Such assets are more liquid than fixed assets *e.g.* farm machinery, equipments etc.

(*c*) **Current Assets :** Such assets are the most liquid assets and are consumable in a year *e.g.* seeds, fertilizers, cash on hand, livestock for sale etc.

Liabilities

(*a*) **Long duration liabilities :** Such liabilities do not require repayment during the current accounting period *e.g.*, long term loans.

(*b*) **Intermediate liabilities :** Such liabilities can be deferred or postponed for the present but fall due within the year *e.g.*, promissory notes and medium term loans.

(*c*) **Current liabilities :** Repayment of these liabilities may be demanded at once *e.g.*, Short term loans, fertilizers, seeds etc.

Efficiency Measures

There are two methods to evaluate efficiency measures for volume of business– Ratio methods and Aggregative measures. Here, ratio methods are discussed :

Assets-Liabilities Ratios

$$\text{Net Capital ratio} = \frac{\text{Total Assets}}{\text{Total Liabilities}}$$

Working Capital ratio

$$= \frac{\text{Working assets and current assets}}{\text{Intermediate \& Current Liabilities}}$$

$$\text{Current ratio} = \frac{\text{Current assets}}{\text{Current liabilities}}$$

Questions From Previous Year's Papers

Q. 1. (a) What is farm plan? What are the characteristics of a good farm plan?

(b) What is cropping scheme? What are its different aspects?

Q. 2. (a) What are different classes of farm labours? What are the special features of Indian farm labourers?

(b) What is depreciation? Explain different methods of computing depreciation with examples.

Q. 3. What is farm management? How is it related to other branches of agricultural science? What are the problems of farm management under Indian conditions? What are your suggestions for its improvement?

Q. 4. (a) Discuss the problems of marketing of agricultural products in India compared to industrial products and the measures taken by the Government to solve it.

(b) How would you test the economic feasibility of a farm credit proposal? Discuss the test process briefly.

Q. 5. (a) What is agricultural economics? How does it differ from general economics under Indian conditions?

(b) How does Indian farming differ from the of North America? Explain.

Q. 6. (a) What is labour saving device? Give five examples of labour saving devices which could be effectively used under India farming conditions.

(b) What is farm capital? Give a broad classification of farm, capital with examples for each class.

Q. 7. (a) What is the difference between cost of cultivation and cost of production of crop?

(b) Prepare a schedule for working out cost of cultivation of sugarcane under irrigated condition in proper sequence.

(c) What are the factors that affect economic success in famring?

Q. 8. Write short notes on :

(a) Laws of diminishing returns in agriculture

(b) Support price in agriculture

(c) Farm inventory

(d) Isoquant

Q. 9. Distinguish between

(a) Fixed cost and Variable cost

(b) Marginal cost and Marginal return

(c) Partial budgeting and Complete budgeting

(d) Distressed sale and Forced sale.

Q. 10. What is dovetailing of farm enterprises? Under what type of farming it is feasible? Elaborate the answer with concrete examples.

Q. 11. (a) What is farming efficiency? Elaborate major parameters of measuring farming efficiency.

(b) Explain broadly the mode of flow of credit from the National Bank for Agriculture and Rural Development (NABARD) for the farm sector in India

Q. 12. Write short notes on the following giving examples :

(a) Lay farming

(b) Farm liabilities and their classification

(c) Non-monitory inputs in crop production

(d) Incremental cost : benefit ratio (ICBR).

Q. 13. What is farm planning? Differentiate it from farm budgeting. Explain the merits of tactical and strategic farm planning which are taken advantage by the majority of farmers.

Q. 14. Enumerate the principles of co-operation and explain them briefly. State the strengths and weaknesses of co-operative credit system.

Q. 15. What are the objectives of farm management? Suggest measures to reverse the trend of population migration from rural to urban areas in India.

Q. 16. What are the factors to be considered in preparation of farm plan and what are the characteristics of a good farm plan?

Q. 17. What are the problems faced by farmers in the existing system of marketing of agricultural produce? Suggest measures for improvement of marketing system in India.

Q. 18. Differentiate between the following pairs in not more than 150 words each.

(a) Partial and Complete budgeting

(b) Diversified farming and Mixed farming

(c) Partial budgeting and complete budgeting

Q. 19. Write short notes on the following :

(a) Processing of black tea

(b) Opportunity test

(c) AGMARK standards.

10. AGRICULTURAL EXTENSION

Introduction :

Extension = Ex + tensis (Latin word)
↓ ↓
Out Stretching

Education : Production of desirable changes in human behaviour through gaining desirable knowledge, attitude and mental and manual skill; is called Education.

The word 'Extension' was used first time in USA. Extension activity was started first time in USA. First extension work was done in 1785 in Philadelphia State of USA when few farmers got together and organised to sell their produce. In 1862, Morril Land Grant Act was passed in USA and signed by the President Lincon. Morril was an educationist. The objective of this act was "All the agricultural institutes would pass on their innovations to rural people." In 1885, the concept of demonstration was given by *Dr. Seeman A. Knapp*. He generated a new variety and demonstrated on one million acre farm in Lausannia. Therefore, he is known as father of method demonstration.

On the basis of American pattern *i.e.,* Land grant college pattern, the first agricultural university at Pant Nagar was established in India. But the study of extension education as a course first time started at Sabour (Bhagalpur) in Bihar in 1956.

Extension Education is an applied behavioural Science to bring about desirable change usually through various strategies and programmes of change and by applying the latest scientific and technological innovations.

Characteristic Features :

(*i*) Participation is purely voluntary.

(*ii*) It is an informal education *i.e.,* out of school and college.

(*iii*) Teacher or extension worker starts with practical first and then after theoretical aspects are to be touched *i.e.,* First Practical then theory.

(*iv*) There is no fixed curriculum or course of study.

(*v*) Farmers study the problems.

(*vi*) Authority rests with the farmers.

(*vii*) It is Bi-directional learning means teacher also learns from the farmers during the course of teaching to the farmers.

(*viii*) Teaching is also through local leaders or lay-leaders.

(*ix*) Teaching is mainly horizontal.

(*x*) Large and heterogenous audience.

(*xi*) It is flexible.

(*xii*) Freedom to develop programmes locally.

(*xiii*) It is based on the needs and expressed desires of the people.

(*xiv*) It is more practical.

(*xv*) It is continuous education *i.e.,* throughout the life.

Objectives of Extension

There are two directions of movement–

1. Fundamental objective : Development of the people.
2. In India there are three main objective of agricultural extension–

(*a*) Dissemination of useful and practical information.

(*b*) Practical application of useful knowledge. The word **'Learning by Doing'** was coined by *John Dewey* in 1966.

(*c*) To improve all aspects of the life of the rural people.

Principles of Extension

(*i*) Principle of interest and Need : means it is based on the needs and interests of the people.

(*ii*) Principle of cultural difference : *i.e.*, based on the cultural back ground of the people.

(*iii*) Principle of Participation:

(*iv*) Principle of Adaptability *i.e.*, Extension programmes should be flexible.

(*v*) Grassroot principle of Organisation : means programmes fit in with the local conditions so that more and more people would participate.

(*vi*) Leadership Principle : Programme is based on full utilisation of local leadership.

(*vii*) The Whole-family Principle : means programme is useful for all the members *i.e.*, male, female and youth of the family.

(*viii*) Principle of co-operarion : Rural people cooperate with their village, block and state officials to pursue a common cause.

(*ix*) Principle of Satisfaction : Satisfaction is the key to success in extension work. A satisfied customer is the best advertisement.

(*x*) Principle of Evaluation : To know the merits and demerits of the programme, analytical study is necessary. Therefore, it needs constant evaluation.

Basic Philosophy of Extension

1. Self help.
2. People are the greatest resource.
3. Programme of change and Cooperative effort.
4. Democratic nature means Development of people by the people and for the people.
5. Two channel of knowledge and experience.
6. Problems : are brought to laboratory.
7. Solutions : are taken to farmers/ villagers.
8. Programme is based on creating interest by seeing and doing.
9. There is voluntarily cooperative participation.
10. Persuation and education of people.
11. Programme is based on attitude and values of the people.

Process of Adoption

(*i*) Adoption is an individual matter or phenomenon or behavioural socio-economical phenomenon or mental process.

(*ii*) Elements of Adoption process :

(*a*) Innovation

(*b*) Diffusion

(*c*) Motivation

(*d*) Adoption

(*iii*) Diffusion is the process between persons.

(*iv*) Stages of Adoption :

(*a*) Awareness

(*b*) Interest

(*c*) Evaluation

(*d*) Trial

(*e*) Adoption

(*v*) Categories of Adopters : There are five groups of adopters.

(*a*) Innovators : Such people are called innovators who adopt immediately after getting knowledge. In India Innovators constitutes only 2.5% of the total population.

(*b*) Early Adopters : Such people adopt through local leaders and constitute only 13.5% of the total Indian population.

(*c*) Early Majority : Such people adopt just before adopting the common people and not through the local leaders and constitute 34% of the total population.

(*d*) Late Majority : Such people adopt after seeing their relatives and neighboures and constitute 34% of the total population.

(*e*) Leggards : Such people adopt in the last and constitute only 16% of the total Indian population.

Communication

1. Teaching and learning is the process of communication.
2. Teacher acts as catalyst.
3. Communication means sharing of ideas and feelings in a mood of mutuality.
4. 'Communication' is derived from latin word 'communis' meaning 'common'. It means to establish commonness between sender and receiver of message is termed as communication.
5. It is a two way or Double way process.
6. Communication involves :

   (*i*) Source and his message

   (*ii*) Receiver and his response
7. The chief emphasis in communication on Target Audience (not on material or medium).
8. Communication systems :

   K → Knowledge G → Generating

   S → System D → Disseminating

   C → Consuming.
9. Key elements of communication :

   (*a*) Sender

   (*b*) Message

   (*c*) Message Treatment *i.e.*, encoding

   (*d*) Communication channel/Medium.

   (*e*) Receiver : It is the most important element because every element is directed towards receiver.

   (*f*) Receiver's response.

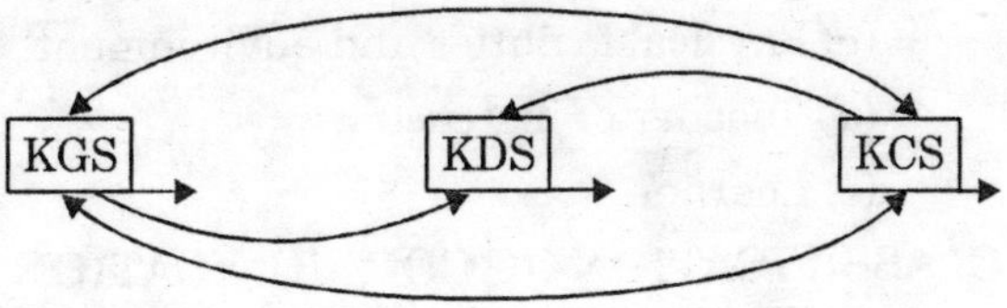

Agencies ⟶

KGS	KDS	KCS
Universities Research Institutes Private Organisation Voluntary Organisation	Mass media Universities Research Instituеs Govt. Agencies Voluntary Organisations	Farmers (in Agriculture)

10. Communication process :

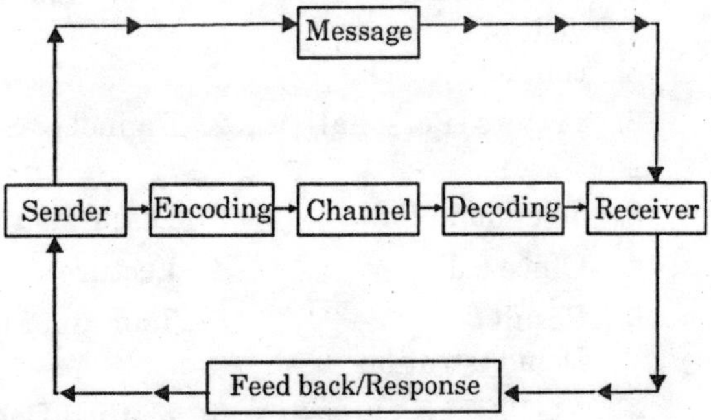

11. Ingredients in communication :

Source → Message → Channel → Receiver

KGS KDS KCS

12. According to Berlo (1960) :

Source → Encoder → Message → Channel→ Decoder → Receiver

Learning & Teaching in Extension & Communication

1. Extension is an educational process to bring about desirable changes.
2. Essential role of an extension worker is to create effective learning situations.
3. Essential elements of effective learning are five in number :

   (*a*) Teaching materials and Plan.

   (*a*) Subject matter

   (*c*) Physical facilities and environment.

   (*d*) Teacher of instructor.

   (*e*) Learner.

CLASSIFICATION OF COMMUNICATION (EXT. TEACHING METHODS)

A. According to use and nature of contact:

On the basis of use and nature of contact, the extension teaching methods are categorised under three groups–

(*i*) **Individual contact method (or Interpersonal channel of communication) :** Here contact is face to face or person to person. It is very effective in teaching, quantum of feedback available is very high but slow communication.

(*ii*) **Group contact method :** Group means a group of 2-30 persons but usually consists of 20-25 persons. Group is usually formed around common interest. Here is face to face contact.

(*iii*) **Mass or community contact method :** It is more useful for making people aware of the new agricultural technology quickly.

Examples of different methods

Individual	*Group (2-30 persons)*	*Mass or Community (More than 30 persons)*
1	*2*	*3*
1. Farm and Home visit of Personal contact	1. Symposium (2-5 speakers)	1. Bulletins
2. Letters (Personal)	2. Pannel (2-8 Speakers)	2. Leaflet/booklet folder/pamphlet
3. Telephone Call	3. Discussion	3. News paper
4. Office call	4. Lecture	4. Magazine
5. Result Demonstration	5. Tour and field days	5. Journal
	6. Method Demonstration (or Demonstration)	6. Exhibition
	7. Meeting	7. Television
	8. Role playing	8. Radio
	9. Puppet show	9. Circular letter
	10. Slide	10. Fairs
	11. PAE set (Public Address equipment)	11. Posters

1	2	3
	12. School	12. Cinema (Film)
	13. Conference	13. Movie
	14. Seminar	14. Drama & Songs
	15. Training camp	
	16. Flash cards	

B. According to Equipments *i.e.*, Projected and Non-projected :

1. Projected Aids : Here projection is controlled by motor and electricity e.g.

(*i*) Film projector

(*ii*) Slide projector : Slide is of 35 mm. and direct projection,

(*iii*) Overhead projector : It is indirect projection and transparencies are used.

(*iv*) Epidiascope/Opaque projector : There is no need of transparency. Epidiascope means both transparent and opaque materials can be seen (or focused) on the screen by magnifying. The image of a picture is made on the screen directly and indirectly. One additional mirror is required in it.

2. Non-Projected Aids : Here no machinery is required *e.g.*, Flash cards, Graphs, Charts, Leaflets, Folders, Blackboard.

C. According to Audio-visual aids:

Examples are

(*i*) Audio : Radio, Taperecorder

(*ii*) Visual : Flash cards, overhead projector, slides etc.

(*iii*) Audio-visual : Puppet, Drama, Television, Cinema etc.

Demonstration :

Demonstration means showing by doing. The basic principle of Demonstration is learning by seeing and doing. There are three types of demonstration–

Method Demonstration :

(*i*) It is short-type demonstration.

(*ii*) It's main purpose is to provide only skill.

(*iii*) It does not compare between the old and new technique or skill. It means comparative study can not be done.

(*iv*) It is the oldest form of teaching.

(*v*) The father of method demonstration was Dr. Seeman. A. Knapp.

(*vi*) It is a single practice demonstration *i.e.*, how to operate tractor, how to apply fertilizer in the field. In this demonstration any process is shown and made clear to the people by doing in a sequence starting from the beginning to the end and zealous person is given opportunity for doing.

Result Demonstration :

(*i*) It is long type demonstration.

(*ii*) It shows the value or worth of the (new) practice.

(*iii*) Comparison between two practices *i.e.*, old and new is always done.

(*iv*) Results of both practices are shown.

(*v*) It is very effective in adoption.

(*vi*) It is conducted by a farmer under direct supervision of an extension worker.

(*vii*) It is used to show the superiority of practices.

National or Composite Demonstration :

(*i*) It is a composite of both method and result demonstration.

(*ii*) It is first line demonstration of Front line extension project.

(*iii*) It is conducted by the researchers on the farmer's field.

(*iv*) The main objective is to show production can be increased per unit area and per unit time.

(*v*) Multiple cropping system are usually followed and High yielding varieties (HYV) are used in this demonstration.

(*vi*) National demonstration was first time started in 1965 by Ministry of Food and Agriculture.

(*vii*) This programme was given to ICAR in 1967.

(*viii*) Now it has become part of agricultural production programme.

TRAINING AND VISIT SYSTEM

1. T and V system is a new extension service approach. The concept of T and V system was evolved in 1973 by Israeli extension expert **Daniel Benor** who was consultant on extension programme in World Bank. This system was first tried in seyhan irrigation project in Turkey.
2. T and V system is also called **Baster and Benor Scheme** and firstly evolved in **Turkey** by incidental learning.
3. T and V system has two phages/stages– (*i*) Training and (*ii*) Visit

   (*i*) **Training :** Training is imparted for transfer of technical knowhow from subject matter specialist (SMS) to extension worker.

   $$\text{SMS} \xrightarrow{\text{Technical knowhow}} \text{Extension worker}$$

   (*ii*) **Visit :** Extension worker has to visit to the farmers for transfers of knowhow obtained at the training.

   $$\text{Ext. worker} \xrightarrow{\text{Technical knowhow}} \text{Farmers}$$

4. It is Govt. sponsored rural development programme.
5. It is also called Reformed Extension or Intensive Agricultural Extension.
6. T and V system is introduced in India in 1974 in Rajsathan canal area and Chambal command area in M.P. to improve the effectiveness of agricultural extension.
7. According to Benor *et. al.* (1984) T and V system is an effective management system of known extension principles.
8. Systematic programme of In-service training of village extension workers and planned schedule of visit to the farmer's field is the basic feature of T and V system.

LAB TO LAND PROGRAMME

This programme was launched in India on the occasion of ICAR golden jubilee celebration year in July 1979 for only one year. But later on this programme was extended further year after year. The objective of LLP is the transfer of proved and visible low cost agricultural technologies to small and marginal farmers and landless laboures to improve their overall socio-economic condition.

The benefits of new technology or technical knowhow of agricultural production were being utilised by the big and rich farmers. Therefore, it was felt that for holistic developmental approach of agricultural sector, the evolved technology in the laboratory (or at the agriculture farm) would be stretched out to the lands of small and marginal farmers. That's why lab to land programme was launched. Under lab to land or land to lab programme, the problems related to the agriculture were brought to the laboratory where the particular solution was to be found out or searched out and later on were communicated to the farmer. But due to agro-climatic regional differences lab to land programme has been changed into Farmer's First Programme where the agricultural problems are sorted out and are solved at the farmer's field itself.

KRISHI VIGYAN KENDRA

- Education committee (1964-66) recommended to establish agricultural polytechnique.
- Finally ICAR mooted the idea to establish Krishi Vigyan Kendra (KVK) and Mohan Singh Mehta Committee was appointed in 1974 by ICAR to formulate KVK scheme.
- First KVK was started at Pondicherry (Puducherry) in 1974 with the aim of transfer to technical literacy to increase agricultural production.
- The main objective of KVK is to impart training (or vocational training) at the kendra (centre) or out of the centre *i.e.*, in the village to the people according to their needs about the Agriculture and allied subjects *viz.* Animal Husbandry, Fisheries, Horticulture, Agriculture Engineering, Home Science etc.
- In the initial five years financial assistance was given to KVK by the Indian Agricultural Research Institute (IARI) and for the next five years it was availed by IARI and State Govt. or State agriculture university in the 50 : 50 ratio. There was a plan to finance full assistance by the state govt. or state agriculture university after the lapse of initial ten years.
- There were 561 KVK in number by the year March 2009 and the plan is to establish one KVK in every district of India.

TECHNOLOGY TRANSFER

The essential and major part of technology is extension. It means technology transfer is broader in meaning than extension *i.e.*,

Technology Transfer ≠ Agl. Extension or Extension.

Technology Transfer includes the additional functions of input supplies and agri-services.

Technology Transfer = Agl. Extn. + Input supplies and agri-services

= Ext. + Supplies and Services.

COMMUNITY DEVELOPMENT PROGRAMME

1. CDP was a Programme/Project/Method/ or a Process means it may be called Community Development Project or CD Method or CD Process.
2. In the formulation of CDP, major role was played by Grow More Food campaign.
3. Initially 15 pilot projects were launched in 1952 with financial assistance from Ford Foundation.
4. On 2nd Oct. 1952, 55 Community Development Projects were started in different parts of the country with Indo-USA agreement for three years.
5. This project covered nearly 25,260 villages and population of 6.4 millions.
6. At outset, each project was consisted of 300 villages, 400-500 square miles area and a population of 2 lakhs.
7. Later on, the project area was divided into three development blocks and thus the whole country has been divided into Development Blocks.

NATIONAL EXTENSION SERVICE

- Due to success of Community Development Project, people demanded more of CDP. Therefore, National Extension Service was inaugurated on 2nd Oct. 1953 owing limited financial and technical manpower resources.
- Later on, NES block was converted into Community Development Block with higher budget to take up more intensive development programmes.
- Under the chairmanship of Balwantrai Mehta one committee was formed in 1957 to revise CDP and the committee was called Committee on Plan Project. And the pattern of CDP was revised with effect from 1 April 1958.
- A block is the Unit of Planning and Development. The entire country has been covered with CDP by the year 1963.

- Under CDP, intensive development work was required in all fields but scheme of National Extension Service (NES) was to provide essential basic staff and a small fund for people to start development work essentially on the basis of self-help.
- The operational unit of NES block was 100 villages comprising of 60,000-70,000 people.

Young Farmer's Association :

4H-club was established in 1900 in America to provide training to youth for agricultural and home development. It was first govt. step. 4H means Heart, Head, Hand and Health as explained by A.B. Graham. On the basis of 4H-club of USA, Young Farmer's Association of India was started by P.S. Deshmukh in 1956.

TRYSEM : Training of Rural Youth for Self Employment. TRYSEM was launched in 1979 (Sixth five year plan) with the basic principle of knowledge by doing or learning by doing to provide technical skills to the rural youth from families below the poverty line. The target group comprises rural youth between the age of 18 and 35 years old.

IRDP : Integrated Rural Development Programme is a non–plan programme which means IRDP comes under five year plan. The main aim of IRDP is the all round development of family. IRDP was launched on 2nd Oct. 1980 (sixth five year plan) by integrating following programmes–

(*i*) SFDA : Small Farmers Development Agency.

(*ii*) DPAP : Drought Prone Area Programme.

(*iii*) Operation Flood II : Development of Dairy, Poultry, Piggery etc. in Gujarat and Haryana.

(*iv*) NREP : National Rural Employment Programme.

(*v*) MNP : Minimum Need Programme.

SWARNA JYANTHI GRAMA SWAROZGAR YOJANA

Govt. of India have launched 'Swarna Jyanthi Grama Swarozgar Yojana' (SGSY) with effect from 1st April 1999 (1999-2000) as the main programme for promoting poverty alleviation through self employment. SGSY is a holistic package and replaces the earlier IRDP, TRYSEM, DWCRA (Development of Women and Children for Rural Areas), SITRA (Supply of Improved Tools Kits for Rural Artisans), Ganga Welfare Plan and Million Wells Scheme (MWS). Unlike in the earlier programmes where the approach adopted was one of selecting the beneficieries first and then deciding on the activity for which assistance should be given to them; in the SGSY the emphasis is on selecting key activities and activity clusters under which beneficieries are selected keeping in view their suitability for the activities. The requirement of assisting only below poverty line households will continue.

Objective of SGSY : Swarozgari should be able to cross the poverty line within 3 years. A minimum net income of Rs. 2000 P. M. is anticipated.

Rural Welfare Activities and Other Programmes in India

S. No.	*Name of Activity of Programme*	*Name of the Worker*	*Starting Year*
	1	*2*	*3*
1.	Cooperative Movement	F. Nicholso	1904
2.	Sri Niketan (W. Bengal)	Rabindra Nath Tagore	1908 (1921)
3.	Gurgaon Project (Haryana)	F.L. Brayne	1920 (1927)

1	*2*	*3*
4. Sevagram (near Wardha in) Maharashtra)	M.K. Gandhi	1927
5. Marthandom Project (Kerala)	**Spencer Hatch**	1928
6. Social Legislation	Govt. of Indian (British)	1929
7. Rural Development	Rural Development Department of British India	1935
8. Grow More Food Campaign	Rural Development Department of British India	1942 (1947)
9. Firka Development Scheme	Madras Govt.	1947 (1943)
10. Nilokheri Project (Haryana)	S.K. Dubey	1943 (1948)
11. Indian Village Service	W.H. Wisher	1948
12. Etawah Pilot Project	Alert Mayer	1948
13. FAO (Food Agriculture Organisation)	International Organisation	1948
14. UNICEF	International Organisation	1948
15. Planning Commission	Govt. of India	**1950**
16. Sarvodaya (from Bombay)	**Acharya Vinoba Bhave**	1950
17. Five year plan	Govt. of India	**1951**
18. Training and Development Centres	Govt. of India	1951
19. Bhoodan Movement	**Acharaya Vinoba Bhave**	**1951**
20. Gramdan Movement	**Acharaya Vinoba Bhave**	1952
21. Community Development Project	Govt. of India	**2nd Oct. 1952**
22. Grow More Food Enquiry Committee	Govt. of India	**1952**
23. National Extension Service	Govt. of India	2nd Oct. 1953
24. UNESCO	International Organisation	1955
25. Family Planning Programme	Govt. of India	1956
26. Kharif and Rabi Movement	Govt. of India	1958
27 **Nalagarh Committee** Report (or Agricultural Administrative Committee)	Govt. of India	1958
28. Intensive Agriculture District Programme (IADP)	Govt. of India	1960-61
29. Multiple Cropping Scheme	Govt. of India	1960
30. Democratic Decentralisation (Panchayati raj)	Govt. of India	1958

1	*2*	*3*
31. National Seed Corporation	Govt. of India	1963
32. Agricultural Refinance Corporation (Later Agriculture Refinance and Development Corporation)	Govt. of India	July 1963
33. Intensive Agriculture Area Programme (IAAP) except Kerala	Govt. of India	1964
34. National Demonstration Project	Ministry of Food and Agriculture	1965
35. High Yielding Variety Programme (HYVP)	Govt. of India	1966-67
36. Administrative Reforms Commission	Govt. of India	1966
37. Agricultural Administration Team Report	Govt. of India	1967
38. State Farms Corporation of India	Govt. of India	1969
39. Small Farmers Development Agency (SFDA) and Marginal Farmers and Agriculture Labour (MEAL)	Govt. of India	1970-71
40. Command Area Development Programme (CADP)	Govt. of India	1974-75
41. 20-Point Programme	Indira Gandhi	1975
42. National Seed Programme	Govt. of India	1975-76
43. Special Livestock Production Programme	Govt. of India	1975-76
44. Regional Rural Banks (RRBs)		1976 Act
45. Antyodaya Programme	Govt. of Rajasthan	1977
46. Desert Development Programme	Govt. of India	1977-78
47. Lab to Land Programme	ICAR	1979
48. TRYSEM (Training of Rural Youth for self Employment)	Govt. of India	1979
49. National Rural Employment	Govt. of India	1980
50. Integrated Rural Development Programme (IRDP)	Govt. of India	2nd Oct. 1980

	2	3
51. Special Component Plan	Govt. of India	2nd Oct. 1980
52. National Bank for Agriculture and Rural Development (NABARD)	Govt. of India	12 July 1982
53. Drought Prone Area Programme (DPAP)	Govt. of India	1982-83
54. Rural Landless Employment Guarantee Programme (RLEGP)	Govt. of India	1983-84
55. Indira Awas Yojna	Govt. of India	1986-87

Questions From Previous Year's Papers

Q. 1. Indicate the meaning and important of extension programmes. Briefly discuss different methods of evaluation. Critically explain the merits of evaluation of extension programmes.

Q. 2. (a) Discuss the steps to be considered for a successful result demonstration and organization of method demonstration.

(b) Distinguish between result demonstration and method demonstration.

Q. 3. What are the main principles of extension programme planning? Discuss the steps involved in programme planning process.

Q. 4. Give a general account of storage and preservation of mushroom, mango and cabbage. What are their export potential?

Q. 5. Write short notes on the following, each not exceeding 150 words :

(a) Lab-to-Land programme

(b) Organisation and function of I.C.A.R.

(c) ICRISAT

Q. 6. Write short critical notes, in about 150 words each on the following :

(a) Small Farmers Development Agency

(b) Jawahar Rojgar Yojana

IFS AGRICULTURE

PAPER-II

1. CELLS

Cell : The cell has been defined as the smallest unit of biological activity which shows full range of properties associated with life. It was discovered by Robert Hooke (1665). He wrote a book 'Micrographia' and coined the term *cell*. Leeuwenhoek (1672) was the first to see *free cells*. He observed bacteria, protozoa, red blood cells, sperms etc. under his microscope. In 1809, Lamarck came to the conclusion that all living beings are formed of cells. Dutrochet (1824) believed in individuality of cells. Living substances was first observed by Corti (1772) and was named *sarcode* by Dujardin (1836). Robert Brown (1831) discovered nucleus while Von Mohl (1838, 1846) & Purkinje (1839) named the jelly-like living substance or sarcode of the cell as *protoplasm.*

On the basis of presence or absence of the nuclear membrane, the cells are classified into two basic types *i.e.,*

(*i*) Prokaryotic cell

(*ii*) Eukaryotic cell

The Prokaryotic cell is characteristic of bacteria and blue green algae (BGA). Due to the absence of nuclear membrane the nucleus is not separable from the cytoplasm as a distinct structure and there are no membranous organelles in the cytoplasm. The smallest cell known is the prokaryotic, *i.e.,* PPLO (*Pleuropneumonia like organism*).

The Eukaryotic cells are characteristic of animals, plants and microorganisms except bacteria and blue green algae. The nuclear material is enclosed with a nuclear membrane and takes the form of a distinct nucleus. The cytoplasm contains many organelles to carry out various cellular function.

Comparision between Prokaryotes and Eukaryotes cells :

Prokaryotes	*Eukaryotes*
1. Protoplasm	
Relatively rigid, usually non-vacuolate gel; relatively resistant to desiccation, osmotic shock and thermal denaturation.	Typically more fluid, generally vacuolate, more sensitive to desiccation, osmotic shock and thermal denaturation.
2. Organelles	
Membrane bound organelles, like Golgi bodies, plastids, mitochondria ER, etc., are absent.	Organelles like Golgi bodies plastids, mitochondria, ER., etc., are present.
3. Nucleus	
True nucleus absent; nuclear membrane and nucleolus not present, nucleoplasm undifferentiated from cytoplasm.	True nucleus present; nuclear membrane, nucleolus and nucleoplasm distinct.
4. DNA	
Scattered in the protoplasm, without histone proteins.	Organised with histone proteins to form distinct chromosomes.
5. Sexual process	
Typical sexual process lacking, but genetic material is exchanged by parasexual processes.	Typeical sexual process (with alternating nuclear fusion and reduction division) often present.

Prokaryotes	*Eukaryotes*
6. Cell division	
Mostly ámitotic.	Typically mitotic.
7. Mitotic apparatus	
Absent.	Present
8. Ribosomes	
70 S type.	80 S type.

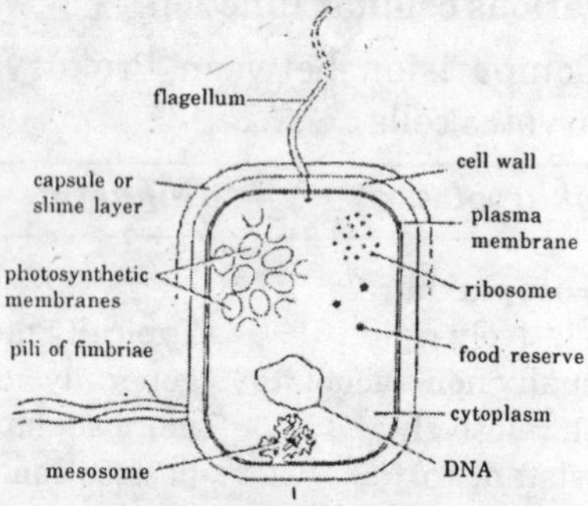

Prokaryotic cell

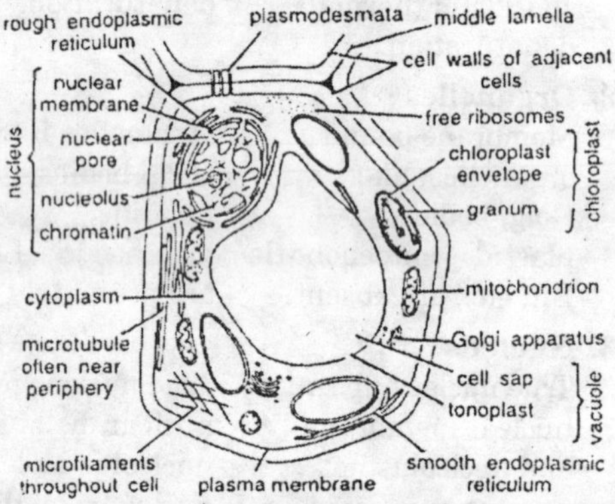

Eukaryotic cell

Fig. 1 Structure of Prokaryotic and Eukaryotic cells.

CELL THEORY

The credit of forming the cell theory goes to German scientist M.J.Schleiden (1838) and German Zoologist T. Schwann (1839).

Schleiden found that all plant cells have essentially similar structure. Schwann (1838) working independently observed that animal cells do not have cell wall but are otherwise similar amongst themselves. He put forward cell hypothesis bodies of animals and plants are made up of cells and their products. Schleiden and Schwann (1839) compared their findings and formulated *cell theory* which states that :

(*i*) Living beings are made of one or more cells.

(*ii*) A cell is a mass of protoplasm having a nucleus.

(*iii*) Cells are similar in basic structure and metabolism.

(*iv*) The functions of an organism are due to activities and interactions of its cells.

MODIFICATION OF CELL THEORY

Cell theory was first modified in the light of Virchow's findings (1855, 1858) that cells develop from pre-existing cell-*Omnis cellula-e-cellula*. It is known as law of other modifications were carried out in the cells theory. The modern cell theory is called 'cell principle.'

***Protoplasm Theory* :** It was proposed by Max Schultze (1861) which states that living matter of an organism in protoplasm and the cell is simply an accumulation of protoplasm limited by an outer membrane and containing a nucleus.

***Organismal Theory* :** Sachs (1874) proposed that the whole organism functions as a single entity which is made of a continuous mass of protoplasm incompletely divided into cells.

***Cellular Autonomy and Multicellularity* :** Cells are autonomous or self contained unit because :

(*i*) They obtain or manufacture food

(*ii*) All cells require energy for overcoming entropy, performing body activities and biosynthesis. For this they oxidise food materials in respiration.

(*iii*) Cells convert non-living materials into components of living protoplasm.

(*iv*) Worn out parts are replaced by news ones.

(*v*) There is exchange of gases.

(*vi*) Cells discard waste materials.

(*vii*) They are able to regulate their activities through flow of energy and information.

(*viii*) Cells maintain their own internal physico-chemical environment.

(*ix*) They may divide and form daughter cells.

(*x*) There is a definite life span. Cells of unicellular organisms lead independent existence with no dependent on others for any function, material or information. They depend upon their own intrinsic information. Irritability is, of course present. Cells of multicellular organisms possess autonomy but show various interactions and specialities.

Cellular Totipotency and Survival : Somatic nucleated cells are totipotent or able to produce a complete organism. This is especially so in case of plant cells. It was first suggested by Haberlandt (1902) and proved by Steward *et al* in 1957, through tissue or cell culture experiments. For its survival and proper functioning, a cell always requires :

(*i*) Flow of Energy for overcoming entropy (tendency for disorderliness) and performing various life activities.

(*ii*) Flow of *information* which is of two types, *intrinsic* or genetic and *extrinsic* through nerves and hormones. Intrinsic or genetic information is contained in DNA. Specific triggers activate DNA segments to transcribe mRNAs which then help synthesise specific polypeptides/proteins/enzymes, etc. Stimulated nerves secrete chemicals to activate certain cells. Hormones are recognised by either membrane receptors or intracellular receptors. The complexes allow particular activities.

Surface Volume Ratio : Metabolically active cells are small since small cells have higher nucleo-cytoplasmic ratio for better control and higher surface-volume ratio for quicker exchange of materials. Larger cells can be efficient only if they are elongated, branched or posses membrane extensions like microvilli. Large sized animals do not posses large sized cells but more numerous small cells.

Shape and Size of Cells :

The cells ranges from 0.5 μ to 20 μ (1μ = 0.001 mm). The largest known cell is the egg of an Ostrich which can be as long as 170 mm. The smallest cell is perhaps yet to be discovered. The shape also is varied and depends upon the environmental conditions; surroundings, function and need of the organism.

Animals are capable of changing their shapes; but the shape of plant cell is fixed due to the presence of cellulose cell-wall.

Simple bacteria can be rod shaped, spiral, oval, round etc. The shapes of desmids and diatoms are varied. Amoeba keeps on changing its shape. The body of unicellular marine alga, *Acetabularia* is differentiated into a rhizoid like base, a long and slender stalk and an umbrella like cap. The RBCs of human beings are rounds, whereas, the muscle cells are long and with pointed ends.

CELL ORGANELLES AND THEIR FUNCTIONS

1. Cell Wall :

In plants (including bacteria) a cell is always surrounded by a cell wall throughout with plasmalemma. Many plants may become heterotrophic due to the loss of chlorophyll, but they still have a definite cell wall. In case of animal cells, the outermost layer of cell is plasmalemma, which is occasionally also called 'cell membrane' or 'plasma membrane'. Morphologically the cell wall consists :

(i) Middle lamella,
(ii) Primary wall,
(iii) Secondary wall, and
(iv) Tertiary wall.

Ultrastructure

Cell wall when studied with the help of an electron microscope after maceration, is found to consists of two main parts, namely.

(i) the fibrils which are left if hemicellulose and pectic materials are removed and
(ii) the ground substance or matrix in which the fibrils are embedded.

In cell plate, cellulose microfibrils are absent, while in bust fibres or cotton hairs, 95% of cellulose is present. Also the orientation of these fibrils in cell wall with respect to the axis of the cell varies. These could be parallel to the cell axis, oblique, perpendicular or may be randomly distributed.

Chemical Composition

Cell wall mainly composed of cellulose produced by cell. Adjacent cell walls are cemented with pectin. Primary and secondary walls are composed mainly of polysaccharide cellulose, but other substances may be incorporated especially in secondary walls.

Substances of plant cell wall are :

(i) Cellulose
(ii) Hemicellulose
(iii) Pectin
(iv) Lignin
(v) Cuticular substances fatty acids
(vi) Mineral deposits (Ca and Mg or carbonates or silicates).

Functions

The function of cell wall in plants is mainly considered to provide mechanical strenghts. In higher plants having vascular system, cell wall provide main supporting framework.

Therefore, besides other main function of cell wall is the same as that of skeleton in animals.

PLASMA MEMBRANE

The term "plasmalemma" was coined by J.Q. Plower in 1931.

Structure of plasma membrane has been studied by their isolation from living systems and also by their artifical synthesis using its constituents.

Variety of cells including liver cells, muscles, amoeba and sea urchin eggs have been used for the isolation of plasma membrane. To obtain plasma membrane from erythrocytes, the cells are treated with hypotonic solution, so that the cell will swell and lose hemoglobin.

The chemical constitution of plasma membrane includes : (i) protein (iii) lipid (iii) small proportion of oligosaccharides.

Structure

Definite plasma membrane of 6nm to 10 nm (10 nm = 100 Å, 1 nm = 10^{-6} mn) was observed on surface of all cell. Plasma membranes of two cells were found to be separated by a space of 11-15 nm.

Plasma membrane of most of the cells appeared to be three layered. The outer dense layers are about 2.00 nm thick and the middle layer about 3.5 nm. This strucutre is called the "unit membrane".

Functions

It performs variety of functions. Diversity of function is reflected in diversity in structure of plasma membrane. It controls cellular semipermeability, resorption, excretion and secretion. Plasma membrane thus represents a selective path way for transport of substances into outside the cell, controlling cell form and cell activity. Another means by which material can be transported into the cell is "pinocytosis" or phagocytosis.

A reserve process to pinocytosis may occur for throwing material out through the plasma membrane.

Most important function of the cell membrane is transport of individual molecules or ions. This can be bought about by :

(*i*) Passive transport

(*ii*) Active transport

In passive transport, movement of molecules or ions, is from high to low concentration in a chemical gradient or an electrochemical gradient (in case of charged molecules) on the other hand in active transport, although movement may take place in the direction of gradient as well, but it should be able to effect the net transfer against the direction of gradient.

RIBOSOMES

These are small granular particles which contain RNA and measure 150 – 250 Å in diameter. They consists of a 40 s and 60 s subunits which together make upon 80 s ribosome.

Functions

Ribosomes serve in the protein synthesis, thus, also known as protein factories of the cell.

MITOCHONDRIA

The first evidence of the presence of mitochondria in plant cells (*Nymphaea*) was given by F. Meves in 1904. However, an important advancement in the study of mitochondria was made with the isolation of liver mitochondria for the first time by Bensley and Hoerr in 1934.

The morphology of mitochondria varies from one cell to another but may remain stable in cells performing same function. The mitochondria normally vary in size from 0.5μ to 2.0μ and are therefore not easy to detect in light microscope. The number of mitochondria per cell varies according to the function and volume of cell, they may be 50-5000 in a cell.

Mitochondria has a double membrane envelope, the two membranes being separated by a space of 6-8 nm. The inner membrane is not smooth and forms mitochondrial crests. This inner membrane divides the mitochondria into two chambers, namely (*i*) the perimitochondrial space between outer membrane and inner membrane, which is continuous into the core of the crests and (*ii*) the inner chamber inside the inner membrane which is occupied by a relatively dense material called the mitochondrial matrix.

Functions

Mitochondria is the power house of the cell and is the source of an energy needed for life on earth. From this organelle, energy is made available to the energy consuming processes of the cell in the form of ATP.

In vitro experiments have now shown that the enzyme of tricarboxylic acid cycle (Kreb's cycle) as well as flavoprotein and cytochrome occur in mitochondria. Several enzymes are found both in mitochondria and cytoplasm. However, α (alpha) oxoglutarate dehydrogenase succinic dehydrogenase are found exclusively in mitochondria, indicating that a functional citric acid cycle is active only in mitochondria. Mitochondria are also respiratory centers of the cell.

It has also been observed that, when cells are removed from aerobic conditions and placed in anaerobic conditions (absence of O_2), the Kreb's cycle stops, mitochondria disappear and a remarkable ER network develop. These observation suggest that the glycolysis (conversion of carbohydrates into pyruvic acid) occurs outside mitochondria. Therefore in anaerobic conditions not only O_2 is absent, but mitochondria are also absent.

The substrate of Kreb's cycle *i.e.,* pyruvic acid is usually found in the perimitochondrial space, while enzymes are found in a series on inner membrane. The combination of O_2 and H_2 and the transfer of energy to ATP perhaps occur on the inner side of mitochondrial inner wall (M face) where the energy rich ATP molecules would be formed.

GOLGI APPARATUS

Golgi complex is also called dictyosome in plant cell. It is known after its discover Camillo Golgi in 1898. It is consists a stack of 20 or more flattened smooth sacs enclosed by membrane. The sacs are curved to assume a convex appearance called the cis-face on one side and a concave, known as trans-face, on the other side. The enzyme thiamine pyrophosphatase is present in the Golgi complex which serves as marker because it is rarely found in other organelles.

Functions

Golgi complex produces lysosomes and secretory granules. New synthesized proteins, lipids and carbohydrates in association with E.R. are transported to cis origin of the complex.

LYSOSOMES

The term lysosomes (hydrolytic particle) was coined by De Duve in 1955.

These are vesicles and contain hydrolytic enzymes which are associated with the digestion of macromolecules within the cell and autolysis of cell organelles. The various components of lysosome are :

Pre-lysosomes,

Primary lysosomes,

Autophagosomes,

Secondary lysosomes, and

Post-lysosomes.

Plastids

The term "Plastids" is derived from the Greek word "Plastikas" (= found or moulded) and was used in 1855 by A.F.W. Schimper to include the cell organelles which are primarily involved in the formation and storage of soluble and insoluble carbohydrates. A. Meyer in 1883, F. Schmitz in 1884 and A.F.W. Schimper in 1885 made detailed cytological studies of these cell organelles and showed that green plastids now known as chloroplasts could bot be formed from cytoplasm, but only from existing chloroplasts.

Depending on the presence or absence of pigment, Schimper classfied the plastids into colourless, "leucoplasts" (lenkos = white), coloured (colours other than green), "chromoplasts" (chroma = colour) and green "chromoplasts" (chloros = green).

The plastid system carrying the genetic information is collectively called "Plastidome" (Dangeard. 1920).

CHLOROPLASTS

Choloroplasts are discrete membrane bound structures found in eukaryotes for carrying out photosynthesis. Such discrete chloroplasts are absent in prokaryotes, where the photosynthetic apparatus consists of internal membranes associated with photosynthetic pigments.

Three dimensional view of chloroplast : A chloroplast is enclosed in two smooth membranes separated from one another by a distinct space known as the "periplastidial space" like the "perimito-chondrial space" in case of mitochondria. Under light microscope the internal structure of a chloroplast can be differentiated into "grana" where the light reaction of photosynthesis takes place and the "stroma", where the dark reaction is completed. While "grana" consists of the lamellar system "stroma" is non-membranous and should have multienzyme complexes associated with it.

Different views have been expressed concerning the relationship of grana lamellae and stroma lamellae. Steinmann and Sjostrand (1955) thought that stroma lamellae grow from those of grana. Hodge *et al* (1955) expressed that granum discs are locally swollen thylakoids. However, grana lamellae and stroma lamellae are similar so far as their origin is concerned.

The grana lamellae contain the light absorbing pigments. The inner surface of the two layers is granular in organization due to spheroids which are called "quantasomes". These quantasomes are the smalles units capable of carrying out the photochemical reaction and each of them contains about 200 chlorophyll molecules.

Grana lamellae and stroma lamellae also differ in thickness. Steinmann and Sjostrand (1955) found the stroma lamellae to be 3 nm and granum lamellae to be 6.5 nm in thickness. It is also known that these lamellae have the character of a unit membrane. Another main component of chloroplast is chlorophyll which can be found either as chlorophyll *a* and *b*, the latter having a aldehyde (– CHO) group in place of – CH_2 group of chlorophyll *a*. Chlorophyll formation takes place during the growth of the prolameller bodies and during the differentiation of the stacks of grana.

Functions

The most important function of chloroplasts is to carry out the process of photosynthesis. The light reaction and the dark reaction takes place at different sites in the chloroplast. While the phosphorylation and the Hill reaction will proceed only in the presence of the quantasomes containing chlorophyll, the H_2 transfer system is perhaps located in the stroma. It has found that the broken chloroplasts containing only grana thylakoids will carry out only the phosphorylation and the Hill reaction.

ENDOPLASMIC RETICULUM

In the cytoplasmic matrix, there is (a) vast net work of closed and open cavities in the form of membrane bound tubules, vesicles and ovoid sacs. This membranous organization travelling the matrix in sometimes called cytoplasmic vacuolar system, of which endoplasmic reticulum forms only a part. The name endoplasmic reticulum was used for the first time by K.R. Porter in 1948 to identify a fine-reticulum which observed in the endoplasm of the cells.

Ultrastructure

ER appear as double membrane with variable spaces. These strands form tubes and vesicles in the cytoplasm. Sometimes, these may be found chains of vesicles which are connected to one another by canalicules of large vesicles.

It is usually continuous system, connected on one side to the nuclear envelop and on the other side to the cell membrane. The ER consists of a double membrane would mean that there is a pair of unit membranes separated by a narrow lumen. The double membrane of ER on their external surface carry granular structures known as ribosomes. The ER rigions carrying ribosomes are, therefore, called as rough endoplasmic reticulum and those devoid of ribosomes are known as smooth ER.

(*i*) **Rough ER (granular) :** The rough ER is particularly well-developed in cell actively engaged in protein synthesis. Rough ER is particularly well developed in pancreatic and liver cells where secretory proteins are synthesized on the attached ribosomes and are translocated through cisternae to different sites in the cells.

(*ii*) **Smooth ER (agranular) :** Smooth ER forms a continuous system with rough ER, but has a different morphology. It consist of smooth membrane segments and found in regions rich in glycogen. Smooth ER is also related to peroxisomes (organelles containing peroxidase, catalase and other oxidases) and to the Golgi complex.

Chemical Composition : ER has a high lipid content. There is more lipid in relation to proteins in the smooth ER than in the rough ER. The latter also contains less sphingomyelin and cholesterol. The membrane proteins of ER have also been stiched by polyacrylamide gel electrophoresis. As many as 30 polypeptide bands.

Functions

There are several possible functions, which endoplasmic reticulum performs. These functions include mechanical support, exhange and translocation of substances, protein synthesis, and the synthesis of lipoprotein and glycogen.

(*i*) **Mechanical Support :** ER forms a network in cytoplasmic matrix and thus divides it into a number of chambers giving it the structure of a vacuolar system. In other words ER forms the skeleton of the cell.

(*ii*) **Exchange and Translocation :** ER also act as a kind of circulatory system for intracellular circulation of various substances. It may help translocation of substances from the cytoplasm to outside the cell and *vice versa.*

(*iii*) **Protein Synthesis :** Protien may be synthesized to be utilized within the cell or these may have to be exported outside the cell to the site of their utility. It is the latter kind of protein in whose synthesis, ER plays an important role.

(*iv*) **Synthesis of Liporprotein and Glycogen :** ER due to ribsomes, is engaged in synthesis of protein. On the other hand smooth ER is engaged in synthesis of lipids in collaboration with Golgi complex. The smooth ER is also known to be involved in the synthesis of glycogen.

NUCLEUS

It is most significant component of the cell which controls various activities of the cell and contain the genetic material DNA.

It was first of all discovered by Robert Brown in 1831.

Occurrence : The nucleus is found in all the eukaryotic cell of the plants and animals. However, certain eukaryotic cells such as the mature tubes or higher plants and mammalian erythrocytes contain no nucleus. Usually the nucleus remains located in the centre, but its position may change from time to time accroding to the metabolic states of the cell.

Number : Usually the cell contain single nucleus but the number of the nucleus may vary from cell to cell. According to the number of the nuclei following types of cell have been recognized.

(*i*) **Mononucleate Cells** : Most plant and animal cells contain single nucleus, such cells are knwon as mononucleate cells.

(*ii*) **Binucleate Cells** : The cells which contain two nucleus are knwon as binucleate cells. Such cells occur in certain protozoans such as *Paramecium* and cell of cartilage and liver.

(*iii*) **Polynucleate Cells** : The cell which contain many (from 2 to 100) nuclei are known as polynucleate cells.

Shape : The size of the nucleus normally remains related with the shape of the cell, but certain nuclei are almost irregular in shape. The spheroid, cuboid or polyhedral cell (Isodiameterical cells) contain the spheroid nuclear.

Size : The size of the nucleus of various cell is also variable. The size of the nucleus is directly proportional to that of the cytoplasm.

Ultrastructure : The nucleus is composed of following structures :

(*i*) The nuclear membrane or karyotheca

(*ii*) The number sap or nucleoplasm

(*iii*) The chromatin fibres

(*iv*) Nucleolus

(*i*) **Nuclear membrane :** If forms an envelope like structure around the nucleus contents and commonly known as the nuclear envelope. It separates nucleoplasm from the cytoplasm.

(*ii*) **Nuclearpores** : The nuclear membrane are not altogether continuous but at several places they are broken by the nuclear openings or pores. The number of the pores for a particular nucleus is variable and often depends on the species and the type of the cell.

The nuclear membrane performs various important function for the nucleus, such as in certain cells (oocyte) the nuclear membrane allow free exchange of ions between the nucleus and the cytoplasm.

The nuclear pores are the pathways for the exchange of the macromolecules, ribonucleus, protein granules and other particles. The permeability of the pore complex depends on the type and metabolic state of the cell.

(*iii*) **The Nuclear sap or Nucleoplasm:** The space between the nuclear envelope and the nucleolus is filled by a transparent, semi-solid, granular and slightly acidophilic ground substance or the matrix known as the nuclear sap or nucleoplasm or karyolymph.

It has a complex chemical composition. It is composed of mainly the nucleoproteins but it also contains other inorganic and organic substances *viz.*, nucleic acids, proteins, enzymes, etc.

(*a*) ***Nucleic acids :*** The most common nucleic acids of the nucleoplasm are the DNA and RNA.

(*b*) ***Proteins :*** The nucleoplasm contains many types of complex proteins. The nucleoproteins can be categorized into two types *i.e.* Basic and Active proteins.

(*c*) **Enzymes :** Nucleoplasm contains many enzymes which are necessary for the synthesis of DNA and RNA. The nucleoplasm also contains cofactors and coezymes such as ATP and acetyl Co A.

(*d*) ***Lipids :*** According to Stoneberg (1937) and Dounce (1955) the nucleoplasm contains small lipid contents.

(*e*) ***Minerals :*** The nucleoplasm also contains several inorganic compounds such as phosphorus, potassium, sodium, calcium, magnesium, *etc.*

(*f*) ***Chromatin fibres :*** The nucleoplasm contains many thread like coiled and much elongated structure. These fibres of the chromatin are twisted and uniformly distributed in the nucleoplasm. Two types of chromatin material have been recognized, *i.e.*, Heterochromatin and Euchromatin.

(*iv*) **Nucleolus :** It contain large spherical and acidophilic dense granule. It was discovered by Fentona.

The main function of nucleolus is the biogenesis of ribosomes. It stores all the proteins of ribosomes and also r-RNA which is transcribed by r-DNA of nucleolar organizer. The newly transcribed r-RNA remains in nucleolus for short time.

CHROMOSOMES

The chromosomes are the most significant biological components of the cell. They control most of the biological and genetical activities. They contains DNA as genetical material, which ultimately influence all the biological phenomena at molecular, physiological and morphological levels. They are the nuclear component of special organization individually and functionally. They are capable of self reproduction and play a vital role in heredity, mutation, variation and evolutionary development of the species.

W.Fleming (1874) first of all described the splitting of chromosomes and coined the term chromatin for stainable material of the nucleus. W. Roux (1883) suspected the involvement of the chromosomes in the machanism of inheritance. Benden and Bovery (1887) reported that number of chromosomes for each species was constant. The present name chromosome (Gr. Chrom = color, soma = body) was coined by W. Waldeyer (1888) to darkly stained bodies of nucleus.

Chromosome Number : The number of chromosomes is constant for particular species. Therefore, these are of great importance in the determination of phylogeny and taxonomy of the species. The nematodes shows the lowest number of chromosomes *e.g. Ascaris megalocephalus.*

Haploid and Diploid

The number of the chromosomes of the genetic cells such as sperm and ova is known as the genetic reduced or haploid sets of chromosomes. The haploid set of the chromosomes is also known as the genome. The somatic or body cells of most organisms contain two haploid sets or genomes and are knwon as the diploid cells. The diploid cells achieve the diploid set of the chromosomes by the union of the haploid male and female gametes in the sexual reproduction.

Morphology

Size : The size varies from species to species and relatively remains constant for a particular species. The length of the chromosomes may vary 0.2 to 5μ. The monocotyledonous plants contain large sized chromosomes then the dicotyledonous plants.

The plants in general have large size chromosomes in comparison to the animals. Further the chromosomes in cell are never alike in size, some may be excetionally large and other may be small. The largest chromosomes are lampbrush chromosomes of certain vertebrate oocytes and polytene chromosomes of certain dipteran insects.

Shape : The shape of the chromosomes is changeable from phase to phase in the continuous process of the cell growth and cell division. Each chromosomes contains a clear zone known as centromere or kinetocore along their length. The centromere divides the chromosomes into two parts, each part is called chromosome arm. The position of centromere vary from chromosome to chromosome and provides different shapes of the latter which are called as Telocentric, Acrocentric and Submetacentric.

Structure : According to classical cytology the chromosome are composed of the chromonema and the centromeres.

Chromonema : In less compact chromosomes, under the optical microscope, a coiled filament is seen in the chromosome. The coiled filament was called chromonema by Vejdovsky in 1912.

The chromonema may be composed of two, four or more fibres according to the species. Further the number of threads in the chromonema may depend on the different phases because at one phase the chromonema may contain one thread and at other phase it may contain three or four threads. The coils, of chromonema may be of two types *i.e.* Paranemic coils and Plectonemic coils.

Centromere : The centromere consists of small granules of spherules. The centromere of the chromosome of the *Trillium* has the diameter of 3μ and the spherules have the diameter of 0.2μ.

The chromosomes of most organisms contain only one centromere and are known as monocentric chromosomes. Certain chromosomes may have two or more centromeres and can be termed as dicentric and polycentric chromosomes.

Giant Chromosomes

Some cells at certain particular stages contain large nuclei with giant or large sized chromosomes. The giant chromosomes are the polytene and lampbrush chromosomes.

Polytene Chromosomes

It occurs in the tissue of salivary glands, gut, trachea, fat body cells and mepighian tubles of many insects of the order Diptera. It is first of all reported by E.G. Ballbiani in 1881 and the name polytene was suggested by Kollan due to the occurrence of many chromosome in them. The polytene chromosomes are larger in size in comparison to other somatic chromosomes.

Lampbrush Chromosomes

In diplotene stage of the meiosis the yolk rich oocytes of many vertebrates such as- fishes, amphibians, reptiles and birds contain exceptionally large sized chromosomes known as the lampbrush chromosomes. It was discovered by Ruckest in 1892.

The lampbrush chromosomes are much larger than the polytene chromosomes and the loops of these chromosomes are rich in RNA and proteins. The RNA appears to be m-RNA.

Chromosomal Variations

The chromosome of each species has a characteristic morphology and number. But sometimes due to certain accidents or irregularities at the time of cell division, crossing over or fertilization, some alteration in the morphology and number of chromosomes takes place. Mainly, two types of variations occurs.

(*i*) Variation in chromosome number

(*ii*) Variation in chromosome morphology

Euploidy : The term euploidy (Gr. Eu = even or true, ploid = unit) designates genomes containing whole sets of chromosomes. The euploids are those organisms which contain balanced set or sets of chromosomes in any number.

Aneuploidy : Variation in chromosome number may occur which do not involve whole sets of chromosome, but only parts of a set. The term aneuploidy (Gr Aneu = uneven, ploid-unit) is given to variations of this nature.

Table 1 : Structure and Functions of Cell Organelles

S.No	*Structure of Organelle*	*Functions*
1.	**Cell-wall** A rigid cell wall surrounding the cell, made up of cellulose, microfibrils running through a matrix of other complex polysaccharides.	Cell-wall provides rigidity, mechanical support and protection to tissues and organs and gives a definite shape to the cell. It is totally permeable and hence pathway for movement of water and mineral salt. It also helps in development of turgor and plays other specialised roles.
2.	**Plasma membrane or Cell membrane** It encloses the cytoplasm. Plasma membrane consists of lipid and protiens. The lipids found in membrane are of three kinds *i.e.*, phospholipids, glycolipids	Plasmamembrane protects the cell from external environment. It is differentially permeable barrier controlling exchange of water and minerals between the cells and

S.No	Structure of organelle	Functions
	and steroids. These three layer together are called as trilaminar.	its outer environment.
3.	**Chloroplast**	
	Large chloroplast containing chlorophyll pigment. It carrying out photosynthesis. It is surrounded by an envelope of two membranes and contains a gel like stroma through which runs a system of membrances that are stacked in places to form grana. Stroma also has ribosomes, lipid droplets and a circular DNA molecule.	It is the site for photosynthesis. The sunlight is trapped and converted to chemical energy in grana which houses light reactions. The products are then used in dark reactions housed in stroma to synthesise sugar and other substances from carbon dioxide.
4.	**Endoplasmic Reticulum**	
	It consists of three types of membrane enclosed elements *i.e.,* vesicles of 25 to 500 mm diameter, tubules of 50 to 100 mm diameter and 40 to 50 mm thick cisterns of variable length and width.	Rought E.R. provide the place for ribosome attachment which are the site of protein synthesis. Smooth E.R. is the place where most of the lipids and polysaccharides are synthesized besides this it provide route for intracellular transport and storage.
5.	**Mitochondria**	
	Mitochondria is a large organelle surrounded by two membranes, the inner being folded to form cristae. Each of two inner and outer membranes is 60 Å thick. The space between cristae into the inner chamber is called matrix.	Mitochondria is regarded as the power house of the cell as it is the site of aerobic respiration. The cristae are the site of electron transport and oxidative phosphorylation.
6.	**Golgi appartus**	
	It is also called Dictyosome in plant cell. A Gogi body consists of a stack of 20 or more flattened smooth sacs enclosed by membrane.	Processing in cisternae and transport in vesicles of many cells materials such as enzymes from ER. It is also involved in secretion and lysosome formation.
7.	**Ribosomes**	
	Very small cell organelles consisting of small sub-unit. They are roughly equal amount of protein and RNA. They are found in mitochondria and chloroplast in plants.	The main function of ribosomes is to carry out protein synthesis with the help of mRNA.

S.No	Structure of organelle	Functions
8.	**Lysosomes** Lysosomes are simple, spherical sac bounded by single membrane and containing hydrolytic enzymes, which are active at acidic pH.	Function concerned with intracellular digestion, break down of molecules, autophagy endocytosis and autolysis.
9.	**Microbodies (Peroxisomes and Glyoxisomes)** Spherical sacs bounded by single membrane which contents appear finely granular and may have crystalloid or filamentous deposits.	Functions concerned with oxidation reactions. The plants cells are the site of the glyoxylate cycle. It contains enzyme catalase that break down hydrogen peroxide.
10.	**Microtubules** Hollow cylindrical and unbranched, which is made up of globular protein subunit *i.e.,* known as tubulin.	Involved in spindle formation intracellular transport of vesicles, larger organelles. It also provide cytoskeletal support to cell to maintain its shape.
11.	**Microfilaments** Microfilaments is very fine protein filaments. It is made up of actin.	Microfilaments are involved in the endocytosis and exocytosis, contractility and motility of the cells.
12.	**Centrosome** It is mostly found in animals and a few plants. It is a cylindrical structure without limiting membrane. It consists of the two centrioles lying at right angles to each other. A centriole contains nine triplet fibres.	Centrosome is the major-microtubule centre of the cell. It take part in formation of basal bodies and mitotic spindle.
13.	**Flagellum/Cilium** The cell organelle is made 11 (9 + 2) fibrils. In which 9 fibirls are doublet and peripheral and two fibrils are single and central in positions.	It is the organelle which help in the locomotion, formation of water current and besides this it also help in elimination of solid particles.
14.	**Nucleus** It is the largest cell organelle and spherical in shape enclosed by envelope of two membranes that perforated and nuclear pores. It also contains a nucleolus. A network of chromatin fibres and a nucleolus are presnet in side suspended in granular matrix called nucleoplasm.	Chromatin fibres are extended chromosomes which are carrier of hereditary characters. Nuclear division is the basis of cell multiplication/reproduction. It manufactures ribosomes. Hence, it nucleus is the repository of genetic information and control all the activities of the cell.

S.No	Structure of organelle	Functions
15.	**Large Central Vacoule** A large fluid filled sac bounded by single membrane called tonoplast. The fluid contains the solution of various substances such as sugars minerals salts, pigments, enzyme and organic acids.	It serve as storage of various substances and waste products towards osmotic properties of the cells.

CELL DIVISION

It was first reported by Prevost and Dumas in 1924, when they studied the cleavage in fertilised egg of frog.

Rudolf Virchow (1855, 1859) reported that new cells arise by division of pre-existing one—*omnis cellulaecellula.* Strasburger (1873) found the new nuclei develop from pre-existing ones. The details were worked out by Strasburger (1875) and Flemming (1879). The term of *mistosis* was coined by Flemming (1882). Meiosis was studied by Sutton (1900) and to some extent by Strasburger (1888) and Winiwater (1900). The term meiosis was coined by Farmer and Moore (1705).

1. *Cell Cycle* : Cell cycle is a series of cyclic changes through which a cell passes during its growth and divisions. Time interval between two surccessive divisions is called *generation time.* Cell cycle has two parts : long non-dividing I-phase and short dividing M-phase.

   INTERPHASE (*I-phase*) : It is complex of changes that occur in newly fomed cell before it is able to divide. Interphase has three stages.

   (*i*) G_1-*Phase.* In this, first growth or post mitotic gap phase, the cell and its nucleus grow in size, RNA and protein (including histone) synthesis occurs.

   (*ii*) *S-Phase.* Chromosomes replicate. Therefore, it is called invisible stage of M-phase.

   (*iii*) G_2-*Phase.* It is the second growth or premitotic gap phase where macro-molecules including protein tubulin are synthesised for cell division. A new centriole pair is formed.

   M-Phase. it is the phase of cell division. Cell division consists of nuclear division of *karyokinesis* and protoplast division or *cytokinesis.* Cell division or M-phase is of three types-amitosis, mitosis, meiosis.

2. *Amitosis* : (Direct Division, Robert Remark, 1841). During amitosis, nucleus elongates, constricts in the middle divides directly into two daughter nuclei. This is followed by division of cytoplasm through constriction, e.g. cartilage cells, degenerate cells.

3. *Mitosis* : It occurs during formation of somatic cells hence it is also called somatic divison. Mitosis is equatorial division in which a parent cell divides into two identical daughter cells; each of which contains the same number and kind of chromosomes as are present in the parent cell. Mitosis occurs in two steps, karyokinesis & cytokinesis.

(A) Karyokinesis : It is the stage of nuclear division (indirect nuclear division) which is continuous but is divided into four stages for the sake of convenience—prophase, metaphase, anaphase and telophase.

(*a*) *Prophase* : In early prophase, the chromatin fibres condense to form elongated chromosomes. The nucleus appears as ball of wool. Centrosome has already divided. The daughter centrosome begin to move away from each other. In *mid prophase,* chromosome shorten and become distinct with each having two chromatids attached to narrow point called CENTROMERE. The centrosomes devlop astral rays and migrate farther. In *late prophase,* the centrosome reach the poles, form asters and begins to develop spindle fibres. Nucleolus degenerates and nuclear envelope starts breaking. In plant cells, centrosomes are absent, spindle fibres develop without them.

(*b*) *Metaphase* : A bipolar spindle is produced. It is anastral (without asters) in plants and *amphiaster* in animals. Spindle is observable with the help of polarising microscope. Spindle has three types of fibres (I) Continuous (pole to pole) (II) Discontinuous (come out of one pole) but do not reach the other pole, (III) Chromosome Fibre (Firbres that attach made of 4-20 microtubules. The middle part of spindle having the maximum diameter is called *equator.* Chromosomes move to the equatorial plane and form equatorial or *metaphasic plate* with their centrosomes attached to both the poles by chromosomal fibres. *Colchicine arrests cell division at metaphase stage. Metaphase is the best time to see chromosomes.*

(*c*) *Anaphase* : The centromere of each chromosome divides. This converts the two chromatids into daughter chromosomes each being attached to the spindle pole of its side by independent chromosomal fibre. The chromosomes move towards the spindle poles.

(*d*) *Telophase* : Chromosome again unfold, elongate forming chromatin fibres. Nucleolus, nucleoplasm and nuclear envelope appear form ER so that two daughter unclei are formed.

(B) Cytokinesis : It is the process of separation of the cytoplasm. In animal cells, there is constriction at the equator that finally results in the separation of the daughter cells. It is of two types.

(*a*) *Cleavage Cytokinesis* : The cell membrane constricts and develops a centripetal furrow or cleavage in the middle. The furrow deepens and divides the parent protoplast into two uninucleate protoplasts or cells.

(*b*) *Cell Plate Cytokinesis* : It occurs in plants vesicles having pectic compounds and other wall materials appear in the middle of persisting spindle called 'Phragmoplast.'

(*iv*) **Meiosis** : Meiosis is a special type of cell division present in germ cells of sexually reproducing organisms. Sexual reproduction occurs by way of sexual cells or gametes (eggs & sperms), which after fertilization constitute the Zygote. Meiosis consists of a single duplication divisions.

Meiosis is Divided into Division I & II

(A) Meiosis I : Meiosis I is the actual reduction division which is also called heterotypic division (the two chromatids of a chromosome often become different due to crossing over.)

(*a*) *Prophase I* : It is longest phase which is complex and divisible into five stages-leptotene, zygotene, pachytene, diplotene and diakinesis.

(b) *Metaphase I* : A bipolar fibrous spindle appears in the area of nucleus. It has asters at the two poles in animal cells (amphiaster) while the same are absent in plant cells (anastral). The chromosome pairs shift to the equator of spindle forming two or double metaphasic plate with the help of their centromeres. Each chromosome gets attached to spindle pole of its side by a chromosome fibre.

(c) *Anaphase I* : Chiasmata disappear completely and the homologous chromosome separate. The process is called *disjunction*. The separated chromosomes (univalents) show divergent chromatids and are called *dyads*. They move towards the spindle poles and ultimately form two groups of haploid chromosomes.

(d) *Telophase I* : Chromosomes elongate. Nucleolus, nucleoplasm and nuclear envelope appear over each chromosome group froming nuclei.

(B) Meiosis II : It is homotypic or equational division which is meant for maintaining the haploid number and separating the two chromatids of a chromosome which have become different due to crossing over. DNA replication is absent.

(a) *Prophase II* : The chromatin fibres shorten to form chromosomes. Nucleolus and nuclear envelop break down. Spindle is formed in the area of each nucleus. Both telophase I and prophase II are omitted in some organisms where anaphase I directly leads to metaphase II; e.g. Trillium.

(b) *Metaphase II* : Chromosomes come to lie at the equator of the spindle forming a single metaphasic plate. The centromere of each chromosome gets attached by both its surfaces to the spindle poles of their sides by distinct chromosome fibres.

(c) *Anaphase II* : Centromere of each chromosome divides into two. This separates the two chromatids of a chromosome into two independent daughter chromosomes. Each daughter chromosome is attached to spindle pole of its side by a chromosome fibre. Chromosomes move towards the spindle poles forming two groups. Since there were two spindle, a total of four groups are formed.

(d) *Telophase II* : The four groups of chromosomes organise themselves into four haploid nuclei.

(C) **Cytokinesis :** Cytokinesis may occur after each division (successive type) or simultaneously at the end of meiosis.

Comparision between Meiosis and Mitosis:

(i) Mitosis occurs in all somatic cells while meiosis is limited to germinal cells only.

(ii) In mitosis, one replication cycle of DNA is followed by one division, resulting in diploid cells. In Meiosis, one replication of DNA is followed by two divisions, resulting in haploid cells.

(iii) In mitosis DNA replication occurs in the 'S' phase, which is followed by G_2. In meiosis there is a premeiotic DNA synthesis, which is very long and followed immediately by meiosis.

(iv) In mitosis, each chromosome behaves independently, while in meiosis there is pairing of homologous chromosomes.

(v) Mitosis last 1 to 2 hours and meiosis losts longer; in the male it may last 24 days and in the female, several years.

(vi) In mitosis, the genetic material remains constant, and in meiosis there is genetic variability.

Questions From Previous Year's Papers

Q. 1. Answer the following in about 150 words each :

(a) Give an illustrated account of ultrastructure and function of chloroplast.

(b) Describe briefly the external morphology of eukaryotic chromosome. How do they behave during zygotene and diplotene stages of meiosis?

Q. 2. Answer the following in about 150 words each :

(a) What are cell organelles? Describe the structure and functions of Mitochondria and Golgi bodies.

(b) What are ergastic substances? Write a note on them.

(c) How ribosomes differ from microsomes?

Q. 3. Write short notes on the following in about 150 words.

(a) Package of practices for wheat cultivation.

(b) Mitosis.

Q. 4. Distinguish between the following in about 150 words each :

(a) Grafting and layering.

(b) RNA and DNA of a plant cell.

Q. 5. Answer the following in about 150 words each :

(a) Draw the structure of typical mitochondria and write its role in plant cell.

(b) What are Plastids? Describe different types of Plastids and their functions.

2. GENETICS AND MUTATIONS

GENETICS

Genetics is a branch of biology dealing with the mechanism of transmission of hereditary characters from generation to generation. The role of nucleus in heredity was established by Hammerling and Boveri. F. Griffith (1928) disovered the role of DNA in genetics.

NUCLEIC ACIDS

Nucleic Acids Structure : Nucleic acids are formed of C, H, O, N and P. Nucleic acids were first discovered by Miescher (1868-69) as *nuclein* and named *nucleic acid by Altman* (1889). Nucleic acids are of two types, DNA and RNA.

Nucleic acids are genetic material mainly located in chromosomes of cell nucleus. Besides, they are also present in ribosomes, mitochondria, plastids and chloroplasts of living organisms. In chromosomes, nucleic acids are associated with basic proteins such as protamins and histones in the form of nucleoproteins.

Chemically, nucleic acids are high molecular weight, polymeric macro molecules composed of thousands of nucleotide units linked with each other through $3' \rightarrow 5'$ phosphodiester bonds.

Classififcation

(*i*) **Deoxy-ribonucleic acids (DNA):** Contain deoxy-ribose and thymine (T) in addition to adenine (A), guanine (G) and Cytosine (C).

(*ii*) **Ribonucleic acids (RNA):** Contain ribose and uracil in addition to A, G and C. They are further divided in to three sub classes on the basis of their functions :

(*a*) **Ribosomal ribonucleic acids (r-RNA):**

(Mol. Wt. 1.3 × 106; 125 to 4000 nucleotide units) 80%.

(*b*) **Messenger ribonucleic acids (m-RNA):**

(Mol. Wt. 4 × 105; 130 to 5000 nucleotide units), 5%.

(c) **Transfer ribonucleic acids (t-RNA):**

(Mol. Wt. 2.5 × 104; 70 to 87 nucleotide units) 15%.

Hydrolysis : Nucleic acids are hydrolyzed by enzyme nuclease to give several nucleotides which on further hydrolysis by the same enzyme ultimately give:

(*a*) Pentose sugars

(*b*) Nitrogen bases and

(*c*) Phosphoric acid

(*a*) Pentose sugars

(1) D-ribose (in RNA)

(2) D-2-deoxy ribose (in DNA)

In nucleic acid strucutre both sugars are present in β-D furanose form.

(*b*) Nitrogen bases :

(1) Purine bases : adenine and guanine

(2) Pyrimidine bases : cytosine, uracil and thymine

(*c*) Phosphoric acid (H_3PO_4): It is present in the form of mono and di-phosphate in nucleic acids and as mono–, di-and triphophate groups in nucleotides.

Nucleosides

- Nucleosides are condensation products of pentose sugar and nitrogen base. Deoxy-ribose containing nucleosides are known as deoxy-ribonucleosides while ribose containing products are known as ribonucleosides.
- Purine bases are linked through its N-9 to C-1' of sugar by β-N-glycosidic bond while pyrimidine bases are attached through their N-3 to C-1' of sugars.
- Nucleosides are named on the basis of N-bases present in them such as adenosine, guanosine, uridine, cytidine and thymidine are the examples of ribonucleosides. In the case of deoxy-nucleosides, the term deoxy' is prefixed to these names.

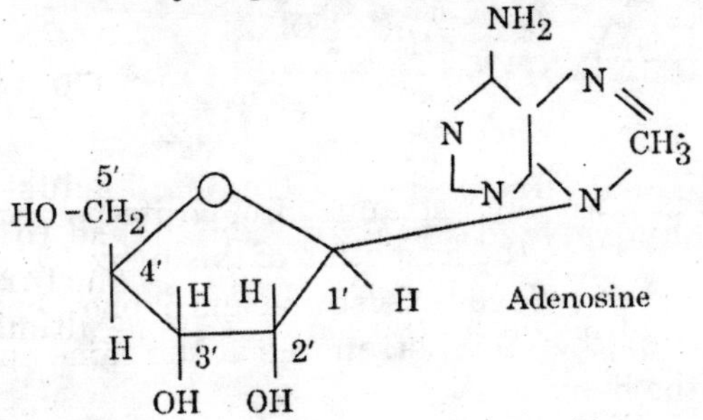

Adenosine

Nucleotides :

- Nucleotides are phosphate esters of nucleosides. Thus, they are made up of N-base, pentose sugar and phosphoric acid which are building blocks of nucleic acids.
- Like nucleosides, nucleotides also form two series *i.e.,* ribonucleotides and deoxy-ribonucleotides.
- Since ribose has three - OH groups (at 2', 3' and 5' positions) and deoxy-ribose has two -OH groups (at 3' and 5'-positions) available for esterification with phosphoric acid 2' 3' and 5'-mono phosphates of ribonucleosides and 3' and 5'-monophosphates of deoxy-ribo nucleotides are known to exist in biological systems. However, 5'-monoposphates or ribo-& deoxy-ribonucleosides are of more significance because they form monomeric units of nucleic acid structure.
- In addition, the existence of mono phosphate, diphosphate and triphosphate groupings at the 5'-position of adenosine to form a series of AMP, ADP and ATP is well known because of their important role in the intermediary metabolism in the conservation and utilization of the energy during oxidation of foodstuffs.
- Nucleotides are named as a phosphate or as an acid of corresponding nucleosides as given below:

Nucleoside	Nucleotide named as phosphate	Nucleotide named as an acid
Adenosine	Adenosine-5'-monophosphate	5'-Adenylic acid
Guanosine	Guanosine-5'-monophosphate	5'-Guanylic acid
Uridine	Uridine-5'-monophosphate	5'-Uridylic acid
Cytidine	Cytidine-5'-monophosphate	5'-Cytidylic acid
Thymidine	Thymidine-5'-monophosphate	5'-Thymidylic acid

- In the case of deoxy-ribonucleotides, the term, 'deoxy' is prefixed to these names.

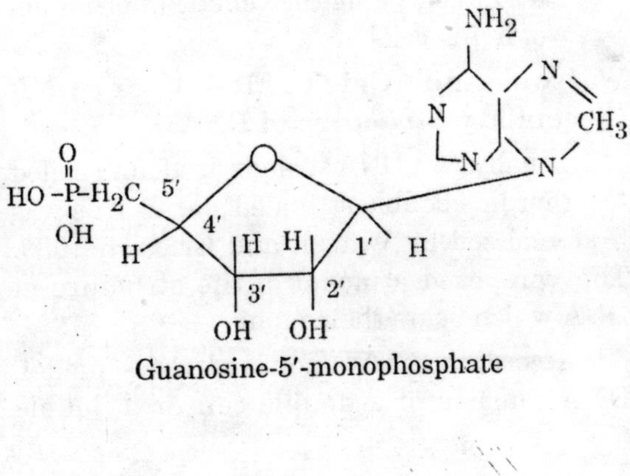

Guanosine-5'-monophosphate

Primary Structure of Nucleic Acids

- Nucleic acids are high molecular weight polymers of nucleotides and are often termed as polynucleotides. The polynucleotides are composed of many 5′-monophosphate nucleotides linked together by phosphodiester bonds.
- Since the diester bond involves 3′ and 5′-positions of the pentose unit in adjacent nucleotides, it is designated as 3′ → 5′ phosphodiester bond.
- The polynucleotide chain is thus formed by alternate pentose and phosphate groups. The various bases are free to project from the chain.

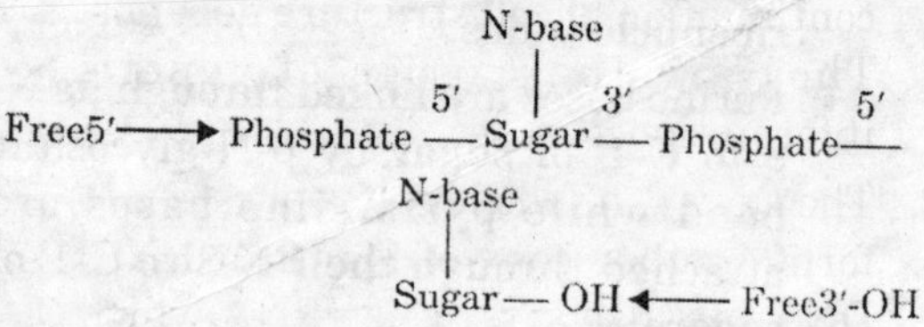

- By inclusion of all the building blocks, the structure of nucleic acid can be shown as :

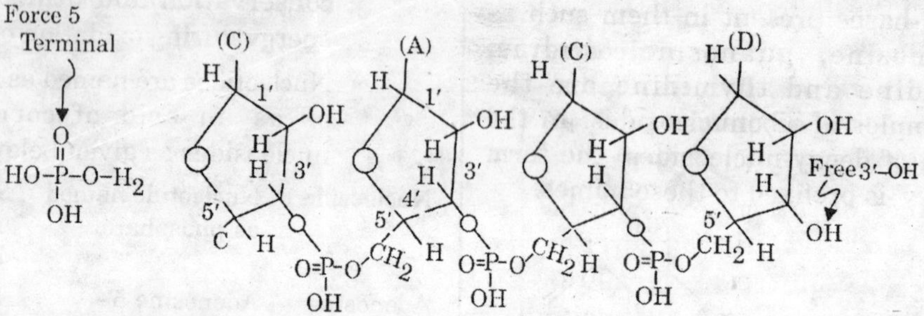

- From left to right, the structure starts with 5′-terminus (with a free phosphate group) and terminates at 3′-OH end.
- AT pH 7, the phosphate groups get ionized (pKa6) and, therefore, the nucleic acids are polyanioninc in nature.
- The sequential arrangement of N-bases in nucleotides of nucleic acids is of prime significance and determines the characteristics of a particular nucleic acid in encoding the genetic information of living cells.

Watson and Crick Model of DNA (Secondary Structure of DNA)

Usually, two DNA strands are found coiled together in a double stranded spiral. This was first realized by Watson and Crick in 1953. They proposed a model of the structure of DNA which bears their name.

According the Watson and Crick model, DNA consists of a double coil or a double helix. Two DNA strands of opposite polarity take part in the formation of this helix. Thus, 3′-OH end of one DNA strand and 5′-phosphate end of other DNA strand lie at the same end of the helix.

The two strands are held together by hydrogen bonds between purine and pyrimidine bases. The bases project from the back-bone of the helix towards inside. Hence, there is an opportunity of H-bonds to be formed between the bases of both strands. This phenomenon is known as base - pairing and follows a strict rule known as base pairing rule.

Cytosine of one strand always pairs with guanine of the other and thymine of one strand always pairs with an adenine of the other. In this process, 2H - bonds are formed in A = T and 3H-bonds are formed in G°C base pairs.

As a result of base pairing rule, the base

sequence of the two strands of DNA are complementary to each other.

Functions of Nucleic Acids

The main functions of nucleic acids are :-

1. Storage, transmission and use of genetic information up on which continuation of cell structure depends. They are the carries of genetic information.
2. The DNA can induce self replication to form another copy of identical DNA. DNA can also synthesize RNA which under take the synthesis of specific protein on the direction of DNA.
3. Nucleic acids are master molecules and directors of all biochemical reactions in living systems.

CHROMOSOME STRUCTURE

The importance of chromosomes in the genetic make-up of an organism can never be overemphasized. Generally speaking, all the members of a species have a typcial caryogram. Not only the number of chromosomes per cell but even the type, size and form of chromosomes are similar throughout the species. Any deviation, in the form of absence of a chromosome, or presence of an additional chromosome or the presence of an additional set or sets of chromosomes, is reflected in the physical or physiological make-up of the individual. Among other things, it is this fact which led to the postulation of the chromosome theory of heredity. This threw open the floodgates of the modern science of molecular biology, which in turn led to genetic engineering, biotechnology, all of which hold out a great promise for the future.

Many lower plants have in the nuclei of their body cells, the same number of chromosomes as the gametes: these are haploid. On the other hand, in the vascular plants, the number of chromosomes present in the nuclei of their body cells, is the same as in zygote: these are diploid. So often, speciation occurs by more than a double multiplication of the haploid number of chromosmes : they are polyploids – tetraploids, hexdaploids, octaploids and so on. The importance of chromosomes can be guaged from the following chromosomes cycle observed in all sexually reproducing organisms.

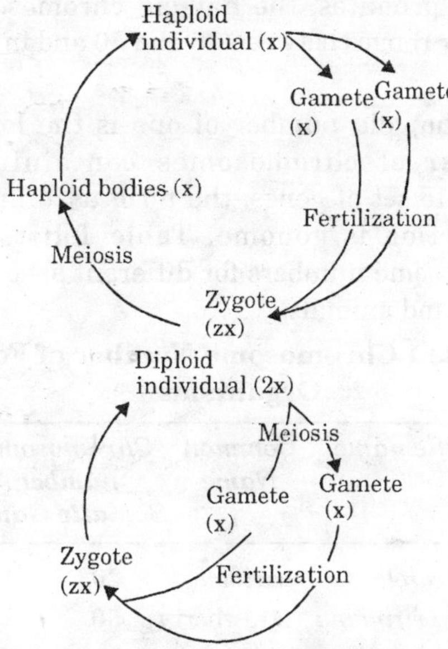

where X is haploid and 2X is diploid.

Fig. 1 Cromosome cycle.

Number

As already pointed out, the chromosomes number is constant for a species. In animals, the lowest number of chromosomes (2) is found in Ascaris ***Megacephala univalens*** and in plants, in a member of Compositae, ***Haplopappus gracilis,*** with a haploid number of 1. On the other hand, there may be several hundred chromosomes in a diploid cell. For example, in the Phylum Protozoa, the Aggregata have over 300 chromosomes and the Aulacantha, which include Radiolaria the diploid number is as high as 1600. In some Pteridophytes (of the plant kingdom) the diploid number is more than 1200. In Ophioglossum, a fern, the diploid number is 1262.

In angiosperms, the most frequent number of chromosomes is 12 and members of this group have, on the average, a haploid number of 8 to 16. Similarly, there is a definite range of chromosome numbers in fungi, the haploid number most often falling between 3 and 8. Similarly, there is a definite range of chromosome numbers in fungi, the haploid number most often falling between 3 and 8. In the primates, the haploid chromosomes number ranges between 16 and 30 and in man it is 23.

A haploid number of one is the lowest number of chromosomes containing a complete set of genes: the term used in this connection is genome. Table 1 lists out chromosome numbers for different species of plants and animals.

Table 1 Chromosome Number of Few Organisms

Scientific name	*Common Name*	*Chromosome number*	
		Somatic	*Gametic*
Daucus carota	carrot	20	10
Fragaria viriniana	strawberry	56	28
Haplopappus gracilis		4	2
Haplopappus ravenii		8	4
Hordeum vulgare	barley	14	7
Lycopersicon esculentum	tomato	24	12
Neurospora crassa	bread mold	14	7
Nicotiana tobacum	tobacco	48	24
Oryza sativa	rice	24	12
Pennisetum americana	pearl millet	14	7
Phaseolus vulgaris	rajma, kidney bean	22	11
Piper nigrum	pepper	128	64
Pisum sativum	pear	14	7
Secale cereale	rye	14	7
Solanum tuberosum	potato	48	24
Sorghum bicolor	jowar, sorghum	20	10
Spinacea oleracea	spinach	12	6
Trillium grandiflorum	wake-robin	10	5
Triticum monococcum	diploid wheat	14	7
Triticum durum	durum wheat	28	14
Triticum asestivum	bread wheat	42	21
Vicia faba	faba bean	12	6
Zea mays	maize	20	10
Apis mellifera	honey bee	32	16
Ascaris megalocephala	round worm	2	1
Bombyx mori	silk worm	56	28
Bufo viridis	toad	22	11
Bos taurus	cattle(cow)	60	30
Canis familiaris	dog	78	39
Columbia livia	pigeon	80	40
Drosophilia melanogaster	fruit fly	8	4
Equus asinus	donkey	62	31
Equus caballus	horse	64	32
Felis domesticus	cat	38	19
Gallus gallus domesticus	chicken	78	39
Homo sapiens	man	46	23
Macaca mulatta	rhesus monkey	48	24
Musca domestica	house fly	12	6
Rattus norvegicus	rat	42	21

Morphology

On the average, chromosomes range in length from 0.5 to 30μ and from 0.2 to 3μ in diameter. Major exceptions are found in insects and other organisms where giant chromosomes, reaching a length of 300 μ and a breadth of 10 μ occur. However, these giant chromosomes show out only in a premetaphase stage.

The smallest chromosomes is approximately 1/80,000 the size of the largest found among living organisms. Generally speaking, plants have larger chromosomes than animals. Trillium sps. have chromosomes reaching a length of 32 μ at metaphase. Plants with many chromosomes have smaller chromosomes than plants with few, through there are a few exceptions. In a single set, the largest chromosome could be 50 times larger than the smallest. But there are many plants, which have all the chromosomes of about the same length. This aspect of chromosomes study has an evolutionary significance and is not germane to our present purposes.

Fig. 2 Structure of Chromosome (Diagrammatic)

A metaphase chromosme is the most suitable material for a study of the structure. During metaphase, the chromosome shows maximum coiling and therefore looks shorter and thicker than at any other time. The chromosomes appears to be made up of two chromatids, which are 'held together' at a point along their lengths, in a region called kinetochore. The kinetochore appears as a constriction in the chromosome: it is the primary constriction. During metaphase, it stains lighter than most other portions of the chromosome, very possibly, this is due to the fact that the regions adjacent to kinetochore are heterochromatic. The kinetochore can also be identified by the fact of the spindle fibres attaching themselves to it during cell division. Indeed, its main portion during cell division lies in its role in the movement of chromosomes. Of course, there is a view that chromosome movement is autonomous, the kinetochore simply providing the force for that movement.

Levan et al suggested a nomenclature for describing chromosomes according to the position of the kinetochore:

(*a*) Metacentric, when the kinetochore is at or near the midpoint of the chromosome, *i.e.,* median, so that the arm ratio is 1:1 or nearly so;

(*b*) Sub-metacentric, when the kinetochore is to either side of the midpoint, *i.e.,* submedian;

(*c*) Acrocentric, when the kinetochore is located close to the end of chromosome, *i.e.,* subterminal and

(*d*) Telocentric, when the kinetochore is located at the end of a chromosome, *i.e.,* terminal.

Position of kinetochore	Types of chromosome
Median	Metacentric
Submedian	Sub-metacentric
Subterminal	Acrocentric
Terminal	Telocentric

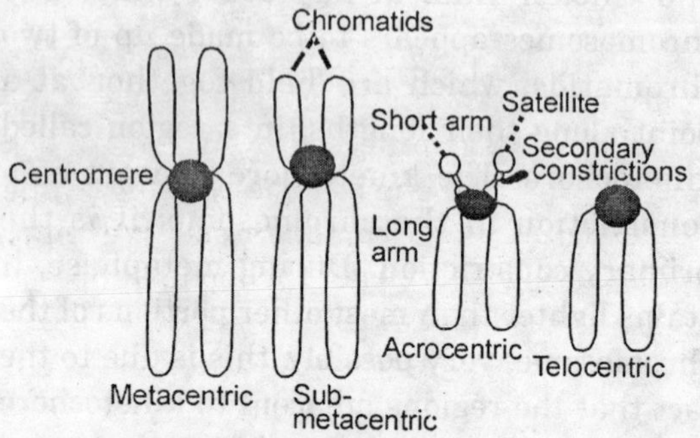

Fig. 3. Chromosomes are classified according to the position of the centromere.

The location of the kinetochore is fixed throughout the lifetime of the chromosome and provides a basis for the identifications of a particular chromosome.

Telocentric chromosomes are sometimes unstable. Occasionally, a telocentric chromosome can get one of its arms swing around the kinetochore, producing an isochromosome: when this happens, the isochromosomes will come to have two genetically idential chromosomes. Normally, the kinetochore of a metacentric chromosome divides in a place parallel to the axis of the chromosomes. Sometimes, however, a misdivision occurs, *i.e.*, the division may take place at right angles to the axis of the chromosome and this will result in two telocentric chromosomes.

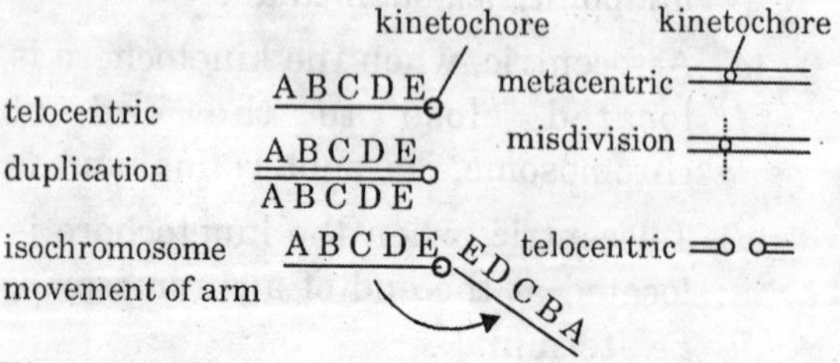

Fig. 4. (a) Formation of an isochromosome. (b) Origin of telocentric chromosmes by misdivision

Secondary Constrictions

A secondary constriction in the chromosome is a constriction other than the kinetochore. These are visible under the light microscope. Often it is associated with the nucleolus during interphase and may take part in the reorgnization of the nucleolus at the end of cell division. It is therefore, also called nucleolus-organising region. It appears as a heterochromatic region (light staining) with an additional segment of the chromosome extending beyond it. This extension is called the satellite body and varies in size depending upon the position of the secondary constriction. Ordinarily, at least one chromosome in every haploid set has a secondary constriction and satellite. Rarely, a single chromosome has two satellites. If the secondary constriction is terminal or subterminal, it is always found in the same chromosome or chromosomes and serves as a diagnostic character of the particular genome (haploid set).

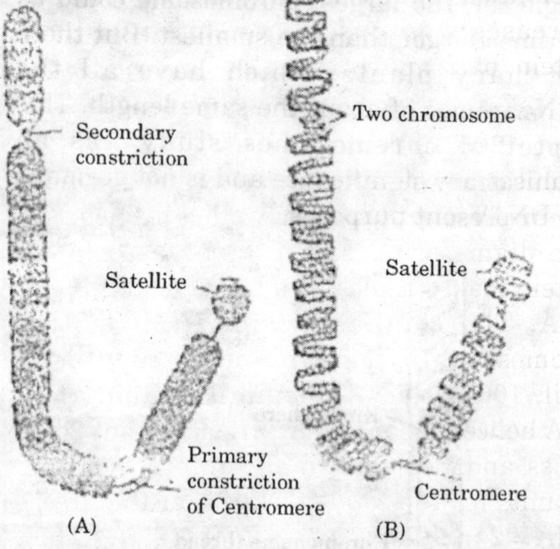

Fig. 5. Diagram of metacentric chromosome. (A) External structure; (B) Internal structure.

Fine Structure of Chromosome

There are two models proposed for explaining chromosomal fine structure. One view is that it is multistranded body. The other view is that it is an enormously long, but highly coiled, arrangement of nucleoprotein fibrils. Let us go on to consider these two viewpoints and their validity.

In Tradescantia, for example, is a chromonema representing a quarter chromatid. So one may say that four chromonemata go to form a chromatid and eight chromosomes. The lymphocyte chromosomes of humans, examined at metaphase suggest that 16 strands, each a double helix of DNA and its associated protein. make up a chromatid. Thus, four such strands comprise a quarter chromatid with with a diameter of 2000 Å. Further, at each level of organisation, there is coiling. Specific arrangement of protein and the presence of divalent cations such as Ca^{++} and Mg^{++} seem to play a part at the lower-levels of coiling. That is, DNA helices and protein are held together by cations while the DNA helices depend upon the protein and its binding to DNA. This interpretation is supported by the observation that the length of the DNA fibrils decreases when associated with histone protein, particularly the one rich in arginine.

Now, the basic super coiled chromatin is 100 to 200 Å thick. Let us see how this organisation could have come into existence. The DNA molecule consists of double helix 20 Å in diameter. Addition of the associated protein makes the basic molecular unit 35 to 40 Å. The smallest visible unit of the chromosome (by electron microscopy) is a fibril, 100 Å thick. This fibril contains two DNA helices separated by a space about 25 Å across and the associated protein. All this accounts for the total thickness of the fibril. (DNA = 2 × 20 Å = 40 Å --- Total 105 Å). This is the basic cytological unit, which can be used as a point of reference. From this macromolecular level, we reach up to the quarter chromatid, consisting of four 100 Å fibrils, so that it is 400 Å thick made up of eight double helices of DNA and the associated proteins. Two quarter chromatids make up the half chromatid, containing about 16 double helices of DNA. A chromatid contains two half chromatids, bringing the total number of helices in chromatid to 32, bringing the diameter to 3,200 Å. The thickness varies cell to cell and from organism to organism. All this is consistent with the model of DNA as proposed by Watson, Crick and Wilkins, and the scheme relating to the replication of chromosomes. We may summarise all this as per the model proposed by E.S.Osgood and other.

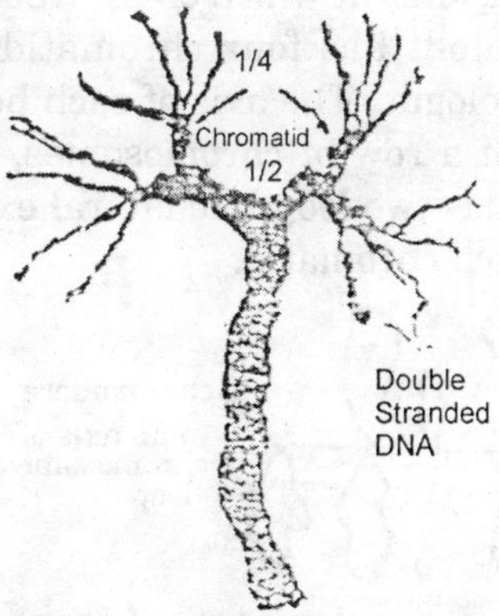

Fig. 6 Model of a metaphase chromosome based on a multistranded organization.

Lampbrush Chromosomes

Lampbrush chromosomes were first observed by Flemming in 1882 and latter in 1892 Ruckert described it in detail in the oocytes of shark. They have been given this name because they looked like brushes used in these days to clean the chimneys of oil lamps. H.G.Gallan came out with an account in their functional terms.

Lampbrush chromosomes occur at the diplotene stage of the meiotic prophase in oocytes of all animals, in spermatocytes of several species and in giant nucleus of the unicellular alga, *Acetabularia*. These have many fine lateral projections, giving them a 'hairy' appearance. They are best seen in the oocytes of Salamander because they have a very high DNA content and therefore very large chromosomes. In some newts, the total length of a lampbrush chromosome set is 5900 μm, about 3 times longer than the polytene chromosomes of Drosophila. Species with lower DNA-content have small lampbrushes and so, it is not quite correct to classify them under giant chromosomes.

Lampbrush chromosomes are found in the meiotic prophase. So, they are always present in the form of bivalents, with the maternal and paternal chromosomes held together by chiasmata, sites at which cross-over occurred. Each bivalent has four chromatids, two in each homologue. The axis of each homologue consists of a row of chromosomes, each one of which has two loop-like lateral extensions, one for each chromatid.

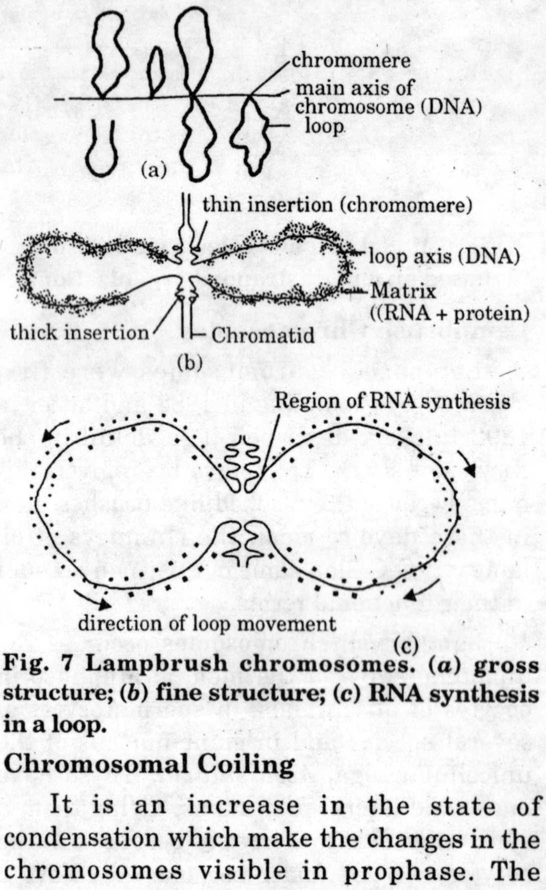

Fig. 7 Lampbrush chromosomes. (*a*) gross structure; (*b*) fine structure; (*c*) RNA synthesis in a loop.

Chromosomal Coiling

It is an increase in the state of condensation which make the changes in the chromosomes visible in prophase. The chromosome that has duplicated itself, now consists of two chromatids. Each of these undergoes a regular cycle of coiling. In fact, condensation is the result of coiling of each chromatid as well as coiling of the two chromatids about each other. There are two levels of coiling: large somatic coils and small minor coils. The somatic coils are small at first. As prophase progresses, they decrease in number but increase in diameter, rendering the chromosome thicker. In the early stages of prophase, the chromatids of each chromosome are coiled about each other; this is called relational coiling. In most cells, they are so closely twisted, that they can not be easily separated.This type of coiling is described as plectonemic. In the meiotic prophase, the coiling is paranemic, and the chromatids are easily separated laterally.

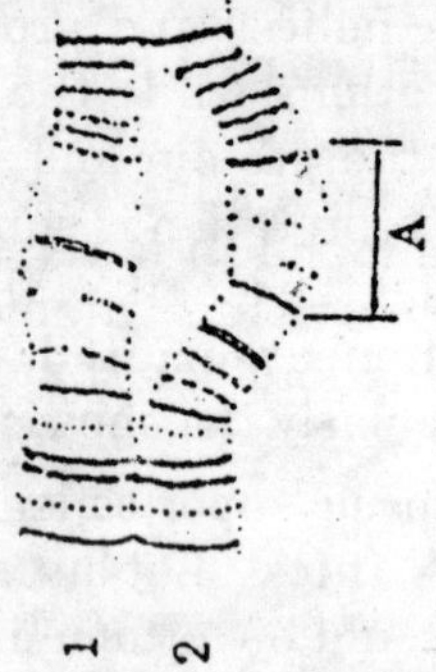

Fig. 8 Levels of chromatid coiling during prophase.

CHROMOSOMAL ABERRATIONS

The term chromosomal aberration, as such is better applied to indicate a gross change in the chromosomal organisation, though some authors are inclined to include mutations and polyploidy. We'll confine ourselves to a consideration of gross changes in the chromosomal organisation, which also result in a changed phenotypic expression.

Chromosomal aberrations are found in a variety of plants and animals. They may be considered under the following headings: Spontaneous and Induced.

Spontaneous Aberrations

Naturally occurring rearrangements of chromosomes are spontaneous aberrations. No definite cause could be attributed to them, though a variety of them have been mentioned: Cosmic radiations, nutritional insufficiencies, environmental changes, such as sudden temperature changes. X-ray irradiated cells sometimes suffer a break in the chromosome and the breaks get bridged again by fusion in the course of cell cycle. Such a bridge-breakage-fusion cycle had been observed in the chromosome 9 of corn.

The four principal, types of spontaneous, aberrations are deficiencies, duplications, translocations and inversions. Most of them involve one or more breaks in the chromosome.

Spontaneous aberrations are infrequent and a majority of organisms, rare. Yet, they played an important part in the evolution of some species, and occur regulary in their population. In most plants and animals, aberrations are found in fewer than 10% of the cells in a given tissue. Often age plays an important role: the older the organism or tissue, the greater is the likelihood of the occurrence of aberrations. Thus in the seedlings that germinated from very old seeds, more of such aberrations are found. Temperature, availability of oxygen and the metabolic state of the cell are the other factors which play a part in the appearance of chromosomal aberrations.

Deficiencies

The loss of a part of a chromosome results in deficiency. There are two types of deficiencies: **terminal** and **interstitial**. A terminal ueficiency is produced by a single break near the end of the chromosome, resulting in the appearance of a small acentric fragment. The interstitial deficiency, on the other hand, is produced by two breaks in an acentric region of chromosome and this also produces an acentric fragment. Such a loss naturally entails loss of genes and this is reflected in the phenotype. The fragment is lost because it lacks a kinetochore and therefore, unstable. It may move to one of the poles during cell division but essentially disintegrates. If by any chance, such a fragment gets to be included in a daughter nucleus, it is lost from the cell in a later division. Often these are recognised as rounded bodies, called micronuclei.

The deficiency may vary in size it may be minute or a major portion of a chromosome. A major loss results in a genetic effect that is often injurious to the organism. The effect may fall far short of death and in such cases, a servere metabolic disorder passed on through generations may be the consequence. But often, the deficiency, may have minimal consequences and indeed, some organisms may even survive the loss of a whole chromosome, without much damage. It can also happen that, of a homologous pair one chromosome can be lost and then a heterozygous deficiency results: this might serve as a recessive mutations. In the polytene chromosomes of Diptera, heterozygous deficiencies are readily identifiabale, because there is an observable alternation in the pattern of the bands, with one or more bands missing from the deficient chromosome. If both the members of a homologous pair are lost, the cell dies: naturally, a cytological observation of such a deficiency is not possible.

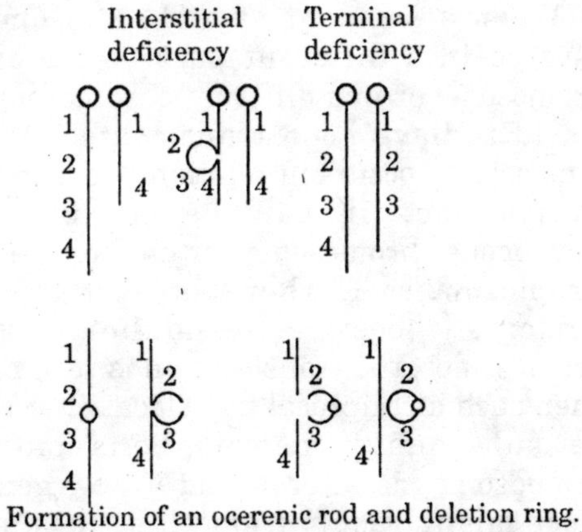

Fig. 9 Illustrating the origin of various types of deficiencies.

Duplications

One type of duplication results from the addition of a segment of a chromosome to a chromosome. Segments differ in size and so, have different genetic constitutions. A second type of duplication arises as a result of the addition of a small centric piece of chromosome to a genome. In a polytene chromosone, duplications can be detected cytologically as an extra band or bands .

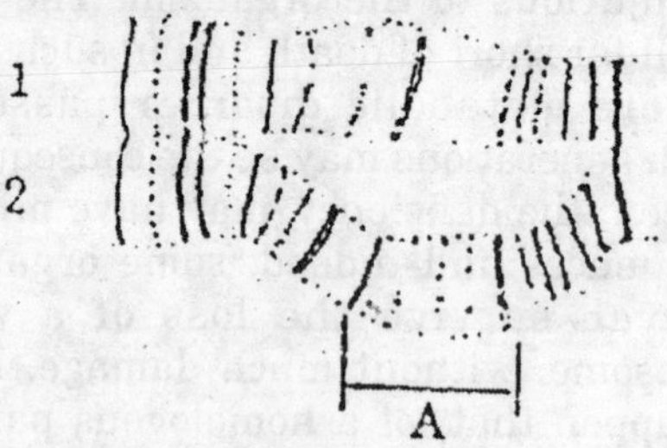

Fig. 10. Heterozygous deficiency, shown by the pairing of homologous chromosomes in a dipteran salivary gland cell. Note the differences in the patterns of bands: segment A is absent from homologue 1 and loop occurs in homologue 2.

Three basic types of segment Duplications are recognised. They are: (1) Tandem duplication (2) Reverse tandem duplication and (3) Displaced duplication.

Translocations

When a segment of a chromosome is inserted in a different part of the same chromosome or in a different chromosome, it is said to have been translocated. When translocation occurs in relation to a different chromosome, it can be as between homologous chromosomes or nonhomologous chromosomes. If there is exchange of segments between nonhomologous chromosomes, the translocation is reciprocal. When such a reciprocal translocation occurs, the subsequent meiotic behaviour of chromosomes is altered and a new genetic effect might result from this. In simple translocation, a small terminal segment of the chromosome is added to the end of a chromosome, homologous or nonhomologous. But this kind of translocation is rather rare becauae of the inability of a normal chromosome end to fuse with any other chromosomes end. Shift is the third type of translocation. It involves the insertion of an interstitial piece of a chromosome into a different portion of the same chromosome or into the interstitial portion of a nonhomologous chromosome. Shift translocation requires a minimum of three breaks in the chromosomes. Reciprocal and shift translocations are the most common types of translocations.

ABC ABC DEF (*a*)   ABC CBA DEF (*b*)

A B C D E F
LMN ABC OPQR
(*c*)

Fig. 11. Basic types of duplications : (*a*) tandem;(*b*)reverse tandem; (*c*) displaced. A segment of a chromsome is represented by letters for the genes it carries.

A B CD E → A C D B E
↑ ↑ ↑
(*a*)

A B CD E
↑ ↑
→ F G B H I
F G H I
↑
(*b*)

Fig. 12. Shift translocation: (*a*) shift within a chromosome; (*b*) shift into a non-homologous chromosome. Vertical arrows indicate breaks.

Inversions

Inversions are the most complex type of chromosomal aberration. They result from the realignment of an interstitial segment of a chromosome. An inversion occurs through two breaks within the chromosome and then a reinsertion of the segment between the breaks in a direction opposite to its original position in the chromosome. The linear order of the genes gets to be reversed in the particular section of the chromosome. Supposing the original order of arrangment of the genes were A B C D E F G H I J K, and inversion occured between D and H, the inverted chromosome would have the gene sequence of A B C D E F H I J K. The length of inversion depends upon the location of the two breaks in the chromosome and can affect any part of the chromosome. There are two kinds of inversions: paracentric and pericentric. In the paracentric inversion, kinetochore is not included and in the pericentric inversion, kinetochore is involved.

Homologous chromosomes which undergo identical inversions, undergo normal meiotic pairing and distribution. But, if only one homologue has an inversion, pairing relations are affected and the chromosomes take on a characteristic appearance. Heterozygous inversions are clearly seen in the polytene dipteran chromosomes because specific segments are clearly identifiable on account of their banding patterns.

The consequences of a heterozygous inversions are varied depending upon whether it is paracentric or pericentric, the number of chiasmata within the inversion and the distribution of the meiotic products in the gametes. The consequences of chiasma formation in the inverted segment. In a case of paracentric inversion, with crossing over, a bridge is produced in anaphase I of meiosis and an acentric fragment is lost. The bridge may break up at any point, giving rise to duplications and deficiencies in the meiotic products. The fragment associated with the bridge causes a deficiency, whose size determines the reduction in fertility imposed. Supposing the meiotic product is a gamete, it becomes nonviable and sterile because it lacks a portion of the chromosome. Figure 13 also explains the nature of the products of pericentric heterozygous inversions, the variations due to chromatids exchanged during crossing over and also the relationship between inversion and the number of chiasmata.

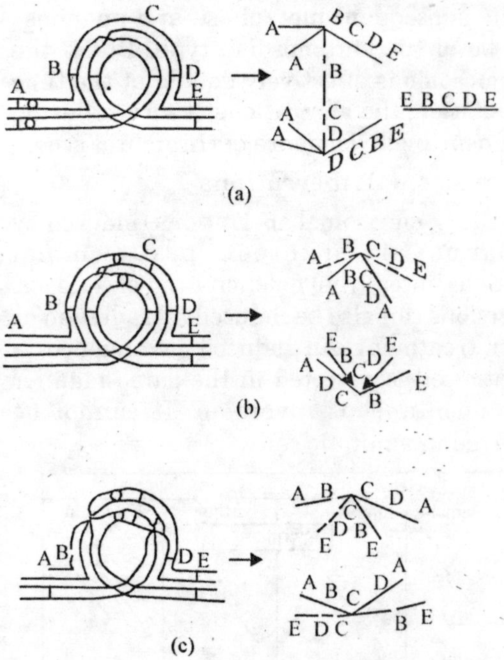

Fig. 13 Configurations and meiotic results of crossing over in heterozygous inversions.

Induced Aberrations

When a chromosomal aberration is mediated by the employment of a chemical substance or irradiation, it is called an induced aberration.

Radiation is often employed to induce chromosomal aberration. Indeed, these aberrations might be the result of gene or point mutations or might be the result of a chromosomal aberration. Generally speaking, the frequency with which gene mutations occur on account of irradiation is so much greater than chromosomal aberrations, the fact can be employed to decide whether an observed change is the result of a mutation or a chromosomal disturbance.

Radiation Induced Chromosomal Aberrations

There are two types of radiation induced chromosomal aberrations: chromosomal and chromatid. If the chromosome is irradiated before duplication, the aberrations observed in the subsequent metaphase and anaphase will be of the chromosome type. But if the chromosome is effectively double at the time of radiation, the aberrations observed during the ensuring division are of chromatid type.

Chromosomal Aberrations

The chromosomal aberrations (induced by radiation) are of three types: terminal deletions, interstitial deletions and exchanges. Inversions can also be induced by radiation or other treatment. An induced inversion in a meiotic cell is detected in the same manner as a spontaneous inversion. It cannot be detected in a mitotic cell.

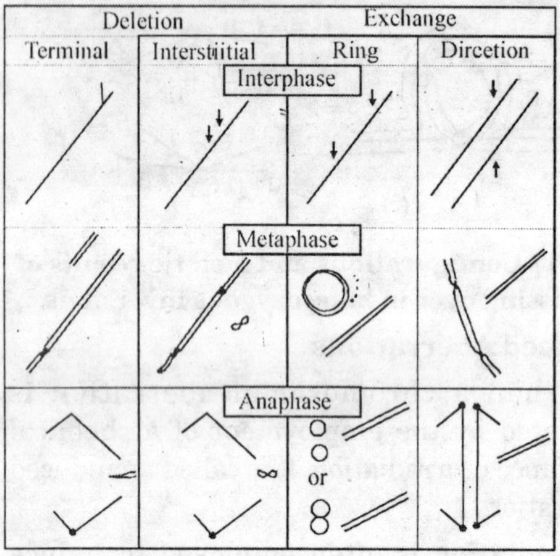

Fig. 14. Radiation induced chromosomal aberrations : the chromosomal type.

LINKAGE AND CROSSING OVER

The linkage is a *phenomenon of close association between two or more genes which tend to be transmitted together disobeying the law of independent assortment.* In otherwords, it can be defined as the tendency of certain genes to enter the gametes in parental combinations. This occurs because recombination or crossing over between such genes is prevented. In a cross involving linked genes, the parental types in the F_2 progeny become far numerous than their expected ratio.

Linkage was first observed by Bateson in 1905 in sweet pea in the cross outlined below:

Parents....... Purple flower-long pollen **BB Ll** × Red flower round pollen **bb ll**

F_1.................................... Purple long **Bb Ll**

F_2......	Purlple-long	Purple-round	Red-long	Red-round
Actual ratio.......	11	1	1	3
Expected ratio......	9	3	3	1

From test cross between the F_1 hybrid of a dihybrid cross and recessive homozygous parent a 1 : 1 : 1 : 1 ratio is expected. When the F_1 hybrid purple flowered long pollened sweet pea is test crossed with recessive parent the result is :

Test cross........ F_1 hybrid Purple-long **Bb Ll** × Recessive parent Red-round **bb ll**

Test cross progeny...	Purlple-long	Purple-round	Red-long	Red-round
	7 :	1 :	1 :	7

The crosses cited show that gametes containing parental gene combinations (**BL** and **bl**) are produced in much greater numbers than the new combinations. From test cross it is proved that both the parental types of gametes, **BL** and **bl** are produced in equal numbers. Therefore we infer that in sweet pea the gene for flower colour and pollen shape are linked. They tend to be inherited together.

The explanation of the mechanism of linkage was provided by Thomas-Hunt Morgan in 1910. The chromosomes are the bearers of the hereditary units or genes.

Their number in a species is constant. It is however far less in comparison to the number of genes in a species which is far numerous. Therefore each chromosome contains several genes. They are arranged linearly on chromosomes. Alleles occupy the same position or locus on homologous chromosomes. Different alleles occupy different loci. Gamete formation follows meiosis. During meiosis segmental exchange of chromatids or crossing over takes place between homologous chromosomes. Due to crossing over genes move from one chromosomes to other forming new combinations. Sometimes different alleles are placed very closely. The closeness does not permit crossing over to occur freely. Therefore, the chance of forming new combination between them reduces and they are said to be in linkage. The linkage between two genes is said to be complete when the chance of crossing over between them is nil. Otherwise it is incomplete.

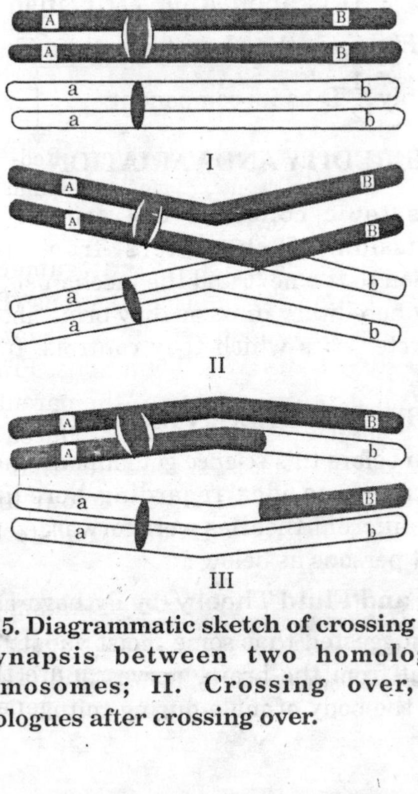

Fig. 15. Diagrammatic sketch of crossing over. I. Synapsis between two homologous chromosomes; II. Crossing over, III. Homologues after crossing over.

SIGNIFICANCE IN RECOMBINATION BREEDING

In plant breeding, linkage has considerable value. When the linkage is between the favourable genes, they tend to be transmitted together to the progeny. In case of tight linkage selection for only one of the characters would suffice. This is very advantageous in cases where selection for one of the traits is easier than that of the other. But when a linkage is observed between a desirable and an undesirable gene, the crop improvement becomes difficult and gets delayed. In such cases, the breeder has to grow sufficiently large F_2 population to get desirable recombinats.The size of the F_2 population required depends on the closeness of linkage; the closer the linkage, the larger the size of F_2 populations.

VARIATION-COMPONENTS OF VARIATION-HERITABILITY

The term genetics was coined by Bateson (1906). It deals with that branch of biology which deals with heredity and variation. While heredity deals with the genetic continuity of germinal material between parent and offspring, variation accounts for the differences between organisms related by descent. Variations are of two kinds, genetic and non-genetic. The former are caused by mutation and recombination of genes during sexual reproduction and are inherited. Non-genetic variation on the other hand is not inherited. It is caused by the effect of the environment on inherited characters. Together, heredity and environment determine the nature of an individual plant, animal and human being. No two sexually reproduced individuals except monozygotic twins are identical in all respects. In other words, each individual has a distinct genotype which is unique to it only. It interacts with the environment to produce the phenotype. Such Genotype × environment interaction is an important consideration in crop improvement. Thus for example, a rice variety of Japan when raised under Indian conditions, may become stunted, though its genetic constitution remains unaltered. Also, the essential features of a rice plant high distinguishes it from any other species is not altered by the variations due to the environment.

Genetics in Relation to Other Sciences : The science of genetics has occupied a key position among modern sciences. Its field of study extends over a wide-horizon. It exhibits either direct or indirect relationships with many other branches of science.

Practical Applications of Genetics : Genetics has many important applications, which are great value for human beings, application of genetics in the fields of (1) improvement of domestic animals, (2) improvement of crop plants, (3) in medicine, (4) legal applications and (5) eugenics.

Heritability

In crop improvement, the genetic component of variation is more important as this component only is transmitted to the next gereration. Hece the ratio of genetic variance to the total variance *i.e.*, phonotypic variance, is known as heritability.

The heritablility may be represented as follows:

$$\text{Heritability (H)} = V_g / V_p$$

$$\text{(or)} \quad V_g (V_p/V_e)$$

Where V_g, V_p and V_e are the genetic, phenotypic and environmental components of variance, respectively.

Heritability is estimated by the following three methods :

(1) From the analysis of variance of a trial consisting of a large number of geontypes.

(2) Estimation of V_g and V_e from the variances of F_2, P_1, P_2 and F_1 generations.

(3) Parent-offspring regression on doubling gives an estimate of heritability

Thus H = 2b, where 'b' is the regression of progeny means on parental values.

Heritability, thus estimated from the above three methods is known as broad sense heritability. Broad sense heritability estimates are very useful when homozygous lines are studied. But in the segregating generations, genetic variance consists of additive and dominance components. Since only homozygous lines are produced in self pollinated crops, the dominance component will not contribute to the phenotype and as such only the additive component (D) of the genetic variance becomes relevent. Therefore the ratio of additive component (D) of variance to the total phenotypic variance is the more appropriate estimate of heritability and is referred to as the narrow sense heritability.

The narrow sense heritability is calculated as follows :

$$H(ns) = \frac{1}{2}\frac{D}{V_{F_2}}$$

Only $\frac{1}{2}$D is applied for estimation of heritability since the phenotypic variance of F_2 has only $\frac{1}{2}$D as its component.

HEREDITY AND VARIATION

This topic concerns the science of transmission of characters from one generation to the next and the mechanism of action of hereditary units as they bring about the charcteristics which they controls. It is genetics.

PRE-MENDELIAN HISTORY

Even before this science got founded, man had some vague idea regarding heredity. Several different theories were forwarded by different persons as below :

Vapour and Fluid Theory (by Pythogoras)

He suggested that some moist vapour is given out from the brain, nerves and other parts of the body of male during coitus. One account of these vapours, the off-springs exhibit similarities with the male parent.

Semen Theory (by Empedocles)

He suggested that both parents produce semen which arises directly from its various body parts. The semen from both parent mixes and produces a new individual.

Aristotle's Idea (by Aristotle)

He suggested that the semen of male is highly purified blood and possesses life-giving pcwer. The semen of female was its menstrual fluid which furnishes nourishing material to the developing off-spring.

Preformation Theory (by Swammerdam)

According to this theory the gametes had the minature copy of adults and the development of embryo was actually only the enlargement of parts that were already present in the sperm or egg. He got support from Hartsoeker (1694) and Dalemponus (1699) who called the miniature human being, *Homunculus*.

Particulate Theory (by Maupertuis)

According to this theory the body of each parent gives rise to minute particles. In sexual reproduction, these particles from both the parents unite together to form the daughter individuals.

Encasement Theory (by Charles Bonnet)

According to this theory every female contains within her body miniature prototypes of all the creatures.

MENDELIAN GENETICS

G. J. Mendel conducted hybridization experiments with garden pea *Pisum sativum*. Though first published in 1866, such valuable work of Mendel remained unnoticed, as it was published in an obscure Journal by an unknown monk. His work was rediscovered after 35 years, in 1900, when three botanists, Hugo de Vries from Holland, C. Correns from Germany and E.V. Tschermak from Austria independently discovered Mendel's paper and reviewed Mendel's laws of inheritance.

VARIATIONS

Variations are difference found amongst individuals of the same species, race and family.

Sources of Variation

Replication of RNA is so nearly perfect that there is almost nil possibility of variations occurring in the genotypes of asexually reproducing organisms, except, may be as the result of environment influences. In case of sexually reproducing organisms there however is ample opportunity for genetic variation to arise. Two processes occurring during meiosis and the fusion of gametes during fertilisation provide for introducing unlimited genetic variation into the population.

Classification of Variation

Variations are classified into the following types on many basis :

I. Basis : *Affected trait*

1. **Morphological Variations :** They are the differences that are found in form and structure.
2. **Physiological Variations :** They are the variations observed in various functions of the body like basal metabolic rate etc.
3. **Cytological Variations :** They are those variations which occur in the number of cells, cell constituents and their products.
4. **Behaviouristic Variations :** The variations are connected with behaviour of the organisms towards different conditions.

II. Basis : ***Impact***

1. **Beneficial Variations :** They are variations which help the organism in adapting to a particular environment.
2. **Harmful Variations :** These variations make organism unfit to its environment.

3. **Neutral Variations :** They do not affect organism in any way.

III. Basis : ***Parts***

1. **Meristic Variations :** These are the variations which involve changes in the number of parts, segments etc, *e.g.*, in human beings hands and feet can have extra digits (6 instead of 5). The phenomenon is known as polydactyly. The number of digits can be less due to fusion called as syndactyly.
2. **Substanctive Variations :** They are variations which affect whole of the organism. *e.g.* In human beings, substantive variations are found in height and weight of individuals belonging to same age.

IV. Basis : Cells affected

1. **Blastogenic or Germinal Variations :** The variations which affect the germ cells of an organism and are inheritable. They are transmitted from one generation to the next. They are caused because of number of factors as :
   (*a*) Chance separation of chromosomes
   (*b*) Chance combination of chromosomes
   (*c*) Crossing over
   (*d*) Chromosome aberrations
   (*e*) Change in chromosomes number
   (*d*) Gene mutations
2. **Somantogenic or Somatic Variations :** They are the variations which affect only the somatic cells of the organisms. They are neither inherited nor transmitted to the next generation, *e.g.*, well developed body muscles of an athlete, boring of pinna etc. Somatogenic variations are caused by three types of factors:
   (*a*) *Environmental factors* : They include temperature, light, nutrition, water supply, humidity, medium or habitat, wind, topography, enemies, etc. Such variations are called as environmental variations.
   (*b*) *Use and disuse of organs* : *e.g.* vocal organs are more developed in singer than a nonsinger.
   (*c*) *Conscious efforts* : Variations produced in human beings due to conscious efforts include reveiving of education, learning of an art, development of some habits, boring of pinnae etc.

MENDELIAN GENETICS

Any inherited trait such as eye colour is referred to as a phenotype. All phenotypes result from the presence of a specific gene or combination of genes, the genotype. In hybrids, one phenotype may be dominant to another. Pure-breeding lines are strains of a species which have been bred for many generations and have maintained the same phenotype. The first clear evidence pointing to what we now call genes came from the work of G. J. Mendel who carried out experiments on inheritance in pea plants in the middle of the 19th century.

SYMBOLS AND TERMINOLOGY

Symbols

English alphabets were used by Mendel to represent the factors. A capital letter like 'A' signified dominant member and lower case like 'a' signified recessive member. The alphabet is chosen on the basis of the mutant character (mutant character is one which deviates from wild type character which is most common) for example, since garden pea is normally tall, the dwarf, which is considered to be mutant is represented by letter 'd'. The tall will then automatically receive the designation 'D'.

Terminology

Gene : A hereditary determiner specifying a biological function a unit of inheritance (DNA) located in a fixed place on the chromosome.

Allelomorphs or alleles : A alleles, the abbreviated form of the term "Allelomrphs" (meaning one form of the other) indicates alternative form of the same gene.

Homozygous and heterozygous : Zygotes or individual organism carrying two units of one allele (DD or dd) are homozygous. Similarly an individual having two different allels will be called heterozygous of hybrid (Dd).

Phenotype and genotype : Two useful terms, phenotype and genotype refer to visible expression of trait and actual gene constitution, respectively.

Monohybrid, dihybrid and trihybrid: Single character each controlled by a single pair of gene of alleles was considered. Such crosses are known as monohybrid crosses and F_2 ratio of 3 : 1 is known as the monohybrid ratio. Similarly, crosses can be considered when two or three pairs of genes or alleles are involved. Such crosses will be called dihybrid and trihybrid crosses and the respective ratios as dihybrid and trihybrid ratios.

Reciprocal crosses : A set of two reciprocal crosses means that the same two parents are used in two experiments in such a way that if in one experiment "A" is used as the female parent and 'B' is used as the male parent in other experiment 'A' will be used as male and 'B' as the female parent.

Back cross and Test cross : The F_1 individuals obtained in a cross are usually selfed to get the F_2 progeny. They can also be crossed with one of the two parents from which they were derived. Such a cross of F_1 individual with either of the two parents is known as back cross. On the other hand, when it is crossed with recessive parent, it is called as test cross. It is called a test cross because it is used to test whether an individual homozygous or heterozygous.

The Laws of Mendel

On the basis of his finding, Mendel proposed the first of the two following fundamental principle of genetics :

(*i*) Law of Segregation : The law of segregation can be explained more clearly by making following suppositions.

(*a*) A character is produced by a specific gene.

(*b*) Each gene has two alternative forms; these forms are known as alleles.

(*c*) The two alleles of a gene govern the development of constrasting forms of the character governed by gene.

(*d*) Each somatic cell of an organism has two copies of each gene.

Law of segregation states that, "the two alleles of a gene present in F_1 do not contaminate each other; they separate and pass into different gametes in their original form producing two different types of gametes in equal frequencies."

The random union between male and female gametes thus produced yields the typical 3 : 1 ratio which is often referred to as monohybrid ratio (since it is observed in F_2 generation of crosses segregating for a single character of gene).

The net consequence of law of segregation assuming single gene with complete dominance is a 3 : 1 ratio in F_2 generation as shown in following figure :

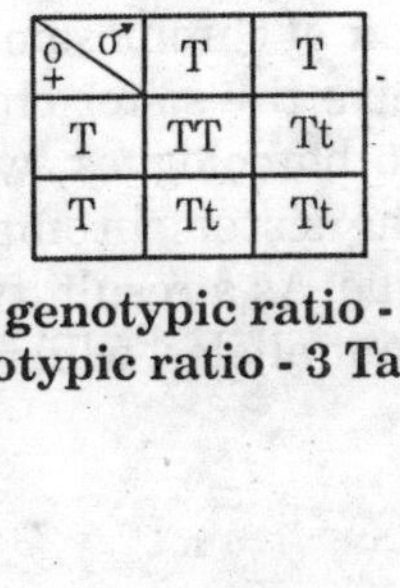

Fig. 16. F_2 genotypic ratio - TT : 2 Tt : 1tt
F_2 phenotypic ratio - 3 Tall : 1 Dwarf

Assumptions Involved in Segregation as an Explanation for the 3 : 1 Ratio :

1. The production of two types of gametes in equal frequencies in F1.
2. Equal survival of different gametes.
3. Random union of male and female gametes, and
4. Equal survival of different zygotes thus produced.

Mendel himself was aware of the first and the third assumptions, and he devised the test cross to test equal frequencies of gametes from the F_1. A failure of the second and fourth assumptions may occur in some cases. Which may lead to significant deviation from the typical 3 : 1 ratio. Fortunately, the failure of these assumptions is not common and it did not occur in the cases studied by Mendel.

Physical Basis of Segregation

The phenomenon of segregation can be easily explained on the basis of the behaviour of homologous chromosomes during meiosis. In F_1 hybrids or a heterozygote, one of the two alleles of gene is located in one chromosome, while the other allele is present in the homologue of this chromosome. The two homologous chromosomes pair during prophase I and orient at the metaphase plate during metaphse I. At anaphase I, one of the two homologous chromosomes move to one pole, while the other chromosomes of the pair moves to the opposite pole. Thus, each pole receives only one member of a homologous pair of chromosome. As a result, one of the two alleles goes to one pole, while the other allele goes to the opposite pole. At anaphase II, the two sister chromatids of each chromosome separate and move to the opposite poles producing four daughter cells each having a single chromatid from each homologous pair of chromosome. Two of these four cells receive the sister chromatids from one of the two homologues, while the other two receive the sister chromatids from the other homologue. As a result, two of four cells receive dominant alleles, while the remaining two cells receive the recessive alleles of the allelic pair. Thus, the separation of homologous chromosomes during meiosis may be regarded as the reason of segregation of two alleles of a gene since the alleles are located in identical position in the homologous chromosomes.

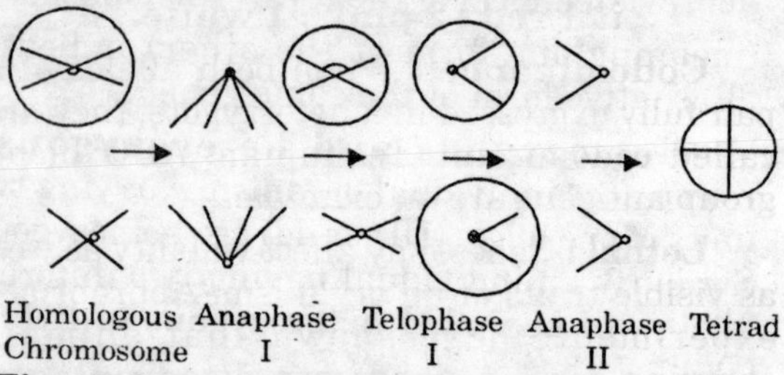

Fig. 17. Segregation of a pair of alleles (Aa) as a result of the movement of homologous chromosomes and of sister chromatids during meiosis. In this case, the first meiotic division is the reduction division.

Variations of the 3 : 1 Ratios :

The simple 3 : 1 monohybrid ratio is not always observe in instances where only one gene is responsible for a particular phenotype. This may be due to a number of factors.

Partial or Incomplete Dominance

When the phenotype of F_1 is intermediate between two parents, it is called incomplete dominance *e.g.* Petal colour in snapdragons.

(*a*)

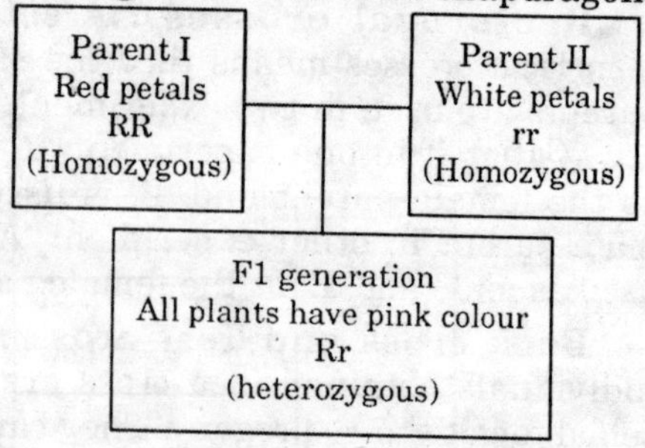

(*b*)

0 \ 0	R	r
R	RR Red	Rr Pink
r	Rr Pink	rr White

Fig. 18 (a) and (b)

Fig. (*a*) Gametes produced of F1 plants carry R or r and those fuse at random to give offspring with genotypes RR, Rr and rr as shown in (b)

(*b*) The genotypic ratio is the same as in Figure 1. Phenotypic ratio is 1 red : 2 pink : 1 white.

Codominance : When both alleles of a pair fully expressed in a heterzygote, they are called codominant. In human, ABO blood group antigens are an example.

Lethal : Genes may affect viability as well as visible traits of an organism. Appropriate experiments have shown that animals carrying certain genes are disadvantaged through impaired biochemical as well as physical functioning. White eyed and vestigial winged Drosophila, for example, have lower viabilities than the wild type. Thus a lethal gene causes the death of all individuals carrying this gene in an appropriate genotype before these individuals reach adulthood. An appropriate genotype for an allele would depend upon its dominant relationship with its another allele. For an allele producing a recessive effect on survival, an appropriate genotype would be in homozygous recessive state while for an allele having a dominant allele effect on survival, both homozygous and heterozygous states would be an appropriate genotypes. *e.g.* yellow coat colour in mice.

Parents Yy Yellow   Yy Yellow

Gametes Y y   Y y

♀ \ ♂	Y	y
Y	YY Die	Yy Yellow
Y	Yy Yellow	yy Grey

Fig. 19. Inheritance of yellow coat colour in mice. It may be noted that mice with yellow coat are always heterozygotes.

(*ii*) Law of Independent Assortment : Independent assortment is defined as random distribution of alleles to the gametes that occur when genes are located on different chromosomes. The distribution of one pair of allele is independent of that of other gene located on non-homologous chromosome. The principle is as a matter of fact, an extension of law of segregation to 2 or more genes situations provided the genes are located on different chromosomes. However similar results are possible when two genes are located on same chromosome provided they are so for apart that there is always crossing over between two genes. The diagrammatic representation of this principle is shown below :

♀ × ♂

Parents YYRR (Yellow, Round)   yyrr (Green, wrinkled)

Gametes YR   yr

F_1 yr Rr (All yellow, Round)

F_2 ♀ yY Rr X ♂ Yy Rr

♀ \ ♂	YR	Yr	yR	yr
YR	YYRR	YYRe	YyRR	YyRr
Yr	YYRr	Yyrr	YyRr	Yyrr
yR	YyRR	YyRr	YyRR	YyRr
yr	YyRr	Yyrr	yyRr	yyrr

Phenotypes	*Genotypes*	*Genotypic Frequency*	*Phenotypic ratio*
Yellow, round	YYRR	1	
	YYRr	2	
	YYRR	2	9
	YrRr	4	
Yellow, wrinkled	YYrr	1	
	Yyrr	2	3
Green, round	yyRR	1	

Phenotypes	*Genotypes*	*Genotypic Frequency*	*Phenotypic ratio*
	yyRr	2	3
Green, wrinkled	yyrr	1	1

Fig. 20. Cross between a variety of garden peas with yellow, round seeds and a variety with green, wrinkled seeds. The F_1 X F_1 illustrates a dihybrid cross.

Test cross of dihybrid : In a test cross, the F_1 hybrid (YyRr) is crossed with a variety or strain having the recessive forms of both the characters (double recessive) *i.e.,* wrinkled, green. According to independent segregation of two genes (Yy and Rr), the F_1 should produce four kinds of gametes; viz., YR, Yr, yR and yr, in equal frequencies *i.e.,* in the ratio 1 : 1 : 1 : 1. A deviation from this ratio does not necessarily mean failure of independent assortment. It may arise to one or more of the following reasons :

1. a lethal action of one or both the genes involved in the cross.
2. an interaction of two or more genes in producing one or both the traits under study.
3. the presence of modifying genes for one or both the genes.
4. pleiotropic effect of one or both the genes.
5. incomplete penetrance and/or expressivity of one or both the genes, and
6. a threshold requirement for the development of one or both the genes.

♀ × ♂

Yellow, round YyRr × Green wrinkled yyrr

		yr	
Phenotypic ratio	YR	YyRr,	Yellow, round
1 : 1 : 1 :1	Yr	Yyrr	Yellow, wrinkled
Genotypic ratio	YR	yyRr	Green, round
1 : 1 : 1	Yr	yyrr	Green, wrinkled

Fig. 21. Result from a test cross of F_1 hybrid (YyRr) heterozy-gous for seed shape and cotyledon colour in pea

Trihybrid ratios : Virtually all cross fertilizing plants or animals differ from other members of the species *i.e.* more than one or two pairs of alleles. Therefore matings in natural breeding populations usually produce new combinations of many genes. The following three pairs of characters may be considered :

(*i*) Tall plants vs. dwarf plant

(*ii*) Yellow seed vs. green seed

(*iii*) Round seed vs. wrinkled seed.

The parent (DD GG WW and dd gg ww) will give rise to the F_1 hybrids (Dd Gg Ww) which are heterozygous for three genes. Eight different types of gametes will be available in equal proportion both on the male side as well as on female side. A checkerboard technique will involve the drawing of 64 combinations. Therefore, for the study of three or more genes, checkerboard is rather difficult and, therefore, forked line method is utilized. The result is given below :

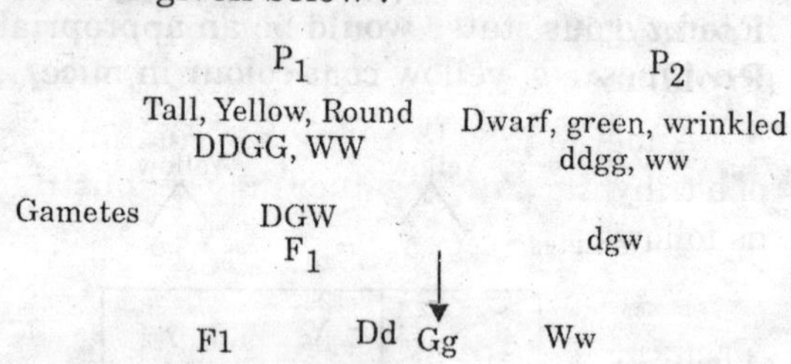

Fig. 22. A trihybrid cross showing the production of eight knids of gametes by F_1

Trihybrid test cross : The trihybrid test cross will involve crossing of a trihybrid (Dd Gg Ww) with triple recessive (dd gg ww). The eight different phenotypes described as above will be obtained in 1:1:1:1:1:1:1:1.

P_1		P_2
Dd Gg WW	X	dd gg ww
(Tall Plant Yellow Round Seeds)		(dwarf plants green wrinkled seeds)

♀ \ ♂	*dgw*	*Phenotypes*	*Phenotypic ratio*
DGW	Dd Gd Ww	Tall, yellow, round	1
DGw	Dd Gg ww	Tall, yellow, wrinkled	1
Dg W	Dd gg Ww	Tall, green, round	1
Dgw	Dg gg ww	Tall, green, wrinkled	1
dGW	dd Gg Ww	Dwarf, yellow, round	1
dGw	dd Gg ww	Dwarf, yellow, wrinkled	1
dgW	dd gg Ww	Dwarf, green, round	1
dgw	dd gg ww	Dwarf, green, wrinkled	1

Fig. 23 A checkerboard showing a trihybrid test cross

Forked Line Method for Genetic Problems

A method for bringing the combinations of a trihybrid cross together may be illustrated as follows :

3 Tall
- 3 yellow
  - 3 Round = 27 Tall, yellow, round
  - 1wrinkled = 9 Tall, yellow, wrinkled
- 1 green
  - 3Round = Tall, green, round
  - 1 wrinkled = 3 Tall, green, wrinkled

1 Dwarf
- 3 yellow
  - 3 Round = = 9 Dwarf, yellow, round
  - 1 Wrinkled = 3 Dwarf, yellow, wrinkled
- 1 Green
  - 3 Round = 3 Dwarf, green, round
  - 1 Wrinkled = 1 Dwarf, green, wrinkled

Fig. 24. Forked line method for solving genetic problems in which independent assortment is involved. Only phenotypes of progeny are listed in this example.

Mathematical method for genetic problems : The expected F_2 result from a trihybrid cross that involves independent assortment and dominance of one allele in each pair is the product of three pairs, such as

$$(A : a)\ (B : b)\ (C : c)$$

Written algebracally,

$(3 + 1)\quad (3 + 1)\quad (3 + 1)$ or $(3+1)^3$, which expands to

$27 + 9 + 9 : 9 : 3 + 3 + 3 + 1$ or $27:9:9:9:3:3:3 : 1$

A cross with four gene pairs under the same condition would result in (3 + 1)4, five gene pair (3 + 1)5, and so on. Number of gametes, genotypes and phenotypes expected from different number of heterozygous pairs of genes are summarized below :

Table 2 : Relationship among pairs of independent alleles, gametes, F_2 phenotypes when dominance is present

Number of Heterozygous pairs	*Number of individuals in perfect F_2*	*Number of kinds of gametes*	*Number of F_2 genotypes**	*Number of F_2 pheno-types*
1	4	2	3	2
2	16	4	9	4
3	64	8	27	8
4	256	16	81	16
:	:	:	:	:
:	:	:	:	:
10	1084576	1024	59049	1024
n	n^4	2^n	3^n	2^n

*Number of different phenotypes in case of partial, co– or over dominance

Gene Interaction

The phenomenon of two or more genes affecting the expression of each other in various ways in the development of a single character of an organism is known as gene interaction. A classical example of gene interaction based on the result of crosses between different breeds of chickens was reported by William Bateson and his associate. R.C. Punnett.

In chickens, comb shape is governed by two genes, p and r. The dominant allele of gene p (P) alone (with rr) produced pea comb, while dominant allele of gene r (R) alone (with pp) produces rose comb. But when both the dominant genes are present together *e.g.* PPRR, they give rise to walnut comb. Recessive condition of both the loci, *i.e.* pprr, gives rise to a distinct comb shape called single. When a breed homozygous for pea comb was crossed with another breed homozygous for rose comb F_1 had walnut comb which is explained below :

Parents PPrr × ppRR
Pea Rose

Gametes Pr Pr

PpRr
Walnut

♀ \ ♂	PR	Pr	pR	pr
PR	PPRR Walnut	PPRr Walnut	PpPR Walnut	PpRr Walnut
Pr	PPRr Walnut	PPrr Pea	PpRr Walnut	Pprr pea
pR	PpRR Walnut	PpRr Walnut	ppRR Rose	ppRr Rose
pr	PpRr Walnut	Pprr Pea	ppRr Rose	pprr Single

Phenotypic ratio-9 walnut: pea 3 Rose : 1 single
Genotypic ratio - 1:2:1:2:4:2:1:2:1

Fig. 25. A typical dihybrid ratio (9:3:3:1) in case of a single character *e.g.*, comb shape in poultry.

Epistasis : The functional interactions of different (non-allelic) genes is called epistasis. The epistasis should not be confused with dominance. Epistasis is the interaction between different genes but dominance is the interaction between different alleles of the same gene.

In sweet peas, the anthocyanin pigment resulting in coloured flower, requires the presence of two dominant genes, 'C' and 'R' *e.g.* CCRR. When either 'C' (*e.g.* CC rr) or 'R' (*e.g.* ccRR) or both the genes (*e.g.* cc rr) are present in the homozygous recessive condition, purple flower colour can not be produced as a result of which white flowers are obtained.

Parents ♀ X ♂
Phenotyeps White White
Genotypes CCpp CcPp ccPP
F_1 Purple
F_2
Phenotypic ratio-9 purple-7 white

♀ \ ♂	CP	Cp	cP	cp
CP	CCPP Purple	CCPp Purple	CcPP Purple	CcPp Purple
Cp	CCPp Purple	CCpp Purple	CcPp Purple	Ccpp White
cP	CcPP Purple	CcPp Purple	CcPP White	ccPp White
cp	CcPp Purple	Ccpp White	ccPp White	ccpp White

Phenotypic ratio-9 purple : 7 White

Fig. 26. Complementary gene action in the development of flower colour in sweet pea giving rise to 9 : 7 ratio in F_2.

Probability in Mendelian inheritance :

Probability is the ratio of a specified event to total events. Limits of probability are from O if an event never occurs to 1 if it always occurs. The law of probability is applied for the solution of expectation of events. If two or more events are independent, the chance that they will occur together is the produce of their separate probabilities. On the basis of law of probability, Mendel predicted that 9/16 (3/4 × 3/4) of the F_2 would be round, yellow; and 3/16 (3/4 × 1/4) round green, 3/16 (1/4 × 3/4) wrinkled, yellow; and 1/16 (1/4 × 1/4) wrinkled, green. Probability of given combination of two independent events is determine according to following formula:

$$P = \frac{n!}{s!t!} \times P^s q^t$$

Where,

P = Probability of a combination in dependent events.

n = total number of independent events.

s = number of one of two mutually exclusive event in the combination.

t = number of other mutually exculsive event in the combination.

p = Probability of first two mutually exclusive event.

q = Probability of the other mutually exclusive event, and

! = factorial 4 = 4 × 3 × 2 × 1

Chi-square Test :

In genetic experiments, certain numerical values are expected based on segregation ratios involved. However, in actual field experiments exact values may not be obtained due to invialability of certain pollen grains, zygotes, no germination of some seeds or even death of few plants after germination. This leads to some deviation between the actual results and the expected ones under given hypothesis. The chi-square (x^2) test is a statistical test to determine whether the deviation is within the limits of experimental error or large enough to reject the hypothesis involved. The formula of chi-square is symbolized as follows :

$$X^2 = \sum \frac{(0 - E)^2}{E}$$

Where,

0 = the observed number

E = the expected number, and

Σ = sigma, the summation sign

The calculated value is compared with the table value of x^2 for the degree of freedom n-1 where n is the number of classes.

Limitations of x^2 Test

1. It is used only on the numerical data, not on the percentages or ratios.
2. It can not properly be used when expected frequency within any phenotypic class is less than 5.

MUTATION

Definition : Mutation refers to sudden heritable and descret changes in any living organism. In the molecular term, mutation is defined as the permanent and relatively rare change in the number of sequence of nucleotides.

Mutation was first discovered by **Seth Wright** in **1791** in the **male lamb** which had **short legs.**

Later on mutation term was coined by "Hugo de Vries in **1900** in **onethera Lamarkiana. Muller 1927 discovered the mutagenic action of X-rays** on **Drosophila**. The life cycle of Drosophila is only 30 minutes and obtained the **noble prize** in **1946.**

Stadler (1928) studied the **effect of gamma rays** and **X-rays in barley and maize.**

Auerbach and **Robson 1946** discovered the many **chemical mutagens.**

Characteristics :

1. Mutation are **generally recessive** but **dominant mutations also occur.**
2. Mutations are generally **harmful** to the organism. Most of the mutations have **deleterious effect** but small proportions **(0.1%)** of them are **beneficial.**
3. Mutations are random, that is they may occur in any gene. However some genes show higher mutation rate than other.
4. Mutations are recurrent that is the same muations may occur again and again.
5. Induced mutations commonly show pleotrophy often due to mutation in closely linked genes.

TYPES OF MUTATIONS

Mutations do occur in nature (Spontaneous mutations) as well as can be artificially induced by various mutagenic agents (induced mutations). Induced mutations are of two types . ***viz.,*** (1) macro-mutations, and (2) micro-mutations. These are defined below :

1. Macro-Mutations

Mutations with distinct morphological changes in the phenotype are referred to as macro-mutations. Such mutations are found for qualititave characters and, therfore, are also called oilgogenic mutations. Identifications of such mutations is easy.

2. Micro-Mutations

Mutations with **invisible phenotypic changes are called micro-mutations**. Such mutations are observed in quantitative characters and, hence are also referred to as polygenic mutations. Indentification of such mutations is very difficult. Micro-mutations are of economic value in plant breeding.

1. Euploidy

Euploidy involves loss or gain of whole sets of chromosomes. Organisms having only one set of chromosomes are **haploids.** Bacteria, fungi and many algae are haploid (n). Most of sexually reproducing animals and higher plants are normally **diploid** (2n). However, haploids occur regularly among diploid species of insects such as ants, rotifers and mites. Haploidy is also seen in plants having a clear alternation of generation where the gametophyte is haploid. Haploids mostly arise from gametes through parthenogenesis in species that are normally diploid.

Additional of whole sets of chromosome greater than 2n is called **polyploidy** *e.g.,* 3n, 4n etc. If the added sets are similar to the existing ones it is called **autopolyploidy**. If they are dissimilar it is called allopolyploidy. Polyploids, possessing even-numbered sets of chromosomes have better chance of equal pairing and separation of chromosomes during meiosis. Their chances of survival is therefore greater. Polyploids with odd numbered sets raise complications in pairing during meiosis and are mostly sterile.

Polyploidy in animals is generally harmful but it has played a big role in evolution of many new species of plants. More than one-third of all flowering plants are considered to be polyploids. The proportion of polyploids may be as high as 70 per cent among grasses.

In animals, polyploidy disturbs the sex-determination mechanism by duplication of sex chromosomes. This usually results in sterility and is therefore, harmful.

Polyploidy in plants can be induced easily by a drug called **Colchicine**. It is an alkaloid obtained from autumn corcus plant *Colchicum autumnale* of Liliaceae family. The drug inhibits the formation of mitotic spindle. As a result, chromosomes duplicate but they remain within the same cell thus increasing their number. Colchincine is now widely used in polyploid breeding for crop improvement.

II. Aneuploidy

Aneuploidy involves a variation in number within a whole set of chromosome *e.g.* 2n + 1, 2n + 2, 2n – 1, 2n – 2 etc. It produces many harmful effects.

The terminology of various types of aneuploidy is given in Table 3.

Although all types of aneuploidy are harmful, the loss of a chromosome or chromosomes has a greater deleterious effect than addition. Generally it is lethal and causes death unless the chromosome involved is very small.

Table 3.2 : Terminology of Aneuploidy compared with the diploid

Type	*Chromosome formula*	*Example*
Diploid		2n AA BB CC DD
Aneuploid		
Monosomic	2n – 1	AA BB CC D
Nullisomic	2n – 2	AA BB CC
Trisomic	2n + 1	AA BB CC DDD
Tetrasomic	2n + 2	AA BB CC DD DD
Doubletri-somic.	2n + 1 +1	AA BB CCC DDD

APPLICATIONS IN CROP IMPROVEMENT

Induced mutations play an important role in crop improvement. The main uses of induced mutations are :

1. Development of improved varieties,
2. Induction of male sterility,
3. Production of haploids,
4. Creation of genetic variability,
5. Overcoming self incompatibility, and
6. Improvement in adaptation.

These are briefly discussed below:

1. Development of Improved Varieties

All over the world, 1542 improved varieties have been developed through induced mutations in different crops (*IAEA*, 1991). Some have been released as mutant varieties and others have been used in crosses for developing improved varieties. In India, improved varieties have been developed through mutation breeding in wheat, rice, barley, sorghum, cotton, surgarcane, blackgram, pigeonpea, field pea, castor bean, papaya, tomato and brinjal Table 4. Besides high yield, varieties with better quality, earliness, dwarfness, disease resistance and low toxin contents have been developed in various crops in different countries. Improvement in quality has been achieved for protein content in rice, oil content in mustard and sugar content in surgarecane. Earliness has been achieved in castor (from 270 days to 140 days), rice, soybean, cotton, greengram, blackgram, pigeonpea and sugarcane. Dwarf varieties have been developed through the use of mutant parents in wheat, rice, *Sorghum* and pearl millet. Disease resistance has been induced in oats to victoria blight and crown rust; in wheat for strip rust; in barley for mildew; in groundnut for leaf spot and stem rust; in sugarcane for red rot; in apple for mildew etc. Low toxin content mutants have been developed in rapeseed and mustard for erucic acid and in *Lathyrus sativa* for neurotoxin content.

2. Induction of Male Sterility

Induced mutations have been useful in induction of male sterility in some crop plants Genetic male sterility has been induced in durum wheat using radiations. CMS mutants have been induced in barley, sugarbeets, pearl millet and cotton. Use of GMS and CMS lines helps in reducing the cost of hybrid seed production. Ethidium bromide has been effectively used for induction of male sterility in pearl millet and barley.

3. Production of Haploids

Use of X-rays irradiated pollens has helped in production of haploids in many crops. Chromosomes doubling of these haploids results in the development of inbred lines which can be utilized either in the development of commercial hybrids or in crossing programmes.

4. Creation of Genetic Variability

Induced mutations are very effective in creating vast genetic variability for various economic characters in crop plants. Induced mutations have been used for increasing the range of genetic variabiiity in barley, oats, wheat and many other crops. In a sexually propagated crops like sugarcane and potato, somatic mutations may be useful, because the mutant plant can be multiplied as a clone.

5. Overcoming Self Incompatibility

Mutation of *S* gene by irradiation leads to restoration of self fertility in self incompatible species (Lewis, 1954). This has been successful in *Prunus ovium* and some other species.

6. Improvement in Adaptation

Induced mutations play an important role in improving adaptation of some crop species. For example, induced mutations helped in improving the adaptation of *Hibiscus subdarifa.* Induced mutants of this species could be successfully grown 1600 km north of its normal habitat (Gregory, 1960).

Table 4. Some mutant varieties developed in India through various mutagens in different crops

Crop species	*Varieties developed and mutagens used*		
	X-rays	*Gamma rays*	*Others*
Wheat	NP 836, JRC 7447	Pusa Lerma Sharbati Sonora	—
Rice	Biraj, CNM 20, LNM 25, CNM 31, Jagnnath, CNM 6	AU 1, AU 4, K 84 Hybrid mutant Mohan, Padmini Rasmi, Sattari,	PL, 56 (EMS) IIT 60 (EMS) Indira (EMS) Prabhavati (EMS)
Barley	—	DL. 253	PL 56 (EMS) RDB (*N*)
Sorghum	Co 21	—	—
Sugarcane	—	Co 6608. Co 8153 Co 997	—
Cotton	Indore 2. MA 9, MCU 7	MCU 10, Rasmi	—
Chickpea	—	Pusa Ageti	
Chickpea	—	Pusa 408, Pusa 413 Pusa 417	Kiran (*N*)
Sesame	—	—	Kalika (EMS)
Groundnut	TG 3, TG 4, TG 17 Vikram	BP_1, BP_2	Co 2 (EMS)
Cowpea	—	—	V 16, V 37, V 38, V 240 (all dMS)
Mungbean	—	Co 4, ML 26—10—3 Pant Mung—2, TAP7	— —
Bean	Pusa Parvati	—	—
Blackgram	—	—	
Pigeonpea	—	Co 5	Co 4 (MMS) Co 3 (EMS). TAT 5 (FN) Trombay (FN)
Pea	—	—	Hans (El)
Castor bean	—	RC 8	Aruna (th *N*)
Payaya	—	Pusa Nanha	—
Tomato	—	P K M 1, S-12 Pusalal Meeruti	Co 3 (EMS) Co 3 (EMS)
Brinjal	—	MDU 1	

Questions From Previous Year's Papers

Q. 1. Answer the following in about 150 words each :

(a) How cytoplasmic inheritance differs from chromosomal inheritance? Explain cytoplasmic inheritance with the help of suitable example.

(b) How can you establish that genes are arranged in linear order on the chromosomes?

Q. 2. Answer the following in about 150 words each :

(a) Distinguish between dicliny and dichogamy. Explain their types with examples.

(b) Differentiate between sexual and asexual reproduction.

Q. 3. Write short notes on the following in 150 words each :

(a) Overcoming weather hazards to avoid crop damage.

(b) Meiosis

(c) Male sterility

Q. 4. What is clonal selection? Describe the methods of clonal selection.

Q. 5. 'Genetic resistance is the most desirable and useful method of controlling a pest.' Discuss critically.

Q. 6. Write short notes on the following in about 150 words each :

(a) Chromosomal abberation

(b) Plant propagation of fruit crops.

3. PLANT BREEDING

HISTORY OF PLANT BREEDING

Plant Breeding, can be reasonably assumed to have commenced, when man first chose certain plants for cultivation. The process by which the wild species were brought under cultivation can be referred to as domestication. Thus domestication can be regarded as a method of plant breeding.

During domestication, it is likely that man exerted some selection, based on his preference, leading to better types (cultivated types) than the wild ones. The movement of man from one place to another has brought about the movement of cultivated plants from one area to another leading to plant introduction in the new area.

Artificial pollination was known to Babylonians and Assyrians. as early as 700 B.C. First artificial hybrid was produced by Thomas Fairchild (1717) while Joseph Koeleruter made extensive crosses in tobacco between 1760 and 1766. However, Knight (1759-1835) was perhaps the first man to develop several new fruit varieties, through artificial hybridization. Nilsson and his associates (1900) have developed the individual plant selection method in detail. Johannsen (1903) proposed the pure line theroy which provided the genetic basis for individual plant selection.

Now the modern methods of plant breeding are based on the genetic and cytogenetic principles. With the rediscovery of Mendel's work in 1900, genetics, the new branch of science began to develop. Mendel's law of inheritance has provided the basis for the development of genetics. With the realisation of the fact that the chromosomes are the carriers of genes, specialised plant breeding methods have developed. G.H. Shull, while working in maize, found that inbreeding resulted in loss of vigour. When the crossed the weak inbred lines, the hybrids were found to be more vigorous than the original variety. This observation has now led to the production of several hybrid varieties as in the case of maize, jowar *(Sorghum bicolor),* bajra *(Pennisetum americanum)* and any other economically useful crops.

New varieties of cultivated plants can result only from genetic reorganisation that gives rise to improvements over the existing varieties in particular characteristics or in combination of characteristic. Thus, plant breeding can be regarded as branch of applied genetics, but it also makes use of the knowledge and techinque of many aspects of plant science, specially physiology and pathology. Plant breeding began when man first chose certain plants for cultivation.

Poehlman defined plant breeding as "*the art and science of changing and improving the heredity of plants*". According to Smith (1961) "*Plant breeding is art and science of improving the genetic patterns of plants in relation to their economic values*".

Objectives of Plant Breeding

The chief aims and objectives of plant breeding are to improve the qualities of plants so that they are much desirable agronomically and economically. The main objectives of plant breeding are as follows :

(*i*) To increase the production of desired plant produces such as grains, oils, fodder, fibres etc.

(*ii*) To yield fungal, bacterial and insect resistance varieties.

(*iii*) To increase the qualities of crops with regard to size, shape, taste, nutrient contents of grains, vegetables and fruits.

(*iv*) To eliminate toxic substances in the consumable parts to make them safe for human consumption.

(*v*) To produce suitable varieties for particular agroclimatic region, which should also be tolerant to storage conditions.

Table 1. Historical Background/Significant Landmarks in Plant Breeding

Year	*Name of Scientist*	*Outstanding contribution*
700 BC	Babylonians and Assyrians	First of all pollinated date palm artificially.
1717	Thomas Fairchild	Developed first interspecific hybrid between sweet william and carnation species of Dianthus (*Dianthus barbatus* × *D. Caryophyllus*).
1800	Knight, T.A. (English)	First used artificial hybridization in fruit crops.
1840	John Le Couteur (English) and Patric Shirref (Scottish)	They developed the concept of progeny test and individual plant selection in cereals.
1856	De Vilmorin (French Biologist)	Further elaborated the concept of progeny test and used same in sugarbeet.
1866	Mendel, G.J. (Austria)	Discovered principles of inheritance working with garden pea.
1890	Rimpu (Sweden)	First made intergeneric cross between bread wheat (*Triticum aestivum*) and rye (*Secale cereale*), which later on gave birth to triticale.
1900	De Vries (Holland) Correns (Germany) Tschermak (Austria)	Rediscovered Mendel's laws of inheritance independently.
1900	Nilssion, H. (Swedish)	Further elaborated individual plant selection method.
1903	Johannsen, W. L. (Danish botanist)	Developed the concept of pureline. In 1909 coined the terms genotype and phenotype.
1908	Shull, G.H. (US) East E.M. (US)	Proposed overdominance hypothesis of East, heterosis independently working with maize
1908	Hardy, G. H. Weingberg, W.	Developed concept of Hardy-Weinberg law in population genetics.

Year	*Name of Scientist*	*Outstanding contribution*
1908	Davenport C. B.	First proposed dominance hypothesis of heterosis.
1910	Bruce, A. B. Keeble, F and Pellew, C.	Elaborated the dominance hypothesis proposed by Davenport.
1914	Shull, G.H.	First used the term heterosis for hybrid vigour.
1917	Jones, D.F.	Proposed dominance of linked gene hypothesis as explanation for heterosis. He first made double cross in maize and also first used genetic male sterility in the development of maize hybrids.
1919	Hays, H.K. Garber, R. J.	Gave initial idea about recurrent selection. Then first suggested use of synthetic varieties for commercial cultivation in maize.
1920	East E.M. and Jones. D.F.	Also gave initial about recurrent selection.
1921	Swell Wright (English)	Gave five systems of mating namely random, genetic assortative, phenotypic assortative, genetic disassortative and phenotypic disassortative.
1925	East, E.M. and Mangelsdorf. A.J.	First discovered gametophytic system of self incompatibility in *Nicotiana sanderae.*
1926	Vavilov. N.I. (Russian Geneticist)	Identified 8 main centres and 3 sub centres of crop diversity. He also developed concept of parallel series of variation or law of homologous series of variation.
1927	Karpechenko (Russian Geneticist)	Fist developed intergeneric hybrid between radish and cabbage which had undersirable features of both species.
1928	Stadler, L.J. (US)	First used X-ray for induction of mutations in crop plants.
1935	Nagaharu, U.	Proposed the origin of tetraploid species of *brassica* using a triangle which is popularly known as U's triangle.
1936	East, E.M.	Supported overdominance hypothesis of heterosis proposed by East and Shull in 1908.
1937	Harrington, J.B.	Proposed mass pedigree method of breeding which is a modification of pedigree method.
1939	Goulden, C.H.	First suggested the use of single seed desecent method for advancing segregating generations of self pollinated crops.

Year	*Name of Scientist*	*Outstanding contribution*
1940	Jenkins, M.T.	Described the procedure of recurrent selection
1944	Stadler, L.J.	Proposed use of gamete selection for improvememnt of inbreds in maize.
1945	Hull, F.H.	Coined the terms recurrent selection and over-dominance working with maize.
1950	Hughes M.B and Babcock, E.B. Gerstel, D.V.	First discovered sporophytic system of self incompatiability in *Crepis foetida. Gerstel* discovered the same independently in *Parthenium argenatum.*
1951	Painter, R.H.	Gave three mechanisms, viz., non-preference, anthibiosis and tolerance of insect resistance in crop plants.
1952	Jensen, N.F.	First suggested the use of multilines in oats.
1953	Borlaug, N.E.	First outlined the method of developing multilines in wheat.
1953	Mather, K.	Developed the concept of disruptive selection.
1956	Flor, H.H.	First developed the concept of gene for gene hypothesis in flax for flax rust caused by *Malampsora lini.*
1958	Thoday, J.M.	Further elaborated the concept of disruptive selection.
1963	Vander Plank, J.E.	Developed the concept of vertical & horizontal resistance.
1964	Borlaug, N.E.	Developed high yielding semidwarf varieties of wheat which resulted in green revolution.
1965	Grafius, J.E.	First applied Single Seed Descent (SSD) method in oats.
1968	Donald, C.M.	Developed the concept of crop ideotype working with wheat.
1970	Patel, C.T.	Developed world's first cotton hybrid for commerical cultivation in India.
1976	Yuan Long ping *et al.*	Developed world's first rice hybrid (CMS based) for commercial cultivation in China.
1983	Fraley *et. al.*	Developed first transgenic (genetically engineered) tobacco plants in USA.
1987	Monsanto	Developed first transgenic cotton plant in USA.

Year	Name of Scientist	Outstanding contribution
1991	ICRISAT	Developed world's first pigeon pea hybrid (ICPH 8 GMS based) for commercial cultivation in India.
1997	Monsanto, USA	First identified terminator gene, which allows germination of seed for one generation only.
1998	Monsanto, USA	Identification of trait or gene, which responds to specific brand of fertilizers and insecticides.

EMINENT INDIAN PLANT BREEDERS

T.S. VENKATRAMAN

He was an eminent sugarcane breeder. He transferred thick stem and high sugar contents from tropical noble cane to North Indian Canes. This process is knwon as noblization of sugarcane. He developed several varieties of sugarcane having high yield and high sugar content. He was Director of Sugarcane Breeding Institute, Coimbatore.

B.P. PAL

He was an eminent breeder known for his contributions to the breeding of superior disease resistant NP. varities of wheat. He was the first Director General of ICAR.

M.S. SWAMINATHAN

He is a famous plant breeder responsible for green revolution in India. He developed high yielding varieties of wheat and rice. He was Director General ICAR and later Director General of IRRI. Philippines from 1982-1988.

PUSHKARNATH

A famous potato breeder who developed several high yielding varieties of potato. He was Director of CPRI, Shimla.

N.G.P. RAO

He is an eminent sorghum breeder. He developed several high yielding hybrids of grain sorghum. He was Chairman of ASRB and Vice-Chancellor of Marathwada Agricultural University, Parbhani.

K. RAMIAH

He was a renowned rice breeder. He developed several high yielding varieties of rice when he was Director of CRRI, cuttack.

RAM DHAN SINGH

He was an inborn plant breeder who developed several superior varieties of wheat in Punjab. His famous variety was C591.

D.S. ATHWAL

He is a famous pearlmillet breeder. He worked in PAU, Ludhiana and developed several superior varieties of Pearlmillet (bajra).

BOSISEN

He was an eminent maize breeder. He developed several varieties of maize for Hill region of Uttarakhand. He established the Vivekanand Parvatiya Krishi Anusandhan Shala at Almora, Uttarakhand and was Director of the same till his death.

DHARAMPAL SINGH

He is an eminent oil-seed breeder. He released several varieties of oil-seeds (rapeseed and mustard) from Kanpur. He was Vice-Chancellor of G.B. Pant University of Agriculture & Technology, Pantnagar.

C.T. PATEL

He was a famous cotton breeder who developed world's first cotton hybrid in 1970 for commercial cultivation in India. He is known as father of hybrid cotton.

V. SANTHANAM

He is a famous cotton breeder who has developed several high yielding varieties of upland cotton and two varieties of Egyptain cotton. He was the first Project Coordinator for All India Coordinated Cotton Improvement Project and later worked in FAO as cotton consultant.

MODES OF REPRODUCTION

Origin of new individuals (called progeny) from pre-existing individuals (called parents) is known as reproduction.

The process of reproduction is also called propagation and the plant part used for the purpose is called propagule.

The manner in which new individuals originate is termed as mole of reproduction.

Mode of reproduction determines :

1. The genetic constitution
2. The extent of inbreeding depression
3. The ease in controlled pollination, and
4. The genetic stability of varieties after release.

Modes of Reproduction : Mainly depending on the involvement of gametes and their fusion, reproduction is classified into two groups.

1. Asexual reproduction
2. Sexual reproduction

1. Asexual Reproduction : Asexual reproduction does not involve fusion of male and female gametes, new individuals arise either from somatic cells or from unfertilized gametes (but not from zygotes). It is of two types

(*i*) Vegetative reproduction

(*ii*) Apomixis

(*i*) Vegetative Reproduction : When a new individual arises from a somatic cell (*i.e.* a cell which does not give rise to gametes) without formation of a seed, it is called vegetative reproduction.

(A) Natural Vegetative Reproduction : In nature vegetative reproduction occurs through undergound stems, sub-aerial stems, bulbils, leaves and even roots *i.e.,* all main parts of plants.

Underground stems : Tuber Potato, bulb (onion, garlic), rhizome (ginger, turmeric) and corn (arwi bunda).

Sub-aerial stems : Like runner, sucker, stolon etc. *e.g*;- banana, mint (mentha sp.), oil palm, date palm etc.

Bulbils : Bulbils are modified flowers, (*i.e.,* vegetative bodies) which give rise to new plants with out fertilization, and seed formation, *e.g*;-Lower flowers in the inflorescence of garlic.

In several species new plants originate from roots (sweet potato) or leaves.

(B) Aritificial Vegetative Reproduction: Vegetative propagation of plants by man using either conventional or biotechnological techniques.

Conventional Approaches : These approaches are based on sections of modified stems (Potato), stem cuttings (sugarcane, grapes, roses, sweet potato etc.) Root cutting, grafting (mango), budding (rose etc.) Layering, copicing, suckering (Banana, Palms, etc). They have been widely used for commercial propagation of fruit trees, ornamental and field crops like sugarcane, sweet potato etc.

Biotechnological Approaches : Large number of plantlets can be produced from small pieces of tissues cultured *in Vitro*. This is called Micropropagation. New plants may arise from pre-existing shoot buds, adventitious shoot buds, adventitious bulbs etc. and somatic embryos. These approaches produce very large number of plants in a very short time and these plants can be kept free from pathogens.

(*ii*) Apomixis : When embryos and seeds develop without fertilization it is termed as apomixis. It is two types :

(A) Obligate Apomixis : When sexual reproduction is totally absent.

(B) Facultative Apomixis : When sexual reproduction also takes place.

Classification of Apomixis :

***(i)* Adventive embryony :** In this case embryos develop directly from a vegetative cell of the ovule (e.g. nucellus) and there is no embryo sac formation. Adventive embryos are generally produced in addition to the zygotic embryos of seeds, this situation is called polyembryony e.g. in mango, citrus etc.

***(ii)* Apospory** : Embryos develop from unreduced egg cells or some other cells of embryo sacs derived from vegetative cells of ovules e.g. in Malus, Crepis, Ranunculus etc.

***(iii)* Diplospory :** Embryo sacs are produced from megaspores which are generally diploid but may be haploid. It is of two types.

(A) Parthenogenesis

(B) Apogamy.

(A) Parthenogenesis : Embryos develop from egg cells. Which may be haploid or diploid.

Diploid parthenogesis occur naturally in many grasses.

Haploid parthnogensis occurs accidentally in low frequencies in many species *e.g;* Maize, tobacco, barley etc. produced Haploid plants.

Haploid plants are produced from pollen grains of cultured anthers this is called *in vitro* androgensis

(B) Apogamy : Embryos develop from **synergids or antipodals** of the embryo sacs and they may be diploid or haploid. Diploid Apogamy occurs in -Antennaria, Alchemilla, Allium etc. Haploid Apogamy can be induced in many species by culture of unfertilized ovaries.

SIGNIFICANCE OF ASEXUAL REPRODUCTION

Merit (Advantage) of Asexual Reproduction

1. Asexual reproduction produces progeny plants identical in genotype to the parent plant. Asexual progeny of single plant are called clone. Clones are used as variety in many crop species.
2. Any desirable plant/mutant can be used as a variety.
3. Diploid apomixis can be utilised to multiply/maintain hybrid varieties.
4. Haploid apomixis especially through *in vitro* ovary culture and through anther culture produces haploid plants.

Chromosome doubling of such plants allows rapid isolation of homozygous lines from heterozygous plants/hybrids.

Demerit (Disadvantage) of Asexuar Reproduction

1. It is does not enable the genes present in two different individuals/ clones to the combined into a single clone. It does not allow gene transfers.
2. Apomixis creates confusion during hybridization.

Sexual Reproduction : In sexual reproduction fusion of a male gamete (n) with a female gamete (n) produces a zygote (2n) which develops into an embryo and ultimately into a new plant.

In crop plants the male and female gametes are produced in specialisd structures known as flowers.

The process of sexual reproduction may be described as under-

1. Sporogenesis
2. Gametogenesis
3. Pollination
4. Fertilisation
5. Embryogenesis.

Flower : In crop plants the male and female gametes are produced in specialised structure known as flowers. A flower is a modified short bud having the following :-

(i) Calyx or Sepals

(ii) Corolla or Petals

(iii) Androecium (Male reproductive organ) and Gynoecium (Female reproductive organ).

Bisexual or Hermaphrodite Flowers : A flower having both androecium and gynoecium is called Bisexual or hermaphrodite.

Unisexual Flowers : Flowers have either male or female reproductive organs.

Staminate : A flower having only androecium is known as staminate.

Pistillate : A flower contain only gynoecium is known as Pistillate.

— Staminate and Pistillate flowers occur on the same plant in a monoecious species such as maize, colocasia, castor, coconut etc.

— But in dioecious species staminate and Pistillate flowers occur on different plants e.g. Papaya, date palm.

— Male gamete is produced in stamen.

— While pistil produces the female gamete.

The male gamete are produced in microspores.

The female gamete are produced in megaspores.

1. Sporogenesis : Production of microspores and megaspores is known as sporogenesis or production of spores is called sporogenesis. Microspores are produced in anthers called microsporogenesis. While megaspores are produced in ovules called megasporogenesis.

Types of Sporogenesis

Sporogenesis is of two types :

(i) Microsporogenesis : Microspores are produced in anthers. Each anther has four pollen sacs that contain numerous pollen mother cells PMC's. Each PMC undergoes meiosis to produce four haploid cells or microspores. This process is known as microsporogenesis. The microspores mature into pollen grains by thickening of their walls.

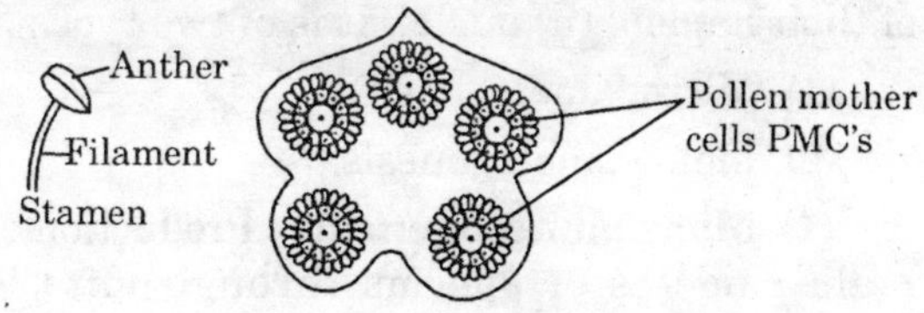

Fig. 1. T.S. of a young Anther

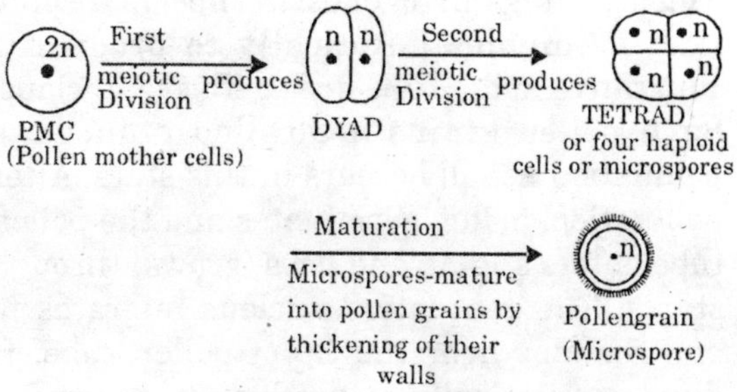

Fig. 2. Microsporogenesis

(ii) Megasporogenesis : Megaspores are produced in ovules present inside the ovary of a pistil. A single cell in each ovule differentiates into a megaspore mother cell, which undergoes meiosis to produce four haploid megaspores.Three of the megaspores degenerate leaving only one functional megaspore per ovule.

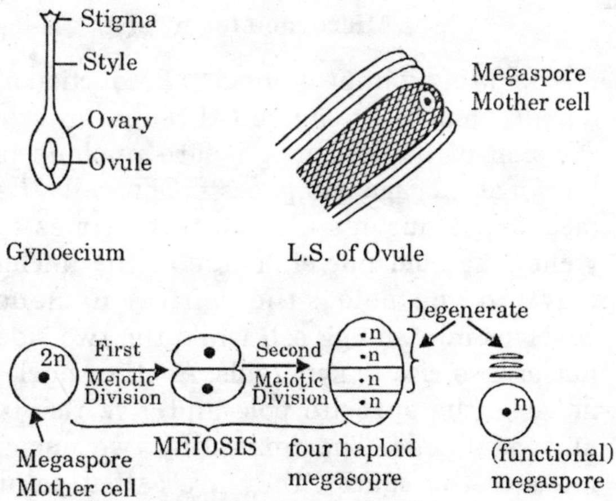

Fig. 3. Megasporogenesis

Gametogenesis : The production of male and female gametes is known as gametogenesis. It occurs within micro and megaspores and involves only mitotic division of their haploid (n) nuclei. It is of two types :-

(1) Microgametogenesis

(2) Megagametogenesis.

(1) Microgametogenesis : Production of male gametes or sperms through mitotic division of haploid nuclei of microspores is called microgametogenesis. The microspore nucleus divides mitotically to produce a generative and a tube or vegetative nucleus. Such pollen grains are called binucleate pollination usually occurs in this state. After pollination, pollen germinates and the pollen tube enters stigma and goes (grows) through styple. The generative nucleus migrates to and remains near the tip of pollen tube. It divides mitotically to produce two sperms. The pollen together with the pollen tube constitute the microgametophyte.

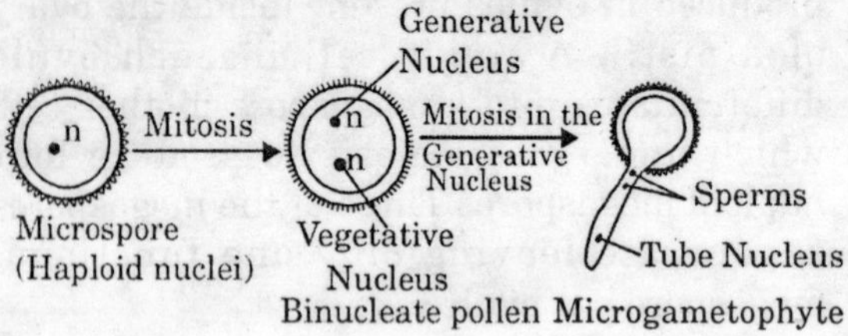

Fig. 4. Microgametogenesis

(2) Megagametogenesis : Production of female gamete or egg cell through mitotic division of haploid megaspore nucleus is known as megagametogenesis. Generally the megaspore nucleus divides three times to yield 8 haploid nuclei. Three of the nuclei move to one pole : the central nucleus develops into an egg cell while the two side nuclei give rise to synergids. Another nuclei move to the opposite pole and give rise to antipodal cells. The remaining two nuclei move to the center, they are called polar nuclei and ultimately fuse to form a 2n secondary nucleus. This elaborate cell housing the egg cell, two synergids, three antipodals and a secondary nucleus is known as embryo sac or megagametophyte.

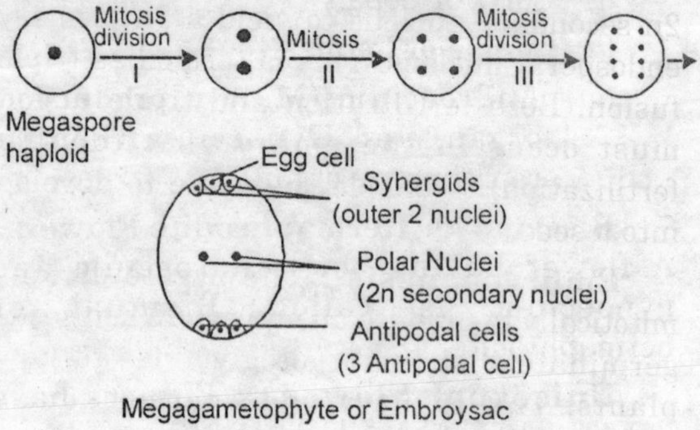

Fig. 5. Megagametogenesis

Pollination : Landing of active or live pollen on a receptive stigma is known as pollination.

or

Pollination refers to the transfer of pollen grains from anthers to stigma. Generally, at the time of pollination pollen grains are in the binucleate stage. Now the pollen germinates and the pollen tube enters the stigma. It travels through the style, finally enters the ovule through the micropyle (a small pore in the ovule) and discharges the two sperms into the embryo sac.

Pollination is grouped into two types :-

(1) Self pollination

(2) Cross pollination.

1. Self pollination or Autogamy : Pollen from an anther may fall on stigma of the same flower leading to self pollination.

2. Cross pollination or Allogamy : When pollen from flowers of one plant are transmitted to stigmas of flowers of another plant it is known as cross pollination.

3. Geitonogamy : When pollen from a flower of one plant falls on the stigmas of the other flower of the same plant known as Geitonogamy *e.g.* In maize (genetic consequences are same as Autogamy).

Fertilization : Fusion of one sperms with the egg cell is called fertilization. It produces a 2n zygote. The other sperm fuses with the

2n secondary nucleus to yield a 3n primary endosperm nucleus. This is termed as triple fusion. Both fertilization and triple fusion must occur in the embryo sac (double fertilization) to enable the ovule to develop into a seed.

Embryogenesis : The zygote divides mitotically to produce an embryo. When seeds germinate their embryos give rise to new plants. The primary endosperm nucleus divides repeatedly to produce endosperm. Endosperm provides nutrition to the young developing embryos of all plants.

Significance of Sexual Reproduction :

1. It creates genetic variation and new gene combinations by segregation and recombination.
2. Genes present in two or more different strains/varieties can be brought together into a single strain/variety. This is achieved by hybridization.
3. Hybrid varieties can be produced and commercially used.
4. It is the basis of almost all breeding schemes/programmes.

Anthesis : The first opening of a flower is called anthesis. It occurs in the morning. It is affected by environmental factors like, tomeperature, humidity etc. The stigma is fully receptive at the time of anthesis. Generally pollen grains are shed from the anthers at this time. Knowledge of anthesis is helpful in making of crosses.

Emasculation is ordinarily done one day before anthesis and pollination of the emasculated flowers is done on the day of anthesis.

Modes of Pollination : Pollination refers to the transfer of pollen grains from anthers to stigmas.

Pollination is grouped into two types.

1. Self pollination (Autogamy)
2. Cross pollination (Allogamy)

Self pollination or Autogamy : Pollen from an anther may fall on stigma of the same flower knwon as self pollination. Many crops show > 95% self pollination but in most of these species self pollination is not complete and cross pollination may occur to 5% due to varietal or Environmental factors.

Mechanisms Promoting Self-Pollination: Self pollinated species must necessarily have bisexual flowers and their anther mature at the same time when their stigmas become receptive.

The following mechanisms promote self pollination.

1. **Cleistogamy :** The flowers do not open at all. This ensures complete self pollination since foreign pollen can not reach the stigma of the closed flower. e.g. some varieties of wheat, rice, oat etc.
2. **Chasmogamy :** Flowers do open, but self pollination occurs just before anthesis. In such cases some cross pollination may occur. e.g. wheat, barley, rice, etc.
3. In some crops the stigma is closely surrounded by anthers or Anthers are located around and slightly above the stigma. Pollination occurs after anthesis but the location of anthers ensures self-pollination. e.g. Brinjal, Tomato, etc.
4. In legumes, flowers open but the anthers and stigma remain enclosed a boat like structure formed by two petals). This ensures self pollination e.g. Pea, gram, soyabean, mungbean etc. (The stamens and the stigma are enclosed by the two petals forming keel).
5. In some species stigmas become receptive and elongate through the staminal column; this results in predominant self pollination.

Genetic Consequences of Self-Pollination :

1. It causes a rapid increase in homozygosity. Therefore, self pollinated populations are normally highly homozygous.
2. Self pollinated species do not show inbreeding depression, but may exihibit considerable heterosis.
3. Therefore, the aim of the breeding methods generally is to develop homozygous varieties. They constitute a pure line.

Cross Pollination or Allogamy :

When a flower is pollinated by pollen produced on another plant, called cross pollination. It is brought about by wind, or transmitted by water or insects.

Mechanisms Promoting Cross Pollinations

1. **Unisexuality :** Unisexual flowers are either staminate or pistillate.

   A. **Monoecy :** Both staminate and pistillate flowers occur in the same plant. e.g. maize, cucurbits, mango, castor etc.

   B. **Dioecy :** Male and female flowers are present on different plants. e.g. papaya, spinach, asparagus.

2. **Dichogamy :** When anthers of hermaphrodite (bisexual) flower mature at a time different from that when its stigma is receptive. This condition is called dichogamy.

   It is of two types :

   A. Protogyny

   B. Protandry.

   (A) **Protogyny :** Stigma of a flower becomes receptive before its anthers are mature, e.g. In Bajra.

   (B) **Protandry :** Stamens mature before stigma becomes receptive. e.g. in maize, sugar beats.

3. In alfalfa stigmas are covered with a waxy film, stigma become receptive only when this film is broken. The film is broken by the visit of honeybees. Which also effect cross pollination.
4. **Self Incompatibility :** In many species active pollen fails to effect fertilization on self pollination. This is known as self incompatibility.
5. In many species a combination of two or more factors is found; this increases the efficieny of the system. e.g. In maize, monoecy and protandry occur together.

Genetic Consequences of Cross Pollination

1. It preserves and promotes heterozygosity in a population.
2. Cross pollinated species are highly heterozygous. They show severe to high inbreeding depression and having high heterosis. Therefore, varieties of such crops should be as heterozygous as possible. e.g. hybrid varieties.
3. Such populations are random mating. Their gene and genotype frequencies follow the Hardy-Weinberg Law. This makes the consequences of selection in such populations very different from those obtained in self pollinated populations.

The Hardy-Weinberg Law : It was proposed independently by Hardy in 1908 and Weinberg in 1909.

"Gene" and genotype frequencies in a random mating population remain constant generation after generation if there is no selection, mutation, migration or random drift.

Genetic Diversity and Centres of Origin

Genetic diversity refers to genetic variablity present within and among species of the living oraganism. Genetic diversity is of great significance for further improvement of crop plants to provide an insurance against the possible crop-classes.

Evidences indicate that cultivated plants are not uniformly distributed throughout the world. Certain areas are rich in genetic diversity than others. N.I. Variator (1916-35) credited for providing knowledge about the global distribution of the crop plants and their wild relatives. He proposed Primary & Secondary Centres of Origin.

Primary Centres of Origin

Primary centres of origin are the areas which shows greatest diversity and are supposed to be orign place of the crop-plants and are generally uncultivated crops e.g. mountains, river-beds, valley, hill.

Secondary Centres of Origin

Secondary centres of origin are the areas in which crop-plants are not supposed to have originated but exibit great diversity of forms.

Centres of origin are the areas with rich genetic diversity and are potential areas for germplasm explorations both at present and for future.

Micro Centres of origin are the areas which shows maximum diversity.

Centres	*Areas*	*Crops*
1. Chinese	Mountaneous regions of Central and West China.	Radish, Opium-poppy, some species of Brassica, Pears, Beaches, Palm Maize, Razma, Cow-pea, Turnip, Secale.
2. Hindustan (a) Indo-Burma (b) Siam-Malaya-Java	North-East India & Burma Sumatra, Bornco, Phillipines, Siam, Malaya, Java	Cucumber, Mango, Cotton, Rice & Sugarcane. Banana, Coconut & Yarn.
3. Central-Asia (Afghanistan)	N-W India, Afganistan, Tazekistan, Uzbakistan, Tian-Sian	*Triticum aestivum, T.compactum,* Pea, Lentil, Flakes, Garlic, Onion, Almond, Apple, Carrot.
4. Asia-Minor (Near-Eastern)	Asia-minor, Transcane asia Iran and part of Turk-manistan	Alfa-Alfa, Cabbage, Rye, oat *B. compestris, B. nigra.* *B. japonica, B. rapa.*
5. Mediterranian	Mediterranian regions	Durum-wheat, Emmer wheat, Peppermint,
6. Abyssinian (Ethopian)	Ethopia, hilly areas of Eritrea	Barley, Castor, Coffee, Grain, Sorghum, Bajra, Broad bean.
7. Central American (Mexican)	South Mexico, Central America	Maize, Razma, Lima bean, Pappaya, Upland Cotton, Guvava, Auagado.
8. South-American		

Centres	Areas	Crops
(a) Peru C.o Peruvian-Equatorian-Bolivian	Peru, Bolivia, Equator	Egyptian Cotton, Pumpkin, Tomato.
(b) Chile	Chile	Potato.
(c) Brazilian-Peru-Guayan	Brazil, Peru, Guayana	Ground nut, Rubber, tree, Pine-apple.
(9) U.S.A (C.o)	USA	Sunflower, Jeruselumarti.

Main Features of Primary Centres :

(*i*) They have large number of dominant genes.

(*ii*) They have wide range of genetic diversity/variability.

(*iii*) Mostly have wild characters.

(*iv*) Shows less crossing over.

(*v*) Natural selection operates.

Secondary Centres of Diversity : Vavilor suggested that various forms of crop plants introduced far away from their primary areas of origin which is called secondary centre of origin.

Main Features of Secondary Centres :

(*i*) They have lesser genetic diversity than primary centres.

(*ii*) They have large number of recessive genes.

(*iii*) Mostly have desirable characters.

(*iv*) Exhibit more crossing over.

(*v*) Both natural and artificial selection operates.

Micro-Centre : In some cases small areas within the centres of diversity show more genetic diversity of some crops is called micro centres.

Gene-Senctury : An area within C.O. diversity protected from human interferance.

Activity or Germplasm or Genetic Resources

(*i*) Exploration or visit and collection

(*ii*) Conservation

(*iii*) Evaluation

(*iv*) Documentation

(*v*) Distribution, Multiplication and Distribution

(*vi*) Ultilisation.

Domestication : It is the process of bringing wild species under human management is called domestication.

Significant changes in the plant species during domestication are :-

(*i*) Almost all the characteristics of plant species have been affected under domestication.

(*ii*) Changes in dormancy.

(*iii*) Decrease in toxins another undesirable substances. e.g. bitter-guard.

(*iv*) Changes in Plant-type e.g. high tillering, high branching, plant height.

(*v*) Reproduction in shattering of parts and spikes.

(*vi*) Changes in size of grains and fruits.

(*vii*) Changes in life-cycle.

(*viii*) Promoted asexual reproduction.

Kinds of Domestication

(*i*) Cultivated type

(*ii*) Wild type.

Acclimatization

The process that leads to adoptation of a variety in a new environment is called acclimatization.

Adoptation : It is a process by which organism become more suited to survive and function in a given environment.

Plant Introduction : It consists of taking a genotype or a group of genotypes or species into an area where they were not grown before even within a country.

or

It is a process of introducting crop-plants into new areas.

Types of Introduction :

1. Primary Introduction : When the introduced variety is well suited to the new environment and directly released as a variety for commercial cultivation without any changes.

e.g. in wheat crop, *Lerma rojo*, Sonora-64

In rice, Tai-chung native-1 (TN1), IR-8, IR-36, IR-28, Tai-chung-65, Maisoori.

2. Secondary Introduction : The introduced variety may be subjected to selection to isolate a superior variety under breeding programme means it may be used in hybridization with a local variety to transfer one or few genes or characters from this variety to local variety. This process is called secondary introduction.

e.g. Kalyan Sona, Sonalika in wheat

Rice - Ratna, Jaya, Saryu-52

These varieties are selected from meterials introduced from CIMMYT, Mexico.

Plant Introduction Agencies : In 1946, plant introduction Agency was started at I.A.R.I, New Delhi founded by ICAR in 1961 division of plant introduction in IARI.

In 1976 a separate institute NBPGR (National Bureau of Plant Genetic Resources, New Delhi) was established.

Sub Stations of NBPGR

(*i*) Shimla (H.P.) for temperate zone.

(*ii*) Jodhpur (Rajasthan) for arid zone.

(*iii*) Kanyakumari (Tamil Nadu) as tropical zone.

(*iv*) Akola (Maharastra) as mid-climatic zone.

Procedure of Plant Introduction

1. Procurement of Germplasm : The Indian scientists send their requirementr to NBPGR, it required germplasm is not available at NBPGR then they collect them from other countries through (IBPGR) International Bureau of Plant Genetic Resources, Rome (Italy). Now called IPGRI (International Plant Genetic Resources Institute) Rome.

2. Plant Quarantine : Quarantine means to keep materials in isolation to prevent spreading of new diseases, insects and weeds.

When the material is collected and introduced from other countries, this act was formulated in India in 1914 as destructive insects and pest acts.

Plant Quarantins Stations are :

(*i*) NBPGR, New Delhi : National Bureau of Plant Genetic Resources.

(*ii*) FRI, (Forest Research Institute) Dehradun.

(*iii*) BSI, (Botanical Survey of India), Kolkatta.

(*iv*) Directorate of Plant Protection, Quarantine and Storage, Faridabad, Haryana.

(*v*) Port of Entry, Delhi, Mumbai, Kolkata, Chennai.

3. Cataloguing : Introduced material is catalogued with following information and classfied into 3 types :-

(*i*) Name of species and variety.

(*ii*) Place of origin.

(*iii*) Adaptation.

(*iv*) Specific characters.

And Classified as :

(*i*) Exotic Collection (E.C.).

(*ii*) Indigenous Collection (I.C.).

(*iii*) Indigenous Wild Collection (I.W.C.).

4. **Evaluation :** To access the potential of new introduced plant material collected from different places.

Research Centres

National Level :

Rice : CRRI–Central Rice Research Institute Cuttak, Orrisa.)

DRR-Directorate of Rice Research, Hyderabad, Andhra Pradesh.

Sugarcane : IISR–(Indian Institute of Sugarcane Research, Lucknow.

SBI–(Sugarcane Breeding Institute, Coimbatare, Tamil Nadu.

Wheat and Barley : DWR (Directorate of Wheat Research, Karnal, Haryana.

Pulses - I.I.P.R. Indian Institute of Pulses Research Kalyanpur; Kanpur, U.P.

Oil seed - Rape Seed Mustard

NRC - National Research Centre for Rape seed, Mustard Bharatpur, Rajasthan.

NRC - for Ground nut - Junagarh, Gujarat.

DOR - (other oilseed) - Directorate for Oilseed Research Hyderabad.

Soyabean - NRC - Indore

Maize - IARI

Potato - CPRI - Central Potato Research Institute, Khufri, Shimla

Cotton - CICR - Central Institute for Cotton Research, Nagpur, Maharashtra.

Tobacco - CTRI - Central Tobacco Research Institute, Raja Mundri, A.P.

Forage Crop - IGFRI - Indian Grassland and Fodder Research Institute, Jhansi, U.P.

Tuber Crop - CTCRI - Central Tuber Crop Research Institute Trivendram, Kerala.

Horticultural Crop - IIHR - Indian Institute of Horticultural Research, Banglore.

CROP IMPROVEMENT

Crop improvement means combining desirable characters in one plant and then multiplying if for mass cultivation. The art of combining useful characters in a single plant is called **plant breeding**. It is specialized technology based on the knowledge of genetics.

Crop improvement through plant breeding has made significant progress in the last seventy five years with phenomenal achievements in the past two decades. It has relsulted in introduction of improved crop plants having higher yield and better qualities with respect to taste, nutrition, disease resistance, stress tolerance, keeping quality etc. In recent years embryo rescue and cell hybridization through tissue culture and production of genetically engineered transgenic plants have added new dimensions to crop improvement. It is now clearly understood that within a given environment crop improvement can be achieved through superior heredity. The variouis aspects of crop improvement are selection, hybridization, polyploid breedig, induced mutation, tissue culture and genetic engineering.

SELECTION

Selection is the choice of certain individual plants based on useful characters from a population. It can be natural and artificial.

I. Natural Selection

It is the process by which those organisms that appear physically, physiologically and behaviourally better adapted to the environment survive and reproduce. They pass on their successful characteristics to the next generation. Those that are not so well adapted either fail to reproduce or die. Thus selection operates through differential mortality and differential reproductive potential. As a process it perpetuates that ensure the survival of species in a given environment.

In nature, environmental limiting factor and population size both operate together to produce a selection pressure. It determines the advantageous alleles when they are expressed in phenotypes for selection. Thus selection pressure determines the spread of an allele within the gene pool. There operate in nature three types of selection process as follows :

(*i*) **Stabilizing Selection :** This operates when phenotypic features coincide with the requirements under optimal environmental conditions. It occurs in all populations. It therefore helps to maintain phenotypic stability within the population over generations.

(*ii*) **Directional Selection :** This operates in response to gradual changes in environmental conditions and moves the mean phenotypes towards one extreme of population.

(*iii*) **Disruptive Selection :** This is rarest form of selection where selection pressure acting from within the population because of extreme intraspecific competition pushes the population away from phenotypic mean towards the extremes of population. This form of selection results in polymorphism and fomation of ecotypes.

II. Artificial Selection

Human beings have used artificial selection in the form of domestication of plants and animals from prehistoric times. The basis of artificial selection is the isolation of natural populations and selective breeding of organisms showing characters useful for man. In artificial selection the humans exert the directional selection pressure which changes the genotype frequencies within the population. Ultimately it results in the formation of new breeds, strains, varieties, races and subspecies of domesticated plants and animals.

SELECTION IN CROP IMPROVEMENT

Selection in crop improvement is a type of artificial selection where plants having desirable characters are separated from their natural populations and propagated for human use. It is practised in three different ways as follows:

I. Pure Line Selection

In this method a population of homozygous plants having desirable characters is raised from a single homozygous plant. Therefore this is often called **single plant selection**. For pure line production several individual plants having the desired characters are selected from a natural population. Each of these plants is then selfed and its seeds are collected and sown separately. The progeny is then subjected to single plant selection for desirable characters. The process is repeated for several generations till true breeding homozygous plants with the desired characters are obtained. Once this is achieved the pure line is multiplied on a commercial scale for cultivation. Thus pure line is a collection of true breeding plants resulting from self pollination of a single homozygous individual. Usually considerable homozygosity can be achieved after ten generations. Once pure lines are obtained for different characters they can be crossed and selected out to introduce several desirable characters into single plant which is then multiplied for commercial use.

Pure line selection is very important in selection of quantitative characters such as grain weight, sugar content, oil content, protein content, vitamins content, lint length etc. Several improved varieties of rice, wheat, sugar beet, oil seeds and cotton have been developed by pure line selection.

II. Mass Selection

The process of selection of large number of plants having similar morphological characters from the field is called mass selection. Seeds of the selected plants are mixed together and sown to raise a population. From the progeny population plants are again selected having desirable characters. The process is repeated till the desired characters are retained. The purpose of mass selection is to eliminate inferior genotypes and to improve the general level of performance by bulking of superior genotype already present in the population. It is the oldest practice employed in crop improvement. Though its use in self pollinated plants is limited it is particularly useful for cross pollinated plants.

The greatest demerit of this method is the chance selection of genetically inferior plants which may appear phenotypically superior because of the availability of more nuturients and growth substances.

III. Clonal Selection

This is the process of selecting a plant having desired characters and vegetatively multiplying it for mass cultivation. This process is particularly important for plants propagated by vegetative means such as sugarcane, banana, potato etc.

PEDIGREE ANALYSIS

Inheritance of characters in humans is reconstructed by tracing the lineages. A table, chart or diagram representing the ancestry of an individual is called **pedigree**. Movement and distribution of certain genetic traits can be studied through pedigree analysis. It is necessary because controlled genetic experiments are not possible in man.

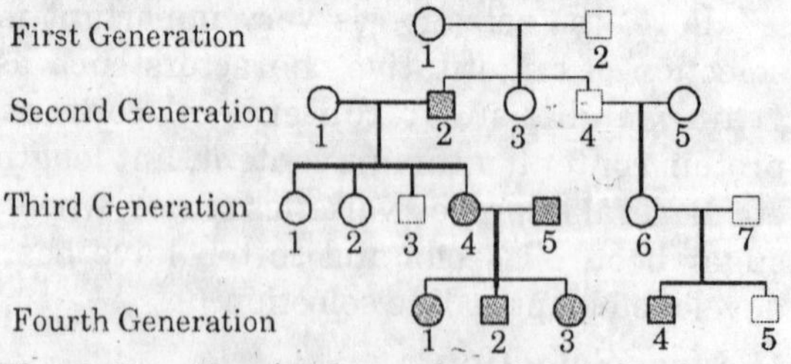

Fig. 6. A pedigree chart showing inheritance of adherent ear lobes which is governed by a recessive gene. From the pedigree chart try to find out the individuals in generations I, II and III for the recessive gene.

Conventionally pedigree analysis is made through a chart. In pedigree chart it is conventional to use circles (○) for females and squares for males (□). The normal characters is represented in (empty symbols (○ or □) and the character to be studied is represented in bold (● or ■). The parents are joined by a horizontal marriage line. The symbols of their children are placed below the parents in order of birth and are joined by a horizontal line, which is joined to the marriage line through a vertical line.

Three basic steps are followed in all pedigree analysis. They are :

1. What is the chance that one parent is a carrier of the gene in question.
2. What is the chance that other parent is a carrier for the same gene.
3. What is the chance that child of these two parents would express the trait in question.

Pedigree analysis is helpful in genetic counselling.

HYBRIDIZATION

Hybridization is the crossing between individuals of genetically different populations. It brings about new gene combinations in the progeny. Such progeny are known as **hybrids** and often have phenoytpic characters that are superior to either of the parental stocks. This phenomenon is called **hybrid vigour** or **heterosis.**

Although particulary useful in plant breeding, hybridization among domestic animals and birds is now widely practised to increase commercial production of meat, eggs, milk and wool. The desired genes of two or more individuals, varieties, or even species can be brought together through hybridization. Selected parents that differ in one or more genes artificially crossed and the progeny are grown for several generations. During this time new gene combinations are brought about by crossing over and independent assortment.

Ultimately, forms with desired phenotype and genotype are selected for propagation on commercial scale. Hybridization thus does not create new genes. It only makes available combinations of gene available in the parental stock. After a time, the limit of such desirable combinations, hence selection, is reached. Then it becomes necessary to introduce new and different genes from other closely related stocks.

Hybridization is applicable to both self and cross pollinated plants. It can be of different types as follows based on the parents involved in crossing.

1. Intraspecific hybridization : In this type both the parents belong to same species. The intraspecific hybridization can be intravarietal involving parents of same variety or intervarietal involving parents of different varieties of a species.

2. Interspecific hybridization : In interspecific hybridization parents crossed belong to related species of a genus.

3. Intergeneric hybridization : In this type the parents belong to different related genera.

Intraspecific hybridizations are common in nature. They are higly successful when done artificially. Interspecific crosses are rare in nature and result in very little success when done artificially. Intergeneric crosses generally result in failures. This happens because in such wide crosses between distantly related species, the haploid sets of chromosomes in the uniting gametes are no longer homologous. Consequently, the zygote contains two distinct haploid chromosomes sets. It either aborts or develops into an infertile, hence biologically unsuccessful adult. However, in distant crosses the progeny becomes fertile and biologically successful if the cromosomes in zygotes are somehow double making two diploid (2n + 2n) sets. Artificial doubling of chromosomes in plants can be induced by drug **clochicine**. The plants having more than one diploid chromosome set are called polyploids. Most of our crops have evolved though polyploidy in nature.

Crop improvement by hybridization takes a long time. It requires a difinite objective, careful progamming and selection of proper germplasm to be successful. The basic aim of hybridization is to:

(*i*) Combine all good characters into a single variety

(*ii*) Increase genetic variability and

(*iii*) Exploit and utilize hybrid vigour.

HYRBID VIGOUR

The increased vigour, growth, productiviy or other functions of the F_1 hybrids over their parents resulting from cross between genetically unlike parents is called **hybrid vigour** or **heterosis**. The F_1 progeny being heterozygous, the harmful effects of recessive alleles are masked by their dominant alleles. This results in hybrid vigour. In some varieties the heterosis results from interaction between particular combination of alleles in heterozygotes.

Heterosis is lost by continuous inbreeding as it increases homozygosity. Hence it becomes necessary to maintain parental lines for continued hybrid seed production. However, heterosis is maintained in vegetative propagation where there is no genetic recombination or segregation of characters. For example, in plants like potato, dahlias, chrysanthemum, roses etc. the hybrids are easily maintained by vegetative propagation.

Hybrid vigour has been successfully employed to increase yield of many crop plants such as maize, sorghum, bajra, wheat, cotton, tomato etc. it is also used in animals for producing better varieties of cattle, silkworms, poultry, pigs etc.

ORIGIN OF NEW PLANT VARIETIES AND SPECIES THROUGH HYBRIDIZATION AND POLYPLOIDY

All dwarf wheat varieties of wheat are derived from crosses with mexican dwarf wheat. Most dwarf rice varieties are produced by incorporation of dwarfing gene *Dee-geo-gen* either from 'Taichung native 1' or 'IR 8' through hybridization. All sugarcane varieties have been derived from introduced noble canes. The 'Pusa Ruby' tomato is obtained from a cross between 'Meerut' and 'Sioux'. Potato variety 'Kufri Kuber' was developed from a complex interspecific hybridization between : (*Solanum curtilobum* × *Solanum tuberosum*) × *Solanum andigena*. The list of such new improved varieties produced through hybridization is endless.

Sometimes new species are created when the chromosome number of F_1 hybrid of a interspecific cross is doubled. This is called polyploidy. This was first demonstrated by Karpechenko by artificial production of a new species *Raphanobrassica* from a cross between cabbage and radish as outlined.

Cabbage (*Brassica oleracea*) 2n = 18 X Raddish (*Raphanus sativus*) 2n = 18

↓

F_1 (Sterile plants) 2n = 18

↓

Chromosome doubling

↓

F_2 hybrids (*Raphanobrassica*) 4n = 36

In nature such hybridization followed by chromosome doubling was responsible for origin of bread wheat which is a hexaploid plant. The course followed in nature which was arrived at through breeding is :

Eincorn Wheat (*Triticum monococcum*) 2n = 14 X Goat grass (*Aegilops speltoides*) 2*n* = 14

↓

Sterilie F_1 2n = 14

↓

Chromosome doubling

↓

Fertile Emmer Wheat (*Triticum durum*) 2*n* = 28

Emmer Wheat 2n = 28 X Wild grass (*Aegilops squarossa*) 2n = 14

↓

Sterile F_1, a triploid 2n = 21

↓

Chromosome doubling

↓

Fertile hexaploid plant Bread wheat (*Triticum aestivum*) 2*n* = 42

Like wheat, many species of our crop plants have evolved in nature through hybridization followed by polyploidy.

ROLE OF BIOTECHNLOGOY IN PLANT BREEDING

Biotechnology uses a package of powerful techniques for manipulation and alteration of life forms and applies engineering principles to such life forms for the processing of materials to provide the desired end products and services. With the recent developments in genetic engineering, molecular biology, cell-to-cell fusion and culture, protein engineering, immunology and immuno-diagnostics and fermentation technology, biotechnology has emerged as a strong multi-disciplinary field where basic and applied sciences have come together.

The induction of foreign genes into cells has made it possible to bypass conventional barriers of genetic incompatibilities and create a variety with entirely new characteristics and functions. Over a wide range of areas like agriculture, industry, health care, population control, energy production, environment control, veterinary sciences and aquaculture, biotechnology has revolutionary implications in resolving problems, improving, productivity, making new products and providing services.

Spinoff from New Techniques

The recombinant DNA technique as well as technologies such as somaclonal variations, protoplast fusion, clonal propagation, including micro-propagation, organogenesis and somatic embryogenesis provide opportunities to bring in new value-added, stress-tolerant, disease and pest-resistant varieties of crops. Similarly, transgenic animals can now produced and there are new opportunities for genetic improvement of traditionally important livestock, Immuno-diagnostics for detection of diseases in plants and animals, embryo transfer technology for berd improvement and better milk production are available in agricultural biotechnology for improving the quality and quantity of production.

Agriculture is a major sector of the Indian economy. About 70 per cent of the population depends on it. Agricultural production contributes nearly a third of the national income and about 35 per cent of the total exports. From the time people began to cultivate land, they have looked for ways to improve productivity and reduce costs. In this century, modern plant breeding has provided farmers with crop varieties that are high yielding, resistant to diseases and pests, and can grow in stress conditions.

Chemicals have been developed to control weeds and pests and to raise the level of nitrogen in the soil. In spite of this, damage to field crops has been very heavy.

Various types of diseases, insects, drought, high salinity, high temperature as well as frost, have cost the country heavily in terms of crop and income losses. It is difficult to eliminate such losses through the use of conventional agricultural practices, which do not help beyond a certain limit in increasing crop productivity. Large quantities of edible oils continue to be imported. India which has more than 30 per cent of the world's cattle population, does not produce even 10 per cent of useful products from these animals. Even with a coastline stretching over 7,000 km and over 27000 km. length of rivers and 100,000 km length of canals and channels, only a little over 30 lakh tonnes of fish are harvested. In spite of the recent good performance in cereals production, it will be difficult to reach the target of sustained production of 240 million tonnes of foodgrains by the turn of the century. Pulses production is stagnating at the level of about 33 million tonnes. Production of fertilizers, milk and milk products is far behind the requirements.

Priorities in Agriculture

Agricultural production continues to be severely affected by the vagaries of monsoon. Greater attention has to be paid to evolve more integrated management of water, soil, soil moisture and soil fertility. It is also necessary to make farming less dependent on water and to utilize increasingly marginal and less productive land for agricultural purposes. Greater fertilizer efficiency has to be achieved and dependence on chemcial pesticides reduced. These requirements and limitations have set the national priorities in biotechnology in the field of agriculture.

These Priorities are :

1. Development and greater use of biological fertilizer;
2. Development and better use of biological pest control;

3. Development of new varieties of cultivars with greater stress tolerance to factors such as :

   (*a*) Insufficient soil moisture;

   (*b*) Salinity and

   (*c*) Pests and diseases;
4. Large-scale production of seeds of high-yielding varieties, hybrid seeds and other propagules;
5. Large-scale production of elite plants of economic improtance, through micro-propagation and tissue culture.
6. Introduction of high-yielding crops for production of edible oils such as oil palm amd elite coconut through tissue culture;
7. use of fast growing multi-purpose trees and other species that can grow on waste degraded land for biomass production, and
8. Introduction of high-yielding commercial crops such as oil palm, coconut, rubber, tea, coffee, coco and tree fruits and fuel, fodder and timber species;

The following are some of the programmes taken up by the Department of Biotechnology (DHT) in the field of agriculture:

Tissue culture micro-propagation of elite tress :

(*i*) Bamboos : A project on tissue culture of bamboo has been initiated by the Department of Biotechnology (DBT) at the University of Delhi. The objectives are to develop and standardise methods for mass propagation of various species of bamboo available in India, using tissue culture techniques. About 1,500 tissue culture bamboo plantlets have been produced and planted in Uttar Pradesh, Orissa, Karnataka and Delhi for evaluation in terms of fast growth enhanced biomass production.

(*ii*) Pilot plants for teak, eucalyptus and sandalwood : Two pilot plant facilities - one at the Tata Energy Research Institute, New Delhi, and the other at the National Chemical Laboratory, Pune, - are being set up for mass scale micro-propagation of certified planting material from the elites of important forest tree species of teak, eucalyptus and sandalwood.

Bio-pesticides : The Government of India has taken up projects to exploit the naturally occurring biological agents for efficient management of insects, pests and diseases. Biotechnology will be a tool to develop them as effective control agents. Mass production techniques, on a pilot scale first, and then on a large-scale, will be standardised. Under this programme, viral, bacterial and fungal agents will be produced to control several important insect pests affecting agriculture and health.

Biofertilizers

(*i*) A major programme for large-scale fermenter-based Rhizobia inoculants productions with high quality control and inhouse R and D back-up is being taken up. The objective is to make available Rhizobium biofertilizer for use in some of the major oilseeds and pulse crops.

(*ii*) Blue-green algal (BGA) biofertilizer : The DBT has also set up a National Facility for blue-green algal collection at the Indian Agricultural Research Institute, New Delhi. This facility is collecting, screening and identifying nitrogen-fixing BGA strains suitable for rice cultivation in different agro-climatic regions. it has also developed as economic, rural-oriented, algal biofertilizer technology for rice. It is also supplying soil-based BGA starter culture to farmers for use as biofertilizer in rice crops.

Tissue culture of cadramom : Cardamom is an export-oriented spice cultivated over one lakh hectares in Kerala,

Karnataka and Tamil Nadu. The productivity, however, is very low at around 60 kg as against 250 kg per hectare to Güatemala. The tissue culture propagation method for cardamom has been standardised and techniques for large-scale multiplication are available within the country. The DBT has taken up a project to demonstrate the performance of elite *in vitro* clones of cardamom throughout the cardamom growing areas, dividing them into 100 units of one hectare each.

Genetic Engineering and Plant Cell Transformation

Genetic engineering simulates genetic recombination at the DNA level outside the cell, it involves isolation of a DNA stretch corresponding to a particular function of a donor and hooking it to a vector for the purpose of transference. It can also involve, when the amino acid sequence of the protein product of a gene is known, synthesizing a gene artificially on the basis of genetic code dictionary and transferring it to the desired recipient.

The following steps of the recombinant DNA technology, also referred to as genetic engineering, are improtant.

1. Gene identification : There are several methods of isolating a particular gene. The first one is applicable when the gene produces a large enough amount of mRNA that can be isolated. The mRNA is copied, by reverse transcriptase, into corresponding cDNA which is turn is used as a probe to fish out the gene from genomic libraries. Genomic library refers to the pool of DNA fragments of a genome produced by the action of restriction enzymes and maintained as clones in a suitable host, usually *E. coli*. In the second method, the protein product of the gene is used as the starting material to artificially synthesize DNA segments based on amino acid sequence of the protein. These DNA segments can be used as probes for identifying the gene from genomic libraries. These two methods have been most widely used. Other mothods of gene identification are chromosome walking, as practical in Drosophila, and use of transposable or mobile elements in plants.

2. Gene transfer : Once the desired gene has been identified and isolated, it needs to be transferred to the recipient. Two major avenues are currenty used for this purpose :

(*i*) Vector mediated transfer which uses the agency of plasmids and viral vectors. Among the plasmids, T_1 of Agrobacterium luminaciens is the most extensively used and the most promising one. It affects gene transfer in dicotyledenous species with high frequency. Attempts are also underway to develop plant viruses, like cauliflower mosaic virus (CaMV), as vectors for gene transfer.

(*ii*) Plant Transformation : This procedure aims as direct introduction of DNA segment into the plant cell. Protoplasts and pollen are considered suitable material for DNA introduction. Among the methods tried for achieving this are co-cultivation (incubating the recipient cells with purified or gene enriched DNA), electroporation (carried out by applying high electric potential for microseconds to change the porosity of the cells to allow intake of DNA molecules) and microinjection (using very find glass needles to inject the desired tranforming DNA directly into the nucleus).

3. Gene integration and expression : For a change to be heritable, stable integration of the donor DNA into the recipient genome is essential. The basic mechanism for this integration is through breakage and reunion following pairing of homologous regions. Even after integration, a foreign gene will express only when it receives relvant signals. When integrated segment is complete (structural plus regulatory elements), the transferred genes are normally expressed. If complete regulatory signals are not available in the donor DNA, the genes will express only when brought under control of the host regulatory elements.

Genetic engineering has tremendous potentials for improving crop plants and has opened up avenues of genetic manipulation which were unthinkable even a couple of decades ago. The complexity of organization of the genetic material in eukaryotes, inadequate knowledge of gene expression and the wide gap in our understanding of the biochemical pathways between the initial steps of gene action and realization of the phenotypes necessitates considerable more work before recombinant DNA technology finds general application for field crop improvement. It is also important to keep in mind that the major contribution of the new technology will be to reach the stage of a stabilized recombinant in the conventional plant breeding procedure. For attaining the maximum gains from this procedure, therefore, conventional plant breeding will still retain relevance when all the methodologies of genetic engineering are perfected. An integrate approach involving the techniques of new biology and the time-tested procedures of agricultural improvement would be the most profitable option for the future.

Biotechnology and Ribulose Bisphosphate Carboxylase-Oxygenase

The balance between photosynthesis and photorespiration controls agricultural production and the balance is determined by the properties of the enzyme bisphophate carboxylase oxygenase. This enzyme is, therefore, a major target for genetic engineering because, if it were possible to alter its properties to favour photosynthesis, major improvements in agricultural productivity could result. All aspects of this important enzyme, from its structure, synthesis and genetic manipulations have attracted the attention of scientists engaged in bio-engineering research.

New Bio-pesticides

Two new bio-pesticides developed by the Centre for Biotechnology at Anna University, Chennai are to be manufactured on a semi-commercial scale by the Tuticorin Allied Chemicals and Fertilizers Ltd.

The formulation containing *Bacillius sphaericus* will be effective against mosquito larvae and will be sold as 'Spic Biomass'. The other formulation containing *Bacillus thuringiensis* called 'Spic Twins' can be used against a host of crop plants.

Cloning

This refers to the practise of repeated propagation of desired foreign genes after inserting them into the DNA of plasmids of bacteria. Chang and Kohen have done pioneering works on the cloning of DNA. They isolated pieces of main chromosome DNA from Staphylococcus. They spliced individual pieces into non-conjugal plasmids. These recombinant plasmids were introduced into *E. coli*. It was found that *E. coli* (host) correctly expressed genes of Staphylococcus. It was concluded that any one clone of *E. coli* host cells would probably carry only one recombinant plasmid and only one piece of Staphylococcus DNA. In this way, large number of particular *E. coli* give rise to large quantities of a particular segment of the staphylococcal genome. This technique is known as DNA cloning.

Seed Production of Cross-pollinated (hybrid) Maize, Jowar, Bajra, etc.

Maize (*Zea mays*) : The presently grown maize hybrids in India are double-crossed. Foundation seeds of two single-crossed are supplied for production of double-crossed hybrid seed. One of these single-crossed is used as the female or seed parent. This is tagged with a yellow label. The other single-cross is the male parent and is marked with a red label. The foundation seed is very valuable and produced at high cost. It is sold on a viable kernel basis. One hectare of land requires 50,000 viable kernels.

Single-Cross Seed Production : Single-cross seed is produced on inbred lines. In the crossing block, the usual planting pattern is two rows of the female inbred (a) to one row of male inbred (b). Detasseling of the female line is done as soon as the tassels are seen emerging out of the flag leaves.

Double-Cross Seed : The double-cross seed is produced on a high yielding female single cross. The double-cross seeds are certified and sold to the farmers for commercial cultivation.

Planting Ratio : The seed-crop must be planted in rows. The usual planting ratio for double-cross seed production is two male rows for every six female rows. Out of the 50,000 viable kernels that are supplied 12,500 are of the male parent and 37,500 of the female parent. Row to row spacing may be 75-90 cm and plant to plant within row is 20-25 cm. Seed should be sown not more than 4-5 cm deep. Male rows are marked at both ends with flags, tagged pegs or marked plants (Sunnhemp or Dhaincha, etc.).

Questions From Previous Year's Papers

Q. 1. What are Back cross and Test cross? Explain their significance in plant breeding.

Q. 2. Answer the following in about 150 words each :

(a) Give a concise account of common method exployed for breeding a typical cross-pollinated crop for higheryield.

(b) What are the causes of male sterility? How could it be exploited for varietal improvement programme?

Q. 3. (a) What is self-incompatibility? Describe its mechanism and relevance in plant breeding.

(b) Give an illustrated account of linkage of genes and its significance in crop improvement.

(c) Describe multi-line varieties with their merits and demerits.

(d) What are distant hybrids? Describe briefly the methods followed to produce distant hybrids and assess their use in crop improvement with suitable examples.

Q. 4. Answer the following in about 150 words each :

(a) What do you mean by mass selection? Discuss its merits and demerits.

(b) What is a clone? Describe the various characteristics of clones.

(c) Briefly describe the various mechanisms of disease resistance in plants.

(d) Explain the genetic basis of breeding of high-yielding varieties in rice. Indicate the present status of the breeding programme.

Q. 5. Answer the following in about 150 words each :

(a) Write the brief the role of biotechnology in plant breeding.

(b) What is drought resistance? Give the methods followed for screening germ plasm in crop species for drought resistance.

Q. 6. Answer the following in about 150 words each :

Define breeding methods, procedure for the following:

(a) Mass selection

(b) Pure line selection

(c) Pedigree method

(d) Backcross method

Q. 7. Answer the following in about 150 words each :

(a) Define heritability. Mention its laws and their significance in plant breeding.

(b) Explain hybrid vigour and its exploitation in crops.

(c) Differentiate between pure line selection and recurrent selection

(d) Give physological importance of diffusion and osmosis.

Q. 8. How a method of plant breeding differs with a breeding technique?

Q. 9. Why back cross method of breeding is used for incorporating disease resistance in plants? How will you transfer resistance when the resistance controlling gene is recessive?

Q. 10. Comment on the following in about 150 words each :

(a) A multi line variety compared to a pure line variety can resist disease spread better but it lacks purity of seed.

(b) Auxins and hormones play important role in plant development and growth.

(c) Processed fruits and flower products fetch higher gains than the unprocessed ones, provided quality standards are maintained.

(d) Agriculture is a gamble in the dark.

(e) High yielding crop varieties boosted food grain production besides saving foreign exchange.

Q. 11. Answer the following in about 150 words :

(a) What is progeny test? Discuss its significance in plant breeding.

(b) Define emasculation. Describe various methods of emasculation.

(c) What is inbreeding? Summarise the effects of inbreeding.

(d) Describe in brief the merits and demerits of mass selection.

(e) Incorporation of novel genes through genetic engineering.

Q. 12. Define hybrid. Give the merits and demerits of hybrids.

Q. 13. (a) Write short notes on the following in about 150 words each :

(a) International institutes for crop improvement.

(b) Multiline varieties.

(c) Micropropagation

Q. 14. Compare the following in about 150 words each:

(a) Pedigree method and bulk method of breeding.

(b) Inbreeds and hybrids.

4. SEED TECHNOLOGY

Seed is defined either Agronomically or Botanically. Agronomically a seed or seed material or propagule is the living organ of the crop in rudimentary form that is used for propagation or in other words, any part of the crop from which a new crop will grow.

Botanically seed is a fertilized ovule consisting of intact embryo stored food and seed coat which is viable and has got the capacity to germinate.

Agronomically germination means the capacity of seeds to give rise to normal sprouts within a definite period fixed for each crop under optimum field conditions.

Four essential factors for germination of seeds—

(*i*) Capacity of seed to germinate.

(*ii*) Moisture

(*iii*) Temperature (suitable)

(*iv*) Oxygen-supply.

Factors governing growth of plants—

(*i*) Parental feature

(*ii*) Air

(*iii*) Moisture

(*iv*) Temperature

(*v*) Light, and

(*vi*) Minerals.

Real Value of Seed : Real value of seed is the percentage of germinability of percentage of purity of seed lot of a crop plant.

$$RV = \frac{\text{Purity \%} \times \text{Germination \%}}{100}$$

RV is expressed in percentage and also known as Utility percentage of seed.

Conditions affecting the real value of seeds are the method of production, the method of handling and the method of storage. Seeds having a real value lower than 70% are usually not preferred for sowing purposes because of poor germination and purity values.

$$\text{Purity \%} = \frac{\text{Wt. of pure seed}}{\text{Wt. of bulk sample}} \times 100$$

(*i.e.* seed + impurities)

$$\text{Impurity \%} = \frac{\text{Wt. of Impurities present in bulk sample}}{\text{Wt. of bulk sample}} \times 100$$

(or Dockage) Impurity percentage is called Dockage.

Genetic Purity

Genetic purity is required 100% as far as impurities by seeds of other varieties of same crop is concerned but in case of Impurity by seeds of other crop species; it is permitted upto 0.1% only.

Types of Pure Seeds

There are four classes recognized by the International Crop Improvement Association.

1. Breeder/Nucleus Seed : Such seeds are produced directly under the supervision of plant breeder and possessed all the required genetic characters. Such seeds have high genetic value and are costly due to very little in quantity. It may be produced by the breeder's concerned Institution when breeder is not available. Breeder seed is used to produce foundation seed. In case of self pollinated species, mass selection may be regularly practiced to retain the genetic purity of the variety.

2. Foundation Seed : Produced from breeder seed and is the source of all other certified seed classes either directly or through registered seed. It is also known as Mother seed. Production of foundation seed is the responsibility of National Seeds Corporation. It is produced on Government farms, at experiment stations, Agriculture Universities or on cultivators' field under strict supervision of research scientists and experts from NSC or SSC. It has specific genetic identity and purity. White tag denotes foundation seed.

3. Registered Seed : Produced from FS or Registered seed itself. It is the parent of certified seed or RS. It has satisfactory genetic identity and purity and is usually produced by progressive farmers under technical guidance and supervision from SSC. It is often omitted and certified seed is produced directly from FS. It is general practice in India. It has purple tag.

4. Certified Seed : Progeny of RS, FS or CS itself. It has satisfactory genetic identity and purity. It is approved and certified by the state seed certifying agency; annually produced by progressive farmers according to standard seed production practices. It has blue tag. It is available for general distribution to farmers for commercial crop production. It is generally produced by SSC but NSC also undertakes its production, if required. Two classes of CS are produced *i.e.,* F_1 and F_2. Recertification is not permitted from F_2 generation (second) of seeds.

Other types of seeds in Agronomic use are —

Improved Seed : Is a better seed substitute for pure seed but is not so good with respect to genetic and physical factors. It has at least 10-15% more genetic potential than the local seed and are resistant to pest and diseases, well adapted to agro-climatic conditions of the locality, high in response to better condition of growth.

HYBRID SEED, COMPOSITE SEED AND MUTANT SEEDS

Viability Test

Seed's viability is defined as the capacity of the seed to remain capable of germination for some specific period of time. When the seeds are dormant or very slow in germination, the rapid test is extremely useful.

1. Respiration Test : Respiration is an indication of life but such tests are complicated.

2. Electrical Conductance Method : Seeds are soaked in distilled water and electrical conductance of such water is tested. The increase in conductance is roughly proportional to the percentage of dead tissues. The increase in the conductivity is due to leaching of metabolites from dead seeds.

3. Potassium permaganate Method: It is a qualitative test to find out whether seeds are viable. Increase in the proportion of dead seed, increases the discolouration of the solution since leaching from living cells is very less.

4. Indigocarmine Method : Portion of dead seeds is determined by counting the number of stained.

5. Embryo Culture Method : Takes about 7-10 days, Judged by counting the number of germinated embryos.

6. Tetrazolium Chloride Test : Known as Biochemical test. Seeds are soaked in 0.5-2% solution of 2, 3, 5 **triphenyl tetrazolium chloride.** The viable or living seeds take bright colouration and the colouration becomes more intense in the embryo. It can be made quicker by cutting kernels, using vacuum and maintaining a temperature of 40-

45° C, it takes only 4-5 minutes to complete a test of 100 kernels.

7. Grodex Test : Grodex is a seed germination indicator and is a brand name of triphenyl tertrazolum bromide in powder form.

Seed Moisture

Germination occurs when seed moisture is above 40-60%.

The moisture determination in seeds by—

1. Traditional bite test
2. Electrical moisture meters
3. Infra-red moisture meters
4. Oil distillation method
5. The lab oven method, and
6. Karl Fisher reagent method.

Seed Dormancy

Dormancy is the arrested development and reversible rest period of plant organs either of a seed or of any vegetative part. The formation of dormant structures is commonly associated with the suspension of metabolic, synthetic and morphogenetic activities that are associated with the minimum physiological activities and a minimum moisture content. During this period, there is very poor or total suspension of respiration or rather anaerobic respiration with higher respiration quotient.

Dormancy is due to lack or inactivity of hydrolytic enzymes. Gibberellins are the predominant germination agents found in the germination phase during the food reserve degradation stage. Cytokinins exert their influence later on the initiation of cell proliferation and expansion. Red light (660 mu) promotes and blue specially far-red light (735 mu) inhibits germination.

Dormancy can be broken artificially by various special treatments which may be grouped into two groups.

(*i*) Physical Treatment

1. Heat treatment at 40-45° C for different duration.
2. Low temperature treatment at 2-8° C for 12-24 hours but seeds should be presoaked for 36 hours before they are given the low temperature treatment.
3. Alternate heating and cooling for several times.
4. Alternate drying and wetting for several times.
5. Exposure for 24 hours of water soaked seed to red light for 1-2 hrs at 15-25° C temperature.
6. Dehusking or removal of seed coats (scarification) by rubbing to make it permeable to water.

(*ii*) Chemicals Treatment :

(1) Inorganic Chemicals

(*a*) *By acid treatment* : Dilute solutions of HNO_3, HCl or H_2SO_4 (0.1-0.5%) for different durations in minutes

(*b*) *KNO_3 (1-3%)* : Strongest and used for immediate dormancy break after harvesting; NH_4NO_3 (1-3%), H_2O_2, H_3BO_4 etc.

(*c*) *By Gases* : By increasing O_2 concentration.

(2) Organic Chemicals

(*a*) *Non-hormonal* : Thiourea, Ascorbic acid.

(*b*) *Hormonal* : GA_3 (1-1000 ppm);- Commonly used hormone to break dormancy; Others are Kinetin (1-100 ppm), Ethylene (Ethrel solution of 100-300 ppm).

Dehumidification : Removal of water-vapour from the air in storage. Silica gel is the most common desiccant used as chemical dehumidifier.

Tempering : Process of bringing grains or other products to a desired moisture or temperature for processing.

Matriclal is the heterogeneity in the quality due to location of the seeds in the inflorescence *e.g.* difference in flowering pattern.

Indian Seeds Act passed in 1966.

Seed Treatment

Besides breaking seed dormancy, seed treatment is also done before sowing the seed for the following purposes—

1. To protect from seed borne and soil borne diseases and insect-pests' damage.
2. To hasten nitrogen fixation capacity in case of pulses.
3. For easy sowing.
4. To promote germination.

(1) TREATMENT FOR DISEASES AND INSECTS CONTROL

(A) Physical Treatment

(a) *Hot water treatment :* Seeds are kept in hot water at a certain temp. for certain period. Later on, after cooling in cold water such seeds are dried in shade.

This method is successful in controlling following diseases—

Loose smut of Wheat (54° C for 10 minutes)

Loose smut of Barley (54° C for 13 minutes)

Alternaria blight of Wheat (38° C for 10 minutes)

Leaf spot of Til (54° C for one hour)

(b) *Solar treatment :* After soaking the seeds in water for some hours, seeds are dried in schorching sun in the month of May-June by keeping on cemented floor metal-sheet.

This method is used to control loose smut of Wheat and Barley.

(B) Chemical Treatment

Different fungicides *e.g.* Agrosan G.N., Çeresan, Captan Thiram etc. are used for the same.

(2) SEED INNOCULATION IN LEGUMES

Before sowing the legume crops in the new area, the legume seeds are to be inoculated with Rhizobium culture.

Seed Plot Technique of Potato

Objective : To produce seeds free from virus Y, A, X and S. These viruses are transmitted by aphids. Aphid population is low in hills during April to August while it is low in the plains during October to early January.

Nucleus seed of potato is produced in the hills during April to August when aphid population is low. It is brought to plains and is stored in cold-storage for planting the seed crop in October. The seed production practices are :

1. Start with disease free seed stocks.
2. Select suitable locations *i.e.,* aphids free during crop growth.
3. Adopt lands isolation and other requirement of certified seed production.
4. Rogueing and inspection of crops.

National Seed Corporation (NSC)

NSC was registered in 1963 having two main objectives —

1. To promote development of a seed industry in India.
2. To produce and supply foundation seeds of various crops.

State Seed Corporation (SSC)

SSCs are chiefly concerned with production and supply of certified seed.

To reduce the workload of NSC and to stimulate a faster growth of seed industry, SSCs were established in view of great success of and the impact made by the Tarai Development Corporation (TDC) Pantnagar, Uttarakhand.

State Seed Certification Agency : It is responsible for seed certification. SSCA makes field inspections and conducts seed tests required for seed certification.

WEED

Weed may be defined as unwanted and undesirable plant which interfere with the utilization of land and water resources and adversely affect human welfare.

Criteria of to be a Weed :

Whether a plant is weed or not, depends upon following :

(*i*) Characteristics and habit of plant

(*ii*) Relative position

(*iii*) Time of occurrence of plant.

Classification of Weed :

A. On the basis of site of Predominance

(A_1) ***Obligate weeds :*** Such weeds are grown only in association with man and his agriculture. It is never found in wild form *e.g. Chenopodium. Anagallis* etc.

(A_2) ***Facultative weeds :*** Such weeds are grown both as wild and in cultivated habitats *e.g. Argemone mexicana, Euphorbia hirta.*

B. On the basis of Dependence on Host

(B_1) Total Root parasite/Holo root parasite *e.g.* Orobanche

(B_2) Total stem parasite/Holo stem parasite *e.g.* Cuscuta

(B_3) Semi-root parasite *e.g.* Striga

(B_4) Semi-stem parasite *e.g. Loranthus* (birdvine).

Seed Testing and Standardization

Accurate and repeatable tests of seed quality are vitally important in several steps of the seed marketing process. The seed grower must have test results to determine if the seed meets contract requirements and to label the seed correctly. Certification agencies rely on a laboratory test to determine if the seed meets the required quality standards, Seed traders rely on the seed test to determine monetary value of the seed lot. Government officials require test results to determine if the seed meets the legal requirements for sale. Most countries impose import standards, and the seed test determines if the seed meets those import requirements. And for the consumer who buys the seed, test results indicate the planting value of the seed. To satisfy these needs, the seed lot may be sampled and tested several times in different laboratories.

TYPES OF SEED QUALITY TESTS

The tests normally required for labeling and selling of seed are purity, noxious weed seed content, and germination. Other tests frequently conducted for various purposes include moisture, vigor, variety indentification, seed health, tetrazolium, and mechanical damage, plus other more specialized tests such as seed size and plantability.

TYPES OF SEED TESTING LABORATORIES

Ownership and management of seed testing laboratories take several forms, within and between countries. In the U.S., for example, there are at least five categories of laboratories. The federal government laboratory tests seed to be imported and also seed lots which are in dispute in interstate shipment. State regulatory laboratories test seed within a state to determine if it is labeled correctly. Seed grown for certification may be tested in state laboratories or in laboratories operated by the state certification agency. Many seed companies maintain their own seed testing laboratories for quality assurance and labeling purposes. And there are numerous private laboratories that operate independently as commercial enterprises. It is extremely important to the orderly marketing of seeds that test procedures are standardized between laboratories so they all obtain the same results. Differing test results between laboratories can lead to costly disruption and delays in the marketing process.

WHY TEST RESULTS MAY VARY

Although seed testing laboratories generally obtain uniform test results, differences occasionally occur. Some of the most common reasons are the following :

1. ***Non-uniform seed lots :*** If improper sampling procedures are used, the samples drawn may not be representative of the lot and the samples received by the laboratories may not be equivalent.
2. ***Different test methods :*** The germination testing Rules frequently allow the use of optional substrate, temperatures, and dormancy-breaking treatments, the choice being left up to the individual analyst. The use of various optional methods may lead to different results, particularly if the seed lots are freshly harvested and partially dormant.
3. ***Different interpretation of the Rules :*** It is extremely difficult to describe certain test procedures unambigu-ously in writing, particularly when they are translated into several languages. Pure seed definitions and interpretation of abnormal seedlings would fall into this category.
4. ***Changes in physiological seed quality :*** Seeds are living organisms, and their response to germination test conditions may change if the tests are conducted several months apart. This is particularly true when the seeds are after-ripening and their dormancy status changes. Low viability may also lead to variable results since deteriorated seed are more sensitive to test conditions such as moisture content of the substrate and the presence of microorganisms.
5. ***Laboratory facilities :*** The quality of germinators, moisture testers, and other equipment, as well as their maintenance and calibration, may lead to undetected differences in test conditions.
6. ***Analyst knowledge and experience:*** The analyst must be able to recognize and control the various factors that lead to unreliable data.

STANDARDIZATION PROCEDURES

Numerous seed organization have been formed with the expressed purpose of promoting uniformity in testing. The International Seed Testing Association (ISTA), formed in 1924, is organization of 59 participating countries. Membership in the Association of Official Seed Analysts (AOSA), formed in 1908, is limited to the official laboratories in the United States and Canada. Membership in the Society of Commercial Seed Technologists (SCST), formed in 1922 consists of private commercial and company laboratories in the U.S. Many other national and regional association exist. Efforts to promote standardization of testing take the following forms :

1. ***Seed testing Rules :*** These Rules specify sample size and testing procedures for most species important in commerce. However, the Rules followed by different organization may differ is some aspects, and they are in constant need of refinement and revision as new information is gained.
2. ***Workshops, training courses, and conferences :*** The AOSA holds two 2-week Beginning Seed Analyst Short Courses a year. ISTA holds occasional workshops in various parts of the world.
3. ***Handbooks and training manuals :*** The AOSA published a seed analyst training manual in 1993 which will be used in conjunction with training courses. ISTA and AOSA have published handbooks on specific topics such as seedling classification, vigor testing, tetrazolium testing and others.
4. ***Referee testing programmes :*** Seed testing organization regularly conduct

referee tests among member laboratories on purity, seed identification, and germination. Laboratories whose results fall outside the norm are contacted to determine the causes of test variations.

5. ***Uniform report forms :*** ISTA laboratories issue international analysis certificates which expedite the international shipment of seeds. AOSA recently adopted a recommended Report of Seed Analysis Forum, which many laboratories have adopted, and which will help alleviate differences in methods of reporting.
6. ***Research on methods :*** Factors affecting differences in test results are often the subject of research projects. One popular topic is seed dormancy. The AOSA annually supports small research projects on seed testing.
7. ***Liasion between seed testing organizations :*** Because of the extensive international seed trade between Europe and North America, considerable effort has been expanded by ISTA and AOSA to reduce the variation in test methods of the two organizations. A joint committee is currently studying ways to harmonize 18 important differences in their Rules.
8. ***Internal quality assurance programmes :*** Most laboratories have some methods of monitoring test procedures to see that they are done correctly. ISTA is currently in the process of formalizing procedures for authorizing laboratories to issue ISTA international analysis certificates. The authorization protocol, based on ISO Guide 25, is designed to ensure that member laboratories, no matter what their size, have the necessary organization, laboratory management practices, and resources to produce accurate and reliable ISTA seed analysis certificates.

LABORATORY QUALITY ASSURANCE PROGRAMMES

For a laboratory to be recognized as technically competent, it must meet several general requirements under the proposed ISTA guidelines. It must have a well-trained staff. It must have all the items of equipment needed to perform the tests and measurements. Periodical maintenance of the equipment must be performed. The equipment should be calibrated at proper time intervals. Germinator temperatures should be monitored. Proper test methods and procedures should be followed.

The laboratory environment should be clean and conducive to good test performance. A systematic procedure for identifying and handling samples should be followed.

The laboratory should maintain a record of all procedures followed. Test results should be reported on an ISTA International Analyses Certificate or other appropriate report form.

ORGANIZING A LABORATORY QA PROGRAMMES

Detailed recommendations and suggestion for organizing a QA programme for a testing laboratory are provided in the following publications :

ISO Guide 25—	Requirements for competence of testing laboratories.
ISTA Document 4—	Adaptation of ISO 25 for seed testing laboratories.
ISO Guide 49—	Development of a laboratory quality assurance manual.

TRENDS AFFECTING SEED TESTING INTERNATIONALLY

Substantive changes are underway regarding seed testing on an international scale. A long-range planning committee of ISTA is addressing some of these possibilities. Future accreditation of laboratories will require that the laboratory have a QA programme in effect. ISTA membership, up to this point restricted to countries, may be extended to approved or licensed commercial laboratories. There very probably will be less government support for testing laboratories. And ISTA laboratories may also be involved in testing other reproductive materials such as cuttings, tissues, and synthetic seeds.

BIOCHEMICAL AND CYTOGENETICAL CHANGES DURING SEED STORAGE

1. BIOCHEMICAL CHANGES

Recently, the biochemical basis of ageing in seed has attracted several workers. The investigations on the metabolic changes in ageing seeds not only pave the way for understanding the intricate molecular-biochemical mechanism leading to the ageing of seeds, but also serve as an index of seed quality.

A. Biochemical Changes in Orthodox Seeds

The following qualitative and quantitative changes were reported in macromolecules, memberanous structure and enzymatic activity in orthodox seeds.

(*a*) **Constitutive Changes :** A reduction in the total content of food reserves was observed. The seed constituents which were affected are carbohydrates, total sugars, non-reducing sugars, water soluble sugars in soybean, greengram, pearlmillet, chickpea and wheat (5, 22, 32, 35). However, reducing sugars increases in pearlmillet and greengram whereas it decreased in soybean and maize.

Table. 1 : Changes in biomolecules during storage

Sr. No.	*Biomolecule (s)*	*Trend*	*Crop*
1.	Carbohydrates :		
(*i*)	Total sugars, non-reducing sugars, WSS	Decrease	Chickpea and Wheat, Pearlmillet, Soybean Greengram.
(*ii*)	Reducing sugars	Increase	Pearlmillet, Greengram
		Decrease	Maize, Soybean
2.	Lipids ;		
(*i*)	Total oil, lipids, phospholipids	Decrease	Maize, Sesame, Castor and Cotton
		Negligible	Pearlmillet
(*ii*)	Fat acidity FFA value	Increase	Soybean, Pearlmillet Mustard a and Maize and Greengram
(*iii*)	Lipid peroxidation	Increases slowly	Mustard and Maize
3.	Proteins and Amino-Acids :		
(*i*)	Total proteins	Decrease	Soybean, Sesamum, Cotton, Castor and Greengram
		Constant	Maize and Pearlmillet

Sr. No.	Biomolecule (s)	Trend	Crop
	(ii) Protein synthesis	Reduced Decrease in Coty. and increase in axis	Rice Soybean
	(iii) Amino-acids	Spectrum varied	Pearlmillet
4.	Nucleic acids :		
	(i) RNA	Decrease	Rice, Soybean,
	(ii) DNA	Decrease	Rice, Soybean,
5.	Mobilization Efficiency.	Decrease	Soybean

***(ii)* Enzymatic Changes :** The measurement of enzymatic activity was one of the earliest biochemical techniques tried to assess deterioration and predict seed germinability. Certain enzymes (Table 2) lose their activities with loss of viability of seeds *e.g.* dehydrogenases, peroxidases and catalases in rice, soybean safflower, pearlmillet, mustard and maize.

Table 2 : Changes in activity of Enzymes

Sr. No.	Enzyme (s)	Trend	Crop
1.	Dehydrogenases, Peroxidases, Catalase	Decrease	Soybean, Maize, Mustard, Safflower, Rice and Pearlmillet
2.	Amylase	Decrease	Rice
	(i) α-amylase	Decrease	Safflower, Soybean
	(ii) β-amylase	Increase	Soybean
3.	Protease	No detectable Increase	Rice
		Decrease	Safflower
4.	RNAse	Increase	Rice
		Decrease	Soybean
5.	Phytase, ATPase and lipase	Decrease	Safflower, Rice

***(iii)* Membrane Permeability :** Most frequently studied aspect is membrane permeability which is evident by leakage of electrolytes and water soluble compounds from the seeds upon imbibition. The leakage of electrolytes, water soluble sugars as well as amino acids significantly increased with duration of storage in all the crops studied including vegetable crops (Table 3). A gradual decrease in pH of the seed leachates was recorded with the increase in the magnitude of deterioration. This may be linked with the increase in the amount of soluble metabolites specially the acidic components.

Table 3 : Changes in membrane permeability after ageing

Sr. No.	Quantitiative change	Trend	Crop
1.	Amount of electrolytes, sugars (WSS) and Amino-acids	Increase	All crops studied including vegetable crops.
2.	Correlation with germination	Negative	Soybean, Maize and Mustard
3.	EC of leachates	Increase	All crops studied
4.	pH of leachates	Gradually decrease	Soybean

B. Biochemical Changes in Recalcitrant Seeds

The Citrus seed viability declined rapidly in open storage. Total phenolic substances have been found to be the cause of loss of viability in rough lemon.

Table 4 : Changes in membrane permeability after ageing

Sr. No.	Molecule (s)	Trend	Crop
1.	Total phenolic substances	Increase	Rough lemon, grapefruit and mandarin
2.	Leaching of Sugars and FFA	Increase	Trifoliate orange and pummelo
3.	Moisture and α-amylase	Decrease	Trifoliate orange and pummelo

2. CYTOGENETICAL CHANGES

The loss of viability is directly proportional of the increase in chromosomal abnormalities. Mitotic and meiotic studies in different species of Triticum showed that aberrant cells percentage increased with the period of storage. The chromosomal aberrations such as breaks, dicentric bridges and laggards were more frequent in the root-tips of ages seeds than those of normal seeds. The nuclear damage caused by ageing was found to be similar to that caused by 10 Kr of X-radiation (Table 5).

Table 5 : Cytogenetical changes during seed ageing

Sr. No.	Cytogenetical change	Trend	Crop
1.	Aberrant cells and chromosomal aberrations	Increase	Wheat
2.	Micromutations	Increase	Wheat
3.	Pollen viability	Decrease	Pea and Wheat
4.	Yield characters	Variations increased	Pea and wheat

DETECTION AND MANAGEMENT OF SEED-BORNE FUNGI FOR QUALITY SEED PRODUCTION

Introduction

Seed is the basic input of crop production. Healthy and viable seed is the first prerequisite for increasing crop production and productivity. The majority of the world food and vegetable crops are grown through seeds. These crops are attacked by a large number of seed-borne plant pathogens such as fungi, bacteria, viruses and nematodes, which cause seed-borne diseases. Among these pathogens, seed borne fungi are very important. Majority of the fungal plant pathogens are disseminated through seeds.

A list of some of the important seed-borne fungal diseases of major food and vegetable crops in India is given in table 6.

DETECTION METHODS

Examination of Dry Seeds

Examination of dry seeds is a quick method for detection of seed-borne fungal pathogens. It provides partial to complete information about health status of a seed sample where pathogen is detectable. It is applied for detection of seed-borne fungal plant pathogens which causes discolouration of the seed or change the size or shape of seed. Also applicable for detecting fungal structures, present in on or with seed. Insect and mechanically damaged seed can also be detected by this method.

Procedure

No standard working sample has been worked out. However, a sample size equal to the one being employed in the purity analysis in seed certification can be used. In India, a sample of 2000-seeds is generally used. Individual seed is examined carefully by naked eye or low magnified hand lense or stereomicroscope. Infected seeds and other non-seed matters are removed, identified, counted and per cent infection is calculated. The following diseases can be detected and identified by this method.

Table 6 : Important Seed-borne Fungal Diseases of Major Food and Vegetable Crops in India

Crop	*Disease*	*Pathogen*
Cereals Wheat *Triticum aestivum*	Black point	*Alternaria alternata Helminthosporium sativum, Curvularia spp*
	Flag smut	*Urocystis agropyri*
	Hill bunt, smooth spored bunt, stinking or covered smut	*Tilletia foetida*
	Hill bunt, stinking smut or reticulate spore smut	*Tilletia caries*
	Kernel bunt	*Neovossia indica, T. indica*
	Loose smut	*Ustilago nuda tritici*
	Leaf blight,	*Alternaria triticina*
	Crown and root rot	*Drechslera sorokiniana*
	Yellow leaf spot, tan spot,	*Drechslera triticirepentis.*
	Ear cockle	*Anguina tritici*

Crop	*Disease*	*Pathogen*
Rice, Paddy		*Pyricularia oryzae*
(*Oryza sativa*)	Blast	*Drechslera oryzae*
	Brown spot	*Ustillaginoidea virens*
	False smut	*Neovossia horrida*,
	Kernel bunt,	*Tilletia barclayana*
	Kernel smut,	
	Black smut,	
	Covered smut	*Rhizoctonia solani*
	Sheath blight	*Trichoconiella padwickii*
	Stackburn	*padwickii*
		Ephelis oryzae
	Udbatta, incense rod	
Maize		*Cephalosporium*
(*Zea mays*)	Black bundle	*acremonium*
		Botryodiplodia
	Black kernel rot	*theobromae*
		Fusarium moniliforme
	Cob rot	*Drechslera maydis*
Pearlmillet, Bajra	Southern leaf blight	*Sclerospora graminicola*
(*Pennisetum*	Downy mildew, green ear	*Claviceps fusiformis*
typhoides)	Ergot	
		Tolyposporium
	Smut	*penicillariae*
Sorghum,		*Colletotrichum*
	Anthrachose	*graminicola*
Jowar, Cholam		
Carrot	Black root rot,	*Alterniaradicina*
(*Daucus carota*)	Seedling blight	
	Leaf blight	*Alternaria dauci*
Onion		
(*Allium cepa*)	Dampling off,	*Botrytis allii*
	Grey mould	
	Downey mildew	*Peronospora destructor*
	Purple blotch	*Alternaria porri*
Pepper, chilli	Anthracnose, ripe fruit	*Colletotricum capsici*,
	Rot and die back	C. *dematium*
(Capsicum *annum*)		
Radish	Grey leaf spot	*Alternaria brassicae*
(*Raphanus sativus*)	Leaf spot	*Alternaria raphani*
	Black eye spot,	*Phytophthora parasitica*,
	Buck-eye rot	*Phytophthora nicotianae*
		var *parasitica*

Crop	*Disease*	*Pathogen*
Tomato (*Lycopersicon esculentum*)	Damping-off Early blight Fruit rot, Leaf blight	*Pythium aphenidematum* *Alternaria solani* *Pytophthora infestans*
Kernel bunt of wheat Ear cockle of wheat Black point of wheat		*Neovossia indica* *Anguina tritici* *Alternaria altrenata* *Drechslera sorokiniana* *Curvularia* spp.
Ergot of pearlmillet (bajra)		*Claviceps fusiformis*
Bunt of rice or Kernel smut		*Neovossia horrida*
False smut of rice Purple blotch of soybean Downy mildew of soybean Wilt of chickpea Kernel rot or stalk rot of maize.		*Ustilaginoidea virens* *Cercospora kikuchii* *Peronospora manshurica* *Fusarium oxysporum* *F. moniliforme*
(*Sorghum vulgare*)	Covered smut, Kernel smut, Short smut, Grain smut,	*Sphacelotheca sorghi*
	Downy mildew	*Peronosclerospora sorghi*
	Loose smut	*Sphacelotheca cruenta*
Oilseeds Rape and mustard (*Brassica spp*)	Black leaf spot, Wire stem Grey leaf spot Drop, watery, soft rot, White blight	*Alternaria brassicicola* *A. brassicae* *Sclerotinia sclerotiorum*
Fibre Cotton (Gossypium spp.)	Anthracnose, seedling blight, boll rot Verticillium wilt Wilt	*Colletotrichum indicum* *Verticillium dahliae* *Fusarium axysporum* of sp. *vasinfectum*
Pulses Chickpea, gram (*Cicer arietinum*)	Ascochyta blight Botrytis grey mould Colletotrichum	*Ascochyta rabiei* *Botrytis cinerea* *Colletotrichum*

Crop	Disease	Pathogen
	Blight	*dematium*
	Wilt	*Fusarium oxysporum* sp. cicer
Soybean (*Glycine max*)	Anthracnose	*Colletotrichum dematium*
	Downy mildew	*Peronospora manshurica*
	Pod and stem blight	*Phomopsis sojae*
	Purple seed stain, purple blotch, Cercospora leaf spot and blight	*Cercospora kikuchii*
Vegetables		
Bottle gourd (*Lagenaria sicenaria*)	Anthracnose	*Colletotrichum lagenarium*
Cucumber (*Cucumis sativus*)	Anthracnose	*C. lagenarium*
Muskmelon (*Cucumis melo*)	Anthracnose	*C. lagenarium*
Water melon) (*Citrullus lanatus)*	Anthracnose	*C. lagenarium*
Brinjal, eggplant (*Solanum melongena*)	Fruit rot	*Phomopsis vexans*

WASHING TEST

The washing test is a qualitative test. This test is a quick procedure used only for detection of those type of pathogens which adhere to the seed surface in the form of identifiable spores. Hence, it does not have a wide application.

This method is used particularly for the fungi, causing smut and bunt in gramineous hosts, except loose smut of wheat and barley. It can also be used for detection of *Peronospora manshurica*, downy mildew of soybean and *Protomyces macrosporus* tumour disease of coriander.

PROCEDURE

For this test no standard working sample has been prescribed so far by ISTA. Therefore, sample size *i.e.,* number of seeds vary from crop to crop. A fixed number of seeds are placed in a flask containing sufficient water and a few drops of detergent. Then the flasks is shaken by hand or on a mechanical shaker for 5-10 minutes depending upon the facilities available. Seeds and washing water are separated by passing through cheese cloth into a beaker. The filtrate may be examined directly or transferred in equal amount into centrifuge tubes and centrifuged at 1500 to 3000 rpm for about 3 to 15 minutes. The pellet is suspended in water and examined under a bright field microscope. A haemocytometer can be used for counting the number of spores per ml. Similarly, spore load per seed is calculated. The following diseases can be detected and identified by this method.

Hill bunt of Wheat	*Tilletia foetida, T. caries*
Kernel bunt of wheat	*Neovossia indica*
Flag smut of wheat	*Urocystis agropyri*
Covered smut of barley	*Ustilagao hordei*
Smut of pearlmillet	*Tolyposporium penc-illariae*

BLOTTER METHOD

The method is most widely practiced seed health testing method. The blotter method is one of the incubation methods. It is used for detecting those fungi which are able to produce mycelial growth and fruiting structures under incubation. Identification of fungi is done based on habit characters under steremicroscope. The fungi which are not identifiable under stereomicroscope, can be identified under compound microscope at higher magnification for their confirmation. All kind of seeds, cereals, forests, legumes, ornamentals and vegetable seeds can be tested by this method.

PROCEDURE

Generally, a working sample of 400 seeds is tested. However, if sample size is less than 400 seeds, then whole sample or part of it may be tested. The number of seeds are to be plated depending upon the size of the plate, seed and type of infection. In a Petri plate of 9 cm. diameter, 10, 25 or even more seeds per plate depending on the size of the seed are plated. The seeds are placed equidistantly on three layers of well water soaked filter papers (blotters). Excessive water is drained off before placing the seeds. The plates are incubated at 20+2°C usually for 7 days in alternating cycles of 12h Nuv or fluorescent light and 12h darkness. After incubation, all seeds are examined under steromicroscope at different magnification (6-60 times) for the identification of the fungi. Sometimes some fungi are not identifical under stereomicroscope. Under such conditions, the fungi can be identified by making slides under compound microscope at higher magnification. Infected seeds with fungi are counted and per cent infection is calculated.

While using this method, some problems are encountered. For example, in crops of crucifers, seed coats are lifted from the blotter surface due to fast germination. The seed coat displacement results in difficulties in evaluation and identification of pathogens. To overcome this problem 0.1-0.2% solution of sodium salt of 2, 4-D (dichlorophenoxy acetic acid) is used instead of pure water for testing seeds for *Phoma lingam*. However, this method is not popular due to its limited applications. Therefore, this method has now been replaced by the deep-freeze blotter method. In this method the Petri plates containing seeds are incubated for one day at 20°C, for the second day at–20°C and then for 5 days under 12h alternating cycle of dark and light at 24h freezing can be reduced to 8h. This method is used for graminicolous fungi *i.e. Drechslera avenae, D. dictyoides, D. siccans* and *D. teres* ; *Plenodomus lingam* in cabbage seeds and *Alternaria* and *Stemphylium* in carrot seeds. This method is not suitable for bean and pea seeds, because decaying occurs on blotters.

The following diseases can be detected and identified by this method.

Black and grey leaf spot of crucifers	*Alternaria brassicicola*
	A. brassicae
Alternaria leaf spot of radish	*A. raphani*
Ascochyta blight of gram	*Ascohyta rabiei*
Botrytis grey mould of gram	*Botrytis cinerea*
Purple seeds stain or purple blotch of soyabean	*Cercospora kikuchii*

Anthracnose of fruit rot of chilli	*Colletotrichum capsici*
Brown spot of rice	*Drechslera oryzae*
Blast of Rice	*Pyricularia oryzae*
Stack burn of rice	*Trichoconiella padwickii.*

AGAR-PLATE METHOD

Agar plate method can be used for detection of the same type of seed-borne fungal pathogens as in the blotter method. However, certain fungi which are not easily detectable in blotter method can be detected by this method. This method is costlier, however, less time consuming than blotter test.

In this method, specific agar media, for specific fungi are used, because of different growing ability of different fungi, under specific incubation conditions. This method provides quick identification of seed with specific fungi. The identification of fungal colonies is done on the basis of colony and growth habit.

PROCEDURE

In general standard working sample of 400 seeds is tested. Two nutrient agar media, malt extract agar (MEA) and potato dextrose agar (PDA) are generally used for seed health testing. The medium is prepared, sterilized and poured into sterilized petriplates. Seeds are treated with 1 to 2% sodium hypochlorite (NaOCl) and placed in petriplates, usually 5-10 seed are placed per 9 cm diameter petriplates. The seeds may be treated with 0.1% mercuric chloride ($HgCl_2$). Instead of Sodiumhypochlorite. However, merceuric chloride treated seeds are washed in sterilized distilled water, 3 to 4 time to remove excess mercuric chloride. The following fungi can be easily detected by this method.

Pathogen	*Medium*
Alternaria triticina	Nutrient Agar
Botrytis cinerea	Nutrient Agar
Fusarium oxysporun	Nutrient Agar (Czapek-Dox Agar)
Drechslera oryzae	Guaiacol Agar
Pyricularia oryzae	Guaiacol Agar
D. sorkiniane	Potato Dextrose Agar

SEEDLING-SYMPTOM TEST

This method is applied for detecting those fungi, which are capable of producing symptoms on the root or shoot of the young seedling. It is used for screening of germplasm in post entry quarantine control, demonstrating seed transmission of certain pathogens that cause symptoms on seedlings and testing and evaluating the efficacy of fungicides for seed treatment. This test can predict the field performance of the seed lot, infected by certain pathogens.

PROCEDURE

This test can be conducted in laboratories, growth chambers or glass houses, using a variety of containers such as test tubes, petriplates, trays, earthen/plastic pots and are sterilized by autoclaving at 15 pound pressure (121°C for 15 minutes) and seeds are sown on them. The containers containing seeds are incubated under optimum conditions (temperature, light and humidity) for developing seedling symptoms of seed borne infection by pathogens which may be comparable with those produced under field conditions. The incubation period and conditions vary from crop to crop and fungus to fungus. At the end of incubation, seedlings for the symptoms are examined and per cent infection is calculated. The following fungi can be detected in crops given below by this method.

Alternaria spp. in crucifers and carrots.

Colletotrichum spp. in sorghum and chilli.

Drechslera spp. in rice and wheat.

Fusarium spp. in chickpea and other hosts.

Pyricularia oryzae in rice.

Septoria nodorum in wheat.

EMBRYO COUNT METHOD

This method is specifically used to detect loose smut fungus in wheat and barley. *Sclerospora graminicola*, downy mildew of bajra (pearlmillet) can also be detected by this method. The method described here is for loose smut of wheat. This method consists of 4 steps viz., embryo staining and extraction, separation, cleaning and examination for loose smut fungal hyphae.

PROCEDURE

Soak 100g of wheat seed in IL of 5% solution of sodium hydroxide (NaOH) or potassium hydroxide (KOH), and 0.15 g trypan blue for 22h at 22-24°C.

The sample is transferred to eelworm flotation vessel (Fenwick can) connected by a tube to hot water tap. A steam of hot water (at 60-65°C) agitates the grain, allows separated embryos to float and pass over the lip with the flow of water, where they are collected into series of 3 graded sieve arranged in descending order of 3.5, 2.0 and 1.0 mm perforations. The embryos are collected in 1 mm sieve.

In some laboratories where Fenwick can is not available, extraction of embryos can be achieved by using flask, tap water shower and the sieves. The process is repeated 3 to 4 times. The embryos are washed into wire basket or tea stainer and dehydrated in methylated spirit or 95% ethyl alcohol for 2 minutes.

The embryos are transferred to a filter funnel connected with a stopper. Then 200ml of lactic acid + glycerol + water mixture (1: 2: 1) is added. The embryos float, the chaff sinks and embryos are collected. This process is repeated until clean embryos are obtained.

The embryos are then transferred into a 250 ml beaker having 75ml of lactic acid + 150ml glycerol (1: 2). The embryos are boiled for 2 minutes. This process clears the embryos. Then the mixture is allowed to cool down. Embryos submerged in lactic acid + glycerol mixture are examined in special grooved 9 cm diameter plates or in plain Petri plates or on glass slides at 12-25 magnification under stereomicroscope with sub stage illumination.

For uniform distribution of embryos in the grooves or plain plates or on glass slides dropper should be used. In infected embryos, the bluish stained mycelium of *Ustilago tritici* may be seen in scutellum, plumule buds or the whole embryo. Infected and healthy embryos are counted and per cent infection is calculated.

This technique has been simplified into embryo floatation technique. The seeds are soaked in a 5% NaOH and 0.02% trypan blue solution for 18h at 25°C. The embryos are recovered through floatation by adding 5% sodium chloride (NaCl) Solution. The embryos are then washed in water, boiled in lactophenol and examined under stereomicroscope.

DISEASE MANAGEMENT

The aim of plant disease control is to prevent economic losses and increase the value of the crop. Control of a plant disease may be achieved by a single method such as immunization and seed treatment in loose smut of wheat. However, satisfactory control of most plant diseases requires more than one measure in disease control strategy. It can be achieved through integration of methods directed against the pathogen, in favour of the host and for modification of environment.

LOCATION OF SEED PRODUCTION

Selection of Geographic Area

Selection of geographic area for any seed crop is made on the basis of suitability of prevailing temperature and humidity in the area for the crop. These factors also influence the seed-borne disease or parasitic fungus flora. Many seed borne fungal diseases are more severe in wet areas than dry areas. Smut and ergot diseases of pearlmillet are serious in wet areas, where rains occur for long duration during flowering period of the crop. The incidence of such diseases can be avoided by growing crops in dry areas with the help of irrigation. In India, Kernel bunt of wheat is prevalent in northern wheat growing states, whereas southern states are free from it.

Selection of Planting Site/field

Within small areas, selection of planting site is important. Many soil-borne diseases can be avoided by proper selection of site. The field infested with pathogens of diseases like wilt of arhar, smut and ergot or pearlmillet and ear cockle of wheat etc. should not be selected for seed production of a particular crop. Kernel bunt disease free seed be produced in dry districts of Haryana, India. The water logged site should not be selected for production of downy mildew disease free seed of pearlmillet.

In Denmark, crucifer seed crops are grown on certain small islands and in coastal areas, where sample ventilation is provided by wind in the crop fields, which reduces the development of *Alternaria brassicicola*.

ERADICATION OR REDUCTION OF SOIL BORNE PATHOGEN

Eradication or reduction of soil borne inoculum from the field can be achieved through the following practices :

Crop Rotation

Crop rotation is essential to avoid soil borne inoculum because many seed borne fungi such as *Phomopsis vexans*, phomopsis blight of eggplant, *Tilletia controversa* dwarf bunt of wheat, *Claviceps fusiformis,* ergot of pearlmillet and *Tolyposporium penicillariae,* smut of pearlmillet and many other survive only for limited number of year. In U.S.A., 3 years crop rotations against *Phomopsis vexans* in eggplant, 3 years or logner for *Alternaria porrif.* sp. *dauci* in carrot are recommended. In India, 3 year crop rotations as a control measure to downy mildew of bajra is recommended.

Fallow

Keeping the fields fallow helps in reduction of inoculum of soil invaders in absence of host. In India, summer fallow decreases *Fusarium oxysporum* f. sp. *cumini,* Fusarium wilt of cumin. In Australia, crown rot of wheat, *Fusarium graminearum* was less severe in crop following a long fallow.

Burning

Now-a-days it has become a common practice to burn straw and stubble, where crops particularly cereals are harvested by combine.

Burning of straw and stubble of perennial rye grass seed crops in the field in the State of Oregan, U.S.A. destroys the inoculum of *Gloeatinia temulenta*, blind seed disease and *Claviceps purpurea*, ergot.

Water Management

Irrigation time and amount of water, influence (influences) disease development. In certain regions, some disease may be controlled by flooding the fields.

In Florida soils, sclerotia of *Sclerotinia sclerotiorum* can be destroyed by flooding continuously or at 3-day intervals for a period of 3-6 weeks. This pathogen may also be controlled through summer planting of lowland rice. Irrigation prior to seedling increases the incidence of flag smut of wheat, *Urocystis agropyri* to a higher level, where as, the incidence of covered smut of barley, *Ustillago hordei* and millet smut, *Sphacelotheca destruens* decreases to a lowest level, if flooding of soil is followed by broad casting the seed one hour later.

MODIFICATION OF CULTURAL PRACTICES

Preparation of the Seed Bed :

The soil structure is of importance to the development of plants and reduction in the development of diseases. Therefore, seed should be sown in well aerated soil and not in packed soil. Packed soil reduced the emergence of seedlings/plants.

In Barely crop, packed soil causes a significant reduction in emergence of seedlings and an increase in the amount of blight and stunting produced by *Drechslera sorokiniana*.

Preparation of seed bed also plays a vital role in controlling diseases of various crops. Sowing on ridges with furrows on either side reduces damping off of sugarbeet, because of better soil drainage in the immediate vicinity of the seedling. Bunt of wheat in early stages of growth is favoured on the flat as against ridged rows.

Date of Sowing

The selection of the sowing date depends upon the prevailing temperature and humidity requirements of the host and parasite.

In England, it has been established that autumn sown seed crops of carrot became heavily infected by black rot, *Alternaria radicina*, whereas spring-sown carrot showed little infection either in the succeeding autumn or after storage.

In Madhya Pradesh, India, five cultivars of soybean showed clear response in seed quality to planting date from June 1 to September 2, during Monsoon season. The number of discoloured seeds and seeds infected by fungi decreased, and the germination capacity increased gradually with delay of planting, because of reduction of rainy period. Some research workers observed the influence of sowing dates on smut severity in smut susceptible pearlmillet hybrid Bj 104. Higher (67%) smut severity was observed on 6th July sown crop, whereas the severity was lower (40%) on 15th July sown crop.

Depth of Sowing

The depth of sowing influences germination, development of seedling and transmission of disease. Proper depth depends upon the size of the seed, the time of seeding and the type of soils. The shallow sowing gives rapidly growing, vigorous plants and the susceptible phase is shortened. The heavy soils require shallow sowing. The shallow sowing usually decreases the incidence of loose smut, *U. avenae* in oats and covered smut, *U. hordei* in barley.

Rate of Seeding

The seeding rate may be a cardinal factor, where it adversely affects plants growth and favours development and spread of pathogens.

In Flax crop, damping off, caused by *Colletotrichum lini* is increased by thick sowing.

In wheat, rate of sowing has no effect on the percentage of plants, infected by *Ustilago, tritici*, smut. However, excessive tillering reduces percentage of infected ears because of limited amount of mycelium is available for infection of tillers.

Dense stands of witner rye with limited tillering, reduce secondary infection by Conidia of honeydew of *Claviceps purpurea*, ergot, while in more widely spaced plants, the infection increased due to prolongation of the flowering period.

Proper Dose of Fertilizers

Adequate and balance dose of fertilizers are important in reduction of seed infection, improving seed quality and maximizing yield. Plants are more susceptible to diseases in soils with excessive or deficient nutrients than those grown in soil with well balanced fertility.

In general, heavy doses of nitrogenous fertilizers increase the disease incidence. The excessive application of nitrogenous fertilizers increases the susceptibility of rice plants to *Pyricularia* blast, *Pyricularia oryzae*. The brown leaf spot (*Drechslera oryzae*) of rice may become severe both by deficient or excess of nitrogen in the fields of poor farming conditions.

Cotton wilt, *Fusarium oxysporum* f. sp. *vasinfectum* is known often to be more serious in potassium deficient soils.

Insufficient phosphorous or potash in soybean can increase losses from the chorocoal rot, pod and stem blight and several root and stem decay pathogens.

The deficiency of calcium and to some extent the deficiency of nitrogen and potassium results in reduction of wheat flag smut *Urocystis agropyri*.

Selection of Disease Escaping Varieties

Certain varieties, in different crops escape damage, because of their growth characters. This is not due to genetic resistance, but because of characteristics of their growth and time of maturity. In Denmark, early maturing cultivars of cauliflower escape from attack of *Alternaria brassicicola*, while late cultivars often are severly attacked because of prevailing humidity.

In Uttar Pradesh, India, early varieties-NCH 20 and Russ, 2877; medium varieties – HR22 and MCH7 and late varieties-T-36 and T-38 of rice have been reported to escape from bunt due to environment.

REDUCTION OR ELIMINATION OF SEED BORNE INOCULUM

Seed Certification and Field Inspection of Seed Crops

The objective of certification is to ensure that as far as possible, only certified seeds are allowed to enter the country or supplied to the growers.

Seed certification is a legally sanctioned system for maintaining the quality of the seed in the seed production programme, involving a series of field and laboratory inspections and evaluation. Quality control of seed is fundamental in seed production.

The entire process of seed production is followed through successive multiplication from nucleus seed to certified seed, ultimately provided for commercial crop production. In certification programmes, minimum certification standards must be strictly followed to the maximum degree. These standards are different and valid for each class. Through certification, certain seed borne pathogens have been controlled and spread to new areas has been checked.

Diseases exclusively seed-borne can be eradicated by using healthy seed stock. Healthy seed stock can be obtained either by eliminating diseased seed crops from seed production through appropriate certification or by effective seed treatment.

Loose smut of wheat and barley is controlled through seed certification programme in India and Sweden.

Two fungicides, Vitavax and Plantvax give complete control of internally seed borne infection of loose smut, *Ustilago nuda* of barley.

In seed production programmes, seed crops are periodically inspected for the presence of diseases that are disseminated by seed and necessary precautions are taken to remove the diseased plants. A minimum of two inspections are needed. Field inspections not only useful in removing the infected plants from seed crop but also act as indicator for initiation of chemical spray programme.

Seed Treatment in Seed Production

Seed treatment is usually given as precautionary measure in seed production. The main aim of seed treatment is to control unnoticed infections, infestations or contaminations, particularly in Breeder and Foundation seed to keep the inoculum at zero level. Seed treatment also prevents the entry of seed borne pathogen in new areas.

Seed treatment in early generations like breeder and foundation seed is less expensive, less hazardous, more effective and causes less pollution as compared to bigger quantities of seed in subsequent generations.

For the eradications of inoculum of specific pathogen, highly selective fungicides, mostly systemics are useful. Presently breeder and foundation seed treatment with Vitavax or Bavistin is a common practice in India for the control of loose smut of wheat and barley.

Ascohyta rabiei in chickpea seeds can be checked by treating seed with 0.3% tridemorph and thiabenzimidazole.

Seed treatment with iprodione controls the seed borne inoculum of *A. brassicicola* in *Brassica spp*.

Seed treatment with Dithane M-45 and Ceresan gives complete control of brown spot and stack burn of rice.

Application of chlorothalonil (1.5 kg/ha), mancozeb (5kg/ha), carboxin (2.5 1/ha) and sisthane (0.64 1/ha) reduce *A. padwickii* and *D. oryzae*, when applied before dough stage in rice crop.

Copper fungicides like Blitox-50, Blue-copper or fytolan are used as effective spray against leaf spot diseases. Foliar spray of copper oxychloride in maize reduces seed borne infection of *Fusarium moniliforme* and *Curvularia pallescens*.

Weekly application of benomyl + captan (0.5kg + 0.5 kg/ha) from boot to physiological maturity significantly reduces *C. lunata* and completely controls F. *monilifrome* in sorghum seeds. Fungicide application increases seed yield, 1000seed. Weight and germination.

Wheat seed infection by *F. graminearum* can be reduced by spraying the plants with benomyl + mancozeb or benomyl or methyl benzimidazole carbamate alone.

Three sprays of iprodione (50% *a.i.*) at 0.5 to 1 kg *a.i.* per ha on cabbage (*Brassica oleracea*) seed crops at 3 weeks interval from the young green pod stage until cutting, control pod and seed infection by *A. brassicicola*. Seed yield and germination is increased and only few seeds are infected.

Eradication of Other Host Plants

Many diseases perpetuate on weed hosts or wild plants in the absence of the main cultivated host. Hence the eradication of such hosts from the field or locality is helpful in preventing perpetuation and spread of diseases. In India, eradication of collateral hosts such as *Panicum antidotale*, *Cenchrus cilaris* and *Setaria verticillata* (personal communication) around pearlmillet (bajra) crop is recommended for reducing the incidence of ergot.

Chemical Protection of Seed Crops

The chemical protection is inseparable from an integrated control strategy against seed-borne diseases. For maintaining the health of the seed crop, raised from pathogen free seeds, on pathogen free land, chemical protection is unavoidable in the standing crop, unless true resistance in the crop is assured.

The aim of the use of chemical in plant disease control is to create, a toxic barrier between the host surface or tissues and the pathogen, present at a particular site on the host.

Hundred of compounds such as sulphur, copper zinc, nickel, manganese etc. are available for crop protection as spray, dust, fumigants, systemics and other categories. For effective spray, selection of fungicides, time of spray and weather conditions are important.

Sulphur and copper fungicides are widely used than others, as they are highly effective.

The organic sulphur compounds such as nabam, dithane, zineb, manab, zerlate, fermate, arasan, thiram and captan are used against many diseases. Manab, ziram and captan are quite effective against cucurbit anthracnose, *Colletotrichum lagenarium*.

Spraying rice crop with fungicides like triphenyltin chloride, fentin hydroxide, kitazin, zineb and manocozeb reduces seed infection of *Alternaria longissima*, *A. padwickii, Curvularia lunata, Drechslera oryzae, Phoma* spp. and *Sclerotium spp.*

MANAGEMENT OF SEED BORNE BACTERIA

Management of seed borne bacteria is a very difficult task. As mentioned earlier, plant pathogenic bacteria can spread very quickly under congenial weather condition. Even a very low level of seed borne inoculum can result in a severe epiphytotic. The transmission of bacteria from seed to seedling is also a complex phenomenon. This generally depends upon several factors, viz., crop species, environmental conditions, amount of inoculum and its survival in infected/infested seeds, types of seed germination and their interactions with other microorganisms associated with seed. We should thus develop a system for controlling the plant bacterioses by keeping in view these factors. Some preventive measures can minimize the losses caused by seed borne bacteria. An integrated disease management programme must be followed for this purpose. Some preventive measures are summarised here :

1. Management by plant quarantine.
2. Management by using certified seed.
3. Management by using disease resistant/tolerant cultivars.
4. Management by raising healthy seed crop.
5. Management by improving seed storage.
6. Management by adequate seed treatment.

Table 7 : Seed-borne Phytobacteria Intercepted at Plant Quarantine and Fumigation station in India from imported seed material

Bacteria	*Host*	*Geographical Distribution*
Clavibacter michiganensis Sub sp. *michiganensis*	*Lycopersicon esculentum*	North America
Erwinia herbicola	*Helianthus*	Europe
Pseudomonas syringae pv. *maculicola*	*Brassica oleracea* var. *capitata*	Europe and North America
P. syringae pv. pisi	*Pisum sativum*	Europe, North America
P. syringae pv. syringae	*Cucumis sativus*	North America
P. woodsii	*Dianthus* caryophyllus	Europe
Xanthomonas campestris pv. campestris	*Brassica oleracea* var. *capitata*	Europe

Table 8 : Important Seed-Borne Phytobacteria of Quarantine Significance in India

Pathogen	*Disease*	*Distribution*
1. *Agrobacterium rhizogenes*	Hairy root of rose	Japan, Australia, France, Italy, U.S.A.
2. *A. tumefaciens*	Crown gall of Gladiolus	Hungary
3. *Erwinia amylovora*	Fire blight of Apple and pear	U.S.A., Europe.
4. *E. chrysanthemi* pv. *partheni*	Carnation blight	Europe
5. *E. rubrifacines*	Phloem canker of walnut	U.S.A.
6. *Pseudomonas caryophylli*	Carnation wilt	Europe, Japan, U.S.A. and Argentina
7. *P. syringae pv. Gladioli*	Gladiolus blight	Australia, Europe, Egypt, New Zealand, U.S.S.R.
8. *Rhodococcus faciens*	Canker of gladiolus	Iran, Europe, Canada
9. *Xanthomonas campestris* pv. *gummisudans*	Gladiols blight	
10. *X.c.* pv. *juglandis*	Walnut blight	U.S.A.
11. *X. c.* pv. *fragriae*	Angular leaf spot of strawberry	North America
12. *Xylophilus ampelins*	Bacterial necrosis of grapevines	Greece, France, South Africa.

Seed-Borne Plant Viruses

Seed is an important basic component of production technology. Among the various Seed borne pathogens, Viruses are unique in that they infect seeds without producing apparent physical damage to the seed. Seed transmission helps in perpetuation of viruses. Plants raised from seeds carrying viruses are potential source of infection right from the very early stage. The problem becomes more complex if the virus in question is present in latent form in the seed.

The important seed-borne viruses reported from India are listed in Table 9.

Table 9 : Seed-borne viruses occurring in India

Virus	*Host*
1	*2*
Bean common mosaic	*Vigna unguiculata*
Potyvirus	*Vigna mungo*
Bean Yellow	*Pisum sativum*
Potyvirus	*V. unquiculata*
Blacke cowpea mosaic	V. unquiculata
Potyvirus	*V. unquiculata*

1	*2*
Blackgram leaf crinkle	*V. mungo*
	V. mungo
Blackgram mottle Carmovirus	*V. mungo*
Eggplant mosaic tymovirus	*Solanum melongena*
Carlavirus	*Arachls hypogea*
Cowpea aphid borne	*V. unquiculata*
Mosaic potyvirus	*V. unquiculata*
Cowpea banding mosaic cucumovirus.	*V. sinensis*
Cowpea chlorotic spot.	*V. sinensis*
Cowpea mosaic	*V. unquiculata*
Cowpea mild mottle carlavirus	*V. unquiculata*
Cucumber green mottle	*Laqeneria siceraria*
mosaic tobamovirus	
Cucumber mosaic	*Beninccse hispida*
Cucumovirus	*Cucurbita moschata*
	C. pepo
	V. unquiculata
Limabean mosaic	*Phaseolus lunatus*
Mung and Urdbean mosaic-I virus	*V. mungo*
	V. radiata
Mung and urdbean Mosaic-2 virus	*V. mungo*
Mosaic-2 virus	*V. radiata*
Peanut clump Furovirus	*A. hypogae*
Peanut mottle potyvirus	*A. hypogae*
Peanut stripe potyvirus	*A. hypogae*
Pea seed-borne mosaic potyvirus	*Pisum sativum*
Southern bean mosaic	*V. unquiculata*
sobomoviruscowpea strain	
Soybean mosaic potyvirus	*Glycine max.*
Sunnhemp mosaic tobamovirus	*V. unquiculata*
Tobacco mosaic tobamovirus	*V. unquiculata*

Table 10 : Morphological seed abnormalities due to infection of some seed-transmitted viruses

Plant species	*Seed abnormality*	*Responsible virus*
Arachis hypogaea	Small size, disco *loured seed-coat*	Peanut mottle *Potyvirus*
Glycine max.	Discoloured seed-coat	Soybean mosaic Potyvirus
Glycine max.	Diffused dark brown spots	Tobacco streak ilarvirus
Hordeum vulgare	Small, shrivelled, light-weight	barley stripe mosaic hordeivirus
Lycopersicon esculentum	Necrotic, blackened	Tobacco mosaic tobamovirus
Phaseolus aureus (syn. *Vigna radiata* Var. *radiata*)	Wrinkled Shrivelled	Mungbean mosaic Potyvirus
Pisum sativum	Wrinkled, greeni -shgrey seed-coat	Pea early browing tobravirus
Pisum sativum	Cracked but "healed" seed-coat Small size, or abonormal shaped	Pea seed-borne mosaic potyvirus
Vicia faba	Discoloured seed-coat	Bean yellow-mosaic Potyvirus
Vigna unguiculata	Shrunken, shrivelled	Cowpea aphid-borne mosaic Potyvirus

MANAGEMENT

The knowledge of mechanism of seed transmission of viral pathogens is helpful in devising suitable control measures and improve seed health testing. A virus may be carried in or on the seed. When a virus is on the seed, one can eliminate it by using appropriate disinfectants or physical method. But when the virus is within the seed especially in embryo, the chance for its transmission to the next generation is assured. The seed borne viruses can be managed by calculation.

***(i)* Visual Observation :** A careful and close look at the seed in certain cases may give some indication of the presence of viruses. Morphological abnormalities on seed like shrivelled seed coat, shrinkenness, discoloration, necrotic spots or bands cracking size and weight are the criteria used for detecting the presence of virus in seed. Normal seed cleaning techniques may help in reducing the seed transmission by removal of morphologically abnormal seeds.

***(ii)* Chemical Treatment :** Seed treatment of tobacco mosaic tobamovrius infecting tomato seeds proved very effective.

Treating the tomato seeds with 10% or higher concentration of trisodium phosphate (TSP) for 10 min. or 20% Hydrochloric acid (HCl) for 30 min. has already become a routine practice.

(iii) **Heat Therapy :** The virus may be eliminated from the infested seed through heat (hot water/dry heat) treatment at high temperatures for relatively shorter period or at low temperature for longer periods. Tobacco mosaic tobamovirus was eliminated from Tomato seeds by subjecting the dry seeds to temperatures at 70 and 80°C for 3 and 1 day respectively

(iv) **Storage Effect :** Long term storage of infected seeds also makes the seed virus free and chances of inactivation are more in externally seed-borne viruses then internally seed-borne viruses.

(v) **Biocontrol :** In cross protection technique the crop plants are deliberately inoculated with avirulent strain, which gives protection against severe strain of the same virus.

(vi) **Certified Seed :** Use of certified virus free seed by the farmers is the most dependable and reliable method for maintaining reasonable seed health standards, and it does not affect seed germination. Seed certification programme against seed-borne viruses must start at the basic level of the germplasm collection available to the plant breeder and continue through the subsequent development of varieties and increase of seed through breeder seed, foundation seed and certified seed. The major method of monitoring the presence of seed-borne viruses is periodic visual examination of the standing crop followed by testing the presence of virus in seeds usually by a growing on test. The lettuce seed certification practiced in USA is an excellent example. In this programme, lettuce mosaic potyvirus and the standard fixed for approval of a seed lot for certification was 1 : 10000 *i.e.,* not more than one infected seeds in 10000 seeds. This limit has been further raised to 1 : 30000.

PHYSICAL DAMAGE OF SEED DURING HARVESTING AND PROCESSING

Seed quality is one of the most important factor affecting the performance and productivity of most agricultural crops. The production of nearly all agricultural crops depends on seed to establish the initial stand. Seed of low germination and vigour perform poorly even under ideal planting conditions, while seed of high vigour generally perform well even under relatively unfavourable conditions. Any loss in quality of seed is a direct economic loss to agricultural industry. Quality loss of seed starts early in the field due to poor agronomical practices, and during combine harvesting. The high speed of threshing action of threshing cylinder of combine or thresher damage the protective cover of seed and reduce their overall strength. This initial damage is further aggravated by a series of handling and transporting operations during processing and marketing procedures. Furthermore poor drying practices also add to the quality loss with the development of cracks and rupturing of seed coat due to thermal stresses developed in the seed by poor drying. Poor storing practices increase the quality loss as the mould and insect infestation is more in the seed already damaged during harvesting, threshing and handling operations. High level of these damages significantly lower the vigour and quality of the seed.

Physical damage to the seed occurs at the following stages/operations.

1. Damage in the field due to poor agronomical practices and unfavourable weather.
2. Seed damage during harvesting and threshing.
3. Seed damage during processing and handling.

4. Seed damage during storage.
5. Seed damage during marketing.

CHANNEL OF SEED MARKETING

The important channels of seed marketing being commonly followed in the country are summarized in flow chart (Fig. 1). In general the most important channels in operation are : State Seed Corporations – their sale counters – farmers; State Seed Corporations – State government – farmers; State Seed Corporations – Cooperative societies-farmers; National Seed Corporation – State Seed Corporations – farmers; Private Seed Firms-dealers-retailers- farmers.

The most important feature of the seed distribution is the absence of agricultural produce dealers (specially wholesaler) from its network. Agricultural produce wholesale dealers operating in the agricultural produce markets are the closest persons of the farmers in general. In most of the situation they arrange sale of the products by the farmers as well as arrange almost all other supplies. Farmers through generations have developed immense confidence and faith over wholesalers. Thus, if this closest friend and guide of the farmer is given priority in seed distribution channel, use of quality seed may take a quantum jump.

The findings of the study call for a through review of the seed sector starting from production planning to final marketing. While planning for seed production, varietal coverage and farmers preference should be given due attention. Similarly, while planning for seed distribution, varietal coverage need to be taken in to consideration. In case of selection/formation of seed distribution channel, the closest person/agency to the farmer should be given first priority.

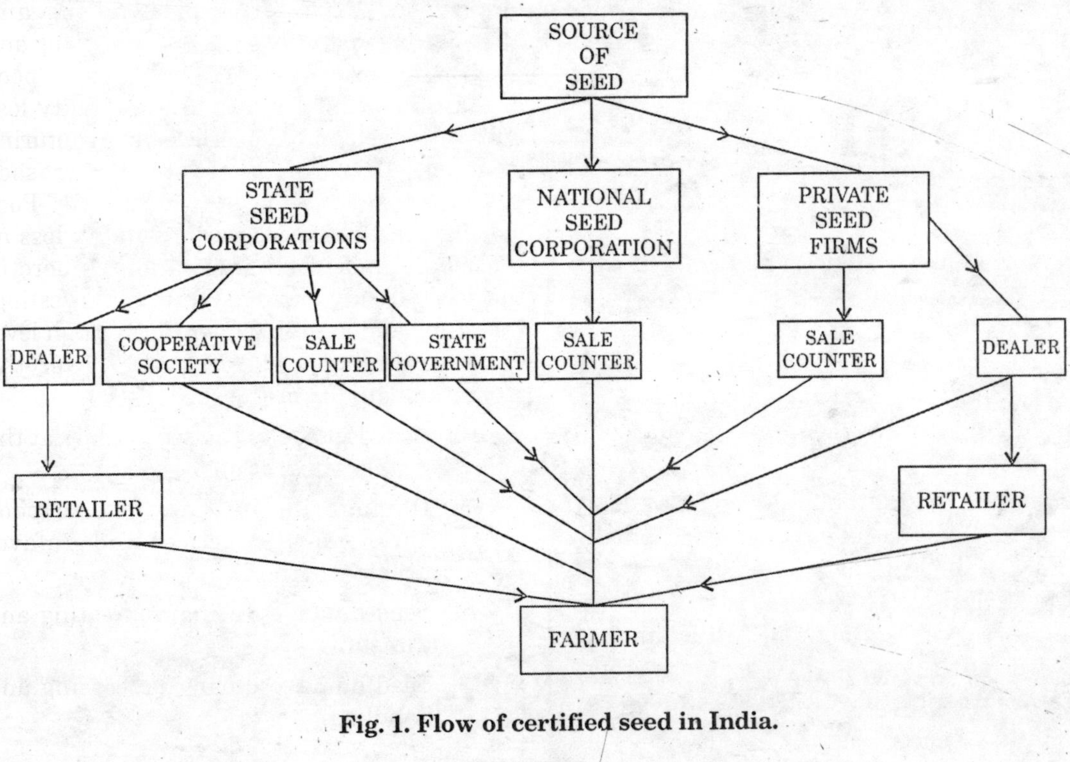

Fig. 1. Flow of certified seed in India.

Questions From Previous Year's Papers

Q. 1. Mention the structural components of albuninous and exalbuminous dicotyledonous seeds. Briefly discuss the major constraints of quality seed production.

Q. 2. Write short notes on::

(a) Sundrying of seeds

(b) Huller scarifier

(c) Mercurials in seed treatment

(d) Types of seed treatment and precautions observed in seed treatment. (Condition under which seed must be treated).

(e) Seed certification.

(f) Foundation seed.

Q. 3. (a) Enlist the qualities of a good seed. What happens when inferior quality seed is used for sowing of a field crop?

(b) Suggest the ideal conditions which should be met while sowing of seeds in the field.

Q. 5. Distinguish between the two in 150 words each :

(a) Certified and registered seeds.

(b) Sex linked and sex influenced characters.

(c) Inter-specific and inter-generic hybridisation.

(d) Breeder seed and certified seed.

Q. 6. Compare the following in about 150 words each:

(a) Registered seed and breeder seed.

(b) Disease tolerance and resistance.

5. PLANT PHYSIOLOGY

DIFFUSION

Diffusion is the movement of molecules or ions of gases, liquids or solutes from regions of higher concentration to regions of lower concentration till they are evenly distributed throughout the available space. The molecules are in high partial pressure. When concentrated. Diffusion therefore occurs from region of high partial pressure to region of low partial pressure. When two substances are diffusing simultaneously the direction of one is independent of the other.

Diffusion occurs due to kinetic nature of matter. At temperature above absolute zero (0°K or –273°C) all components of matter are in a constant random motion. It is due to certain amount of kinetic energy possessed by the molecules. As a result, greater number of molecules move out of their higher concentration than those that re-enter it. The direction of overall molecular movement of a substance occurs from a *region of higher free energy of its molecules to a region of lower free energy. The free energy is the energy available to do work.* It depends on (*i*) the rate of motion of molecules, and (*ii*) the number of molecules per unit volume. Free energy of one mole (6×10^{23} molecules) of a substance is its **chemical potential**. Therefore the diffusion of a substance occurs from a *region of its higher chemical potential to a region of its lower chemical potential.*

The rate of diffusion is inversely proportional to the square root of density of the diffusing substance.

$D \propto \frac{1}{\sqrt{d}}$ Where D = diffusion, and d = density

Temperature and pressure increase the rate of diffusion due to increase in motion energy. An increase in concentration of medium in which diffusion occurs decreases the rate of diffusion. The greater the concentration gradient more rapid is the diffusion of molecules.

OSMOSIS

The movement of water (or any other solvent) across a semipermeable membrane from a region of its higher concentration to a region of its lower concentration is called Osmosis. It is a process of diffusion. A semipermeable membrane allows solvent molecules to diffuse but prevents the diffusion of solute molecules. However, a truly semipermeable membrane is never encountered in nature. Biological membranes are only differentially permeable or selectively permeable. They only restrict but never stop the diffusion of molucules. The osmotic flow occurs from a region of higher chemical potential of solvent to a region of its lower chemical potential. The chemical potential of water is called **water potential**. It can be defined as the difference between free energy of water in a system and the free energy of pure water at atmospheric pressure and a defined temperature. Usually, the water potential in living systems is denoted by greek letter ψ. Techinically, ψ means potential and water potential should be ψw. But in living systems the solvent is always water. Therefore, it is simpler to use ψ and assume the *w* when describing the water potential in living systems. Water potential is always negative in sign and is commonly expressed by biologists in pressure units such as bars. Its maximum value is '0' for pure water at constant temperature and pressure water potential is equivalent by opposite in sign to the term *diffusion pressure deficil* (DPD) or *suction pressure* (SP) used in the earlier texts.

Water potential of pure water is lowered by solutes due to attraction between solute and solvent molecules. All solutions therefore have water potentials less than '0'. The *decrease in water potential brought about by the solute in solution is called* **solute potential** (ψs). It is also expressed in bars with a negative sign. It depends on the toal number of solute particles either molecules or ions in solutions and not on their kind or charge. For example, one mol of sodium chloride in solution dissociates into 2 mol of ions. Therefore, 0.5 molal solution of sodium chloride has same solute potential as 1.0 molal sucrose solution which is –26.9 bars at NTP. At atmospheric pressure the ψ of a solution is determined by its solute potential. For a solution at atmospheric pressure. $\psi = \psi s$. Solute potential has replaced the term *osmotic pressure* (OP) used earlier. The osmotic pressure is expressed either in bars or in atmospheres with a (+) positive sign. It increases as ψs decreases. It can be defined as *the pressure which when applied to an aqueous solution prevents the osmotic flow of pure water into it.*

IMBIBITION

The absorbtion of water or any other liquid by materials without forming a true solution is called imbibition. Imbibition invariably results in swelling of the imbibant. For example dry seeds, wood, gelatin etc., absorb water and swell. Similarly, rubber absorbs ether and swells. Imbibition involves both diffusion and capillary action. In a plant cell the hydrophilic macromolecules in cell wall and protoplasm act as imbibants. The imbibed water molecules are bound to them by intermolecular cohesive forces. In the process some of the kinetic energy of molecules is lost as heat and it causes a rise in temperature. The pressure developed due to swelling imbibants is enormous. It is called *imbibition pressure* (IP). In recent years IP is replaced by term **matric potential** (ψ_m) with a negative sign for studying cell water relations.

SURFACE TENSION

Like a stretched membrane, the surface of a liquid tend to contract as much as – possible. This phenomenon is called surface tension. Water has the highest surface tension of any known liquid. And it is reason why water rises to – unusually high levels in narrow capillary tubes. The surface tension of water is 72.8. This has great significance in physiology.

TRANSPIRATON

The loss of water in the form of vapours from the living tissues of aerial parts of the plant is called transpiration.

- About 98% of water absorbed by land plant is transpired.

Types of Transpiration

(1) **Cuticular :** Cuticle provides a relatively impermeable covering. If cuticle is thin and green, about 20% of the total transpiration takes place through it, but if its thickness is increased, the extent of water vapour loss is significantly reduced.

(2) **Lenticular :** Lenticels are small regions on bark etc, and possess small loosely arranged cells called as complementary cells.

According to Huber, this loss through lenticels is only 1.0 per cent of the total transpiration.

(3) **Stomatal :** Stomata are tiny pores present on the epidermal surface of leaves, young stems and in certain truits. Nearly 97 per cent of the total transpiration takes place through these stomata.

STOMATA

Help in aseous exchange at the time of respiration and photosynthesis.

- There are two kidney shaped guard cells which bound a minute elliptical pore in a stoma. Guard cells are modified epidermal cells.

  The wall of guard cells near the pore is thick.

  The outer wall is thin, elastic and semipermeable.

- Loftfield classified stomata on the basis of their daily movement into four main types—

  (*a*) **Alfalfa type :** Open throughout the day and closed all night *e.g.*, radish, mustard, turnip, apple, pea.

  (*b*) **Potato type :** Open throughout the day and night except few hours following sunset *e.g.*, cabbage, pumpkin, onion.

  (*c*) **Barley type :** Open only for a few hours in day *e.g.*, barley, maize, oat, wheat.

  (*d*) **Equisetum type :** Always open throughout day and night *e.g.*, *Equisetum*.

Distribution of Stomata on the Leaves

1. **Apple or mulberry type :** On the under surface of leaves only *e.g. apple*.
2. **Potato type :** More on under surface than upperside. *e.g. Potato, brinjal.*
3. **Oat type :** Equally distributed on both the surfaces. *e.g. rice, wheat.*
4. **Water lily type :** Only on the upper surface. *e.g. water lily*.
5. **Potamogeton type :** Either absent or if present, they are functionless, present mostly in submerged aquatic plants. *e.g. Potamogeton*.

Significance of Transpiration

(*i*) Removal of water in the form of vapours has a cooling effect on the leaves. So it does not allow the leaf temperature to rise to detrimental levels.

(*ii*) It helps in movement of xylem sap which simultaneously increases the absorption of mineral nutrients by the roots from the soil. It enhances extensive development of root system that supports the heavy aerial growth against wind.

Curtis (1926) called transpiration as necessary evil.

FACTORS AFFECTING TRANSPIRATION

(A) External Factors

1. **Atmospheric humidity :** If atmosphere is humid, it reduces the rate of transpiration. When the air is dry, the rate of transpiration increases.
2. **Wind :** A high wind speed or a dry breeze will greatly increase transpiration.
3. **Atmospheric pressure :** Low atomospheric pressure increases the rate of transpiration.
4. **Soil temperature :** Plants growing in warm regions exhibit less transpiration at a temperature lower than 5 – 8°C.
5. **Air temperature :** The rate of evaporation doubles with every rise in temperature by 10°C. High temperature affects the closure of stomata, reduces transpiration.
6. **Water :** Less amount of soil water decreases the rate of transpiration. If

the rate of transpiration exceeds the rate of absorption, the stomata get closed and plant wilts.

(B) Internal Factors

1. **Leaf structure :** Presence of thick cuticle and sunken stomata reduces the rate of transpiration.
2. **Leaf orientation :** Transpiration is low in north-south orientation as compared to other crientation.
3. **leaf area :** Directly proportional to the transpiration rate.
4. **Plant age :** Germinating seeds exhibit a slow rate of transpiration. It becomes maximum at maturity and decreases at senescence stage.
5. **Root shoot ratio :** The increase in ratio of root and shoot enhances the rate of transpiration.
6. **Water contents of the leaves :** Directly proportional to the rate of transpiration.

ENZYMES

Enzymes are protein substances which act as biological catalysts with a high degree of specificity produced within the cell having enormous ability to catalyse all metabolic reactions in a highly effective manner. Enzymes may be simple protein or conjugated protein formed of apoenzyme (protein part) and cofactor (prosthetic group or coenzymes or metallic cofactor).

Edward Buchner (1897) showed that juice of groundnut and preserved yeast cells ferment sugar.

The term enzyme was coined by **W. Kuhne**.

J.B. Sumner purified and crystallised urease enzymes from Jack beans. He also suggested that enzymes are proteins.

Properties

Enzymes act catalysts, are required in small amount, highly specific, act best at a temperature between 25—40°C and at low temperature action slows down and at high temperature get denatured. Enzymes require optimum pH specific for each enzyme. The relative concentration of enzyme and substrate affect the velocity of the reaction. Certain inhibitors check the enzymatic action. Extracellular enzymes are produced in the inactive forms called proenzymes. Certain enzymes are slightly different in molecular structure but perform identical activities, they are known as isoenzyme or **isozymes**

NOMENCLATURE AND CLASSIFICATION OF ENZYMES

According to International Union of Biochemistry (**I.U.B—1961**) system of classification.

1. Reactions and enzymes catalyzing them are divided into 6 major classes each with 4-13 subclasses.
2. The enzyme name has two parts—first name is of substrate. The second ending in *–ase* indicates types of reaction.
3. The enzyme has a systematic Code No. (E.C.). The first digit denote the class, the second sub-class, the third sub-sub class and fourth one is for the particular enzyme name. Thus E.C.2.7.1.1 dentoes class two (transferases)-subclass-7 sub-subclass 1 (an alcohol function as phosphate acceptor). The fourth digit indicate hexokinase.

Major Classes of Enzymes

1. **Oxidoreductases.** Formerly known as oxidases and dehydrogenase.
2. **Transferases.** Catalyze transfer of one carbon group, aldehyde or ketone or functional group.
3. **Hydrolases.** These enzymes cause cleavage of variety of bonds by addition of water.
4. **Lyases** result in direct removal of groups from substrate or break the bonds without addition of water.

5. **Isomerases.** Which catalyse isomeric changes.
6. **Ligases or Synthetases.** Ctalyze linking together of different types of bonds.

MICHAELIS-MENTEN EQUATION

According to **Michaelis-Menten** equation K_m is equal to substrate concentration at which the half of maximum velocity is achieved. **Michaelis** and **Menten** proposed a hypothesis for enzyme action according to which the enzyme molecule combines with a substrate complex which further dissociates to form product and enzyme back

$$E + S \underset{K_2}{\xrightarrow{K_1}} E - S \xrightarrow{K_3} E + P;$$

$$K_m \text{ (Michaelis – Menten Constant)} = \frac{K_3 + K_2}{K_1}$$

They gave the following equation :

$$V_o = \frac{V_{max}(S)}{(S) + K_m}$$

It is the statement of the quantitative relationship between the initial velocity V_o, the maximum velocity V_{max} and the initial substrate concentrations : all related through Michaelis Menten constant K_m.

E = free enzyme

S = Substrate

ES = enzyme substarte complex

P = product

K_1 = the rate constant for ES formation

K_2 = the rate constant for dissociation of ES into E and S

K_3 = the rate constant for dissociation of ES complex into E and P.

Lock and Key Hypothesis of Enzyme Action Mechanism

(Template Hypothesis, Emil Fischer, 1894). The active sites of the enzyme have a specific geometric shape wherein the substarte molecules fit in just like a key in a particular lock. The subsrate molecules undergo change forming products. The products are released and the active sites of enzyme become free to pick up more substrate molecules.

Induced Fit Theory (Koshland, 1959)

The active site of enzyme posseses two groups, **buttressing** or **supporting** and **catalytic**. As the substrate gets associated with buttressing region, the active site changes configuration so that the catalytic group comes to lie in opposite area where substrate bonds are to be changed.

Enzymes differ from catalysts in being proteinaceous, having high molecular weight, high efficiency, narrow range of pH, narrow range of effective temperature, susceptibility to poisons and short wave radiations.

Optimum pH varies for enzymes to enzymes, *e.g.* 2 for pepsin, 8.5 for trypsin. Most intracellular enzymes function at near neutral pH. High temperature denatures enzymes. Lower temperature inactivates them. Within limits. Q_{10} is 2-3. *Time factor* (initial rise followed by fall) also operates. Enzymes inhibition can be due to protein poisons (*e.g.* cyanide, lead, nickel), end products (allosteric, feedback or retro-inhibition, *e.g.* excess of glucose phosphate inhibits hexokinase or glucokinase activity, excess of isoleucine inhibits threonine deaminase) and specific enzyme inhibitors.

FACTORS AFFECTING ENZYME ACTIVITY

(*i*) Substrate Concentration

Enzyme activity increases with increase in concentration of the substrate to a maximum and then it levels off. Probably at this concentration of substrate, amount of enzyme becomes limiting. Some enzymes are inhibited even by high substrate concentration. This phenomenon is called 'substrate inhibitions'.

Two types of graphs are obtained with substrate concentration and enzyme activity plot. Straight line or Michaelis type of curve is obtained with the enzymes which are made up of one unit. The enzymes which are made up of several subunits and show interaction amongst subunits (called **allosteric enzymes**), exhibit sigmoidal type of curve.

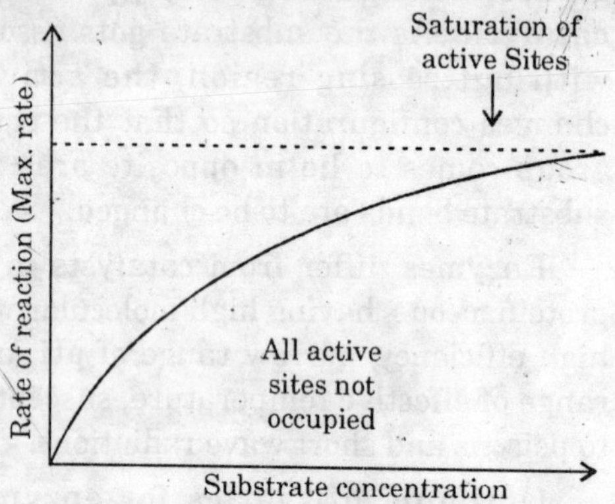

(ii) Enzyme Concentration

In general, the rate of reaction will increase with increasing enzyme concentration, provided substrate concentration is maintained at a high level and other conditions such as pH and temperature are kept constant. Increase in enzyme concentration increases the rate of reaction by providing more active sites to the substrates.

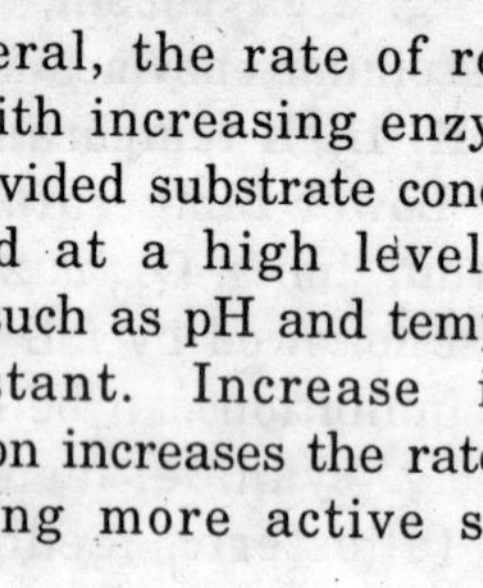

(iii) Temperature

In most of the enzymatic reactions, rise of 10°C in the temperature doubles the rate of reaction between 5-40°C. At higher temperature Q_{10} drops to 1° or lower. Enzymes are denatured irreversibly at 50°C to 60°C, because of their proteinaceous nature. But a few enzymes continue to be active above 60°C also *e.g.*, the enzymes of dry tissues, such as seeds and spores are more resistant to high temperature.

The increased activity of enzyme at high temperature is because the heat increases molecular motions due to which substrate molecules move more quickly and chances of their bumping into each other are increased. As a result, there is a greater probability of a reaction being caused.

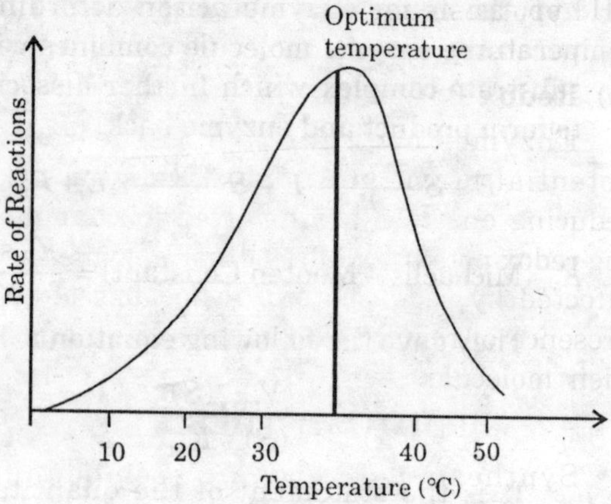

Deep freezing of food for preserving them for long periods is done not only to prevent the growth and multiplication of micro-organisms, but also to inactivate enzymes. It makes impossible for the micro-organisms to digest the food.

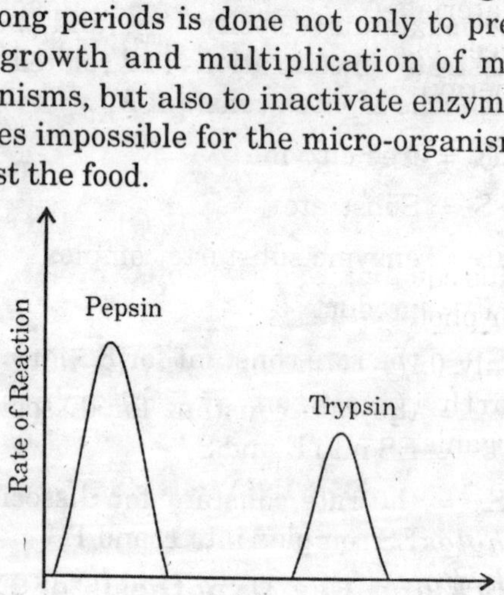

(iv) pH

Enzymes normally function most effectively at particular hydrogen ion concentrations. Each one of them shows reduced activity outside its own optimum pH range. Certain enzymes like *pepsin* have very low pH requirements, whereas enzymes like trypsin are active at high pH. Enzymes like urease are active only near neutrality.

The hydrogen ion concentration may alter the ionization and solubility of the enzymes, the substrates, inhibitors and activators. It may also change the enzymes susceptibility to heat. This may explain why the optimum pH of an enzymes varies with the temperature.

(v) Redox Potential

Enzymes are sensitive to the redox potential of the cell also. Oxidizing and reducing enzymes are involved in changing the redox potential. Many other enzymes are affected by redox potential because of the presence of readily oxidisable –SH group in their molecule.

PHOTOSYNTHESIS

- Synthesis of organic compounds (carbohydrates) from inorganic raw materials (CO_2 and Hydrogen donor) by green plants in the presence of light (solar energy)

$$CO_2 + 2H_2O \xrightarrow[\text{Green plants}]{\text{Light energy}} (CH_2O)_n + H_2O + O_2$$

This equation was given by **C.B. Van Niel** for photosynthesis.

- Only 0.2% of the light energy falling on earth is utilized by photosynthetic organisms.

DEFINITION

Photosynthesis is the synthesis of carbohydrates by green plants in the presence of light by utilizing CO_2 *and* H_2O'. By this process solar energy is trapped by autotrophic organisms, and is stored in the form of chemical energy.

Photosynthesis is anabolic, endothermic and reduction process. Photosynthesis in green plant (but not bacterial plant) can be represented as :

$$6CO_2 + 12H_2O \xrightarrow[\text{Chlorophyll}]{\text{Light}} C_6H_{12}O_6 + 6H_2O + 6O_2$$

Of the world's total photosynthesis, 90% is carried by marine water algae and aquatic plants.

During the process of photosynthesis, the light energy is converted into chemical energy.

Photosynthesis is an oxidation-reduction process. In this process water is oxidized to form sugars. It has two phases :

(A) Light Reaction

(B) Dark Reaction

(A) *Light Reaction :* It is light sensititive process, therefore, photochemical reaction occurs in the granum of chloroplast. This process includes absorption of light energy, conversion of light energy into chemical energy, and synthesis of reducing power or assimilatory power. Light reaction is also known as *Hill reaction*. This reaction includes following main processes :

(a) *Excitation of electron :* When P-680 or P-700 forms of a chlorophyll molecule receive a photon of light they becomes excited

$$Chl + h\nu = chl^*$$

(b) *Photolysis of water and O_2 evolution:* After excitation of electron, photolysis of water takes place and oxygen evolves.

(c) *Formation of $NADPH_2$:* The hydrogen of water that evolves after photolysis of water taken up by hydrogen acceptor molecule NADP (Nicotinamide Adenine Dinucleotide Phosphate). After accepting hydrogen, $NADPH_2$ is formed. Light reaction is divided in two parts :

I. Photosystem I

II. Photosystem II

I. *Photosystem I :* Chlorophyll molecule absorbs photon and get excited releasing electron. These electrons are accepted by A (FeS) and passing through cytochrome of return to chlorophyll. In this photosystem energy of photon is stored in ATP. This process is called cyclic *photophosphorylation*.

(i) Chl + $h\upsilon$ = Chl* ...(1)
(ground state of chlorophyll) (quantum of light) (excited state of Chlorophyll)

(*ii*) $4H_2O \longrightarrow 4OH + 4H$

$4OH \longrightarrow 2H_2O + O_2\uparrow$ ...2

(*iii*) $2NADP + 4H + 4e \longrightarrow 2NADPH_2$
(from eq. 1) (from eq. 2)

(*iv*) Chl*

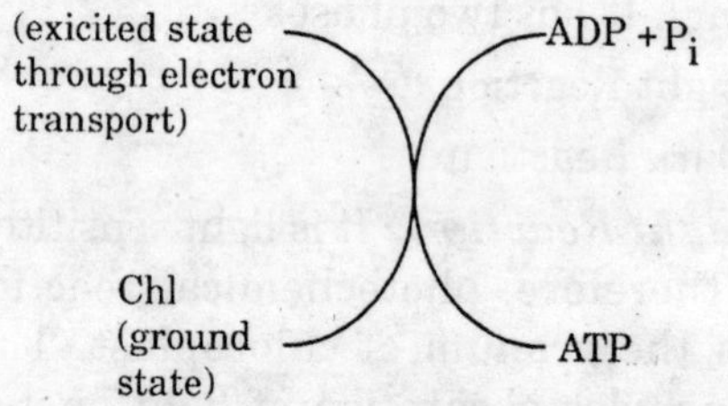

(II) *Photosystem II* : Chlorophyl molecules absorb photons and get excited releasing electrons. These electrons are excited by 'Q' and passing through ETS, reenter PS I. In this systems ATP is also synthesized. As electrons released from PS II do not return to PS II, it is called non-cyclic photophosphorylation. In this act, photolysis of water takes place and oxygen evolves.

(B) *Dark Reaction* : This process does not require light. This process takes place in stroma of chloroplast. In dark reaction, CO_2 combines with many molecules and after several steps form sugar Calvin traced out the path of CO_2 fixation into sugar by using radio isotope of carbon C^{14} in CO_2 molecule.

In presence of RuBP carboxylase enzymes (also called *Rubisco*) CO_2 combines with ribulose 1-5 biphosphate to form 3-phosphoglyceric acid which is first stable compound.

With the help of assimilatory power (ATP and $NADPH_2$) phosphoglyceric acid is changed into 3 phosphoglyceraldehyde. This phosphoglyceraldehye is immediately converted to sugars. Glucose is end product of photosynthesis but they accumulate in the form of starch. Above pathway of CO_2 fixtation is called C_3 cycle because first stable product **phosphoglyceric acid (PGA)** is 3-carbon compound. The plants in which C_3 cycle occurs are called **C_3 plants**. These plants are mainly dicots.

Hatch and Slack (1967) discovered an alternate pathway of CO_2 fixation and is called **C_4 pathway**. This pathway occurs mainly in monocots.

In C_4 cycle, CO_2 combines with phosophoenol pyruvic (PEP) acid in presence of enzyme PEP carboxylase. The first stable compound is oxaloacetic acid (OAA) which is a 4 carbon compound and so the name of pathway is C_4 cycle.

In C_3 Plants :

(*i*) CO_2 acceptor is RUBP

(*ii*) Carbon pathway in Photosynthesis is Calvin cycle (C_3)

(*iii*) First stable product is PGA

(*iv*) Kranz's anatomy is absent

(*v*) Photorespiration occurs

(*vi*) CO_2 compensation point is high.

In C_4 Plants :

(*i*) CO_2 acceptor is PEP

(*ii*) Carbon pathway in PS is Hatch-Slack pathway

(*iii*) First stable product is OAA

(*iv*) Leaves have Kranz's anatony

(*v*) No photorespiration

(*vi*) Low CO_2 compensation point.

Bacterial Photosynthesis : In bacterial photosynthesis, oxygen does not evolve and water is not used as hydrogen donor. Instead of H_2O, bacteria uses H_2S. Photosynthetic bacteria are green sulphur bacteria, *e.g.*

Chlorobium purple sulphur bacteria, Chromatium and non sulphur bacteria *e.g. Rhodospirillum.* Photosynthetic pigments in bacteria are bacteriochlorophyll.

Blackman's law of limiting factor (1905) : "When a process is conditioned as to its rapidity by a number of separate factor, the rate of process is limiting by the pace of slowing factor".

Note :

(A) Each leaf contain 60-100 chloroplast

(B) Photosynthetic pigments are embedded in the thylakoid membrane of chloroplast.

(C) Most plants contain 2 or 3 times more cholorophyll *a* than chlorophyll *b*.

(D) The formula of chlorophyll *a* is $C_{55}H_{72}O_5N_4Mg$.

(E) The formula of chlorophyll *b* is $C_{55}H_{70}O_5N_4Mg$.

(F) Red light is most suitable for photosynthesis.

(G) Carotenes are of three types α, β, and γ.

Major Scientists Related with PHOTOSYNTHESIS are :

(A) *Von Helmont (1648) :* Stated that plants derive food fro soil and water.

(B) *J. Priestley (1772) :* Reported that green plants purify the air.

(C) *J. Ingenhousz (1779) :* Reported that green plants purify air in presence of sunlight only.

(D) *J.R. Mayer (1845) :* Established the fact that plants store the energy of sunlight in the form of chemical energy.

(E) *Sachs etal (1862) :* Reported that starch is the first visible product of photosynthesis.

(F) *Blackman (1905) :* (*i*) Established that photosynthesis is a two step process. A dark reactions also occurs along with photochemical reactions.

(*ii*) Proposed law of limiting factors in (1905).

(G) *Warburg (1920) :* Found green alga *Chlorella*, to be useful for photosynthesis experiments.

(H) *Emerson and Arnold (1932) :* Proved that light reaction consists of two distinct photochemical processes.

(I) *Robert Hill (1937) :* Discovered production of oxygen without accompanying CO_2 fixation by isolated chloroplasts.

(J) *Ruben, hassid* and *Kamen (1941) :* Proved that oxygen evolved in photosynthesis comes from water.

(K) *Arnon, Allen and Whatley (1954) :* Demonstrated fixation of CO_2 by chloroplast using $^{14}CO_2$.

(L) *Malvin Calvin (1854) :* Using unicellular alga—*Chlorella*—as experimental material traced steps in the fixation of CO_2 (Calvin cycle/C_3 cycle, he got Nobel Prize for the same in 1961).

(M) *Hatch and Slack (1967) :* Established C_4 pathway for fixation of CO_2.

(N) *Haber, Michel and Dissenhofer (1985) :* Crystallised photosynthetic reaction centre of bacterium *Rhodobacter.* Got Nobel Prize in 1980 for the same.

(O) *Bousingault :* Proved that the volume of CO_2 absorbed is equal to the volume of O_2 evolved.

PHOTOSYNTHETIC PIGMENTS

Photosynthesis is a photobiochemical reaction and needs absorption of light by photosynthetic pigments. The most important pigments required in the process are the chlorophyll an in addition to chlorophyll the carotenoid and phycobilin pigments also actively participate in photosynthesis.

Chlorophylls : A light absorbing green pigments found in chloroplasts, a methyl-phytol ester of the chlorophyllins; responsible for trapping light energy in the primary events of photosynthesis. Chlorophyll *a* is bluish green with empirical formula of $C_{55}H_{72}O_5N_4Mg$ while chlorophyll *b* is olive green with empirical formula of $C_{55}H_{70}O_6N_4Mg$.

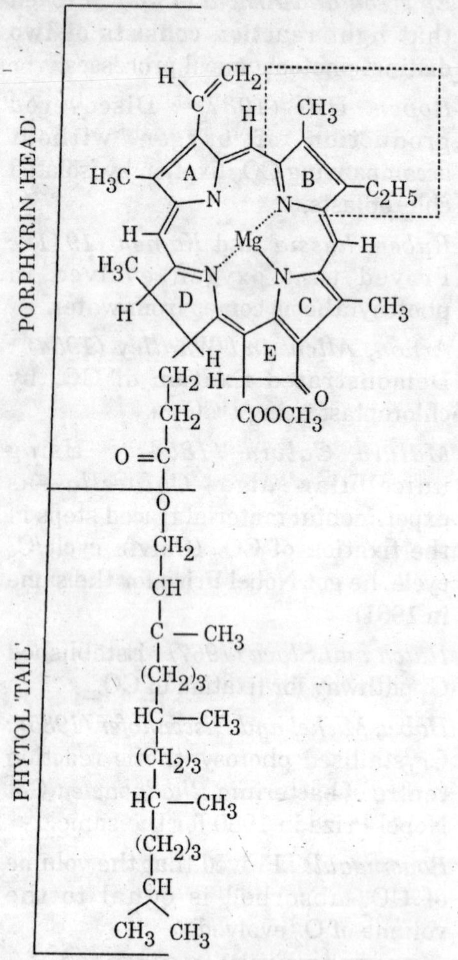

Fig. 1. Structure of chlorophyll *a* molecule

Hill Oxidants : They are hydrogen acceptors like ferricyanide, chromate, benzoquinone, dichlorophenol, indophenol. The oxidants were employed by Hill (1937) to study the effect of light on isolated chloroplasts in CO_2 free environment. The oxidants got reduced and O_2 evolved, showing that evolution of O_2 does not require carbondioxide.

Absorption Spectrum : The graphic representation of curve depicting the various wavelengths of light absorbed by a substance is known as absorption spectrum. Chlorophylls mostly absorb light radiations in blue (more) and red parts of light spectrum (430 nm and 662 nm for chlorophyll *a*, 455 nm and 644 nm for chlorophyll *b*).

Action Spectrum : It is a graphic representation or curve depicting the rate of photosynthesis in various wavelengths of light.

Carotenoids : It is a groups of accessory photosynthetic pigments of yellowish to reddish colour which possess conjugate double bonds (commonly tetraterpens). They are of two types, *carotenes* ($C_{40}H_{56}$ *e.g.* β carotene) and *xanthophylls* ($C_{40}H_{56}O_x$) oxygen containing carotenoids absorb light radiation in the mid region of light spectrum, convert nascent oxygen to molecular oxygen and protect various chloroplast constitutents from nascent oxygen.

Phycobilins : They are water soluble, open tetrapyrrole pigments found in red algae and blue green algae. Usually they occur in phycobilisomes attached to thylakoids and hand over their absorbed light energy to chlorophyll. Phycobilins are of three types—plycocyanin (blue), allophycocyanin (blue) and phycoerythrin (red).

Photosynthetic Unit : The smallest group of photosynthetic pigement molecule which can pick up light energy and convert it into chemical forms. It has a photocentre (= reaction centre = trap centre) of chlorophyll *a* molecule (*e.g.* p_{700}, P_{680}) surrounded by harvesting molecules differentiated into core molecules and antenna molecules.

Photosystems : They are groupings of photosynthetic units which posses photocentres and are surrounded by specific light harvesting pigment molecules. They are of two types. PS I and PS II. Photosystem I is present in stroma thylakoids and nonappressed parts of granal thylakoids. Photocentre is P_{700}. It can perform cyclic photophosphorylation independently and alongwith PS II it transfers electrons to $NADP^+$, PS II is present in appressed part of granal thylakoids. Photocentre is P_{680}. It picks up electrons emitted during photolysis of water and perform noncyclic photophosphorylation. PS I contains a reducing agent X, Fe S centre, ferredoxin, cytochrome *f* and cytochrome b_{563}. PS II contains ($Mn^{+2}Cl^-$) for photolysis), quencher Q, plastoquinone (PQ), cytochrome b_{559}, cytochrome *f* and copper containing plastocyanin (PC). PS II is more strongly fluorescent than PS I.

Photophosphorylation : It is the process of enzymatic formation of ATP from ADP and inorganic phosphate with the help of energy of solar radiations. Photophosphorylation is of two types. *Cyclic* and *Noncyclic.*

Cyclic photophorsphorylation : It is that type of light energized ATP synthesis in which electron expelled by exited photocentre is returned to it after passing over a chain of electron carriers.

Noncyclic photophosphorylation: It is that type of light energized ATP synthesis in which the eletron expelled by excited photocentres does not return to them. Both PS I and PS II are involved in it. They coordinate their activities to produce assimilatory power (ATP and NADPH).

Light Phase : (Hill Reaction, Photochemical phase). It is first stage of photosynthesis which consists of light driven splitting of water or photolysis, evolution of oxygen and synthesis of assimilatory power (ATP and NADPH). An enzyme complex X, Mn and Cl are required for photolysis.

Quantum Yield : (*i*) It is the number of oxygen molecules produced per quantum (h_2) or photon of light. The value is 0.125 (*ii*) It is the number of light quanta or photons used up for evolution of one molecule of oxygen. 8 quanta of light are required for one molecule of O_2.

Dark Phase : (Biosynthetic Phase, Blackman's Reaction). In this phase carbon dioxide is assimilated with the help of assimilatory power to produce organic substances. It is of two types, Calvin cycle and Hatch Slack cycle.

Calvin Cycle

(*i*) ***Carboxylation :*** In the presence of *Rubisco* (Ru BP carboxylase, most abundant protein), carbon dioxide combines with ribulose biphosphate (acceptor molecule) to form first a transitory 2-carboxy 3-keto-1, 6 biphosphoribotol and then two molecules of 3-phosphoglyceric acid or PGA (*First stable product*).

(*ii*) ***Glycolytic Reversal :*** With the help of assimilatory power (ATP and NADPH), PGA is changed to glyceraldehydes 3-phosphate (3-phosphoglyceraldehyde). Some of the molecules of glyceradehyde 3-phosphate are transformed into their isomer dihydroxy acetone 3-phosphate. The two combine giving rise to fructose 1, 6-diphosphate from which glucose and its polymers are produced.

(*iii*) ***Regeneration of RuBP :*** RuBP is regenerated through the formation of 4-C, 5-C and 7-C intermediates. For this fructose 6-phosphate reacts with glyceraldehydes 3-phosphate to form erythrose 4-phosphate and xylulose- 5-phosphate to form erythrose 4-phosphate and dihydroxyacetone phosphate condense to produce sedoheptulose 1 : 7 diphosphate from which sedoheptulose- 7-phosphate is formed. The latter reacts with glyceraldehydes- 3-phosphate to produce ribose- 5-phosphate and xylulose 5-phosphate.

Both then undergo isomerisation to produce ribulose- 5-phosphate. When required ribulose- 5-phosphate, is changed to ribulose 1, 5-biphosphate (RuBP, RuDP).

Hatch-Slack Pathway (C_4 Pathway, Dicarboxylic Acid Pathway) : It occurs in some tropical plants like maize, sugarcane, *Atriplex, Amaranthus* having Kranz anatomy (concentric undifferentiated mesophyll around vascular bundles with chloroplast containing bundle sheath). Bundle sheath chloroplasts are larger, agranal and without PS II acivity. Mesophyll cell fix carbon dioxide with the help of 'Phosphoenol pyruvate' (first acceptor_in the presence of *pepco* (PEP carboxylase) is an unstable compound oxaloacetic acid (first product). Oxaloacetic acid is changed to malic acid/aspartic acid for transport to bundle sheath cells. In bundle sheath cells, carbon dioxide is released and is assimilated through Calvin cycle. Pyruvate is released which passes back into mesophyll cells where PEP is regenerated.

For synthesis of one molecule of glucose, C_3 plants require 18 ATP and 12 NADPH while C_4 plants need additional 12 ATP molecules. C_4 plants are more efficient in picking up carbon dioxide and tolerating drought conditions. Photorespiration is little in them. They are not harmed even at full summer sunlight. CO_2 compensation point is 0-10 ppm (as compared to 10-100 ppm for C_3 plants). Photosynthetic rate is 40-90 mg CO_2/ dm^2/hr (as compared to 15-35 CO_2/dm^2/hr in C_3 plants).

CAM Photosynthesis : Sacculent (Cactus, *sedum*, Kalanchoe) have a photosynthetic pathway similar to C_4 plants. Their stomata open during night when CO_2 is taken from outside and fixed as malic acid with the help of phosphoenol pyruvate. Calvin cycle occurs during the day when stomata are closed.

Bacterial Photosynthesis : It is ANOXYGENIC (without evolution of O_2) because water is not employed as hydrogen donor. Instead H_2, H_2S and other compounds are employed.

Trap centre is usually B 890 of bacteriochlorophyll *a*. It absorbs radiations between 870-890 nm of infra-red range. Though both cyclic and non-cyclic photophosphorylations occur, there is only one photosystem. Assimilatory power consists of ATP and NADH.

Photorespiration : (Dicker and Tio, 1959). It is light induce oxidation of photosynthetic intermediates with the help of oxygen. For this rubisco functions as RuBP oxygenase. RuBP is oxidized to form PGA and phosphoglycolate. Phosphoglycolate is dephosphorylated to form glycolate. Glycolate is considered to the *substrate* for photorespiration though one oxidation has already occurred in chloroplasts. Glycolate passes into peroxisomes where it is changed to glyoxylate in the presence of oxygen and catalase. Glyoxylate is aminated to form glycine. Glyoxylate/glycine is considered to be first product of photorespiration. Two molecules of glycine combine to form one molecule of serine with the evolution of CO_2. Serine is deaminated and the 3-C product enters Calvin cycle.

Principle of Limiting Factors : (Blackman, 1905). When a process is conditioned as to its rapidity by a number of separate factors, the rate of the process is limited by the pace of the slowest factor. In other words, at one time, only one factor limits the rate of the process. It is called limiting factor. A *limiting factor* is that factor which is deficient to such an extent that increase in its value directly increases the rate of the process.

Questions From Previous Year's Papers

Q. 1. Answer the following in about 150 words each:

(a) Distinguish between C_3 and C_4 plants. Why are C_4 plants considered photosynthetically more efficient?

(b) Define Respiratory Quotient (R.Q.). With the help of suitable chemical reactions show where R.Q. will be 1, > 1, > 1 and α.

(c) Explain the theories of ascent of sap. How can you prove that translocation of sap takes place through xylem tissue.

(d) State how IAA can be distinguished from GA, by their specific action on higher plants. Describe the role of IAA in Agriculture.

Q. 2. Write short notes on :

(a) Storage of potato tuber

(b) Vernalization

(c) Photoperiodisin

(d) Anaerobic respiration

Q. 3. What are phytohormones? How are they used in plant propagation and breaking dormancy?

Q. 4. What is a polyhouse? What are the benefits of polyhouses?

Q. 5. List out commonly grown jasmine varieties and their methods of propagation.

Q. 6. Answer the following in about 150 words each :

(a) Distinguish between auxins and gibberellins.

(b) Discuss on the physiological effects of Gibberellins.

(c) What factors affects and rate of respiration in plants?

(d) How do aerobic and anerobic respirations differ?

Q. 7. Answer the following in about 150 words each :

(a) What are colloids? Explain their properties.

(b) Define diffusion. What factors influence the rate of diffusion?

(c) Define and differentiate between transpiration and guttation.

(d) What are cytokinins and their physiological effects?

Q. 8. Describe factors responsible for poor seed germination and methods to improve germination.

Q. 9. (a) Define synthetic variety. What measures would you suggest for the improvement of the performance of synthetic varieties.

(b) Briefly discuss the factors influencing photosynthesis.

(c) What are phytohomones? Describe in brief the role of gibberellins in plants.

Q. 10. Answer the following in about 150 words each :

(a) What are enzymes? State their characteristics and discuss their role in plant cell.

(b) Write about the plant growth regulators? Discuss the factors influencing plant growth.

(c) Write briefly methods of breaking seed dormancy.

6. METABOLISM

The metabolism applies to the assembly of biochemical reactions which are employed by the organisms for the synthesis of cell materials and for the utilization of energy from their environments. Metabolism may be defined as 'the sum total of all the enzyme-catalyzed reactions that occur in an organism. The large number of reactions in a cell are organized into a relatively small number of sequences or pathways. It is a highly coordinated and purposeful cell activity, in which multienzyme systems cooperate. This obviously points out to the fact that the metabolism of even a simple unicellular organism is time variant.

Metabolism in micro-organisms and the human beings :

(a) Micro-organisms like bacteria (*e.g., Escherichia coli*) can double in number every 40 minutes in a culture medium containing only glucose and inorganic salts, or in 20 minutes in a rich broth. The components of the medium are depleted and very little is added to the medium by the cells. Each cell contains hundreds to thousands of molecules of each of about 2,500 different proteins, about 1,000 types of organic compounds and a variety of nucleic acids. It is, thus, apparent that the bacterial cells participate in a variety of metabolic activities.

(b) Human adults maintain a constant weight for about 40 years, during which period a total of about 60 quintals of solid food and 45,000 litres of water are metabolized. And yet both body weight and body composition remain almost constant.

CARBOHYDRATE METABOLISM

The constant formation, transformation and degradation of the carbohydrates in the organism is carbohydrate metabolism. The most important reactions of it are :

(i) Interconversions of polymeric storage forms (glycogen and starch) and monomeric transport and substrate forms (glucose).

(ii) Reactions of carbohydrate degradation and interconversions.

(iii) Reactions for the synthesis of glucose from non-carbohydrate substances (glucogenic amino acids, fats). Glucose 6-phosphate has a central position in the entire carbohydrate metabolism.

THE CITRIC ACID CYCLE

The citric acid cycle (Kreb's cycle or Tricarboxylic acid cycle) is a series of reactions in mitrochondria that brings about the catabolism of acetyl residues; liberating hydrogen equivalents, which upon oxidation lead to the release and capture as ATP of most of the available energy of tissue fuels. The acetyl residues are in the form of acetyl-CoA (CH_3-CO~S – CoA, active acetate), and ester of co-enzyme A. CoA contains the vitamin pantothenic acid. (Fig. 1).

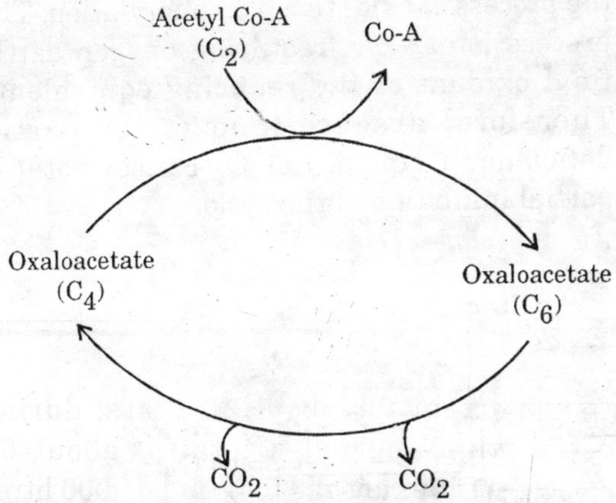

Fig. 1. Citric Acid Cycle-illustrating the catalytic role of oxalocetate.

The major function of the citric acid cycle is to act as the final common pathway for the oxidation of carbohydrate, lipids and protein. This is because glucose, fatty acids and many amino acids are all metabolized to acetyl-CoA or intermediates of the cycle Fig. 2. It also plays a major role is gluconeogenesis, transmination, demination and lipogenesis.

Essentially, the cycle comprises the combination of a molecule of acetyl-CoA with the pure carbon dicarboxylic acid oxaloacetate, resulting in the formation of a six-carbon tricarboxylic acid, citrate. There follows a series of reactions in the course of which two molecules of CO_2 are released and oxaloacetate is regenerated.

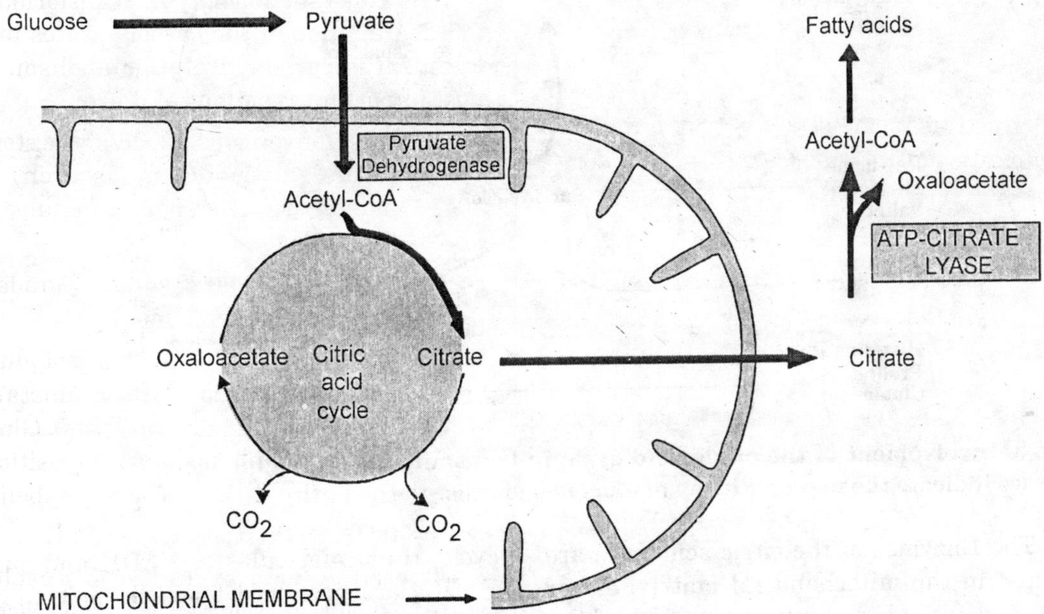

Fig. 2. Participation of the citric acid cycle in fatty acid synthesis from glucose.

Since only a small quantity of oxaloacetate is needed to facilitate the conversion of a large quantity of acetyl units to CO_2 oxaloacetate may be considered to play a CATALYTIC ROLE.

The citric acid cycle is an integral part of the process by which much of free energy liberated during the oxidation of carbohydrate, lipids and amino acids is made available. During the course of oxidation of acetyl-CoA in the cycle, *reducing, equivalents* in the form of hydrogen or of electrons are formed as a result of the activity of specific dehydrogenases Fig. 3. These reducing equivalents then enter the respiratory chain, where large amounts of ATP are generated in the process of oxidative phosphorylation. This process is *aerobic*, requiring oxygen as the final oxidant of the reducing equivalents. Therefore, absence (anoxia) or partial deficiency (hypoxia) of O_2 causes total or partial inhibition of the cycle.

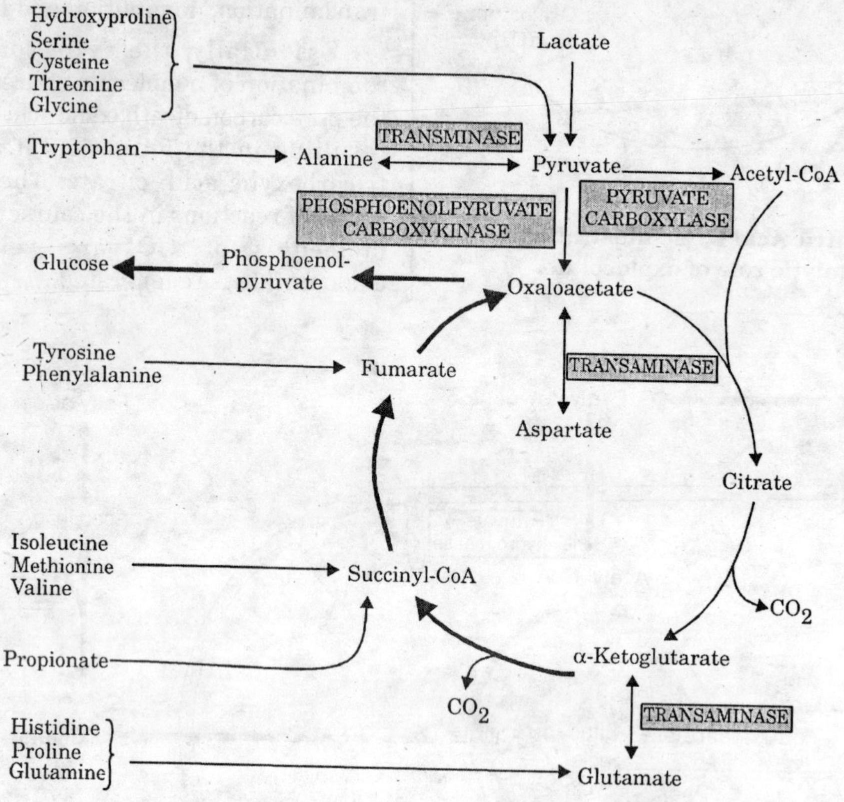

Fig. 3. Involvement of the citric acid cycle in transmination and gluconeogenesis. The bold arrows indicate the main pathway of gluconeogenesis.

The Enzymes of the citric acid cycle are located in the mitochondrial matrix; either free or attached to the inner surface of the inner mitochondrial membrane, which facilitates the transfer of reducing equivalents to the adjacent enzymes of the respiratory chain; situated in the inner mitrochondrial membrane.

As a result of oxidations catalyzed by dehydrogenase enzymes of the citric acid cycle, three molecules of NADH and one of $FADH_2$ are produced for each molecules of acetyl-CoA catabolized in one revolution of the cycle see Fig. 4. These reducing equivalents are transferred to the respiratory chain in the inner mitochondrial membrane. During passage along the chain, reducing equivalents from NADH generate three high-energy phosphate bonds by the esterification of ADP to ATP in the process of oxidative

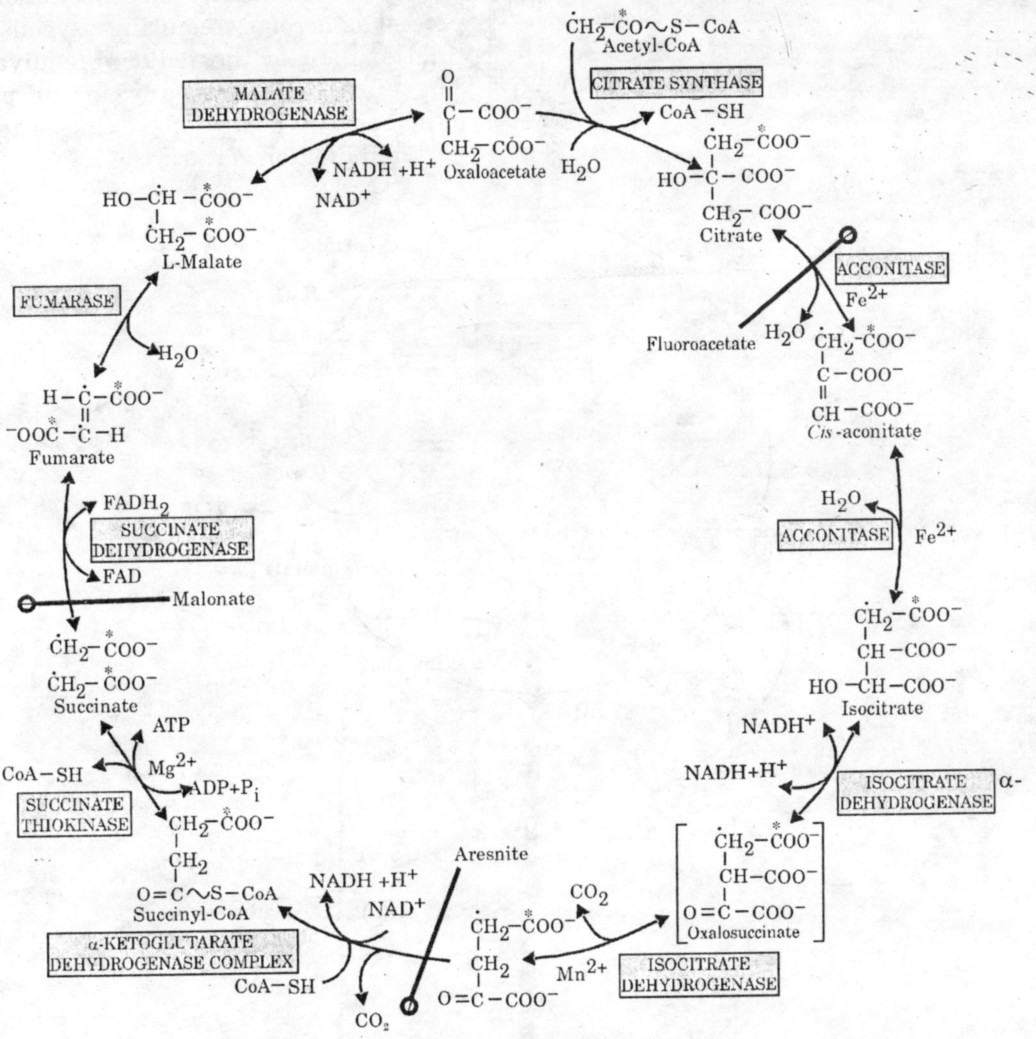

α-ketoglutrate

Fig. 4. The citric acid (Krebs) cycle. Oxidation of NADH and $FADH_2$ in the respiratory chain leads to the generation of ATP via oxidative phosphorylation. In order to follow the passage of acetyl-CoA through the cycle, the two carbon atoms of the acetyl radical are shown labeled on the carboxyl carbon (designated by asterisk) and on the methyl carbon (using the designation*). Although two carbon atoms are lost as CO_2 in one revolution of the cycle, these atoms are not derived from the acetyl-CoA that has immediately entered the cycle but form that portion of the citrate molecule which was derived from oxaloacetate. However, on completion of a single turn of the cycle, the oxaloacetate that is regenerated is now labeled, which leads to labeled CO_2 being evolved during the second turn of the cycle. Because succinate is a symmetric compound and because succinate dehydrogenase does not differentiate between its two carboxyl groups, "randomization" of label occurs at this step such that all four carbon atoms of oxaloacetate appear to be labeled after one turn of the cycle. During gluconeogenesis, some of the label in oxaloacetate is incorporated into glucose and glycogen. The sites of inhibition (O) by fluoroacetate, malonate, and arsenite are indicated.

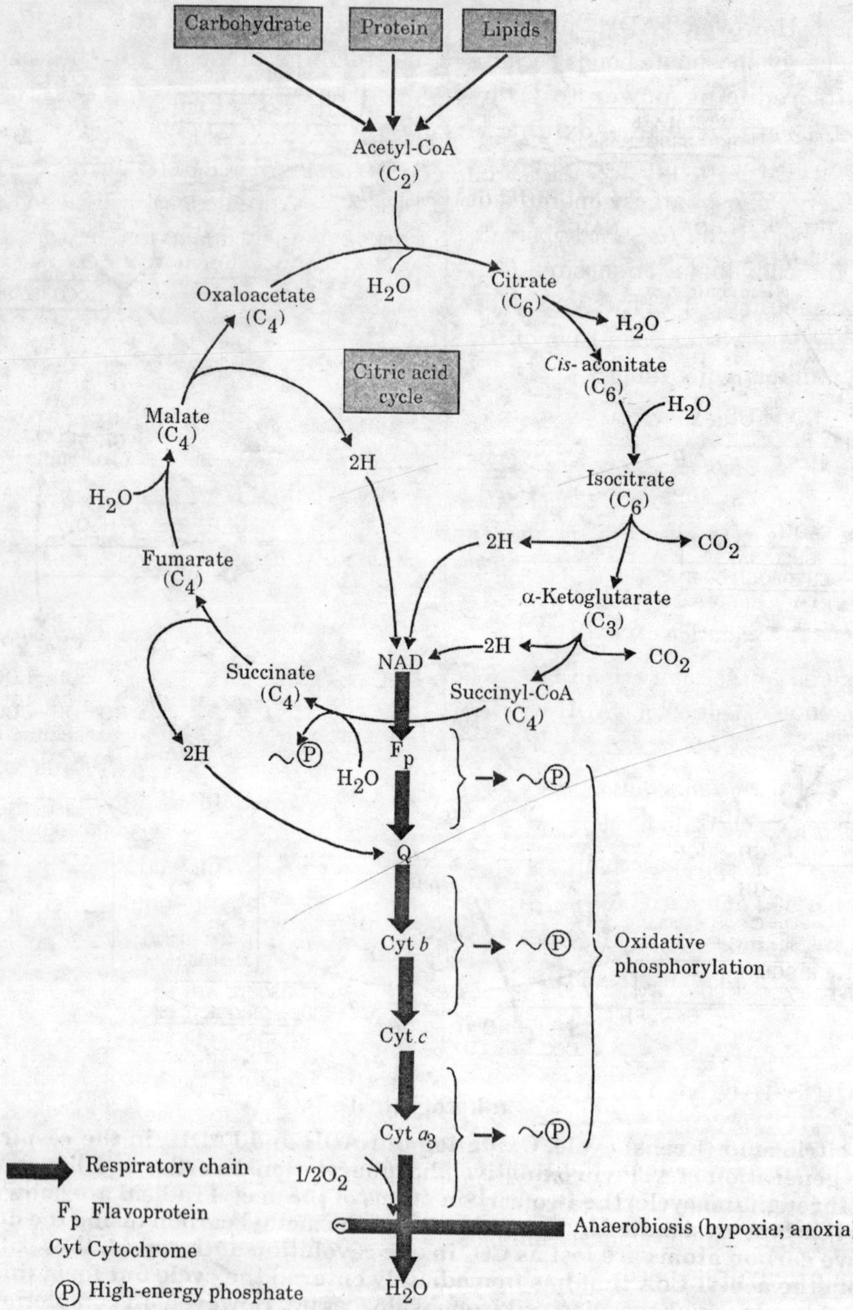

Fig. 5. The citric acid cycle : the major catabolic pathway for acetyl-CoA in aerobic organisms. Acetyl-CoA, the product of carbohydrate, protein, and lipid catabolism, is taken into the cycle, together with H_2O, and oxidized to CO_2 with the release of reducing equivalents (2H). Subsequent oxidation of 2H in the respiratory chain leads to coupled phosphorylation of ADP to ATP. For one turn of the cycle, 11~(P) are generated via oxidative phosphorylation and one ~(P) arises at substrate level from the conversion of succinyl-CoA to succinate.

phosphorylation. However, $FADH_2$ produces only two high-energy phosphate bonds because it transfers its reducing power to Q, by passing the first site for oxidative phosphorylation in the respiratory chain. A further high-energy phosphate is generated at the level of the cycle itself (*i.e.*, at substrate level) during the conversion of succinyl CoA to succinate see Fig. 5. Thus, 12 ATP molecules are generated for each turn of the cycle, as shown in following table 1.

Table–1

	Enzyme	*Method of ~(P) Production*	*ATP molecules formed*
(*i*)	Isocitrate dehydrogenase	Respiratory chain oxidation of NADH	3
(*ii*)	2-Ketoglutera-te dehydrogenase	Respiratory chain oxidation of NADH	3
(*iii*)	Succinate thiokinase	Phosphorylation at substrate level	1
(*iv*)	Succinate dehydrogenase	Respiratory chain oxidation of $FADH_2$	2
(*v*)	Malate dehydrogenase	Respiratory chain oxidation of NADH	3
			Net = 12

VITAMINS TAKING PART IN TCA CYCLE

(*i*) Riboflavin : Present in the form of flavin adenine dinucleotide (FAD), a cofactor in the α-ketoglutarate dehydrogenase complex and in succinate dehydrogenase.

(*ii*) Niacin : Found in the form of nicotinamide adenine dinucleotide (NAD), the coenzyme for three dehydrogenases in the cycle; isocitrate dehydrogenase; α-Ketoglutarate dehydorgenase and malate dehydrogenase.

(*iii*) Thiamine (Vitamin B_1) : Present as thiamine diphosphate, the coenzyme for decarboxylation in α-ketoglutarate dehydrogenase reaction; and

(*iv*) Pantothenic acid : As a part of coenzyme A, the cofactor attached to "active" carboxylic acid residues such as acetyl-CoA and succinyl- CoA.

Some metabolic pathways end in a constituent of the citric acid cycle; while other pathways originate from the cycle. These pathways concern the processes of gluconeogenesis, transmination, deamination, fatty acid synthesis. Therefore, the citric acid cycle plays roles in both oxidative and synthetic processes *i.e.*, it is amphibolic.

In most tissues, where the primary function of the citric acid cycle is to provide energy, there is little doubt that *Respiratory control* via the respiratory chain and oxidative phosphorylation is the overriding control on citric acid cycle activity. Thus, activity, is immediately dependent on the supply of oxidized dehydrogenases cofactors (*e.g.* NAD^+), which in turn, because of the tight coupling between oxidation and phosphorylation is dependent on the availability of ADP and ultimately, on the rate of utilization of ATP. Therefore, provided there is adequate O_2, the rate of doing work via utilization of ATP determines both the rate of respiration and the activity of the citric acid cycle. In addition to this overall or coarse control, the properties of some enzymes of the cycle indicate that control might also be exerted at the level of the cycle itself to reinforce the coarse control.

The most likely sites for regulation of TCA cycle are the non-equilibrium reactions.

These are catalyzed by pyruvate dehydrogenase, citrate synthase, NAD-linked isocitrate dehydrogenase and α-ketoglutarate dehydrogenase

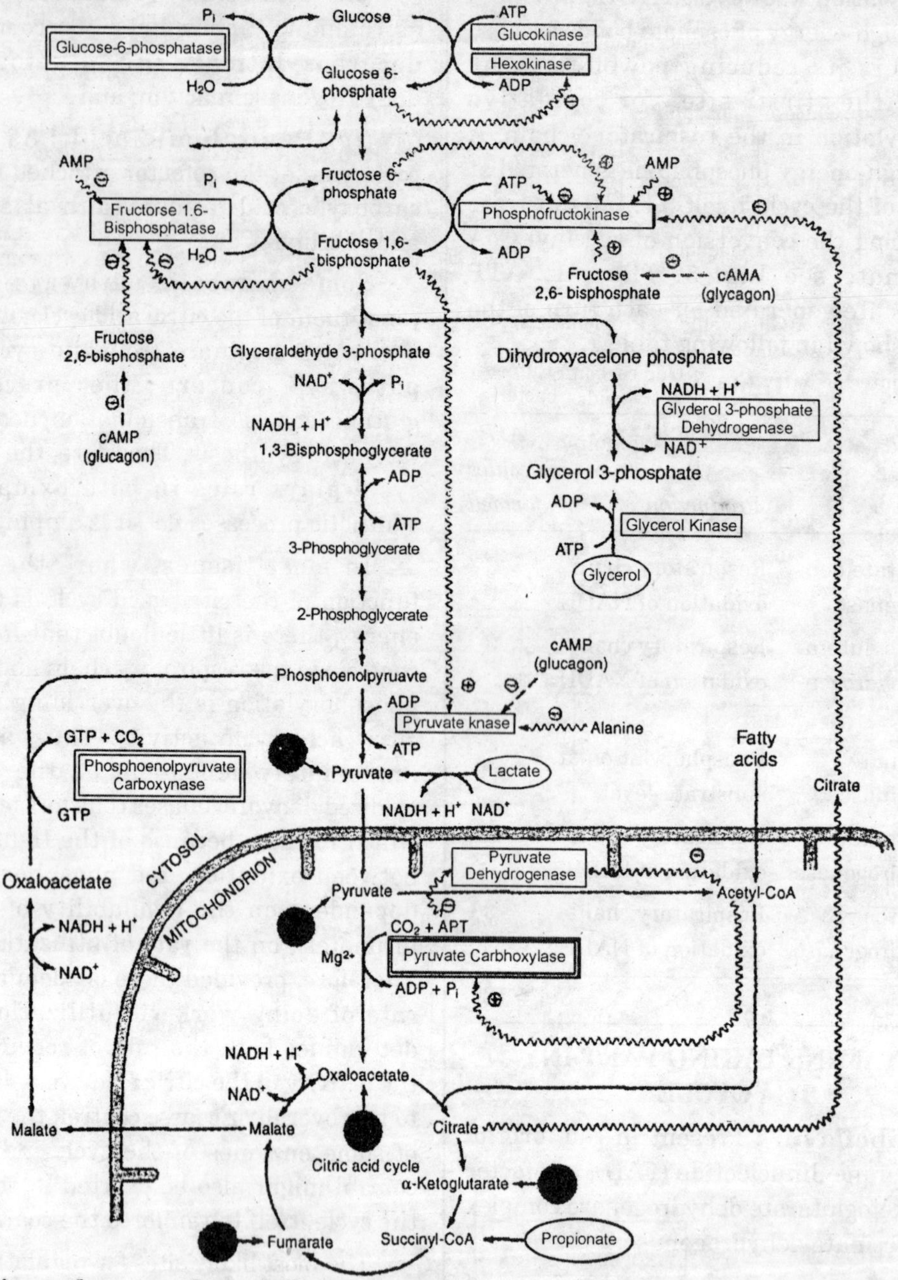

Fig. 6. Major pathways and regulation of gluconeogenesis and glycolysis in the liver. Entry points of glucogenic amino acids after transmination are indicated by arrows extended from circles. The key gluconeogenic enzymes are enclosed in double-bordered boxes. The ATP required for gluconeogenesis is supplied by the oxidation of long-chain fatty acids. Propionate is of quantitative importance only in ruminants. Arrows with wavy shafts signify allosteric effects dash-shafted arrows, covalent modification by reversible phosphorylation. High concentrations of alanine act as a "gluconeogenic signal" by inhibiting glycolysis at the pyruvate kinase step.

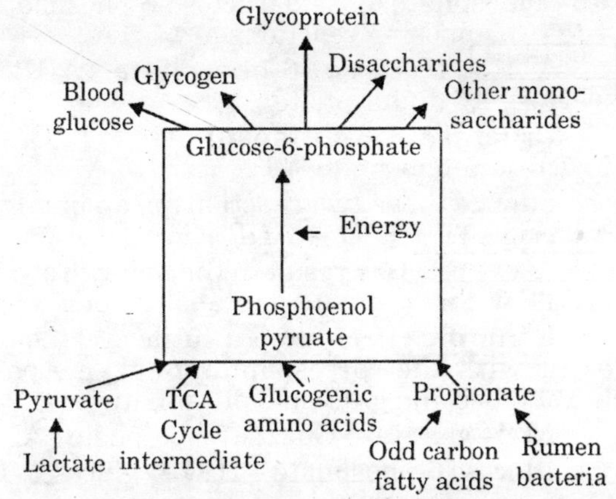

Fig. 7. The pathway from phosphoenolpyruvate to glucose-6-phosphate is common to the biosynthetic conversion of many different precursors into various carbohydrates in animal tissues.

Liver glycogen serves as a reservoir of glucose readily converted into blood glucose, whereas muscle glycogen is an important source of ATP energy for muscular contraction through its break down via glycolysis. In animals the formation of D-glucose form non-carbohydrate precursors is called *gluconeogenesis* ("formation of new sugar"). The important precursors of D-glucose in animals are lactate, pyruvate, glycerol, most of the amino acids, and the intermediates of the citric acid cycle. In animals, gluconegenesis occurs largely in the liver and to a much smaller extent in kidney cortex. In plants photosynthesis makes glucose and other carbohydrate.

Gluconeogenesis

As it is true for all biosynthetic pathways, gluconeogenesis proceeds by an enzymatic pathways, that differs from the corresponding catabolic pathway, that is independently regulated, and that requires input of chemical

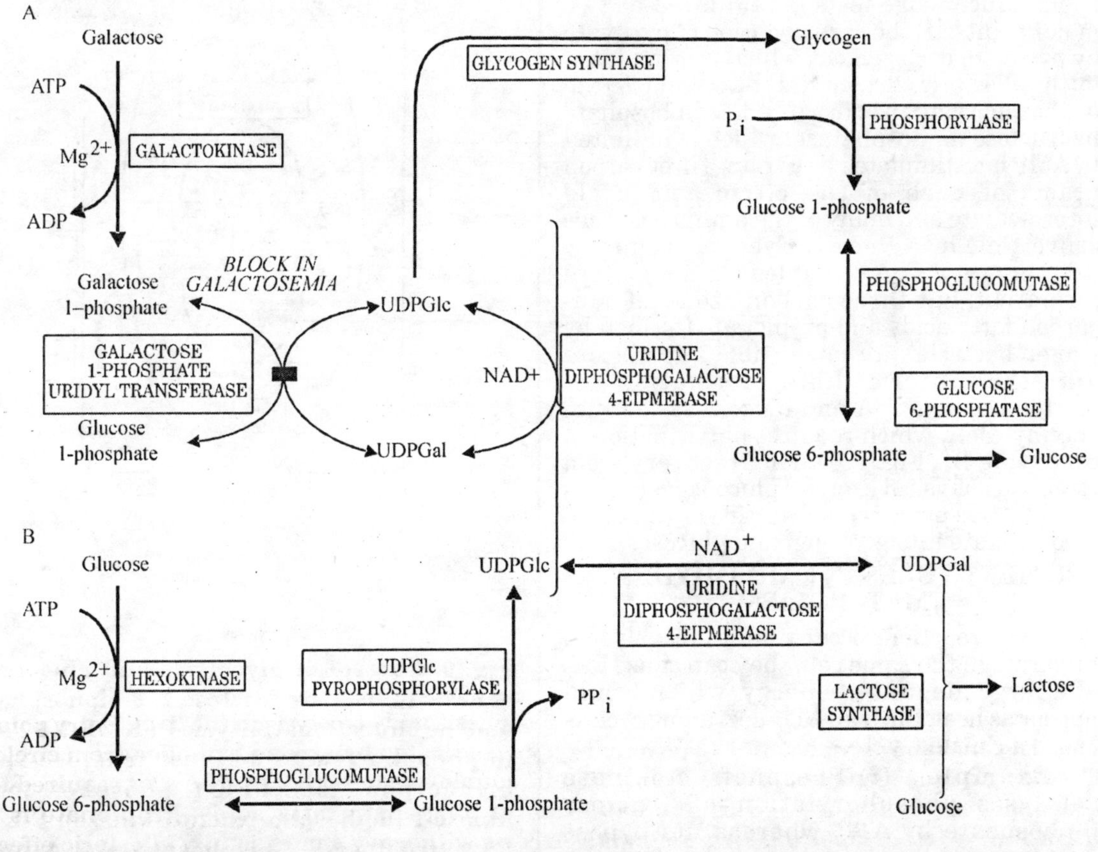

Fig. 8. Pathway of conversion of (A) galactose of glucose in the liver and (B) glucose to lactose in the lactating mammary gland.

energy in the form of ATP. The pathway of gluconeogenesis shares seven steps with the pathway of glycolysis. The biosynthetic pathway from pyruvate to glucose, which in vertebrates takes place largely in the liver and secondarly in the kidney, employs eight of the glycolytic enzymes which function reversibly and are present in large excess. These are, however, three irreversible steps in the downhill glycolytic pathway that cannot be used in gluconeogenesis and are bypassed by alternative reactions catalyzed by quite different enzymes. The first bypass consists of the conversion of pyruvate into phosphoenol pyruvate via the formation of oxaloacetate; the second is the dephosphorylation of fructose 1,6-diphosphate by fructose diphosphatase; and the third is the dephosphorylation of glucose 6-phosphate by glucose—6—phosphatase Fig. 7. For each molecule of D-glucose made from pyruvate, the terminal phosphate groups of four molecules of ATP and two of GTP must be used. Gluconeogenesis is regulated at two major points; (*i*) the carboxylation of pyruvate by pyruvate carboxylase, which is stimulated by the allosteric effector acetyl-CoA and (*ii*) the dephosphorylation of fructose 1,6-diphosphate by fructose diphosphatase; which is inhibited by AMP but stimulated by citrate. Three carbon atoms of each of the citric acid cycle intermediate and many of the amino acids are convertible into glucose. Even-car-bon fatty acids or acetyl CoA do not lead to net glucose formation; but three carbon atoms of odd-carbon fatty acids and propionate (formed by rumen bacteria) are convertible into glucose via the intermediate formation of methylmalonyl CoA and its conversion into succinyl CoA, which requires participation of coenzyme B_{12} Fig. 8. During recovery from strenuous physical exercise gluconeogenesis is a very active process resulting in conversion of blood lactate into glycogen and glucose.

FUTILE CYCLES IN CARBOHYDRATE METABOLISM

If two reactions occur simultaneously at a high rate in the same cell; they can cause loss of a large amount of energy, which would appear as heat. Such an ATP-degrading cycle is called a **Futile Cycle**.

Example : (*i*) Phosphofructokinase catalyses phosphorylation of fructose 6-phosphate by ATP, whereas, its bypass counterparts is gluconeogenesis, fructose diphosphatase, catalyses hydrolysis of fructose 1,6-diphosphate to yield fructose-6-phosphate. The two opposing reactions are

ATP + fructose -6-phosphate→ADP + fructose 1,6 diphosphate

Fructose 1,6-diphosphate + H_2O → Fructose-6-phosphate + Pi

Sum o these two reactions is an energy-wasting ATP + H_2O → ADP + Pi

Above reaction result in the net hydrolysis of ATP without any net metabolic work.

Example : (*ii*) A similar futile cycle could occur with the corresponding enzyme pair hexokinase and glucose-6 phosphatase.

ATP + glucose → Glucose 6-phosphate + ADP

Glucose 6-phosphate + H_2O → glucose + Pi

Sum : ATP + H_2O → ADP + Pi

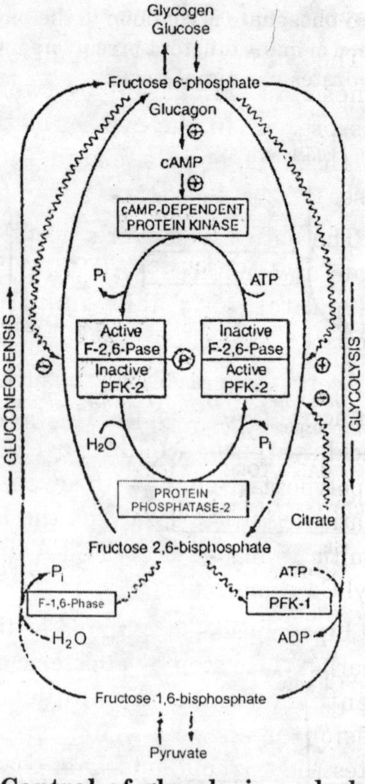

Fig. 9. Control of glycolysis and gluconeogenesis in liver by fructose 2, 6-biphosphate and the bifunctional enzyme PFK-2/F-2, 6-Pase (6-phospho fructo-2-kinase/fructose-2, 6-bisphospha-tase). PFK-1, phosphofructokinase-1 [6-phospho fructo-1-kinase]; F-1, 6-Pase, fructose-1, 6-bisphosphatase. Arrows with way shafts indicate allosteric effects).

LIPIDS METABOLISM

Lipids : The compounds in this group are characterized by their relative insolubility in water and solubility in organic solvents. The cause of this general property of lipids and related compounds is the predominance of long hydrocarbon chains or benzene rings. There structures are non-polar and hydrophobic. In many lipids, there chains may be attached at one end to a polar group, rendering it capable of binding water by hydrogen bonds. Lipids may be simple or compound.

A. Biosynthesis of Fatty Acids

(a) The synthesis of long chain fatty acids (lipogenesis) is carried out by two enzyme systems present in the cytosol of the cell : Acetyl Co-A carboxylase and fatty acid synthase.

(b) The pathway converts acetyl Co-A to palmitate and requires NADPH, ATP, Mn^{+2}, biotin, pantothenic acid and HCO_3^- as cofactors.

(c) Acetyl Co-A carboxylase is required to convert acetyl Co-A to malonyl Co-A. In turn, fatty acid synthase, a multienzyme complex of one polypeptide chain with seven separate enzymatic activities, catalyzes the assembly of palmitic from one acetyl Co-A and seven malonyl Co-A molecules.

(d) Lipogenesis is regulated at the acetyl Co-A carboxylase step by allosteric modifiers covalent modification, induction and repression of enzyme synthesis. Citrate activates the enzyme, and long chain acetyl Co-A inhibits its activity. Insulin activates acetyl Co-A carboxylase in the short term by dephosphorylation and in long term by induction of synthesis. Glucagon and epinephrine have opposite actions to insulin.

(e) Lengthening of long chain fatty acids takes place in the endoplasmic reticulum catalyzed by a microsomal elongase enzyme system.

B. Oxidation of Fatty Acids (KETOGENESIS)

(a) Fatty acid oxidation in mitochondria leads to the generation of large quantities of ATP by a process called β-oxidation that cleaves acetyl Co-A units sequentially from fatty acyl chains. The acetyl Co-A is oxidized in the citric acid cycle, generating further ATP. (Fig. 11).

(b) Oxidation of odd-numbered carbon fatty acid yield acetyl Co-A plus one molecule of propionyl Co-A, which is glucogenic.

(c) Peroxisomes are capable of oxidizing very long chain fatty acid but only as far as octanoyl Co-A, which must then be transferred to mitochondria for further oxidation.

(d) The ketone bodies (acetoacetate, 3-hydroxy butyrate and acetone) are formed in hepatic mitochondria when there is a high rate of fatty acid oxidation. (Fig. 14). The pathway of ketogenesis involves synthesis and breakdown of 3-hydroxy-3 methylglutaryl-Co-A (HMG-Co-A) by two key ketogenic enzymes, HMG Co-A synthase and HMG-Co-A lyase (Fig. 11).

(e) Ketone bodies are important fules in extrahepatic tissues.

(f) Ketogenesis is regulated at three crucial steps: *(i)* Control of free fatty acid mobilization from adipose tissue *(ii)* the activity of carnitine palmitoyl transferase-I in liver, which determines the proportion of the fatty acid flux that is oxidized rather than esterified and *(iii)* partition of acetyl Co-A between the pathway of ketogensis and citric acid cycle (Fig. 13).

(g) Disease associated with impairment of fatty acid oxidation lead to hypoglycemia, fatty infiltration of organs and hypoketonemia.

(h) Ketosis is mild in starvation but severe in **diabetes mellitus** and ruminant ketosis (Fig. 12).

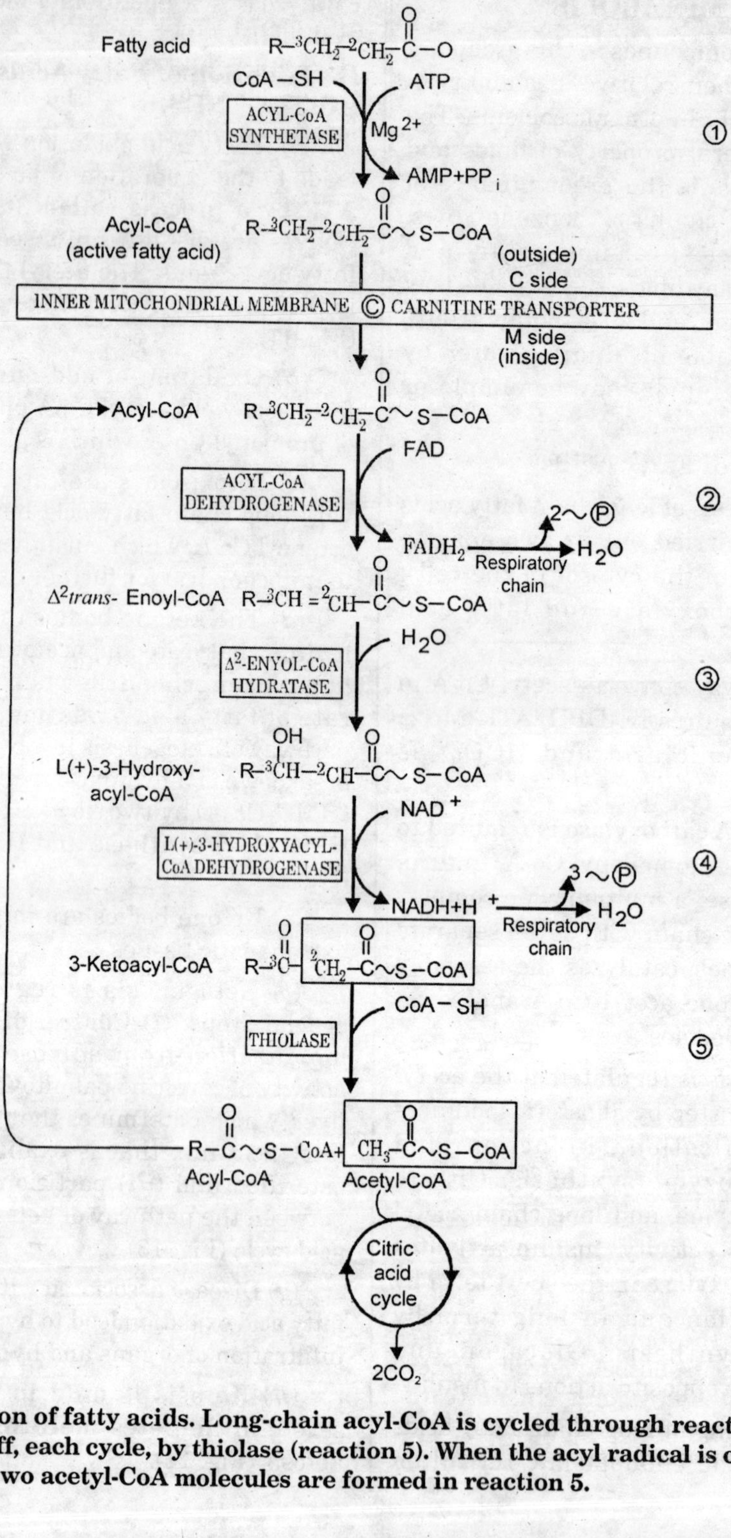

Fig. 10. β-Oxidation of fatty acids. Long-chain acyl-CoA is cycled through reactions 2-5, acetyl-Co A being split off, each cycle, by thiolase (reaction 5). When the acyl radical is only four carbon atoms in length, two acetyl-CoA molecules are formed in reaction 5.

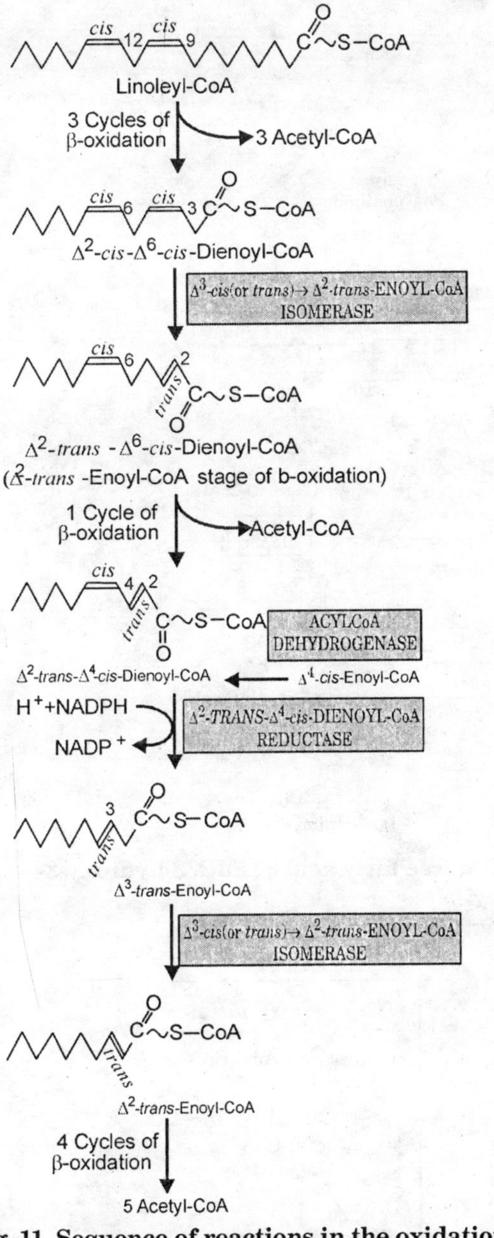

Fig. 11. Sequence of reactions in the oxidation of unsaturated fatty acids. *e.g.*, linoleic acid. Δ^4-cis-fatty acid or fatty acids forming Δ^4-cis-enoyl-CoA enter the pathway at the position shown. NADPH for the dienoyl-CoA reductase step is supplied by intramitochondrial sources so as glutamate dehydrogenase, isocitrate dehydrogenase and NAD(P) H transhydrogenase.

C. Metabolism of Unsaturated Fatty Acids and Eicosanoids

(*a*) Biosynthesis of unsaturated long-chain fatty acids is achieved by a combination of desaturase enzymes, which introduce double bonds, and elongase enzymes, which lengthen existing acyl chain by 2 carbons at a time.

(*b*) Higher animals are restricted to Δ^4, Δ^5, Δ^6 and Δ^9 desaturases, which does not allow for insertion of new double bonds beyond the 9 position of fatty acids. As a result, linolenic (ω_6) and α-linolenic (ω_3) acids cannot be synthesized and must be provided in the diet. They are called the **essential fatty acids**.

(*c*) The essential fatty acids give rise C_{20} (eicosanoic) fatty acids from which are synthesized every important groups of physiologically and pharmacologically active compounds, the **eicosanoids**. They comprise the prostaglandins, thromboxanes, leukotrienes and lipoxins. Prostaglandins and thromboxanes are synthesized via the cyclo-oxygenase pathway (inhibited by aspirin), leuko-trienes and lipoxins are synthesized via the lipoxygenase pathway.

(*d*) Since different groups of eicosanoids are synthesized from the essential fatty acids, the balance between the physiologic effects of the various eicosanoids may be manipulated by changing the fatty acid composition of the diet.

D. Metabolism of Acylglycerols and Sphingolipids

(*a*) Triglycerols are the major energy-storing lipids, whereas phosphoglycerols, sphingomyelin, and glycosphingolipids are amphipathic and fulfil many roles, ranging from structural functions in cell membranes to specialized functions, *e.g.* precursors for hormone second messengers long surfactants, and platelet-activating factor (PAF).

(*b*) Triacylglycerols and some phosphoglycerols are synthesized by progressive acylation of glycerol 3-phosphate. The pathway bifurcates at phosphatidate, forming

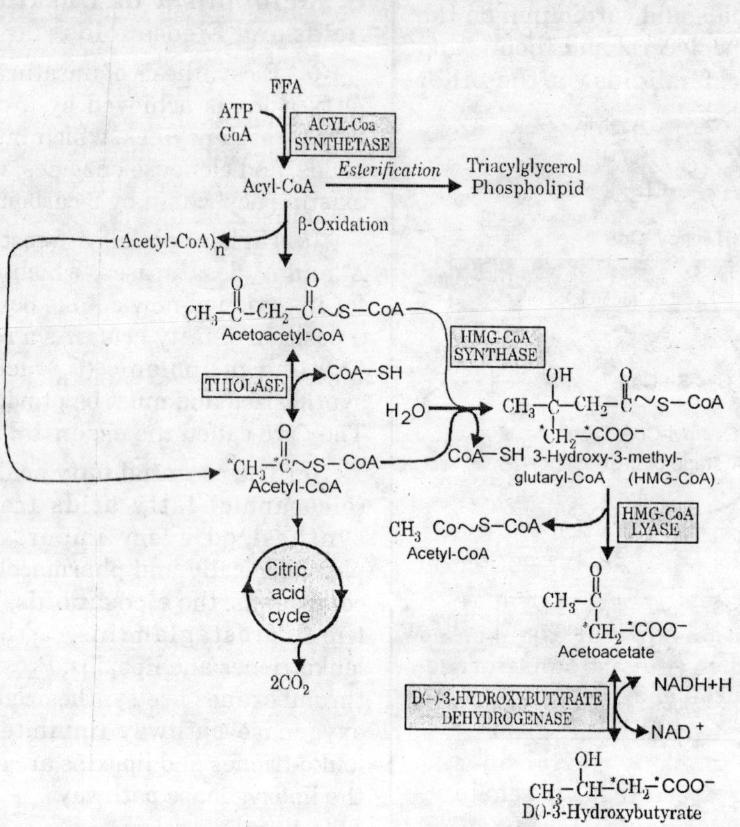

Fig. 12. Pathways of ketogenesis in the liver. (FFA, free fatty acids; HMG, 3-hydroxy-3-methylglutaryl.)

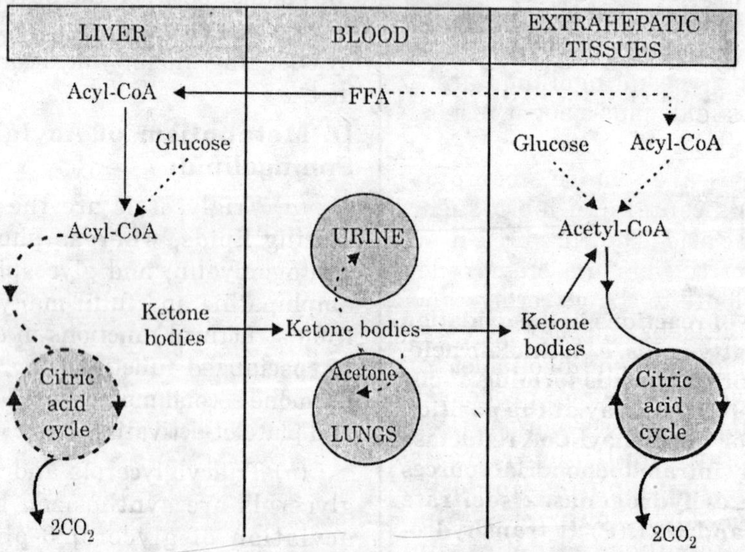

Fig. 13. Formation, utilization, and excretion of ketone bodies. (The main pathway is indicated by the solid arrows.)

inositol phospholipids and cardiolipin on the one hand and triacylglycerol and choline and ethanolamine phospholipids on the other hand.

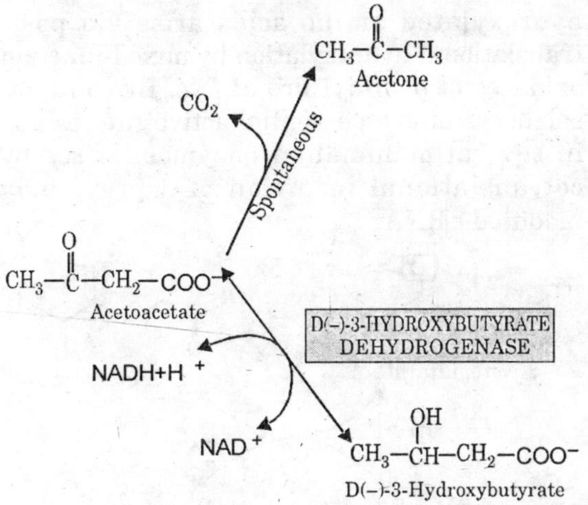

Fig. 14. Interrelationships of the ketone bodies. D (-)-3-Hydroxybutyrate dehydrogenase is a mitochondrial enzyme.

(*c*) Plasmalogens and PAF are either phospholipids formed by acylation and alkylation of dihydroxy-acetone phosphate.

(*d*) All sphingolipids are formed from ceramide (N-acylsphingosine). Spingomyelin is a phospholipid present characteristically in membranes of organelles involved in secretory processes (*e.g.* Golgi apparatus).

The simplest glycosphingolipids are a combination of ceramide plus a sugar residue (*e.g.* Galcerin myelin).

Gangliosides are more complex glycosphingolipids containing more sugar residues plus sialic acid. They are present in the outer layer of the plasma membrane, where they contribute to the glycocalyx and are important as antigens and cell receptors.

(*f*) Phospholipids and sphingolipids are involved in several disease processes including respiratory distress syndrome (lack of lung surfactant), multiple sclerosis (demyelination), and sphingolipidoses (inability to breakdown sphingolipids in lysosomes), due to inherited defects in hydrolase enzymes.

PROTEINS METABOLISM

***Proteins* :** They are amino acid polymers formed of one or more polypeptides (monomeric proteins and oligomeric proteins). The minimum molecular weight of a protein is 4500 (Adrenocorticotrophin hormone with 39 amino acids), 5733 (bovine insulin, two polypeptides, 51 amino acids A 21, B 30 in bovine and 53 with 22 + 31 amino acids in human) and 6000 (bacterial ferredoxin). Haemoglobin has 4 polypeptides with 574 amino acid residues and molecular weight of 64,500. Glutamate dehydrogenase has a molecular weight of about 1 million with 40 polypeptides and 8300 amino acids.

A polpeptide is formed of a linear row of amino acids joined by peptide bonds. This constituted the primary structure. Secondary structure is of two main types, α-helix and β-pleated. In α-helix, a single amino acid chain is coiled spirally by establishing hydrogen bonds between first and fourth amino acids. In β-pleated arrangement a sheet is produced by holding of two or more polypeptide chains in parallel or antiparallel manner by means of hydrogen bonds. The polypeptide chains are folded variously in tertiary structure. The bonds formed during tertiary structure can easily be broken by high temperature, high energy radiations and salts of heavy metals.

The process is called *denaturation*, quaternary structure is present in case of oligomeric proteins. In shape, proteins can be fibrous (elastin, collagen, actin, myosin, keratin) or *globular* (histone, haemoglobin, egg albumin, serum globulin). In function they can be *structural* (*e.g.* Elastin in ligaments, collagen in tendons and cartilage, tubulin in microtubules, chondrin in cartilage, osseinin bone, fibroin in silk, keratin in hair skin and nails.) *contractive* (*e.g.* actin, myosin), *carrier / transport proteins* (haemoglobin for oxygen, lipoprotein of plasma for lipids from liver to other organs), visual pigments (*e.g.* rhodopsin), *receptor* (*e.g.* adrenaline receptor), *hormones*, (*e.g.* insulin, GH, parathormone), *blood clotting* (*viz.* fibrinogen, thrombin), *protective* (immunglobulin) enzymatic (*e.g.* amylase) and storage (*e.g.* glutelin, albumins, globulins, prolamines). Proteins can be *simple* (*e.g.* most storage proteins like hordein, zeatin, glutenin of wheat, oryzenin) or *conjugated* (with additional groups). Conjugated proteins include nucleoproteins (with DNA, RNA), chromoproteins (flavoproteins with FMN or FAD, haemocyanin and cytochrome with Fe, rhodopsin with vitamin A, haemocyanin and cytochrome oxidase with Cu, Chloroplastin with chrolophyll, biliproteins with phycobilins), metaprotein (Fe in Ferritin), lipoprotein (with lipid like lipovitellin of egg yolk), phosphoprotein (phosphate as in casein, ovovitellin of egg yolk), glycoprotein, mucoprotein (*e.g.* mucin of saliva) etc. Derived proteins include proteoses, peptones as also a protein called monellin. Proteins present in meat, egg and milk are called *complete proteins* as they contain all the essential amino acids. Amongst plant foods, only soybean protein is nearly complete. The *most abundant* protein is *rubisco* (RuBP carboxylase) present in chloroplasts.

All vertebrates, including humans, can form the 12 nutritionally non-essential amino acids from amphibolic intermediates or from other dietary amino acids. Vertebrates cannot, however, biosynthesize the 10 nutritionally essential amino acids. Vertebrates biosynthesize amino acids from amphibolic intermediates via metabolic pathways that involve 5 or fewer enzyme-catalyzed reactions. The parent amphibolic intermediates and the amino acids to which they give rise are citric acid cycle intermediates α-ketoglutarate (Glu, Gln, Pro, Hyp) oxaloacetate (Asp, Asn) and the glycolytic intermediate 3 phosphoglycerate (Ser, Gly), Three other amino acids (Cys, Tyr, Hyl) are formed from nutritionally essential amino acids. Serine provides the carbon skeleton and homocysteine, the sulphur for cysteine biosynthesis, while phenylalanine hydroxylase converts phenylalanine to tyrosine. Since no codon or tRNA dictates the insertion of Hyp or Hyl into peptides, neither dietary hydroxyproline nor dietary hydroxylysine is incorporated into proteins. There hydroxylated amino acids arise via post-translational hydroxylation by mixed-function oxidases of peptidyl Pro or Lys. By contrast, selenocysteine an essential active site residue in several mammalian enzymes, arises by cotranslational insertion of a previously modified t RNA.

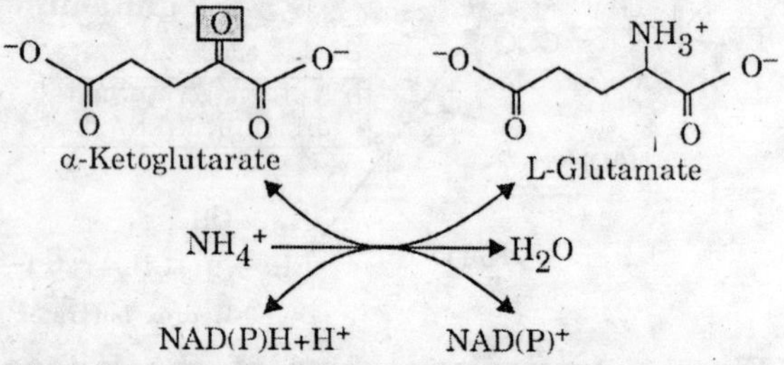

Fig. 15. The glutamate dehydrogenase reaction. Reductive amination of α-ketoglutarate by NH_4^+ rpceeds at the expense of NAD(P)H.

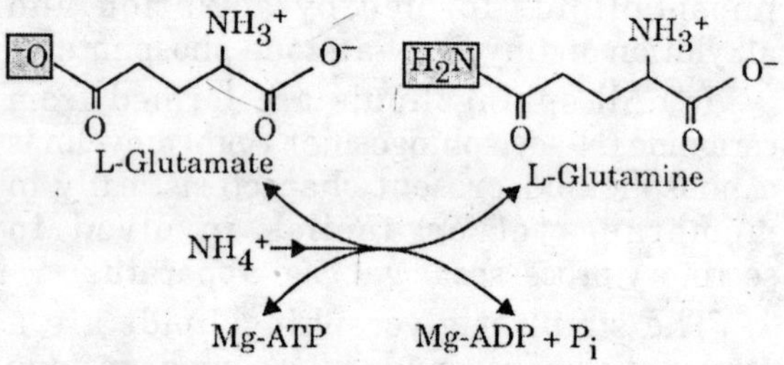

Fig. 16. The glutamine synthetase reaction.

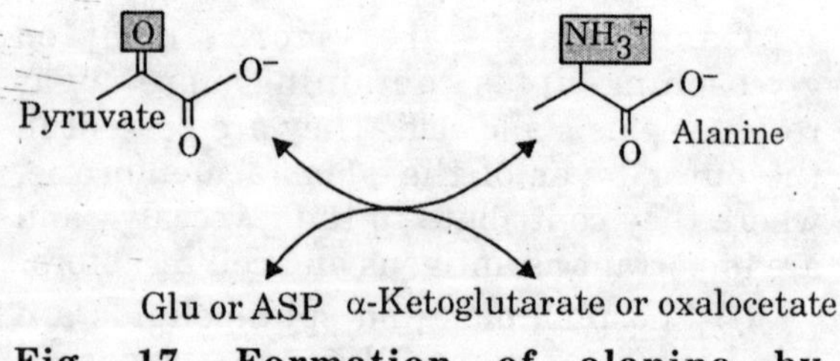

Fig. 17. Formation of alanine by transamination of pyruvate. The amino donor may be glutamate or aspartate. The other product thus is α-ketoglutarate or oxaloacetate. If oxaloacetate rather then pyruvate is the ox acid, acceptance of the amino group of glutamate form asparate.

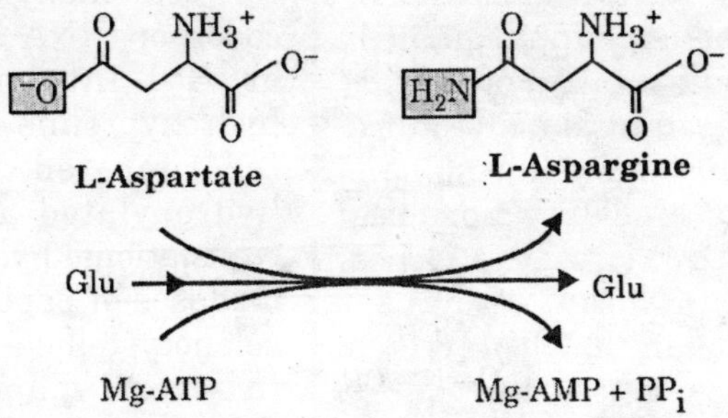

Fig. 18. The asparagine synthetase reaction. Note similarities to and differences from the glutamine synthetase reaction.

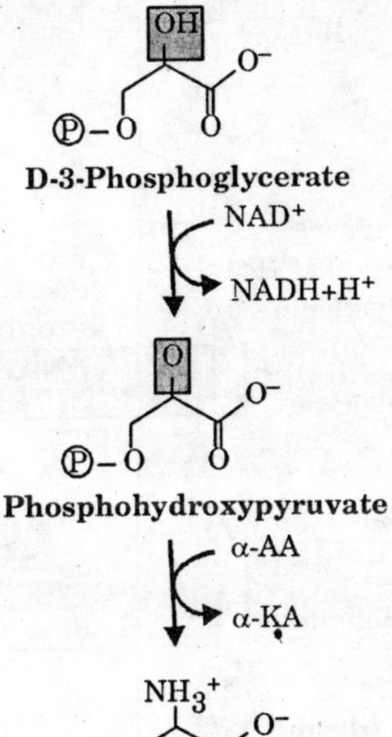

Fig. 19. Serine biosynthesis. (α-AA, α-amino acids; α-KA, α-keto acids.)

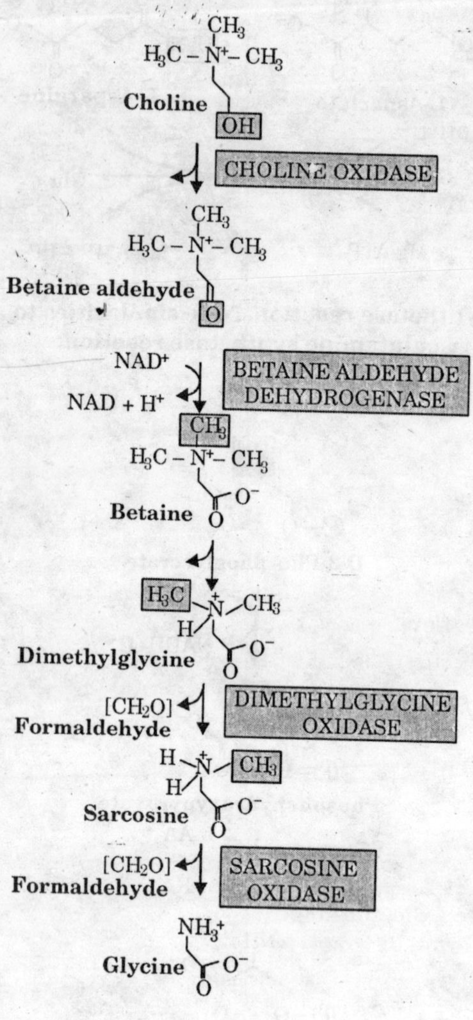

Fig. 20. Formation of glycine from choline.

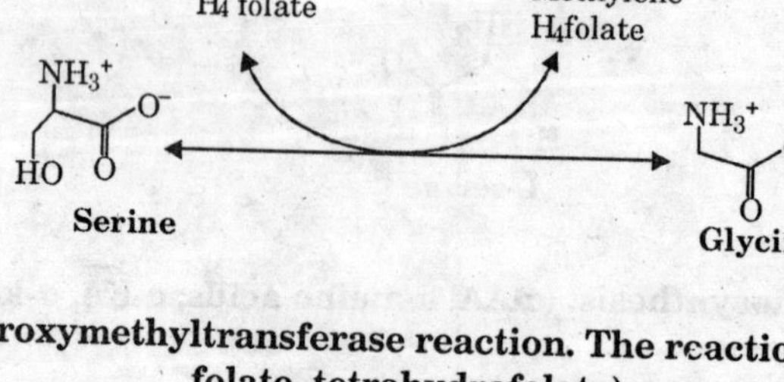

Fig. 21. The serine hydroxymethyltransferase reaction. The reaction is freely reversible. (H_4 folate, tetrahydrofolate).

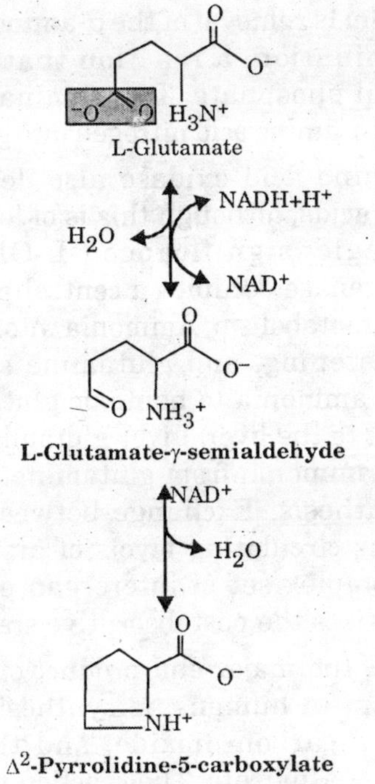

Fig. 22. Biosynthesis of proline from glutamate by reversal of the reactions of proline catabolism.

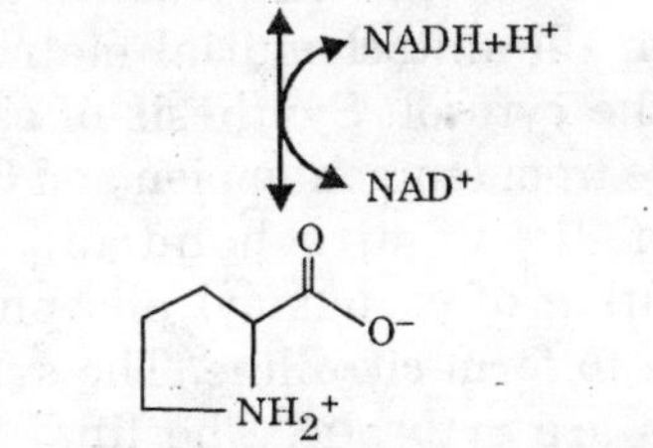

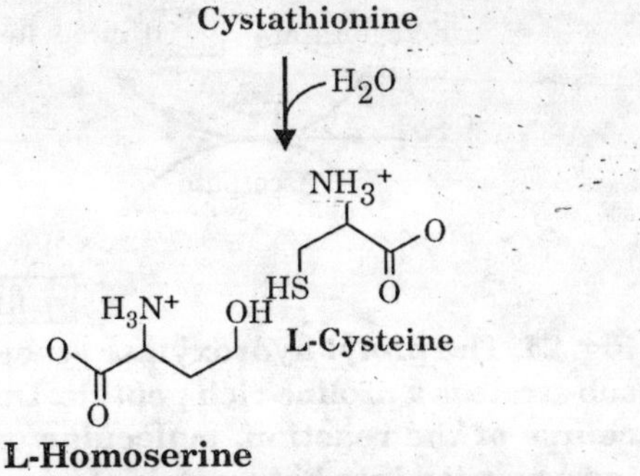

Fig. 23. Conversion of homocysteine and serine to homoserine and cysteine. Note that while the sulfur of cysteine derives from methionine by transsulfuration, the carbon skeleton is provided by serine.

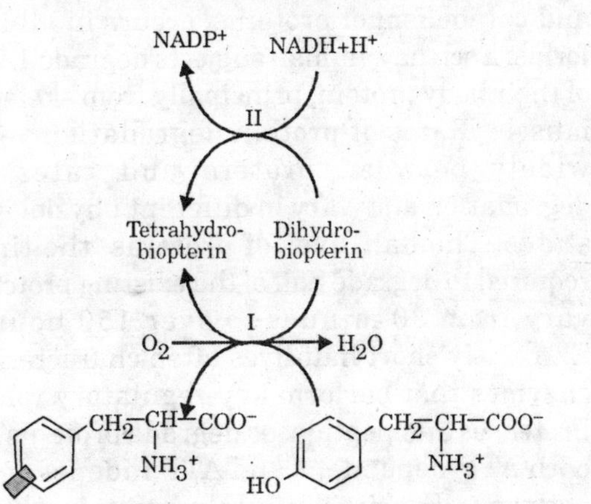

Fig. 24. The phenyl hydroxylase reaction. Two distinct enzymatic activities are involved. Activity II catalyzes reduction of dihydrobiopterin by NADPH, and activity I the reduction of O_2 to H_2O and phenylalanine to tyrosine. This reaction is associated with several defects of phenylalanine metabolism.

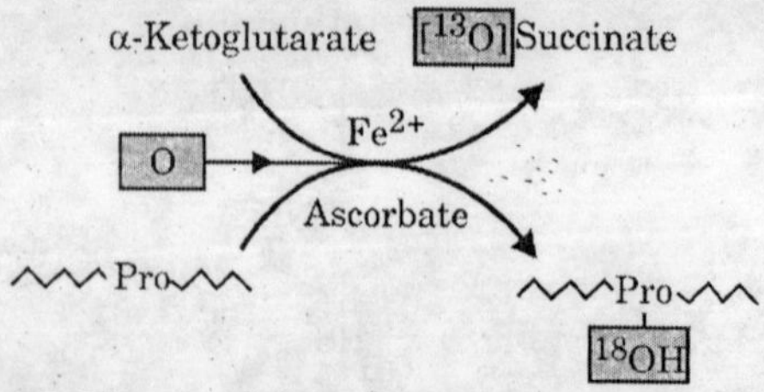

Fig. 25. The prolyl hydroxylase reaction. The sub-strate is a proline-rich peptide. During the course of the reaction, molecular oxygen is incorporated into both succinate and proline (shown by the use of heavy oxygen, $^{18}O_2$). Lysyl hydroxylase catalyzes an analogous reaction.

CATABOLISM OF PROTEIN

Protein turnover, the continual synthesis and catabolism of proteins, occurs in all life forms. Each day, human subjects degrade 1-2% of their body protein, principally from skeletal muscle. Rates of protein degradation vary widely between protein and rates of degradation may vary in different physiologic states. The half-lives of proteins, the time required to degrade half of the existing protein, vary from 30 minues to over 150 hours. Extremely short half-lives often characterize enzymes that perform key-regulatory roles. Proteases and peptidases degrade proteins by both ATP-dependent and ATP independent pathways. For circulating glycoproteins, liver cell-surface asialoglycoprotein receptors bind and internalize asialoglycoproteins destined for degradation by lysosomal proteases. For many intracellular proteins attachment of several molecules of ubiquitin targets them for degradation. Amino acids liberated by protein catabolism or ingested in excees of need are then degraded, not stored.

Ammonia is highly toxic to all animals. While fish excrete ammonia directly, the need to conserve water precludes this as a major route of nitrogen elimination in birds or land animals. Birds detoxify ammonia by converting it to uric acid. Humans and other higher vertebrates convert ammonia to urea. In either case, the initial reaction in amino acids catabolism is removal of the α-amino group by transamination, a reaction that requires pyridoxal phosphate. Transamination thus channels α-amino acid nitrogen into glutamate.

L-amino acid oxidase also deaminates α-amino acids, although this is of less certain physiologic significance. L-Glutamate dehydrogenase occupies a central position in nitrogen metabolism. Ammonia intoxication is life threatening, and glutamine synthasae converts ammonia to nontoxic glutamine for transport to the liver. Liver glutaminase then releases ammonia from glutamine for use in urea synthesis. Exchange between organs maintains circulating levels of amino-acids, and a complex set of interorgan exchanges characterizes the postabsorptive state.

Urea, the major end product of nitrogen catabolism in humans, is synthesized from ammonia, carbon dioxide, and the amide nitrogen of aspartate. The reaction take place in part in the mitochondrial matrix and in part in the cytosol. Synthesis of carbamoyl phosphate from ammonium ion and CO_2 takes place in liver mitochondria, as does condensation of carbamoyl phosphate with ornithine to form citrulline. The subsequent reactions are cytosolic. The final reaction, catalyzed by arginase, cleaves arginine to urea and ornithine and completes the cycle. Regulation of urea bisoynethesis involves both, changes in enzyme levels and allosteric regulation of carbamoyl phosphate synthase activity by N-acetylglutamate. Inborn errors of metabolism are associated with each reaction of the urea cycle. There include **hyperammonemia** types 1 & 2, **citrullinemia, argininosuccinicaciduria & hyperargininemia.**

When amino acids are present in excess of metabolic needs, their carbon skeletons are catabolized to amphibolic intermediates for use as sources of energy or as substrates for carbohydrate and lipid biosynthesis. Removal of the α-amino nitrogen by transmination is most often the initial reaction of amino acid

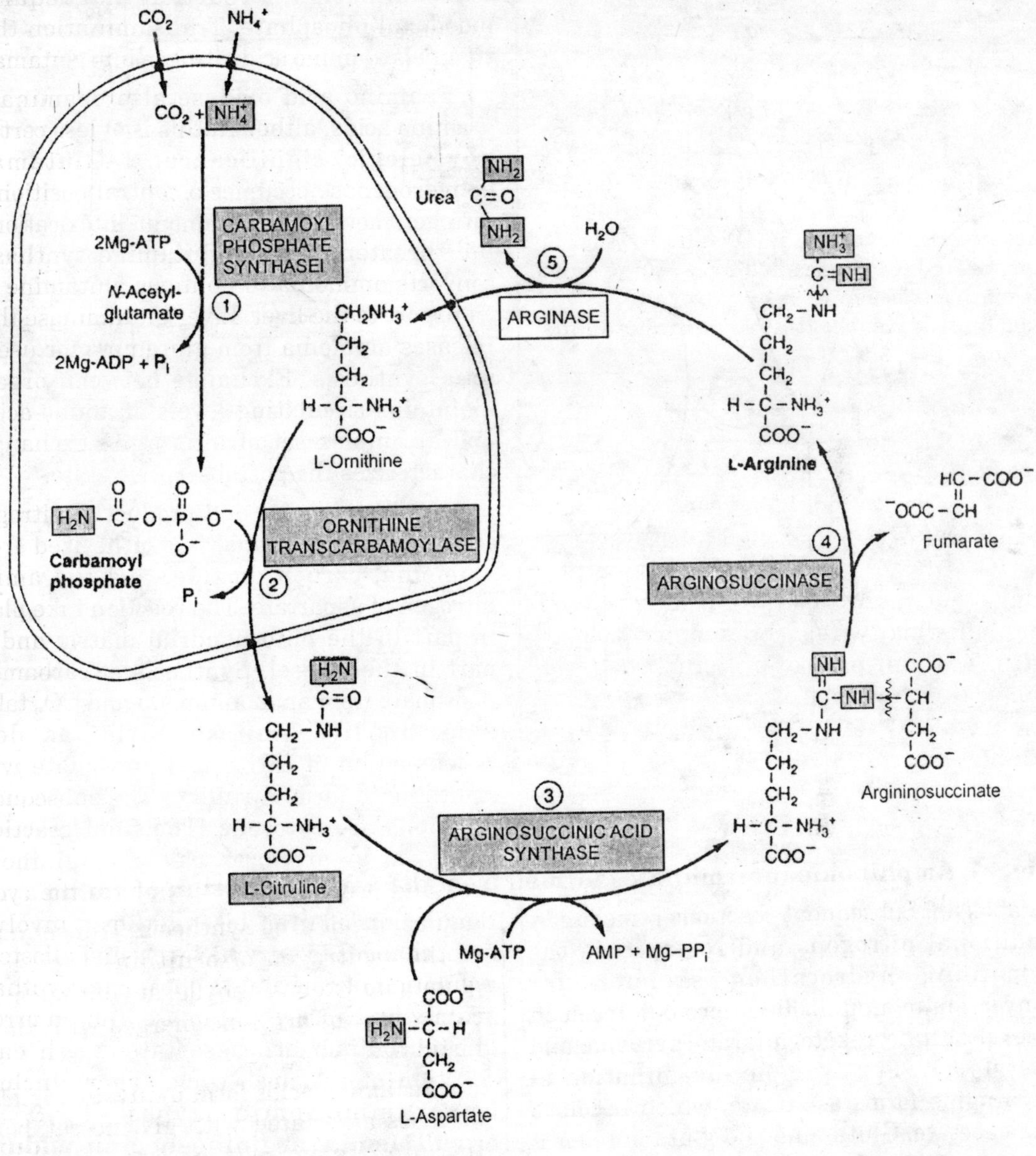

Fig. 26. Reactions and intermediates of urea bisoynthesis. The nitrogen-containing groups that contribute to the formation of urea are shaded. Reaction (1) and (2) occur in the matrix of liver mitochondria and reaction (3), (4) and (5) in liver cytosol. CO_2 (as bicarbonate, ammonium ion, ornithine, and citrulline enter the mitochondrial matrix via specific carriers (•) present in the inner membrane of liver mitochondria.

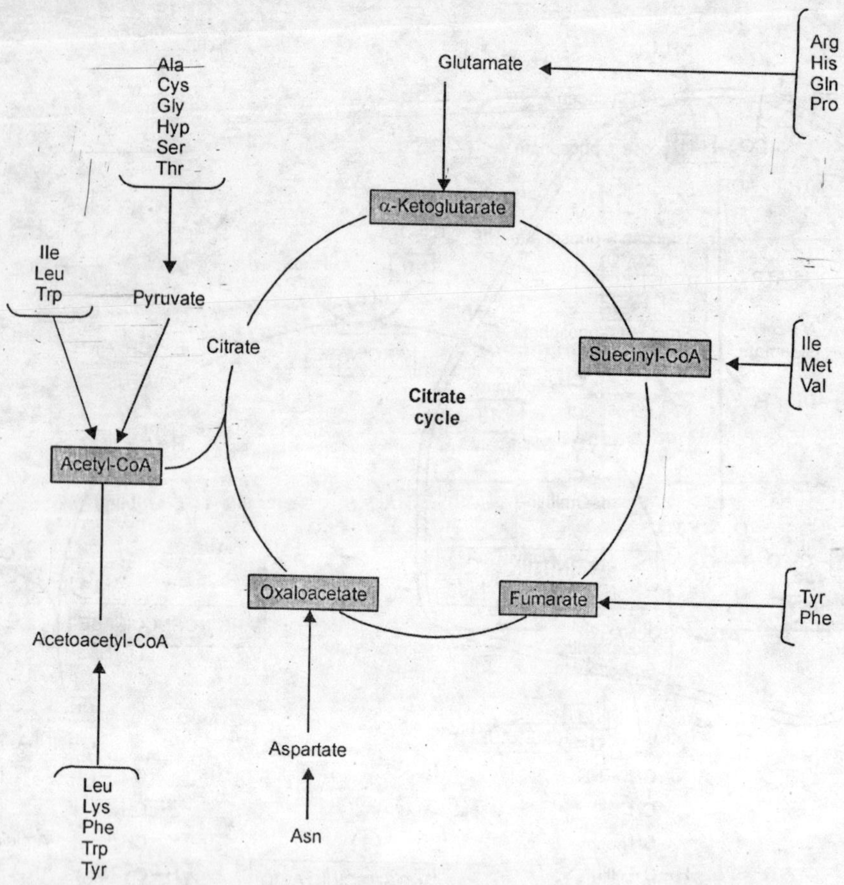

Fig. 27. Amphibokic intermidiates formed from the carbon skeleton of amino acids.

catabolism. Subsequent reactions remove any additional nitrogens and restructure the remaining hydrocarbon skeleton for conversion to amphibolic intermediates such as oxaloacetate, α-ketoglutarate, pyruvate and acetyl CoA. For example, deamination of asparagine forms aspartate, which becomes oxaloacetate. Glutamine and glutamate form α-ketoglutarate by analogous reactions. No known metabolic disorders are associated with the catabolism of these four amino acids. Two **hyperprolinemias** are associated with the catabolic pathway that converts proline to α-ketoglutarate. The initial reaction of arginine catabolism is catalyzed by arginase, an enzyme of urea synthesis. Transmination of the δ-nitrogen of ornithine then forms glutamate-γ-semialdehyde, at which point the catabolism of arginine merges with that of histidine.

Six amino acids form pyruvate. Metabolic diseases associated with glycine catabolism include **glycinuria** and primary **hyperoxaluria.** Transamination of alanine forms pyruvate directly, while serine is catabolized by glycine. Following reduction of cystine to cysteine, two sets of catabolic reactions convert cysteine to pyruvate. Metabolic diseases associated with cysteine catabolism include **cystine-lysinuria**, cystine

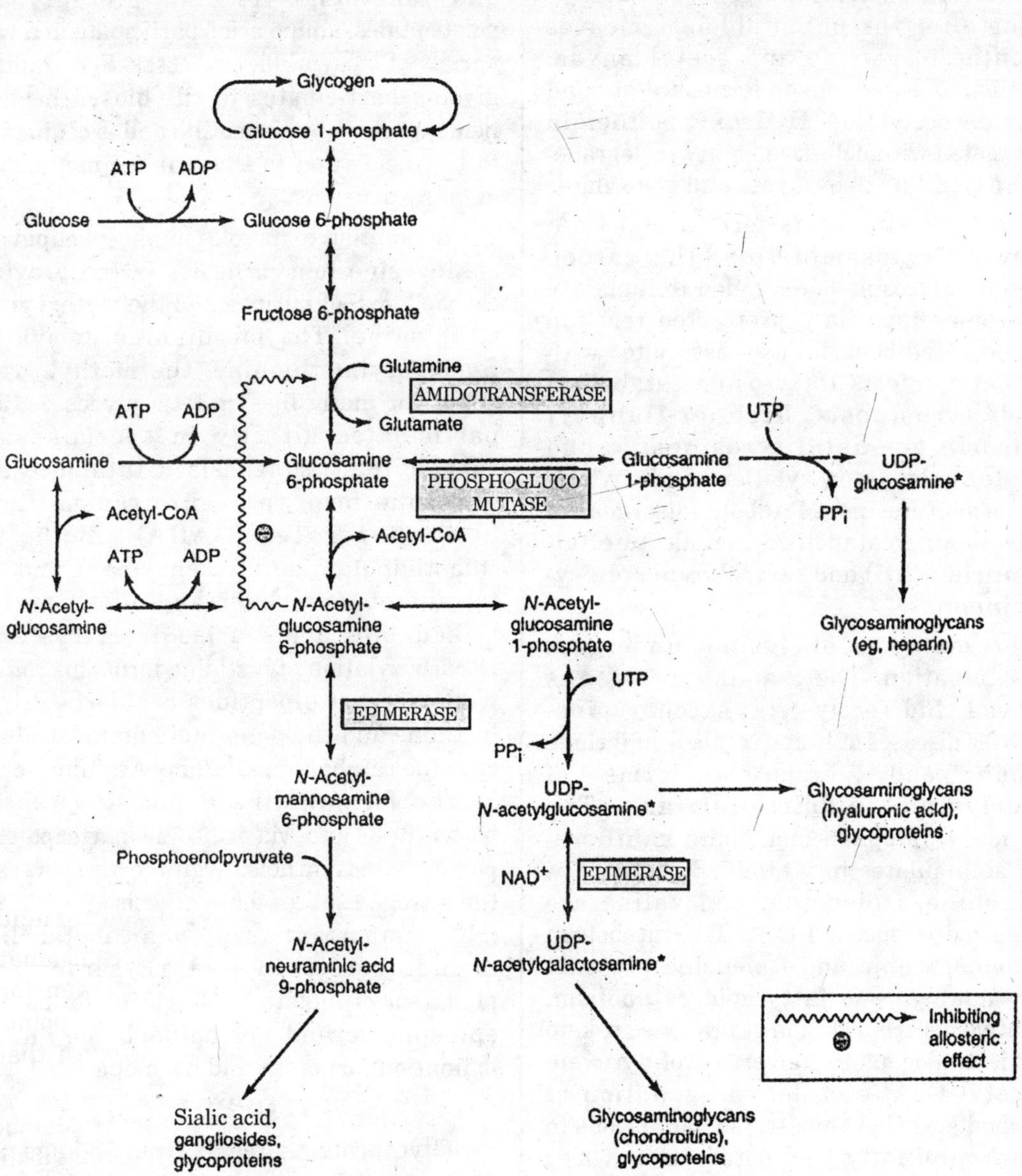

Fig. 28. Summary of the interrelationships in metabolism of amino sugars. (At asterisk : Analogous to UDPGlc.) Other purine of pyrimidine nucleotides may be similarly linked to sugars or amino sugars. Examples are thymidine diphosphate (TDP)- glucosamine and TDP-N-acetylglucosamine.

storage diseases, and the **homocystinurias.** Thremine catabolism merges with that of glycine after threonine aldolase cleaves threonine to glycine and acetaldehyde. Oxidation of acetaldehyde forms acetate and ultimately acetyl CoA. **Hydroxyprolinemia** is associated with defective ability to degrade-4-hydroxyproline to pyruvate and glyoxylate.

Twelve amino acids form acetyl CoA. Following transamination, the carbon skeleton of tyrosine is degraded to fumarate and acetoacetate via a protracted reaction sequence. Metabolic diseases associated with enzymatic defects in tyrosine catabolism include **tyrosinosis, Richner-Hanhart syndrome, neonatal tyrosinemia,** and **alkaptonuria.** Hydroxylation of phenylalanine forms tyrosine. Metabolic disorders of phenylalanine catabolism include **phenylketonuria** (PKU) and several **hyperpherylalaninemias.**

No nitrogen of lysine undergoes transamination. The α-amino nitrogen is removed indirectly via saccharopine. Metabolic diseases of lysine catabolism include periodic and persistant forms of **hyperlysinemia/ammonemia.** The abnormal tryptophan metabolite **xantherenate** accumulates in vitamin B_6 deficinecy. Methionine, isoleucine, and valine are catabolized to succinyl CoA. The catabolsim of leucine, valine and isoleucine presents many analogies to fatty acid catabolism. Oxidative decarboxylation of branched α-keto acids is analogous to conversion of pyruvate to acetyl CoA, and dehydrogenation of branched acyl CoA thioesters is analogous to a reaction of fatty acid catabolsim. Three reactions are specific to leucine catabolism, four to valine catabolism, and three to isoleucine catabolsim. Metabolic disorders of branched-chain amino acid catabolism include **hypervalinemia, maple syrup urine disease,** intermittent **branched chain ketonuria, isovaleric acidemia,** and **methylmalonic aciduria.**

In addition to fulfilling specific structural and functional roles in proteins and polypeptides, amino acids participate in a wide variety of biosyntheic processes. For example, glycine participates in the biosynthesis of heme, purines, and creatine and is conjugated to bile acids and to the urinary metabolites of many drugs.

In addition to its roles in phospholipid and sphingosine biosynthesis, serine provides carbon 2 & 8 of purines and the methyl group of thymine. The methionine derivative S-adenosylmethionine, the methyl group donor for many biosynthetic processes, also participates directly in spermine and spermidine bisynthesis. Glutamate and ornithine form the neurotransmitter γ-**aminobutyrate (GABA).** Both the thioethanolamine of coenzyme A and the taurine of taurocholic and other taurine-linked bile acids arise from cysteine. Decarboxylation of histidine forms histamine, while several dipeptides are derived from histidine and the nonprotein amino acid and cytosine catabolite β-alanine. Arginine serves as the formanidine donor for creatine biosynthesis and, via ornithine, participates in polymine biosyntheis. Arginine also serves as the nitrogen source for synthesis of nitric acid (NO). Important tryptophan metabolites include serotonin in turn serves as a precursor of melatonin. Tyrosine forms both epinephrine and nor-epinephrine and its iodination forms thyroid hormone.

GLYCOPROTEINS

Glycoproteins result from linkage of a protein with a carbohydrate moiety of variable molecular weight, called **Glycan**. They belong to the group of glycoproteins with glyco-amino acids (association of a glycon with an amino acids) and glycopeptides (glycan associates with a peptide). Together with the glycolipids they form the family of *glycoconjugates*.

I. Nature of the Carbohydrates Part

Monosaccharide Constituent : The monosaccharides constituting glycans are neutral; osamines, uronic acids and sialic acids. The most common are :

—Netural Monosaccharides : D-galactose; D-mannose; L-fucose, L-rhamnose, D-xylose.

—Osamines : (in N-acetylated form): D-glucosamine : D-galactosamine; D-muranic acid.

—Uronic acid : D-glucuronic acid; L-iduronic acid.

—Sialic acids : N-acetylneuraminic acid;

N = glycolylneuraminic acid,

N.O–acetylneuraminic acids

Structure of Glycans : These are linear and branched glycans.

A. Sub-maxillary mucin : One of the best known is the submaxillary mucin of sheep which contains about 40% carbohydrates; mainly consisting of N-acetyl, neuraminic acid and N-acetylgalactosamine. These two sugars are conjugated in disaccharide units and about 800 of these units are linked to the peptide chain in the following manner.

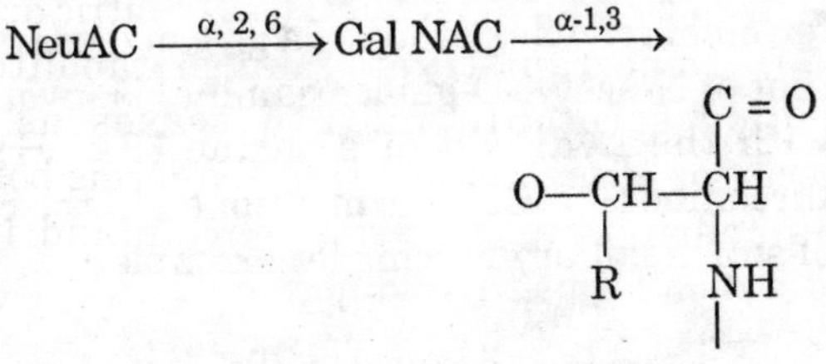

R = H (series) or CH_3 (threonine)

Mucins give highly viscous solutions, but this viscosity disappear under the action of a neuraminidase (or sialidase).

B. Proteoglycans of the fundamental Substance : They result from the association-by O-glycosidic linkages with serine residues of proteins; with glycans having an acids character, and are called acid *mucoploy-saccharides*, These glycans are composed of linear chains of molecular weight-varying from 50,000 (chondrotin sulphuric acid A) to several million (hyaluronic acid), resulting from the polymerization of disaccharide units. These units always contain a N-acetylhexosamine, associated either with a neutral monosaccharide (galactose in keratin sulphate) or with a uronic acid. Esterification by sulphuric acid confers on these molecules a highly acid character which reinforces that of uronic acid.

As an indication, one may represent the structure of the disaccharide repetition units called hyalobiuronic acid) of hyaluronic acid

$$\xrightarrow{\beta\,1,3} \Big[\text{D} - \text{GlcNAcp} \xrightarrow{\beta\,1,4} \text{D} - \text{GlcAUp} \xrightarrow{\beta\,1,3}\Big]_n$$

and the general diagram of the proteoglycan or **chondroitin sulphuric** acid A (or chondroitin-4-sulphate) :

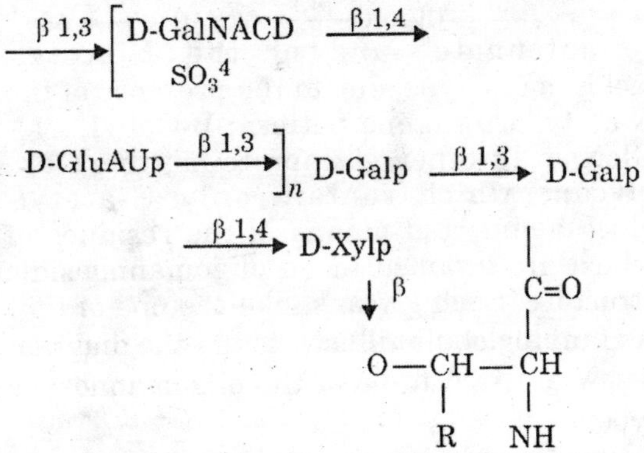

C. Mucopeptides of Murein : Murein is one of the constituents of bacterial cell walls. It is composed of muropeptides joined by their peptide chains. These muropeptides result from the linkage of short peptides with glycan chains; consisting of disaccharide repetition units; these units are composed, for example; of N-acetyl-D-glucosamine and N-acetyl-muramic acid in the case of the muropeptide of *Staphylococcus aureus*.

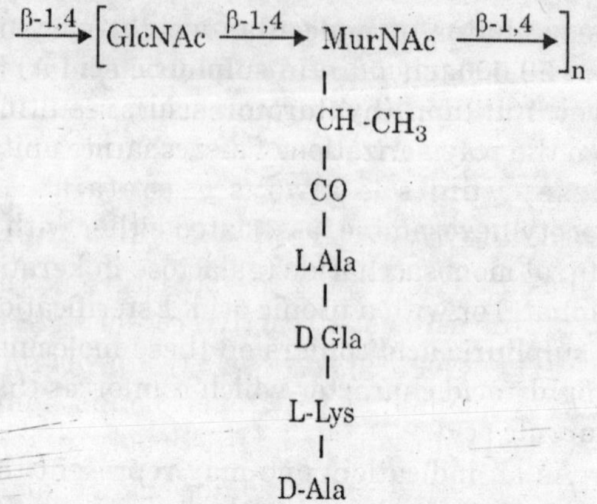

D. Complex Glycans : Glycans of very complex structure are found in numerous animal glycoproteins; like ovalbumin, human serum transferrin, thyroglobulin etc. In transferrin; there are two identical glycans having the following structure. Such a structure is called

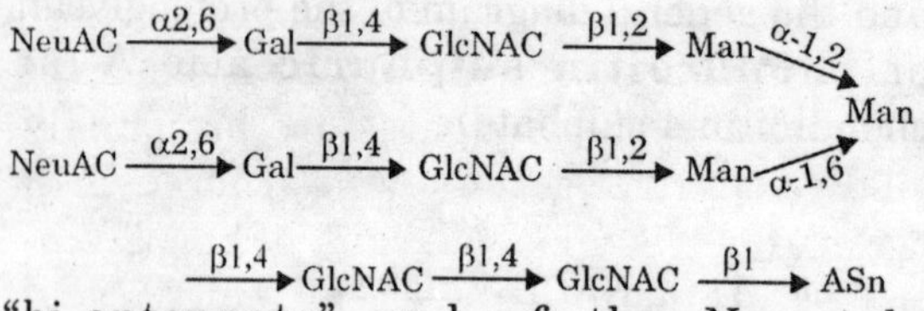

"bi-antennate" and of the N-acetyllactosaminic type; due to the presence of the N-acetyllactosamine pattern; B-Gal (1, 4)—GlcNac. In other glycoproteins; there are glycans which contain only N-acetylglucosamine and mannose; the residues of which are grouped in an oligomannaosidic structure. Such glycans, like the one of unit A of thyroglobulin illustrated in the diagram below are said to be of the oligomannosidic type.

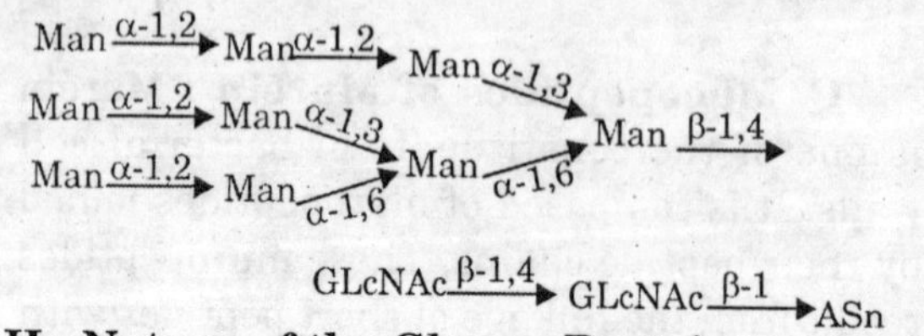

II. Nature of the Glycan-Protein Linkage

The above examples show that there are mainly two types of linkages.

(*a*) Amide Linkage : On the one hand, in numerous animal glycoproteins, where it results from the conjugation of the reducing group of N-acetyl glucosamine with the amide group of asparagine.

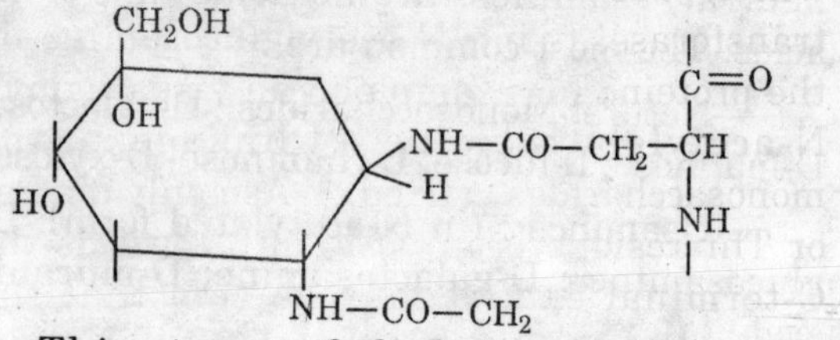

This type of linkage; called "N-glycosylaminic" linkage defines the class of N-glycosylproteins; on the other hand, in the murein of bacterial cell walls, where it results from the condensation of the carbonyl group of N-acetylmuramic acid with the amino group of alanine.

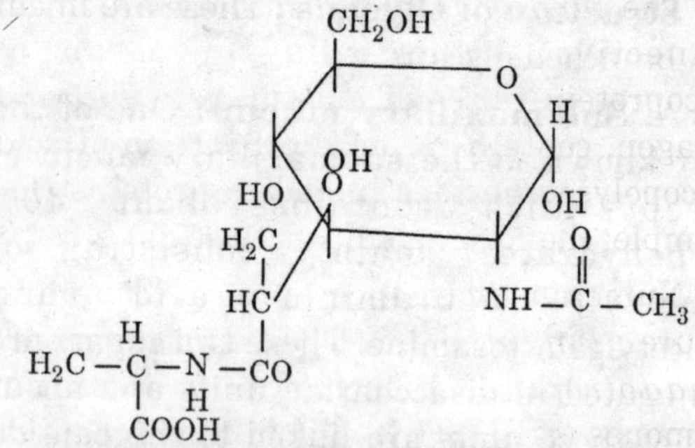

(*b*) O-Glycosidic Linkage : Characteristic of O-glycosyl proteins; where the terminal reducing group of a glycan (generally, that of N-acetyl-D-galactosamine) is involved with the hydroxyl of a serine (R = H) or threonine (R = CH_3) as mentioned in the case of sub-maxillary mucins for example

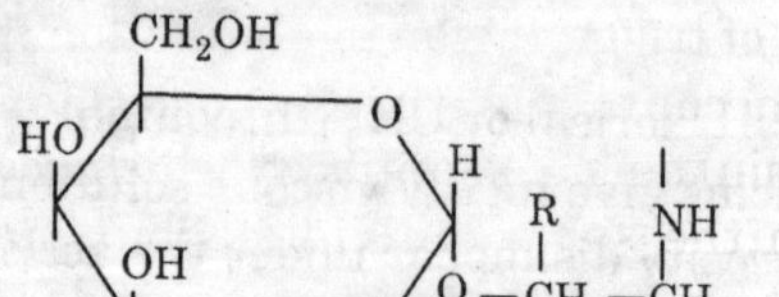

III. Biosynthesis of Glycoproteins

The biosynthesis of glycan groups involves glycosyltransferases and nucleotides-monosaccharides; which are common to the synthesis of free and conjugated polysaccharides.

There are signals on the peptide chain, which are recognized by the glycosyl transferase, fixing N-acetylglucosamine on the protein. For example in an "asparaginyl-N-acetylglucosamine" linkage, the monosaccharides is fixed on Asn only if a Ser or Thr residue is in position β towards the C-terminal end. It may be said that the recognition sequence is therefore, Asn-X-ser-Thr.

IV. Importance of Glycoproteins

Glycoproteins are very widely distributed in animal and plant tissues, as well as in micro-organisms and viruses.

The *fundamental substances* which, in connective tissue, fills the mesh of glycoprotein fibres of elastin, reticulin and collagen, contains a large proportion of acid mucopolysaccharides linked to proteins (for example; chondroitia sulphuric acids).

Numerous hormones are of glycoprotein nature : *Pituitury* (LH, FSH) and *Chorionic gonadotropins* pituitary *thyreotropic* hormones (TSH). Thyroglobulin, precuses or of the thyroid hormone is also a glycoprotein. In cell-membrane there are numerous glycoproteins which play an important role in the social life of the cell and in the immune phenomenon for example, the specific antigens of blood groups, A, B and O, present in the walls of human erythrocytes (and capable of triggering an agglutination if they come in contact with the corresponding agglutinin) a plasma antibody which does not exist in the same individual, but may be present in the plasma of an individual belonging to another blood group are glycoprotein or glycolipids.

Biological fluids are generally very rich in glycoproteins (saliva, urine, bile, milk, tears, blood). For example, in blood, practically all protein-except serum albumin are glycoproteins. Antibodies, or osomucoid, transferrin (form of transport-of iron), ceruleoplasmin, haptoglobins, prothrombin and fibrinogen (the later two substances play a fundamental role in blood coagulation.)

V. Role of Glycan Groups

(*i*) Maintenance of the structure of the protein in biologically active conformation, through glycan-glycan or glycan-protein secondary linkages (hydrogen bonds, ionic bonds and hydrophobic interactions).

(*ii*) Protection of the peptide chain against attack by proteoloytic enzymes.

(*iii*) Decrease in antigenic power of proteins by the masking of epitopes.

(*iv*) Control of the inhibition of membranes by water, and consequently, of the diamembrane passage of mineral ions and small organic molecules. In this connection, the observation that the glycan fractions of membrane glycoconjugates are profoundly modified in cancerous cells (increase in molecular weight of glycans of the glycoproteins and in their rate of sialylation) could explain the modifications noted in the permeability of the membranes of these cells.

(*v*) Action in the cellular phenomenon of recognition : Recognition and association of cells involving peptides which specifically recognize oligosaccharides structures and are called *lectins*. Recognition of target cells by hormones, toxins, bacteria and virus and also by other glycoproteins the desialylation of circulating glycoproteins causes their instantaneous capture by a lectin present in the memberanes of hepatocytes and which specifically recognize the residues of galactose in non-reducing terminal position, this capture being followed by the internalization of asialoglycoproteins and their destruction by the lysosomial enzymes). The above mentioned fact that glycans of the glycoconjugates of cancerous cell membranes undergo profound modifications on the one hand and the observation that glycans play a role in the contact inhibition phenomenon (arrest of mitosis when normal cells come in contact with each other) and on the other hand, could explain (*a*) the perturbations manifest in the social life of cancerous cells, loss of contact inhibition and metastatic diffusion and (*b*) the appearance of surface neo-antigens, capable of inducing the immune reaction of the organisms.

COORDINATION OF METABOLISM

The basic strategy of metabolism is to form ATP, reducing power and building blocks for biosyntheis. Central themes of it are as follows :

(*i*) ATP is the Universal Currency of Energy : The high phosphoryl transfer potential of ATP enables it to serve as the energy source in muscle contraction, active transport, signal amplification and biosynthesis. The hydrolysis of an ATP molecule changes the equilibrium ratio of products to reactants in a coupled reaction by a factor of about 10^6. Hence, a thermodynamically unfavourable reaction sequence can be made highly favourable by coupling it to the hydrolysis of a sufficient number of ATP molecules. For example, three molecules of ATP are consumed in the conversion of mevalonate into isopentenyl pyrophosphate, the activated five-carbon unit in the synthesis of cholesterol.

(*ii*) ATP is generated by the oxidation of fuel molecules such as glucose, fatty acids and amino acids : The common intermediate in most of these oxidations is Acetyl CoA. The carbons of the acyl unit are completely oxidized to CO_2 by the citric acid cylcle with the concomitant formation of NADH and $FADH_2$. These electron carriers then transfer their high-potential electrons to the respiratory chain. The subsequent flow of electrons to O_2 leads to the pumping of protons across the inner mitochondrial membranes. This proton gradient is then used to synthesize ATP. Glycolysis also generates ATP, but the amount formed is much smaller than in oxidative phosphorylation. The oxidation of glucose to pyruvate yields only 2ATP; whereas, 30 (or 32) ATPs are formed when glucose is completely oxidized to CO_2. However, glycolysis can proceed rapidly for a short time under anaerobic conditions; in contrast with oxidative phosphorylation which requires a continuous supply of O_2.

(*iii*) NADPH is the major electron donor in reductive biosynthesis : The most bisynthesis the products are more reduced than the precurosors; and so reductive power is needed as well as ATP. The high-potential electrons required to drive these reactions are usually provided by NADPH. For example, in fatty acid bisynthesis, the keto group of an added two carbon unit is reduced to a methylene group by the input of four electrons from two molecules of NADPH. The activation of O_2 by mixed function of P_{450} oxygenases in hydroxylation reactios also illustrates the pervasive role of NADPH as a reductant. The pentose phosphate pathway suplies much of the required NADPH. This reductant is also formed by the tandem operation of the mitrochondrial citrate-pyruvate shuttle and the malate enzyme in the cytosol.

(*iv*) Biomolecules are constructed from a relatively small set of building blocks : The highly diverse molecules of life are synthesized from a much smaller number of precursors. The metabolic pathways that generate ATP and NADPH also provide building blocks for the bisynthesis of more complex molecules. For example dihydroxy acetone phosphate formed in glycolysis gives rise to the glycerol backbone of phosphatidyl choline and other phosphoglycerides. Phosphoenolpyruvate, another glycolytic intermediate provides part of the carbon skeleton of the aromatic amino acids. Acetyl CoA, the common intermediate in the breakdown of most fuels, supplies a two carbon unit in a wide variety of biosynthesis. Succinyl CoA, formed in the citric acid cycle, is one of the precursors of porphyrins. Ribose-5 phosphate, which is formed in addition to NADPH by the pentose phosphate pathway, is the source of the sugar unit of nucleotides. Many biosynthesis also require one carbon units. Tetrahydrofolate is a source of these units at several oxidation levels. The formations of these derivatives and of S-adenosyl-methionine, the major donor of methyl groups, is closely tied to amino acid metabolism. Thus, the central metabolic pathways have ANABOLIC as well as CATABOLIC roles.

(*v*) Bisoynthetic and degradative pathways are almost distinct : For example, the pathway for the synthesis of fatty acids is different from that of their degradation. Likewise, glycogen is synthesized and degraded by different sets of reactions. This separations enables both bisoynthetic and degradative pathways to be thermodynamically favourable at all times. A bisoynthetic pathway is made exergonic by coupling it to the hydrolysis of sufficient number of ATP. For example, four more ~(P) are spent in converting pyruvate into glucose in gluconeogenesis than are gained in coverting glucose into pyruvate in glucolysis. The four additional ~(P) assume that glyconeogenesis like glycolysis, is highly exergonic under all cellular conditions. The essential point is that the rate of metabolic pathways are governed more by the activities of key enzymes than by mass action. The separation of biosynthetic and degradative pathways contributes greatly to the effectiveness of metabolic control.

Recurring Motifs in Metabolic Regulation : The complex network of reactions in a cell is precisely regulated and coordinated. Metabolism is controlled in several ways :

(*i*) Allosteric Interactions : The flow of molecules in most metabolic pathways is determined primarily by the amounts and activities of certain enzymes rather than by the amount of substrate available. Essentially irreversible reaction are potential control sites. The first irreversible reaction in a pathway (the committed step) is nearly always tightly controlled enzymes catalysing committed steps are allosterically regulated, as exemplified by phosphofructokinase in glycolysis and acetyl CoA carboxylase in fatty acid synthesis. Subsequent irreversible reactions in a pathway also may be controlled. Allosteric interactions enable such enzymes to rapidly detect diverse signals and to integrate this information.

(*ii*) Covalent Modifications : Some regulatory enzymes are controlled by covalent modifcation in addition to allosteric interactions. For example, the catalytic activity of glycogen phosphorylase is enhanced by phosphorylation, whereas, that of glycogen synthase is diminished. There covalent modifications are catalyzed by specific enzymes. Another example is glutamine synthetase, which is rendered less active by the covalent insertion of an AMP unit. Again, addition and removal of this modifying group are catalyzed by specific enzymes. Why is covalent modifcation used in addition to non covalent allosteric control? Covalent modification of key enzymes in metabolism are the final stage of amplifying cascades. Consequently metabolic pathways can be rapidy swtiched on or off by very small triggering signals, as shown by the action of epinephrine in stimulating the breakdown of glycogen. Also, covalent modifcations usually last longer (seconds to minutes) than do reversible allosteric interactions (milliseconds to seconds).

(*iii*) Enzyme Levels : The amounts of enzymes, as well as their activities, are controlled. The rate of synthesis and degradation of many regulatory enzymes are altered by hormones.

***(iv)* Compartmentation :** The metabolic patterns of eukaryotic cells are markedly affected by the presence of comparments. Glycolysis; the pentose phosphate pathway, and fatty acid synthesis take place in the cytosol, whereas, fatty acid oxidation, the TCA cycle and oxidative phosphorylation are carried out in mitochondria. Some processes, such as gluconeogenesis and urea synthesis depend on the interplay of reactions that occur in both compartments. The fates of certain molecules depend on whether they are in the cytosol or in mitochondria, and so their flow across the inner mitochondrial membranes is often regulated. For example, fatty acids transported into mitochondria are rapidly degraded, in contrast-with fatty acids in the cytosol, which are esterified or exported. Long-chain fatty acids are transported into the mitochondrial matrix as esters of carnitine a carrier that enables these molecules to traverse the inner mitchondrial matrix.

***(v)* Metabolic Specializations of Organs :** Regulation in higher eukaryotes is profoundly affected and enhanced by the existence of organs with different metabolic roles.

7. GROWTH AND DEVELOPMENT

Definition : In a generalized way growth can be *defined as an irreversible increase in size*. It involves multiplication, expansion and differentiation of cells. The *differentiation is a change in form and physiological activity*.

Plants typically continues to grow throughout their lives. Growth in a plant is the result of cell division, enlargement of the new cells and their differentiation into different types of tissues. Thus, growth can be defined as the permanent and irreversible change in any dimension (like size and volume) of an organism accompanying an increase in the dry weight.

PHYSIOLOGICAL CHANGES DURING GROWTH

The physiological change taking place during the *cell division*, *cell enlargement* and *cell differentiation* (*maturation*) are given as under.

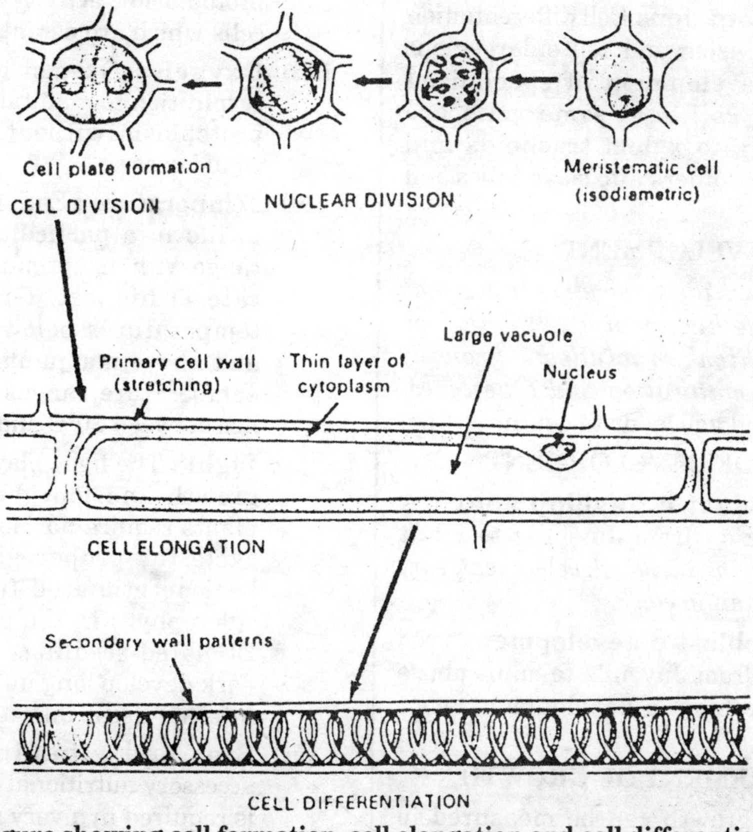

Fig. 1. Figure showing cell formation, cell elongation and cell differentiation

Cell division : A cell is metabolically highly active at the time of cell division. Its cellular mass increases and replication of genetic material (nucleic acids) takes place. Growth as a result of division is based on mitotic cell division. In the stage of mitosis each chromosome is split lengthwise into two homologous chromatids which pass equally into daughter cells. As a result of division each cell is only half the size of parent cell. These cells then proceed to enlarge.

Cell enlargement : Cell division is followed by cell enlargement. The cell increases in size due to vacuolation (by absorption of water). A big central vacuole appears which pushes the cytoplasm to be limited to a thin boundary layer against the cell wall. The new cell material is synthesized to cope with the enlargement.

Cell differentiation : Cell differentiation following cell division and cell enlargement leads to the development of specialized mature tissue cell, *e.g.* some cells are differentiated into xylem tracheids and trachea and some others into sieve tubes and companion cells.

DEVELOPMENT

Development is the sequence of events that occurs in the life history of a cell, organ or organism which includes growth, differentiation, maturation and senescence. Senescence or old age leads to death.

TYPES OF DEVELOPMENT

(*i*) **Homoblastic development :** A gradual transition from Juvenile to adult phase is called *homoblastic development. e.g., Ipomoea, Delphinium etc.*

(*ii*) **Heteroblastic development :** An abrubt change from Juvenile to adult phase is called heteroblastic development. *e.g., Hedera* (Ivy).

MEASUREMENT OF GROWTH

The plant growth can be measured in terms of :

(*i*) Increase in volume

(*ii*) Increase in weight

(*iii*) Increase in height *or* diameter

(*iv*) Increase in area *etc.*

FACTORS AFFECTING GROWTH

Growth in plants is affected by the following factors ones are :

(*i*) **Nutrient supply :** Green plants are dependent on nutrients from soil to manufacture food. Growth ceased when the nutrient supply becomes limiting. Heterotrophic plants and animals also require food for growth, which provides energy and materials needed for the process. Growth occurs when food supply is in excess of catabolic need.

(*ii*) **Water supply :** Water maintains protoplasmic activity and turgidity of cells which are essential to growth.

(*iii*) **Oxygen :** Oxygen is required for respiration to maintain the vitality of protoplasm without which growth would cease.

(*iv*) **Temperature :** Each plant is adapted to life in a particular temperature range with an optimum when growth rate is highest. Growth stops at temperatures below the minimum and above maximum of this range. Temperature ranges of most plants lies between 20°C and 40°C.

(*v*) **Light :** The light plays a vital role in growth and morphogenesis. Most plants require normal day and night cycle for proper growth. Leaves become etiolated (do not develop chlorophyll) in the absence of light. Etiolated seedlings growing in the dark develop long internodes without internal tissue differentiation.

(*vi*) **Bios and vitamins :** Bios is an accessory nutritional substance which is required in a very minute quantity for the healthy growth of a plant body, in addition to normal nutrition. Vitamins also play a very important role in the development of plant body.

(*vii*) Growth hormones : They are now well known as the internal factors contributing largely to the growth of the plants.

PHOTOPERIODISM

Photoperiodism is the response of plants to relative lengths of day and night for their flowering. Angiosperms are divided into the following three categories based on such responses.

W.W. Garner and **H.A. Allard (1920)** observed the effect of day length on the flowering of plants and established the concept of critical photoperiod (exposure to plants to light less or more than a certain period each day).

CLASSIFICATION ON THE BASIS OF PHOTOPERIODIC RESPONSE

Short Day Plants (SDP) : Flowering in plants take place only when day length is shorter than a critical day length. Typical short-day plants do not flower unless they are subjected to dark periods of about 11-14 hours, *e.g., Bryophyllum, Chrysanthemum, Xanthium, Solanum, Nicotiana tabaccum,* Strawberries, Rice, Dahlias, Sorghum, Soybean *etc.*

Long Day Plants (LDP) : Flowering in plants take place only when day length is longer than a critical day length. Long day plants need shorter night of about 11-12 hours, *e.g.,* Barley, black henbane, larkspur, lettuce, *oat,* potatoes, spinach, wheat, radish, sugarbeet *etc.*

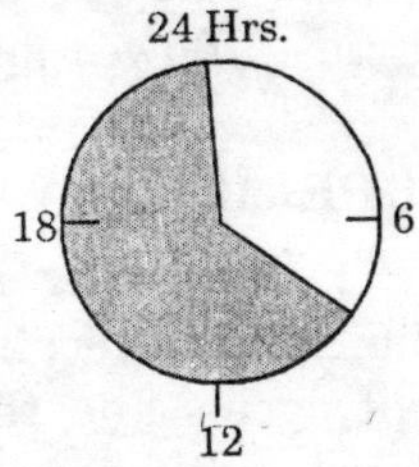

Short Day Plants

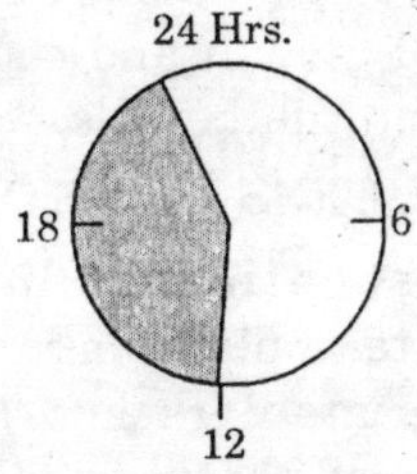

Long Day Plants

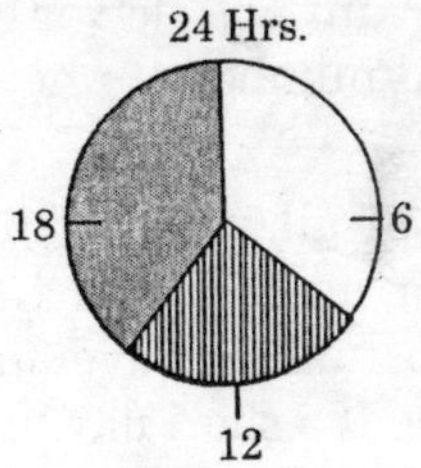

Day Neutral Plants

The short day and long-day plants do not imply that all long-day plants require period of light that are longer than those needed by short-day plant. Critical times for some long-day plants are either almost equal *or* even shorter than these of some short-day plants, *e.g., Xanthium* (SDP) and *Hyoscyamus niger* (LDP) required 12-13 hours photoperiod for flowering. *Xanthium* has a critical day length of 11 hr. and both flower when these values are not exceeded.

Short day plants (SDP)	*Long day plants (LDP)*
1. Plants need a photoperiod of less than critical day length to produce flowers.	Plants need a photoperiod of more than critical day length to produce flowers.
2. Long dark period is critical for flowering.	Long dark period is not critical for flowering.
3. No flowering occurs if the dark period is interrupted mid-way by a flash of light.	Flowering occurs even if the dark period is interrupted by a flash of light.
4. Interruption in light period does not inhibit flowering.	Interruption in light period inhibits flowering.
5. No flowering occurs under alternating cycles of short light and long dark periods.	Flowering occurs under alternating cycles of short light and still shorter dark periods.

Day Neutral Plants (DNP): Plants which are uneffected by dark *or* light cycle, *e.g.,* Tomatoes, sunflower, cotton, four O'clock plant, pea, roses *etc.*

These plants start to flower at a certain stage of growth and continue to flower and bear fruit till they die.

PROCESS OF PHOTOPERIODISM

Absorption of light : Flowering in plants take place only when plants receive appropriate dark and light cycles and the number of photoperiodic cycles differ from species to species *i.e.,* it is a species specific characteristics. Plant will flower only after it received required number of photo inductive cycles.

Wavelength of all types of light do not stimulate flowering. For the induction of flowering the most effect wavelengths range is 560 nm-640 nm. If a short day plant is given red light (660 nm), there is an inhibition in flowering and when it is followed by far red light (730 nm), flowering get stimulated. If far red is again, followed by the induction of red light, flowering will again get inhibited.

ROLE OF PHYTOCHROME IN FLOWERING AND GERMINATION

Phytochrome

Phytochrome is a plasma membrane bound red-light (low energy) receptor pigment system involved in photomorphogenetic responses of plants. It is universally present in green plants except some alage. It is a phycobilin bound to protein and exists in two interconvertible forms. One called phytochrome-red (Pr.) has absorption maxima around 660 nm. It is the stable form. The other, phytohormone-far red (Pr), has maxima near 730 nm. On absorbing red light Pi changes to Pfr. The Pfr changes to Pr either rapidly by absorbing far-red light or slowly in darkness. The Pfr is considered as the active form. Most probably a Pfr to Pr ratio determines a morphogenetic response. It initiates reactions accompanying the morphogenetic changes by activating specific genes.

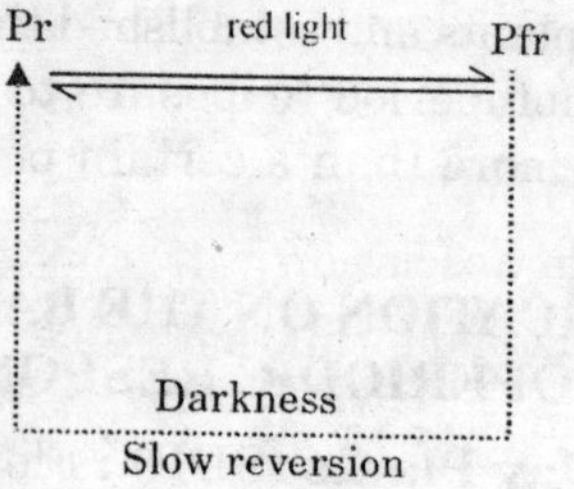

A. Phytochrome and Flowering

Involvement of phytochrome in flowering is seen from night interruption experiments. Short-day plants remain vegetative when exposed to red (660 nm) night break but flower under far-red. Long-day plants growing in short-day conditions flower under red but remain vegetative under far-red. When red and far-red exposures are given in close succession, the nature of light in the last exposure determines the response as follows:

Night break under short-day condition	*Response of short-day plants*	*Response of long-day plants*
R	Vegetative	Flower
R + FR	Flower	Vegetative
R + FR + R	Vegetative	Flower
R + FR + R + FR	Flower	Vegetative

B. Phytochrome and Germination

Hydrated positively photoblastic seeds respond to exposures of red and far-red illumination indicating involvement of phytochrome. Red exposure triggers germination and far red inhibits it. In light sensitive lettuce seeds the last exposure determines germination as follows :

R	germination
R + FR	no germination
R + FR + R	germination
R + FR + R + FR	no germination

C. Other phytochrome mediated physiological responses occur in plants besides flowering and germination. Some of these are given below :

1. Bud dormancy
2. Leaf abscission
3. Rhizome formation
4. Epinasty
5. Differentiation of primary leaves
6. Plastid orientation
7. Synthesis of anthocyanin
8. Elongation of leaf petiole and stem
9. Bulb formation

VERNALIZATION

Several plants flower only when exposed to extreme cold for several weeks. The inductive exposure may be required at seed germination phase as in Petukus rye or at a very late stage of growth as in henbane. This *requirement of low temperature for flowering is called vernalization.* As a process, vernalization does not induce flowering. It only modulates growth in a way that prepares the plant to flower. The effective temperature for vernalization usually lies between few degrees above zero and 15°C.

Vernalisation was first studied in Europe on the winter varieties of cereals such as wheat, barley, oats and rye. The winter varieties are sown in winter and are harvested in spring. However, when these were sown in spring, these do not flower in the spring. If these are kept alive, these bloom only in the next spring after passing through a winter season. If these seeds are exposed to low temperature (0-4°C) for a few weeks, these produce flowers in the same spring.

PHASES OF VERNALIZATION

(*i*) **Thermophase :** It requires a temperature ranging between 10-20°C along with moisture and oxygen. This phase has to be completed prior to the initiation of primordial of reproductive organs.

(*ii*) The period of low temperature treatment varies from a days to 90 days and it is species character.

Photophase : It is the period of illumination with a high temperature after thermophase.

Vernalin is produced when a plant is treated with, low temperature. Vernalin is supposed to be a kind of gibberellin as the vernalized plants have higher level of gibberellin than non-vernalized plants.

In photophase, vernalin helps in the synthesis of a flowering hormone called *florigen.*

APPLICATIONS OF VERNALIZATION

It is beneficial in the reduction of time period between germination and flowering. so yield of plants is increased besides this it is also beneficial in the protection of spring season plants due to freezing injury due to very low winter temperature.

Therefore, vernalization is beneficial in reducing the period between germination and flowering. Thus more than one crop can be obtained during a year.

SENESCENCE

Senescence can be defined as the collective progressive and deteriorative process that ultimately *terminate the functional life of an organism.* It is the period between reproductive maturity and death of a plant or plant part. The onset of sensescene in plants in marked by **decline** in photosynthetic rate. **Negative growth** is the term sometimes used for senescence.

Types of Senescence

Senescence in plants is manifested in various types as follows :

(*a*) **Whole plant senescence :** Here senescence begins with reproductive maturity like **rice, wheat, gram** and **mustard, the** whole plant dies after seed production. Such type of senescence is also observed in **monocarpic** plants (the plants that live for several years but flower only once) such as certain **bamboos** and **sago palm.** This is seen in annuals, biennials and monocarpic plants.

(*b*) **Sequential senescence : In many perennial plants,** the apical merstems continue to produce new buds and leaves, while the older leaves and lateral organs senesce and die.

(*c*) **Shoot senescence :** In some perenials like **banana** and **gladiolus**, the above ground part of the shoot dies every year after producing flowers and fruits. However, the underground parts (shoot and root) survive and give rise to new shoots again in the following year. *e.g.*, Banana, dahlia, onion, gladiolus etc.

(*d*) **Simultaneous or synchronous senescence :** In some trees like elm and **maples**, all the leaves are shed in late autumn (October).

(*e*) **Control of senescence :** In many cases, senescence could be delayed by removing flowers from the plants. Roots produce cytokinins. It promotoes leaf abscission and ripening of fruits. Thus senescence seems to be under the **control of hormones,** ABA and ethylene, and is retarded by cytolanins.

Plant Movements

Movements in higher plants are chiefly in the form of bending, twisting, elongation of certain parts, etc. These movements are not as noticeable as in animals. Thus difference between the movements of plants and animals is only of degree and is related to the fundamental difference in their modes of nutrition.

Plants being autotrophic need not move bodily from place to place while animals depend for their nutrition readymade food and therefore, move about in search of it. Movements in plants are chiefly in response to certain external or internal stimuli. A stimulus may be defined as an environmental agent or change that induces a reaction in the living organisms. The reaction plants to the stimulus is called response.

The response to any stimulus is due to the ability of protoplasm to appreciate and react to the change in the environment. This property of the protoplasm is called irritability or sensitiveness. The stimuli may be :

(*i*) Mechanial (*e.g.*, touch or pressure),

(*ii*) Chemical (*e.g.*, auxins, poisons),

(*iii*) Environmental (*e.g.*, light, temperature, moisture) and

(*iv*) Gravitational etc.

All parts of the plant are not sensitive to stimuli. There are often certain localized regions called perceptive regions or perceptive organs which receive a stimulus *i.e.*, known as responsive region.

Autonomic Movements

The movement in plants induced by internal factors are called autonomic movements.

Paratonic Movements

The movements in plants induced by external factors are known as paratonic movements.

Kinds of Movements

Plant movements occur due to four types of changes : (*i*) Physical, (*ii*) locomotion, (*iii*) growth, and (*iv*) turgor.

Classification of Plant Movements

The plant movements are broadly classified into two categories (*i*) vital and (*ii*) physical.

I. Vital Movements

They are shown by living cells or plants. They have been subdivided as under :

(A) Movements of Locomotion

(*a*) Autonomous or spontaneous :
- (*i*) Ciliary
- (*ii*) Amoeboid
- (*iii*) Cyclosis

(*b*) Paratonic or autogenic or induced or tactic :
- (*i*) Phostotactic
- (*ii*) Thermotactic
- (*iii*) Chemotactic
- (*iv*) Rheotactic
- (*v*) Galvanotactic

(B) Movements of Growth

(*a*) Autonomous
- (*i*) Nastic
- (*ii*) Nutational

(*b*) Paratonic or Tropic
- (*i*) Phototropism
- (*ii*) Geotropism
- (*iii*) Hydrotropism
- (*iv*) Chemotropism
- (*v*) Thigmotropism
- (*vi*) Aerotropism
- (*vii*) Thermotropism
- (*viii*) Rheotropism
- (*ix*) Galvanotropism
- (*x*) Traumatotropism

(C) Movement of Variation

(*a*) Autonomous

(*b*) Paratonic or Nastic
- (*i*) Nyctinasty
- (*ii*) Thigmonasty
- (*iii*) Hydronasty
- (*iv*) Chemonasty
- (*v*) Seismonasty

(A) Movements of Locomotion

Physically or bodily movements of the whole plant body or of an organ or of material within the plant cell which occur in response to inherent factors and are free and spontaneous from one place to another in some medium is called *movements of locomotion*. Movements of locomotion may be:

A. Autonomous or Paratonic Movements of Locomotion :

(*i*) Ciliary movements : Some algal forms like, *Chlamydomonas, Volvox* and many other Volvocales, move about bodily in water with the help of their cilia. Such ciliary movements are also shown by their zoospores or zoogametes.

(*ii*) Amoeboid movement : The plasmodia of myxomycetes, gametes of *Spirogyra* and protoplasts of tapetum show amoeboid movement. They form pseudopodia like processes. Certain zoospores also show amoeboid movements.

(*iii*) Cyclosis : The movement of protoplasm is called as *cyclosis*. It is of the following two types :

(*a*) Rotation : The circular movement of protoplasm is called as *rotation*. It is seen in the young leaf cells of *Hydrilla, Vallisneria, Chara* and *Eoldea*. This movement may be clockwise or anticlock-wise.

(*b*) Circulation : It is radial movement of protoplasm occurring in the form of eddies around different vacuoles of a cell. It is seen in the staminal hairs of *Tradescantia, Rhoeo* and young hairs on the vegetative part of many cucurbitaceae.

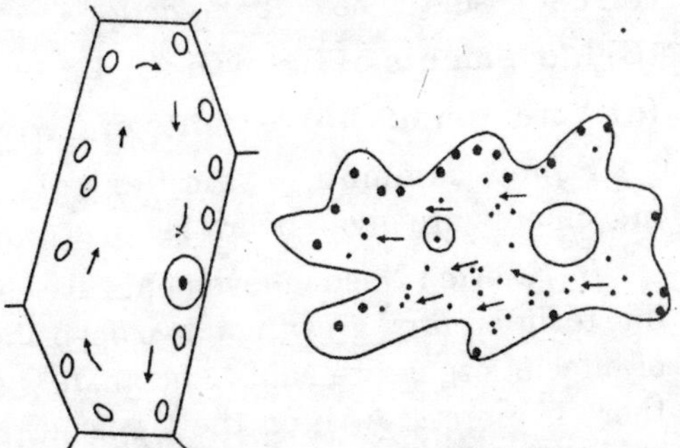

A. Rotation B. Circulation

Fig. 2 Autonomic movements of locomotion

B. Paratonic or Tactic (Taxis) Movements of Locomotion

They are produced in response to some external stimulus. They are said to be positive if directed towards the stimulus and negative if away from the stimulus. These movements are sub-divided as under:

(i) Phototactic (light) : Light induced locomotion movements are called as *phototactic. e.g., Chlamydomonas.*

(ii) Thermotactic (temperature) : Temperature induced locomotion movements are said to be *thermotactic. e.g., Flagellated organisms.*

(iii) Chemotactic (chemicals) : Chemical stimulus induced locomotion movements are said to be *chemotactic e.g.*, movement of antherozoids towards the egg in bryophytes, pteridophytes etc. The chemical stimulus is supplied in the form of sugars (bryophytes) or malic acid (pteridophytes) formed by the degeneration of neck canal cells and ventral canal cells. This movement confirms to positive chemotropism. The bacteria are sensitive to peptone and K-salts.

(iv) Rheotactic : Locomotion movement performed in response to running water current is called as rheotactic.

(v) Galvanotactic : The locomotion movement performed in response to electric current is said to be *galvanotactic.*

(B) Movements of Growth

(a) Autonomous Movements of Growth

Some common examples of such movements are given below :

(i) Nastic : Nastic movements are caused due to differential growth on two opposite side of bifacial organ are said to be *nastic*. When there is more growth on the Upper or inner side, the phenomenon is called as *epinasty*. Similarly, if there is more growth on the lower or outer side, the phenomenon is called as *hyponasty*. The flower bud of poppy becomes inverted due to epinasty but the flower once again becomes upright due to hyponasty. In the same way, the opening of a flower bud occurs due to epinasty whereas it closes due to hyponasty. These movements are observed not only in dorsiventral organs but also in hypocotyls, epicotyls, roots, stems, pedicles and stamens. Those autonomic growth movements which occur only once in the lifetime are sometimes described as *ephemeral.*

(ii) Nutational : Such autonomic growth movement is shown by the growing shoot apex in several plants shows zigzag movement perhaps due to change in growth rates at two opposite points. Such a type of movement is said to be as *nutational*. In some plants this type of growth allows the shoot apex to grow in a helical path in upward direction. This movement has been described as *circumnutation.*

(b) Paratonic or Tropic Movement of Growth

Growth movements which occur in response to unidirectional external stimuli and result in positioning of the plant part in the direction of stimulus, are described as *tropic movements*. Here the stimulus acts on the protoplasm from one side. Movement of stem, petiole, floral axis, etc. are good examples of paratonic movements. They are of the following types :

(i) Phototropism (heliotropism) : Light induced growth movements are called as *phototropic*. The stem grows towards the source of light, hence called *positively phototropic*. The root, on the other hand, grows away from the source of light, hence-described as *negatively phototropic*. The leaves of many plants grow at right angles to the incident light, hence they are called as *diaphototropic.*

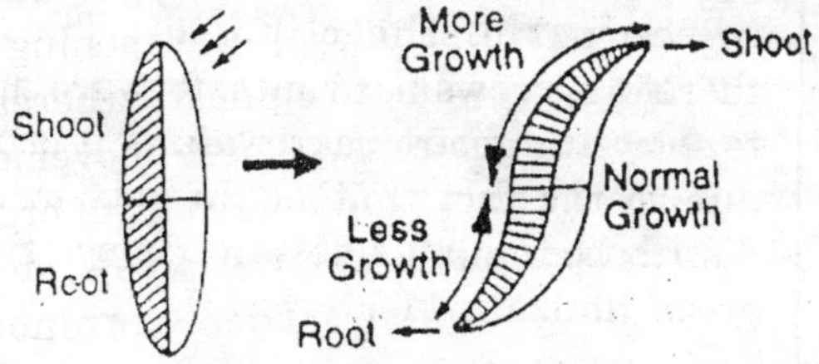

Fig. 3. Phototropism : Effect of light on auxin accumulation, and root, growth

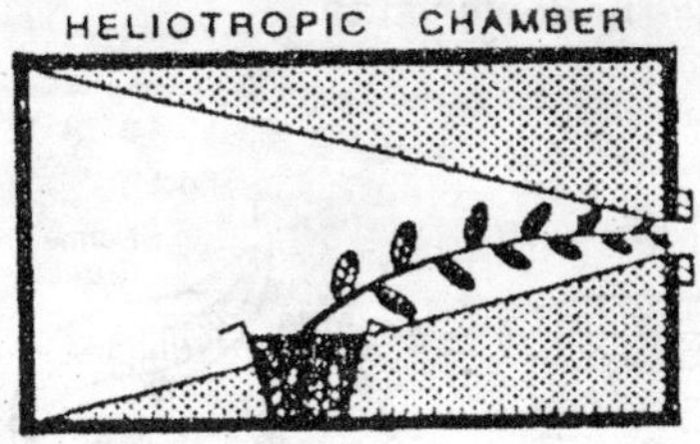

Fig. 4 Positive Phototropism : Chamber used to demonstrate phototropism

A vertically placed embryonic axis, on unilateral illumination shows auxin synthesis in the apex which gets unequally distributed. It is more on the shaded side. According to **Gaiston**, light induced inhibition of auxin synthesis occurs in the shoot apex *i.e.*, less auxin precursor is converted into auxin on the illuminated side. Thus, more growth occurs on the shaded side of stem, as a result of which it curves towards the source of light. The concentration of auxin that induced growth in stem, retards or inhibits growth in roots. As a result, the root curves away from the source of light.

(*ii*) Geotropism : Frank (1868) was first to establish this phenomenon and also proposed the term. More terms such as *gravitropism* and *barytropism* were coined but the term geotropism was preferred over others. Gravity induced growth is called as *geotropism*. The root grows towards the force of gravitation, hence called as *positively geotropic*. On the contrary, the stem grows away from the force of gravitation, hence described as *negatively geotropic*.

The geotropic behaviour can be precisely subdivided into four categories.

(*i*) The main root grows vertically downward exactly towards the force of gravitation (earth's centre), hence it is termed as *positively orthogeotropic*.

(*ii*) The main-stem, on the other hand, grows in the reverse direction, hence called as *negatively orthogeotropic*.

(*iii*) The rhizomes and runners growing at right angles to the force of gravitation are described as *diageotropic*.

(*iv*) The stem and root branches growing at an angle of 45° from the vertical axis are termed as *plageotropic* (or *plagiogeotropic*). The leaves and root hair are immune to gravitational stimulus. They are described as *apogeotropic*.

Perception of geotropic stimulus : The geotropic stimulus is perceived by the root tip. Even the root cap can capture this stimulus. Then a series of reactions start which ultimately result in the curvature. Several veiws have been put forward to explain the mechanism of perception of geotropic stimulus.

Cholodny-Went theory : This is based on gravity induced lateral polarization of organs and unequal distribution of auxins on illuminated and dark sides. The horizontal placement of embryonic axis gets illuminations on the upper side. The auxins synthesized in the shoot apex get accumulated on the lower side. This induces growth on the shaded side in stem. As a result the stem curves to upper side. The concentration of auxins that induces growth in stem retards growth in the roots. As a result the root curves to the lower side.

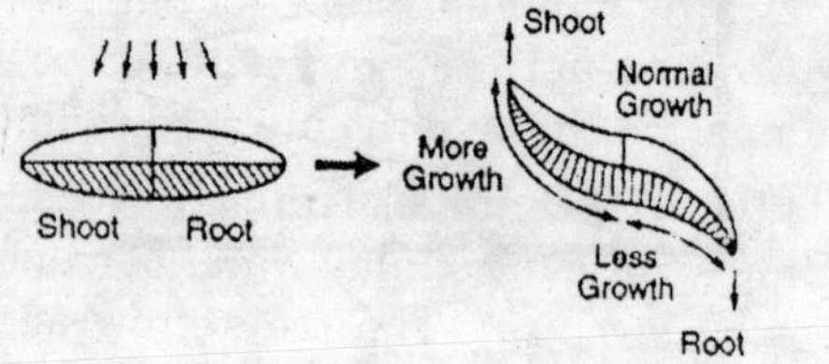

Fig. 5 Cholodny-Went's theory

Statolith theory : The earlier workers believed that the gravitational stimulus is perceived by large starch grains called *statoliths*. The cells containing these grains are called as *statocyts* or *statocyte*. Some workers believed that the statoliths are plastids containing several starch grains. Usually they rest on the lower cell wall. Any change or displacment of cell organ initiates a series of changes in the cell culminating in geotropic curvature.

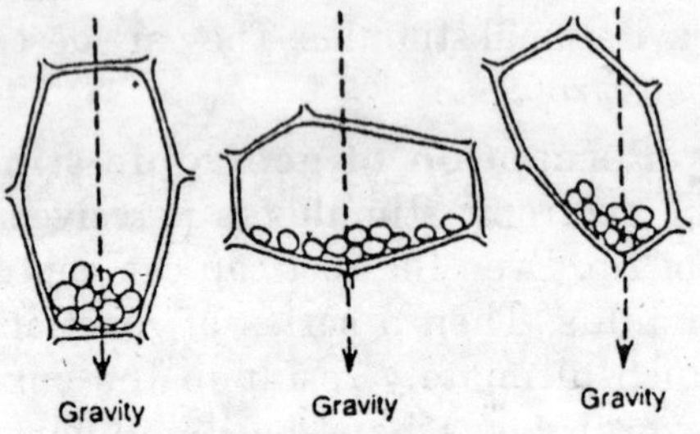

Fig. 6 Statolith's theory

Besides, the microsomes are also thought to be responsible for capturing the geotropic stimulus resulting in the movement of Ca^+ and K^+. This finally results in a geotropic curvature.

Clinostat : It comprises a disc with which are rotated by a axial rod with the help of a motor. The axial rod bears a pointer which tells about the angular rotation with the help of a circular scale placed on the top of the motor. With the help of this device the pot can be rotated very slowly, say fifteen minutes per round. The geotropic stimulus is nullified if a plant is rotated horizontally along its long axis in the pot of the clinostat. The shoot, therefore, grows horizontal forward and fails to show any geotropic curvature. It is perhaps due to the fact that auxin gets uniformly distributed on all sides and, hence the stem grows horizontal forward.

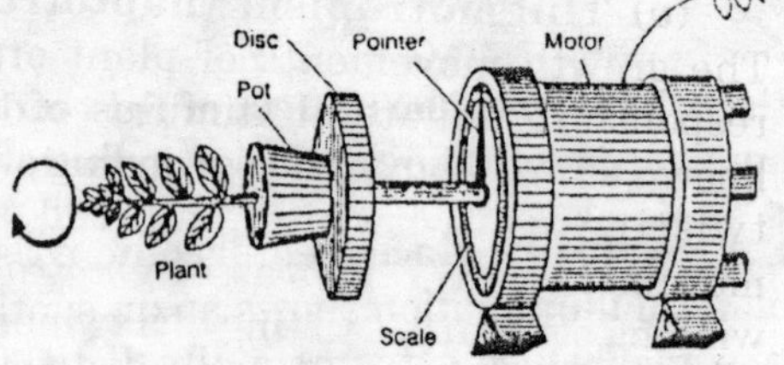

Fig. 7 The clinostat

(*iii*) **Hydrotropism :** Water stimulus induced growth movements are called as hydrotropic. This phenomenon was first observed by **Johnson (1829)**. In fact, it is a sort of chemotropism. Some seeds are placed on moist saw dust spread over a wire gauge. The wire gauge is placed over a through. The seeds now germinate producing the radicle which grows vertically downward through the pore of the wire gauge due to positive geotropism. The tip of the radicle then curves upward due to positive hydrotropism.

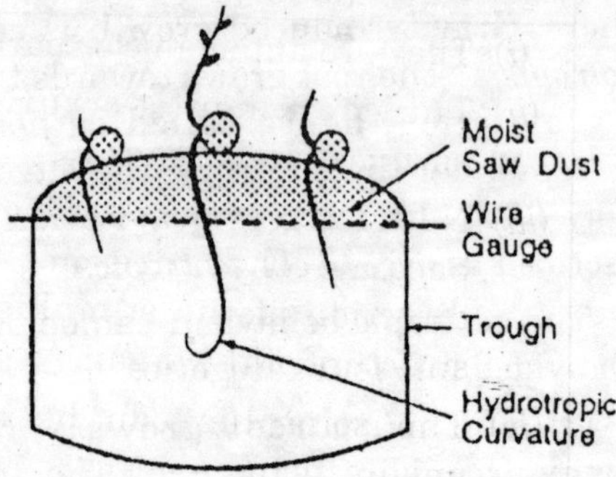

Fig. 8 Hydrotropism

***(iv)* Chemotropism :** The movement of plant organs due to unilateral stimulus of chemicals is called as *chemotropism i.e.,* growth of pollen tube towards the micropyle (*positive chemotropism*). The chemical stimulus is supplied in the form of Ca^{++}. The roots of *Lupinus albus* show positive chemotropism with sodium monohydrogen phosphate and negative chemotropism with KNO_3, $Ca(NO_3)_2$, NH_4NO_3.

***(v)* Thigmotropism (haptotropism):** The growth movements of plant organs in response to unilateral stimulus of touch is known as *thigmotropic e.g.,* winding of tendril, twisting of a twiner induced growth movements are called as *thigmotropic e.g.,* winding of tendril, twisting of a twiner around a solid support. It is also seen in the stem of *Cuscuta* and roots of *Vanilla*. When the tip of the tendril comes in contact with a solid object having uneven surface, it coils around the support. This is due to differential growth in the tendril.

***(vi)* Aerotropism :** Air (particularly oxygen) stimulus induced growth movements are called as aerotropic. This is also a type of chemotropism. The pneumatophores grow against the geotropic stimulus due to aerotropism. The roots are described as positively aerotropic whereas the pollen tubes as *negatively aerotropic*.

***(vii)* Thermotropism :** Temperature induced growth movements are called as *thermotropism*. The peduncles of *Tulipa sylvestris* and *Anemone nemerosa* bend towards sun and follow its path throughout the day, perhaps in response to its heat imparted through the infrared radiations.

***(viii)* Rheotropism :** Growth movement in response to running water current is called as *rheotropism*. The roots grow against the direction of water current and they are, therefore, described as *positively rheotropic*. The root of the seeding is more sensitive to rheotropic stimulus than the mature plant.

***(ix)* Galvanotropism :** Growth movements made in response to electric current are described as Galvanotropic. Such movements have been observed in the roots of some plants.

***(x)* Traumatotropism :** Injury induced growth movements are called as *traumatotropism*. The growing root tip, if injured, grows away from the injured side amounting to negative traumatotropism. Injury in the lamina induces traumatotropic curvature in the lamina and petiole of the leaf towards the injured side. This amounts to *positive traumatotropism*. It is also seen in the epicotyls and hypocotyls.

Differences between Nastic and Tropic Movements

Nastic Movements	Tropic Movements
(i) They are autonomic or paratonic.	*(i)* They are always paratonic.
(ii) The movements occur in flat or asymmetrical organs.	*(ii)* The movements are commonly found in cylindrical organs.
(iii) Nastic movements are nondirectional because they are not related to direction of the stimulus but to the structure of the organ.	*(iii)* Tropic movements are called directional movements because the direction of movement is related to the direction of the stimulus.
(iv) The stimulus can be diffused or unidirectional.	*(iv)* The stimulus must be unidirectional or unilateral.
(v) They are curvature movements of growth or variation (Turgor).	*(v)* They are curvature movements of growth only.

(C) Movements of Variations

Movements shown by mature organs of the plants are normally not due to growth. Very often such movements are the results of the changes in the turgidity of the cells and are, therefore called movements of variation. Movements of variation are of two types :

(a) Autonomous Movement of Variation

The most common example of such movement is seen in the leaves of Indian telegraph plant *(Desmodium gyrans)*, *Trifolium pretense, Eleiotis soratia* etc. In these plants the leaves are trifoliate. When the environmental conditions are favourable, the lateral leaflets perform to-and-fro movement.

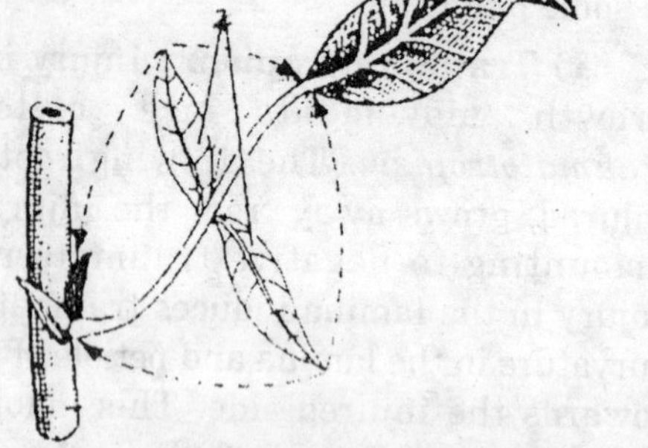

Fig. 9 Autonomic movements of Variation in Indian telegraph plant (*Desmodium gyrans*).

(b) Paratonic or Nastic Movement of Variation

(i) Nyctinasty : Certain leaves as well as flowers open during the day and closed at night. These so called sleep movements, brought about by the alteration of day and night, are called nyctinasty. When these movements are induced by light, they are described as *photonastic* and when induced by temperature, they are *thermonastic*. Photonasty is seen in several plants. In *Impatients, Marsilea* and *Oxalis*, the leaves are expanded horizontal in the day and droop at night. On the contrary, the leaves of *Chenopodium album, Polygonum aviculare,* and *Delonix regia* are horizontally expanded in the day but folded vertically upward at night. Thermonasty is seen in the flower of *Tullipa*.

(ii) Thigmonasty (Haptonasty) : These movements occur due to stimulus of touch and can be observed in insectivorous plants. The tentacles of *Drosera* leaf curve and the lamina lobes of *Dionaea* fold on coming in contact with an insect. Similar response to touch stimulus is seen in the leaf margins of *Pinguicula*.

(iii) Hydronasty : Humidity induced variation movements called as *hydronastic*. An increase in the humidity induces sleep movement in the leaves. *e.g., Myriophyllum* and *Oxalis*.

(iv) Chemonasty : Chemical stimulus induced variation movements are called as *chemonastic*. The leaves of *Mimosa pudica* exhibit sleep movement in chloroform environment whereas the leaves of *Callisia repens* show curvature in coal gas environment.

(v) Seismonasty : Such movements are seen in the leaves of sensitive plants, *Mimosa pudica* and *M. spegazzinii*. The leaves of these plants droop rapidly and the leaflets fold in response to touch stimulus, stock, rain, wind, electric current and sudden change in temperature.

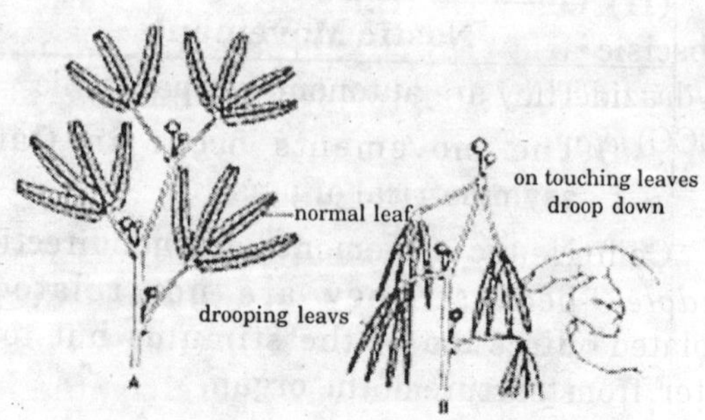

A. Before touch and B. After touch

Fig. 10 *Mimosa pudica* (sensitive plant) showing seismonasty.

Physical Movements

They are also called as *hygroscopic movements*. They are mechanical in nature occurring in dead parts of the plant. Such movements are performed during dispersal of spores, pollen grains and seeds.

Types of Physical Movements

(*i*) **Hydrochasy :** The hygroscopic movement performed due to imbibition of water is called as *hydrochasy e.g.*, movement in the peristomial teeth of moss, elators of *Equisetum etc.*

(*ii*) **Xerochasy :** The hygroscopic movement performed due to loss of water is called xerochasy *e.g.*, movement performed during dehiscence of follicles, pods, and some capsule, elaters of *Marchantia etc.*

GROWTH HORMONES

The physiological activities of plants to a greater extent are regulated by a variety of internally synthesized substances called *hormones*. These hormones provide regulatory effect to the growth of the plants *i.e.,* either promote the growth *or* hamper it, when they are present even in minute quantities.

Growth hormones *or* growth regulators are of two types :

(I) Growth promoters : Auxins, Gibberellins (GA) and Cytokinins.

(II) Growth inhibitors : Ethylene, Abscisic acid (ABA), Morphactins, Maleic hydrazide (MH) and Chlorocholine chloride (CCC), *etc.*

AUXINS

Commonly occurring natural auxin is *Indole-3-acetic acid* or **IAA**. It was first isolated by Kogl in human urine in 1934 and later from higher plants. Several synthetic compounds or growth regulators having auxin-like activities are also known. These synthetic auxins include *Indole butyric acid* (**IBA**), *Dichlorophenoxyacetic acid* (**2, 4 D**), *Trichlorophenoxyacetic acid* (**2, 4-5-T**), and *Indole propionic acid.*

Natural auxin, **IAA**, is synthesized from an amino acid called tryptophan. The IAA is produced in apical meristems and is translocated to other parts. Its movement is always polar and away from apex to other zones even if the position of the organ is inverted. Certain chemicals like *triiodobenzoic acid* (**TIBA**) inhibit the auxin activity. They are called **antiauxins**.

PHYSIOLOGICAL FUNCTIONS OF IAA

(*i*) It induces cell enlargement and longitudinal growth.

(*ii*) It inhibits abscission or shedding of leaves and fruits.

(*iii*) Higher concentrations of IAA induce parthenocarpy.

(*iv*) It induces and promotes growth of adventitious roots.

(*v*) It promotes cell division in the cambium.

(*vi*) It inhibits the growth of lateral buds and accelerates the growth of apical bud. This phenomenon is called **apical dominance**.

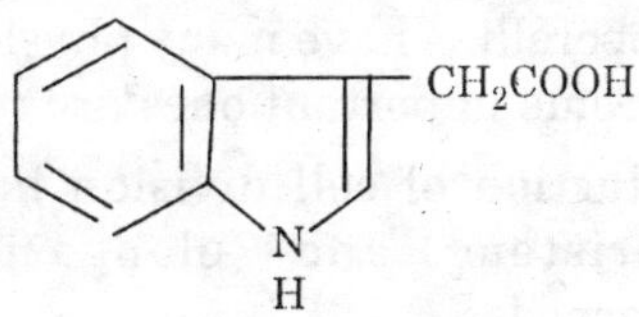

Structure of IAA

GIBBERELLINS

The gibberellins are plant growth hormones which enhance the longitudinal growth of stem when applied to intact plants. However, they do not enhance the growth of isolated plant parts. The presence of meristematic cell is essential for the elongation and growth caused by gibberellins. E. Kurosawa discovered them in 1926 as the active substance produced by fungus

Gibberella fujikuroi (*Syn. Fusarium moniliforme*) responsible for *Bacanae* or "Foolish" disease of rice. This disease is marked by excessive growth in height of infected plants.

MECHANISM OF ACTION

It stimulates cell division in shoot tip. The cell growth is promoted by the increase in the hydrolysis of starch, fructose and sucrose. It further increases wall plasticity. Most of the worker are of the opinion that the effect of gibberellins is indirect since they act by altering the auxin status. In the aleurone layer of barley the gibberellins increase the transcription of genes that code for protease and amylase enzymes. The protease activity produce tryptophan, which is translocated to coleoptile tip where it is converted to IAA.

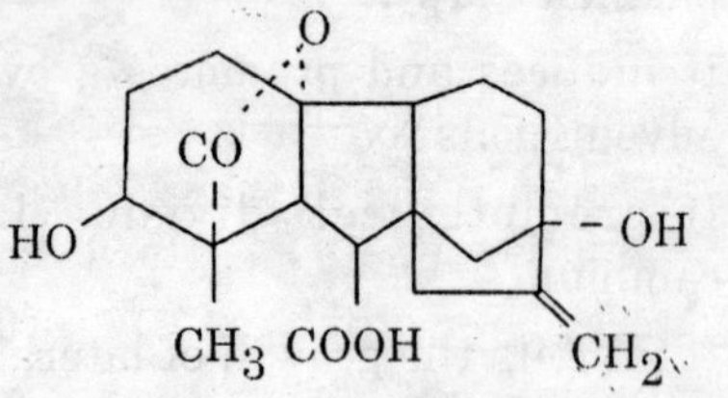

Structure of Gibberellins or Gibberellic acid.

PHYSIOLOGICAL EFFECTS

The gibberellins have many physiological functions. Some important ones are :

(*i*) Induction of cell division in apical meristem and elongation of internodes.

(*ii*) Triggering of cell division in cambium insome decidous trees.

(*iii*) Stimulation of development of parthenocarpic fruits.

(*iv*) Breaking of dormancy in seeds and buds.

(*v*) Induction of synthesis of enzymes like amylase and several other hydrolases.

(*vi*) Induction of flowering in long day plants and a number of cold requiring plants.

CYTOKININS (KINETINS)

The cytokinins are plant growth substances which act primarily on cell division and have little or no effect on extension growth. Cytokinins are compounds derived from a nitrogen containing compound adenine.

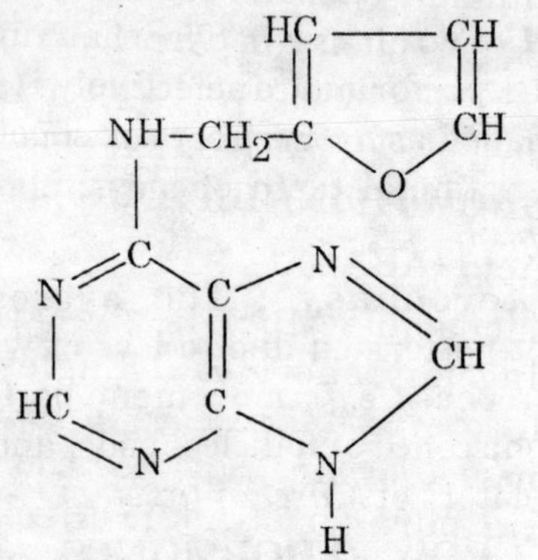

Kinetin (6 Furfuryl aminopurine)

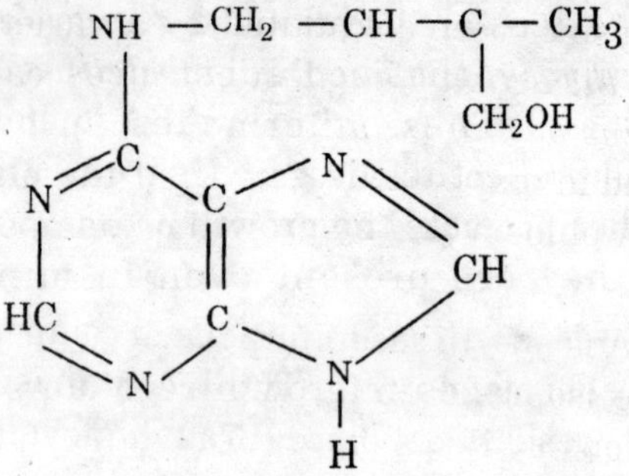

Zeatin

Structure of Various cytokinins

The synthesis of cytokinins occurs in root tips. It is then transported to different parts of the plant through xylem elements. According to Osborne and Black (1964), the movement of CK is polar and basipetal. It moves very slowly.

PHYSIOLOGICAL EFFECTS OF CYTOKININS ON PLANTS

Cytokinins are produced in roots and translocated to aerial parts through xylem. Besides enhancing cell division they prevent senescence of leaves. They interact with auxins to overcome apical dominance.

Hormonal interaction involving cytokinins also play roles in flowering and seed germination processes.

Cytokinins play a part in controlling the initiation of plant organs. In tissue culture, the cells of tobacoo pith form some callus if supplied with nutrients and sugars. However, by varying the balance between auxin and cytokinins it is possible to selectively initiate the development of either roots *or* shoots.

GROWTH INHIBITORS

Abscisic Acid (ABA)

Abscisic acid (ABA) is the growth suppressing phytohormone. Eagles and Wareing discovered its presence in 1936 and used the name *dormin*. But they could not isolate it in pure form. Addicott and his coworkers in 1965 isolated it from cotton fruit and called it *abscisin*. Use of these old names has long since been discontinued. *Abscisic acid opposes the action of auxins, gibberellins and cytokinins within plant body.* ABA is mostly produced in mature leaves and is translocated through phloem and xylem to shoot tips and roots.

ABA is a C-15 sesquiterpene, a compound of three isoprene units. The biosynthesis of ABA probably takes place through mevalonic acid pathway. Most of this hormone is synthesized in leaves and fruits.

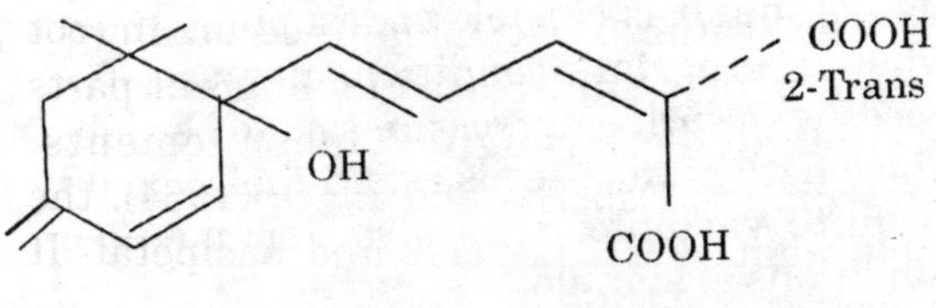

2-Cis Abscissic acid

PHYSIOLOGICAL EFFECTS

Higher concentrations of ABA promotes senescence and abscission of organs; induces dormancy in buds and seeds; and initiates flowering in short-day plants. Recent studies indicate it as the phytohormone responsible for geotropism in roots. It also causes stomatal closure when it is produced in wilting leaves. It therefore contributes to the defense of the plant against water stress conditions.

In certain short day plants like *S. nigrum*, it induces flowering during long days. But in typical short day plants it is ineffective.

ETHYLENE

Ethylene is the smallest phytohormone. It was observed in 1864 that the gas illuminating the streets in German cities, due to leakage in pipes caused leaf fall in the road side shade trees.

Ethylene gas ($CH_2 = CH_2$) is produced in certain plant tissues. Ripening fruits in particular synthesize large quantities of ethylene. It is also produced in leaves, flowers, stems, roots, tubers and seeds.

The ethylene is synthesized from the amino acid, methionine in many plants like apple, cauliflower, tomato *etc*. However, it is also thought to be synthesized from isoamyl alcohol, methional, ethyl acetate *or* glutamate. Its synthesis from glucose via methionine *or* its aldehyde methional occurs in the following manner:

Glucose → Oxaloacetate → Asparate → Homocysteine → Methicnine → Ethylene

$$\text{Methionine} \xrightarrow[NH_3 + CO_2]{\text{FMN, light}} \text{Methional}$$

$$\xrightarrow[CH_3SH\ +\ HCOOH]{\text{Peroxidase } H_2O_2} \text{Ethylene}$$

PHYSIOLOGICAL EFFECTS

It promotes abscission, fruit ripening and transverse cell wall formation. It can break dormancy of several plant organs but inhibits lateral bud growth. It is also involved in epinastic and geotropic movements in plants.

It induces *cellulase* activity leading to promotion of leaf abscission and suppresses the growth of buds in decapitated stem.

Table : 1 Comparison of the Activities of Various Phytohormones

S. No.	Plant Character	Phytohormones Auxins	Gibberellins	Cytokinins	AbscisicAcid
1.	Abscission (Fall of leaves & fruits)	Inhibition	Inhibition	Inhibition	Stimulation
2.	Dormancy of apical buds	No effect	Breaks dormancy	Breaks dormancy	Induces
3.	Apical dominance	Promotes (indirect effect)	Promotes	Inhibits	Inhibits
4.	Seed dormancy	No effect	Suppresses	Suppresses	Induces
5.	Seed germination	No effect	Stimulates	Stimulates	Inhibits
6.	Cell division	Stimulates	Stimulates	Stimulates	Inhibits
7.	Flower initiation in LDPs	Stimulates	Stimulates	No effect	Inhibits
8.	Flower initiation in SDPs	Inhibits	No effect	No effect	Stimulation in few plants
9.	Senescence	Inhibits	Inhibits	Inhibits	Stimulates
10.	Synthesis of hydrolytic enzymes (α-amylase)	No effect	Stimulates	No effect	Inhibits
11.	Gene activity	Stimulates	Stimulates	Stimulates	Inhibits
12.	Parthenocarpy	Stimulates	Stimulates	No effect	No effect
13.	Growth	Promotes	Promotes	Promotes	Inhibits

PHYSIOLOGICAL CHANGES DURING SEED DEVELOPMENT

The seed is a unit of dispersal. Ovule develops into the seed after fertilization. The process begins with a flurry of metabolic activities. Cell divisions begin. Embryo develops. Food reserves are laid down in the endosperm or in the cotyledons of developing embryo. Then all activities stop. Growth of embryo ceases. Many of the cells outside of the embryo die. Water evaporates or is drained away. Seed coat becomes increasingly impermeable to water and oxygen. Metabolic activities are almost reduced to a stand still. At this stage the seed is usually dispersed. It is dry and inactive. Water content of most dry seed is around 10%.

Dry seed is usually referred to as **quiescent** or **dormant. Quiescence** refers to *suppression of embryo growth imposed by factors external to seed*. **Dormancy** refers to *suppression of embryo growth by internal factors* Embryo of a quiescent or dormant seed remains in a state of suspended animation. It is alive without any apparent sign of life. It is capable of resuming growth when appropriate conditions are satisfied. Seeds with such embryos are said to be viable. The length of time seeds retain their viability is quite variable. It is also dependent on conditions of storage.

SEED GERMINATION

(I) Epigeal germination : In this type of germination the cotyledons come above the soil surface into air and light, due to rapid growth and elongation of hypocotyls. The cotyledons are green and make food to be used by stem during growing season. They finally dry off and seedlings become independent *e.g., bean, gourd, castor, cotton, etc.*

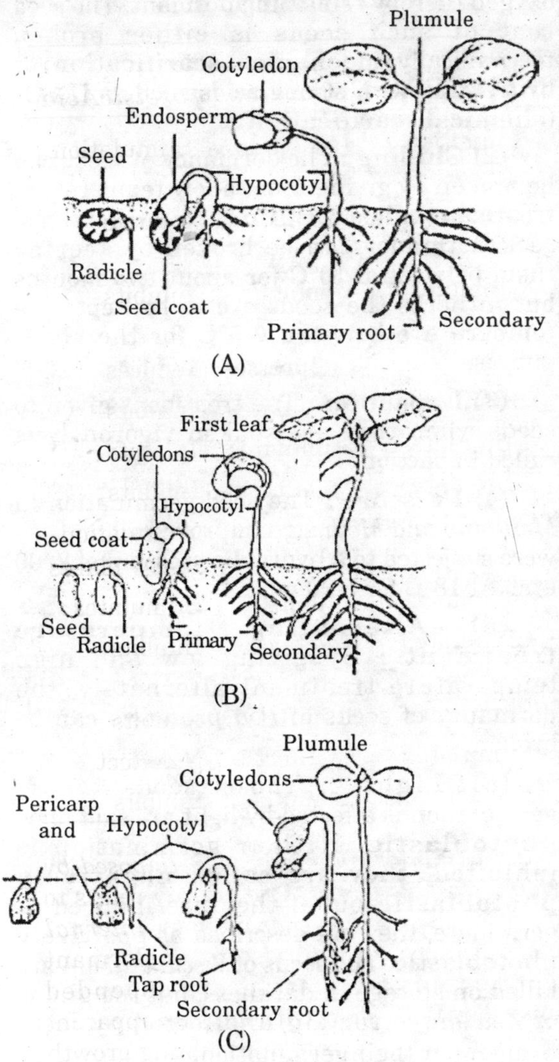

A. Castor Bean Seed B. Bean Seed

C. Sunflower Seed

Fig. 11. Epigeal germination. Stages in the germination of A : castor bean seed; B : bean seed and C : sunflower seed.

(II) Hypogeal germination : In this type, the cotyledons remain in soil or just above the surface. Here the epicotyl elongates, pushing plumule upwards. Cotyledons do not turn green and gradually dry up and fall off *e.g., pea, mango, groundnut etc.*

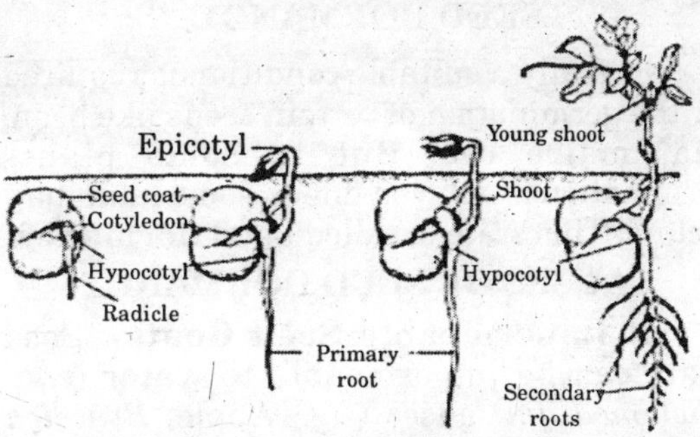

Fig. 12. Successive stages of hypogeal germination of dicotyledonous exalbuminous seed of pea.

FACTORS FOR SEED GERMINATION

Essential factors for seed germination are :

(1) Moisture : Initially the reserve food is high and so the protoplasm is highly concentrated and no vital activity is possible at this concentration. Adequate water absorption converts insoluble stored food into soluble form. This food is transferred to growing parts.

- It brings about activation of dormant protoplasm. It is necessary for respiration as it is the mode of transfer of oxygen.
- Moisture softens seed coat and testa. Seed swells up and embryo breaks through softened seed coat and comes out easily.

(2) Oxygen : As the seed germinates it is not in the position to synthesises of its own food and so is dependent upon reserved food. This is metabolized through respiration which required oxygen. So oxygen is required in large quantities. For this reason the seeds which are deeply sown, fail to germinate.

(3) Temperature : There is a particular range of temperature for each seed beyond which it does not germinate.

(4) Light : Germination of a number of seeds is favoured by light except in onion while some are totally indifferent to the effect of light *e.g., maize, bean* etc.

SEED DORMANCY

Normally a suitable condition is required for the germination of certain seeds like bean, pea, maize etc. But in some plants germination is delayed due to some inhibitory factors. This state is called **seed dormancy.**

CAUSES OF SEED DORMANCY

(1) Impermeable Seed Coats : Seed coats can be impermeable to water *(e.g., Chenopodium)* gases (*e.g.*, Apple, *Brassica alba*) or chemicals (*e.g., Xanthium*).

(2) Excess Salts : They cause dormancy in seeds of *Atriplex*.

(3) After-Ripening : The embryo is mature but the seed requires a period for gaining the ability to germinate *e.g.,* Oat, Barley, Wheat etc.

(4) Immature Embryo : In *Eranthis hiemalis* the embryo is immature at the time of seed shedding. Dormancy is the period required for embryo to develop fully.

(5) Tough Seed Coats : *e.g., Capsella, Lepidium etc.*

(6) Inhibitors : Ferulic acid present in Tomato juice does not allow seeds to germinate. Other inhibitor are ABA (most common), secondary plant products like phenolic inhibitors and cyanogenic inhibitors *e.g.,* ferulic acid. They may occur in seed coats (*Cucurbita,* endosperm (*Iris*) or embryo.

METHODS FOR BREAKING THE SEED DORMANCY

(1) Scarification : Seeds with hard seed coats may remain impermeable to water and oxygen thereby remaining dormant. The seed coat of such seeds is either broken mechanically (**mechanical scarification**) or by treating with strong acids such as H_2SO_4 (**chemical scarification**).

(2) Chilling : The dormancy of seeds can be broken by giving them a low temperature treatment called **Chilling**. In conifers, the seed dormancy can be broken by keeping them between 5-10°C for about two months but in herbs the seeds are to be kept at a temperature between 0-5°C for the above purpose.

(3) Impaction : The treatment given to seeds when they are shaken vigorously is called impaction.

(4) Pressure : The seed germination in *Melilotus* and *Medicago* improved when they were subjected to a hydraulic pressure of 2000 atm. At 18°C for 5-20 mts.

(5) Alternating temperature treatment : By giving low and high temperature treatment alternately, the dormancy of seeds of *Poa pratensis* can be broken.

(6) Light : Those seeds whose germination is affected by light are said to be **photoblastic.** If their germination is inhibited, they are called **negatively photoblastic** but if they are induced to germinate, they are described as **positively photoblastic.** The seeds of *Viscum album* are killed on storage in darkness, but the grains of *Zea mays* remain unaffected by light throughout their germination.

Questions From Previous Year's Papers

Q. 1. Answer the following in about 150 words each :

(a) What are plant regulators? Describe their mode of action and importance in agriculture.

(b) Explain polyploidy and its applications in crop improvement.

Q. 2. Describe the following in about 50 words each :

(a) Hormones and phermones.

(b) Endocrine and exocrine glands.

Q. 4. Explain about the causes of seed dormancy. Suggest the methods of breaking seed dormancy.

8. DISEASES OF VARIOUS CROPS AND ITS CONTROL

PLANT DISEASES

The term disease refers to the disorders produced in the body by the harmful physiological changes. The normal physiological process (or chemical reaction) can be altered or inhibited by a causal agent, such as fungus, bacterium or a virus.

Disease has been defined as a malfunction of a process that caused by continuous irritation. It naturally results in some sufferings while producing distinctive symptoms. Diseases result in loss of substantial amount of plant products in the field and/or in store. There are records of enormous loss of plant and animal lives due to plant diseases in different parts of the world. Famine in England and Ireland in 1845 is a famous example. It was due to late blight of potato. The economic crisis in Sri Lanka during 1871-1893 was due to attack of rust in coffee plantations and Bengal famine in 1943 was due to leaf spot disease of paddy. These and many other examples force us to realise the importance of understanding plant diseases and their control.

Stages in Disease Development

The process of infection and development of disease involve many stages. This chain of events is called disease cycle. The main stages of the disease cycle are described as under :

I. Inoculation

A disease develops when an inoculum comes in contact with the host. This process is called inoculation. Inoculum may be a bacterial cell, virus, mycoplasma, nematode, fungal hypha, oospore, etc.

II. Pre-penetration Changes

The spores of the pathogen, after landing on the surface of the host, germinate and form one or more filamentous germ tubes. Germination is affected by a number of factors, such as temperature, moisture, humidity, pH, oxygen concentration and non-pathogenic micro-organisms present on the surface of the host. Besides these, certain chemicals secreted on the surface of the roots (rhizosphere) and leaves (phyllosphere) inhibit the germination process.

III. Post-penetration Changes

Once the pathogen has entered the host, it secretes substances like enzymes, toxins and growth regulators. These substances bring out physiological, anatomical and morphological changes in the host.

Enzymes like cutinase, pectinases, ligninases, polygalacturonase and cellulytases secreted by the pathogen are helpful in breaking the cell wall, thus facilitating its entry into the host. Toxins like alternaric acid, fusaric acid, colletonin, periconin and pircularin are secreted by fungi. These are poisonous proteins or protein-like substances.

GENERAL SYMPTOMS OF PLANT DISEASES

The biochemical changes in the host tissue caused by infection finally change morphological and anatomical characteristics. These visible changes are known as disease symptoms. Some of the symptoms like chlorosis, necrosis, galls, curls, wilting, etc., are common to many diseases whereas others like smuts, rusts and mildew are specific.

On the basis of the morphological and anatomical changes occurring after infection, the symptoms are broadly classified into following categories.

I. Necrosis

The pathogen, after entering the host, secretes some enzymes and toxins which kill the host tissue. This is known as necrosis and the dead tissues as necrotic areas. The pathogens which derive their nutrition from such dead tissue are called necroptrophs. Necrosis may be caused by fungal as well as bacterial pathogens.

Necrotic areas may appear as spots (*e.g.*, leaf spot of mango caused by *Xanthomonas campestris*) or stripes (*e.g.*, stripe disease of barley caused by *Helminthosporium*).

II. Canker

These are dead and corky areas with definite margins occurring on the stems, branches, twigs or fruits of woody trees. Example–citrus canker caused by *Xanthomonas citri*.

III. Scab

Scabs are rough, crust-like lesions developed on the infected surface. These are more or less circular in outline. Examples–apple scab caused by *Venturia inaequalis*.

IV. Rusts

The rusts appear as small pustules of red, brown, black or yellow colour on stem or leaf epidermis of the host. Examples–black or stem rust of wheat caused by *Puccinia graminis tritici*, rust of gram caused by *Uromyces ciceris-arietini*.

V. Mildews

In mildew, the mycelium and spores of pathogen (fungus) are seen as a whitish growth on the host surface. When the tangled mycelium, sporangiophores and sporangia appear like a downy growth, it is called downy mildew examples–downy mildew of jowar caused by *Sclerospora graminicola*, downy mildew of maize caused by *S. maydis*. On the other hand, when fungal mycelium along with conidia and conidiophores appear as dull or white powder, it is known as powdery mildew. Examples–powdery mildew of peas caused by *Erysiphe polygoni*, powdery mildew of cucurbits caused by *Erysiphe cichoracearum*.

VI. Galls

These are globose or irregular outgrowths produced on the infected parts of the host. Smaller galls are called warts or tubercles whereas large ones are known as excrescence. Examples–wart disease of potato caused by *Synchytrium endobioticum*, stem galls of coriander caused by *Protomyces macrosporus*.

VII. Curls

Some pathogens cause abnormal increase (hypertrophy) in the size of infected cells of the leaf. As a result the diseased leaf becomes curled, arched or distorted. This disease is known as curl disease. Example–leaf curl of papaya caused by virus.

VIII. Floral Abnormalities

In some diseases the infected floral parts become abnormally enlarged, green, fleshy and leaf-like.

IX. Blights

Blight is characterized by rapid killing of leaves, stem and flowers. It gives a burnt appearance. Examples–leaf blight of wheat caused by *Alternaria tenuis*, early blight of potato caused by *Alternaria solani*.

X. Rots

Softening, discolouration and often disnitegration of the succulent plant tissues as a result of fungal or bacterial infection is known as rot. Rot causing pathogens may affect any plant organ like root (root rot), stem (stem rot), fruit (fruit rot), etc. Examples—stem rot of paddy caused by *Sclerotium oryzae,* fruit rot of cucurbits, caused by *Pythium aphanidermatum.*

XI. Damping Off

This symptom is caused by soil inhabiting fungi. The pathogen attacks the base of the stem near the soil surface and due to disintegration of tissue of the basal portion of the stem or seedling, the plant topples down. Example–damping off of seedlings caused by species of *Pythium, Sclerotinia, Fusarium, Rhizoctonia,* etc.

XII. Chlorosis

This is a very common symptom causing the discolouration or yellowing of leaves. Chlorosis is caused by destruction of chlorophyll in the cells or failure of infected cells to form chlorophyll. A variety of fungi, bacteria and viruses are known to caused chlorosis.

XIII. Smuts

It refers to sooty charcoal-like mass of spores of fungal pathogens. Smut spores usually develop on the floral organs of the host. Examples–loose smut of wheat caused by *Ustilago tritici, covered* smut of barley caused by *Ustilago hordei.*

Apple Scab

Mildew

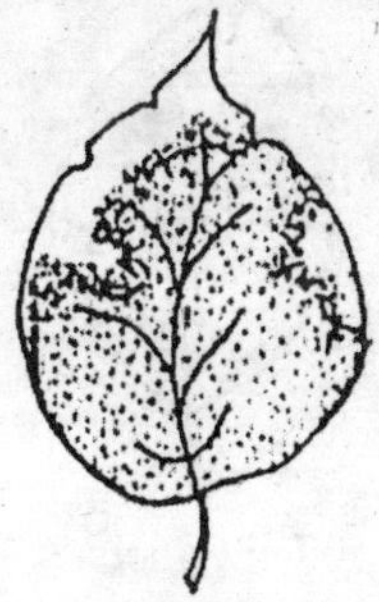

Necrosis

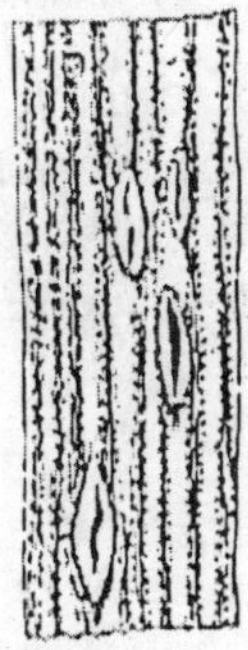

Rust

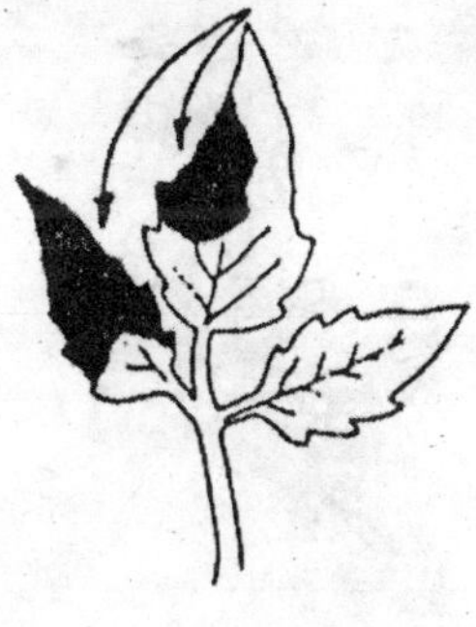

Leaf Blight

Canker

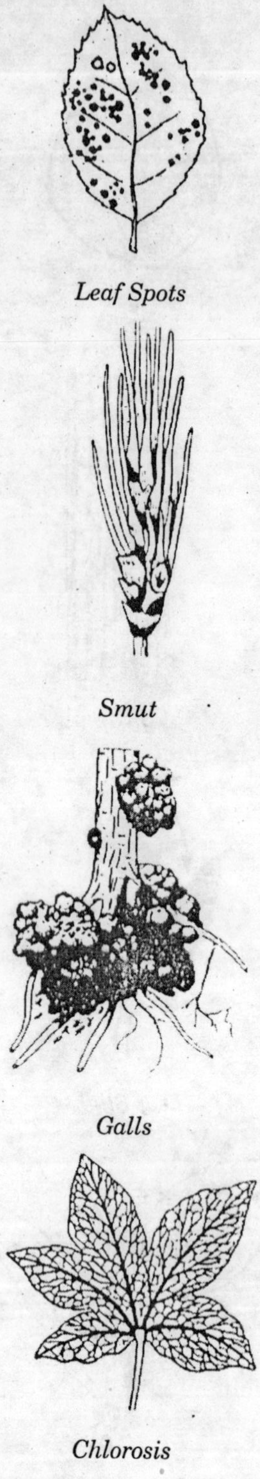

Fig. 1. Some common plant diseases.

IMPORTANT DISEASES OF VEGETABLE CROPS

(*i*) Cole Crops

Cabbage	Clubrot, yellow cabbage, Black rot.
Cauliflower	Damping off, Black leg, Black spot, Black rot, Bacterial soft rot, Brown rot.

(*ii*) Fruit Vegetable

Brinjal	Phomopsis blight, Fusarium wilt, Damping off, Bacterial wilt.
Chillies	Damping off, Fusarium wilt, Fruit rot, Leaf spot, Bacterial leaf spot.
Tomato	Damping off, Early blight, Fruit rot, Fusarium wilt, Bacterial wilt, Bacterial canker, Bacterial spot, Bacterial speek, Bacterial soft rot.
Okra	Dampring off, Powdery mildew, Fusarium wilt, Yellow Vein Mosaic.

(*iii*) Cucurbits

Cucurbits	Powdery mildew, Downey mildew, Anthracnose, Fusarium wilt, Fruit rot, scab, Bacterial wilt, Bacterial soft rot.

(*iv*) Beans and Peas

	Cowpea Cercospora leaf spot, Seedling mortality, Stem rot, Pod rot, Anthracnose, Powdery mildew, Bacterial blight.
French bean	Anthracnose, Ashy stem blight, Bacterial blight.
Peas	Powdery mildew, Downey mildew, Fusarium wilt, Bacterial blight.
Lima bean	Downey mildew.
Indian bean/ cluster bean	As per cowpea and French bean.

(v) Bulbous, Tuber and Root Vegetables

Onion	Downey mildew, Onion smut, Purple blotch, Bacterial soft rot.
Potato	Early blight, Late blight, Black scruf, wart, Bacterial brown rot, soft rot, scab.
Carrot	Cercospora blight or leaf spot, Bacterial blight and Root scab, Bacterial soft rot.
Radish	Damping off, White rust.
Turnip	Powdery mildew, Downey mildew.
Beet root	Downey mildew, Damping off, Selerotium root rot.
Turmeric	Soft rot, Leaf spot, Bacterial wilt.
Ginger	Soft rot, Leaf spot, Bacterial wilt.

Table 1. Some viral diseases, their insect vectors and prominent symptoms

Disease	*Vector*	*Symptoms*
Potato leaf roll	Aphids *(Myzus persicae)*	Inward rolling of lower leaves, they become, thick, leathery and upright.
Potato rugose mosaic	Aphids (*Myzus persicae)*	Wrinkling, puckering of leaves, leaflet margins rolled downward, growth stunted.
Tomato leaf roll	Whitefly *(Bemisia tabaci)*	Stunting of the plants downward rolling and crinkling of the leaves.
Tomato spotted wilt virus	Thrips *(Thrips tabaci, Frankliniella occidentalis, F. fusca Scirtothrips dorsalis*	Browning of leaves, concentric circular spots on fruits; stunted plant growth.
Little leaf of brinjal	Leaf hopper *(Hishimonus physicits)*	Leaf size is reduced considerably which gives "rosette' appearance.
Chilli leaf curl	Whitefly (*Bemisia tabaci*)	Abaxial and adaxial curling of the leaves, stunted growth, flowers and fruits are few and small in size.
Melon mosaic	Aphids (*Myzus persicae*)	Tips of the runners and shoots from the crown protude above the ground. Leaves are smaller and malformed. Only a few fruits term with abnormal appearance.
Pumpkin mosaic virus	Aphids (*Aphids gossypii, A. craccivora, Myzus persicae*	Leaves show vein-clearing and vein-banding. Size of leaves and fruits is reduced.

Table 2. Some Important Fungal Diseases of Economically Important Plants

Pathogen	Host	Disease
I. Myxomycetes		
1. *Plasmodiophora brassicae*	*Brassica oleraceae* var. *capitata* (Cabbage, Patta Gobhi) Fam. Cruciferae	Club root disease Finger and toe disease White rust of Crucifers
II. Phycomycetes		
2. *Albugo candida* = *Cystopus candidus*	*Brassica campestris* (Mustard; Sarson) *Raphanus sativus* (Radish; Mooli) and other members of Fam. Cruciferae	Downy mildew
3. *Peronospora arborescens*	*Papaver somniferum* (Poppy : Afim) Fam. Papaveraceae)	Damping off
4. *Phytophthora infestans*	*Solanum tuberosum* (Potato; Aaloo) Fam. Solanaceae	Late blight of Potato
5. *Sclerospora graminicola*	*Pennisetum typhoides* (Perl Millet; Bajra) Fam. Poaceae	Green ear disease of Bajra
6. *Sclerospora sorghii*	*Sorghum vulgare* (Sorghum; Jowar) Fam. Poaceae	Downy Mildew of Sorghum
III. Ascomycetes		
7. *Claviceps microcephala*	*Pennisetum typhoides* (Pearl millet; Bajra) Fam. Poaceae	Ergot of Bajra
8. *Erysiphe cichoracearum*	Members of family Cucurbitaceae	
IV. Basidiomycetes		
9. *Puccinia graminis tritici*	*Triticum aestivum* (Wheat; Gehoon) Fam. Poaceae	Stem rust or black rust of Wheat
10. *Puccinia glumarum*	*Triticum aestivum* (Wheat; Gehoon) Fam. Poaceae.	Stripe rust or yellow rust of Wheat
11. *Puccinia triticina*	*Triticum aestivum* (Wheat; Gehoon) Fam. Poaceae.	Leaf rust or brown rust of wheat
12. *Ustilago hordei*	*Hordeum vulgare* (Barley; Joan) Fam. Poaceae	Covered smut of Barley
13. *Ustilago hordei*	*Hordeum vulgare* (Barley; Joan) Fam. Poaceae	Loose smut of Barley.
V. Deuteromycetes		
14. *Alternaria solani*	*Solanum tuberosum* (Potato; Aaloo) Fam. Solanaceae	Early blight of Potato
15. *Cercospora personata*	*Arachis hypogaea* (Ground nut; Moongphali) Fam. Papilionaceae	Tikka disease of Groundnut

Pathogen	Host	Disease
16. *Colletotrichum falcatum*	*Saccharum officinarum* (Sugarcane; Ganna) Fam. Poaceae	Red rot of Sugarcane
17. *Fusarium udum*	*Cajanus cajan* (Pigeon pea; Arhar) Fam. Papilionaceae	Wilt of Arhar
18. *Fusarium vasinfectum*	*Gossypium* sp. (Cotton; Kapas) Fam. Malvaceae	Wilt of Cotton
19. *Helminthosporium oryzae*	*Oryza sativa* (Rice; Dhaan) Fam. Poaceae	Sesame leaf spot or brown leaf spot of Rice

Table 3. Some Important Bacterial Diseases of Economically Important Plants

Pathagen	Host	Disease
1. *Corynebacterium tritici*	*Triticum aestivum* (Wheat; Gehoon) Fam. Poaceae	Tondu or bacterial ear rot
2. *Pseudomonas mangiferae-indiceae*	*Mangifera indica* (Mango; Aam) Fam. Anacardiaceae	Bacterial leaf spot
3. *Pseudomonas rubrilineans*	*Saccharum officinarum* (Sugarcane; Ganna) Fam. Poaceae	Red stripe of Sugarcane
4. *Pseudomonas solanacearum*	*Lycopersicum esculentum* (Tobacco; Tambaku) Fam. Solanaceae	Bacterial wilt of Tomato
5. *Pseudomonas solanacearum*	*Nicotiana tabacum* (Tobacco; Tambaku) Fam. Solanaceae	Bacterial wilt of Tobacco
6. *Xanthomonas campestris* var. *armoriaceae*	*Brassica oleraceae* var. *captitata* (Cabbage; Patta gobhi) Fam. Cruciferae	Bacterial leaf spot of Cabbage
7. *Xanthomonas malvacearum*	*Gossypium sp.* (Cotton; Kapas) Fam. Malvaceae	Black arm or angular leaf spot of Cotton
8. *Xanthomonas oryzae*	*Oryza sativa* (Rice; Dhaan. Chawal) Fam. Poaceae	Bacterial blight of Rice
9. *Xanthomonas vasculorum*	*Saccharum officinarum* (Sugarcane; Ganna) Fam. Poaceae	Gummosis of Sugarcane
10. *Xanthomonas vesicatoria*	*Capsicum annum* (Chillies; Hari mirch) Fam. Solanaceae	Bacterial leaf spot of Chillies

Table 4. Some Important Viral Diseases of Economically Important Plants

Host	Disease
1. *Abelmoschus esculentus* (Lady's finger; Bhindi) Fam. Malvaceae	Yellow vein mosaic of Bhindi
2. *Arachis hypogaea* (Ground nut; Moongphali) Fam. Papilionaceae	Rosette disease of Groundnut
3. *Elettaria cardamomum* (Cardamom; Chhoti elaichi) Fam. Zingiberaceae	Chirke

Host	Disease
4. *Gossypium* sp. (Cotton; Kapas) Fam. Malvaceae	Stenosis
5. *Musa* sp. (Banana; Kela) Fam. Musaceae	Bunchy top of Banana
6. *Pyrus malus* (Apple; Sev) Fam. Rosaceae	Mosaic of Apple
7. *Saccharum officinarum* (Sugarcane; Ganna) Fam. Poaceae	Grassy shoot of Sugarcane

CLASSIFICATION OF PLANT DISEASES

Various classifications of plant diseases are available. These have been based on different criteria such as severity of infection and its geographical distribution, nature of causal organism, mode of primary infection and perpetuation and extent of infection on host.

A brief outline of some important classifications of plant diseases is given below.

I. Classification based on severity of infection and geographical distribution

On this basis, diseases have been classified into following four categories.

1. Endemic diseases : These are the diseases occurring more or less regularly from year to year in a particular region or locality in mild or severe form.

2. Epidemic diseases : These diseases occur in a severe form particularly in all regions where the crop is grown. Thus, epidemic diseases are widespread (while endemic are restricted to an area).

3. Sporadic diseases : Such diseases break out occasionally and at different locations. Sporadic diseases may not always be destructive.

4. Pandemic diseases : Diseases which occur all over the world and cause large scale destruction of crops are said to be pandemic.

II. Classification based on nature of causal organism

On this basis diseases are classified into following two categories :

1. Infectious or parasitic diseases : These diseases are caused by living parasites. Thus for infectious or parasitic diseases to occur, contact or association of pathogen with the host is essential. They can be easily transmitted from one pathogen to another. Depending upon the pathogen, these diseases have been further classified into viral, bacterial, mycoplasmal or fungal diseases.

2. Non-infections or non-parasitic diseases : Such diseases are not caused by any living agent, hence, they remain non-infectious and are not transmitted from one diseased plant to another, Non-infectious diseases may be caused by improper conditions of soil and air, unfavourable temperature, oxygen concentration and atmospheric humidity, air pollution, deficiency or excesses of minerals in the soil and unfavourable soil pH. All these factor cause physiological disorders in the plants which appear in the form of diseases.

III. Classification based on mode of primary infection and perpetuation

On the basis of mode of primary infection and perpetuation, diseases have been classified into following three categories.

1. Soil-borne diseases : Pathogens of such diseases survive in the soil in the form of spores, mycelium or rhizomorph. Under favourable conditions the pathogens infect roots either at seedling or an adult stage of the plant.

2. Air-borne diseases : Spores of many fungi (*e.g.,* rusts and mildews) survive in air. Such pathogens are easily disseminated by wind and infect shoot of the plant.

3. Seed borne diseases : Some pathogens survive as dormant mycelium or spores in the seeds and other propagative organs of the host plants.

CONTROL OF PLANT DISEASES

Control of plant diseases is essential to prevent qualitative and economic losses. One of the major difference in controlling plant and human diseases is that the plants are generally treated as populations and the aim is to protect the entire crop rather than an individual plant (except for some ornamental plants and trees), whereas in human and animal diseases care is taken to save each individual. In nature pathogens of many diseases are present, hence to make the programme cost effective steps are taken to control more than one disease at a time.

Plant disease control measures can be classified into following three categories :

(1) Prophylactic measures,

(2) Curative measures, and

(3) Biological measures.

I. Prophylactic Measures

These are preventive measures aimed to protect the host from exposure to pathogens and environmental conditions favourable to disease development. Some prophylactic measures are listed below.

1. Quarantine : It is a legal control on import and export of diseased plants and plant parts to prevent the spread of diseases and pests. All countries of the world have their own Plant Quarantine Acts which allow import of propagating materials (such as seeds, tubers, bulbs, rhizomes, etc.) only when it is accompanied by a certificate from the Agriculture Ministry of the exporting country that the material is pathogen free. Pathogen reaches new areas along with infected seeds, fruits, vegetables, etc., therefore, food stuff should always be imported from disease free areas. In India there are 16 quarantine centres along various sea, road and air routes where all living/dormant plant materials are checked.

2. Eradication of alternate host : Many pathogenic fungi complete their life cycle on two host (*e.g.*, wheat rusts) and the alternate host provides shelter to the pathogen under unfavourable conditions. An effective method of controlling the pathogen would be, therefore, to eradicate the alternate host, so that the pathogen does not complete its life cycle.

3. Crop rotation : Growing a particular crop year after year in the same field increases the chances of infection. Spores and mycelia of the pathogens present in the soil are good inoculum for the infection of the subsequent crops. If the same crop is grown continuously for many years, the soil becomes heavily infested with the pathogen and it is rather impossible to get disease free crop in such fields.

However, if an alternate crop is grown in the field the chances of survival of the pathogen are reduced significantly (due to absence of suitable host) and next time when main crop is sown, infection is usually insignificant.

4. Chemical prophylaxins : A variety of compounds of sulphur, mercury, arsenic, zinc and copper are used to control plant diseases. Majority of these compounds protect the above ground part of the plant. Some of these chemicals are protective in nature, *i.e.*, they are usually effective only in the plant area to which they have been applied and are not translocated in the plant body. A few are systemic, *i.e.*, they are translocated to different body parts. Such chemicals besides being preventive are also therapeutic, *i.e.*, they from a protective cover on the plant surface and do not allow the pathogen the grow on the plant.

II. Curative Measures

These measures involve treatment of individual plants after the appearance of disease symptoms. Curative measures involve physical and chemical therapy of diseased plants and their eradication.

BIOLOGICAL MEASURES OF PEST CONTROL

Chemicals used as pesticides often produce harmful effects on living organisms. It has, therefore, become necessary to find alternatives to these chemicals which do not produce undesirable effects. Biological control by using plant or animal materials has been found useful in controlling many harmful pests. Some of these are mentioned below.

I. Biological Control of Weeds and Bioherbicides

It is practically impossible to manually remove the weeds in a crop field. Use of chemicals as weedicides with selective action on unwanted plants alone was itself a great discovery. But this too was not without its harmful effects. These chemicals if not used in appropriate doses may even harm the crop or may even stimulate the growth of weeds themselves. A search was then made for alternative to chemical weedicides. It was found that certain living organisms such as insects, micro-organisms, etc., are useful as weedicides. The insects which have selective feeding habits and micro-organisms causing diseases only on specific weeds and kill them could be very useful as pesticides. The insects to be used as bioherbicide must be thoroughly tested for its host specificity before being put to commercial use. In India and Australia, prodigious spread of prickly pear *(Opuntia)* was controlled by introduction of cochineal insects *(Cactoblastis cactorum)*.

The first bioherbicides, called *de vine*, is being commercially used since 1981. It is a mycoherbicide based on fungus *Phytophthora palmivra*. It controls the growth of milkweed vines *(Morrenia odorata)* in citrus orchards. Another mycoherbicide called *collego* has been developed from conidia of fungus *Colletortichum gloeosporioides*.

II. Bioinsecticides

The most suitable insecticide should show following characteristics.

(1) It should completely control only the specific or target organism,

(2) It must be biodegradable, non-persistent, non-toxic and,

(3) It should be cost effective.

None of the chemical pesticides being used presently meet these qualities. Hence, like bioherbicides, a search was conducted to identify organisms which could be used as bioinsecticides. The following are some of the biological methods of control.

1. Pathogens, parasites and predators : This method of insect control consists of use of other insects, diseases, parasites or predators. The commonest example is the control of aphids (homopterous insects) by the introduction of ladybug or praying mantis (*Mantis*).

Another bioinsecticide, based on mutant strains of bacterium *Bacillus thuringiensis* (BT) has been successfully tested on insects affecting cotton, maize, cabbage, sunflower, safflower and pigeon pea.

Table 5. Some Microbial Insecticides

	Target insects	*Biocontrol agents*
	I. Fungi	
1.	Glasshouse white fly *(Trialeurodes vaporaviorum)*	*Aschersonia aleyrodis* (Aseranija)
2.	Range of insects	*Beaveria bassiana* (Boverin, Boverol)
3.	Citrus rust mite	*Hirsutella thompsonii* (Mycar)
4.	Range of insect	*Metarhizium anisopliae* (Metaquino, Metabiol)
5.	Lepidopteran insects	*Nomuraea rileyi*
6.	Range of insects	*Verticillium lecanii* (Vertalec Mycotal)
	II. Bacteria	
1.	Range of insects and mites	*Bacillus thuringiensis* (Dipel, Thuricide, Novabac, etc.)
	III. Virus	
1.	Boll worms	Heliothis nuclear (Elcar) Polyhedrosis virus

2. Sterilization strategy : This is a method where the insect itself is used for its control. The screw worm *Cochliomyia hominivorax* was eliminated by releasing sterile male insect (produced by irradiation) at the time of mating. The natural fertile population was greatly reduced by this technique.

3. Insect hormones : The insect hormones have also been found useful in controlling insects. Pheromones are hormones with such a potentiality. These are the chemicals which transmit information from one individual to another of the same species. Pheromones are useful in sending signals to individuals to come together for sexual activities, etc.

If the mating behaviour or sexual activities could be controlled by using pheromones, population size of these insects can be reduced. Pheromones which attract males of appropriate species are secreted by females. If the traps are made by using synthetic analogs of female pheromones, the males are attracted and could be eventually eliminated. The males are now not available for reproduction. This has been found useful in controlling the population of gypsy moth.

In another case, molting hormone ecdysone and the juvenile hormone have been used to control insect population. Molting or shedding of insect cuticle at regular intervals is required for early growth. Juvenile hormone should be present in the early stages to prevent early maturation. If this hormone is given at a later stage, the insects get transformed into giant larvae and immature adults which die quickly. Thus, application of juvenile hormones at unsuitable times causes death of insect pests.

Male flour beeltes have special glands which produce ethylquinone. This inhibits egg laying in females. Hence, ethylquinone is useful as a population control pheromone.

4. Natural insecticides : Natural insecticides are extracted from plants and sometimes from micro-organisms also. Such insecticides have low toxicity for animals and are not injurious to organisms in the food chain.

Romans and Chinese are known to have used natural insecticides in the past. The Chinese are reported to be the first to find out the insecticidal properties of rotenones present in the roots of *Derris elliptica.*

Alkaloids like nicotine from tobacco (tambaku; *Nacotiana* spp.) and pyrethrum and cinerin from pyrethrum inflorescence *(Chrysanthemum cinerifalium)* have been used as plant insecticides. Pyrethrin is an important ingredient of preparations used against a wide range of insect pests, as mosquito coils, fly sprays and aerosols.

Neem (margosa; *Azadirachta indica*) is considered to be one of the most useful nature insecticides. Biologically active chemicals have been isolated from its oil, seeds, bark and leaves. Azadirachtin and other limonoids such as meliantiol and salanin are very effective against insects, even in minute quantities. Azadirachtin repels insects (repellant), inhibits their feeding and affects their hormonal balance. It also affects metamorphosis of several insect larvae and thereby, prevents the increase of new insect population. Neem is known to resist more than 200 species of insects, mites and nematodes.

INTEGRATED PEST MANAGEMENT (IPM)

This involves a variety of pest control methods employed together in a way that there is less dependence on chemical pesticides and greater application of biological control methods.

Some simple methods like soil conditioning, to rotation and improved sanitation are known to reduce pest problems.

Another method of protection of crops from pests is the starvation. A target crop is grown away from the major crop so that insects are attracted to the former and are thus kept away from the useful or major crop. Pest attracting crop may also be mixed planted with the major crop to reduce the concentration on the former.

Besides these, chemicals may also be sprayed at the same time after desirable control is obtained by biological methods. A comparatively better method of ultra-low volume spraying is now used. This consists of spraying a very small but most effective concentration of chemical pesticide. Such a low amount does not cause pollution which is a major harm caused by chemical pesticides.

PESTICIDES

Pesticides are the substances used for killing animals and plant pests. A pest is an organism that causes an epidemic disease associated with high mortality. Hence, pests are harmful to man physically and also to his crops causing economic losses. Pests, therefore, include bacteria, fungi, nematodes, insects, etc. Even the weeds are now being considered as pests. Each pesticide is given a name starting with the pest that it kills and ending into 'cide' (killer). Thus, a pesticide for killing bacteria is termed bacteriocide, for fungi–fungicide and so on. Since all pests are living organisms, therefore, pesticides could be more effectively placed under a broader category 'biocides'–killer of living organisms.

Pesticides are substances which kill certain living organisms. These are broadly categorised as follows on the basis of organisms killed by them.

(1) Bacteriocides,

(2) Fungicides,

(3) Herbicides,

(4) Weedicides,

(5) Insecticides,

(6) Nematicides, and

(7) Rodenticides.

Pesticides are required for protecting the crops and thus reducing commercial and economic losses. About 30% of the agricultural productivity is estimated to have been lost due to pests and diseases. Pesticides have been in use since long. DDT, an important pesticide came into use during World War. II. So also 2, 4 D (2, 4 Dichloro phenoxy acetic acid–a herbicide) was being very widely used at the same time.

1. Classes of Pesticides

Following are some of the major classes of pesticides based on their chemical structure.

1. Organochlorines : These are chlorinated organic compounds. They are lipophilic and thus, have great affinity for fatty animal tissues. Some commonly used organochlorines are **DDT** (dichloro-diphenyl trichloroethane), **BHC** (benzene hexachloride), **aldrin, dieldrin, endrin, endosulphan**, etc.

2. Organophosphates : These are organic esters of phosphoric, triphosphoric and other phosphoric acids. They affect nervous system very severely. Some of the organophosphates commonly used in India are **malathion** (one of the active ingradient of Flit), **parathion, fenitrothion**, etc.

3. Carbamates : These are organic esters of carbanic acid. They are structurally similar to acetyl choline–a natural chemical which is a neurotransmitter. Hence, these show a great affinity for an enzyme acetylcholine esterase. Some of the common carbamates include **carbofuran** (commercially) known as Furadan), **propoxur** (Baygon) and **aldicarb** (Temik). All these carbamates are effective insecticides and their derivatives are also used as herbicides (*e.g.*, phenylcarbamates) and fungicides (dithiocarbamates).

4. Pyrethoids : These are the derivatives of a chemical called **pyrethrin**. It is obtained from an annual plant *Chrysanthemum cinerarifolium* (fam. Compositae). The flowers are the main source of pyrethrum of commerce. Highest pyrethrin contents occur in inflorescence when in full bloom.

5. Triazines : These are the derivatives of urea. They are used as herbicides in the control of weeds in cotton, tea and tobacco plantations. The common triazines include atrazine, simazine, etc.

Degradations of Different Chemicals in the Soil

There are a large number of agrochemicals available in the market–chemical fertilizers (phosphate and nitrates), pesticides, insecticides, fungicides, and defoliants. Many of the organopesticide (that include insecticides, herbicides, and fungicides) are: halogenated-hydrocarbons (aldrin, dieldrin, DDT, chlordane, heptachlor, endrin, and lindane); organophosphorus (malathion, parathion, diazinon); organosulphur; carbamates (carbaryl, aldicarb, cabofuran); and phenol-based (2, dichloro-phenol (2, 4-D); 2, 4, 5-trichlorophenoxy acetic acid (2, 4, 5-T) compounds.

Mode of Action of Pesticides

There is a glut of industrially produced pesticides in the market. Pesticides are used to kill pests and they are neurotoxic. Many of the agrochemicals are not only toxic to the organisms against which they are supposed to act on, but also to other organisms and ecological systems, directly or indirectly. Chemical fertilizers affect the soil pH-balance and stimulate weed growth. Insecticides. herbicides and fungicides are agrochemical compounds that are highly toxic and bring about drastic ecological imbalance in plant kingdom. Most of them come under banned chemicals. They cause paralysis, loss of balance of motor functions. Many polynuclear organic hydrocarbons are carcinogenic. Pesticides cause heavy loss to pollinators; like honeybees and butterflies. They interfere with avian ecology–growth, egg production, shell-thickness, hatching ability and fertility.

Organochlorines

DDT (dichlorodiphenyltrichloroethane) is the oldest of the organochlorine insecticides. DDT interferes with the action of Na/K-ion channels, and prevents the normal transmission of nerve impulses. It inhibits the absorption of Ca^{2+} by bones and it produces enzymes; which decompose sex hormone steroids, thus creating hormonal imbalance.

DDT has several drawbacks and environmental impact.

(1) Persistence : It is one of the most persistent pesticides (half-life ~5-10 years). DDT is not readily absorbed through the skin when it is in a powder form. Its main entry points are respiratory and digestive tracks. As it is fat-soluble, large amounts accumulate in the brain, liver, and kidneys.

(2) Bioaccumulation : Effects of DDT are amplified due to fat-solubility and its accumulation in the living tissues. The chemical accumulates in fish, and when birds eat such fisth, the chemical accumulates in their fat tissue, resulting in fragile eggs. The thinning of eggshells and breakage of eggs are attributed to the effects of DDT upon the enzyme *carbonic anhydrase*.

Some other organochlorine pesticides are aldrin, chlordane, dieldrin, endrin, methoxychlor. Aldrin, dieldrin and other chloro-pesticides are metabolized in a manner similar to DDT. Aldrin is oxidized to dieldrin in the metabolic process and the latter is even more toxic to fish. That is, in some causes pollutants are converted metabolically in the environment to more toxic chemical species. Chlordane is a more potent pesticide than DDT. Like DDT, Chlordane is not readily decomposed and persists for long periods of time in the soil, foodstuffs etc. Unlike DDT, it can enter the body through the skin, respiratory and digestive tracts. Its effect is cumulative. Derivative chlordane is heptachlor, which is fat-soluble. Endrin is the most toxic of all the chlorinated hydrocarbons. It is about fifteen times as toxic as DDT to mammals, thirty times as poisonous to aquatic life, and about three hundred times as poisonous to birds.

Organophosphate

Organophosphates (OPs) are the currently used generic term that includes all insecticides containing phosphorus. All organophosphates are derived from one of the phosphorus acids, and as a class are generally the most toxic of all pesticides to vertebrates. The OPs have two distinctive features they are generally much more toxic to vertebrates than other classes of insecticides, and most are chemically unstable or non-persistent. It is this latter characteristic that brought them into agricultural use as substitutes for the persistent organocholrines.

Phenolic Pesticides

Dinitrophenol and its derivatives have broad range of insecticidal, herbicidal and fungicidal toxicities.

Herbicides, such as Na-arsinite, Na-chlorate, paraquat (1, 1'-dimethyl-4-4'-bipyridynium ion), simazin, mecocrop, dalapon, monuron, alachlor, 2,4-D (2, 4-Dichlorophenoxy acetic acid), and 2, 4, 5-T (2, 4, 5-Trichlorphenoxy acetic acid; Agent Orange) are used to kill 'unwanted' herbs and foliants. These chemicals interfere with photosynthesis causing plant death. Defoliation of vegetation and forests lead to increased soil erosion and leaching of nutrients. The ecological implications are long ranging and far-reaching. The pathological effects on plants of herbicides such as Agent Orange, and malathion (*O,O*-dimethyl S-(1, 2-dicarbethoxyethyl phosphorodithioate)) in chemical warfare by the USA forces in Vietnam had drastically affected the ecology in that contry. Forests have been defoliated, agricultural crops were completely destroyed and fauna has been affected. Spraying in mangroves with 2, 4,-D and 2, 4 5-T has completely destroyed the vegetation and fauna.

Fungicides are used to kill fungal pathogens of plants. Some of these are alkylmercury, benomyl, captan, carboxin karathene, maneb, misterm, rovral, thiram, zineb and ziram. All fungicides the toxic.

All pesticides that are dangerous for the pests are also dangerous to other organisms. Organophosphorus pesticides kill the pests by attacking the nervous system and causing the inactivation of the synaptic enzyme, acetylcholinesterase (AChE). Organophosphorus esters, carbamates and ureas are metabolized by enzymes in the human liver and are converted to predominantly water-soluble products and eliminated in the urine. But organochlorine compounds, lacking metabolizing enzymes, are more persistent in the environment. Pesticides that persists in the environment for longer periods are, naturally, more dangerous.

Advantages of Pesticides

Following are the advantages of using pesticides :

(1) Protection of high yielding and useful varieties of plants from pests, thus increasing production of food and other crops to feed the increasing world population.

(2) In public health programmes pesticides are used to control the carriers of vector borne diseases like, malaria, filaria, sleeping sickness, dengue fever, etc.

Hazards of Pesticides

Pesticides are harmful in the following ways

(1) Pesticides are in fact poisons. These are generally non-selective in their action and, therefore, kill both harmful and harmless organisms. Sometimes only a few harmful organisms are killed while more harmless organisms are eliminated. This often disturbs the balance of ecosystem.

(2) Some of the pests which can tolerate high concentration of pesticides, survive, multiply and produce genetically more resistant varieties.

(3) Amount of pesticides in each trophic level increases progressively through the food chain (biomagnification or bioconcentration). This often becomes more than the normal and tolerable limits. Hence, fruits, vegetables, etc., do not remain safe for consumption.

(4) Pesticides are often used carelessly resulting into serious health problem. They may also cause the death of large number of unrelated organisms.

Alternative to Pesticides

Advantages and hazards of pesticides need to be balanced and managed. There appears to be no way to stop using pesticides. A solution has now, however, been found having considered different aspects of pesticide management. The pesticides are now expected to be safe for use. This programme is called Integrated Pest Management (IPM).

EPIDEMIOLOGY

Epidemiology is the science dealing with disease dynamics. Epidemics of plant disease occur only when certain conditions are fulfilled. There must be a source of inoculum, availability of susceptible hosts and the occurrence of approapriate environmental conditions over a sufficient period of time to allow infection, development of the parasite within the host, reproduction and dissemination. Weather may play a decisive role in plant-disease epidemics since many parasites require a narrow range of environmental conditions for infection, development, reproduction and dissemination.

Three types of pathogen behaviour have been recognized in the development of plant disease epidemics: mono-cyclic in which there is only one parasitic generation each cropping season, polycyclic when there is more than one generation each cropping season and polyetic in which parasite is monocyclic but the incidence of diseased plants increases over several seasons. Epidemics may arise from discrete sources of infection known as foci or from a more general distribution of inoculum.

Inoculum may arise from many different sources, the most important generally being host material. Vectors which may be insects, fungi or nematodes are normally required for the dissemination of viruses and viroids. Severe epidemics usually occur only when there is a large population of susceptible hosts, aggressive parasite with a high reproductive rate and suitable environmental conditions such as high moisture and temperatures which favour the pathogen.

e.g., Rice Tungro, Wheat rust and Rice Blast.

$$D_t = \sum_{i=0} f\,(p_i, h_i, c_i)$$

D_t – is a measure of disease at time t, p_i, h_i and e_i summarize respectively, all the parasite, host and environmental factors that contribute to an increase in disease and f is the factor that relates the interaction of p, h and e over the period $i = 0$ to t to the amount of disease at time t.

PEST FORECASTING AND PEST SURVEILIANCE

Pest forecasting and pest surveillance are key to successful implementation of Integrated Pest Management which enable the prediction of pest incidence and allow the farmer to take pest control measures in advance. Pest forecasting is a long time process requiring systematic collection of data on pest activity and weather data for several years and the relationship between the two entities is established. Pest surveillance relates to short time forecasting which is based on keeping close vigil on a crop in the season and alerting the farmer to take appropriate action.

Three major components involved in the development and implementation of forecasting schemes are :

(*i*) define the economic threshold for pest attack,

(*ii*) develop relevant monitoring and forecasting procedures, and

(*iii*) Provide means for implementing the forecasting programme with the crop production schemes.

Many short term forecasts are based on direct counts of the pest on a particular crop shortly before damage may occur. Many sampling techniques have been developed for estimating insect population on the host plant. The chosen method should be quick, inexpensive and simple to execute as well as should provide an accurate evaluation of the field situation. Choice depends on pest and crop characteristics. A knowledge is required of the distribution of a particular pest species within the crop and on individual plants.

Chemical monitoring is based on either host plant or sex attractants. Aerial monitoring using suction traps has many advantages for sampling randomly distributed populations of small flying insects. The pest surveillance programme encompasses (i) fixed plot survey and (ii) roving survey. Both involve *insitu* assessment of pests and diseases in the standing crop. The supporting methodlogy includes observations on the activity of pests by setting light traps, pheromone traps, spore trap etc. The weather parameters of the respective areas are also recorded to study their influence on the pests and diseases.

Fixed Plot Survey : Two fields of about one acre in size are selected into two different villages in the jurisdiction of each Agricultural Officer. Five microplots each of the size of 1 m^2 area are fixed in each field. The microplots are laid one each in four quarters of the field and one in the middle. The microplots should be fixed about 10 m away from the bunds. The observations for most of the pests and diseases are confined to the five microplots in each field.

Roving Survey : Conducted every weak at the rate of two fields in each of the four villages in the jurisdiction of each Agricultural Officer. In each field observations are recorded from the south west corner by a diagonal walk.

COMPATIBILITY OF SPRAY CHEMICALS

When two chemicals are brought together in a single spray mixture, a compound differing from either parent may be formed. A knowledge of the effects of such compounds on the plants when applied is essential to avoid improper use. The incompatibility in such cases may be :

(1) Chemical incompatibility : Different compounds are formed due to reaction of various chemicals as in synthetic organic compounds with an alkaline material.

(2) Phytotoxic incompatibility : The component parts though by themselves are not injurious to the plants and do not show any chemical reaction when mixed, the mixture causes injury to the plants.

(3) Physical compatibility : In which the chemicals used change their physical form to one that is unstable and hazardous to application.

(4) Biological compatibility : The mixtures should be more toxic to the insects in killing, rather than either of them used alone.

On no account insecticides should be mixed with plant growth regulators or micronutrients. Always avoid mixing of two insecticides. Combinations of sevin and malathion causes injury to cotton.

Particular micro-organisms in soil degrades particular pesticides. *e.g.*, A strain of the Bacillus *Nocardia alba* degrades parathion to the extent of 61% in 8 days under optimum conditions.

Pesticides belonging to the group carbamates and OP are compatible with biofertlizers like Azotobacter and Rhizobium and they derive nutrition from the pesticides.

MICROBIAL TOXINS

Microbial toxins are the compounds produced by the fungi, some of which are known to be highly toxic. The toxins produced by the fungi found as contaminants on food grains and food stuffs such as Aflatoxins are of great significance. The metabolism of *Aspergillus niger* on groundnut known as Aflatoxin was first discovered in 1961 when lakhs of turkeys died in England after being fed with groundnut meal. It is a powerful hepatotoxic and it is a powerful carcinogen. In general consumption of contaminated feed by an animal may result in an unhealthy situation due to aflatoxins causing liver damage, marked bile duct proliferation and a decreased production or even death.

Proper harvesting, drying and storage are important factors in lessening alfatoxins contamination and toxic production. Propionic acid and acetic acids will inhibit mould growth. Treatment with ammonia or ammonium hydroxide will detoxify feeds.

STORAGE PESTS OF CEREALS AND PULSES, HYGIENE OF STORAGE GODOWNS, PRESERVATION AND REMEDIAL MEASURES

Introduction : Grain is a living biological product. It respires and can germinate under optimum environmental conditions. The respiration process in the grain is externally manifested by a decrease in dry weight utilization of oxygen, evolution of carbon dioxide and release of heat. The rate of respiration is dependent upon the moisture content of the grain and the temperature of the grain. The maximum moisture content permissible for different grains for safe storage varies to some extent. Also, a low temperature is conducive to good storage.

The important factors that influence storage grains and pulses, are:

(*i*) Kind and variety of seed

(*ii*) Initial condition of the grain at the time of storage

(*iii*) Moisture content of the grains

(*iv*) Temperature at which grains are stored, and sanitation and suitability of the storage godown.

Moisture content of the grains is a very important factor. The Table 6 below gives an idea of the relationship between moisture content and storage life.

Table 6 : Moisture content and storage life of cereal seeds: (Harrington and Douglas, 1970)

Seed moisture content per cent	*Storage life*
11 to 13	1/2 Year
10 to 12	One Year
9 to 11	Two Years
8 to 10	Four Years

At moisture contents above 13%, the losses could be very rapid due to mould growth. Also, within the normal range, biological activity of seeds, insects and moulds further increase as the temperature increases.

In view of the considerations, grains of cereals and pulses should be dried to safe moisture contents. For cereals in ordinary storage conditions for 12 to 18 months, drying grains upto 10% moisture content is quite satisfactory.

STORAGE PESTS OF CEREALS AND PULSES: There are numerous insect pests of stored grains. They damage the stored grains and often make them unfit for human consumption.

Damage caused by stored grain pests may be :

(*a*) direct damage (damage due to destruction of grains by pests)

or (*b*) indirect damage.

Direct damage may be in the form of (*i*) loss of weight, (*ii*) loss of germinating capacity of (*iii*) damage to containers in which grains are stored.

Indirect damage may be in the form of (*i*) contamination with foreign matter such as insect excreta, eggs, mould, spores, etc. (*ii*) heating of the grain causing fermentation, acidification, etc, and (*iii*) loss of nutritional value through organoleptic modifications.

Both the direct and indirect damages lower the commercial value of the stored grains, resulting in financial loss. The more important pests affecting cereals and pulses are described below.

CEREAL PESTS

1. Rice weevil (*Sitophilus oryzae* L.)

The weevil measuring 4mm long is dark brown and has four light reddish or yellowish spots on elytra. The female makes a small hole on the grain, deposits an egg and covers it with a gelatinous fluid. In a period of 4-5 months female may lay from 60 to 400 eggs. The apodous grub feeds inside the grains, pupates there itself and emerges through an irregular hole made on the grain. The life-cycle ranges from 26-28 days.

This is one of the most destructive pests of stored grains throughout India. It damages many cereals *viz.*, wheat, rice, maize, barley and also jowar and bajra.

Distribution : This is a cosmopolitan pest and occurs wherever cereal grains are stored.

Damage: Both adults and grubs feed on the grains, the former making cavities for laying eggs and the latter eating inside the grain and making it hollow.

2. Lesser Grain Borer (*Rhyzopertha dominica* Fabt.)

This is the most destructive pest of nearly all cereal grains in India. The beetle has also been found to breed in flour and dry fruits.

Distribution : It is found almost all over India.

Damage : The larvae bores into the grains and feed inside throughout their larval stage. The damaged grains are hollow and unfit for consumption.

3. Khapra beetle (*Trogoderma granarium* Events)

This is a major pest of wheat but also thrives on oats, rice, maize, jowar, etc. This is found all over India.

Damage : The larvae damage the grains by feeding on the outer sufrace, generally the embryo portion. If the infestation is heavy, the larvae also feed on the inside of the grains. The pest is most active during active during the rainy season, when it causes the maximum damage.

4. Rust-red flour beetle (*Tribolium castaneum* Herbst.)

This is found in association with other, pests of stored grains in stores, mills, granaries, werehouses, etc. attacking rice, wheat, barley, millets, etc. The larvae and the adults generally feed mostly on the broken grains, flour dust or on grains already damaged by other pests. It is present all over India.

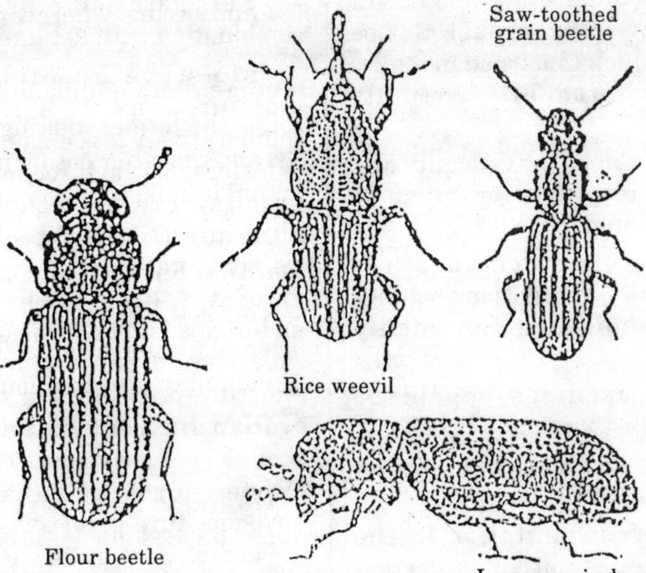

Fig. 2 Stored grain pests

Hygiene of Storage Godowns, Preservation and Remedial Measures

General principles for grains and pulses storage : For safe storage of grains and pulses, the following principles need to be borne in mind:

(*i*) The atmosphere in the grain storage godown should be dry and cool.

(*ii*) Before placing grains into storage, they should be dried to safe moisture limits, appropriate to the grain.

(*iii*) Only well-cleaned grain in good condition should be stored.

(*iv*) Effective storage pest control, and

(*v*) Proper sanitation in seed stores should be ensured.

In warm, humid areas, proper insulation of storage houses is necessary to keep the storage as cool as possible. This could be achieved by providing a false ceiling with ventilation between ceiling and roof by constructing thick stone or brick walls: or by a layer of insulation in walls or ceiling ventilating fans to bring in the cool night air can be done provided it is not so humid as to raise the seed moisture content to a level when it can be attacked by storage fungi.

The grains should be maintained dry. Storage in moisture proof bags will solve the problem of moisture penetration.

Storage structures should have the following features:

(*i*) They should have built in protection against thefts, rodents, birds, insects and fungi, that might enter the storage and destroy the grains.

(*ii*) They should have arrangements to control temperature and relative humidity to minimise losses in grain quality.

Pest and Disease Control

For protection of stored grains/pulses, the godown / warehouse intended for this purpose should have the following constructional features:

(*i*) Warehouse should have no windows and should have only one metal door, which can be sealed properly and locked.

(*ii*) The foundation should be made of stone or concrete and should extend 90 cm above the ground level.

(*iii*) A lip around building at 90 cm height extending out 15 cm should also be constructed. Such construction makes entrance by rodents virtually impossible.

(*iv*) The floor must be paved and any cracks that may develop must be promptly repaired.

(*v*) All cracks around openings like electric conduits, ventilation openings and doors should be thoroughly sealed.

(*vi*) Ventilation openings should be screened against birds and insects.

Other Measures for Preservation of Grains in Good Condition

Sanitation : Good Sanitation in the grains store is very essential for protection from insects and rodents. Toss grain bags should either be repaired immediately or replaced with new bags to avoid spillage in the warehouse. All spilled grains, or floor sweepings should be immediately removed. Discarded seeds and cleanings should be carried away, not just dumped outside the door to harbour and multiply storage pests. Besides cleaning, the floor and walls should be sprayed with a residual insecticide as often as required. In well-maintained grain godowns, spraying once a year is satisfactory.

Fumigation : The most serious source of reinfestation is a grain store maintained free of insects is infested grain that may be brought in. Such infestation can be controlled by fumigation. It is better to fumigate the lot separately in a fumigation room before bringing it inside the main godown.

Temperature Control : As pointed out earlier, temperature is one of the most important environmental factors which influence grain quality during storage. The lower the temperature, the better the storage and condition of the grains.

Temperature control may be achieved by (*i*) ventilation, (*ii*) insulation or (*iii*) refrigeration.

Refrigeration storage must be used combination with dehumidification.

Moisture Proofing : It is better to moisture proof a storage. This is comparatively less expensive than insulation of a storage. The three most useful moisture-proofing are polyethylene, asphalt and aluminium foil. Whichever material is selected, the entire storage must be moisture-proofed. A layer of the moisture-proofing material is laid underneath the concrete floor. This should be overlapped with the wall moisture-proofing and this inturn, should overlap the ceiling moisture-proofing. All should be overlapped. The doors should be moisture-proofed. Ventilation opening should have moisture-proof covering over them they are not in use. A grain storage that is properly moisture-proofed will ensure that there is no leakage of moisture from outside into the grain storage.

Electromagnetic Energy in Insect Control: In recent times, it has been found that electromagnetic energy can be made use of in insect control. The use of radio-frequency (RF) portion of electromagnetic spectrum in controlling insects, particularly those infesting grain, foodstuff and wood is of interest. The possibilities of controlling certain wood boring species have been demonstrated. Mites infesting grain and flour have been controlled by exposure to RF field; adult insects have been found to be more susceptible than the immature stages. It may be due to the fact that the early stages are spent inside the grain and are thus effectively shielded. Rice weevil infesting wheat is controlled effectively when exposed to RF treatment for a few seconds. The lethal effect appears to be due to tissue heating and it has been shown that the thoracic ganglia are affected by the treatment. So far, however, no practical scale applications of significance have been developed. Perhaps, it may assume a more decisive role in control of pests of stored grains in the future.

Damage : When the infestation is acute, wheat flour, suji or maida, are rendered unfit fot human consumption. The insect-infested products turn yellow and become mouldy with excreta and start's smelling.

5. **Saw-toothed Grain beetle (*Oryzaephilus surinamensis* L.)**

This pest is cosmopolitan in distribution and is found all over India on cereal products like flour, maida, biscuits, etc. The presence of this beetle in the products renders them unfit for consumption.

Damage : The beetle and the larvae feed on the food particles and forms cells by gluing them up with its secretion.

6. **Angoumois grain moth (*Sitotroga cerealella* Olire)**

This is a serious pest of unmilled grains like wheat, barley, rice, maize and millets. It is distributed all over India. Infestation of this pest starts from the field and is passed on to the granaries through the grains and straw.

Damage : The larvae is responsible for causing damage to the grains. In early stages, it bores into the grain through a minute hole and feeds on the kernel inside. The grains containing larvae are passed unnoticed and the infestation is detected only with the emergence of the moth.

The effected grains are rendered hollow and are full of larvae excrements.

The loss caused by the pest to stored grains may run up to ten per cent or so.

7. **Rice moth (*Coreyra cephatonica* Staint)**

This is found all over India. This is a serious pest of stored paddy, rice, suji, wheat flour, jowar, etc.

Damage: The larvae bore into the grains and feed inside. They also web cocoons enclosing broken grains, which indicate their presence.

8. **Almond moth (*Ephestia cautella* Walker)**

This is a pest of stored wheat, rice, almonds, walnut, niger, cashewnut, tamarind seeds, pistachio, raisins, etc.

Damage : The caterpillars weave silken tubes in the flour and over the food materials, with the result, that their keeping quality is reduced. When the infection is heavy, the product is unfit for consumption.

PESTS OF STORED PULSES

1. **Pulse beetle (*Callosobruchus chinensis* L.)**

This is a very serious pest of gram, pea, cow-pea, bean, arhar, lentil, mung, urad and soyabean in storage all over India. The infestation starts from the field and also from the infested godowns.

Damage : The larvae bore into the grains, feed and develop inside till they come out as adults. The infestation cannot be detected in the early stages, since the hole through which the larvae enter is very minute. The damaged grains are hollow inside, bear small holes and are unfit for consumption or seed purposes.

2. ***Bruchu analis* Fabr.**

This is found in association with C. chinensis in almost all parts of India. The pest damages pulses in storage.

3. ***B. phaseoli* Gyll.**

This attacks cow-pea, beans, mung, pigeon-pea and soyabean in the store. The damage caused by this pest is similar to that caused by *C. chinensis.*

4. ***Laria affinis* Frol.**

This is known as pea beetle, because it prefers to attack peas in the store. It does not breed freely in dry grains.

Damage : The grub bores into the pod and attacks the green grain inside. Such grains are rendered useless.

Preservation and Remedial Measures: The infestation by most of the insect pestes takes place either in the field or on the threshing floor or in the store godown. Many control measures cannot be carried out in the field. Therefore, these measures, whether prophylactic or curative can only be carried out in the storage godown.

1. Keep store godowns clean. Before storing fresh grains, sweep out all dirt and rubbish material and burn the refuse. Store only fully dried and pest-free grains.
2. Close up all cracks, crevices in the floor ceiling and walls.
3. Spray godowns thoroughly with 0.2% DDT as an extra precaution against the pest sheltering inside.
4. Grains for seed can be stored by mixing pyrenone (pyrethrum dust and pipropnyl butoxide mixture) with, the grain at the rate of 50 g per 30 kg of grain or 3% DDT at the rate of 40 g per 20 kg of grain. This grain should not be consumed.
5. Do not mix grains for consumption with insecticides. Only bags containing grains should be dusted lightly on the outer surface with 5% BHC or DDT or malathion dust at the rate of 150 kg per 10 m^2.
6. Fumigate infested grains, bags or store rooms with aluminium phosphide, ethylene dichloride and carbon tetrachloride mixture or methyl bromide or ethylene dibromide. Fumigate only in closed rooms or under gasproof tarpaulins.
7. As far as possible, use improved storage structures for storing foodgrains, where no or minimum infestation and loss can take place.

After fumigation, ensure that the room is well aerated by opening all doors and windows.

Questions From Previous Year's Papers

Q. 1. Answer of the following in about 150 words each :

(a) What do you understand by biological control? How can you aim at biological control to check rice pests under Indian situation.

(b) What type of mouth parts does a boring insect have? How can knowledge of mouth parts be helpful in chemical control of insects?

(c) Why have thiocarbamate fungicides gained popularity in recent years? what are the modes of action thicarbamate fungicides?

(d) What is a citrus canker? What are the symptoms observed? How can you control the disease?

Q. 2. What are the advantages of cutting over the seeded plant in mango cultivation? How can you control

(i) Mango mealy bug, and

(ii) Red ant in mango orchard?

Q. 3. Answer the following in about 150 words each :

(a) Describe the common pests and diseases of brinjal. Suggest plant protection measures to control these pests and diseases.

(b) What are pheromones? Which pheromones appear to be more effective in the control of insects? How can pheromones be used for the suppression of insect?

(c) Name the causal organism of powdery mildew of cucuribts. Describe the symptoms and suitable methods to control the disease.

(d) Name important stored grain pests of rice and pea. Discuss methods to control these pests.

Q. 4. Answer any four of the following in about 150 words each :

(a) What precautions are necessary for introducing a parasitoid or a predator in a locality?

(b) Name some important insect pathogenic fungi. How the insects are killed by fungal infection?

(c) Mention viral diseases of rice and their management.

(d) Define biopesticides and their mertis and demerits.

Q. 5.Describe the climatic requirements, varieties and pest management of mango and tomato.

Q. 6. Answer the following in about 150 words each :

(a) Give a list of important pests and diseases of potato, and suggest an integrated management module for the major pest and disease complex.

(b) What are prophylactic and curative measures for the stored grain pests in godowns?

(c) What are insect hormones? Discuss their significance in insect pest management.

(d) Give systematic position, nature of damage, life history and control measures of rice gundhi bug and gram pod borer.

Q. 7. Write short notes on :

(a) Systemic pesticides

(b) Remote sensing

(c) Integrated pest management

(d) Mulching

(e) Classify plant diseases

(f) Seed borne diseases

Q. 8. Enumerate the methods of preservation of fruits and vegetables.

Q. 9. Write short notes on :

(a) Diseases favoured by soil

(b) Plant and leaf hoppers as vectors

(c) Management of vector borne diseases

(d) Saw-toothed grain beetle.

Q. 10. Answer the following in about 150 words each :

(a) Bring out five important pests on crucifers, their nature of damage and management.

(b) Bring out different pesticide formulations with a short note on each.

(c) What are the qualities expected of a successful parasitoid?

(d) Explain the advantages and disadvantages of systemic diseases. 5 + 5 = 10

(e) List out 10 Pod borers on pulses with their systematic position. (Common name, Scientific name, Family, Order and describe their adults.)

Q. 11. Describe the following in about 150 words each :

(a) Mode of action of pesticides.

(b) Cultivation and export significance of Chrysanthemum.

(c) How evolution takes places in nature? Give its signifcance.

Q. 12. Write short notes on the following in about 150 words.

(a) Package of practices for wheat cultivation.

(b) Biopesticides.

(c) Diseases of tomato.

Q. 13. Give scientific name, nature of damage, life cycle and control measures of the following pests :

(a) Mustard aphid

(b) paddy grasshopper.

Q. 14. Describe the Eco-friendly management of pests and diseases.

Q. 15. Compare the following in about 150 words each:

(a) Nematicides and rodenticides.

(b) I.P.M. and I.R.M.

Q. 16. Answer the following in about 150 words each :

(a) Discuss the principles and methods of preservation of fruits and their products.

(b) What is biological control? Explain the mode of actions and characteristics of an effective biological control agent.

(c) How you will suggest the management practices of the following pests with an integrated approach :

(i) Citrus trunk border

(ii) Citrus leaf miner.

(d) Give a concise account of molecular diagnostics used for disease diagnosis.

Q. 17. (a) Name four important stored grain pests of rice. Describe briefly the biology and management of any one of them.

(b) Write in brief the management of insect-pests by using genes from Bacillus thuringiensis in transgenic plants.

(c) Write the symptoms, causal organism, disease cycle and management of wart disease of potatol.

Q. 18. Write about the mode of action of organophosphatic insecticides. Give few examples of systemic and non-systemic insecticides.

Q. 19. Give the diagnostic symptoms, causal organism, disease cycle, predisposing factors and management of bacterial wilt of solanaceous crop plants.

Q. 20. Discuss in brief the role of computers in plant disease forecasting with special reference to late blight of potato.

Q. 21. Write short notes on the following in about 150 words each :

(a) Bimodal transmission of plant viruses by insect vectors.

(b) Peach leaf curl and papaya leaf curl.

(c) Cultivation practices of chrysanthemum.

(d) Cleistothecium and Perithecium.

9. STORAGE PESTS AND THEIR CONTROL

CLIMATIC REQUIREMENTS OF VEGETABLE CROPS

In fact, climate of a region is the total of long-time performance of its various components *viz.*, temperature, light (sunshine), humidity, rainfall, wind direction, wind velocity, and such phenomena as fog, frost, thunder, gale etc.

The climate of a region is mainly influenced by the factors as under :

(*i*) latitude,

(*ii*) altitude,

(*iii*) topography,

(*iv*) position related to continents and oceans,

(*v*) position related to large scale atmospheric circulation patterns.

Almost all components of the climate influence vegetable crops. All are closely interrelated. The effect of each is modified by others. All crops have certain natural threshold limits of the climatic components beyond which they do not grow normally but breeding and selection are gradually extending these threshold for many crops.

Following is a brief account on important climatic components which are affecting vegetable production most.

(A) Temperature

Temperature is one of the most important components of climate. It plays vital role in the production of vegetable crops. Temperature affects rate of plant growth, mineral and water uptake by roots, flowering and pollen viability, blossom fertilization and fruitset, carbohydrate and growth regulator balance, rate of maturation and senescence, and quality, yield and shelf-life of the edible products. The temperature of the air and soil affects, all growth processes of plants.

Seed germination, root primodia initiation, leaf initiation, anthocyanin synthesis, plastid formation, photo-periodism, flower induction, leaf abscission, bud dormancy and sex expression are altered because temperature changes rate of metabolic activity; others reflect physical or structural impairment of functions of tissues; still other relate to differentiation of reproductive growth.

Most of biennial vegetables initiate reproductive growth after extended exposure to low temperature and/or a specific day length. This stimulus is more effective as plants reach adult growth. The duration of exposure needed to initiate reproductive growth. The duration of exposure needed to initiate reproductive growth declines as the temperature declines.

(*i*) Effects of Temperature on Germination

The effect of temperature on germination has received much attention. Some vegetable seeds such as onion, will germinate at freezing temperatures but the rate of growth is extremely slow. At 32°F, it takes 135 days for the appearance of an onion seedling when planted one-half inch deep. This emphasizes that some seeds can withstand cold temperatures and seed will be alive when the soil temperature increases. Some seeds, such as sweet corn and beans will rot if planted at low temperatures for long period of time. The minimum temperature for germination of some vegetable seeds are given in Table 1. This minimum temperature can be used as an indication of when to plant the crops in the spring. When the temperatures have reached the minimum, the vegetables may be planted. It is assumed that the soil temperatures will continue to increase, however, planting vegetables before the minimum temperature required to germination is reached, does not produce an earlier crop. Instead, the seed will not germinate and it will give more time for soil organisms to destroy the seeds, resulting in reduced stand.

There is a maximum temperature at which vegetable seeds will germinate and high temperature may kill many vegetable seeds. High soil temperature is also damaging at the time of seedling emergence, and seedling may die due to heat injury at the soil surface. Lettuce and endive, however, will not germinate at high temperature and if the soil temperature has not reached the maximum and killed the seed, the seeds will germinate when the soil temperature has cooled. This is particularly important in summer planting for a fall crop.

Table 1. Soil temperatures for vegetable seed germination.

MINIMUM TEMPERATURES (F)

32°F	*40°F*	*50°F*	*60°F*	*65°F*
Endive	Beet	Asparagus	Limabean	Eggplant
Lettuce	Parsley	Sweet corn	Snap bean	Muskmelon
Onion	Broccoli	Tomato	Cucumber	Pumpkin
Parsnip	Pea	Turnip	Okra	Squash
Spinach	Cabbage		Pepper	Watermelon
	Radish			
	Carrot			
	Swiss chard			
	Cauliflower			
	Celery			

OPTIMUM TEMPERATURES (°F)

70°F	*75°F*	*80°F*	*85°F*	*95°F*
Celery	Asparagus	Limabean	Snap bean	Cucumber
Parsnip	Endive	Radish	Parsley	Muskmelon
Spinach	Lettuce	Carrot	Beet	Carrot
	Pea	Tomato	Pepper	Okra
		Cauliflower	Broccoli	Cauliflower
		Turnip	Sweet corn	Pumpkin
		Onion	Cabbage	Onion
			Swish chard	Squash
				Radish

MAXIMUM TEMPERATURES

75°F	*85°F*	*95°F*	*105°F*
Celery	Limabean	Asparagus	Cucumber
Endive	Parsnip	Eggplant	Muskmelon
Lettuce	Pea	Beet	Okra
Spinach		Onion	Pumpkin
		Broccoli	Squash
		Parsley	Sweetcorn
		Cabbage	Turnip
		Pepper	Watermelon

Effects of Temperature on Flowering

Temperature is one critical environmental factor which affects flowering. Many vegetables are induced to flower by low temperatures, particularly biennial and perennial plants, such as spinach, are induced to flower at high temperatures. Tomatoes will produce more flowers if grown at 80°F during the day and 65°F at night than at higher or lower night temperatures.

The induction of flowering due to low temperature is called vernalization. Biennial plants normally grew one year are induced to flower during the winter and flower the next year. They may, however, be induced to flower the first year and if this happens; the plant does not produce a satisfactory edible plant parts.

Effect of Temperature on Fertilization and Fruit Set

Excessively high temperature or low temperature may reduce pollen viability or germinability and receptivity of the stigma. Poor fertilization usually is characterized by abortion of the flower or premature abscission of the fruit.

Generally, average monthly temperature of 21-23°C is optimum for fruit setting in tomato.

The critical factor in setting of tomato fruit is the night temperature. The optimum range being 59 to 68°F (15 to 20°C). Fruits fail to set at 55°F or below. When average maximum day temperature is above 70°F, tomato fruit set is low.

High light intensity accompanied by high temperature is harmful to tomato fruit set. In higher or lower temperatures, blossom drops due to poor pollen germination and pollen tube growth.

Even cultivars differ in their temperature sensitivity for fruit setting in certain vegetable crops. Some of the brinjal cultivars with round fruits are known to set well under lower temperature compared to long fruited cultivars. Similarly in capsicums, bell peppers require cooler weather compared to hot peppers while most of cucurbits can set under higher temperature. Pumpkins need cooler weather for good fruit setting.

Effects of Temperature on Quality of Vegetables

Temperature affects vegetable quality, not only through respiration, but also because of tissue damage or altered morphology following exposure to excessive heat or chilling and because of changes in relative amounts of sugar and starch in the edible product. Warm season vegetables-tomato, pepper and squash are especially sensitive to chilling, normally at temperature below 45°F to 50°F (7°C to

10°C). The consequence of chilling is surface pitting or spotting and poor colour development. High temperatures in these and other vegetables also cause physical damage (sunburn) or may affect pigmentation. For example when tomato fruits are exposed to direct sun radiation fruit temperatures may increase by 10°C or more above ambient air temperature. If the fruit temperature exceeds 30°C for long periods, the affected part of the fruits becomes yellowish and remains so during ripening. When temperature of an exposed fruit portion exceeds 40°C, it becomes white and sunken (sun-scald, sunburn), pungency of onion and radish develop rapidly at high temperatures. Temperature stress at the time of fruit set or during late fruit development may cause defects (blossom scarpuffy fruit in tomato) that render product unmarketable.

Effect of Temperature on Growth and Development of Edible Portion

Development of edible part is highly dependent on temperature in many crops. In case of potato, a temperature range of 20-24°C is favourable for sprouting and initial growth. For subsequent growth and tuberization a temperature of 18-20°C is optimum. Above 30°C tubers do not form. Thus, potatoes are best cultivated in a season when the temperature gradually drops to synchronize the period of tuberization. In onion formation of bulb is favoured by higher temperature (20-22°C) whereas in garlic exposure to cooler weather helps in the production of large bulbs. Carrot shows good root development at 15-21°C. In ranges they become tapered which may cause considerable loss. The optimum temperature for curd formation in cauliflower is 17°C.

Effect of Temperature on Root Processes

A decrease in root temperature decreases water absorption (as the temperature of water decreases its viscosity increases). There is increase in hydrogen bonding).

A decrease in temperature also decreases permeability of membranes to water. Since gases are more soluble in water at low temperatures there is an increase in dissolved CO_2 and O_2 that decrease pH, which reduce water absorption.

At low temperature, the activity of solutes decrease and there is higher osmotic potential in the cell, which reduces the active transport system in the root cells.

At low temperature, nutrient uptake is reduced because there is reduction in the amounts of nutrient release in the soil solution from parent material so supply of nutrient is less and reduced activity of micro-organisms that release the nutrients.

Effect of Temperature on Photosynthesis and Respiration

During daylight, photosynthetic activity normally exceeds that of respiration, resulting in net accumulation of carbohydrates. In the absence of light, however, respiration utilizes these reserves. The higher the night temperature greater is the loss of reserves. High night temperatures therefore, limit both yield and quality of such vegetables as root crops and potatoes.

Respiration is also a major factor affecting ripening and post harvest quality of vegetables.

Light

Light is an electromagnetic radiation which is a form of kinetic energy. It comes from the sun to the earth as discrete particles called quanta or photons at the speed of 3,00,000 km per second. Light is one of most important factors affecting plant life very effectively.

Light is an integral part of the photosynthetic reaction in that it provides the energy of the combination of carbondioxide (CO_2) and water (H_2O) in the green cells having chlorophyll for the formation of carbohydrates with the release of oxygen. Kluyur (1928) gave the following equation to explain the oxidation of water in photosynthesis.

$$CO_2 + 2H_2O \longrightarrow CH_3O + H_2O + O_2$$

Ruben, Hassid and Kamen (1941) using radioactive O^{18} in water supplied to the plants found that oxygen released in photosynthesis came from water molecule and not from CO_2 and that was confirmed by Dole and Jenks (1944). The correct overall reaction is therefore

$$6CO_2 + 12H_2O \xrightarrow[\text{Chlorophyll}]{\text{680 K cal of radiant energy}} C_6H_{12}O_6 + 6H_2O + 6O_2$$

Besides oxygen, the light reaction gives rise to two very important products (*a*) reducing agent $NADP_2$ (*b*) an energy rich compound ATP; these two product of the light reaction are utilized in the dark phase of photosynthesis.

The main sites of carbohydrate production are leaves but stems and buds are also capable of photosynthesis. Many plants thrive in complete light, whereas other some require a partial or complete shade.

The performance of crops is influenced by three aspects of light *viz.*, light intensity, light quality and light duration.

Effect of Light on Seed Germination

Though for a large number of species light is not essential for germination of seed. But certain species of plants require exposure to light before germination. According to light sensitivity seed of many species are classified as:

(1) Germination is favoured by light

(2) Germination is favoured by dark

(3) Germination is unaffected by light or dark

Photoblastic

Seeds in first category are said to be 'photoblastic'.

Effect of Light on Vegetative Growth

Light furnishes the necessary energy for photosynthesis and the length of day or number of daylight hours affects the growth and flowering of plants. Light has a pronounced effect on stem growth.

Effect of Light (Photoperiod) on Flowering

The effect of duration of light or photoperiodism can be defined as the developmental responses of plants to the relative lengths of the light and dark periods. The striking effect of photoperiod on flowering was discovered in 1920 by Garmer and Allard.

Humidity

Water affects plants growth primarily through the soil solution. The relative humidity within a plant canopy, however, does influence transpiration rate and turgor of leaves and the intensity of related physiological disorders, such as tipburn. Humidity also affects plant growth indirectly by supporting development of disease and insect infestations. In some species (*e.g.* beans) low humidity seems to increase flower abortion, and pollen viability is decreased in many plants.

Rainfall

Rainfall is a very important factor in vegetable cultivation, and if a market garden is to be established in a new area it is essential that the pattern of rainfall in the region be studied before any decision is taken concerning the types of crop to be cultivated. Hills or ridges of high land favour uneven distribution of rainfall. Local variations of rainfall in a humid tropics can be important and, in some hilly areas, can influence the methods of cultivation to be practiced and the types of crop which can be successfully grown.

Wind

The effect of high wind on crops can be appreciable. Complete physical destruction may result because little can stand against winds of the order of 100 km/hour, even large trees become uprooted. Some crops have quite low damage even due to high wind speed. In many regions high winds can destroy the flowers, or strip the crops.

High wind speed increases evaporation and transpiration processes and need for more available water. Strong winds interfere with the activities of insects during pollination times, but they also assist directly in the transport of pollen and seeds, including the seeds of undesirable vegetation such as weeds.

Wind erosion of soil is of prime importance in some regions of the world where the dry topsoil is eroded into tiny particles and removed from the region in the form of dense clouds of dust.

Frost and Dew

Most plants tolerate temperatures 2 to 4°F (1 to 2°C) below freezing without physical damage. The freezing points of most cells are depressed because of dissolved solutes, and most cell solutions tend to supercool 2 to 4°F (1-2°C) more. Supercooled cell sap will form ice in response to enucleation by cell inclusions or by external factors such as bacteria. Ice formation within a cell generally is lethal. Plants that tolerate freezing do so because they tolerate extracellular ice formation. Tender plants that have been preconditioned (Hardened) also tolerate extracellular freezing, but species vary in the degree to which they can be preconditioned.

Chilling damage occurs at temperatures above freezing and primarily affects plants of tropical or subtropical origin. Only corn, among the warm season crops, is resistance to chilling effects. Chilling results in a number of changes in plant function. Movement of water and solute into root is slowed, and permeability of cellular membranes may be altered after plants have been returned to normal growing temperatures. Visible effect of chilling on plant organs vary, from surface lesions to abnormal pigmentation, stored produce may be predisposed to pathogen infection by field chilling prior to stage.

Post-harvest Handling

Post-harvest handling of vegetables play very important role in earning remunerative Income. As soon as vegetables are harvested with whole plant or part(s) thereof, they immediately undergo certain physiological and biochemical changes and certain losses with respect to loss in weight, appearance, colour, texture, nutritive values etc. The extent of losses can be avoided by sending them to the market as soon as possible or by storing them in cold storage. Unfortunately cold storage facilities are not available for various vegetables in India except for potato, onion etc., which of course are stored in cold storage.

After harvesting, vegetables are subjected to the following essential operations which prepare vegetables for markets (local as well as distant markets) and storage.

Essential Operations after Harvesting

1. Trimming
2. Curing
3. Sorting
4. Washing
5. Grading
6. Packing
7. Labeling
8. Precooling

1. Trimming

During harvesting, additional portion remains with harvested produce which is in fact undesirable and need to be trimmed. Outer leaves of cabbage and cauliflower should be removed. Top portion of carrot is trimmed at the base of the root. All the feeding roots from tuberous roots are trimmed to improve quality.

2. Curing

Onion, garlic, potato and sweet potato require curing for a couple of days. These are spread or heaped under shade in order to harden skin, cut portions are suberized, and soil which remained adhered get separated automatically during curing. Extra water is also lost.

3. Sorting

Under this operation, injured, bruised, cut, over-sized undersized, decayed, shrivelled vegetables are sorted out. After sorting, healthy lot is left free from any unwanted subject. Vegetables are subjected for sorting manually or mechanically placing them on running belt.

4. Washing

If necessary, healthy lot is washed in running water. Sprinkling of water can also be done for washing. Washing removes all soil, dust and dirt. While washing some weed plants are also removed which is very common in leafy vegetables like palak, methi, amaranths, coriander, mint etc.

5. Grading

Healthy lot which is obtained after sorting is graded into different grades as per demand in the market. Graded vegetables have good demand in the market and also fetches high prices.

6. Packing

After grading, it is essential to put the vegetables into suitable containers of required and desired sizes. In India, vegetable marketing is not so sophisticated. Many vegetables are transported in gunny bags or bamboo baskets or loose. Generally packing is done as per demands of the local market and transport facilities and distance of markets. Types of packing also depend on types of vegetable grown.

Merits of Packing

1. Packed vegetables are not subjected to immediate losses.
2. They maintain their freshness for considerable period.
3. Packed vegetables have good demand and fetch comparatively high prices.
4. Packed vegetables are conveniently transported.

Causes of Post-harvest Losses

(A) Primary Causes

1. Mechanical injury
2. Physio-biochemical losses
3. Microbial losses
4. Physical losses

(B) Secondary Causes

1. State of maturity
2. Time of harvesting
3. Storage facilities
4. Bruishing caused due to transportation and distribution.

Post-harvest Losses :

1. Shrivelling and shrinkage
2. Physiological loss in weight
3. Sprouting (in onion and potatoes)
4. Rotting or losses through spoilage

Control of Post-harvest Losses

The extent of post-harvest losses in vegetables can be minimized by :

(*i*) Careful harvesting
(*ii*) Harvesting of vegetables at the right stage of maturity
(*iii*) Adequate and suitable storage facilities
(*iv*) Pre-and post-harvest treatment
(*v*) Proper sorting, grading and packing
(*vi*) Careful transportation and distribution.

Kinds of Packing

In India, much attention is not given on packing of vegetables for home consumption. However, for export marketing it is done in proper manner because good packing carry good impression on good quality. Most commonly in India, packing is done in the following:

(*i*) Gunny bags
(*ii*) baskets made of bamboo and arhar sticks
(*iii*) wooden boxes,
(*iv*) plastics containers
(*v*) polythene bags
(*vi*) cartons made of cardboard.

Packing is done for whom ?

(*a*) Packing for distant markets : For sending vegetables to distant markets, they are packed in bamboo baskets for vegetables like okra, guar, chillies, cabbage and cauliflower. Dry grasses and leaves are used as lining material inside the containers. Potato, sweet potato, onion and garlic are packed in gunny bags and paper cutting are used as packing material. The top of basket or gunny bags is stitched.

(*b*) **Packing for consumers :** In India, no packing is done for consumers. People go to market for purchasing vegetables along with hand bag.

(*c*) **Packing for local markets :** Practically, vegetables are not packed for selling in local markets. Vegetables are carried in full of baskets and gunny bags.

Labelling

Labelling is done for identification of the item without opening the packet. It indicate, the weight, price, date of packing, name and the address of producer. Some precautions and warnings are also included wherever they are applicable.

Labelling is accomplished by (*i*) printing directly on packing, (*ii*) pasting a printed label on the package and (*iii*) wrapping with material or using printed bags. Both colour and design make labelling impressive and informative.

Precooling

Precooling is a method of removing field heat from harvested vegetables especially during hot weather which prevents decay, retard the ripening and senescence, and loss in quality. Precooling is done particularly when vegetables are transported to long distance or stored for a long time. Precooling is done after harvesting and prior to storage. It is economical to do precooling with cold water. Vegetables like tomato, runner bean, lettuce, carrot, celery, asparagus, okra, artichokes etc. respond well to precooling in terms of less physiological weight loss during storage.

MARKETING

Once vegetable is produced either it has to be consumed by the grower and/or its surplus quantity has to be sold or disposed off to the consumer through a particular channel of marketing.

Hanson (1971) describes, marketing is the process of discovering and translating consumer needs and wants into product and service specifications, beating demand for these products and services and then in turn expanding this demand.

Disposal of Vegetables in Short Time

1. Most of the vegetables, especially leafy ones are highly perishable in nature.
2. Storage facilities are inadequate.
3. Processing facilities are inadequate.
4. Market prices are very fluctuating.
5. Lack of cooperative marketing net work in India.
6. Crops are not insured.

CHANNELS OF VEGETABLE MARKETING

They are described briefly as under :

(A) Selling Vegetables to Retailers

This involves small quantity vegetables that are sold to various buyers. It is done at

(*a*) Mandies

This is the place where the growers and commission agents or their representatives assemble for selling and purchasing of vegetables, commission agents purchase vegetables for resell. Commission agents may sell vegetables to the retailers in Mandy itself or they may carry the produce and may sell it somewhere else too.

(*b*) Selling at the Farm

Sometimes, the wholesaler or his agents or merchant come to the field of the producer, and settle the price for the whole field on the standing crop. This is, in fact, a type of auction in the absence of auctioneers.

(*c*) Auction Market

It is the place where growers or producers bring their produce which is auctioned by Brokers or Dalals. Retailers purchase vegetables from brokers for selling them in different location of city of town. In this system, vegetables are collected in heaps and then sold by auction. Each lot or heap concerned lot is purchased by the highest bidder.

(B) Selling Vegetables to Wholesaler

Vegetables which are comparatively less perishable like potato, sweet potato, onion, garlic etc. are sold to wholesalers that involves large scale movement of vegetables from one region to another. Wholesalers may store and sell the vegetables by consignment to city or town's commission merchant or agent.

(C) Selling Vegetables to Cooperatives

Only a few vegetables at some places are being marketed through cooperative societies wherever these are available. These organizations, solicit business, maintain records of vegetable collection of money, payment records, provide facilities for storage for short period and help growers many ways. Growers get remunerative prices of vegetables because there is no involvement of any middleman.

(D) Selling of Vegetables to Consumers

This involves selling of vegetables house to house or selling by the side of roads.

(*a*) House to House Selling

In fact, producers do not involve in selling of their vegetables house to house except in some big cities where the producers from very nearest fields carry vegetables and do selling door to door. Such vegetables are fresh and usually sold very easily. Producers are able to sell their vegetables in the morning hours and they return to their homes within three to four hours at noon.

(*b*) Road Side Selling

It is also commonly seen that some vegetables are sold on highway road side by growers to the consumers. The fields are attached or nearer to roads. Growers harvest their vegetables fresh and sell them. At this point, some retailers may also buy vegetables and sell them there itself or carry them to other nearby localities.

(E) Selling Vegetables in Weekly Bazars

In small town or large village or among a few villages, weekly bazars are arranged. Vegetables are brought by growers there and they are sold directly to consumers. Usually, retailers and commission agents are not there. However, their presence in weekly bazars is also not uncommon.

In weekly bazars, vegetables are available a fresh. These are brought by bullock carts, camel carts, Auto Reksha, bycles, head loads etc., Growers are producers. They start assembling before noon and return to their homes by evening.

(F) Marketing Yards

This is the place where producers carry their vegetables in bulk and sale them to wholesalers. Here prices do not fluctuate much at least for the period of 7-10 days. From wholesalers, vegetables are purchased by retailers who usually sell their vegetables in small markets. By this way vegetables reach to the consumers.

(G) Export and Import Market

The methods of selling vegetables are more or less similar. But quality remain main consideration in terms of appearance, shape, size, texture, nutrient etc. and then comes to quality packing in suitable size. In these markets usually perishable vegetables have little place. However, daily fresh vegetables may be sent by air to nearby countries.

(H) Processing Market

This involves production of certain vegetables on large scale maintaining continuity in their supply. Producers can directly contact the processor for getting all information about the production. Sometimes, processor want to have vegetable of a particular variety, with which the producer should be well acquainted. Processor also provides guidance for cultivation practices and take responsibility to accept produce. It is usually contractual agreements between the processor and the grower. Even the processor pays a sizeable percentage of money in advance to the grower. Doing so, processor becomes sure of getting vegetables and the grower has no disposal problem, though settlement of the final prices is done later.

The main use of vegetables in processing units is for freezing, canning, pickling and dehydration. Few examples of marketing channels are being adopted in the marketing of the following vegetable crops in India.

(*i*) Tomato

Channel 1 : Producer – Commission agent – Retailer – Consumer

Channel 2 : Producer – Commission agent – Wholesaler – Retailer – Consumer

Channel 3 : Producer – Wholesaler – Retailer – Consumer

Channel 4 : Producer – Commission agent – Shipper – Terminal market – Wholesaler – Retailer – Consumer

Channel 5 : Producer – Cooperative society – wholesaler/retailer – consumer

Channel 6 : Producer – Retailer – Consumer

(*ii*) Brinjal

Channel 1 : Producer – Commission agent – Wholesaler – Retailer – Consumer

Channel 2 : Producer – Commission agent – Retailer – Consumer

Channel 3 : Producer – Retailer – Consumer

(*iii*) Chillies

Channel 1 : Producer – Commission agent – Wholesaler – Retailer – Consumer

Channel 2 : Producer – Retailer – Consumer

Channel 3 : Producer – Consumer

(*iv*) Onion

Channel 1 : Producer – Commission agent – Wholesaler – Retailer – Consumer

Channel 2 : Producer – NAFED – Wholesaler – Retailer – Consumer

Channel 3 : Producer – Cooperative – Consumer

(*v*) Potato

Channel 1 : Producer – Consumer

Channel 2 : Producer – Wholesaler – Retailer – Consumer.

Channel 3 : Producer – Cooperative society – Consumer

Channel 4 : Producer – Local dealers Warehouse – Retailer – Consumer

(*vi*) Leafy Vegetables

Channel 1 : Producer – Consumer

Channel 2 : Producer – Retailer – Consumer

Channel 3 : Producer – Commission agent – Retailer – Consumer

Methods of Marketing of Vegetables

The prices of vegetables are settled by the commission agents on behalf of the seller with the buyer in the following ways.

(*a*) Private Negotiation

In this method, the purchaser make his offer personally to the commission agent and the bargain is settled. This method is common all over the country.

(*b*) Open Auction

In this method, almost all buyers assemble at a particular time in the market or at shop of the commission agent. Each plot of vegetables is kept for auction separately by the auctioneer. The highest bid is accepted for approval of the seller.

Quality Parameters of Vegetables

These are given as below :

(*a*) Appearance

Good shape, colour and freedom from blemishes and dirt.

(*b*) Texture

Crispness in cucumbers, mealiness in potatoes and juiceness in melons. These properties depend on the stage of maturity, inherited characters, cultural conditions, and moisture.

(*c*) Flavour

Pleasant flavour is always preferred.

(*d*) Nutritive Value

This is known after under taking tests. High chemical constituents lead to good nutritive value of vegetables.

Factors Affecting Quality of Vegetables

1. Treatment before harvesting
2. Maturity at harvest
3. Method of harvesting
4. Curing
5. Trimming
6. Washing
7. Sorting or grading
8. Suitable packing

Owing to lack of vegetable cooperative market network in India, the vegetable cultivation on large scale seems to be a risky proposition.

STORAGE

Methods of Vegetables Storage

The following methods of storing vegetables are common in India.

1. Country Method

In order to keep vegetables for future use growers follow various way to store their vegetables after harvest. Under ambient temperature conditions perishable vegetables cannot be stored 3 to 10 days, meanwhile, a good percentage of vegetables Retailers keep their vegetables in turgid conditions by sprinkling of tape water for 2-3 days, particularly leafy vegetables, fruit vegetables (okra, tomato, brinjal, green chillies), root crops (radish, carrot) and cucurbits (cucumber, sponge gourd, ridge gourd, bitter gourd, bottle gourd, little gourd, spine gourd, pointed gourd) dipped in water, cabbage heads are kept fresh by removing outer leaf at alternate days, doing so, the size and the weight of head decreases but retailers do not go in loss because they increase the price accordingly.

Vegetables like onion, garlic, potato, sweet potato and fully ripen pumpkins and fully matured wax gourd can be stored for longer period though losses are higher under ordinary conditions. For storing onion, with the help of a rope onion bulbs are tied on their neck arranged in spirally manner around the rope and hanged in the well ventilated shed. The another way is to spread onion bulbs on the floor in the shed making layer of 10 to 15 cm thick. The bulbs are turned time to time and rotten, damaged and sprouted bulbs are removed. Onion bulbs can also be stored safely for long period by keeping them in trays or tiers are arranged in well ventilated room or shed. Bulbs are checked time to time and unwanted bulbs are removed. In similar ways, garlic bulbs can also be stored under ordinary conditions. Potato and sweet potato tubers are stored with dry river sand. A thick layer of sand is made on the floor of the shed and potato/sweet potato tubers are arranged 15-20 cm thick layer and covered with 3-4 cm and sand layer and then again tubers are arranged. In this way 4 to 5 layers of tubers are arranged. Time to time checking may be done and any rotting tuber if found is removed.

Under well ventilated room or shed fully ripen pumpkins and wax gourd can be stored for about 4 to 5 months.

2. Storing Vegetables in Cold Storage

Vegetables in cold storage can be stored as fresh for longer period of time which help in stretching the vegetables marketing seasons all the year round and it will also go a long way in avoiding seasonal gluts, distress sales and price crashes.

Unfortunately, in India cold storage facility for storing vegetables is meager except for a number of cold storage plants that are available particularly in potato growing areas of Bengal, Bihar, Madhya Pradesh, Uttar Pradesh, Punjab and Gujarat. The largest cold storage for potato is at Kufri, Shimla. A number of multipurpose large-sized cold storage warehouses have also been started in big cities like Delhi, Kolkata, Mumbai, Jalandhar and Chennai for storing perishables.

In cold storage low temperature (0 to 10°C) and high humidity (70-84%) are maintained. Under these conditions, physiological and biochemical changes in side the stored vegetables slow down resulting in prolonging shelf-life. Nutritive values of vegetables remain unaltered (Table 2).

Table 2. Storage temperature and relative humidity for Vegetables(s)

Vegetables	*Temperature (°C)*	*RH (%)*	*Storage life (weeks)*
Onion, leaves	0.0	90-95	2
Onion bulbs	0.0	70-75	20-24
Pea, green	0.0	88-92	2-3
Pepper, green	7.2	85-90	3-5
Pepper, ripe	5.6-.7.2	90-95	2
Potato	3.0-4.4	85	34
Pumpkin	1.7-11.6	70.75	24-36
Radish, topped	0.0	88-92	3-5
Squash, winter	12.8-15.6	70-75	24-36
Sweet corn	6.0-1.7	90-95	1
Sweet potato	10.0-12.8	80-90	13-20
Tapioca, root	0.0-1.7	85	23
Tomato, unripe	8.9-10.0	85-90	4-5
Tomato, ripe	7.2	90	1
Turnip	0.0	90-95	8-16
Watermelon	7.2-15.6	80-90	2
Asparagus	0.0	95	3-4
Brinjal	10.0-11.1	92	3-4
Dolichus lablab, pod	0.6-1.7	90	3
Beet, topped	0.0-1.7	90-95	8-14
Beet, bunched	0.0	92	1-5
Bitter gourd	0.6-1.7	85-90	4
Cabbage, early	0.0-1.7	92-95	4-6
Cabbage, late	0.0-1.7	92-95	12
Carrot, topped	0.0	95	20-24
Cauliflower (Snowball)	0.0-1.7	85-95	7
Celery	0.6-0.0	92-95	8
Colocacia	11.1-12.8	85-90	21

Vegetables	Temperature (°C)	RH (%)	Storage life (weeks)
Coriander, leaves	0.0-1.7	90	5
Cucumber	10.0-11.7	92	2
Garlic	0.0	65	28-36
Ginger	7.2-10.0	75	16-24
Lettuce, head	0.0	90-95	3
Lettuce, leaves	0.0	95	1
Lima bean, pods	4.4-7.2	90-95	1.5-2.0
Muskmelon			
(Canta loupe)	1.7-3.3	90-95	1.5
(honey dew)	7.2	85	4.5
Okra	8.9	90	2

Factors Affecting Storage Life of Vegetables

1. Harvested at right maturity
2. Properly sorted and graded
3. Free from injuries
4. Humidity of storage
5. Right packing
6. Temperature of storage
7. Cleanliness of storage
8. Chemical composition of produce
9. Duration of storage
10. Kind and type of crop and variety

Role of Fruits and Vegetables : Nutritive Value and Role in Human Nutrition

Fruits and vegetables form the nutritive part of human diet being rich in vitamins and minerals. As such, they come under the category of 'protective foods'. The Indian Council of Medical Research has recommended a balanced diet to contain 90 gm of fruits and 284 gm of vegetables. Whereas, the present availability works out to 55 gm of fruits and 125 gm of vegetables per day per person. In addition to vitamins and minerals, a balanced diet should contain calorie yielding foods (carbohydrates) and body building foods (proteins) for the normal growth and wellbeing of a person. The importance of these constituents with suitable examples follows.

(1) Carbohydrates : These provide energy so that a person can carry out his work satisfactorily. Most of the fruits are high in sugars mostly dextrose and levulose and other sugars also. Sugars are important calorie yielding foods being easily digested and yield energy quickly, *e.g.* Mango, Potato, Sweet potato.

(2) Proteins : These are body building foods essential for growth. Deficiency of proteins causes retarded growth and increased susceptibility to diseases. In children kwashiorkor is frequent and often fatal. In adults, lack of protein leads to apathy and lethargy. Most of the fruits are low in proteins except guava and banana which contain 1 to 1.5% protein. Amongst vegetables, peas and beans are rich in proteins.

(3) Vitamin A : Vitamin A is present in fruits and vegetables in the form of provitamin A or carotene. Carotene is converted into Vitamin A in the body. Carotene is only 50%

as potent as Vitamin A. This vitamin is necessary for vision. Deficiency of Vitamin A causes night blindness and a serious deficiency causes an eye disease known as 'xerophthalmia'. Further, vitamin A promotes growth in young age and offers resistance to diseases. Mango, Papaya and Persimmon are rich in Vitamin A. Amongst vegetables, Carrot, Pumpkin (*Arkachandan*), Leafy green vegetables, Tomato, Green beans and Cucumber are rich in this vitamin.

(4*a*) **Vitamin B_1** (Thiamine) : Lack of this vitamin causes beriberi, paralysis and loss of sensitivity of skin. It is abundant in Orange, Pineapple, Jackfruit, Cashewnut, Green chilli, Beans, Onion, Sweet potato, Agati.

(4*b*) **Vitamin B_2** (Riboflavin) : It is required for growth and health of skin. Deficiency causes loss of appetite, reduction in body-weight and sore throat. It is abundant in *Bael,* Papaya, Banana, Apricot, Litchi, Pomegranate, Cabbage, Cauliflower, Potato, Beans, etc.

(5) Vitamin C : Deficiency of vitamin C causes scurvy, bleeding of gums, tooth decay, rheumatism. *Aonla* and guava are richest source of vitamin C which is also present in Grape, Lemon, Orange, Pineapple, Tomato, Leafy green vegetables, Cabbage, Chilli, Drumstick leaves, etc.

(6) Source of Fibre or Roughages : The fibrous portion of fruits and vegetables is found to exert beneficial effects by increasing the intestinal peristalsis and consequent relief from constipation. The fibre content in fruits is low. However, Guava, Grapes and *Aonla* contain fairly good amount of fibre (3.0 to 6.9%).

(7) Calcium : Calcium is essential for development of bones and its deficiency causes osteomalacia, caries of teeth, etc. Fruits and vegetables rich in calcium are : Acid lime, Orange, Cabbage, Leafy vegetables, Cauliflower, Onion, Agati, Drumstick leaves.

(8) Phosphorus : It is essential for maintaining the moisture content of tissues. Fruits rich in phosphorus are : Guava, Grape, Jackfruti, Passion fruit, Orange; while vegetables rich in phosphorus are : Carrot, Chilli, Drumstick leaves, Beans, Onion.

(9) Iron : It is essential for maintaining haemoglobin content of red blood corpuscles. Its deficiency causes nutritional anaemia. Fruits, rich in iron are : Custard apple, Guava, Pineapple, Strawberry, Grape. Vegetables rich in iron are : Carrot, Drumstick leaves, Beans, Agati.

(10) Nutritive Significance of Flavonoids: All fruits, citrus in particular, contain flavonoids which operate in infective conditions.

DESIGN, LAYOUT AND PLANTING

Planning the Orchard

Before undertaking the actual planting of fruit trees, it is advisable to prepare a plan which will enable the grower to provide for not only the most economic orchard management but also an economic layout and location of roads, drains, irrigation channels, hedges and windbreaks, etc.

Roads and Buildings

The buildings such as owner's residence, shed and labourers' quarters should be located near a public road or in the centre or near the well. The area necessary for construction should be left unplanted even if the construction is delayed. Straight roads, at right angles to each other, or about 2.5-3.0 m (8-10 ft) width should be made for easy movement of carts and machinery. The roads should be given a slope to drain off water.

Well Digging

If the source of irrigation is to be a well, it should be dug before planting as the trees require water as soon as they are planted. The well should be located as far as possible at the highest point to facilitate easy distribution of water at less cost.

Fencing

To prevent destruction of the trees from stray cattle and also to protect the orchard from thieves, it is necessary to provide some kind of fencing on all sides of the garden and this should be done preferably before planting the fruit trees.

Fences may be using thorns and dead bushes, but these are not satisfactory and require frequent repair and replacement. Barbed wire fencing is very good but its initial cost is rather high.

The best protection is, however, a construction of live fence. Some of the plants very useful as live fence are :

(*i*) *Prosopis juliflora and Caesalpinia sepiaria (Chillari)* : These can be established in May-June. The seed should be sown in a trench 30 cm (1 ft.) wide and 22.8 cm (9 in.) deep, all around the orchard boundary.

(*ii*) *Carissa carandas (Karonda)* : This makes an effective, dense hedge. In addition, it bears fruits if not pruned too closely.

Windbreaks

Windbreaks consist of planting of trees, shrubs or raising of artificial barriers on the windward side of an orchard for protection from wind. The most effective windbreak is a double row of tall trees, alternately placed. Plants like Eucalyptus, *Dalbergia sisoo, Carambola, Jambul,* and mulberry are found good. *Shelter belts* are wide and long belts of several rows or tall trees and shrubs planted across the prevailing wind direction to deflect wind currents, to reduce wind velocity and to give general protection against sand movement on vast agricultural fields/orchards, canals, highways, railway lines, etc. Effective shelter belts generally consist of 5 to 10 rows. Shelter belts are of great value in arid zones.

There should be at least as much space between the windbreaks and first row of trees as between the fruit trees. The windbreaks has its maximum effect to a distance of about four times as great as its height but has the same effect over about twice the distance.

IMPORTANCE OF WINDBREAKS

(1) High winds cause breakage of branches or loss of whole limb. High winds during summer from south-west whip the banana leaves and shred them completely. As such, *shevri (Sesbania egyptica)* is grown as a windbreaks all around banana orchard.

(2) Water loss is more in wind than in still air. Transpiration losses are considerably increased in exposed orchard than in trees protected by windbreaks.

(3) There is reduction in water requirement of fruit trees. In California, unprotected citrus orchards required 5 years to attain the size which was attained in two years in other orchards having windbreaks.

(4) Windbreaks provide protection from winter injury. Windbreaks raise the temperature on cold night by 2-3°C. They protect tree tops from high desiccating cold winds of winter.

(5) It has been found that the rate of soil moisture evaporation decreased towards leeward side.

(6) Windbreaks protect the blossoms, small fruitlets from strong winds preventing their desiccation resulting in high yields.

Systems of Planting Orchards

Lay-out means locating the position of trees, roads and buildings in the orchard being established, and systems of lay-out refer to the orderly ways of planting the trees. It is desirable to have the trees planted in systematic way because :

(1) Orchard operations like interculture and irrigation are carried out easily.

(2) It enables equal distribution of area under each tree.

(3) It results in least wastage of land.

(4) It makes supervision more easy and effective.

(5) There is room for systematic extension of the orchard.

The six systems of planting in which the fruit trees are commonly planted are as follows :

(*i*) Rectangle system

(*ii*) Square system

(*iii*) Quincunx or diagonal system

(*iv*) Hexagonal system

(*v*) Triangle system

(*vi*) Contour system

Short description of each system with diagram follows :

(*i*) Rectangle System : Trees are planted in straight rows running at right angles on one side of the field. Distance from plant to plant and row to row is not the same and four trees joined at the base give a rectangle. Cultivation and irrigation can be done in two directions. (Fig. 1).

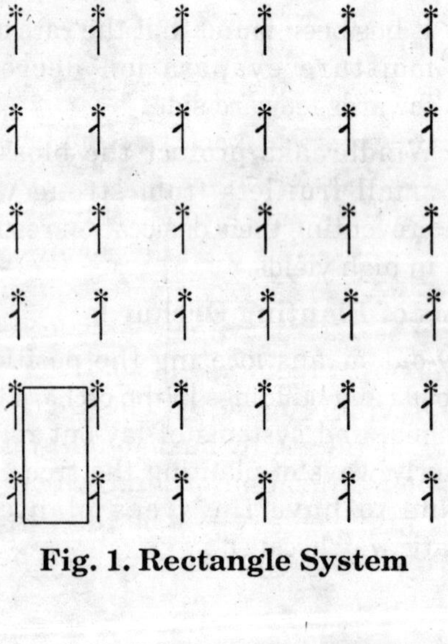

Fig. 1. Rectangle System

(*ii*) The Square System : The square system of planting is the simplest and the most convenient for lay-out. Trees are set at the corners of squarers formed by intersecting lengthwise parallel lines with crosswise parallel lines. This system of planting is universally adopted all over India. It has many advantages. Irrigation channels can run straight. Operations like ploughing, harrowing, cultivation, spraying, harvesting, etc. become easy when trees are planted at equal distances from each other in regular lines.

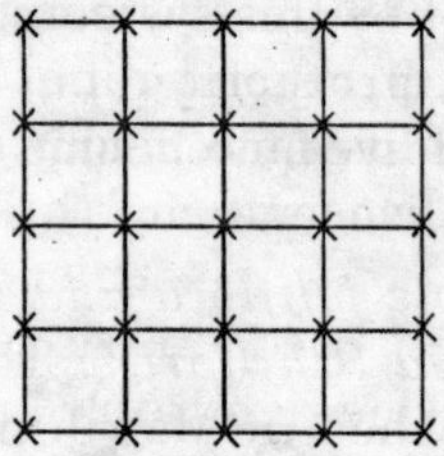

Fig. 2. Square System

(*iii*) Quincunx or Diagonal System : It is same as the square system with the addition of a tree in the centre of each square, that is, at the points of diagonal cut. In this case, the number of trees is almost doubled but the distance between the trees in the centre and at the corner is much reduced. For this reason, the central tree is usually not a permanent tree and is planted to fill the central space. This is known as a "Filler". Filler serves as a source of additional income till the main trees come into bearing. It should be removed if it hinders the growth of main plants in any way. Obviously, fillers are planted when plant to plant distance is much and the plants are expected to come into bearing after a number of years (Fig. 3).

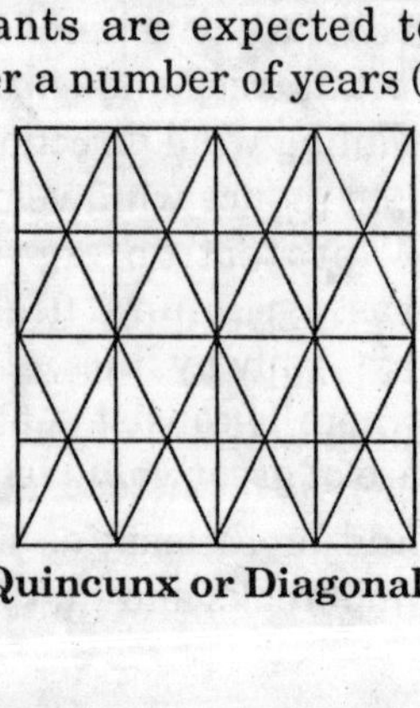

Fig. 3. Quincunx or Diagonal System

***(iv)* The Hexagonal System :** In this system, the trees are set at the corners of equilateral triangles. This system differs from the square system in that the distance between the rows is less than the distance between the trees in the rows, but distance from tree to tree in six directions, remains the same. Besides permitting cultivation in three directions, this system allows planting of 15% more trees than can be planted by square system in a given area.

For lay-out by this system, the base line is first set up after staking it at the required distance; the rest of the field is marked by a simple device consisting of three iron rings and two pieces of wire each equal in length to the distance between the stakes marked on the base line. One righ is fixed at one end of each piece of wire. The remaining ring is fixed at the other ends of the two pieces of the wire. Thus, there are two end rings and one central ring on the wires. The end rings are slipped over the first two pegs and the wires are pulled tight in order to drive a peg through the central ring, in the second row. The end rings are then slipped over the next peg and a second peg is fixed in the second row through the third or central ring. This system is not commonly followed as it is difficult to lay-out (Fig. 4).

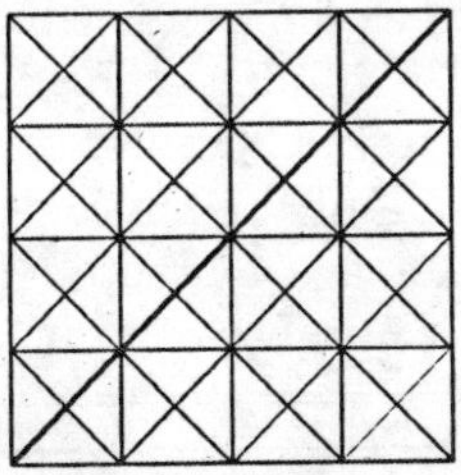

Fig. 4. Hexagonal System

***(v)* Triangle System :** In this system, the trees are plated as in the square system except that those in the even numbered rows are midway between, instead of opposite to those in the odd numbered.

This system is not of much practical importance. The number of trees is also less than those in the square system and the plants are not placed at equal distance from all sides (Fig. 5).

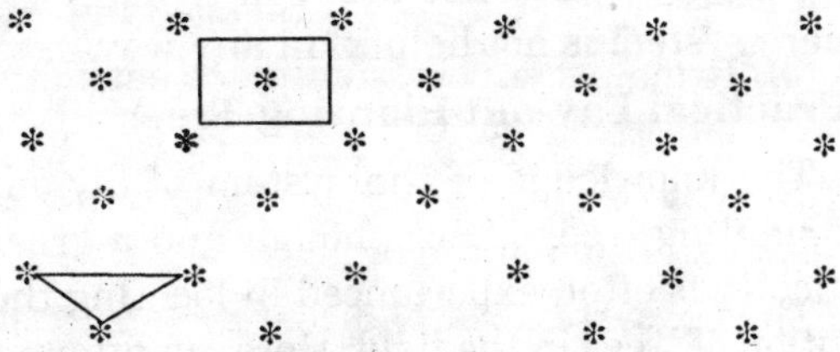

Fig. 5. Triangle System

***(vi)* Contour System :** This system is meant for hilly tracts only. Pegs are marked at various heights from mean sea level and the points having the same altitude are connected together by a line and the trees are given spacing on this line. This retards the ill-effects of erosion. The trees will be in a straight line from one side only. The rows are represented by lines passing through the same contour. (Fig. 6).

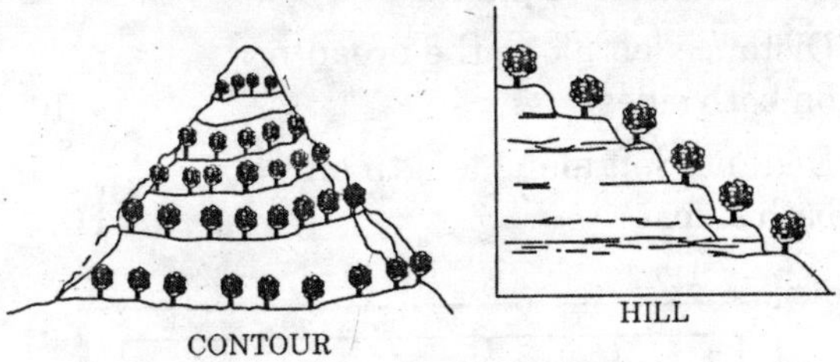

Fig. 6. Contour System

Though the square system of lay-out for planting the trees is the most popular one and it claims to be easy to practice and facilitates inter-cultivation, the hexagonal system is certainly better, as it accommodates about 15 per cent more plants than the square system. This means 15 per cent increase in income from the same area without any decrease in the land (area) requirements of trees. This is an appreciable benefit. The increase in number of plants in hexagonal system is because of utilization of land which is not utilized in the square system (Fig. 2 and 4). The argument that the plants become overcrowded in the hexagonal system is not very convincing, because in the square system also the trees are placed at the same distance on four sides as in the hexagonal system. More diagonal distance between trees in the square system is not helpful in any way.

A Practical Lay-out Planting Trees

The knowledge of the system of lay-out for planting trees is not enough and a great difficulty is often experienced in locating the position of trees in the field. Here, an attempt has been made to outline the procedure for lay-out by common systems of planting.

Number of plants in each row	...	9
Number of rows	...	8
Total number of plants	...	72
Number of rows lengthwise	...	8
Number of plants in each row	...	9
Number of rows breadthwise	...	9
Number of plants in each row	...	8
Total number of plants	...	72
Distance left along the breadth on both sides	...	10′
Distance left along length on both sides	...	$11^1/_2$′

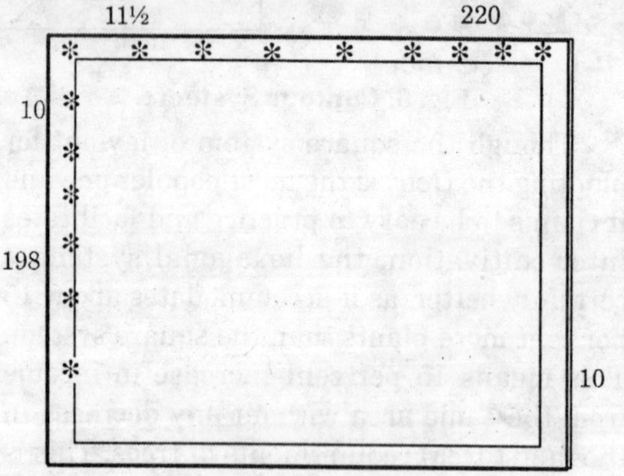

Fig. 7. Actual Field Lay-out by Square System

From the plan and above information, it is quite evident that after leaving $12^1/_2$ feet along both the breadthwise sides of the field, length of 8 × 25 ft + 25 ft. = 225′ would be required; but the field measures only 220 feet. This shortage of 5 ft should be adjusted at the ends of the first row. That is, instead of the first tree being placed at a distance of 25/2 feet (half the plant to plant distance) from the boundary mark it will be—

$$\frac{25}{2} - \frac{5}{2} = 10 \text{ ft from the boundary.}$$

The lay-out plans of square and hexagonal systems thus prepared for a field of one acre measuring 220′ × 198′ with plant distance as 25 ft. will indicate the following information (Fig. 7) :

Square System

Length of the field	...	220 ft
Breadth of the field	...	198 ft
Plant to plant distance	...	25 ft
Row to row distance	...	25 ft

Similarly, adjustment for rows running perpendicular to the lengthwise sides should be made by leaving 11½, instead of 12½′ on either side (Fig. 8)

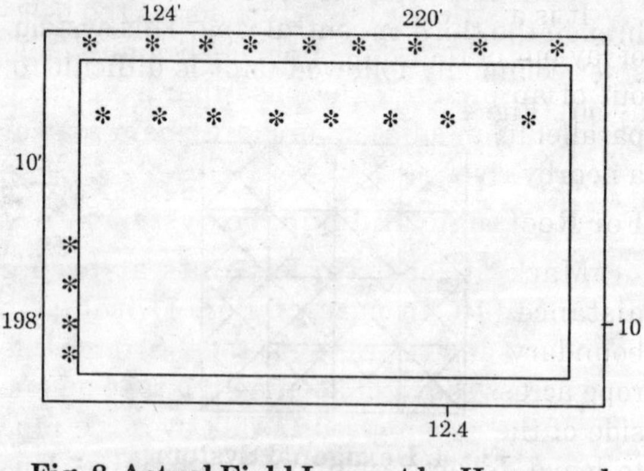

Fig. 8. Actual Field Lay-out by Hexagonal System

Number of plants in each odd row, 9. Number of plants in each even row 8..Number row, 9. Total number of plants 77.

Number of trees in

the first row $\frac{220}{25}$	=	9 (with 5′ deficit. Refer above)
Row to row distance	:	0.866* × P ft Where P is the tree to tree distance – 0.866 × 25 ft = 21.65 ft.
Breadth of the field	:	198 ft.
Total number of rows	:	$\frac{198}{21.65}$ = 9 (with 3.15 ft surplus)
Number of odd rows	:	1, 3, 5, 7, 9, ..4
Total number of plants in odd rows	:	5 × 9 = 45
Number of even rows	:	2, 4, 6, 8 ..4
Total number of plants in even rows	:	4 × 8 = 32
Total number of plants by hexagonal system	:	45 + 32 = 77

Selection of Base Line

It is a straight line which forms the basis of lay-out of the whole field. To begin the lay-out of an orchard, the base line is selected parallel to an adjacent orchard, main road or a nearby river.

For Rectangle and Square Systems

Mark at least three points at proper distance (10′ in case of Fig. 1) from the boundary and fix ranging rods. Stretch the rope across the field keeping the rope on one side of the ranging rods. Walk over the rope to leave an impression on the ground. This represents the first row as well as the base line. Now stretch the measuring tape along this row and fix wooden pegs to locate the positions of trees leaving proper distance from the ends ($11^1/_2$ ft in case of Fig. 2). Make a right angle on this row at the position of the first plant by fixing at least three ranging rods on the other side and looking through the grooves of the cross-staff.

Ranging rods should always be kept straight. Stretch the rope across the field through the same side of the ranging rods. Make sure that this is right angle by measuring 30 feet on one side, 40 feet on the other and 50' as the third side (Fig. 9). Similarly, make a right angle at the point of the last plant. Mark the position of the side trees on the last row on both the perpendiculars and join the two corresponding points. Check that all the four corners are at right angles. Mark the positions of rows towards either side of the boundary and of trees on the first and last rows. Stretch rope across the corresponding points on the sides leaving impressions on the ground and get the positions of the plants. Fix wooden pegs to represent their position.

For Quincunx System

Lay-out of the field as in the case of square system. Stretch rope through the diagonal points of squares and fix additional pegs at the points where diagonals cross.

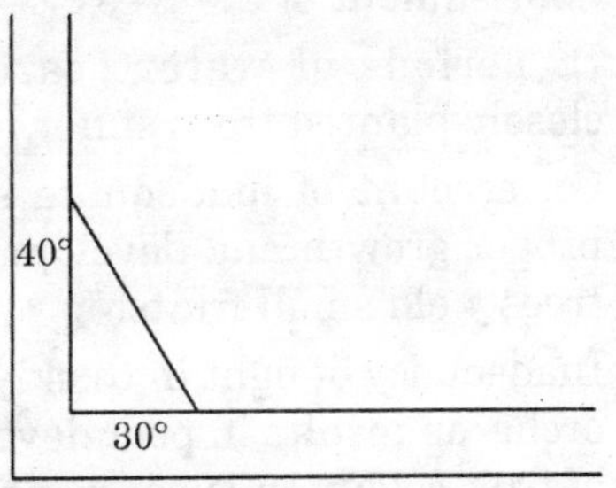

Fig. 9. Checking a Right Angle

For Hexagonal System

Mark the four sides as in the case of square system with the distance shown in the stretch. Locate the position of plants also on the first row.

Take rope slightly more in length than double the distance between the plants. Put a knot in the centre so that the length of the rope on either side of the knot is as much as the tree to tree distance. An iron chain or rod (3/8″ dia) with a ring in the centre and either arm equal in length to the tree to tree distance is often used. Hold the ends of the ropes, each at the positions of two consecutive plants on the first row, and stretch from the centre to give an equilateral triangle and thereby the position of a plant on the second row is fixed. In this way, the field can be laid out.

Every first and the last plant in the odd row should fall on the lines representing the perpendiculars on the first row. This serves as a check for the correctness of the lay-out.

Spacing of Fruit Plants

The spacing depends primarily on the size, the full grown tree is expected to attain. It must be borne in mind that when the trees are full grown, there should not be any overcrowding of the trees.

The main disadvantages of the overcrowding are :

(*i*) When the trees are planted too close to each other, their roots become crowded, and this leads to under-nourishment of the trees.

(*ii*) In periods of water scarcity, the closely planted trees suffer more.

(*iii*) On account of inadequate scope for proper growth and development, the trees yield small fruits.

(*iv*) Inadequacy of light in thickly planted orchards results in poor development of fruit colour on lower regions of the trees.

(*v*) Close planting hinders proper cultural operations.

(*vi*) The closely planted trees naturally tend to grow tall thereby increasing the difficulty in pruning, spraying, harvesting, etc.

From the above discussion, it is clear that, for proper development and better yields, the fruit trees must be spaced properly. The two important factors which determine the spacing of fruit plants are :

(*i*) Natural habit of the plant, and

(*ii*) Soil and climatic conditions.

Trees which have a natural big spread, *e.g.* mango; which is bigger in size than *santra or mosambi,* would require more spacing.

Under favourable soil and climatic conditions, the trees would grow to their best and as such would require more spacing as compared to the same trees growing under unfavourable soil and climatic conditions.

The grafted or budded trees in general, being smaller than seedling trees, would require less spacing as compared to the seedling trees.

The best guide to determine the spacing would be the observation of the size attained by full grown trees, in a well managed orchard in the vicinity of the selected site.

The distance of the selected site.

The distance for various fruit trees is given the Table 3.

Table : 3 The distance of various fruit trees

Fruits	Distance
1. Mango	30′ to 45′
2. *Chiku*	25′ to 30′
3. Santra	20′ to 25′
4. *Mosambi*	20′ to 25′
5. *Kagdi limbu*	15′ to 18′
6. Grape fruit	20′ to 25′
7. Guava	18′ to 24′
8. Banana/dwarf	5′ to 6′
9. Banana/tall	8′ to 10′
10. Papaya	8′ to 18′
11. Custard apple	15′ to 18′
12. Pomegranate	15′ to 18′
13. Jackfruit	30′ to 40′

Digging the Pits

The plot where the trees are to be planted should be laid out by marking the position of fruit trees by fixing the pegs. While digging the pits, these stakes are required to be removed and thus the exact position of the tree is lost.

To overcome this, use of planting board is advised. Planting board is a plank 5′ long, 2′ wide and 1″ thick with central notch and two more notches on its either sides at equal distance as shown in the Fig. 10. This distance should be larger that half the size of the pit required.

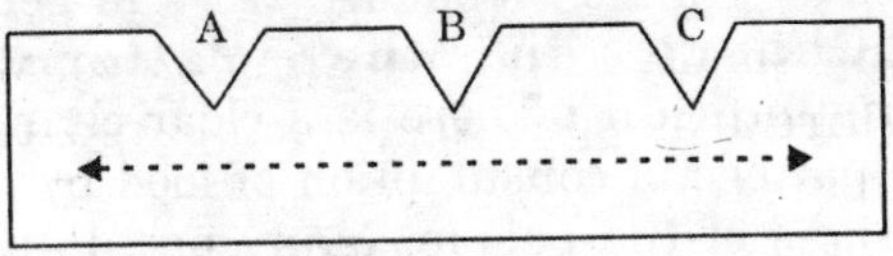

Fig. 10. Planting Board

The central notch 'A' is placed on a peg, marking the position of the tree. Two pegs are inserted in notches 'B' and 'C' pegs. While planting the trees, the side notches are fixed in the pegs at 'B' and 'C' and the plant is held in the notch 'A'. Later on, the pegs 'B' and 'C' are removed.

If planting is to be done in June, then the pits should be dug during summer so that the planting could be taken up with the onset of monsoon. In the heavy rainfall areas, it is advisable to take up the planting after the monsoon so that the planted young plants are not required to remain in waterlogged condition.

It is convenient to dig pits of 3′ × 3′ × 3′ or 2′ × 2′ × 2′. If the soil is having a uniform texture, it may not be necessary to dig pits of such a big size. In such cases, the soil may be scooped out with a digging fork and the plant set in. When the pits are dug, they should be refilled by mixing well rotten F.Y.M. with the soil and should be watered, before planting.

Questions From Previous Year's Papers

Q. 1. Answer any four of the following in about 150 words each :

(a) Discuss in brief about semiochemicals in pest control.

(b) Management of storage pests

Q. 2. Answer the following in about 150 words each :

(a) What are prophylactic and curative measures for the stored grain pests in godowns?

(b) Do the climatic requirements and the cultural practices of crop production carry the same meaning or differ with one another? Explain in brief.

Q. 3. Write short notes on the control measures of diseases of food grains during storage.

10. FOODS

FOOD PRODUCTION AND DIETARY PATTERN

A. Food Production and Consumption Trends in India

Introduction : India is predominantly an agricultural country. Till about three decades ago traditional agricultural practices were in vogue. Agriculture was in a primitive stage for several decades and the rural population was left with no alternative but to depend on land. For want of employment opportunities in the non-agricultural sectors, there is excessive pressure on land.

In India about 66 per cent of the total working population is engaged in agriculture. A decade ago, the percentage of the total population engaged in agriculture in the developed countries like U.K., U.S.A., Canada and Australia was 2.2, 2.4, 5.6 and 6.2 respectively. The percentage of land-man ratio is the highest in India which leads to low productivity. The percentage of the population active in agriculture in Pakistan is 54.5 and in Bangladesh 84.8.

Cropping pattern has diversified and non-traditional crops like summer moong, soyabean, summer groundnut, sunflower etc., are gaining importance. In order to utilize scarce resources optimally, a short duration third crop is also being raised, utilizing residual, moisture, available from post-kharif and post-rabi.

Change in the Pattern of Consumption : There is a clear change in the pattern of consumption of food by many sections of the people. Many people prefer superior grains to coarse millets with the result that wheat and rice have to an extent displaced the minor millets.

The department of Food and Public distribution undertakes various activities such as procurement of food items, their storage, movement and delivery to the distributing agencies, besides this it is responsible for management of the the ford economy of the nation.

A close watch is kept on production and efforts are made to ensure their adequate availability of foodgrains etc at reasonable prices in different parts of the country. The details of production of foodgrains for last 10 years are summarised in the following table.

Table 1. Production of foodgrains (in lakh tonnes)

Crop	1998-99	1999-2000	2000-2001	2001-02	2002-03	2003-04	2004-05	2005-06	2006-07	2007*-08
Rice	860.8	896.8	849.8	933.4	718.2	885.3	853.1	917.9	933.5	956.8
Wheat	712.9	763.7	696.8	727.7	657.6	721.5	720.0	693.5	758.1	767.8
Coarse Cereals	313.3	303.4	310.8	333.7	260.7	376.0	339.2	346.7	339.2	396.7
Pulses	149.1	134.1	110.7	133.7	111.3	149.1	133.8	133.9	142.0	151.9
Total	2036.1	2098.0	1968.1	2128.5	1747.8	2131.9	2046.1	2092.0	2172.8	2273.2

*as per advanced estimates as on 22.4.2008.

Table 2. Procurement of Foodgrains (in lakh tonnes)

Marketing Season	1998-99	1999-2000	2000-2001	2001-02	2002-03	2003-04	2004-05	2005-06	2006-07	2007-08*
Rice[1]	125.99	182.28	212.81	221.27	164.10	228.28	217.93	276.56	251.07	259.54
Wheat[2]	126.52	141.44	163.55	206.30	190.54	158.01	165.95	147.85	92.26	111.27

[1] Marketing season : October-September
[2] Marketing season : April-March
* As on 26.6.2008.

There are two aspects of foodgrains consumption policy. One aspect is, to control increasing rate of population so that the pressure of demand on foodgrains may be reduced to an extent (Population policy). The second is to change the consumption pattern in favour of non-cereals (Nutrition policy).

1. Population Policy : The Family Welfare Planning Programme is the Government's population policy through which steps are taken to bring down the fertility rate which is relfected in family size and ultimately in the population of the country.

2. Nutrition Policy : Among the various socio-economic groups those who are below the poverty line, landless agricultural labourers, those who live in slum and remote tribal areas, people exposed to natural calamities are found to be vulnerable to malnutrition.

Children, pregnant women and nursing mothers also are exposed to malnutrition. The aim of nutrition policy of the Government is to divert the people from the fine-grained cereal diet to a non-cereal *i.e.*, millets (coarse grains) diet with high nutrient content. For this purpose, a Food and Nutrition Board has been set up.

(*i*) Special Nutrition Progammes (SNP) : The Board organises various, nutrition programmes for the benefit of vulnerable groups like pre-school and school going children. Highly nutritive varieties of food have been evolved as supplementary nutrition for children, pregnant women and nursing mothers from 1970-1971.

This special food provides 300 calories with 10-12 grams of protein for the age group up to 6 years for 300 days in a year. For pregnant women and nursing mothers this food provides 500 calories with 25 grams of protein for 300 days.

Foodgrains versus Fruits and Vegetables : It is known that for most Indians the calorie intake is insufficient. To reduce calorie insufficiency, what is required would be higher incomes for the poor and the availability of cheap sources of calories. The accompanying Table on the calorie and protein content of different types of food and the price per unit calorie and proteins portrays what should be an obvious picture. Cereals and pulses are by far the cheapest sources of calories and protein. Fruits and vegetables contain other valuable ingredients, but so far as calories are concerned, they cannot replace cereals and pulses.

Those who suffer from an inadequacy in calorie consumption cannot, therefore, be expected to turn to fruits, vegetables, nuts and eggs. Such food sources are more expensive. A healthy food, no doubt, requires, besides calories and protein, other essential nutrients like vitamins, minerals, dietary fibre, etc. The recommendations of the Indian Council of Medical Research almost two decades ago, covered cereals, pulses, green and other vegetables, tubers, milk, oils and sugar.

Surveys conducted during 1988-90 show, that in poor households, the consumption of cereals is much higher and consumption of vegetables, fruits, milk, oil, etc., are very much lower, while the converse is true with the affluent classes. In view of these facts, what is called for, is to continue the drive for production of cereals, fruits, vegetables, milk, eggs, oil, and simultaneously steadily improve the purchasing power of the poorer sections.

Table 3. Calorie and Protein Content in Different Foods

Type of Food	Food Contents	
	Calories a kg	Protein in gm a kg
I. Fine cereals		
Rice	3,400	75
Wheat	3,460	118
II. Coarse grains		
Jowar	3,490	104
Bajra	3,032	97
III. Pulses		
Tur	3,350	223
Moong	3,480	245
IV. Vegetables		
Brinjals	218	12.7
Cabbage	238	15.8
Potatoes	970	16.0
V. Fruits		
Bananas	84/each	0.8/each
VI. Nuts		
Groundnut	5,490	267
Copra	6,620	68
VII. Eggs	100/each	7.5/each

Sources : 1. Calorie and food content from National Sample Survey Organisation, Report No. 238, 1978.

B. NATIONAL AND INTERNATIONAL FOOD POLICIES

Agriculture takes care of producing food, food problem arises when there is a deficit production or improper marketing or distribution. To monitor the proper functioning of the above factors, food policies are propounded by the Government at the national and state levels. At the global level alsc food policy originates when serious calamities crop up in certain countries and large sections of the population face starvation. Several countries rushed food to Ethiopia a few years ago.

It is of interest to know that on the separation of Burma (now Myanmar) in 1937 from India, imports of 15 to 20 lakh tonnes of rice diminished and food problem in India originated. When Burma fell to Japan in the World War II, the supplies were completely cut off and the food crisis worsened. Bengal famine of 1943 is still fresh in our memory.

After the War ended in 1945, India was partitioned in 1947 giving rise to Pakistan. 82 per cent of the population remained in India, only 68 per cent of the irrigated area and 75 per cent of the cropped area came to India's share and the rest went to Pakistan. Rice and wheat had to be imported from foreign countries. The food policy adopted was :

(*a*) Food rationing and the consequent commitment by the Government to feed millions of people.

(*b*) Procurement of internal supplies was found inadequate and foodgrains were imported.

(*c*) Depending upon the requirement, and local production, the imports were increased.

(*d*) Imported foodgrains were costlier than locally produced grains, and therefore Government had to subsidise while distributing them to make the price come within the reach of the common man.

In 1947, the Food Policy Committee recommended a new approach to the food problem to be adopted immediately.

(*a*) In stages, it should be planned to do away with import of foodgrains.

(b) The commitment to the consumers given by the Government in the rationing system to be liquidated in stages.

(c) A substantial internal procurement should be pursued to solve the food problem.

The Food Procurement Committee of 1950 made suggestions for complete decontrol and free market. This was not acceptable to the Government as risks involved were very many.

Food Policy During 1950-51

The Government of India was anxious to reduce imports and food-aid and self-sufficiency in food was focussed in the First-Year Plan. The seasons were favourable, harvests were good and there was a comfortable food position. Food prices came down by 23 per cent during the first plan period. The increase in production contained the inflation, and stabilised the economy. Decontrol of food was under consideration towards the end of the plan.

National Food For Work Programme (NFFWP) :

The scheme for National Food for Work Programme has been launched with effect from 13-10-2004. This programme is being implemented in 150 most backward districts of the country so that the generation of supplementary wage employment and providing for food security through creation of need based economic, social and community assets in these districts, is further intensified. Most of the backward districts, which would be benefit from the scheme are in the tribal belts. The scheme will provide 100 days of employment at minimum wages for at least one able-bodied person from each house hold in the country. Allocation and offtake of foodgrains under the scheme during 2004-05, 2005-06 and 2006-07 is as under.

Table 4. Allocation and offtake of foodgrains under the scheme in lakh tonnes.

S.No.	Year	Allocation	offtake	% of offtake	Allocation	offtake	% of offtake
1	2004-05	14.25	3.06	21.48	5.75	0.65	11.30
2	2005 – 06	6.65	6.59	99.09	2.53	4.08	161.26
3	2006 – 07	0.00	1.22	0.00	0.00	0.21	0.00

* Offtake include backlog quota.

Targetted Public Distribution System

In order to ensure availability of minimum quantity of foodgrains to the families living below the poverty line, the Government launched the TPDS in June 1997. It was intended to benefit about six crore poor families in the country for whom a quantum of 72 lakh tonnes of foodgrains was earmarked annually at the rate of 10 kg per family per month.

The allocation was increased from 10 kg to 20 kg from 1 April 2000. This was increased from 20 to 25 kg per family per month from July 2001. From 1 April 2002, this allocation has been further increased from 25 to 35 kg per family per month. The Central Issue Price (CIP) for BPL families is Rs. 4.15 per kg for wheat and Rs. 5.45 per kg for rice.

Table 5. Allocation and offtake of Foodgrains in lakh tonnes

S.No.	Year	Allocation	Offtake
1	2003-04	712.52	239.31
2	2004-05	717	293.55
3	2005-06	716.21	311.06
4	2006-07	576.56	313.69
5	2007-08	392.98	332.8

Processing and Production Constraints

Processing Foodgrains (Cereals and Pulses) : The post-harvest technology includes the operations commencing with the harvest and as such includes the process of harvesting and threshing of crop as well as cleaning, grading, packing and storage of grains. The processing of raw materials into finished or ready to use products is yet another aspect.

Processing wheat crop has been mechanised but only in selected areas where combination have been pressed into service. Scientific storage of grains is another aspect which has received considerable attention. In crops like oilseeds and pulses very little progress has been made in this direction. This is because for the operations to be mechanised synchrony in time and space is essential. Further, the operation to be economical, the fields should be contiguous and crop spread over large areas.

The majority of pulse crops of India are grown either as mixed crops or raised on relatively small areas in the nooks and corners of fields. Hence, the mechanical operations are of not much relevance today though some progress has been made outside India specially in Australia both in chickpea and pigeonpea. Care of plants immediately after harvest till the threshing operation and bruchid infestation during storage are the major problems with pulses.

The pulse crops exhibit indeterminate growth habits where vegetative growth continues side by side even after the reproductive phase is in progress. This has resulted in what is known as production in "flushes". Fortunately, this phenomenon is confined predominantly in kharif pulses like pigeonpea, greengram, blackgram and cowpea. Hand-picking is the only way to collect the mature pods. However, we have now varieties which give one major flush and such varieties are harvested at the stage of pod maturity. But the major constraint is the fact that though pods are dry, the rest of the plant is still green and before threshing operations could commence, these plants have to be sun-dried.

During the process of drying when the plants are stacked on the ground, conditions are favourable for the saprophytic fungi to multiply rapidly with plenty of moisture, optimum temperature and relatively dim light. This commences the process of rotting the specially those plants in contact with the soil are badly damaged. This not only reduces the overall grain yield but the quality of left-over seed is affected adversely, resulting in the formation of 'hard' seeds. Rotting after harvest could be eliminated in pigeonpea by stacking the bundles upright but this is not possible in the rest of the crops. The losses could be reduced if the harvested material is kept on hard-dry ground and turned over regularly. Further, the plants should never be roped tightly in bundles but left loose so as to permit some aeration. In rabi pulses like gram, lentil and peas the entire plant is dry at the time of harvest, and normally no such problem exists. But unusual rains cause havoc as it happened in 1982, and under such situations it is best to leave the crop standing in the field for some more time.

The bruchid infestation accounts for major losses during storage and sometimes grain losses are total. The adult lays eggs which are visible as white dots on the seed coat. After the eggs hatch the larvae move into the seed which serves as the nutrition for their growth. The adults emerge out through a pore rendering such seeds unfit for human consumption. This storage pest belongs to genus *Cailosobruchus* and at least two species *C. maculatus* and *C. chinensis* are common. The rate of multiplication is very fast and it roughly takes four weeks from egg to egg. High humidity and the temperature around 30°C appears to be optimum. With rapid rate of multiplication even a pair of adults can cause considerable damage in course of time.

They often appear in the crop in low numbers just prior to harvest. The spray of endosulfan at this stage gives partial control, besides it can prove a health hazard due to carry-over effect. The bruchid infestation also occurs in harvested material and on threshing floors though the major spot appears to be storage godown. Some of the preventive measures are :

1. Spray of insecticide prior to harvest. This practice could be used where the crop is raised for seed purpose only.
2. Stacking and threshing operations should be carried out on clear places possible free or away from insects.
3. Drying seeds appears to be the best preventive measure. Hatching of egg and development into the adult insect is dependent on the percentage moisture of seed. Fifteen per cent and above is most ideal for multiplication whereas ten per cent and lower seems to be safe.
4. Bruchid essentially is a creeper and once available makes its way through the holes in the packing material. An experiment was conducted by storing seed material in different packing material. Gunny bags proved to be poor whereas thick lined cloth bags proved ideal. Storing of grain in double cloth bags has given fairly good protection, though it has to be kept in mind that this practice will not be foolproof. This combination of polythene bag inside and thick cloth bag outside is also satisfactory though this may cause some loss in germination-percentage.
5. Though seed material could be treated with insecticides including DDT, BHC or even Captan, for consumption purpose Malathion has been suggested. But this is controversial and no insecticide appears to be safe.
6. Fumigation with either aluminium phosphide or ethylene dichloride or carbon tetrachloride is effective. However, these fumigants are insecticides and not ovicides and hence fumigation has to be done at least twice. Another disadvantage is that small farmers may not be in a position to use this method.
7. Storage in proper containers is yet another method where Pusa Bin has proved fairly effective.

Methods of Processing

(*a*) Drying : This refers to the removal of small amounts of moisture from a solid or nearly solid material by evaporation by spreading the material in a thin or thick layer.

Depending upon the mode of heat transfer, drying methods are divided into (a) conduction drying (b) convection drying and (c) radiation drying. There are other methods also known as 'dielectric drying', chemical or absorption drying, vacuum drying, freeze drying, etc. Convection drying is adopted for all types of grains and conduction drying for parboiled grains.

In 'Conduction drying', heat transfer to the wet solid takes places through a metallic solid surface. The source of heat may be hot water, steam, flue gases, hot oil, etc. The surface temperatures vary widely. Contact dryers can be operated under low pressure and in inert atmosphere. Dust and dusty materials can be removed.

In 'Convection drying', hot gases are used to dry the wet solid which carry away the vaporised moisture. The process of transferring the heat to the solid is by convection. This is a costlier method than the conduction drying as fuel consumption per kg of moisture evaporated is higher.

'Radiation Drying' : This is based on the absorption of radiant energy of the sun and its transformation into heat energy by the grain. The effectiveness of the sun drying depends upto the temperature, relative humidity of the atmospheric air, speed of the wind, type and condition of the grain. Sun drying is the traditional method in tropical countries.

Grain parameters : The factors which affect the rate of drying are as follows :

(*a*) Type, variety and condition of the grain'

(*b*) Initial moisture content at harvest;

(*c*) Structure and chemical composition of the kernel, seed coat, husk, etc.

(*d*) Foreign materials present in the grain.

These factors should be considered in designing a suitable grain dryer.

(*b*) Parboiling : This process is in vogue for centuries in the East. Nearly 50 per cent of paddy is parboiled and milled into rice in India. Parboiling is a hydrothermal treatment of paddy followed by drying before milling into rice. Since 1940, parboiling is practised on a commercial scale in the U.S.A., Italy and British Guiana.

During parboiling, gelatinisation of starch and disintergration of protein in the endosperm takes place. The starch and protein expand and fill the internal air spaces. The fissures and cracks in the endosperm are sealed, making the grain translucent and hard; thus minimising the breakage of grain during milling. The colour of rice changes to yellow or yellowish-brown depending upon the variety of the paddy, soaking time, temperature, steaming time, drying time, etc.

Water soluble B-vitamins and other water soluble nutrients diffuse into the endosperm during parboiling and therefore the loss of nutrients is less in parboiled rice even after polishing. Vitamin E is also found in parboiled rice. The heat treatment, during parboiling destroys some natural anti-oxidants. This causes increased rancidity during storage. Scented and slender varieties are not parboiled. Long and slender varieties which are more fragile are boiled to make them hard and minimise breakage during milling. The moisture content of the parboiled paddy is retained between 14 and 16 per cent.

(*c*) Grain Milling Operations : Foodgrains have an outer protective husk/bran layer composed of rough, fibrous, pigmented and waxy substances which are not suitable for edible purposes. The oily fraction of the grain reduces the storage life of grains. Removal of these components of the grains by suitable processing techniques is a prerequisite prior to milling or flour making. Milling consists in reduction of size and separation of inedible forms prior to processing the foodgrains into edible form. Milling includes cleaning, husking, sorting, whitening, polishing, grinding, sifting, etc. To increase the milling quality of foodgrains and improve the quantity and quality of the end products, some of the foodgrains are subjected to hydrothermal treatment which is called 'conditioning' prior to milling.

Flow chart of the two methods of milling pulses is given below.

Wet milliing	**Dry milling**
Pulses	Pulses
Cleaning (chaff, dirt, etc.)	Cleaning (chaff, dirt, etc.)
Soaking	Pitting (mixture of husk and broken kernels)

Mixing with red earth	Pretreatment with oil
↓	↓
Conditioning	Conditioning
↓	↓
Dehusking and splitting (mixture of husk small brokens and powder)	Dehusking and splitting (mixture of husk, brokens and powder)
↓	↓
Grading-brokens	Grading
↓	↓
Dehusked split pulses (grade 1 pulses)	Polishing (grade 1 pulses).

There are two modern methods of milling corn; 'dry milling' and 'wet milling'. In dry milling, corn germ (for corn oil extraction), corn husk and deoiled germ (for feed) and broken corn (for breakfast preparations) are the products obtained. In wet milling, pure starch, germ and feed are got.

Milling of pulses involves removal of outer husk and splitting the grain into two equal halves. The husk is more tightly held by the kernel of pulses than in the case of cereals. Greengram, redgram, bengalgram, horsegram, fieldpea are the common pulses. Even in the case of pulses, there are two milling methods viz. wet milling and dry milling.

Storage Properties of Legumes : During long periods of storage, undesirable changes in the colour of seed coat, reduced digestibility and acceptability, toughening of seeds leading to prolonged cooking time, take place. Insect infestation and contamination by mycotoxins, also result in qualitative and quantitative loss of food legumes. It is necessary to correlate storage conditions like temperature, relative humidity and duration of cooking and fix optimum conditions of storage for different pulses. Research studies should investigate physico-chemical treatments to inhibit undesirable changes or enhance desirable changes. Development of pulses with easier cooking quality, and better digestibility characteristics, better storage and keeping qualities, milling and processing characteristics pose a serious challenge to plant breeders and post-harvest technologists.

Cooking and Consumer Acceptance of Food Legumes : Cooking of pulses for long period results in increased fuel consumption which is wasteful and is also a constraint in the rural households. It also results in reduction and modification of nutrients by lowering the availability of lysine and biological value. Therefore, cooking quality of legumes should be precisely defined followed by standardised methods to test quality determinants like flavour, cooking time, seed textures and colour, palatability, etc., to enable comparison and evaluation.

Varietal and agro-climatic characteristics modify the milling quality of grain legumes. Loose husked varieties with less gumminess and bold seeded varieties, require miniumm pre-milling operations and yield better. Small-sized pulses are not advantageous if they are to be converted into flour or used as split dal. In legume improvement programme, these factors have to receive attention.

In warm humid climate insect infestation and mould attacks bring about qualitative and quantitative changes and hence high priority should be accorded in storage programmes to avoid these damages.

Technological Considerations of Processing Pulses : Conventional and traditional milling of pulses remove anything between 10 and 25 per cent of edible portion and according to some estimates, 1.5 million tonnes of pulses valued at Rs. 750 crores are lost. This huge loss is a challenge to the plant breeders and food technologists since it should be possible to recover as much of the milling losses by a technology-oriented approach. It will be worthwhile to examine the possibility of designing and fabricating equipments common to both cereal and pulse milling. Pulses are eaten as puffed tasted snacks in a ready-to-eat form in a traditional manner.

Prolonged heat treatments during processing, result in reduction of nutritive value and process parameters should be standardised to minimise processing losses and promote increased consumption of pulse products.

New systems of processing legumes have been developed in some countries including India and they are :

(*a*) Improved decortication and milling;

(*b*) Development of quick cooking methods;

(*c*) Manufacture of instant legume powder;

(*d*) Multi-mixes containing cereals, pulses and oilseeds;

(*e*) Preparation of legume protein isolates and concentrates.

Pulses are an important source of protein for large segments of the population and attempts should be made to identify and establish amino acid patterns of diet for different ecological zones to facilitiate die improvement. Practical and fast screening techniques-*in vitro* and bio-assays for determining digestibility, nutritive value are to be developed. Standardisation and definition of screening procedures is a primary requisite to accelerate the nutritional importance of food legumes. Final assessment of nutritional qualities must be made on living organisms or with highly correlated *in vitro* techniques. Cost reduction of processed lagume preparations will determine the acceptability and use of the product.

Factors Affecting Crop Production :

Crop growth

Internal factors (Genetic or Hereditary)	External factors (Environmental)
	1. Climatic
	2. Edaphic
	3. Biotic
	4. Physiographic
	5. Man (Anthropic)

In food processing the other common constraints are heavy loss in transit and storage. Especially 50 per cent of the harvested fruits are lost during the post harvest stages due to :

(*a*) Lack of knowledge of maturity standards and not harvesting fruits is the correct stages;

(*b*) Improper harvesting at harvest time causing damages and lack of cooling facilities;

(*c*) Lack of post-harvest treatment with fungicides;

(*d*) Non-availability of suitable transport;

(*e*) Production units being small and not properly equipped;

(*f*) Monoculture of varieties and crops leading to glut; and

(*g*) Limited utilisation for processing.

The Atmospheric Factors which Affect the Crop Plants are Called Climatic Factors

1. Precipitation;
2. Temperature;
3. Atmospheric humidity;

4. Solar radiation;
5. Wind velocity;
6. Atomospheric gases.

Next in importance is the Soil reaction : Soils may be neutral, acidic or alkaline depending upon their content of the basic salts and acidic components. Neutral soils are best for the growth of most crops.

Soil acidity beyond a particular limit is injurious to plant growth due to the following reasons :

1. High acidity (particularly high alumina content) is toxic to plants.
2. High acidity interferes with the absorptions of several nutrients particularly the cations such as K, Ca and Mg due to their low content in soil. Nutrients like P are fixed in acidic soils.
3. Decomposition of organic matter by micro-organisms may be reduced.
4. The activities of nitrifying and nitrogen fixing bacteria may be checked.
5. Certain types of fungoid diseases like potato scab may be favoured.

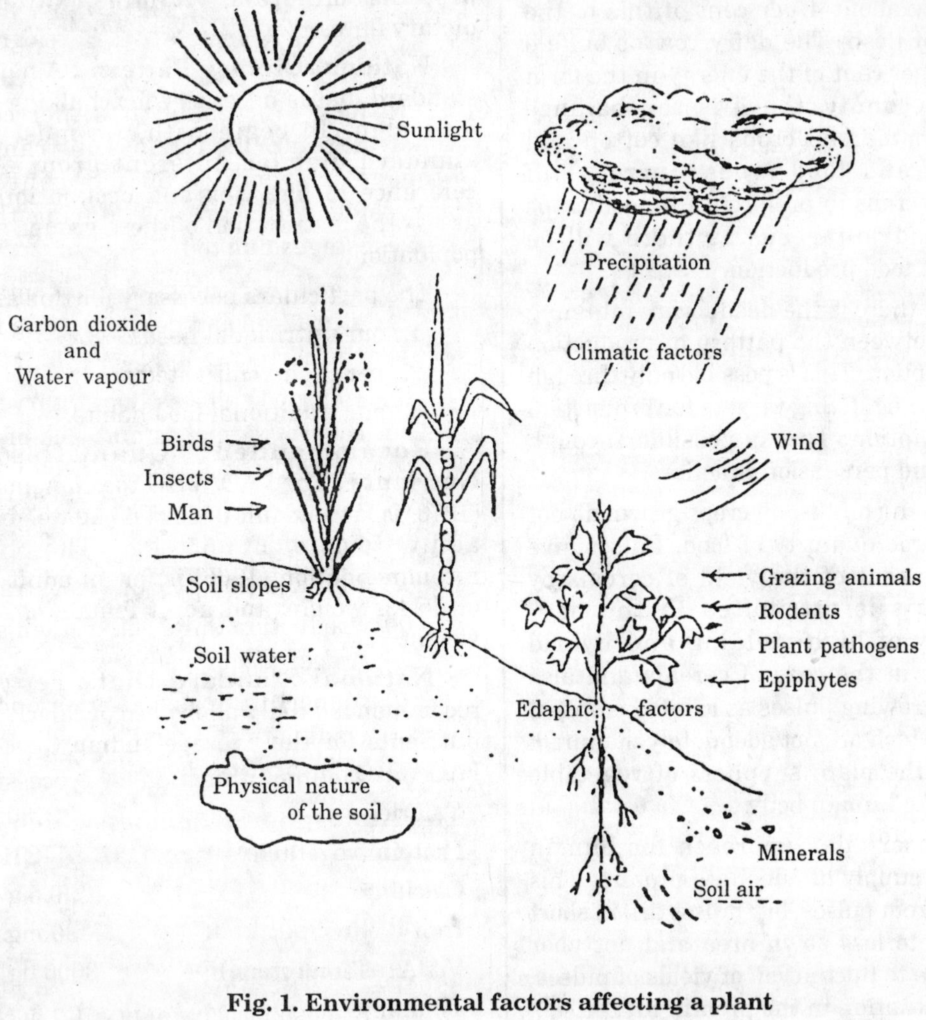

Fig. 1. Environmental factors affecting a plant

D. RELATION OF FOOD PRODUCTION TO NATIONAL DIETARY PATTERN

National Standard Diet : Human diet consists of vegetarian and non-vegetarian components. Crops that are grown yield staple food crops; horticultural plants supply fruits and vegetables. These two comprise vegetarian diet while the poultry and the animals reared on farms yield eggs, milk and meat. Meat of the fowls, sheep, goat and other livestock form the non-vegetarian part of human diet.

The animal retains a major portion of the energy consumed by it through feeds and returns only about 4 per cent of this to the consumer of flesh. The dairy cow or buffalo returns 20 per cent of the energy in the form of milk. Secondly, there is the balance between commercial crops like cotton and sugarcane and food crops. Increase of commercial crops in preference to food crops will be disadvantageous as there will be reduction in food production.

Thirdly, there is the need for maintaining a balance between the pattern of production and consumption. This is possible only through proper planning, fixing targets for production and consumption. This is possible through education and persuasion practices.

The fourth point is, all crops grown do not yield the same quantity of food. Pulses give only 50 per cent of the yield of cereals by weight. This is attributed to the non-availability of high yielding and hybrid varieties as in the case of cereals and also because of growing pulses as rainfed crops on poor lands which are not adequately manured. Pulses are the main suppliers of vegetable protein to the human body.

The present day approach for human nutrition is supply of adequate protein. This can be had from pulses, but pulses are in short supply due to less sown area and not poor outturn. Due to fluctuation of yields of pulses, there is fluctuation in the protein intake.

Planning is neccessary in growing different crops like cereals, pulses, oilseeds, sugarcane, vegetables and horticultural crops on pre-determined areas for each crop to obtain a diet that will provide balanced nutrients for the human system. There should be no violent displacement of other crops to the extent of seriously reducing the yield and upsetting the programme of balanced production.

Balanced Food : Food has many different components and each component is necessary for one function or other. The major components are : Carbohydrates, fats, proteins, minerals, vitamins, water and dietary fibres.

National Dietary Pattern : A national standard diet is necessary for chalking out a food plan. To begin with, we must have standard diet for different groups with reference to age, sex and occupation and assess the distribution of these groups in the population.

The particulars necessary for this are :

1. our nutritional needs
2. per capita cultivated area
3. our traditional food habits.

Recommended Quantities of Nutrients : The FAO/WHO recommendation (1973) is for an adult male of 65 kg weight and adult female of 55 kg. The ICMR recommendation (1966) is for an adult male of 55 kg weight and adult female of 45 kg weight.

National Standard Diet : Per caput recommended daily allowance of calories and nutrients for the average Indian (based on FAO/WHO data).

Calories	2280
Protein (vegetable)	12 g
Calcium	0.5 g
Iron	30 mg
Vit. A (as β carotene)	3000 μg
Thiamine	1.5 mg

Riboflavin	1.35 mg
Nicotinic acid	14.0 mg
Ascorbic acid (Vitamin C)	50 mg

The appended Tables provide data on the following :

A. Per caput recommendation of protein in India
B. Balanced diet for adult men
C. Balanced diet for adult women
D. Balanced diet for adolescent boys and girls
E. Balanced diet for children
F. Standard diet for the average Indian and land requirement for the standard diet.

Dietician's Five-Food Groups : Priority grouping of food is as follows :

I. Milk group	– including milk and milk products
II. Meat group	– this includes meat, eggs, fish, beans, peas, pulses and nuts
III. Vegetable and fruit group	– includes all vegetables and fruits except those included under item II above
IV. Bread and cereal group	– staple food cereals and millets
V. Other foods	– used for seasoning including fats and oils, sugar and sweets.

Table 6. Calculation of per caput daily requirement of protein in India on the basis of ICMR recommendations (1968)

Age/sex-group	*Number per thousand of Population (approximate)*	*Recommended daily allowance (g)*	*Total requirement for the group (g)*
Infants*			
< 1 year	35	–	–
Children			
1-3 years	95	18.5	1756
4-6 years	85	22.0	1870
7-9 years	80	33.0	2640
Adolescents, males			
10-12 years	43	41.0	1763
13-15 years	33	55.0	1815
16-19 years	35	60.0	2100
Adolescents, females			
10-12 years	38	41.0	1558
13-15 years	30	50.0	1500
16-19 years	31	50.0	1550
Adults			
Men	255	55	14025
Women	240	45	10800
Allowance for pregancy (latter half))	20	10	200

Age/sex-group	Number per thousand of Population (approximate)	Recommended daily allowance (g)	Total requirement for the group (g)
Allowance for lactation	35	20	700
Whole population	1000		42277
Per caput daily requirement = 42.3 g or, say, 42 g			

*According to the FAO/WHO Expert Committee, it is not necessary to consier infant requirements when we are making allowance for lactation.

Table 7. Balanced Diets for Adult Men
(Recommended by the Indian Council of Medical Research)

	Sedentary		Moderate work		Heavy work	
	Veg. (g)	Non-veg. (g)	Veg. (g)	Non-veg (g)	Veg. (g)	Non-veg (g)
Cereals	400	400	475	475	650	650
Pulses	70	55	80	65	80	65
Green leafy vegetables	100	100	125	125	125	125
Other vegetables	75	75	75	75	100	100
Roots and tubers	75	75	100	100	100	100
Fruits	30	30	30	30	30	30
Milk	200	100	200	100	200	100
Fats and oils	35	40	40	40	50	50
Meat and fish	–	30	–	30	–	30
Eggs	–	30	–	30	–	30
Sugar and jaggery	30	30	40	40	55	55
Groundnut	–	–	–	–	50*	50*

*Additional 30 g of fats and oils can be included in the diet in place of groundnut.

Table 8. Balanced Diets for Adult Women
(Recommended by the Indian Council of Medical Research)

	Sedentary		Moderate work		Heavy work		Additional allowances during	
	Veg. (g)	Non-veg. (g)	Veg. (g)	Non-veg (g)	Veg. (g)	Non-veg (g)	Pregnancy (g)	Lactation (g)
Cereals	300	300	350	350	475	475	50	100
Pulses	60	45	70	55	70	55	–	10
Green leafy vegetables	125	125	125	125	125	125	25	25

	Sedentary		*Moderate work*		*Heavy work*		*Additional allowances during*	
	Veg. (g)	***Non-veg. (g)***	***Veg. (g)***	***Non-veg***	***Veg.***	***Non-veg***	***pregnancy***	***Lactation***
Other Vegetables	75	75	75	75	100	100	–	–
Roots and tubers	50	50	75	75	100	100	–	–
Fruits	30	30	30	30	30	30	–	–
Milk	200	100	200	100	200	100	125	125
Fats and oils	30	35	35	40	40	45	–	15
Sugar and jaggery	30	30	30	30	40	40	10	20
Meat and fish	–	30	–	30	–	30	–	–
Eggs	–	30	–	30	–	30	–	–
Groundnut	–	–	–	–	40*	40*	–	–

*Additional 25 g of fats and oils can be included in the diet in place of groundnut.

Table 9. Balanced Diets for Adolescent Boys and Girls
(Recommended by the Indian Council of Medical Research)

	Boys				*Girls*	
	13-15 years		*16-18 years*		*13-18 years*	
	Veg. (g)	***Non-veg. (g)***	***Veg. (g)***	***Non-veg (g)***	***Veg. (g)***	***Non-veg. (g)***
Cereals	430	430	450	450	350	350
Pulses	70	50	70	50	70	50
Green leafy vegetables	100	100	100	100	150	150
Other vegetables	75	75	75	75	75	75
Roots and tubers	75	75	100	100	75	75
Fruits	30	30	30	30	30	30
Milk	250	150	250	150	250	150
Fats and oils	35	40	45	50	35	40
Meat and fish	–	30	–	30	–	30
Eggs	–	30	–	30	–	30
Sugar and jaggery	30	30	40	40	30	30
Groundnut	–	–	50*	50*	–	–

* Additional 30 g of fats and oils can be included in the diet in place of groundnut.

Table 10. Balanced Diets for Children (Recommended by the Indian Council of Medical Research)

	1-3 years		*4-5 years*		*7-9 years*		*10-12 years*	
	Veg. (g)	*Non-veg. (g)*	*Veg. (g)*	*Non-veg (g)*	*Veg. (g)*	*Non-veg (g)*	*Veg. (g)*	*Non-veg (g)*
Cereals	150	150	200	200	250	250	320	320
Pulses	50	40	60	50	70	60	70	60
Green leafy vegetables	50	50	75	75	75	75	100	100
Other vegetables / Roots and tubers	30	30	50	50	50	50	75	75
Fruits	50	50	50	50	50	50	50	50
Milk	300	200	250	200	250	200	250	200
Fats and oils	20	20	25	25	30	30	35	35
Meat and fish	–	30	–	30	–	30	–	30
Sugar and jaggery	30	30	40	40	50	50	50	50

Table 11. Standard Diet for the Average Indian (Recommended by Nutrition Expert Group, 1968)

Article of food	*Recommended per caput daily allowance (g)*	*Per caput daily consumption (1969/70) (g)*
Cereals	370	384
Pulses (including nuts and oilseeds)	70	53
Milk	180	116
Meat, fish and eggs	35	8
All vegetables	235	58
All fruits	37	48
Fats and oils	38	10
Sugar and jaggery	40	49
Total	1005	726

Management of Foodgrains

Save Grain Campaign : The scheme is implemented through network of 12 SGC offices in close collaboration with the State Govt. and NGOs. The main objective of the scheme is to transfer the technical know-how developed by IGMRI to the farmers for minimising the post-harvest losses in foodgrains. Under the scheme an assistance for purchasing the metal beans and other inputs Rs. 10,000 per nucleus village is provided to the farmers.

During 2006-2007, 29250 farmers were trained in stipendary/non-stipendary training-programmes. 15,977 metals bins distributed, 15,711 non-metallic storage structures improved/constructed and 336 nucleus villages developed.

Quality Standards for Foodgrains

The Govt. exercises due control over the quality of foodgrains procured for the central/

state pool. The Quality Control Cell of the ministry at New Delhi, Kolkata and Hyderabad monitor the quality of foodgrains being procured by FCI and state agencies for central pool as well as at the time of storage and distribution. During 2005-2006, 521 Food Storage Depots.

Indian Grain Storage Management and Research Institute : Indian Grain Storage Management and Research Institute (IGMRI), Hapur is engaged in the training and R & D work relating to grain storage management. This Institute has three field stations at Hyderabad, Jorhat and Ludhiana. The IGMRI also conducts various training courses on storage, inspection of foodgrains, pest control, etc. for the officers of storage agencies, pest control operators etc.

During 2006-07, 30 long/short-term training courses and 13 artisan training were conducted, 2282 foodgrains sample for physical quality parameters, 712 samples for pesticide residue and 380 samples for mycotoxin contamination were analysed by IGMRI, Hapur and its field stations.

Questions From Previous Year's Papers

Q. 1. Discuss in brief the principles and methods of preservation of fruits and vegetables.

Q. 2. Compare the nutritive value of mango, apple and banana. Give three common high-yielding varieties of each of them cultivated in India

Q. 3. Give the contribution of different categories of food crops to the total food production in India. How can the existing balance between food production and population growth be, at least maintained in the coming decades?

Q. 4. Disuss the trend of production and consumption of food grain in India what policies have been adopted for procurement and distribution of foodgrain in the country?

Q. 5. What are the major contraints in food production in India? Discuss briefly.

Q. 6. Answer the following in about 150 words each :

(a) Write on the technique of preparation of pineapple squash.

(b) Give the procurement and processing contraints of food grains.

Q. 7. Write short notes on :

(a) Protein-energy malnutrition

(b) Intersex in Papaya.

YOUR SPACE